The Day The Dollar Dies

Willard Cantelon

16

EasyRead Large

RHYW

Copyright Page from the Original Book

Bridge-Logos
Alachua, FL 32615 USA

The Day the Dollar Dies
by Willard Cantelon

Printed in the United States of America.

Library of Congress Catalog Card Number: 2009925711
International Standard Book Number 978-0-88270-969-7

Scripture quotations in this book are from the *King James Version* of the Bible.

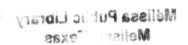

G163.317.N.m904.35230

This optimized ReadHowYouWant edition contains the complete, unabridged text of the original publisher's edition. Other aspects of the book may vary from the original edition.

Set in 16 pt. Verdana

TABLE OF CONTENTS

FOREWORD

In the Seventies, while home in Germany on furlough from Africa, I read with fascination and awe my friend's book *The Day the Dollar Dies.* I remember not being able to put it down till I had reached the last page. Here was unfolding before me the height of biblical end-time prophecy in such detailed fashion that it made me hold my breath. The tremendous foresight of this Christian statesman and writer, the intensive research invested, his access to high calibre sources, his knowledge of global affairs—all of that showed me: here God himself had anointed the writer's pen in warning to coming generations.

The US Dollar in those days was *the* currency, opening doors the world over. Its demise was unthinkable, unless you had heard from God himself. The Book of the Revelation, the Book of Daniel, both were now no longer an ancient, dust covered, writ, but supra relevant revelation of the political state of affairs in our very lifetime! Prosperous merchants now weeping; wealthy tycoons now plunged into deepest despair; happy young speculators and seasoned fortune hunters, polished, suave scoundrels at the end of their wheeler-dealer tether! Unbelievable! The audacity of such a forecast!

The fall of the great divide of Iron and Bamboo Curtains, one global monetary system, the Council of Europe, the European Union, the EURO, Europe's ascendancy to become a united global player, who could—after the "Wirtschaftswunder"[1] of Ludwig Erhard[2]—foresee such rapid developments, almost within the twinkling of an eye? Eastern and Western Europe fused into one powerful body! Revelation's Bull with the Woman[3] on it surfacing in the United Europe, in Strasburg and Brussels!

Meanwhile I have read and re-read Dr. Cantelon's book many times; in English and in German. And each time I read it more eagerly—if this were possible—than before. Each time, fresh light was shed on our day and age that clearly shows the pitfalls at the very brink of which we are standing today. It makes me tremble, but also look up as our Redemption is drawing nigh. Nobody should neglect the pages of this prophetic book with its biblical global end-time scope, a book compiled by an obedient servant of God with a listening ear, an understanding heart, and a courageous, gifted, pen!

Presently, I am back in Kenya, more precisely in the Nyanza Province where the cradle of the father of US President Barack Obama stood, in Alego Kogelo. I see with my own eyes the consequences of the dying dollar, just as Willard had seen it decades ago. If we want to fathom the present and prepare for the future, we must read yesterday's book with its urgent message for today.

Herbert Ros[4]
Awasi, February 2009

PREFACE

Berlin was in shambles, Frankfurt and Stuttgart in ruins. Millions of refugees wandered the streets of West German cities where the ghostly remains of bombed buildings stared without sympathy at the homeless seeking shelter.

The war was over, but the wounds remained. They would take time to heal.

Years would be required to remove the rubble, and memories of Adolph Hitler would never be erased. Germany's rebuilding would require more than brick and mortar. Faith once firm in the hearts of older Germans had been severely shaken by 19 years of Nazi domination.

On the edge of Frankfurt, I stood with a friend, J.P. Kolenda. Together we stared at the squat gray buildings surrounded by tall grass and weeds.

"So you plan to establish a school in this place to train young Germans for the ministry," I said slowly.

"I know the buildings are drab and inadequate," replied my friend. "We would build better if we had the funds."

Slowly I reached out my hand and shook his in agreement. Then for a moment I stared at my hand, as if it belonged to someone other than myself. Why had I pledged my help so impulsively? How much money would I have to raise? And where? And how?

The weeks that followed my commitment at Frankfurt were rainy ones. The skies of Germany continued to mourn the millions of lives lost in the war.

On the rain-soaked hills of Wurttemberg we gathered together an unusual group of men. There was a platoon of special police who, at our request, had donned uniforms resembling the SS guards of the Third Reich. Then there were the two pathetic-looking figures who stood shackled and blindfolded, awaiting execution. Next to me stood my closest friend and cameraman, Colonel Alfred Garr.

The rain stopped falling. I shouted, "Scene 1, Take 1," and we began shooting the final scene of our film, *Three Germanys.* The film would portray the old Germany of the past, war-torn Germany, and a rebuilt Germany. Hopefully, the film would be as acceptable as the first documentaries we had done in India and Africa.

Later that year, the film won not only a film-festival award, but the hearts of the viewers, and proved valuable in raising the needed funds for the German ministerial school.

No scene in the film, however, was as dramatic or sobering as the expression on the face of a little German mother who viewed the film on a special occasion. Moved with a desire to assist the German school, she brought a gift of 10,000 marks for the building program. She held her money with pride and tenderness, as though it was part of her very life. And in a very literal sense, it was exactly that; she had earned the money with the sweat of her brow, and had guarded it constantly in the war's destructive years. Now she was investing it in a worthy cause and she beamed with pride as she offered her contribution.

How could I tell her she had held this money too long'? Why did it fall to my lot to shock this sensitive soul with the news that her money was virtually worthless? Why had she not read the morning paper, or heard the announcement that the new government at Bonn had canceled this currency?

If I told her the truth, how would she react? The *Stars and Stripes,* official paper of the Occupation Forces in Europe, would later list the staggering number of German suicides on that June Sunday in 1948. Millions of Germans were aware that their marks were inflated, but few realized that they were to be so suddenly canceled altogether. Marks that would have bought a house on Saturday would not be sufficient in value to buy a winter coat on Sunday.

"Madam," I said slowly, "I'm awfully sorry, but I cannot accept your money."

"And why not?" she asked, perplexity written on her face.

"Because it has been canceled," I said, as gently as I could.

"But, how could they cancel it? And why?" she cried with dismay.

In those two words rested two great questions! How and why? It was not possible in a single sentence to give this honest heart the answer to her questions, but there were longer answers that could be given to her, and to anyone who cared to listen—how and why money was canceled in the past, and would again be canceled in the future.

Early in life, I had become interested in money. Not in possessing it, but in understanding its power, its influence, its origin, and its destiny. Why did the German mark become so inflated in 1923 that it took a wagonload to buy a frankfurter? Why did Hitler blame the Jews for much of Germany's economic woes and destroy millions at Auschwitz[5] and Dachau?[6] Why was the German mark again canceled in June of 1948? Why, with World War II so far behind us, is the Western world now talking daily about a new money system? If a new system would shortly be established, who would control it?

In my early youth, I had been given copies of the documents entitled, *The Protocols of the Learned Elders of Zion.* These articles supposedly contained the plot of a few men representing the financial wizards of the world, who not only controlled the financial resources of men and nations, but planned to control completely every man and nation through a monopoly of the world's finances.

With awakened interest, I found myself researching the works of anyone who wrote on the subject, and listening to every speaker who spoke on this theme.

I was amazed to learn that many leaders in government both at home and abroad firmly believed that there was a small group of international bankers—totally different in nature and office from the men who served the public in smaller private banks—who were responsible for setting up and removing kings and financing wars throughout history. These men were frequently referred to as the *Illuminati,* or the Luciferian Society, because they received their power and wisdom directly from Lucifer, the prince of this world.

Extreme as it sounded, I was amazed at the ever-increasing reference to such a society and to the growing general acceptance of the idea of a world government.

While reading *Great Ideas Today: 1971* (published by the *Encyclopaedia Britannica),* I was surprised to find so much of this volume devoted to world government. Space was given to the writings of Dostoevsky, who refers to Christ returning to Earth and being rejected by those who had pledged their loyalties to Lucifer. They were promised by Lucifer that they would be given his wisdom and power, and with him rule mankind.

As I traveled from country to country and studied the trends toward a world government, I saw two forces at work. On one hand, I saw honest and sincere men who felt that only a world government under the control of a strong leader could save the world from poisoning itself through pollution, from famine brought on by exploding population, and from the danger of annihilation by atomic war. These men worked feverishly for the establishment of a world government under the banner of humanitarianism, or concern for man's survival. Along with these, there were also the honest men who daily struggled in the world of finance where world trade had far outgrown the volume of money available, men frustrated by the inadequacies of the old money systems that had their origins in the medieval centuries.

Apart from these honest and sincere men, however, I was forced to the conclusion that there was a small group of men who seemed indeed to be endowed with almost supernatural power, who worked behind the scenes making the key economic—and therefore directive—decisions of many countries. For instance, one of the world's most powerful banking dynasties sprung up in Europe under the name of Rothschild. Its center was in Frankfurt, Germany. On scores of occasions, I had stood in the heart of Frankfurt, gazing up at the mammoth banking houses rising high into the sky. These were tied in a very real and powerful manner to other great banking houses of the world.

In my youth, it seemed that the skylines of the cities were dominated by the church spires pointing heavenward. Now, in every town and city, it was the bank buildings that towered over all else. They seemed like temples indeed, temples built by men who had chosen to serve not God but mammon.

I determined that I would learn not merely how a world government would be formed, and how a new world money system would be established, but also why.

The subject was not one that could be mastered in a four-or-seven-year span of study at an institution of higher learning. All over the world, each new day brought new developments and broader fulfillments of what men of old declared through inspiration would be fulfilled in our day.

I am humbly grateful to God for the opportunities He has given me to pursue this subject for many years in many places, writing books, producing films, delivering messages.

I am especially grateful for a girl, once known to her Philadelphia friends as Verna Jones.

I met her at the close of a month of meetings in the old Metropolitan Opera House in Philadelphia over a quarter of a century ago. After a twenty-minute conversation and six months of prayer, I gave her an engagement ring. We were married in Philadelphia on a Saturday, I spoke in Chicago the next day and have missed very few days speaking publicly since. The honorariums from speaking engagements have cared for the family and enabled me to keep us together. Even when our sons, Lee and Paul, were babies, Verna kept them with us in our journeys over continents and oceans.

One day recently in Brussels, my friend, Charles Greenaway, was quoting our mutual friend, J. Philip Hogan. "There's only one girl in all the wide world who could be happily married to a man like Willard," he said. "Any morning of the week, he may announce at breakfast time, 'We're going to move,' and Verna's reply would usually be the same, 'When? This morning or this afternoon?'" Thus was I ideally equipped for a quest that would take me into the council chambers of a dozen foreign lands—and into the mentality of the international banker as an archetype.

Willard Cantelon
Glendale, California

CHAPTER 1

THE SEARCH

My search to know the how and why of an impending new world money system took me to the halls of the United Nations and to the galleries of the U.S. Senate. It took me to the capitals of Europe, where we viewed the economic scene through the eyes of the Gnomes of Zurich. And to Brussels, where I listened to the world's leading voices describe a new number system which would soon replace the gold and silver and the currencies of the hour. Frequently, I heard advocates of the new money system lauding its virtues and extolling its advantages over the old systems. But in my mind there always remained one great question: If the new system was universal, who would control it?

This was a question of supreme importance. If I believed the pages of history and the statements made by leaders of yesterday, then surely I must believe that those who controlled money would play a major role in the affairs of men.

BRITAIN'S LEADERS

Reginald McKenna, who had served as Chancellor of England's Exchequer, said in January, 1924, "I am afraid that the ordinary citizen will not like to be told that the banks can and do create money, and they who control the credit of a nation direct the policy of the governments and hold in the hollow of their hands, the destiny of the people.

Sir Drummond Fraser, Vice President of the Institute of Bankers, also stated in 1924, "The Governor of the Bank of England must be the autocrat who dictates the terms upon which alone the government can obtain money."

Lord Gladstone, who also served as Chancellor of Britain's Exchequer, said in 1852, "The government ... in the matters of finance was to leave the money power supreme and unquestioned."

America's Leaders

President James Garfield said in 1881, "He who controls the money of a nation controls the nation."

In 1933, Vice-President John Garner said in referring to international bankers, "You see, gentlemen, who owns the United States."

Congressman Charles Lindbergh of Minnesota said in 1920, "Financial panics are scientifically created."

An International Banker

In the book entitled, *The Federal Reserve Bank* by H.S. Kenan, Meyer Amschel Rothschild is quoted as saying, "Give me control over a nation's economy, and I care not who writes its laws."

The Father of Communism

In his *Communist Manifesto,* Karl Marx declared, "Money plays the largest part in determining the course of history."

Leaders of the Common Market

In Brussels, I listened to the leaders of Europe's Common Market declare their intentions and plans to establish a new money system replacing the old. What then would be the fate of the present currencies of the Western world when they would be replaced with a new number system?

Would there be a rash of suicides and a cry of despair from the lips of millions, as there was when the stock market crashed in 1929, or when the German mark was canceled in 1948?

Anxiety of Americans Today

Today, Americans are anxious about their future security. They long to know the future. In the November, 1970, issue of *Today's Health,* published by the American Medical Association, reference was made to:

- 40 million Americans who pay 200 million dollars annually to 5,000 astrologers in seeking to know the future.

- The interest in astrology continues to increase. Most newspapers in America carry astrology columns.
- Untold thousands of people profess to believe in witchcraft. In one year alone, Americans purchased over 2,000,000 Ouija boards.

Christ Warned Against False Prophets

"There shall arise ... false prophets, and ... they shall deceive.... Behold, I have told you before" (Matthew 24:24-25).

The Bible Tells Men They Can Know the Future

The Prophet Isaiah declared God's message in strong language: "I am God, and there is none like me, Declaring the end from the beginning, and from ancient times the things that are not yet done, saying, My counsel shall stand" (Isaiah 46:9-10).

The Apostle Peter declared: "We have also a more sure word of prophecy; whereunto ye do well that ye take heed, as unto a light that shineth in a dark place" (2 Peter 1:19).

Some people not fully conversant with the writings of the prophets of the Bible suggest that they predicted only gloom and doom. But actually, their voices unite in predicting a day of ultimate peace and prosperity.

They are in complete agreement that there will be a day of order and justice when wars cease and there dawns a golden age of world harmony. As man approaches that day, it seems far away, even as the darkest hour is just before the dawn.

The Prophet John tells in great detail of world events that will transpire at the close of this age. Man will face some dark and difficult years when the world comes under a world government and a leader who controls men with a new money system described by John.

And he causeth all, both small and great, rich and poor, free and bond, to receive a mark in their right hand, or in their foreheads: And that no man might buy or sell, save he that had the mark ... or the number (Revelation 13:16-17).

Repeatedly, I read with amazement the statements penned by the John the fisherman. From a lonely island almost 2,000 years ago, he foretold a day when men, great and small of all nations, would see their old currencies suddenly canceled and replaced with a Universal Number System.

I committed the words of the prophets to memory and quoted them before audiences, civic and religious, large and small. From the Debating Hall of Oxford to the Cathedral of Calcutta; from London's Royal Albert Hall to Nairobi, the capital of Kenya; I spoke through the years, not as a bigot or dogmatist with a strange doctrine, but with an honest heart. I spoke as one seeking to understand a changing world in the light of prophecy.

CHAPTER 2

A SECRET OF POWER

One still, cold, winter night I stood high on the south bank of the Potomac, gazing across the river at the city of Washington, which sparkled in a covering of new-fallen snow.

For a third of a century, America had been the land of my adoption, and for several years Washington had been my home. To me, she was the very heart of the nation, and my own heart was part of her.

If Paris to many spelled pleasure and Rome to others represented religion, then surely Washington was a symbol of power. Was there any place in the world where her voice was not heard and her influence not felt?

Discovering America

In my early years in America, however, I had given little thought or consideration to America's place in world affairs. I was too occupied with the wonder and excitement of discovering America itself.

During a single decade, I drove over half a million miles in America, and traveled still more in the air and on the water. The sheer size of this country was staggering. I once added the territories of two dozen nations and compared their size to that of the U.S.A.

To my amazement, I found that the territories of England, Ireland, Scotland, Wales, Norway, Sweden, Denmark, Holland, Germany, Switzerland, France, Belgium, Spain, Portugal, Greece, Italy, Austria, Hungary, Czechoslovakia, Poland, Romania, Cuba, Ceylon, and Japan combined covered less than one half of the area of the U.S.A. In fact, one could place all of these in America twice over and still have 114,740 square miles to spare.

A Multi-Race Population

As America's population grew, so did the variety of nationalities within her borders. By the time her population reached 200 million, the races within America represented almost every land on earth.

Wealth in Few Hands

At the conclusion of World War II, the contrast between the wealth of America and the poverty of other nations stood in sharp contrast. In 1945, Americans found themselves possessing:

- 70% of the free world's gold
- 50% of the productive power
- 65% of the world's telephones, radios, and automobiles

All of this wealth was in the hands of 6 1/2% of the world's people, but it was not destined to remain this way for long.

Postwar Europe

At the close of World War II, I had walked in silence down the streets of London and Coventry beholding the skeletons of the buildings bombed in the blitzkriegs. In Rotterdam I gazed with awe at the endless acres of rubble. The proud Dutch city had been literally pulverized by the merciless assaults of the Luftwaffe.

With Colonel Garr I drove across France. The factories in many cities were idle. The spirits of the people seemed as shattered as their towns and villages.

In Stuttgart, I looked from the window of a bombed abode, gazing incredulously at the once-beautiful city of Wurttemberg, now 70% in ruins.

In Berlin, I walked on what had been called the Victory Parade. I did not hear the click of the heel, nor see the Elite Guard of Hitler strutting with their proud goose step. The Victory Parade seemed lonely and empty. Berlin was 90% in ruins.

European Bankruptcy

During the many weeks we spent in Berlin, we learned firsthand some of the sorrows of war. Fran Kleist told us how she traded her treasured piano for a sack of potatoes to keep from starving and burned her furniture to keep from freezing.

In Frankfurt, Amandus Frotcher, the industrialist builder, told how he offered his valuable rings for a quarter pound of margarine.

A Picture Reversed

In a few short years, the contrast between America's prosperity and Europe's postwar poverty vanished. Out of the war ruins of European cities, skyscrapers and modern buildings arose almost overnight.

The autobahns and expressways of Europe, once so devoid of cars, became congested with traffic; and hotels in the holiday seasons invariably hung out signs reading, "No Vacancy."

The four-word plea, "Take me to America," once familiar on almost every European's lips began to vanish. There was no mistake. Europe along with other nations was growing richer and America was grower poorer.

CHAPTER 3

THE EMERGING PICTURE

Increasingly I was being invited to address audiences, civic and religious, on the subject of the New World Money System. One of the most challenging and interesting groups to which I was asked to speak was the Research Department of the United States Air Force. On December 14, 1970, I was invited to deliver a two-hour address to these men who had devoted much of their lives to science and physics.

How well I recall that bleak December evening. I could not help but contrast it with my first visit to Washington two decades earlier. Then I came in the springtime, when the cherry blossoms gave the city a beautiful dress of pink. I remembered how I had stood in the bright spring sunshine on the steps of the U.S. Capitol which cost over $24 million to erect. So quickly the calendar had brought me to 1970.

As I drove by the majestic building, I said, "You look a bit older tonight, old Capitol. You have sought to bear the burdens of a third of the world and in so doing have been unable to adequately bear your own. The men abroad who once seemed satisfied to hold your paper money became fearful that you could not redeem it, so they claimed your precious metal. But if those who have profited by your generosity predict a death of the dollar, one thing is certain: their currencies will be canceled also, and the new system will affect everyone."

A New World System Predicted

Passing the Capitol, I came to the building in which I was to speak. As I studied the faces of the men assembled around the conference table, I saw that all were strangers, with one exception, Colonel Glen Balmer. Colonel Balmer was a quiet man for whom I held profound respect. His name occupied more space in America's *Who's Who* than any other man I knew.

I knew that the colonel had a deep faith in God and also a keen interest in the subject I was to discuss. As for the other men, I presumed some would be Protestant, some Catholic, some Jewish, and others with no profession of faith at all.

I suggested in my introduction that the prophecies of the Bible could shed light on America's future and bring to light some significant truths concerning the New World Money System.

I reminded the men that in our nation, 1,665 persons suffered nervous breakdowns daily. In spite of the fact that $25 million were spent on tranquilizers and nerve medicine annually, someone was admitted to a mental institution every three minutes. According to Dr. Boggs, mental illness in America was increasing 100% faster than the population, even though science and medicine had made great progress. That very month, spokesmen for the Food and Drug Administration had suggested on national television that 70% of all American expenditures on medicine were an effort to calm the nation's ragged nerves. A recent headline had declared the economic uncertainties of the hour to be the major cause of America's nervous breakdown.

I told my audience, "I do not come as a religious bigot seeking to force some extreme doctrine as a biased dogmatist. I will merely review the familiar facts of the day and quote some words written by men thousands of years ago."

I told them of John's prophecy of a day when the world would not buy and sell with silver and gold nor any other currency but only with a number system.

The audience of Air Force career men grew attentive and sympathetic as I reminded them that the highly esteemed Robert Morris Page, inventor of pulsation radar, wrote, "The prediction of highly significant events far in the future could be accomplished only through knowledge obtained from a realm which is not subject to the laws of time as we know them."

For two hours I quoted statistics and statements made by leaders strong in faith. I concluded by quoting the utterances written by prophets of the Bible long ago and asked the audience, in the words of Christ, "What think ye?"

At the close of my address, a strange hush came over the entire audience. It was as though a light had penetrated a room that shortly before had been filled with the blue patterns of cigar and cigarette smoke and the pessimism of men.

"Yes," I said firmly, "the message of the New World Money System is not a dark message. It is indeed very bright. For those who understand prophecy, these are days of amazing meaning in man's destiny."

The two hours in the conference hall had passed like so many minutes. I received an ovation, along with a unanimous invitation to return.

"It is no credit to me," I told Colonel Balmer as I was leaving. "It was really not my message. The most thrilling part of my address had been written by men over 2,000 years ago, and I merely quoted it."

CHAPTER 4

AN EARLY BEGINNING

I shivered a little from a breeze blowing up from the Potomac. "Yes, Washington," I said to the sleeping city, turning back to my car, "your sun may have set, but a bright new day is soon to dawn."

In a few minutes, I was at the front door of my home at 308 Old Courthouse Road. My wife and boys had retired for the night; but burning coals on the hearth smiled cheerfully, and flickering fingers of fire beckoned to me to sit down and reminisce, and so I did.

"When did you first start speaking on the New World Money System?" I recalled Colonel Balmer asking.

"It was before World War II was fought or the United Nations, the International Monetary Fund, and the World Bank were formed," I had said. "It was before computers were invented or 'paper gold' was introduced."

"What prompted you to speak on this subject?" he asked.

The answer took me back many years.

Pulling my chair closer to the fire, I stared at the coals on the hearth. Then came a miracle that man cannot explain. Memory, with its mystical power, reconstructed in the fire the scenes of yesterday.

No, they were not merely pages from a man's diary. They were scenes of great events that pertained to all the people of the world, scenes that had continuity and order. It was as though some master mind had eliminated all of the personal incidents that had once seemed important to me in earlier life. I saw only the events that contributed to the formation of a one-world government and a new world money system.

I sat with bated breath, realizing that it was almost finished. The old currencies that had served for so many centuries would soon be canceled, and the new number system would take their place.

As I saw with clarity the scene of the final world government and the new money system, I was reminded of the paintings I had sought to place on the canvas with brush and oils. From Mombasa to the Matterhorn I had striven to capture on canvas some of the wonders of nature. I had learned that one rule in art was basic. The artist must not start with a leaf or pebble. He must close his eyes, and then open them just enough to allow a little light to fall on the object of interest. In that partial light, he first sees a horizon where the earth and sky meet. Then the profile of the mountains stand in bold relief as they touch the plains.

A Thirty-Year-Old Notebook

I thought of the sheafs of notes I had written on the subject of the New World Money System, and saw myself writing them through the years. On the sunny deck of the old *Queen Elizabeth,* I wrote in the mid-Atlantic. On the same ship, I wrote in the February storms while clinging to the side of the bunk or berth, striving to make the pen and paper meet, in a ship that groaned and tossed in the tempest. I saw myself writing on the veranda of a bomb-ruined hotel in Germany or in the back of an Indian warehouse in Calcutta. From Ottawa to Oxford, from Boston to Berlin, I wrote notes on the one subject that grew ever bigger and more exciting. After a time, I had a thirty-year-old notebook.

My files would have been worthless to a stranger. Cards, clippings, books, and reams of paper all went into the precious collection of facts and truths. "Old fire," I said as I gazed into its glowing embers, "your friends across the world have collected most of my notes. Fires and fireplaces in a score of lands have turned most of them to ashes, and I have deigned it so. I have sought to retain, primarily, only the bold outline, the basic principles that all can understand."

My First Public Appearance

My first public utterance on the subject was in the summer of 1939, from the platform of the United Church of Canada. Dr. Robinson, the pastor, had suddenly resigned to seek a seat in the House of Parliament. The church board asked me to be the interim speaker. The black robe and high pulpit seemed a bit out of keeping with my customary surroundings, but for many weeks I kept speaking.

My message on "Current Events in the Light of Bible Prophecy" was somewhat different from what the congregation had been accustomed to hearing under Dr. Robinson.

When I concluded my weeks in the church, I walked home where friends had gathered to help me make an important decision. Of course, I had only one choice—in their judgment. I was to go to seminary to become a clergyman. Some even suggested the giving of money in an effort to persuade me to accept their well-meant advice.

"But I am not a pastor, and I never shall be," I replied. And the following Sunday found me on the platform of the theater, seeking to reach an audience that I had not reached in the sanctuary of the church. There, when I made the statement, "I may live to see the day when the world will not use silver, gold, or currencies as legal tender; but only a universal number system," Attorney Schultz winked.

My cheeks flushed with momentary embarrassment as I caught the message he conveyed to Postmaster Winram who was seated across the aisle. I was embarrassed, but not angry. My better judgment told me that the realistic attorney considered my statement too extreme to be taken seriously. And indeed, it had been made before World War II was declared, before nations plunged deeper into debt, before "rationing" became a household word in the Western world, before pollution brought its alarm signals to the entire globe, before a world bank was formed, and before computers were invented.

A Higher Wisdom

There was one basic difference between Attorney Schultz and myself. He undoubtedly had filled his mind with the recitation of the *Laws of Evidence;* and the available evidence in that hour did not seem, in his judgment, to point toward a one-world money system, let alone a one-world government. In contrast, my life had been filled with the words of the prophets of the Bible. Even in that hour, I had read and re-read the words of the Prophet John, concerning a coming world government under the control of one who, according to John (Revelation 13:16), would cause all, small and great, rich and poor, free and bond, to receive a mark ... that no man might buy or sell, save he that had the mark ... or the number.

John did not make this amazing prediction because of his super-intelligence. He very honestly explained, "I heard [a voice] ... which said ... I will shew thee things which must be hereafter" (Revelation 4:1).

The Prophet Daniel, like John, did not take credit for the prophecies he uttered concerning future events. He said, "There is a God ... that revealeth secrets, and maketh known ... what shall be in the latter days" (Daniel 2:28). And he added, "This secret is not revealed to me for any wisdom that I have more than any living" (Daniel 2:30).

Regarding the message of the prophets, Peter wrote, "We have also a more sure word of prophecy; whereunto ye do well that ye take heed, as unto a light that shineth in a dark place" (2 Peter 1:19).

A light in a dark place? This was my great reason for declaring the message of the prophets. It was not a message of judgment written on the blackboard of destruction with the chalk of fire and brimstone. It was a message of hope, a message of assurance. It was the dawn of day, a day when the sun of man's hopes would not sink into the western skies of endless wars or a silent cemetery of the dead. It was a light, the only light that could pierce the war clouds of the centuries and promise man a dawn of peace.

On the Threshold

Little did that audience realize on that quiet afternoon in 1939 that we were already on the verge of a war that would violently alter, almost overnight, many of the principles and patterns of life in the free world. There would be the amassing of astronomical debt, the introduction of a rationing system, and a hundred other factors propelling the old world rapidly toward the formation of the new one-world system. The prophets of the Bible, too, not only predicted a one-world system in our day, they also described the forces that would influence its establishment; and one of the forces bringing it to pass would be the horrors of war.

Nation Against Nation

The voice of King George VI trembled with emotion when on September 3, 1939, he announced the declaration of war. A strange sensation swept over me when I heard the king say: "This war cannot be compared to any conflict in past history when army met army on the battlefield. For the first time in man's history, it is a war of nation against nation, and kingdom against kingdom."

Reaching for the Bible on my desk, I opened quickly to the passage where Christ described the events at the end of the age:

> "And ye shall hear of wars and rumours of wars: see that ye be not troubled: for all these things must come to pass, but the end is not yet. For nation shall rise against nation, and kingdom against kingdom" (Matthew 24:6-7).

CHAPTER 5

A WHOLE WORLD AT WAR

I rose from my chair by the fireplace to throw another log on the fire, and I said to myself, "How little do my sons, sleeping peacefully in the rooms above, know of the horrors of World War II." Over half the generation now living was not alive when World War II came to its close. Few, indeed, care to glance at the calendar of yesterday, with its vivid reminder of the awful expanse of World War II.

September 1, 1939—Hitler invaded Poland

September 3, 1939—Britain, Australia, New Zealand, France declared war on Germany

September 6, 1939—South Africa declared war on Germany

September 10, 1939—Canada declared war on Germany

April 9, 1940—Germany invaded Norway and Denmark

May 10, 1940—Germany invaded the Netherlands, Belgium, and Luxembourg

June 10, 1940—Italy declared war on France and Britain

June 11, 1940—France and Britain declared war on Italy

June 22, 1941—Germany and Romania invaded Russia

December 7, 1941—Britain declared war on Finland, Hungary, and Romania

December 7, 1941—Japan declared war on the United States, Great Britain, Australia, New Zealand, Canada, and South Africa

December 8, 1941—United States, France, and Great Britain declared war on Japan

December 11, 1941—Italy and Germany declared war against the United States

December 11, 1941—the United States declared war against Italy and Germany

December 13, 1941—Britain declared war on the Netherlands

June 5, 1942—United States declared war against Bulgaria, Hungary, and Romania

December 25, 1942—Britain declared war on Thailand

October 13, 1943—Italy declared war against Germany

July 14, 1945—Italy declared war on Japan

August 8, 1945—Russia declared war on Japan

The World's Greatest Armada

On June 6, 1944, my friend Colonel Al Garr crossed the English Channel on D-day morning. Ernest Hemingway was at his side in the assault craft. Garr, a chief ordinance officer with the First Army, described the amazing sight:

- 1,000 planes and gliders
- 2,400 U.S. and British bombers
- 5,049 fighter planes
- 3,467 heavy bombers
- 1,645 light and medium bombers
- 2,316 transport aircraft
- 2,591 gliders 4,000 ships
- 2,876,439 troops

For 60 miles, the coast of France was wet with blood of men dying on the beachheads.

Fulfilled Prophecy

In the opening hours of World War II, the king had said, "Unlike wars of the past when army met army, this, for the first time in man's history, is nation against nation and kingdom against kingdom."

The death toll of World War II bore ghastly evidence that his statement was true. In wars of the past, it was soldiers who died in greatest number, but in this war it was the civilians.

- 16,933,000 soldiers died in combat
- 34,305,000 civilians perished

Parents and children, infants and aged perished in numbers totaling twice the toll of the battlefield. While the dead paid with their lives, the living must pay with their dollars. The astronomic cost of war—both during and after—forced fathers and mothers to literally mortgage their children's future for decades.

Counting the Cost

Twenty-five years previously, the European nations had fought the First World War. In order to complete that conflict, a score of nations had come to America for economic aid.

Now, at the close of World War II, the nations once again turned to America for assistance. Were they denied? No!

America to the Rescue

On June 5, 1947, George Marshall, Secretary of State, spoke at Harvard University, outlining a plan to rebuild Europe, Congress accepted the plan and authorized $12 billion for Europe, but this was only the beginning. Eleven billion had already been given to Russia under "lend-lease."

Soon it seemed that almost every nation on earth was standing on the doorstep of Washington. None seemed to apologize for their appeals for loans or outright gifts.

Friend and foe alike went away with his requests granted, whether he was worthy or unworthy. By 1962, America had given away over $80 billion. But the giving did not end. Soon it was 100 billion, and then 200 billion.

Too Many Creditors

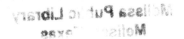

Deeper and deeper America sank into debt. Prior to World War I, we prospered like no other nation on earth. Our national debt was only two million dollars. Now it was so great that it would take a path of dollar bills reaching to the moon seventy times to pay it. The interest alone on the national debt was costing the American public $500 per second. [As of February 2009, our National Debt was nearly eleven trillion dollars.) Cries of "Unfair!" were increasing in volume and number from those who understood the unbelievable truth of America's bankruptcy.

By signing seven treaties, America was pledged to assist 43 countries of the world whose populations represented almost *1/3* of the world's total population.

In less than a quarter of a century following World War II, America had scattered over the world enough wealth to equal the total worth of fifty of the nation's leading cities.

$341 Billion

World War II was the most expensive war in history. It cost the United States $250 million for each day of war.

The war was declared on December 7, 1941, and continued until the Japanese surrendered on September 2, 1945. The war lasted 1,364 days. No average mind could comprehend the total cost of the war. Multiplying $250 million by 1,364 days, we see that the American people spent $341 billion as their part alone in World War II. If one sought to pay that figure at the rate of $1,000 per day, it would take almost 1,000,000 years of payments. [As of February 2009, the Iraqi war had cost nearly $600 billion.]

World War II brought suddenly and violently into the world an increased money supply, increased debts, and expanded rationing, which paved the way for the new number system. But still the cost of war was not ended. It would go on.

War Costs Continued

Peace did not end the arms race. Great nations, small nations, rich and poor, all seemed to be caught up in a mad frenzy of military spending. A spokesman in the United Nations who had studied the spiraling costs of military investments over the last decade predicted that the day was not far distant when the world would be spending $10 billion every 24 hours, if the present rate of increase continued unchecked. And strange as it seems, even with all of the attempts of peace talks and arms limitations, military investments still continue to increase.

In a day when men become calloused to crises, and insulated against emergencies, they fail to ponder the momentous affairs in which they are caught up and carried forward to the point of no return. The daily war costs of our world have reached such astronomical proportions, few indeed are capable of comprehending it. Only by illustration could one grasp in even a small measure the magnitude of man's financial problems. If a man dropped into his cash register a silver dollar every second, for a period of approximately 172 years, the total would equal the world's military expenditures for only *one* day. If 1/3 of all the poor people of the world gave their total paychecks, the amount would be insufficient to pay the yearly costs of war.

In 1867, Russia sold Alaska to the United States for $7.2 million. Thirteen years later, the Alaskan gold rush broke out, and men came from around the globe to dig gold from Alaskan soil and wash it from her rivers. After 41 years of the Alaska Gold Rush, the total yield of the precious metal was $320 million.

In 1851, gold was discovered in Australia, the continent down under. Between 1851 and 1861, Australia produced only half a billion dollars in gold, enough to finance the modern world's military might for only one single day!

The Meaning of Money

With a hostile world daily building bigger armies, and demanding more costly weapons, how did man manufacture money in such astronomical amounts to fly the armadas of the air, and sail his ships and submarines of war? To build his bombs, and feed and clothe his armies? If he was doing this on credit, to whom was he indebted, and where and when would it all end?

To my amazement, almost no one paused to consider or ponder the meaning of money. To me, it was not a materialistic message. Money was a man's life. He earned it by the brilliance of his brain, or the sweat of his brow. Money built roads to develop lands, schools to educate children, hospitals to care for the sick. Money was bread for the children, and security for the aged. In the spiritual realm, money built churches, and gave the message of Christ to the nations of the world.

Some reflected the attitude that money was some sacred shrine which must be approached with fear and trembling, a power from a plane beyond the understanding of modern man, a system he must never question. Others took the attitude that money was a system too complicated to be understood. Early in life, I was persuaded that money was neither mystical nor mysterious. History revealed the origin of money and its progressive use to the present hour. The prophets of the Bible foretold the ultimate end of the money system, with unmistakable detail and clarity. To understand the history of the past, and the prophecy of the future, was to have complete comprehension and understanding of the present. It was not confusing. It could be understood and explained in a layman's language.

The Power of Money

In January, 1972, I stopped on the street in Brussels and picked up a copy of the *International Herald Tribune.* In it was a quarter-page ad which had been placed by the committee promoting George McGovern for President of the United States. The caption of the ad read:

GIVE TO THE MCGOVERN-FOR-PRESIDENT CAMPAIGN BECAUSE YOU KNOW MONEY ELECTS THE PRESIDENT.

Regardless of my attitude toward the candidates, I had to agree that this statement was correct. The power of money was fantastic. It had removed kings and set up kings through the centuries. It had played a part in war and peace. It could set men free, or bind them as slaves. The Bible had much to say on the theme of money. It was a drama without end. The characters who controlled money were among the most colorful on the stage of the world.

Spectacular headlines of the world's news media that shocked and startled certain people with the announcements of the coming New World Money System were no surprise to those who had watched the progressive development through the years toward a new system. In one sense, the action internationally was like a giant chess game. Much had happened even in my own lifetime. Indeed, the international manipulation of money does resemble a chess game with its kings and queens, its bishops, knights, and pawns. Early in my life, it seemed that the board was full of players, but each passing year saw the removal of the smaller men, one by one.

To me, it was exciting to watch the international moves. As the players on the board of the world became fewer, like an eager spectator, I found myself anticipating the next move in advance of its occurrence. Contemporary students of the New World Money System sometimes seem prone to place the reason for the coming system on a single factor or two. In some respects, this was an oversimplification, but I had to admit that war certainly played a major part in moving the world toward a central government and a one-world money system.

CHAPTER 6

HOW WILL THE DOLLAR DIE?

If we have come to the final days of the dollar era, it is natural to ask how money began and how it will end.

What Is Money?

Man might simply define money by saying it is, a standard of value for goods received and service rendered. Money was anything that people would accept in exchange for goods or services, in belief that they may in turn exchange it later for other goods or services.

Origin of Money

Everyone at some time or other hears interesting expressions related to money, such as "shell out" or "he paid his fee" or "not worth his salt," etc. The words "shell out" date back to the time when men used shells for money. The little cowrie or ornamental shell spread as money from China and India eastward to the islands of the Pacific Ocean and became a medium of exchange in many parts of Africa and even the Americas. Cowrie money still circulates today among the Dahomeans of the west coast of Africa. The only form of this money that ever gained international usage was this delicate pea-to-walnut size seashell that was carried around the world by the sailing traders of yesterday. In some countries, even after metal coins were introduced, the already existing cowrie shells were preferred. They were cleaner, more pleasant to handle, and impossible to counterfeit.

The expression, "paying a fee," had its origin in Germany. There the word for cattle is *Vieh,* pronounced "fee." Long ago, if a farmer wished to pay his debt to his local doctor or landlord, he would take him one of his cattle.

On occasion, we hear that someone "was not worth his salt." In India in the ninth century, salt was so scarce, it became more precious than the fabled Indian sapphires. Before the days of refrigeration, salt was used as a preserver of foodstuffs. It was placed in quills and bamboo tubes of varying lengths and sizes. About the first century A.D., salt was scarce in the Roman Empire. Mankind had not yet found a way to extract it in sufficiently large quantities from the earth or from the sea. The Roman soldiers of that time were often paid a *salarium* or "salt money." From the Latin *salarium* we receive our modern word "salary."

The Shilling

The Anglo-Saxons who invaded Britain in the sixth century came from Norway, Sweden, Denmark, and northern Germany. From 517 on through the sixth century, they moved across England from the Bristol Channel to the Irish Sea. These invaders wore metal rings and ornaments known as *schellingas.* They traded these ornaments for bread and the other necessities of life, and gradually these pieces of metal became a recognized medium of exchange. With the passing of time, the *schellingas* became the shilling of England.

The Dollar

The origin of the dollar was equally interesting. The first dollar was coined by the counts of Schlik in 1519. It was called the "Joachimsthaler," after Joachimsthal, the place in Bohemia where the silver was mined and the mint was located. The name was too long, and eventually it became shortened to "thaler." Its name changed phonetically according to the language of the country in which it was circulated. When the German Reich officially authorized the coin, it was called the "Reichsthaler." In Scandinavia, it became known as the "rigsdaler," in Holland it was the "rijksdaalder," and in Poland it was simply the "taler." Later in the eighteenth century, it became known in America as the dollar.

Money in America

When the early settlers came to America, they brought with them quite a variety of currencies from the continent. Naturally this paper money was only as good as the integrity of those who issued it. The value of that money might rise or fall in proportion to the financial strength of the institution in back of the paper currency. In olden days, communication lines were long and often interrupted. Sometimes colonists found themselves possessing paper currencies of supposed value, only to learn later that they were virtually worthless. In an effort to avoid this problem, pioneers petitioned the British government for the privilege of creating their own currency. It was denied by George III of England. Benjamin Franklin said, "We would gladly have borne the tax on tea if we could have been granted the power to create our own money."

When the American colonists were short of money, they used almost anything as a medium of exchange. They traded with corn and codfish and coonskins. They exchanged whiskey and musket-balls, tobacco and cattle. It was all legal tender.

America's Tobacco Money

With the winning of the War of Independence, the colonists were free to create their own money. Naturally, there was not enough gold in their reserves to represent sufficient backing for their paper currency. So, in states like Virginia, Maryland, and North Carolina, tobacco was adopted as a money standard and became a legal tender.

When plantation owners harvested their tobacco crops and placed them in the warehouses awaiting sale, the warehouse operators issued to the owners paper receipts for the tobacco. These receipts became transferable and were circulated from one hand to another and even from state to state. The tobacco receipts, indeed, became legal tender, and in a very true sense, a form of money.

But when the price of tobacco rose and fell, the value of the paper rose and fell accordingly. When men held paper for any length of time, they might find the value of their tobacco receipts greatly altered from the time when they were first issued.

Gold

The most intriguing and by far the most universal substance used as money through the centuries is gold. In spite of the fact that gold does not pay interest to those who hoard it or possess it, a recent poll revealed that most of the people of the world still crave gold. It is beautiful to the eye. It does not rust or tarnish. In the hands of the craftsman, it is pliable. An ounce of gold will make a wire 50 miles long or may be pounded out in a film so thin it can cover 100 square feet. The ancient Egyptians knew how to hammer gold into leaves so thin that 367,000 made a pile only one inch high.

No one knows when gold was first discovered by man. At the site of Ur in Mesopotamia (now

Iraq) archaeologists have discovered gold vessels made as early as 3500B.C.

The Gold Standard

In 1870, America's banks went on the gold standard. This meant that any American could come to the bank with his paper money and exchange it for gold. In 1933, however, this was changed. In the aftermath of the crash of 1929 and the depression that followed, the morale of the nation was such that it was willing to accept any revisions or suggestions which might point to a way out of their misery. Mr. Roosevelt asked the government to pass legislation demanding that the American people give up their gold. This they did, receiving in exchange paper money showing they had received $20.67 an ounce for their precious metal. Immediately, however, the government raised the price of gold to $35.00 an ounce, realizing a $3 billion profit. When asked his opinion on this particular action, Senator Carter Glass replied to President Roosevelt on April 27, 1933, "I think it is worse than anything Ali Baba's forty thieves ever perpetrated."

Elusive Gold

Thirty miles south of Louisville, Kentucky, out on the open prairie, Uncle Sam sought to prepare a storehouse for his golden billions. An army of government men blasted a mighty hole in the ground.

A wall of mirrors was constructed to reflect every shadow of anything that would pass by—an airplane in the sky or a mouse crawling on the ground. Fifteen hundred soldiers stood at attention nearby, guarding night and day the steel vault containing America's gold.

But in spite of the physical guard placed on the gold at Fort Knox, America's gold steadily drained away. If the gold could speak, it might impart quite a story of the miles it had traveled from country to country and from one hand to another. At the height of her power, Britain took much of the gold from the Spanish. The Spanish took it from the colonies that they invaded. At the close of World War I, when the leaders of the Western world met in the beautiful Hall of Mirrors to sign the Treaty of Versailles, Germany was compelled to deliver up all the gold she possessed in the Reich Bank of the nation. It would not be long, however, before much of America's gold would move back again to Germany and to western Europe.

In 1934, when legislation was passed prohibiting the American public from owning gold currency, the door was left wide open to the foreign holders of American dollars to claim gold in exchange for their paper. But even before this international stage was set, Representative Louis T. McFadden (Republican-PA.), Chairman of the Committee on Banking and Currency, made statements on June 10 of 1932 which indicated America's gold was already moving back to Europe. His statements were recorded in the *Congres-*

sional Record and pages 140-174 in H.S. Kenan's book entitled *The Federal Reserve Bank.* Representative McFadden speaks of those on the other side of the water with a strong banking "fence getting the currency of the Federal Reserve Banks—exchanging that currency for gold and transmitting the gold to the foreign confederates." McFadden named the dates on which America's gold was shipped to Germany: "On April 27, 1932, $750 thousand in gold was sent to Germany. One week later another $300 thousand in gold was shipped to Germany the same way. In the middle of May of that year, $12 million in gold was shipped to Germany.... Almost every week there was a shipment of gold to Germany—these shipments are not made for profit."

Representative McFadden referred also to the comments of Senator Elihu Root:

> "Long before we wake up from our dreams of prosperity through an inflated currency, our gold which could have kept us from catastrophe will have vanished, and no rate of interest will tempt it to return."

In his report to Congress, Louis McFadden asked the question, "Why should our depositors and our government be forced to finance the munition factories of Germany and Soviet Russia?"

Representative McFadden continued:

> "Gold was taken from the entrusting American people and was sent to Europe. In the last several months $1,300,000,000 in gold has been sent to

> Europe—every dollar of that gold once belonged to the people of United States and was unlawfully taken from them."

As I weighed the words of Louis McFadden and other lawmakers, I also witnessed the fantastic scene of America's vanishing gold. The record was unbelievable:

- 1949—$24,500,000,000
- 1958—$21,593,000,000
- 1959—$20,478,483,000
- 1960—$19,420,997,000
- 1961—$17,667,587,000
- 1962—$15,997,647,000
- 1965—$13,733,000,000

On and on the gold drain went, unabated. Then came the crisis in the spring of 1968. We were living in Europe at that particular time. On March 14, hysterical crowds of people crowded, screamed, and scrambled their ways to the windows of the banks of England, and to the bank windows of the sub-basements of Paris to exchange their paper for gold. On one single day, the crude and the cultured, the peer and the peasant, carried off 200 tons of the precious metal. They stored it in secret places of their homes and deposited it in various banks in strongboxes labeled with fictitious names.

On that day Senator Everett Dirksen in conversation with Secretary of the Treasury Fowler, William McChesney Martin, and a dozen other senators said, "We have reached the bottom of the barrel."

It seemed like only yesterday when I spoke on monetary matters when America had $26 billion in gold in her treasuries. By June 30 of 1971, it had been reduced to $10.5 billion. [As of July 2008, the United States held approximately $241 billion in gold.]

Inflation

Why did the people of Europe and Britain crowd hysterically into their banks on March 14, 1968, to exchange $240 million in paper for 200 tons of gold? They could not eat their gold for food. They could not wear it for clothes. It was too heavy to carry on the streets as a legal tender or medium of exchange. Why did they prefer to have the precious metal in place of their paper money?

The answer was extremely clear. They were afraid that their paper would be canceled with the stroke of a legislative pen. It would be as worthless as the German marks of 1923 when it took a wheelbarrow load to buy a simple sandwich or hot dog. The average man knew his paper money was becoming of less and less value. Americans could recall 1937 when $30 a month would put food on the table for a family of four. By 1947, the same food would cost $43. By 1957, it would cost $72. Then $100, and inflation continued unchecked.

The British, too, looked at their paper with its diminishing value. The record was indeed far from encouraging. The monetary facts offered little hope for the survival of their paper. In 1930, the official value of the pound was $4.86. In 1952, $2.82; in 1967, $2.40.

In May of 1973 on the streets of Tokyo, I stared with incredulity at the spectre of inflation in Japan. Ground beef that was selling in October for $1.40 per pound was now $2.87; orange juice was over $3.00 per glass; steak, $16.00 per pound. In less than a year the price of real estate had doubled, and wool had tripled. Hashimoto, Secretary General of the ruling Liberal Democratic Party tried in vain to reason with the financial giants of his country. He concluded that those in a position to affect the inflation were too strong and beyond control.

The problem of inflation was worldwide. Since World War II, the currencies of over 100 nations had been devalued, some many times. I recalled a 1959 address by Robert Anderson, Secretary of the Treasury. He bluntly spelled out the technique of inflation:

Suppose tomorrow morning I want to write a check for $100 million, and the treasury does not have the money. I call the Federal Reserve Bank and ask, "Will you loan us $100 million at 3 1/2% for six months if I send you over our note to that effect?" The officer of the Federal Reserve Bank would naturally say, "I will." He would merely create that much money subject to Reserve requirements by crediting our account in the sum and accepting the government note as an asset. When I finished writing checks for $100 million, we would have added 100 million to the nation's money supply. This, he added, is one of the principles by which the 1940 dollar has shrunken to $.41 with a quadrupling of our money supply.

Nations continuing programs of war and welfare and other costly programs, were forced to continue borrowing money. America increased her federal budget 84% in a five-year period. By going deeper in debt, she also increased her money supply 47%. Consequently, the buying power of the dollar continued to fall ever lower. In certain countries of the world, it was overwhelming. In Argentina, inflation increased 289% in a five-year period. In Brazil, over 500%. In Java, 1,000%. As the cry of inflation was heard around the world and received with genuine alarm, governmental leaders strove in vain to curb this economic disease that would spell death to all systems eventually.

Ludvig Erhard, Germany's Minister of Finance at the close of World War II, had said, "Give us depression or problems, but not inflation, for it spells eventually certain death to any economy."

Erhard knew that inflation, allowed to continue, was like sending a pilot across the ocean with a plane in which was insufficient fuel. There came unavoidably a point of no return when the pilot found he had insufficient fuel to take him to either shore.

Too Much or Not Enough

In spite of the fact that the U.S. government had increased its money supply 47% in a five-year period, and other nations were doing the same thing, still there were those who cried it was not enough. Between 1954 and 1965, world trade had doubled. I sat with a thousand delegates in the International Board of Trade in the Waldorf Astoria Hotel of New York listening to the speakers struggle with their unsolved problems. World trade had reached the staggering figure of $159.2 billion. The currencies and credits with which they had to carry on this volume of trade was little more than $67.3 billion. By 1973, the volume of trade in the free world was $367 billion. I talked with Mitchell Sharpe, then Minister of Finance for Canada, and some of the American leaders. These men realized that the currencies being used were outmoded and insufficient for the modern day. They pointed out that the system was medieval, serving acceptably in the olden days when communities were small and self-contained, but thoroughly inadequate for the present. The leaders of the nations involved in trade spoke of the nightmarish task of trying daily to adjust the varying exchange rates between the currencies from country to country on a day-to-day basis. They clamored for a single system of standardized value large enough in volume to allow world trade to move forward in an orderly fashion.

In 1967, two years following that International Board of Trade meeting in New York, the world leaders met in Rio. In discussing the inadequacy of the present world money systems to carry on world trade, Guido Carli from Rome suggested ersatz money which would resemble paper gold that was to be presented to the world the following year. I was back in America when the announcement came. It was March 31, 1968. Most of the world reacted with amazement at the announcement that came from Europe stating that the nations of the world were ready to transact business with a new medium of exchange known as "paper gold." But to all who follow the trend of monetary matters, the announcement was no surprise. For days there was a feeling in the air that something momentous was coming. An editor wrote in the *Financial Times,* "Something sinister is going on."

With great interest, I followed the comments and reactions of world leaders.

Carl Schiller, Germany's financier, stated, "There's a worm in the apple somewhere."

Pierre Paul Schweitzer seemed pleased. Schweitzer, the nephew of Albert Schweitzer, was an elite Protestant, born in Alsace-Lorraine, who had served as number-three man in the Bank of France, and had been elected managing director of the International Monetary Fund. Some declared that when paper gold was presented to the world on that March morning, Schweitzer declared, "Gentlemen, we are right on schedule."

Seventy-two percent of the nations in the IMF were considered underdeveloped. Schweitzer seemed especially dedicated to the task or policy of taking from the rich to give to the poor. This naturally made him popular with the majority in the IMF, who were elated at the prospect of acquiring some of America's wealth regardless of the measures.

Why the Announcement From Europe?

Many Americans, startled by the announcement of paper gold, were asking, "Why has this declaration come to us from the bankers of Europe? Why did we have to hear it first from the lips of the spokesmen representing the gold pool so integrated with the World Bank and the International Monetary Fund?"

The attitude of the average man on the street was one of absolute helplessness. In olden days, banking had been a rather personal matter between himself and a trusted friend. It had changed with the passing of time until it was with an institution equally trusted and respected. The local banker was indeed his friend and would discuss with sincerity the personal financial needs of any of his clients. But banking had become much more than a localized or even nationalized institution. In a single lifetime it had seemingly taken on an ominous new form of world control.

A question began to arise in the hearts of millions of Americans. "Why can't we retain our financial destiny in our own hands? Why can't banking be a personal matter between man and his banker as in the past? Why must it be in the international courts and the arenas of the world?"

In searching for the answers to those questions, I seemed to find a twofold answer. Logic and wisdom could explain with clarity the reasons for a world bank. But there was a dark side, which, when properly considered, revealed an invisible government with an amazing power that planned world control in a sinister fashion.

CHAPTER 7

BANKS AND BANKERS—YESTERDAY AND TODAY

The Origin of Banking

Banking may have been born in Babylon 3,000 years ago. The first banking transactions may well have been carried on by two men. A possessor of gold might find it undesirable to carry the heavy metal with him on a journey. If unable to carry his treasure conveniently, he found it most desirable to leave it in the custody of a trusted friend. The custodian of the gold would stamp his signet on a piece of parchment or leather which represented a receipt for the precious metal. At a later date, anyone presenting this receipt to the guardian of the gold could retrieve the treasure. This system in the beginning was as simple as the present-day policy of leaving one's car on the parking lot and retrieving it by presenting the ticket to the parking lot attendant.

As the system grew more popular, qualified personalities found themselves guarding the gold for numerous men who trusted them with their treasures.

Fractional Money Lending

With the passing of time, these owners of gold traded their receipts between each other in business transactions. But seldom did they come to collect in bags the heavy metal which was impractical to carry from place to place. After much experience, the guardians of gold were able to ascertain the percentage of gold that would actually be collected by the owners under normal circumstances. Although the precious metal did not belong to them (it was still the property of those who had entrusted it to their care), these guardians of gold began to lend the precious metal to others who were willing to pay a percentage, called "usury," for the use of it. It was not long until these guardians of gold became known as "lenders" as well as guardians. And because they would lend as much as 80% of the gold they were guarding, they became known as "fractional moneylenders." Like most programs developed by man, the system could prove to be of great worth and benefit if properly used, but it could also be a monster of evil if abused.

Banks in America

Our founding fathers and early colonists faced an impossible situation in monetary matters.

As banks sprang up in the New World and issued their own paper money, they operated under state laws and licenses granted them by their local state government. Confusion began to reign as people moved from state to state carrying various forms of paper of diverse value.

The National Bank Act

In 1863, Abraham Lincoln influenced the passing of the National Bank Act. This provided for a system of private banks that would receive their charters only from the government and operate on a given standard of values and regulations.

The Federal Reserve Bank

On December 23, 1913, Woodrow Wilson influenced legislation that established the Federal Reserve Bank or the Federal Reserve System. With the establishment of the Federal Reserve System, the United States government forfeited the right to create its own money. The government retained the power only of issuing government bonds upon which the taxpayers paid interest to the Federal Reserve System which alone had the power to issue the currency known as Federal Reserve Notes. The attitude of government men toward the Federal Reserve System was interesting, to say the least. Some lauded its virtues, and others deplored its dangers. Some referred to the Federal Reserve System as "the banks' bank" and declared it was necessary to safeguard the local bankers in times of crisis.

Financial Crisis, June 19-23, 1970

On June 19, 1970, the American people escaped a national economic crisis by a mere hairline. The sixth largest enterprise in the United States, the largest railroad of the country, the Pennsylvania Central, went bankrupt. The bankers were confident that the government would bail them out. They gathered in the northwest conference room of the tenth floor of the Federal Reserve Bank of New York to sign the papers as soon as the word came from Washington.

But Congressional disapproval had been hardening. Wright Patman, chairman of the House Banking Committee, refused to grant the $200 million loan, declaring it would be "only the beginning of a welfare program for the giant corporation." What could be done? The Federal Reserve System had been criticized for cutting off money too abruptly in 1966 and of increasing it too fast in 1967 and early 1968.

If stockholders across the nation became concerned that their stocks in this or any other company were to lose their value, they could commence a run on banks in seeking to cash in their stocks that would deplete the reserves of the banks of America and throw the entire nation into chaos. Needless to say, tension was high, and furious action was taken to stave off a national panic that could have created havoc in those days between June 19 and 23.

Bankers of the nation lined up for loans of $1.7 billion, hoping to be able to meet the demands for money that would be brought to them by fearful stockholders wishing to exchange their paper stock for money.

Too few Americans realize that the banks of the nation operate much the same as the "Fractional Money Lenders" of the past. If a large number of people were to desire their money from the bank at one time, the banks would have only a fraction of the amount needed. A national scare like the collapse of the Pennsylvania Central Railroad could have started such a situation. This is why private banks strove to borrow extra money from the Federal Reserve in the face of such an impending crisis.

The World Bank

In 1944 a World Bank was born, an infant that soon grew into a mighty giant. The national problems that had brought into existence a National Banking Act and the Federal Reserve System were identical in many respects to the problems that brought about the establishment of the World Bank. In the early pioneer days, men could do business with a local bank because few traveled far from home and seldom crossed the borders of another state. Even by the turn of the century, few men had traveled more than three hundred miles.

Overnight, the entire scene changed. With the age of automation, world travel became common.

Men traveled across the oceans seemingly as easily as they walked across the street. In a single year, 108 million Americans took 360 million trips totaling 312 billion miles.

International Monetary Fund

In Europe, I watched the frustrations of people moving from one country to another carrying in their pockets a variety of currencies, each with a different value and a changing exchange rate from day to day. From the Bon Marché of Brussels to the American Express Office of Frankfurt or the Hilton Hotel of Rome, I have heard angry voices at the cashier's window declaring their currency to be worth more than the exchange rate they were being quoted.

If the inconveniences and the frustrations of the individual were obvious, the merchants of the world were a thousand times more agitated. They dealt in multi-million-dollar transactions. If they bought or sold on a given day when the exchange rate was at one figure, only to find days or hours later the exchange rate had varied, they might face either exorbitant profit or total bankruptcy.

They cried for an International Monetary Fund that would guarantee stabilization and protect them against the daily fluctuations on a violent scale. Just as the local pioneers wanted their local banks to be governed by a national banking act, now various nations of the world were asking for some form of international control. They turned their eyes to the United Nations and to the agency that had been established within the UN, an agency called the International Monetary Fund.

The International Monetary Fund was established in 1944 at the Bretton Woods Conference in the United States. At the outset, it was viewed with suspicion by some of the countries reluctant to forego their national sovereignty. At first the membership was only 27 nations, then it grew to 45, finally to 100, and on to 124. Certain rules were laid down and nations were expected to follow them.

The Fund, for example, refused to lend to countries that would alter their exchange rates by more than 10% without the approval of the International Monetary Fund. With the formation of the IMF, other names began to appear prominently in the world arena, names such as the World Bank, the G-10 (standing for Great Ten), and the Gold Pool. It was a spokesman from the latter, on March 31, 1968, who introduced "paper gold."

"Paper gold"—the name was indeed intriguing, but it was a misnomer. It was neither paper nor gold but only a number placed by the name of the nation. The amount of that number was called a "drawing right" and was abbreviated with three initials "SDR" standing for "Special Drawing Right." With the announcement of paper gold, and the proposal that some $10.5 billion of it be issued in the first sixty-month period, the spokesman for the world body emphasized it was only for international use. Behind the closed doors of the conference room, however, other world leaders reputedly said it would be the system in the near future for every individual on earth.

Only twelve months and seventeen days prior to the announcement of paper gold, I was flying into Denver, Colorado. I was scarcely conscious of the plane touching the runway, for I found myself engrossed in an article in the February 14, 1967, issue of the *U.S. News & World Report.* The article was written by George Mitchell of the Federal Reserve System. It pictured a telephone in every home attached to a computer that carried the owner's name or number. The phone was not installed for social or business reasons. It was merely a connecting line to the computer or the data center that carried the homeowner's number and his drawing right. When a personal need arose for himself or for his family, the owner would pick up the phone and learn from the computer at the other end what he could or could not have. This was called his special drawing right. So the system introduced on March 31, 1968, would indeed expand until it became universal and all-inclusive. As I pondered the fearful possibility of the financial control of men and nations in the hands of an international committee, I found myself remembering again the words of Meyer Amschel Rothschild: "Give me control over a nation's economy and I care not who writes its laws."

And the words of Lord Gladstone:

> "The government ... in the matters of finance must leave the money power supreme and unquestioned."

And the words of Chancellor Reginald McKenna:

> "They who control the credit of a nation direct the policy of the governments and hold in the hollow of their hand the destiny of the people."

In addition, Karl Marx, who said in his *Manifesto:*

> "Money plays the largest part in determining the course of history."

Who Will Control the Money?

Communist or capitalist, banker or president of the nation, all men seemed to agree that those who controlled the finance of a nation represented a power greater than any other legislative body.

I recalled an afternoon in Brussels when I addressed an international group in the Metropole Hotel. Apart from John Bains of the *Brussels-Phoenix Press,* the members of the audience were strangers to me. Most of the men present held high office in various departments and were favorably disposed toward the new system on which I was to speak. I concluded my luncheon address by saying, "Gentlemen, you look with approval upon this coming new order and the new system it will bring. You believe it has the answers to some of the frustrations and unanswered problems of the present moment, but I, in all sincerity, would like to ask you one basic question before leaving you today: who will control it?"

A hush fell over the room. I looked from face to face in search of an answer. On one side sat a four-star general, on the other, an attorney. None offered to speak.

"Perhaps," I said, "you feel that none of us has the answer to this question: Who will hold in his hand your future in this new international government with its new world money system? But there is an answer. It is spelled out clearly by a man who lived 2,000 years ago and described these very days."

Opening my Bible, I read once again the familiar words of John, the prophet, who wrote concerning a world government and its leader who would hold power over all kindreds, and tongues, and nations:

> "...and causeth all, both small and great, rich and poor, free and bond, to receive a mark in their right hand, or in their foreheads: And that no man might buy or sell, save he that had that mark ... or the number" (Revelation 13:7, 16-17)

The Invisible Government

On March 22, 1922, John F. Hylan, Mayor of New York City, made the following statement: "The real menace of our republic is the invisible government which, like a giant octopus, sprawls its slimy length over our city, state, and nation. At the head is a small group of banking houses, generally referred to as 'international bankers.'"

To what extent did international bankers exercise ownership or control over America's Federal Reserve System?

The public in general assumed that the stock in the Federal Reserve System was owned by America's private banks, but apparently this was not voting stock. For years I observed those who were genuinely concerned over this very grave question. The men concerned were often the most astute businessmen and lawmakers of our land, some as prominent as Wright Patman, Chairman of Banking and Currency. In 1941, Congressman Patman wrote concerning this question to Marriner S. Eccles, Chairman of the Board of Governors for the Federal Reserve Bank. On April 18th of that same year Congressman Patman received a reply from Eccles which read, "This so-called stock ownership, however, is more in the nature of enforced subscription to the capital of the Federal Reserve Bank than an ownership in the usual sense."

More than a quarter of a century later, Mr. Patman was still trying to get an answer from the chairman of the Board of Governors of the Federal Reserve, then William McChesney Martin: "The stock, or that word 'stock' is a misnomer, is it not?"

Mr. Martin's answer: "If you were talking about stock in terms of proprietorship ownership—yes."

Mr. Patman continued, "Then the word 'stock' is a misnomer. It is not correct at all. It is just an involuntary assessment that has been made on the banks as long as they are members. Therefore, the statement that the banks own the Federal Reserve System is not a correct statement, is it?"

Mr. Martin: "The banks do not own the Federal Reserve System."

As I pondered the words of Wright Patman and the statements of many other prominent lawmakers on Capitol Hill through the years, it seemed that a great number of prominent senators and congressmen had expressed their concern that the financial power of America was held not in the hands of its local bankers or its lawmakers, but rather in the hands of a few international bankers who exercise their control over not only America but also western Europe.

Is there, in truth, a small group of international bankers controlling the world's financial destiny, even as Mayor Hylan of New York declared?

Paul Warburg

Who *was* responsible for the formation of the Federal Reserve? None other than the scion of Hamburg's famed banking House of Warburg—Paul Warburg. Regarding Mr. Warburg, Professor E.R.A. Seligman, himself of the international banking family and head of the Department of Economics at Columbia University, said, "The Federal Reserve Act is the work of Mr. Warburg more than of any other man."

The Honorable Louis McFadden, Chairman of Banking and Currency Committee, seemed to reach the same conclusion. On March 4, 1933, he said to Congress:

> "We know from assertions made here by the Honorable John Garner, Vice-President of United States, Paul Warburg did come here from Hamburg, Germany, for one purpose—to take over the treasury of the United States as the international bankers have done with the treasuries of Europe."

Regarding the so-called group of international bankers, Mr. McFadden said further on June 10, 1932, "It controls everything here, and it controls all our foreign relations. It makes and breaks governments at will."

Paul Warburg had a son named James P. Warburg. On February 17, 1950, he stood before the U.S. Senate and declared, "We shall have world government whether or not we like it. The only question is, whether world government will be achieved by conquest or consent."

The House of Rothschild

Meyer Amschel Rothschild (1743-1812) of Frankfurt, Germany, studied originally to be a rabbi. Later, however, he turned his interests to finance and, with his five sons, established the famous banking house in Frankfurt. Four of the sons were later sent to Vienna, London, Paris, and Naples to set up branches of their family bank. This combine soon became the most powerful banking establishment of Europe.

Amschel Rothschild, the eldest son, remained with his father in Frankfurt and became the treasurer of the German Confederation. Salomon, the second son, founder of the Vienna branch, became a leading personality in the Austro-Hungarian Empire. Nathan, the third son, founder of the London branch, became the most powerful man in English finance. Carl, the fourth son, founder of the Naples branch, became one of the most powerful men in Italy. James (Jacob), the fifth son, founder of the Paris branch, soon dominated the financial destiny of France. By 1850, the House of Rothschild represented more wealth than all the royal families of Europe and Britain combined.

International Bankers

The House of Warburg, the House of Rothschild, the few other powerful banking houses became known as "the international bankers." They are described best by Dr. Carroll Quigley who taught at Princeton and Harvard. He did research in the archives of France, Italy, and England and authored several widely read books. When Dr. Quigley decided to write *Tragedy and Hope* (Macmillan, 1966), he knew he would be exposing one of the best-kept secrets in the world. Regarding the international bankers, Dr. Quigley states:

> "They remained different from ordinary bankers in distinctive ways: (1) they were cosmopolitan and international; (2) they were close to governments and were particularly concerned

with questions of government debts; (3) their interests were almost exclusively in bonds and very rarely in goods; (4) they were, accordingly, fanatical devotees of inflation; (5) they were almost equally devoted to secrecy and the secret use of financial influence in political life. These bankers came to be called the international bankers."

In quoting Dr. Quigley, W. Cleon Skousen comments on page 4 of his book entitled *The Naked Capitalist:*

"Dr. Quigley makes it clear throughout his book that, by and large, he warmly supports the goals and the purposes of the network. If that be the case, why should he want to expose a worldwide conspiracy and disclose many of its most secret operations? Obviously disclosing the existence of a mammoth power network that is trying to take over the world could not help but arouse the vigorous resistance of the people who are its intended victims, so why did Dr. Quigley write this book?"

Quigley's answer appears in a number of places, but it is especially forceful and clear on pages 979-980. He says, in effect, that now it is too late for the little people to turn back the tide. In a spirit of kindness, he is therefore urging them not to fight a power that is already established. All through his book, Dr. Quigley assures us that we can trust these benevolent well-meaning men who are secretly operating behind the scenes. They, he declares, are the hope of the world. All who resist them represent tragedy, hence the title of his book. Dr. Quigley states:

> "I know of the operations of this network because I have studied it for twenty years, and was permitted for two years in the early 1960's to examine its papers and its secret records. I have no aversion to it, nor to most of its aims, and have for much of my life been close to it, and to many of its instruments."

According to W. Cleon Skousen, "Dr. Quigley expresses the utmost contempt for members of the American middle class, who think they can preserve what he calls their 'petty bourgeois' property rights and constitutional privileges."

After pondering these writings, I asked myself how far back one could trace this organized plan for control of world finance. On July 4, 1856, Benjamin Disraeli declared before the British House of Commons, "The world is governed by very different personages from what is imagined by those who are not behind the scenes."

Some of the strongest words that came to my attention were those of Curtis B. Dall, written in Philadelphia, Pennsylvania, on April 1968, as an introduction to H.S. Kenan's book on the Federal Reserve Bank. In reference to the international bankers, Mr. Dall writes:

> "They are driving toward complete control of the world's long-range monetary policy and principal world markets for their own profit.

> They foment foreign wars to aid this objective."

It did not take a brilliant mathematician long to prove with simple arithmetic that war debts allowed to continue would soon burden the people of the world with such indebtedness that it would take most of the earning power of the masses simply to pay the compounding interest. Was it possible, I asked myself repeatedly, that men could so crave power that they would be willing to sacrifice millions of lives to the god of war in order to achieve their goals?

If it were true, were they so deluded or deceived that they justified the mass slaughter of the innocent as a socalled stepping-stone to a better world they were seeking to build? Regardless of the questions, or their answers, there was one certain fact: the world was swiftly moving toward centralized government and universal control. The General Assembly of the United Nations frequently echoed with accusations and dissension. But there was one power that seemed even stronger than man's endless legislation. It was the power of money. Whoever controlled it, controlled man's destiny. The path toward world control seemed to be indeed a divided highway. On one side, there were the shadowy personalities representing the high priests of finance, who visualized the wealth of the world in few hands—their hands. On the other side of the road, there were a number of men, honest and sincere, who pointed out that the total commitment to a world government was man's only hope of escaping a nuclear holocaust. Or famine from exploding population, or poison from pollution.

Checks Obsolete

Members of the Federal Reserve warned that the nations' banks could strangle on the billions of checks the Americans wrote each year, pointing out that in a hundred months the number of checks would double. They urged the adoption of a computer system which would automatically transfer funds between bank accounts. A person's pay would automatically be credited to his bank account by his employer, without the writing of a check. And the regular payments that the worker owed—car payments, rent, etc.—would automatically be sent to his creditors' accounts when due. George Mitchell of the Federal Reserve declared it was most urgent to reform the checking system before the economy smothered under a pile of paper.

I did not know George Mitchell personally, but I did know many honest and sincere bankers who shared his sentiments. There was Carlos Verheek of the Kredietbank of Belgium, and Banker Keller of Germany.

Mountains of Paper

As I sat with Banker Keller in his Stuttgart office, I heard him heave a weary sigh. "We are being buried under paper," he said sadly. From the doorway of his office I could see the lines of people standing impatiently before the bank tellers.

I knew that back home our government was spending $350,000 a minute. The welfare program alone was costing the taxpayers more than a billion dollars a month. In a four-year period, the federal budget had increased 84% and in five years the money supply 47%.

In America, I had talked with my banker friends. Without exception, every banker realized we were coming to the end of an old regime and the dawn of a new era. Our early ancestors had used shells, iron, cotton, or cattle as a medium of exchange. Then gold. Now, the paper currencies were becoming as antiquated as all of the obsolete systems that man had used. A new system was about to dawn over the western world and it would be a number system, made possible by the birth of the computer in 1946.

CHAPTER 8

THE COMPUTER AGE

What fantastic progress computer technology has made! On February 15, 1971, I pondered the words spoken by Dr. Brainard, as he described the first computer at Penns Morre School of Engineering. It weighed 30 tons, and occupied 1,500 square feet of space. Today, infinitely more complicated computations are done by common garden-variety computers, occupying no more office space than a junior executive. [Today, of course, we have desktop, laptop, and hand-held computers that are vastly smaller.}

Computers that could register one character per second had been made obsolete by those that could register a thousand characters per second (or one character per millisecond). The progression went from milliseconds to micro-seconds to nanoseconds. When computers reached the place of registering in nanoseconds, or one billion characters per second, I said, "Surely this is the ultimate. Nothing in this world will ever exceed that speed of computation."

But by New Year's Day of 1973, IBM technicians were speaking of picoseconds, which would mean the computer would register one trillion characters per second.

[In 2008, IBM and scientists at Los Alamos National Laboratory built the world's fastest supercomputer. The supercomputer called Roadrunner has broken a speed barrier—a petaflop of sustained performance—that eluded computer makers for several years. A petaflop is 1,000 trillion operations per second.]

For the Nation and the World

A virtual network of computers began to be tied together in unity over the nation. Large computers drove small ones, which in turn drove a multitude of terminal units which would be placed in every home and place of business. [Using various statistics, AMD, the second-largest global supplier of microprocessors, estimated the population of internet users to be 1.5 billion as of January 2009.]

Connected with Telstar, a man could be in any country or island of the sea where a mechanical device was within reach of his hand and by registering his own number on the mechanical device, he could send a message to Telstar and on to his local bank, and receive it back again in his corner of the world—all in ten seconds of time. Surely the stage was set for the marvelous and mysterious operation of a universal number system.

TRW Credit Data was adding 50,000 names a week to its data center, and claimed they would soon have a complete record of everyone who had ever used credit.

Increased Concern

Along with the wonders of the developing system, more and more people became alarmed that they were being homogenized into a maze of wheels and tapes. This concern was not the expression of the emotional or the illiterate; qualified speakers spoke openly, and brilliant writers wrote freely on the dangers of being swallowed up in a great machine. Senator Ed V. Long of Missouri said, "I must report to you that the right to privacy is being dangerously and recklessly ignored and violated."

Dr. Orville G. Brim, Jr., head of the Russell Sage Foundation, said, "There is no doubt that we can run the society better with this information but doing this could well be in conflict with all our fears of having privacy invaded."

Every American's Record on One Roll of Tape

I recalled the day that NASA gave the contract to Honeywell for the production of the laser computer. It was reported that this computer could document on a single roll of tape all of the vital statistics of every American in the nation. The claim was also made that this marvelous machine had instant playback.

This would mean that a stranger from Savannah, Georgia, could walk into an office in San Diego, or

Seattle, and give them his number. Before he could cross the street, the office would have all the vital statistics concerning that stranger. His place of birth, his education, his training, his profession, his criminal record, his health record, and his religious inclinations.

A Machine With No Heart

While pondering the power of the computer age, I recalled a moment in a travel agency on Lake Street in Pasadena, California. I stepped to the counter on a beautiful June afternoon to pick up my air tickets. On leaving the building, I heard the troubled voice of a little mother, which caused me to pause and listen to her problem.

"I am sorry, ma'am," said the airline officer, "but you have no tickets."

"But I made my reservations over two weeks ago. Only yesterday I phoned in to reconfirm the fact you were holding my reservations for me."

"I'm sorry," replied the clerk again, "but you have no tickets on this particular flight, and no space is available."

I watched the mother's face cloud with anxiety, and the children by her side blinking to hold back their tears. It was the beginning of the holiday season, the rush had already begun, and all flights going from Los Angeles to Atlanta that day were fully booked.

"It was so important that we leave this evening," said the little mother in great distress. "Please, is there no one I can talk to personally?"

Then came an answer that rang in my ears for many days, an answer I would never forget.

The clerk looked blankly into the face of the troubled customer, and replied, "Ma'am, the computer apparently canceled your reservations, and no one talks back to the computer."

I turned down the street saying to myself that the new era is both fantastic and fearful. Men have created a machine that has almost supernatural brains but no heart at all.

One Card—One Number

When I arrived at our home back in Washington, D.C., in the summer of 1968, my telephone rang. I answered the call, and a stranger in New York introduced himself as Mr. White and said he would like to ask me some questions. He asked my place of birth, and also regarding my employment, how long I had been engaged in my particular profession.

The speaker had a congenial voice and chatted as leisurely as though he were in my living room. I watched the minutes tick off the clock. I knew that he was calling long-distance and every minute was costing money.

With a warm, reassuring, voice, the party from New York answered my eventual queries, "No, sir, we are just updating our credit files."

"Yes, your credit record is perfect, but we feel we must keep in step with the times."

When the phone conversation finally concluded, I turned the plastic pockets of my wallet. There was the Diners Club card, the Carte Blanche, the American Express, the Bank of America, the Master Charge, the telephone card, the Standard Oil, Texaco, Shell Oil, and Gulf Oil cards, the Sheraton Hotel card, and the Ambassador TWA card. Laughingly, I said to myself, "My wallet is almost too heavy to carry and contains everything but money." Every card represented a number, and I could easily understand why the move was on to consolidate all of these into a single number. Even as I thought about the significance of the computer system, I realized the government was spending $2 billion every twelve months in operating 2,500 computers that soon would have complete mastery of man's privacy and control of his every action. In spite of the well-grounded fears of millions of people, the number system had dawned and would dominate their immediate future.

It seemed indeed to make a lot of sense to consolidate all of man's cards and numbers into one. Men who discussed the number system went beyond the suggestion of a single card. They declared this, too, could be lost or stolen.

Almost daily we began to hear suggestions that each man be given a lifetime number that could be permanently impressed on his flesh. In Europe I had heard the spokesman on the Frankfurt radio station discussing the idea of tattooing man's number on the face. When placed on the flesh, they said, a number could not be lost, nor could it be stolen from the owner.

In America, I talked with a friend who was with the Northwest National Bank. He spoke of the progress being made in the laboratories in developing an invisible, nontoxic ink which would be tattooed on man's flesh, invisible in normal light, but clearly legible in a special light.

One of my friends in the news media said even the president pointed out the value of such a system. If man merely had a number, it would not only reduce to almost zero the causes for crime on the street, but would also prove to be a deterrent to major crimes such as plane hijacking. Why would a man try to rob a man or bank or hijack a plane if all he could collect would be a number?

Imagine, life without money ... No more checkbooks to balance, no more debts to refinance (presumably the computer would automatically stop our credit if we were about to exceed our earning capacity), no more worries about inflation or devaluation. What freedom, what bliss!

There was only one small prerequisite: for such a system to work, it would require every man to have a number. Were a man to refuse to wear his number, there would be no way to incorporate him into the system.

As the prophet had predicted almost two thousand years previously, "No man might buy or sell, save he that had ... the number" (Revelation 13:17).

CHAPTER 9

COMING TO THE END

In the spring of 1939, two things seemed extremely secure: the dignity of the individual and the sovereignty of his money. Almost overnight, however, everything changed. With the declaration of war, man's own interests were ignored. The interest of the nation came first, and rules and regulations were not made in the interest of individuals; they were made in the interest of the nation's survival.

Raw materials and manufactured goods were being channeled into war usage. Domestic demands ran much higher than supply. Rationing was immediately established. Men were issued little books of paper coupons on which were printed numbers.

I watched the power of this system in effect in almost every walk of life, and in several lands.

Rationing in Britain was extremely severe. For thirteen years, the British knew the miseries of rationing. During the most extreme years, the English people received one egg per week, and two ounces of beef per week, per person. Bad as his plight was, the last days of the war and the immediate postwar years were even worse for the Germans. Amandus Frotcher in Frankfurt told me of cases in Germany where men were shot to death for the crime of possessing a pig.

In spite of the fact they lived in a land that was large and rich, Americans, too, tasted the restrictions of the ration system. They obtained their tea and coffee, sugar and shoes, clothes and gasoline, and many other commodities only with their ration coupon. The money they possessed was no longer the most powerful medium of exchange, no longer stood alone as legal tender. Times without number, I watched men seek to bribe the butcher, or the grocer, or the service-station attendant to give them more than their share. If a rich man was honest, however, he received the same commodities of life as the poorest servant in his employ.

With the Japanese surrender on September 2, 1945, World War II came to a close. People turned their faces with hope toward the eastern sky, longing for the dawn of universal peace. They threw into the fire the ration coupon books that had bound them to limited provisions for so many years and heaved a sigh of relief. "Here's hoping," they said, "that we will never see this system again in our land.

With the dawn of 1973, rationing was once again in headlines all across America.

Fuel Shortage

On Friday morning, January 19, 1973, I was in Dallas, Texas. Picking up my copy of the Dallas *Morning News,* I read the bold headlines on the front page: FUEL SHORTAGE TURNING INTO CRISIS.

Later that day, the *Times-Herald* carried a similar headline: SHORTAGE OF HEATING OIL CAUSES NATIONAL CRISIS.

When in Charlotte, N.C. on May 10, 1973, I picked up the evening paper, The *Charlotte News,* and read the headline: 9 FILLING STATIONS CLOSE, GAS SHORTAGE LINK DENIED

Headlines of this nature were being seen more and more frequently in many areas of the nation.

In studying the various articles, I discovered that the announcement was received by many Americans with mingled consternation and confusion. One article read as follows:

> The national energy "crisis," here yesterday and gone tomorrow, seems almost elusive, and the experts disagree even on its existence. Now it seems the people directly affected by the current fuel shortages give different opinions, as two stories by Associated Press at left, and International Press at right, reflect. Is there an Energy Crisis? Facts are facts, but it depends on who you ask and when.

As I followed the reactions of our nation's leaders, I turned my eyes and interest again to the Dallas *Morning News,* January 16. The top half of 11-A was devoted to an article headlined, PRODUCERS ASK HIGHER GAS PRICES.

And on the bottom half of the same page, ran a second headline: KOSYGIN TOURS OIL GAS AREA IN USSR TO BOOST DEVELOPMENT PLANS.

The two stories on the same page did not come as a total surprise to some of us who had followed the developments of these events for several months. On November 12, 1972, I was in Eugene, Oregon. I picked up the daily paper, the *Register Guard,* and read an article reprinted from the Washington *Star,* which said,

Washington *Star News* reports U.S. may buy as much as forty billion dollars' worth of natural gas from Russia during the next twenty-five years. U.S. companies backed by federal financing would buy 36.5 trillion cubic feet of liquefied natural gas.

The head of one of the oil and gas producers' groups said Russian gas would cost six times more than the wholesale price of U.S. gas.

In response to that announcement in November, Tom Medders, Jr., head of the Independent Petroleum Association of America, said, "It is disturbing that our government is willing to encourage development of the Soviet Union's gas at such a cost, when it is pursuing regulatory policies that are discouraging the needful capital expenditures to develop our own natural gas resources at home."

Serious-minded leaders, such as Senator Henry Jackson and Commerce Secretary Peter Peterson, and others, raised the question, "Would it not be unwise to make our nation dependent on an energy source that was held in the hands of a foreign nation?"

In spite of the fact the alarms were being sounded, there was every indication that Americans would be subjected to gas rationing in the near future. Men as prominent as Mr. O'Leary, member of the Atomic Energy Commission, predicted rationing in the near future.

Russian Wheat

While America was discussing the purchasing of thirty-six trillion cubic feet of Russian gas, the Russians were occupied with the task of importing twenty million tons of wheat, which they had purchased from the United States, at a price of over one billion dollars. Although the Russian press sought to keep this tremendous importation of wheat a secret from their own people, the free world was told it was because of a drought in the USSR.

Some indicated the drought in Russia was the worst in a hundred years, and affected 27.5 million acres of land.

Several years previously, I recalled reading an article by Sterling Slappey. His article carried the headline, SOVIET WHEAT PURCHASES LINKED TO ALCOHOL NEEDS.

Mr. Slappey quoted a report from the reputable German Institute of Industries. They declared the Soviets had greater need for wheat to distill into industrial alcohol than to turn into bread. They said that it took nine tons of wheat to make two tons of alcohol, which in turn would make one ton of synthetic rubber. They also declared the Russians needed 550,000 tons of industrial alcohol for the purposes mentioned. Some who read Slappey's article and his quotations from the Institute of German Industries, said, "We do not mind as taxpayers subsidizing cheap wheat for Russian bread, but we would resent subsidizing the wheat purchase to the USSR if it were to be used for military production."

Was the fuel crisis in America genuine, or was it somehow linked to the possible purchase of Russian gas? If the suggested deal with Russia should develop as outlined, the twenty-five-year contract for forty billion worth of Russian gas would be the biggest transaction in the history of man.

Preparation for Shortage

Right or wrong, true or false, one thing seemed certain: the world was moving toward a ration system in the immediate future. Many people living only for the day awakened to the announced crisis with dismay. But others prepared for the future.

I remembered in 1955 when I had returned to Europe from Africa. I paused to rest a few days in the little Swiss village of Beatenberg, nestled in the Alps, high above Thunersee. As I basked in the warm sunshine on the veranda of the Beau Regard Hotel, I was suddenly disturbed by a deep, rolling, sound resembling thunder in the distance. My friend, Herr Bhent, owner of the hotel, surprised me with a strange explanation. The Swiss, he said, were storing wheat in preparation for the days of shortages that could be ahead.

I realized how typically Swiss this action was. By 1984, the world would have another billion mouths to feed, and what would that mean? It would require an *additional* 300 million tons of grain to feed another billion people. This would be more grain than was presently being grown by the United States, Canada, and Western Europe combined.

In my youth, South America exported more grain than the United States and Canada. Now, because of her increased population, she was forced to import grain. China, too, had ordered 20 million bushels of wheat, and others were out shopping in the world markets.

The Black Horse

The Prophet John described a dark hour coming on the earth when there would be shortage of food. In symbolical language, he likened this to a rider on a black horse, and wrote:

> "And I beheld, and to a black horse; and he that sat on him had a pair of balances in his hand. And I heard a voice ... say, A measure of wheat for a penny ... and see thou hurt not the oil" (Revelation 6:5-6).

The Pale Horse

Following John's description of the black horse and famine, he described the rider on a pale horse:

> "And I looked, and behold a pale horse: and his name that sat on him was Death" (Revelation 6:8).

Often, after reading these words of John the Prophet, I pondered the statements of some of our leading social scientists and demographers. Dr. Paul Ehrlich, departmental head of biological sciences at Stanford University, had repeatedly addressed America on national television. He spoke of the possibility of water being rationed in 1974. He suggested that as many as 20 million may die of starvation in the next 12 months, and millions, if not billions, may perish with hunger in the near future.

Dr. Raymond Ewell served as vice-president of the Research Department in the State University of New York. He, also, portrayed a world where millions, if not billions, would be starving to death within a very few years of time.

Danger of Famine—True or False?

While addressing the collective group of U.S. Army chaplains in Europe on March 27, 1970, I alluded to the remarks made by Dr. Ehrlich and Dr. Ewell. At the conclusion of my address, a veteran officer asked if I did not think the comments concerning starvation were merely propaganda. I asked the officer if he had ever been in Asia. And he replied, no. "Then," I said, "Sir, I am afraid you have never seen poverty."

The chaplain had spent most of his years in America or Western Europe. I reminded him that Western Europe and Canada and America were in what we termed the food belt of the world, which lies between latitudes 30 and 55. Outside of the food belt, there are millions of acres of steaming jungle, burning desert, and desolate mountain waste. Some estimated that over 60% of the world's people lived outside of the food belt.

Exploding Population

It was the poor nations of the world also that were facing the grim threat of a population explosion. This was a term seldom mentioned in my youth. Some felt the sudden emphasis on exploding population was propaganda produced by men in favor of a one-world government, in an effort to persuade people that it was either unite or perish. Those disturbed over the exploding population painted a rather alarming picture, however:

- A.D.1 world population, ¼ billion
- 1850 world population, one billion
- Today, 3.5 billion

[July 2008, the world's population was 6,706,993,152]

The contrast between the past and present was impressive—18 centuries for the world to grow from 1/4 billion to one billion. Only 80 years required to add a second billion. Thirty years needed to add a third billion. A fourth billion would be added to world population in 14 years. That world population increase is 2% in one year does not sound disturbing. But to those who take time to ponder the true meaning, a world is seen with a population doubling every 35 years.

Demographers pointed out that the increase of population in the next 12 months would equal the combined populations of Canada, Australia, New Zealand, Switzerland, Israel, Denmark, Norway, and Sweden.

I stared at the fire for a few minutes trying to comprehend what the future would hold if the increase in population should continue unabated. During the five hours I had been sitting by the fire, the world population had increased another 65,000. Doctor Harrison Brown of California declared that if the population increase continued at its present rate, in seven centuries there would literally not be standing room on the surface of the Earth.

Naturally, the average American could not comprehend this. He lived in a land where there were fewer than a dozen people per square mile in some communities. He could not visualize the crowded congestion of Asia where some countries had an average of 700 people per square mile. Were the predictions overstated? Were they true or false?

I could not say for certain, but one thing I did know: I had walked the streets of Calcutta and of other cities of the East. I had seen the crowds of hungry people who had little or nothing of earthly goods and scarcely room to lay their head. Doctor Earl Butz, formerly of Purdue University, declared:

> "I am convinced that most of the arable land of the world is now under cultivation. We have presently in our world about 3.3 billion acres suitable for food production. This represents about one acre per person at present, but in approximately three decades, the world population will double."

A Double Problem

Many naive Americans, considering the population problem, say, "Technology will solve our crisis." But the more serious-minded point to the solemn facts that world food productivity is declining, not increasing. This, they declare, is the result of polluted air and water and impoverished soil.

When the ecologists met in Los Angeles, the *Los Angeles Herald Examiner* carried the headline, CAN HUMANITY SURVIVE FIVE YEARS?

It was most impressive to listen to the arguments of these scientific men. "Corn," they said, "does not grow in Iowa merely from what it draws from the soil or sod. It must receive its carbon from the carbon dioxide in the heavens above. To grow 100 bushels of corn, 20,000 pounds of carbon dioxide is required to provide the 5,500 pounds of carbon needed by the plants." I listened with interest to men discussing the delicate balance of the atmosphere which was: 78% nitrogen, 21% oxygen, with another dozen gases making up the 1% remaining. What happens, even in a land as big and free as America, when the people pour into the heavens annually:

- 100 million tons of carbon monoxide
- 32.2 million tons of sulfur oxide
- 32 million tons of hydrocarbon compounds
- 28.3 million tons of particulate matter
- 20.6 million tons of nitrogen oxide?

The result is death. I stood in the airport of Orlando, Florida, listening to a Floridian lamenting the loss of their pure air and pointing to the fact that the Spanish moss was already dying in the trees. I drove in the beautiful mountain range of Lake Arrowhead in California. The ranger pointed to the pine trees that were dying at the 5,000-foot level. The people of Denver, Colorado, feared they were losing their 400,000elm trees, and in less than a decade, the people of Florida saw 15,000 palm trees die.

As I viewed the world picture and listened to the comments of the scientists, my thoughts turned again to the words of the Prophet John. In Revelation 8:7, he spoke of a third part of the trees on Earth dying: "The third part of trees was burnt up."

An astronaut predicted in 10 years' time the sun's rays would be diminished by 50% if man continued to pour into the heavens his ceaseless clouds of poison. But polluted air was not the only problem. Polluted water was equally alarming.

Water Pollution

Man poured into the oceans annually 7,422,000 tons of waste. This did not include the dredge spoils or the radio-active waste from plants along the shore. In a single year, America saw signs posted on ninety-one bathing beaches that read, "Unfit for Bathing" or "Closed Because of Pollution."

The problem was certainly not confined to America. It was worldwide. A traveler going abroad for the first time stared in wonder at warning signs placed in Hawaii, Samoa, Guam, Puerto Rico, and Europe; signs that read, "Polluted Water."

As I traveled over Europe, I was saddened to hear the beautiful Mediterranean referred to as "the sick sea," while up in the north of Europe they spoke of the North Sea as the "Dying Sea."

Across the world, the sea life was sick and dying in many areas. Forty million dead fish were taken out of the Rhine River, poisoned with the 6,000 pollutants that were being poured into the waters of Europe's most picturesque and historical waterway. The *International Herald Tribune,* published in Europe, showed pictures of men in Amsterdam who had developed their photographs in the waters of the river. They declared there was enough acid in the water to develop film without adding any further chemicals. Similar pictures depicting like circumstances were published in faraway Japan. On the banks of Escambia Bay in Florida, the big fishery was closed down. It was as dead as the sea life in the polluted waters. Men as prominent as Doctor Ripley predicted that the Pacific Ocean might be as devoid of life as Lake Erie in another two decades.

As I read these statistics, I turned again to the Prophet John:

> "And the third part of the creatures which were in the sea, and had life, died" (Revelation 8:9).

Fear of Pollution Drives Men to World Government

Not surprisingly, the leaders of the world viewed the conditions with concern. On December 3, 1968, leaders from Sweden introduced in the United Nations, Resolution 3298. They suggested pollution be solved through inter-national agreement and cooperation. In 1970 the leaders of the world met in Strasbourg, France, to consider control of industry. In 1971, another meeting was conducted in Prague. On June 5, 1972, more than 1,200 delegates gathered in Stockholm, Sweden. They represented a hundred nations. They urged the government with global authority to police the nations of the world to save the planet from poison due to pollution. Back in Washington, Richard Nixon declared in his address on the state of the union, "The threat to our environment demands action. It is literally now or never."

The Secretary-General of the United Nations was even more outspoken. In his address delivered in

Texas he said, "We now face a worldwide crisis involving all living creatures."

Without doubt, the average man seemed to become more and more bewildered. When he turned his eyes to the heavens at noonday and saw nothing but a brown pall of ugly smog, he cried for laws that would clear the atmosphere and save him from the poison of pollution. The large oil refineries of America, failing to deliver the needed fuel and energy during the crisis weeks of 1973, declared one of the reasons for the shortage was the limitations imposed upon their production because of environmental control laws. Civic leaders accused the owners of the oil refineries of using the oil shortage as a deliberate influence to cause them to relax their environmental control. What could men do? Americans claimed they had lost $132 million in their fruit and vegetable crops because of poisoned air. Yet if they imposed laws strict enough to clear the atmosphere, then the economy was apparently endangered, and the necessary production of oil and energy reached a crisis point. The problem was not confined to the United States alone. Countries as spacious as Canada were faced with similar situations. In the city of Toronto, leaders forced 43 industries to close their operation for three days because the pollution in Canadian skies had reached a crisis point.

Poison or Famine

Two ugly words had become part of modern man's vocabulary, "poison" and "famine." Ugly as these words appeared, I could not conceive an honest person pushing them aside as mere propaganda of the one-world federalists. Anyone discounting the dangers of pollution would indeed have to close his eyes deliberately to the facts of the day. In 1941 there were thirty-three rivers in America which boasted of salmon. Today there are six. Forest rangers told me of lookout stations being simply abandoned, useless because of the ugly pall of smog that hung so persistently over hills and valleys.

An astronaut ventured to declare that already 50% of the valuable rays of the sun were being denied to Mother Earth by an ugly specter named pollution.

Could it be purely accidental that the Prophet Amos long ago wrote concerning this day and said, "I will darken the earth in the clear day" (Amos 8:9).

Could it be mere chance that he added in the next breath, "I will send a famine in the land" (Amos 8:11).

If the earth was being clouded with pollution, so were the minds of men. As I pored over the comments made by world-renowned scientists, their statements grew ever darker and more pessimistic. One wrote, "Mankind is racing toward extinction."

A group of British scientists published a so-called blueprint for survival. The central theme or thesis of their document read:

> "Growth in the world is self-defeating, and the planet cannot any longer sustain additional life. We are now moving toward social and biological collapse."

Certain people refuse to acknowledge such printed statements and brush them aside with disdain or deliberate disinterest. I could not. I was exposed too often to the confirmation of personal interviews and involvements with other men.

In Manchester, England, I spoke in the Free Trade Hall in the heart of the city. Not only were the hall's 2,500 seats filled, but another 1,200 persons gathered in the overflow Albert Hall across the street. I spoke on the words of the prophets and their description of our day, closing my address, as always, with the assurance that prophecy was not a doomsday message. It was a light in a dark place, promising a bright tomorrow and a permanent end to man's evils and woes.

On Sunday I said farewell to our Manchester audience, but remained in the city on Monday. That evening, one of Britain's best-known scientists, Dr. Robinson, spoke in the same hall. At the close of his address, his Manchester audience was left paralyzed with fear and deep despair. He offered them practically no hope for the future. On Tuesday morning, following his address, the *Manchester Guardian* carried the headline, DOCTOR ROBINSON, NEVER AGAIN VISIT MANCHESTER.

Dr. Robinson's words reminded me of those of Dr. Rene Dubos, Pulitzer Prize winner, retired microbiologist from Rockefeller University of New York, who said, "We used to speak of the atomic bomb as a threat. Now we might consider it as a relief."

Three ugly forces seemed to have suddenly arisen like giants on man's horizon: exploding population threatened famine, increased pollution threatened poison, atomic weapons threatened destruction. These three seemed to have joined in an unholy alliance to drive all of humanity into a one-world government. More and more men were turning in this direction as the only chance of survival. Even as the prophet had declared, men through fear would say "a federation, a federation."

The room in which I sat contemplating all these things was aglow with the flames from the fireplace. The embers on the hearth that had warmed and cheered me now reminded me of the glow of atomic radiation.

CHAPTER 10

THE EARTH WILL SHAKE

On August 6, 1945, the B-29 bomber known as the Enola Gay was flying in Japanese skies with the first atomic bomb to be dropped on mankind. Like most of the rest of the world, I was totally ignorant as to what was about to take place.

Early on that August morning, I had mounted a horse at Red Lodge, Montana, and had spent the day climbing Black Pyramid Mountain.

I had recently returned from visiting the disabled veterans who had come back from Okinawa and Iwo Jima. While the sound of the battle had died away in Europe, blood still flowed unceasingly in the Far Pacific regions. On the island of Iwo Jima, 6,825 American boys had died and 21,703 Japanese.

Saddened with the sorrows of war, I sought on this particular day to remove myself for a few hours from man's materialistic world and refresh my body and mind in God's great outdoors.

On top of Pyramid Mountain in the late August afternoon, I looked out across the valley with a sigh. How sad that men could not live in peace as the Creator intended them to live.

While I was standing alone in the silence of God's outdoor cathedral the most fearful experience known to man was taking place in the Pacific.

A bomb weighing approximately 400 pounds was dropped on the city of Hiroshima, whose population was 343,969, and the whole world was shaken with the awful introduction of atomic destruction. Seven thousand acres of ground were scorched by the radiation of the blast. The Japanese newspaper, *Chugoku Shimbun,* estimated 280,000 Japanese were killed by the bomb, more than half the population of the city.

Late that evening when I drove into Billings, every channel of the news media was announcing the awful introduction to the atomic age.

Within three days, another atomic bomb was dropped—on the city of Nagasaki. Five days later Japan surrendered. War in the Pacific ended, but the mad arms race had only begun.

The atomic bomb was no accident that happened overnight. Over 40 years before the explosion in Japan, Einstein, a student in Switzerland, had told the scientific world that energy equaled mc^2. Most men chose to ignore his findings, and a few openly ridiculed his statement. How could one kilo of matter be equal to 25 billion kilowatt-hours of energy? But Einstein's theory was not a myth, and the fearful power of the universe had been discovered by man. Over $2 billion had been spent in research, developing a bomb capable of destroying man's world.

At my request, Colonel Garr went to Japan with his camera to document on film the destruction of Hiroshima. As he returned with the footage which we placed on the television stations of America, I was saddened at the sight of the destruction of life and property. Hiroshima had been scorched by the radiation of the blast. In the Peace Park at Hiroshima, the Japanese erected a memorial that read, "The mistake shall not be repeated."

The Atomic Bomb Race

The passing of time did little to substantiate the hopes of the Japanese.

- September 23, 1949, Russia detonated an atomic bomb.
- November 1, 1952, America exploded the first hydrogen bomb.
- August 12, 1953, Russia released a hydrogen bomb.
- May 15, 1957, Britain exploded an atom bomb.
- February 13, 1960, France displayed her atomic power.
- October 16, 1964, China joined the great powers possessing atom bombs.

[Several other nations now possess nuclear weapons. These include India, Pakistan, and Israel. North Korea and Iran appear to be developing such weaponry, as well.]

The atomic scientists watched the buildup with dismay. In June, 1947, the Bulletin of the Atomic Scientists carried a picture on the cover with the clock of the world showing the hands reading seven minutes to midnight. In October, 1949, the same bulletin showed the same clock with the hands at four minutes to midnight. In 1953, the Bulletin of the Atomic Scientists magazine showed the clock with the hands at two minutes to midnight.

[The minute hand of the Doomsday clock is reset in accordance with international and global events and circumstances, such as nuclear proliferation and climate changes. In the past it has been as far as seventeen minutes from midnight (1991) and as close as two minutes to midnight (1953). In 2002, the clock was set at seven minutes to midnight. Then on January 17, 2007, the Bulletin of the Atomic Scientists moved the minute hand of the Doomsday Clock two minutes closer to midnight. It is now 5 minutes to midnight.]

The Hydrogen Bomb

In San Diego, I talked with Captain Eddy. He had been with the expedition in the Marshall Islands on November 1, 1952, when America exploded her first hydrogen bomb. In a sober voice, Captain Eddy said, "No one could visualize the awfulness of that sight unless he were there in person." Two hundred miles above the Pacific, the mighty hydrogen bomb was detonated. The blast lighted up thousands of miles of Pacific sky. At Auckland, New Zealand, 3,800 miles away from the scene of the blast, New Zealanders said the ocean showed a reflection that was blood-red.

"The scientists present at the scene were dreadfully shaken," said Eddy. "They thought they had set the heavens aflame with a chain reaction of exploding atoms that would surely go around the world." On returning from his mission, Captain Eddy asked to be transferred to another department of service, and was given a position in the field of seismology, studying earthquakes back in the South Pacific.

Earthquakes and Atom Bombs

That there is a connection between atom bombs and earthquakes might sound humorous to some, but the facts allow little room for humor or ridicule.

On an island called Amchitka, southwest of Anchorage, Alaska, a 53-inch shaft was sunk deep into the heart of the ground. On September 6, 1971, man created the largest man-made earthquake in history. The bomb that was detonated on the island of Amchitka was 250 times more powerful than the one that had been dropped on Hiroshima. The explosion rocked not only the island of Amchitka; it caused earth tremors on the opposite side of the globe.

Professor Marcus Baath in Uppsala, Sweden, declared that the underground blast from Alaska caused his Richter scale to show a 7.4 earth tremor—in *Sweden.*

Increase of Earthquakes

Each year the United States government was spending $7.5 million on the study of earthquakes. The research revealed an amazing increase in earthquakes through the ages.

- Fifteenth century—150 recorded earthquakes
- Sixteenth century—153 recorded earthquakes
- Seventeenth century—378 recorded earthquakes
- Eighteenth century—640 recorded earthquakes
- Nineteenth century—2,119 recorded earthquakes

The twentieth century has broken all records of the past. In this century alone, more than a million people have died in earthquakes.

- Yugoslavia—1,000 deaths
- Alaska—114 deaths
- Chile—hundreds die
- Iran—1,000 die
- Turkey—many killed by earthquakes
- Peru—50,000 died in earthquakes

At Christmas of 1972, destruction and death was experienced in Managua, Nicaragua. One U.S. government report declared that by the year 2000, one out of four Americans will be living near an active earthquake fault.

The Great Earthquake of the Past

In past years, I have frequently paused to view the lava rock that covers much of the western

U.S.A. How could one explain the thousands of acres of lava rock in Eastern California, New Mexico, Arizona, Utah, Nevada, Wyoming, Nebraska, Eastern Washington, and Idaho? One day, surely, the face of Mother Earth must have broken and buckled in a thousand places while lava rock ran like rivers over much of the globe. The Prophet Isaiah, in chapter 14, alludes to such an hour in the dim, distant, past when the earth trembled and became a desolate wilderness.

A Great Earthquake Still to Come

When describing the end of this age, Christ declared: "There shall be ... earthquakes" (Matthew 24:7), earthquakes not comparable to anything of the past history, but a great earthquake even as described by John in his prophetic Book of the Revelation: "There was a great earthquake, such as was not since men were upon the earth, so mighty an earthquake, and so great ... and the cities of the nations fell" (Revelation 16:18-19).

John describes this earthquake in the same chapter in which he discusses the battle of Armageddon and seemingly suggests when the heavens flame with atomic weaponry the earth will also reel and rock.

Scientists Warn of a Great Earthquake

With bated breath I reflected upon the statements of certain scientific men suggesting that a salvo of bombs exploded in the heavens above the surface of the Earth could well cause the entire globe to shake. True, they said, the world weighs 6,600 billion times a billion tons. But it is not dead weight. The Earth that spins on its axis at 1,000 miles an hour also moves through space in its elliptical orbit around the sun at 67,000 miles an hour.

The great globe spinning on its axis in delicate balance could be rocked and shaken by a fearful blast of atomic weapons in the heavens, said the scientific group. This seems to be exactly what the Prophet Isaiah saw long ago when he wrote, "The windows from on high are open, and the foundations of the earth do shake" (Isaiah 24:18).

And the writer of Hebrews adds, "Yet once more I shake not the earth only, but also heaven" (Hebrews 12:26).

The Powers of the Heaven Shall Be Shaken

Apart from the war and danger of earthquakes, the atomic bombs pose still another threat to man's survival on the Earth.

In May, 1966, I picked up a copy of *Science and Mechanics,* and read a feature article by A.I. Schutzer. It quoted men of scientific knowledge, such as Henry G. Houghton of M.I.T., who gave his report to the U.S. Senate. It also quoted Captain Howard T. Orville, former head of the President's Advisory Committee on Weather Control. In discussing radioactive fallout from atomic bombs, Captain Orville said, "The results could even be more disastrous than nuclear warfare."

Why would Captain Orville and Professor Henry Houghton, and men like Dr. Edward Teller express alarm over the weather patterns of the world being disrupted by man's detonating atomic bombs? The scientists pointed out that the Earth's weather is manufactured in an envelope of atmosphere about eight miles high that encloses the world. The machine that makes the weather is the radiation that comes from the sun. Tamper with any one of the basic forces that mold our weather picture, said the scientists; and you change the weather somewhere in the world.

Why? First of all, because the amount of precipitation in the form of rain in any given area appears to be affected by the electrical balance between earth and air. The earth carries a negative charge. The air carries a positive charge. This is constantly being ionized by cosmic rays from the sun. Nature has set up an amazing system of re-balancing the positive-negative balance between earth and air. But, said the scientists, men seem to have upset this balance with the radioactive fallout.

As I moved across the world and kept interest in the changing weather patterns from nation to nation, the irregularities seemed endless. In 1965 for instance, for the first time to man's knowledge, four inches of snow fell in England in August. On the Tiber River in Rome, ice chunks were floating for the first time in over 500 years. While Russia was experiencing the worst drought in a century, torrential rains flooded eastern U.S.A. in 1972. Prior to 1945, the number of hurricanes and tornadoes in America averaged approximately 300 per year. Now, the number was almost double. [From 1950–2004, the average number of tornadoes in the United States was 910 a year. May 2003 had 543 tornatoes, the most ever recorded in one month.]

MANY NATIONS PLAGUED BY TOPSY TURVY WINTER, read the headline in the January 6, 1973, edition of the *Los Angeles Times.* The news media reported strange weather everywhere:

- Sweden warm, Israel cold, South Africa dry; fluridden Russia too balmy for crops.
- "It was cold where it should have been warm, warm where it should have been cold, and dry where it should have been wet."
- Europe is undergoing its most bizarre winter in recent times.
- Drought-stricken South Africa has lost millions of dollars on crop loss.
- Subtropical Israel lost $12 million in agriculture from unseasonable cold.
- Crop losses in Rhodesia in the middle of the southern hemisphere summer have amounted to at least $30 million thus far. South African Agricultural Minister Hendrik Schoeman estimated crop losses at $318.5 million because of a three-month summer drought.

- Norway, Sweden and Finland, normally blanketed by snow, all reported grass fires sparked New Year's Eve. Nils Tymark, Stockholm weather observer, said, "The situation is idiotic, I have never seen anything like it in all my life."

As I gathered data from the news media from the world relative to the disrupted weather patterns of the nations, and viewed them in the light of scientific statements made by men who felt it was brought about by the disruption of the balance in the atmosphere, I recalled the prophetic words of Christ: "The powers of heaven shall be shaken (Luke 21:26). The most literal translation of this line from the original Greek reads, "The powers of the heaven shall be disrupted."

The Atomic Bomb—A Threefold Threat

When the atomic bomb was dropped on August 6, 1945, man considered it only a weapon of war. Now men saw the atomic bomb threaten civilization in a threefold manner. There were indeed the dangers of destruction in war. To this had been added the scientific warnings that atomic explosions could disturb the balance of the globe and contribute to earthquakes, and thirdly, and not to be ignored, the disruption of the weather patterns of the world by pollution of radioactive fallout.

The Cry for World Government

Harold Urey said, "The only escape from total destruction of civilization will be a world government."

Robert J. Oppenheimer stated, "In the field of atomic energy, there must be set up a world power."

Arthur Compton added his word: "World government has become inevitable."

Dr. Ralph Barton Perry of Harvard said, "One-world government is in the making. Whether we like it or not, we are moving toward a one-world government."

Professor Hocking wrote, "Therefore the alternative is that we vest all political power in one agency and resign that power ourselves."

When President Nixon was asked by a news writer about his attitude toward Russia's superiority in the heavy missile race, he replied, "Gentlemen, we have enough weapons already stock-piled to destroy several civilizations such as this."

And before him, President Johnson had said, "In the event of a nuclear war between Russia and America, 100 million Americans and 100 million Russians would be dead in the first nuclear exchange. The great cities would be in ashes, and the fields would be barren. The industrial world would be destroyed, and man's dreams vanished."

One-man Government?

I sat in Brussels in March, 1972, with my friend, Dave Oliver, who had devoted 28 years of his life to tirelessly working with the Atomic Energy Commission. In recalling the atomic bomb that was dropped on Hiroshima on August 6, 1945, we were impressed that it was the voice signal of the U.S. President, Harry Truman, that released that bomb from the B-29 that flew over Hiroshima on that memorable day. With knowledge of that amazing incident, we turned in the prophetic Scriptures to the prophecies of John in the Book of the Revelation. Here the prophet not only spoke of a one-world government, canceling the old monetary currencies of the past and establishing a new number system, the prophet also spoke of a world leader, having authority over the military power of the world, and declared, "Power was given him over all kindreds, and tongues, and nations [and he adds], He maketh fire come down from heaven on the earth in the sight of men (Revelation 13:7, 13).

If a man became head of a world government and possessed such power, surely it would be greater than what any man in history had ever possessed before him.

What would happen if such power was invested in a man who should turn into a maniac like Adolph Hitler? Was there such a danger? Of course there was, and most sober-minded leaders of government realized it. But man seemed to be caught between two undesirable alternatives. The old paths behind him pointed back to Hiroshima, Nagasaki, and 50 million dead from World War II. The other path offered the forfeiture of rights by individuals and nations being pushed daily nearer to a form of world government.

Grenville Clark said, "Perhaps it may take a few nuclear bombs and several million deaths."

And Joseph Clark added, "The people will follow when the leaders tell them there is no alternative."

CHAPTER 11

TWO MAN-MADE SOLUTIONS: COMMUNISM AND THE UN

Time and again, man had sought to establish his temple of peace. There was the Tribunal Palace in the Hague. For weeks, we had lived on Scheveningsweg street in the shadow of the Peace Palace. To walk in its echoing corridors was to be impressed that it resembled a mausoleum more than a monument.

Then there was the League of Nations established in Geneva at the close of World War One. Forty-six nations participated there at the cost of $190 million before its final demise in 1946. From the ashes of destruction and the blood of the beachheads, man turned his face to San Francisco's Golden Gate, hoping to build on American shores an organization that would guarantee peace to the world.

The Birth of the UN

It was a beautiful June day in San Francisco in 1945. The flags were flying and a stiff breeze was blowing in from the Pacific. I watched the delegates from fifty nations gather in the world's most important meeting. Over fifty million had been left dead on the battlefields of the world. With smoke still rising from the ruined cities of Europe and Asia, and tears still wet on the cheeks of widows and orphans, the delegates of the world sat around the peace tables to discuss one more attempt at universal peace.

One American delegate asked if it would be in order to suggest prayer, asking God's guidance on the opening with an invocation. His suggestion was immediately brushed aside by those who stated it would be offensive to the atheistic delegates who had congregated for the meeting.

When Woodrow Wilson, supported by many young intellectuals of America, had sought to influence the U.S. government in 1920 to support the League of Nations, he failed. Why, then, 26 years later, were American people ready to join the United Nations, which, in a sense, was the tree that grew from the roots of the League of Nations?

Men pointed out that the two obstacles which prevented America from joining the League of Nations were old-fashioned ideas pertaining to patriotism and religion. In the book entitled *Great Ideas Today: 1971,* published by the *Encyclopaedia Britannica,* Joseph Clark says, "Old fashioned patriotism is surely an obstacle to world government."

But the so-called old-fashioned ideas of patriotism and religion seemed to be waning in America. By a vote of eight to one, the Supreme Court expressed their disfavor toward compulsory prayer in the public schools, and with a vote of six to one denied students public Bible reading in the classroom.

When a survey was made of 1,150 high school students, only one in 39 could name three books written by Saint Paul. Only one student in 38 could name three Old Testament prophets. Only one in 8 could name three of the Ten Commandments. A survey made in the colleges showed 60% could not name one parable that was delivered by Jesus, and 53% of Americans were unable to name even one of the four gospels.

Russia was spending more than a billion dollars on literature and propaganda outside of the USSR each year. The doctrines of socialism were not only being taught in the classrooms of the colleges, but were also being heard from the pulpits of many churches, and from the pens of religious leaders.

I wonder, I said to myself, how many Americans have studied the charter of the UN sufficiently to realize that it commits each member nation to a program of total socialism for itself and for all other nations. Alger Hiss was a major architect of the UN charter and served as the secretary general of the San Francisco conference for the organization of the United Nations. Twenty-five years later, U Thant was quoted as praising Lenin as a political leader whose ideals were reflected in the United Nations' charter.

Wealth and Poverty

Why, I asked myself repeatedly, did so many American leaders, both in church and in the classrooms of colleges, speak strongly in favor of world socialism? E. Stanley Jones, in his *The Choice Before Us,* declared, "God reached out and put his hand on the Russian Communist. Communism is the only political position that really holds the Christian position."

In one sense, I found it very difficult to comprehend a man like E. Stanley Jones writing lines that seemed to endorse Communism.

On the other hand, I reminded myself of the years that he had spent in India. In 1953, speaking for many days on the club grounds of Lucknow, I saw the results of this man's work in that city of north central India. Undoubtedly Jones was moved by the scenes of squalor and poverty that plagued the masses of that great nation. He must have contrasted the poor and the hungry with the abnormal wealth of such men as the Nizam of Hyderabad, a descendant of the Mogul emperors, who ruled over fifteen million poverty-stricken subjects for decades. Reputedly, he had more wealth than any other man in the world, with a net income of $15 million annually. Much of his wealth came from the fabulous valley of Golconda, one of the world's richest diamond mines.

The Nizam had 500 wives, and he gave his favorite one a gold Rolls Royce. He ate all of his meals off golden plates, and boasted that the English displayed 24 golden plates in London, while he had golden place settings for 150 guests. One of his favorite diamonds was the 182 1/2-carat diamond he used for a paperweight. He sat in chairs and relaxed on couches of solid gold, and had a carriage of gold built that was not usable because of its weight.

If Stanley Jones endorsed socialism, it was perhaps because he had stood among the beggars and hungry children in the shadow of the Taj Mahal. It was without doubt the most beautiful tomb in the world. It was built by the Indian ruler, Shah Jahan, as a memorial to his favorite wife, Muntaz-i-Mahal, which means "Bride of the Palace." It took 20,000 workmen twenty-one years to erect the Taj, and when the workmen finished the delicate tasks of carving their marble and alabaster into seventy-foot domes rising 150 feet high, they undoubtedly gazed at the slender minarets, supposedly built as towers for prayer, mirrored in the reflecting pools beside the tomb, and then turned to Shah Jahan for their reward. Did he give them a smile of appreciation or a hand of gratitude? No, the payment they received for creating one of the beauties of the world was the ugly point of the soldier's knife that pierced their eyes. Shah Jahan wanted to make sure no other monarch would ever again have a Taj as beautiful as his.

Communism in Egypt

If there were Communists in Egypt, it, too, might be understandable. The Great Pyramid of Gizeh served as a perpetual reminder of the days when masters with a stroke of the whip compelled men to serve them as slaves. As I climbed the Great Pyramid, and walked around its perimeter, my mind seethed with a thousand questions. How could this monument be built on desert sand, towering 484 feet high, with a base that measured 761 feet? Where could they have quarried the granite which they had piled in 201 concourses, some blocks of granite weighing as much as twenty tons?

Some felt the immense blocks of granite were brought from Syene, a distance of 500 miles. The total weight of the pyramid was estimated to be six million tons. A mathematician calculated that the volume of the pyramid was eighty-five million cubic feet. Should a monument as large as the pyramid be converted into a wall four feet high and one foot thick, it would extend from New York City to San Francisco.

The ancient record tells us that 100,000 men, laboring in relays of three months, worked thirty years to complete the Great Pyramid. Were modern engineers to build such a monument today, the contract price would be over five billion dollars.

Men might be able to compute the weight and the measurements of the pyramid, but they would never be able to measure the cries and the tears of the laborers who bore the heavy burdens and built the monument on the desert sand, only to pass and be forgotten by everyone but God.

Communism in Germany

While in the Alps of Southern Germany, I visited the beautiful palace built by Ludwig of Bavaria. "He was a genius," said our guide, with a touch of German pride. "The fountain that erupts in the reflecting pool in front of the palace is the product of Ludwig's ingenuity. He captured the mountain stream far back in the hills and brought it down to the reflecting pool to erupt in regular intervals like a giant geyser." The genius of Ludwig was equally displayed inside the palace. The dining-room table was prepared for his own self-indulgence. He preferred to eat in total solitude. A touch of a button lowered the table to a room below where the waiters and chefs loaded it with the various dainties of the land. Another touch of the button brought the table back up to the king, who preferred to live in a fantasy world.

"He was a dreamer," said our guide. "He seemed detached from the people of his land." I walked through another castle built by Ludwig. It was called the Neuschwanstein. From room to room I wandered, beholding the beauty, and contemplating the genius of this man who built this castle with the symbol of the swan, which had been the theme of Wagner's composition. In one room was Wagner's personal piano, a gift to the king, who had been an admirer of the great composer. And what happiness did Ludwig derive from all of this? Enough to cause him to take his own life in a lonely mountain lake. In order to build his dream castles, he had taxed the Bavarians so unmercifully that they scarcely had money for food.

In the bright Bavarian sunlight, I could see the Neuschwanstein shining majestically in the green forest and outlined against the sky. And yonder in the distance, I could see a tiny lake, the last resting-place of a leader who dedicated his life to serving himself, rather than his people.

The Story of the Ages

The story of the ages changes little. With monotonous repetition it reveals the struggles between the poorest of the poor, and the richest of the rich. When Attila of the Huns was buried in Hungary, he had his body encased in a coffin of gold, a second coffin of silver, and a third coffin of iron. In the midst of a vast plain, a host of prisoners dug a huge grave and buried him in the night. His coffin was covered with the spoils and riches from many nations, and when all was finally and carefully hidden underground, the workmen were murdered so that the resting place of the king might never be known.

The same procedure was basically followed at the death of Alaric, the all-conquering Goth, who conquered Rome. At his death, multitudes of captives were set to work to turn the mighty river out of its course. When this was done, they laid the tyrant in a huge sepulcher adorned with the spoils and trophies of vanquished armies. They buried him in the river bed, and then turned the waters again in their natural course, so that all might be hidden from view. These workmen, too, were put to death, so that the location of the grave of the tyrant would be kept a secret.

On the banks of the Thames, I visited the Tower of London. It was begun in the year 1000, and the British had filled it with valuable things belonging to every age. The Tower of London had beheld some of the bitterest tragedies in history. In the Tower, kings and princes, queens and princesses had been murdered. Great and good men were imprisoned, tortured, and killed. Had Gundulf the Weeper known what a place of agony he was creating, when he built the Tower, he would have wept still more and with far better reason.

I stood with an endless line of tourists watching men and women with eager faces gaze with excitement on the gold and jewels that had been gathered for the Empire. My mind went back through history, recalling vividly some of the events of the past and the names of the famous men that had come down as immortal from Britain's golden age. There was Francis Drake, who, to the British of his day, was the greatest hero of all.

On the high seas, Drake, time and again, challenged the mighty ships of Spain. Time after time, he set their towering ships aflame. In his own ship, the *Golden Hind,* he brought back to England $200 thousand worth of gold.

From years of traveling abroad, I turned my thoughts again to my homeland where so many were preaching the doctrine of socialism. The American public, according to H.R. Gross, was in debt to the tune of $1.7 trillion, which means that every child born a U.S. citizen inherits the equivalent of a personal debt of $8,500. [As of 2009, the personal debt has topped two trillion dollars.]

Some pointed to the weaknesses of Capitalism and declared that Communism was preferable. Some uninformed speakers and writers suggested that the leaders and founders of Communism had a love for the laborer and were seeking to build a wonderful world of brotherly love. Was this true? There was only one way to find out: examine the records.

Marx

Because Karl Marx is considered to be one of the early fathers of Communism, I became interested in learning what I could about his own early life. Carl Schurz, a political leader of the nineteenth century, wrote concerning Marx:

> "I have never seen a man whose bearing was so provoking and intolerable.... Everyone who contradicted him, he treated with abject contempt. It is said of those who knew Marx that he hated people as individuals."

Stalin

Svetlana Alliluyeva, the daughter of Joseph Stalin, writes on pages 140-42 of her book *Only One Year* (Harper & Row, 1969):

> "Twenty-seven of those years I lived under a heavy weight ... a time of singlehanded despotism, bloody terror, economic hardships, the cruelest of wars, and ideological reaction.... I lived at the very top of the pyramid, where truth hardly reached one at all.... In the family in which I was born and bred nothing was normal, everything was oppressive, my mother's suicide was most eloquent testimony to the hopelessness of the situation. Kremlin walls all around me, secret police in the house, in the kitchen, at school. And over it all a wasted, obdurate man, fenced in from his former colleagues, his old friends, from all those who had been close to him, in fact from the entire world, who with his accomplices had turned the country into a prison, in which everyone with a breath of spirit and mind was being extinguished; a man who aroused fear and hatred in millions of men—this was my father."

The leaders of Communism make no effort to conceal their attitude toward truth. Lenin said, "Promises are piecrusts, made to be broken," and "The best revolutionary is a youth without morals."

Joseph Stalin said, "Honest diplomacy is as impossible as iron wood or dry water."

When Dwight D. Eisenhower was in office as president, he declared in a State of the Union message, "We have learned the bitter lesson that international agreements, historically considered by us as sacred, are regarded in Communist doctrine and practice to be mere scraps of paper."

Communism and God

The attitude of Marx and Lenin toward God was clearly expressed in the language, "I hate all gods."

Karl Marx declared, "The idea of God is the keystone of a perverted civilization. It must be destroyed."

This attitude seemed to permeate all who embraced the doctrines of Communism. Khrushchev's son-in-law, Alexei Adzhubei, said, "Every flirtation with God is an unutterable abomination."

All who read the words of Lenin were indeed aware of his hatred of God and religion. He wrote:

"Religion is the opium of the people. Religion is a kind of spiritual gin, in which the slaves of capitalism drown their human shape and their claim to any decent human life."

Communism and the Home

Long ago God gave to Moses the Ten Commandments. These became the foundation stones of all advanced civilization of the western world. One of those commandments read, "Honour thy father and thy mother: that thy days may be long upon the land which the Lord thy God giveth thee" Exodus 20:12).

Repeatedly, Moses reminded the people of this solemn command from the Almighty (e.g., Deuteronomy 5:16). Christ, too, repeatedly referred to this commandment, and Paul, in writing to the Ephesian church, said:

> "Children, obey your parents in the Lord: for this is right. Honour thy father and mother; which is the first commandment with promise; That it may be well with thee, and thou mayest live long on the earth" (Ephesians 6:1-3).

The words of Moses, Jesus, and Paul were in direct contrast to those of the *Communist Manifesto:* "The bourgeois clap-trap about the family and education, about the hallowed co-relation of parent and child becomes all the more disgusting."

Paul in writing to Titus concerning motherhood said, "Teach the young women ... to love their husbands, to love their children, to be ... keepers of the home" (Titus 2:4-5).

Communism and Their Enemies

Jesus said, "I say unto you which hear, Love your enemies, do good to them which hate you, Bless them that curse you, and pray for them which despitefully use you. And unto him that smiteth thee on the one cheek offer also the other" (Luke 6:27-29).

Marx and Engels stated in the Communist Manifesto, "Their ends can be attained only by the forceable overthrow of all existing social conditions."

During the Stalin purges, it is estimated that 374 generals and 30,000 line officers were put to death.

Dr. Nicholas Zermov, professor at the University of Moscow, declared, "Four or five million Christians perished since the Revolution (not including those put to death for political reasons)."

Zermov also said that in 1935 the government closed 14,000 churches and convicted 3,687 clergymen in criminal courts. Some of these were executed by firing squads.

China's record was no better. On October 1, 1949, Mao, in order to crush resistance on the home front, ordered what he called Mass Shock, in which 12 million were wiped out. (Western statistics put the number at 20 million.)

In February, 1950, Mao called all identified with the previous national government to register. They were promised forgiveness. Three months later they were the victims of a mass purge.

Communism and the Weak

In writing to the Romans, the Apostle Paul said, "We then that are strong ought to bear the infirmities of the weak, and not to please ourselves" (Romans 15:1).

In contrast, Joseph Stalin said, "In our time it is not our custom to give any consideration to the weak."

On March 26, 1959, Peter Chu Pong, former Minister of Nanking, China, appeared before the House Committee on Un-American Activities, and testified:

> "We were placed in classes for brainwashing. From morning till night, they taught Communism. They wanted me to reject Christ and give up the church and admit that the only God was Mao-Tsetung, head of the Communistic Government."

A former Communist said:

> "They asked me to forget Katyn Forest. Forget the slave labor camps, forget the genocide of the captive nations, forget the butchery of Budapest, forget the annihilation of thirty million people, forget their anti-God, anti-Christ, anti-church, and anti-home doctrines, and to forget all that is dear and place our faith in them."

With amazing courage some of Russia's finest writers have dared to express the true feelings of their hearts. Alexander Solzhenitsyn, considered by many to be Russia's greatest author, writes, "The USSR is guilty of committing *spiritual murder,* a variant of the gas chamber but more cruel."

In an edition of the *Los Angeles Times* in April, 1973, Murray Seeger tells how the government leaders in Russia seek to control men's minds and spirits. He describes the heavy volume of anti-religious action and propaganda that have been continued in all parts of Russia against many different faiths ever since the Bolshevik Revolution took place fifty-five years ago.

In light of the Communist attitude toward Christians and Jews, are men not justified in asking why this government should receive favored treatment?

Why should American taxpayers pay $300 million in taxes to subsidize cheap wheat for the USSR? Or why should Russia get 200,000 tons of butter from The European Common Market for twenty cents per pound, when the British pay sixty cents for the same butter?

Perhaps some of the international bankers might shed some light on this. They might tell us how the Communist banks were able to borrow forty billion Eurodollars six months before the dollar was devalued 10% on February 6th of 1973, and comment on the extraordinary good fortune of their timing. For when this debt is repaid, it will be repaid with dollars valued at ninety cents, which means a net profit of four billion dollars for the borrowers.

"Only one thing is clear," wrote one economist from Europe, "and that is the mystery that surrounds these strange actions."

That Russia was receiving favored treatment was beyond any question. It had been, ever since the birth of the United Nations. When it was organized in 1945, there were only fifty nations of the world represented in the UN. In the ten years following its birth, however, Communism had spread across the world at the rate of forty-four square miles per hour.

As new nations were being born and being admitted to the UN, the roster clearly revealed the young and struggling nations being admitted were often those who had accepted the doctrines and principles of Communism. This doctrine thrived especially in undeveloped areas, estimated to be at least 72% of the whole.

With the apparent domination of Communistic personalities in control of UNESCO and the International Police Force, reflected in the UN charter, it was difficult to understand how the United States could be removed much further from the position of leadership.

In the twenty-one years following the establishment of the UN there were twenty-two presidents of the UN General Assembly. Not one was an American. The same could be said about the highest office, that of Secretary-General.

Representation in the UN

As I sat by the fire on this particular evening, allowing memory to take me back through the milestones that man had passed in his momentum toward a one-world government I pondered the possibilities of the United Nations holding supreme control of the entire world. If 95% of the world's population was already in the UN and other nations such as East and West Germany were to be admitted, it had already reached the place of world representation. But was it capable of bringing man what man most desired, world peace and order?

I stood once in the general assembly hall in the UN and counted the number of seats being filled with the respective nations of the world, trying to estimate the population of the various countries. There was Iceland and Barbados whose populations together were smaller than that of Albuquerque, New Mexico.

There was Luxembourg and Swaziland, Fiji and Gabon, whose populations were less than that of Columbus, Ohio. Cyprus and Kuwait had populations smaller than Louisville, Kentucky.

Mauritania, Jamaica, and Mongolia had fewer people than Houston, Texas.

Costa Rica and Nicaragua, Albania, Sierra Leone, Somalia, Dahomey, Honduras, had populations only half of that of Philadelphia, Pennsylvania.

No one in honesty or kindness would want to exclude or deny a small nation its rightful place. But serious minded people are prone to ask whether it is fair for nations as small as these to have a vote in the General Assembly of the UN which would equal the vote of the United States with over 200 million people. Did the vote in the General Assembly of the UN really represent the people of the world with equity?

The Financial Record of the UN

When the United Nations chose to place its headquarters on the banks of the Hudson River in New

York, the American government loaned sixty-five million dollars tax-free toward the center. John D. Rockefeller, Jr., gave eight million dollars toward the land. The City of New York gave $26.5 million to prepare the site. The Ford Foundation gave over six million dollars toward a library to contain 400,000 books. Within a quarter of a century, the expenditures of the United Nations reached $9.2 billion. Of this amount, the United States has provided 41%. The financial records in a single year revealed Americans paid 31.8% of the annual UN budget.

The picture grew more discouraging when one gazed at the financial records of a single year and saw that Russia was $66.9 million in the red. Apparently not content to have the United States carry the heavy financial burden of the United Nations, the Russians wanted her to do even more. On Friday, November 17, 1972, the *Los Angeles Times* carried an article which read:

> Russia urges U.S. to increase UN aid. The normally humdrum budgetary committee broke into oratorical fireworks.... V.S. Safronchuk speaking to the General Assembly said, "The U.S. should be assessed 38.4% instead of its present 31.52%." This brought U.S. Ambassador George Bush to his feet; pointing to Safronchuk, Bush asserted that his government pays 40% of the overall costs, those outside as well as inside the regular budget, compared with the Soviets' contribution of 7%.

A look at the program within the UN that was supposed to be carried on as a humanitarian effort for the needy of the world—UNICEF (United Nations International Children's Emergency Fund)—revealed in 1970 that Russia gave $5.2 million compared to America's $159 million. This meant that Russia gave 1.47% compared to America's 45%.

Where, I asked myself, were the men who said the doctrines of Communism were closest to those of the early Christians? If the early church shared things in common, it was with the spirit of love which said, "What I have is yours." But the doctrine of Marx and Lenin was as different from Christianity as darkness is from light. Their spirit of greed and selfishness declared, "What you have is mine, and if you do not give it freely, we will take it from you by force."

The Justice of the United Nations

Foundations of the United Nations were laid by the United States, the United Kingdom, and the Soviet Union, from August 21 to September 28, 1944, in the Dumbarton Oaks Conference in Washington. Immediately afterward, the Republic of China became one of the five founding nations, and was given lifetime membership in the Security Council. Her population was larger than ¾ of the nations who held membership in the UN. Even in Taiwan, she maintained diplomatic relationship with sixties countries of the world. In the field of commerce, she exported over a billion dollars' worth of merchandise annually, and yet when Albania, with a population half the size of Philadelphia, made a motion that the Republic of China be expelled, the smaller nations rallied to the suggestion in a demonstration of emotionalism and bias that left a permanent blemish on the record of the UN. Ambassador Bush said on October 25, 1971, "Never have I seen such hate."

The late David Lawrence, respected news journalist and editor of the *U.S. News & World Report,* said, "Can any nation be safe in an atmosphere of such irresponsible and emotional action?"

The Chinese leaders returned to Taiwan in tears. They carried with them a record free from blot or blemish. Their dues had been paid. Their position had been held with honor. But without a single grievance against them, they were expelled and not even granted the courtesy of being permitted to speak for themselves. Someone dared to suggest before their departure that perhaps Communist China and Nationalist China could each have a seat. The pro-Communist block pounded their desks and shouted down the proposal. A few days later, they were willing to talk about two seats being given to both West Germany and Communist East Germany, to sit side by side.

The UN and Peace

When asked if the UN hoped to end all wars, international lawyer Ambassador J. Reuben Clark, Jr., said:

> "There seems no reason to doubt that such real approval as the Charter has among the people

> is based upon the belief that if the Charter is put into effect, wars will end.... The Charter will not certainly end war. The Charter provides for force to bring peace, but such use of force is itself war.... The Charter does take from us the power to declare war and to choose the side on which one must fight."

If men hoped the United Nations would bring peace to the world, their hopes proved groundless. The list of wars fought since 1945 seemed almost endless:

Indonesia, 1945-1947
China, 1945-1949
Kashmir, 1947-1949
Greece, 1946-1949
Israel, 1948-1949
Philippines, 1948-1952
Indo-China, 1945-1954
Malaya, 1945-1954
Korea, 1950-1953
Formosa, 1950
Kenya, 1952-1953
Sinai, 1956
Suez, 1956
Hungary, 1956
Quemoi-Matsu, 1954-1958
Lebanon, 1958
Tibet, 1950-1959
Cyprus, 1955-1959
Algeria, 1956-1962

Cuba, 1958-1959
Laos, 1959
Kuwait, 1961
Goa, 1961
Yemen, 1962
Congo, 1960-1962
Cuba, 1961
South Vietnam, 1959-1973
Himalayas, 1959-1962
Angola, 1960
West Guinea, 1962
Colombia, 1960
Cuba, 1962
Algeria-Morocco, 1963
Venezuela, 1963
Malaysia, 1963
Congo, 1964
Thailand, 1964
Dominican Republic, 1965
Peru, 1965
Pakistan, India, 1965-1972
[Israel, Six-Day War 1967
Israel Yom Kippur War, 1973
Israel Invasion of Lebanon, 1978, 1982-2000
Afghanistan Soviet Invasion, 1979-1989
Iraq Iran-Iraq War, 1980-1989
Argentina Falklands/Malvinas War, 1982
Iraq Gulf War, 1990-1991
Russia Chechen Uprising, 1994-1996
Afghanistan, 2001-

Iraq, 2003-]

On August 10, 1962, Herbert Hoover said:

"I urged the ratification of the United Nations by the senate, but now we must realize the United Nations has failed to give us even a remote hope of lasting peace. Instead it adds to the dangers of wars, which now surround us."

The United Nations and God

What has been the attitude of the United Nations toward God? Dr. Julian Huxley, who had served as Director of UNESCO, said, "While a faint trace of God still broods over the world like the smile of a cosmic Cheshire cat, science and knowledge will soon rub that trace away."

UN Leaders Ask for More Power

On August 23, 1970, U Thant addressed the Fourteenth World Congress of the World Association of World Federalists in Ottawa, Canada, and said, "A world under law is realistic and obtainable. The ultimate crisis before the UN is the crisis of authority."

The convention conducted by the lawyers and judges of the world in the interest of world law was a solemn sight indeed. There were 263 judges from every continent, Africans in red robes, sitting by Indians and Pakistanis, and Israelis, and five justices from the U.S. Supreme Court. Even a copy of the Magna

Carta was on hand. And banners across the platform read "Pax Orbis ex Jure," meaning "World Peace by World Law."

There were 119 countries represented. The main decision was to recommend that the UN Charter be amended to provide compulsory jurisdiction for individuals, as well as nations. Joseph Clark called for:

> "An executive with substantially greater powers than those now exercised by the Secretary-General of the UN. A judiciary system modeled after the world court. Decisions enforced by a world police force, under the command of a world executive."

Would man be willing to resign such power to the United Nations, knowing it was under Communistic domination? For many the answer was yes. One person said, "If the price of avoiding all-out thermal nuclear wars should prove to be acquiescence in the Communistic domination of the world, it seems probable that such a price would be paid."

And if the question was asked, "Why?" perhaps the answer would best be expressed by Adlai Stevenson, who in a speech to the United Nations Correspondents' Association said, "Interpret us ... as puzzled, yet aspiring men, struggling on the possible brink of Armageddon."

Why would men who are members of a strong and a free democracy vote in favor of a world organization which would include the explosive characteristics of South America, the turbulence of the Middle East, the tyranny of Russia, and the violence of Asia? One speaker answered the question by saying sadly, "No, it is not desirable; but we have no alternative. There is no other way out."

CHAPTER 12

THE MARCH TOWARD ARMAGEDDON

Intercontinental Ballistic Missiles

USSR	USA
1,590	1,054

Surface-to-Air Missiles

USSR	USA
10,000	500

Nuclear Missile Submarines

USSR	USA
48	41

Interceptor Aircraft

USSR	USA
3,000	600

Anti-Ballistic Missile Systems

USSR	USA
64	0

Time and again America sought to reduce her military strength and atomic weaponry. But they found that the formula did not work. It was impossible to disarm for peace.

On the evening of Tuesday, May 27, 1969, I went to the postbox in front of our Washington home, and picked up the newspaper, *The Evening Star.* The entire back page was devoted to an article by Secretary of

Defense Melvin Laird and others, entitled, THE REAL TRUTH ABOUT HOW MANY U.S. SENATORS ARE BEING TRICKED BY RUSSIA.

The subtitles were equally startling: "Russia is racing to a five-to-one first-strike nuclear superiority over America. Here is how they tricked America into letting it happen ... and how they are now tricking many U.S. Senators into leaving us defenseless."

In 1958, the United States had a five-to-one nuclear superiority over Russia. To keep its lead, the U.S. was testing bigger and bigger nuclear bombs, and so was Russia. Suddenly Russia announced she would like a moratorium on these tests. Radiation fallout was alarming the world, so the U.S. and Russia agreed to explode no more test bombs in the air. In the spirit of that moratorium, the U.S. began dismantling its testing installations, and stopped developing bigger bombs.

Russia did just the opposite. It secretly raced ahead. Suddenly, in September, 1961, Russia violated the moratorium with a series of tests in which it exploded the world's biggest hydrogen bomb, an incredible hundred-megaton monster vastly more powerful than anything the U.S. had. Overnight, Russia went years ahead of the U.S. in vital knowledge.

Tricked and dismayed, the U.S. then negotiated the famous test-ban treaty. It was approved by the U.S. Senate. President Kennedy acclaimed a new era of successful cooperation between the two countries.

In that spirit, the U.S. started cutting back on our missiles, taking the largest ones out of our stockpiles.

Russia again did just the opposite. It raced ahead. Suddenly, in June, 1967, a special study ordered by the Congress showed that while the U.S. had gone backward, the Soviets had forged ahead in total megatonnage.

By April of 1973, *U.S. News & World Report* showed Russian supremacy in many areas of the arms race:

So forboding was the prospect of atomic annihilation that many people sought to build around the sensitivities of their inner soul an insulation of indifference. But they could not shut entirely from their minds the sobering truths of their day. Dope addiction became rampant across the nation. The younger generation, seemingly in hopeless despair, sought to drown their normal sensitivities in a sea of hallucinogens. Yes, the arms race would continue unabated.

For years I had followed with interest efforts made by leaders of Russia and America in the SALT Talks. After endless months and thousands of dollars had been spent in these discussions, suddenly the Strategic Arms Limitations Talks became virtually meaningless, because China had reached the place where she too had become a major atomic power threat.

Senator Stuart Symington, addressing the Senate Armed Services Committee on January 9, 1973, said:

> "China is expected in 1975 to have an operational intercontinental ballistic missile which could be capable of striking the U.S.... I was shocked to find out how close another power is to becoming a super-power in missiles. This to me reduces the practical effect of the Strategic Arms Limitations Talks with the Soviet Union."

It seemed that the entire world was on the march toward Armageddon and knew it. I picked up a copy of the *Reader's Digest* and read thirteen references to the Battle of Armageddon. On the cover of the *Post,* one word was splashed across the front of the bright red cover: ARMAGEDDON. At a newsstand on the streets of Barcelona, Spain, I picked up a newspaper with the bold headline discussing Armageddon. In his dying hours, Douglas MacArthur said, "We are now entering Armageddon."

Vietnam

Weary of war and fearing for his future, man was willing to cling to any thin thread of hope. Willing, indeed, he was to sit in the tension-filled halls of the UN and indulge in the divisive arguments which continued endlessly between the opposing blocks of power. For ten years, the nations had discussed the war in Vietnam with bitter accusations, while presidential envoy Henry Kissinger traversed a well-beaten path between Peking, Moscow, Washington, and Paris to obtain an uneasy peace.

The years had taken a tremendous toll of American life and property. Reportedly, 304,000 American boys had been wounded, and 56,000 had been killed. Since 1966, America had dropped 7.1 million tons of bombs on Vietnam. She had lost 1,647 planes and 2,281 helicopters. The war had cost as much as $70 million per day to wage.

World War I

I was too young to remember another peace, earlier in the century, the end of "the war that was to end all wars." The armistice was signed on the eleventh hour of the eleventh day of the eleventh month in the year, bringing to a close the fearful struggle of World War I.

I was two years old on that fateful day in 1918. Spending the first 12 years of my life in a Canadian town west of Winnipeg, I recalled, as a lad, pausing at the monument erected on the main street of the town, and reading the names engraved in marble. As I stood in reverence reading the names of those who had died in conflict, older men of the village would pat my head and say softly, "These, son, are the names of those who died to make your world safe. They died that no more would ever have to die in battle." How wrong they proved to be. With the passing of time, wars not only became more frequent, but weapons more destructive.

Futile Quest for Peace

Rivers of ink and acres of paper would be required to record man's futile quest for peace. In the thirteenth century, the wild horsemen of Genghis Khan Swept out of Mongolia across the steppes of Central Asia, and burned the capital Kiev. The Tatar yoke lasted 240 years. The Russians have never forgotten the rule that finally ended in 1480. The pages of history reveal that Russia has been at war 75% of the time during the past seven centuries. France and Britain have been involved in Wars over 50% of the last seven centuries. In 3,358 years of man's history, he could point to only 227 years of global peace. From 1500B.C. to A.D.1860, man had signed 8,000 treaties—with an average life expectancy of less than two years.

A Norwegian statistician goes even further and says that in 5,560 years of history, man has fought 14,531 wars. This represents 2.6 wars per year. In 885 generations, we have witnessed only *10 years* of unsullied peace. More than 600 million men have matched to the battlefields of the world never to return.

CHAPTER 13

MAN LOSES HOPE IN MAN

In God we trust. So widespread and deep was that conviction in the American colonies that the founding fathers never even thought twice before affixing it to the coin of the realm. There was no doubt in their minds as to who *the* Founding Father was, to whom they owed everything, and whose advice and consent they invariably sought before making any federal, local, or personal decision.

But somewhere along the way, with the dawn of the scientific revolution and the Age of Reason, with its unprecedented affluence, we began to think that we *had done* it ourselves, that we *could* do it ourselves. More and more intellectuals and teachers were assuring us that God did not exist, that with the elevation of man's mind, even the concept of God was no longer essential.

And for those of us who did not already know Him, this suited our emerging frame of mind, as we made idols of self-reliance, self-confidence, self-centeredness. Look at all we have accomplished; see what *we* can do.

And the scientists and the planners, flush with the first-fruits of the new technology, said, "Come to us with all your problems. Given enough time and goodwill, there is nothing we cannot solve."

But somehow there was never enough time, and goodwill was little more than a Christmas-card sentiment, and for every problem they sought to solve, they seemed to create ten more that no one had been able to foresee.

And now, as the voices of the increasingly disillusioned are raised against them, they eschew the enormous responsibility they once so lightly assumed, retorting, "Well, we're not God, are we?" No, they are not. But they were more than willing to be in the beginning.

So man has come to the end of his resources. He has risked everything on his ability to do it himself, and all he has succeeded in doing is pulling his world down around his ears. In the enormity of what he has done, at last he is beginning to see that in his own strength he can do nothing.

The result? For some, a turning back to the God once trusted, and a joyous rediscovery that He never changed. He can be absolutely trusted yesterday, today, and forever.

But for the majority, utter despair—on a scale the world has never known. Hedonism, hatred of morality, mindless violence—and amongst our youth, bitter rejection of authority and a blaming of "those in charge" for the hopeless mess the world is in. And escape—into alcohol, drugs, Eastern religions, anything to get as far away from reality as possible. But there is no permanent escape, save one.

It has been estimated that 1,000 American college students will succeed in taking their own lives this year, 9,000 will attempt suicide, and 90,000 will threaten to take their lives. And further, that one hundred young people attempt suicide for every one that is officially recorded. The despair at the degenerating world seems to be reflected even in the lives of some of the smaller children. On the front page of the *Los Angeles Herald Examiner,* there appeared a story. It read as follows:

A gruesome little ditty called "Suicide Song" intended as a parody for a Parent-Teachers' Association skit was briefly Number One on the third grade Hit Parade in the Beach Community's schools. Teachers were aghast when they heard the words:

"Oh, come with me to the kitchen,
to the kitchen, to the kitchen.
Oh, come with me to the kitchen
and there a date with death we both will keep.
Turn on the gas in the oven,
in the oven, in the oven.
It will gently lull us both to sleep.
Listen to the hissing sound.
Listen to the hissing sound.
They are calling, gently calling you and me.
Listen to the hissing sound.
Listen to the hissing sound.
We'll say good-bye and die in ecstasy."

It was sung to the tune of "Listen to the Mocking Bird."

While some American children sang such songs of tragedy, across the other side of the ocean in the USSR, school children were singing, "The Blight of the World Is Jesus."

The Source of Earth's Sorrow

What had happened to man's world? Why did he find himself in the enlightenment of intellectualism stumbling in the darkness of his own confusion with morals too low and taxes too high, power groups arrogant, crime rampant, and extremists violent? With his ability to put a billion characters a second on the computer tape, man had succeeded also in generalizing humanity—identity was stifled and individuals had been transformed into IBM cards. The environment of violence had become natural. Man had changed his world into a psychedelic asylum.

Where was the utopia that was to have been born of Hegel's dialectic triads? Marx and Engels had embraced the words of Hegel who wrote that the individual exists only for the state, the state is divine, the absolute end, the true God, the divinity which enjoys an authority and majesty absolute. Marx and Engels echoed in their *Manifesto* the writings of Kant who began with man rather than God and was followed by Nietzsche who presented the *Übermensch* or "Superman." These doctrines had not only filled the hearts of millions of the lower levels of society, they had been echoed time and again in the halls of the Security Council and the General Assembly of the UN even by the highest leaders of the world bodies. *Newsweek* published an interview with U Thant in which he said, "I believe in the philosophy of thesis, antithesis and synthesis. From its present antithesis, I believe the world is moving toward a new synthesis."

Those who knew the basic philosophy and doctrine of Communism heard in these words the words of Hegel, Engels, and Karl Marx.

But, any honest man could see that something was sadly lacking. The words of the world leaders reminded the listener of those spoken long ago by Cicero, who read the *Phaedo* and sighingly said, "Plato ... thou reasonest well, but..."

From the days of Cicero and Plato to the present leaders like U Thant there remains the one problem word—"BUT..."

A world of plenty and a day of peace so near, so possible, "BUT..."

The truth is that our world *is* a world of plenty. The world's finest scientists estimate Earth's real riches to be her grain and her gold, her fruit and gems, her timber and treasures, almost limitless in minerals and resources. Some suggest that Earth's combined wealth would conservatively total one decillion dollars. Divide this equally among Earth's present population and every man, woman, and child would be a billionaire a billion times over.

Divide the fifty-eight million square miles of land equally and every person alive today would have ten acres each. Many good men today dream and discuss a world that man could live in if he were free from wars and deception and self-destruction.

Dr. Peter Goldmark, who was President and Research Director of CBS Laboratories for thirty-six years, shows, for example, how a hundred million Americans could build model communities of 3000, and use only 4% of America's land.

R. Buckminster Fuller is called by U. Thant one of the greatest philosopher-scientists of our time. On April 26, 1973, when flying from Dallas to Los Angeles, I picked up the airline magazine and read in the *American Way* the interview between the architect, Michael Ben Eli and Buckminster Fuller. Mr. Fuller said:

> Sadly, we see enormous numbers of stranded poverty-stricken people while potential abundance is being deliberately curtailed by governments subservient to the landlord's will.
>
> Humanity is so accustomed to failure it still assumes failure to be normal, and does not realize that it has literally earned—and actually acquired—the capability to take care of everyone on earth at a higher standard of living than ever heretofore experienced by anyone.

> The really big fact is that we are going to have to go through a complete mental resorting of what it is all about. Then we are going to have to go about taking care of everybody not as on relief, but with the same spontaneous welcome and love accorded a newborn baby.
>
> Landlordism will no longer be able to extract a ransom. *Money too will become obsolete,* with the ability to produce enough to take care of all.
>
> The fact that we now have the capability to support all life and are not doing so means we have to introduce a *new* system. One that can make the world work.

The flight time between Dallas and Los Angeles was devoted primarily to the consideration of the words of Buckminster Fuller. It was not my first introduction to this philosopher-scientist. In past occasions, our paths had crossed in American cities where each of us had been speaking under different auspices. I agreed with his conviction that the world was large enough and sufficiently rich to sustain all men on the highest level, under ideal conditions. But I could not agree that man alone, without God, could ever realize its potential.

After reading the "Master Plan for Living" provided by Peter Goldmark, and studying the blueprint for the future drawn by Buckminster Fuller, I had to sigh with Cicero and say, "Thou reasonest well, but..."

Something was missing. I knew it, they knew it, and all the leaders of the world knew it. The Kremlin was confused. The U.S. Senate was perplexed. The leaders of Europe were distressed. What was man's future, his ultimate end?

Distress with Perplexity

When disciples long ago discussed with Christ the conditions that would climax this age, He said there would be "Upon the earth distress of nations, with perplexity" (Luke 21:25).

The Greek word for "distress" is *aporia,* meaning "unable to discover a way out" or "coming to an impasse."

The prophecies of the Bible, indeed, portray every detail that we could visualize in this present hour, but do not leave us in the valley of doom or in the darkness of the present moment. In discussing these days, Jesus added with a triumphant note, "And when these things begin to come to pass, then look up, and lift up your heads; for your redemption draweth nigh" (Luke 21:28).

Surely the prophets of old promised God would come to man's side in the hour of his darkest trial. The day would dawn when His Son would sweep away the failures of the past centuries and establish law and order and usher in a kingdom of peace. But man still had not reached that moment when he was willing to lift his eyes and look up. No, he would still continue on the spiraling downward pathway of human failure.

In the famous conversation between Raymond Swing and Albert Einstein, Mr. Swing said, "Either we will find a way to establish world government, or we will perish in a war of the atom."

Doctor Einstein replied, "The secret of the bomb should be committed to a world government, and the USA should immediately announce its readiness to give it to a world government."

Commenting on this 1945 exchange, Sumner Wells, in *The Atomic Bomb and World Government,* wrote, "No world government of the character envisaged by Professor Einstein would function unless it possessed the power to exercise complete control over the armaments of each constituent state."

As men began to move more rapidly toward world government, fear was expressed by some of the world's finest intellectuals. Doctor Charles Merriam, for many years professor of political economy in the University of Chicago, said, "I raise my voice to warn—human liberty may be lost."

But most intellectuals were not only willing to concede that liberty would be lost, they were in favor of disposing of it. Professor Laski of Oxford, England, declared, "Sovereignty must go; that means also the interests which sovereignty protects must be recognized as outmoded in character and dangerous in operation."

As I moved from country to country, I was astonished at the amazing political phenomena of the times, the continued trend toward totalitarian controls. A world government of unprecedented size and power would still of necessity demand a world leader. Men had reached the place where they were not only willing to accept such a suggestion, but were willing to cry for strong individual leadership in this hour.

Few men expressed themselves more firmly in this respect than Paul Henri Spaak. A European statesman born in Brussels, Spaak led the Socialist Party of Belgium and was the first president of the Council of Europe. One of the planners of the European Common Market, he also served as president of the United Nations' General Assembly and as Secretary-General of NATO. In addition, he served as Prime Minister of Belgium and as Minister of Foreign Affairs for his country. Few men had filled such a roster of important offices. Spaak repeatedly expressed his desire to see a strong man arise on the world horizon to lead men out of the confusion of their present dilemma: "Let that man be a military man or a layman, it matters not."

Spaak's cry for strong, one-man, rule was echoed on the lips of many leaders. Roswell Gilpatric, former Deputy Secretary of Defense, said, "Strong, one-man, civilian control of America's giant military establishment is vital to the nation's well-being. The concentration of authority is inevitable."

Crisis Measures

In America, at the time of the Cuban Missile Crisis in 1962, a series of emergency measures were formulated, to be followed in the event of a full confrontation, and they were signed into law by the late John

F. Kennedy. They stand today exactly as they were signed on February 16 and February 27, 1962. Those emergency documents provide that the president should have complete and final dictatorial control, the authority to undertake immediate and decisive action. His executive orders are to be carried out through the Office of Emergency Planning and they are to be put into effect, "...in any time of increased international tension or economic or financial crisis."

These orders are all-inclusive:

- *Executive Order 10995* – to take over all communication media.
- *Executive Order 10997*—take over all electric power, petroleum, gas, fuels, and minerals.
- *Executive Order 10998*—take over all food resources and farms.
- *Executive Order 10999*—take over all methods of transportation, highways, and seaports.
- *Executive Order 11000*—mobilization of civilians and work forces under governmental supervision.
- *Executive Order 11001*—take over all health, welfare, and educational functions.
- *Executive Order 11002*—the Postmaster-General, a member of the President's Cabinet, will operate a nationwide registration of all persons.
- *Executive Order 11003*—to take over all airports and aircraft.

- *Executive Order 11004*—take over housing and finance authorities—to relocate communities—to build new housing with public funds—designate areas to be abandoned as unsafe—establish new locations for populations.
- *Executive Order 11005*—take over all railroads, inland waterways, and public storage facilities.
- *Executive Order 11051*—designate responsibilities of Office of Emergency Planning, give authorization to put all other executive orders in effect in times of increased international tension or economic or financial crises.

The word "crisis" seemed to be appearing almost weekly in the headlines of the news media—population crisis, war crisis, fuel and energy crisis. If man was willing under crisis to commit total and absolute power to an individual leader of the nation or the world, how sudden and complete could be the revolutionary new methods swept in by such a man!

Who could administer such an instant world government?

H.G. Wells expressed the sentiments of millions when he wrote, "It is necessary to discover a head capable of directing it, endowed with an intelligence surpassing the most elevated human level."

Over and over I found myself quoting those statements of Wells—"endowed with an intelligence surpassing the most elevated human level ... surpassing the most elevated human level."

The Leader

Did Wells actually visualize a world leader with supernatural power? If so, from whom would such a ruler receive his power? Were there other men as prominent as Wells who entertained similar thoughts? I soon discovered that there were.

One U.S. poll revealed that over 60% of the population believed in supernatural powers outside the human realm.

In May of 1973, *Reader's Digest* featured an article relating to the discovery of life in outer space. It suggested that the scientific pendulum since 1963 had been swinging toward the side of evidence of life beyond the boundaries of our planet.

I recalled the words of the Astronomer Gibson Reeves who referred to "...a rebelling mind somewhere in the universe having its effect on our planet earth." I wondered when I read the words of Gibson Reeves if he was referring to Lucifer who long ago, according to the prophets of the Bible, led a rebellion in his desire to be equal with Christ.

Again I pondered the words of Isaiah who wrote:

> "How art thou fallen from heaven, O Lucifer, son of the morning!... For thou hast said in thine heart, I will ascend into heaven ... I will be like the most high" (Isaiah 14:12-14).

John, Jude, Peter, Ezekiel, and Isaiah all wrote concerning the rebellion led by Lucifer. The prophets defined the cause of his rebellion, named the number that followed him and described his ultimate destruction. Of utmost importance was the effect this had on men on Earth.

On November 16, 1972, Pope Paul VI, addressing an audience of 6,000 people said, "We are all under an obscure domination. It is by Satan, the prince of this world."

Dr. Billy Graham, addressing thousands, said, "The devil is very real. Everyone knows that there are supernatural powers in the world."

One might expect Dr. Graham or Pope Paul to believe in Satan, but references to Lucifer or Satan were beginning to appear more frequently in unexpected places.

I recalled a sleepless night in the Admiral Benbow Inn in Memphis, Tennessee. It was not bad food nor a bad dream that kept me awake, it was a volume published by Encyclopedia Britannica entitled *Great Ideas of 1971.*

Much of the volume was devoted to the words of men who wrote in favor of world government. I weighed carefully their comments and compared particularly the blueprint drawn by Dr. Hutchinson and his committee to the description of world government written by the Prophet John almost 2,000 years earlier. I was fascinated at the similarities.

Suddenly I came to page 118 and stared with amazement at what I read. From book 5, chapter 5, quotations were printed from Dostoevsky's *The Brothers Karamazov.* Here the Russian writer depicted Jesus returning to Earth, being rejected by a world leader who said:

> "Why hast Thou come now to hinder us? ... We are working not with Thee but with him (Satan) ... We took from him what Thou didst reject with scorn, that last gift he offered Thee, showing Thee all the kingdoms of the earth. We took from him Rome and the sword of Caesar, and proclaimed ourselves sole rulers of the earth ... We shall triumph and shall be Caesars, and then we shall plan the universal happiness of man ... Hadst Thou accepted that last counsel of the mighty spirit (Satan), Thou wouldst have accomplished all that man seeks on earth—that is, someone to worship ... Who can rule men if not he who holds their conscience and their bread in his hands?"

And I recalled those haunting words in the Gospel of Luke:

> "And the devil taking him [Jesus] up into an high mountain, shewed unto him all the kingdoms of the world in a moment of time. And the devil said unto him, All this power will I give thee, and the glory of them: for that is delivered unto me; and to whomsoever I will I give it. If thou therefore wilt worship me, all

> shall be thine. And Jesus answered and said unto him, Get thee behind me, Satan: for it is written, Thou shalt worship the Lord thy God, and him only shalt thou serve" (Luke 4:5-8).

Jesus did not bow down to Satan, but neither did He discount Satan's claim to the glories of this world when he said, "That is delivered unto me; and to whomsoever I will I give it."

No, Christ did not refute the claim of Lucifer that the glories of earth had been delivered unto him, nor did he deny that he could give the same to any who would follow or worship him.

Christ referred to him as, "The prince of this world" (John 14:30).

Somewhere, apparently in the distant past, Lucifer had been given a certain authority over the planet Earth. One day, according to the prophets of the Bible, his jurisdiction over Earth would end and he would be judged and destroyed.

No one knew this better than Lucifer himself. The Prophet John says he has "great wrath, because he knoweth that he hath but a short time" (Revelation 12:12).

The aspiration which prompted him to lead his first rebellion was the desire to be like the Most High who was worshiped.

Lucifer longed to be worshiped. He offered Christ the power and glory of Earth in exchange for just one thing—His worship.

The words of Dostoevsky were much more than foolish fiction. They resembled all too literally the words of the prophet John who declared in the thirteenth Chapter of the Revelation that Lucifer would give his wisdom and power to those who would be leaders of the final form of government in which sinful man would rule the world.

The Prophet John, however, does not conclude his message as Dostoevsky does. John agrees that men of Satanic power will hold world authority for a brief time, but that they will be overthrown by Christ who will establish righteousness and universal peace and order.

This final act will be the glorious climax, the grand finale of all that has been written by the prophets. The Book of the Revelation closes in a blaze of glory where truth triumphs and men live in a new Earth wherein dwells righteousness.

The log on the hearth had almost turned to ashes. Only a few red embers still lingered on the grate. The night hours had virtually slipped away, and I shivered a little as I stirred the last of the coals with an effort to encourage them to one final flame.

What scenes had unfolded before me in that fire during those night hours of reverie and meditation!

The battle of the ages had been reenacted before my eyes. The symbolic dove of peace had not yet found a resting place on Earth, nor would it until the Prince of Peace would come. But the hour was drawing near. I could see the rosy rays of promise breaking over the pages of the inspired writings of the prophets who said, "He that shall come will come, and will not tarry" (Hebrews 10:37).

If a thousand inspired utterances penned in the past had already been miraculously fulfilled, the few remaining prophecies would surely be fulfilled as well.

Lucifer's rebellion against God had continued through the centuries. Men on Earth had also been included in a conflict which seemed endless.

The story of this struggle had been written with the ink of blood and tears. The concluding chapter was now being penned.

The final scene of battle would be in the Middle East. According to the prophet Ezekiel, Russia and her allies would march against Israel. He writes: "And thou shalt come up against my people of Israel, as a cloud to cover the land; it shall be in the latter days" (Ezekiel 38:16).

How little do the Russian leaders know the destruction that awaits them in their coming invasion of Israel! They have for many years opposed the church, oppressed the Jews, and hurled insults in the face of God and His Son. I had seen posters produced by the anti-God artists of Communism depicting the workingman dumping Jesus Christ in a sewer, and others mocking the sacrament, showing men eating the dismembered body of Jesus in a suggested orgy of cannibalism.

God is not ignorant of the insults and attacks made against Him and His followers by the leaders of

Communism who cry, "We hate all gods." There is a day of reckoning coming, and God's prophets tell how, when, and where it will take place.

The Prophet Ezekiel, who sees Russia in the latter days turning her face toward Israel, writes:

> "Thus saith the Lord GOD; It shall come to pass, that at the same time shall things come into thy mind, and thou shalt think an evil thought: And thou shalt say, I will go ... To take a spoil" (Ezekiel 38:10-12).

No where in the world is there greater spoil than the oil of the Middle East.

In Saudi Arabia alone, Ahmed Zaki Yamani, Minister of Oil, estimates their reserves at 150 billion barrels which is 30% of the world's known reserves. Some estimate that in less than seven years the oil of the Middle East could represent as much as $250 billion in value. [As of 2008, Saudi Arabia had proven oil reserves of 267 billion barrels, and is expected by some to have an estimated reserve by 2025 of 900 billion barrels.]

There is also the wealth of the Dead Sea with its limitless deposits of potash and other chemicals. Added to all of this is the importance of the Middle East geographically. Some have crudely but aptly referred to the Middle East, in the center of the globe as "the jugular vein of the World."

If Lucifer declared he would grant the riches of Earth to those who would follow him, this promise should surely apply to the anti-God leaders of Communism.

Little do the armies of Russia realize as they march toward Palestine, that they are marching toward their own destruction. Lucifer's reign as prince of this world is about to end. His time has finally run out. The prophet Ezekiel tells how God views this final act and says:

> "Thus saith the Lord GOD; in that day when my people of Israel dwelleth safely, shalt thou not know it? And thou shalt come from thy place out of the north parts ... a great company, and a mighty army: And thou shalt come against my people of Israel, as a cloud to cover the land; it shall be in the latter days" (Ezekiel 38:14-16).

Two verses later, the prophet describes God's fury and in verse 22, he tells of the fire from Heaven that destroys the armies of Russia and her allies.

As I studied these stupendous statements, I found myself wondering whether the destruction of the Russian armies would be caused by an atomic holocaust or by divine intervention. Perhaps, I said to myself, it was each.

As I read into the next chapter, one thing was extremely clear, God had declared His opposition to this invasion and through the pen of His prophet wrote, "And I will turn thee back, and leave but a sixth part of thee ... and seven months shall the house of Israel be burying of them" (Ezekiel 39:2, 12).

No, I said slowly, God is neither unjust nor unmerciful. He cannot allow Lucifer to succeed in this final act of aggression, nor can He allow those who follow the prince of this world to triumph in their march against Israel and gain world control.

World control? Ah, yes, that has been the dream and desire of Lucifer through all of the ages. "Follow me!" he cried, "Obey me! Worship me! Ye shall be as Gods, and the glories of this world shall be thine."

Among those willing to follow Lucifer were the money changers whose God was mammon. Though Christ drove them from the temple, they did not disappear from Earth. The Luciferian Society of money changers became the unseen rulers over kings and princes.

The cry of the dying soldiers and the blood of a hundred battlefields meant nothing to those who saw an opportunity to gain wealth through war.

How clear, I thought, how very clear is the strategy of Lucifer when explained by the prophets of the Bible. He deceives the world leaders and leads them to the battlefields to fight wars that cost billions of dollars to fight. To obtain the vast sums of money essential to waging wars, the governments of the world were forced to borrow from the moneylenders who were the High Priests of Finance. On these astronomical war debts the taxpayers were forced to pay interest.

Presently, the annual cost of arms and armies demanded payments equaling all of the paychecks of one-third of the world's poorer people. With the arms race continuing unabated, a spokesman for the UN predicted an annual price tag of a trillion dollars by 1980. Nations would continue to sink deeper in debt, and taxpayers would continue to pay interest to international bankers, who according to Dr. Quigley, "...were different from ordinary bankers and were concerned with questions of government debts. They were devoted to secrecy and financial influence in political life."

I thought on these words and repeated again the words written by Curtis B. Dall concerning the international bankers when he wrote, "They are driving toward complete control of the world's long-range monetary policy—for their own profit. They foment foreign wars to aid this objective."

The objective? Yes, the objective of those gaining control of the world's wealth was to have total authority over all mankind.

My thoughts turned one more time to the writings of the Russian Dostoevsky who said, "We shall triumph—we shall plan the universal happiness of man."

This, said Dostoevsky, would be accomplished by the one who would hold control of man's conscience and his bread.

The only happiness sought by Lucifer, however, was not man's good but his own Satanic desire to have men worship him. If he controlled man's bread he could force men to bow to him.

The Prophet John tells how this world leader who will have power over "all kindreds, and tongues, and nations" (Revelation 13:7), and "cause that as many as would not worship the image of the beast should be killed" (Revelation 13:15).

And again I recalled the fantastic passage of Scripture that I had repeated so many times before:

> "He causeth all small and great, rich and poor, free and bond, to receive a mark in their right hand, or in their foreheads: And that no man might buy or sell save he that had the mark ... or the number" (Revelation 13:16-17).

This would seem to be Lucifer's hour of triumph. He has struggled many long centuries to reach this goal. He has deceived the nations in leading them to battle. He has imparted his cunning and power to the moneychangers of the world who have stripped the masses of their wealth and have brought all mankind under a number system.

"Now," he cries, "men must worship me or be put to death. No man can buy or sell or live in my one-world society, unless he takes the number of our universe."

I had seen wars bring debts and rationing. I had seen certain natural circumstances contribute to the establishment of the International Monetary Fund and the World Bank. I had witnessed the computer age transform our world into IBM cards on which men were filed as digits rather than people. I had viewed the skylines of the world's leading cities, where bank buildings rose heavenward like giant cathedrals.

Unbelievable, I thought, as I studied these superstructures dominating the horizons of the world. Unbelievable that some of these great banking houses will be devoid of vaults. They will have no need of such, for in place of money will be only computers that carry a man's number and determine his allowance in a worldwide ration system.

Even while I thought on these truths, I was moved with the knowledge that banking houses were perfecting the non-toxic ink with which a number could be implanted for life on man's flesh.

The world system will be praised and promoted by brilliant men. With eloquence and apparent logic they will persuade men that this is the path to peace and security.

The world leader will rise to power with flattery and gain complete control of the military and monetary powers of all nations.

A dark picture? Yes, indeed. But hardly the conclusion of man's drama.

John the Revelator did not conclude his book of the Revelation with the universal number system described in chapter 13, nor the Battle of Armageddon in chapter 16, nor the anti-Christ system under Lucifer mentioned in chapters 17 through 19. Thank God, the Prophet John writes chapter 20 describing the overthrow of Lucifer and his forces. Chapters 20 and 21 describe with inspired eloquence a new

Heaven and Earth, where blood no longer is shed, where tears no longer flow, where war clouds no longer darken the sky.

The glorious daybreak of deliverance dawning on a world which had suffered for so many centuries the deception and destruction brought to Earth by Lucifer, the archenemy of God and man.

When Christ was on Earth as the Savior of men, Lucifer sought to tempt Him by offering Him Earth's glories. He knew Christ had come for one express purpose that was described by John who wrote, "For this purpose the Son of God was manifested, that He might destroy the works of the devil" (1 John 3:8).

Satan's demons recognized Christ as the Son of God even when men looked on Him only as the carpenter's son. On one occasion, they cried, "What have we to do with thee, Jesus, thou Son of God? art thou come hither to torment us before the time?" (Matthew 8:29).

Lucifer knew that Christ had said, "I will come again" (John 14:3). "Ye shall see the Son of man sitting on the right hand of power." (Mark 14:42).

Jude also writes, and Enoch, the seventh from Adam, prophesied: "the Lord cometh with ten thousands of his saints" (Jude 14).

When doing a documentary film on the United Nations, I paused outside the UN and gazed with incredulity at the huge marble slab on which had been engraved a message from the USSR.

It was a quotation from the Prophet Isaiah pertaining to the return of Christ. Some read this and asked if some miracle had caused the atheistic leaders of Communism to acknowledge their own failures and the world's only hope in the return of Christ, when they chiseled in marble for the world to read, "And they shall beat their swords into ploughshares, and their spears into pruninghooks: nation shall not lift sword against nation, neither shall they learn war any more" (Isaiah 2:4).

The presentation of Scripture by the Communists to the UN was really no miracle, but merely another example of deception. When Lucifer tempted Christ, he, too, quoted Scripture—broken Scripture and half-truth Scriptures taken out of context.

The words chiseled in marble by the Communists spoke of universal peace, but the inference was a peace that would be brought to mankind by the UN, not by God.

If the Communist leaders had presented to the UN a plaque bearing the complete Scripture written by Isaiah rather than a half-truth, it would have commenced with the statement:

> "And it shall come to pass in the last days, that the mountains of the LORD's house shall be established ... And many people shall go and say, ... we will walk in His paths: ... And He shall judge among the nations, and shall rebuke many people" (Isaiah 2:2-4). And would have concluded with

> the words, "and let us walk in the light of the LORD" (Isaiah 2:5).

The Prophet Micah penned words identical to Isaiah and added the glorious statements:

> "But they shall sit every man under his vine and under his fig tree; and none shall make him afraid; for the mouth of the LORD of hosts hath spoken it ... and we will walk in the name of the LORD our God for ever and ever" (Micah 4:4-5).

This indeed is the glorious truth that all the prophets of the Bible emphasize. The Prophet Daniel speaks of the hour when the God of heaven shall "set up a kingdom, which shall never be destroyed; and the kingdom shall not be left to other people ... it shall stand forever." (Daniel 2:44)

But what will it take to deliver man from the greed and lust and hatred which flow from sinful hearts? God's Word declares it will take the final and complete destruction of Lucifer and his legions, which through the centuries have blinded the minds of men, even as the Apostle Paul declares. (See 2 Corinthians 4:4.)

When Lord Gladstone was Prime Minister of England, he said, "More and more I find my thoughts turning to the great statement—when the Son of Man cometh."

This indeed is man's great hope. I sat in the heart of London with one of Britain's brilliant writers, Kenneth DeCoursey, and he told of a conversation with Winston Churchill who referred to the return of Christ as man's only hope.

It is indeed a hope that soon will be fulfilled. Man need not, however, wait only for the physical return of Christ to overthrow the kingdom of evil. His Spirit, which is already in the world, will enter the heart of everyone who is willing to bow humbly in recognizing Him as Lord and Master.

Christ not only spoke of his coming Kingdom, He also declared that the Kingdom of God can be within you. This is not only a privilege, *it is imperative* if one will inhabit the Kingdom to come.

Christ said to Nicodemus, "Except a man be born again he cannot see the kingdom of God" (John 3:3).

These words sounded strange to the ruler of the Jews, and he asked how could these things be? But the mystery did not hinder him from accepting by faith the realities of the spiritual kingdom which would lead him into the literal kingdom of God.

One day Christ will reign as Lord and Master on the throne of every heart, and righteousness will cover the earth as the waters cover the sea.

I turned to the window with amazement and realized the sun was now breaking on the eastern horizon. The birds were singing in the light of dawn; the world was awakening to a new day. The last glowing embers had died on the hearth; the hours of the night had passed. I walked to the front door, threw it open, and stepping outside, I faced the sun. "Prophecy," I cried, "is truly a light in a dark place." Even in the shadows of the present confusion we have, as Peter declared, a sure word of prophecy: "Where unto ye do well that ye take heed, as unto a light that shineth in a dark place, until the day dawns, and the day star arise in your hearts" (2 Peter 1:19).

ENDNOTES

[1] The term *Wirtschaftswunder* (help·info) (German for "economic miracle") describes the rapid reconstruction and development of the economies of West Germany and Austria after World War II.

[2] Ludvig Erhard was called the "father of economic miracle" in Germany after World War II and became Chancellor of Germany from 1963-1966.

[3] Revelation 17:3

[4] Herbert Ros is a published theologian living in Stuttgart, Germany.

[5] A Nazi concentration camp located in Poland.

[6] A Nazi concentration camp located in Germany in the Bavarian region about 20 miles northwest of Munich.

BACK COVER MATERIAL

WHEN AND HOW WILL TIIK DOLLAR DIE?

The founder of the Rothschild dynasty said, "Give me control of a nation's economy, and I care not who writes its laws."

Is the economy out of control? Has it died already? Are we headed toward a one-world government and a one-world economy?

The global recession has caused many to seek answers to all these questions. World finance and world prophecy are two of the most fascinating and timely topics in today's news. Willard Cantelon was an expert in both fields, and this book—a rerelease of a best-selling Logos classic—presents the findings of his life-long research.

The Day the Dollar Dies is as relevant today as it was in the seventies, when it was first published. Many of its statistics have been updated, and the focus of the book remains timely. It speaks directly and prophetically to the world's current economic situation.

The provocative insights you will read in this book shed light on what the Bible has to say about the perilous times in which we live. You will discover behind-the-scenes information that is based on careful research.

Without question, *The Day the Dollar Dies* will profoundly affect the way you feel about the future of the world's economy. You will be surprised, challenged, and inspired by the urgent message of this book, which ends on a note of hope.

WILLARD CANTELON (1916-1999) was well-recognized and the author of three books on global economics and Bible prophecy: *The Day the Dollar Dies, New Money or None?,* and *Money Master of the World,* all published by Logos International Fellowship, which became Bridge-Logos. He spent years lecturing at civic, university, and church gatherings. Cantelon was fascinated by the ancient prophets of the Bible, and he was convinced that their writings contained answers for the present day.

Books For ALL Kinds of Readers

At ReadHowYouWant we understand that one size does not fit all types of readers. Our innovative, patent pending technology allows us to design new formats to make reading easier and more enjoyable for you. This helps improve your speed of reading and your comprehension. Our EasyRead printed books have been optimized to improve word recognition, ease eye tracking by adjusting word and line spacing as well as minimizing hyphenation. Our EasyRead SuperLarge editions have been developed to make reading easier and more accessible for vision-impaired readers. We offer Braille and DAISY formats of our books and all popular E-Book formats.

Made in the USA
Coppell, TX
28 December 2019

13768335R00109

TENTH CANADIAN EDITION

UNDERSTANDING CANADIAN BUSINESS

William G. Nickels
University of Maryland

James M. McHugh
St. Louis Community College at Forest Park

Susan M. McHugh
Applied Learning System

Rita Cossa
DeGroote School of Business, McMaster University

Julie Stevens
Brock University

McGraw Hill Education

Understanding Canadian Business
Tenth Canadian Edition

ISBN-13: 978-1-25-965495-4
ISBN-10: 1-25-965495-8

2 3 4 5 6 7 TCP 22 21 20

Printed and bound in Canada.

Product Director, Canada: Rhondda McNabb
Portfolio Manager: Amy Clarke-Spencley
Marketing Manager: Emily Park
Senior Content Developer: Amy Rydzanicz
Senior Portfolio Associate: Stephanie Giles
Supervising Editor: Janie Deneau
Photo/Permissions Editor: Monika Schurmann
Copy Editor: Margaret Henderson
Plant Production Coordinator: Michelle Saddler
Manufacturing Production Coordinator: Jason Stubner
Cover Design: Jodie Bernard, Lightbox Communications, Inc.
Cover Image: © Rob Ball
Interior Design: Liz Harasymczuk
Page Layout: SPi Global
Printer: Transcontinental Printing Group

mheducation.ca

About the Authors

Bill Nickels is emeritus professor of business at the University of Maryland, College Park. He has over 30 years' experience teaching graduate and undergraduate business courses, including introduction to business, marketing, and promotion. He has won the Outstanding Teacher on Campus Award four times and was nominated for the award many other times. He received his MBA degree from Western Reserve University and his PhD from The Ohio State University. He has written a marketing communications text and two marketing principles texts in addition to many articles in business publications. He has taught many seminars to business people on subjects such as power communications, marketing, non-business marketing, and stress and life management.

Jim McHugh holds an MBA degree from Lindenwood University and has had broad experience in education, business, and government. As chairman of the Business and Economics Department of St. Louis Community College–Forest Park, Jim coordinated and directed the development of the business curriculum. In addition to teaching several sections of Introduction to Business each semester for nearly 30 years, Jim taught in the marketing and management areas at both the undergraduate and graduate levels. Jim enjoys conducting business seminars and consulting with small and large businesses. He is actively involved in the public service sector and served as chief of staff to the St. Louis County Executive.

Susan McHugh is a learning specialist with extensive training and experience in adult learning and curriculum development. She holds an MEd degree from the University of Missouri and completed her coursework for a PhD in education administration with a specialty in adult learning theory. As a professional curriculum developer, she has directed numerous curriculum projects and educator training programs. She has worked in the public and private sectors as a consultant in training and employee development.

Rita Cossa is an Assistant Professor at the DeGroote School of Business, McMaster University. This textbook marks her seventh edition as an author for *Understanding Canadian Business.* She primarily teaches introduction to business courses to undergraduate students. Other courses taught include Business Policy & Strategic Management, as well as Marketing courses at both the undergraduate and graduate levels. Teaching highlights include a nomination to *TV Ontario's Best Lecturer Competition,* multiple nominations for a McMaster Student Union Teaching Award, and notations in the *Maclean's Guide to Canadian Universities* as a Popular Prof for Marketing. Her pedagogical interests include active learning, student engagement, and self-reflection. Prior to teaching, Rita held management-level positions in the banking industry.

Julie Stevens is an Associate Professor in the Department of Sport Management at Brock University. During the past twenty years she has taught several graduate and undergraduate management courses related to organization theory, policy, change and innovation, governance, and professionalism within commercial, non-profit, and public sectors. She holds Instructional Skills Workshop training and has served on various teaching and learning committees. Her teaching philosophy, which emphasizes critical commentary and active learner engagement, is enacted through a diverse range of practices within classroom and online forums. Drawing upon her background as a Research Fellow with the North American Society for Sport Management, she integrates current affairs and scholarship to provide relevant, problem-based learning opportunities for students.

Dedication

To my children, Leila and Mattia, and my husband, Stephen, for their support during the creation of this edition. And to my students whose questions and discussions have contributed to a textbook with their learning in mind.

Rita Cossa

To Ron, my husband, and our children, Nolan and Turner, for their support, encouragement, and patience. For my past and present students whose dreams for the future inspired much of my writing.

Julie Stevens

To our families – Marsha, Joel, Carrie, Claire, Casey, Dan, Molly, Michael, Patrick, and Quinn. Thank you for making everything worth doing and giving us the support to do it well!

Bill Nickels, Jim McHugh, Susan McHugh

Brief Contents

Contents

PART 3
LEADERSHIP, ORGANIZATION, AND PRODUCTION TO SATISFY CUSTOMERS *286*

Preface

Understanding Canadian Business has been created with you and your students in mind. We've listened and that's helped us offer you:

Resources that were developed based directly on your feedback—all geared to make the most of your time and to help students succeed in this course. The supplemental resources have been reviewed to ensure cohesion with the text.

Technology that leads the way and is consistently updated to keep pace with you and your students. Connect offers students a truly interactive and adaptive study arena. Interactive applications, SmartBook, and Connect Insight are designed to engage students and have been proven to increase grades by a full letter.

Support that is always available to help you plan your course, work with technology, and meet the needs of you and your students.

Keeping up with What's New

Users of *Understanding Canadian Business* have always appreciated the currency of the material and the large number of examples from for-profit and non-profit companies of *all* sizes and industries in Canada and around the world. Accordingly, this edition features the latest business practices and other developments affecting business including:

- Sustainability
- Humanistic management
- Social enterprise
- Crowdfunding
- The gig economy
- Social media examples
- The mobile/on-demand marketing era
- Big data, data analytics, and data mining
- Green procurement and green marketing
- Ethical consumerism
- Global freelancing and virtual professionals
- Trade agreements and trade protectionism
- Public-private partnerships
- Digital currencies
- The living wage
- Violence and bullying in the workplace
- And much more

We remain dedicated to listening vigilantly to what you tell us you need in this course. We have made changes and enhancements in this revision that are all based on what we heard from you. As you look through the next few pages, you'll find what you need to navigate your way most effectively through this book and its supplements.

Integration of Important Concepts Throughout the Text

Understanding Canadian Business, Tenth Canadian Edition, is revised, updated, and filled with new examples of business in Canada and around the world.

LEARNING OBJECTIVES

Tied directly to the summaries at the end of the chapter and to the test bank questions, the learning objectives help students preview what they should know after reading the chapter, and then test that knowledge by answering the questions in the summary. These learning objectives are also incorporated in the margins throughout the chapter, at the start of the discussion that pertains to the learning objective. This way, students can quickly see where the content aligns with each objective.

LEARNING OBJECTIVES

After you have read and studied this chapter, you should be able to:

LO1 Describe basic economics.

LO2 Explain what capitalism is and how free markets work.

LO3 Compare the benefits and negative consequences of socialism and communism.

LO4 Describe the mixed economy of Canada.

LO5 Illustrate the significance of key economic indicators and the business cycle.

GETTING TO KNOW BUSINESS PROFESSIONALS

Each chapter begins with a profile of a business person whose career relates closely to the material covered in that chapter. Not all of the personalities are famous, since some of them work in small businesses and non-profit organizations. Take some time to consider their career choices and how they spend their time applying the business principles discussed in the text.

A wide variety of analytical tools is available for data scientists. Their work is also creating a new field of marketing research that focuses on data visualization, or the presentation of the results of the analysis. Are there any courses that you could take in your program that would support a career as a data scientist?

Source: Courtesy of Fox 40 International Inc. Used with permission.

PHOTO AND ILLUSTRATION ESSAYS

More and more students have expressed that they are visually oriented learners; therefore, increased emphasis on the pedagogical value of illustrations is essential. Some photos and illustrations are accompanied by a short caption that highlights the relevance of the visuals to the material in the text.

© Monty Rakusen/Image Source

A wide variety of analytical tools is available for data scientists. Their work is also creating a new field of marketing research that focuses on data visualization, or the presentation of the results of the analysis. Are there any courses that you could take in your program that would support a career as a data scientist?

BOXED FEATURES

Important business concepts and themes are incorporated throughout the text. Certain topics deserve special emphasis and are highlighted in feature boxes titled "Spotlight on Small Business," "Making Ethical Decisions," "Seeking Sustainability," "Reaching Beyond Our Borders," and "Adapting to Change" appearing throughout the chapters.

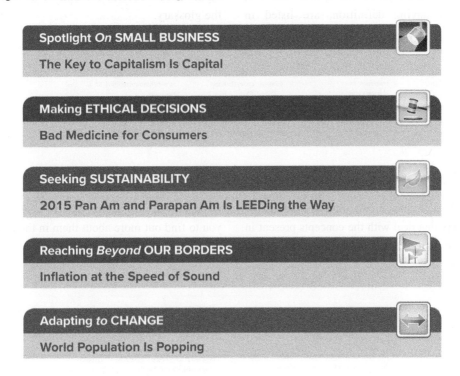

Spotlight *On* SMALL BUSINESS

The Key to Capitalism Is Capital

Making ETHICAL DECISIONS

Bad Medicine for Consumers

Seeking SUSTAINABILITY

2015 Pan Am and Parapan Am Is LEEDing the Way

Reaching *Beyond* OUR BORDERS

Inflation at the Speed of Sound

Adapting *to* CHANGE

World Population Is Popping

PROGRESS ASSESSMENTS

To ensure that students understand and retain the material, Progress Assessments stop them and show them what they need to review before proceeding. The Progress Assessment is a proven learning tool that helps students comprehend and retain material.

PROGRESS ASSESSMENT

- What is the difference between revenue and profit?
- What is risk, and how is it related to profit?
- What is the difference between standard of living and quality of life?
- What do the terms stakeholders, offshoring, outsourcing, and insourcing mean?

INTERACTIVE SUMMARIES

The end-of-chapter summaries are directly tied to the Learning Objectives and are written in a question-and-answer format—great for chapter review and studying.

SUMMARY

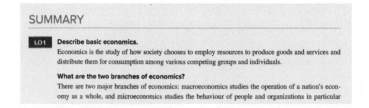

LO1 Describe basic economics.
Economics is the study of how society chooses to employ resources to produce goods and services and distribute them for consumption among various competing groups and individuals.

What are the two branches of economics?
There are two major branches of economics: macroeconomics studies the operation of a nation's economy as a whole, and microeconomics studies the behaviour of people and organizations in particular

KEY TERMS

Important terms, highlighted throughout the text with an accompanying definition, are listed in alphabetical order at the end of the chapter and in the glossary.

KEY TERMS

boom 95	disinflation 94	mixed economies 86
brain drain 84	economic cycles (business cycles) 95	monopolistic competition 81
business cycles (economic cycles) 95	economics 70	monopoly 82
capitalism 76	free-market economy 85	oligopoly 81
command economy 86	gross domestic product (GDP) 89	perfect competition 81
communism 85	human development index 95	recession 95
		recovery 96

CAREER EXPLORATION

At the end of each chapter, we offer a brief list of potential careers that deal with the concepts present in the chapter. The examples are drawn from the Canadian Occupational Projection System and we encourage you to find out more about them in the Government of Canada Job Bank.

CAREER EXPLORATION

If you are interested in pursuing a career in economics, here are a few to consider. Find out about the tasks performed, skills needed, pay, and opportunity outlook in these fields through Internet sites that include the Government of Canada Job Bank, Workopolis, Monster, CareerBuilder, Glassdoor, and Indeed, as well as through the Career Centre at your school.

- **Statistican**—applies mathematical or statistical theory and methods to collect, organize, interpret, and summarize numerical data to provide useful information.
- **Marketing research analyst**—studies market conditions and helps companies understand what products people want, who will buy them, and at what price.

CRITICAL THINKING QUESTIONS

Found in each chapter, Critical Thinking Questions ask students to pause and think about how the material they are reading applies to their own lives.

> CRITICAL THINKING
>
> Many say that business people do not do enough for society. Some students choose to work for non-profit organizations instead of for-profit organizations because they want to help others. However, business people say that they do more to help others than non-profit groups because they provide jobs for people rather than giving them charity, which often they believe that businesses create all the wealth that non-profit groups distribute. Can you find some middle ground in this debate that demonstrates how both business people and those who work for non-profit organizations contribute to society and need to work together more closely to help people? Could you use the concepts of Adam Smith to help illustrate your

DEVELOPING CAREER SKILLS

The Developing Career Skills section has activities designed to increase student involvement in the learning process. The exercises develop analytical communication, technological, and team-based skills. Some of these mini-projects require library or online searches, while others can be used as team activities either in or out of the classroom.

> DEVELOPING CAREER SKILLS
>
> **Key:** ● **Team** ★ **Analytic** ▲ **Communication** ⊡ **Technology**
>
> ▲ **1.** Find out firsthand the impact of global trade on your life. How many different countries' names appear on the labels in your clothes? How many languages do your classmates speak? List the ethnic restaurants in your community. Are they family-owned or corpo-
>
> ●★⊡▲ **4.** In a group of four, list the top five Canadian-based multinationals. When researching, create a table that will include the following pieces of information: the company names, the year each was created, the number of global employees, the industry or indus-

ANALYZING MANAGEMENT DECISIONS

Each chapter concludes with a case that allows students to analyze management decision making. These cases are intentionally brief and are meant to initiate discussion rather than take up the entire class period.

> ANALYZING MANAGEMENT DECISIONS
>
> **The Rule of 72**
>
> No formula is more useful for understanding inflation than the rule of 72. In fact, The Rule of 72 was highlighted in the Reaching Beyond Our Borders box in this chapter.

END-OF-PART RUNNING CASE

The chapters in this edition are divided in six parts. A six-part running case has been created based on Fox 40 International Inc., a proudly Canadian company that dominates the global whistle industry. For successful Canadian entrepreneur and inventor Ron Foxcroft, it all started with a dream for a pealess whistle. Read the case at the end of each part to learn how Ron, his son Dave, and their management team apply the business principles introduced in the chapters for each part. The discussion questions encourage students to further evaluate these business concepts.

> RUNNING CASE
>
> **Fox 40 International Inc.: A Family Business**
>
> For successful Canadian entrepreneur and inventor Ron Foxcroft, it all started in 1982 when he purchased Fluke Transport, a Southern Ontario trucking business. The company slogan—If It's On Time . . . It's A "FLUKE"—was soon recognized throughout North believed that it would only be used by a few hundred referee friends. Despite the critics, Ron managed to put together $150,000 from his own private funds and in 1987 he created Fox 40. Ron risked everything as he pursued this dream: his family's financial future (only

Market Leading Technology

connect

Learn Without Limits

McGraw-Hill Connect® is an award-winning digital teaching and learning platform that gives students the means to better connect with their coursework, with their instructors, and with the important concepts that they will need to know for success now and in the future. With Connect, instructors can take advantage of McGraw-Hill's trusted content to seamlessly deliver assignments, quizzes and tests online. McGraw-Hill Connect is a learning platform that continually adapts to each student, delivering precisely what they need, when they need it, so class time is more engaging and effective. Connect makes teaching and learning personal, easy, and proven.

Connect Key Features:

SMARTBOOK®

As the first and only adaptive reading experience, SmartBook is changing the way students read and learn. SmartBook creates a personalized reading experience by highlighting the most important concepts a student needs to learn at that moment in time. As a student engages with SmartBook, the reading experience continuously adapts by highlighting content based on what each student knows and doesn't know. This ensures that he or she is focused on the content needed to close specific knowledge gaps, while it simultaneously promotes long-term learning.

CONNECT INSIGHT®

Connect Insight is Connect's new one-of-a-kind visual analytics dashboard—now available for instructors—that provides at-a-glance information regarding student performance, which is immediately actionable. By presenting assignment, assessment, and topical performance results together with a time metric that is easily visible for aggregate or individual results, Connect Insight gives instructors the ability to take a just-in-time approach to teaching and learning, which was never before available. Connect Insight presents data that empowers instructors improve class performance in a way that is efficient and effective.

SIMPLE ASSIGNMENT MANAGEMENT

With Connect, creating assignments is easier than ever, so instructors can spend more time teaching and less time managing.

- Assign SmartBook learning modules.
- Edit existing questions and create their own questions.
- Draw from a variety of text-specific questions, resources, and test bank material to assign online.
- Streamline lesson planning, student progress reporting, and assignment grading to make classroom management more efficient than ever.

SMART GRADING

When it comes to studying, time is precious. Connect helps students learn more effectively by providing feedback and practice material when they need it and where they need it. This is done in several ways.

- Automatically score assignments, giving students immediate feedback on their work and comparisons with correct answers.
- Access and review each response; manually change grades or leave comments for students to review.
- Track individual student performance—by question, assignment or in relation to the class overall—with detailed grade reports.
- Reinforce classroom concepts with practice tests and instant quizzes.
- Integrate grade reports easily with Learning Management Systems including Blackboard, D2L, and Moodle.

MOBILE ACCESS

Connect makes it easy for students to read and learn using their smartphones and tablets. With the mobile app, students can study on the go—including reading and listening using the audio functionality—without constant need for Internet access.

INSTRUCTOR LIBRARY

The Connect Instructor Library is a repository for additional resources to improve student engagement in and out of the class. It provides all the critical resources instructors need to build their course.

- Access Instructor resources.
- View assignments and resources created for past sections.
- Post your own resources for students to use.

Instructors' Resources

Understanding Canadian Business, Tenth Edition, offers a complete, integrated supplements package for instructors to address all of their needs.

Connect assets have been prepared by Grace O'Farrell from the University of Winnipeg.

Instructor's Manual:

The instructor's manual, prepared by Peter Mombourquette, Mount Saint Vincent University, accurately represents the text's content and supports instructors' needs. Each chapter includes the learning objectives, the glossary of key terms, a chapter synopsis, a lecture outline, and solutions to the end-of-chapter discussion questions and videos.

Computerized Test Bank:

This flexible and easy-to-use electronic testing program allows instructors to create tests from book-specific items. Created by Sandra Wellman, Seneca College, the test bank has undergone a rigorous auditing and revision process for the tenth edition. It contains a broad selection of multiple choice, true/false, and essay questions. Instructors may add their own questions as well. Each question identifies the relevant page reference and difficulty level. Multiple versions of the test can be created and printed.

PowerPoint Presentations:

These robust presentations offer high-quality visuals from the text and highlight key concepts from each chapter to bring key business concepts to life. Two different presentations offer instructors choice on how they like to present the material to their classes. Both the basic and enhanced sets were authored by Michael Wade, Seneca College.

Videos for All Chapters:

Customized business segments from the McGraw-Hill Management Library filmed specifically for the Nickels text can be accessed on the password-protected area of Connect. Detailed teaching notes are available in the instructor's manual and on the instructor area of Connect.

MANAGER'S HOTSEAT

The **Manager's HotSeat** video cases allow students to watch real managers apply their years of experience to confront daily issues, such as ethics, diversity, teamwork, and the virtual workplace. The Manager's HotSeat videos are ideal for group or classroom discussion.

APPLICATION-BASED ACTIVITIES

The Connect Application-Based Activities are highly interactive and automatically graded, application- and analysis-based exercises wherein students immerse themselves in a business environment, analyze the situation, and apply their knowledge of business strategies to real-world situations. Students progress from understanding basic concepts to using their own knowledge to analyze complex scenarios and solve problems.

SUPERIOR LEARNING SOLUTIONS AND SUPPORT

The McGraw-Hill Education team is ready to help instructors assess and integrate any of our products, technology, and services into your course for optimal teaching and learning performance. Whether it's helping your students improve their grades, or putting your entire course online, the McGraw-Hill Education team is here to help you do it. Contact your Learning Solutions Consultant today to learn how to maximize all of McGraw-Hill Education's resources.

For more information, please visit us online: **http://www.mheducation.ca/he/solutions.**

Acknowledgements

Development of the Text and Supplements Package

To ensure continuous improvement of our product, we have used an extensive review and development process for each of our editions. Building on that history, the development process for this tenth edition included evaluation by a broad panel of instructors where new ideas were exchanged. The tenth Canadian edition continues to be the market's gold standard due to involvement of these committed instructors. We thank them all for their help, support, and friendship—your suggestions to improve the quality, coverage, and the supplements package were invaluable.

Reviewers who were vital in helping us develop the tenth edition include:

Ramon Baltazar, *Dalhousie University*
Rod Hayward, *University of the Fraser Valley*
Tannys Laughren, *Laurentian University*
Josephine McMurray, *Wilfrid Laurier University*
Zorana Svedic, *University of British Columbia*
Dave Swanston, *University of Toronto*

Many thanks are also due to the following people who worked hard to make this book a reality: Alwynn Pinard and Amy Clarke-Spencley, Portfolio Managers; Amy Rydzanicz, Senior Content Developer; Jeanette McCurdy and Janie Deneau, Supervising Editors; Michelle Saddler, Production Coordinator; Margaret Henderson, Copy Editor; Monika Schurmann, Permissions and Photo Researcher; and Jodie Bernard, Designer.

The authors would also like to extend their appreciation to Ron Foxcroft for allowing them to highlight Fox40 International Inc. as this edition's running case. Started over twenty-five years ago, this privately held, family-run organization exemplifies many of the business principles introduced in this edition.

PART 1

CHAPTER 1

The Dynamic Business Environment

LEARNING OBJECTIVES

After you have read and studied this chapter, you should be able to:

LO1 Illustrate the importance of key business fundamentals to wealth generation.

LO2 Identify business stakeholders and their importance to non-profit organizations and business activities.

LO3 Explain how entrepreneurship is critical to the wealth of an economy, and list the five factors of production that contribute to wealth.

LO4 State the six elements that make up the business environment and explain why the business environment is important to organizations.

LO5 Give examples of how the service sector has replaced manufacturing as the principal provider of jobs, but why manufacturing remains vital for Canada.

PROFILE

GETTING TO KNOW: RON FOXCROFT, CEO, FOX 40 INTERNATIONAL INC.

For successful Canadian entrepreneur and inventor Ron Foxcroft, it all started in 1982 when he purchased Fluke Transport, a Southern Ontario trucking business. The company slogan—If It's On Time . . . t's A "FLUKE"—was soon recognized throughout North America. Over the years, Foxcroft diversified into new ventures and the Foxcroft Group of Companies now includes Fluke Transportation Group, Fluke Warehousing Inc., Foxcroft Capital Corp., Fox 40 International Inc., and Fox 40 USA Inc.

The formation of Fox 40 International Inc. is the result of a dream for a pealess whistle. When Foxcroft began developing the whistle, he was motivated by his knowledge and experience as an international basketball referee. Frustrated with faulty pea whistles, he spent three years of development with design consultant Chuck Shepherd, resulting in the creation of the Fox 40 Classic Whistle. (The whistle was named for Foxcroft, who was 40 when his invention was being developed). Introduced in

Source: Courtesy of Fox 40 International Inc. Used with permission.

1987, this finely tuned precision instrument does not use a pea to generate sound. In fact, there are no moving parts whatsoever. There is nothing to obstruct sound, nothing to stick, freeze, or fail. The patented design moves the air blast through three tuned chambers. Fox 40 whistles are constructed entirely of high-impact ABS plastic so they are impervious to moisture. A quick rinse in disinfectant eliminates bacteria. Every time, they deliver on faultless performance (e.g., loudness), and they never fail.

In 1987, Shepherd said to Foxcroft, "Ron, we have just developed the 'best whistle in the world.' You must pledge to me that you will dedicate your life to making the Fox 40 whistle better." To this day, Foxcroft and the company employees continue to honour this pledge.

Fox 40 International Inc., a proudly Canadian company, dominates the global whistle industry. Tens of thousands of Fox 40 whistles are produced monthly for shipment to 140 countries. They are sold to referees, coaches, water safety, search and rescue teams, personal security, animal trainers, all sport enthusiasts, as well as the outdoor and premium incentive markets. The complete line of Fox 40 products has grown substantially with over 900 active stock-keeping units (SKUs) that include the following: 21 styles of Fox 40 Whistles; lanyards & attachments; Fox 40 gear; SmartCoach coaching boards; the SICK Self Impression Custom Kit and Heat Alert mouthguards; marine & outdoor products; pink products; and logo-imprinted products.

An avid sportsman, Foxcroft's philosophy of "be the best at what you do" has contributed to his success both on and off the basketball court. He has been named one of the 52 most influential persons in North American Officiating of all time. In 2010, the National Association of Sports Officials named him—the only Canadian—to a group of 30 who have made a difference in the world of sports officials. He spent fourteen seasons as a game observer for the National Basketball League (NBA). Off the court, PROFIT magazine voted him to be one of the top ten Canadian businessmen of the decade. He has been honoured as Entrepreneur of the Year by the Burlington Economic Development Corporation. More recently, he has been featured in the New York Times, CBC ESPN, the History Channel, he's had an audience with the Queen at Buckingham Palace and received the prestigious NASO Gold Whistle Award, this honour is considered the highest distinction bestowed on a referee in the world. He was also gratified to receive an Honourary Graduation Diploma from Mohawk College. Today, Foxcroft continues his active role as Founder and Chief Executive Officer (CEO) of Fox 40 International Inc. and Chairman and CEO of Fluke Transportation.

Foxcroft credits his customers and employees for the improvements to the original whistle. In his words, "When you are the best, you need to be better." This all starts with watching people to understand their needs. It involves developing products and services that customers might want. Making decisions along the way is challenging, but if you are successful, you can make a lot of customers very happy. Throughout this process, you need to have a vision, be focused, adapt to change, and never give up. His advice for future entrepreneurs, in the words of Walt Disney, is to "Get a good idea and stay with it. Dog it, and work it until it's done and done right."

The purpose of this text is to introduce you to the exciting and challenging world of business. Each chapter will begin with a story similar to this one. You will meet more successful entrepreneurs who have started a business. You will also learn about people who work for companies and have succeeded far beyond their original expectations. You will learn about all aspects of business: management, human resource management, marketing, accounting, finance, and more. You will also learn about businesses of all sizes. We begin by looking at some key terms and exploring the rapidly changing business environment so that you can prepare to meet tomorrow's challenges today.

Sources: Ron Foxcroft, CEO of Fox 40 International Inc. and Chairman and CEO of Fluke Transportation, and Juliana Child, VP Promotional Sales & Events, Fox40 International Inc., September 22, 2017; "The Story of Fox 40," Fox 40 International Inc., February 21, 2014, http://www.fox40world.com/index.cfm?id=55884l; "Ron Foxcroft presented with prestigious Queen Elizabeth II Diamond Jubilee Medal," Fox 40 International Inc., August 15, 2012, http://www.fox40world.com/index.cfm?returnid=56106&newsid=3393&pagepath=KEEPING_IN_TOUCH/News_Releases&id=57428; Ron Foxcroft, Founder and CEO, Fox 40 International Inc., in-person interview, December 19, 2011; "BEDC Inducts Mr. Ron Foxcroft into the Entrepreneur Hall of Fame," Burlington Economic Development Corporation, June 10, 2011, www.bedc.ca/sites/default/files/PDF/businessnews/MediaRelease—BEDCInductsMr.RonFoxcroftintotheEntrepreneurHallofFame.pdf; John Kernaghan, "Fox 40 founder Foxcroft feted," *The Hamilton Spectator*, October 18, 2010, www.thespec.com/sports/local/article/268488—fox-40-founder-foxcroft-feted; Referee Staff, "Not An Inadvertent Whistle," *Referee Magazine*, July 2007, 45–47; and Global TV, "Ron Foxcroft," *The Globe and Mail*, June 29, 2005.

Using this Course to Prepare for Your Career

Since you have signed up for this course, we are guessing you already know the value of higher education. When averaged across gender and fields of study, the holders of a post-secondary education make a cumulated average of about $1,000,000 over 20 years compared to a cumulated average of about $670,000 for high school graduates.[1] That is nearly 60 percent more for post-secondary graduates compared to those with just a high school diploma. Thus, what you invest in a post-secondary education is likely to pay you back many times.

See Figure 1.1 for more of an idea of the earnings of a business post-secondary education after 20 years compared to an overall post-secondary and high school education. That does not mean there are not good careers available to non–post-secondary graduates. It just means those with an education are more likely to have higher earnings over their lifetime. In addition, for both men and women, a degree is associated with more years of coverage in an employer-sponsored pension plan and fewer layoffs than a person with a high school diploma.[2]

The value of a post-secondary education is more than just a larger paycheque. Other benefits include increasing your ability to think critically and communicate your ideas to others, improving your ability to use technology, and preparing yourself to live in a diverse and competitive world. Knowing you have met your goals and earned a degree also gives you the self-confidence to work toward future goals.

Experts say today's post-secondary graduates will likely hold seven or eight different jobs (often in several different careers) in their lifetime.[3] You too may want to

FIGURE 1.1

EARNINGS COMPARISON OF POST-SECONDARY AND HIGH SCHOOL GRADUATES OVER 20 YEARS

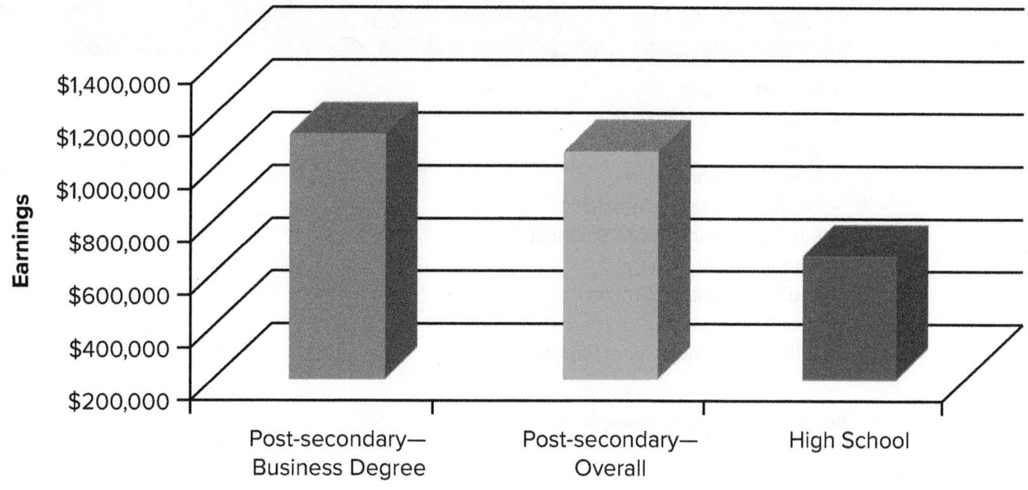

Note: Earnings are averaged across men and women; Post-secondary-Overall earnings is averaged across nine areas of study.

Source: Yuri Ostrovsky and Marc Frenette, "The Cumulative Earnings of Postsecondary Graduate Over 20 Years: Results by Field of Study," Statistics Canada, October 2014, Catalogue no. 11–626–X, accessed March 15, 2015, http://www.statcan.gc.ca/pub/11-626-x/11-626-x2014040-eng.htm.

change careers someday. It can be the path to long-term happiness and success. That means you will have to be flexible and adjust your strengths and talents to new opportunities. Learning has become a lifelong job. You will need to constantly update your skills to achieve high competence and remain competitive.

If you are typical of many post-secondary students, you may not have any idea what career you would like to pursue. That is not necessarily a big disadvantage in today's fast-changing job market. After all, many of the best jobs of the future do not even exist today. Figure 1.2 lists 10 careers that did not exist 10 years ago. There are no perfect or certain ways to prepare for the most interesting and challenging jobs of tomorrow. Rather, you should continue your education, develop strong technology and Internet skills, improve your verbal and written communication skills, and remain flexible and forward thinking while you explore the job market. But without a doubt, business knowledge will be valuable in the future.

© Laura Doss/Getty Images

The rewards of post-secondary education are well worth the effort for graduates, who can expect to earn nearly 60 percent more than high school graduates over the 20 years. Businesses like graduates too, because the growing needs of a global workplace require knowledgeable workers to fill the jobs of the future. What other benefits do you see from earning a degree?

FIGURE 1.2

NEW CAREERS

These careers did not exist 10 years ago:
• App Developer • Social Media Manager • Uber Driver • Driverless Car Engineer • Cloud Computing Specialist • Big Data Analyst/Data Scientist • Sustainability Manager • YouTube Content Creator • Drone Operator • Millennial Generational Expert

Source: World Economic Forum, weforum.org, accessed June 2018.

One of the objectives of this class, and this book, is to help you choose an area in which you might enjoy working and have a strong chance to succeed. You will learn about economics, global business, ethics, entrepreneurship, management, marketing, accounting, finance, and more. At the end of the course, you should have a much better idea which careers would be best for you and which you would not enjoy. But you do not have to be in business to use business principles. You can use marketing principles to get a job and to sell your ideas to others. You can use your knowledge of investments to make money in the stock market. You will use your management skills and general business knowledge wherever you go and in whatever career you pursue including government agencies, charities, and social causes.

© Sam Edwards/age fotostock

There are many opportunities for you to gain knowledge from industry experts. You may work in a company, volunteer in an organization, or plan to take a placement or internship course. What programs are offered at the career services office at your university or college that will help you learn more about possible career options directly from those who work in the field?

Post-secondary courses are best at teaching you concepts and ways of thinking about business. However, to learn first-hand how to apply those ideas to real business situations, you need to explore and interact with other resources. You can extend your understanding and awareness of the business world through contact with others who have business experience. For example, many post-secondary students have had experience working in business or non-profit organizations. Hearing and talking about those experiences exposes you to many real-life examples that are invaluable for understanding business. Outside contact also offers a wealth of information. Who can tell you more about what it is like to start a career in accounting than someone who is doing it now? One of the best ways to learn about different businesses is to visit them in person. The world can be your classroom.

Business Fundamentals

LO1

Illustrate the importance of key business fundamentals to wealth generation.

One thing that you can learn from the chapter-opening Profile is that success in business is often based on the strategy of finding a need and filling it. Ron Foxcroft saw the need for a pealess whistle and he filled it. This strategy lets you help the community in several ways. You provide needed goods, jobs, and services to people in the area. **Goods** are tangible products such as computers, food, clothing, cars, and appliances. **Services** are intangible products (i.e., items that cannot be held in your hand) such as education, health care, insurance, recreation, and travel and tourism.

Although you do not need to have wealth as a primary goal, one result of successfully filling a market need is that you can make money for yourself, sometimes a great deal, by giving customers what they want. A **business** is any activity that seeks to provide goods and services to others while operating at a profit. An **entrepreneur** is a person who risks time and money to start and manage a business. You will read more about successful entrepreneurs throughout this text.

An entrepreneur learns early that a business needs a reliable accountant, a good lawyer, and strong managers. Entrepreneurs may have to go to financial institutions (e.g., banks) or to venture capital firms to borrow money. In today's economy, borrowing from a financial institution is harder than usual.[4] Therefore, later on in the text, we will talk about ways to get closer to financial institutions so that they will be more inclined to give you a loan. Entrepreneurs will also need to learn more about business, including how to deal with unions, what kind of insurance to buy, and how to find the right people to hire. Usually that means studying business at a post-secondary institution.[5] Access to a college or university education is much easier today now that so many courses are available online.[6]

goods
Tangible products such as computers, food, clothing, cars, and appliances.

services
Intangible products (i.e., products that can't be held in your hand) such as education, health care, insurance, recreation, and travel and tourism.

business
Any activity that seeks to provide goods and services to others while operating at a profit.

Revenues, Profits, and Losses

Revenue is the total amount of money received during a given period for goods sold and services rendered and from other financial sources. **Profit** is the amount of money a business earns above and beyond what it spends for salaries and other expenses. Since not all businesses make a profit, starting a business can be risky. A **loss** occurs when a business' expenses are more than its revenues. If a business loses money over time, it will likely have to close, putting its employees out of work. It should be no surprise, therefore, that thousands of businesses enter and exit the marketplace throughout the year.[7] Some owners close down one business to start another one or to retire.

Even though such closings are not failures, they are reported as exits by Innovation, Science and Economic Development Canada. A 2016 report indicated a net decrease of approximately 4,800

© Tom Hauck/AP Images

In 1979, Geral Fauss took 5000 oversized foam fingers to the Sugar Bowl in New Orleans not knowing if he would sell a single one. The former high school shop teacher created the now-famous fingers a few years earlier and they became a big hit with his students. Fortunately, the Sugar Bowl crowd liked them, too. He sold every last finger and launched a company that is still going strong. What risks and rewards did Fauss face when starting his business?

entrepreneur
A person who risks time and money to start and manage a business.

revenue
The total amount of money received during a given period for goods sold and services rendered, and from other financial sources.

profit
The amount a business earns above and beyond what it spends for salaries and other expenses.

loss
When a business's expenses are more than its revenues.

risk
The chance of loss, the degree of probability of loss, and the amount of possible loss (i.e., time and money).

small a medium-sized businesses in Canada.[8] Only a small proportion of firms that exit the marketplace end up filing for *bankruptcy,* which refers to the liquidation of the business debtor's assets and the end of the commercial entity's operations.[9] As discussed later in this text, most business failures are due to poor management or problems associated with cash flow.

The business environment is constantly changing. What seems like a great opportunity one day—for example, online grocery shopping—may become a failure when the economy changes. Starting a business may come with huge risks. But huge risks can result in huge profits. We'll explore that concept next.

Matching Risk with Profit

Starting a business involves risk. Generally speaking, **risk** refers to the chance of loss, the degree of probability of loss, and the amount of possible loss. Risk is the chance an entrepreneur takes of losing time and money on a business that may not prove profitable. Profit, remember, is the amount of money a business earns *above and beyond* what it pays out for salaries and other expenses. For example, if you were to start a business selling hot dogs in the summer, you would have to pay for the cart rental, for the hot dogs and other materials, and for someone to run the cart while you were away. After you paid your employee and yourself, paid for the food and materials you used, paid the rent on the cart, and paid your taxes, any money left over would be profit.

Keep in mind that profit is over and above the money you pay yourself in salary. You could use any profit you make to rent or buy a second cart and hire other employees. After a few summers, you might have a dozen carts employing dozens of workers.

Even among companies that do make a profit, not all make the same amount. Those companies that take the most risk may make the most profit. There is high risk, for example, in making a new kind of automobile.[10] Elon Musk, CEO of Tesla Motors, has experienced both success and failure as the company tries to move the automotive industry toward electric cars. Regardless of production concerns, Tesla has grown its revenues five-fold from 2013–2018.[11]

As a potential business owner, you need to do research (e.g., talk to other business people and read business publications) to find the right balance between risk and profit for you. Different people have different tolerances for risk. To decide which is the best choice for you, you have to calculate the risks and the potential rewards of each decision. The more risks you take, the higher the rewards may be. In Chapter 7, you will learn more about the risks and rewards that come with starting a business.

Standard of Living and Quality of Life

Entrepreneurs such as Elon Musk, the founder of Tesla Motors and SpaceX, not only became wealthy themselves, they also provide employment for many other people. Businesses and their employees pay taxes to the different levels of government (federal, provincial, and municipal). This money is used to build hospitals, schools, libraries, playgrounds, roads, and other public facilities. Taxes also help to keep the environment clean, support people in need, and provide police and fire protection. Thus, the wealth businesses generate and the taxes they pay help everyone in their communities. A country's businesses are part of an economic system that contributes to the standard of living and quality of life for everyone in the country (and, potentially, the world). How has the most recent economic slowdown affected the standard of living and quality of life in Canada?

The term **standard of living** refers to the amount of goods and services people can buy with the money they have. For example, Canada has one of the highest standards of living in the world, even though workers in some other countries may on average make more money per hour. How can that be? Prices for goods and services might be higher than in Canada, so a person in that country can buy less than what a person in Canada can buy with the same amount of money. For example, a kilogram of local cheese may cost $20.65 in Japan and $11.60 in Canada.[12]

© Skip Brown/National Geographic/Getty Images

When Nick Woodman wanted to show off videos of his stunts to other surfers, he used rubber bands and a surfboard leash to attach cameras to his wrist. His early attempts did not work, but after a lot of work and a $235,000 investment, his GoPro cameras are now the gold standard for self-documenting extreme sports. Today, Woodman's company brings in $526 million in annual revenue. What risks and rewards did Woodward face when starting his business?

Often, goods cost more in one country than another because of higher taxes and stricter government regulations. Finding the right level of taxes and regulation is important in making a country or city prosperous. We'll explore that issue more deeply in Chapter 2. At this point, it is enough to understand that Canada enjoys a high standard of living partly because of the wealth created by its businesses.

The term **quality of life** refers to the general well-being of a society in terms of its political freedom, natural environment, education, health care, safety, amount of leisure, and rewards that add to the satisfaction and joy that other goods and services provide. Maintaining a high quality of life requires the combined efforts of businesses, non-profit organizations (to be discussed soon), and government agencies. The more money businesses create, the more is potentially available to improve the quality of life for everyone. It's important to be careful, however. Working to build a higher standard of living may lower the quality of life if it means less time with family or more stress.[13]

standard of living The amount of goods and services people can buy with the money they have.

quality of life The general well-being of a society in terms of its political freedom, natural environment, education, health care, safety, amount of leisure, and rewards that add to the satisfaction and joy that other goods and services provide.

Responding to the Various Business Stakeholders

LO2 Identify business stakeholders and their importance to non-profit organizations to business activities.

Stakeholders are all of the people who stand to gain or lose by the policies and activities of a business and whose concerns the business needs to address. As noted in Figure 1.3, stakeholders include many different groups such as customers, employees, financial institutions (e.g., banks and credit unions), investors (e.g., shareholders), environmentalists, and government. Stakeholders may also have direct and indirect impact upon a business or organization. Each of the stakeholder types shown in Figure 1.3 can be considered either primary, those who without their participation the business would not exist, or secondary, those whose influence is not essential to the survival of a business. Don't forget that businesses can also influence government policies through the activities and efforts of their associations, lobbyists, and trade unions.

FIGURE 1.3

A BUSINESS AND ITS STAKEHOLDER

Often the needs of a firm's various stakeholders will conflict. For example, paying employees more may cut into shareholders' profits. Balancing such demands is a major role of business managers.

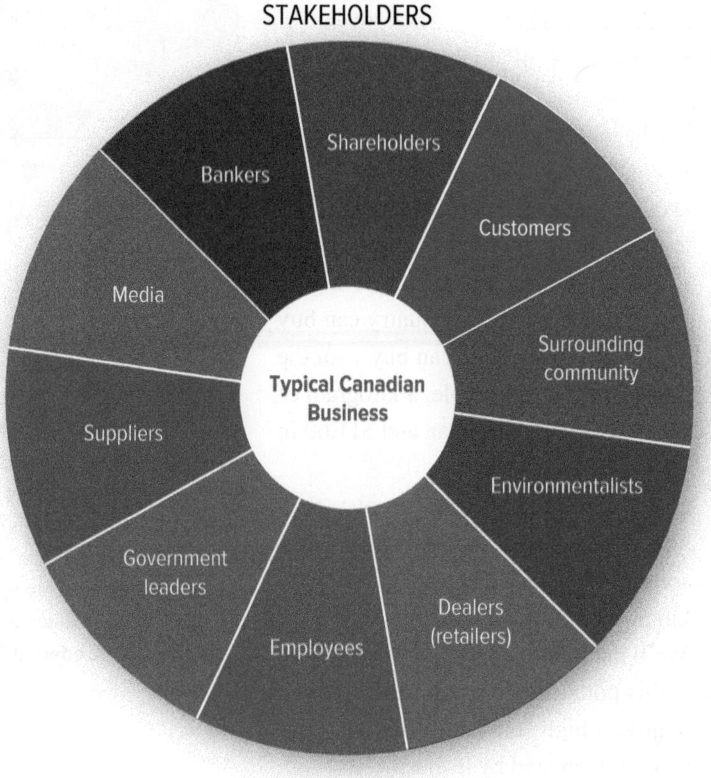

Source: John Mackey and Raj Sisodia, *Conscious Capitalism* (Boston, MA: Harvard Business Review Press, 2013).

stakeholders
All the people who stand to gain or lose by the policies and activities of a business.

offshoring
Sourcing part of the purchased inputs outside of the country.

outsourcing
Assigning various functions, such as accounting, production, security, maintenance, and / or legal work, to outside organizations.

The challenge of the twenty-first century will be for organizations to balance, as much as possible, the needs of all stakeholders. For example, the need for the business to make profits must be balanced against the needs of employees for sufficient income. Ignore the media, and they might attack your business with articles that hurt sales. Oppose the local community, and it may stop you from expanding. The need to stay competitive may call for offshoring jobs to other countries, recognizing that this sound business strategy might do harm to the community because jobs would be lost.[14] **Offshoring** entails sourcing part of the purchased inputs outside of the country.[15] **Outsourcing** means contracting with other companies to do some or all of the functions of a firm, such as production or accounting.[16]

You may be wondering, how are the terms insourcing, outsourcing, and offshoring different? A Statistics Canada report highlights the distinction. As stated, "Outsourcing decisions affect the boundaries of the firm—what production takes place within the firm and what is purchased from outside the firm. Changes in offshoring may be, but are not necessarily, related to changes in outsourcing. They involve decisions both to purchase outside of the firm and to do so from abroad. Considerations to do the latter are at the heart of the study of international trade. Interest in outsourcing arises because it may foretell changes in industrial structure. Interest in offshoring arises because it may signify changes in international trading patterns."[17]

Companies have gone from outsourcing production jobs to offshoring research and development and design functions. Such decisions may prove disastrous to these firms doing the offshoring if the overseas companies use the information to produce their own competitive products.[18] In Canada, most of the offshoring that occurs is with the United States, though there has been some increase over the last decade with developing countries.[19]

A recent study indicated outsourcing will continue to grow at 12 to 26 percent across functions such as information technology, legal services, and human resource management.[20] It is also expected that governments will create legislation to reduce offshoring. **Insourcing** initiatives to return jobs to companies exist in various industries, such as the automotive sector, where Ford Motor Company advanced workers to higher pay scales and as a result, hired more entry-level employees.[21]

insourcing
Assigning various functions that could go to an outside organization to employees in the company.

It is legal to outsource and offshore, but is that best for all stakeholders, including workers? Business leaders must make decisions based on all factors, including the need to make a profit. As you can see, pleasing all stakeholders is not easy and it calls for trade-offs that are not always acceptable to one or another stakeholder. Keep in mind that regardless of temptations, company officials do have a responsibility to their stakeholders.

non-profit organization
An organization whose goals do not include making a personal profit for its owners or organizers.

Such trade-offs are also apparent in the political arena. As will be discussed in Chapter 4, governments make policies that affect many stakeholders. However, budget limitations force governments to make difficult choices, and these decisions are often not popular. Consequently, after years of insufficient funding, any changes in the areas of the environment, health care, and education generate a great deal of attention. As you will learn, balancing the demands of stakeholders is not limited to for-profit businesses.

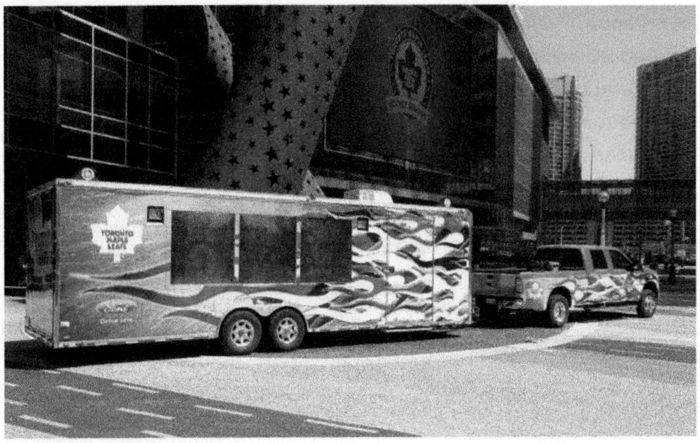

© ValeStock/Thinkstock

Media have also become an important stakeholder in the business environment. Two telecommunications conglomerates, Bell and Rogers, paid CAD$1.32 billion to acquire a 75 percent share of Maple Leaf Sports and Entertainment. The purchase gave them a majority share of the corporation that owns and manages the Toronto Maples Leafs, Marlies, Raptors, Toronto FC, real estate such as the Air Canada Centre, and television properties. What media stakeholders impact business in other industries? How do they impact the business? Are they primary or secondary stakeholders?[22]

Using Business Principles in Non-Profit Organizations

Despite their efforts to satisfy all of their stakeholders, businesses cannot do everything that is needed to make a community all it can be. Non-profit organizations—such as schools, hospitals, charities like the United Way and the Salvation Army, and groups devoted to social causes—also make a major contribution to the welfare of society, as well as economic activity and jobs. A **non-profit organization** is an organization whose goals do not include making a personal profit for its owners

© Jorge Guerrero/AFP/Getty Images

The goals of non-profit organizations are social and educational, not profit-oriented. The Red Cross, for example, is a national, not-for-profit charitable organization whose mission is to manage the blood and blood products supply for Canadians. The organization employs approximately 2800 full-time employees and generates over CAD$1 million in revenue?[25] The organization provides assistance to around 30 million people annually, from refugees to victims of natural disasters. Why do good management principles apply equally to profit-seeking businesses and non-profit organizations?

or organizers. Non-profit organizations strive for financial gains because revenue is needed to operate, but such gains are used to meet their social or educational goals rather than for personal or shareholder profit.

Non-profit organizations also include the different levels of government in our country. They are increasingly involved in business decisions and operations even though the primary purpose is not to generate a profit. We will consider the role of government in business in Chapter 4.

Social entrepreneurs are people who use business principles to start and manage non-profit organizations and help address social issues. Muhammad Yunus won the Nobel Prize for starting the Grameen Bank, a microlending organization that provides small loans to entrepreneurs too poor to qualify for traditional loans. Yunus has started 30 of what he calls social businesses that do not have profit as their goal. One, for example, provides cataract operations for a fraction of the usual cost.[23] The Adapting to Change box in Chapter 5 features the Canadian Social Entrepreneurship Foundation. Would you consider becoming a social entrepreneur?

Your interests may lead you to work for a non-profit organization. Two million people, including professionals and staffers, work for Canada's approximately 170 000 charities and non-profit organizations.[24] This does not mean, however, that you should not study business. If you want to start or work in a non-profit organization, you will need to learn business skills such as information management, leadership, marketing, and financial management. Therefore, the knowledge and skills you acquire in this and other business courses will be useful for careers in any organization, including non-profits. We shall explore entrepreneurship right after the Progress Assessment.

PROGRESS ASSESSMENT

- What is the difference between revenue and profit?
- What is risk, and how is it related to profit?
- What is the difference between standard of living and quality of life?
- What do the terms stakeholders, offshoring, outsourcing, and insourcing mean?

Entrepreneurship Versus Working for Others

LO3

Explain how entrepreneurship is critical to the wealth of an economy, and list the five factors of production that contribute to wealth.

There are two ways to succeed in business. One is to rise up through the ranks of large companies such as Royal Bank of Canada or Manulife Financial. The advantage of working for others is that somebody else assumes the entrepreneurial risk and provides you with benefits such as paid vacation time and health insurance. It's a good option and many people choose it.

The other, riskier, path is to start your own business and become an entrepreneur. While you may hear about success stories, keep in mind that many small businesses fail each year; thus, it takes a brave person to start a small business or to turn a business around. Furthermore, as an entrepreneur you do not receive any benefits such as paid vacation time and health insurance. You have to provide them for yourself!

Before you take on the challenge of entrepreneurship, it makes sense to study the experiences of those who have succeeded to learn the process. Consider the example of Ron Joyce, who purchased a Dairy Queen outlet in 1963. Two years later, he invested $10,000 to become a franchisee in the first Tim Hortons (we will discuss franchising in Chapter 6). By 1967, he became a full partner in the company with Tim Horton. In the early years, both partners worked on expanding the business. When Horton died in 1974, Joyce became the sole owner of the chain. In the following years, he continued to develop the business, spending hundreds of hours piloting his plane in search of new franchise opportunities and doing everything from training new store owners to baking donuts. When Joyce sold the chain to Wendy's for US$450 million in 1995, there were more than 1000 Tim Hortons restaurants. Tim Hortons became Canada's largest quick-service restaurant chain, with 5515 systemwide restaurants, including 4590 in Canada, 869 in the United States, and 56 in the Gulf Cooperation Council, an alliance of six Middle Eastern countries.[26] In 2014, the company merged with Burger King to form a new Canadian-based parent company, called Restaurant Brands International, and become the third-largest fast-food chain in the world.[27]

© AndreyPopov/iStock/Thinkstock

How well do you know yourself? Are you more excited at the prospect of starting your own small business or would you prefer to work for a large- or medium-sized business? The answer to this question may start with understanding your personal risk tolerance.

What you can learn from successful entrepreneurs like Ron Joyce is that you need to find something that you love to do. Before he became an entrepreneur, Joyce was a police officer. He started to get experience in business with his Dairy Queen outlet, and from there went on to great success with his Tim Hortons restaurants. While there were many challenges along the way, he was willing to put in the long hours needed to be successful. In addition to the original coffee and donut offerings, he continuously added new products to the restaurants to meet his customers' needs.

This is also the case for Ron Foxcroft, the focus of the chapter-opening Profile. Nearly 30 years after introducing the Fox 40 Classic Whistle, Fox 40 International Inc. sells an expanded whistle product line, pro coaching boards, mouthguards, and Fox 40 marine products (e.g., first aid and safety kits).

Small businesses and entrepreneurs contribute enormously to the Canadian economy. While these terms have been briefly mentioned in this chapter, be aware that more time will be spent discussing their significance in Chapters 6 and 7. After all, without the initial ideas and risks taken by entrepreneurs, we would not have successful businesses today.

The Importance of Entrepreneurs to the Creation of Wealth

Have you ever wondered why some countries are relatively wealthy and others are poor? Economists have been studying the issue of wealth creation for many years. They began the process by studying potential sources of wealth to determine which are the most important. Over time, they came up with five factors that seemed to contribute to wealth, which they called **factors of production**. Figure 1.4 describes those five factors, which are:

factors of production
The resources used to create wealth: land, labour, capital goods, entrepreneurship, and knowledge.

1. *Land (or natural resources).* Land and other natural resources are used to make homes, cars, and other products.
2. *Labour (workers).* People have always been an important resource in producing goods and services, but many people are now being replaced by technology.

FIGURE 1.4

THE FIVE FACTORS OF PRODUCTION

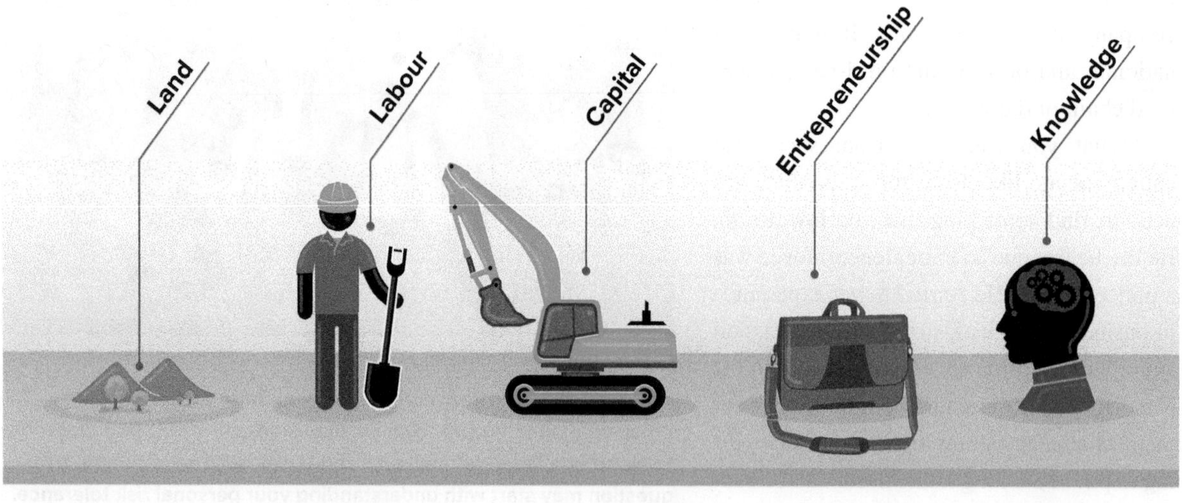

Source: Drucker Institute, druckerinstitute.com, April 2017.

3. *Capital Goods.* This includes machines, tools, buildings, or whatever else is used in the production of goods. It does not include money. Money is used to buy factors of production but is not always considered to be a factor by itself.
4. *Entrepreneurship.* All the resources in the world have little value unless entrepreneurs are willing to take the risk of starting businesses to use those resources.
5. *Knowledge.* Information technology has revolutionized business, making it possible to quickly determine wants and needs and to respond with desired goods and services.

© Rosemarie Gearhart/E+/Getty Images RF

To create wealth for its citizens, a country requires more than natural resources like timber. No matter how vast its forests or other inputs, like labour, fuel, and waterways, a country needs the efforts of entrepreneurs, and the skill and knowledge to produce goods and services. How can the government support entrepreneurship and the spread of knowledge?

Traditionally, business and economics textbooks have emphasized only four factors of production: land, labour, capital, and entrepreneurship. But management expert and business consultant Peter Drucker said that the most important factor of production in our economy is and always will be *knowledge.*

What do we find when we compare the factors of production in rich and poor countries? Some poor countries often have plenty of land and natural resources. Russia, for example, has vast areas of land with many resources such as timber and oil, but it is not considered a rich country (yet). In contrast, Japan is a relatively rich country but is poor in land and other natural resources. Therefore, land is not the critical element for wealth creation.

Most poor countries, such as Mexico, have many labourers, so labour is not the primary source of wealth today. Labourers need to find work to make a contribution; that is, they need entrepreneurs to provide jobs for them. Furthermore, capital—machinery and tools—is now easy for firms to find in world markets, so capital is not the missing ingredient. Capital is not productive without entrepreneurs to put it to use.

What makes countries rich today is a combination of *entrepreneurship* and the effective use of *knowledge.* Entrepreneurs use what they have learned (knowledge) to grow their businesses and increase wealth. Economic and political freedom also matter.

The business environment either encourages or discourages entrepreneurship. That helps explain why some provinces and cities in Canada grow rich while others remain relatively poor. In the following section, we'll explore what makes up the business environment and how to build an environment that encourages growth and job creation.

PROGRESS ASSESSMENT

- What are some of the advantages of working for others?
- What benefits do you lose by being an entrepreneur, and what do you gain?
- What are the five factors of production? Which ones seem to be the most important for creating wealth?

LO4

State the six elements that make up the business environment and explain why the business environment is important to organizations.

The Business Environment

business environment The surrounding factors that either help or hinder the development of businesses.

The **business environment** consists of the surrounding factors that either help or hinder the development of businesses. Figure 1.5, which summarizes some of the points discussed in this chapter, shows the six elements in the business environment:

1. The legal environment
2. The economic environment
3. The technological environment
4. The competitive environment
5. The social environment
6. The global environment

Businesses that create wealth and jobs grow and prosper in a healthy environment. Thus, creating the right business environment is the foundation for social benefits of all kinds, including good schools, clean air and water, good health care, and low rates of

FIGURE 1.5

TODAY'S DYNAMIC BUSINESS ENVIRONMENT

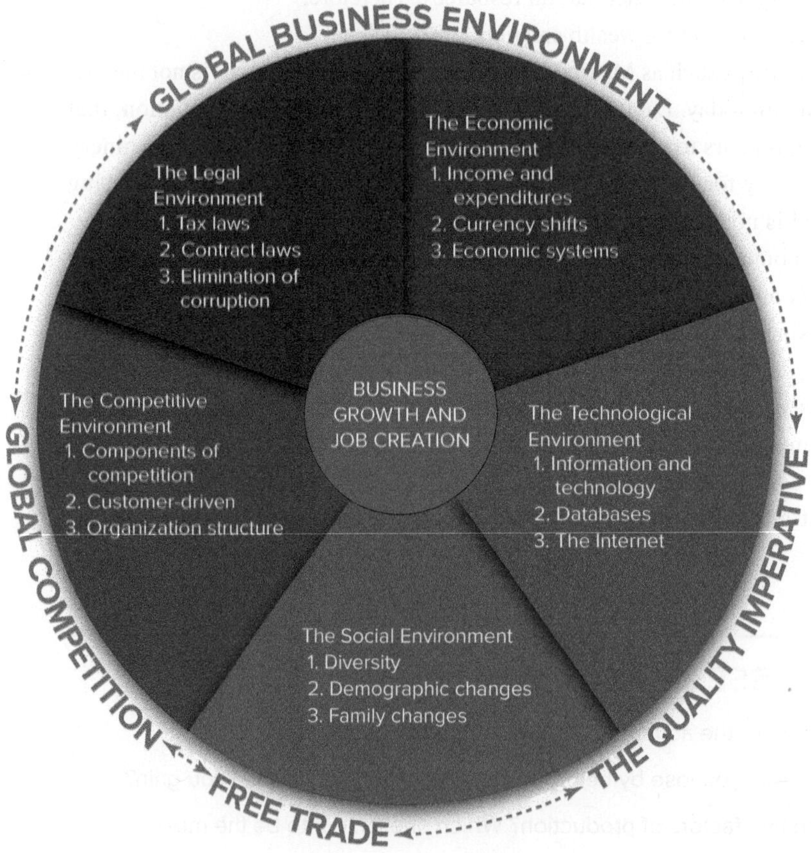

crime. Businesses normally cannot control their environment, but they need to monitor it carefully and do what they can to adapt as it changes.

The Legal Environment

People are willing to start new businesses if they believe that the risk of losing their money is not too great. Part of that decision is affected by how governments work with businesses. Governments can do a lot to lessen the risk of starting and running a business through the laws (also known as Acts) that are passed by its elected officials. The Constitution Act defines the powers that can be exercised by the different levels of government. In Chapter 4, we will review some of the responsibilities of these different levels.

Each piece of legislation authorizes an agency (such as Innovation, Science and Economic Development Canada) to write regulations that interpret the law in more detail and indicate how it will be implemented and enforced. Consequently, **regulations** consist of restrictions that provincial and federal laws place on businesses with respect to the conduct of their activities.[28] Regulations exist to protect consumers as well as businesses.[29] In Chapter 4, you will be introduced to some government departments that deal with businesses.

regulations
Restrictions that provincial and federal laws place on businesses with respect to the conduct of their activities.

LAWS AFFECT BUSINESS

Businesses need to be aware of the laws that are in place (or that may be passed) that will affect their operations. For example, government can keep taxes and regulations to a minimum, thereby encouraging entrepreneurship and increasing wealth. Entrepreneurs are looking for a high return on investment (ROI), including the investment of their time. If the government takes away much of what the business earns through high taxes, the ROI may no longer be worth the risk. Provinces and territories that have high taxes and restrictive regulations tend to drive entrepreneurs out, while areas with low taxes and less restrictive regulations can attract entrepreneurs.

The government can also lessen the risks of entrepreneurship by passing laws that enable business people to write contracts that are enforceable in court. You can read more about the importance of business law in Canada in an online supplement to this text.

There are many laws in Canada that are intended to minimize corruption, and businesses can flourish when these laws are followed. Nonetheless, corrupt and illegal activities at some companies do negatively affect the business community and the economy as a whole.[30] Ethics is so important to the success of businesses and the economy as a whole that we feature Making Ethical Decisions boxes in each chapter and devote Chapter 5 to the subject.

The capitalist system relies heavily on honesty, integrity, and high ethical standards. Failure of those fundamentals can weaken the whole system as was the case with the subprime mortgage scandal in the United States.[31] The faltering economy of 2008–2009 was due in large part to such failure. Some mortgage lenders, for instance, failed to do the research necessary to ensure their borrowers' creditworthiness. Many subprime borrowers forfeited their loans. The ripple effects of these unpaid debts not only cost many people their homes but also reduced the value of housing across the country and made it difficult for even business borrowers to get new loans. Part of the blame for this economic disaster can be placed on the borrowers who did not tell the truth about their income or who

Making ETHICAL DECISIONS

How Ethical Are You?

It is easy to criticize the ethics of people whose names appear in the headlines. It is more difficult to see the moral and ethical misbehaviour of your own social group. Do you find some of the behaviours of your friends morally or ethically questionable?

A survey found that the number of employees calling in sick had reached a five-year high, and three-fifths were not sick at all. Other employees have been caught conducting personal business at work, such as paying their bills or going on Facebook. And others play video games on their work computers. We are sure you can add many more examples.

Several companies today are creating ethics codes to guide their employees' behaviour. We believe the trend toward improving ethical behaviour is so important that we have made it a major theme of this book. Throughout the text you will see boxes like this one, called Making Ethical Decisions, that pose ethical dilemmas and ask what you would do to resolve them. The idea is for you to think about the moral and ethical dimensions of every decision you make.

© shironosov/iStock/Thinkstock

Here is your ethical dilemma. You have become addicted to your electronic gadgets. Some days at work you spend most of the time playing games, watching TV, texting, sending e-mails to friends, or reading a book or magazine on your devices. What is the problem in this situation? What are your alternatives? What are the consequences of each alternative? Which alternative will you choose? Is your choice ethical?

otherwise deceived the lenders. Financiers also assume blame for irresponsible lending decisions that exposed their bank or financial institution to significant risk.[32] This subprime mortgage crisis will be discussed in Chapter 4.

It is easy to see the damage caused by the poor moral and ethical behaviour of some business people. What is not so obvious is the damage caused by the moral and ethical lapses of the everyday consumer—that is, you and me. The Making Ethical Decisions box discusses that issue in more depth.

Governments from different countries can work together to create an environment that allows entrepreneurship to thrive. For example, in 2015 the United Nations adopted what it calls Sustainable Development Goals (SDGs) that list specific targets for ending poverty and improving the lives of the disadvantaged in the next 15 years. The ultimate goal is to move toward prosperity by partnering governments, businesses, and non-profits in order to solve problems at the ground level in developing countries.

The Economic Environment

The economic environment affects both businesses and consumers. For our discussion, the focus will be on businesses. The economic environment looks at income, expenditures, and resources that affect the cost of running a business. Businesses review the results of major economic indicators such as consumer spending, employment levels, and productivity. This analysis will give them a sense of what is happening in the marketplace and what actions they may need to take. Since Chapter 2 is dedicated to how economic issues affect businesses, the discussion here will be very brief.

© Partha Pal/The Image Bank/Getty Images

Starting a business is more difficult in some countries than in others. In India, for example, it is a time-consuming and bureaucratic process to obtain government permission. Nonetheless, new businesses can become a major source of wealth and employment. This sari shop is one small example. What do you think would be the effect of a little more freedom to create business opportunities in this country of over a billion people?

The movement of a country's currency relative to other currencies also pertains to this environment. Currency movements are especially critical for countries that generate a great deal of business activity from exports, such as Canada. For instance, in the late 2000s the Ontario economy was negatively impacted as a result of the strong Canadian dollar, which surpassed parity with the U.S. dollar in the fall of 2007. The province lost tens of thousands of manufacturing jobs in just a few years as manufacturers shifted operations overseas. Some of the province's flagship employers, like General Motors, closed factories and trimmed production at other manufacturing facilities.[33] The opposite is also true. For example, a lower Canadian dollar value relative to the U.S. dollar makes our exports cheaper and more attractive to the U.S. market, as consumers can buy more products with their higher-valued currency. What is the value of the Canadian dollar compared to other currencies today? How does it compare to the value of the U.S. dollar? What is the impact of the currency difference upon the Canadian economy?

Another aspect of the economic environment is the degree of entrepreneurship that is present. One way for governments to actively promote entrepreneurship is to allow private ownership of businesses. In some countries, the government owns most businesses and there is little incentive for people to work hard or create a profit. Around the world today, however, some governments are selling those businesses to private individuals to create more wealth. In Chapter 2, we will discuss the different economic systems around the world.

You should soon realize, as we continue with our brief introduction to the other business environments, that the activities occurring in one environment have an impact on the others. In short, all of the environments are linked. For example, if a new government regulation decreases business taxes, then the impact will be seen in the economic environment when one considers expenditures. As a business person you need to scan all of the environments to make good business decisions.

The Technological Environment

Since prehistoric times, humans have felt the need to create tools that make work easier. Few technological changes have had a more comprehensive and lasting impact on businesses, however, than the emergence of information technology (IT): computers, networks,

© danlefeb/Getty Images

Vivametrica, a Calgary-based data analytics platform company, is a new entrant in the wearable intelligence industry. The Canadian firm is taking advantage of the emerging wearable technology market, which is expected to reach US$2 billion by 2018. While its services target consumers, health-care providers, and researchers, the company's immediate appeal is to corporate wellness programs for various enterprises that seek to improve employee productivity. Companies in the manufacturing, financial, oil and gas, insurance, education, and health industries see the value data analytics can serve to improve their return on investment for employee wellness initiatives.[38]

smartphones, and the Internet. The Adapting to Change box discusses how one form of technology, drones, can make businesses more effective and efficient.

Smartphones and other mobile devices, as well as social media like Facebook and Twitter, have completely changed the way people communicate with one another. Advertisers and other business people have created ways of using these tools to reach their suppliers and customers. Even politicians have harnessed the power of the Internet to advance their causes.[34]

IT is such a major force in business today that we discuss its impact on businesses throughout the entire text. New technologies are dramatically changing business practices and the way businesses and customers buy and sell.[35]

HOW TECHNOLOGY BENEFITS WORKERS AND YOU

One of the advantages of working for others is that the company often provides the tools and technology to make your job more productive. **Technology** means everything from phones and copiers to computers, mobile devices, medical imaging machines, and the various software programs and apps that make business processes more effective, efficient, and productive. Applied science or engineering research often leads to new technology. *Effectiveness* means producing the desired result. *Efficiency* means producing goods and services using the least amount of resources. Effectiveness is usually more important than efficiency.

Productivity is the amount of output you generate given the amount of input, such as the number of hours you work. The more you can produce in any given period, the more money you are worth to companies. Today, the high rate of productivity means employers need fewer workers, which in turn, contributes to the high unemployment rate we are now experiencing.[36]

technology
Everything from phones and copiers to computers, mobile devices, medical imaging machines, and the various software programs and apps that make business processes more effective, efficient, and productive.

productivity
The amount of output that is generated given the amount of input (e.g., hours worked).

Technology affects how and where people work. For example, in the years since the recession of 2007–2009, freelancers have become more important to the business world than ever before. Rather than spend money on recruiting and retaining full-time employees, many companies prefer to hire temporary workers to cut costs. In fact, thanks to the Internet, freelance employees do not even need to live in the same country as their employers to do good, lucrative work.

The company Elance acts as an online marketplace that connects freelancers with companies looking for contractors.[37] For instance, if a Silicon Valley start-up is looking for an affordable engineer, Elance can introduce the company to a qualified candidate from Eastern Europe or India. Elance then collects an 8.75 percent transaction fee from the company. With more than 8 million registered individuals, in 2013 Elance saw its revenues grow to $300 million. Following a merger with its former rival oDesk, Elance expects billings to increase by more than $1 billion annually as businesses become more dependent on freelance labour, and workers adapt to its flexible structure. "Millennials want to work

Adapting *to* CHANGE

Up, Up, and Away

Sure drones can deliver a wide variety of things—everything from your Amazon order to a precisely targeted bomb. But they can also help businesses be more productive and efficient. Drones can scan, map, and gather data, tasks that used to require satellites, planes, and helicopters that only the deepest-pocketed companies could afford. Today even small businesses can pick up a drone for a few hundred dollars.

Construction companies can use drones to collect data far more frequently and accurately than they can with manned aircraft and human surveyors. Farmers can survey their fields of crops. Communication companies can inspect lofty cell towers. Property inspectors can inspect buildings. And this can all be done at much lower costs than traditional methods. For example, building inspectors usually charge $200–$300 for a typical home roof inspection that can take six hours. However, if the inspector uses a drone, the cost is $10 and takes only an hour. And piloting a drone is much less risky than climbing ladders or cell towers.

© Jochen Tack/Alamy

Of course, there are many concerns about the use of drones. Drones have been used to buzz planes, endanger military aircraft, and spy on neighbours' property with tiny video cameras. To combat these threats, the U.S. Congress has proposed giving the Federal Aviation Administration (FAA) more authority to regulate the use of drones. The drone industry is concerned that the lawmakers will inhibit the development and use of drones in their effort to rein in the people who misuse them. What do you think the government should do to regulate drones?

Sources: Mark Sundeen, "Welcome to Drone-Kota," *Popular Science,* May/June 2016; Ashley Halsey III, "Senate Considers Ramping Up FAA Oversight of Drone Use," *The Washington Post,* March 16, 2016; Mikal E. Belicove, "How Will Drones Change My Business?" *Entrepreneur,* April 16, 2016; Clay Dillow, "A Drone for Every Job Site," *Fortune,* September 15, 2016; Chris Anderson, "Drones Go to Work," *Harvard Business Review,* May 2017.

independently and control their careers," says Elance founder Fabio Rosati. "If I had to give advice to anybody about their careers, I would say your number one priority should be to remain employable as opposed to remaining employed."

THE GROWTH OF ELECTRONIC COMMERCE (E-COMMERCE)

e-commerce
The buying and selling of goods and services over the Internet.

E-commerce is the buying and selling of goods and services online. There are two major types of e-commerce transactions: business-to-business (B2B) and business-to-consumer (B2C). In 2013, Canadian enterprises sold $136 billion in goods and services over the Internet. Approximately 61 percent of the sales involved wholesale trade, manufacturing, and retail trade.[39] The increase resulted from more online shoppers (B2C) as well as a higher volume of Internet B2B orders. In 2017, estimates showed Canadian retailer e-commerce sales reached $18 billion.[40]

As important as the Internet has been in the consumer market to retailers like Amazon, it has become even more important in the B2B market, which consists of selling goods and services from one business to another, such as IBM selling consulting services to a local bank. Websites have become the new stores.

Traditional businesses have been learning how to deal with the competition from B2B and B2C firms, and vice versa. People would just as soon sell used items posted on Kijiji and Craigslist than throw away unwanted household items.[41] Many entrepreneurs use e-commerce to start a business and are recognized by eBay through its Entrepreneur of the Year awards.[42] Just consider one country: over 215 million Chinese citizens are using the Internet.[43] And what did people do before they could Google? E-commerce has become so important that we will discuss it throughout the text.

Do not confuse e-commerce with electronic business (e-business). Mostly done with web technologies, the term **e-business** refers to any information system or application (e.g., business software) that empowers business processes. While e-commerce is frequently mixed up with the term e-business, e-commerce only covers one aspect of e-business (i.e., the use of an electronic support for the commercial relationship between a company and individuals).[44]

e-business
Any information system or application that empowers business processes.

database
An electronic storage file for information.

identity theft
Obtaining an individual's personal information, such as Social Insurance Number and credit card numbers, for illegal purposes.

USING TECHNOLOGY TO BE RESPONSIVE TO CUSTOMERS

A major theme of this text is that those businesses most responsive to customer wants and needs will succeed. That realization points to one way in which even traditional retailers can use Internet technology. For example, businesses use bar codes to identify products that customers buy and their size, quantity, and colour. The scanner at the checkout counter can read that information and put it into a **database**, an electronic storage file in which information is kept.

Databases enable stores to carry only the merchandise their local population wants. But because companies routinely trade database information, many retailers know what you buy and from whom you buy it. Thus they can send you catalogues and other direct mail advertising offering the kind of products you might want, as indicated by your past purchases. We discuss other ways businesses use technology to be responsive to consumers throughout the text and in more detail in Appendix A.

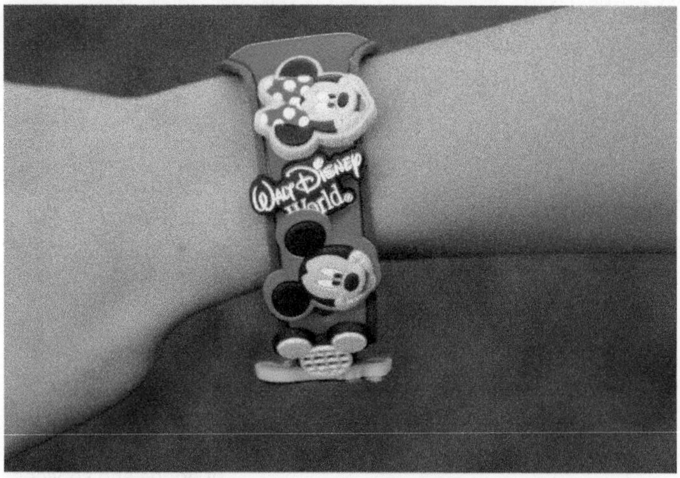

© Jennifer Blankenship RF

Walt Disney World introduced MyMagic+, a convenient way for guests to create their ideal vacation experience. The key element is the MagicBand, providing an all-in-one way to effortlessly connect all the vacation choices guests make online. The MagicBand uses RF technology and serves as park ticket, hotel room key, access to FastPass+ advance reservation of attraction times, and Disney's PhotoPass. Disney hotel guests may use the bands to charge meals and merchandise to their hotel account.

Unfortunately, the legitimate collection of personal customer information also opens the door to identity theft. **Identity theft** is the act of obtaining personal information about a person, such as social insurance number and/or credit card numbers, and using that information for illegal purposes, such as making purchases. For example, in 2017 even though Apple itself was not hacked, it reported that some Apple customers who secured their iCloud accounts with the same passwords they use on other sites that *were* hacked (especially accounts on LinkedIn, Yahoo!, and Dropbox) suffered breaches to their Apple accounts as well.[45] Experts advise us to create new passwords for each account so that if the password on one account is stolen, the hackers can't access the rest of your accounts too. They also recommend storing them in a password manager, and activating two-factor authentication, which is an additional layer of security, when possible.[46]

In response to consumer complaints, federal privacy laws have been created. The *Personal Information Protection and Electronic Documents Act* (PIPEDA) sets out ground rules for how private sector organizations may collect, use, or disclose personal information in the course of commercial activities.[47] If you think an organization covered by the Act is not living up to its responsibilities under the law, you have the right to lodge an official complaint. The Office of the Privacy Commissioner of Canada advocates privacy rights for Canadians.

What you should learn from this example is to limit those to whom you give personal information.[48] You also need antivirus software on your computer as well as a firewall and antispyware software. You may also want to monitor your credit report. It is important for you to understand identity theft, security, privacy, stability, and other important IT issues.

SOCIAL MEDIA MARKETING[49]

In Chapter 14 you will read how some Canadian companies are in the midst of the emergence of the social media marketing era. The most common tools or platforms used by both consumers and organizations are social networking sites (e.g., Twitter, Facebook, and Instagram), blogs, wikis, podcasts, and other shared media sites (e.g., YouTube). To survive in this social media world, organizations must understand, navigate, and adapt to this new landscape. Some organizations are heeding this advice. A recent report found 57 percent of small business owners use social media, and Facebook and LinkedIn are the most common tools.[50] In particular, small businesses and entrepreneurs are leveraging social media as a way to connect and communicate with current and potential customers.

Social media is also used for **crowdsourcing**, which helps a business find solutions to challenges. It is a valuable tool to better understand the dynamics of a business market.[51] The future may also utilize crowdsourcing to build better collaboration between government and citizens, students and universities, patients and hospitals.[52]

crowdsourcing
Using the expertise of a large group of people to solve a business problem.

PROGRESS ASSESSMENT

- List the six elements of the business environment.
- What are four ways in which the government can foster entrepreneurship?
- How does technology benefit workers and customers?

The Competitive Environment

Competition among businesses has never been greater than it is today. Some companies have found a competitive edge by focusing on quality. The goal for many companies is zero defects—no mistakes in making the product. However, simply making a high-quality product is not enough to allow a company to stay competitive in world markets. Companies now have to offer both high-quality products and good value—that is, outstanding services and products at competitive prices. Figure 1.6 shows how competition has evolved to a new, world-class model.

COMPONENTS OF COMPETITION[53]

When developing their strategies, companies must consider the factors that drive competition: entry, bargaining power of buyers and suppliers, existing rivalries, and substitution possibilities. Scanning the competitive environment requires a look at all of these factors.

Entry In considering the competition, a firm must assess the likelihood of new entrants.. Additional producers increase industry capacity and tend to lower prices. *Barriers to entry* are business practices or conditions that make it difficult for new firms to enter the market. Barriers to entry can be in the form of capital requirements, product identity, distribution access, or switching costs. The higher the expense of the barrier, the more likely it will deter new entrants, and vice versa (e.g., barriers to exit).

Power of Buyers and Suppliers Powerful buyers exist when they are few in number, there are low switching costs, or the product represents a significant share of the buyer's total costs. This last factor leads the buyer to exert significant pressure for price competition. A supplier gains power when the product is critical to the buyer and when it has built up switching costs.

Existing Competitors and Substitutes Competitive pressure among existing firms depends on the rate of industry growth. In slow-growth settings, competition is more heated for any possible gains in market share. High fixed costs also create competitive pressures for firms to fill production capacity. (We will discuss production in Chapter 10.) For example, airlines offer discounts for making early reservations and

FIGURE 1.6

HOW COMPETITION HAS CHANGED BUSINESS

Traditional Businesses	Modern Businesses
Customer satisfaction	Delighting the customer*
Customer orientation	Customer and stakeholder orientation**
Profit orientation	Profit and social orientation†
Reactive ethics	Proactive ethics‡
Product orientation	Quality and service orientation
Managerial focus	Customer focus

* *Delight* is a term from total quality management. *Bewitch and fascinate* are alternative terms.
** Stakeholders include customers, employees, investors, suppliers, dealers (e.g., retailers), and the community; the goal is to please *all* stakeholders.
† A social orientation goes beyond profit to do what is right and good for others.

charge penalties for changes or cancellations in an effort to fill seats, which represent a high fixed cost.

COMPETING BY EXCEEDING CUSTOMER EXPECTATIONS

Manufacturers and service organizations throughout the world have learned that today's customers are very demanding. Companies have to offer both high-quality products and outstanding service at competitive prices (value). Business is becoming customer-driven, not management-driven as in the past. This means that customers' wants and needs must come first. Read the Spotlight on Small Business box to discover how one company tracks their customers' needs to remain vital.

Customer-driven organizations include Disney amusement parks, where the parks are kept clean and appeal to all ages, and Moto Photo, which does its best to please customers

Spotlight *On* SMALL BUSINESS

Fighting for Air Space: Chinook Helicopters Ltd.

When it comes to services we purchase on a daily basis, helicopter pilot certification isn't one that normally comes to mind. But for Chinook Helicopters Ltd., teaching people how to fly helicopters is a core competence.

Formed in 1982, Chinook Helicopters is privately owned and holds 25 percent of the Canadian market in helicopter training. The company has become a national leader in helicopter pilot and helicopter maintenance certification. Although Chinook is based in Abbotsford, British Columbia, the company notes 30 percent of its 2017 student admissions came from beyond Canadian borders. This is one indication of how the company sets its expertise apart from others in the global environment.

Its success is dependent upon how well the company can keep pace with change in the technological environment, such as innovation in robotics and Unmanned Aerial Vehicles (UAVs). The competition environment is also challenging as commercial piloted unmanned aircraft systems often get contracts for pipeline surveillance. Nevertheless, the demand for helicopter pilots in all regions of the world means the company must remain up to date on domestic and international standards so it can set its service apart from others in a competitive landscape.

© Chinook Helicopters

At a meeting of the Helicopter Association of Canada in 2011, an expert panel discussed the impact of economic cycles on business. Flight training is dependent upon the economy so when industries such as forestry, oils and gas, mining and exploration, resource management, and aerial media work experience growth, Chinook's needs to outmaneuvre its competitors.

Tracking the dynamic business environment is what makes Chinook's training opportunities cutting edge and attractive to anyone looking to have a career in the helicopter industry.

Sources: Chinook Helicopters Ltd., accessed May 22, 2018, chinookhelicopters.com; Woodrow Bellamy III, "Canadian Helicopters: Operating, Training for Challenging Missions," Rotor and Wing International, April/May 2018, accessed May 22, 2018 http://digitaledition.rotorandwing.com/april-may-2018/canadian-helicopters-operating-training-for-challenging-missions/; Matt Nichols, "Forecasting the Future: Industry Experts Discuss Key Issues at Helicopter's First Roundtable," *Helicopters Magazine*, July, 18, 2011, accessed May 22, 2018, https://www.helicoptersmagazine.com/standards-regulations/forecasting-the-future-2884.

with fast, friendly service. Such companies can successfully compete against Internet firms if they continue to offer better and friendlier service. Successful organizations must now listen more closely to customers to determine their wants and needs, then adjust the firm's products, policies, and practices to meet those demands. We will explore these concepts in more depth in Chapter 14.

COMPETING BY RESTRUCTURING AND EMPOWERMENT

To meet the needs of customers, firms must give their front-line workers (e.g., office clerks, front-desk people at hotels, and salespeople) the responsibility, authority, freedom, training, and equipment they need to respond quickly to customer requests. They must allow workers to make other decisions essential to producing high-quality goods and services. The process is called **empowerment**, and we'll be talking about it throughout this book. To implement a policy of empowerment, managers must train front-line people to make decisions within certain limits, without the need to consult managers.

empowerment
Giving front-line workers the responsibility, authority, and freedom to respond quickly to customer requests.

As many companies have discovered, it sometimes takes years to restructure an organization so that managers are willing to give up some of their authority and employees are willing to assume more responsibility. We'll discuss such organizational changes and models in Chapter 9.

The Social Environment

demography
The statistical study of the human population with regard to its size, density, and other characteristics, such as age, race, gender, and income.

Demography is the statistical study of the human population with regard to its size, density, and other characteristics such as age, race, gender, and income. In this book, we are particularly interested in the demographic trends that most affect businesses and career choices (see Chapter 11 for more details on generational trends and employees). The Canadian population is going through major changes that are dramatically affecting how people live, where they live, what they buy, and how they spend their time. Furthermore, tremendous population shifts are leading to new opportunities for some firms and to declining opportunities for others. For example, there are many more retired workers than in the past, creating new markets for all kinds of goods and services.

Generation X
A demographic group of Canadians who were born in the period from 1965 to 1976.

Generation Y (Millennials)
A demographic group of Canadians who were born in the period from 1977 to 1994; the children of the Baby Boomers.

Baby Boomers
A demographic group of Canadians who were born in the period from 1946 to 1964.

Generation Z
A demographic group of Canadians who were born in the period from 1995 onward.

THE AGING POPULATION

The Canadian population has been aging for several decades.[54] More people are living longer due to better medical knowledge and technology, better health habits, more exercise, and a reduction in the number of people who smoke. The portion of the population that is very young continues to decrease because of birth rates that have declined since the mid-1960s. **Generation X** represents the demographic group that were born in the period 1965-1976. **Generation Y**, also known as Millennials (those born in the period from 1977 to 1994) represents the children of the large number of **Baby Boomers** (those born in the period from 1946 to 1964). Some students are part of Generation Y while others may be part of **Generation Z**, who include those born from 1995 onward.

Figure 1.7 shows the population projections for Canada. You will notice that the 20–34 years and 35–64 years age groups are declining, while the 65 years and over age

FIGURE 1.7

POPULATION DISTRIBUTION BY AGE GROUP

YEAR	0–4	5–19	20–34	35–64	65 AND ABOVE
2016	5.7%	16.3%	20.5%	41.2%	16.3%
2021	5.6%	16.5%	19.3%	40.1%	18.5%
2026	5.5%	16.9%	18%	38.8%	20.8%
2031	5.2%	16.8%	17.5%	37.7%	22.8%
2036	5%	16.5%	17.7%	37.1%	23.7%

Source: Adapted from "Population Projections for Canada, Provinces and Territories 2009–2036," Cat. No. 91–520–X, June 2010. Retrieved from http://www.statcan.gc.ca/pub/91–520–x/2010001/t370-eng.htm.

group is increasing steadily. Based on these projections, it is expected that seniors will become more numerous than children sometime around 2021. According to Statistics Canada, by 2036 nearly one quarter of the population will be Generation Z.[55]

WORKFORCE TRENDS

What do such demographics mean for you and for businesses in the future? In his book *Boom Bust & Echo: Profiting from the Demographic Shift in the 21st Century,* economist and demographer David Foot writes that demographics play a pivotal role in the economic and social life of our country. According to Foot, demographics explain about two-thirds of everything—including which products will be in demand in five years.[56] According to Statistics Canada, by 2031 seniors will account for nearly 25 percent of the Canadian population. This amount continues to grow through to 2036.[57] Immigration and the projected birth rates are not expected to balance the workforce losses created by the aging population, either in Canada or globally.[58] We will discuss some of the human resource management issues related to an aging population in Chapter 12.

© Monkey Business Images Ltd./photolibrary RF

Canada boasts enormous ethnic and racial diversity. Its workforce is also widely diverse in terms of age, which means that managers must adapt to the generational demographics of the workplace. In addition to changes in the demand of goods and services the demographic shift also impacts labour supply. What are some challenges of working with someone much younger or much older than you?

Think of the products and services that middle-aged and elderly people will need—anything from travel and recreation to medicine, nursing homes, assisted-living facilities, adult day care, home health care, and the like—and you will see opportunities for successful businesses of the twenty-first century. Don't rule out computer games and online services. Don't forget the impact of aging baby boomers: more grandparents with extra money in their pockets will buy extra gifts for their grandchildren. Businesses that cater to older consumers will have the opportunity for exceptional growth in the near future. The market is huge.

MANAGING DIVERSITY[59]

Canada has a strong multicultural population. In the last ten years, it has welcomed close to 2.7 million permanent residents. The high level of annual admission of immigrants and the relatively slow rate of natural growth of the population explain why the proportion of the foreign-born in the Canadian population has been increasing since the 1990s.

Citizenship and Immigration Canada's plan is to admit approximately 250 000 immigrants each year.[60] In order to meet this target, the government manages a number of immigration programs to enable people from other countries to become Canadian citizens. Approximately 62 percent of immigrants come to Canada through economic categories, such as the skilled worker, skilled trade, and business immigrant. The remaining 38 percent gain citizenship through family and humanitarian categories.

While this information is not exhaustive, it should give you an idea of some of the demographic trends that business people track as they develop their products and services. Can you think of some opportunities that are not currently being met as a result of some of these trends?

PROGRESS ASSESSMENT

- Describe the components of competition.
- What is empowerment?
- What social trends are evident in Canada?

The Global Environment

The global environment of business is so important that we show it as surrounding all other environmental influences in Figure 1.5. Two important environmental changes in recent years have been the growth of global competition and the increase of free trade among nations.

World trade, or *globalization,* has grown thanks to the development of efficient distribution systems (we'll talk about these later in the text) and communication advances such as the Internet. Globalization has greatly improved living standards around the world. China and India have become major competitors. For example, Lenovo, a Chinese firm, bought IBM's PC unit. Shop at Walmart and most other retail stores, and you cannot help but notice the number of "Made in China" stickers you see. Call for computer help, and you are as likely to be talking with someone in India as someone in Canada. As the Reaching Beyond our Borders box discusses, China has become a key to success for even Hollywood and the movie business.

Reaching *Beyond* OUR BORDERS

Hollywood Climbs the Great Wall

In late 2016, the producers of the remake of the movie *Jumanji* put out a casting call to talent agencies across Hollywood. Their quest was to find a Chinese actor to play a major role in the film. Like many others, this casting of Chinese actors in U.S. films was an obvious effort to appeal to audiences in China. Today, China is the world's second-largest movie market, with over $5 billion in ticket sales in 2016. It is expected to surpass the world leader, the United States, in the next few years. Studios also note that even though China limits the number of foreign films that can be shown in the country, more than half of the top 10 grossing films in China are from Hollywood.

Chinese investors today are not just interested in distributing Hollywood films in their country. They intend to become major players in the entire film industry. For example, Wang Jianlin, the wealthiest man in China, is a major buyer in Hollywood. His Dalian Wanda Group has interests in every stage of the entertainment industry including ownership of the theatre chain AMC Entertainment Holdings, which he purchased in 2012 for $1 billion. He intends to make AMC the largest theatre chain in the United States. Wang also actively sought to buy a stake in Paramount Pictures until the company decided not to sell. Wang promises to pursue his goal of being a key part of the movie business and has a personal goal to make China a movie-making power in its own right.

© Photo 12/Alamy

Sources: Jacky Wong, "Wanda-Sony Pictures: China Coming to Theater Near You," *The Wall Street Journal*, September 24, 2016; Erich Schwartzel, Kathy Chu, and Wayne Ma, "China's Play for Hollywood," *The Wall Street Journal*, October 2, 2016; Michal Lev-Ram, "Can China Save Hollywood?" *Fortune*, May 22, 2017.

World trade has its benefits and costs. You will read much more about its importance in Chapter 3 and in the Reaching Beyond Our Borders boxes in each chapter.

HOW GLOBAL CHANGES AFFECT YOU

As businesses expand to serve global markets, new jobs will be created in both manufacturing and service industries. Global trade also means global competition. The students who will prosper will be those prepared for the markets of tomorrow. Rapid changes create a need for continuous learning, so be prepared to pursue your education throughout your career. You will have every reason to be optimistic about job opportunities in the future if you prepare yourself well.

climate change
The movement of the temperature of the planet up or down over time.

greening
The trend toward saving energy and producing products that cause less harm to the environment.

sustainability
Social perspectives focus on quality of human life; economic views emphasize a steady-state economy.

THE ECOLOGICAL ENVIRONMENT

Few issues have captured the attention of the international business community more than climate change.[61] **Climate change** is the movement of the temperature of the planet up or down over time. The issue now is global warming. Some of the world's largest firms—including General Electric, Coca-Cola, Shell, Nestlé, DuPont, Johnson & Johnson, British Airways, and Shanghai Electric — say the evidence for climate change is overwhelming. Saving energy and producing products that cause less harm to the environment is a trend called **greening**. Greening has become such a pervasive issue that impacts every type of business decisions.

The term **sustainability** has different meanings depending upon the context in which it is used. Social perspectives of sustainability focus upon the quality of human life over time while economic views of sustainability emphasize a steady-state economy.[62] We shall discuss business and sustainability issues in the Seeking Sustainability boxes throughout the text and in Chapter 5.

Seeking SUSTAINABILITY

Services Expand the Circular Economy and Reduce Waste

Have you ever bought a movie on DVD? Today most of us watch movies on Netflix or some other on-demand service. it is the same with music—why store stacks of CDs when you can use services like Spotify? All sorts of products are becoming services. For example, you can store files in the cloud instead of your computer. You can take Ubers or Lyfts instead of owning a car. Businesses can rent office carpets by the month, rent lighting, or print by the page.

Technology enables a large variety of products to be offered as services. The Internet of Things put sensors on all sorts of things that allow companies to track usage, measure performance, and develop new business models. For example, GPS enables car companies to provide "mobility services" (such as BMW's ReachNow, General Motor's Maven, and Zipcar's car-sharing services). Some ride-sharing services are beginning to use technology called *telematics* to track drivers' performance. Sensors in the drivers' cell phones can track when they speed, cut corners, brake suddenly, or send texts while driving.

© Brian Snyder/Reuters/Alamy.

The product-as-service model is one way to move away from a "take-make-dispose" economy (i.e., take raw materials, make a product, and dispose of it when you're finished with it) toward a more *circular economy* that reduces waste. Companies that retain ownership of their products maintain them and extend their life cycles. Instead of planning for obsolescence so we buy new versions of the products more often, companies that provide products as services have an incentive to make products that last as long as possible and that can be repaired easily and cheaply. Think of all the landfill space that would save.

Sources: Greg Gardner, "GM Launches Shared-Ride Service Called Maven," *USA Today*, January 22, 2016; Douglas MacMillian, "Car Apps Test Tracking of Drivers," *The Wall Street Journal*, January 27, 2016; Ben Schiller, "How Netflixication Can Deliver a Waste-Free Circular Economy," *Fast Company*, March 13, 2017.

The Evolution of Canadian Business

LO5

Give examples of how the service sector has replaced manufacturing as the principal provider of jobs, but why manufacturing remains vital for Canada.

Many managers and workers are losing their jobs in major manufacturing firms. Businesses in Canada have become so productive that, compared to the past, fewer workers are needed in industries that produce goods. If global competition and improved technology are putting skilled people out of work, should we be concerned about the prospect of high unemployment rates and low incomes? Where will the jobs be when you graduate? These important questions prompt us to look briefly at the manufacturing and service sectors.

Progress in the Agricultural and Manufacturing Industries

Canada has seen strong economic development since the nineteenth century. The agricultural industry led the way, providing food for Canadians and people in other parts of the world. Inventions such as the harvester and cotton gin did much to make farming successful, as did ongoing improvements to such equipment. The modern farming industry has become so efficient through the use of technology that the number of farms has dropped. Due to increased competition, many of the farms that existed even 50 years ago have been replaced by some huge farms, some merely large farms, and some small but highly specialized farms. The loss of farm workers over the past century is not a negative sign. It is instead an indication that Canadian agricultural workers are more productive.

Most farmers who lost their jobs went to work in factories. The manufacturing industry, much like agriculture, used technology to become more productive. The consequence, as in farming, was the elimination of many jobs. Again, the loss to society is minimal if the wealth created by increased productivity and efficiency creates new jobs elsewhere. This is exactly what has happened over the past 50 years. Many workers in the industrial sector found jobs in the service sector. Most of those who cannot find work today are people who need retraining and education to become qualified for jobs that now exist.

CANADA'S MANUFACTURING INDUSTRY

The goods-producing sector includes the manufacturing, construction, utilities, agriculture, forestry, fishing, mining, quarrying, and the oil and gas industries. Of this sector, manufacturing employs just under ten percent of Canada's working population, as noted in Figure 1.8. Manufacturing is diverse in Canada and it includes food, beverage, clothing, chemical, machinery, wood, and petroleum and coal products manufacturing.[63]

Tens of thousands of Canadian jobs were lost in the late 2000s. The rising Canadian dollar and increasing global competition were two of the reasons for these losses. Despite such losses, manufacturing still remains an important contributor to the Canadian economy.

The Canadian Manufacturers & Exporters highlights some of the reasons why this sector is important to Canada:

- Employs 1.8 million Canadian and represented 10.5 percent of the workforce in 2012;[64]
- Generates $3.15 in economic spin-off of every for every $1.00 in manufacturing output;[65]

FIGURE 1.8

THE IMPORTANCE OF THE SERVICES-PRODUCING AND GOODS-PRODUCING SECTORS IN CANADA

Canada is a service economy, where the majority of jobs are generated in the services-providing sector. This table highlights the importance of each sector, as well as the three largest-employer industries in each.

	Number of Employed (thousands)	Total Workforce (percent)
TOTAL EMPLOYED IN CANADA	18,464	100.0
Services-Producing Sector	14,541	79
Trade	2,809.6	15.2
Health Care and Social Assistance	2,383.2	12.9
Professional, Scientific & Technical Services	1,448.8	9.9
Goods-Producing Sector	3,876	21
Manufacturing	1,724.8	9.3
Construction	1,409.3	7.6
Forestry, Fishing, Mining, Quarrying, Oil & Gas	329.6	1.7

Source: Statistics Canada. Employment by Industry and Sex, 2017, accessed May 19, 2018, http://www.statcan.gc.ca/tables-tableaux/sum-som/l01/cst01/labor10a-eng.htm.

- 45 percent of manufacturers and exporters foresee a 1 to 10 percent rise in their workforce;[66] and
- 59 percent of manufacturers and exporters plan to increase research and development investments.[67]

While the manufacturing sector is much smaller today than it was 25 years ago, it is still clearly an integral part of our business economy. We will discuss the manufacturing sector and production in more detail in Chapter 10.

Progress in Service Industries

In the past, the dominant industries in Canada produced goods such as steel, railroads, and machine tools. The shift in Canada's employment profile began slowly in the early twentieth century, and has accelerated rapidly since the 1950s. Today, the leading firms are in services (such as legal, health and wellness, telecommunications, entertainment, financial services, etc.). As noted in Figure 1.8, the services-producing sector employs almost 79 percent of the working population.

There are several reasons why there has been growth in this sector. First, technological improvements have enabled businesses to reduce their payrolls while increasing their output. Since staffing has been downsized by many companies, business has become more complex and specialized companies have relied more heavily on outside services firms. Secondly, as large manufacturing companies seek to become more efficient, they contract out an increasing number of services, creating more opportunities for business people. Other service firms have risen or expanded rapidly to provide traditional services that used to be performed by women at home. Since many women have entered the workforce, there is increased demand for food preparation, child care, and household maintenance, to name just a few services.

Chances are very high that you will work in a service job at some point in your career. Another bit of good news is that there are *more* high-paying jobs in the services-producing sector than in the goods-producing sector. High-paying service-sector jobs abound in health care, accounting, finance, entertainment, telecommunications, architecture, law, software engineering, and more. Projections are that some areas of the service sector will grow rapidly, while others may have much slower growth. Figure 1.9 lists many service-sector jobs; look it over to see where the careers of the future are likely to be. Retailers like SportChek are part of the service sector. Each new retail store can create managerial jobs for post-secondary graduates.

The strategy for graduates is to remain flexible, find out where jobs are being created, and move when appropriate. Such was the case for Edmonton-based FourQuest Energy, which was singled out by PROFIT 200 as Canada's Fastest-Growing Company. The company provides mechanical pre-commissioning, shutdown, and maintenance services for oil-and-gas facilities. "I just felt the business had such a great probability of success. I couldn't see any potential for failure if we could just get it started." says Nik Grgic, President. He and fellow entrepreneur, Karl Gannon, Executive Vice President, decided it was worth abandoning a steady paycheque with a multinational energy firm to start this company.[68]

© Erik Isakson/Blend Images LLC

The entire process of growing food and getting it to our tables is so smooth that it's easy to take the agriculture industry for granted. But behind those well-stocked supermarkets is an army of farmers and distributors who supply our needs. The use of technology has led to increased productivity and made farmers more efficient, resulting in larger farms. This trend has meant less expensive food for us, but a continual reduction in the number of small, family-run farms. Is it still possible for small farms to be successful, and if so, how?

Your Future in Business

Despite the growth in the service sector, the service era now seems to be coming to a close as a new era is beginning. We are now in the midst of an information-based global revolution that will alter all sectors of the economy. It's exciting to think about the role you will play in that revolution.

As mentioned earlier in this chapter, business is an activity that seeks to provide goods and services to others while operating at a profit. This text introduces you to areas such as business trends, business ownership, leadership and organizations, management of human resources, marketing and accounting and financial activities. As you learn more about business, it is important to keep in mind there are two management approaches that influence these fundamental areas—scientific and humanistic management.

FIGURE 1.9

WHAT IS THE SERVICE SECTOR?

There's much talk about the service sector, but few discussions actually list what it includes. Here are examples of businesses in the service sector.

Amusement and Recreation Services	Amusement parks	Ice skating rinks	Bowling alleys	Pool halls	Botanical gardens	Infotainment	Carnivals
	Race tracks	Circuses	Golf courses	Symphony orchestras	Restaurants	Fairs	Video rentals
Business Services	Collection agencies	Management services	Equipment rental	Trash collection	Computer programming	Exterminating	Research & development labs
	Window cleaning	Tax preparation	Web design	Commercial photography	Accounting	Commercial art	Ad agencies
	Public relations	Consulting	Detective agencies	Interior design	Stenographic services	Employment agencies	
Legal Services	Lawyers	Paralegals	Notary public				
Educational Services	Schools	Libraries	Online schools	Computer schools			
Health Services	Chiropractors	Nursery care	Dentists	Physicians	Medical labs	Dental labs	
Motion Picture Industry	Production	Distribution	Theatres	Drive-ins			
Social Services	Job training	Elder care	Family services	Child care			
Automotive Repair Services and Garages	Transmission repair	Tire retreading	Exhaust system shops	Truck rental	Auto rental	Paint shops	Parking lots
	Car washes						
Financial Services	Banking	Real estate agencies	Investment firms (brokers)	Insurance			
Personal Services	Photographic studios	Shoe repair	Tax preparation	Laundries	Funeral homes	Linen supply	
	Beauty shops	Child care	Health clubs	Diaper service	Carpet cleaning		
Lodging Services	Hotels, rooming houses, and other lodging places	Sporting and recreation camps	Trailer parks and campsites for transients				
Cultural Institutions	Non-commercial museums	Art galleries	Botanical and zoological gardens				
Selected Membership Organizations	Civic associations	Business associations					
Miscellaneous Services	Telecommunications	Architectural	Engineering	Utilities	Lawn care	Vending	Delivery
	Surveying	Septic tank cleaning	Radio and television	Sharpening	Reuphoistery	Watch repair	Welding

Scientific management studies work to find the most efficient ways of doing things and then teach people those techniques. As we will discuss in Chapter 11, Frederick Taylor, referred to as the father of scientific management, sought to increase worker productivity. His views became the dominant strategy for how business operates. But according to the International Humanistic Management Association, the consequence of thinking exclusively in terms of productivity is that "those things that have a price take priority over those that do not, [such as] human integrity, environmental beauty, or quality of life."[69]

However, the second type of management, **humanistic management**, presents a different view where a worker is not viewed simply as a machine for efficiency, but as person who really matters. It is often referred to as *people-oriented management* because rather than treat people as a simple resource for profits, the approach seeks profits for human ends.[70] It may be said that this type of management, which focuses upon human dignity and well-being, presents a new perspective where issues of inequality, poverty, environmental destruction, and mass migration force us to change the way we do business.[71]

humanistic management
A people-oriented management approach that emphasizes the dignity and well-being of employees.

As you read the chapters in this textbook, keep in mind how each of the business fundamentals you learn might be impacted by humanistic management. How might such an approach change they was we do business? Given what you have learned in this chapter about the dynamic business environment, Is this approach going to play an important role in the future economy?

You may be a leader, that is, you may be one of the people who will implement the changes and accept the challenges of world competition based on world quality standards. This text will introduce you to some of the concepts that will make such leadership possible, not just in business but also in government agencies and non-profit organizations. Business cannot prosper in the future without the co-operation of government and social leaders throughout the world.

PROGRESS ASSESSMENT

- What changes have affected the global environment?
- Give examples of how the service sector has replaced manufacturing as the principal provider of jobs, but why manufacturing remains vital for Canada.
- Why is the services-producing sector important to the economy?

SUMMARY

LO1 **Illustrate the importance of key business fundamentals to wealth generation.**

A business is any activity that seeks to provide goods and services to others while operating at a profit.

What are the relationships between risk, profit, and loss?

Profit is money a business earns above and beyond the money that it spends for salaries and other expenses. Business people make profits by taking risks. *Risk* is the chance an entrepreneur takes of losing time and money on a business that may not prove profitable. A loss occurs when a business' costs and expenses are higher than its revenues.

LO2 **Identify business stakeholders and their importance to non-profit organizations and business activities.**

Stakeholders include customers, employees, shareholders, suppliers, dealers, bankers, the media, people in the local community, environmentalists, and elected government leaders. The goal of business leaders is to try to recognize and respond to the needs of these stakeholders and still make a profit.

How do non-profit organizations differ from profit-seeking organizations?

A non-profit organization is an organization whose goals do not include making a personal profit for its owners or organizers.

Which stakeholders are most important to a business?

The goal of business leaders is to try to balance the needs of all stakeholders and still make a profit. Some businesses put the needs of shareholders above the other interests, but most businesses today seek a balance among the needs of the various stakeholders.

LO3 **Explain how entrepreneurship is critical to the wealth of an economy, and list the five factors of production that contribute to wealth.**

Working for others means getting benefits like paid vacations and health insurance. Entrepreneurs are people who risk time and money to start and manage a business. They gain the freedom to make their own decisions, more opportunity, and possible wealth.

What are the five factors of production?

Businesses use five factors of production: land (natural resources), labour (workers), capital goods (buildings and machinery), entrepreneurship, and knowledge. Of these, the most important are entrepreneurship and knowledge, because without them land, labour, and capital are not of much use. What makes rich countries rich today is a combination of *entrepreneurship* and the effective use of *knowledge.*

LO4 **State the six elements that make up the business environment and explain why the business environment is important to organizations.**

The business environment consists of the surrounding factors that either help or hinder the development of businesses. The six elements are the legal environment, the economic environment, the technological environment, the competitive environment, the social environment, and the global environment.

The legal environment in influenced by government who may allow private ownership of businesses, pass laws that enable business people to write contracts that are enforceable in court, establish a currency that is tradable in world markets, help to lessen corruption in business and government, and keep taxes and regulations to a minimum. From a business perspective, lower taxes mean lower risks, more growth, and thus more money for workers and the government.

Technology enables workers to be more effective, efficient, and productive. *Effectiveness* means doing the right thing in the right way. *Efficiency* means producing items using the least amount of resources. *Productivity* is the amount of output you generate given the amount of input (e.g., hours worked).

Within the social environment, diversity has come to mean much more than recruiting and keeping minority and female employees. Diversity efforts now include seniors, disabled people, people with different sexual orientations, atheists, extroverts, introverts, married people, singles, and the devout. Managing diversity means dealing sensitively with workers and cultures around the world.

Explain why the business environment is important to organizations.

Scanning the business environment on a continual basis is important to organizations so that they can take advantage of trends. These trends could affect the organization's ability to achieve its objectives, steer clear of threats, or take advantage of new opportunities.

LO5 **Give examples of how the service sector has replaced manufacturing as the principal provider of jobs, but why manufacturing remains vital for Canada.**

Canada has evolved from an economy based on manufacturing to one based on services.

Why is manufacturing still a vital industry for Canada?

While the services-producing sector employs almost 78 percent of the working population, the manufacturing industry employs approximately 9.6 percent of workers. Every $1 of manufacturing in Canada generates $3.15 in total economic activity. Forty-five percent of manufacturers foresee a growth in their workforce and nearly 60 percent plan to increase research and development investment.

KEY TERMS

CAREER EXPLORATION

Since this first chapter is an overview of all the different fields of business, we thought we'd concentrate on identifying a few careers in the sector with the most jobs: services. If you are interested in pursuing a career in the services sector, here are a few to consider. Find out about the tasks performed, skills needed, pay, and opportunity outlook in these fields through Internet sites that include the Government of Canada Job Bank, Workopolis, Monster, CareerBuilder, Glassdoor, and Indeed, as well as through the Career Centre at your school.

- **Lodging manager**—ensures that guests on vacation or business travel have a pleasant experience at a hotel, motel, or other type of establishment with accommodations and that the business is run efficiently and profitably.
- **Meeting and event planner**—coordinate all aspects of events and professional meetings, including arranging meeting locations, transportation, and other details.
- **Interior designer**—select and specify colors, furniture, and other materials to create useful and stylish interiors for buildings.
- **Network and computer systems administrator**—responsible for the day-to-day operation of computer networks.

CRITICAL THINKING

Imagine that you are thinking of starting a restaurant in your community. Answer the following questions.

1. Who will be the various stakeholders of your business?
2. How will you establish good relationships with your suppliers? With your employees?
3. You need to consider whether you will purchase locally grown produce versus foreign-grown produce. What are the advantages and disadvantages of using either, especially if the foreign-grown produce is cheaper or of better quality?
4. What are some of the things you could do to benefit your community other than provide jobs and generate tax revenue?
5. You are considering paying your employees the minimum wage. Do you think that you would attract better employees if you offered higher wages?
6. How might you be affected by the six environmental factors outlined in this chapter? Which factor(s) might have the biggest impact on your business?

DEVELOPING CAREER SKILLS

Key: ● **Team** ★ **Analytic** ▲ **Communication** ⊡ **Technology**

●★⊡▲ 1. Make a list of non-profit organizations in your community that might offer you a chance to learn some of the skills you will need in the job you hope to have when you graduate. How could you make time in your schedule to volunteer or work at one or more of those organizations? Write a letter to a non-profit organization to inquire about such opportunities. Hint: You can identify organizations and events in your city by going to 411 Local Search and inputting "non-profit organizations and events *your city name*" in the cell under Business, near the top. A less-targeted source is the Charity Village website. Charity Village supports Canada's charities and non-profit organizations as well as the stakeholders who support them.

●★ 2. Form into teams of four or five and discuss creating an entirely new product or service. What value does this new product or service create? Who are the stakeholders for this new product or service? Could an entrepreneur readily produce it or would its chance of success be higher if it was produced by a large company? Explain.

⊡★ 3. Imagine that you are a local business person who has to deal with the various issues involved with outsourcing. You want to begin with the facts. How many jobs have been lost to outsourcing in your area, if any? Are there any foreign firms in your area that are creating jobs (insourcing)? You will need to use the Internet to find the data you need.

●⊡▲ 4. Form into teams of four or five and discuss the technological and e-commerce revolutions. How many students now shop for goods and services online? What have been their experiences? What other high-tech equipment do they use to make purchases (smartphones, tablets, laptops, etc.)? What products do they plan on buying in the next year?

●⊡▲ 5. Use Yelp to find five businesses that provide services in your area. List those businesses and, for each, describe how social trends might affect them in both positive and negative ways. Be prepared to explain your descriptions to your team or the whole class, as your instructor directs.

ANALYZING MANAGEMENT DECISIONS

Canada's Fastest-Growing Companies

Every year, *PROFIT* magazine publishes a list of Canada's fastest-growing companies. The importance of many of the points we discussed in this chapter is evident in a recent issue, especially when one considers the breakdown among the types of companies. Service providers dominate the marketplace, which reinforces that Canada is a service economy. Here is a breakdown of the Top 100:

Focus	Number of Firms
Software	31
Manufacturing	12
Marketing and Media	11
Retail	8
Construction	6
Consumer Service	5
Industrial Service	5
Financial Services	5
Information Technology	4
Wholesale and Distribution	3
Human Resources	3
Professional Service	2
Transportation and Logistics	2
Real Estate	1
Agriculture	1
Telecommunication	1

While the companies were located across Canada, Ontario continued to support the largest share of these companies.

What makes these companies leaders is that they grew rapidly. It does not matter whether they are high-tech or old-economy companies, manufacturing or service companies, they all are exceptional. A remarkable assortment of products and services are offered by these companies. Examples include trucking, car parts, exterior painting services, steeped tea, gaming, sustainable office furniture, business performance consultants, and construction management.

Province/Territory	Number of Firms
Ontario	58
British Columbia	16
Quebec	16
Alberta	5
Saskatchewan	2
Manitoba	2
Nova Scotia	1

Source: "Profit 500: A complete ranking of Canada's fastest growing companies," *Canadian Business,* September 14, 2017, accessed June 24, 2018, http://www.canadianbusiness.com/profit500/2017-ranking-p500/.

Discussion Questions

1. Which of these data support the information discussed in the chapter? Explain your answer.
2. Why do certain provinces or regions have so many (e.g., Ontario) or few (e.g., Atlantic Canada) companies?
3. Review the most recent edition of PROFIT 500 for information on the companies that have made the list. Are there any surprises? How much has changed since these results were posted?

APPENDIX A

Using Technology to Manage Information

PROFILE

GETTING TO KNOW: BEN FRIED, CIO, GOOGLE

Since its founding in the late 1990s, Google has aimed to change the way that people communicate and manage information over the Internet. And judging from the billions of dollars that the search giant earns each year, it's safe to say it has been successful in its mission. Still, setting the standard for innovation is no easy task. In order to develop the latest online tools that consumers depend on, Google must make certain that its employees can use the most innovative procedures and have the most up-to-date technology they need for their work.

That's where chief information officer Ben Fried comes in. As CIO, it's his job to manage how the company uses information technology (IT) and data to accomplish its goals. Although he is an executive, Fried considers his job to be more about employee empowerment rather than strict management. "The overwhelming philosophy of my organization is to empower Googlers with world-leading technology," said Fried. "But the important part is that we view our role as empowerment, and not standard-setting or constraining or dictating or something like that. We define our role as an IT department in helping people get their work done better than they could without us."

© David Paul Morris/Bloomberg/Getty Images.

Before he became the head of IT at one of the most technologically advanced organizations in history, Fried graduated from Columbia University and worked as a researcher there for several years. As a top computer engineer, he developed software programs for some of the world's leading scientific institutions. One of his most distinguished accomplishments includes designing a mission-scheduling system for NASA's orbital telescopes. Fried eventually left academia and joined the technology department of the investment bank Morgan Stanley. During his 13 years with the company, Fried oversaw essential IT tasks like e-commerce, organization of market data, computer programming, e-mail management, videoconferencing, employee productivity, and much more.

In 2008 Fried joined Google as its CIO and faced his greatest challenge yet. After all, the company's employees knew plenty about technology themselves. In order to win the confidence and respect of these expert colleagues, Fried knew he had to staff his IT department with people who were just as informed and eager to work as he was. "When the people you deliver technology to are technology experts . . . it's really important that you make sure that that daily impression, that first impression they get of IT, is a good impression," said Fried. "To do this you have to have IT people who are more knowledgeable about the technology and the best ways to use it than the average employee."

Part of what drew Fried to Google was the company's policy of granting employees the freedom to use technology in the ways that's best for them. In fact, Google employees can spend as much as 20 percent of their time on passion projects. As CIO, though, Fried must also ensure that people follow the rules. For instance, a colossal business like Google requires many security measures to stay safe. So while the IT department lets employees work with whatever devices they choose, staffers also need to comply with certain security protocols. And with tens of thousands of employees at Google, managing this aspect of the business is a full-time pursuit.

For Fried and his colleagues in Google's IT department, this task is just one small part of a constantly evolving and expanding operation. "Technology moves very fast, and enterprises often feel the rational need to have a slower pace of change, so they can get a better return on investment, or so they don't need to make people learn new things all the time," said Fried. "But if you slow things down too much, you have no change at all."

As CIOs like Ben Fried and tech companies continue to change the face of the digital landscape, it's possible that even the most entrenched technologies could become obsolete in a few years. In this chapter you'll learn about how this ever-changing tech world affects business.

Sources: Peter High, "Google CIO Ben Fried Makes Change a Core Competency," *Forbes*, March 14, 2016; Scott Matteson, "Meet Google CIO Ben Fried," *TechRepublic*, November 26, 2013; Walter Frick, "Google's CIO on How to Make Your IT Department Great," *Harvard Business Review*, August 13, 2013; "Learn from a CIO: 6 Lessons from Google CIO Ben Fried," *Nerdio*, October 6, 2016; "Benjamin Fried," www.columbia.edu, accessed October 2017.

The Role of Information Technology

The importance of business knowledge is not new; however, what is new is the recognizing the need to manage it like any other asset. To manage knowledge, a company needs to share information efficiently throughout the organization and to implement systems for creating new knowledge. This need is constantly leading to new technologies that support the exchange of information among staff, suppliers, and customers. Studies have shown that data-driven decision making (i.e., collecting data, analyzing them, and using them to make crucial decisions, like whether to create a new product or service) can lift productivity

5 percent higher than decision making based on experience and intuition.[1] Who wins and who loses will be decided by who harnesses the technology that provides the pipeline of interaction and information flows between and among individuals and organizations.

Evolution from Data Processing to Business Intelligence

What has been the role of information technology? To understand technology today it is helpful to understand how we reached this stage.

data processing (DP)
Name for business technology in the 1970s; included technology that supported an existing business and was primarily used to improve the flow of financial information.

information systems (IS)
Technology that helps companies do business; includes such tools as automated teller machines (ATMs) and voice mail.

information technology (IT)
Technology that helps companies change business by allowing them to use new methods.

business intelligence (BI) (or analytics)
The use of data analytic tools to analyze an organization's raw data and derive useful insights.

- In the 1970s, business technology was known as **data processing (DP)**. (Although many people use the words *data* and *information* interchangeably, they mean different things. *Data* are raw, unanalyzed, and unorganized facts and figures. *Information* is processed and organized data that managers can use for decision making.) The primary purpose of data processing was to improve the flow of financial information. Employees who performed data-processing tasks were support staff who rarely came into contact with customers.
- In the 1980s, business technology became known as **information systems (IS)** when it moved out of the back room and into the centre of the business. Its role changed from *supporting* the business to *doing* business. Customers began to interact with a wide array of technological tools, from automated teller machines (ATMs) to voice mail. As business increased its use of information systems, it became more dependent on them.
- Until the late 1980s, business technology was just an addition to the existing way of doing business. Keeping up to date was a matter of using new technology on old methods. But things started to change when businesses applied new technology to new methods. Business technology then became known as **information technology (IT)**, and its role became to *change* business by sorting, retrieving, and sending information efficiently.
- In the 1990s, the introduction of the World Wide Web changed the way that people interacted with one another and information. Online services such as Google offered a new way of accessing information. In addition, Bluetooth technology created conveniences by providing wireless communication systems to replace cables that typically connected devices, thus freeing people to access information wherever they wanted.
- During the 2000s, as technology became more sophisticated, it became better known as **business intelligence (BI)**. BI refers to a variety of software applications used to analyze an organization's raw data and derive useful insights from the data. BI activities include data mining (which we discuss later in this appendix), online analytical processes, querying, and reporting.[2] Knowledge is information charged with enough intelligence to make it relevant and useful. Knowledge technology adds a layer of intelligence to filter appropriate information and deliver it when it is needed.

BI changes the traditional flow of information. Instead of an individual going to the database, the database comes to the individual. Managers can put a new employee at a workstation using BI training software and let the system take over everything from laying out a checklist of the tasks required on a shift to providing answers and insights that once would have taken up a supervisor's time.

BI helps businesspeople focus on what's important: deciding how to react to problems and opportunities. For example, imagine you're a sales rep who just closed an important deal. While you celebrate your success, the finance department is upset because your customer never pays on time, which costs the company a lot of money. BI could provide you that insight so that you could negotiate different payment terms with the customer, thus connecting sales activity to financial requirements in a seamless process.

Technology changes react with one another to create more change. Maintaining the flexibility to successfully integrate these changes is crucial to business survival. For instance, Kodak once dominated the camera industry but failed to compete effectively and lost market share. Even though it invented the first digital camera, the company was concerned that digital photography would eat into its traditional film business. So Kodak decided to continue focusing on film rather than digital cameras, a decision that eventually led to the company's bankruptcy.[3] Despite its size and money, Kodak wasn't flexible enough to adapt to changing trends.

Knowledge sharing is at the heart of keeping pace with change. Of course, it can be difficult to predict which new technologies will be successful. For a fun look at the worst technology predictions of all time, see Figure A.1.

Obviously, the role of the IT staff has changed as technology itself has improved and evolved. The chief information officer (CIO) has moved out of the back room and into the boardroom, and now spends less time worrying about keeping systems running and more time finding ways to boost business by applying technology to purchasing decisions, operational strategy, and marketing and sales. Today the role of the CIO is to help the business use technology to communicate better with others, while offering better service and lower costs.[4]

© Michael Ventura/Alamy

The Amazon Echo is more than just an ordinary sound system: the hands-free device is powered by Alexa, Amazon's artificial intelligence software. All a user has to do is say "Alexa" and he or she has the device's attention. From there the user can ask Alexa to play music, check the weather, or even order groceries. But software glitches occur, as in one case where Alexa sent a family's personal conversations to a third party without their knowledge.[5] Do you think voice-activated appliances like this will become more popular in the future?

How Information Technology Changes Business

Time and place have always been at the centre of business. Customers once had to go to the business during certain hours to satisfy their needs. For example, people went to the store to buy clothes. They went to the bank to arrange for a loan. Businesses decided when and where they did business with them. Today, IT allows businesses to deliver goods and services whenever and wherever the customer wants them. You can order books and clothes, arrange a home mortgage loan, and buy music or a car online, anytime you choose.

Consider how IT has changed the entertainment industry. Fifty years ago, you had to go to a movie theatre if you wanted to see a movie. Forty years ago, you could wait for it to be on television. Thirty years ago, you could wait for it to be on cable television. Twenty-five years ago, you could go to a video store and rent it. Now you can order video on demand by satellite, cable, or streaming services that let you watch on your TV, computer, smartphone, tablet, or other device whenever and wherever you wish.

FIGURE A.1

THE WORST TECHNOLOGY PREDICTIONS OF ALL TIME

You cannot be right all the time. Here are a few quotes from technology leaders who got it wrong.

"Television won't be able to hold onto any market it captures after the first six months. People will soon get tired of staring at a plywood box every night."
—Darryl Zanuck, executive at 20th Century Fox, 1946
"I predict the Internet will soon go spectacularly supernova and in 1996 catastrophically collapse."
—Robert Metcalfe, founder of 3Com, 1995
"This 'telephone' has too many shortcomings to be seriously considered as a means of communication."
— Western Union internal memo, 1876
"Inventions have long since reached their limit, and I see no hope for further developments."
—Roman engineer Julius Sextus Frontinus, 10 A.D.
"Who the hell wants to hear actors talk?"
—H. M. Warner, Warner Brothers, 1927
"I think there is a world market for maybe five computers."
—Thomas Watson, president of IBM, 1943
"Do not bother to sell your gas shares. The electric light has no future."
—Professor John Henry Pepper, scientist, 1870s
"Remote shopping, while entirely feasible, will flop."
—*Time*, 1966
"There is no reason anyone would want a computer in their home."
—Ken Olsen, founder of Digital Equipment Corporation, 1977

Sources: Entrepreneur Staff, "10 of the Worst Tech Predictions of All Time," *Entrepreneur,* July 1, 2016; "Worst Tech Predictions of All Time," *The Telegraph,* June 29, 2016.

As IT broke time and location barriers, it created new organizations and services that were independent of location. That independence brought work to people instead of people to work. Smartphones, laptop computers, netbooks, and personal digital assistants allow employees to have access to people and information as if they were in the office. For example, the TSX Venture Exchange is an electronic stock exchange where buyers and sellers make trades electronically.

The way people do business drastically changes when companies increase their technological capabilities. Electronic communications can provide substantial time savings. E-mail and texting have put an end to tedious games of telephone tag and are far faster than paper-based correspondence. Internet and intranet communications using shared documents and other methods allow contributors to work on a common document without time-consuming meetings. See Figure A.2 for other examples of how IT changes business.

■ **FIGURE A.2**

HOW INFORMATION TECHNOLOGY IS CHANGING BUSINESS

Organization

Technology is breaking down corporate barriers, allowing functional departments or product groups (even factory workers) to share critical information instantly.

Operations

Technology shrinks cycle times, reduces defects, and cuts waste. Service companies use technology to streamline ordering and communication with suppliers and customers.

Staffing

Technology eliminates layers of management and reduces the number of employees. Companies use computers and telecommunication equipment to create "virtual offices" with employees in various locations.

New products

Information technology shortens development cycles by feeding customer and marketing comments to product development teams quickly so that they can revive products and target specific customers.

Customer relations

Customer service representatives can solve customers' problems instantly by using company-wide databases to complete tasks from changing addresses to adjusting bills. Information gathered from customer service interactions can further strengthen customer relationships.

New markets

Since it is no longer necessary for customers to walk down the street to get to stores, online businesses can attract customers to whom they would not otherwise have access.

Types of Information

Today, information flows into and through an organization from many different directions. The types of information available to businesses today include:

- *Business Process Information.* This includes all transaction data gathered at the point of sale as well as information gained through operations like enterprise resource planning, supply chain management (these are discussed in Chapter 10), and customer relationship management systems.
- *Physical-World Observations.* These result from the use of radio frequency identification (RFID) devices, miniature cameras, wireless access, global positioning systems (GPSs), and sensor technology—all of which have to do with where people or items are located and what they are doing.

Computer chips cost pennies apiece and can be found in a wide range of products including credit cards, printer ink cartridges, baseballs, tire valves, running shoes, and

The Economic Concept of Demand

Demand refers to the quantity of products that people are willing to buy at different prices at a specific time. Generally speaking, the quantity demanded will increase as the price decreases. Again, the relationship between price and quantity demanded can be shown in a graph. Figure 2.2 shows a simple demand curve for T-shirts. The various points on the graph indicate the quantity demanded at various prices. For example, at a price of $45, the quantity demanded is just five T-shirts, but if the price were $5, the quantity demanded would increase to 35 T-shirts. All things being equal, the lower the price, the more buyers are willing to buy. The line connecting the dots is called a demand curve. It shows the relationship between quantity demanded and price.

demand
The quantity of products that people are willing to buy at different prices at a specific time.

The Equilibrium Point and the Market Price

It should be clear to you after reviewing Figures 2.1 and 2.2 that the key factor in determining the quantity supplied and the quantity demanded is *price.* Sellers prefer a high price, and buyers prefer a low price. If you were to lay one of the two graphs on top of the other, the supply curve and the demand curve would cross. At that crossing point, the quantity demanded and the quantity supplied are equal. Figure 2.3 illustrates that point. At a price of $15, the quantity of T-shirts demanded and the quantity supplied are equal (25 shirts). That crossing point is known as the *equilibrium point* or the *equilibrium price.* In the long run, that price will become the market price. **Market price**, then, is determined by supply and demand.

market price
The price determined by supply and demand.

Supporters of a free market would argue that because supply and demand interactions determine prices, there is no need for government involvement or government planning. If surpluses develop (i.e., if quantity supplied exceeds quantity demanded), a signal is sent to sellers to lower the price. If shortages develop (i.e., if quantity supplied is less than

FIGURE 2.2

THE DEMAND CURVE AT VARIOUS PRICES

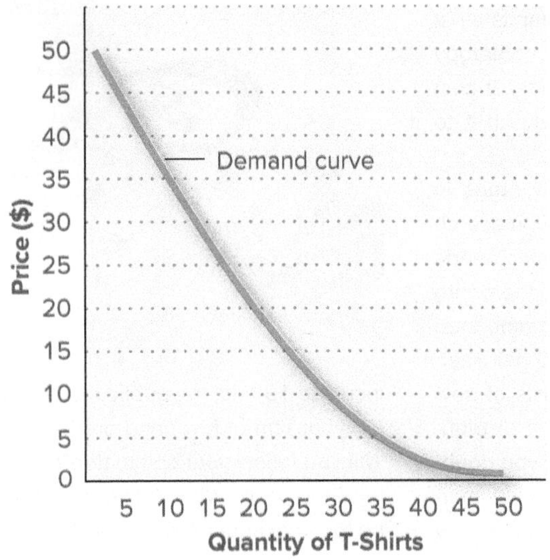

This is a simple demand curve showing the quantity of T-shirts demanded at different prices. The demand curve falls from left to right. It is easy to understand why. The lower the price of T-shirts, the higher the quantity demanded.

■ **FIGURE 2.3**

THE EQUILIBRIUM POINT

The place where quantity demanded and supplied meet is called the equilibrium point. When we put both the supply and demand curves on the same graph, we find that they intersect at a price where the quantity supplied and the quantity demanded are equal. In the long run, the market price will trend toward the equilibrium point.

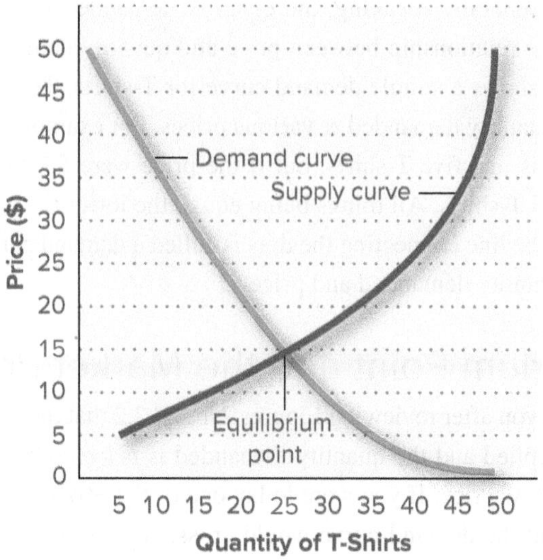

quantity demanded), a signal is sent to sellers to increase the price. Eventually, supply will again equal demand if nothing interferes with market forces.

The Making Ethical Decisions box raises an interesting question about when pricing may be a bit out of control and what to do about it.

Making ETHICAL DECISIONS

Bad Medicine for Consumers

Your company, a large pharmaceutical firm, acquired a drug called Relivoform when it bought a generic drugmaker. The purchased company was the market's leading supplier of the drug, and it was by far its most profitable product. Relivoform is a major chemotherapy drug important in the treatment of liver cancer. It cost $300 per treatment, and many patients rely on it to control the spread of their cancer.

Currently, your company has many new drugs in development costing the company millions in research and testing. It may be years before Health Canada approves the new drugs and you can get them into the market. Your finance committee has recommended increasing the price of Relivoform to $3,000 per treatment to help alleviate the development costs of new drugs. Since your company now controls the distribution of the drug (even though it's a generic), you doubt any competitors could immediately impact your market. When word leaked out that Relivoform's price may increase 10-fold, the public reacted with a rage, accusing your firm of favouring profits over patients' needs. Will you follow your committee's recommendation and raise the price? What are your alternatives? What might be the consequences of each?

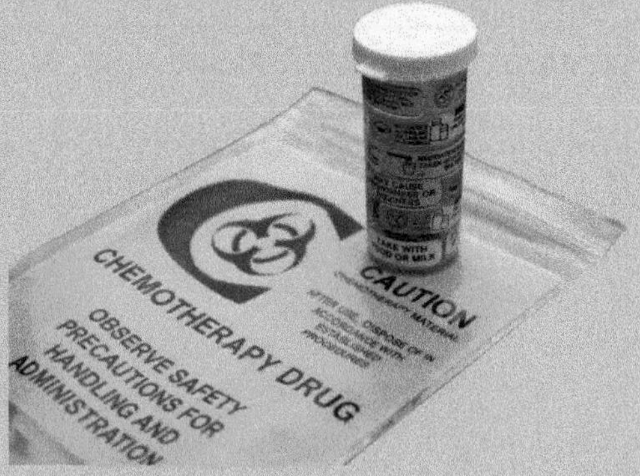

© fluxfoto/Getty Images RF

In countries without a free market, there is no mechanism to reveal to businesses (via price) what to produce and in what amounts, so there are often shortages (not enough products) or surpluses (too many products). In such countries, the government decides what to produce and in what quantity, but without price signals it has no way of knowing what the proper quantities are. Furthermore, when the government interferes in otherwise free markets, such as when it subsidizes farm goods, surpluses and shortages may develop. Competition differs in free markets, too. We shall explore that concept next.

Competition Within Free Markets

Economists generally agree that four different degrees of competition exist: (1) perfect competition, (2) monopolistic competition, (3) oligopoly, and (4) monopoly.

Perfect competition exists when there are many sellers in a market and no seller is large enough to dictate the price of a product. Under perfect competition, sellers' products appear to be identical. Agricultural products (e.g., apples, corn, potatoes) are often considered to be the closest examples of such products. You should know, however, that there are no true examples of perfect competition. Today, government price supports and drastic reductions in the number of farms make it hard to argue that even farming is an example of perfect competition.

perfect competition
The market situation in which there are many sellers in a market and no seller is large enough to dictate the price of a product.

Monopolistic competition exists when a large number of sellers produce goods that are very similar but are perceived by buyers as different (e.g., personal computers, candy, and T-shirts). Under monopolistic competition, *product differentiation* (the creation of real or perceived product differences) is a key to success. Through advertising and packaging, sellers try to convince buyers that their products are different from competitors', though they may be very similar or even interchangeable. The fast-food industry, in which there are often promotional battles between hamburger restaurants, offers a good example of monopolistic competition.

monopolistic competition
The market situation in which a large number of sellers produce very similar products that buyers nevertheless perceive as different.

An **oligopoly** occurs when a few sellers dominate a market. Oligopolies exist in industries that produce goods in the areas of oil and gas, tobacco, automobiles, aluminum, and aircraft. One reason some industries remain in the hands of a few sellers is that the initial investment required to enter the business is tremendous. In an oligopoly, prices for products from different companies tend to be close to the same. The reason for this is simple. Intense price competition would lower profits for all competitors, since a price cut on the part of one producer would most likely be matched by the others. Note, for example, that most cereals are priced about the same, as are soft drinks. Thus, advertising is a major factor determining which of the few available brands consumers buy, because often it is advertising that creates the perceived differences. As in monopolistic competition, product differentiation, rather than price, is usually the major factor in market success.

oligopoly
A form of competition in which just a few sellers dominate the market.

Although WestJet Airlines Ltd. operates within an oligopoly in Canada, it still has to listen to the needs of its customers and try to be innovative. As a result, customers can choose to check in at the counter, on the web, on mobile devices, at kiosks, and they can tag their own bags.

monopoly
A market in which there is only one seller for a product or service.

A **monopoly** occurs when there is only one seller for a good or service, and that one seller controls the total supply of a product and the price. Traditionally, monopolies were common in areas such as water, electricity, and telephone services that were considered essential to a community. Legislation has ended the monopoly status of utilities in some areas, letting consumers choose among providers. The intention of such *deregulation* is to increase competition among utility companies and, ultimately, lower prices for consumers. Figure 2.4 highlights where these forms of free-market competition fall when one considers the number of sellers (i.e., competitors) in the marketplace.

Benefits and Limitations of Free Markets

One benefit of the free market is that it allows open competition among companies. Businesses must provide customers with quality products at fair prices with good service. If they do not, they lose customers to businesses that do. Do government services have the same incentives?

The free market—with its competition and incentives—was a major factor in creating the wealth that industrialized countries now enjoy. Some people even talk of the free market as an economic miracle. Free-market capitalism, more than any other economic system, provides opportunities for poor people to work their way out of poverty. Capitalism also encourages businesses to be more efficient so they can successfully compete on price and quality. Would you say that Canada is increasing or decreasing the emphasis on capitalism? Why?

Yet even as free-market capitalism has brought prosperity, it has brought inequality as well. Business owners and managers make more money and have more wealth than workers. There is much poverty, unemployment, and homelessness. People who are old, disabled, or sick may not be able to support themselves. What should society do about such inequality?[24]

Smith assumed that as people became wealthier, they would naturally reach out and help the less fortunate in the community. As was discussed earlier, while this has not always happened, business people are becoming more concerned about social issues and their obligation to return to society some of what they have earned. For example, Warren Buffet, Chairman and Chief Executive Officer of Berkshire Hathaway and ranked as one of the world's wealthiest people, and Bill and Melinda Gates, who formed the Bill and Melinda Gates Foundation, signed the Giving Pledge which promises to give away at

FIGURE 2.4

FREE-MARKET COMPETITION BASED ON THE NUMBER OF SELLERS

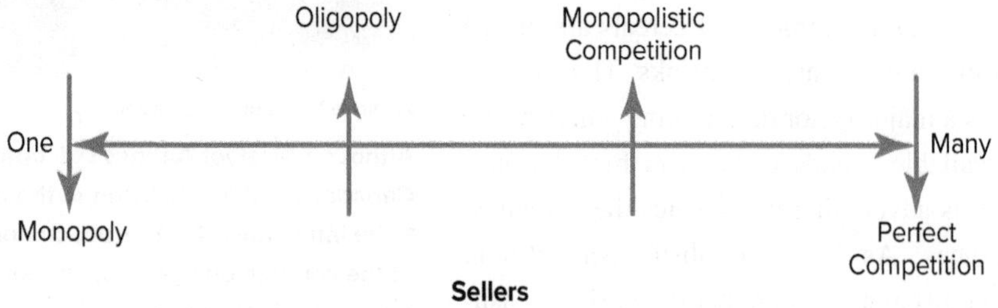

least half of their vast wealth to philanthropic causes.[25] In another example, every year an amount equivalent to 1 percent of Cirque du Soleil's earnings is dedicated to environmental policies for sustainable development managed by Cirque, as well as to the ONE DROP Foundation.[26]

An example of the limitation of a free market is also illustrated through the case of the North American professional sport industry. Revenue for this industry is expected to reach $73.5 billion by 2019.[27] Given the industry operates within the United States and Canada, it is fair to believe it is subject to the forces of a free market economy. But when you look closely at the leagues who manage the big four sports – Major League Baseball, the National Basketball Association, the National Football League, and the National Hockey League, the form of competition is far from perfect.

Consider the profit generated by these four leagues – revenues sources include sponsorship, merchandise, gate receipts (tickets), and broadcast/media rights. One would believe that these profits are distributed through perfect competition among businesses that operate within each of the professional sports, but that is not the case. The North American professional sport leagues operate as a monopoly and as a result the market fails to be competitive.[28]

For example, The National Hockey League (NHL) is the only seller of premiere professional hockey in North America. The league, through its owners who sit on the Board of Governors, and its Commissioner, control the supply of the product through decisions about franchise expansion. This is why few Canadian franchises exist.[29] The NHL also controls the price as each team owner has exclusivity within a specific city or market, and can set its ticket price as desired. How strong is the monopoly of a North American professional sport league, such as the NHL? Do you believe open competition among many premiere professional leagues would improve the quality of professional hockey for consumers? Do you believe a rival league is possible?

One of the dangers of free markets is that some people let greed dictate how they act. Criminal charges brought against some big businesses in banking, oil, accounting, telecommunications, insurance, and pharmaceuticals indicate the scope of the potential problem. Some business people have deceived the public about their products; others have deceived shareholders about the value of their stock, all in order to increase executives' personal assets. Clearly, some government rules and regulations are necessary to make sure that all of a business' stakeholders are protected and that people who are unable to work get the basic care they need. To overcome the limitations of capitalism, some countries have adopted an economic system called socialism. It, too, has its good and bad points. We explore the advantages and disadvantages of socialism after the Progress Assessment questions.

PROGRESS ASSESSMENT

- How do business people know what to produce and in what quantity?
- How are prices determined?
- Describe the four degrees of competition.
- What are some of the limitations of free markets?

LO3

Compare the benefits and negative consequences of socialism and communism.

Understanding Socialism

socialism
An economic system based on the premise that some, if not most, basic businesses should be owned by the government so that profits can be evenly distributed among the people.

Socialism is an economic system based on the premise that some, if not most, basic businesses—such as steel mills, coal mines, and utilities—should be owned by the government so that profits can be evenly distributed among the people. Entrepreneurs often own and run the smaller businesses, and individuals are often taxed relatively steeply to pay for social programs.

Socialists acknowledge the major benefit of capitalism—wealth creation—but believe that wealth should be more evenly distributed than occurs in free-market capitalism. They believe that the government should be the agency that carries out the distribution and be much more involved in protecting the environment and providing for the poor.[30]

The Benefits of Socialism

The major benefit of socialism is supposed to be social equality. Ideally, it comes about because the government takes income from wealthier people, in the form of taxes, and redistributes it to poorer people through various government programs. Free education, free health care, and free child care are some of the benefits socialist governments, using the money from taxes, may provide to their people. Workers in socialist countries usually get longer vacations, work fewer hours per week, and have more employee benefits (e.g., generous sick leave) than those in countries where free-market capitalism prevails.

© Kathy deWitt/Alamy

Socialism has been more successful in some countries than in others. This photo shows Denmark's clean and modern public transportation system. In Greece, overspending caused a debt crisis that forced the government to impose austerity measures that many Greeks oppose. What other factors might lead to slower growth in socialist countries?

The Negative Consequences of Socialism

Socialism may create more equality than capitalism, but it takes away some of business people's incentives to work hard, as their profits will be heavily taxed. For example, tax rates in some nations once reached 85 percent.

Today, doctors, lawyers, business owners, and others who earn a lot of money pay very high tax rates. As a consequence, some of them leave socialist countries for capitalistic countries with lower taxes, such as the United States. This loss of these educated people to other countries is called a **brain drain**.

Imagine an experiment in socialism in your own class. Imagine that after the first exam, those with grades of 90 and above have to give some of their points to those who make 70 and below so that everyone ends up with grades in the 80s. Would those who got 90s study as hard for the second exam? What about those who got 70s? Can you see why workers may not work as hard or as well if they all get the same benefits regardless of how hard they work?

brain drain
The loss of educated people to other countries.

Socialism also results in fewer inventions and less innovation because those who come up with new ideas usually do not receive as much reward as they would in a capitalist system. Generally speaking, over the past decade or so, most socialist countries have simply not kept up with more capitalist countries in new inventions, job creation, or wealth creation.[31]

Communism may be considered a more intensive version of socialism. We shall explore that system next.

Understanding Communism

Communism is an economic and political system in which the state (the government) makes almost all economic decisions and owns almost all of the major factors of production. Communism affects personal choices more than socialism does. For example, some communist countries have not allowed their citizens to practice certain religions, change jobs, or move to the town of their choice.

communism
An economic and political system in which the state (the government) makes all economic decisions and owns almost all of the major factors of production.

One problem with communism is that the government has no way of knowing what to produce because prices do not reflect supply and demand as they do in free markets. As a result, shortages of many items may develop, including shortages of food and basic clothing. Another problem with communism is that it does not inspire business people to work hard, because the government takes most of their earnings. Therefore, although communists once held power in many nations around the world, communism is slowly disappearing as an economic form.

Most communist countries today are suffering severe economic depression. In North Korea, many people are starving. In Cuba, people suffer from a lack of goods and services readily available in most other countries, and some fear the government. While some parts of the former Soviet Union remain under communist ideals, Russia itself now has a flat tax of 13 percent. Even this low tax rate increased the government's tax revenues by nearly 30 percent, because more people were willing to pay.

The Trend Toward Mixed Economies

The nations of the world have largely been divided between those that followed the concepts of capitalism and those that adopted the concepts of communism or socialism. Thus, to sum up the preceding discussion, the two major economic systems vying for dominance in the world today can be defined as follows:

free-market economy
An economy in which the market largely determines what goods and services are produced, who gets them, and how the economy grows.

1. A **free-market economy** exists when the market largely determines what goods and services are produced, who gets them, and how the economy grows. *Capitalism* is the popular term used to describe this economic system.

© Dmitry Lovetsky/AP Images

Russia has been moving away from communism toward a viable market economy. As poverty begins to decline, a middle class is emerging, but many of the country's vast natural resources are difficult to tap. Laws that promote business are few, and an active black market for goods exists. Many observers are optimistic that Russia can prosper. What do you think?

2. A **command economy** exists when the government largely decides what goods and services are produced, who gets them, and how the economy will grow. *Socialism* and *communism* are the popular terms used to describe variations of this economic system.

Experience has shown that neither of these systems has resulted in optimum economic conditions. Free-market mechanisms have not been responsive enough to the needs of the poor, the old, or the disabled. Some people also believe that businesses in free-market economies have not done enough to protect the environment. Over time, voters in free-market countries, such as Canada, have therefore elected officials who have adopted social and environmental programs such as medicare, unemployment compensation, and various clean air and water acts. What new or enhanced social policies do you know of that have been enacted or are being considered today?

command economy
An economy in which the government largely decides what goods and services are produced, who gets them, and how the economy will grow.

Socialism and communism, for their part, have not always created enough jobs or wealth to keep economies growing fast enough. As a consequence, communist governments are disappearing and socialist governments have been cutting back on social programs and lowering taxes for businesses and workers. The idea is to generate more business growth and thus generate more revenue.[32]

The trend, then, has been for so-called capitalist countries to move toward socialism and so-called socialist countries to move toward more capitalism. We say "so-called" because no country in the world is purely capitalist or purely socialist. All countries have some mix of the two systems. Thus, the long-term global trend is toward a blend of capitalism and socialism. This trend likely will increase with the opening of global markets as a result of the Internet. The net effect of capitalist systems moving toward socialism and socialist systems moving toward capitalism is the emergence throughout the world of mixed economies.

mixed economies
Economic systems in which some allocation of resources is made by the market and some by the government.

Mixed economies exist where some allocation of resources is made by the market and some is made by the government. Most countries do not have a name for such a system. If the dominant way of allocating resources is by free-market mechanisms, then the leaders of such countries still call their system capitalism. If the dominant way of allocating resources is by the government, then the leaders call their system socialism. Figure 2.5 compares the various economic systems.

PROGRESS ASSESSMENT

- What led to the emergence of socialism?
- What are the benefits and drawbacks of socialism?
- What are the characteristics of a mixed economy?

■ **FIGURE 2.5**

COMPARISONS OF KEY ECONOMIC SYSTEMS

	Capitalism (U.S.A.)	Socialism (Sweden)	Communism (North Korea)	Mixed Economy (Canada)
Social and Economic Goals	Private ownership of land and business. Freedom and the pursuit of happiness. Free trade. Emphasis on freedom and the profit motive for economic growth.	Public ownership of major businesses. Some private ownership of smaller businesses and shops. Government control of education, health care, utilities, mining, transportation, and media. Very high taxation. Emphasis on equality.	Public ownership of all businesses. Government-run education and health care. Emphasis on equality. Many limitations on freedom, including freedom to own businesses, change jobs, buy and sell homes, and assemble to protest government actions.	Private ownership of land and business with government regulation. Government control of some institutions (e.g., mail). High taxation for the common welfare. Emphasis on a balance between freedom and equality.
Motivation of Workers	Much incentive to work efficiently and hard, because profits are retained by owners. Workers are rewarded for high productivity.	Capitalist incentives exist in private businesses. Government control of wages in public institutions limits incentives.	Very little incentive to work hard or to produce quality products.	Incentives are similar to capitalism except in government-owned enterprises, which have few incentives.
Control over Markets	Complete freedom of trade within and among nations. No government control of markets.	Some markets are controlled by the government and some are free. Trade restrictions among nations vary and include some free trade agreements.	Total government control over markets except for illegal transactions.	Some government control of trade within and among nations (trade protectionism).
Choices in the Market	A wide variety of products is available. Almost no scarcity or oversupply exists for long because supply and demand control the market.	Variety in the marketplace varies considerably from country to country. Choice is directly related to government involvement in markets.	Very little choice among competing products.	Similar to capitalism, but scarcity and oversupply may be caused by government involvement in the market (e.g., subsidies for farms).
Social Freedoms	Freedom of speech, press, assembly, religion, job choice, movement, and elections	Similar to mixed economy. Government may restrict job choice, movement among countries, and who may attend upper-level schools (i.e., post-secondary institution).	Very limited freedom to protest the government, practice religion, or change houses or jobs.	Some restriction on freedoms of assembly and speech. Separation of church and state may limit religious practice in schools.

LO4

Describe the mixed economy of Canada.

Canada's Mixed Economy

Like most other nations of the world, Canada has a mixed economy. The degree of government involvement in the economy today—in areas such as health care, education, and business regulation, just to name a few—is a matter of some debate. (In Chapter 4, we will discuss the role of government in more detail.) The government's perceived goal is to grow the economy while maintaining some measure of social equality. The goal is very hard to attain. Nonetheless, the basic principles of freedom and opportunity should lead to economic growth that is sustainable.

Several features have played a major role in Canada becoming an independent economic entity with high government involvement in the economy. First, we are one of the largest countries in the world geographically, but we have a small population (over 35 million).[33] We have one of the lowest population densities in the world.

Most important, our neighbour to the south has ten times the population and an economy even greater than that proportion, speaks our language, is very aggressive economically, and is the most powerful country in the world. The United States exerts a very powerful influence on Canada as our largest trading partner. (We will discuss details in Chapter 3.) To control our destiny, Canadian governments have passed many laws and regulations to ensure that significant economic and cultural institutions, such as banks, insurance companies, and radio and TV stations, remain under Canadian control. (Even powerful countries like the United States and Japan have similar regulations.)

All of these factors led to the Canadian capitalist system taking on many characteristics of a mixed economy. Massive government support was necessary to build our first national rail line, the CPR, in the 1880s. When air transport was beginning in the 1930s no company wanted to risk investing heavily in such a large country with only 10 million people spread thinly across the land. So the government set up Air Canada (then called Trans Canada Airlines) to transport mail, people, and freight. There are many such examples of government action to protect the national interest.

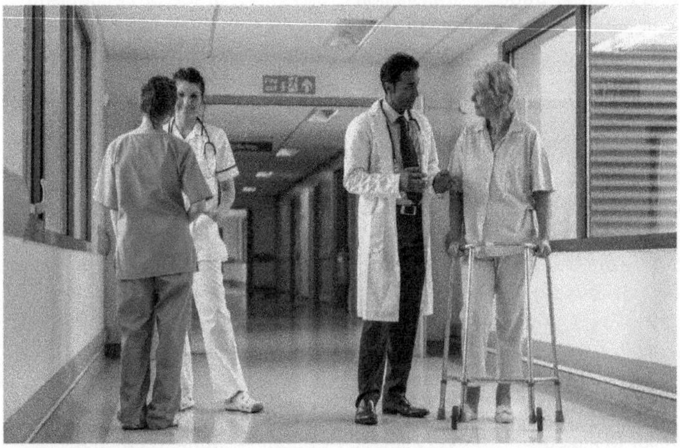

© Spotmatik Ltd/Shutterstock

Governed by the Canada Health Act, public care is designed to make sure that all eligible people in the country have reasonable access to insured health services on a prepaid basis, without direct charges at the point of service. Private care covers anything beyond what the public system will pay for. Who would benefit from private health coverage? What happens if someone is not eligible for private coverage?

In the 1980s, many countries, including Canada, began to reduce government involvement in, and regulation of, the economy. This trend toward deregulation was widespread. In Canada, airlines, banks, and the trucking industry have all seen a marked reduction in regulatory control.

This trend continues today as groups lobby the government to relax regulations to allow them to be more competitive. For example, to encourage competitiveness, the Competition Policy Review Panel recommends lowering barriers to foreign investment in a number of industries, including telecommunications and air transportation.[34]

The Conference Board of Canada has released a report that warns that Canadian industries need to do a better job competing for global investment dollars, attracting foreign investors, and establishing new investments overseas.[35]

There are also many new players entering the Canadian marketplace that are competing with publicly funded (i.e., government-funded) institutions. One such industry is health care, where private health care supporters continue to lobby for a greater presence in Canada.

In the years to come, we can expect to see more examples of our mixed economy moving toward a more capitalist system, as the private sector will play a greater role in delivering some goods and services (e.g., health care) that have historically been managed by public institutions. Keep in mind that during tough economic times, voters demand more government involvement. Thus, it is a traditional and desirable role of government to increase expenditures (e.g., provide financial aid to industries, increase spending on infrastructure, etc.) to support and stabilize the economy. The question is how much involvement, debt, etc. is appropriate.

Understanding Canada's Economic System

LO5

Illustrate the significance of key economic indicators and the business cycle.

The strength of the economy has a tremendous effect on business. When the economy is strong and growing, most businesses prosper and almost everyone benefits through plentiful jobs, reasonably good wages, and sufficient revenues for the government to provide needed goods and services. When the economy is weak, however, businesses are weakened, employment and wages fall, and government revenues decline as a result.

Because business and the economy are so closely linked, business literature is full of economic concepts. It is virtually impossible to read business reports with much understanding unless you are familiar with the economic terms being used. One purpose of this chapter is to help you learn additional economic concepts, terms, and issues—the kinds that you will be seeing daily if you read the business press, as we encourage you to do.

Key Economic Indicators

Three major indicators of economic conditions are (1) the gross domestic product (GDP), (2) the unemployment rate, and (3) the price indexes. Another important statistic is the increase or decrease in productivity. When you read business literature, you will see these terms used again and again. It will greatly increase your understanding if you learn the terms now.

GROSS DOMESTIC PRODUCT

Gross domestic product (GDP) is the total value of final goods and services produced in a country in a given year. Either a domestic company or a foreign-owned company may produce the goods and services included in the GDP as long as the companies are located within the country's boundaries. For example, production values from Japanese automaker Toyota's factory in Cambridge, Ontario, would be included in the Canadian GDP. Likewise, revenue generated by Magna International's manufacturing and assembly

gross domestic product (GDP)
The total value of goods and services produced in a country in a given year.

REPORT CARD

Economy Indicators

	Income per capita	GDP growth	Labour productivity growth	Inflation	Unemployment rate	Employment growth	Inward FDI Performance Index	Outward FDI Performance Index
Australia	C	A	A	A	A	B	D	D
Austria	C	C	C	A	A	B	D	B
Belgium	D	D	C	A	B	C	A	A
Canada	C	B	B	A	B	B	D	C
Denmark	D	D	B	A	B	C	C	B
Finland	D	C	C	A	B	C	D	D
France	D	D	C	A	C	C	D	C
Germany	C	C	C	A	A	B	D	D
Ireland	C	C	B	A	D	D	C	D
Japan	D	B	B	B	A	C	D	D
Netherlands	C	D	D	A	A	C	D	C
Norway	A	A	B	B	A	A	D	C
Sweden	C	C	B	A	B	B	D	C
Switzerland	B	C	C	C	A	B	D	A
U.K.	D	D	D	A	B	B	D	C
U.S.	B	B	C	A	B	A	D	D

Note: Data for the most recent year available used. For details on data sources, see the Methodology section of this website.
Source: The Conference Board of Canada.

Courtesy of The Conference Board of Canada. Used with permission.

According to the Conference Board of Canada (www.conferenceboard.ca), businesses need to work smarter to improve productivity. This includes producing higher-value-added products and services that are worth more in the marketplace. This report card summarizes country ratings in a variety of areas.

plants in Brazil would be included in Brazil's GDP, even though Magna is a Canadian company.

If GDP growth slows or declines, there are often many negative effects on business. What can account for increases in GDP? A major influence on the growth of GDP is how productive the workforce is—that is, how much output workers create with a given amount of input. This is linked to the combination of creating jobs, working longer hours, or working smarter. Working smarter means being more productive through the use of better technology and processes and employing a more educated and efficient workforce. In the past, GDP growth has been affected by rising employment (to be discussed soon), low inflation, and low interest rates.[36]

The more you produce, the higher the GDP and vice versa. The economy benefits from a strong GDP. Money that is earned from producing goods and services goes to the employees that produce them in the form of wages. People who own the business generate a return on their investment, and government benefits from tax collection.

A strong economy usually leads to a high standard of living for Canadians. In your opinion, have too many people in Canada sacrificed their quality of life to have a higher standard of living by working more? Since productivity is central to a country's GDP, we will look at this next.

PRODUCTIVITY IN CANADA

An increase in productivity means a worker can produce more goods and services than before in the same time period, usually thanks to machinery or other equipment. Productivity in Canada has risen because computers and other technology have made production faster and easier. Improved productivity can decrease production costs which can then result in lower prices. Therefore, business people are eager to increase productivity.

The Canadian economy is a service economy. Productivity is an issue because service firms are very labour-intensive. Spurred by foreign competition, productivity in the goods-producing sector is rising rapidly. In the service sector, however, productivity is growing more slowly because service workers—like teachers, clerks, lawyers, and barbers—have fewer new technologies available than there are for factory workers.

PRODUCTIVITY IN THE SERVICES-PRODUCING SECTOR

One problem with the services-producing sector is that an influx of machinery may add to the *quality* of the service provided but not to the *output per worker.* For example, you have probably noticed how many computers there are on campus. They add to the quality of education but they do not necessarily boost professors' productivity. The same is true of some equipment in hospitals, such as CAT scanners, PET scanners (more modern versions of the X-ray machine), and MRI scanners. They improve patient care but they do not necessarily increase the number of patients doctors can see. In other words, today's productivity measures in the services-producing sector fail to capture the improvement in quality created by new technology.

unemployment rate
The percentage of the labour force that actively seeks work but is unable to find work at a given time.

Clearly Canada and other countries need to develop new measures of productivity for the service economy, measures that include quality as well as quantity of output. Productivity is extremely important to a country, as it is a measure of its economic prosperity. Canadian businesses are criticized for not spending enough on research and development, relative to other advanced countries. By not doing so, these businesses will fall behind in the fierce global competitive battle. We will discuss the importance of research and development in Chapter 10.

Of course, technological advances usually lead to people being replaced by machines, often contributing to unemployment. We will now examine this important issue.

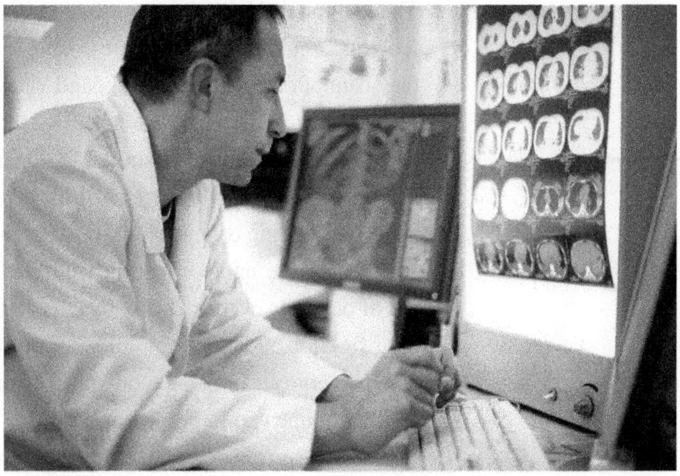

© logoboom/Getty Images RF

It can be difficult to measure productivity in the service sector. New technology can improve the quality of services without necessarily increasing the number of people served. A doctor can make more-accurate diagnoses with scans, for instance, but still can see only so many patients in a day. How can productivity measures capture improvements in the quality of service?

THE UNEMPLOYMENT RATE

The **unemployment rate** refers to the percentage of the labour force (15 years and over) that actively seeks work but is unable to find work at a given time.[37] Figure 2.6 describes different

FIGURE 2.6

FOUR TYPES OF UNEMPLOYMENT

The types of unemployment are:

Frictional unemployment

Frictional unemployment refers to those people who have quit work because they didn't like the job, the boss, or the working conditions and who haven't yet found a new job. It also refers to those people who are entering the labour force for the first time (e.g., new graduates) or are returning to the labour force after significant time away (e.g., parents who reared children). There will always be some frictional unemployment because it takes some time to find a first job or a new job.

Structural unemployment

Structural unemployment refers to unemployment caused by the restructuring of firms or by a mismatch between the skills (or location) of job seekers and the requirements (or location) of available jobs (e.g., coal miners in an area where mines have been closed).

Cyclical unemployment

Cyclical unemployment occurs because of a recession or a similar downturn in the business cycle (the ups and downs of business growth and decline over time). This type of unemployment is the most serious.

Seasonal unemployment

Seasonal unemployment occurs where demand for labour varies over the year, as with the harvesting of crops.

types of unemployment. Figure 2.7 highlights Canada's unemployment rate over 25 years. The real rate is higher because Statistics Canada does not include people who have given up looking for jobs, those who were unable to work, those who stay in or return to school because they cannot find full-time work, and various other categories of people. The unemployment rate is a key indicator of the health of the economy and of society more generally. That is, when economic growth is strong, the unemployment rate tends to be low and a person who wants a job is likely to experience little trouble finding one. On the other hand, when the economy is stagnating or in recession (to be discussed soon), unemployment tends to be higher.[38]

People are unemployed in Canada for various reasons. Perhaps their employer goes out of business or their company cuts staff. Young persons enter the job market looking for their first job and other employees quit their jobs but have trouble finding new ones. Companies merge and jobs are consolidated or trimmed. Companies transfer their operations to another country, or a branch of a foreign company is closed down. When a job is lost, not only is it a loss to society and the economy, but the loss of income can also create hardship for individuals and families.

According to Statistics Canada, the unemployed include persons who (during the reference period) were as follows: (1) on temporary layoff during the reference week with an expectation of recall and were available for work; (2) without work, had looked for work in the past four weeks, and were available for work; or (3) about to start a new job within four weeks from reference week, and were available for work.[39] Unemployment insurance only goes so far to relieve such unemployment. Which type(s) of unemployment seems to be the most serious to the economy?

FIGURE 2.7

THE UNEMPLOYMENT RATE IN CANADA 1989–2014

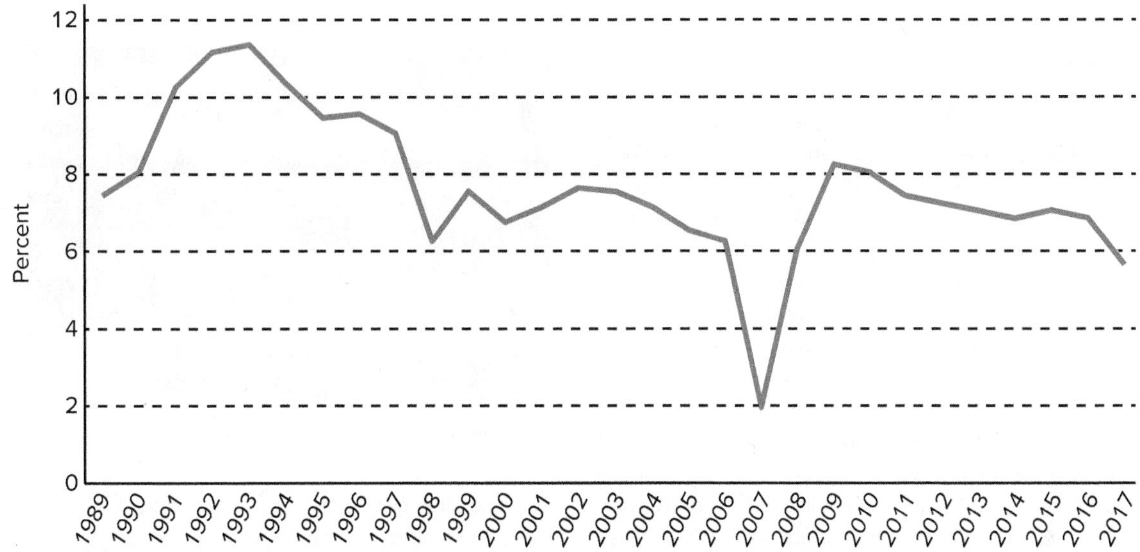

Source: Statistics Canada. Table 282-0087 - Labour force survey estimates (LFS), by sex and detailed age group, annual (persons unless otherwise noted), CANSIM (database), accessed 2017-01-27; Statistics Canada, Labour Force Survey, http://www.stats.gov.nl.ca/statistics/Labour/PDF/UnempRate.pdf.

THE PRICE INDEXES

The price indexes indicate the health of the economy by measuring the levels of inflation, disinflation, deflation, and stagflation. **Inflation** refers to a general rise in the prices of goods and services over time. The official definition is "a persistent increase in the level of consumer prices or a persistent decline in the purchasing power of money, caused by an increase in available currency and credit beyond the proportion of goods and services." Thus, it is also described as "too many dollars chasing too few goods." Go back and review the laws of supply and demand to see how that works. Rapid inflation is scary.

inflation
A general rise in the prices of goods and services over time.

If the cost of goods and services goes up by just 7 percent a year, everything will double in cost in just ten years or so. Inflation increases the cost of doing business. When a company borrows money, interest costs are higher, employees demand increases to keep up with the rise in the cost of living, suppliers raise their prices, and as a result the company is forced to raise its prices. If other countries succeed in keeping their inflation rates down, then Canadian companies will become less competitive in the world market. The Reaching Beyond Our Borders box highlights several examples of inflation out of control.

© Paul Sakuma/ AP Images/CP Images

The overall unemployment rate in Canada fluctuates. Over the last decade, it has been as low as 6 percent and as high as 8 percent. Unemployment insurance goes only so far to relieve the loss of income caused by losing your job. How high is the unemployment rate in your area today?

Reaching *Beyond* OUR BORDERS

Inflation at the Speed of Sound

If you are familiar with the Rule of 72, you know it's a simple way to measure how long it would take for prices to double at a given rate of inflation. For example, if inflation is growing at 6 percent a year, prices would double in 12 years (6 divided into 72). This would be an unacceptable inflation rate in Canada, where the Bank of Canada targets keeping price increases at 2 percent (or less) a year. Well, what if prices went up 221 percent in one month? Impossible? Unfortunately, not in Venezuela, which is the most recent example of hyperinflation.

© Manaure Quintero/Bloomberg/Getty Images

Hyperinflation is when the price of goods and services rises by 50 percent a month. It often starts when a country's government prints more money to pay for excess spending. In Venezuela, prices increased by 63 percent in 2014, 121 percent in 2015, and 481 percent in 2016. Expectations are that prices will increase by 1,600 percent in 2017. In fact, things got so bad that Venezuela's currency, the Bolivar, collapsed. It's value was so low that cash to pay for goods and services was being weighed instead of counted. The country is now facing shortages of food and medicine, with children being affected harshly.

Venezuela is not the first country to suffer the ravages of hyperinflation. German hyperinflation was a classic example after World War I, when prices were doubling every three days. Pictures of Germans pushing wheelbarrows full of marks (German currency) to buy a loaf of bread were common. Zimbabwe had hyperinflation from 2004 to 2009. Its economy faced an inflation rate of 98 percent a day, with prices doubling every 24 hours.

The price of a Big Mac or cup of Starbucks coffee doubling every day doesn't sound great to us. Let's hope the Bank of Canada stays vigilant against inflation and keeps our rate at or below 2 percent.

Sources: Luke Graham, "Inflation in Venezuela Seen Hitting 1,500% in 2017 as Crisis Goes from Bad to Worse," CNBC, accessed September 2017; Ben Bartenstein and Mark Glassman, "Hyperinflation," *Bloomberg Businessweek*, January 8, 2017; Kimberly Amadeo, "What Is Hyperinflation: Its Causes, Effects, and Examples," *The Balance*, accessed September 2017; Guillermo Garcia Montenegro, "The Case for Currency Substitution in Venezuela," *Forbes*, January 11, 2017.

disinflation
A situation in which price increases are slowing (the inflation rate is declining).

deflation
A situation in which prices are declining.

stagflation
A situation in which the economy is slowing but prices are going up regardless.

consumer price index (CPI)
A monthly statistic that measures the pace of inflation or deflation.

Disinflation describes a condition where price increases are slowing (the inflation rate is declining). **Deflation** means that prices are actually declining.[40] It occurs when countries produce so many goods that people cannot afford to buy them all. That is, too few dollars are chasing too many goods. While declining prices might sound good, it's an indication that economic conditions are deteriorating.[41] **Stagflation** occurs when the economy is slowing but prices are going up regardless.[42]

The **consumer price index (CPI)** is a monthly statistic that measures the pace of inflation or deflation. To determine the CPI, costs of a "basket" of goods and services for an average family—including food, shelter, transportation, and clothing and footwear—are calculated to see if they are going up or down. For example, Canadian consumers paid, on average, 1.9 percent more for such a basket in December 2017, than twelve months earlier; this was led by increases in the costs of fresh vegetables (6.9 percent).[43] The CPI is an important figure because it affects nearly all Canadians, either directly or indirectly. For example, government benefits (such as Old Age Security and Canada Pension Plan), rental agreements, some labour contracts, and interest rates are based on the CPI.

Other indicators of the economy's condition include housing starts, retail sales, motor vehicle sales, consumer confidence, and changes in personal income. You can learn more about such indicators by reading business periodicals, contacting government agencies, listening to business broadcasts, and exploring the Internet.

The United Nations suggests the development of a country cannot be based only upon economic measures. Some indexes measure social factors that are considered along with economic information. One example is the **human development index (HDI)**, which examines the wealth, health, and education of a country according to incomes, life expectancy, and years of schooling. A recent United Nations report identifies the HDI for many countries throughout the world is slowing down.[44]

human development index
A measure of a country's progress that includes wealth, health, and education.

The Business Cycle

Business cycles (also known as **economic cycles**) are the periodic rises and falls that occur in economies over time.[45] These fluctuations are often measured using the real GDP.[46] Economists look at a number of types of cycles, from seasonal cycles that occur within a year to cycles that occur every 48 to 60 years. Economist Joseph Schumpeter identified the four phases of long-term business cycles as boom, recession, depression, recovery, as illustrated in Figure 2.8.

business cycles (economic cycles)
The periodic rises and falls that occur in economies over time.

boom
A period that brings jobs, growth, and economic prosperity.

recession
Two or more consecutive quarters of decline in the GDP.

1. An economic **boom** is just what it sounds like—business is booming. Periods of economic boom bring jobs, growth, and economic prosperity.
2. Two or more consecutive quarters of decline in the GDP result in a **recession**. In a recession, prices fall, people purchase fewer products, and businesses fail. A recession has many negative consequences for an economy: high unemployment, increased business failures, and an overall drop in living standards. The 2009 recession is an example.

FIGURE 2.8

THE BUSINESS CYCLE

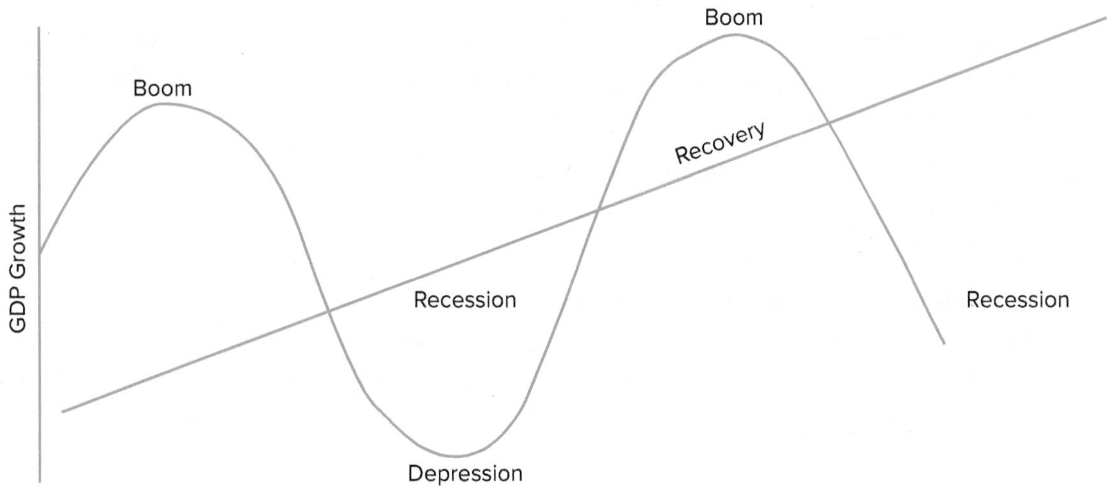

depression
A severe recession.

3. A **depression** is a severe recession usually accompanied by deflation. Business cycles rarely go through a depression phase. In fact, while there were many business cycles during the twentieth century, there was only one severe depression (in the 1930s).

recovery
When the economy stabilizes and starts to grow.

4. A **recovery** occurs when the economy stabilizes and starts to grow. This eventually leads to an economic boom, starting the cycle all over again.

One goal of some economists is to predict such ups and downs. That is very difficult to do. Business cycles are identified according to facts, but we can explain those facts only by using theories. Therefore, one cannot predict with certainty. But one thing is certain: over time, the economy will rise and fall as it has done in recent years.

Since dramatic swings up and down in the economy cause all kinds of disruptions to businesses, the government tries to minimize such changes. The government uses fiscal policy and monetary policy to try to keep the economy from slowing too much or growing too rapidly. We will discuss both of these policies in Chapter 4.

PROGRESS ASSESSMENT

- What factors have contributed to the decision to have a mixed economy in Canada?
- Name three economic indicators and describe how well Canada is doing using each one.
- What is the difference between a recession and a depression?

SUMMARY

LO1 **Describe basic economics.**

Economics is the study of how society chooses to employ resources to produce goods and services and distribute them for consumption among various competing groups and individuals.

What are the two branches of economics?

There are two major branches of economics: macroeconomics studies the operation of a nation's economy as a whole, and microeconomics studies the behaviour of people and organizations in particular markets (e.g., why people buy smaller cars when gas prices go up).

LO2 **Explain what capitalism is and how free markets work.**

Capitalism is an economic system in which all or most of the means of production and distribution (e.g., land, factories, railroads, and stores) are privately owned and operated for profit.

Who decides what to produce under capitalism?

In capitalist countries, business people decide what to produce; how much to pay workers; how much to charge for goods and services; whether to produce certain goods in their own countries, import those goods, or have them made in other countries; and so on.

How does the free market work?

The free market is one in which decisions about what to produce and in what quantities are made by the market—that is, by buyers and sellers negotiating prices for goods and services. Buyers' decisions in the marketplace tell sellers what to produce and in what quantity. When buyers demand more goods, the price goes up, signalling suppliers to produce more. The higher the price, the more goods and services suppliers are willing to produce. Price, then, is the mechanism that allows free markets to work.

What is supply and demand?

Supply refers to the quantity of products that manufacturers or owners are willing to sell at different prices at a specific time. Demand refers to the quantity of products that people are willing to buy at different prices at a specific time. The key factor in determining the quantity supplied and the quantity demanded is price.

What is the relevance of the equilibrium point?

The equilibrium point, also referred to as the equilibrium price, is the point where the quantity demanded is the same as the quantity supplied. In the long run, that price becomes the market price.

LO3 **Compare the benefits and negative consequences of socialism and communism.**

Socialism is an economic system based on the premise that some businesses should be owned by the government. Socialism creates more social equality. Compared to workers in capitalist countries, workers in socialist countries not only receive more education and health care benefits but also work fewer hours, have longer vacations, and receive more benefits in general, such as child care. The major disadvantage of socialism is that it lowers the profits of owners, thus cutting the incentive to start a business or to work hard. Socialist economies tend to have a higher unemployment rate and a slower growth rate than capitalist economies.

Under communism, the government owns almost all major production facilities and dictates what gets produced and by whom. Communism is more restrictive when it comes to personal freedoms, such as religious freedom. With communism, one can see shortages in items such as food and clothing, and business people may not work as hard as the government takes most of their earnings. While many countries practice socialism, only a few (e.g., North Korea) still practice communism.

LO4 **Describe the mixed economy of Canada.**

A mixed economy is one that is part capitalist and part socialist. That is, some businesses are privately owned, but taxes tend to be high to distribute income more evenly among the population.

What countries have mixed economies?

Canada has a mixed economy, as do most other countries of the world.

What does it mean to have a mixed economy?

A mixed economy has most of the benefits of wealth creation that free markets bring plus the benefits of greater social equality and concern for the environment that socialism offers.

LO5 **Illustrate the significance of key economic indicators and the business cycle.**

Three major indicators of economic conditions are (1) the gross domestic product (GDP), (2) the unemployment rate, and (3) the price indexes.

What are the key terms used to describe the Canadian economic system?

Gross domestic product (GDP) is the total value of goods and services produced in a country in a given year. The unemployment rate represents the number of unemployed persons expressed as a percentage of the labour force. The consumer price index (CPI) measures changes in the prices of a basket of goods and services that consumers buy. It is a monthly statistic that measures the pace of inflation (consumer prices going up) or deflation (consumer prices going down). Productivity is the total volume of goods and services one worker can produce in a given period. Productivity in Canada has increased over the years due to the use of computers and other technologies.

What are the four phases of business cycles?

In an economic boom, businesses do well. A recession occurs when two or more quarters show declines in the GDP, prices fall, people purchase fewer products, and businesses fail. A depression is a severe recession. Finally, recovery is when the economy stabilizes and starts to grow.

KEY TERMS

CAREER EXPLORATION

If you are interested in pursuing a career in economics, here are a few to consider. Find out about the tasks performed, skills needed, pay, and opportunity outlook in these fields through Internet sites that include the Government of Canada Job Bank, Workopolis, Monster, CareerBuilder, Glassdoor, and Indeed, as well as through the Career Centre at your school.

- **Economist**—studies the production and distribution of resources, goods, and services by collecting and analyzing data, researching trends, and evaluating economic issues.
- **Statistican**—applies mathematical or statistical theory and methods to collect, organize, interpret, and summarize numerical data to provide useful information.
- **Marketing research analyst**—studies market conditions and helps companies understand what products people want, who will buy them, and at what price.
- **Actuary**—analyzes the financial costs of risk and uncertainty and uses mathematics, statistics, and financial theory to assess the risk that an event will occur.

CRITICAL THINKING

Many say that business people do not do enough for society. Some students choose to work for non-profit organizations instead of for-profit organizations because they want to help others. However, business people say that they do more to help others than non-profit groups because they provide jobs for people rather than giving them charity, which often precludes them from searching for work. Furthermore, they believe that businesses create all the wealth that non-profit groups distribute. Can you find some middle ground in this debate that demonstrates how both business people and those who work for non-profit organizations contribute to society and need to work together more closely to help people? Could you use the concepts of Adam Smith to help illustrate your position?

DEVELOPING CAREER SKILLS

Key: ● **Team** ★ **Analytic** ▲ **Communication** ⊡ **Technology**

●★▲ **1.** In teams, develop a list of the advantages of living in a capitalist society. Then develop lists headed "What are the disadvantages?" and "How could such disadvantages be minimized?" Describe why a person in a socialist country might reject capitalism and prefer a socialist state.

⊡★ **2.** Show your understanding of the principles of supply and demand by looking at the oil market today. Go online and search for a chart of oil prices for the last few years. Why does the price of oil fluctuate so greatly? What will happen as more and more people in China and India decide to buy automobiles? What would happen if most Canadian consumers decided to drive electric cars?

●★▲ **3.** This exercise will help you understand socialism from different perspectives. Form three groups. Each group should adopt a different role in a socialist economy: one group will be the business owners, another group will be workers, and another will be government leaders. Within your group discuss and list the advantages and disadvantages to you of lowering taxes on businesses. Then have each group choose a representative to go to the front of the class and debate the tax issue with the representatives from the other groups.

▲★ **4.** Draw a line and mark one end "capitalism" and the other end "socialism." Mark where Canada is now on that line. Explain why you marked the spot you did. Students from other countries may want to do this exercise for their own countries and explain the differences to the class.

●★▲ **5.** Break into small groups. In your group, discuss how the following have affected people's purchasing behaviours and attitudes toward Canada and its economy: development of the Alberta oil sands; the Atlantic seal hunt; mad cow disease; and the growth of the Internet. Have a group member prepare a short summary for the class.

ANALYZING MANAGEMENT DECISIONS

The Rule of 72

No formula is more useful for understanding inflation than the rule of 72. In fact, The Rule of 72 was highlighted in the Reaching Beyond Our Borders box in this chapter.

Basically, the rule allows you to quickly compute how long it takes the cost of goods and services to double at various compounded rates of growth. For example, if houses were increasing in cost at 9 percent a year, how long would it take for the price of a home to double? The answer is easy to calculate. Simply divide 72 by the annual increase (9 percent) and you get the approximate number of years it takes to double the price (eight years). Of course, the same calculation can be used to predict how high food prices or auto prices will be 10 years from now.

Here is an example of how you can use the rule of 72. If the cost of attending a post-secondary institution increases by 6 percent a year, how much might you have to pay to send your child to a post-secondary institution in 24 years (this assumes you will have a child six years from now) if costs are now $10,000 a year? To find the answer, you divide 72 by 6, which shows that the cost of an education would double in 12 years. It would double twice in 24 years. Your son or daughter can expect to pay $40,000 per year to attend college.

Discussion Questions

1. If the cost of a post-secondary institution education is about $20,000 per year now, what will it cost your children per year if costs go up 9 percent a year and your children go to a post-secondary institution 16 years from now?
2. If the value of a home doubles in 12 years, what is the annual rate of return? (Hint: Use the rule of 72 in reverse.)
3. If you put $1,000 into a savings account and earned 6 percent per year, how much money would you have in the account after 48 years?

CHAPTER 3

Competing in Global Markets

LEARNING OBJECTIVES

After you have read and studied this chapter, you should be able to:

LO1 Describe the importance of the global market and the roles of comparative advantage and absolute advantage in global trade.

LO2 Explain the importance of importing and exporting, and define key terms used in global business.

LO3 Illustrate the strategies used in reaching global markets, and explain the role of multinational corporations in global markets.

LO4 Evaluate the forces that affect trading in global markets.

LO5 Debate the advantages and disadvantages of trade protectionism, define tariff and non-tariff barriers, and give examples of common markets.

LO6 Discuss the changing landscape of the global market.

P R O F I L E

GETTING TO KNOW: INDRA KRISHNAMURTHY NOOYI, CEO, PEPSICO

Indra Nooyi grew up in southeast India, the daughter of an accountant and a stay-at-home mother. Every night at dinner her mother would present a world problem to Indra and her sister, and they would compete to solve it as if they were prime minister or president. As a schoolgirl, she was on the debate team, played cricket, and was part of an all-girl rock band in which she played guitar (an instrument she still enjoys.)

She earned a bachelor's degree in physics, chemistry, and mathematics before receiving master's degrees in business from the Indian School of Management in Calcutta and the Yale School of Management in Connecticut. After completing graduate school, Nooyi worked for the Boston Consulting Group before moving on to a strategic-planning position at Motorola. She was prepared to move on

© Monica Schipper/Getty Images

to a management position with General Electric in 1994 when PepsiCo was able to lure her away. By 1996, Pepsi's sales had slowed and the company was losing the global market to competitor Coca-Cola big time. Coca-Cola was earning over 70 percent of its revenue from global sales while Pepsi generated only 29 percent. As strategy chief and head of mergers and acquisitions, Nooyi advised the company to buy Tropicana and Quaker Oats (which would bring Gatorade to Pepsi) and to sell company restaurant subsidiaries Pizza Hut, Taco Bell, and KFC. Her goal was to increase global sales.

In 2001, Nooyi became CFO of PepsiCo. Five years later she became PepsiCo's first female CEO, as well as its first CEO not born in the United States. As CEO, she proclaimed a new theme of "Performance with purpose," Pepsi's promise to do what's right for the business by doing what's right for people and the planet. She reclassified the company's products into three categories: "fun for you" (such as potato chips and regular sodas), "better for you" (diet or low-fat versions of snacks and sodas), and "good for you" (products such as oatmeal). She put a good deal of Pepsi's money behind the effort to help global customers develop healthier lifestyles. The company has made some progress in making unhealthy products less so by removing 400 000 tons of sugar from its drinks over the past 10 years and reducing salt and saturated fats from Lay's and Ruffles chips.

PepsiCo has grown substantially under Nooyi's leadership. Today, PepsiCo is a $66 billion global company that boasts 22 brands that generate over $1 billion each. The company has over 264 000 employees worldwide and is sold in more than 200 countries and territories around the globe. Nooyi recently announced the company would expand the corporate global agenda she had started, emphasizing health and social accountability. She pledged PepsiCo would continue to focus on making its products healthier, empowering the company's global employees, and encouraging environmental responsibility.

Indra Nooyi is an example of a successful global businessperson who has proven that it doesn't matter who you are or where you come from if you have the will and determination to succeed. She understands cultural and economic differences, and knows how to adapt her company to global changes successfully. This chapter explains the opportunities and challenges businesspeople like Indra Nooyi face every day in dealing with the dynamic environment of global business.

Sources: Lyndon Driver, "How Indra Nooyi Changed the Face of PepsiCo," *World Finance*, October 14, 2016; Jennifer Reingold, "Indra Nooyi Was Right. Now What?" *Fortune*, June 15, 2015; Robert Safian, "How PepsiCo CEO Indra Nooyi Is Steering the Company to a Purpose-Driven Future," *Fast Company*, January 19, 2017; www.pepsico.com, accessed September 2017.

LO1

Describe the importance of the global market and the roles of comparative advantage and absolute advantage in global trade.

The Dynamic Global Market

Have you ever dreamed of travelling to exotic cities such as Paris, Tokyo, Rio de Janeiro, or Cairo? Today, over 90 percent of the companies doing business globally believe it is important for their employees to have experience working in other countries.[1] The reason is not surprising. Although Canada is a market of more than 37 million people, there are over 7 billion potential customers in the 194 independent countries that make up the global market.[2] (See Figure 3.1 for a map of the world and important statistics about the world's population.[3]) That is too many people to ignore.

In 2017, Canadian consumers bought nearly $70.9 billion in merchandise from China.[4] Canadian companies, both large and small, continuously look for opportunities to grow their businesses. For example, Rogers Communication signed a 12-year, $5.2 billion deal with the National Hockey League (NHL) for the league's broadcast and media rights.[5] TSN and Sportsnet paid an undisclosed amount to share the multimedia rights for 380 Barclays Premiere League football matches.[6]

More broadly, other companies actively seek opportunities around the globe. United Parcel Service (UPS) has experienced solid market growth in its global operations and Walmart and Starbucks have opened stores in South Africa. Major League Baseball is broadcast in hundreds of countries in 17 languages.[7] The National Basketball Association (NBA) and the National Football League (NFL) played regular season games in London and Mexico in 2017.[8] NBC paid $1 billion to telecast six full seasons of England's Barclays Premier Soccer League in the United States.[9] American film stars Matt Damon, Tom Cruise, and Meryl Streep draw crowds to movie theatres around the globe.

Bombardier Inc. is a world-leading manufacturer of innovative transportation solutions in the areas of aerospace and rail transportation.[10] Headquartered in Montreal, the company has 80 production and engineering sites in 28 countries, and a worldwide network of service centres.[11]

FIGURE 3.1

WORLD POPULATION BY CONTINENT

As shown on this map, 60.2 percent of the world's population lives in Asia while only 7.4 percent lives in North America.

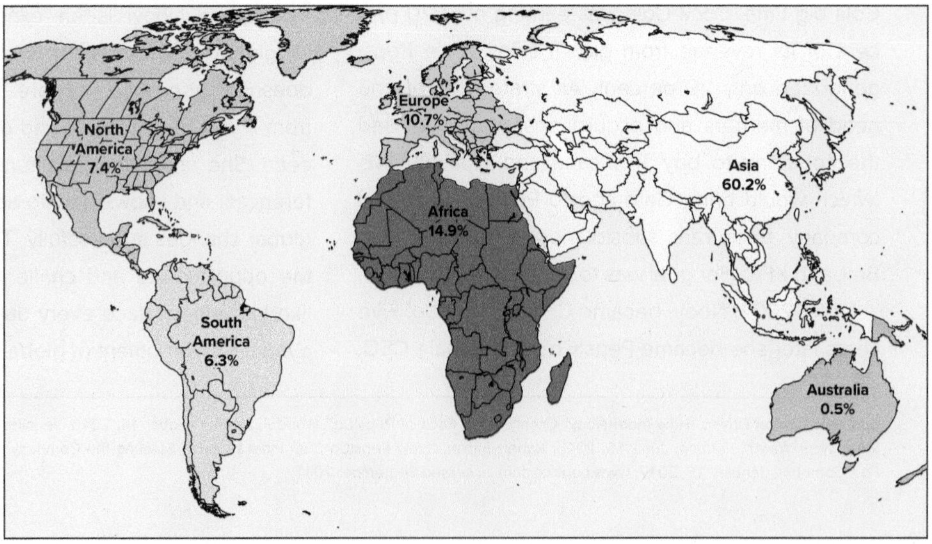

Companies also continuously review their global operations to ensure that they are operating at a profit. One Canadian industry that has been particularly hard hit as a result of global trends is the auto industry. Factors such as the increasing price of gas and weakening demand for trucks and sport utility vehicles (SUVs) have forced companies to consider restructuring plans. As a result, thousands of Canadian jobs have been eliminated. Layoffs have occurred at General Motors Canada, Fiat Chrysler Automobiles, Ford Motor Company of Canada, and many parts suppliers.[12] Canada's share of North American auto production fell to a record low of 14 percent in 2013.[13] The global market is truly dynamic, and progressive companies continuously scan the business environment to ensure that they take advantage of the opportunities and minimize the impact of threats.

© Gerry Penny/EPA/Newscom

It may not be what the rest of the world calls "football," but American football is attracting an audience outside the United States. London's Wembley Stadium has been home to the NFL's International Series since 2007. What cultural factors must U.S. sports franchises overcome in order to increase popularity abroad?

Because the global market is so large, it is important to understand the language of international trade. Canada is a large exporting nation. **Exporting** is selling products (i.e., goods and services) to another country. **Importing** is buying products from another country. Competition in exporting is very intense and Canadian companies face aggressive rivalry from exporters around the world who also have the same objectives of growing their businesses.

This chapter will familiarize you with global business and its many challenges. As competition in global markets increases, the demand for students with training in global business is almost certain to grow. If you choose such a career, prepare yourself to work hard and always be ready for new challenges.

exporting
Selling products to another country.

importing
Buying products from another country.

Why Trade with Other Nations?

No country, not even a technologically advanced one, can produce all of the goods that its people want and need. Even if a country did become self-sufficient, other nations would seek to trade with that country to meet the needs of their citizens. Some nations, like Venezuela and Russia, have an abundance of natural resources but have limited technological know-how. Other countries, such as Japan and Switzerland, have sophisticated technology but few natural resources. Global trade enables a nation to produce what it is most capable of producing and to buy what it needs from others in a mutually beneficial exchange relationship. This happens through the process of free trade.

Free trade is the movement of goods and services among nations without political or economic barriers. It is often a hotly debated concept.[14] Figure 3.2 offers some of the pros and cons of free trade.

free trade
The movement of goods and services among nations without political or economic barriers.

The Theories of Comparative and Absolute Advantage

Global trade is the exchange of goods and services across national borders. Exchanges between and among countries involve more than goods and services, however. Countries also exchange art, sports, cultural events, medical advances, space exploration, and labour.

FIGURE 3.2

THE PROS AND CONS OF FREE TRADE

PROS	CONS
• The global market contains more than 7 billion potential customers for goods and services.	• Domestic workers (particularly in manufacturing-based jobs) can lose their jobs due to increased imports or production shifts to low-wage global markets.
• Productivity improves when countries produce goods and services in which they have a comparative advantage.	• Workers may be forced to accept pay cuts from employers who can threaten to move their jobs to lower-cost global markets.
• Global competition and less-costly imports keep prices down, so inflation does not curtail economic growth.	• Moving operations overseas because of intense competitive pressure often means the loss of service jobs and white-collar jobs.
• Free trade inspires innovation for new products and keeps firms competitively challenged.	• Domestic companies can lose their comparative advantage when competitors build advanced production operations in low-wage countries.
• The uninterrupted flow of capital gives countries access to foreign investments, which helps keep interest rates low.	

Comparative advantage theory, suggested in the early nineteenth century by English economist David Ricardo, was the guiding principle that supported this idea of free economic exchange.[15]

comparative advantage theory
A theory that states that a country should sell to other countries those products that it produces most effectively and efficiently, and buy from other countries those products that it cannot produce as effectively or efficiently trade.

Comparative advantage theory states that a country should sell to other countries those products that it produces most effectively and efficiently, and buy from other countries those products it cannot produce as effectively or efficiently. Japan has shown this ability with cars and electronic items. Canada has such an advantage with certain forestry and agricultural products, and various minerals. In contrast, Canada lacks a comparative advantage in growing coffee; thus, we import most of the coffee we consume. By specializing and trading, Canada and its trading partners can realize mutually beneficial exchanges.[16]

In practice, the comparative advantage theory does not work so neatly. For various reasons, many countries decide to produce certain agricultural, industrial, or consumer products despite a lack of comparative advantage. To facilitate this plan, they restrict imports of competing products from countries that can produce them at lower costs. The net result is that the free movement of goods and services is restricted. We will return to the topic of trade protectionism later in the chapter.

absolute advantage
The advantage that exists when a country has a monopoly on producing a specific product or is able to produce it more efficiently than all other countries.

A country has an **absolute advantage** if it has a monopoly on producing a specific product or is able to produce it more efficiently than all other countries. However, an absolute advantage in natural resources does not last forever. For instance, South Africa once had an absolute advantage in diamond production but this is no longer the case.

Global competition also causes other absolute advantages to fade. Today there are very few instances of absolute advantage in global markets.

Getting Involved in Global Trade

People interested in finding a job in global business often think of firms like Bombardier, Magna International, and Sony, which have large multinational accounts. The real job potential, however, may be with small businesses. Small businesses contribute between 25 and 41 percent to Canada's gross domestic product and employ approximately seven million individuals (or 69.7 percent of the total labour force in the private sector). As well, small businesses account for about 90 percent of Canadian exporters.[18] With the help of government agencies, such as Foreign Affairs and International Trade Canada and Export Development Canada, many small businesses are becoming more involved in global markets.

Getting started globally is often a matter of observation, determination, and risk. What does that mean? First, it is important to observe and study global markets. Your library, the Internet, and your fellow classmates are good starting points for doing your research. Second, if you have the opportunity, travelling to different countries is a great way to observe foreign cultures and lifestyles and see if doing business globally appeals to you. A poll of Canadian small business owners between 25 and 39 years of age found that 72 percent export their goods and services.[19] Global trade is an effective strategy for businesses of any size.

Canada became a diamond producer in 1998 when the Ekati diamond mine opened about 300 kilometres northeast of Yellowknife. Here you see the Diavik Diamond Mine, located on a 20-square-kilometre island in the same area. With the opening of new mines, Canada's global diamond market share is expected to grow to a world-leading 25.2 percent in 2018.[17]

LO2

Explain the importance of importing and exporting, and define key terms used in global business.

Importing Goods and Services[20]

The Canada Border Services Agency deals with importers across the whole range of goods and services that enter our country. These products (also referred to as articles) are subject to compliance with certain conditions imposed by the federal and, sometimes, provincial government(s). Some of the conditions may include the following:

- Is the article prohibited entry into Canada (e.g., baby walkers are prohibited due to Canadian safety standards)?
- Is the article allowed to be imported only under the authority of an import permit? Examples include textiles and clothing, steel, wheat, barley and their products, certain farm products (e.g., dairy, chicken, eggs, and turkey), and firearms.
- Is the article subject to some other federally-imposed condition? For example, goods for retail sale have to comply with labelling laws; motor vehicles have to meet emission control standards; and food and agricultural products have to pass the necessary health and sanitary checks.

© Top Photo Corporation /Alamy

China produces and exports 80 percent of the toys manufactured in the world. What products do you use that are imported from China?

- Is the article subject to some privately-certified standard? For example, all electrical appliances and equipment must be certified by a recognized certification body before they can be sold in Canada.
- Is there a provincial rule to comply with? For example, imports of liquor, wine, and beer require prior authorization from the appropriate liquor commission.

Review Figure 3.3 for categories and examples of goods and services that are imported as well as exported.

Exporting Goods and Services[21]

You may be surprised at what you can sell in other countries. The fact is, you can sell just about any good or service that is used in Canada to other countries—and often the competition is not nearly as intense for

FIGURE 3.3

CATEGORIES AND EXAMPLES OF CANADA'S GOODS AND SERVICE TRADE

Categories	Examples
Merchandise Trade Categories	
Industrial Goods and Materials	Metals and metal ores, chemicals and plastics, and other industrial goods and materials
Machinery and Equipment	Industrial and agricultural machinery, aircraft and other transportation equipment, and other machinery and equipment
Energy Products	Crude petroleum and other energy products such as natural gas, petroleum, and coal products
Automotive Products	Passenger autos and chassis, trucks and other motor vehicles, and motor vehicle parts
Agricultural and Fishing Products	Wheat, fruits and vegetables, and other agricultural and fishing products such as live animals, feed, beverages, and tobacco
Forestry Products	Lumber and sawmill products, wood pulp and other wood products, and newsprint and other paper products
Other Consumer Goods	Apparel and footwear, and miscellaneous consumer goods such as watches, sporting goods and toys, and television and radio sets
Service Trade Categories	
Travel Services	Business travel and personal travel
Transport Services	Air transport, water transport, land, and other transport
Commercial Services	Communication, construction, insurance, computer and information, architectural, engineering, research and development, and other financial services
Government Services	Military activities and business support

Sources: "Canada's International Trade in Services, 2013," Statistics Canada, October 1, 2014, http://www.statcan.gc.ca/daily-quotidien/141001/dq141001b-eng.pdf; Canadian International Merchandise Trade, Statistics Canada, January 2015, Catalogue no. 65-001-X.

producers in global markets as it is at home. You can, for example, sell snowplows to Saudi Arabians who use them to clear sand off their driveways. Don't forget that services can be exported as well.

Why is trade so important? Trade with other countries enhances the quality of life for Canadians and contributes to our country's economic well-being. Exports alone account for one in five Canadian jobs.

Canadian goods and services can be sold abroad directly as an export from a Canadian company or they can be sold indirectly via a foreign-located subsidiary of a Canadian company. Sales by majority-owned foreign affiliates of Canadian businesses are an important means by which Canadian companies engage in international commerce.

Spend some time reviewing Figure 3.4. By understanding this information, you will realize why you hear so much about imports and exports in the news. After all, such activities are vital to our economy. What questions might you ask about Canada's trade performance?

Shania Twain began singing in clubs and community events in her hometown of Timmins, Ontario, and to date has sold millions of records worldwide. Other Canadian-born entertainers that have global appeal include Justin Bieber, Celine Dion, Drake, and Michael Bublé. Do you prefer to support Canadian talent?

It is also important for businesses to be aware of these great opportunities. But don't be misled. Selling in global markets is not by any means easy. (Review the Spotlight on Small Business box for an example of one export area where Canadian businesses thrive.) Adapting goods and services to specific global markets is potentially profitable but can be very difficult. We shall discuss a number of forces that affect global trading later in this chapter.

balance of trade
A nation's ratio of exports to imports.

trade surplus
A favourable balance of trade; occurs when the value of a country's exports exceeds that of its imports.

trade deficit
An unfavourable balance of trade; occurs when the value of a country's imports exceeds that of its exports.

Measuring Global Trade

In measuring the effectiveness of global trade, nations carefully follow two key indicators: balance of trade and balance of payments. The **balance of trade** is a nation's ratio of exports to imports. A *favourable* balance of trade, or **trade surplus**, occurs when the value of the country's exports exceeds that of its imports. An unfavourable balance of trade, or **trade deficit**, occurs when the value of the country's imports exceeds that of its exports.

FIGURE 3.4

CANADA'S GOODS AND SERVICES IMPORT/EXPORT PERFORMANCE, 2016

	SERVICES		GOODS	
	Exports	Imports	Exports	Imports
Value (billions)	$107,164	$129,261	$521,368	$547,237
Annual Growth (%)	4.8%	2.0%	0.1%	0.1%

Source: "Canada's State of Trade: Trade and Investment Update—2017," Office of the Chief Economist, Global Affairs Canada, accessed May 20, 2018, http://www.international.gc.ca/economist-economiste/performance/state-point/state_2017_point/index.aspx?lang=eng#1_0.

Spotlight *On* SMALL BUSINESS

Let the Games Begin

Members of Generation Z, a demographic group born between 1995 and the present, love to play video games. Statistics show they multitask across five screens daily and spend 41 percent of their time outside of school with computers or mobile devices. While many of the video gaming platforms have big business names, such as Sony, Apple, and Nintendo, much of the work to design the games comes from small businesses. In 2013, Canada's video gaming industry ranked third in the world and contributed $2.3 billion in GDP to the Canadian economy.

© Lorenzo Rossi/Hemera/Thinkstock

The Canadian companies are primarily small and micro-sized businesses based in urban centres. But there are exceptions: Other Ocean Interactive, which operates from offices in Charlottetown, Prince Edward Island, and St. John's, Newfoundland, is best known for the development of Konami's award-winning Xbox LIVE™ Arcade download, *Castlevania™; Symphony of the Night™*, Midway's Nintendo DS release of the popular franchise *Ultimate™ Mortal Kombat®*; and the highly popular *Sega's Super.* While a location away from the California gaming hub may seem a challenge, studio head Deidre Ayre sees the choice a different way, "I am proud to say we have created 75 jobs in the Atlantic region so far and that number is still growing."

Bight Games, also in PEI, built success on "freemium" games (apps that are free with fees for virtual goods) *Trade Nation,* a perennial top-grossing game in the App Store, and *The Simpsons: Tapped,* a popular mobile video game. The business was so successful Electronic Arts (EA) acquired the indie mobile games developer. "Video games are not IT in the traditional sense. We're in the entertainment business," says Stuart Duncan, founder of Bight Games. "We employ as many artists as programmers, and deal with original intellectual property, as well as patents. And, we make more money than Hollywood."

With these products, both companies gain an edge in the competitive environment of the global gaming industry that has an estimated value of $30 billion. According to the Entertainment Software Association of Canada, 65 percent of Canadians believe the video gaming industry has a positive effect on the Canadian economy. Thanks to small businesses like these, it's true.

Source: Matthew Bambach, "Canada's video-game industry ranks No. 3 worldwide," *The Globe and Mail,* March 18, 2013, http://www.theglobeandmail.com/report-on-business/small-business/sb-digital/biz-categories-technology/canadas-video-game-industry-ranks-no-3-worldwide/article9875545/; "Our Industry is Thriving," Entertainment Software Association of Canada, accessed June 27, 2018, theesa.ca; Hayley Peterson, "Millennials are old news – Here's everything you should know about Generation Z," Business Insider, June 25. 2014, http://www.businessinsider.com/generation-z-spending-habits-2014-6; "Prince Edward Island's Video Gaming Industry Showing Signs of Making Serious Noise," *The Guardian,* January 8, 2008, http://www.gameplan.ca/documents/guardianstory1.pdf; Dean Takahashi, "EA acquires mobile game developer Bight Games," VB, August 15, 2011, http://venturebeat.com/2011/08/15/ea-acquires-mobile-game-developer-bight-games/.

In 2009, Canada registered its first trade deficit in 15 years and this continued to be the case in 2014.[22] It is easy to understand why countries prefer to export more than they import. If I sell you $200 worth of goods and buy only $100 worth, I have an extra $100 available to buy other things. However, I'm in an unfavourable position if I buy $200 worth of goods from you and sell you only $100.

The **balance of payments** is the difference between money coming into a country (from exports) and money leaving the country (for imports) plus money flows coming into or leaving a country from other factors such as tourism, foreign aid, military expenditures, and foreign investment. The goal is always to have more money flowing into the country than flowing out of the country; in other words, a *favourable* balance of payments. Conversely, an *unfavourable* balance of payments is when more money is flowing out of a country than coming in.

© Ollie Millington/WireImage/Getty Images

Although Funko's Pop! line of toys aren't very lifelike, that hasn't stopped these big-headed figurines from becoming a global sensation. Funko's toys usually take on the appearance of famous fictional characters or pop culture icons, giving them widespread appeal to collectors around the world. As a result, each year Funko earns tens of millions from sales of its Pop! toys. Does a career in the global collectibles market seem appealing to you?

Trading in Global Markets: The Canadian Experience

At first glance, Canada's foreign trade statistics seem impressive. While our abundant natural resources are a major area for exports, developing countries continue to give Canada stiff competition in these areas. When we look carefully at the numbers in Figure 3.5, we see that we are dependent on one country, the United States. Over the long-term, Derek Burleton, Deputy Chief Economist with Toronto-Dominion Bank (TD), expects that Canada's economic prosperity will be increasingly driven by trade with economies other than the United States'. He predicts that by 2020, the United States will account for only two-thirds of Canada's exports, down from a peak of 85 percent in 2002.[23] Read the next section to learn about these priority markets.

Canada's Priority Markets[24]

Technological advances in most fields, primarily in the area of transmission and storage of information, have shattered the archaic notions of how things ought to function, from production and trade to war and politics. The new ways of communicating, organizing, and working are inviting the most remote corners of the world to be actors on the global economic stage. These *emerging economies* are enjoying high growth rates, rapid increases in their living standards, and a rising global prominence. Tapping into these markets is crucial. For example, in 30 years a gain of just 0.1 percent in the Canadian share of the import markets of Brazil, Russia, India, and China (BRIC countries) would mean an export gain of $29 billion.

balance of payments
The difference between money coming into a country (from exports) and money leaving the country (for imports) plus money flows from other factors such as tourism, foreign aid, military expenditures, and foreign investment.

Based on extensive consultation with government, academic, and Canadian business and industry representatives, the federal government developed its Global Markets Action Plan. The plan identifies three priority market types: emerging markets with broad Canadian interests, emerging markets with specific opportunities for Canadian businesses, and established markets with broad Canadian interests. These emerging market types include 21 countries and focus upon Asia Pacific (ten countries),

FIGURE 3.5

CANADA'S GOODS AND SERVICES TRADE BY REGION, 2016

	SERVICES		GOODS	
	Exports %	Imports %	Exports %	Imports %
United States	55.1	54.4	75.3	65.8
European Union	16.8	16.8	8	9.5
China	–*	–	4.3	6.9
Japan	1.6	1.6	2.1	2.1
Mexico	–	–	1.7	3.5
India	–	–	0.8	0.5
South Korea	–	–	0.9	1.6
Rest of World	26.5	26.5	6.9	10.1

* indicates no services export or import values for the region were provided in the federal government report.

Source: "Canada's State of Trade: Trade and Investment Update—2017," Table 4.2-"Goods Exports 2016", Table 4.3-"Goods Imports 2016", and Table 4.6-"Services Exports and Imports by Region 2016", Global Affairs Canada, accessed May 20, 2018, http://www.international.gc.ca/economist-economiste/performance/state-point/state_2017_point/index.aspx?lang=eng#1_0.

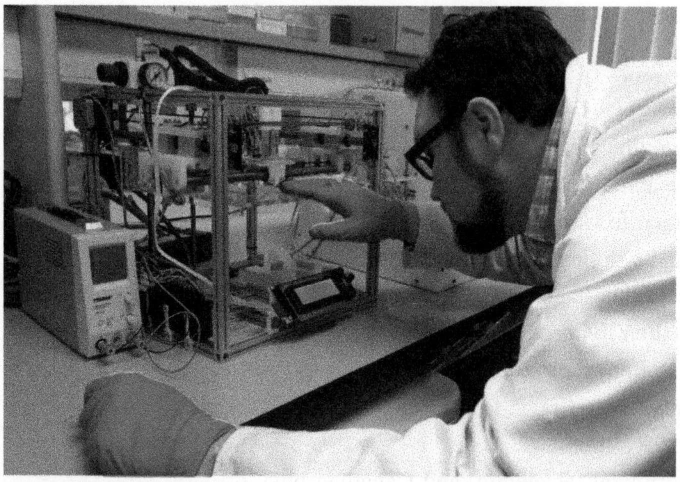

© Andrew Milligan/CP Images

One objective of the federal government's Science and Technology program is to identify and incorporate world-leading research into the development of innovative processes, goods, and services in Canada. What are some other benefits of such initiatives?

Latin America and Caribbean (four countries), North America (one country), Middle East and Africa (four countries), and Europe (two countries).[25]

China and India are of particular interest as they are growing and emerging markets due to their size and economic transformation. A Conference Board of Canada report notes that by 2050, India will be the world's third-largest economy, with a GDP approaching US$30 trillion, behind only the United States and China, which will top the list. Steps already taken to encourage a stronger Canadian presence in the global marketplace include tax cuts, increased support for research and development, and critical investments in infrastructure at Canada–U.S. border crossings and Canada's Asia-Pacific Gateway.

PROGRESS ASSESSMENT

- How do world population and market statistics support the expansion of Canadian businesses into global markets?
- What is comparative advantage? How does this differ from absolute advantage?
- How are a country's balance of trade and balance of payments determined?

Strategies for Reaching Global Markets

LO3

Illustrate the strategies used in reaching global markets, and explain the role of multinational corporations in global markets.

Businesses use many different strategies to compete in global markets. The key strategies include licensing, exporting, franchising, contract manufacturing, creating international joint ventures and strategic alliances, and engaging in foreign direct investment. Each of these strategies provides opportunities for becoming involved in global markets, along with specific commitments and risks. Figure 3.6 places the strategies discussed on a continuum showing the amount of commitment, control, risk, and profit potential associated with each one. Take a few minutes to look it over before you continue.

Licensing

A firm (the licensor) may decide to compete in a global market by **licensing** the right to manufacture its product or use its trademark to a foreign company (the licensee) for a fee (a royalty). A company with an interest in licensing generally needs to send company representatives to the foreign producer to help set up the production process. The licensor may also assist or work with a licensee in such areas as distribution, promotion, and consulting.

licensing
A global strategy in which a firm (the licensor) allows a foreign company (the licensee) to produce its product in exchange for a fee (a royalty).

A licensing agreement can benefit a firm in several ways. First, the firm can gain revenues it would not otherwise have generated in its home market. Also, foreign licensees

FIGURE 3.6

STRATEGIES FOR REACHING GLOBAL MARKETS

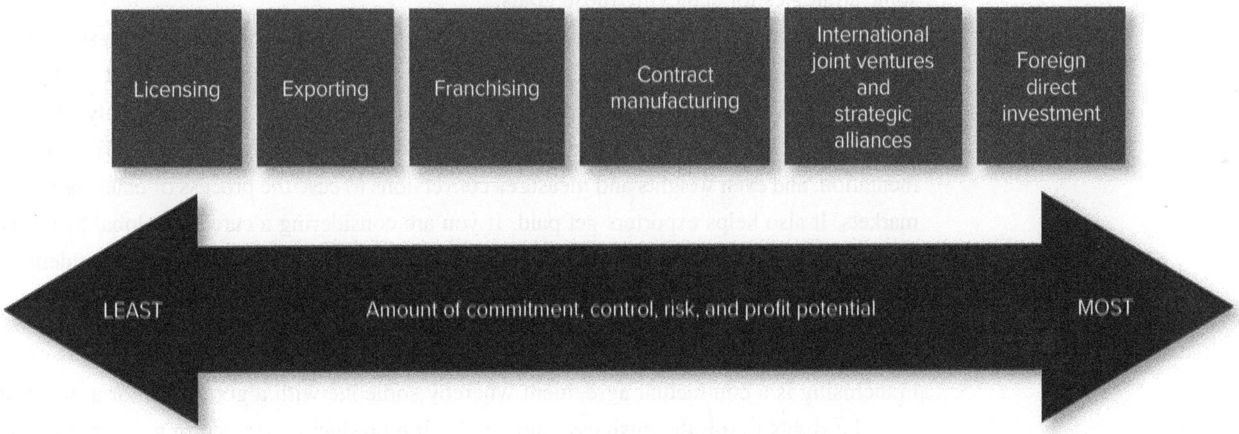

© Albert L. Ortega/Getty Images

Marvel has licensed many companies to make products related to successful film franchises like *Guardians of the Galaxy*. Do you think Marvel-licensed products will maintain their global popularity with new generations of viewers?

must often purchase start-up supplies, component materials, and consulting services from the licensing firm. Coca-Cola has entered into global licensing agreements with over 300 licensees that have extended into long-term service contracts that sell over $1 billion of the company's products each year. Service-based companies are also active in licensing. For example, Tokyo Disneyland, the first Disney theme park opened outside the United States, is operated by Oriental Land Company under a licensing agreement with the Walt Disney Company. In fact, Disney is the largest licensor of consumer products globally, with over $50 billion of licensed products.[26]

A final advantage of licensing is that licensors spend little or no money to produce and market their products. These costs come from the licensee's pocket. Therefore, licensees generally work hard to succeed. However, licensors may also experience some problems. Often, a firm must grant licensing rights to its product for an extended period, 20 years or longer. If a product experiences remarkable growth in the foreign market, the bulk of the revenues earned belong to the licensee. Perhaps even more threatening is that a licensing firm is actually selling its expertise. If a foreign licensee learns the company's technology or product secrets, it may break the agreement and begin to produce a similar product on its own. If legal remedies are not available, the licensing firm may lose its trade secrets, not to mention promised royalties.

Exporting

Canadian companies export goods and services (e.g., call centres, IT consultants, and cultural and performing artists). As you will see in the chapters on marketing, many decisions have to be made when a company markets a new product or goes into new markets with existing products. Often the first export sales occur as a result of unsolicited orders received. Regardless of how a company starts exporting, it must develop some goals and some strategies for achieving those goals.

Canadian firms that are still hesitant can engage in indirect exporting through specialists called export-trading companies (or export-management companies) that assist in negotiating and establishing trading relationships. An export-trading company not only matches buyers and sellers from different countries but also deals with foreign customs offices, documentation, and even weights and measures conversions to ease the process of entering global markets. It also helps exporters get paid. If you are considering a career in global business, export-trading companies often provide internships or part-time opportunities for students.

Franchising

Franchising is a contractual agreement whereby someone with a good idea for a business sells the rights to use the business name and sell a product or service in a given territory in a specified manner. Franchising is popular domestically and internationally. (We will discuss it in depth in Chapter 6.) Canadian franchisors such as Molly Maid and Tim Hortons have global units operated by foreign franchisees.

In 1986, brothers Michael and Aaron Serruya, then aged 19 and 20, wanted to buy a franchise, but no one would take a chance on them. So, they started their own frozen yogourt shop, Yogen Früz. Today, Yogen Früz has grown to be a world leader in the frozen yogourt category, with over 1300 locations worldwide and a 20-year Top 500 Global Franchise rating.[27] Another Canadian business, BeaverTails Pastry, was started in 1978. The company produces whole-wheat pastries that are stretched by hand to resemble the tail of a beaver, one of Canada's best-known national symbols. The pastries are then float cooked on high-quality canola oil and served piping hot, topped with butter and a choice of delectable flavours. The company operates over 80 franchised and licensed outlets across Canada, together with two locations in Saudi Arabia and two stores in Colorado's ski country.[28]

© Aneta_Gu/Getty Images RF

Tired of studying and want a quick snack? How about a piping hot pizza topped with pickled peppers and cucumbers drizzled with mayo like the one above. International chains like Pizza Hut serve pies like these around the globe in order to appeal to different tastes. How can franchises ensure their products are appropriate for global markets?

Franchisors have to be careful to adapt their product or service to the countries they serve. Yum! Brands' has 40 000 of its KFC, Taco Bell, and Pizza Hut restaurants in 130 countries around the world.[29] They learned quickly that preferences in pizza toppings differ globally. Japanese customers, for example, enjoy squid and sweet mayonnaise pizza. In the company's KFC restaurants in China, the menu is chicken with Sichuan spicy sauce and rice, egg soup, and a "dragon twister" (KFC's version of a traditional Beijing duck wrap).[30]

Dunkin' Donuts' donut holes might look the same in its 3200 franchises in 36 countries across the globe, but local taste preferences are anything but the same. For example, in the company's donut shops in China, the donut of choice is dry pork and seaweed. Read the Adapting to Change box that highlights another global franchise champion, McDonald's.

Contract Manufacturing

Contract manufacturing involves a foreign company's production of private-label goods to which a domestic company then attaches its own brand name or trademark. (This practice falls under the broad category of *outsourcing,* which we introduced in Chapter 1 and which will be discussed in more depth later in this chapter.) For example, contract manufacturers make circuit boards and components used in computers, printers, smartphones, medical products, airplanes, and consumer electronics for companies such as Dell, Apple, and IBM. Foxconn is the world's largest contract manufacturer and makes such well-known products as the iPhone and Microsoft's XBox One. Nike has more than 800 contract factories around the world that manufacture all its footwear and apparel. The pharmaceutical industry also makes use of contract manufacturing and is expected to grow to an $84 billion market by 2020.[31] Worldwide contract manufacturing is estimated to be an over $300 billion industry.

contract manufacturing
A foreign country's production of private-label goods to which a domestic company then attaches its brand name or trademark; also called outsourcing.

Adapting *to* CHANGE

Many Flags Fly Over the Golden Arches

For decades McDonald's has been the undisputed king of global food franchising. With almost 39 000 restaurants in 120 countries, Mickey D's serves more than 68 million customers every day.

So how did McDonald's become such a global powerhouse? It certainly didn't get there through hamburgers alone. Since it first began expanding overseas, McDonald's has been careful to include regional tastes on its menus along with the usual Big Mac and french fries. For instance, in Thailand patrons can order the Samurai Burger, a pork-patty sandwich marinated in teriyaki sauce and topped with mayonnaise and a pickle and salmon rice. In Germany, a McNurnburger is three bratwurst served on a bun with mustard and onions. Japanese customers can have their famous fries drizzled with pumpkin and chocolate sauces.

McDonald's is also careful to adapt its menus to local customs and culture. In India, the company pays respect to religious sentiments by not including any beef or pork on its menu. Mickey D's recently launched a meatless Big Mac for India's many vegetarian customers, using two corn and cheese patties. This complements its best-selling Maharaja Mac, a chicken patty with jalapenos and habanero sauce. In Israel, all meat served in the chain's restaurants is 100 percent kosher beef. The company also closes many of its restaurants on the Sabbath and religious holidays. For more examples, go to *www.mcdonalds.com* and explore the various McDonald's international franchises websites. Notice how the company blends the culture of each country into the restaurant's image.

© Zhang Peng/LightRocket/Getty Images

McDonald's is also determined to stay on top as the premier global franchisor. Starting in 1961, McDonald's became the first restaurant company in the world to develop a training center, Hamburger University. Today, McDonald's has campuses in Oak Brook, Illinois, Tokyo, London, Sydney, Munich, Sao Paolo, Moscow, and Shanghai. Globally, over 275 000 students have graduated. In Shanghai, the company's Hamburger University attracts top-level college graduates to be trained for management positions. Only about 8 out of every 1000 applicants makes it into the program, an acceptance rate even lower than Harvard University's. Today, over 40 percent of the senior managers at McDonald's are graduates of Hamburger University.

By successfully mixing its image with many cultures, McDonald's has woven itself into the world's fabric. Going forward, McDonald's remains dedicated to quality as it continues adapting and expanding further into the global market.

Sources: Newley Purnell, "McDonald's Fan Scours the Globe to Dish on Menu Variations," *The Wall Street Journal*, February 19, 2016; Natalie Walters, "McDonald's Hamburger University an Be Harder to Get into Than Harvard and Is Even Cooler Than You'd Imagine," AOL.com, October 24, 2015; Preetika Rana, "U.S. Chains Redo Menus in India," *The Wall Street Journal*, March 23, 2016; McDonald's, www.mcdonalds.com, accessed September 2017.

Contract manufacturing enables a company to experiment in a new market without incurring heavy start-up costs such as building a manufacturing plant. If the brand name becomes a success, the company has penetrated a new market with relatively low risk. A firm can also use contract manufacturing temporarily to meet an unexpected increase in orders and, of course, labour costs are often very low.

One company, featured in *PROFIT* magazine's ranking of Canada's emerging growth companies, has used contract manufacturing successfully. FouFou Dog is a dog apparel company whose collection includes canine track suits, hoodies, jewelled collars and leashes, as well as chew toys. At the age of 24, Cheryl Ng, owner of a Maltese dog named Ernie, started the company because she liked how Paris Hilton dressed her dog. Today, the company exports 95 percent of its products. According to Ng, "All our stuff is made in Argentina. In China, quality control can be hit-and-miss or downright sloppy—you could have a disaster on your hands—but it's been consistently good from my suppliers." And she has other reasons for heading south instead of east: "My suppliers will make me a small quantity if I want to try something out. You can't get that from China anymore, and I don't want to be stuck with a colour or style nobody wants; besides, they let me check out the textiles before I buy and they always have good stuff." She also likes the shorter flights and the fact that she only has to cross two time zones.[32]

© Johann Brandstatter/Alamy

Bombardier Transportation was awarded a contract to supply Bombardier Flexity Swift high-floor light rail vehicles to the Bursa Metropolitan Municipality, Turkey. The vehicles will be built at Bombardier's manufacturing facility in Bautzen, Germany. Train cars will come from the Siegen site, while the electrical equipment will be supplied by the Mannheim plant.

International Joint Ventures and Strategic Alliances

A **joint venture** is a partnership in which two or more companies (often from different countries) join to undertake a major project. Joint ventures are often mandated by governments as a condition of doing business in their country, as often occurs in China. For example, Disney and state-owned Shanghai Shendi Group's $5.5 billion joint venture created the first Disneyland theme park in China, which opened in 2016.[33]

joint venture
A partnership in which two or more companies (often from different countries) join to undertake a major project.

Joint ventures are developed for many different reasons. Marriott International and AC Hotels in Spain entered a joint venture to create AC Hotels by Marriott in order to increase their global footprint and future growth.[34] PepsiCo, as part of its Performance with Purpose global vision, agreed to joint ventures with Tata Global Beverages of India to develop packaged health and wellness beverages for the mass consumer market in India and the Strauss Group in Mexico to provide fresh dips and spreads.[35]

The benefits of international joint ventures are clear:

1. Shared technology and risk.
2. Shared marketing and management expertise.
3. Entry into markets where foreign companies are often not allowed unless goods are produced locally.

The drawbacks are not so obvious but are important.[36] One partner can learn the other's technology and practices, and then use what it learned to its own advantage. Also, a shared technology may become obsolete or the joint venture may become too large to be as flexible as needed.

© FRED LUM/THE GLOBE AND MAIL DIGITAL IMAGE/CP Images

The Bank of Nova Scotia formed a joint venture with the Bank of Beijing. The Bank of Beijing Scotiabank Asset Management Co. Ltd. markets mutual funds to retail and institutional customers through the Chinese bank's national branch network.

strategic alliance A long-term partnership between two or more companies established to help each company build competitive market advantages.

The global market is also fuelling the growth of strategic alliances. A **strategic alliance** is a long-term partnership between two or more companies established to help each company build competitive market advantages. Unlike joint ventures, strategic alliances do not share costs, risks, management, or even profits. Thanks to their flexibility, strategic alliances can effectively link firms from different countries and firms of vastly different sizes. Strategic alliances with Daimler AG and Toyota were crucial to Tesla helping to ensure early success for the company. A later alliance with Panasonic was a major boost in assisting with the company's battery technology.[37]

Foreign Direct Investment

foreign direct investment (FDI) The buying of permanent property and businesses in foreign nations.

foreign subsidiary A company owned in a foreign country by the parent company.

Foreign direct investment (FDI) is buying permanent property and businesses in foreign nations. As the size of a foreign market expands, many firms increase FDI and establish a foreign subsidiary. A **foreign subsidiary** is a company owned in a foreign country by another company (called the *parent company*). The subsidiary operates like a domestic firm, with production, distribution, promotion, pricing, and other business functions under the control of the subsidiary's management. The subsidiary must observe the legal requirements of both the country where the parent firm is located (called the *home country*) and the foreign country where the subsidiary is located (called the *host country*).

The primary advantage of a subsidiary is that the company maintains complete control over any technology or expertise it may possess. The major shortcoming is the need to commit funds and technology within foreign boundaries. Should relationships with a host country falter, the firm's assets could be *expropriated* (taken over by the foreign government). Swiss-based Nestlé has many foreign subsidiaries. The consumer-products giant spent billions of dollars acquiring foreign subsidiaries such as Jenny Craig (weight management), Gerber Baby Foods, Ralston Purina, Chef America (maker of Hot Pockets), Libby Foods, and Dreyer's and Häagen-Dazs Ice Cream in the United States as well as Perrier in France. Nestlé employs over 333 000 people in 86 countries and has operations in almost every country in the world.[38]

multinational corporation An organization that manufactures and markets products in many different countries and has multinational stock ownership and multinational management.

Nestlé is a **multinational corporation**, one that manufactures and markets products in many different countries and has multinational stock ownership and management. Multinational corporations are typically extremely large corporations like Nestlé, but not all large global businesses are multinationals. A business could export everything it produces, deriving 100 percent of its sales and profits globally, and still not be a multinational corporation. Only firms that have *manufacturing capacity* or some other physical presence in different nations, such as Magna International, can truly be called multinational. Figure 3.7 lists the ten largest multinational corporations in the world.

Canadian subsidiaries of foreign-based companies have played a major role in developing the Canadian economy. There are, however, several disadvantages to foreign investment. One is that Canada has been criticized for having a "branch plant economy." This occurs when many subsidiaries are owned by foreign companies and profits are returned to the home country rather than reinvested in Canada. A second concern is the outright purchase of Canadian companies, where non-Canadian companies gain more control of the economic activity within Canada.

Investment Canada Act Legislation that provides rules to review significant investment in Canada by non-Canadians.

During the past decade the degree of Chinese ownership among Canadian companies has increased, particularly in sensitive industries such as health care, oil and gas, natural resources, and technology. However, questions have been raised whether this change is best for Canada's economic interests.[39] The **Investment Canada Act** provides the rules

■ **FIGURE 3.7**

THE LARGEST MULTINATIONAL CORPORATIONS IN THE WORLD (USD)

Company	Country	Revenue
1. Walmart Stores	United States	$482,130,000
2. State Grid	China	$329,691,000
3. China National Petroleum	China	$299,271,000
4. Sinopec Group	China	$294,344,000
5. Royal Dutch Shell	Netherlands	$272,156,000
6. Exxon Mobil	United States	$246,204,000
7. Volkswagon	Germany	$236,600,000
8. Toyota Motor	Japan	$236,592,000
9. Apple	United States	$233,715,000
10. BP	Great Britain	$225,982,000

Source: *Fortune*, www.fortune.com, accessed June 2017.

to review significant investments in Canada by non-Canadians.[40] However, the federal government has loosened these rules and approved various purchases.

There are several examples of non-Canadian purchases of shares in Canadian companies in the past decade. For example, the 2017 purchase of Retirement Concepts, a Vancouver-based retirement home chain, by Cedar Tree Investments Canada (owned by China's Anbang Insurance), which gave Chinese owners an entry into the Canadian healthcare sector.[41] In 2013, Nexen Inc., a Canadian oil and gas company, was sold to the Chinese National Offshore Oil Corporation (CNOOC).[42] PetroChina purchased Encana Corporation's shale gas property in northern British Columbia in 2011, which raised concerns that the deal was designed to lock up the supply of gas, at a relatively low price, and move it to China.[43] Finally, the purchase of Norsat International, a high-tech firm that sells satellite equipment, by Chinese-owned Hytera Communications was approved in 2017.[44] Should the federal government be flexible or firm on the foreign ownership of Canada in companies? Should certain industries be protected more than others?

© Cole Burston/Bloomberg via Getty Images

While Chinese ownership of Canadian companies has increased during the past decade, the federal government does have the power to reject purchases by non-Canadians. The decision to veto the purchase of Aecon Group Inc., a Canadian construction company, by China Communications Construction Co. Ltd. (CCCC) demonstrates the sensitive nature of these transactions.[45] Do you consider federal government review of foreign ownership a deals important to protect Canadian interests?

In the early 1990s, Michael Porter, the competition guru from Harvard University Business School, released a report titled *The Competitive Advantage of Nations* that was commissioned by the Canadian government. While this report is now 25 years old, some of his points still ring true today:

> *One of Canada's competitive problems is the high concentration of foreign-owned firms that perform little sophisticated production or R&D. It matters a lot where a multinational calls home, because a company's home base is where the best jobs exist, where core R&D is undertaken, and where strategic control rests. . . . Home bases are important to an economy because they support high productivity and productivity growth.*

Regardless of these concerns, more countries are welcoming subsidiaries as a way to develop their economies.

Getting involved in global business requires selecting an entry strategy that best fits your business goals. The different strategies discussed reflect different levels of ownership, financial commitment, and risk. However, this is just the beginning. You should also be aware of market forces that affect a business' ability to trade in global markets. After the Progress Assessment, we will discuss them.

PROGRESS ASSESSMENT

- What are the advantages to a firm of using licensing as a method of entry in global markets? What are the disadvantages?
- What is the key difference between a joint venture and a strategic alliance?
- What makes a company a multinational corporation?

LO4

Evaluate the forces that affect trading in global markets.

Forces Affecting Trading in Global Markets

The hurdles to success are higher and more complex in global markets than in domestic markets. Such hurdles include dealing with differences in sociocultural forces, economic and financial forces, legal forces, and physical and environmental forces. Let's take a look at each of these global market forces to see how they challenge even the most established and experienced global businesses.

culture
The set of values, beliefs, rules, and institutions held by a specific group of people.

ethnocentricity
An attitude that one's own culture is superior to all others.

Sociocultural Forces

The word **culture** refers to the set of values, beliefs, rules, and institutions held by a specific group of people.[46] Culture can also include social structures, religion, manners and customs, values and attitudes, language, and personal communication. An attitude that one's own culture is superior to all others is known as **ethnocentricity**. If you hope to get involved in global trade, it is critical to be aware of the cultural differences among nations.

Different nations have very different ways of conducting business. Canadian businesses that wish to compete globally must adapt to those ways. In North America, we like to do things quickly. We tend to call each other by our first names and try to get friendly even on the first encounter. In Japan, China, and other countries these actions would be considered surprising and even rude. Canadian negotiators will say no if they mean no, but Japanese negotiators usually say maybe when they mean no.

Religion is an important part of any society's culture and can have a significant impact on business operations. Consider the violent clashes between religious communities in India, Pakistan, Northern Ireland, and the Middle East—clashes that have wounded these areas' economies. Companies sometimes ignore religious implications in business decisions. Both McDonald's and Coca-Cola offended Muslims in Saudi Arabia by putting the Saudi Arabian flag on their packaging. The flag's design contains a passage from the Quran (Islam's sacred scripture), and Muslims feel that their holy writ should never be wadded up and thrown away.

© Keith Homan/Alamy Stock Photo

Formed in 1994, Spin Master Toys is the 4th largest toy manufacturer in the United States. The company was formed in 1994 by two young entrepreneurs straight out of university. Since then they have grown from a "single product toy company into a leading global, diversified, multi-platform and highly innovative children's entertainment company." What social trends do you think impact the toy industry? How might demographic trends around the world influence Spin Master Toys' future marketplace?[47]

Successful companies are those that can understand these differences and develop goods and services accordingly. Regardless of whether the focus is a large or small global market, understanding sociocultural differences is important when managing employees. In Latin American countries, workers believe that managers are placed in positions of authority to make decisions and be responsible for the well-being of their workers. Consider what happened to one North American manager in Peru who was unaware of this characteristic and believed that workers should participate in managerial functions. This manager was convinced that he could motivate his workers to higher levels of productivity by instituting a more democratic decision-making style than the one already in place. Soon workers began quitting their jobs in droves. When asked why, the workers said the new manager did not know his job and was asking the workers what to do. All stated that they wanted to find new jobs, since obviously this company was doomed due to incompetent managers.

Many companies still fail to think globally. A sound philosophy is: *Never assume that what works in one country will work in another.* Companies such as Roots, Nike, and Toyota have developed brand names with widespread global appeal and recognition. However, even these successful global marketers often face difficulties.[48] To get an idea of the problems companies have faced with advertising translations, take a look at Figure 3.8.

■ **FIGURE 3.8**

OOPS, DID WE SAY THAT?

A global marketing strategy can be very difficult to implement. Look at the problems these well-known companies encountered in global markets.

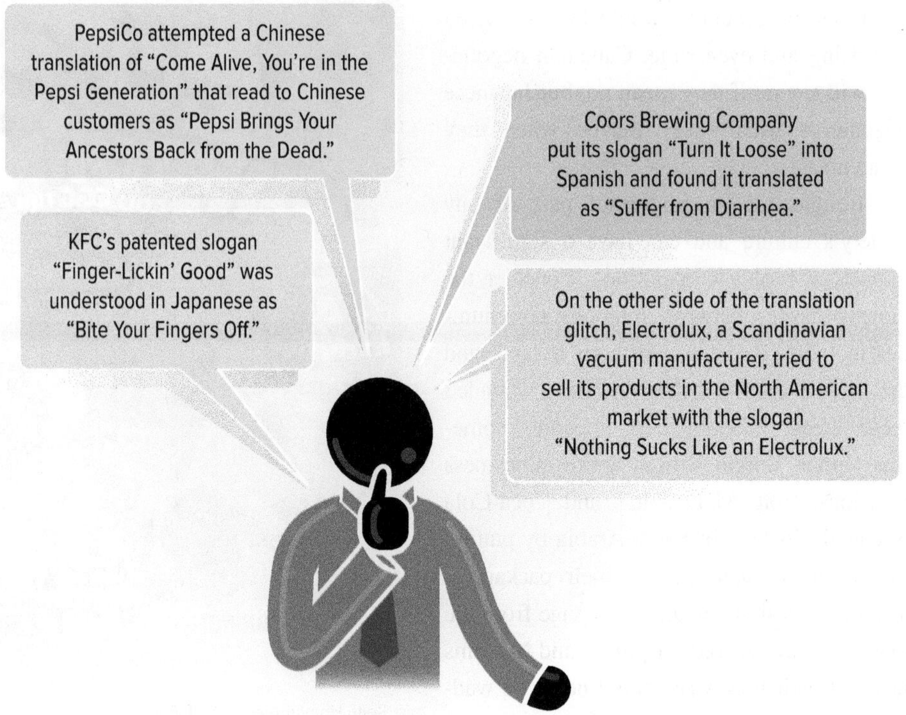
PepsiCo attempted a Chinese translation of "Come Alive, You're in the Pepsi Generation" that read to Chinese customers as "Pepsi Brings Your Ancestors Back from the Dead."
KFC's patented slogan "Finger-Lickin' Good" was understood in Japanese as "Bite Your Fingers Off."
Coors Brewing Company put its slogan "Turn It Loose" into Spanish and found it translated as "Suffer from Diarrhea."
On the other side of the translation glitch, Electrolux, a Scandinavian vacuum manufacturer, tried to sell its products in the North American market with the slogan "Nothing Sucks Like an Electrolux."

Economic and Financial Forces

Economic differences can also make entering global markets more challenging. In Qatar, annual per capita income is almost $130,000, the highest in the world. In economically strapped Haiti, per capita income is barely over $1,800.[49] It is hard for us to imagine buying chewing gum by the stick instead of by the package. Yet this buying behaviour is commonplace in economically depressed nations like Haiti, where customers can afford only small quantities. You might suspect with over 1.2 billion potential customers, India would be a dream market for Coca-Cola. Unfortunately, Indians consume only 12 eight-ounce bottles of Coke per person a year due to low per-capita income. The same is true in the booming beauty and personal care market in India. Cosmetic giant L'Oréal sells primarily small, sample sizes of shampoo, tiny tubes of men's face wash, and petite pouches of Garnier hair colour due to low incomes.[50]

Global financial markets unfortunately do not have a worldwide currency. Mexicans shop with pesos, South Koreans with won, Japanese with yen, and Canadians with dollars. Globally, the U.S. dollar is considered a dominant and stable currency.[51] However, it does not always retain the same market value.[52] In an international transaction today, one dollar may be exchanged for eight pesos; tomorrow, you may only get seven. The **exchange rate** is the value of one nation's currency relative to the currencies of other countries.

exchange rate The value of one nation's currency relative to the currencies of other countries.

Changes in a nation's exchange rates can have important implications in global markets. A *high value of the dollar* means that a dollar would be traded for more foreign currency than normal. The products of foreign producers would be cheaper because it takes fewer dollars to buy them, but the cost of Canadian-produced goods would become more expensive to foreign purchasers because of the dollar's high value. Conversely, a *low value of the dollar* means that a dollar is traded for less foreign currency than normal. Therefore, foreign goods become more expensive because it takes more dollars to buy them, but Canadian goods become cheaper to foreign buyers because it takes less foreign currency to buy Canadian goods.

Global financial markets operate under a system called *floating exchange rates,* in which currencies "float" according to the supply and demand for them in the global market for the currency. This supply and demand is created by global currency traders, who develop a market for a nation's currency based on the perceived trade and investment potential of the country.

devaluation
Lowering the value of a nation's currency relative to other currencies.

countertrading
A complex form of bartering in which several countries may be involved, each trading goods for goods or services for services.

Changes in currency values cause many problems globally.[53] For instance, labour costs for multinational corporations like Bombardier, Nestlé, General Electric, and Sony can vary considerably as currency values shift, causing them to juggle production from one country to another.

Currency valuation problems can be especially harsh on developing economies. At certain times a nation's government will intervene and adjust the value of its currency, often to increase the export potential of its products. **Devaluation** is lowering the value of a nation's currency relative to other currencies. Argentina and Venezuela both devalued their currencies in 2014 to try to alleviate severe economic problems in each country.[54] Unfortunately, the move did little to solve the country's problems. Inflation in Venezuela is expected to hit 1600 percent in 2017[55] (see Chapter 2). Sometimes, due to a nation's weak currency, the only way to trade is *bartering,* which is the exchange of merchandise for other merchandise, or service for other service, with no money involved.[56]

Countertrading is a complex form of bartering in which several countries may be involved, each trading goods for goods or services for services. Let's say that a developing country such as Jamaica wants to buy vehicles from Ford Motor Company in exchange for bauxite, a mineral compound that is a source of aluminum ore. Ford does not need Jamaican bauxite, but does need compressors. In a counter-trade agreement, Ford may trade vehicles to Jamaica, which then trades bauxite to another country —say, India—which then exchanges compressors with Ford. All three parties benefit in the process, and avoid some of the financial problems and currency constraints in global markets. Estimates are that countertrading accounts for over 20 percent of all global exchanges, especially with developing countries.[57]

© SkyF/iStock/Thinkstock

When the dollar is "up," foreign goods and travel are a bargain for Canadian consumers. When the dollar trades for less foreign currency, however, foreign tourists (like these viewing Niagara Falls) often flock to Canadian cities to enjoy relatively cheaper vacations and shopping trips. Do Canadian exporters profit more when the dollar is up or when it is down?

Legal Forces

In any economy, the conduct and the direction of business are firmly tied to the legal environment. In Canada, federal and provincial laws heavily affect business practices. In global markets, the absence of a central system of law means many different systems of laws may apply. This makes conducting global business difficult as business people navigate a sea of laws that are often inconsistent. Antitrust rules, labour relations, patents, copyrights, trade practices, taxes, child labour, product liability, and other issues are governed differently country by country. The Making Ethical Decisions box questions selling products in a global market with a different legal system.

Canadian businesses must follow Canadian laws in conducting business globally. For example, bribery is not considered legal in Canada. The problem is that this runs contrary to beliefs and practices in many countries where corporate or government bribery not only is acceptable, but also may be the only way to secure a lucrative contract. The Organisation for Economic Co-operation and Development (OECD) and Transparency International have led a global effort to fight corruption and bribery in foreign markets, with limited success.[58] Figure 3.9 shows a partial list of countries where bribery or other unethical business practices are most common.

The co-operation and sponsorship of local business people can help a company penetrate the market and deal with laws and bureaucratic barriers in their country.

Physical and Environmental Forces

Certain technological forces can also have an important impact on a company's ability to conduct business in global markets. In fact, technological constraints may make it difficult given the nature of exportable products. For example, houses in most developing countries do not have electrical systems that match those of Canadian homes, in kind or in capacity. How would the differences in electricity available (110 versus 220 volts) affect a Canadian appliance manufacturer wishing to export?

Also, computer and Internet usage in many developing countries is rare or nonexistent. You can see how this would make for a challenging business environment in general and would make e-commerce difficult, especially as this is becoming a critical element of business. After the Progress Assessment, we will explore how trade protectionism affects global business.

FIGURE 3.9

COUNTRIES RATED HIGHEST ON CORRUPT BUSINESS

The corruption perceptions index ranks countries and territories according to their perceived level of public sector (government) corruption. This list starts with the most corrupt countries.

1. Somalia
2. South Sudan
3. North Korea
4. Syria
5. Yemen
6. Sudan
7. Libya
8. Afganistan
9. Venezuela
10. Iraq
165. Canada (9th least corrupt country in the world)
174. Denmark (least corrupt country in the world)

Source: Transparency International, 2017.

Making ETHICAL DECISIONS

Exporting Your Problems Away

As the top manager of Nighty Nite, a maker of children's sleepwear, you received notification from the Health Canada that the fabric you use in your girl's nightgowns has been deemed unsafe. A study of the product was conducted after a child was seriously burned while wearing a nightgown that burst into flames when she ventured too close to a gas stove. Health Canada ruled the material used did not have sufficient flame-retardant capabilities to meet Canadian standards. Your company was instructed to immediately remove the product from store shelves and issue a product recall.

© Blend Images - Erik Isakson/Getty Images

This is a tough blow for the company since the nightgowns are popular and sell well in the market. Plus, you have a large supply of the product in your warehouse that now is just taking up space. A big financial loss for the company is likely.

Your sales manager reminds you that many countries do not have such strict product laws as Canada. He suggests the product could be exported to a country with less stringent product safety rules. Exporting the product to another country would solve your inventory and profit concerns, but you wonder about sending a product deemed unsafe in Canada to children in another market. What are the consequences of each alternative? What will you do?

PROGRESS ASSESSMENT

- What are the major hurdles to successful global trade?
- What does ethnocentricity mean, and how can it affect global success?
- How would the low value of the dollar affect Canadian exports?

LO5

Debate the advantages and disadvantages of trade protectionism, define tariff and non-tariff barriers, and give examples of common markets.

Trade Protectionism

As we discussed in the previous section, sociocultural, economic and financial, legal, and physical and environmental forces are all challenges to global trade. What is often a much greater barrier to global trade, however, is trade protectionism. **Trade protectionism** is the use of government regulations to limit the import of goods and services. Supporters of trade protectionism believe that it allows domestic producers to survive and grow, producing more jobs. Those against trade protectionism argue that it not only impedes global trade, but that it also adds millions of dollars to the price of products, costing consumers billions of dollars.

trade protectionism
The use of government regulations to limit the import of goods and services.

Countries often use protectionist measures to guard against practices such as dumping. **Dumping** is selling products in a foreign country at lower prices than those charged in the producing country. This tactic is sometimes used to reduce surplus products in foreign markets or to gain a foothold in a new market. Some governments may offer financial

dumping
Selling products in a foreign country at lower prices than those charged in the producing country.

© Elenathewise/Getty Images

Business leaders believe that too many sales have been lost due to the growing number of imported products. This is the case in the renewable energy industry where Canada placed a tariff on cheap Chinese-made solar panels.[60] While the change protects Canadian companies, will it slow the development of solar projects in Canada?

incentives to certain industries to sell goods in global markets for less than they sell them at home. China and Taiwan for example, were found guilty of dumping solar panels in the United States.[59] To understand how trade protectionism affects global business, let's briefly review some global economic history.

Business, economics, and politics have always been closely linked. What we now call economics was once referred to as the *political* economy, indicating the close ties between politics (government) and economics. In the seventeenth and eighteenth centuries, business people and governments advocated an economic policy called *mercantilism.* The overriding idea of mercantilism was for a nation to sell more goods to other nations than it bought from them; that is, to have a favourable balance of trade. According to the mercantilists, this resulted in a flow of money to the country that sold the most globally. This philosophy led governments to implement **tariffs**, which are taxes on imports, thus making imported goods more expensive to buy.

tariff
A tax imposed on imports.

There are two kinds of tariffs: protective and revenue. *Protective tariffs* (import taxes) are designed to raise the retail price of imported products so that domestic products will have a more competitive price. These tariffs are meant to save jobs for domestic workers and to keep industries—especially infant industries that have companies in the early stages of growth—from closing down entirely because of foreign competition. Such tariffs are usually met with resistance. Sometimes a tariff affects products and services indirectly. For example, in a dispute over labelling laws the World Trade Organization has ruled that American beef producers have an unfair advantage over Canadian producers. As discussed early in this chapter, Canada needs to increase its exports to other countries but in doing so Canadian businesses may be subject to tariffs. For example, past U.S. protective tariff policy, which raised the price of Canadian-made beef sold in the United States, reduced sales and costs Canada's beef and pork industries more than $1 billion a year.[61] *Revenue tariffs,* the second kind of tariff, are designed to raise money for the government.

© REUTERS/Paul Darrow

Believing that the annual seal hunt off the East Coast is inhumane, the European Union has imposed an import ban (or trade embargo) on all products from Canada's seal hunt. The Canadian government believes that it is a trade law violation and has appealed this decision to the World Trade Organization. Which perspective do you support?

An **import quota** limits the number of products in certain categories that a nation can import. Canada has import quotas on a number of products including textiles and clothing, agricultural products, steel, and softwood lumber.[62] The goal is to protect Canadian companies and to preserve jobs. Products subject to export controls include softwood lumber, firearms, sugar and sugar-containing products, peanut butter, and B.C. logs.[63] The Canadian Export and Import Control Bureau sets various regulations regarding import controls (goods and services entering Canada) and export controls (goods and services exiting Canada) in accordance with the Export and Import Permits Act (EIPA).

import quota
A limit on the number of products in certain categories that a nation can import.

An **embargo** is a complete ban on the import or export of a certain product or the stopping of all trade with a particular country. Political disagreements have caused many countries to establish embargoes, such as Canada's embargo against North Korea, reflecting its condemnation of the North Korean regime's complete disregard for human rights and ongoing repression of the democratic movement.[64]

embargo
A complete ban on the import or export of a certain product or the stopping of all trade with a particular country.

Non-tariff barriers are not as specific or formal as tariffs, import quotas, and embargoes but can be as detrimental to free trade.[65] Such barriers include restrictive standards that detail exactly how a product must be sold in a country. For example, India imposes a number of restrictive standards like import licensing, burdensome product testing requirements, and lengthy customs procedures that inhibit the sale of imported products. The discovery of mad cow disease resulted in a temporary import ban of Canadian beef by Taiwan, Peru, Belarus, China, and other countries.[66]

General Agreement on Tariffs and Trade (GATT)
A 1948 agreement that established an international forum for negotiating mutual reductions in trade restrictions.

Would-be exporters might view trade barriers as good reasons to avoid global trade, but overcoming trade constraints creates business opportunities. Next, we'll look at organizations and agreements that attempt to eliminate barriers.

The GATT and the WTO

In 1948, government leaders from 23 nations formed the **General Agreement on Tariffs and Trade (GATT)**, a global forum for reducing trade restrictions on goods, services, ideas, and cultural programs. In 1986, the Uruguay Round of the GATT convened to renegotiate trade agreements. After eight years of meetings, 124 nations voted to lower tariffs an average of 38 percent worldwide, and expand new trade rules to areas such as agriculture, services, and the protection of patents.

The Uruguay Round also established the **World Trade Organization (WTO)** to mediate trade disputes among nations. The WTO, headquartered in Geneva, Switzerland, is an independent entity of 164 member nations, and its purpose is to oversee cross-border trade issues and global business practices among those nations.[67] Trade disputes are presented by member nations with decisions made within a year, rather than languishing for years, as in the past.

The WTO has not solved all global trade problems. Legal differences (discussed earlier) often impede

© Jonathan Hayward/TCPI/The Canadian Press

Canada's long dispute with the United States over softwood lumber cost the economy billions of dollars and thousands of jobs. In 2002, the United States imposed duties of 27 percent on Canadian softwood lumber, arguing that Canada unfairly subsidized producers of spruce, pine, and fir lumber. While international trade tribunals sided with Canada, it was not until 2006 that an agreement between both countries was signed. The United States agreed to return over $4.5 billion in duties it had collected and remove tariffs on lumber. In 2017, the ongoing challenges of the softwood lumber dispute led Canada to file a wide-ranging complaint with other trade concerns to the WTO.[68]

© Sam Panthaky/AFP/Getty Images

In the past, this Indian family used to use bullocks to pull their plow, but had to sell them because the cost to maintain the animals is now too high. Do you think a Doha resolution regarding tariff protection would help families like these?

trade expansion. And a wide gap separates developing nations (80 percent of the WTO membership) and industrialized nations like Canada. The WTO meetings in Doha, Qatar, began in 2001 to address dismantling protection of manufactured goods, eliminating subsidies on agricultural products, and overturning temporary protectionist measures. Unfortunately, the Doha Round ended in 2008 with no significant agreements.[69]

The IMF and the World Bank

The **International Monetary Fund (IMF)** was created in 1944. The IMF is an international bank supported by its members that usually makes short-term loans to countries experiencing problems with their balance of trade. The IMF's basic objectives are to promote exchange stability, maintain orderly exchange arrangements, avoid competitive currency depreciation, establish a multilateral system of payments, eliminate exchange restrictions, and create standby reserves. The IMF makes long-term loans at low interest rates to the world's most destitute nations to help them strengthen their economies. The function of the IMF is very similar to that of the World Bank.

The **World Bank**, an autonomous United Nations agency, is concerned with developing infrastructure (e.g., roads, schools, hospitals, power plants, etc.) in less-developed countries. The World Bank borrows from more prosperous countries and lends at favourable rates to less-developed countries. (In recent years, the IMF and the World Bank have forgiven some loans to highly indebted countries, such as Guinea.) To qualify for the program, numerous macroeconomic policies (such as inflation and poverty reduction) have to be implemented. These new requirements allow the lending organizations to continue to fulfill their objectives.

Some countries believe that their economies will be strengthened if they establish formal trade agreements with other countries. Some of these agreements, involving forming producers' cartels and common markets, are discussed next.

World Trade Organization (WTO)
The international organization that replaced the General Agreement on Tariffs and Trade, and was assigned the duty to mediate trade disputes among nations.

International Monetary Fund (IMF)
An international bank that makes short-term loans to countries experiencing problems with their balance of trade.

World Bank
An autonomous United Nations agency that borrows money from the more prosperous countries and lends it to less-developed countries to develop their infrastructure.

producers' cartels
Organizations of commodity-producing countries that are formed to stabilize or increase prices to optimize overall profits in the long run.

Producers' Cartels

Producers' cartels are organizations of commodity-producing countries. They are formed to stabilize or increase prices, in order to optimize profits over the long term. The most obvious example today is the Organization of the Petroleum Exporting Countries (OPEC). Similar attempts have been made to manage prices for copper, iron ore, bauxite, bananas, tungsten, rubber, and other important commodities. These cartels are all contradictions to unrestricted free trade and letting the market set prices.

Common Markets

An issue not resolved by the GATT or the WTO is whether common markets create regional alliances at the expense of global expansion. A **common market** (also called a **trading bloc**) is a regional group of countries that have a common external tariff, no internal tariffs, and the coordination of laws to facilitate exchange among member countries. Two examples are the United States-Mexico-Canada Agreement and the European Union. Let's look briefly at both.

common market (trading bloc)
A regional group of countries that have a common external tariff, no internal tariffs, and a coordination of laws to facilitate exchange; also called a trading bloc. An example is the European Union.

THE UNITED STATES-MEXICO-CANADA AGREEMENT (FORMERLY THE NORTH AMERICAN FREE TRADE AGREEMENT)

In North America, the **United States-Mexico-Canada Agreement (USMCA)** exists to coordinate trade among the three member countries—Canada, the United States, and Mexico. In order to examine how the USMCA impacts the Canadian economy, it is important to understand the origin of the agreement and trade issues that have arisen over time. These points are discussed next.

United States-Mexico-Canada Agreement (USMCA)
The agreement among three member-countries that coordinates trade. Replaces the NAFTA agreement.

A widely debated issue of the early 1990s was the ratification of the North American Free Trade Agreement (NAFTA), which created a free-trade area among Canada, the United States, and Mexico. In January 1993, NAFTA came into effect, replacing the previous Free Trade Agreement between Canada and the United States. The objectives of NAFTA were to (1) eliminate trade barriers and facilitate cross-border movement of goods and services among the three countries; (2) promote conditions of fair competition in this free-trade area; (3) increase investment opportunities in the territories of the three nations; (4) provide effective protection and enforcement of intellectual property rights (e.g., patents, copyrights, etc.) in each nation's territory; (5) establish a framework for further regional trade co-operation; and (6) improve working conditions in North America.

NAFTA was driven by the desire of Mexico to have greater access to the U.S. market. Improved access would spur economic growth, provide more employment for Mexicans, and raise the low standard of living in Mexico. The U.S. government hoped creating more jobs in Mexico would stop the flow of illegal immigrants who were crossing their border. Canada was really a minor player in the deal, but the Canadian government was concerned that it would be left out or penalized indirectly unless it joined the bloc. Canadians would see a small gain with freer access to the growing Mexican market, but the country was still a minor customer for Canada.

The NAFTA agreement permitted all three countries to reduce trade barriers with one another while maintaining independent trade agreements with other countries. The NAFTA timetable also set a date when the agreement would expire. During the time leading up to the expiry deadline, the three countries negotiated to work out exemptions, tariffs, and dispute-resolution procedures to handle trade disagreements. The politics of free trade change and the desire for a government to protect or open its economy through trade will vary, and that was the case as the agreement's expiry date approached.[70]

Officially, almost all trade in the region now flows tariff-free. Leaders from Canada, the United States, and Mexico meet to discuss several major areas of dispute. Many areas have yet to be resolved including trucking, immigration, the environment, and agricultural tariffs.

There was concern by some groups (e.g., unions) in Canada and the United States that NAFTA had contributed to employment losses and that economic benefits were not realized. Some Canadian business people remained opposed because they did not like many of the details in NAFTA. In addition, Mexico had a weak policy on environmental problems, poor working conditions, and a questionable record on human rights and political freedom. That country had repeatedly been condemned by many organizations in North America and abroad for serious flaws on all these counts. Some believed NAFTA had forced Mexico to gradually improve these conditions and saw signs of this happening, albeit slowly.

In was within this climate of both approval and disapproval for NAFTA that negotiations to renew the trade agreement began in 2017. In September 2018, NAFTA was replaced with a new free trade agreement called the United States-Mexico-Canada Agreement (USMCA). During the 14-month negotiation period, Canadian businesses were hesitant to implement long-term commitments because future access to the United States market was unclear. But when the agreement was finally reached, many argued it provided the certainty necessary to motivate investors to begin supporting the Canadian economy.[71]

At the time of this writing, the USMCA is a new trade agreement, and early reviews of its impact for Canada are both positive and negative. On one hand, the renewed agreement maintains the dispute-resolution system and the protection of cultural industries that were important to Canada within the previous NAFTA agreement.[72] It also provides Canadian consumers with more choice through easier access to goods and services from the U.S. along with lower duties.[73] On the other hand, the USMCA still allows protective tariffs, such as those the U.S. has imposed upon aluminum and steel from Canada, and import quotas in relation to the automotive industry.[74] In addition, the requirement that Canada must inform the United States of intentions to pursue trade negotiations with a non-market country raises alarms that Canada's autonomy to strengthen relations with existing trading partners, such as China, and new trading partners is reduced.[75]

In any trade agreement it is difficult to ensure all the interests of a country are met. Usually, trade negotiations strive for a balance, with negotiators, business leaders, and citizens understanding that there will be both benefits and costs to an agreement. In the early days of the new agreement, Canadian businesses will be looking to answer many questions. Does the USMCA open the American and Mexican markets for Canadian businesses? Or are the partner countries, particularly the U.S., able to implement a protectionist trade policy? What might be the overall impact of the USMCA upon the Canadian economy or upon specific industries, such as automotive and agriculture? The USMCA is a 16-year agreement with an option to extend it for an additional six years. The answers to these questions, and many others related to the original objectives of NAFTA—such as the elimination of trade barriers, free competition, and better working conditions—will only become evident over time.

THE EUROPEAN UNION

The EU began in the late 1950s as an alliance of six trading partners (then known as the Common Market and later the European Economic Community). Today it is a group of 28 nations (see Figure 3.10) with a combined population of over 510 million and a GDP of $16.5 trillion. Though the EU is represented as a unified body in the WTO, the economies of six members (Germany, France, United Kingdom, Italy, Spain, and the Netherlands) account for over three-fourths of the EU's GDP.

European unification was not easy, but in 1999 the EU took a significant step by adopting the euro as a common currency. The euro has helped EU businesses save billions by eliminating currency conversions and has challenged the U.S. dollar's dominance in

FIGURE 3.10

MEMBERS OF THE EUROPEAN UNION

Current EU members are highlighted in yellow. Countries that have applied for membership are in orange.

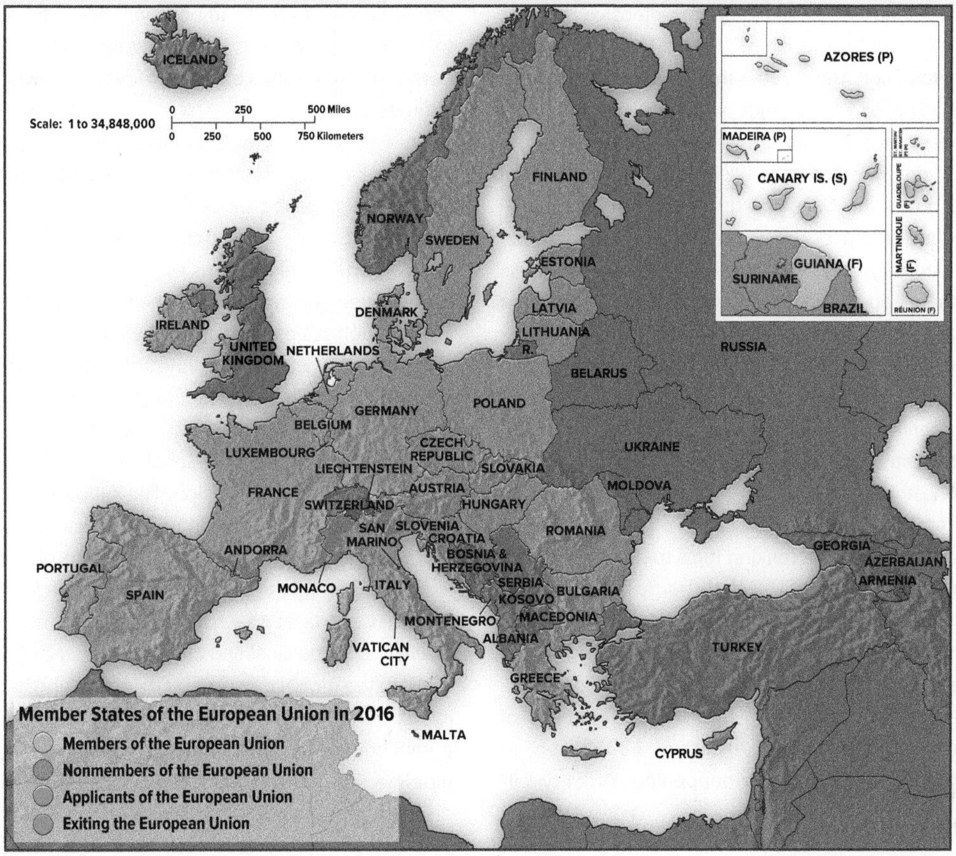

global markets. Eighteen member nations now use the euro as their common currency. In 2013, the EU faced debt, deficit, and growth problems due to financial difficulties in member nations Greece, Italy, Portugal, and Spain that required bailout assistance.[76] EU officials moved forward with broad economic policies to ensure the financial stability of the union.

The EU is facing the loss of a major member, the United Kingdom (UK). In 2016, the UK voted to leave the EU (an action called *Brexit,* a combination of the words *Britain* and *exit*). As of this writing, the UK has begun the process of exiting the EU. The UK is the first nation to withdraw from the EU.[77]

Even though the EU faces challenges going forward, it still considers continued economic integration among member nations as the way to compete globally against major competitors like the United States and China.

Just as it did with NAFTA, Canada negotiated the Canada–European Union Comprehensive Economic Trade Agreement (CETA) in order to provide preferential treatment for Canadian goods and services to enter the EU market[78] The Seeking Sustainability box

Seeking SUSTAINABILITY

The Politics of Oil

The tar-like bitumen has to be melted out of the ground and processed in a highly energy-intensive manner before it can be refined like regular oil. The U.S. Environmental Protection Agency says that "GHG emissions from the Canadian oil sands crude would be approximately 82 percent greater than the average crude refined in the U.S. on a well-to-tank basis." And in confidential briefing notes, the Canadian government has acknowledged that the emissions-per-barrel will likely increase as the industry is forced to pursue harder-to-access reserves deeper underground. Further expansion of the oil sands—which are the fastest growing source of greenhouse gas emissions in Canada, and the biggest energy project in the world—would lock Canada into a high-carbon economy for decades to come.

The EU has adopted a "Fuel Quality Directive" aimed at making those who sell and supply fuel reduce the carbon footprint of their products by 6 percent over the next decade. The EU is ranking fuels to help sellers and buyers identify those fuels with the largest carbon footprint. In line with that position, some members of the EU are pushing to rate oil sands fuel as more environmentally damaging than fuel from conventional crude oil.

The federal government and the government of Alberta lobbied the EU, at a cost of $30 million, to prevent the EU rating from happening. A "dirty oil" classification would amount to a European ban on oil sands crude. It would impose financial disincentives to discourage refiners and marketers from using fuel derived from oil sands bitumen in favour of lower-carbon sources of fuel.

In Fall 2014, the Canadian government's effort paid off. The EU voted not to impose a veto on Alberta bitumen (also called tar sands) oil. The decision was a setback in Europe and North America for supporters of low-carbon fuel regulations that are aimed at reducing greenhouse gas emissions in the transportation sector.

Although Canadian oil companies gained better access to the EU market, the ability to move Alberta bitumen deposits to other global markets remains delayed. U.S. President Barack Obama vetoed the Keystone pipeline and a U.S. Senate vote in March 2015 failed to overturn his decision. The Alberta government also faces difficulty in getting political leaders in British Columbia to support the Trans Mountain pipeline. The federal government purchased the pipeline from Kinder Morgan Canada, at a $4.5 million price tag, in an effort to alleviate both political and crude oil supply bottlenecks.

With the global demand for oil increasing, the inability of Canadian companies to access the market is a challenge. The debate of the merits of any type of pipeline creates opposing views. On one hand, government leaders could capitalize on the situation and create higher standards that ensure regulations are in place to keep oil companies honest while at the same time enable them to sell to global markets. On the other hand, environmental lobbyists believe the decision not to permit the pipeline will delay further oil sands investment and generate momentum toward a clean energy future.

How have the Canadian government and environmentalists reacted to the EU, United States, and interprovincial decisions? What are the economic and environmental implications of each decision?

© TODD KOROL/Reuters

Sources: Julie Gordon and Rod Nickel, "Canada dreams of sending its oil to Asia via Trans Mountain, but most of it will end up in California," *Financial Post*, June 27, 2018, accessed July 30, 2018, https://business.financialpost.com/commodities/energy/canada-dreams-of-oil-exports-to-asia-but-california-beckons; Glen Hodgson, "Can Canada remain an energy 'superpower'?" *The Globe and Mail*, September 26, 2017; Jonathan Waldman, "Don't kill Keystone XL. Regulate It," *The New York Times*, March 6, 2015, http://www.nytimes.com/2015/03/06/opinion/dont-kill-keystone-xl-regulate-it.html?ref=topics; Coral Davenport, "Senate fails to override Obama's Keystone Pipeline veto," *The New York Times*, March 4, 2015, http://www.nytimes.com/2015/03/05/us/senate-fails-to-override-obamas-keystone-pipeline-veto.html?ref=topics&_r=0; Mark Downie, "Keystone and the Riddle if the Tar Sands," *Newsweek*, February 25, 2015, http://www.newsweek.com/keystone-and-riddle-tar-sands-309522; Barbara Lewis, "EU lawmakers fail to approve tar sands oil veto," Reuters, December 17, 2014, http://www.reuters.com/article/2014/12/17/eu-energy-canada-idUSL6N0U12Q820141217; "Stopping the Keystone XL," Natural Resources Defense Council, accessed March 27, 2015, http://www.nrdc.org/; Lorne Gunter, "A European reprieve for Canada's oil sands," *The Globe and Mail*, February 24, 2012, A14.

outlines just some of the complexities of these agreements. For example, Canadian shrimp faced up to a 20 percent duty, making it more expensive for consumers and, therefore, less competitive compared to shrimp products from other countries. CETA eliminates this duty, making Canadian-produced shrimp more affordable in the EU and giving these businesses a 20 percent boost in competitiveness.[79]

OTHER TRADE AGREEMENTS [80]

According to Foreign Affairs, Trade and Development Canada, Canada is involved in 11 free-trade agreements (FTA) including the Canada–Korea FTA effective in 2015 and the Canada–Honduras FTA brought into effect in 2014. Negotiations for new FTAs are ongoing with many countries. For example, a Canada–Caribbean Community (CARICOM) agreement seeks to create new opportunities for Canadian business in sectors including manufacturing, agriculture and financial services. A Canada–India FTA presents estimated GDP gains from US$6–$15 billion for Canada and US$6–$12 billion for India with potential exports gains ranging between 36 to 60 percent for each country.

PROGRESS ASSESSMENT

- What are the advantages and disadvantages of trade protectionism?
- What is the difference between protective tariffs and revenue tariffs?
- What is the primary purpose of the WTO?
- State four objectives of NAFTA.
- What is the primary objective of a common market like the EU?

Globalization and Your Future

LO6 Discuss the changing landscape of the global market.

Not long ago, FDI in China was considered to be not worth the risk, but the value of Chinese trade has roughly doubled every four years over the last three decades.[81] In 2013, China attracted US$117 billion in FDI.[82] Today, over 400 of the Fortune 500 companies (the world's largest companies) have invested in China. According to Goldman Sachs Group and the London Center for Economic and Business Research, China could overtake the United States as the world's largest economy by 2028.[83]

Since 2009, China has been the largest motor vehicle market in the world with sales and production topping nearly 22 million vehicles in 2013.[84] It is estimated that by 2030, there could be more cars on the road in China than all the cars in the world today. Walmart began operations in China in 1996 and now has 443 stores with plans to open more. Even newcomers like IMAX Corporation are expanding in this fast-growing market. By 2021, it is expected that China will have 80 000 movie screens, which is twice the number in the United States, of which 575 will be IMAX 3D screens.[85]

Many view China as a free trader's dream, where global investment and entrepreneurship will lead to wealth. However, concerns remain about China's one-party political system, human rights abuses, currency issues, and increasing urban population growth. China's underground economy also generates significant product piracy and counterfeiting, although the country has been more responsive to these problems since its admission

© MIKE CASSESE/Reuters

Bombardier Inc. is the world's largest manufacturer of planes and trains. Its 2012–2033 market forecast shows a strategy to expand in markets including China, the Middle East, and Africa.[86] What challenges will the company have to address in order to enter these markets?

to the WTO. With the global economy continuing to grow, China will be a key driver of the world economy along with the United States, the EU, and Japan.

While China attracts most of the attention in Asia, India's population of 1.3 billion presents a tremendous opportunity. With nearly 575 million of its population under 25, India's working-age population will continue to grow while Canada expects a decline in the 2020s. Already India has seen huge growth in information technology and biotechnology, and its pharmaceutical business is expected to grow to $30 billion, a jump of over 150 percent by 2020. Still, it remains a nation with difficult trade laws and an inflexible bureaucracy.[87]

Russia is an industrialized nation with large reserves of oil, gas, and gold that became a member of the WTO in 2012. Multinationals like Chevron, ExxonMobil, and BP have invested heavily in developing Russia's oil reserves. However, Russia's economy slowed when world oil prices declined and the government admitted that growth prospects for the economy were not strong for the next two decades.[88] Unfortunately, Russia is plagued by political, currency, and social problems.

Brazil is an emerging nation that, along with China, India, and Russia, was projected to be one of the wealthier global economies by 2030. In fact, the term *BRIC* has been used as an acronym for the economies of Brazil, Russia, India, and China. Today, Brazil is the largest economy in South America and the seventh-largest economy in the world with well-developed agriculture, mining, manufacturing, and service sectors. Along with Russia, Brazil was expected to dominate the global market as a supplier of raw materials. China and India were predicted to be leading global suppliers of manufactured goods and services. Unfortunately, the past few years have been difficult for Brazil's economy with increasing inflation and slow growth. Still, its expanding consumer market of over 200 million people is a target for major exporters like the United States and China.

The BRIC economies are certainly not the only areas of opportunity in the global market. The developing nations of Asia, including Indonesia, Thailand, Singapore, the Philippines, Korea, Malaysia, and Vietnam, also offer great potential for Canadian businesses. Africa, especially South Africa, has only begun to emerge as a centre for global economic growth. Business today is truly global and your role in it is up to you.

As you learned in Chapter 1, outsourcing means contracting with other companies to do some or all of the functions of a firm, rather than providing them within the company. In Canada, companies have outsourced payroll functions, accounting, and some manufacturing operations for many years. However, the shift in outsourcing manufacturing and services from domestic businesses to primarily low-wage markets outside of Canada is getting more attention. This shift is referred to as offshoring. Take a look at the pros and cons of offshore outsourcing in Figure 3.11.

© Imaginechina/AP Images

China's economy is booming, and a highly educated middle class with money to spend is emerging, especially in the cities. Many observers believe China will continue its rapid growth and play a major role in the global economy. Are Canadian firms prepared to compete?

To remain competitive, Canada must focus on innovation and entrepreneurship. It is increasingly important for Canadian workers to obtain the proper education and training needed to stay ahead in the future. Whether you aspire to be an entrepreneur, a manager, or some other type of business leader, think globally in planning your career.

FIGURE 3.11

THE PROS AND CONS OF OFFSHORE OUTSOURCING

PROS	CONS
• Less strategic tasks can be outsourced globally so companies can focus on where they can excel and grow.	• Jobs are lost permanently and wages fall due to low-cost competition offshore.
• Outsource work allows companies to create efficiencies that in fact let them hire more workers.	• Offshoring may reduce product quality, which can cause permanent damage to a company's reputation.
• Consumers benefit from lower prices generated by effective use of global resources and developing nations grow, thus fuelling global economic growth.	• Communication within the company, with its suppliers, and with its customers becomes much more difficult.

Reaching *Beyond* OUR BORDERS

My Home Is Your Home

"Share your homes, but also share your world." This short statement formed the mission statement of Airbnb's founder Brian Chesky. He started Airbnb in San Francisco, targeting customers wanting to list or book accommodations as part of the growing sharing economy that allows owners to rent their homes or rooms to strangers. He believed his competitors in the travel industry had lost touch with their customers by providing only "cookie cutter" rooms in downtown areas. He felt such accommodations didn't allow travelers a real chance to "experience" the cities they visited. Today, Airbnb has 2 million listings across the globe with a company valuation of $25.5 billion, making it (on paper) the largest hotel chain in the world.

The company initially did extensive research to test if its "don't just go there, live there" message would resonate with potential users. The "live there" campaign focused on encouraging travelers to live like locals and experience the cities they visit like local residents. A social media marketing campaign using 3D technology delivered a new style of visual advertising. The video received 11 million views on Facebook, 56 000 "likes," and 5200 comments. The company also made effective use of Instagram by partnering with professional photographers to create images that had a smart design and message that clearly spoke to its target customers.

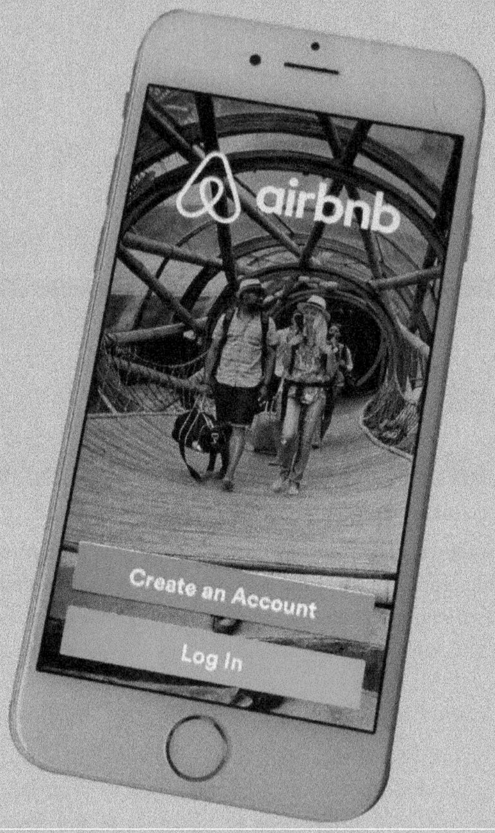

© digitallife/Alamy

This year, Airbnb is on track to book almost $1 billion in revenue, with projections rising to $10 billion per year by 2020. If you haven't already, check out Airbnb promotions and offers on its website.

Sources: Max Chafkin, "Airbnb Opens Up the World," *Fast Company,* February 2016; Katie Richards, "Put Away the Selfie-Stick and Act Like a Local, Urges Airbnb's New Campaign," *Ad Week,* April 19, 2016; Thales Teixeira and Michael Blanding, "How Uber, Airbnb, and Etsy Turned 1,000 Customers into a $1 Million," *Forbes,* November 16, 2016; www.airbnb.com, accessed September 2017.

By studying foreign languages, learning about foreign cultures, and taking business courses (including a global business course), you can develop a global perspective on your future. As you progress through this text, keep two things in mind: globalization is real, and economic competition promises to intensify.

Also keep in mind that global market potential does not belong only to large, multinational corporations, as the Reaching Beyond Our Borders box describes. Small and medium-sized businesses have a world of opportunity in front of them. In fact, these firms are often better prepared to leap into global markets and react quickly to opportunities than are large firms. Finally, don't forget the potential of franchising, which we will examine in more detail in Chapter 6.

PROGRESS ASSESSMENT

- How has the Internet affected doing business in global markets?
- What are the economic risks of doing business in countries like China?
- What might be some important factors that will have an impact on global trading?
- What can you do in the next few years to ready yourself for a career in global business?

SUMMARY

LO1 **Describe the importance of the global market and the roles of comparative advantage and absolute advantage in global trade.**

Canada has a population of more than 37 million people. The world market for trade is huge. Over 99 percent of the people in the world live outside Canada. Major Canadian companies routinely cite expansion to global markets as a route to future growth.

Why should nations trade with other nations?

Nations should trade globally as (1) no country is self-sufficient, (2) other countries need products that prosperous countries produce, and (3) natural resources and technological skills are not distributed evenly around the world.

What is the theory of comparative advantage?

The theory of comparative advantage contends that a country should make and then sell those products it produces most efficiently but buy those it cannot produce as efficiently.

What is absolute advantage?

Absolute advantage means that a country has a monopoly on a certain product or can produce the product more efficiently than any other country. There are few examples of absolute advantage in the global market today.

LO2 **Explain the importance of importing and exporting, and define key terms used in global business.**

Anyone can get involved in world trade through importing and exporting. Business people do not have to work for big multinational corporations.

What kinds of products can be imported and exported?

Just about any kind of product can be imported and exported. Companies can sometimes find surprising ways to succeed in either activity. Selling in global markets is not necessarily easy, though.

What terms are important in understanding world trade?

Exporting is selling goods and services to other countries. Importing is buying goods and services from other countries. The balance of trade is the relationship of exports to imports. The balance of payments is the balance of trade plus other money flows such as tourism and foreign aid. Dumping is selling products for less in a foreign country than in your own country. See the Key Terms list after this Summary to be sure you know the other important terms.

LO3 **Illustrate the strategies used in reaching global markets, and explain the role of multinational corporations in global markets.**

A company can participate in world trade in a number of ways.

What are some ways in which a company can get involved in global business?

Ways of entering world trade include licensing, exporting, franchising, contract manufacturing, joint ventures and strategic alliances, foreign direct investment, and sovereign wealth funds.

How do multinational corporations differ from other companies that participate in global business?

Unlike other companies that are involved in exporting or importing, multinational corporations also have manufacturing facilities or some other type of physical presence in different nations.

LO4 **Evaluate the forces that affect trading in global markets.**

The forces include sociocultural, economic and financial, and legal. Each can be examined in detail to determine their impact in various global markets.

What are some of the forces that can discourage participation in global business?

Potential stumbling blocks to global trade include sociocultural forces (e.g., religion), economic and financial forces (e.g., disposable income), legal forces (e.g., laws on bribery), and physical and environmental forces (e.g., Internet usage).

LO5 **Debate the advantages and disadvantages of trade protectionism, define tariff and non-tariff barriers, and give examples of common markets.**

Political differences are often the most difficult hurdles to international trade.

What is trade protectionism?

Trade protectionism is the use of government regulations to limit the import of goods and services. Supporters believe that it allows domestic producers to survive and grow, producing more jobs. The key tools of protectionism are tariffs, import quotas, and embargoes.

What are tariff and non-tariff barriers?

Tariffs are taxes on foreign products. There are two kinds of tariffs: (1) protective tariffs, which are used to raise the price of foreign products, and (2) revenue tariffs, which are used to raise money for the government. Non-tariff barriers include safety, health, and labelling standards.

What are some examples of trade organizations that try to eliminate trade barriers and facilitate trade among nations?

The World Trade Organization (WTO) replaced the General Agreement on Tariffs and Trade (GATT). The purpose of the WTO is to mediate trade disputes among nations. The International Monetary Fund (IMF) is an international bank that makes short-term loans to countries experiencing problems with their balance of trade. The World Bank is a United Nations agency that borrows money from the more prosperous countries and lends it to less-developed countries to develop their infrastructures.

What is a common market? State some examples.

A common market is a regional group of countries that have a common external tariff, no internal tariff, and a coordination of laws to facilitate exchange. The idea behind a common market is the elimination of trade barriers that existed prior to the creation of this bloc. Examples include USMCA and the EU.

LO6 **Discuss the changing landscape of the global market.**

The landscape of global business is changing and it is important for graduates to learn about global market trends in order to consider possible career options.

How is business changing?

New and expanding markets present great potential for trade and development. For example, changes in technology, especially through the Internet, allow access to global customers.

What countries offer opportunities for Canadian businesses?

Expanding markets such as China, India, Brazil, and Russia present great potential for trade and development.

KEY TERMS

absolute advantage 106
balance of payments 111
balance of trade 109
common market (trading bloc) 128
comparative advantage theory 106
contract manufacturing 115
countertrading 123
culture 120
devaluation 123
dumping 125
embargo 127
ethnocentricity 120
exchange rate 122
exporting 105
foreign direct investment (FDI) 118
foreign subsidiary 118
free trade 105
General Agreement on Tariffs and Trade (GATT) 127
import quota 127
importing 105
Investment Canada Act 118
International Monetary Fund (IMF) 128
joint venture 117
licensing 113
multinational corporation 118
producers' cartels 128
strategic alliance 118
tariff 126
trade deficit 109
trade protectionism 125
trade surplus 109
trading bloc (common market) 128
United States-Mexico-Canada Agreement (USMCA) 129
World Bank 128
World Trade Organization (WTO) 127

CAREER EXPLORATION

If you are interested in pursuing a career in international business, here are a few to consider. Find out about the tasks performed, skills needed, pay, and opportunity outlook in these fields through Internet sites that include the Government of Canada Job Bank, Workopolis, Monster, CareerBuilder, Glassdoor, and Indeed, as well as through the Career Centre at your school.

- **Customs broker**—acts as a liaison between the federal government and import/export firms; handles the logistics of moving products across borders.
- **Translator**—converts information from one language into another language
- **Wholesale and manufacturing sales representative**—sells goods for wholesalers or manufacturers to businesses, government agencies, and other organizations in global markets.
- **Buyer and purchasing agent**—buys products and services for organizations to use or resell; evaluates suppliers, negotiates contracts, and reviews the quality of products.
- **Trade analyst**—researchers market data, analyzes trade data to generate strategic plans and policy within private and public sectors.

CRITICAL THINKING

1. About 99 percent of the world's population lives outside Canada, but many Canadian companies, especially small businesses, still do not engage in global trade. Why not? Do you think more small businesses will participate in global markets in the future? Why or why not?
2. What can businesses do to prevent unexpected problems in dealing with sociocultural, economic and financial, legal, and physical and environmental forces in global markets?
3. Countries like Canada that have a high standard of living are referred to as industrialized nations. Countries with a low standard of living and quality of life are called developing countries. (Terms formerly used were *underdeveloped* or *less-developed countries.*) What factors prevent developing nations from becoming industrialized nations?
4. How would you justify the use of revenue or protective tariffs in today's global market?

DEVELOPING CAREER SKILLS

Key: ● **Team** ★ **Analytic** ▲ **Communication** ⊡ **Technology**

▲ 1. Find out firsthand the impact of global trade on your life. How many different countries' names appear on the labels in your clothes? How many languages do your classmates speak? List the ethnic restaurants in your community. Are they family-owned or corporate chains?

★▲ 2. Prepare a short list of the advantages and disadvantages of trade protectionism. Share your ideas with others in the class and debate the following statement: Canada should increase trade protectionism to save Canadian jobs and companies.

●★⊡▲ 3. The economies of Ontario and British Columbia depend heavily on exports. Ontario relies primarily on trade to the United States and Europe, while British Columbia relies heavily on trade with Asia. In a group of four, research these statements. Use Excel to develop two graphs that break down the exporting countries that trade with each of these provinces. Present your findings to the class.

●★⊡▲ 4. In a group of four, list the top five Canadian-based multinationals. When researching, create a table that will include the following pieces of information: the company names, the year each was created, the number of global employees, the industry or industries in which they operate, annual revenues, and number of countries in which they have offices. Present your findings to the class.

●★▲ 5. Form an imaginary joint venture with three classmates and select a product, service, or idea to market to a specific country. Have each team member select a key global market force in that country (sociocultural, economic and financial, legal and regulatory, or physical and environmental) to research. Have each report his or her findings. Then, as a group, prepare a short explanation of whether the market is worth pursuing.

ANALYZING MANAGEMENT DECISIONS

The Challenge of Offshoring

Outsourcing, as noted in Chapter 1, is the process of assigning various functions, such as accounting, production, security, maintenance, and legal work to outside organizations. In Canada, companies have outsourced payroll functions, accounting, and some manufacturing operations for many years. However, the shift to primarily low-wage global markets, called offshoring (or offshore outsourcing), has become a major issue. Export Development Canada believes that there are about 4000 Canadian companies with some sort of overseas presence, an increase from 10 years ago.

Canadian companies such as Bombardier Inc. (manufactures state-of-the-art planes and trains) and Gildan Activewear Inc. (one of the world's largest T-shirt makers) have outsourced manufacturing offshore for years. Fundamentally, as lower-level manufacturing became more simplified, Canadian companies shifted focus from assembling products to design and architecture. Today, economists agree that we are moving into the "second wave" of offshoring that involves sizable numbers of skilled, well-educated middle-income workers in service-sector jobs such as accounting, law, financial and risk management, health care, and information technology that were thought to be safe from foreign market competition.

For example, the financial sector, including the Royal Bank of Canada, has been criticized for making its employees train the foreign workers hired to replace them. This shift is potentially more disruptive to the Canadian job market than was the first, which primarily involved manufacturing jobs. The pros and cons of offshoring were identified earlier in this chapter (see Figure 3.11). China and India are oftentimes named as country providers of offshoring. Currently, China is primarily involved with manufacturing at the low end of the technology scale, and India focuses on call centres, telemarketing, data entry, billing, and low-end software development. However, China is intent on developing advanced manufacturing technology and India has a deep pool of scientists, software engineers, chemists, accountants, lawyers, and physicians. The technology talent in these nations also keeps growing: China graduates 250 000 engineers each year and India about 150 000.

When you consider the impact of offshoring on Canada, research supports that more than two-thirds of imported services are from the United States, not China and India. A Statistics Canada paper finds that globalization and technology are the two key factors driving offshoring by Canadian companies. Services offshoring does not seem to affect productivity or employment. It does seem to reduce wages in the services-producing sector, though not in the goods-producing sector. Finally, on an industry-by-industry basis, rising offshoring of services seems to be associated with rising value-added activities. In the financial sector, for instance, low value-added activities such as general accounting are outsourced while high value-added activities such as strategizing are kept in-house and in-country.

Sources: "RBC Foreign Workers Controversy: No more replacing Canadians, bank vows," *Huffington Post Canada,* May 24, 2013, http://www.huffingtonpost.ca/2013/05/24/rbc-foreign-workers-hire-canadians_n_3332240.html; John Baldwin and Wulong Gu, "Offshoring and Outsourcing in Canada," Economic Analysis Research Paper Series, 11F0027M No. 055, Statistics Canada, http://www.statcan.gc.ca/pub/11f0027m/2008055/s7-eng.htm; Christine Dobby, "Offshore opportunities 'too good to pass up'," *The Financial* Post, November 22, 2011, FP16; William Watson, "Myth-Busting Offshoring," *National Post,* May 30, 2008, http://network.nationalpost.com/np/blogs/fpcomment/archive/2008/5/30/myth-busting-offshoring.aspx; Pete Engardio, "The Future of Outsourcing," *BusinessWeek,* January 30, 2006, 50–58; and Richard Ernsberger, "The Big Squeeze: A 'Second Wave' of Offshoring Could Threaten Middle-Income, White-Collar and Skilled Blue-Collar Jobs," *Newsweek International,* May 30, 2005.

Discussion Questions

1. Why are more Canadian companies investigating offshoring as a possible business strategy?
2. Do you think that offshoring is detrimental to the Canadian economy? Explain.
3. In your opinion, what are some business activities that should not be offshored? Explain.

CHAPTER 4

The Role of Government in Business

LEARNING OBJECTIVES

After you have read and studied this chapter, you should be able to:

LO1 List the seven categories of government activities that can affect business.

LO2 Trace the historical role of government in the Canadian economy, and explain why Crown corporations were created.

LO3 Demonstrate why understanding laws and regulations at all levels of government is critical to business success.

LO4 Describe how the Bank of Canada influences monetary policy.

LO5 Explain how taxation and fiscal policy affect the Canadian economy.

LO6 Describe how government expenditures benefit consumers and businesses alike.

LO7 Illustrate how purchasing policies and services assist Canadian businesses.

PROFILE

GETTING TO KNOW: LISA VON STURMER, CEO/FOUNDER, GROWING CITY

In this chapter, you will learn how government activities can assist businesses of all sizes. To this end, there are many government agencies mandated to provide support for entrepreneurs. One example is Futurpreneur Canada, where Lisa von Sturmer obtained a start-up loan of $15,000 for her company, Growing City.

Based in Vancouver, Growing City is the first company in North America to offer a corporate organics composting program. Like many entrepreneurs, von Sturmer got the idea from personal experience. While vacationing on Savary Island in British Columbia, where recycling and composting are mandatory, she realized the opportunity of

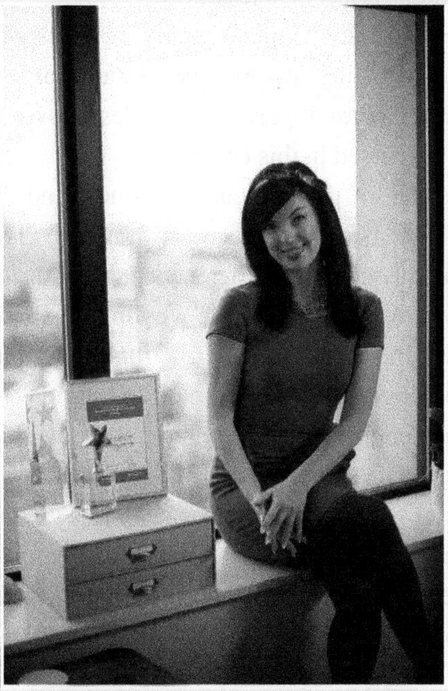

Source: © Ben Nelms

social enterprise. Social enterprise is a small but growing segment of the Canadian economy. Social enterprises are organizations that make money and deliver social or environmental benefits. They may be not-for-profits organizations or profit-making companies.

The company provides office composting, recycling, and event services. It also puts sustainability into its own business practices through supportable uniforms, ethically-made bins, and soil donation programs to non-profit organizations.

In 2012, Growing City won the National Best Green Business Award from the Canadian Youth Business Foundation followed by an appearance on CBC's *Dragon's Den* in 2013. At the time, von Sturmer serviced 82 offices in Vancouver, but the television exposure generated so much interest that Growing City considered a franchise model to meet global demand. As of 2014, the company was expanding its 10-person workforce and already had 200 clients in Metro Vancouver. Corporate customers are the target and current clients include BC Hydro and the South Terminal of the Vancouver International Airport.

von Sturmer was an official Canadian Delegate for the 2014 G20 Young Entrepreneurs Alliance Summit in Sydney, Australia. She, along with other young Canadians, have found a niche in social enterprise. "I wanted to create a business where I knew I was making a tangible, positive impact," von Sturmer said. What's the key to success? "I think the thing that makes Growing City so special and different is that we really look at the problem of waste production from a service standpoint."

Five years ago, reports indicated Canada was lagging behind in social enterprise activity. With small businesses like Growing City, the gap is closing.

Sources: Rhea Seymour, "The Rise of Social Enterprise," Women of Influence, November 3, 2014, http://www.womenofinfluence.ca/2014/11/03/rise-social-enterprise/; Brian Morten, "Turning garbage into gold – Vancouver organics recycling program growing like a weed," *The Vancouver Sun*, July 18, 2014, http://www.vancouversun.com/technology/Turning+garbage+into+gold/10043546/story.html; Mary Teresa Bitti, "Growing City composting company put the brakes on franchising after dragon's Den appearance," *Financial* Post, January 28, 2013, http://business.financialpost.com/2013/01/28/growing-city-composting-company-puts-the-brakes-on-franchising-after-dragons-den-appearance/; "About Us," Growing City, accessed June 28, 2018, http://www.growingcity.com/; Simon Avery, "Canada playing catch-up in social enterprise," *The Globe and Mail*, October 19, 2010, http://www.theglobeandmail.com/report-on-business/small-business/sb-growth/sustainability/canada-playing-catch-up-in-social-enterprise/article1316055/.

Government Affects Business

LO1

List the seven categories of government activities that can affect business.

Government activities that affect business may be divided into seven categories: Crown corporations, laws and regulations, the Bank of Canada, taxation, government expenditures, purchasing policies, and services. Because all of these activities are scattered among different levels of government and many departments, agencies, and corporations, it is not possible to present this information in such neatly divided categories. However, as you make your way through the rest of the chapter you will be able to see how elements of these different aspects of government actions affect business.

It should become obvious as you read that governments are trying to respond to businesses' needs. This includes anything from creating laws that create a level playing field to providing services that support business initiatives. Figure 4.1 provides an overview of the seven categories of government activity discussed in this chapter.

The focus of this chapter is on the role of government in business and this knowledge can open up discussion about how business affects government. The general government-business connection is important but will be different depending on the country. As discussed in Chapter 2, economic systems vary around the world. This also means the extent to which a government intervenes in the economy will vary from country to country.

The seven government activities highlighted in this chapter provide the basis upon which you may compare and contrast different governments around the world and their impact on business. As you read this chapter about the role of Canadian government in business, you can also consider the role of government in other countries with which you are familiar, whether you are an international student, a first-generation student from an immigrant family, or simply have an interest in international business. You can also choose a country and specifically explore its government and business dynamic—you never know if your future career will take you there one day!

FIGURE 4.1

GOVERNMENT INVOLVEMENT WITH BUSINESS

Government activities that affect business can be divided into seven categories. (LO1)

1. **Crown Corporations.** There are hundreds of such companies, and they play an important role in the economy. Crown corporations sometimes compete with for-profit businesses. (LO2)
2. **Laws and Regulations.** These cover a wide range, from taxation and consumer protection to environmental controls, working conditions, and labour–management relations. Review Online Supplement 1: Working Within the Legal Environment of Business for some examples. (LO3)
3. **The Bank of Canada.** Canada's central bank promotes the economic and financial welfare of the country. The bank is responsible for areas such as monetary policy and currency. (LO4)
4. **Taxation.** All levels of government collect taxes—income taxes, the GST or HST, provincial sales taxes, and property taxes. Taxation is also fine-tuned by government to achieve certain goals or to give effect to certain policies. This is called fiscal policy. (LO5)
5. **Government Expenditures.** Governments pay out billions of dollars to Canadians. When these recipients spend this money, businesses benefit. All levels of government provide a host of direct and indirect aid packages as incentives to achieve certain goals. These packages consist of tax reductions, grants, loans, and loan guarantees. (LO6)
6. **Purchasing Policies.** Governments are very large purchasers of ordinary supplies, services, and materials to operate the country. Because the federal government is the single largest purchaser in Canada, its policies regarding where to purchase have a major effect on particular businesses and the economy. (LO7)
7. **Services.** These include a vast array of direct and indirect activities, among them helping companies go international, bringing companies to Canada, and training and retraining the workforce. (LO7)

Government Involvement in the Economy

LO2

Trace the historical role of government in the Canadian economy, and explain why Crown corporations were created.

As noted in Chapter 2, the Canadian economic system is described as a mixed economy—that is, an economic system in which some allocation of resources is made by the market and some is made by the government. Every country's government is involved in its economy, but the specific ways in which the governments participate vary a great deal. There are particular historical reasons why Canada developed into a nation in which governments play very important roles.

When Canada was formed as a country in 1867, the federal government was given the power to "regulate trade and commerce." When the western provinces later joined this Confederation, it became clear that it would take special efforts to build a unified Canada. The very small population was scattered across a huge country, and there was no railway to connect it. Trading patterns were in a north to south configuration because, like today, most people lived near the U.S. border. The United States developed much faster and with a larger population and a bigger economy—which provided products not available in the provinces, either because they were not made in Canada or because there was no transportation to distribute them.

This led the Canadian governments, starting with our first prime minister, Sir John A. Macdonald, to develop what was called a **National Policy**. The policy placed high tariffs on imports from the United States to protect Canadian manufacturing, which had higher costs. In addition, the federal government began to grapple with the difficult question of building a costly rail line from the east coast to the west coast.

National Policy
Government directive that placed high tariffs on imports from the United States to protect Canadian manufacturing, which had higher costs.

These two issues set the tone for the continuous and substantial involvement of Canadian governments in developing and maintaining the Canadian economy. As you make your way through this chapter and read about these complex activities, you should

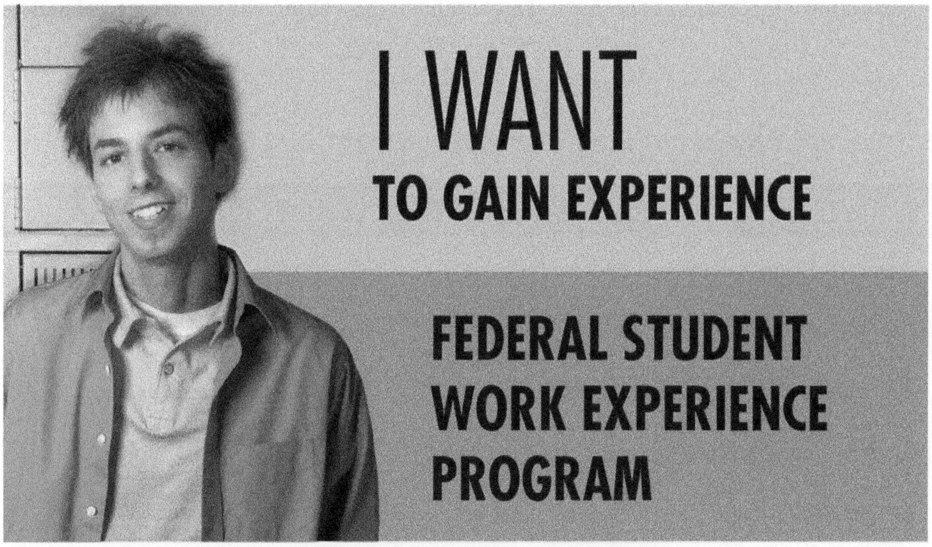

Reproduced with the permission of the Public Service Commission of Canada, 2012

Various government programs support student employment opportunities. For example, the Federal Student Work Experience Program provides thousands of full-time students with work experience. With only one application, you can be considered for temporary jobs in various federal organizations across the country.

not be surprised to learn that the different levels of government are large employers in the country. The federal government and the provinces with the largest populations and levels of economic activity—namely, Ontario, Quebec, British Columbia, and Alberta—have been excellent sources of employment for graduates in the past.

As you will see in this chapter, we also have an interventionist government that, through its activities (e.g., regulatory and fiscal policy), tries to create a stable economy for businesses. In Chapter 3, you learned that trade agreements, such as the North American Free Trade Agreement (NAFTA) and the European Union (EU) have focused on eliminating tariffs between countries. But the work has not stopped, and the federal government is in the midst of negotiating 34 international investment and free trade agreements.[1]

Before we explore the seven government activities within the Canadian context in more detail, let us briefly review how the Canadian government affects business as a whole. You never know, one day you may have a job in one of these areas.

PROGRESS ASSESSMENT

- What are the seven categories of government involvement with business?

Crown Corporations

Crown corporations Companies that are owned by the federal or a provincial government.

In Canada, an important aspect of the role of government is expressed through **Crown corporations**, which are companies that are owned by the federal or provincial government. Review Figure 4.2 for a brief list of the top federal and provincial Crown corporations in Canada. The federal government has Crown corporations related to

FIGURE 4.2

CANADA'S LARGEST FEDERAL AND PROVINCIAL CROWN CORPORATIONS BY REVENUE

Rank	Federal Crown Corporation	2017 Revenue ($ billions)
1	Canada Pension Plan Investment Board	$36.273
2	Canadian Commercial Corporation	$ 2.657
3	Public Sector Pension Investment Board	$15.913
4	Canadian Mortgage and Housing Corporation	$ 9.159
5	Canada Post Corporation	$ 7.891
6	Export Development Canada	$ 2.072

Source: "Consolidated Financial Information for Crown Corporations (Annual Report 2016-2017)," Government of Canada, accessed June 28, 2018, https://www.canada.ca/en/treasury-board-secretariat/services/reporting-government-spending/inventory-government-organizations/consolidated-financial-information-crown-corporations-annual-report-2016-2017.html.

13 portfolios.[2] These include the Canadian Broadcasting Corporation (CBC) in Canadian Heritage, the Royal Canadian Mint in Finance, Canadian Tourism Commission in Industry, and VIA Rail Canada Inc. in Transport.

Crown corporations are set up for several reasons. First, they provided services that were not being provided by businesses, which is how Air Canada came into being in the 1930s. Crown corporations were also created to bail out a major industry in trouble, which is how the Canadian National Railway (CNR) was formed in 1919. Lastly, they provided some special services that could not otherwise be made available, as in the case of the Bank of Canada (discussed later in this chapter).

Each province also owns a variety of Crown corporations. Typically, a Crown corporation owns the province's electric power company but this is changing in some cases (see next section that discusses privatization). Quebec has the Caisse de dépôt et placement du Québec (which means Quebec Deposit and Investment Fund), a giant fund that was established to handle the monies collected by the Quebec Pension Plan. With $298.5 billion in total net assets, it is one of the largest pools of funds in North America.[3] This plan was set up parallel to the Canada Pension Plan in 1966. The fund also handles other Quebec government funds, and it is a very powerful investment vehicle that is used to guide economic development in Quebec. Although it, too, must operate on a sound financial basis, it has a broad scope to make decisions that will benefit the Quebec economy.

Canada's nuclear industry faces challenges as the federal government reduces its role in research and waste management. The Crown corporation Atomic Energy of Canada was downsized when its responsibilities were shifted to a predominantly foreign-owned multinational corporation. What do you think should be the government's role in the nuclear industry? Are there industries that require more government intervention compared to others?

The Role for Crown Corporations

Since the 1990s, federal and provincial governments have embarked upon a series of measures designed to reduce the role of government in the economy. Over the years, large Crown corporations like Teleglobe Canada, Air Canada, and CNR were sold. The national system of air traffic control, the management of airports, hundreds of ports and ferries, and other Maritime installations were also sold. The whole process of selling publicly-owned corporations is called **privatization**.

This disposal of government assets and companies signalled a minor revolution in Canadian history. Also during this time, industries that had been regulated, such as airlines, oil and gas, and trucking, were partially or completely deregulated. **Deregulation** means that the government withdraws certain laws and regulations that seem to hinder competition. Review Online Supplement 1: Working Within the Legal Environment of Business supplement for a discussion on deregulation.

The federal government sold its remaining stake in Petro-Canada, an oil and gas company, in 2005. Analysts claim the decision has made the company more efficient and profitable.

privatization
The process of governments selling Crown corporations.

deregulation
Government withdrawal of certain laws and regulations that seem to hinder competition.

Similar activities were undertaken by provincial governments. The Ontario provincial government partially privatized the Crown corporation Hydro One Inc., However, a long history of mismanagement resulted in heavy debt for the corporation, which will still mean high costs ratepayers.[4] In this case, taxpayers will still pay even though part of the corporation was sold to business. Privatization may create a greater sense of accountability to the public, who become customers, but this may not be the case with the privatization of Hydro One.[5] Should government intervene when it comes to public utilities such as electricity? Should they do so through a Crown corporation or through laws and regulations (covered in the next section)?

Municipal governments are also looking to privatize services such as water systems, garbage collection, and cleaning. Everywhere you look, government agencies, like for-profit organizations, are looking at ways to lower costs and improve efficiencies.

It may seem odd that this introduction on the role of government includes a discussion on how the different levels of government are selling some of their Crown corporations and getting out of these services. A key reason for privatization is to increase revenue for the government when facing pressure to pay down the national debt. (Deficits will be discussed later in this chapter). Nevertheless, it is important to note that Crown corporations exist and that they provide important services to both businesses and consumers. The question is—what should be the role of government Crown corporations in the Canadian economy.

LO3

Demonstrate why understanding laws and regulations at all levels of government is critical to business success.

PROGRESS ASSESSMENT

- What are Crown corporations? Why were they created?
- What does privatization refer to? Can you cite any examples?

© Supreme Court of Canada

The Supreme Court of Canada has the final decision on constitutional questions and on important cases of civil and criminal law. It also deals with appeals from decisions of the provincial courts of appeal. It is comprised of nine Supreme Court Justices (seen here in February 2015) who are recommended by the prime minister and appointed by the governor general.

Laws and Regulations

In Chapter 1 you were introduced to the importance of the legal environment. These laws (and resulting regulations) are created by elected politicians. Consequently, the political parties in power can greatly affect the business environment. This is why it is important to be aware of the beliefs of the different political parties. As stated at the start of this chapter, some think the government should have more say in business, while others think that less government intervention is best. Regardless of the political party, public perception and changing opinion can affect government policy making. This is why all stakeholders should be considered when laws and regulations are created, modified, approved, and implemented.

The power to make laws is based on the British North America Act, 1867 (BNA Act). The BNA Act was passed by the British Parliament in 1867. It is the law that created the Canadian Confederation and it sets the legal ground rules for Canada. In 1982, the BNA Act became part of the new Constitution and was renamed the Constitution Act, 1867.

Laws are derived from four sources: the Constitution, precedents established by judges, provincial and federal statutes, and federal and provincial administrative agencies.[6] Canada has a legislature in each province and territory to deal with local matters. The Parliament in Ottawa makes laws for all Canadians. The Constitution defines the powers that can be exercised by the federal and provincial governments. In the event of a conflict, federal powers prevail.

As a business person, you will be affected by current (and potential) laws and regulations. Online Supplement 1: Working Within the Legal Environment of Business outlines various laws that affect business. As you progress through the chapters in this textbook you will learn how different areas, such as the ecological issues within the global environment or human resource management, integrates with laws, such as environmental laws and labour laws.

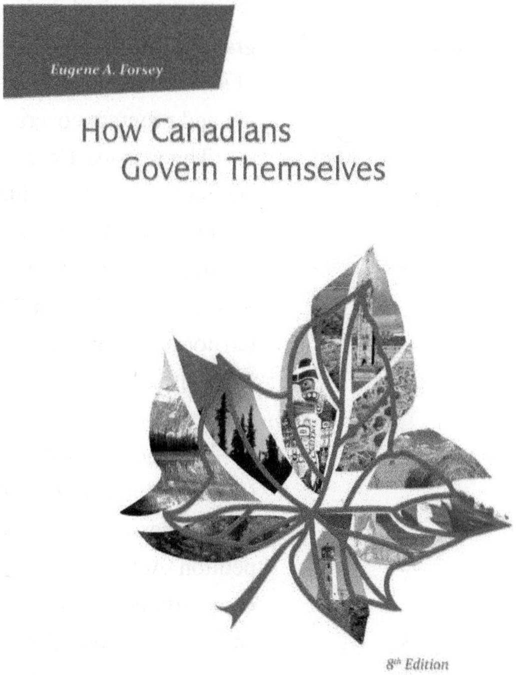

***How Canadians Govern Themselves* is a publication that describes Canada's Constitution, the judicial system, and government powers. It is an excellent resource tool if you wish to learn more about Canada's system of government.**

Federal Government Responsibilities[7]

The federal government is responsible for issues that affect citizens across Canada. Its primary responsibility is to ensure and support the country's economic performance. This includes overseeing such industries as aeronautics, shipping, railways, telecommunications, and nuclear energy. Some other responsibilities that have an impact on business operations are listed below:

- trade regulations (interprovincial and international)
- incorporation of federal companies
- taxation (both direct and indirect)
- the banking and monetary system
- hospital insurance and medicare
- the public debt and property
- national defence
- unemployment
- immigration
- criminal law
- fisheries

Let us consider hospital insurance and medicare, as here we see some overlap with federal, provincial, and territorial government responsibilities. The national Parliament, in effect, established nationwide systems of hospital insurance and medical care by making grants to the provinces and territories on condition that their plans reach certain standards of service. This has been largely successful, despite some differences in modes of financing and program coverage.

The Canada Health Transfer (CHT) is the largest major funds transfer to provinces and territories. It provides long-term predictable funding for health care and supports the principles of the federally regulated Canada Health Act, which are universality, comprehensiveness, portability, accessibility, and public administration. The CHT cash transfer was $37.15 billion in 2017–2018 and is expected to reach 42 percent of provincial and territorial expenditure by 2020.[8] In summary, while the federal government is responsible for health care, it is still up to the provinces and territories to implement these policies, and their co-operation is critical for success.

Another example, Innovation, Science and Economic Development Canada (ISEDC) (formally Industry Canada) is the federal agency that administers a variety of laws affecting businesses and consumers. One of the most relevant pieces of legislation is the Competition Act, which aims to ensure that mergers of large corporations will not restrict competition and that fair competition exists among businesses. (Some of the major consumer protection laws are shown in Figure 4.3.) The Act covers many areas, including discriminatory pricing, price fixing, misleading advertising, and the refusal to deal with certain companies. The Act is administered and enforced by Competition Bureau Canada, an independent law enforcement bureau within ISEDC.

Consider the clothes you wear. They are required to have a label showing the country of origin, size, type of fabric, and washing instructions. When you buy 25 litres of gasoline, you can feel confident that you have received a true measure because of the sticker on the equipment showing when it was last inspected. There are laws that give consumers the

FIGURE 4.3

SOME MAJOR FEDERAL CONSUMER PROTECTION LAWS

These laws all provide consumers with information and protection in various ways. There are also provincial consumer protection laws.

Personal Information Protection and Electronics Document Act: sets rules for how private-sector organizations collect, use, and disclose personal information for commercial activities.

Canadian Agricultural Products Standards Act: covers a wide range of farm products such as organic, meat, poultry, eggs, maple syrup, honey, and dairy products.

Consumer Packaging and Labelling Act: applies to all products not specifically included in other Acts.

Food and Drugs Act: covers a whole range of regulations pertaining to quality, testing approval, packaging, and labelling.

Hazardous Products Act: covers all hazardous products.

Textile Labelling Act: includes apparel sizing and many other special areas.

Weights and Measures Act: applies to all equipment that measures quantities such as scales, gas pumps, and so forth.

right to cancel contracts or return goods within a certain period of time. It is not possible to go through a day and not find an instance where laws have helped you in some way.

As noted in Chapter 1, competition has never been greater than it is today, both internationally and domestically. Within Canada, the "Canadian Free Trade Agreement" (discussed later in this chapter), limits the movement of products such as chicken, dairy, and egg products among provinces and territories, and can create barriers to trade.[9] Beyond Canada, the federal government lobbies the governments of other countries to decrease trade barriers in an attempt to create business opportunities for Canadian firms. The following two examples highlight each of these responsibilities in relation to competition and trade.

THE COMPETITION BUREAU: CHOCOLATE CONSPIRACY[10]

The Competition Bureau probed whether competitors were colluding to control the prices of chocolate bars in Canada. The investigation involved Canada's largest candy bar makers and provided the basis for a class-action lawsuit based upon the claim consumers paid inflated prices for products such as Twix, Mars, Oh Henry, Dairy Milk, Crispy Crunch, Aero, and Smarties between 2001 and 2008. In 2013, four companies, Cadbury Adams Canada Inc., Nestlé Canada Inc., Mars Canada Inc., and Hershey Canada Inc. paid $23.2 million to settle a class-action lawsuit regarding the matter.

The candy bar example demonstrates how the Competition Bureau helps protect Canadian consumers from artificially high prices for goods and services. However, critics claim the Competition Bureau is anti-consumer because it is just as likely to force companies to raise the price of a good or service as lower the price. For example, the bureau recently initiated legal action against the Hudson's Bay Co. (HBC) for offering low prices for an excessive period of time in its mattress businesses. The bureau claimed HBC inflated regular prices to then claim discounts reflected significant deals for consumers.[11] According to competition law, a store must offer regular pricing for a substantial period of time, normally 50 percent of the time, when it comes to low-price practices.

What do you think? Does the Competition Bureau protect shoppers or harass stores that have low prices?

marketing boards Organizations that control the supply or pricing of certain agricultural products in Canada.

MARKETING BOARDS

In Canada, we have a special system of **marketing boards** that control the supply or pricing of certain agricultural products. Consequently, they often control trade. This supply management is designed to give some stability to an important area of the economy that is normally very volatile. Farmers are subject to unique conditions and that have a great effect on their business and on our food supply. Weather and disease are major factors in the operation of farms and are beyond the control of the individual farmer. The same is true for unstable prices, changes in supply resulting from uncoordinated decision making by millions of farmers around the world, and the exercise of market power by concentrated business organizations.

© Radu Bercan / Shutterstock.com

Do you eat Cadbury, Hershey, Nestlé, or Mars chocolate products? Maybe the chocolate bar prices aren't as low as they should be.

In the past farmers have experienced periods of severe drought, flooding, severe cold, and diseases that affected crops, livestock, and poultry. The situation regarding international markets and supply has a serious impact on Canada's grain farmers, since Canada exports much more wheat than it consumes domestically. This market fluctuates greatly depending on the supply in other major grain-exporting countries such as the United States, Argentina, and Australia. The market also depends on demand from major importers such as China and Russia, whose abilities to meet their own requirements are subject to wide variation. Often the Canadian government (like other governments) grants substantial loans with favourable conditions to enable these countries to pay for their imports of our wheat and other agricultural products.

Because we export billions of dollars of agricultural products annually, the ability to hold our own in international markets has a major impact on the state of the Canadian economy. When farmers are flourishing, they buy new equipment and consumer goods and their communities feel the effects of ample cash flow. So does the transportation industry. Conversely, when farmers are suffering, all of these sectors hurt as well.

To smooth out the effects of these unusual conditions on this sector of our economy, and to ensure a steady supply of food to consumers at reasonable prices, some government agencies were set up to control dairy products and poultry. The Canadian Dairy Commission controls the output and pricing of milk and other dairy products. The Egg Farmers of Canada, Chicken Farmers of Canada, the Turkey Farmers of Canada, and the Canadian Hatching Egg Producers consist of representatives from the provinces that produce these items. These organizations control the amount of production for all of the goods under their supervision by allocating quotas to each province that produces them. Provincial agencies administer these quotas and set prices for their province. Each agency controls products that are sold only in its province.

The Canadian system of marketing boards has been under attack by various organizations because it does not permit normal competitive conditions to operate in this field. It is argued that this distorts the whole industry and raises prices for Canadian consumers. Defenders of the system argue that other countries have different systems that create the same effect as our marketing boards but are just less visible. The EU spends billions of dollars on subsidies for their farmers. The United States, which often complains about other countries' unreasonable trade barriers, has its own restrictions, such as on sugar imports.

Provincial Government Responsibilities[12]

Each province and territory has its own government. Issues that affect provincial residents but do not necessarily affect all Canadians are governed at the provincial level. Provincial government responsibilities include the following areas:

- regulation of provincial trade and commerce
- natural resources within their boundaries
- incorporation of provincial companies
- direct taxation for provincial purposes
- licensing for revenue purposes
- the administration of justice
- health and social services

- municipal affairs
- property law
- labour law
- education

The retention of a high degree of provincial autonomy in the provision of elementary and secondary school education and the accommodation of religious and linguistic preferences has resulted in a variation in school systems. Both government levels also fund programs for post-secondary education.

PUBLIC-PRIVATE PARTNERSHIPS (P3s OR PPPs)

One trend that we are seeing today is the merging of public and private philosophies in **public-private partnerships** (P3s or PPPs). P3s represent a method of privatizing public services or public infrastructure. Figure 4.4 indicates the extent and estimated value of public–private partnerships in Canada. In a Nanos Research Poll, 62 percent of Canadians were open to the private sector delivering services in partnership with the government in areas such as roads, hospitals, transit systems, and public housing.

public-private partnerships (P3s or PPPs)
A method of privatizing public services or public infrastructure.

Recent statistics indicate Canada has over 270 P3 projects valued at $127.7 trillion.[13] Let us consider health care facilities (e.g., hospitals). In a typical P3 deal, the government

FIGURE 4.4

NUMBER OF P3 PROJECTS IN CANADA, 2018

	Number
Health	97
Transportation	78
Justice	23
Water and Wastewater	19
Recreation and Culture	15
Education	14
Energy	11
Accommodation	10
Information Technology	5
Government Services	4
Total	276

Source: "Canadian PPP Project database," Canadian Council for Public-Private Partnerships, accessed May 31, 2018, http://projects.pppcouncil.ca/ccppp/src/public/search-project?pageid=3d067bedfe2f4677470dd6ccf64d05ed; and http://p3spectrum.ca/project/.

allows for-profit private corporations to finance, design, build, and operate health facilities. The government commits to lease the facility and use certain services for a period of as much as 30 years or more. Some provinces enter into P3 arrangements to build needed hospitals, promising that the P3s will save money and be more efficient. P3 opponents say that some P3s cost more to build and operate, take private profits from the public health budget, hide their costs, and erode the quality of services. With more than 80 P3 hospitals in operation or development, governments, health care leaders, and communities are clearly P3 supporters.

FREE TRADE BETWEEN PROVINCES[14]

While interprovincial trade is a $300-billion industry in Canada, many Canadian companies and individuals face obstacles when trying to do business outside of their home province or territory. Estimates on the costs of these interprovincial barriers in Canada are $14 billion per year. Interprovincial trade barriers are damaging to the economy and to Canadians' standards of living. While it is clear why they were created (i.e., to protect provincial jobs), these protectionist barriers discourage competition, distort market forces, and reduce efficiency.

The Canadian Free Trade Agreement (CFTA) (formerly the Agreement on Internal Trade) is an intergovernmental trade agreement signed by Canadian First Ministers. Its purpose is to reduce and eliminate barriers to the free movement of persons, goods, services, and investment within Canada. The objective is to reduce extra costs to Canadian businesses by making internal trade more efficient, increasing market access for Canadian companies, and facilitating work mobility for tradespeople and professionals. For example, the Certified General Accountants of New Brunswick successfully appealed to the Internal Trade Secretariat to have the government of Quebec stop restricting access to those who were recognized as qualified to practice accounting in that province.

CFTA amendments have removed barriers that have made it difficult, and sometimes impossible, for workers from one province or territory to work in another. It is reported that over $1 billion, moves between provinces each day. The CFTA is intended to enable even more interprovincial economic activity in the future. While it is not expected that such amendments will address all barriers, it is a step in the right direction.

© PATRICK FULGENCIO/CP Images

The federal government spends billions of dollars on post-secondary education. This includes the Canada Student Grants Program, the Canada Student Loans Program, and Mitacs, a work placement program. Education is one area where government impacts you directly. How much does your provincial government spend on education? How much do you think government should support post-secondary education?

Municipal Government Responsibilities[15]

Municipal governments—cities, towns, villages, counties, districts, and metropolitan regions—are set up by the provincial legislatures. Their authority is defined by the specific province in which they operate. There are roughly 4000 municipal governments in Canada that provide a variety of services. Municipalities provide services such as water supply, sewage and garbage disposal, roads, sidewalks, street lighting, building codes, parks, playgrounds, libraries, and so forth. Schools are generally looked after by school boards or commissions elected under provincial education acts.

Municipalities also play a role in consumer protection. For example, they have regulations and laws regarding any establishment that serves food. Inspectors regularly examine the premises of all restaurants for cleanliness. Local newspapers often publish lists of restaurants fined for failing to maintain required standards. There are similar laws (called zoning laws) about noise, odours, signs, and other activities that may affect a neighbourhood. Certain zones are restricted to residences, and others permit only certain quiet businesses to operate.

Zoning requirements also limit the height of buildings and define how far they must be set back from the road. Most Canadian cities require that all high-rise buildings have a certain ratio of garage space so that cars have off-street parking spots. Parking problems in residential areas due to overflow of vehicles from adjacent businesses have led to parking being limited to residential permit holders on certain streets, so that stores and other places of business must offer commercial parking lots for their customers. And, of course, there are speed limits set by municipal or provincial authorities.

All businesses usually must obtain a municipal licence to operate so the appropriate department can track them to ensure they are following regulations. Many municipalities also have a business tax and a charge for water consumption.

In summary, each level of government has its own roles and responsibilities. Sometimes there is overlap and in other instances there is downloading of responsibilities. Such is the case with some municipal services. An understanding of these responsibilities will contribute to a better understanding of who is responsible for developing, implementing, and overseeing policies that are important to business.

PROGRESS ASSESSMENT

- What are responsibilities of the federal government?
- What are responsibilities of the provincial governments?
- Why are there interprovincial trade barriers?
- What are responsibilities of the municipal governments?

The Bank of Canada[16]

LO4 Describe how the Bank of Canada influences monetary policy.

The Bank of Canada (BoC), a federal Crown corporation, is Canada's central bank. As a financial institution, it provides banking services on behalf of the federal government; however, it does not offer banking services to the public.

Have you ever wondered who lends the federal government money when it spends more than it collects in taxes? One source is the BoC since its role is to promote the economic and financial well-being of Canada. The day-to-day administration of monetary policy (to be discussed next) is the responsibility of the BoC, in co-operation and in consultation with the federal finance minister. In addition, the BoC is also responsible for Canada's bank notes, financial system (to be discussed in Chapter 18), funds management, and retail debt.

© Susan Mcarthur-letellier I Dreamstime

The BoC opened its doors in 1935 as a privately owned institution, with shares sold to the public. By 1938, it became a Crown corporation and it remains so today. What would be the risks if the BoC were a private institution?

Using Monetary Policy to Keep the Economy Growing

Monetary policy is the management of the money supply and interest rates. The **money supply** is the amount of money the BoC makes available for people to buy goods and services. You may wonder why it can't directly increase or decrease the money supply at will since it regulates the supply of paper currency in circulation. The answer is that the bank notes issued by the BoC represent only a small portion of all the money circulating in the economy at any one time; the bulk of the money supply consists of deposits that the public holds at financial institutions.[17]

The second part of monetary policy is interest rates. When the economy is booming, the BoC tends to raise interest rates in an attempt to control inflation. This makes money more expensive to borrow. Thus, businesses borrow less, and the economy slows as business people spend less money on everything, including labour and machinery. The opposite is true when the BoC lowers interest rates as businesses tend to borrow more, and the economy improves. Raising and lowering interest rates should therefore help control the business cycles.

monetary policy
The management of the money supply and interest rates.

Before we consider how the BoC influences the money supply, let us first consider why the money supply needs to be controlled.

money supply
The amount of money the Bank of Canada makes available for people to buy goods and services.

MANAGING INFLATION AND THE MONEY SUPPLY

Imagine what would happen if governments or nongovernmental organizations were to generate twice as much money as exists now. There would be twice as much money available, but still the same amount of products. What would happen to prices? (Hint: Remember the laws of supply and demand from Chapter 2.) Prices would go *up,* because more people would try to buy goods and services with their money and bid up the price to get what they wanted. This rise in price is called *inflation,* which some people call "too much money chasing too few goods."

© Chris Wattie/Reuters

The Governor of the Bank of Canada is its Chief Executive Officer and the Governor has full authority over the business. In the picture above, Governor Stephen Poloz speaks at a press conference about the BoC's activities.

Now think about the opposite: What would happen if the BoC took money out of the economy, or put less money in? Prices would go *down* because there would be an oversupply of goods and services compared to the money available to buy them; as introduced in Chapter 2, this decrease in prices is called *deflation.* If too much money is taken out of the economy, a recession might occur. That is, people would lose jobs and the economy would stop growing.

Now we come to another question about the money supply: Why does it need to be controlled? The reason is that doing so allows us to manage, somewhat, the prices of goods and services. The size of the money supply also affects employment and economic growth or decline. The global money supply is controlled by central banks like the BoC, the U.S. Federal Reserve Bank, and the European Central Bank (ECB). Decisions made by central banks affect the economies of the world. For example, the ECB has enacted quantitative easing (increasing the money supply) to combat lacklustre growth, low inflation, and political uncertainty that has been plaguing Europe.[18]

CONTROL OF THE MONEY SUPPLY[19]

As already mentioned, the BoC is in charge of monetary policy, and the country's money supply influences monetary policy. The objective of the monetary policy is to support a level of spending by Canadians that is consistent with the BoC's goal of price stability. With this in mind, the BoC will conduct monetary policy aimed at keeping inflation within the inflation-control target range of 1 to 3 percent. By influencing the rate at which the supply of money and credit is growing, total spending on goods and services in the economy can be stabilized. The availability of money and credit must expand over time, and the BoC is responsible for ensuring that the rate at which more money is introduced into the economy is consistent with long-term stable growth.

The BoC carries out monetary policy by influencing short-term interest rates. It does this by raising and lowering the target for the overnight rate, also called the BoC's *policy interest rate.* The **overnight rate** is the interest rate at which major financial institutions borrow and lend one-day (or overnight) funds among themselves. Changes in the target rate for the overnight rate then influence the **prime rate** which is the interest rate that banks charge their most creditworthy customers. The prime rate serves as a benchmark for other interest rates, such as those for consumer loans and mortgages, and interest paid on bank accounts, term deposits, and other savings.

overnight rate
The interest rate at which major financial institutions borrow and lend one-day (or overnight) funds among themselves.

prime rate
The interest rate that banks charge their most creditworthy customers.

There is a common misconception that the cost of credit provided by banks to their customers is driven by the BoC's overnight rate. While the overnight rate does influence the pricing of very short-term credit, this is less than 1 percent of funding that banks use for lending. Banks obtain funding from a wide variety of short- and long-term funding sources, certificates of deposit, and bonds. You will learn about these funding sources in Chapters 17 and 18.

Transmission of Monetary Policy[20]

The transmission of monetary policy is the process by which changes in the BoC's policy interest rate work their way through the economy, ultimately to affect the rate of inflation. Changes in this interest rate affect various kinds of economic activity (and over time, inflation) through four main channels, as shown in Figure 4.5.

When interest rates go down, people and businesses are encouraged to borrow more from commercial banks (the first channel), and thus spend more. This behaviour then boosts the economy as the demand for goods and services increases. But if the economy grows too fast, it can lead to inflation. The BoC may then raise the overnight rate (which then increases the prime rate and other interest rates) to slow down borrowing and spending by putting a brake on inflation. When interest rates rise, consumers and businesses tend to hold less money, to borrow less, and to pay back existing loans.

The second channel for the transmission of monetary policy is the effect that changes in interest rates have on the prices of various assets such as bonds, stocks, and houses.

FIGURE 4.5

THE TRANSMISSION OF MONETARY POLICY

It can take six to eight quarters for a change in the policy interest rate to have its full effect on inflation. While changes can affect commercial interest rates, asset prices, and the exchange rate quite quickly, there can be a significant lag before interest rate changes influence expectations (i.e., spending and saving decisions).

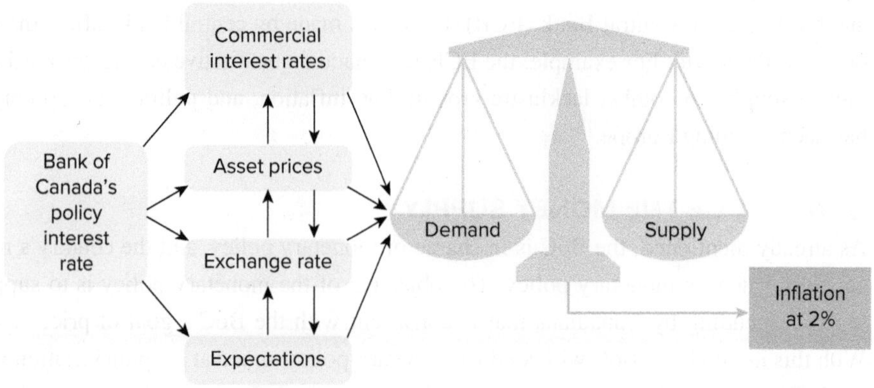

Source: Based on "Canada's Money Supply," Bank of Canada, October 2011, www.bankofcanada.ca/wp-content/uploads/2010/11/canada_money_supply.pdf.

An increase in interest rates can put a damper on the prices of these assets, thus decreasing household wealth, which in turn may discourage borrowing and spending.

The third channel considers the exchange rate, a concept introduced in Chapter 3. A *falling dollar value* means that the amount of goods and services you can buy with a dollar decreases. A *rising dollar value* means that the amount of goods and services you can buy with a dollar goes up. Thus, the price in U.S. dollars you pay for a pair of jeans you buy at an outlet mall in the United States will be lower if the Canadian dollar rises relative to the U.S. dollar, and vice versa. What makes the dollar weak (falling dollar value) or strong (rising dollar value) is the position of the Canadian economy relative to other economies. When the economy is strong, the demand for dollars is high, and the value of the dollar rises. When the economy is perceived as weakening, however, the demand for dollars declines, and the value of the dollar falls. The value of the dollar thus depends on a relatively strong economy.

The fourth channel is the effect of changes in interest rates on people's expectations of future interest rates, growth, and inflation. These expectations often affect decisions of firms and households about current saving and investment choices, and they affect wages, the prices of goods and services, and asset prices.

In choosing a target for the overnight rate, the BoC picks a level that it feels will keep future inflation low, stable, and predictable. Keeping inflation low and stable helps provide a good climate for sustainable economic growth, investment, and job creation.

PROGRESS ASSESSMENT

- Describe the BoC and its role in the Canadian economy.
- Define monetary policy. What actions can be taken to influence the economy?
- Compare the overnight rate and the prime rate.
- Through what four channels can the monetary policy be transmitted? Describe each.

Taxation

LO5

Explain how taxation and fiscal policy affect the Canadian economy.

Mention the word taxes and most people frown. That's because taxes affect almost every individual and business in the country. Taxes are how all levels of government redistribute wealth. The largest sources of federal government revenues come from personal income taxes (49.0 percent) and corporate income taxes (14.4 percent).[21] Revenues collected allows governments to discharge their legal obligations. This revenue is used to pay for public services (e.g., fire, police, and libraries), pay down debt, and fund government operations and programs.

Taxes have also been used as a method of encouraging or discouraging taxpayers. For example, if the government wishes to reduce the use of certain classes of products (e.g., cigarettes and alcohol), it passes what is referred to as a *sin tax.* It is hoped that the additional cost of the product from increased taxes discourages additional consumption.

Figure 4.6 summarizes the average family's total expenditures as a percentage of cash income. After looking at the chart, were you surprised to learn that the average Canadian family now spends more of its income on taxes (42.5 percent) than it does on basic necessities such as food, shelter, and clothing combined (37.4 percent)?[22]

Figure 4.7 considers the breakdown of the various taxes that the average Canadian family pays. The largest component was income taxes (31.1 percent).[23] Queen's University Faculty of Law Professor Kathleen Lahey believes that focussing on income taxes alone is limited as it looks at only one component of the tax system. She believes that the impact that corporate tax cuts had on tax revenue is frequently ignored.[24] On the one hand, public outcry at personal income tax rates could make it easier for the government to cut these rates; however, the result would shift more of the tax burden to taxes such as sales taxes, employment insurance premiums, and Canada Pension Plan (CPP) contributions. Those forms of taxation weigh most heavily on low-income families, couples and individuals,

FIGURE 4.6

THE AVERAGE CANADIAN FAMILY'S TOTAL EXPENDITURES AS A PERCENTAGE OF CASH INCOME, 2016

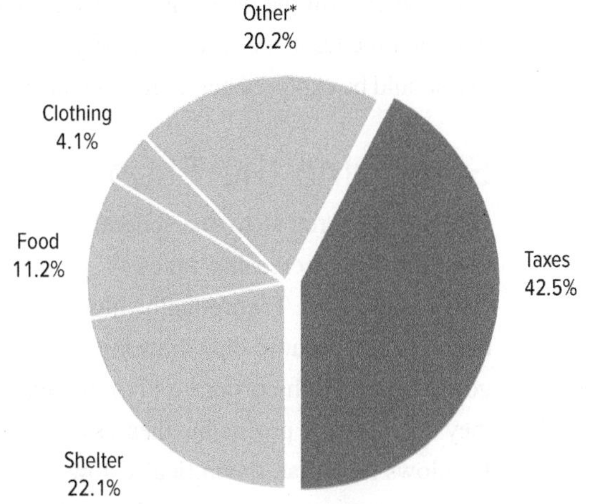

*"Other expenditures" include household operations (communications, child care expenses, pet expenses), transportation, health care, recreation, education, tobacco products, and alcoholic beverages.

Source: Milagros Palacios, Feixue Ren, and Charles Lammam, "Taxes versus the Necessities of Life: The Canadian Consumer Tax Index 2017 Edition," The Fraser Institute, August 2017, https://www.fraserinstitute.org/sites/default/files/canadian-consumer-tax-index-2017.pdf.

FIGURE 4.7

TAX BILL OF THE AVERAGE CANADIAN FAMILY, 2016

The average Canadian family pays total taxes of $35,283 based on total cash income of $83,105.

Taxes	As % of Total Taxes
Income taxes	31.1%
Payroll & health taxes	20.3%
Sales tax	14.4%
Property tax	11.3%
Profit tax	11.2%
Liquor, tobacco, amusement, & other excise taxes	5.2%
Fuel, motor vehicle licence, & carbon taxes	2.7%
Other taxes	2.4%
Import duties	0.9%
Natural resource taxes	0.6%

Source: Milagros Palacios, Feixue Ren, and Charles Lammam, "Taxes versus the Necessities of Life: The Canadian Consumer Tax Index 2017 Edition," The Fraser Institute, August 2017, https://www.fraserinstitute.org/sites/default/files/canadian-consumer-tax-index-2017.pdf.

disabled people, and those with unequal access to well-paying jobs, such as women, and Aboriginal and immigrant workers, says Lahey.[25]

Can you see how it's important to consider all aspects when information about taxation is released? Start by asking yourself some questions. What is the purpose of the tax? What stakeholders will the decision to change the tax impact the most? What stakeholders will be impacted the least? As you can read from the above, there are always different perspectives that should be explored before making business decisions that will impact many stakeholders.

Stabilizing the Economy Through Fiscal Policy

fiscal policy
The federal government's effort to keep the economy stable by increasing or decreasing taxes or government spending.

Fiscal policy refers to the federal government's effort to keep the economy stable by increasing or decreasing taxes or government spending. The first half of fiscal policy involves taxation. Theoretically, high personal income and corporate tax rates tend to slow the economy because they draw money away from the private sector and are remitted to the government. High corporate tax rates may discourage small business ownership because they decrease the profits businesses can make, and this can make the effort less rewarding. It follows then that, theoretically, low tax rates would tend to give the economy a boost.[26] The government can use taxation to help move the economy in a desired direction. For example, taxes may be lowered to stimulate the economy when it is weak. Similarly, taxes may be raised when the economy is booming to cool it off and slow down inflation.

Federal and provincial governments constantly use the lever of fiscal policy to stimulate specific geographic and industrial areas. They offer special tax credits to companies that open plants in areas of chronically high unemployment, such as Cape Breton or Newfoundland and Labrador. All companies that invest in specific activities considered desirable by the government (such as the technology sector) may be eligible to receive a tax credit that reduces the income tax they have to pay. Unfortunately, some of these programs have been scaled back or eliminated due to budget constraints.

© Rachel Frank/Corbis/Glow Images

The Canadian Federation of Students (CFS) wants to eliminate interest charges on federal and provincial student loans. Students collectively owe over $28 billion in student loans to governments, and the CFS claims that the federal government is using these interest charges as a source of revenue, projected to be approximately $862.6 million from the Canada Student Loans Program in 2018.[27] What are the pros and cons of this suggestion? Is waiving student interest fees the same as when a government offers interest-free loans to businesses?

The second half of fiscal policy involves government spending. Governments spend money in many areas, including social programs, the environment, highways, etc. If the government's spending exceeds the amount gathered in taxes for a specific period of time (namely, a fiscal year), then it has a **deficit**.

One way to lessen annual deficits is to cut government spending, which is difficult to do. Every year, there is demand by the provinces and territories for increased transfer payments, the need for funds due to unexpected situations (such as the massive floods in Quebec and New Brunswick), more pressure from international bodies to increase peacekeeping support, and so on. Some believe that government spending helps the economy grow. Others believe that this money comes out of the pockets of consumers and business people—especially when taxes have been increased—and that this slows growth. What do you think?

THE NATIONAL DEBT (FEDERAL DEBT)

The **national debt (also known as the public debt)** is the accumulation of federal government borrowing (deficits) over time. It captures the federal government's estimated total liabilities (debts) and what must be borrowed from the markets.[28] The national debt increases when the government spends more than it receives in revenues, and it has to borrow heavily. If it doesn't reduce spending and pay back these loans when the economy is booming, the debt keeps rising. Canada's national debt is over $637 billion and deficits are projected to persist until 2050.[29] Combined federal and provincial net debt is over $1.4 trillion.[30]

Increased government borrowing and spending stimulates an economy. Cuts in spending have the

© THE CANADIAN PRESS/Jonathan Hayward

Fort McMurray, Alberta was evacuated in May 2016 due to a wildfire that destroyed 1595 buildings, which included 2579 living spaces and 22 commercial spaces. According to the Insurance Bureau of Canada, it was the costliest disaster in Canadian history.[31] Have there been any disasters in your area that required government support?

Making ETHICAL DECISIONS

Fiscal Policy Decisions

In the late 1990s, the federal government was under strong pressure from the business community to reduce or wipe out the annual deficit in the annual budget. Business was convinced that these constant deficits and the resulting accumulated debt were dragging the Canadian economy down and making Canada less competitive with other major countries. As a result, the federal government drastically cut its expenditures.

There were significant reductions in funding to the provinces for health care, post-secondary education, and other important activities. Combined with other budget-cutting measures (e.g., lower and fewer payments to the unemployed and laying off employees), the result was an increase in poverty levels, especially among children and women.

These facts lead to some ethical questions. How could such severe budget cuts have been avoided? Does the business community bear some responsibility for the increase in poverty in Canada? In other words, was it ethical for businesses to allow our national debt to grow so large and not challenge the government's annual deficits much earlier? What do you think?

© lightwise/123RF

deficit
Occurs when a government spends over and above the amount it gathers in taxes for a specific period of time (namely, a fiscal year).

national debt (also known as public debt)
The accumulation of the federal government's borrowing (deficits) over time.

surplus
An excess of revenues over expenditures.

opposite effect as they slow down the economy. Such decisions influence many stakeholders. The Making Ethical Decisions box highlights how cuts in government spending can negatively impact individuals.

Reductions in the national debt have been the result of surpluses—a **surplus** is an excess of revenues over expenditures. As the debt comes down, the annual interest costs are also reduced. This reduction in the national debt can translate into a savings of millions of dollars each year on debt interest payments.

Controlling the debt means improved financial security, commitment to social programs, and more room to lower taxes. The latter may then stimulate the economy. A country with stable and well-funded government social programs also encourages business development, including hiring, because there is less risk that the business will be asked to increase employee benefits. A lower debt also means that in times of economic slowdown or when unexpected events occur (such as the global financial crisis) the government may have funds available to alleviate the ensuing pressures.

If the debt is high, there is less money that can be dedicated to social programs and initiatives to assist businesses in becoming more competitive. According to Aaron Wudrick, federal director of the Canadian Taxpayers Federation, "Rising public debt means a higher tax burden on future taxpayers, especially given an ageing population with a shrinking proportion of working-age Canadians. Interest rates are currently at record lows and we are still spending more on public debt interest payments alone than we do on our armed forces. When rates rise, the cost could balloon rapidly, squeezing programs and services."[32]

Do you better understand how the combined levels of government debt (e.g., national, provincial, and territorial) can impact your future?

THE FEDERAL BUDGET

On an annual basis (around springtime), the federal finance minister releases a blueprint for how the government wants to set the country's annual economic agenda. This document, called the **federal budget**, is a comprehensive report that reveals government financial policies and priorities for the coming year.

federal budget
A comprehensive report that reveals government financial policies for the coming year.

The budget is reviewed carefully by businesses, Canadians, and other stakeholders. Through this document, one learns about revenues (from taxation) and expenditures (e.g., Canada Pension Plan payments) for the past year. In addition, the government will communicate program changes for the future, as well as forecasted growth projections. It answers questions such as: How much money will go to pay down the debt? How much money will go to social programs such as health care? Will there be more money for research and development? Will taxes go up or down?

Provincial and territorial governments also release their own budgets. Their financial stability affects political decisions and, ultimately, the business environment within their boundaries.

PROGRESS ASSESSMENT

- Explain the purpose of taxation.
- How does the government stabilize the economy through fiscal policy?
- What are the benefits of a controlled national debt?

Government Expenditures

LO6

Describe how government expenditures benefit consumers and businesses alike.

In 2018, the Governments in Canada provided $75.4 billion to the provinces and territories.[33] These transfer and equalization payments cover areas such as health care, secondary education, old-age pensions, allowances to low-income families or individuals, employment insurance, welfare, workers' compensation, child care, and various other payments to individuals. The payments give Canadians more purchasing power and, therefore, the creation of a more viable market for businesses.

As people spend their money, large numbers of Canadian companies and their employees benefit as a result of this purchasing power. Increasing or lowering the rates or eligibility for these payments results in further fine-tuning of the economy. Again, government cutbacks have resulted in the reduction of such payments in recent years.

Governments also spend huge sums of money on education, health, roads, ports, waterways, airports, and various other services required by businesses and individuals. They also provide aid through direct and indirect government programs designed to help businesses. The Canadian Subsidy Directory lists more than 4185 sources of financing and government programs for anyone searching for Canadian grants, loans, and government programs.[34] Governments also intervene on an ad hoc (special or unplanned) basis in important cases. For example, as of 2017, government funding to the National Angel Capital Organization, which provides capital and coaching to early-stage businesses, supported $722.8 million worth of investment in 1918 investments by 1124 companies throughout the country.[35]

Financial Aid

All levels of government offer a variety of direct assistance programs to businesses, including grants, loans, loan guarantees, consulting advice, information, and other aids that are designed to achieve certain purposes (see Figure 4.8). Some government aid is designed to help industries or companies that are deemed to be very important—at the cutting edge of technology, providing highly skilled jobs, and oriented toward exports. Other programs focus upon small-scale businesses, For example, the federal government funds the Aboriginal Business Entrepreneurship Development where you can apply for up to $99,999 in business development support if you are Aboriginal or have a majority-owned Aboriginal business.[36] Discover some other businesses in which the federal government invests in the Spotlight on Small Business box.

© The Canadian Press Images/Larry MacDougal

It is estimated that government provides $3.3 billion in subsidies to oil and gas producers in Canada. This amount would pay for the education of 260 000 students based upon Canada's average annual spending of $12,700 per student. Are fossil fuel subsidies good for the Canadian economy? What other strategies could the government implement to help the economy?[41]

Fossil fuel subsidies are common in almost every country of the world.[37] They include subsidies for petroleum products, electricity, natural gas, and coal. The International Monetary Fund identified the worldwide cost of fossil fuel subsidies in 2011 as $480 billion for "pre-tax" subsidies and $1.9 trillion for "post-tax" subsidies.[38] This represents a range of two to eight percent of government spending. Both "pre" and "post" tax subsidies enable fossil fuel energy to be offered at a lower-than-cost price through support to energy producers (pre) and consumers (post).

In 2011, Canada expended $26 billion to subsidize energy, which reflects four percent of government revenues.[39] Based upon Canada's population that year, the subsidies represented $787 for each person. Fossil fuel subsidies include a number of federal and provincial programs. For example, the Alberta government offered Energy Industry Drilling Stimulus, which cost $1.7 billion in 2011, to reduce royalty costs to oil and gas producers in the province. The Ontario government's Fuel Tax Exemption for Coloured Fuel, which cost $285 million in 2011, exempts fuel tax for this type of gas, which is used in forestry, agriculture, and fishing. Over time, these subsidies may increase or decrease depending upon public opinion and economic trends.

There is world recognition that fossil fuel subsidies need to adapt to current and future energy needs.[40] Governments provide support to the fossil fuel industry, which has both costs and benefits. On one hand, subsidies generate economic

■ **FIGURE 4.8**

TOP TEN RECIPIENTS, CANADIAN GOVERNMENT FUNDING, 2016 (MILLIONS)

Rank	Company name	Amount	Industry
1	FCA Canada Inc. (Chrysler)	85.8	Manufacturing
2	AE Côte-Nord Canada Bioenergy Inc.	76.5	Cleantech
3	Enerken Alberta Biofuels LP	67.1	Cleantech
4	Bombardier Inc.	54.15	Manufacturing
5	MDA Systems Ltd.	54	Telecom
6	Tata Steel Minerals Ltd.	50	Mining and Natural Resources
7	IAMGOLD Corporation	50	Mining and Natural Resources
8	Calfrac Well Services	46.4	Energy
9	TransAlta Renewable	45.9	Cleantech
10	C.T.M.A. Tanverserie Ltée	43.18	Transportation
	Total	**$573.03**	

Source: "Top 50 companies that received Canadian government funding," *The Globe and Mail,* July 19, 2017, accessed May 31, 2018, https://www.theglobeandmail.com/report-on-business/top-50-report-on-business-the-funding-portal/article19192109/.

growth in the fossil fuel industry, which in turn provide jobs and stimulates further business of other companies that service the industry. On the other hand, the subsidies can have a significant drain on government budgets and intensify climate change through higher energy consumption because energy costs are artificially low.

Major Federal Programs[42]

Canada is a very large country with uneven resources, climate, and geography, which has led to uneven economic development. **Transfer payments** are direct payments from governments to other governments or to individuals. Federal transfer payments to individuals include elderly benefits and employment insurance. Such payments provide social security and income support.

transfer payments Direct payments from governments to other governments or to individuals.

Equalization is the federal government's transfer program for reducing fiscal disparities among provinces and territories. This payment enables less-prosperous provincial governments to provide their residents with public services that are roughly comparable to those in other provinces, at roughly comparable levels of taxation. For example, in 2017–2018 the federal government allotted $38.6 billion to the Canadian Health Transfer which supports health care. While provinces are free to spend the funds on public services

equalization A federal government program for reducing fiscal disparities among provinces.

Spotlight *On* SMALL BUSINESS

Sustainable Development Technology Canada

The federal government invests billions of dollars in grants and programs that stimulate innovation to benefit the Canadian economy. One such program is Sustainable Development Technology Canada (SDTC) whose mandate is to "fund Canadian cleantech projects and coach the companies that lead them as they move their ground-breaking technologies to market." The cleantech industry represents and estimated value of $4 trillion worldwide. In Canada, the industry consists of over 856 mainly small and medium-sized firms involved with oil and gas, mining, power generation, transportation, agriculture, forestry and forest products, and water and energy efficiency. The Canadian cleantech industry generates $13.27 billion in revenues and employs over 55 200 people.

SUSTAINABLE DEVELOPMENT TECHNOLOGY CANADA

© Sustainable Development Technology Canada (SDTC)

To date the SDTC has supported 347 projects for a total of $989 million in government support. SDTC-funded companies have generated an additional $2.18 billion in follow-up financing dollars from the private sector.

The SDTC impacts many regions of Canada. The Vancouver Economic Council (VEC) ran a SDTC workshop to promote the cleantech industry to entrepreneurs and small businesses in the city. According to Bryan Buggy, VEC's Director, Strategic Initiatives and Sector Development, 33 400 people, or the equivalent of one in twenty jobs in Vancouver, are green jobs, including positions in sustainable building design and development; waste management and recycling; land and water remediation; agriculture management; and sustainability consulting. In Manitoba, a 2004 project involved Prairie Pulp and Paper Inc. and the Straw Producers Co-op of Manitoba for a tree-free agriculture-fibre paper mill that created paper products from farm residue.

The salmon aquaculture industry on Vancouver Island also involves cleantech projects; the Middle Bay Sustainable Aquaculture Institute is developing a commercial-scale solid wall containment system to improve salmon production in a way that reduces interference with the marine environment. The Namgis Land-Based Atlantic Salmon Recirculating Aquaculture System (RAS) Pilot Project will reduce the risk of disease for the salmon and treat the solid and liquid waste generated from the salmon rearing. Each of these projects support sustainable business.

Does support to this industry make good business sense? What are some other benefits to supporting cleantech small businesses?

Sources: "Celebrating 15 Years of Canadian Cleantech - 2016-2017 annual report," Sustainable Development Technology Canada, accessed May 31, 2018, https://www.sdtc.ca/sites/default/files/sdtc_2016_ar_en_r14.pdf; "Canada's Economic Action Plan," Sustainable Development Technology Canada, accessed April 5, 2015, http://actionplan.gc.ca/en/initiative/sustainable-development-technology-canada; "Projects 2015," Sustainable Development Technology Canada, accessed April 5, 2015, https://www.sdtc.ca/en/about-sdtc/about-us; "Green entrepreneurs attend Sustainable Development Technology Canada Workshop," PR Associates, September 29, 2014, http://www.prassociates.com/blog/2014/green-entrepreneurs-attend-sustainable-development-technology-canada-workshop.

according to their own priorities, these payments are intended to fund medicare, post-secondary education, and smaller programs.

In 2017–2018, the federal government will provide $18.96 billion in equalization payments to the provinces. Did you notice that this program does not include the territories? The Territorial Formula Financing program provides territorial governments with funding to support public services, in recognition of the higher cost of living in the north.

PROGRESS ASSESSMENT

- Explain how governments in Canada spend tax dollars to help Canadians.
- Give two examples of how government has provided financial aid to businesses.
- Who benefits from equalization transfer payments?

Purchasing Policies

LO7

Illustrate how purchasing policies and services assist Canadian businesses.

Most governments are very large purchasers and consumers of goods and services; indeed, in Canada they are the largest buyers. Procurement policies guide how governments buy and sell goods and services for various department and agencies; the intent is to have the best interest of Canadians in mind. The federal and provincial governments use this enormous purchasing power to favour Canadian companies. The provinces favour those companies within their boundaries and have even set up trade barriers between provinces (as discussed earlier). When advanced technology items—civilian or military—must be obtained from foreign companies, our governments usually insist that a certain minimum portion be manufactured in Canada. This enables Canadian companies to acquire advanced technology know-how and to provide employment.

Contracts are often awarded to help Canadian businesses even if they are sometimes more expensive than bids by non-Canadian companies. This is particularly true in the military acquisitions programs. Whatever can be produced or serviced in Canada—ships, electronics, trucks, artillery, ammunition—is acquired from Canadian companies. (See the Seeking Sustainability box for an example of pro-environment government purchasing policies).

Be aware that government procurement has some challenges. It is a demanding bidding process that is strictly regulated. In some provinces, government organizations may also include government boards, councils, committees, commissions, and publicly funded academic, health, and social service organizations.[43] It can be demanding to fully understand government procurement and to properly target potential niches. In large cities alone—such as Montreal, Toronto, and Vancouver—there are several hundred public organizations that function differently for their procurement. If a firm is interested in conducting business in the Canadian public sector, MERX Canadian Public Tenders service is an easy, fast, and efficient prospecting tool. New opportunities are listed daily for access to billions of dollars in Canadian public-sector business opportunities. They range from the private sector to all levels of government, and include the MASH (Municipal, Academic, School Boards and Hospitals) sector from across Canada.[44]

Services

The federal government has departments that provide services to businesses and consumers. We will look at two of these important departments: Innovation, Science and Economic Development Canada and the Department of Foreign Affairs, Trade and Development. There are corresponding departments in many of the provinces, especially the four largest and most developed ones (British Columbia, Alberta, Ontario, and Quebec).

Seeking SUSTAINABILITY

Procurement for the Planet

Governments spend a great deal of money to purchase goods and services. While exact figures are hard to determine, total government programs expenditures totalled $240.4 billion in 2011–2012 and this value will continue to rise. It is estimated that the fifteen largest municipalities in Canada spend in excess of $10 billion dollars annually on goods, services, and capital projects. By the sheer volume of purchases, governments of all level are able to influence environmental sustainability through policies referred to as "green procurement." These policies ensure environmental considerations are included when governments make purchase decisions.

© Radharc Images/Alamy

The objective of the federal government policy on green procurement is to advance the protection of the environment and support sustainable development. At the provincial level, sustainable procurement policies, such as the one for Nova Scotia, integrate environmental, economic, and social considerations in procurement decisions in order to obtain the best value for government and the people it serves. But it is at the municipal level where green procurement is most important since these governments have direct or indirect control over 45 percent of greenhouse gas emissions in Canada.

Municipal governments have developed strategic sustainability plans that include areas such as buildings and facilities, municipal vehicle fleets (including transit), street lighting, and waste management. Dawson Creek, British Columbia, is on its way to becoming a "solar city"; the lighting systems for fire and police stations and City Hall were retrofitted, and solar panels for traffic signs, bus stops, and trail lights were installed throughout the community. The Canadian Urban Transit Association noted there are 14 000 transit buses across Canada, of which nearly 90 percent run on diesel. In an effort to address this significant ecological footprint, several environmental transit fleet initiatives exist in cities across the country to identify the best options for electric and hybrid vehicle purchases.

Does the city or town where you live have an environmental sustainability plan? Does the council follow a green procurement policy? What are the advantages and disadvantages of these initiatives?

Sources: "Policy on Green Procurement," Public Works and Government Services Canada, February 18, 2015, http://www.tpsgc-pwgsc.gc.ca/ecologisation-greening/achats-procurement/politique-policy-eng.html; "Environmental technology verification for municipal fleets: a public transit perspective," Canadian Urban Transit Association, 2013, http://www.fcm.ca/Documents/presentations/2013/SCC2013/Environmental_Technology_Verification_for_Municipal_Fleets_EN.pdf; "The State of Municipal Sustainable Procurement in Canada Best Practices & Current Trends," Reeve Consulting, 2012, accessed https://reeveconsulting.files.wordpress.com/2011/05/2012-state-of-munic-sust-proc-canada.pdf; "Federal Expenditures by Year and Item (Total), 1061-1962 to 2011-2012," Government Spending: Canadian Taxpayers Association, January 2013, http://www.taxpayer.com/media/Federal%20Expenditures%20by%20Year%20and%20Item%20%28Total%29,%201961-1962%20to%202011-2012%281%29.pdf; "Highlighting best practices – sustainable procurement resources for municipal, academic, schools and health and social service (MASH) organizations," Office of Sustainability, Dalhousie University, 2012; "Dawson Creek – a near carbon neutral city in the idle of northeastern B.C.'s shale gas boom," Green Energy Futures, June 23, 2012, http://www.greenenergyfutures.ca/episode/08/awesome-dawson-creek-northern-oil-and-gas-town-bets-big-renewable-energy; "Building Canada's green economy: the municipal role," Federation of Canadian Municipalities, 2011, https://fcm.ca/Documents/reports/Building_Canadas_green_economy_the_municipal_role_EN.pdf.

Innovation, Science and Economic Development Canada

For many years, the federal government has implemented a variety of programs to help small businesses get started. These programs are part of a larger one, called Canada

Business Network, that involves setting up Canada Business service centres in every province and territory. These centres are operated jointly with provincial governments and certain local organizations. Innovation, Science and Economic Development Canada (ISEDC) publishes brochures, booklets, and guides informing business people of the help available and how and where to get it. ISEDC also participates in the production of publications to promote Canadian businesses internationally.

Other programs are designed to encourage businesses to establish themselves or expand in economically depressed areas of the country. These are populated regions that are industrially underdeveloped, have high unemployment, and have lower standards of living. The programs include help for the tourism industry and for Aboriginal residents of remote areas who want to establish businesses.

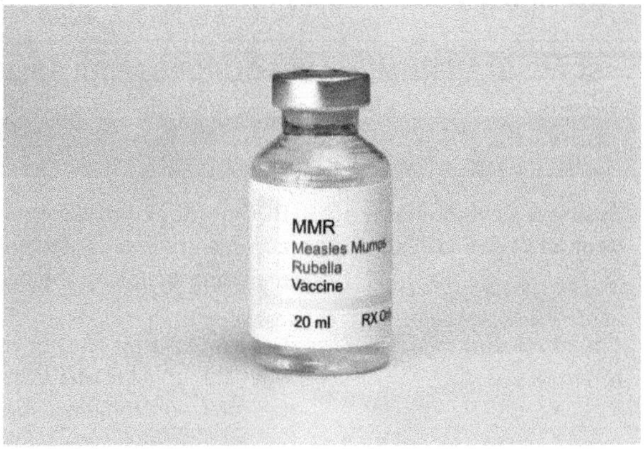

NRC researchers recently signed an agreement with the China National Biotech Group for three collaborative projects related to vaccine development for specific populations. The goal of the NRC is to increase Canada's innovation capacity and translate new science and technology initiatives to profits for businesses and gains for the Canadian economy.

NATIONAL RESEARCH COUNCIL

The National Research Council (NRC) is a federal agency that began in 1916. It reports to Parliament through ISEDC. The NRC plays a significant role in research that helps Canadian industry remain competitive and innovative. Its vision is to be the most effective research and development organization in the world, stimulating sustainable domestic prosperity.[45]

This organization includes four umbrella divisions in transportation and manufacturing, engineering, life sciences and emerging technologies which are divided further across fourteen key industry research centres.[46] Located in every province, areas of research and industry support include aerospace, biotechnology, engineering and construction, fundamental sciences, information and communications technologies, and manufacturing.

Global Affairs Canada

Because exports are particularly important to Canada's economic well-being, the government has a very large and elaborate system to assist companies in their exporting and foreign-investment activities. The federal government, most provincial governments, and all large municipal governments have various ministries, departments, and agencies that provide a variety of such services. These include information, marketing, financial aid, insurance and guarantees, publications, and contracts. All major trading countries provide similar support to their exporters.

See Figure 4.9 for a list of government sources that are available to assist Canadian businesses. Most of them also provide some support for those that wish to succeed in global markets. We have discussed some of these organizations already in this textbook.

FIGURE 4.9

SOME GOVERNMENT RESOURCES AVAILABLE TO ASSIST CANADIAN BUSINESSES

Government Source	Mission
Business Development Bank of Canada (BDC)	BDC provides small and medium-sized businesses with flexible financing, affordable consulting services, and venture capital. BDC has a particular focus on the emerging and exporting sectors of the economy.
Canada Business Network	Canada Business Network is a government information service for businesses and start-up entrepreneurs in Canada. It serves as a single point of access for federal and provincial/territorial government services, programs, and regulatory requirements for business.
Export Development Canada (EDC)	EDC provides Canadian exporters with financing, insurance, and bonding services as well as foreign market expertise.
National Research Council (NRC)	NRC helps turn ideas and knowledge into new processes and products. Businesses work with partners from industry, government, and universities.

PROGRESS ASSESSMENT

- Why do federal and provincial governments tend to favour Canadian companies when contracts are approved?
- How does the NRC contribute to technology advancement in Canada?
- List some organizations that aim to help exporters.

Role of the Canadian Government—Some Final Thoughts

industrial policy
A comprehensive, coordinated government plan to guide and revitalize the economy.

Some people believe that the best way to protect the Canadian economy is for the federal government to withdraw from active direction and participation in the economy. Instead, government should develop a long-term industrial policy of leadership and take an active role in shaping the future of the economy. An **industrial policy** is a comprehensive, coordinated government plan to guide and revitalize the economy. An industrial policy requires close consultation with business and labour to develop a program for long-term sustainable industrial development.

What should be clear is that government always has a critical role to play. While this is contrary to free-market principles, troubled times are usually followed by calls for more government involvement in the economy. As we move forward, the federal government will continue to focus on international trade initiatives to provide opportunities for Canadian businesses. Others are opposed in principle to such government intervention and instead would support deregulation, privatization, and less government involvement within Canada and other countries. Now that you understand the seven categories of government activities, you can examine both sides of this issue.

SUMMARY

LO1 **List the seven categories of government activities that can affect business.**

The seven categories of government activities are Crown corporations, laws and regulations, the Bank of Canada, taxation and financial policies, government expenditures, purchasing policies, and services. See Figure 4.1 for a brief description of each activity.

What is the relationship between Canada's economic system and government involvement?

As noted in Chapter 2, Canada has a mixed economy, which is an economic system in which some allocation of resources is made by the market and some by the government. As a result of the Constitution Act, the different levels of government have responsibilities and jurisdiction over certain matters of the economy and population.

LO2 **Trace the historical role of government in the Canadian economy, and explain why Crown corporations were created.**

The Canadian government played a key role from the beginning of the country in 1867 in protecting young manufacturing industries and getting the railroad built to the west coast, helping to join the country together.

Why did the government have to do what it did?

It had the legal power and responsibility to do so as a result of the Constitution Act. The United States threatened to overwhelm our industries, which were not strong enough by themselves to resist or to build the railway.

Why were Crown corporations necessary?

Companies were not willing or able to assume certain responsibilities or fill some needs in the marketplace. CNR, Air Canada, and Hydro-Québec are some important examples. (CNR and Air Canada are no longer Crown corporations.)

What is the recent trend with Crown corporations?

In recent years, we have seen an increasing trend where governments (both federal and provincial) have been selling Crown corporations. This is called privatization. Some examples include the sale of remaining Petro-Canada shares and the sale of BC Rail Ltd.

LO3 **Demonstrate why understanding laws and regulations at all levels of government is critical to business success.**

Businesses need to understand the laws and regulations that affect them. The Constitution Act defines the powers that can be exercised by the federal government and provincial governments. In the event of a conflict, federal powers prevail.

What are some federal government responsibilities?

The federal government's responsibilities include trade regulations, the incorporation of federal companies, national defence, immigration, and the fisheries.

What are some provincial government responsibilities?

Among other areas, provincial governments oversee natural resources within their boundaries, the administration of justice, municipal affairs, and education.

What are some municipal government responsibilities?

Municipal governments—cities, towns, villages, counties, districts, metropolitan regions—are set up by the provincial legislatures. Municipalities provide services such as water supply, sewage and garbage disposal, roads, sidewalks, street lighting, building codes, parks, playgrounds, libraries, and so forth. They play a role in consumer protection (e.g., inspectors examine restaurants) and the establishment of zoning requirements.

LO4 Describe how the Bank of Canada influences monetary policy.

The Bank of Canada (BoC), a federal crown corporation, is Canada's central bank. Its role is to promote the economic and financial well-being of Canada.

What is monetary policy?

Monetary policy is the management of the money supply and interest rates.

Why does the money supply need to be controlled?

The value of money depends on the money supply; that is, how much money is available to buy goods and services. Too much money in circulation causes inflation. Too little money causes deflation, recession, and unemployment. Controlling the money supply allows us to manage, somewhat, the prices of goods and services. The size of the money supply also affects employment and economic growth or decline.

How is the money supply controlled?

The BoC is in charge of monetary policy, and the country's money supply influences monetary policy. The BoC carries out monetary policy by influencing short-term interest rates. It does this by raising and lowering the target for the overnight rate.

LO5 Explain how taxation and fiscal policy affect the Canadian economy.

Each level of government collects taxes. These taxes allow governments to discharge their legal obligations and to fund social programs.

What is fiscal policy?

Fiscal policy refers to the federal government's effort to keep the economy stable by increasing or decreasing taxes or government spending. Federal and provincial governments constantly use the lever of fiscal policy to stimulate specific geographic and industrial areas.

What is the national debt?

The national debt, also known as the public debt, is the accumulation of federal government borrowing (deficits) over time. The national debt increases when the government spends more than it receives in revenues, and it has to borrow heavily. If it doesn't reduce spending and pay back these loans when the economy is booming, the debt keeps rising.

How is monetary policy different from fiscal policy?

Controlled by the BoC, monetary policy is the management of the money supply and interest rates. When the economy is booming, the BoC tends to raise interest rates in an attempt to control inflation. Since money is more expensive to borrow, businesses borrow less, and the economy slows as business people spend less money on everything. Fiscal policy involves broader government efforts to ensure a stable economy.

LO6 Describe how government expenditures benefit consumers and businesses alike.

Government expenditures benefit consumers and businesses alike. Some expenditures specifically target business subsidies, such as research and development initiatives for Canadian manufacturers, or support for agriculture, cleantech, and forestry that enables companies to be competitive in global markets. For consumers, expenditures for a stable income, such as old age security and employment insurance, are important, as is government support for education and job creation, which help people establish a stable income.

How do governments assist consumers with their tax dollars?

Governments disburse tens of millions of dollars annually in social program spending (e.g., old-age pensions, employment insurance, allowances to low-income families, etc.). These transfers give consumers more purchasing power.

How do businesses benefit from government expenditures?

All levels of government provide direct and indirect aid packages as incentives to achieve certain goals. These packages can consist of tax reductions, tariffs and quotas on imports, and subsidies including grants, loans, and loan guarantees.

LO7 **Illustrate how purchasing policies and services assist Canadian businesses**

Purchasing policies and services assist Canadian businesses. The purchasing power of government is very high when considered across the federal, provincial, territorial, and municipal levels. In many instances, Canadian businesses are targeted for opportunities to obtain government contracts or sell goods and services to government departments.

Why is preferential treatment given to Canadian companies when they bid for a government contract?

Contracts are often awarded to help Canadian businesses. This way, companies are employing Canadians and contributing to a strong economy.

What are two government departments that are particularly focused on assisting Canadian businesses?

Industry Canada and the Department of Foreign Affairs, Trade and Development assist businesses domestically and internationally.

KEY TERMS

Crown corporation 146
deficit 161
deregulation 147
equalization 165
federal budget 163
fiscal policy 160
industrial policy 170
marketing boards 151
money supply 156
monetary policy 156
national debt (also known as public debt) 161
National Policy 145
overnight rate 157
prime rate 157
privatization 147
public-private partnerships (P3s or PPPs) 153
surplus 162
transfer payments 165

CAREER EXPLORATION

If you are interested in pursuing a career in public service (government), here are a few to consider. Find out about the tasks performed, skills needed, pay, and opportunity outlook in these fields through Internet sites that include the Government of Canada Job Bank, Workopolis, Monster, CareerBuilder, Glassdoor, and Indeed, as well as through the Career Centre at your school.

Senior government manager—oversee the management and administration of a government department, agency or program; apply leadership and strategic planning expertise to create and implement government services to Canadians.

Policy officer—works with Ministers and senior officials across many areas of government; informs government decision making by providing sound advice, recommendations and analysis.

Financial or budget officer—financial management and administration as it relates to a particular government department or program; develop and prepare budgets as well as other areas of procurement and forecasting.

CRITICAL THINKING

1. The issue of how much government should be involved in the economy has been the subject of much debate in Canada. In the United States, ideology has played a major role in influencing Americans to believe that, in principle, government should "butt out." This thinking ignores the significant role that the U.S. government has played and continues to play in the country's economy. In comparison, the governments in France and Sweden are more socialistic in nature and government involvement is more common. In Canada, we are less negative and perhaps more pragmatic: If it works, let's do it. But where do we go from here? Do we need less or more government involvement? Is it a question of the quality of that involvement? Could it be smarter rather than just less? How can the cost of government involvement decrease?
2. What are the implications of a majority federal government to the Canadian political scene? How does this differ from a minority government? (A minority government exists when no one party has a majority of seats in a legislative assembly. To pass legislation and other measures, that government would need the support of at least some members of other parties in the assembly.[47]) Explain.
3. If you represented the federal government, how would you respond to industries that have been seeking government action (e.g., subsidies or changes to policies) but to no avail? For example, take the position of the Canadian forestry industry, which in ten years lost about 114 000 jobs.[48] Keep in mind that other industries (e.g., aircraft manufacturing and automotive) have received such support (i.e., subsidies and bailout money).
4. The overnight bank rate, set by the Bank of Canada, is currently very low. What circumstance(s) would cause the Governor of the Bank of Canada to raise this rate? What impact would this increase have on individuals and businesses with debt?

DEVELOPING CAREER SKILLS

Key: ● **Team** ★ **Analytic** ▲ **Communication** ⊡ **Technology**

▲⊡ 1. Scan your local newspapers, *The Globe and Mail*, the *National Post*, or a Canadian magazine such as *Canadian Business* for references to government programs that help Canadian businesses or have assisted a specific company. Bring these articles to class and discuss.

★▲⊡ 2. Many foreign governments have developed strong marketing campaigns to attract Canadian businesses. They also offer many incentives, including financial ones, to lure businesses to move there. Should anything be done about this? Many provincial and municipal governments have similar programs to attract foreign companies to their jurisdictions. Check out your provincial and municipal governments' websites for examples. Bring your information to class to discuss this kind of government expenditure.

●★▲⊡ 3. In a group of four, choose an industry (e.g., telecommunications, auto, health care, etc.). Find out if there have been any recent changes in federal and/or provincial legislation that will impact businesses. For example, has the Canadian Radio-television and Telecommunications Commission (CRTC) deregulated the industry? What are advantages and disadvantages of these changes? Have any of the provinces moved closer to a two-tier heath care system? Present your findings in a report or to the class.

★● **4.** Although unemployment remains high, especially among young people, business people complain that they cannot find trained employees to fill existing vacancies. Job candidates lack math and science backgrounds and their written English-language skills are weak. (In Quebec, there are similar complaints, but the language problems are with French.) Further, too many candidates are high-school dropouts. What can be done about this serious problem? Should business or government be working harder on it? What exactly should they be doing? Discuss this in a group of three.

ANALYZING MANAGEMENT DECISIONS

Gambling: A Cash Cow for Provincial Governments

Starting slowly in Quebec in the late 1960s, but catching on quickly across the country, lotteries, casinos, bingo, video lottery terminals (VLTs), and other forms of gambling had become, by the end of the twentieth century, a major source of revenue for many provincial governments.

You can get some idea of how large the gambling business has become by looking at the revenues and profits for the Ontario and Quebec governments for their respective 2014 year ends. The Ontario Lottery and Gaming (OLG) Corporation generated $6.6 billion in economic activity. Total revenue at Loto-Québec was approximately $3.5 billion. The OLG and its contracted companies employ 17 000 people. Over the years, both organizations have generated billions of dollars for their respective governments. Both operations also allot millions of dollars to help gamblers whose obsession with gambling has proven destructive to themselves or their families.

Sources: Public Accounts of Ontario – 2013-2014, Volume 2c, Ministry of Finance, Government of Ontario, 2014, pp. 2–83, http://www.fin.gov.on.ca/en/budget/paccts/2014/14vol2cEng.pdf; Loto Quebec 2014 Annual Report, accessed April 5, 2015, http://lotoquebec.com/cms/dms/Corporatif/en/the-corporation/annual-report/2014_annual_report_pages_C1-C12.pdf.

Discussion Questions

1. Some people and organizations argue that governments should not be in the gambling business, that encouraging gambling is a bad idea. Others argue that private enterprise should run that kind of business, and argue further that companies would generate more profit compared to government run gambling operations, leading to more tax revenues for governments. Governments reply that they want to prevent organized crime from controlling gambling, so they must own and run such operations. What do you think? Is it okay for governments to be in the gambling business?
2. Governments seem to believe that gambling is a great way to raise money because Canadians don't seem to mind creating revenue by having some fun and a chance at big winnings, instead of just paying higher taxes. Besides, they argue, nobody is forced to gamble, so it's a kind of voluntary tax. How do you feel about that? Do you agree with this argument? Explain.
3. Some churches and other institutions concerned with personal and family welfare point to the rising number of family and personal breakdowns caused by people becoming gambling addicts. Also, easy access to video lottery terminals (VLTs) is very bad for young persons. Do you agree with either of these concerns? Why? What can be done to improve the situation?
4. Suppose that you agree with those who are totally opposed to governments encouraging gambling. Wouldn't taxes have to be raised to replace these revenues? Would you mind paying more taxes? Do you think your parents or family members would mind? Do you have any other suggestions for how government can generate this level of revenue?

CHAPTER 5

Ethics and Social Responsibility

LEARNING OBJECTIVES

After you have read and studied this chapter, you should be able to:

LO1 Explain why obeying the law is only the first step in behaving ethically.

LO2 Ask the three questions to answer when faced with a potentially unethical action.

LO3 Describe management's role in setting ethical standards.

LO4 Distinguish between compliance-based and integrity-based ethics codes, and list the six steps that can be considered when setting up a corporate ethics code.

LO5 Define corporate social responsibility, and compare corporations' responsibilities to various stakeholders.

LO6 Discuss the importance of ethical behaviour and social responsibility in global markets.

PROFILE

GETTING TO KNOW: MATTHEW FLANNERY, CEO/FOUNDER, BRANCH, FORMER CEO/CO-FOUNDER, KIVA

People talk about the state of "the economy" so much that it can seem as if economics only deals with big, world-shaking financial issues. In reality, though, economics can be found all around us in daily life. From a family saving money for the future to a major corporation measuring its revenue, the world is full of economies both large and small.

It's these small economies that are the major concern of Matt Flannery, founder and CEO of Branch, a socially conscious financial services company, and former co-founder of the non-profit microlending company Kiva.

Kiva offers small loans to entrepreneurs working in developing countries in Africa, Asia, and South America, as well as to borrowers in more established nations in North America and Europe. Unlike business people operating in the United States, these entrepreneurs don't need thousands

© Kiva

upon thousands of dollars to see their dreams become reality. Instead, many loans issued by Kiva are little more than a few hundred dollars.

But it's not the size of the loans that makes Flannery's work notable. In fact, microlending has been a common source of financing for the developing world since the early 1980s. What sets Kiva apart from the rest is the organization's approach. Kiva operates in a similar way to crowdfunding sites like Kickstarter or Indiegogo. These companies rely on small donations from many people in order to fund a larger goal. At Kiva, users first go to the site to select the person or family they'd like to fund. Next, they lend $25 to the entrepreneur of their choice. If the funding goal is reached, then Kiva covers the loan arranged by field partners who work with the entrepreneurs. The borrowers gradually make repayments to the field partners who transfer them back to Kiva so it may distribute the money back to the lenders.

Although lenders don't earn any interest, the satisfaction of helping another human being thousands of miles away is enough to ensure that 78 percent of people who put their money into Kiva come back to lend again. Today Kiva has distributed more than $1.15 billion in loans to entrepreneurs throughout the world "Small loans used for business growth encourage self-respect, accountability, and hope among loan recipients," says Flannery. "Primarily, the challenges they [entrepreneurs in Africa] face are very similar to the challenges we face . . . a story about a woman selling fish on the side of the street in Uganda, you can get into profit margins, inventory management, the same things that businesses here think about. There's a commonality that can unify people. Which is exciting."

Flannery took a winding road to reach this point in his career. Interestingly enough, prior to Kiva, he did not have any previous background in either financing or the non-profit sector. After getting a degree from Stanford University, Flannery got a job developing software at TiVo, but he really wanted a business of his own. "I tried to start maybe ten companies," says Flannery. "It was like I had a midlife crisis at 22." For example, Flannery attempted to start a DVD-machine-rental business years before Redbox existed. He also tried his hand at starting an online luxury clothes rental company. "A lot of those other ideas for me were a little empty . . . they weren't proactive movements towards something I loved. This idea is different. The actual content of the idea I enjoy every day . . . this is my dream job."

The inspiration for Kiva didn't hit him until he spent a few months working in rural communities throughout Africa. The same experience drove him to leave Kiva in 2014 and found a new company, Branch, in 2015. Branch is a socially conscious business that focuses upon the personal loan market in emerging economies. The company initially competed in sub-Saharan African countries such as Kenya, Tanzania, and Nigeria, but has attracted enough attention to expand into other regions, such as India. Branch competes with financial institutions in these markets by providing a quick, customer-oriented approach that combines financial services and technology. The company's mission is "to deliver world-class financial services to the mobile generation."

Many people don't realize the importance of the economic environment to the success of business. That is what this chapter is all about. You will learn to compare different economic systems to see the benefits and the drawbacks of each. You will learn how the free-market system of Canada works. And you will learn more about what makes some countries rich and other countries poor. By the end of the chapter, you should understand the direct effect economic systems have on the wealth and happiness of communities throughout the world.

Sources: "About Us," Branch, accessed June 6, 2018, https://branch.co/about; Connie Loizos, "This young lending startup just secured $70 million to lend $2 at a time," TechCrunch, March 28, 2018, accessed June 6, 2018, https://techcrunch.com/2018/03/28/this-young-lending-startup-just-secured-70-million-to-lend-2-at-a-time/; Aswin Manipelli, "Tested by adversity, Fintech Branch emerges stronger and better at risk management," *Forbes,* July 24, 2017, accessed June 6, 2018, https://www.forbes.com/sites/aswinmannepalli/2017/07/24/tested-by-adversity-fintech-branch-emerges-stronger-and-better-at-risk-management/#1ffe8e4bfdd3; Mohana Ravindranath, "Microfinance Nonprofit Kiva Launches in D.C.," The *Washington Post,* January 8, 2013; Interview, "Why Purpose Matters For Matt Flannery of Kiva.org," Yscouts, September 11, 2013; Charles Blass, "Matt Flannery: Co-Founder and CEO, Kiva Microfunds," Thefuturemakers.net, May 2, 2013; and www.kiva.org.

LO1

Explain why obeying the law is only the first step in behaving ethically.

Ethics Is More Than Legality

It is not uncommon to hear of instances where business people are involved in unethical behaviour. Some examples of Canadian companies that have been caught in such scandals include Livent, CIBC World Markets, Nortel, and WestJet. After two years of denying accusations, WestJet Airlines Ltd. admitted to spying on Air Canada. In a news release, WestJet apologized for accessing a confidential Air Canada website designated for reservations: "This practice was undertaken with the knowledge and direction of the highest management levels of WestJet and was not halted until discovered by Air Canada. This conduct was both unethical and unacceptable and WestJet accepts full responsibility for such misconduct."[1] As part of the settlement, WestJet paid Air Canada's investigation and litigation costs of $5.5 million and it made a $10 million donation in the name of both airlines to children's charities across Canada.[2] The Canadian business environment has also been impacted by notable scandals in other countries such as Enron, Arthur Andersen, Tyco, and Parmalat, just to name a few.

© Sean Gallup/Getty Images

Volkswagen agreed to a $290.5 million settlement related to its emissions cheating scandal. The Canadian deal covered 20 000 vehicles. In addition, Volkswagen Canada Group will pay an additional $2.5 million civil penalty. All together, Volkswagen's attempt to bypass environmental regulations cost the company more than $23 billion.[3]

It is not just for-profit business people who are accused of unethical behaviour. Government employees have also been implicated. For example, Elections Canada launched an investigation after the 2011 federal election. Voters complained that they had received phone calls on behalf of Elections

Canada directing them to the wrong polling stations.[4] A pattern of phone calls was reported in which voters identified as not supporting the Conservatives were targeted with robocalls or live calls directing them to the wrong polling stations.[5] People from seven ridings went to court asking that the election results in their constituency be overturned.[6] A Federal Court Judge found fraud was a factor but no election results were overturned. In 2014, a Conservative Party staffer was found guilty under the Elections Act of willfully preventing a voter from casting a ballot. However, the judge also stated the convicted person did not act alone.[7] Review Figure 5.1 for a brief summary of some of the most-publicized scandals in recent years.

© THE CANADIAN PRESS/Fred Chartrand

The Ontario government faced 50 land claims in 2015. The largest, The Algonquin Land Claim, covers 32 000 km² in Eastern Ontario that is populated by more than 1.2 million people. A key factor in many land claims across Canada is ownership of natural resources.[8]

Given the ethical lapses that are so prevalent today, what can be done to restore trust in the free- market system and leaders in general? First, those who have broken the law need to be punished accordingly. New laws making accounting records more transparent

FIGURE 5.1

BRIEF SUMMARY OF SOME CORPORATE SCANDALS

Lottery Corporations: Ontario Ombudsman Andre Marin's Report blasted the Ontario Lottery and Gaming Corporation for not cracking down on retailers who collected tens of millions of dollars in jackpots between 1999 and 2006, some of them fraudulently. As a result, police began probing allegations of fraudulent lottery prize claims by retailers. The Atlantic Lottery Corporation announced it was turning over its files to police over similar concerns of retailers stealing winning tickets from customers. The British Columbia government announced an audit of the province's lottery system following a negative report by its Ombudsman that found it was open to fraud.

Research In Motion (RIM) Stock Option Scandal: An Ontario court approved a settlement between the company and the Ironworkers of Ontario Pension Fund over allegations RIM had backdated stock options to company executives. Under terms of the settlement, RIM's co-founders Jim Balsillie and Mike Lazaridis agreed to pay $2.5 million each (in addition to the $5 million the executives had each agreed to repay earlier). The company has also ceased giving stock options to directors, added more independent directors to the board, and tightened up its executive compensation practices.

Federal Government Sponsorship Scandal: The Auditor General's 2004 Report found that $100 million was paid to a variety of communications agencies in the form of fees and commissions, and said that the program was basically designed to generate commissions for these companies rather than to produce any benefit for Canadians. Implicated in this scandal were high-level officials. Charles Guité, a former senior bureaucrat, was sentenced to 42 months in prison for defrauding the federal government. Other scandal participants who received prison sentences include Jean Brault (30 months) and Paul Coffin (18 months). Gilles-André Gosselin was charged in 2008 with 19 criminal charges, including fraud.

Hollinger International Inc.: Conrad Black, who once headed the Hollinger International Inc. media empire, was convicted of obstruction of justice in 2007. In addition to three other former Hollinger executives, he was found guilty of fraud for funnelling US$6.1 million from the media company. Black was sentenced to 6½ years in federal prison and ordered to pay a six-figure fine plus restitution of $6.1 million. Three former Hollinger executives also received sentences: Jack Boultbee (27 months), Peter Atkinson (24 months), and Mark Kipnis (placed on probation with six months of house arrest). David Radler, one-time CEO of Hollinger International, plead guilty to mail fraud. He received a 29-month sentence and agreed to pay a US$250,000 fine.

(easy to read and understand) and more laws making business people and others more accountable may help. But laws do not make people honest, reliable, or truthful. If they did, crime would disappear.

One danger in writing new laws to correct behaviour is that people may begin to think that any behaviour that is within the law is also acceptable. The measure of behaviour, then, becomes: "Is it legal?" A society gets in trouble when people consider only what is illegal and not also what is unethical. Ethics and legality are two very different things. Although following the law is an important first step, ethical behaviour requires more than that. Ethics reflects people's proper relations with one another: How should people treat others? What responsibility should they feel for others? Legality is narrower. It refers to laws we have written to protect ourselves from fraud, theft, and violence. Many immoral and unethical acts fall well within our laws.[9] For example, gossiping about your neighbour or sharing something told to you in confidence is unethical, but not illegal.

Ethical Standards Are Fundamental

ethics
Standards of moral behaviour; that is, behaviour that is accepted by society as right versus wrong.

We define **ethics** as the standards of moral behaviour; that is, behaviour that is accepted by society as right versus wrong. Many people today have few moral absolutes. Many decide situationally whether it's okay to steal, lie, or text and drive. They seem to think that what is right is whatever works best for the individual, and that each person has to work out for himself or herself the difference between right and wrong. That is the kind of thinking that has led to the recent scandals in government and business. This is not the way it always was. However, in the past decade there has been a rising tide of criticism in Canada (and other countries) of various business practices that many Canadians consider unacceptable.

In a country like Canada, with so many diverse cultures, you might think it would be impossible to identify common standards of ethical behaviour. However, among sources from many different times and places—such as the Bible, Aristotle's *Ethics,* William Shakespeare's *King Lear,* the Quran, and the *Analects* of Confucius—you will find the following basic moral values: integrity, respect for human life, self-control, honesty, courage, and self-sacrifice are right; cheating, cowardice, and cruelty are wrong. Furthermore, all of the world's major religions support a version of the Golden Rule: Do unto others as you would have them do unto you.[10]

Ethics Begins with Each of Us

LO2

Ask the three questions to answer when faced with a potentially unethical action.

It is easy to criticize business and political leaders for their moral and ethical shortcomings, but we must be careful in our criticism to note that ethics begins with each of us. Ethical behaviour should be exhibited in our daily lives, not just in a business environment.

Plagiarizing material from the Internet, including cutting and pasting information from websites without giving credit, is the most common form of cheating in post-secondary institutions today. To fight this problem, many instructors now use services like Turnitin, which scans students' papers against more than 40 billion online sources to provide evidence of copying in seconds.[11] Have you seen students cheat on assignments or exams? How did this make you feel? Students use many reasons to rationalize such behaviour, such as "Everyone else is doing it" or "I ran out of time to prepare, but I will do all my own work next time." What do you think of these reasons?

In a study, most teens said they were prepared to make ethical decisions in the workforce, but an alarming 51 percent of high school students admit that they have cheated on tests in the last year. Studies have found a strong relationship between academic dishonesty among undergraduates and dishonesty at work.[12] A more recent article reported statistics related to academic integrity across Canadian universities. Figures indicated the highest percentage for a school in different plagiarism categories as follows; repeat offenders (four or more occasions) was 13.5 percent. collaboration on independent assignments was 66 percent, bought an assignment was 5.4 percent, and business programs was 11.5 percent.[13]

© imageBROKER / Alamy Stock Photo

In 2017, Harvard University rescinded offers to students as a result of offensive posts in a Facebook group. The university also cancelled the men's soccer team season when student-athlete conduct on Facebook was deemed sexist. Reactions varied from views the students were unfairly punished to the punishment was deserved.[14] How do you feel about students being held accountable by a university for their personal social media behaviour?

In response, many schools are establishing heavier consequences for cheating and requiring students to perform a certain number of hours of community service to graduate. Do you think such policies make a difference in student behaviour?

It is always healthy when discussing moral and ethical issues to remember that ethical behaviour begins with you and me. We cannot expect society to become more moral and ethical unless we as individuals commit to being moral and ethical ourselves.

The Making Ethical Decisions boxes throughout the text—like the accompanying one on Ponzi schemes—remind you to keep ethics in mind whenever you are making a business decision. The choices are not always easy. Sometimes the obvious solution from an ethical point of view has drawbacks from a personal or professional point of view. For example, imagine that your supervisor at work has asked you to do something you feel is unethical. You have just taken out a mortgage on a new house to make room for your first baby, due in two months. Not carrying out your supervisor's request may

© hafakot/Shutterstock RF

Plagiarizing from the Internet is one of the most common forms of cheating in colleges today. Remember, even if you copy and paste information from a site like Wikipedia, it's still plagiarism! Have you ever been tempted to plagiarize a paper or project? What are the possible consequences of copying someone else's material?

Making ETHICAL DECISIONS

Canadian Ponzi Schemes

News stories of corporate fraud and corruption are all too common. White-collar criminals often assume the complexity of the financial system will hide their crimes, leaving them free to embezzle to their heart's content. But people tend to notice when a few billion dollars suddenly go missing. Eventually, even the most careful corporate criminal gets caught.

Canadian convictions related to money managers are becoming more prevalent. The managers tell clients they will invest their money in various ventures and pay them back on their returns, minus a commission. With a Ponzi scheme, however, the fraudsters don't invest the money. They simply pass money contributed by new investors on to early investors (minus a healthy sum held back for their own personal use, of course), claiming the money as profits from the existing clients' "investments." The steady income fools the investors into thinking their wealth is growing when in reality it is being siphoned off from other people. Obviously the scheme depends upon being able to continuously attract new "investors."

© Devonyu/iStock/Thinkstock

In 2014, Gary Sorenson and Milowe Brost, owners of a Calgary company, were convicted for what RCMP claim is the largest Ponzi scheme in Canadian history. Their lucrative scam defrauded 3000 investors from around the world of $300 to $400 million. The money was intended for mining and investment companies but the owners funnelled the cash to themselves. The two men were fined $54 million by the Alberta Securities Commission and prosecutors are seeking the maximum 14 year sentence for the fraudsters.

Do you think the punishment fits the crime in this case?

Sources: Barrie McKenna, "Largest Ponzi scheme in Canadian history exploited boom time Alberta," *The Globe and Mail,* February 15, 2015, updated May 12, 2018, accessed June 29, 2018, http://www.theglobeandmail.com/report-on-business/largest-ponzi-scheme-in-canadian-history-exploited-boom-time-alberta/article23010870/; Annalise Klingbeil, "What's next for Sorenson and Brost? Multi-year sentences common for Canadian Ponzi schemes," *Calgary Herald,* February 15, 2015, updated February 17, 2015, accessed June 29, 2018, http://calgaryherald.com/news/local-news/whats-next-for-sorenson-and-brost-multi-year-sentences-common-for-canadian-ponzi-schemes; Lauren Krugel, "Trial begins into alleged Ponzi scheme called largest in Canadian history," *Maclean's,* September 8, 2014, accessed June 29, 2018, http://www.macleans.ca/news/canada/trial-begins-into-alleged-ponzi-scheme-called-largest-in-canadian-history/.

get you fired. What would you do? Sometimes there is no easy alternative in such *ethical dilemmas* because you must choose between equally unsatisfactory alternatives.

It can be difficult to balance between ethics and other goals such as pleasing stakeholders or advancing in your career. According to management writer Ken Blanchard and religious leader Norman Vincent Peale, it helps to ask yourself the following questions when facing an ethical dilemma:[15]

1. *Is my proposed action legal?* Am I violating any law or company policy? Whether you're thinking about having a drink and driving home, gathering marketing intelligence, designing a product, hiring or firing employees, getting rid of industrial waste, or using a questionable nickname for an employee, think about the legal implications. This is the most basic question in business ethics, but it is only the first.
2. *Is it balanced?* Am I acting fairly? Would I want to be treated this way? Will I win everything at the expense of another? Win–lose situations often become lose–lose situations and generate retaliation from the loser. Not every situation can be completely

balanced, but the health of our relationships requires us to avoid major imbalances over time. An ethical business person has a win–win attitude and tries to make decisions that benefit all.

3. *How will it make me feel about myself?* Would I feel proud if my family learned of my decision? My friends? Could I discuss the proposed situation or action with my supervisor? The company's clients? Will I have to hide my actions? Has someone warned me not to disclose them? What if my decision was announced on the evening news? Am I feeling unusually nervous? Decisions that go against our sense of right and wrong make us feel bad—they erode our self-esteem. That is why an ethical business person does what is proper as well as what is profitable.

© Shutterstock / eldeiv

A new provision under Canada's Copyright Modernization Act, called the "notice and notice" program, allows copyright holders such as a movie studio to send notices for illegal Internet downloads. The government's intent is to educate people about copyright infringement. Do you think this is an effective way to curtail Internet piracy?

PROGRESS ASSESSMENT

- What is ethics?
- How do ethics differ from legality?
- When faced with ethical dilemmas, what questions can you ask yourself that might help you make ethical decisions?

Managing Businesses Ethically and Responsibly

LO3

Describe management's role in setting ethical standards.

Ethics is caught more than it is taught. That is, people learn their standards and values from observing what others do, not from hearing what they say. This is as true in business as it is at home. Organizational ethics begins at the top, and the leadership and example of strong managers can help instil corporate values in employees. A great example can be found in the Spotlight on Small Business.

Trust and co-operation between workers and managers must be based on fairness, honesty, openness, and moral integrity. The same applies to relationships among businesses and among nations. A business should be managed ethically for many reasons: to maintain a good reputation; to keep existing customers and attract new ones; to avoid lawsuits; to reduce employee turnover; to avoid government intervention in the form of new laws and regulations controlling business activities; to please customers, employees, and society; and simply to do the right thing.

Spotlight *On* SMALL BUSINESS

MEATHEAD MOVERS

Being a mover seems like a fairly straightforward job: carry someone's stuff out to a truck, then drive to his or her new place and unload. But this simple process is more personal than you might think. After all, movers spend large amounts of time in the homes of strangers. As a result, they get brief but intimate looks into the lives of their customers, and sometimes the view is not pleasant.

Aaron Steed found himself in a dangerous situation while working as a mover in high school. He had been carrying a young woman's stuff to his truck when the customer's abusive boyfriend showed up in a rage. The intensity of the event also made Aaron think about other women that he moved out of similar circumstances. He and his brother Evan received numerous calls from survivors of domestic abuse after the pair placed their first ad in a local paper.

Courtesy of Meathead Movers

Knowing they could do more to help, he and Evan agreed that their new company, Meathead Movers, would relocate survivors of domestic violence for free. The brothers recognized they had a unique opportunity to help people escape from their horrible home lives. The charitable policy didn't damage the company's growth. As the years went on Meathead Movers expanded beyond the Steeds' hometown of San Luis Obispo, California, to branches located throughout the state. This has led to rave reviews of Meathead Movers' staff from people involved in non-profits. "They're wonderful, sensitive, caring and enthusiastic," said Kathleen Buczko, executive director of the Los Angeles–based Good Shepherd Shelter. "They help turn something that had been associated with something that was so incredibly traumatic into a celebration of moving to their new homes and to a new life."

For ethical entrepreneurs like Aaron and Evan Steed, receiving feedback like this is one of the best parts about business. What responsibility does a businesses have to it stakeholders: customers, investors, employees, and society?

Sources: Nick Wilson, "Moving Out? Meathead Movers Will Help You Donate to Local Nonprofits as You Pack," *San Luis Obispo Tribune*, December 5, 2016; Jessica Kwong, "Moving Company Comes to the Aid of Domestic Violence Victims," *Orange County Register*, August 1, 2016; Brittany Woolsey, "Meathead Movers Offers Services for Free to Victims of Domestic Abuse," *Los Angeles Times*, December 6, 2015; Dennis Romero, "Moving Company Will Help You Leave an Abusive Partner for Free," *LA Weekly*, September 4, 2015; Sydney Maki, "Ex-Fresno State Star Dwayne Wright Starts Gig at Meathead Movers," *Fresno Bee*, June 11, 2016; Anne Kallas, Meathead Moves into Helping Nonprofits," *Ventura County Star*, March 4, 2017.

Some managers think that ethics is a personal matter—either individuals have ethical principles or they don't. These managers feel that they are not responsible for an individual's misdeeds and that ethics has nothing to do with management. But a growing number of people think that ethics has everything to do with management. Individuals do not usually act alone; they need the implied, if not direct, co-operation of others to behave unethically in a corporation.

For example, there have been reports of cell phone service sales representatives who actually lie to get customers to extend their contracts—or even extend their contracts without the customers' knowledge. Some phone reps intentionally hang up on callers to prevent them from cancelling their contracts. Why do these sales reps sometimes resort to overly aggressive tactics? Because poorly designed incentive programs reward them for meeting certain goals, sometimes doubling or tripling their salaries with incentives. Do their managers say directly, "Deceive the customers"? No, but the message is clear. Overly ambitious goals and incentives can create an environment in which unethical actions like this can occur.

LO4

Distinguish between compliance-based and integrity-based ethics codes, and list the six steps that can be considered when setting up a corporate ethics code.

Setting Corporate Ethical Standards

More and more companies have adopted written codes of conduct. Figure 5.2 offers Hershey Company's code of conduct as a sample. Although ethics codes vary greatly, they can be classified into two categories: compliance-based and integrity-based. **Compliance-based ethics codes** emphasize the prevention of unlawful behaviour by increasing control and penalizing wrongdoers. Where compliance-based ethics codes are based on avoiding legal punishment, **integrity-based ethics codes** define the organization's guiding values, create an environment that supports ethically sound behaviour, and stress shared accountability among employees. See Figure 5.3 for a comparison of compliance-based and integrity-based ethics codes.

compliance-based ethics codes
Ethical standards that emphasize preventing unlawful behaviour by increasing control and by penalizing wrongdoers.

The following six-step process can help improve business ethics:[16]

1. Top management must adopt and unconditionally support an explicit corporate code of conduct.
2. Employees must understand that expectations for ethical behaviour begin at the top and that senior management expects all employees to act accordingly.

FIGURE 5.2

OVERVIEW OF THE HERSHEY COMPANY'S CODE OF ETHICS

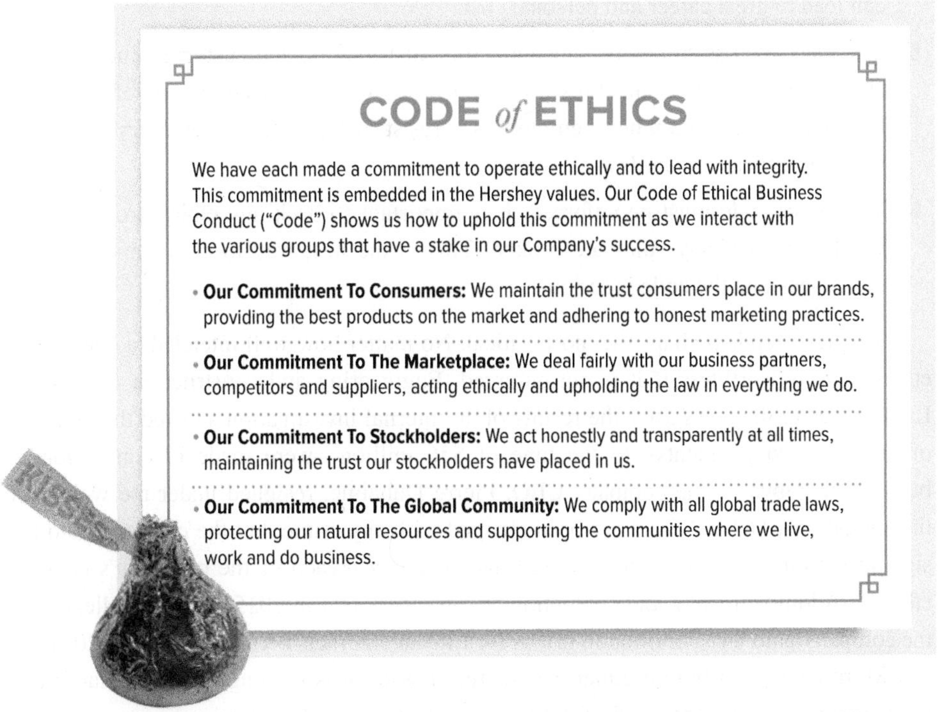

CODE *of* ETHICS

We have each made a commitment to operate ethically and to lead with integrity. This commitment is embedded in the Hershey values. Our Code of Ethical Business Conduct ("Code") shows us how to uphold this commitment as we interact with the various groups that have a stake in our Company's success.

- **Our Commitment To Consumers:** We maintain the trust consumers place in our brands, providing the best products on the market and adhering to honest marketing practices.
- **Our Commitment To The Marketplace:** We deal fairly with our business partners, competitors and suppliers, acting ethically and upholding the law in everything we do.
- **Our Commitment To Stockholders:** We act honestly and transparently at all times, maintaining the trust our stockholders have placed in us.
- **Our Commitment To The Global Community:** We comply with all global trade laws, protecting our natural resources and supporting the communities where we live, work and do business.

More and more companies have adopted written codes of ethics. Here is the Hershey Company's Code of Ethics, which directs the company's road map.

Note: This is an overview of Hershey's code of ethics. To see the company's complete ethics code, go to www.thehersheycompany.com.

FIGURE 5.3

STRATEGIES FOR ETHICS MANAGEMENT

Both codes have a concern for the law and use penalties as enforcement. Integrity-based ethics codes move beyond legal compliance to create a "do-it-right" climate that emphasizes core values such as honesty, fair play, good service to customers, a commitment to diversity, and involvement in the community. These values are ethically desirable, but not necessarily legally mandatory.

Features of Compliance-Based Ethics Codes		Features of Integrity-Based Ethics Codes	
Ideal	Conform to outside standards (laws and regulations)	Ideal	Conform to outside standards (laws and regulations) and chosen internal standards
Objective	Avoid criminal misconduct	Objective	Enable responsible employee conduct
Leaders	Lawyers	Leaders	Managers with aid of lawyers and others
Methods	Education, reduced employee discretion, controls, and penalties	Methods	Education, leadership, accountability, decision processes, controls, and penalties

integrity-based ethics codes
Ethical standards that define the organization's guiding values, create an environment that supports ethically sound behaviour, and stress a shared accountability among employees.

whistleblowers
People who report illegal or unethical behaviour.

3. Managers and others must be trained to consider the ethical implications of all business decisions.
4. An ethics office must be set up. Phone lines to the office should be established so that employees who don't necessarily want to be seen with an ethics officer can inquire about ethical matters anonymously. **Whistleblowers** (people who report illegal or unethical behaviour) must feel protected from retaliation as oftentimes this exposure can lead to great career and personal cost.
5. Outsiders such as suppliers, subcontractors, distributors, and customers must be told about the ethics program. Pressure to put aside ethical considerations often comes from the outside, and it helps employees to resist such pressure when everyone knows what the ethical standards are.
6. The ethics code must be enforced. It is important to back any ethics program with timely action if any rules are broken. This is the best way to communicate to all employees that the code is serious.

This last step is perhaps the most critical. No matter how well intended, a company's ethics code is worthless if it is not enforced. Engineering and construction firm SNC-Lavalin was in the news after the results of an internal investigation showed that a series of unauthorized payments—to the tune of $56 million—were made in connection to business in Libya.[17] The company CEO, Pierre Duhaime, resigned under the weight of the allegations; Duhaime had not been charged with any crime, but the company said his signing off on payments to undisclosed agents was a breach of the company's code of ethics.[18] Additional fraud and corruption charges were laid in 2015 related to allegations the company paid $47.7 million in bribes for Libyan contracts between 2001 and 2011.[19]

More recently, a billion dollar class-action lawsuit was filed against Canadian bread producers and grocers accused of a 14-year, industry-wide bread price fixing scheme.[20] In its 2017 Code of Conduct, Loblaw Companies Ltd., the CEO, Chairman and President,

Galen Weston Jr., stated "Our customers, colleagues and partners have high expectations of our conduct." However, the company is one of 12 named in the suit and is part of a criminal investigation by the Competition Bureau Canada.[21]

An important factor in the success of enforcing an ethics code is selecting an ethics officer. The most competent ethics officers set a positive tone, communicate effectively, and relate well to employees at every level. They are equally comfortable as counsellors and investigators, and can be trusted to maintain confidentiality, conduct objective investigations, and ensure fairness. They can demonstrate to stakeholders that ethics are important in everything the company does.

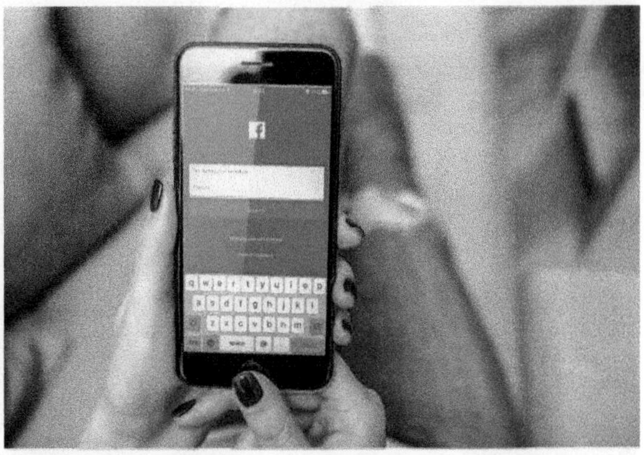

© Denis Rozhnovsky / Alamy Stock Photo

Apple faced backlash when the company admitted it used software updates to limit the performance of iPhone models. The company claimed the adjustment was to address battery life. The U.S. Department of Justice and the Securities and Exchange Commission is investigating.[22] How do you feel about companies interfering with your devices without your knowledge?

As more organizations are recognizing the importance of this role, associations are also providing support for those in these roles. One such example is the Ethics Practitioners' Association of Canada (EPAC). EPAC's mission is "to enable individuals to work successfully in the field of ethics in organizations by enhancing the quality and availability of ethics advice and services across Canada." This organization supports ethics officers, consultants, educators, students, and others who are interested in the field of ethics as applied to organizations of all kinds.

THE SARBANES-OXLEY ACT OF 2002 (SOX)[23]

The major corporate and accounting scandals in the United States in the early 2000s (e.g., Enron, Tyco, Adelphia, and WorldCom) gave rise to the implementation of U.S. federal legislation known as the Sarbanes-Oxley Act (SOX). The legislation established stronger standards to prevent misconduct and improve corporate governance practices. SOX applies to all publicly traded companies whose shares are listed on the stock exchanges under the jurisdiction of the U.S. Securities and Exchange Commission. The goal of SOX is to ensure the accuracy and reliability of published financial information. Requirements deal with the proper administration routines, procedures, and control activities.

SOX also protects whistleblowers from any company retaliation as it requires that all public corporations provide a system that allows employees to submit concerns regarding accounting and auditing issues both confidentially and anonymously. The purpose is to motivate employees to report any wrongdoing. For example, the legislation provides for reinstatement and back pay to people who were punished by their employers for passing information about frauds to authorities.

In response to SOX, Canada also implemented similar corporate governance legislation.

WHISTLEBLOWER LEGISLATION IN CANADA[24]

One might suggest that for the six steps mentioned earlier to work, there must first be protection in place for whistleblowers. Otherwise, how effective can such a process be? Unfortunately, there is no legislation in place that protects all workers—public sector and

© wildpixel/iStock/Thinkstock

The Public Servants Disclosure Protection Act was passed in 2007. The legislation was intended to support "truth telling" by whistleblowers who try to protect the public interest. Critics claim government efforts to impose codes of conduct and nondisclosure agreements place whistleblowers at risk. What do you believe motivates a whistleblower?

private sector—across the country. Regarding public-sector workers, the federal government and some provinces have variations of whistleblower legislation that set up a third-party independent officer, such as the federal integrity commissioner or Saskatchewan's public interest disclosure commissioner, to whom employees can raise concerns. Let us consider one piece of legislation.

The Federal Accountability Act (FAA) applies to approximately 400 000 government employees. It lists a wide range of measures to help make the Canadian federal government more accountable and to increase transparency and oversight in government operations. Among other objectives, it is promoted as protecting federal government employees who come forward, so they need not fear reprisal. This includes direct employee access to the commissioner to report wrongdoing in the workplace. The commissioner has the authority to deal with reprisal complaints, conduct investigations, and attempt to conciliate a settlement between the parties. Democracy Watch, a citizen group advocating democratic reform, government accountability, and corporate responsibility, believes that much more needs to be done to protect whistleblowers. Among some of its criticisms, it maintains that the "FAA established a system that does not provide promised adequate funding for whistleblowers' legal services, and that it requires the whistleblower to prove retaliation has occurred (instead of requiring the government to prove it has not punished the whistleblower)."

© OLIVIER JEAN/Reuters

The Charbonneau Commission examined corruption within the Quebec construction industry. Much of the investigation relied upon whistleblowers who spoke out about collusion that involved connections to organized crime and political parties.

While Canadians who work for corporations listed on a U.S. stock exchange may have some protection under the U.S. Sarbanes-Oxley legislation, there is no provision to protect other, private-sector whistleblowers. In a KPMG survey on private corporations' policies on whistleblowers, almost two-thirds of respondents to the business ethics survey stated that they have a written policy requiring employees to report fraud or misconduct in the workplace. However, only 40 percent of respondents reported having formal systems designed to protect whistleblowers from retaliation. One-fifth of respondents lacked any type of protection system. Yet whistleblowers add value to corporations. A PricewaterhouseCoopers study showed that whistleblowers uncovered far more fraud than internal audit and all other management control systems combined. The study, which polled 5400 senior executives from 40 countries, found that 43 percent of corporate frauds had been initially detected by employee tip-offs.

A high profile example of a whistleblower relates to the misuse of data for profit by companies such as Facebook. While working for Cambridge Analytica, Canadian Christopher Wylie conducted psychological profiling of various users through apps that required the use of Facebook. The data was then used to predict the personal traits and vulnerabilities of millions of Americans and in turn, target political messages for candidates in the 2016 election.

Going public wasn't easy for Wylie, who stated, "Speaking out against social media giants like Facebook is intimidating, particularly when I come forward as a whistleblower,"[25] Since the story broke public unease over the privacy issue has expanded to include many companies, such as Twitter and Google.[26] How do you feel about companies using your personal information for profit?

PROGRESS ASSESSMENT

- How are compliance-based ethics codes different from integrity-based ethics codes?
- What are the six steps to follow in establishing an effective ethics program in a business?
- What laws are in place to protect whistleblowers?

Corporate Social Responsibility

LO5

Define corporate social responsibility, and compare corporations' responsibilities to various stakeholders.

Just as you and I need to be good citizens, contributing what we can to society, corporations need to be good citizens as well. **Corporate social responsibility (CSR)** is the concern businesses have for the welfare of society, not just for their owners. CSR goes well beyond merely being ethical. It is based on a commitment to integrity, fairness, and respect.[27]

It is important to note that both CSR and ethics are often judgment calls, depending on which side of the issue you are on. To clarify, one person's unethical behaviour can be considered another person's sound business decision. Also, do not underestimate the impact of cultural values. Differences from country to country also contribute to varying perspectives on the same issue. This can result in decision making that is not in line with one's personal values but is congruent with what is considered ethical in a country.

corporate social responsibility (CSR)
A business' concern for the welfare of society.

Part of CSR includes the general idea of combining shopping with ethics. This concept, termed **ethical consumerism**, is a strategy where "companies provide products that appeal to people's best selves."[28] While consumers are more aware that they can effect change through their purchase decisions, many companies who adapt this approach face challenges.[29] The sales of ethical brands are often low and it is easy to believe that

ethical consumerism
A strategy where companies provide products that appeal to people's best selves.

© Lannis Waters/Zuma Press/Newscom

Company employees volunteer in their communities for many causes. Here volunteers work to beautify a school through painting, cleanups, landscaping, and rebuilding a volleyball court. Do companies have responsibilities to the communities in which they operate beyond obeying the laws?

corporate philanthropy
Dimension of social responsibility that includes charitable donations.

A-Way Express
THE WHOLE PACKAGE

Courtesy of A-Way Express. Used with permission.

Social enterprises such as A-Way give back to the community in ways that are not found in traditional employee–client business relations. The organization serves both environmental and social purposes. Its couriers use public transit to provide a low-cost carbon neutral delivery service. At the same time, A-Way employs people living with mental health challenges. "Toronto's Social Purpose Transit Courier" may be A-Way's business slogan but its true purpose is the health, well-being, and recovery of its workforce. What are other ways social enterprises can tackle major social issues?

ethical consumerism is not important to consumers. But often, consumers opt to purchase from local crafts people rather than large brands because they know exactly where and how the product was made.[30] The challenge, then, is to shift ethical consumerism from a niche to mainstream so companies with this business philosophy can have enough sales to succeed. This can be done with a little help, as you'll see in the Adapting to Change box. How do you feel about conscientious consumption? Have you ever made a purchase decision based upon this philosophy?

You may be surprised to know that not everyone thinks that CSR is a good thing. Some critics of CSR believe that a manager's sole role is to compete and win in the marketplace. Economist Milton Friedman made a classic statement when he said that the only social responsibility of business is to make money for shareholders. He thought that doing anything else was moving dangerously toward socialism. Other CSR critics believe that managers who pursue CSR are doing so with other people's money—money they invested to make more money, not to improve society. In this view, spending money on CSR activities is stealing from investors.[31]

CSR defenders, in contrast, believe that businesses owe their existence to the societies they serve and cannot succeed in societies that fail.[32] Firms have access to society's labour pool and its natural resources, in which every member of society has a stake. Even Adam Smith, the father of capitalism, believed that the self-interested pursuit of profit was wrong and that benevolence was the highest virtue. CSR defenders acknowledge that businesses have deep obligations to investors, and that businesses should not attempt government-type social responsibility projects. However, they also argue that CSR makes more money for investors in the long run. Studies show that companies with good ethical reputations attract and retain better employees, draw more customers, and enjoy greater employee loyalty.[33]

The social performance of a company has several dimensions:

- **Corporate philanthropy** includes charitable donations to non-profit groups of all kinds. Some make long-term commitments to one cause, such as the Canadian Tire Jumpstart Charities, which has helped more than 1.4 million financially

Adapting *to* CHANGE

Social Entrepreneurship

The Canadian Social Entrepreneurship Foundation (CSEF) site was created by Jason Carvalho to spur innovation and "bridge the gap" that was developing between the non-profit, business, and government sectors. The motto of the CSEF is taken from a famous quote paraphrased by Robert Kennedy which is as follows: "Some men and women see things as they are and say, 'Why?' I dream things that never were and say, 'Why not?'"

To begin to bridge this gap, CSEF looks for social entrepreneurs who are under the age of 40 and who want to develop and take a new service or product to market. Although social entrepreneurs share some characteristics and techniques with traditional business entrepreneurs—for example, an emphasis on innovation and the utilization of time-tested business theories and practices—their work and impact span private, non-profit, and government sectors. In fact, watching what changes in these sectors is what generates social entrepreneurship ideas.

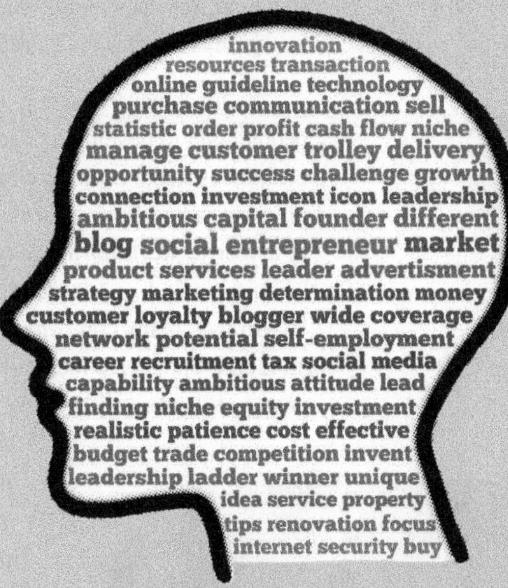

© Zurainy Zain/Shutterstock

CSEF, which is 60 percent a virtual organization, provides access to funding, media resources, mentorship and support, and an online community. It invests in Canadian social enterprises that produce revenue and focus on specific areas such as (social) inventors, children and youth (e.g., employing at-risk youth), the environment (e.g., clean technologies and energy efficiency), and civic engagement.

Can you see yourself as a social entrepreneur? You could become a small business owner in Canada, but you could also use the business skills you learn in this course to be a social entrepreneur in Canada and other countries. Think of the possibilities.

Sources: The Canadian Social Entrepreneurship Foundation. Copyright 2010, www.csef.ca. Used with permission.

disadvantaged kids across Canada since 2005.[34] The charity provides financial support for kids ages four to eight to participate in organized sport and physical activity.

- **Corporate social initiatives** include enhanced forms of corporate philanthropy. Corporate social initiatives differ from traditional philanthropy in that they are more directly related to the company's competencies. For example, three of the largest global logistics and transportation companies, Agility, UPS, and Maersk, work together to support humanitarian efforts during large-scale natural disasters. Their emergency relief teams go anywhere in the world to provide support in aviation, warehousing, transportation, reporting, and communications.[35]

corporate social initiatives
Dimension of social responsibility that includes enhanced forms of corporate philanthropy that are more directly related to the company's competencies.

- **Corporate responsibility** includes everything from hiring minority workers to making safe products, minimizing pollution, using energy wisely, and providing a safe work environment—that is, everything that has to do with acting responsibly within society—for example, treating employees fairly and ethically. This is especially true of businesses that operate in other countries with different labour laws than those in Canada.

corporate responsibility
Dimension of social responsibility that includes everything from hiring minority workers to making safe products.

corporate policy Dimension of social responsibility that refers to the position a firm takes on social and political issues.

- **Corporate policy** refers to the position a firm takes on social and political issues. For example, Patagonia's corporate policy includes this statement: "A love of wild and beautiful places demands participation in the fight to save them, and to help reverse the steep decline in the overall environmental health of our planet. We donate our time, services and at least 1% of our sales to hundreds of grassroots environmental groups all over the world who work to help reverse the tide."[36]

So much news coverage has been devoted to the problems caused by corporations that people tend to develop a negative view of the impact that companies have on society. But businesses make positive contributions too. Few people know, for example, that a Xerox program called Social Service Leave allows employees to take a leave of absence for up to a year to work for a non-profit organization while earning their full Xerox salary and benefits, including job security.[37]

In fact, many companies allow employees to give part-time help to social agencies of all kinds. The recent recession has changed the way that many corporations approach corporate philanthropy. Now they are often likely to give time and goods rather than money. Many companies are now encouraging employees to volunteer more—on company time.[38] For example, Mars Incorporated encourages community involvement by offering paid time off to clean parks, aid medical clinics, and plant gardens. Nearly 10 000 Mars employees volunteer 37 000 hours a year.[39]

© The Canadian Press Images/Lee Brown

Tim Horton's conducts various corporate social responsibility initiatives related to individuals, communities and the planet. The company's community outreach includes the Tim Horton's Children's Foundation, the Timbits Minor Sports Program, the Smile Cookie, and Pitch-In Week. Have you heard about these programs in your hometown?

The Toronto Dominion Bank demonstrates corporate responsibility through community initiatives that focus upon affordable housing, the environment, and volunteerism.[40] The TD Volunteer Network is an online database that allows charities to post volunteer opportunities to more than 60 000 bank employees. The Volunteer Grants Program donates $500 to a charity where a TD employee volunteered more than 40 hours annually. In 2014, Canada's five biggest banks reported a collective annual profit of $31.7 billion.[41] Given the success of the finance sector in Canada, do you expect Canadian banks to do more for communities?

Two-thirds of the MBA students surveyed by a group called Students for Responsible Business said they would take a reduced salary to work for a socially responsible company.[42] But when the same students were asked to define *socially responsible,* articulating a clear answer was complicated. It appears that even those who want to be socially responsible cannot agree on what it is.

Concepts of Social Corporate Responsibility

What should be the guiding philosophy for business in the twenty-first century? For most of the twentieth century, there was uncertainty regarding the position top managers should take, and this question is still debated today. How a company answers this question depends on its fundamental belief of how stakeholders should be treated and its responsibility to society. There are two different views of corporate responsibility to stakeholders:

1. *The Strategic Approach.* The strategic approach requires that management's primary orientation be toward the economic interests of shareholders. The rationale is this: as owners, shareholders have the right to expect management to work in their best interests; that is, to optimize profits. Furthermore, Adam Smith's notion of the invisible hand suggests that the maximum social gain is realized when managers attend only to their shareholders' interests.

   Friedman and others argue that since (in their view) only people can have social responsibilities, corporations are only responsible to their shareholders and not to society as a whole. Although they accept that corporations should obey the laws of the countries within which they work, they assert that corporations have no other obligation to society.[43] Often, the interests of other stakeholders are considered only when they would adversely affect profits if ignored.

© McGraw-Hill Education

Imperial Tobacco Canada promotes itself as a socially responsible company. Among other programs, it supports Operation I.D., a youth smoking prevention program. Overall, what view of corporate responsibility do you believe this company supports?

2. *The Pluralist Approach.* This approach recognizes the special responsibility of management to optimize profits, but not at the expense of employees, suppliers, and members of the community. This approach recognizes the moral responsibilities of management that apply to all human beings. Managers don't have moral immunity when making managerial decisions. This view says that corporations can maintain their economic viability only when they fulfill their moral responsibilities to society as a whole. When shareholders' interests compete with those of the community, as they often do, managers must decide how to act, using ethical and moral principles.

The guiding philosophy for the twenty-first century will be some version of the pluralist approach. Managerial decision making will not be easy, and new ethical guidelines may have to be drawn. But the process toward such guidelines has been started, and a new era of more responsible and responsive management is under way.

Figure 5.4 highlights some examples of responsibility efforts by certain companies. However, the time when ethics matters the most is when the company is tested. That is, when it is in a crisis. This is when a company can prove that it is staying true to its values and ethics, based on its reaction to the crisis. Moving forward in this chapter, you will be introduced to two examples (highlighted in photos with some details in the captions) of companies that were faced with a crisis. Some would argue that one handled the situation much better than the other. Do some research to discover which was which.

Perhaps it would be easier to understand social responsibility if we looked at the concept through the eyes of the stakeholders to whom businesses are responsible: customers, investors, employees, society in general, and the environment.

FIGURE 5.4

EXAMPLES OF CORPORATE RESPONSIBILITY EFFORTS

Company	Social Responsibility Efforts
Starbucks	When the South American coffee crops were dying from coffee-leaf rust in 2014, Starbucks' R&D farm developed rust-resistant coffee plants. The company improved the lives of coffee growers by giving away the superior seeds to more than a million farmers and workers across seven countries and three continents.
Zipline International	Zipline uses drones to distribute medical supplies to clinics hindered by impassable roads and limited storage facilities. The company is 100 percent focused on serving the neediest health care systems and has turned away customers asking it to deliver other goods.
PepsiCo, Panera, McDonald's, Nestlé	These are just a few of the food companies that are providing healthier food and drink options by doing such things as switching to cage-free eggs; adopting stricter antibiotics policy; removing preservatives; reducing fat, sugar, and sodium; and adding more minerals and nutrients.
GlaxoSmithKline	The pharmaceutical company delivers health care to those who are underserved. GSK no longer files drug patents in the lowest-income regions of the world in order to make drugs more accessible. It reinvests 20 percent of any profits it makes in the least-developed countries into training health workers and building medical infrastructure.
General Electric	GE invested $17 billion in research and development of clean technology such as the Digital Wind Farm which can boost a wind farm's energy production by 20 percent.
Mastercard	The credit company is making it easier for charities to get help to the people who really need it quickly. MasterCard distributes cards similar to gift cards that are loaded with points redeemable for groceries, medicine, shelter, building materials, or business supplies. The cards can be made and distributed in a day or two, compared with the weeks needed to create and send paper vouchers.
Coca Cola	The soft drink company has helped 1.2 million women in 60 countries become entrepreneurs by partnering with governments and non-profit organizations to create market-specific entrepreneurship programs.
Intel	The technology giant is helping build a workforce capable of keeping up with the digital revolution. Intel's Teach program helps K–12 teachers integrate technology in classrooms and build critical STEM (science, technology, engineering, and math) skills.

Sources: Erika Fry et al., "Change the World," *Fortune,* September 1, 2016; Beth Donnell, "Free Bird," *Fortune,* September 1, 2016; Lisa Brown, "Panera Challenges Its Fast-Food Rivals to Offer a Healthier Kids' Menu," *St. Louis Post-Dispatch,* August 12, 2016; Mike Esterl, "PepsiCo Boosts Its Health Targets," *The Wall Street Journal,* October 18, 2016; Rachel Syme, "Most Creative People in Business 2016," *Fast Company,* June 2016; Liz Welch, "Sustainability in a Bottle," *Inc.,* June 2016; Adele Peters, "A Higher Calling," *Fast Company,* July–August 2016.

Responsibility to Customers

Consumers have four basic rights: (1) the right to safety, (2) the right to be informed, (3) the right to choose, and (4) the right to be heard. These rights will be achieved only if business and consumers recognize them and take action in the marketplace.

A recurring theme of this book is the importance of pleasing customers by offering them real value. Since three of five new businesses fail, we know this responsibility is not as easy to meet as it seems. One sure way of failing to please customers is to be less than honest with them. The payoff for socially conscious behaviour, however, can be new customers who admire the company's social efforts—a powerful competitive edge. Consumer behaviour studies show that, all else being equal, a socially conscious company is likely to be viewed more favourably than others. In fact, a recent GT Nexus survey showed that 50 percent of the consumers surveyed were willing to pay more for goods from socially responsible companies.[44]

Given the value customers place on social efforts, how do companies make customers aware of such efforts? One tool many companies use to raise awareness of their social responsibility efforts is social media. The primary value of using social media to communicate CSR efforts is that it allows companies to reach broad and diverse groups, allows them to connect directly with customers in a low-cost, efficient way, and enables them to interact with specific groups more easily than through more traditional efforts.[45]

It's not enough for companies to brag about their social responsibility efforts; they must live up to the expectations they raise or face the consequences. When herbal tea maker Celestial Seasonings ignored its advertised image of environmental stewardship by poisoning prairie dogs on its property, it incurred customers' wrath.[46] Customers prefer to do business with companies they trust and, even more important, don't want to do business with those they don't trust. Companies earn customers' trust by demonstrating credibility over time; they can lose it at any point.

Responsibility to Investors[47]

Some people believe that before you can do good, you must do well (i.e., make a lot of money); others believe that by doing good, you can also do well. What we do know is that ethical behaviour is good for shareholder wealth. It does not subtract from the bottom line, but rather adds to it. On the other hand, unethical behaviour does cause financial damage. Those cheated by financial wrongdoing are the shareholders themselves. Unethical behaviour may seem to work for the short term, but it guarantees eventual failure. For example, in the early 2000s, accounting irregularities reported at Nortel Networks Corp., once the most-traded stock in Canada, damaged investor trust and subsequently the company's share

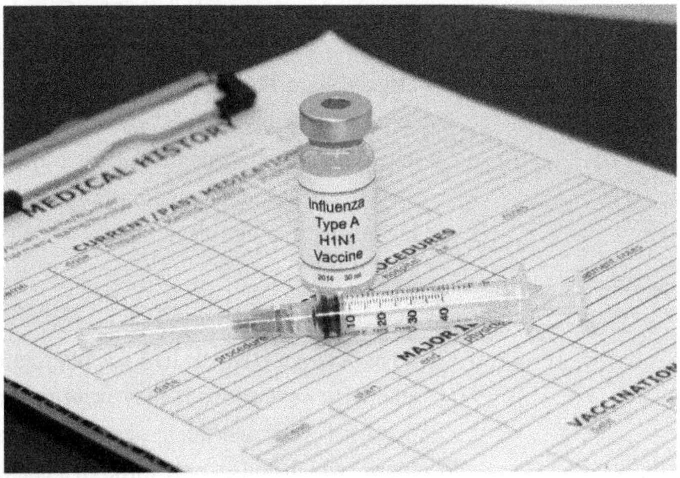

© Sherry Yates Young/Shutterstock

High-risk groups lined up for hours at public clinics when the H1N1 vaccine was released in October 2009, while many non-high-risk Canadians (e.g., some professional athletes and private-clinic members) received the vaccine courtesy of their employers. For weeks following the initial rollout, thousands of those on the priority list did not receive the vaccine due to the shortage. Were the actions of these employers ethical?

value. Years later, the company was still being scrutinized amid rumours of bankruptcy when its share price was under $1. In 2009, the company declared bankruptcy.

Unfortunately, we continue to read of individual business people who abuse the trust that individual investors have placed in them. Some high-profile examples in recent years include financiers Earl Jones and Bernard Madoff. Jones plead guilty to defrauding 158 clients of $50 million in a Ponzi scheme that he operated for more than two decades. He was sentenced to 11 years in prison. Madoff is serving a 150-year sentence after admitting he squandered tens of billions of dollars in investors' money. Madoff's crimes left many investors impoverished and some charities insolvent.

Many investors believe that it makes financial as well as moral sense to invest in companies that plan ahead to create a better environment. By choosing to put their money into companies whose goods and services benefit the community and the environment, investors can improve their own financial health while improving society's health.[48]

INSIDER TRADING[49]

insider trading
An unethical activity in which insiders use private company information to further their own fortunes or those of their family and friends.

A few investors, known as inside traders, have chosen unethical means to improve their own financial health. **Insider trading** uses private company information to further insiders' own fortunes, or those of their family and friends. For example, Andrew Rankin, a former executive with RBC Dominion Securities, was charged by the Ontario Securities Commission (OSC) with 10 counts of tipping off his friend, Daniel Duic. Investigators found that Rankin had alerted Duic to upcoming mergers and acquisitions before they were publicly known. The OSC alleges that, based on this information, Duic bought and sold investments in ten companies and saw his investment increase following the release of the merger and acquisition news. Duic agreed to pay just over $3 million in the form of a penalty, taxes, and lawyer's fees and to testify against Rankin. Under the Ontario Securities Act, Rankin was sentenced to six months in jail for Canada's first conviction for illegal stock tipping.

The OSC also successfully prosecuted Mitchell Finkelstein, a partner at the law firm Davies Ward Phillips & Vineberg LLP, for feeding insider investor tips to Paul Azeff, a former CIBC investment adviser. While Mr. Finkelstein may appeal the OSC ruling, the case demonstrates one of the rare times the regulator has successfully prosecuted various market gatekeepers including lawyers, bankers, brokers, or investment advisors for violating insider trading rules.

Responsibility to Employees

It has been said that the best social program in the world is a job. Businesses have a responsibility to create jobs if they want to grow. Once they have done so, they must see to it that hard work and talent are fairly rewarded. Employees need realistic hope of a better future, which comes only through a chance for upward mobility. One of the most powerful influences on a company's effectiveness and financial performance is responsible human resource management. We'll discuss this in Chapter 12.

If a company treats employees with respect, they usually will respect the company as well. Mutual respect can make a huge difference in a company's bottom line. In their book *Contented Cows Give Better Milk,* Bill Catlette and Richard Hadden compared "contented cow" companies with "common cow" companies. The companies with the contented employees outgrew their counterparts by four to one for more than 10 years. The "contented cow" companies out-earned the "common cow" companies by nearly

$40 billion and generated 800 000 more jobs. The authors attribute this difference in performance to the commitment and caring that the companies demonstrate for their employees.[50]

One way a company can demonstrate commitment and caring is to give its employees salaries and benefits that help them reach their personal goals. The wage and benefit packages offered by warehouse retailer Costco are among the best in hourly retail. Even part-time workers are covered by Costco's health plan, and the workers pay less for their coverage than at other retailers such as Walmart. Increased benefits reduce employee turnover, which at Costco is less than a third of the industry average.[51] Estimates show that replacing employees costs between 150 and 250 percent of their annual salaries, so retaining workers is good for business as well as morale.[52]

When employees feel they have been treated unfairly, they often strike back. Getting even is one of the most powerful incentives for good people to do bad things. Not many disgruntled workers are desperate enough to resort to violence in the workplace, but a great number do relieve their frustrations in more subtle ways, such as blaming mistakes on others, not accepting responsibility for decision making, manipulating budgets and expenses, making commitments they intend to ignore, hoarding resources, doing the minimum needed to get by, making results look better than they are, or even stealing. The loss of employee commitment, confidence, and trust in the company and its management can be very costly indeed. Employee larceny costs Canadian businesses billions of dollars every year. According to a 2014 report by the Association of Certified Fraud Examiners, the average cost of occupational fraud, which includes the misappropriation of assets and financial statement fraud, is approximately $250,000 in Canada.[53] Canadian retailers alone are relieved of approximately $4 billion of merchandise annually, or $10.8 million every day, with employees out-stealing the shoplifters.[54] You will read more about issues that affect employee–management relations in Chapter 13.

© Tupungato / Shutterstock.com

In 2013, over 1000 people died when the Rana Plaza garment factory in Bangladesh collapsed. Loblaws Cos. Ltd. contracted the business that operated the factory for its Joe Fresh apparel line. In response, the company dropped seven garment makers in Bangladesh due to unsafe working conditions and facilities. It has also contributed $5 million to a long-term compensation package for victims of the tragedy, committed $1 million toward global charity Save the Children and a rehabilitation hospital in Bangladesh, and updated its Supplier Code of Conduct. Do the apparel brands you purchase have similar standards for their suppliers?[55]

Responsibility to Society

One of business' responsibilities to society is to create new wealth, which is disbursed to employees, suppliers, shareholders, and other stakeholders. But if businesses don't create wealth, who will? Non-profit organizations play an important role in distributing the funds they receive from donors, governments, and even their own investments in billions of shares in publicly held companies. As those stock prices increase, more funds are available to benefit society. However, for stock prices to increase, the publicly held company must be successful. For companies to prosper, they need to provide customers with safe products. Businesses today, more than ever before, need to develop long-term profitable relationships with their customers. There is no question that repeat business is based on buying safe and value-laden goods and services, at reasonable prices.

Businesses are also partially responsible for promoting social justice. Many companies believe that business has a role in building a community that goes well beyond giving back. To

© Roberto E. Rosales/Zuma Press/Alamy

The wage and benefit packages offered by warehouse retailer Costco are among the best in hourly retail. Even part-time workers are covered by Costco's health plan. Increased benefits reduce Costco employee turnover to less than a third of the industry average. Why do you think Costco is so successful at keeping its employees?

them, charity is not enough. Their social contributions include a variety of social-oriented activities such as cleaning up the environment, providing computer lessons, caring for the elderly, and supporting children from low-income families.

As concern about global warming increased, the green movement emerged in nearly every aspect of daily life. What makes a product "green"? Some believe that a product's carbon footprint (the amount of carbon released during production, distribution, consumption, and disposal) defines how green it is. Many variables contribute to a product's carbon footprint. The carbon footprint of a package of, say, frozen corn includes not only the carbon released by the fertilizer to grow the corn but also the carbon in the fertilizer itself, the gas used to run the farm equipment and transport the corn to market, the electricity to make the plastic packages and power the freezers, and so on (see the Seeking Sustainability box for a story of companies that reduce their carbon footprint by using recycled clothing to manufacture apparel).

No specific guidelines define the carbon footprints of products, businesses, or individuals or outline how to communicate them to consumers. PepsiCo presents carbon information with a label on bags of cheese-and-onion potato chips, for example, that says "75 grams of CO_2."[56] Simple enough, but what does it mean? (We don't know either.)

The focus of this text is on business; however, one should not forget that government decisions also affect business and society. The Walkerton, Ontario, *E. coli* tragedy that killed seven people and made half of the town's 5000 residents ill from contaminated

© Ingram Publishing/SuperStock

Cases of animal cruelty have surfaced in the Canadian dairy and poultry industries. Maple Leaf Foods Inc. was in the spotlight when a video taken by a member of Mercy for Animals Canada showed cruelty at a turkey breeding barn. In response, the company launched an Animal Care Commitment that includes an annual independent audit of all pork and poultry operations.[57] How does a company's animal treatment standards influence your purchase decisions?

© The Organic Box

The Organic Box is owned and operated by an Edmonton farming family. Through a network that covers four regions in Alberta, the company promotes an ethical food philosophy.[58] Finding ways for people to consume local food is also the purpose of Body Fuel Organics in Regina, and Urban Harvest Organic Delivery in Kelowna. Do you think a "buy local" approach is an effective way for a business to be socially responsible? Why or why not?

Seeking SUSTAINABILITY

Green Is the New Black

"Green is the New Black" is the translated name of a Dutch newsletter about organic and sustainable clothing brands. But the slogan also signals a new trend in fashion where apparel companies embrace sustainability in a variety of ways.

Vancouver is a hotbed for small boutique stores that design and sell sustainable clothing. Nicole Bridger Design uses ethically-sourced materials including renewable and biodegradable fabrics from around the world. The owner, Nicole Bridger, intentionally selects fabric suppliers who are Global Organic Textile Standards (GOTS) certified. The business employs over 35 people, including cutters, sewers, and finishers in the local factory, and a management team.

Boardroom Eco© Apparel is an apparel design and manufacturing company also located in Vancouver. Formed in 1996, Boardroom began to sell low-impact recycled polyester fabrics and closed-loop apparel recycling in 2001 and hasn't looked back. They manufacture 90 percent of their goods in their Vancouver factory and 70 percent of the business is exported to the United States. The company promotes closed-loop by recycling used polyester apparel. "If you don't start setting it up now, where you're starting to take back your own product or other people's products and putting it back into new product," says Boardroom President Mark Trotzuk, "you're not going to be able to do business."

© stevanovicigor/iStock/Thinkstock

A recent report projects the Canadian apparel market will grow from $30 billion in 2012 to $50 billion in 2025. China's market is expected to increase from $150 billion to $540 billion, and India's market will increase from $45 billion to $200 billion during the same period of time. With growth this size, sustainable apparel manufacturing may be the only option.

Sources: "About-Transparency," Nicole Bridger, 2015, http://www.nicolebridger.com/pages/transparency, accessed April 7, 2015; "Organizations," Ecofashion World, 2015, http://www.ecofashionworld.com/Organizations/Green-Is-the-New-Black.html, accessed April 7, 2015; Betsy Cummings, "Wearables," Advertising Specialty Institute, July 2010, http://www.asicentral.com/asp/open/content/content.aspx?id=4992&green, accessed April 7, 2015; "Apparel market size projections from 2012 to 2025, by region," Statista, http://www.statista.com/statistics/279757/apparel-market-size-projections-by-region/, accessed April 2015; Dixie Gong, "10 Best Canadian Eco-Shops," *Flare*, March 28, 2013, http://www.flare.com/fashion/10-best-canadian-eco-shops/?gallery_page=8#gallery_top.

water is one such example. After hearing testimony from more than 100 witnesses over nine months, Justice O'Connor concluded that the catastrophe could have been prevented if brothers Stan and Frank Koebel, who ran Walkerton's water system, had properly chlorinated the water and if the Ontario government had heeded warnings that cuts to the provincial environment ministry were resulting in ineffective testing.[59] Clearly, the Koebel brothers were responsible for their individual decisions.

Responsibility to the Environment[60]

Businesses are often criticized for their role in destroying the environment. Such was the case when images of the slow death of 500 ducks on a toxic oil sands tailings pond in northern Alberta flashed around the world. This led to federal and provincial legal action against Syncrude Canada Ltd., which was charged under the Alberta Environmental Enhancement

© Katherine Welles / Shutterstock.com

To date, BP Oil has paid $14 billion in restoration and cleanup efforts to help individuals and businesses affected by the 2010 Gulf of Mexico spill. Considered to be the world's biggest accidental oil leak, the explosion killed 11 oil rig workers and unleashed an estimated 3.2 million barrels of oil before the damaged well was capped three months later. There has also been extensive damage to marine and wildlife habitat.[62] How effective do you think the threat of financial punishment is to curbing the damage of business to the environment?

© paintings / Shutterstock.com

The carbon tax, sometimes called a green tax, can refer to any number of measures designed to increase the cost of burning fossil fuels like oil, gas, and coal. A carbon tax would provide an incentive to stop the social harm and move to more positive alternatives. Quebec was the first province to introduce a carbon tax in 2007 but opposition is strong in Alberta where oil and gas production is vital to the economy. What do you think? Could governments, businesses, and consumers be doing more to protect the environment? Do you agree or disagree with a green tax?[63]

and Protection Act and the federal Migratory Birds Convention Act. While Syncrude attempted to rescue some of the ducks that landed in the tailings pond, only a handful were taken out of the water for cleaning and none survived. The Analyzing Management Decisions case near the end of this chapter discusses the implications of train spills in various regions of Canada.

We are seeing more efforts to reverse years of neglect to the environment. For example, the Sydney Tar Ponds in Nova Scotia are North America's largest hazardous waste site. More than 80 years of discharges from the steel-producing coke ovens near the harbour filled Muggah Creek with contaminated sediments. By 1983, Environment Canada had pinpointed the coke ovens as the major source of pollution in the Sydney area. Fishing was banned and the Sydney lobster fishery was closed. Statistics show that the area has significantly higher levels of cancers and other debilitating diseases than anywhere else in Canada. Two decades later, there have been several attempts and more than $100 million spent to clean up this toxic site. In May 2004, the governments of Canada and Nova Scotia committed $400 million to the cleanup. Citizens of Sydney are still trying to address contamination issues related to their health and private property through a court trial.[61]

The green movement has provided consumers with many product choices. However, making those choices means sorting through the numerous and confusing claims made by manufacturers. The clutter in the marketplace challenges even the most dedicated green activists, but taking the easy route of buying what's most readily available violates the principles of the green movement. Environmental efforts may increase a company's costs, but they also allow the company to charge higher prices, increase market share, or both. Ciba Specialty Chemicals, a Swiss textile-dye manufacturer, developed dyes that require less salt than traditional dyes. Since used dye solutions must be treated before being released into rivers or streams, less salt means lower water-treatment costs. Patents protect Ciba's low-salt dyes, so the company can charge more for its dyes than other companies can charge for theirs. Ciba's experience illustrates that, just as a new machine enhances labour productivity, reducing environmental costs can add value to a business.

Not all environmental strategies are as financially beneficial as Ciba's, however. In the early 1990s, tuna producer StarKist responded to consumer concerns about dolphins in the eastern Pacific dying in nets set out for yellow fin tuna. The company announced it would sell only skip-jack tuna from the western Pacific, which do not swim near dolphins. Unfortunately, customers were unwilling to pay a premium for dolphin-safe tuna and considered the taste of skipjack inferior. Nor was there a clear environmental gain: for every dolphin saved in the eastern Pacific, thousands of immature tuna and dozens of sharks, turtles, and other marine animals died in the western Pacific fishing process.

Environmental quality is a public good; that is, everyone gets to enjoy it regardless of who pays for it. The challenge for companies is to find the right public good that will appeal to their target markets. Many corporations are publishing reports that document their net social contribution. To do that, a company must measure its positive social contributions and subtract its negative social impacts. We will discuss that process next.

© MartinLisner/iStock/Thinkstock

Ethical Funds believes that the best possible returns can be achieved by investing in companies that combine strong financial performance with positive social, environmental, and governance performance. The company does not invest in corporations that derive a significant portion of their income from military weapons, tobacco, or nuclear power. Would you invest in companies on the basis of their environmental, social, and governance performance?

Social Auditing

It is nice to talk about having organizations become more socially responsible. It is also encouraging to see some efforts made toward creating safer products, cleaning up the environment, designing more honest advertising, and treating women and minorities fairly. But is there any way to measure whether organizations are making social responsibility an integral part of top management's decision making? The answer is yes, and the term that represents that measurement is *social auditing*.

A **social audit** is a systematic evaluation of an organization's progress toward implementing programs that are socially responsible and responsive. One of the major problems of conducting a social audit is establishing procedures for measuring a firm's activities and its effects on society. What should a social audit measure? Many social audits consider such things as workplace issues, the environment, product safety, community relations, and respecting the rights of local people. See Figure 5.5 for an outline of business activities that could be considered socially responsible.

social audit
A systematic evaluation of an organization's progress toward implementing programs that are socially responsible and responsive.

A commitment to corporate social responsibility implies a commitment to some form of **triple-bottom line (TBL, 3BL, or People, Planet, Profit)** reporting.[64] TBL is used as a framework for measuring and reporting corporate performance against economic, social, and environmental parameters.[65] Corporations that use TBL focus on the economic value they add, but also on the environmental and social value they add and destroy.[66]

triple-bottom line (TBL, 3BL, or People, Planet, Profit)
A framework for measuring and reporting corporate performance against economic, social, and environmental parameters.

There is some question as to whether positive actions should be added (e.g., charitable donations and pollution control efforts) and negative effects subtracted (e.g., layoffs and overall pollution levels) to get a net social contribution. Or should only positive actions be recorded? What do you think? However they are conducted, social audits force organizations to consider their social responsibility beyond the level of just feeling good or managing public relations.

■ **FIGURE 5.5**

SOCIALLY RESPONSIBLE BUSINESS ACTIVITIES

Community-related activities such as participating in local fundraising campaigns, donating employee time to various non-profit organizations, and participating in urban planning and development
Employee-related activities such as establishing equal opportunity programs, offering flextime and other benefits, promoting job enrichment, ensuring job safety, and conducting employee development programs; you will learn more about such programs in Chapter 12
Political activities such as taking a position on nuclear safety, gun control, pollution control, consumer protection, and other social issues, and working more closely with local, provincial, and federal government officials
Support for higher education, the arts, and other non-profit social agencies
Consumer activities such as ensuring product safety, creating truthful advertising, handling complaints promptly, setting fair prices, and conducting extensive consumer education programs

In addition to the social audits conducted by the companies themselves, there are five types of groups that serve as watchdogs regarding how well companies enforce their ethical and social responsibility policies:

1. *Socially conscious investors* insist that a company extend its own high standards to all its suppliers. Social responsibility investing (SRI) is on the rise. In Canada, investment funds managed by responsible investing strategies represent more than $1.5 trillion.[67] Be aware that SRI is highly subjective. Different people have different values, so what is ethically appropriate for one may not be the case for another.
2. *Socially conscious research organizations,* such as Ethisphere, analyze and report on CSR efforts.[68]
3. *Environmentalists* apply pressure by publicly identifying companies that do not abide by the environmentalists' standards.
4. *Union officials* identify violations and force companies to comply to avoid negative publicity.
5. *Customers* make buying decisions based on their social conscience. Many will take their business elsewhere if a company demonstrates unethical or socially irresponsible practices.

sustainable development
Implementing a process that integrates environmental, economic, and social considerations into decision making.

Courtesy of Rainforest Action Network

The goal of the Rainforest Action Network, an environmental activist group, is to show companies that it is possible to do well by doing good. It conducts public campaigns designed to put consumer pressure on companies that refuse to adopt responsible environmental policies. RAN has helped convince dozens of corporations including Home Depot, to change their practices.

What these groups look for constantly changes as the world view changes. One important thing to remember is that it is not enough for a company to be right when it comes to ethics and social responsibility. It also has to *convince* its customers and society that it's right.

SUSTAINABLE DEVELOPMENT[69]

Sustainable development means implementing a process that integrates environmental, economic, and social considerations into decision making. This reinforces the World Commission on Environment and Development's conclusion that development should be sustainable for the benefit of current and future generations. Such a focus has created opportunities for ventures such as Envirotech Office Systems, based in Mississauga, Ontario. Corporations that wish to replace aged office furniture can deal with Envirotech. The company provides a cost-effective alternative to updating these items through its re-manufacturing process. For example, one re-manufactured workstation prevents 276 pounds of landfill waste and 800 pounds of raw material consumption.[70] This kind of business activity gives the Earth relief from the pressures of expanding population and waste.

PROGRESS ASSESSMENT

- What is CSR, and how does it relate to a business' major stakeholders?
- How does the strategic approach differ from the pluralist approach?
- What is a social audit, and what kinds of activities does it monitor?
- Which company—Loblaws Cos. Ltd. or BP Oil—best demonstrated socially responsible behaviour?

LO6

Discuss the importance of ethical behaviour and social responsibility in global markets.

International Ethics and Social Responsibility

Ethical problems and issues of social responsibility are not unique to Canada. Top business and government leaders have been caught in major "influence-peddling" (read bribery) schemes in Japan, South Korea, Brazil, Pakistan, and Zaire. What is new about the moral and ethical standards by which government leaders are being judged? They are much stricter than in previous years.

Government leaders are not the only ones being held to higher standards. Many businesses are demanding socially responsible behaviour from their international suppliers by ensuring that suppliers do not violate domestic human rights and environmental standards. For example, clothing manufacturer PVH (makers of such brands as Calvin Klein and Tommy Hilfiger) will cancel orders from suppliers that violate its ethical, environmental, and human rights code. McDonald's denied rumours that one of its suppliers grazes cattle on cleared rain-forest land but wrote a ban on the practice anyway.

Fair trade is a growing social movement dedicated to making sure that producers in developing countries are paid a fair price for the goods we consume (rather than exploiting desperately poor people), resulting in more money in their pockets.[71] Put another way, it is a strategy for poverty alleviation and sustainable development with the purpose of creating opportunities for producers who have been disadvantaged or marginalized by the traditional economic model.[72] Fairtrade Canada is responsible for certifying that Canadian products bearing the FAIRTRADE Mark meet international Fairtrade standards. If the product bears the FAIRTRADE Mark on the package, then it means that it has conformed to Fairtrade standards and it has contributed to the development of disadvantaged producers and workers.[73]

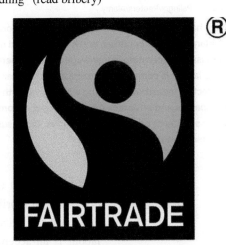

Fairtrade products can include coffee, tea, cocoa, and flowers. The FAIRTRADE Mark has a well-established European and North American base and is becoming recognized in markets such as Brazil, Russia, India, China, and the Middle East. A recent survey found that FAIRTRADE is the most widely recognized ethical label in the world.[74] Do you ever look for goods with a FAIRTRADE distinction?

© Crack Palinggi/Reuters/Alamy

Nike has outsourced the manufacture of its products to plants in other countries and has weathered much criticism for operating in low-wage nations where child labour is common. The company has taken many corrective measures, including working with other companies and advocacy groups on a set of common labor standards and factory guidelines. Can a successful firm overcome past ethical errors?

In contrast are companies criticized for exploiting workers in less-developed countries. Nike, the world's largest athletic shoe company, has been accused by human rights and labour groups of treating its workers poorly while lavishing millions of dollars on star athletes to endorse its products. Cartoonist Garry Trudeau featured an anti-Nike campaign in his popular syndicated series *Doonesbury.*

Nike worked hard to improve its reputation. Nike monitors efforts to improve labour conditions in its 700 contract factories that are subject to local culture and economic conditions. The company released the names and locations of its factories, both as a show of transparency and to encourage its competitors to work on improving conditions as well. While Nike's efforts had little impact at first, conditions have improved significantly in many of its suppliers factories. However, there are still reports of unsafe workplaces.[75]

Why has Nike's monitoring program not been as successful as the company hoped? One reason is that in emerging economies, government regulations tend to be weak, which leaves companies to police their suppliers to ensure they comply with laws and regulations. That's a major task for a company like Nike, which produces 98 percent of its shoes in hundreds of factories in many different countries. Another reason is that as a buyer, Nike has different degrees of leverage. This leverage is based on how long Nike has worked with a supplier or how much of the factory's revenue depends on Nike alone.

The fairness of requiring international suppliers to adhere to domestic ethical standards is not as clear-cut as you might think. For example, what could be considered a gift in one culture is considered a bribe in another. Is it always ethical for companies to demand compliance with the standards of their own countries? What about countries in which child labour is an accepted part of the society and families depend on the children's salaries for survival? What about foreign companies doing business in Canada? Should these companies have to comply with Canadian ethical standards? What about multinational corporations? Since they span different societies, do they have to conform to all of the societies' standards? None of these questions are easy to answer, but they give you some idea of the complexity of social responsibility issues in international markets (see the Reaching Beyond Our Borders box for an example of an ethical culture clash).

Reaching *Beyond* OUR BORDERS

Ethical Culture Clash

The extension of corporations' reach into communities across the globe has led to many questions: For which communities are the companies responsible? Are domestic operations more important than foreign ones? Should the interests of employees be put first, or is the company's image the main priority?

Here's an example of how corporate ethics can clash with cultural ethics. Joe, the oldest son of a poor South American cloth peddler, managed to move to the United States, earn an engineering degree, and get a job with a large telecommunications company. After five years, Joe seemed to have bought into the company culture and was happy to be granted a transfer back to his home country. He was told that the company expected him to live there in a safe and presentable home of his choice. To help him afford such a residence, his employer agreed to reimburse him a maximum of $2,000 a month for the cost of his rent and servants. Each month Joe submitted rental receipts for exactly $2,000. The company later found out that Joe was living in what was, by Western standards, a shack in a dangerous area of town. Such a humble home could not have cost more than $200 a month. The company was concerned for Joe's safety as well as for the effect his residence would have on its image. The human resource manager was also worried about Joe's lack of integrity, given he had submitted false receipts for reimbursement.

© David R. Frazier/Alamy

Joe was upset with what he considered the company's invasion of his privacy. He argued he should receive the full $2,000 monthly reimbursement all employees received. He explained his choice of housing by saying he was making sacrifices so he could send the extra money to his family and put his younger siblings through school. This was especially important since his father had died and his family had no one else to depend on. "Look, my family is poor," Joe said. "So poor that most Westerners wouldn't believe our poverty even if they saw it. This money means the difference between hope and despair for all of us. For me to do anything less for my family would be to defile the honour of my late father. Can't you understand?"

Often it is difficult to understand what others perceive as ethical. Different situations often turn the clear waters of "rightness" downright muddy. Joe was trying to do the honourable thing for his family. Yet the company's wish to have its higher-level people live in safe housing is not unreasonable, given the dangerous conditions of the city in which Joe lived. The policy of housing reimbursement supports the company's intent to make its employees' stay in the country reasonably comfortable and safe, not to increase their salaries. In the United States, where Joe would not receive a housing supplement, it would be unethical for him to falsify expense reports in order to receive more money to send to his family. In South America, though, the issue is not so clear.

Sources: Meghan M. Biro, "Happy Employees = Hefty Profits," *Forbes*, January 19, 2014; Shirley Engelmeir, "Engage a Diverse Work Force to Capture Foreign Markets," *American Banker*, November 13, 2012.

SUMMARY

LO1 **Explain why obeying the law is only the first step in behaving ethically.**

Ethics goes beyond obeying laws. It also involves abiding by the moral standards accepted by society.

How is legality different from ethics?

Ethics reflects people's proper relation with one another. Legality is more limiting; it refers only to laws written to protect people from fraud, theft, and violence.

What influences our ethical decision making?

Ethical behaviour begins with you and me. We are influenced by our society and what it considers to be ethical, the behaviour of others (both socially and in a work setting), and by our own personal values and beliefs.

LO2 **Ask the three questions to answer when faced with a potentially unethical action.**

It can be difficult to maintain a balance between ethics and other goals such as pleasing stakeholders or advancing your career.

How can we tell if our business decisions are ethical?

We can put our business decisions through an ethics check by asking three questions: (1) Is it legal? (2) Is it balanced? and (3) How will it make me feel? Companies (and individuals) that develop strong ethics codes and use these three questions have a better chance than most of behaving ethically.

LO3 **Describe management's role in setting ethical standards.**

Some managers think that ethics is an individual issue that has nothing to do with management, while others believe that ethics has everything to do with management.

What is management's role in setting ethical standards?

Managers often set formal ethical standards, but more important are the messages they send through their actions. Management's tolerance or intolerance of ethical misconduct influences employees more than written ethics codes do.

LO4 **Distinguish between compliance-based and integrity-based ethics codes, and list the six steps that can be considered when setting up a corporate ethics code.**

Business ethics can be improved if companies follow a six-step process.

What is the difference between compliance-based and integrity-based ethics codes?

Whereas compliance-based ethics codes are concerned with avoiding legal punishment, integrity-based ethics codes define the organization's guiding values, create an environment that supports ethically sound behaviour, and stress a shared accountability among employees.

What are the six steps that can improve business ethics?

The six steps are as follows: (1) top management must adopt and support an explicit corporate code of conduct; (2) employees must understand that expectations for ethical behaviour begin at the top and that senior management expects all employees to act accordingly; (3) managers and others must be trained to consider the ethical implications of all business decisions; (4) an ethics office must be set up, and phone lines to the office should be established; (5) outsiders such as suppliers, subcontractors, distributors, and customers must be told about the ethics program; and (6) the ethics code must be enforced.

Which step is the most critical in this six-step process?

The last step is most critical because a company's ethics policy must be enforced to be taken seriously.

LO5 **Define corporate social responsibility, and compare corporations' responsibilities to various stakeholders.**

Corporate social responsibility goes beyond merely being ethical.

Define corporate social responsibility.

Corporate social responsibility is the concern businesses have toward stakeholders.

How do businesses demonstrate corporate responsibility toward stakeholders?

Business is responsible to five types of stakeholders: (1) it must satisfy customers with goods and services of real value; (2) it must make money for its investors; (3) it must create jobs for employees, maintain job security, and see that hard work and talent are fairly rewarded; (4) it must create new wealth for society and promote social justice, and (5) it must contribute to making its environment a better place.

How are a company's social responsibility efforts measured?

A corporate social audit measures an organization's progress toward social responsibility. Some people believe the audit should add together the organization's positive actions and then subtract the negative effects to get a net social benefit.

LO6 **Discuss the importance of ethical behaviour and social responsibility in global markets.**

Social responsibility issues are complex in global markets.

How can companies influence ethical behaviour and social responsibility in global markets?

Many businesses are demanding socially responsible behaviour from their international suppliers by making sure their suppliers do not violate human rights and environmental standards. Companies like Phillips–Van Heusen will not import products from companies that do not meet their ethical and social responsibility standards.

KEY TERMS

compliance-based ethics codes 185
corporate philanthropy 190
corporate policy 192
corporate responsibility 191
corporate social initiatives 191
corporate social responsibility (CSR) 189
ethical consumerism 189
ethics 180
insider trading 196
integrity-based ethics codes 185
social audit 201
sustainable development 202
triple-bottom line (TBL, 3BL, or People, Planet, Profit) 201
whistleblowers 186

CAREER EXPLORATION

If you are interested in pursuing a career focused on helping people, society, and the environment, here are a few to consider. Find out about the tasks performed, skills needed, pay, and opportunity outlook in these fields through Internet sites that include the Government of Canada Job Bank, Workopolis, Monster, CareerBuilder, Glassdoor, and Indeed, as well as through the Career Centre at your school.

- **Compliance officer**—examines, evaluates, and investigates conformity with laws and regulations.
- **Green job**—job that produces goods or provides services that benefit the environment or conserve natural resources. Search in the OOH for careers in water conservation, sustainable forestry, biofuels, geothermal energy, environmental remediation, solar power, recycling, and so on

- **Social and community service manager**—coordinates and supervises social service programs and community organizations; manages staff who provide social services to the public.
- **Fundraising manager**—organizes events and campaigns to raise money and other donations for an organization; increases awareness of an organization's work, goals, and financial needs.
- **Social entrepreneur**—helps people solve and cope with problems in their everyday lives while at the same time seeks social innovation is areas such as education, health, and environment.

CRITICAL THINKING

1. Think of a situation in which you have been involved that tested your ethical behaviour. For example, perhaps your best friend forgot about a term paper due the next day and asked you if he could copy and hand in a paper you wrote for another instructor last semester. What are your alternatives, and what are the consequences of each one? Would it have been easier to resolve the dilemma if you had asked yourself the three questions in the ethics check? Try answering them now and see if you would have made a different choice.
2. Companies appear to act with corporate responsibility but the underlying motive seems to be to increase profits. Does this motive undermine the value of corporate responsibility or is it only the actions that are important? That is, do you think less of a company if you know it is being responsible only to increase its profits?
3. What do you think of the phrase, "It's not personal, it's just business?" Do you agree or disagree with this statement if it were to be used to justify a business decision? Explain.

DEVELOPING CAREER SKILLS

Key: ● **Team** ★ **Analytic** ▲ **Communication** ⊡ **Technology**

★▲ 1. What sources have helped shape your personal code of ethics and morality? What influences, if any, have ever pressured you to compromise those standards? Think of an experience you had at work or school that tested your ethical standards. How did you resolve your dilemma? Now that time has passed, are you comfortable with the decision you made? If not, explain what you would do differently.

⊡ 2. Newspapers and magazines are full of stories about individuals and businesses that are not socially responsible. What about those individuals and organizations that do take social responsibility seriously? We don't normally read or hear about them. Do a little investigative reporting of your own. Identify a public interest group in your community and identify its officers, objectives, amount of financial support, and size and characteristics of membership. List some examples of its recent actions and/or accomplishments. Consider environmental groups, animal protection groups, political action committees, and so on. (If you don't know where to start, call your local Chamber of Commerce, the Better Business Bureau, or local government agencies for help). Try using one of the Internet search engines to help you find more information.

★ 3. You are the manager of a coffee house called the Morning Cup. One of your best employees wants to be promoted to a managerial position; however, the owner is grooming his son for the promotion your employee seeks. The owner's act of nepotism may hurt a valuable employee's chances for advancement, but complaining may hurt your own chances for promotion. What do you do?

★▲ **4.** You are a salesperson at a clothing store. You walk into the storage room to start ticketing some clothes that came in that morning and see a co-worker quickly take some pants from a box and put them into her knapsack. Your colleague does not see you enter the room. What do you do? Do you leave and say nothing to your employer? Do you say something to your colleague? Is your responsibility to your organization, your colleague, or both? What might be the implications of your decision?

□★▲ **5.** Go to the website of a local corporation and search for its written ethics code. Would you classify its code as compliance-based or integrity-based? Explain.

★□ **6.** What effects have the new laws protecting whistleblowers had on the business environment? Go online or to the library to research individuals who reported their employers' illegal and/or unethical behaviour. Did the companies change their policies? If so, what effect have these policies had on the companies' stakeholders? What effect did reporting the problems have on the whistleblowers themselves?

ANALYZING MANAGEMENT DECISIONS

CNR's Poor Environmental Track Record

Canadian National Railway (CNR) has a long history of train spills, which have resulted in significant environmental damage. In 2005, CNR was charged by Alberta Environment with failing to take all reasonable measures to remedy and confine the spill from a train derailment into a northern Alberta lake. In the incident, 43 cars derailed next to Wabamun Lake, west of Edmonton, spilling almost 800 000 litres of heavy fuel and a potentially cancer-causing wood preservative.

Alberta Environment spokeswoman Kim Hunt said the charges were laid by Alberta Justice after a review. "It's the law in Alberta that the polluter pays," Hunt told the Canadian Press. After the spill, Alberta Environment issued an Environmental Protection Order to CNR. The company was ordered to clean up the spill, begin long-term environmental planning and monitoring of the area, and keep the public informed on its progress. Residents of Wabamun were told in June 2006 that they could use the lake again for swimming and boating, but not for washing dishes, cleaning vegetables, or bathing.

CNR offered nearly $7.5 million on a sliding scale to the area's 1600 residents. The payments, which ranged from $1,500 to $27,000 for those closest to the spill, were in recognition of loss of property use as a result of the derailment. The Paul First Nation, whose reserve is on the western shore of the lake, also filed a multi-million-dollar lawsuit against CNR, Ottawa, and the province, alleging that the spill destroyed its traditional way of life. In September 2008, CNR reached a $10 million settlement with the band. Earlier in 2008, three charges were laid by Environment Canada and Fisheries and Oceans Canada against CNR: one for allegedly depositing a substance harmful to migratory birds into a lake and the other two for alleged disruption of a fish habitat.

CNR's poor environmental performance continues today. In early 2015, three train spills occurred in Northern Ontario within the span of one month. In one case, crude oil entered the Mattagami River System. Chief Walter Naveau of the Mattagami First Nation said his community is concerned about smoke inhalation, environmental damage, water safety, and most importantly, the spawning grounds for fish local wildlife habitat upon which the community depends. Environmental activists claim the ecosystem will never be restored to its original health. When asked about CNR's claim that the train spill was cleaned up, Naveau replied, "They may say those things but why should I trust them?" The issue has gained federal government attention as Canadian Transport Minister Lisa Raitt stated CNR should be called to answer questions before a parliamentary committee. "What's going on operationally?" said Raitt. "I can hear from CN, but I think CN should talk to Parliament and should talk to Canadians."

Sources: Raveena Aulakh, "Crude oil spilled in CN derailment will impact ecosystems for long time, activists say," *The Toronto Star,* March 9, 2015, http://www.thestar.com/news/world/2015/03/09/crude-oil-spilled-in-cn-derailment-will-impact-ecosystems-for-long-time-activists-say.html; Adam Miller, "CN crude oil train derailment in Gogama, Ont. 'very concerning', transportation minister says," *The National Post,* March 8, 2015, http://news.nationalpost.com/news/canada/cn-crude-oil-train-derailment-in-gogama-ont-very-concerning-transportation-minister-says; "Canadian National Railway to Pay $10M to Alta. Band in Derailment Along Lake," CANOE Inc., September 12. 2008, http://cnews.canoe.ca/CNEWS/Politics/2008/09/12/6751421-cp.html; "Oil Spill Nets CN Rail Three Charges from Feds," *Canadian Geographic,* March 18, 2008, www.canadiangeographic.ca/cea/archives/news_item.asp?articleid=493; Gordon Kent and Kelly Cryderman, "Wabamun Residents Unhappy with CN Charge," CanWest News Service, June 6, 2006, www.canada.com/topics/news/national/story.html?id=14a77881-cc1b-4ec0-90a7-fd86af5a9c7c&k=58041; and "CN Rail Charged in Oil Spill at Alta. Lake," The Canadian Press, June 6, 2006, http://sympaticomsn.ctv.ca/servlet/ArticleNews/story/CTVNews/20060605/cn_wabamun_060506.

Discussion Questions

1. What stakeholders were impacted by each of these incidents?
2. Conduct some research into these stories. As a result of the 2008 derailment, what changes were implemented by CNR? How did these changes impact what occurred in 2015?
3. Do you feel that the costs associated with train spills are excessive? Explain.

RUNNING CASE

Ron Foxcroft: The Dream for a Pealess Whistle

For successful Canadian entrepreneur and inventor Ron Foxcroft, it all started in 1982 when he purchased Fluke Transport, a Southern Ontario trucking business. The company slogan—If It's On Time . . . It's A "FLUKE"—was soon recognized throughout North America. Over the years, Foxcroft diversified into new ventures and the Foxcroft Group of Companies now includes Fluke Transportation Group, Fluke Warehousing Inc., Foxcroft Capital Corp., Fox 40 International Inc., and Fox 40 USA Inc.

The formation of Fox 40 International Inc. (Fox 40) is the result of a dream for a pealess whistle. When Foxcroft began developing the whistle, he was motivated by his knowledge and experience as an international basketball referee. Frustrated with faulty pea whistles, he spent three years of development with design consultant Chuck Shepherd, resulting in the creation of the Fox 40 Classic Whistle. (The whistle was named for Foxcroft and that he was 40 when his invention was being developed).

Introduced in 1987, this finely tuned, precision instrument doesn't use a pea to generate sound. In fact, there are no moving parts whatsoever. There is nothing to obstruct sound, nothing to stick, freeze, or fail. The patented design moves the air blast through three tuned chambers. Fox 40 whistles are entirely constructed of high-impact ABS plastic so they are impervious to moisture. A quick rinse in disinfectant eliminates bacteria. Every time, they deliver on faultless performance (e.g., loudness), and they never fail.

Fox 40 International Inc., a proudly Canadian company, dominates the global whistle industry. Tens of thousands of Fox 40 whistles are produced monthly for shipment to 140 countries. They are sold to referees, coaches, water safety professionals, search and rescue teams, personal security teams, animal trainers, sport enthusiasts, as well as customers in the outdoor and premium incentive markets. The complete line of Fox 40 products has grown substantially with over 900 active stock-keeping units (SKUs) that include the following: 19 Fox 40 Whistles Styles; Lanyards & Attachments; Fox 40 Gear; SmartCoach Coaching Boards; SICK Self Impression Custom Kit, and Heat Alert Mouthguards; Marine & Outdoor Products; Pink Products; and Logo Imprinted Products.

When you consider the global business environment, the biggest threat is counterfeiters. There are at least thirty-six attempts per year to counterfeit the company's products. In response, Fox 40 aggressively polices its patents and trademarks. This includes monitoring offshore websites and catalogue publications for the misuse of Fox 40 intellectual property (IP). It is the company's responsibility to police and look for infringements to protect its IP and distributors worldwide. In addition, when a new product is introduced, an improvement to the new product is already in the vault, ready to be introduced at the first sign of counterfeiters.

Direct exporting is the strategy used to reach global markets. Rather than hiring someone to represent Fox 40 in a foreign country, Fox 40 employees attend global trade shows that service their targeted countries. At these trade shows, they look for three distributors that will deal directly with Fox 40. Orders are then directly exported to these distributors.

Even though offshoring would result in lower overall costs, the company insists on controlling the quality of its products by manufacturing them domestically. International customers especially value Fox 40's "Made in Canada" products as they connote quality. This is reinforced in international business trade shows where Fox 40 employees are often asked to confirm that their products continue to be made in Canada. At an annual ISPO MUNICH trade show, Ron observed that attendance seemed poorer than in the past in the Sourcing section. (ISPO MUNICH is an international leading sports business trade show. Every year, over 2000 international exhibitors present their latest products to more than 80 000 visitors from over 100 countries. Exhibitors are categorized by segment: Outdoor, Ski, Action, Sportstyle, Performance Sports, and Sourcing.) This part of the trade show included association members from offshore countries such as China, Taiwan, and India. Ron believes that the lower turnout for some of the offshore exhibitors was in recognition of buyers' concerns with the decreasing quality of offshore-produced products. As a result, buyers are increasingly seeking high standard, quality-made products from manufacturers such as Fox 40.

There has been some discussion in this text about the role of government in business. Ron's perspective is as follows: "Government has been a big help to me in business. I simply take what they do and do the exact opposite. They take 12 months to do what I do in 12 minutes. I have learned to have courage, 59-minute stand-up meetings, eliminate large committees, long-winded rhetoric, and keep my company lean and customer focused. If governments practised this, they could be efficient too. However, most politicians are focused on re-election and not customer (citizen) service. Therefore, rather than make correct decisions they make popular decisions. Finally, too many rules in government inhibit innovation."

The company's GREEN PLAN highlights some of the areas where Fox 40 has taken steps to do its part to help to protect the environment. Examples include the following: reusing shipping containers whenever possible; the elimination of all clamshell packaging; bagging whistles and mouthguards in #4 biodegradable packaging; reducing the overall whistle package size by 20 percent to lessen the impact on the environment; and reducing the size of shipping boxes due to package dimension changes, resulting in less boxboard consumed and improved shipping methods. Sustainable packaging solutions include blister packaging made from recycled water and pop bottles, and using print material that contains recyclable and/or recycled post-consumer waste material. Savings over nine months from the use of emission-free electricity in print production includes 93 trees preserved for the future, 128 746 litres of wastewater flow saved, and 15 289 kilograms of air emissions not generated.

Fox 40 is a strong community-conscious company and as a result invests heavily in corporate responsibility initiatives. Over the years, it has helped well over 100 organizations that include non-profits, charities, foundations (e.g., the Foxcroft Family Youth Foundation, which supports disadvantaged youth), hospitals, and educational institutions. Ron also believes that we should support the military and veterans. In recognition of Fox 40's contributions, Ron was appointed as the 2012 Honorary Colonel in The Argyll and Sutherland Highlanders of Canada Reserve Troop.

While Ron has chaired several local high-profile capital campaigns—which include Hillfield Strathallan College, St. Joseph's Hospital, and McMaster University Athletics Capital Campaign—most of the company's contributions are anonymous. These anonymous contributions have often been directed to areas that have been deemed to have the greatest need. The Foxcrofts recognize that there are over 60 000 charities and non-profits in Ontario. By anonymously supporting some of those in need, they do not upset the many worthy ones that are left out.

Ron credits his customers and employees for the improvements to the original whistle. In his words, "When you are the best, you need to be better." This all starts with watching people to understand their needs. It involves developing products and services that customers might want. Making decisions along the way is challenging, but if you are successful, you can make a lot of customers very happy. Throughout this process, you need to have a vision, be focused, adapt to change, and never give up. His advice for future entrepreneurs, in the words of Walt Disney, are to, "Get a good idea and stay with it. Dog it, and work it until it's done and done right."

Sources: Ron Foxcroft, CEO of Fox 40 International Inc. and Chairman and CEO of Fluke Transportation, in-person interview, September 22, 2017, Hamilton; and Dave Foxcroft, President and COO, Fox 40 International Inc., in-person interview, June 25, 2012, Hamilton; "Fox 40 Green Initiatives," Fox 40 International Inc., June 1, 2012, www.fox40world.com/index.cfm?pagepath=ABOUT_US/Green_Initiatives&id=4240; Roy Green, "Roy Green: A Terrifying Moment Leads to a Canadian Global Success," *The Canadian Business Journal,* May 12, 2012, www.cbj.ca/features/may_12_features/roy_green_a_terrifying_moment_leads_to_a_canadian_global_success.html; "Visitors," Messe München International, 2012, www.ispo.com/munich/en/All-Sports/Visitors; "Who We Are: The Fox 40 Story," Fox 40 International Inc., December 18, 2011, www.fox40world.com/index.cfm?pagepath=ABOUT_US/Who_We_Are_The_Fox_40_Story&id=4099; "BEDC Inducts Mr. Ron Foxcroft into the Entrepreneur Hall of Fame," Burlington Economic Development Corporation, June 10, 2011, www.bedc.ca/sites/default/files/PDF/businessnews/MediaRelease-BEDCInductsMr.RonFoxcroftintotheEntrepreneurHallofFame.pdf; John Kernaghan, "Fox 40 founder Foxcroft feted," *The Hamilton Spectator,* October 18, 2010, www.thespec.com/sports/local/article/268488-fox-40-founder-foxcroft-feted; REFEREE Staff, "Not An Inadvertent Whistle," *REFEREE Magazine,* July 2007, 45–47; and "Ron Foxcroft, Summit of Life," Global TV, Summer 2005.

Discussion Questions

1. In addition to employees and customers, what other stakeholders does the company consider as part of its business activities?
2. What is the primary reason why the company is unlikely to consider other global market-entry strategies (e.g., licensing)?
3. Visit the company's website at http://www.fox-40world.com. What are some of its newest green initiatives? Can you recommend any new ones?
4. Do you have a dream for a product that has not yet been produced? If yes, how do you plan to develop this idea and turn it into reality?

PART 2

CHAPTER 6

Forms of Business Ownership

LEARNING OBJECTIVES

After you have read and studied this chapter, you should be able to:

LO1 List the advantages and disadvantages of sole proprietorships.

LO2 Describe the advantages and disadvantages of partnerships. Include the differences between general and limited partners.

LO3 Discuss the advantages and disadvantages of corporations.

LO4 Outline the advantages and disadvantages of franchising. Include the challenges of global franchising.

LO5 Describe the role of co-operatives in Canada.

PROFILE

GETTING TO KNOW: BRIAN SCUDAMORE, CEO/FOUNDER, O2E BRANDS, PARENT COMPANY OF 1-800-GOT-JUNK?, WOW 1 DAY PAINTING, YOU MOVE ME, AND SHACK SHINE

In 1989, 18-year-old college student Brian Scudamore could not find a summer job, so he decided to start his own business in Vancouver, British Columbia. Inspired by a junk-hauling truck he saw at a McDonald's, Scudamore bought a used truck for $700 and began a junk removal company called the Rubbish Boys. His slogan was "We'll Stash Your Trash in a Flash!" Over the following summers Scudamore's business grew, and in 1998 he changed the name to 1-800-GOT-JUNK? and expanded his business.

With uniformed employees and clean, shiny trucks proudly advertising the company's name and telephone number, Scudamore set his company apart from other independent junk haulers, creating an unlikely brand out of hauling people's trash or, as Scudamore sees it, treasure. Servicing both the residential and commercial markets, 1-800-GOT-JUNK? is recognized for outstanding customer service that is based on a simple, yet effective concept: friendly drivers call

© O2E

customers in advance; arrive at the customer site on schedule; and provide a full cleanup after the junk is removed. Whenever possible, items are recycled or donated.

While many companies expand their businesses by transforming into corporations and selling shares on the open market, 1-800-GOT-JUNK? expanded through franchising as a way to achieve rapid market penetration and revenue growth. Today, the company is the world's largest junk removal service.

Scudamore has used his customer-service–focused business model to launch other home service brands. Under the parent company O2E Brands, one will find a collection of companies that include 1-800-GOT-JUNK?, WOW 1 DAY PAINTING, You Move Me (a professional local moving company), and Shack Shine (a company that provides window cleaning, pressure washing or gutter cleaning). O2E Brands projects that it will have 500 franchise partners with system-wide sales of $500 million by the end of 2025.

When asked what the biggest challenge facing his business was, Scudamore responded that it was, "Keeping the right people, keeping them motivated and great. As clichéd as it sounds, having the right people is all a business really is."

Just like Scudamore, all business owners must decide for themselves which form of business is best for them. Whether you dream of starting a business for yourself, going into business with a partner, forming a corporation, or someday being a leading franchisor, it is important to know that each form of ownership has its advantages and disadvantages. You will learn about them all in this chapter.

Sources: "About O2E Brands," O2E Brands, October 12, 2017, http://www.o2ebrands.com/about us; "Brian Scudamore," LinkedIn, February 24, 2015, https://www.linkedin.com/in/scudamore; "Brian Scudamore, Founder and CEO,"1-800 GOT JUNK? [2015?], http://www.1800gotjunk.com/ca_en/about/brian_scudamore.aspx; "Meet Brian Scudamore, You Move Me," Small Business BC, 2015, http://smallbusinessbc.ca/success-story/meet-brian-scudamore-you-move-me/; "Start a Franchise," You Move Me, [2015?], http://www.youmoveme.com/ca/franchising/the-opportunity; "Press Kit," 1-800 GOT JUNK? [2013?], http://www.1800gotjunk.com/sites/default/files/PRKIT_2013_NORTHAMERICA.pdf; "Brian Scudamore, Founder and CEO," 1-800 GOT JUNK?, May 12, 2012, www.1800gotjunk.com/us_en/about/brian_scudamore.aspx; Jeff Beer, "Q&A: Brian Scudamore founder/CEO, 1-800-Got-Junk," *Canadian Business,* May 7, 2012, www.canadianbusiness.com/article/81127-q-a-brian-scudamore-founder-ceo-1-800-got-junk; Eric Stites, "Franchise Relations: Different Ideas, Great Solutions," *Franchising World,* May 1, 2008; and "Junk Removal Founder Awarded Entrepreneur of the Year by International Franchise Association," PR Newswire, February 11, 2008.

Starting a Small Business

Like Brian Scudamore, many people start new businesses in Canada every year. Chances are, you have thought of owning your own business or know someone who has. How you set up your business can make a tremendous difference in your long-term success. The three major forms of business ownership are (1) sole proprietorships, (2) partnerships, and (3) corporations. Each has advantages and disadvantages that we will discuss.

Courtesy of Abeego Designs Inc. Used with permission

With a background in holistic nutrition, Toni Desrosiers, co-founder of Victoria, British Columbia-based Abeego Designs Inc., developed a reusable beeswax wrap.[1] Did you see her pitch on Dragons' Den? Would you try this plastic-free food covering?

It can be easy to get started in your own business. You can begin a lawn mowing service, develop a website, or go about meeting other wants and needs in your community. A business owned, and usually managed, by one person is called a **sole proprietorship**. This is the most common form of business ownership.

Many people do not have the money, time, or desire to run a business on their own. When two or more parties legally agree to become co-owners of a business, the organization is called a **partnership**.

Sole proprietorships and partnerships are relatively easy to form, but there are advantages to creating a business that is separate and distinct from the owners. A legal entity with authority to act and have liability separate from its owners is called a **corporation**.

As you will learn in this chapter, each form of business ownership has advantages and disadvantages. It is important to understand both before attempting to start a business. Keep in mind that just because a business starts in one form of ownership, it does not have to stay in that form. Many companies start out in one form, then add (or drop) a partner or two, and eventually may become corporations or franchisors. The advantages and disadvantages that are highlighted in this chapter may give you an idea of why there may be a change in ownership form as the business grows. Let's begin our discussion by looking at the most basic form of ownership—the sole proprietorship.

sole proprietorship
A business that is owned, and usually managed, by one person.

partnership
A legal form of business with two or more parties.

corporation
A legal entity with authority to act and have liability separate from its owners.

Sole Proprietorships

Advantages of Sole Proprietorships

LO1

List the advantages and disadvantages of sole proprietorships.

Sole proprietorships are the easiest kind of businesses for you to explore in your quest for an interesting career. Every city has sole proprietors you can visit. Talk with some of these business people about the joys and frustrations of being on their own. Some advantages they mention may include the following:

1. *Ease of starting and ending the business.* All you have to do to start a sole proprietorship is to buy or lease the needed equipment (e.g., a saw, a laptop, a tractor, a lawn mower, etc.) and put up some announcements saying you are in business. You may have to get a permit or licence from the local government, but often that is no problem.

Visit Canada Business Network to learn how to register your business with the different levels of government. It's just as easy to get out of business; you simply stop. There is no one to consult or to disagree with about such decisions.

2. *Being your own boss.* Working for others simply does not have the same excitement as working for yourself—at least, that is the way sole proprietors feel. You may make mistakes, but they are your mistakes—and so are the many small victories each day.
3. *Pride of ownership.* People who own and manage their own businesses are rightfully proud of their work. They deserve all the credit for taking the risks and providing needed products.
4. *Retention of company profit.* Owners not only keep the profits earned but also benefit from the increasing value as their businesses grow.
5. *No special taxes.* All profits of a sole proprietorship are taxed as the personal income of the owner, and the owner pays the normal personal income tax rate on that money. Another tax advantage for sole proprietors is that they can claim any business losses against other earned income. These losses would decrease the personal taxes they would need to pay. Understanding tax planning is an important factor in choosing the appropriate form of business organization and often requires the advice of professional accountants. Accounting will be discussed in Chapter 16.
6. *Less regulation.* While proprietorships are regulated by the provincial/territorial governments, and the proprietorship may have to be registered, overall they are less regulated than corporations.[2] As well, the administration of a proprietorship is less costly than that of a corporation.

© dolphfyn / Alamy

Over the last three years, the federal government spent more than $24.4 million on Facebook and Instagram ads, promotions and sponsored posts and videos as a way to promote events and communicate messages and policy initiatives.[3] Would you be more likely to use Facebook to learn about policies that impact your small business or would you go directly to the government's website(s)?

Disadvantages of Sole Proprietorships

Not everyone is equipped to own and manage a business. Disadvantages of owning your own business may include the following:

1. *Unlimited liability—the risk of personal losses.* When you work for others, it is their problem if the business is not profitable. When you own your own business, you and the business are considered one. You have **unlimited liability**; that is, any debts or damages incurred by the business are your debts and you must pay them, even if it means selling your home, your car, or whatever else you own. This is a serious risk, and one that requires not only thought but also discussion with a lawyer, an insurance agent, an accountant, and others.

unlimited liability The responsibility of business owners for all of the debts of the business.

2. *Limited financial resources.* Funds available to the business are limited to the funds that the one (sole) owner can gather. Often it is difficult to save enough money to start a business and keep it going. The costs of inventory, supplies, insurance, advertising, rent, computers, utilities, and so on may be too much to cover alone. Since there are serious limits to how much money one person can raise, partnerships and corporations have a greater probability of obtaining the needed financial backing to start and equip a business and keep it going.
3. *Management difficulties.* All businesses need management; someone must keep inventory records, accounting records, tax records, and so forth. Many people skilled at selling things or providing a service are often not so skilled at keeping records. Sole proprietors often find it difficult to attract good, qualified employees to help run the business because they cannot compete with the salaries and benefits offered by larger companies.
4. *Overwhelming time commitment.* Though sole proprietors may say they set their own hours, it is hard to own a business, manage it, train people, and have time for anything else in life when there is no one with whom to share the burden. The owner of a store, for example, may put in 12 hours a day, at least six days a week—almost twice the hours worked by a non-supervisory employee in a large company. Imagine how this time commitment affects the sole proprietor's family life. Many sole proprietors will tell you, "It's not a job, it's not a career, it's a way of life."[4]
5. *Few fringe benefits.* If you are your own boss, you lose the fringe benefits that often come from working for others. You have no paid health insurance, no paid disability insurance, no pension plan, no sick leave, and no vacation pay. These and other benefits may add up to 30 percent or more of a worker's compensation.
6. *Limited growth.* Expansion is often slow since a sole proprietorship relies on its owner for most of its creativity, business know-how, and funding.
7. *Limited lifespan.* If the sole proprietor dies, is incapacitated, or retires, the business no longer exists (unless it is sold or taken over by the sole proprietor's heirs).
8. *Possibly pay higher taxes.* If the business is profitable, it may be paying higher taxes than if it was incorporated as a Canadian Controlled Private Corporation (CCPC).[5] That is, tax rates are more advantageous if the business is incorporated. We will expand on this point later on in the chapter under the corporations discussion.

© John Lund/Marc Romanelli/Blend Images LLC RF.

Being the sole proprietor of a company, like a clothing boutique, means making a major time commitment to run the business, including constantly seeking out new customers and looking for reliable employees when the time comes to grow. If you were a sole proprietor, what would you need to do if you wanted to take a week's vacation?

Talk with a few local sole proprietors about the challenges they have faced in being on their own. They are likely to have many interesting stories to tell about problems in getting loans from financial institutions, problems with theft, and problems simply keeping up with their businesses. These are reasons why many sole proprietors choose to find partners to share the load.

PROGRESS ASSESSMENT

- What are the three forms of business ownership?
- What are the advantages and disadvantages of sole proprietorships?
- Why would unlimited liability be considered a major drawback of sole proprietorships?

Partnerships

A partnership is a legal form of business with two or more parties. The business can be a partnership of individuals, corporations, trusts, other partnerships, or a combination of these.[6] Two types of partnerships are general partnerships and limited partnerships. In a **general partnership** all owners share in operating the business and in assuming liability for the business' debts. A **limited partnership** has one or more general partners and one or more limited partners.

A **general partner** is an owner (partner) who has unlimited liability and is active in managing the firm. Every partnership must have at least one general partner. A **limited partner** is an owner (partner) who invests money in the business but does not have any management responsibility or liability for losses beyond his or her investment. **Limited liability** means that the limited partner's liability for the debts of the business is *limited* to the amount put into the business; therefore, personal assets are not at risk.

Another type of partnership was created to limit the disadvantage of unlimited liability. A **limited liability partnership (LLP)** limits partners' risk of losing their personal assets to the outcomes of only their own acts and omissions and those of people under their supervision. If you're a limited partner in an LLP, you can operate without fear that one of your partners might commit an act of malpractice resulting in a judgment that takes away your house, car, retirement plans, etc. as would be the case in a general partnership. LLPs, usually only available to groups of professionals (e.g., doctors, lawyers, and accountants), are governed by provincial legislation.[7]

Advantages of Partnerships

Often, it is much easier to own and manage a business with one or more partners. Your partner may be skilled at inventory control and accounting, while you do the selling or servicing. A partner can also provide additional money, support, and expertise as well

general partnership
A partnership in which all owners share in operating the business and in assuming liability for the business' debts.

limited partnership
A partnership with one or more general partners and one or more limited partners.

general partner
An owner (partner) who has unlimited liability and is active in managing the firm.

limited partner
An owner (partner) who invests money in the business but does not have any management responsibility or liability for losses beyond the investment.

LO2

Describe the advantages and disadvantages of partnerships. Include the differences between general and limited partners.

limited liability
The responsibility of a business' owners for losses only up to the amount they invest; limited partners and shareholders have limited liability.

limited liability partnership (LLP)
A partnership that limits partners' risk of losing their personal assets to only their own acts and omissions and to the acts and omissions of people under their supervision.

Christine Magee started Sleep Country Canada with partners Steve Gunn and Gord Lownds based on their dream to give customers what they want. Today, the company is Canada's largest mattress retailer. Do you have any colleagues that you would consider partnering up with to start a business?

as cover for you when you are sick or on vacation. Figure 6.1 suggests several questions to ask yourself when choosing a partner.

Partnerships usually have the following advantages:

1. *More financial resources.* When two or more people pool their money and credit, it's easier to pay the rent, utilities, and other bills incurred by a business. A limited partnership is specially designed to help raise capital (money). As mentioned earlier, a limited partner invests money in the business but cannot legally have any management responsibility, and has limited liability.
2. *Shared management and pooled/complementary skills and knowledge.* It is simply much easier to manage the day-to-day activities of a business with carefully chosen partners. Partners give each other free time from the business and provide different skills and perspectives. Some people find that the best partner is a spouse. Lulu Cohen-Farnell, founder of Real Food for Real Kids, believes that keys to success include good communication and understanding each other's roles. She points out "I am the 'why' and the 'what'," while her husband, David, is the 'who,' the 'how' and the 'when.'[8] Many husband-and-wife teams manage restaurants, service shops, and other businesses.[9]
3. *Longer survival.* Partnerships are more likely to succeed than sole proprietorships because being watched by a partner can help a business person become more disciplined.[10]
4. *Shared risk.* A partnership shares the risk among the owners. This includes financial risk in starting the business and ongoing risks as the business grows. Such was the case for Inder Bedi when he brought on a business partner for Matt & Nat. This was necessary to bring the business to the next level by taking production to Asia in order to decrease costs.[11]
5. *No special taxes.* As with sole proprietorships, all profits of partnerships are taxed as the personal incomes of the owners, and the owners pay the normal income tax rate on that money. Similarly, any business losses can be used to decrease earned income from other sources.

Lara Murphy and Karen Ryan met on a construction site in Banff, Alberta while working as project managers. Today they own Ryan Murphy Construction, a construction, renovation, and project management company. Have you met anyone that would make an ideal business partner?

FIGURE 6.1

QUESTIONS TO ASK WHEN CHOOSING A BUSINESS PARTNER

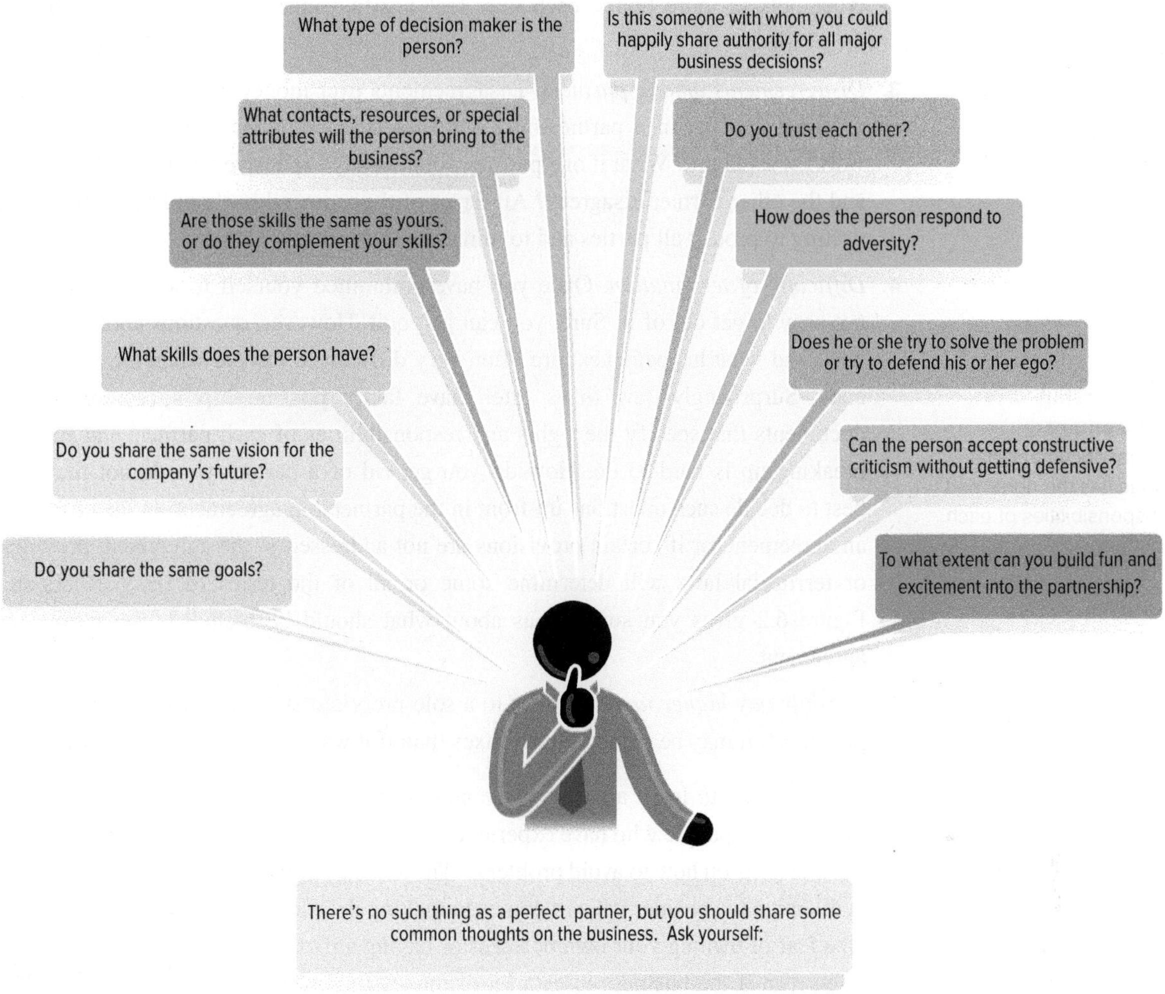
What type of decision maker is the person?
Is this someone with whom you could happily share authority for all major business decisions?
What contacts, resources, or special attributes will the person bring to the business?
Do you trust each other?
Are those skills the same as yours, or do they complement your skills?
How does the person respond to adversity?
What skills does the person have?
Does he or she try to solve the problem or try to defend his or her ego?
Do you share the same vision for the company's future?
Can the person accept constructive criticism without getting defensive?
Do you share the same goals?
To what extent can you build fun and excitement into the partnership?
There's no such thing as a perfect partner, but you should share some common thoughts on the business. Ask yourself:

6. *Less regulation.* Like a sole proprietorship, a partnership is less regulated than a corporation.

Disadvantages of Partnerships

Any time two people must agree, conflict and tension are possible. Partnerships have caused splits between relatives, friends, and spouses. Let's explore the disadvantages of partnerships next.

1. *Unlimited liability.* Each *general* partner is liable for the debts of the firm, no matter who was responsible for causing those debts. You are liable for your partners' mistakes as well as your own. Like sole proprietors, general partners can lose their homes, cars, and everything else they own if the business loses a lawsuit or goes bankrupt.

2. *Division of profits.* Sharing risk means sharing profits, and that can cause conflicts. There is no set system for dividing profits in a partnership, and they are not always divided evenly. For example, if one partner puts in more money and the other puts in more hours, each may feel justified in asking for a bigger share of the profits.
3. *Disagreements among partners.* Disagreements over money are just one example of potential conflict in a partnership. Who has final authority over employees? Who works what hours? What if one partner wants to buy expensive equipment for the firm and the other partner disagrees? All terms of the partnership should be spelled out in writing to protect all parties and to minimize misunderstandings.[12]
4. *Difficulty of termination.* Once you have committed yourself to a partnership, it is not easy to get out of it. Sure, you can just quit. However, questions about who gets what and what happens next are often very difficult to resolve when the partnership ends. Surprisingly, law firms often have faulty **partnership agreements** (legal documents that specify the rights and responsibilities of each partner) and find that breaking up is hard to do. How do you get rid of a partner you do not like? It is best to decide such questions up-front in the partnership agreement. In the absence of an agreement, or if certain provisions are not addressed in the agreement, provincial or territorial laws will determine some or all of the terms of the partnership.[13] Figure 6.2 gives you some ideas about what should be included in a partnership agreement.
5. *Possibly pay higher taxes.* Similar to a sole proprietorship, if the partnership is very profitable, it may be paying higher taxes than if it was incorporated as a CCPC.[14]

partnership agreement
Legal document that specifies the rights and responsibilities of each partner

The best way to learn about the advantages and disadvantages of partnerships is to interview several people who have experience with such arrangements. They will give you insights and hints on how to avoid problems. The Making Ethical Decisions box leaves you with a dilemma to consider when it comes to making decisions in a partnership.

One fear of owning your own business or having a partner is the fear of losing everything you own if the business loses a lot of money or someone sues the business. Many business people try to avoid this and the other disadvantages of sole proprietorships and partnerships by forming corporations. We discuss this basic form of business ownership in the next section.

Making ETHICAL DECISIONS

Outsourcing or Outsmarting?

Imagine that you and your partner own a construction company. You receive a bid from a subcontractor that you know is 20 percent too low. Such a loss to the subcontractor could put him out of business. Accepting the bid will certainly improve your chances of winning the contract for a big shopping centre project. Your partner wants to take the bid and let the subcontractor suffer the consequences of his bad estimate. What do you think you should do? What could be the consequences of your decision?

FIGURE 6.2

PARTNERSHIP AGREEMENT PROVISIONS

It's not hard to form a partnership, but it's wise for each prospective partner to get the counsel of a lawyer experienced with such agreements. Lawyers' services are usually expensive, so would-be partners should read all about partnerships and reach some basic agreements before calling a lawyer.

For your protection, be sure to put your partnership agreement in writing. The following provisions are usually included in a partnership agreement:

1. The name of the business. All provinces require the firm's name to be registered with the province if the firm's name is different from the name of any of the partners.
2. The names and addresses of all partners.
3. The purpose and nature of the business, the location of the principal office(s), and any other locations where business will be conducted.
4. The date the partnership will start and how long it will last. Will it exist for a specific length of time, or will it stop when one of the partners dies or when the partners agree to discontinue?
5. The contributions made by each partner. Will some partners contribute money, while others provide real estate, personal property, expertise, or labour? When are the contributions due?
6. The management responsibilities. Will all partners have equal voices in management, or will there be senior and junior partners?
7. The duties of each partner.
8. The salaries and drawing accounts of each partner.
9. Provision for sharing of profits or losses.
10. Provision for accounting procedures. Who'll keep the accounts? What bookkeeping and accounting methods will be used? Where will the books be kept?
11. The requirements for taking in new partners.
12. Any special restrictions, rights, or duties of any partner.
13. Provision for a retiring partner.
14. Provision for the purchase of a deceased or retiring partner's share of the business.
15. Provision for how grievances will be handled.
16. Provision for how to dissolve the partnership and distribute the assets to the partners.

PROGRESS ASSESSMENT

- What is the difference between a limited partner and a general partner?
- What are some of the advantages and disadvantages of partnerships?
- State four provisions usually included in a partnership agreement.

LO3

Discuss the advantages and disadvantages of corporations.

Corporations

Although the word *corporation* makes people think of big businesses, such as the Bank of Montreal or Irving Oil, it is not necessary to be big to incorporate (start a corporation). Obviously, many corporations are big. However, incorporating may be beneficial for small businesses also.

A corporation is a federally or provincially chartered legal entity with authority to act and have liability separate from its owners. The corporation's owners (called shareholders or stockholders, as they hold shares or stock of ownership in the company) are not liable for the debts or any other problems of the corporation beyond the money they invest. Shareholders do not have to worry about losing their homes, cars, and other personal property if the business cannot pay its bills—a very significant benefit. A corporation not only limits the liability of owners, but it also enables many people to share in the ownership (and profits) of a business without working there or having other commitments to it. We will discuss the rights of shareholders in Chapter 17.

public corporation Corporation that has the right to issue shares to the public, so its shares may be listed on a stock exchange.

In Canada, corporations are divided into two classes: public and private. A **public corporation** has the right to issue stock (ownership in the company through shares) to the public, which means its shares may be listed on a stock exchange. This offers the possibility of raising large amounts of capital, regardless of the size of the company. That is, public corporations can be small and large companies.

© The Jim Pattison Group

Starting with one auto dealership in 1961, the Jim Pattison Group is now the second-largest private company in Canada. With annual sales of $9.6 billion, the company focuses on the automotive, agriculture, media, packaging, food and beverage, magazine distribution, entertainment, export, and financial industries.[15] Do you recognize any of these brands?

There are approximately 1.8 million private corporations in Canada.[16] A **private corporation** is usually controlled by a small number of shareholders and its shares are not listed on a stock exchange.[17] (Go to Chapter 18 to learn how a stock exchange works.) This greatly reduces the costs of incorporating. Many small corporations are in the private category. This is the vehicle employed by individuals or partners who do not anticipate the need for substantial financing but want to take advantage of limited liability. Examples can include family businesses such as farms and restaurants, as well as professional services. Many large corporations are also registered as private corporations. Examples include Apple Canada (owned by Apple Inc.), Walmart Canada Corporation (owned by Wal-Mart Stores, Inc.) and Ford Motor Company of Canada (owned by Ford Motor Company).

© Chapman's Ice Cream

Chapman's Ice Cream is a private corporation started in 1973 by Penny and David Chapman. Today it is Canada's largest independent ice cream manufacturer. Have you tasted company products?

private corporation
Corporation that is usually controlled by a small number of shareholders and its shares are not listed on a stock exchange.

CCPCs have some advantages over public corporations, especially from a taxation perspective. Advantages include the following: a CCPC is eligible for the small-business deduction and as a result, pays a lower rate of federal tax (small-business rate) on the first $500,000 of active business income; CCPCs have an additional month to pay taxes owed; and CCPCs are entitled to enhanced investment tax credits.[18]

Another important advantage for the owner of a private corporation is that he or she can issue stock to a child, or a spouse, making them co-owners of the company. This procedure is not available to a sole proprietor. It is a simple and useful way of recognizing the contribution of these or other family members, or employees, to the company. This procedure may also be a good way for the owner to prepare for retirement by gradually transferring ownership and responsibility to those who will be inheriting the business.

Keep in mind that with any kind of succession planning in private corporations, conflict may arise. In the mid-1990s, brothers Wallace and Harrison McCain of McCain Foods were bitterly divided over who should lead the company when they were gone. Wallace wanted his son Michael to take over, while Harrison preferred outside management. The disagreement ultimately wound up in a New Brunswick court, which sided with Harrison. Ousted from the company, Wallace went to Toronto, where he took over Maple Leaf Foods with sons Michael and Scott.[19] The Adapting to Change box discusses some of the challenges associated with family businesses.

There is a formal procedure for forming a corporation that involves applying to the appropriate federal or provincial agency. It is always recommended that company owners seek the services of a competent lawyer and accountant prior to proceeding with any incorporation. The procedure for large or public corporations is much more complex and expensive and definitely requires hiring a legal firm. These costs can easily run into the thousands of dollars. Figure 6.3 describes various types of corporations.

Adapting to CHANGE

Challenges of Family Businesses

© Dmytro Zinkevych / Alamy Stock Photo

Family-run businesses account for approximately 90 percent of the world's companies. They range from small restaurants and corner stores to large companies such as James Richardson & Sons, Ltd. and Wal-Mart Stores Inc.

According to business-heir-turned-author Thomas William Deans, the biggest problem facing family businesses today is not the business, it is the family. In his book, *Every Family's Business,* he blames the parents for not talking business at the dinner table, not including adult children in the decision-making process, just assuming that their kids want the business, and worst of all, "gifting" the business to unappreciative kids.

Since it's "our business" in a family company, management problems are somewhat different from similar problems in non-family businesses. Conflicts sometimes abound because relatives look upon the business from different viewpoints. Those relatives who are silent partners, shareholders, and directors may only see dollar signs when judging capital expenditures, growth, and other major matters. Relatives who are engaged in daily operations judge major matters from the viewpoint of the production, sales, and personnel necessary to make the company successful. Obviously, these two viewpoints may conflict in some instances. This natural conflict can be aggravated by family members who have no talent for money or business.

While the majority of family business owners would like to see their businesses transferred to the next generation, few survive the transition. According to the Family Business Institute, only about 30 percent of family businesses survive into the second generation, and 12 percent are still viable into the third generation.

Family business failures are primarily due to the lack of family business succession planning. A Canadian Business Insights study found that just 17 percent of family-run businesses have a firm succession plan in place. The key to effective governance for a family business is to recognize when the family business is moving from one stage to another, such as from the controlling owner (i.e., the original owner) to a sibling partnership where siblings have an ownership interest and/or some family shareholders are not working in the business. By designing revisions to the governance structure that will meet the needs of the owners for the next stage, expectations and responsibilities are likely to be clearer, contributing to a more successful business venture.

Sources: Duncan Hood, "Modern Family," *Report on Business,* November 2017, p. 2; "Succession Planning," Family Business Institute, 2017, http://www.familybusinessinstitute.com/index.php/Succession-Planning/; "Succession Planning," The Family Business Institute, Inc., 2017, https://www.familybusinessinstitute.com/consulting/succession-planning/; Graham F. Scott, "The 20 Biggest Family-run Businesses in Canada," *Canadian Business,* June 8, 2015, http://www.canadianbusiness.com/lists-and-rankings/richest-people/2015-family-business-ranking/; "Succession Planning for Family Business," BDO Canada LLP, 2012, www.bdo.ca/library/publications/familybusiness/succession/planning1.cfm; "Governance for the Family Business," KPMG in Canada, 2008, www.kpmg.ca/en/services/enterprise/issuesGrowthGovernance.html; and "The Parent Trap," *PROFIT,* 30 October 2008, http://www.profitguide.com/manage-grow/strategy-operations/family-business-the-parent-trap-29448.

Advantages of Corporations

Most people are not willing to risk everything to go into business. Yet for businesses to grow, prosper, and create economic opportunity, many people need to invest money in them. One way to solve this problem is to create an artificial being, an entity that exists only in the eyes of the law—a corporation. This entity is a technique for involving people in business without risking their other personal assets.

FIGURE 6.3

SOME CORPORATION TYPES

Corporations can fit in more than one category.

A benefit (B) corporation is certified to meet rigorous standards of social and environmental performance, accountability, and transparency. Review the Seeking Sustainability box for an example.

A Crown corporation is one that can only be registered by the provincial or federal government. This was discussed in Chapter 4.

A domestic corporation conducts business in its home country (e.g., Canada only).

A multinational corporation is a firm that operates in several countries.

A non-profit (or not-for-profit) corporation is one that does not seek personal profit for its owners. Review Chapter 1 for more information.

A private (closed) corporation is one whose shares are held by a few people and are not available to the general public.

A professional corporation is a private corporation whose owners provide professional services (e.g., accountants and architects).

A public (open) corporation sells shares to the general public.

Seeking SUSTAINABILITY

B Corporations Let Sustainability Set Sail

While vacationing on the small island of Tobago, Michael Dimin and his sons saw a nasty sight as their boat headed to dock after a day of fishing. Tons of rotting fish littered the water, left there by fishermen who caught too many to sell locally. That gave Dimin an idea: what if they sold the surplus fish directly to New York restaurants? After all, demand for fresh seafood would always be high at the city's many upscale eateries. Plus, with an outside market to sell to, fishermen in Tobago wouldn't need to waste so much of their catch.

Dimin knew this venture was likely to be profitable, but more than that he wanted ocean conservation and sustainability to be the driving force of the business. That's why he registered his company, Sea to Table, as a benefit corporation (or B corporation).

With this business structure, companies are certified to meet rigorous standards of social and environmental performance, accountability, and transparency. They are judged by how well they meet their own set of socially or environmentally beneficial goals. There is a growing community of more than 2100 Certified B corporations from 50 countries and over 130 industries working together toward one unifying goal: to redefine success in business. In Canada, there are more than 150 B corporations.

© Volodymyr Melnyk / Alamy Stock Photo

For Sea to Table, being a B corporation means developing relationships with sustainable fisheries needing better access to markets, thus creating a direct connection between fishermen and chefs. This allows the company to keep its supply lines transparent while eliminating the costly middlemen. Not only do business models like this help society, but their compassionate goals tend to lure in some of the most talented people in the job market. It just goes to show that profits aren't the only way to measure success in the business world.

Sources: "What are B Corps?" B Lab, 2017, http://www.bcorporation.net/what-are-b-corps; "B Lab Canada" B Lab, 2017, https://www.bcorporation.net/Canada; "Our Story," Sea to Table, 2014, www.sea2table.com; "Sean and Michael Dimin," Future of Fish, www.futureoffish.org, accessed February 2014; and Lindsay Gellman and Rachel Feintzeig, "Social Seal of Approval Lures Talent," *The Wall Street Journal*, November 12, 2013.

© THE CANADIAN PRESS/Richard Buchan

Companies can change their status over time. For example, The TDL Group Corp., a private corporation, was the original owner of the Tim Hortons chain. It merged with Wendy's International, Inc. in 1995. In 2006, Tim Hortons was spun off as a separate company. In 2014, Burger King acquired Tim Hortons to create Restaurant Brands International, the third-largest fast-food chain in the world.[20]

A corporation has a separate legal identity from the owners—the shareholders—of the company and files its own tax returns. Let's explore some of the advantages of corporations:

1. *Limited liability.* A major advantage of corporations is the limited liability of owners. Remember, limited liability means that the owners of a business are responsible for losses only up to the amount they invest in it. Many corporations in Canada have the letters *Ltd.* after their name, which speaks to this limited liability. Others end their names with *Inc.* (for incorporated) or *Corp.* (for corporation) to indicate their status.

   Be aware that you should not incorporate if it is your intention to use this ownership form as a way to avoid your debts. As a sole proprietorship or partnership, the debts the business incurs remain personal liabilities even after they are taken over by a corporation. Legally, it is the status existing at the time the debts were incurred that governs, not what happens subsequently.

2. *Ability to raise more money for investment.* To raise money, a corporation can sell ownership (shares) to anyone who is interested. This way, thousands of people can own part of major companies such as Rogers Communications Inc., TD Bank Group, Manulife Financial Corp., EnCana Corp., Loblaw Companies Ltd., and smaller companies as well. If a company sold 1 million shares for $50 each, it would have $50 million available to build plants, buy materials, hire people, manufacture products, and so on. Such a large amount of money would be difficult to raise any other way.

   Corporations can also borrow money by obtaining loans from financial institutions like banks. They can also borrow from individual investors by issuing bonds, which involve paying investors interest until the bonds are repaid sometime in the future.[21] You can read about how corporations raise funds through the sale of shares and bonds in Chapter 17.

3. *Size.* That one word summarizes many of the advantages of some corporations. Because they can raise large amounts of money to work with, big corporations can build modern factories or software development facilities with the latest equipment. They can hire experts or specialists in all areas of operation. They can buy other corporations in different fields to diversify their business risks. (What this means is that a corporation can be involved in many businesses at once so that if one is not doing well, the negative impact on the total corporation is lessened.) In short, a large corporation with numerous resources can take advantage of opportunities anywhere in the world.

   When one considers size, different criteria can be used. This can include the number of employees, revenues, assets, and profits. Note that corporations do not have to be large to enjoy the benefits of incorporation. Professionals (such as physicians and lawyers) can incorporate. Individuals and partnerships can also incorporate. Figure 6.4 lists some of Canada's largest corporations.

4. *Perpetual life.* Because corporations are separate from those who own them, the death of one or more owners does not terminate the corporation.
5. *Ease of ownership change.* It is easy to change the owners of a corporation. All that is necessary is to sell the shares to someone else.
6. *Ease of attracting talented employees.* Corporations can attract skilled employees by offering benefits such as a pension plan, dental plan, and stock options (the right to purchase shares of the corporation for a fixed price). To be competitive, sole proprietorships and partnerships may offer money or other benefits to compete with such plans. Benefits will be discussed in Chapter 12.

© Anderson Ross/Blend Images LLC

As a result of corporate scandals, board members are under increasing scrutiny to ensure that they are effectively fulfilling their roles and responsibilities to their stakeholders. Consequently, companies continue to review their practices by answering questions such as these: Is the board independent from its officers? Does the company have a statement of corporate governance practices? To truly represent the shareholders, are directors elected every year?

FIGURE 6.4

CANADA'S LARGEST CORPORATIONS (2016)

A. Public Corporations Based on Profit			
Rank	**Company**	**Profit ($ billions)**	**Category**
1	Royal Bank of Canada	C$10.41	Banks
2	Toronto-Dominion Bank	C$ 8.82	Banks
3	Bank of Nova Scotia	C$ 7.12	Banks
4	Bank of Montreal	C$ 4.62	Banks
5	CIBC	C$ 4.28	Banks
B. Private Corporations Based on Revenue			
Rank	**Company**	**Revenue ($ billions)**	**Category**
1	Wal-Mart Canada	US$25.40	Retail
2	Costco Wholesale Canada	US$17.94	Retail
3	Direct Energy Marketing Ltd.	C$ 20.69	Utilities
4	Desjardins Group	C$ 16.98	Financial
5	McKesson Canada	US$13.70	Wholesale

Sources: "Top 1000: Public (Top 1000)" and "Top 1000: Private (Top 1000)," *ROB Magazine,* June 27, 2017, https://beta.theglobeandmail.com/report-on-business/rob-magazine/top-1000/top-1000-stocks-rated-canada/article35448077/?ref=http://www.theglobeandmail.com&.

corporate governance
The process and policies that determine how an organization interacts with its stakeholders, both internal and external.

7. *Separation of ownership from management.* **Corporate governance** refers to the process and policies that determine how an organization interacts with its stakeholders. Corporate governance is necessary because of the evolution of public ownership. In public corporations, unlike sole proprietorships and partnerships, there is a separation between ownership and management.[22] As a result, the board of directors was created.

With corporate governance, rules outline how the organization is to be managed by the board of directors and the officers. The board assumes many of the same responsibilities that would typically rest with the sole proprietor, partners, or owners of a private corporation. Board members are often chosen based on their business experience and level of expertise. Those who serve on boards (both for-profit and nonprofit) may be held personally liable for the misconduct of the organization. Having directors insurance is one way to try to limit this risk. Risk will be discussed in Online Supplement 2.

The corporate hierarchy in Figure 6.5 shows how the owners/shareholders are separate from the managers and employees. The owners/shareholders elect a board of directors, who in turn hire the officers of the corporation that oversee major policy issues. The owners/shareholders thus have some say in who runs the corporation but have no real control over the daily operations (e.g., setting the price for a product).[23]

FIGURE 6.5

HOW OWNERS AFFECT MANAGEMENT

Owners have an influence on how business is managed by electing a board of directors. The board hires the top officers (and fires them if necessary). It also sets the pay for those officers. The officers then select other managers and employees with the help of the Human Resource Department.

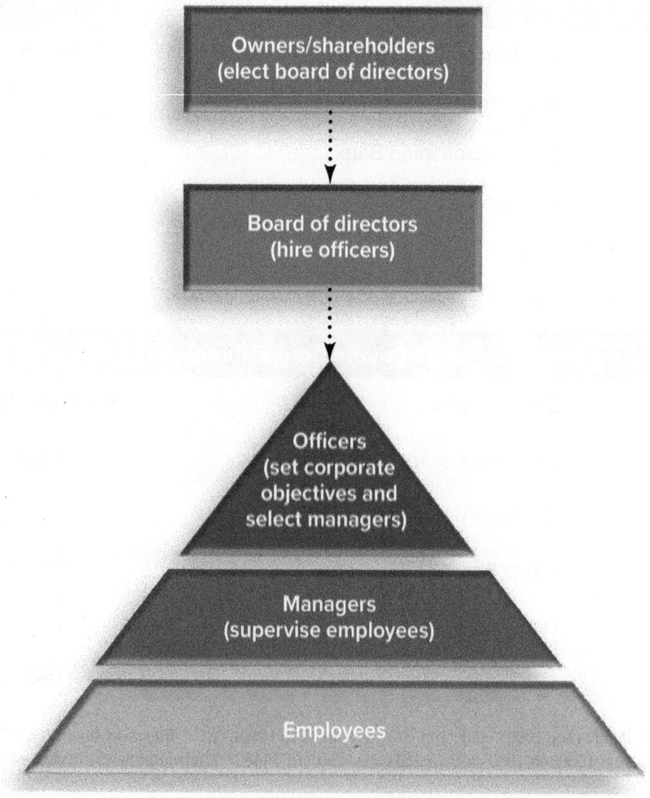

Disadvantages of Corporations

There are so many sole proprietorships and partnerships in Canada that there must be some disadvantages to incorporation. Otherwise, more people would incorporate their businesses. The following are a few of the disadvantages.

1. *Initial cost.* Incorporation may cost thousands of dollars and involve the services of lawyers and accountants.
2. *Extensive paperwork.* The paperwork filed to start a corporation is just the beginning. A sole proprietor or a partnership may keep rather broad accounting records. A corporation, in contrast, must keep detailed financial records, the minutes of meetings, and more.
3. *Double taxation.* Corporate income is taxed twice. First the corporation pays tax on income before it can distribute any net income, as *dividends,* to shareholders. Then the shareholders pay tax on the dividends they receive from the corporation. While this is *double* taxation, it is not excessive taxation, as the tax system is designed to provide some offsetting credits such as the dividend tax credit for investors.
4. *Two tax returns.* An individual who incorporates must file both a corporate tax return and an individual tax return. Depending on the size of the corporation, a corporate return can be quite complex and require the assistance of a chartered professional accountant (CPA).
5. *Size.* Size may be one advantage of corporations, but it can be a disadvantage as well. Large corporations sometimes become too inflexible and tied down in red tape (i.e., have to follow many regulations) to respond quickly to market changes, and their profitability can suffer.
6. *Difficulty of termination.* Once a corporation has started, it is relatively difficult to end. Legal procedures are costly and more complex than for unincorporated companies.
7. *Possible conflict with shareholders and their board of directors.* Conflict may brew if the shareholders elect a board of directors who disagree with management.[24] Since the board of directors chooses the company's officers, entrepreneurs serving as managers can find themselves forced out of the very company they founded. This happened to Tom Freston, one of the founders of MTV, and Steve Jobs, a founder of Apple Computer. (Jobs returned to the company later.)

Some business people are discouraged by the costs, paperwork, and special taxes that corporations must pay. However, many others believe that the advantages of incorporation outweigh the challenges. Figure 6.6 compares the three main types of organizations.

Business Regulations

Companies that wish to operate in Canada must follow federal and provincial/territorial business laws and regulations. Among other things, this applies to registration and to reporting and information.

REGISTRATION

Governments need to know what businesses are in operation to ensure that a wide range of laws and regulations are being followed. Guaranteeing that the names of businesses are not duplicated is important to avoid confusion. Additionally, governments have to be sure

FIGURE 6.6

COMPARISON OF FORMS OF BUSINESS OWNERSHIP

		PARTNERSHIPS		CORPORATION	
	Sole Proprietorship	General Partnership	Limited* Partnership	Public Corporation	Private Corporation
Documents Needed to Start Business	None, may need permit or licence	Partnership agreement (oral or written)	Written agreement; must file certificate of limited partnership	Articles of incorporation, bylaws	Articles of incorporation, bylaws; must meet criteria
Ease of Termination	Easy to terminate: just pay debts and quit	May be hard to terminate, depending on the partnership agreement	Same as general partnership	Hard and expensive to terminate	Not difficult; pay off debts, sell off assets, withdraw cash, and pay taxes
Length of Life	Terminates on the death of owner, sale, or retirement	Terminates on the death or withdrawal of partner	Terminates on the death or withdrawal of partner	Same as general partnership	Perpetual life
Transfer of Ownership	Business can be sold to qualified buyer	Must have agreement of other partner(s)	Same as general partnership	Easy to change owners; just sell shares	Easy—just sell shares†
Financial Resources	Limited to owner's capital and loans	Limited to partners' capital and loans	Same as general partnership	More money to start and operate: sell stock and bonds; loans	Owners' capital and loans; no public stock issue allowed
Risk of Losses	Unlimited liability	Unlimited liability	Limited liability	Limited liability	Limited liability
Taxes	Taxed as personal income	Taxed as personal income	Same as general partnership	Corporate, double taxation	Same as public corporation
Management Responsibilities	Owner manages all areas of the business	Partners share management	Cannot participate in management	Separate management from ownership	Owners usually manage all areas
Employee Benefits	Usually fewer benefits and lower wages	Often fewer benefits and lower wages; promising employee could become a partner	Same as general partnership	Usually better benefits and wages, advancement opportunities	Same as public corporation

*There must be at least one general partner who manages the partnership and has unlimited liability.
†Unless the agreement specifies otherwise.

that taxes are being paid. To ensure these and other goals, every company must register its business. This is a simple, routine, and inexpensive procedure.

Companies wanting to incorporate must fill out articles of incorporation and file these with the appropriate provincial/territorial or federal authority. **Articles of incorporation** are a legal authorization from the federal or provincial/territorial government for a company to use the corporate format. The main advantage of being a federally incorporated company is that incorporation gives the company name added protection and guarantees its usage across Canada. Depending on the type of business you are considering, you may be required to incorporate federally.

articles of incorporation
A legal authorization from the federal or provincial/territorial government for a company to use the corporate format.

REPORTING AND INFORMATION

Businesses receive many documents from the different levels of government during the course of a year. Some are just information about changes in employment insurance, the Canada or Quebec Pension Plan, or tax legislation as it affects them or their employees. Then there are various forms that all companies must complete so that governments can compile statistical reports that businesses, individuals, research organizations, and governments need to operate effectively. For example, Statistics Canada maintains vast databases and creates useful reports from this information.

All public corporations must file annual reports containing basic data about themselves. An annual report should include the name of the officers, how many shares have been issued, and the head office location. Of course, every corporation must also file an annual tax return containing financial statements and pay the necessary taxes during the year. Review Chapter 16 for examples of financial statements.

franchise agreement
An arrangement whereby someone with a good idea for a business sells the rights to use the business name and sell its goods and services in a given territory.

franchisor
A company that develops a product concept and sells others the rights to make and sell the products.

PROGRESS ASSESSMENT

- What are the major advantages and disadvantages of incorporating a business?
- What is the role of owners (shareholders) in the corporate hierarchy?
- If you buy shares in a corporation and someone is injured by one of the corporation's products, can you be sued? Explain.

Franchising

LO4

Outline the advantages and disadvantages of franchising. Include the challenges of global franchising.

In addition to the three basic forms of business ownership, there are two special forms: franchising and co-operatives. Let's look at franchises first. A **franchise agreement** is an arrangement whereby someone with a good idea for a business (the **franchisor**) sells the rights to use the business name and to sell a good or service (the **franchise**) to others (the **franchisee**) in a given territory. As you might suspect, both franchisors and franchisees have a stake in the success of the franchise.

Some people, uncomfortable with the idea of starting their own business, would rather join a business with a proven track record through a franchise agreement. A franchise can be formed as a sole proprietorship, a partnership, or a corporation.

Some students mistakenly identify franchising as an industry. It is not a specific industry. Rather, franchising is a business model; it is a method of distributing a good or service, or both, to achieve a maximum market impact with a minimum investment. It is not a separate form of business ownership from those already summarized in Figure 6.6, and it does not replace a form of business. How the franchisee sets up the franchise business (i.e., sole proprietorship, partnership, or corporation) and operates it, however, is dependent on the advantages and disadvantages of each form of business ownership.

franchise
The right to use a specific business' name and sell its goods or services in a given territory.

franchisee
A person who buys a franchise.

Courtesy of Booster Juice. Used with permission

Promoted as Canada's premium juice and smoothie chain, Booster Juice operates over 400 franchise units.[25] Would you be interested in purchasing a franchise? If not this one, what type of good or service franchise might appeal to you as a business owner?

Often, what looks like a chain of stores—Home Hardware Stores Ltd., Quiznos, and Great Canadian Dollar Stores—is usually a franchise operation with each unit owned by a different person or company. (There are also corporate locations owned by the franchisor.) Sometimes one person or group may own and operate more than one franchise unit. Regardless of the form of business ownership (e.g., partnership), all units are part of a franchise operation. In the following pages you will see the advantages and disadvantages of this type of business operation, and you will learn what to consider before buying a franchise unit.

According to the Canadian Franchise Association, there are over 78 000 franchise units across Canada and they employ more than one million people.[26] Franchising is more than food (e.g., Dairy Queen, Swiss Chalet, Cora, and Pizza Pizza) as 60 percent of franchises can be found in non-food sectors and industries (e.g., Oxford Learning, Mr. Lube Canada, Molly Maid, and First Choice Haircutters).[27] Have you ever considered owning one of these? Review Figure 6.7 for some tips in evaluating franchises.

Advantages of Franchises

Franchising has penetrated every aspect of Canadian and global business life by offering goods and services that are reliable, convenient, and competitively priced. The worldwide growth of franchising could not have been accomplished by accident. Franchising clearly has some advantages.

1. *Management and marketing assistance.* Compared with someone who starts a new business, a franchisee usually has a much greater chance of succeeding because he or she has established products or services to sell, help choosing a location, and assistance in all phases of promotion and operation. It is like having your own store but with full-time consultants when you need them. Franchisors usually provide intensive management training since they want the franchisees to succeed. For example, franchisor Boston Pizza International Inc. provides an extensive seven-week training program for new franchisees and their management teams. Trainers provide in-store staff training two weeks prior to opening and support for two weeks post-opening. After this, the restaurant is assigned a Regional Business Manager for dedicated support.[28]

   Some franchisors help their franchisees with local marketing efforts rather than having franchisees depend solely on national advertising. Franchisees also have a network of fellow franchisees facing similar problems who can share their experiences. The goal is to support franchisees however possible.

2. *Personal ownership.* A franchise operation is still your business, and you enjoy as much of the incentives and profit as any sole proprietor would. You are still your

FIGURE 6.7

BUYING A FRANCHISE

Since buying a franchise is a major investment, be sure to check out a company's financial strength before you get involved. A good source of information about evaluating a franchise deal is the handbook, "Investigate Before Investing," available from International Franchise Association Publications.

Checklist for Evaluating a Franchise

The Franchise

Did your lawyer approve the franchise contract you're considering after he or she studied it paragraph by paragraph?

Does the franchise give you an exclusive territory for the length of the franchise?

Under what circumstances can you terminate the franchise contract and at what cost to you?

If you sell your franchise, will you be compensated for your goodwill (the value of your business' reputation and other intangibles)?

If the franchisor sells the company, will your investment be protected?

The Franchisor

How many years has the firm offering you a franchise been in operation?

Does it have a reputation for honesty and fair dealing among the local firms holding its franchise?

Has the franchisor shown you any certified figures indicating exact net profits of one or more going firms that you personally checked yourself with the franchisee? Ask for the company's disclosure statement.

Will the firm assist you with:
- A management training program?
- An employee training program?
- A public relations program?
- Capital?
- Credit?
- Merchandising ideas?

Will the firm help you find a good location for your new business?

Has the franchisor investigated you carefully enough to assure itself that you can successfully operate one of its franchises at a profit both to itself and to you?

You, the Franchisee

How much capital will you need to purchase the franchise and operate it until your income equals your expenses?

Does the franchisor offer financing for a portion of the franchising fees? On what terms?

Are you prepared to give up some independence of action to secure the advantages offered by the franchise?

Do you have your family's support?

Does the industry appeal to you? Are you ready to spend much or all of the remainder of your business life with this franchisor, offering its products or services to the public?

Your Market

Have you made any study to determine whether the products or services that you propose to sell under the franchise have a market in your territory at the prices you'll have to charge?

Will the population in the territory given to you increase, remain static, or decrease over the next five years?

Will demand for the products or services you're considering be greater, about the same, or less five years from now than it is today?

What competition already exists in your territory for the products or services you contemplate selling?

Sources: U.S. Department of Commerce, Franchise Opportunities Handbook; and Steve Adams, "Buying a Brand," *Patriot Ledger* (Quincy, MA), March 1, 2008.

own boss, although you must follow more rules, regulations, and procedures than you would with your own privately owned business. The Spotlight on Small Business box features an example of a growing franchise that is attracting new franchisees.

3. *Nationally recognized name.* It is one thing to open a gift shop or ice cream store. It is quite another to open a new Hallmark store or a Baskin-Robbins. With an established franchise, you get instant recognition and support from a product group with established customers around the world.
4. *Financial advice and assistance.* Two major problems for small-business owners are arranging financing and learning to keep good records. Franchisees get valuable assistance and periodic advice from people with expertise in these areas. In fact, some

Spotlight *On* SMALL BUSINESS

Unlocking a Growing Franchise

Have you ever locked your keys in your car? Whom did you call? Chances are you called a locksmith you didn't know. Pop-A-Lock, a fast-growing franchise, provides trusted locksmiths 24 hours a day. Although it started out specializing in opening car doors, it has grown into a security firm that works on electronic access to buildings, closed circuit TVs, smart key rekeying, commercial automotive security, and more.

Pop-A-Lock believes that it is critical to support franchisees. It provides a 24/7 hotline for any tech who runs into problems. The in-house marketing team keeps the buzz going through social media. And CEO Don Marks makes twice-a-month calls in which he coaches franchisees on how to grow their businesses. Pop-A-Lock supports the community as well as its franchisees by offering free school security auditing. Through its PAL-SavesKids program, it directs techs immediately to kids left unattended in locked cars. With franchised locations in Canada, Australia, and the United States, the company plans to add 150 units to its 500-unit system in the next two years. Could you hold the keys to one of them?

Courtesy of System Forward America, Inc.

Sources: "About Pop-A-Lock," Pop-A-Lock, accessed October 31, 2017, www.popalock.com; and Jason Daley, "How Franchises Grow Fast," *Entrepreneur*, February 2016.

franchisors, such as Meineke Car Care Centers, Gold's Gym, and UPS Stores, provide financing to potential franchisees they believe will be valuable partners of the franchise system.[29]

5. *Lower failure rate.* Historically, the failure rate for franchises has been lower than that of other business ventures. This is one reason why Canadians find them so attractive. However, franchising has grown so rapidly that many weak franchises have entered the field, so you need to be careful and invest wisely.[30]

Disadvantages of Franchises

There are some potential pitfalls to franchising. Disadvantages of franchising include the following:

1. *Large start-up costs.* Most franchises will demand a fee for the rights to the franchise. Fees for franchises can vary considerably. The startup capital range for College Pro Painters is $0 to $5,000 with $0 investment required.[31] But if you want to own a Boston Pizza franchise, you will need more money. The franchise fee is $60,000 and one needs to have a minimum of $600,000 (unencumbered) for startup capital with between $1.7 to $2.6 million in investment is required.[32]
2. *Shared profit.* The franchisor often demands either a large share of the profits in addition to the start-up fees or a percentage commission based on sales, not profit. This share is called a *royalty.* For example, if a franchisor demands a 10-percent royalty on

a franchise's net sales, 10 cents of every dollar the franchisee collects (before taxes and other expenses) must be paid to the franchisor.[33]

3. *Management regulation.* Management "assistance" has a way of becoming managerial orders, directives, and limitations. Franchisees feeling burdened by the company's rules and regulations may lose the spirit and incentive of being their own bosses with their own businesses. Often franchisees will band together to resolve their grievances with franchisors rather than each fighting their battles alone. For example, some Tim Hortons franchisees created an association, Great White North Franchisee Association, to address their grievances with franchisor, Restaurant Brands International Inc. An $850 million class-action lawsuit alleges that the franchisor is trying to intimidate its restaurant owners and force the franchisees who formed the association out of their restaurants.[34]

Trademarks of Canadian Tire Corporation, Limited use under licence

To become a Canadian Tire Associate Dealer, successful candidates must be well-rounded individuals who have a positive attitude for success and the passion and dedication necessary to excel. Self-motivation is key. Along with a good mix of experience and personal characteristics, candidates must be willing to make a personal and financial investment—a minimum of $125,000 of accessible capital—to become a Dealer.[35] Does this franchise interest you?

4. *Coattail effects.* The actions or failures of other franchisees have an impact on your future growth and profitability. Due to this *coattail effect,* you could be forced out of business even if your particular franchise has been profitable. For example, the customer passion for high-flying franchisor Krispy Kreme sank as the southern Ontario market became flooded with new stores and the availability of the product at retail locations caused overexposure. McDonald's and Subway franchisees complain that due to the company's relentless growth, some new stores have taken business away from existing locations, squeezing franchisees' profits per outlet.

5. *Restrictions on selling.* Unlike owners of private businesses, who can sell their companies to whomever they choose on their own terms, many franchisees face restrictions in the reselling of their franchises. To control quality, franchisors often insist on approving the new owners, who must meet their standards.

6. *Fraudulent franchisors.* Contrary to common belief, most franchisors are not large systems like Liberty Tax Service or Booster Juice. Many are small, rather obscure companies that prospective franchisees may know little about. Most franchisors are honest, but there has been an increase in complaints about franchisors that deliver little or nothing of what they promised. Before you buy a franchise, make certain you check out the facts fully and remember the old adage "You get what you pay for."

E-Commerce in Franchising

The Internet has changed franchising in many ways. Most brick-and-mortar franchises have expanded their businesses online and created virtual storefronts to deliver increased value to customers. Franchisees like Carole Shutts, a Rocky Mountain Chocolate Factory franchisee,

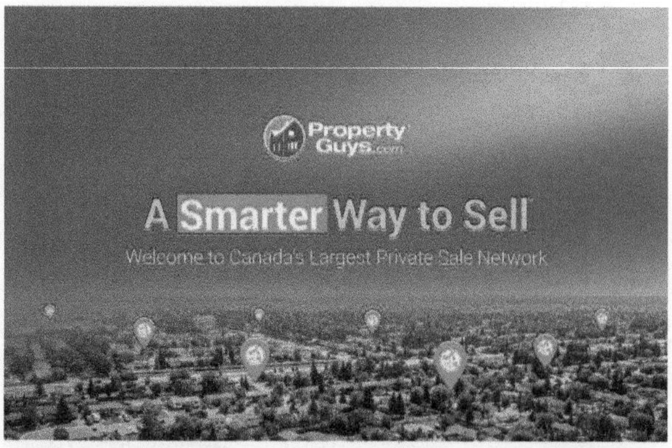

© PropertyGuys.com

No real estate license is required to be a franchisee with part of PropertyGuys.com, Canada's largest private sale franchise network. Would you be willing to list your home with someone from this company?

increased her sales by setting up her own website. Many franchisors, however, prohibit franchisee-sponsored websites because conflicts can erupt if the franchisor creates its own website. Sometimes franchisors send "reverse royalties" to franchisees who believe their sales were hurt by the franchisor's online sales, but that doesn't always bring about peace. Before buying a franchise, read the small print regarding online sales.

Today potential franchisees can make a choice between starting an online business or a business requiring an office or storefront outside of the home. Quite often the decision comes down to financing. Traditional bricks-and-mortar franchises require finding real estate and often require a high franchise fee. Online franchises, like Printinginabox.com, charge no up-front franchise fee and require little training to start a business. Franchisees pay only a set monthly fee. Online franchises also do not set exclusive territories limiting where the franchisee can compete. An online franchisee can literally compete against the world.

Franchisors often use technology, including social media, to extend their brands, to meet the needs of both their customers and their franchisees, and even to expand their businesses. Formed in Moncton, New Brunswick, PropertyGuys.com has built on the "For Sale by Owner (FSBO)" Internet concept. The company offers a high tech / high touch service delivered by its expert online PGPros (also known as the local franchise operator), innovative real estate brokers to connect clients to realtor.ca, certified professional appraisers, a unique answering and appointment booking service, and access to real-estate lawyers.[36]

Home-Based Franchises

Home-based businesses offer many obvious advantages, including relief from the stress of commuting, extra time for family activities, and lower overhead expenses. One disadvantage is the feeling of isolation; however, compared to home-based entrepreneurs, home-based franchisees feel less isolated. Experienced franchisors often share their knowledge of building a profitable enterprise with other franchisees.

Home-based franchises can be started for as little as $2,000. Today you can be a franchisee in areas ranging from cleaning services to tax preparation, child care, pet care, or cruise planning.[37] Before investing in a home-based franchise, it is helpful to ask yourself the following questions: Are you willing to put in long hours? Can you work in a solitary environment? Are you motivated and well organized? Does your home have the space you need for the business? Can your home also be the place you work? It's also important to check out the franchisor carefully.

Franchising in International Markets

Franchising today is truly a global effort. Canadian franchisors are counting their profits in euros, yuan, pesos, won, krona, baht, yen, and many other currencies. For example, McDonald's has more than 36 000 restaurants in more than 100 countries serving over 69 million customers each day.[38]

What makes franchising successful in international markets is what makes it successful domestically: convenience and a predictable level of service and quality. Because of proximity and language, the United States is by far the most popular target for Canadian-based franchises.

© Stephan Gabriel/imageBroker/age fotostock

Holiday Inn's InterContinental Amstel hotel in Amsterdam has been celebrated as the Netherlands' most beautiful and luxurious hotel. Holiday Inn franchises try to complement the environment of the area they serve. This hotel is on the crossroads of Amsterdam's financial and exclusive shopping districts. What do you think would have been the reaction if Holiday Inn built the typical Canadian-style hotel in this area?

Franchisors, though, must be careful and do their homework before entering into global franchise agreements.[39] Three questions to ask before forming a global franchise are: Will your intellectual property be protected? Can you give proper support to global partners? Are you able to adapt to franchise regulations in other countries? If the answer is yes to all three questions, global franchising creates great opportunities. It's also important to remember that adapting products and brand names to different countries creates challenges. In France, people thought a furniture-stripping franchise called Dip 'N Strip was a bar that featured strippers.

In 1986, brothers Michael and Aaron Serruya, then aged 19 and 20, wanted to buy a franchise, but no one would take a chance on them. So, they started their own frozen yogurt shop, Yogen Früz, in Toronto, Ontario. Today, Yogen Früz has grown to be a world leader in the frozen yogurt category, with over 1400 locations operating in 47 countries around the world.[40]

Co-Operatives[41]

LO5

Describe the role of co-operatives in Canada.

Some people dislike the notion of having owners, managers, workers, and buyers as separate individuals with separate goals, so they have formed co-operatives, a different kind of organization to meet their needs for child care, housing, food, and financial services. A **co-operative (co-op)** is an organization owned and controlled by people—producers, consumers, or workers—with similar needs who pool their resources for mutual gain. Co-operatives are locally owned and democratically controlled by the members who use their services. They are founded on the common idea that people know what's best for them and can work together to achieve their goals.

co-operative (co-op)
An organization owned and controlled by people—producers, consumers, or workers—with similar needs who pool their resources for mutual gain.

Worldwide, more than one billion people are members of co-operatives. There are over 9000 co-operatives, credit unions, and mutuals in Canada and over 750 000 across the world. Together, Canadian co-operatives have over 18 million members and employ more than 150 000 people.

Members democratically control these businesses by electing a board of directors that hires professional management. Some co-operatives ask consumer-members to work for a number of hours a month as part of their membership duties. Other co-operatives are made up of members who actually make the product being sold. One example is

© MEC, photographer: Ashley Barker

Mountain Equipment Co-operative (MEC) was formed in Vancouver, British Columbia, in 1971. MEC started with $65 in capital and a goal of providing affordable, good-quality climbing gear to an underserved mountaineering community. It is now Canada's largest retailer co-operative in terms of membership. Have you shopped at a local co-op?

Gay Lea Foods, the second-largest dairy co-operative in Canada, and owned by over 1200 dairy farmers. Others are worker-owned co-operatives, which are self-managed by employees who directly hire and fire their managers.

In their over one-hundred year history in Canada, co-operatives represent a large and diverse heritage of Canadians working together to build better communities based upon co-operative principles. These principles differ from other business principles in several ways:

- *A different purpose.* Co-operatives meet the common needs of their members, whereas most investor-owned businesses exist to maximize profit for their shareholders. Figure 6.8 summarizes some of the philosophical and community benefits of co-operatives.
- *A different control structure.* Co-operatives use a system of one-member/one-vote, not the one-vote-per-share system used by most businesses. This helps the co-operatives serve the common need rather than the individual need.
- *A different allocation of profit.* Co-operatives share profits among their member-owners on the basis of how much they use the organization, not on how many shares they hold. Profits tend to be invested in improving services for the members.

FIGURE 6.8

SOME CO-OPERATIVE BENEFITS

Philosophical Benefits	Community Benefits
People favoured over money in terms of priorities	Ability to change things that do not work
Greater community autonomy	Fair market prices
Product and service development by the people for the people	Strong customer/client loyalty
Opportunities to strengthen community bonds by helping one another	Greater employment opportunities
You can define your own needs instead of letting a conglomerate do it for you	Better access to quality products and services
Modest savings for all instead of the excessive accumulation of profits by a few	Economic and social growth in the community

Source: "The Co-Operative Advantage," CoopZone Developers' Network Co-operative, accessed November 3, 2017, http://www.coopzone.coop/about-co-operatives/the-co-operative-advantage/.

FIGURE 6.9

CO-OPERATIVES IN CANADA BY AREA OF ACTIVITY

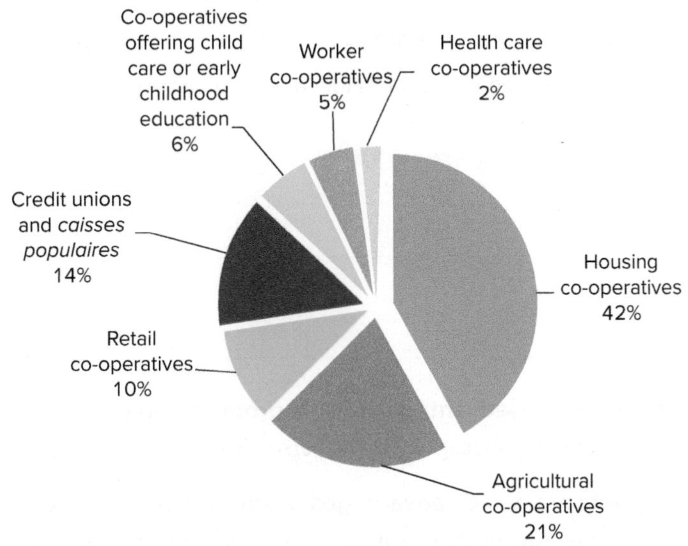

Source: Courtesy of Canadian Co-operative Association, The Power of Co-operation: Co-operatives and Credit Unions in Canada, Ottawa. Used with permission.

Since co-operatives distribute their profits to members as a reduction in members' costs, these profits are not subject to income tax. From time to time, various business organizations assert that many co-operatives are now more like large businesses and should be taxed. So far, this viewpoint does not appear to have extensive support.

Co-operatives are major players in many sectors in Canada. Figure 6.9 provides a breakdown of the number of co-operatives by area of activity. Housing co-operatives form the largest category, followed by agricultural co-operatives, and then credit unions and caisses populaires. You can infer that co-operatives can be found in many industries. The co-operative model has a long history and a proven track record in social and economic development, having served thousands of groups in both urban and rural areas. They are especially important to many rural and remote communities. In some communities, co-operatives are the only providers of retail and financial services, health and home care services, communications and utility services, tourism facilities, and other basic amenities.

Which Form of Ownership Is Best for You?

You can build your own business in a variety of ways. You can start your own sole proprietorship, partnership, or corporation. Or, you can buy a franchise and be part of a larger corporation. Co-operatives are corporations that usually have a different motivation than traditional for-profit businesses. There are advantages and disadvantages to each. However, there are risks no matter which form you choose. Before you decide which form is best for you, you need to evaluate all of the alternatives carefully.

PROGRESS ASSESSMENT

- What are some of the factors to consider before buying a franchise?
- What opportunities are available for starting a global franchise?
- What is a co-operative? How does it differ from a for-profit organization?

SUMMARY

LO1 **List the advantages and disadvantages of sole proprietorships.**

A business owned, and usually managed, by one person is called a sole proprietorship.

What are the advantages and disadvantages of sole proprietorships?

The advantages of sole proprietorships include ease of starting and ending the business, being your own boss, pride of ownership, retention of profits, no special taxes, and less regulation than for corporations. The disadvantages include unlimited liability, limited financial resources, difficulty in management, overwhelming time commitment, few fringe benefits, limited growth, limited lifespan, and the possibility of paying higher taxes depending on the level of income.

LO2 **Describe the advantages and disadvantages of partnerships. Include the differences between general and limited partners.**

When two or more parties legally agree to become co-owners of a business, a partnership is formed.

What are the advantages and disadvantages of partnerships?

The advantages include more financial resources, shared management and pooled knowledge, longer survival than sole proprietorships, and less regulation than corporations. The disadvantages include unlimited liability, division of profits, possible disagreements among partners, difficulty of termination, and the possibility of paying higher taxes depending on the level of income.

What are the main differences between general and limited partners?

General partners are owners (partners) who have unlimited liability and are active in managing the company. Limited partners are owners (partners) who have limited liability and are not active in the company.

LO3 **Discuss the advantages and disadvantages of corporations.**

A corporation is a legal entity with authority to act and have liability separate from its owners.

What are the advantages and disadvantages of corporations?

The advantages include more money for investment, limited liability, size, perpetual life, ease of ownership change, ease of drawing talented employees, and separation of ownership from management. The disadvantages include initial costs, paperwork, size, difficulty of termination, double taxation, and possible conflict with a board of directors.

What are some categories of corporations?

Figure 6.3 lists some corporation types. Organization types include Benefit, Crown, domestic, multinational, private, professional, and public.

LO4 **Outline the advantages and disadvantages of franchising. Include the challenges of global franchising.**

A franchise agreement is an arrangement whereby the franchisor sells the rights to use the business name and to sell a good or service (the franchise) to others (the franchisee) in a given territory.

What are the benefits and drawbacks of being a franchisee?

The benefits include a nationally recognized name and reputation, a proven management system, promotional assistance, and pride of ownership. Drawbacks include high franchise fees, managerial regulation, shared profits, and transfer of adverse effects if other franchisees fail.

What is the major challenge to global franchises?

It may be difficult to transfer an idea or product that worked well in Canada to another culture. It is essential to adapt to the region.

LO5 **Describe the role of co-operatives in Canada.**

A co-operative is an organization that is owned and controlled by people with similar needs who pool their resources for mutual gain.

What is the role of a co-operative?

Co-operatives are organizations owned by members/customers. Some people form co-operatives to give members more economic power than they would have as individuals. Small businesses often form co-operatives to give them more purchasing, marketing, or product development strength.

How do co-operatives' principles differ from other business principles?

Co-operatives have a different purpose, control structure, and allocation of profit than traditional for-profit businesses. Review Figure 6.8 for a discussion of co-operative benefits.

KEY TERMS

CAREER EXPLORATION

Whether you choose to structure your business as a sole proprietorship, partnership, or corporation, you can operate in any industry you like. Find out about the tasks performed, skills needed, pay, and opportunity outlook in these fields through Internet sites that include the Government of Canada Job Bank, Workopolis, Monster, CareerBuilder, Glassdoor, and Indeed, as well as through the Career Centre at your school.

- **Graphic design service**—creates visual concepts to communicate ideas that inspire, inform, and attract consumers; develops the overall layout and production design for various applications such as advertisements, brochures, magazines, and corporate reports.
- **Lawn care service**—makes sure the grounds of houses, businesses, and parks are attractive, orderly, and healthy.

- **Information technology support service—** provides help and advice to people and organizations using computer software or equipment.
- **Pet care service—**feeds, grooms, bathes, and exercises pets and other non-farm animals.

CRITICAL THINKING

1. Have you ever dreamed of opening your own business? If so, what kind of business? Could you start such a business in your own home? How much would it cost to start? Could you begin the business part-time while you attend school? What satisfaction and profit could you get from owning your own business? What could you lose? (Be aware that you must be careful not to use a name for your business that has already been used or registered by someone else. You may face some local restrictions and licence requirements if you operate from your residence such as requiring to have a certain number of parking spaces for your clients, having a limit on the size and type of vehicle and signage permitted, etc.)
2. Is it accurate to say that franchisees have the true entrepreneurial spirit? Could you see yourself as a franchisee or franchisor? Which one? Do you have an idea that you think could eventually grow into a franchise? Explain.

DEVELOPING CAREER SKILLS

Key: ● **Team** ★ **Analytic** ▲ **Communication** ⊡ **Technology**

●⊡★▲ 1. Research businesses in your area and identify two companies that use the following forms of ownership: sole proprietorship, partnership, and corporation. Arrange interviews with managers from each form of ownership and get their impressions about their businesses. (If you are able to work with a team of fellow students, divide the interviews among team members.) Some questions that you might ask include: How much did it cost to start this business? How many hours do you work? What are some drawbacks that you have encountered with the way your business is set up (i.e., business form), if any? What are the specific benefits of this business form? Share the results with your class.

●▲★ 2. Have you thought about starting your own business? What opportunities seem attractive? Think of a friend or friends whom you might want as a partner or partners in the business. List all of the financial resources and personal skills you will need to launch the business. Then make separate lists of the personal skills and the financial resources that you and your friend(s) might bring to your new venture. How much capital and what personal skills do you need but lack? Develop an action plan to obtain them.

▲★ 3. Let's assume you want to open one of the following new businesses. What form of business ownership would you choose for each business? Why?

   a. Wedding planning service
   b. Software development firm
   c. Video game rental store
   d. Online bookstore

⊡★ 4. Find out how much it costs to incorporate a company in your province or territory. Then compare it to the cost of federal incorporation. Is there a significant difference? Why might you choose not to incorporate federally?

⊡★ 5. Find information online about a business co-operative (e.g., Vancouver City Savings Credit Union, Welch's, etc.). Research how it was formed, who can belong to it, and how it operates.

ANALYZING MANAGEMENT DECISIONS

Going Public

George Zegoyan and Amir Gupta face a difficult decision. Their private auto parts manufacturing company has been a great success—too quickly. They cannot keep up with the demand for their product. They must expand their facilities, but have not had time to accumulate sufficient working capital, nor do they want to acquire long-term debt to finance the expansion. Discussions with their accountants, lawyers, and stockbrokers have confronted them with the necessity of going public to raise the required capital.

Zegoyan and Gupta are concerned about maintaining control if they become a public company. They are also worried about loss of privacy because of the required reporting to various regulatory bodies and to their shareholders. Naturally, they are also pleased that the process will enable them to sell some of their shareholdings to the public and realize a fair profit from their past and expected future successes. They will be able to sell 40 percent of the shares for $500,000, which is ten times their total investment in the company. It will also allow them to raise substantial new capital to meet the needs of their current expansion program.

The proposed new structure will allow them to retain 60 percent of the outstanding voting shares, so they will keep control of the company. Nevertheless, they are somewhat uneasy about taking this step, because it will change the nature of the company and the informal method of operating they are used to. They are concerned about having "partners" in their operations and profits. They are wondering whether they should remain as they are and try to grow more slowly, even if it means giving up profitable orders.

Discussion Questions

1. Do they have any other options besides going public? Is the franchise route a viable option? Explain.
2. Do you think they should try to limit their growth to a manageable size to avoid going public, even if it means forgoing profits now? Why?
3. Would you advise them to sell their business now if they can get a good price and then start a new operation? Explain.

CHAPTER 7

Entrepreneurship and Starting a Small Business

LEARNING OBJECTIVES

After you have read and studied this chapter, you should be able to:

LO1 Explain why people are willing to become entrepreneurs, and describe the attributes of successful entrepreneurs.

LO2 Discuss the importance of small business to the Canadian economy.

LO3 Summarize ways to learn how small businesses operate.

LO4 Analyze what it takes to start and run a small business.

LO5 Outline the advantages and disadvantages that small businesses have in entering global markets.

P R O F I L E

GETTING TO KNOW: TONIA JAHSHAN, FOUNDER, STEEPED TEA

On a vacation getaway in 2006 to a bed and breakfast in Mahone Bay, Nova Scotia, Tonia Jahshan and her husband, Hatem, tasted loose-leaf tea for the very first time. They liked it so much that they brought some home to share with friends and family. Before Jahshan knew it, she was holding fifteen tea parties a month.

© Steeped Tea

Started in 2006, Steeped Tea sells loose-leaf tea and accessories. The company began with minimal investment. The couple bought their teas in small quantities and stored them in their garage. They grew the business by using a direct-sales model whereby they sold their tea through independent consultants rather than building their own sales force. Mostly women working part-time, these consultants are independent business owners who run tea parties in people's homes. They earn up to 39 percent commission.

A turning point for the company was when the couple appeared on *Dragons' Den*. Their venture-capital pitch resulted in four offers. Dragons David Chilton and Jim Treliving each invested $125,000 for a 10 percent ownership in the company, resulting in an overall $250,000 offer for 20 percent ownership. The owners chose them as Treliving had great connections in the United States—where the Jahshans wanted to establish a presence—and Chilton showed a solid understanding of the company's business model.

When Jahshan launched the company, it was a one-woman show. Since then, the company has grown exponentially. Her success—annual sales of more than $20 million and 9000 salespeople across North America—earned Jahshan the top spot on the 2016 W100 ranking of Canada's Top Female Entrepreneurs. The vision is to have at least 20 000 representatives in Canada, and 10 000 representatives in the United States, and to keep growing.

Stories about people like Tonia Jahshan, who take on the challenge of starting their own business, are commonplace in this age of the entrepreneur. As you read about more examples in this book, maybe you will become inspired to become an entrepreneur yourself!

Sources: Mai Nguyen, "The Secret of Steeped Tea's Phenomenal Growth," PROFITguide.com, May 16, 2016, http://www.profitguide.com/manage-grow/success-stories/w100-tonia-jahshan-steeped-tea-growth-103020/3; "Our Story," Steeped Tea, 2015, http://www.steepedtea.com/our-story/; "In pictures: Dragons' Den success story feels the summer doldrums," *The Globe and Mail*, August 14, 2014, http://www.theglobeandmail.com/report-on-business/small-business/sb-growth/the-challenge/summer-doldrums-sour-the-milk-for-tea-company/article13736933/; "Stories from the Den: Tonia and Hatem Jahshan, Steeped Tea," *YouInc.com*, April 28, 2014, https://youinc.com/content/lifestyle/stories-from-the-den-tonia-and-hatem-jahshan-steeped-tea; Julia Chapman, "Steeped in Dragons' Den dollars, Hamilton tea firm grows up," CBC News, October 5, 2013, http://www.cbc.ca/news/canada/hamilton/news/steeped-in-dragons-den-dollars-hamilton-tea-firm-grows-up-1.1913049; Dan Misener, "Dragons' Den success story has caught a cold," *The Globe and Mail*, August 14, 2013, http://www.theglobeandmail.com/report-on-business/small-business/sb-growth/the-challenge/dragons-den-success-story-has-caught-a-summer-cold/article13729083/; and Marjo Johne, "How couple's perfect pitch yielded four offers on Dragons' Den," *The Globe and Mail*, December 7, 2012, http://www.theglobeandmail.com/report-on-business/small-business/starting-out/how-couples-perfect-pitch-yielded-four-offers-on-dragons-den/article6007914/.

The Age of the Entrepreneur[1]

Today most young people know that it is unlikely they will get a job in a large corporation and stay there for 30 years. For those who want more control over their destiny, working in or starting a small business makes sense. **Entrepreneurship** is accepting the challenge of starting and running a business. The word entrepreneur originates from the French word, *entreprendre,* which means "to undertake." In a business context, it means to start a business. You can imagine how the concept of entrepreneurship has a wide variety of meanings. On the one extreme, an entrepreneur is a person of very high aptitude who pioneers change, possessing characteristics found in only a very small fraction of the population. On the other extreme, anyone who wants to work for himself or herself is considered an entrepreneur. It is for this reason that we discuss both entrepreneurship and small business in this chapter.

entrepreneurship Accepting the challenge of starting and running a business.

While many people use the terms entrepreneurship and small business interchangeably, there are significant differences. Entrepreneurial ventures differ from small businesses in the following four ways:[2]

1. *Amount of Wealth Creation.* Rather than simply generating an income stream that replaces traditional employment, a successful entrepreneurial venture creates substantial wealth, typically in excess of several million dollars of profit.

Courtesy of Roots Canada

Inspired by their passion for Algonquin Park, Michael Budman and Don Green created Roots Canada in 1973. Since the business was not going to be passed on to their children, they sold a majority stake in their clothing and leather goods company in 2015.[3] Do you know of any other Canadian companies that have gone through ownership changes? What has motivated these changes?

2. *Speed of Wealth Creation.* While a successful small business can generate several million dollars of profit over a lifetime, entrepreneurial wealth creation often is rapid. For example, this may occur within five years.
3. *Risk.* The risk of an entrepreneurial venture must be high. Otherwise, with the incentive of sure profits, many people would pursue the idea of entrepreneurship, making business ventures impossibly competitive.
4. *Innovation.* Entrepreneurship often involves substantial innovation beyond what a small business might exhibit. This innovation gives the venture the competitive advantage that results in wealth creation. Innovation may be in new products, new production methods, new markets, and new forms of organizations.

From this list, you can quickly gather that entrepreneurship is not always small and small business is not always entrepreneurial. While most businesses start small, it is the intent to stay small that separates them from entrepreneurship. Explore this chapter and think about the possibilities. That is, the possibility of entrepreneurship and the possibility of starting a small business in your future.

Well-Known Canadian Entrepreneurs[4]

Entrepreneurs have played a major role in developing the Canadian economy. For example, Kenneth Colin Irving opened Bouctouche, New Brunswick's first garage and service station in 1924. That same year, he opened a Ford dealership in Saint John and established Irving Oil. He was 25 years old. Today, Irving Oil operates Canada's largest refinery, 10 distribution terminals, a fleet of delivery trucks, and over 900 fuelling locations serving its wholesale, commercial, and retail customers. It sells a range of finished energy products including gasoline, diesel, home heating fuel, jet fuel, and complementary products.

Next, consider other examples of entrepreneurs who have created companies that are now household names in Canada. Do you recognize these logos?

Courtesy of Leon's. Used with permission.

Trademarks of Canadian Tire Corporation, Limited use under licence.

- Ablan Leon began his career selling clothing from a suitcase door-to-door. When he had enough money, he bought a small building in Welland, Ontario, and in 1909 the A. Leon Company was established. Today, Leon's Furniture Limited is one of Canada's largest retailers, selling a wide range of merchandise including furniture, major appliances, and home electronics. The company continues to be run by the Leon family.
- In 1922, two brothers, John W. and Alfred J. Billes, purchased the Hamilton Tire and Garage Ltd. store in Toronto, Ontario, with a combined savings of $1800. In 1923, the brothers sold the shop and moved to the corner of Yonge and Gould streets in Toronto under the name Canadian Tire Corporation. Today, Canadian Tire Corporation, Limited (CTC) is a family of companies. They include Canadian Tire, FGL (Sport Chek,

Hockey Experts, Sports Experts, National Sports, Intersport, and Atmosphere), Pro Hockey Life, Mark's, Canadian Tire Financial Services, CT REIT, PartSource, Gas+, and Canadian Tire Jumpstart Charities. The latter is a national charity that is dedicated to helping kids overcome financial and accessibility barriers to sport and recreation in order to provide inclusive play for kids of all abilities.

- In 1907, J. W. Sobey started a meat delivery business in Stellarton, Nova Scotia. With a horse-drawn meat cart, he purchased and collected livestock from local farmers for resale. The first modern Sobeys supermarket opened in 1947. One of Canada's two national grocery retailers with approximately 1500 stores in all 10 provinces, retail banners include Sobeys, Safeway, IGA, Foodland, FreshCo, Price Chopper, Thrifty Foods, and Lawtons Drugs, as well as more than 380 retail fuel locations. Sobeys Inc. is a wholly-owned subsidiary of Empire Company Limited, headquartered in Stellarton.

Courtesy of Sobeys Inc. Used with permission.

- In 1957, Wallace and Harrison McCain, supported by brothers Andrew and Robert, founded McCain Foods Limited in Florenceville, New Brunswick. Today, the privately-owned company is an international leader in the frozen-food industry. While potatoes are at the heart of its offerings, the company also produces other food products that include pizza, appetizers, oven meals, and desserts that are found in more than 160 countries. McCain also owns the Day & Ross Transportation Group, one of the largest transportation companies in Canada.

McCain Foods Limited

- In 1969, Jean Coutu and Louis Michaud opened a discount pharmacy in Montreal, Quebec. They offered a large array of products, high-quality professional services, and longer store-opening hours. Under the banners of PJC Jean Coutu, PJC Clinique, PJC Santé, and PJC Santé Beauté, the company grew to be a leading pharmacy franchisor in Canada with 418 stores in Ontario, Quebec, and New Brunswick. In 2017, the Jean Coutu Group was acquired by Metro Inc. (Canada's third-largest grocer) for $4.5 billion. This acquisition gives Metro an expanded foothold in the drug business, similar to Loblaw Companies Ltd.'s acquisition of Shoppers Drug Mart four years earlier.

Courtesy of The Jean Coutu Group (PJC) Inc. Used with permission.

These stories have much in common. One or a couple of entrepreneurs had a good idea, borrowed some money from friends and family, and started a business. That business now employs thousands of people and helps the country prosper.

Canada has plenty of entrepreneurial talent. Names such as Mike Lazaradis (Research in Motion Limited), Frank Stronach (Magna International), Ratana Stephens (Nature's Path Foods), Guy Laliberté (Cirque du Soleil), and Susan Niczowski (Summer Fresh, Inc.) have become as familiar as those of the great entrepreneurs of that past. Some of our chapter profiles highlight other entrepreneurs, such as this chapter's profile, Tonia Jahshan (Steeped Tea), Canada's Top Female Entrepreneur for 2016. The Spotlight on Small Business box highlights several entrepreneurially minded individuals who created businesses while in school.

© Enactus

Guided by academic advisors and business experts, "the student leaders of Enactus Canada create and implement community empowerment projects and business ventures in communities coast to coast. The focus is advancing the economic, social, and environmental health of Canada."[5] Is there an Enactus group on your campus?

Spotlight *On* SMALL BUSINESS

Student Startups

Although most entrepreneurs wait until they finish their education to make the jump into their own businesses, some aspiring entrepreneurs choose to buck the trend. Here are just a few examples of young entrepreneurs who found success in their post-secondary years.

Jennifer Ger and Suzie Chemel met while studying for their business degrees at the University of Western Ontario. They set out to build their company, Foxy Originals, with a vision: to make high-style fashion jewellery accessible to everyone. Upon graduation, they focused full-time on their business. All pieces are designed and made in Canada with products sold through retailers and online.

Marie Wright is both the owner of Mirror Image Media and a student at St. Francis Xavier University. The company is a video production company that helps to promote businesses, non-profits, and events. It develops stories through concept development, script writing, creative direction, filming and post-production services.

Courtesy of Foxy Originals. Used with permission

Matt Rendall met his Clearpath Robotics co-founders while a student in the University of Waterloo's robotics engineering program. The company develops autonomous mobile robots that will take on the sometimes risky and tedious materials-handling jobs in warehouse operations.

Ann Yang and Phil Wong sought a solution for the waste of billions of pounds of produce that go unharvested or unsold each year because it is the wrong size, shape, or colour to sell in stores. The Georgetown University students' solution was to start Misfit Juicery, a company that makes juice from misfit fruits and vegetables.

Kyle Pham and Nick Nguyen wanted to find a fun and easy way to help the public experience 3D printing technology in their homes. The two University of Southern California students started CubeForme. The company is a subscription-box service that connects designers with the public by shipping a variety of products such as gadgets, games, and art pieces each month.

Diane Fairburn made stained-glass gifts in her first-year college dorm room and sold them at a table near the cafeteria. It has been over 30 years since she started her business, Decorative Glass Solutions. It has survived more than three decades of economic ups and downs.

Sources: "The Foxy Story," Foxy Originals, accessed November 7, 2017, http://www.foxyoriginals.com/Designer-Profile.html; "Our Story," Misfit Juicery, accessed November 6, 2017, https://misfitjuicery.co/about/; Andrew Seale, "Toronto Jewelry Designers Foxy Originals Were Cool Before Made in Canada Was," Startup HERE Toronto, October 3, 2017, http://startupheretoronto.com/type/profiles/toronto-jewelry-designers-foxy-originals-cool-made-canada/; "About Foxy Originals," TalentEgg Inc., 2017, https://talentegg.ca/employer/foxy-originals; "Coolest College Startups 2016," *Inc.*, accessed January 2017, https://www.inc.com/college-startups; Tim Talevich, "Business Class," *The Costco Connection*, August 2016; Jen Falzon, "St. Francis Xavier University Student Entrepreneur Named 2016 Provincial Champion," Enactus Canada, February 16, 2016, http://enactus.ca/st-francis-xavier-university-student-entrepreneur-named-2016-provincial-champion/; and "Support Kitchener's Robot Revolution," The Business Development Bank of Canada, June 3, 2015, https://www.bdc.ca/en/about/mediaroom/news_releases/pages/yea2015_finalist_on.aspx.

LO1

Explain why people are willing to become entrepreneurs, and describe the attributes of successful entrepreneurs.

Why People Take the Entrepreneurial Challenge

Taking the risk of starting a business can be scary and thrilling at the same time. One entrepreneur described it as almost like bungee jumping. You might be scared, but if you watch six other people do it and they survive, you are then able to do it yourself. Here are some reasons why people are willing to take the entrepreneurial challenge:

- *Opportunity.*[6] Many people, including immigrants new to Canada, may not have the skills for today's complex organizations, but they do have the initiative and drive to work the long hours demanded by entrepreneurship. The same is true of many corporate managers who leave corporate life (by choice or after downsizing) to run businesses of their own. The opportunity may arise due to a sudden inheritance whereby some individuals decide to try something different, a change in health may force a career path adjustment, or even disliking a supervisor so much that being self-employed is an attractive option. Others, including an increasing number of Millennials, women, minorities, older people, and people with disabilities, find that starting their own businesses offers them more opportunities than working for others.

© FatCamera/Getty Images

Tops, bottoms, and accessories are produced by lululemon athletica for women, men, and girls. Under what conditions would you prefer to purchase products in-store versus online?

- *New Idea, Process, or Product.* Some entrepreneurs are driven by a firm belief, perhaps even an obsession, that they can produce a better product, or a current product at a lower cost, than anybody else. Perhaps they have gotten hold of a new widget or have conceived of an improvement that they are convinced has a large potential market. Creating eco-friendly, yet effective, cloth diapers, is what encouraged Ilana Grostern and Amy Appleton to start AppleCheeks Cloth Diapers. "We felt we could design something better," says Grostern.[7]
- *Profit.* It is natural for people to benefit monetarily from their ideas and dedication and to be rewarded for the money they risk and their hard work when they run a business. Yet long after a business has produced substantial profits and amassed personal fortunes for its owners, many continue to enjoy the challenge of overcoming the endless problems that every business faces and the satisfaction of continued success.
- *Challenge.* Some people believe that entrepreneurs are excitement junkies who thrive on risk. Entrepreneurs take moderate, calculated risks; they do not just gamble. In general, though, entrepreneurs seek achievement more than power.
- *Independence.* Many entrepreneurs simply do not enjoy working for someone else. They want to be free to roam, create, work, and delegate.
- *Family Pattern.* Some people grow up in an atmosphere in which family members have started their own businesses, perhaps going back several generations. The talk at the dinner table is often about business matters. This background may

© McGraw-Hill Education

Cindy Tran started Sweet Petite Confectioner in Vancouver, British Columbia. She was influenced by watching her father as a child: "Seeing how he navigated the ups and downs that come with owning a business didn't deter me from my own dreams of being an entrepreneur," she says. "I viewed his experiences as lessons I could learn from when I eventually built my company."[8]

predispose young men or women to think along the same lines. Sometimes there is a family business, and the next generation grows up expecting to take its place there in due course.

What Does It Take to Be an Entrepreneur?

Would you succeed as an entrepreneur? You can learn about the managerial and leadership skills needed to run a firm. However, you may not have the personality to assume the risks, take the initiative, create the vision, and rally others to follow your lead. Those traits are harder to learn or acquire. A list of entrepreneurial attributes to look for in yourself includes:[9]

- *Self-directed.* You should be self-disciplined and thoroughly comfortable being your own boss. You alone will be responsible for your success or failure.
- *Self-nurturing.* You must believe in your idea even when no one else does, and be able to replenish your own enthusiasm. Gary Mauris, President and co-founder of Dominion Lending Centres Inc., Canada's top national mortgage company advises, "Prepare yourself for the storm. Everyone, from your family to your competitors, will take a run at you to instill doubt. You have to be passionate and believe in your business model."[10]
- *Action-Oriented.* Great business ideas are not enough. The most important thing is a burning desire to realize, actualize, and build your dream into reality.
- *Highly Energetic.* It is your own business and you must be emotionally, mentally, and physically able to work long and hard. For example, when starting Extreme Pita, brothers Mark and Alex Rechichi were so consumed with work that they often slept on cots in the shop's backroom after their evening shifts. That way, they could get a few hours of sleep before starting all over again the next morning.
- *Tolerant of Uncertainty.* Successful entrepreneurs take only calculated risks (if they can help it). Still, they must be able to take *some* risks. Remember, entrepreneurship is not for the squeamish or those bent on security. You can't be afraid to fail. The late football coach Vince Lombardi summarized the entrepreneurial philosophy when he said, "We didn't lose any games this season, we just ran out of time twice." New entrepreneurs must be prepared to run out of time a few times before they succeed.
- *Able to Learn Quickly.* Making errors is inevitable. Only those who do nothing make no mistakes. What is important is what you learn from them. Good entrepreneurs are quick to learn such lessons.

Courtesy of Megan Gibson, PB&Jams

Megan Gibson has always been a big fan of peanut butter, but it wasn't until she sampled a spicy Haitian variety that she began experimenting with her own recipes. Rave reviews from family and friends inspired Gibson to buy a food truck and start PB&Jams, a company that Gibson operates while also working full-time as a high school health teacher.

They adapt and change direction as required instead of letting pride stand in the way of admitting mistakes.

While courage is not considered a skill, it is nevertheless an important element of an entrepreneur. Courage is required to challenge the status quo, to see an opportunity, and then most importantly, to try to do something about it. Entrepreneurs are doers. They do not just think and talk about an idea, they act on it! Also be aware that even if you possess many (or even all) of these attributes, there is no guarantee that you will be successful with every endeavour.

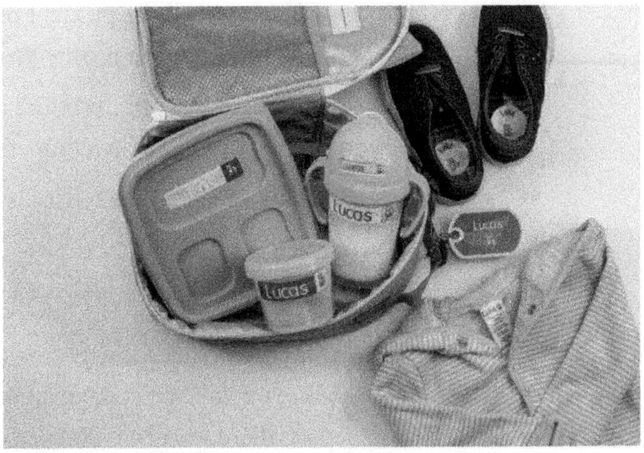

Courtesy of Mabel's Labels. Photo copyright of Mabel's Labels.

Four moms started Mabel's Labels when they got tired of their children losing their belongings or getting them mixed up with those of their friends. Labels go on everything from clothing to containers, for children and adults alike. What items would you label?

Turning Your Passions and Problems into Opportunities

While many entrepreneurs' business ideas are inspired by their passions, many see business opportunities in their problems. For example, while Celtel's founder Mo Ibrahim saw the opportunity to bring mobile phones to over 1 billion people in Africa who had never even used a phone much less owned one, large telecommunication companies saw only poor peasants and logistical hurdles. Celtel became Africa's largest cell provider.[11] Ibrahim sold the company for $3.4 billion.[12]

Most entrepreneurs do not get ideas for products and services from some flash of inspiration. The source of innovation is more like a *flashlight.* Imagine a search party walking in the dark, shining lights, looking around, asking questions, and looking some more. "That's how most creativity happens," says business author Dale Dauten. "Calling around, asking questions, saying 'What if?' till you get blisters on your tongue."

To look at problems or passions and see opportunities in them, ask yourself these questions: What do I want, but can never find? What product or service would improve my life? What really irritates me and what product or service would help?

Keep in mind, however, that not all ideas are opportunities. If your idea does not meet anyone else's needs, the business will not succeed. You may have a business idea that is a good opportunity if:[13]

- It fills customers' needs.
- You have the skills and resources to start a business.

© YAY Media AS / Alamy Stock Photo

Take a survey to find out if you might have the entrepreneurial spirit by going online to the Business Development Bank of Canada (*www.bdc.ca*) and searching for Entrepreneurial Potential Self-Assessment.

- You can sell the product or service at a price customers are willing and able to pay—and still make a profit.
- You can get your product or service to customers before your window of opportunity closes (i.e., before competitors with similar solutions beat you to the marketplace).
- You can keep the business going.

Female Entrepreneurs[14]

In the past few decades, more women have gone into business for themselves. Throughout this book, you will see some examples. According to Statistics Canada's *Labour Force Survey* report, there were 950 000 self-employed women in Canada, accounting for approximately 36 percent of all self-employed persons. A greater concentration of women run **small and medium-sized enterprises (SMEs)**, which are businesses with fewer than 500 employees. SMEs owned by female entrepreneurs are concentrated in the services-producing sector and include industries such as information, administration, health care, and recreation. When a woman does decide to start a business, she tends to stay in business longer. In other words, survival rates are higher. Have these numbers changed since this chapter was written?

SMEs (small and medium-sized enterprises) Refers to all businesses with fewer than 500 employees.

Studies have shown a variety of reasons for the emergence of female entrepreneurs:

- *Financial Need.* Fluctuating employment and drops in average real incomes over the years have encouraged many women to start a business. Steeped Tea, the focus of this chapter's profile, has been successful in attracting consultants who are looking to supplement their incomes.
- *Lack of Promotion Opportunities.* Most positions in higher management are still dominated by men. Although the situation is improving, the pace is extremely slow. Many women who are frustrated by this pace may take the entrepreneurial route.
- *Women Returning to the Workforce.* Many women who return to the job market after raising a family find that their skills are outdated. They also encounter subtle age discrimination. These factors encourage some to try self-employment.
- *Family and Personal Responsibility.* The increased rate of divorced women and single mothers in recent years has created a situation in which many women find themselves with children and little or no financial support. Some even refuse such support to be more independent. Affordable technology has made it possible for women to start home-based businesses.
- *Public Awareness of Women in Business.* As more publicity highlights that growing numbers of

Courtesy of Indigo. Used with permission.

Heather Reisman is the founder, Chair, and CEO of Indigo Books & Music Inc., Canada's largest book, gift, and specialty toy retailer.[15] In addition to offering online sales, the company operates in all 10 provinces and one territory in Canada through 89 superstores under the banners *Chapters* and *Indigo*, and 123 small-format stores under the banners *Coles*, *Indigospirit*, *SmithBooks*, and *The Book Company*.[16] Have you considered following the careers of business people such as Reisman to learn how they became successful?

women have started their own ventures, the idea catches on and gives others the confidence to try. Often two or more women will team up to form a partnership.

- *Part-Time Occupations.* Often women with some particular talent—for example, publicity, writing, designing, making clothes, cooking, organizing, or human relations—are encouraged to develop their hobby or skills on a part-time basis to see how far they can go with it. This focus has resulted in many notable success stories.
- *Higher Rate of Success for Women.* Female entrepreneurs seem to have a better success rate than men. Various factors may account for this. Women feel less pressured than men to achieve quick results. They are a little more cautious, so they make fewer mistakes. They also accept advice more readily than men, who may feel that they need to know it all. It will be interesting to follow this process to see if women continue to start ventures at the same rate and maintain their remarkable track record.

There are many resources available to help female entrepreneurs network and get general support. Some examples include the Canadian Women's Business Network, Women's Enterprise Centre, and the Canadian Association of Women Executives & Entrepreneurs. Financial institutions also offer small-business products and services aimed at women, which often can be accessed on their websites. In the meantime, if you wish to learn about some of Canada's top female entrepreneurs, review the annual *PROFIT/Chatelaine* W100 rankings.

Entrepreneurial Teams

An **entrepreneurial team** is a group of experienced people from different areas of business who join together to form a managerial team with the skills needed to develop, make, and market a new product. A team may be better than an individual entrepreneur because team members can combine creative skills with production and marketing skills right from the start. Having a team also can ensure more co-operation and coordination among functions.

entrepreneurial team
A group of experienced people from different areas of business who join together to form a managerial team with the skills needed to develop, make, and market a new product.

While Steve Jobs was the charismatic folk hero and visionary of Apple Inc., it was Steve Wozniack who invented the first personal computer model, and Mike Markkula who offered the business expertise and access to venture capital. The key to Apple's early success was that the company was built around this "smart team" of entrepreneurs. The team wanted to combine the discipline of a big company with an environment where people could feel they were participating in a successful venture. The trio of entrepreneurs recruited seasoned managers with similar desires. All of the managers worked as a team. Everyone worked together to conceive, develop, and market products.

PROGRESS ASSESSMENT

- What are key differences between entrepreneurial ventures and small businesses?
- Why are people willing to become entrepreneurs?
- What are the advantages of entrepreneurial teams?

© MonkeyBusiness / Image Source

Many small businesses start out as micro-enterprises. Do you know of any local micropreneurs?

Micropreneurs and Home-Based Businesses

Not every person who starts a business wants to grow it into a mammoth corporation. Some are interested in maintaining a balanced lifestyle while doing the kind of work they want to do. The smallest of small businesses are called **micro-enterprises**, most often defined as having one to four employees.[17] While other entrepreneurs are committed to the quest for growth, **micropreneurs** (owners of micro-enterprises) know they can be happy even if their companies never appear on a list of top-ranked businesses.

micro-enterprises
A small business defined as having one to four employees.

micropreneurs
Small-business owners with fewer than five employees who are willing to accept the risk of starting and managing the type of business that remains small, lets them do the kind of work they want to do, and offers them a balanced lifestyle.

Many micropreneurs are owners of home-based businesses. According to Industry Canada, approximately 54 percent of all employer businesses (632 460 in number) were micro-enterprises.[18] Micropreneurs include consultants, video producers, architects, and bookkeepers. Many with professional skills such as graphic design, writing, and translating have found that one way of starting a freelance business is through websites such as Upwork and Freelancer that link clients and freelancers. The sites post job openings and client feedback and serve as secure intermediaries for clients' payments.

Many home-based businesses are owned by people combining career and family. Don't picture just moms with young children; men also run home-based businesses. Here are more reasons for the growth of home-based businesses:

- *Computer Technology.* Computer technology has levelled the competitive playing field, allowing home-based businesses to look and act as big as their corporate competitors. Broadband Internet connections, smartphones, and other technologies are so affordable that setting up a business takes a much smaller initial investment than it once did.
- *Corporate Downsizing.* Downsizing has led some to venture out on their own. Meanwhile, the work of the downsized employees still needs to be done and corporations are outsourcing much of the work to smaller companies.
- *Change in Social Attitudes.* Whereas home-based entrepreneurs used to be asked when they were going to get a "real" job, they are now likely to be asked instead for how-to-do-it advice.

Working at home has its challenges, of course. Here are a few:

- *Getting New Customers.* Getting the word out can be difficult because you do not have a retail storefront.
- *Managing Time.* You save time by not commuting, but it takes self-discipline to use that time wisely.
- *Keeping Work and Family Tasks Separate.* It is great to be able to throw a load of laundry in the washer in the middle of the workday if you need to, but you have to keep such distractions to a minimum. It also takes self-discipline to leave your work at the office if the office is at home.

FIGURE 7.1

POTENTIAL HOME-BASED BUSINESSES

Many businesses can be started at home. To turn a home business into a success, you need to be prepared to work at it and have the appropriate knowledge and skills that you need to run any business.

1. Home Renovation Services	**6.** Wedding Planner Services
2. Pet Products and Services	**7.** E-commerce
3. Catering Services	**8.** In-Home Beauty Services
4. Cleaning Services	**9.** Sewing and Alteration Services
5. Fall Prevention Products - Sales and Service	**10.** Business/Life Coach Services

Source: Susan Ward, "The Best Home Business Opportunities," The Balance, July 20, 2017, https://www.thebalance.com/top-home-business-opportunities-2948561.

- *Abiding by City Ordinances.* Government ordinances restrict the types of businesses that are allowed in certain parts of the community and how much traffic a home-based business can attract to the neighbourhood.
- *Managing Risk.* Home-based entrepreneurs should review their homeowner's insurance policy since not all policies cover business-related claims. Some even void the coverage if there is a business in the home.

Home-based entrepreneurs should focus on finding opportunity instead of accepting security, getting results instead of following routines, earning a profit instead of earning a paycheque, trying new ideas instead of avoiding mistakes, and creating a long-term vision instead of seeking a short-term payoff. Figure 7.1 lists ten ideas for potentially successful home-based businesses. You can find a wealth of online information about starting a home-based business in the "Start a Business" section of *www.entrepreneur.com.*

Online Businesses

There is a multitude of small businesses selling everything online from staplers to refrigerator magnets to wedding dresses. These small businesses compete with other small businesses as well as large web-based and bricks-and-mortar businesses. According to a Forrester Research report, online spending will account for about 9.5 percent of overall retail purchases in Canada by 2019, amounting to $39 billion a year.[19]

Web-based businesses have to offer more than the same merchandise customers can buy at stores—they must offer unique products or services. For example, Marc Resnik started his web-based distribution company after waking up one morning laughing about his business idea. Now *ThrowThings.com* makes money for him as he's shipped products to more than 44 countries. Although the company's offerings seem like a random collection of unrelated items, everything it sells can be thrown. You can buy promotional products in the "Throw Your Name Around!" section, ventriloquist dummies in the "Throw Your

© iofoto/Shutterstock RF

Each year, Canadian couples get married. For soon-to-be newlyweds, TheKnot.com may be an invaluable resource for planning the big day. From sharing gifts registries to creating detailed schedules, the website helps ease the stress that inevitably comes with getting ready for a wedding. What does the site offer that other wedding planners do not?

Voice!" section, and sporting equipment in the "Things to Throw!" section. About two-thirds of the company's revenue comes from the promotional products section, which allows customers to add a logo to thousands of products. Why is Resnik's business so successful? One frequent customer believes it's because of Resnik's exceptional service and quick turnaround time.[20]

A web-based business is not always a fast road to success. It can sometimes be a shortcut to failure. Hundreds of high-flying dotcoms crashed after promising to revolutionize the way we shop. That is the bad news. The good news is that you can learn from someone else's failure and spare yourself some pain. And, of course, you can learn from their successes as well. Many people have started online businesses by following these steps:

1. Find a need and fill it.
2. Write copy that sells.
3. Design and build an easy-to-use website.
4. Use search engines to drive traffic to your site.
5. Establish an expert reputation for yourself.
6. Follow up with your customers and subscribers with e-mail.
7. Increase your income through back-end sales and upselling.

You can learn much more about how to implement each of these steps by going online to *www.entrepreneur.com* and reading the article, "How to Start a Business Online."

Entrepreneurship Within Firms

intrapreneurs
Creative people who work as entrepreneurs within corporations.

Entrepreneurship in a large organization is often reflected in the efforts and achievements of intrapreneurs. **Intrapreneurs** are creative people who work as entrepreneurs within corporations. The idea is to use a company's existing resources—human, financial, and physical—to launch new products and generate new profits.

At 3M, which produces a wide array of products from adhesives like Scotch tape to non-woven materials for industrial use, managers are expected to devote 15 percent of their time to thinking up new products or services.[21] You know those brightly coloured Post-it Notes that people use to write messages on just about everything? That product was developed by Art Fry, a 3M employee. He needed to mark the pages of a hymnal in a way that would not damage or fall out of the book. He came up with the idea of the self-stick, repositionable paper. The 3M labs soon produced a sample, but distributors were unimpressed and market surveys were inconclusive. Nonetheless, 3M kept sending samples to secretaries of top executives. Eventually, after a major sales and marketing program, the orders began pouring in, and Post-it Notes became a big winner. The company continues to update the product; making it from recycled paper is just one of many innovations. Post-it Notes have gone international as well—the notepads sent to Japan are long and narrow to accommodate vertical writing. Now you can even use Post-it Notes electronically—the software program Post-it Software Notes allows you to type messages onto brightly coloured notes and store them on memo boards, embed them in documents, or send them through e-mail.

Other examples of intrapreneurial ventures include Apple's Mac; Google's Gmail, Google News, and Google AdSense; General Motors' Saturn; 3M's Scotch Pop-Up Tape; and Sony's PlayStation.[22]

© Lucidio Studio, Inc./Moment/Getty Images RF

When you come up with a winning idea, stick with it. That has certainly been the motto of the 3M company, the maker of Post-it Notes. 3M encourages intrapreneurship among its employees by requiring them to devote at least 15 percent of their time to thinking about new products. How has this commitment to innovation paid off for 3M and its employees?

Encouraging Entrepreneurship: What Government Can Do

The different levels of government provide many services to help entrepreneurs and small businesses succeed. Canada Business Network promotes entrepreneurship and innovation, and it provides assistance through an organized network of service centres across Canada.[23] This collaborative arrangement among federal departments and agencies, provincial and territorial governments, and not-for-profit entities has the goal to provide businesses with the resources they need to grow and prosper, including a wide range of information on government services, programs, and regulations.

Innovation, Science, and Economic Development Canada (ISED) provides research and business intelligence information. There (*www.ic.gc.ca*) one can find small business research and statistics on Canadian SMEs.

Entrepreneurs and new start-ups can also find assistance from business incubators. **Business incubators** provide space, services, advice, and support to assist new and growing businesses to become established and successful. The business incubator's main goal is to produce successful firms that will leave the program financially viable and freestanding. The other goals of incubation programs are creating jobs, retaining businesses in a community, building or accelerating growth in a local industry, and diversifying local economies.

business incubators Centres that provide space, services, advice, and support to assist new and growing businesses to become established and successful.

The National Business Incubator Association estimates that there are about 7000 business incubators worldwide. Incubator sponsors—organizations or individuals who support an incubation program financially—include academic institutions, economic development organizations, government entities, and for-profit organizations. According to a recent study, 87 percent of incubator graduates remain in business.[24]

Business incubators vary in the way they deliver their services, in their organizational structure, and in the types of clients they serve. Incubators frequently help entrepreneurs prepare plans and proposals, assist them in making contacts to find financing, and assist participants to obtain cheaper insurance. However, most incubators themselves are not investors. The majority of activities are in the form of services and indirect support.

The earliest incubation programs focused on technology companies and service firms. In more recent years, they are targeting industries such as food processing, arts and crafts, telecommunications, and software development. Another focus is micro-enterprise creation.

Photo by Mariane Bulger. Used with permission

The DMZ at Ryerson University is a university-affiliated business incubator. It is Canada's largest incubator and multidisciplinary co-working space for young entrepreneurs. The DMZ helps startups fast-track product launches, grow their companies, and reach customers in a supportive community by connecting them with customers, advisors, industry professionals, and one another. Does your school have an incubator?

PROGRESS ASSESSMENT

- How do micropreneurs differ from other entrepreneurs?
- What are some of the opportunities and risks of web-based businesses?
- List some services for entrepreneurs provided by the federal government.

Getting Started in Small Business

Let's suppose you have a great idea for a new business, you have the attributes of an entrepreneur, and you are ready to take the leap into business for yourself. How do you start? That's what the rest of this chapter is about.

LO2

Discuss the importance of small business to the Canadian economy.

It may be easier to identify with a small neighbourhood business than with a giant global firm, yet the principles of management are similar for each. The management of charities, government agencies, churches, schools, and unions is much the same as the management of small, medium, and large businesses. So, as you learn about small-business management, you will make a giant step toward understanding management in general. All organizations demand capital, good ideas, planning, information management, budgets (and financial management in general), accounting, marketing, good employee relations, and good overall managerial know-how. We shall explore these areas as they relate to small businesses and, later in the book, apply the concepts to large firms, even to global organizations.

Small Versus Big Business[25]

small business
A business that is independently owned and operated, is not dominant in its field, and meets certain standards of size in terms of employees or annual revenues.

It would be helpful to define what is meant by the term *small business*. A **small business** can be defined as a business that is independently owned and operated, is not dominant in its field, and meets certain standards of size in terms of employees or annual revenues. Many institutions define small business according to their own needs. For example, ISED defines a small business as one that has fewer than 100 employees (i.e., 1 to 99 employees).

According to ISED, there are over 1.1 million employer businesses in Canada. Figure 7.2 breaks down the number of businesses by sector and number of employees. Small businesses account for the vast majority (97.9 percent) of all employer businesses.

As you can see, small business is really a big part of the Canadian economy. How big a part? We'll explore that question next.

Small Business Statistics[26]

Small businesses are a dynamic part of the Canadian economy. Nearly all small businesses are Canadian-owned and managed. This is in contrast to large businesses, of which many are foreign-owned and managed. Small businesses thus play a major role in helping to maintain the Canadian identity and Canadian economic independence.

FIGURE 7.2

NUMBER OF EMPLOYER BUSINESSES BY SECTOR AND FIRM SIZE (NUMBER OF EMPLOYEES), DECEMBER 2015

Approximately 98 percent of Canadian employers' businesses are considered small businesses.

		NO. OF BUSINESS LOCATIONS		
	Percentage of Employer Businesses	Total	Goods-Producing Sector	Services-Producing Sector
Small businesses (1–99 employees)	97.9	1,143,630	245,540	898,090
Medium-sized businesses (100–499 employees)	1.8	21,415	5,342	16,073
Large businesses (500 + employees)	0.3	2,933	569	2,364
Total	**100.0**	**1,167,978**	**251,451**	**916,527**

Source: Statistics Canada, "Number of Employer Businesses by Sector and Firm Size (number of employees), December 2015," Innovation, Science and Economic Development Canada, 2, June 2016, https://www.ic.gc.ca/eic/site/061.nsf/vwapj/KSBS-PSRPE_June-Juin_2016_eng-V2.pdf/$file/KSBS-PSRPE_June-Juin_2016_eng-V2.pdf.

Small businesses also continue to be feeders for future large businesses. As they prosper and develop new goods and services, they are often bought out by large companies, which in turn become more competitive. Alternatively, after small businesses establish a good track record, some of them convert from private to public companies, enabling them to obtain significant financing and become larger companies.

According to the most recent *Key Small Business Statistics,* here are some quick facts about small businesses:

- 97.9 percent of businesses in Canada have fewer than 100 employees of which 54.1 percent are micro-enterprises.
- They created approximately 1.1 million jobs between 2005 and 2015.
- They employed 8.2 million individuals (70.5 percent of the total private labour force).
- They contributed an average of 30 percent to the gross domestic product of their province.
- SMEs exported $106 billion (25.2 percent of Canada's total exports).
- 15.7 percent of small businesses were solely owned by females while over 19.7 percent were owned in equal partnerships between male and female owners.

Importance of Small Businesses

Since most of Canada's jobs are in small businesses, there is a very good chance that you will either work in a small business some day or start one. In addition to providing employment opportunities, small firms believe they offer other advantages over

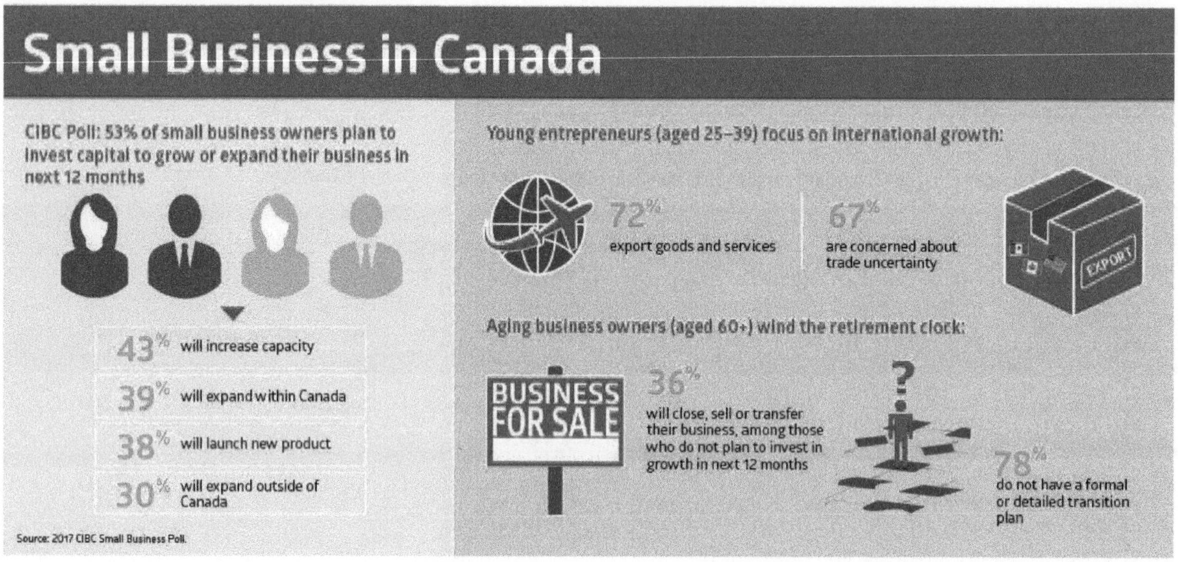
Small Business in Canada
CIBC Poll: 53% of small business owners plan to invest capital to grow or expand their business in next 12 months
43% will increase capacity
39% will expand within Canada
38% will launch new product
30% will expand outside of Canada
Source: 2017 CIBC Small Business Poll.
Young entrepreneurs (aged 25–39) focus on international growth:
72% export goods and services
67% are concerned about trade uncertainty
EXPORT
Aging business owners (aged 60+) wind the retirement clock:
BUSINESS FOR SALE
36% will close, sell or transfer their business, among those who do not plan to invest in growth in next 12 months
?
78% do not have a formal or detailed transition plan

© CIBC

According to a CIBC Small Business Poll, nearly half of Canada's young small business owners (ages 25–39) have increased their focus on international growth in the last five years.[27] Are you surprised by any of the statistics above?

larger companies—more personal customer service and the ability to respond quickly to opportunities.

Bigger is not always better. Picture a hole in the ground. If you fill it with big boulders, there are many empty spaces between them. However, if you fill it with sand, there is no space between the grains. That is how it is in business. Big businesses do not serve all the needs of the market. There is plenty of room for small companies to make a profit filling those niches.

© asiseeit/Getty Images RF

Tutors often operate independently and teach a limited number of pupils at any given time. Despite their small-scale businesses, tutors can have a big impact on the educational development of their clients. Can you see why tutors are considered micropreneurs?

Small-Business Success and Failure

You cannot be naïve about business practices, or you will go broke. There is some debate about how many new small businesses fail each year. There are many false signals about entries and exits. When small-business owners go out of business to start new and different businesses, they may be included in the "failure" category when obviously this is not the case. Similarly, when a business changes its form of ownership from partnership to corporation, it may be counted as a failure. Retirements of sole owners may also be in this category.

Thousands of businesses enter and exit the marketplace throughout the year. *Key Small Business Statistics* discusses survival in the following way:

> Survival is defined as the percentage of new firms that continue to operate when they reach a given age. Geographic location, type of industry, size and age, general economic conditions, and market influences (e.g., the number and size of competitors and new entrants) impact how long a business stays active. Survival reflects their productivity, innovation and resourcefulness, as well as their adaptability to changing market conditions. When considering SMEs, survival rates decline with time. About 80 percent of businesses survive for one year and 72 percent of enterprises that entered the marketplace survived for two years.[28]

Figure 7.3 lists reasons for small-business failure. Managerial incompetence and inadequate financial planning are among them. Keep in mind that when a business fails, it is important that the owners learn from their mistakes. Some who have failed are more realistic than novice business people. Because of the lessons they've learned, they may be more successful in their future ventures. Milton Hershey, for example, tried starting candy businesses in Chicago and New York and failed both times. He could have followed in the footsteps

FIGURE 7.3

CAUSES OF SMALL-BUSINESS FAILURE

Plunging in without first testing the waters on a small scale.	Buying too much on credit.
Underpricing or overpricing goods or services.	Extending credit too freely.
Underestimating how much time it will take to build a market.	Expanding credit too rapidly.
Starting with too little capital.	Failing to keep complete, accurate records so that the owners drift into trouble without realizing it.
Starting with too much capital and being careless in its use.	Carrying habits of personal extravagance into the business.
Going into business with little or no experience and without first learning something about the industry or market.	Not understanding business cycles.
Borrowing money without planning just how and when to pay it back.	Forgetting about taxes, insurance, and other costs of doing business.
Attempting to do too much business with too little capital.	Mistaking the freedom of being in business for oneself for the liberty to work or not, according to whim.
Not allowing for setbacks and unexpected expenses.	

CAUSES OF SMALL-BUSINESS SUCCESS

The customer requires a lot of personal attention, as in a beauty parlour.	A large business sells a franchise operation to local buyers. (Don't forget franchising as an excellent way to enter the world of small business.)
The product is not easily made by mass-production techniques (e.g., custom-tailored clothes or custom auto-body work).	The owner pays attention to new competitors.
Sales are not large enough to appeal to a large firm (e.g., a novelty shop).	The business is in a growth industry (e.g., computer services or web design).

of his father, a dreamer who lacked the perseverance and work ethic to stick to an idea long enough to make it work. Instead Hershey kept trying and eventually built not only the world's largest candy company, but also schools, churches, and housing for his employees.

Arianna Huffington, cofounder of the *Huffington Post,* put learning from failure this way: "I failed, many times in my life . . . but my mother used to tell me, 'failure is not the opposite of success, it's a stepping stone to success.' So at some point, I learned not to dread failure."[29] According to Ranford Neo, author of *The Instant Entrepreneur,* "Most successful entrepreneurs will tell you that they have failed at some point in time. But rather than look at the failure as an assertion of their inability, they chose to look at it objectively, as a learning experience."[30]

Choosing the right type of business is critical. Many of the businesses with the lowest failure rates require advanced training to start—veterinary services, dental practices, medical practices, and so on. While training and degrees may buy security, they do not tend to produce much growth—one dentist can fill only so many cavities. If you want to be both independent and rich, you need to go after growth. Often high-growth businesses, such as technology firms, are not easy to start and are even more difficult to keep going.

The easiest businesses to start have the least growth and the greatest failure rates (like restaurants). The easiest to keep alive are difficult to get started (like manufacturing). And the ones that can make you rich are the ones that are both hard to start and hard to keep going (like automobile assembly). See Figure 7.3 to get an idea of the business situations that are most likely to lead to success.

When you decide to start your own business, think carefully. You are unlikely to find everything you want—easy entry, security, and reward—in one business. Choose those characteristics that matter most to you; accept the absence of the others; plan, plan, plan; and then go for it!

PROGRESS ASSESSMENT

- What are some quick facts about small businesses?
- Why are small businesses important to Canada?
- What are causes of small-business failure?

LO3

Summarize ways to learn how small businesses operate.

Learning About Small-Business Operations

Hundreds of would-be entrepreneurs of all ages have asked the same question: How can I learn to run my own business? There are several ways to get into your first business venture. They are:

1. Learn from others.
2. Get some experience.
3. Buy an existing business.
4. Buy a franchise.
5. Inherit/take over a family business.

Learn from Others

Investigate your local school for classes on small business and entrepreneurship. There are entrepreneurship programs in post-secondary schools throughout Canada. Some entrepreneurs have started businesses as students—see the Analyzing Management Decisions case near the end of the chapter for an example. One of the best things about such courses is that they bring together entrepreneurs from diverse backgrounds who form helpful support networks. Talk to others who have already done it. They will tell you that location is critical and caution you not to be under-capitalized; that is, to start with enough money. "Everything takes twice as long and costs twice as much as you think it will," shares Rene Goehrum, President and CEO of BioSyent Inc., one of Canada's fastest-growing independent pharmaceutical companies.[31] They will warn you about the problems of finding and retaining good workers. And, most of all, they will tell you to keep good records and hire a good accountant and lawyer before you start. Free advice like this is invaluable.

© Nancy Newberry

Sharon Anderson Wright spent her teenage years sorting novels, nonfiction, and newspapers at her family's used bookstore. She knew what her customers liked to read and worked closely with her mother to learn the fine details of the business. This experience served her well as she expanded Half Price Books into a national company earning $240 million in annual revenue. How do you think Wright's experience helped the business succeed?

Get Some Experience

There is no better way to learn small-business management than by becoming an apprentice or working for a successful entrepreneur. Many small-business owners got the idea for their businesses from their prior jobs. An industry standard is to have three years' experience in a comparable business.

By running a small business part-time during your off hours or on weekends, you can experience the rewards of working for yourself while still enjoying a regular paycheque at another job. This is what John Stanton, founder of the Running Room, did when he first started his company. He kept his full-time job as a food industry executive when he opened the Running Room in a house in Edmonton, Alberta. At first, he only sold cotton T-shirts and running shoes. Four years later, he was confident that the company had growth potential.[32] He quit his job and concentrated on building the Running Room chain. Today, the company is North America's largest chain of running stores, operating over 110 stores in Canada and the United States.[33]

Learning a business while working for someone else may also save you money because you are less likely to make "rookie mistakes" when you start your own business. The Making Ethical Decisions box presents ethical questions about using the knowledge you have gained as an employee to start your own business.

Buy an Existing Business

Small-business owners work long hours and rarely take vacations. After many years, they may feel stuck in their businesses. They may think they cannot get out because they have too much time and effort invested. Consequently, there are some small-business owners out there eager to get away, at least for a long vacation.

This is where you come in. Find a successful business person who owns a small business. Tell him or her that you are eager to learn the business and would like to serve an apprenticeship—that is, a training period. State that at the end of the training period (one

Making ETHICAL DECISIONS

Should You Stay or Should You Go?

© abluecup/iStock/Thinkstock

Suppose you have worked for two years in a company and you see signs that the business is beginning to falter. You and a co-worker have ideas about how to make a company similar to your boss' succeed. Rather than share your ideas with your boss, you and your friend are considering quitting your jobs and starting your own company together. Should you approach other co-workers about working for your new venture? Will you try to lure your boss' customers to your own business? What are your alternatives? What are the consequences of each alternative? What is the most ethical choice?

year or so), you would like to help the owner or manager by becoming assistant manager. As assistant manager, you would free the owner to take off weekends and holidays, and to take a long vacation—a good deal for him or her. For another year or so, work very hard to learn all about the business—suppliers, inventory, bookkeeping, customers, promotion, and so on. At the end of two years, make the owner this offer: the owner can retire or work only part-time and you will take over the business. You can establish a profit-sharing plan for yourself plus a salary. Be generous with yourself; you will earn it if you manage the business. You can even ask for 40 percent or more of the profits.

The owner benefits by keeping ownership in the business and making 60 percent of what he or she earned before—without having to work. You benefit by making 40 percent of the profits of a successful firm. This is an excellent deal for an owner about to retire—he or she is able to keep the firm and a healthy profit flow. It is also a clever and successful way to share in the profits of a successful small business without any personal monetary investment. If you think that this is not realistic, be aware that "three-quarters of all small business owners plan to exit their enterprises in the next decade, according to a survey by the Canadian Federation of Independent Business. The vast majority of those departures—85 percent—will result from a desire to retire."[34]

If profit-sharing does not appeal to the owner, you may want to buy the business outright. How do you determine a fair price for a business? Value is based on (1) what the business owns, (2) what it earns, and (3) what makes it unique. Naturally, your accountant will need to help you determine the business' value.[35]

If your efforts to take over the business through either profit-sharing or buying fail, you can quit and start your own business fully trained.

Buy a Franchise

In Chapter 6, you were introduced to franchising. Many business people first get into business via franchising. Recall that franchising is a method of distributing a good or service, or both, to achieve a maximum market impact with a minimum investment. From your investment perspective, you are not creating a product or service from nothing. Rather, you are benefiting from the experience of the franchisor. Franchising is a way that you can start a business venture, especially if you are more comfortable doing so with an established product and process.

When deciding which method is best for you in terms of getting into your first business venture, be sure to weigh the advantages and disadvantages of each option before proceeding. One example of a successful franchise business is Molly Maid International Inc., a leader in the cleaning industry.

® Registered trademark of Recipe Unlimited Corporation and its affiliates. The Ultimate Dining Card artwork as of July 2018.

Recipe Unlimited Corporation (formerly Cara Operations Ltd.) is Canada's oldest and largest full-service restaurant company.[36] It franchises and/or operates the restaurant brands noted above. Have you ever considered buying one of these franchises?

Inherit/Take Over a Family Business[37]

It is not uncommon for the dream of one to evolve into a family business as was the case for Irving Oil (introduced earlier) or Kit and Ace. Husband and wife teams (such as Timothy Snelgrove and Teresa Snelgrove, founders of Timothy's World Coffee, and the Jahshans, highlighted in the chapter profile) are also quite common when you review the Canadian landscape of family businesses.

There are a number of factors that make family businesses unique. One is ownership. Public companies are typically owned by a large number of shareholders whose primary interest in ownership is generating the best return on investment. However, family businesses are often owned by a much smaller group whose ownership often has elements of personal identity, family legacy, and community responsibility entwined with its economic interests. This "emotional ownership" often results in family businesses having a longer-term view. Another factor that tends to separate successful family firms from their public counterparts is the concept of stewardship. Many family businesses have a clear understanding that the business is something to be preserved and grown for future generations. As Bill Ford, the chairman of Ford Motor Company once said, "I'm working for my children and grandchildren and feel I'm working for our employees' children and grandchildren as well."

As with any form of business, there are some challenges associated with a family business. According to the Family Business Institute, only about 30 percent of family businesses survive into the second generation, and 12 percent are still viable into the third generation. For example, Israel (Izzy) Asper, founder of CanWest Global Communications Corp., once dreamed of creating a worldwide media empire. When he died in 2003, his son, Leonard, was left in charge as CanWest's CEO. Leonard stepped down as CEO in 2010 when the company was restructured due to bankruptcy.

There are two common reasons why a family does not retain its business. The first reason is straightforward—there is no qualified successor. The second major reason for unsuccessful business transitions is more unfortunate. In many cases, businesses fail or are sold off due to a lack of planning. The Adapting to Change box in Chapter 6 highlights management problems as another factor. Regardless of such challenges, inheriting or taking over a family business is another way that one can learn about small business.

PROGRESS ASSESSMENT

- What are ways that one can get into a business venture?
- What are benefits of acquiring an existing business?
- What are challenges associated with family businesses?

LO4

Analyze what it takes to start and run a small business.

Managing a Small Business

One of the major causes of small-business failure is poor management. Keep in mind, though, that the term *poor management* covers a number of faults. It could mean poor planning, record keeping, inventory control, promotion, or employee relations. Most likely it includes poor capitalization. To help you succeed as a business owner, in the following sections we explore the five functions of business in a small-business setting, which are as follows:

1. Planning your business
2. Financing your business (finance)
3. Knowing your customers (marketing)
4. Managing your employees (human resources)
5. Keeping records (accounting)

WORK FOR THE BEST BOSS EVER.
you
Start your own summer business. Get hands-on training, mentoring, and awards up to $3,000. Find out how at Ontario.ca/SummerCompany or 1-888-576-4444.
Summer Company
#SummerCompany
Ontario

© Ministry of Economic Growth and Development

Summer Company gives students the opportunity to receive hands-on training and mentoring as well as grants of up to $3,000 to start and operate a summer business. If you do not live in Ontario, is there a similar program in your area?

Although all of the functions are important in both the start-up and management phases of the business, the first two functions—planning and financing—are the primary concerns when you start your business. The others are the heart of your operations once the business is underway.

Planning

Many people eager to start a small business come up with an idea and begin discussing the idea with professors, friends, and other business people. At this stage, the entrepreneur needs a business plan. A **business plan** is a detailed written statement that describes the nature of the business, the target market, the advantages the business will have in relation to competition, and the resources and qualifications of the owner(s). A business plan forces potential owners of small businesses to be quite specific about the goods or services they intend to offer. They must analyze the competition, calculate how much money they need to start, and cover other details of operation. A business plan is also mandatory for talking with bankers or other investors. Put another way, a business plan is a tool that is used to transition the entrepreneur from having an idea to actually developing a strategic and operational framework for the business.

business plan
A detailed written statement that describes the nature of the business, the target market, the advantages the business will have in relation to competition, and the resources and qualifications of the owner(s).

Lenders want to know everything about an aspiring business. First, pick a financial institution, such as a bank, that serves businesses the size of yours. Have a good accountant prepare a complete set of financial statements and a personal balance sheet. Make an appointment before going to the bank, and go to the bank with an accountant and all of the necessary financial information. Demonstrate to the banker that you are a person of good character, civic minded, and respected in business and community circles. Finally, ask for all the money you need, be specific, and be prepared to personally guarantee the loan.

WRITING A BUSINESS PLAN

A good business plan takes a long time to write, but you have got only minutes in the Executive Summary to convince readers not to throw it away. Since bankers receive many business plans every day, the summary has to catch their interest quickly. There's no such thing as a perfect business plan; even the most comprehensive business plan changes as the new business evolves. Figure 7.4 gives you an outline of a comprehensive business plan.

Many software programs can help you get organized. One highly rated business-plan program is Business Plan Pro. You can also review sample business plans and templates on the Canada Business Network.

Getting the completed business plan into the right hands is almost as important as getting the right information into the plan. Finding funding requires research. Next, we discuss sources of money available for new business ventures. All require a comprehensive business plan. The time and effort you invest before starting a business will pay off many times over. The big payoff is survival.

Financing Your Business

When *starting* a business, an entrepreneur can consider different types of financing, as listed in Figure 7.5. Personal financing (84 percent) and credit from financial institutions (45 percent) represent the most frequently used sources for SMEs.[38] You may even want to consider borrowing from a potential supplier to your future business. Helping you get started may be in the supplier's interest if there is a chance you will be a big customer later. This is what Ray Kroc did in the early years of McDonald's. When Kroc didn't have the funds available to keep the company going, he asked his suppliers to help him with the necessary funds. These suppliers grew along with McDonald's. It's usually not a good idea to ask such an investor for money at the outset. Begin by asking for advice; if the supplier likes your plan, he or she may be willing to help you with funding too.

Inder Bedi wrote a business plan for Matt & Nat as his final assignment in an entrepreneurship class during his final semester at Concordia University.[39] See if such a course is available in your program.

■ FIGURE 7.4

SAMPLE OUTLINE OF A BUSINESS PLAN

Length of a Comprehensive Business Plan

A good business plan is between 25 and 50 pages long and takes at least six months to write.

Cover Letter

Only one thing is certain when you go hunting for money to start a business: You will not be the only hunter out there. You need to make potential funders want to read your business plan instead of the hundreds of others on their desks. Your cover letter should summarize the most attractive points of your project in as few words as possible. Be sure to address the letter to the potential investor by name. "To Whom It May Concern" or "Dear Sir" is not the best way to win an investor's support.

Section 1—Executive Summary

Begin with a two-page or three-page management summary of the proposed venture. Include a short description of the business, and discuss major goals and objectives.

Section 2—Company Background

Describe company operations to date (if any), potential legal considerations, and areas of risk and opportunity. Summarize the firm's financial condition, and include past and current balance sheets, income and cash-flow statements, and other relevant financial records. (You will learn about these financial statements in Chapter 16.) It is also wise to include a description of insurance coverage. Investors want to be assured that death or other mishaps do not pose major threats to the company.

Section 3—Management Team

Include an organization chart, job descriptions of listed positions, and detailed resumés of the current and proposed executives. A mediocre idea with a proven management team is funded more often than a great idea with an inexperienced team. Managers should have expertise in all disciplines necessary to start and run a business. If not, mention outside consultants who will serve in these roles and describe their qualifications.

Section 4—Financial Plan

Provide five-year projections for income, expenses, and funding sources. Do not assume the business will grow in a straight line. Adjust your planning to allow for funding at various stages of the company's growth. Explain the rationale and assumptions used to determine the estimates. Assumptions should be reasonable and based on industry/historical trends. Make sure all totals add up and are consistent throughout the plan. If necessary, hire a professional accountant or financial analyst to prepare these statements.

Stay clear of excessively ambitious sales projections; rather, offer best-case, expected, and worst-case scenarios. These not only reveal how sensitive the bottom line is to sales fluctuations but also serve as good management guides.

Section 5—Capital Required

Indicate the amount of capital needed to commence or continue operations, and describe how these funds are to be used. Make sure the totals are the same as the ones on the cash-flow statement. This area will receive a great deal of review from potential investors, so it must be clear and concise.

Section 6—Marketing Plan

Do not underestimate the competition. Review industry size, trends, and the target market segment. Discuss strengths and weaknesses of the good or service. The most important things investors want to know are what makes the product more desirable than what is already available and whether the product can be patented. Compare pricing to the competition's. Forecast sales in dollars and units. Outline sales, advertising, promotion, and public relations programs. Make sure the costs agree with those projected in the financial statements.

Section 7—Location Analysis

In retailing and certain other industries, the location of the business is one of the most important factors. Provide a comprehensive demographic analysis of consumers in the area of the proposed business as well as a traffic-pattern analysis and vehicular and pedestrian counts.

Section 8—Manufacturing Plan

Describe minimum plant size, machinery required, production capacity, inventory and inventory-control methods, quality control, plant personnel requirements, and so on. Estimates of product costs should be based on primary research.

Section 9—Appendix

Include all marketing research on the good or service (off-the-shelf reports, article reprints, etc.) and other information about the product concept or market size. Provide a bibliography of all the reference materials you consulted. This section should demonstrate that the proposed company will not be entering a declining industry or market segment.

FIGURE 7.5

SOURCES OF FINANCING FOR SMES (2014)

Fifty-one percent of Canadian SMEs requested external financing in 2014. Since they often lack both a credit history and the collateral needed to secure a loan, it is not surprising that personal financing represents the largest source (84 percent) of funding.

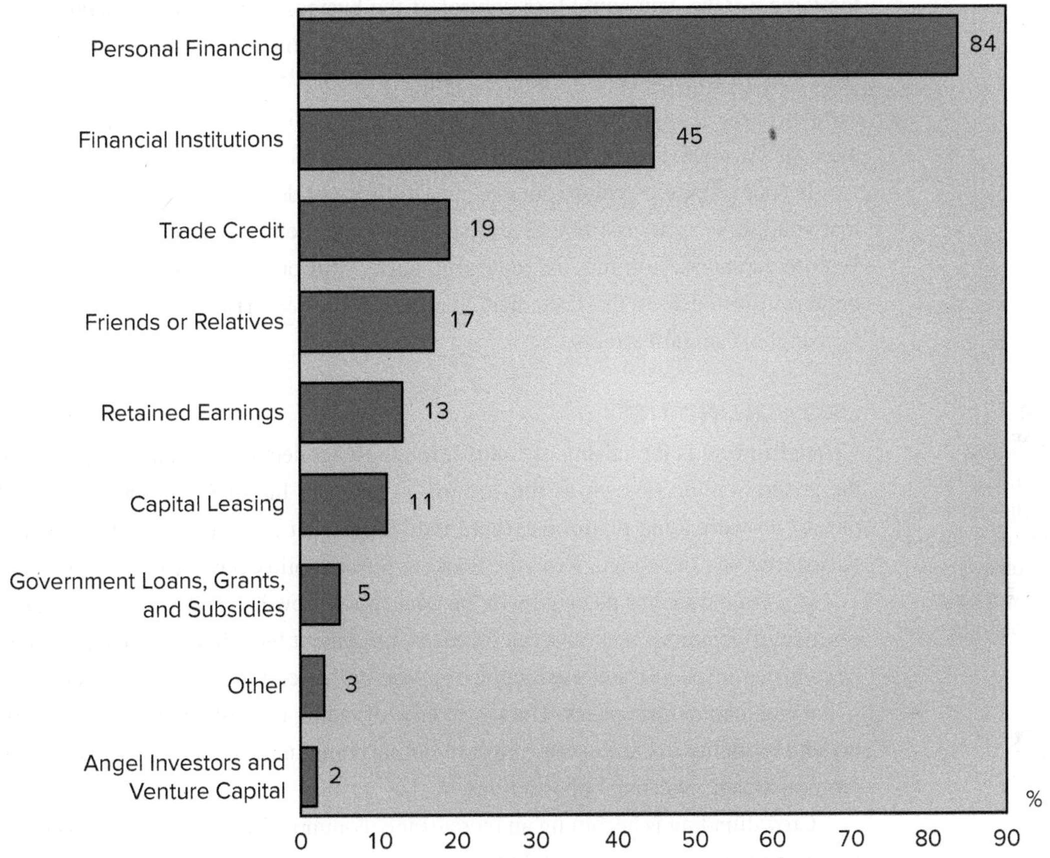

Note: Multiple responses were possible, so estimates will not add up to 100 percent.

Source: Statistics Canada, Survey on Financing and Growth of Small and Medium Enterprises, 2014.

ANGEL INVESTORS AND VENTURE CAPITALISTS

Individual investors are also a frequent source of capital for most entrepreneurs. **Angel investors** are individuals, often successful business people, who invest their own money into a potentially rewarding private company.[40] Angel investors may be willing to invest in early-stage, start-up businesses, and established businesses, as well as have experience and contacts to contribute.[41]

A number of websites match people who want money with those willing to lend it. They include Angel One Investor Network, Canadian Investment Network, and Angel Investment Network.

Venture capitalists may finance your project—for a price. **Venture capitalists** use other firms' money (e.g., money raised through investment banks, insurance companies,

angel investors
Private individuals, often successful business people, who invest their own money into a potentially rewarding private company.

venture capitalists
Individuals or companies that invest in new businesses in exchange for partial ownership of those businesses.

pension funds, and other financial institutions) and other people's money that they then invest in private companies.[42] For example, Disruption Ventures is a woman-led venture fund seeking to invest solely in tech businesses founded or run by women — still a rarity in Canada.[43] Venture capitalists are seldom interested in early-stage companies, unless there are compelling reasons (e.g., a high tech business with already successful founders).

Venture capitalists may ask for a hefty stake (as much as 60 percent) in your company in exchange for the cash to start your business or to expand it. If the venture capitalist takes too large a stake, you could lose control of the business. Since the widespread failure of early web startups, venture capitalists have been willing to invest less and expect more return on their investment if the new company is sold.[44] Therefore, if you're a very small company, you likely won't have a good chance of getting venture capital. You may have more success with an angel investor.

If your proposed venture does require millions of dollars to start, experts recommend that you talk with at least five investment firms and their clients in order to find the right venture capitalist. You may be able to connect with potential investors through various organizations such as the Canadian Venture Capital & Private Equity Association and Kensington Capital Partners.

CROWDFUNDING[45]

crowdfunding
Raising funds through the collection of small contributions from the general public (known as the crowd) using the Internet and social media.

Crowdfunding is the raising of funds through the collection of small contributions from the general public (known as the "crowd") using the Internet and social media. Examples of crowdfunding platforms where individuals can ask for or donate money include Kickstarter and Indiegogo. Read the Seeking Sustainability box for more on Kickstarter.

Crowdfunding has its origins in the concept of crowdsourcing. *Crowdsourcing* is the practice of obtaining needed services, ideas, or content by soliciting contributions from a large group of people and especially from the online community rather than from traditional employees or suppliers. The key to crowdfunding is its link to online social networking and its ability to harness the power of online communities in order to extend a project's promotion and financing opportunities.

Crowdfunding is becoming an increasingly common form of raising funds in the technology and media industries (including music, film, and video games) as these sites tend to work out best for people whose ideas play to an Internet audience. These artists and video game designers may reward contributors with T-shirts or products. Traditionally, crowdfunding is used to raise money to fund the development of a well-defined, singular project. It offers business people a chance at success by showcasing their businesses and projects to the entire world. It also has a unique dual function of providing both private financing and generating publicity and attention for a project.

ONLINE FINANCING SOURCES

There are many information sources for financing. Examples of government grants and programs include the Scientific Research and Experimental Development program and the National Research Council's Industrial Research Assistance Program.

From the comfort of your desk, you can visit government sites, such as the Business Development Bank of Canada or Canada Business Network Industry, to find financing sources. You can discover funding programs for your small business through the Centre for Small Business Financing's Grant Finder program. Another site for federal, provincial,

Seeking SUSTAINABILITY

Kickstarting a Benefit Corporation

The crowdsourcing site, Kickstarter, has helped nearly 10 million people raise more than $2.2 billion to meet all sorts of funding needs. In India, for example, the crowdfunding platform helped a group of artists raise $16,000 to create colourful interior designs for taxis.

© Taxi Fabric/Barcroft India/Getty Images

But while it is great to help Kickstarter's users get the funding they seek, the company has a broader goal than just making money. It wants to make a positive difference to society. The company believes so strongly in doing good that it reincorporated as a benefit corporation in 2015. Benefit corporations, introduced in Chapter 6, are mission-based companies that are judged by how well they meet their own set of socially or environmentally beneficial goals

Kickstarter does not take advantage of tax loopholes and donates 5 percent of its post-tax profit to arts-education programs and organizations fighting inequality. Today there are more than 3000 benefit corporations, including Patagonia and Etsy. It just goes to show that profits aren't the only way to measure success in the business world.

Sources: Jorge Newbery, "Can Millennials, Crowdfunding, and Impact Investing Change the World?" *Huffington Post,* March 10, 2017; "Dawn of the Do-Gooders," *Fast Company,* January 2016; and Nikita Richardson, "Kickstarting a Pro-Social Trend," *Fast Company,* April 2016.

municipal, and private funding is Fundica at *fundica.com*. Financing information can also be found at *profitguide.com* on the "Finances" page. While this list is not exhaustive, it serves to highlight that there are many sources.

Obtaining money from financial institutions, investors, and government sources can be a challenge for most small businesses. (You will learn more about financing in Chapter 17.) Those who do survive the planning and financing of their new ventures are eager to get their businesses up and running. Your success in running a business depends on many factors, especially knowing your customers, managing your employees, and keeping good records. These topics will be discussed next.

Knowing Your Customers

One of the most important elements of small-business success is knowing the market. In business, a **market** consists of people with unsatisfied wants and needs who have both the resources and the willingness to buy. Many of our students have the willingness to own a brand-new Maserati sports car. However, few have the resources necessary to satisfy this want. Would you be a good market for a luxury car dealer?

market
People with unsatisfied wants and needs who have both the resources and the willingness to buy.

Once you have identified your market and its needs, you must set out to fill those needs. The way to meet your customers' needs is to offer top quality at a fair price with great service. Remember, it is not enough to get customers—you have to *keep* them. As sales coach Phil Glosserman says, "People buy in order to experience the feelings they

Adapting *to* CHANGE

Building Relationships by Building Subscribers

It seems every time we use websites to search for information or products, we're asked to subscribe to the site's e-mail list or to provide small bits of information about who we are. Why is that? Marketers are finding that more contact with you and information gathered about you leads to a greater chance of satisfaction on your part, and a far greater chance of sales.

© Ben Rose/Getty Images

The more we engage in discussions of beauty products on Birchbox's Facebook page, the more likely we are to venture over to its site and subscribe to its box service. When interest is shown in the box service, questions are asked about beauty regimens, skin types, colour preferences, and the like. From there, the company designs a box of samples catered to your likes and what will work for you.

Getting users to make the jump into subscription is the hardest part. Marketers need to know the difference between someone "liking" an article, song, video, or product and actually commenting and interacting with other users as well as the content providers. Research has shown people who have a higher level of interaction feel more strongly committed to the company than those who "lurk" or passively consume the information. Discussion needs to be designed to get more users into the conversation and thereby learn what it is users want to see.

This type of engagement is found not just from things we *buy.* When logging in to Spotify or YouTube accounts, users are given songs and videos that closely resemble what they're already interested in. News websites do this as well. What other industries do you think will embrace this type of customer interaction next?

Sources: Marguerite Ward, "Birchbox CEO: Sending Great Cold Emails Was How I First Found Success," CNBC, February 10, 2017; Gerry Smith, "New York Times Offers Free Spotify Service to Boost Subscribers," Bloomberg, February 8, 2017; and Lior Zalmanson and Gal Oestreicher-Singer, "Turning Content Viewers into Subscribers," *MIT Sloan Management Review*, Spring 2016.

get from having their needs met." Sure, your product may meet those needs now. However, if customers tell you they've discovered something they don't like in your product, call them back when you fix it and tell them, "Thanks for the good idea."[46]

Take a look at the Adapting to Change box to see how companies are using interactions with their customer base to improve and tailor offerings to individuals.

One of the greatest advantages that small businesses have over larger ones is the ability to know their customers better and to adapt quickly to their ever-changing needs. The only way to know what your customers' needs are is to listen, listen, listen. Don't let your passion and ego get in the way of changing your products or services to fit what customers really want. The Reaching Beyond Our Borders box discusses how you can let customers and others from around the world help you design your products. You will gain more insights about marketing in Chapters 14 and 15. Now let's consider the importance of effectively managing the employees who help you serve your market.

Reaching *Beyond* OUR BORDERS

Listening to What Your Customers Need

What's better than knowing what your customers need and then designing products to meet those needs? Getting your customers to design the products themselves. That's what Quirky has done. You may be familiar with Quirky's most successful product, Pivot Power, the pivoting power strip that allows you to bend the strip in order to fit large adapters in every outlet.

Pivot Power's creator, Jake Zien, will be the first Quirky inventor to earn $1 million in royalties a year.

© Quirky

When Zien was a college student, he joined the Quirky community and submitted his idea as a simple, basic drawing. A week later, it was selected for development. A year after that, it was on sale at Bed Bath & Beyond. Zien just submitted an idea; everything else was done by the Quirky community (i.e., all inventors, influencers, staff, and customers from around the world). Those who contribute their ideas regarding design, style, enhancing, packaging, naming, taglines, or pricing are called influencers. The influencers don't just get a pat on the back for helping out; if their ideas are used, they are paid a portion of the royalty as well. Once a product is ready for production, Quirky decides which of its 21 suppliers and factories (mostly in Asia) will make the product.

Quirky founder and CEO, Ben Kaufman, knew Quirky would work two years ago when he saw a tweet of a Target advertisement for Quirky products. The tweeter wrote, "I made that." Actually, the person hadn't made that. But he was part of the community that helped create it, an experience that gave him a sense of ownership. You can't build a customer relationship stronger than that!

Sources: Stephanie Mlot, "Quirky's Ben Kaufman Gets GE to Share Its Patents," *Bloomberg Businessweek*, March 20, 2014; "Quirky, GE Unveil Aros Smart Air Conditioner," *PC Magazine*, March 19, 2014; and Josh Dean, "Is This the World's Most Creative Manufacturer?" *Inc.*, October 2013.

Managing Your Employees

As a business grows, it becomes impossible for an entrepreneur to oversee every detail, even if he or she is working 60 hours per week. This means that hiring, training, and motivating employees is critical.

It is not easy to find good, qualified help when you offer less money, fewer benefits, and less room for advancement than larger firms do. That is one reason why employee relations is important for small-business management. Employees of small companies are often more satisfied with their jobs than are their counterparts in big businesses. Why? Quite often they find their jobs more challenging, their ideas more accepted, and their bosses more respectful.[47]

Often entrepreneurs reluctantly face the reality that to keep growing, they must delegate authority to others. To whom should you delegate authority, and how much? "The art of management is delegation," says Andrew Faridani, President and CEO of BreezeMaxWeb Ltd., Canada's leading provider of online solutions. "You've got to be able to relinquish some of the hold or grip that you have on particular departments. And that was the biggest learning curve for me. By nature, I'm fanatic about being in control of the business. You have to realize that when you delegate to people in particular departments, life becomes much easier and everything runs more smoothly. I firmly believe it is the number one thing that makes businesses effective and successful."[48]

This can be a particularly touchy issue in small businesses with long-term employees and in family businesses. As you might expect, entrepreneurs who have built their companies by themselves often feel compelled to promote employees who have been with them from the start—even when they aren't qualified to serve as managers. Common sense probably tells you this could be detrimental to the business.

The same can be true of family-run businesses that are expanding. Attitudes such as "You can't fire family" or "You must promote certain workers because they're family" can hinder growth. Entrepreneurs can best serve themselves and the business if they gradually recruit and groom employees for management positions. By doing this, entrepreneurs can enhance trust and the support of the manager among other employees and themselves. You will learn more about managing employees in Chapters 11, 12, and 13.

Keeping Records

Small-business owners often say that the most important assistance they received in starting and managing the business involved accounting. A business person who sets up an effective accounting system early will save much grief later. Accurate record keeping enables an owner to follow daily sales, expenses, and profits, as well as help owners with inventory control, customer records, and payroll.

Many business failures are caused by poor accounting practices that lead to costly mistakes. A good accountant can help you decide whether to buy or lease equipment and whether to own or rent a building. Help may also be provided for tax planning, financial forecasting, choosing sources of financing, and writing requests for funds.

Other small-business owners may tell you where to find an accountant experienced in small business. It pays to shop around for advice. You will learn more about accounting in Chapter 16.

© Chris Ryan/age fotostock

A necessary and invaluable aide is a competent, experienced lawyer who knows and understands small businesses. Lawyers can help with a variety of matters, including leases, contracts (e.g., partnership agreements), and protection against liabilities. They do not have to be expensive. In fact, several prepaid legal plans offer services such as drafting legal documents for a low annual rate.

Looking for Help

Small-business owners have learned, sometimes the hard way, that they need outside consulting advice early in the process. This is especially true of legal, tax, and accounting advice but may also be true of marketing, finance, and other areas. Most small and medium-sized firms cannot afford to hire such experts as employees, so they must turn to outside assistance.

Make your marketing decisions long before a product is produced or a store is opened. An inexpensive marketing research study may help you determine where to locate, whom to select as your target market, and what would be an effective strategy for reaching those people. Thus, a marketing consultant with small-business experience can be of great help to you, especially one who has had experience with building websites and using social media.

Two other invaluable experts are a commercial account officer and an insurance agent. The commercial account officer can help you design an acceptable business plan and give you valuable financial advice as well as lend you money when you need it. An insurance agent will explain the risks associated with a small business and how to cover them most efficiently with insurance and other means like safety devices and sprinkler systems.

Often business professors from local colleges and universities will advise small-business owners free or for a small fee. Some universities have clubs or programs that provide consulting services by master of business administration (MBA) candidates for a nominal fee. Does your school provide such services?

It also is wise to seek the counsel of other small-business owners. Review small-business articles on marketing, business planning, incorporation, and financial management. Peer groups within specific industries can give you better insights into the challenges and solutions encountered by other business owners in your field.

Other sources of advice include local chambers of commerce, the Better Business Bureau, national and local trade associations (such as the Canadian Federation of Independent Business), the business reference section of your library, and small-business-related sites on the Internet. Some have been noted in this chapter.

LO5

Outline the advantages and disadvantages that small businesses have in entering global markets.

Going Global: Small-Business Prospects

As we noted in Chapter 3, the world market is a much larger, much more lucrative market for small businesses than focusing on Canada alone. Despite that potential, most small businesses still do not think internationally, and only a small percentage of small businesses export.

Technological advances have helped increase small-business exporting. For example, PayPal makes it possible for small businesses to get paid automatically when they conduct global business online. The Internet also helps small businesses find customers without the expense of international travel. As people acquire more wealth, they often demand specialized products that are not mass-produced and are willing to pay more for niche goods that small businesses offer.

Still, many small businesses have difficulty getting started in global business. Why are some companies missing out on the huge global markets? Primarily because getting there involves a few major hurdles: (1) financing is often difficult to find, (2) would-be

Courtesy of Milt Reimer, FXR Racing. Used with permission.

Milt Reimer, founder of FXR Racing, a $50 million-a-year snowmobile and motocross clothing empire, has 600 dealers across 13 countries.[49] Have you thought of a product that can address an unmet need and would be successful not only in Canada, but globally?

exporters do not know how to get started and do not understand the cultural differences between markets, and (3) the bureaucratic paperwork can threaten to bury a small business.

Besides the fact that most of the world's market lies outside of Canada, there are other good reasons for going global. Exporting can absorb excess inventory, soften downturns in the domestic market, and extend product lives. It can also spice up dull routines.

Small businesses have several advantages over large businesses in international trade, which include the following:

- Overseas buyers enjoy dealing with individuals rather than with large corporate bureaucracies.
- Small companies can usually begin shipping much faster.
- Small companies can support a wide variety of suppliers.
- Small companies can give customers more personal service and more undivided attention because each overseas account is a major source of business to them.

The growth potential of small businesses overseas is phenomenal. This is why there are many organizations that offer assistance. Some of these have been cited in this chapter as well as in Chapter 4. Web-based business applications are helping small businesses cross boundaries like never before and, in some instances, levelling some of the advantages that large businesses traditionally have had.

PROGRESS ASSESSMENT

- What are the five functions of business in a small-business setting?
- There are nine sections in the business plan outline in this chapter. Can you describe at least four of those sections?
- What are some of the advantages and challenges that small businesses have over large businesses in selling in global markets?

SUMMARY

LO1 Explain why people are willing to become entrepreneurs, and describe the attributes of successful entrepreneurs.

Entrepreneurship is accepting the challenge of starting and running a business.

What are a few of the reasons people start their own businesses?

Reasons include profit, independence, opportunity, and challenge.

What are the attributes of successful entrepreneurs?

Successful entrepreneurs are self-directed, determined, action-oriented, highly energetic, tolerant of uncertainty, and able to learn quickly.

LO2 Discuss the importance of small business to the Canadian economy.

A small business is often defined as a business that is independently owned and operated, is not dominant in its field, and meets certain standards of size in terms of employees or annual revenues.

Why are small businesses important to the Canadian economy?

In Canada, 97.9 percent of businesses have fewer than 100 employees, of which 54.1 percent are micro-enterprises. SMEs exported goods totalling $106 billion. Perhaps more important to tomorrow's graduates, small businesses employ a large portion (70.5 percent) of the total private labour force.

Why do so many small businesses fail?

Many small businesses fail because of managerial incompetence and inadequate financial planning. See Figure 7.3 for a list of causes of small-business failure. Some of these causes include attempting to do too much business with too little capital, underestimating how much time it will take to build a market, and not allowing for setbacks and unexpected expenses.

What factors increase the chances for success?

Figure 7.3 outlines some situations for small-business success. This includes whether the product is not easily made by mass-production techniques, whether sales are not large enough to appeal to a large firm, and whether the owner pays attention to new competitors.

LO3 **Summarize ways to learn how small businesses operate.**

Most people have no idea how to go about starting a small business.

What hints would you give someone who wants to learn about starting a small business?

An entrepreneur can improve the odds by learning from others. First, take courses and talk with some small-business owners. Second, get some experience working for others. Finally, study the latest in small-business management techniques, including the use of programs for things such as payroll, inventory control, and mailing lists.

LO4 **Analyze what it takes to start and run a small business.**

Writing a business plan is the first step in organizing a business.

What goes into a business plan?

See Figure 7.4 to see what goes into a business plan. A business plan includes a section on company background, the financial plan, and the location analysis.

What sources of funds should someone wanting to start a new business consider investigating?

A new entrepreneur has several sources of capital: personal savings, relatives, banks, finance companies, venture-capital organizations, government agencies, angel investors, and more.

What are some of the special problems that small-business owners have in dealing with employees?

Small-business owners often have difficulty finding competent employees. Grooming employees for management responsibilities can be challenging.

Where can potential entrepreneurs find help in starting their businesses?

Help can be found from many sources: accountants, lawyers, marketing researchers, loan officers, insurance agents, the Business Development Bank of Canada, and your instructors.

What online sources are available to assist entrepreneurs?

Entrepreneurs can start by visiting government sources, such as the Innovation, Science and Economic Development Canada website. Financial services providers also have sites dedicated to small businesses.

LO5 **Outline the advantages and disadvantages that small businesses have in entering global markets.**

The future growth of some small businesses is in foreign markets.

What are some advantages small businesses have over large businesses in global markets?

Some reasons why foreign buyers enjoy dealing with small businesses rather than large corporations include (1) small businesses can support a wide variety of suppliers, (2) they can ship products more quickly, and (3) small businesses give more personal service.

Why don't more small businesses start trading internationally?

Reasons why small businesses don't trade internationally include: (1) financing is often difficult to find, (2) would-be exporters do not know how to get started and do not understand the cultural differences between markets, and (3) the bureaucratic paperwork can threaten to bury small businesses.

KEY TERMS

angel investors 271
business incubators 259
business plan 268
crowdfunding 272
entrepreneurial team 255
entrepreneurship 247
intrapreneurs 258
market 273
micro-enterprise 256
micropreneurs 256
small and medium-sized enterprises (SMEs) 254
small business 260
venture capitalists 271

CAREER EXPLORATION

You can start a small business in any industry you like. We've talked about a few throughout the chapter, but here are a few more with low start-up costs to consider. Find out about the tasks performed, skills needed, pay, and opportunity outlook in these fields through Internet sites that include the Government of Canada Job Bank, Workopolis, Monster, CareerBuilder, Glassdoor, and Indeed, as well as through the Career Centre at your school.

- **Craft and fine artist**—uses a variety of materials and techniques to create art for sale. Craft artists create handmade objects, such as pottery, glassware, textiles, and other objects. Fine artists create original works of art such as paintings and sculptures.
- **Web developer**—designs and creates websites, which means they are responsible for the look of the site and for its technical aspects, and may create content for the site.
- **General repair service**—paints, makes household repairs, works on plumbing and electrical systems, and so on.
- **Small engine mechanic**—inspects, services, and repairs motorized power equipment such as outdoor power equipment (lawnmowers, leaf blowers, etc.).

CRITICAL THINKING

1. Small businesses continue to be feeders for future large businesses. As they prosper and develop new goods and services, they are often bought out by large companies. Is this good or bad? Should we do anything about it? If so, what?
2. Are there any similarities between the characteristics demanded of an entrepreneur and those of a professional athlete? Would an athlete be a good prospect for entrepreneurship? Why or why not? Could teamwork be important in an entrepreneurial effort?
3. Imagine yourself starting a small business. What kind of business would it be? How much competition is there? What could you do to make your business more attractive than those of your competitors? Would you be willing to work 60 to 70 hours a week?

DEVELOPING CAREER SKILLS

Key: ● **Team** ★ **Analytic** ▲ **Communication** ⊡ **Technology**

⊡★ **1.** Find issues of *Canadian Business, Canadian Business Franchise,* and *PROFIT* magazines in the library, your local bookstore, or on the Internet. Read about the entrepreneurs who are heading today's dynamic new businesses. Write a profile about one entrepreneur.

▲★ **2.** Select a small business that looks attractive as a career possibility for you. Talk to at least one person who manages such a business. Ask how he or she started the business. Ask about financing, personnel challenges (e.g., hiring, firing, training, and scheduling), accounting issues, and other managerial matters. Prepare a summary of your findings, including whether the manager found the job to be rewarding, interesting, and challenging—and why.

⊡★ **3.** Contact a government agency such as Export Development Canada or Business Development Bank of Canada. Write a brief summary of the services that they offer small businesses. (Hint: Each organization has a website: *www.edc.ca* and *www.bdc.ca*.)

⊡★▲ **4.** Contact a local financial institution (e.g., bank) and make an appointment to speak with a commercial accounts officer. Ask this person what a small business owner should consider if she or he is looking for financing. (This may include a discussion on the requirements of a business plan and what that institution wishes to see in this document.) Review other sources of financing that might be available. What other resources are available to assist small-business owners. Bring this information to class and share it with your peers.

●▲★ **5.** There has been some discussion in this chapter about entrepreneurship and traits of entrepreneurs. In a group, highlight the differences between a small business owner and an entrepreneur.

ANALYZING MANAGEMENT DECISIONS

Starting a Small Business While in School

Brett Sheffield, full-time student at the University of Manitoba and owner of Sheffield Farms and Stay Fit Health Club, was named the 2012 Student Entrepreneur National Champion by the national charitable organization, Advancing Canadian Entrepreneurship (ACE). Sheffield was triumphant after provincial, regional, and national rounds of competition because of his extraordinary achievements operating one flourishing business and launching a second while attending school full-time.

Sheffield Farms is a grain farm located in rural Manitoba that was founded in 2008, and Stay Fit Health Club is a 24-hour fitness centre in its first year of operation. "Sheffield's determination and proven business achievements, such as expanding his farm from 160 to 1,700 acres and pioneering a second business while maintaining his honour roll status at school, are ideal qualities of a Student Entrepreneur champion," said Amy Harder, President, ACE. "ACE is confident that Brett will make Canada proud at the Global Student Entrepreneur Awards in New York City."

Sheffield competed at the national level against five other regional finalists, to a panel of 50 industry leaders and CEOs. In addition to the national title, he received a $10,000 cash prize. "Competitions like the ACE National Exposition allow students from all corners of Canada to showcase our entrepreneurial talent," said Sheffield. "I'm honoured at being named the Student Entrepreneur National Champion and I look forward to continuing to take my business to new heights."

Sources: Sean Stanleigh, "Manitoba student wins national competition," *The Globe and Mail,* May 10, 2012, www.theglobeandmail.com/report-on-business/smallbusiness/sb-tools/small-business-briefing/manitoba-student-wins-national-competition/article2428615/#in; "University of Manitoba Student Wins 2012 Student Entrepreneur National Champion Title," Advancing Canadian Entrepreneurship Inc., May 9, 2012, www.acecanada.ca/news/newsItem.cfm?cms_news_id5591; and Martin Cash, "U of M student farmer aces biz award," *Winnipeg Free Press,* May 1, 2012, www.winnipegfreepress.com/business/u-of-m-student-farmer-aces-biz-award-149618705.html.

Discussion Questions

1. What are the advantages and potential problems of starting a business while in school?
2. What kinds of small businesses operate around your school? Talk to the owners and learn from their experiences.
3. What opportunities exist for satisfying student needs at your school? Pick one idea, write a business plan, and discuss it in class (unless it is so good you do not want to share it; in that case, good luck).
4. Search and find what other Canadian competitions exist for student entrepreneurs. Would you enter any of them?

RUNNING CASE

Fox 40 International Inc.: A Family Business

For successful Canadian entrepreneur and inventor Ron Foxcroft, it all started in 1982 when he purchased Fluke Transport, a Southern Ontario trucking business. The company slogan—If It's On Time . . . It's A "FLUKE"—was soon recognized throughout North America. Over the years, Ron diversified into new ventures and the Foxcroft Group of Companies now includes Fluke Transportation Group, Fluke Warehousing Inc., Foxcroft Capital Group, and Fox 40 International Inc. (Fox 40).

All of these companies are private corporations. Although the word corporation makes people think of big businesses, it is not necessary to be big to incorporate. As introduced in this text, one of the biggest advantages of incorporation is limited liability. Owners of private corporations can also make decisions more quickly than is typically the case for large, public corporations.

The formation of Fox 40 is the result of a dream for a pealess whistle. When developing his first whistle, Ron was motivated by his knowledge and experience as an international basketball referee. "I always had a problem with whistles," he explains. "They have a cork pea in them and when you blow a pea-whistle really hard, nothing comes out. When they're frozen or wet or get some dirt inside, they lose their efficiency." As a result, Ron, like many other referees, sometimes found himself unable to stop play even though he saw a clear violation take place. In a fast-moving game like basketball, a whistle that fails does not get a second chance to sound. In a really big game, even when the whistle did work, the play occasionally was not stopped because the whistle's sound was drowned out by the noise of the roaring crowds. Frustrated with faulty pea whistles, he spent three years of development with design consultant Chuck Shepherd, resulting in the creation of the Fox 40® Classic Whistle.

Although Ron was convinced a better whistle would sweep the basketball market, he was unable to obtain bank financing for the venture. Very few thought that a pealess whistle would turn out and some believed that it would only be used by a few hundred referee friends. Despite the critics, Ron managed to put together $150,000 from his own private funds and in 1987 he created Fox 40. Ron risked everything as he pursued this dream: his family's financial future (only his wife, Marie, knew how much he was risking), Fluke Transport's reputation, and Fluke Transport's money. While Ron had complete confidence in manufacturing a pealess whistle that would work, he did not know that it would be the commercial success that it is today. Twenty-five years later, Fox 40 remains a proudly Canadian company. It dominates the global whistle industry and tens of thousands of Fox 40® Whistles are produced monthly for shipment to 140 countries.

What about succession planning? Today, Ron plays an active role as Founder and Chief Executive Officer (CEO) of Fox 40, and Chairman and CEO of Fluke Transportation Group. While he has passed the day-to-day running of Fox 40 to his son, Dave, Ron continues to focus on the company's strategic direction. This includes listening to customers and employees (Ron insists that the best ideas still come from them), and concentrating on increasing brand recognition for the Fox 40® brand. While it is up to Ron and Dave to approve a new idea, it is up to Dave and his team to implement it. "Once you have decided on a course of action," says Ron, "failure is not an option."

Dave has listened to whistles all of his life, in addition to the people who use them. As Fox 40's President and Chief Operating Officer, he is responsible for managing Fox 40's global sales, marketing, and operations. This includes overseeing the development of the company's diverse, innovative product base and strategic acquisitions with the company's highly capable team. Outside of the company, he is involved in industry events (e.g., as a delegate for the World Federation of Sporting Goods), he actively supports several charitable associations that support youth, and he works as a professional referee in the Canadian Football League (CFL Referee #30) and the National Football Development League (NFL #167).

To achieve sales and profit growth targets of 10 to 15 percent per year, efforts focus on the development of Fox 40 products. As a take on the "Build a better mousetrap" catchphrase, Dave believes, "You have to build it and then the world will beat a path to your door . . . but you need to still sell it, work it, and be innovative."

While Ron recognizes that very few "seconds in command" (i.e., presidents) are happy, he is quick to point out that these are the individuals who run the show. "Dave is the ideas guy," Ron emphasizes. Examples include new product introductions (e.g., the marine line, the Heat Alert Mouthguard, and the CAUL Fingergrip whistle), and social media initiatives such as Facebook contests. Dave remains modest. "My job is to keep him [Ron] as the face of the company and it will always be the case . . . Maybe it is the referee training. The good one [referee] is never seen."

Ron was motivated to become an entrepreneur for reasons that include, "My fear of working for a dumb boss and fear of being hungry." What is it like for the next generation to work in the family business? "Working for your dad is just like refereeing," says Dave. "The first game you work, they expect you to be perfect. Every game after, they expect you to improve . . . just like working for your dad."

It is evident that there is mutual respect between the Foxcrofts. When asked how they are able to successfully work together, Ron had some answers. "Don't hold grudges," he said. "We do not discuss work outside of the office. When you walk out of the building, it is over until the next morning . . . It cannot be all-consuming in your private life."

Both Ron and Dave are often approached by individuals that seek investment in their ideas or that wish to discuss their ideas. The advice that they routinely give these individuals is: "Don't give away ownership of your business or your product!" Ron adds, "We are not a distributor. We are a manufacturer distributor and we own everything we sell."

Source: Ron Foxcroft, CEO of Fox 40 International Inc. and Chairman and CEO of Fluke Transportation, in-person interview, September 22, 2017, Hamilton, Ontario.

Discussion Questions

1. What are some advantages of Canadian-owned, private corporations over public corporations?
2. What are reasons why people are willing to take the challenge of starting a business?
3. "Immediate family members are given an opportunity to work for the company for a living," says Dave Foxcroft. What are some possible challenges in working with family members? How can these challenges be managed?

PART 3

CHAPTER 8

Management and Leadership

LEARNING OBJECTIVES

After you have read and studied this chapter, you should be able to:

- **LO1** Describe the changes occurring today in the management function.
- **LO2** Describe the four functions of management.
- **LO3** Relate the planning process and decision making to the accomplishment of company goals.
- **LO4** Describe the organizing function of management.
- **LO5** Explain the differences between leaders and managers, and describe the various leadership styles.
- **LO6** Summarize the five steps of the control function of management.

PROFILE

GETTING TO KNOW: KEVIN PLANK, FOUNDER, UNDER ARMOUR

Confidence is an essential quality for any aspiring leader, but that doesn't mean it's an easy thing to maintain. Just ask Kevin Plank, who, as a young college graduate, spent his life savings on starting Under Armour. Plank's path to success was far from smooth. Over the years he has overcome numerous hurdles that tested his confidence both as a businessperson and a leader.

Plank faced one of these setbacks soon after he started selling moisture-wicking athletic shirts from his grandmother's basement in Washington, DC. Along with investing his nest egg, he also racked up thousands of dollars of credit card debt launching the company. With hardly any money left, Plank tried to turn his luck around by betting his last $100 at a blackjack table. He lost it all. Already feeling crushed, Plank's night got worse when he arrived at a toll booth and had no money to pay his way through. "It was the single worst moment of my life, having to face that poor toll booth operator, waiting for her two dollars," said Plank.

He spent the rest of the night in tears, terrified that his business was doomed to fail. Then the next morning he visited the company's PO box and

© Nathaniel Welch/Redux

found a cheque for $7,500 that he had been waiting to receive for a while. "That was the last time I doubted the company," said Plank. He told himself, "Wipe the tears away, stand up, be a man, run your business, find a way." And that's precisely what Plank did as he took Under Armour out of the basement and into locker rooms across the country.

Along with business, sports has been one of Plank's lifelong passions. In fact, the idea for Under Armour came to him while playing football for the University of Maryland. Although quick on his feet, Plank felt weighed down by his sweat-soaked undershirt. So after graduation, he spent weeks searching New York City's Garment District for moisture-removing alternatives to ordinary cotton fabric. Plank found what he was looking for, developed some prototypes, and then sent the items off to a unique test market. "I graduated from college and realized, I know 60 people playing in the NFL who have careers that are going to be somewhere between three and five years," said Plank. "And I either take advantage of it now or lose it forever." Fortunately, the players liked the product and started telling their coaches about it. Soon Plank received orders from college athletic programs as well as professional teams.

While this outside assistance helped build the brand, sales at Under Armour remained low for the first few years. But Plank changed the game in 1999 with a risky decision to place a half-page ad in *ESPN Magazine*. With a price tag of $12,000, the ad cost nearly as much as the company's entire earnings from 1996. But unlike Plank's trip to the blackjack table, this time his gamble worked. The year ended with Under Armour bringing in $1 million in sales. By 2002, revenue topped out at more than $50 million.

Under Armour now earns billions of dollars annually on products ranging from standard shirts and shoes to a growing line of "smart" athletic wear. Plank plans to expand Under Armour into one of the biggest companies in the world. Of course, reaching such a lofty goal will take a confident leader who can make the right decisions at the right time. Given those requirements, Kevin Plank seems like a good bet: "Respect to Silicon Valley and all the great companies that are out there, but we feel we are just getting started, we have a long way to go, and we like our odds."

This chapter is all about leadership and management. You will learn that shared leadership is more widespread than you might have imagined.

You will also learn about the functions of management and how management differs from leadership. All in all, you should get a better idea of what leaders and managers do and how they do it.

Sources: Rachel Monroe, "Under Armour's Quest to Dethrone Nike and Jump-Start Baltimore," *Bloomberg Businessweek*, June 28, 2016; J. D. Harrison, "When We Were Small: Under Armour," *The Washington Post*, November 12, 2014; Parmy Olson, "Silicon Valley's Latest Threat: Under Armour," *Forbes*, October 19, 2015; Richard Feloni, "The Billionaire Founder of Under Armour Was Once So Broke He Couldn't Pay a $2 Toll—Here's What the Experience Taught Him," *Business Insider*, January 26, 2016; Lorraine Mirabella, "Under Armour Brings in New President; Plank Remains CEO," *The Baltimore Sun*, June 27, 2017.

LO1

Describe the changes occurring today in the management function.

Managers' Roles are Evolving

resources
A general term that incorporates human resources, natural resources, and financial resources.

Managers must practise the art of getting things done through organizational resources. **Resources** is a general term that incorporates human resources (e.g., employees), natural resources (e.g., raw materials), and financial resources (e.g., money). Resources include the factors of production, which were introduced in Chapter 1. Every business has scarce resources, and management is about deciding how to effectively use these scarce resources.

At one time, managers were called bosses, and their job consisted of telling people what to do and watching over them to be sure they did it. They were typically more proficient and knew more than the employees they supervised. Bosses tended to reprimand those who did not do things correctly and, generally, were impersonal. Many managers still behave that way. Perhaps you have witnessed such behaviour; some coaches use this style.

© Robert Nicholas / age fotostock

Canada still trails the United States and the rest of the world in developing female leaders. Over 80 percent of organizations don't have a clear strategy for developing female leaders and yet studies have shown that having more senior level women improves company profit.[5] What should be included in leadership development programs for women?

Today, however, most managers tend to be more progressive. For example, they emphasize teams and team building; they create drop-in centres, team spaces, and open work areas. They may change the definition of *work* from a task you do for a specified period in a specific place to something you do anywhere, anytime. They tend to guide, train, support, motivate, and coach employees rather than tell them what to do.[1] Thus most modern managers emphasize teamwork and co-operation rather than discipline and order giving.[2] They may also open their books to employees to share the company's financials.

Managers of high-tech firms, like Google and Apple, realize that many workers often know more about technology than they do. At first, Google tried to get by with no managers. Soon, however, they found that managers were necessary for communicating strategy, helping employees prioritize projects, facilitating co-operation, and ensuring that processes and systems aligned with company goals.[3]

The people entering management today are different from those who entered in the past. Leaders of Fortune 100 companies tend to be younger, more of them are female, and fewer of them were educated at elite universities.[4] Managers in the future are more likely to be working in teams and assuming completely new roles in the firm. For one thing, they'll be

© Paul J. Richards/AFP/Getty Images

Rather than telling employees exactly what to do, managers today tend to give their employees enough independence to make their own informed decisions about how best to please customers. How do you think most employees respond to this empowerment on the job?

doing more expansion overseas.[6] Further, they may be taking a leadership role in adapting to climate change.[7]

Future managers will need to be more globally prepared; that is, they need skills such as adaptability, foreign language skills, and ease in other cultures.[8]

Future changes in the work environment will mean that work will increasingly be completed by teams, and change will come more quickly. Transparency in how managers do their job (in terms of corporate governance, found in Chapter 6) and how they address corporate social responsibility (discussed in Chapter 5) will become increasingly important.

What this means for you and other graduates of tomorrow is that successful management will demand a new kind of person: a skilled communicator and team player as well as a planner, coordinator, organizer, and leader.[9] These trends will be addressed in the next few chapters to help prepare you for your future career in management. In the following sections, management in general and the functions managers perform are discussed.

The Four Functions of Management

LO2

Describe the four functions of management.

Well-known management consultant Peter Drucker says that managers give direction to their organizations, provide leadership, and decide how to use organizational resources to accomplish goals.[10] This description gives you some idea of what managers do. In addition to those tasks, managers today must deal with conflict resolution, create trust in an atmosphere where trust has been badly shaken, and help create balance between work lives and family lives.[11] Managers look at the big picture, and their decisions make a major difference in organizations.[12]

The following definition of management provides the outline of this chapter: **Management** is the process used to accomplish organizational goals through planning, organizing, leading, and controlling people and other organizational resources. (Figure 8.1 provides a comprehensive listing of all the critical tasks in this process.)

management The process used to accomplish organizational goals through planning, organizing, leading, and controlling people and other organizational resources.

FIGURE 8.1

WHAT MANAGERS DO

Some modern managers perform all of these tasks with the full co-operation and participation of workers. Empowering employees means allowing them to participate more fully in decision making.

Planning	**Leading**
• Setting organizational goals. • Developing strategies to reach those goals. • Determining resources needed. • Setting precise standards.	• Guiding and motivating employees to work effectively to accomplish organizational goals and objectives. • Giving assignments. • Explaining routines. • Clarifying policies. • Providing feedback on performance.
Organizing	**Controlling**
• Allocating resources, assigning tasks, and establishing procedures for accomplishing goals. • Preparing a structure (organization chart) showing lines of authority and responsibility. • Recruiting, selecting, training, and developing employees. • Placing employees where they will be most effective.	• Measuring results against corporate objectives. • Monitoring performance relative to standards. • Rewarding outstanding performance. • Taking corrective action when necessary.

planning
A management function that includes anticipating trends and determining the best strategies and tactics to achieve organizational goals and objectives.

organizing
A management function that includes designing the structure of the organization and creating conditions and systems in which everyone and everything work together to achieve the organization's goals and objectives.

leading
Creating a vision for the organization and guiding, training, coaching, and motivating others to work effectively to achieve the organization's goals and objectives.

Planning includes anticipating trends and determining the best strategies and tactics to achieve organizational goals and objectives, for example, pleasing customers. The trend today is to have *planning teams* to help monitor the environment, find business opportunities, and watch for challenges. Planning is a key management function because the other management functions depend heavily on having a good plan. Most often this plan is reflected in a set of budgets, which will be talked about more in Chapter 17.

Organizing includes designing the structure of the organization and creating conditions and systems in which everyone and everything work together to achieve the organization's goals and objectives. Many of today's organizations are being designed to please the customer and in turn, generate a profit. Thus, organizations must remain flexible and adaptable because when customer needs change, organizations must change along with them or risk losing business.[13]

Whole Foods Market, for example, is known for its high-quality, high-priced food items. But it has introduced many lower-cost items to adjust to the financial losses of its customer base. In 2016, Whole Foods launched its first lower-cost store, called 365, to appeal to cash-strapped Millennials. The 365 stores will offer only a quarter of the products carried by the traditional stores and will have no butchers, wine experts, or fishmongers, which will help reduce costs.[14] Amazon purchased Whole Foods in 2017. Do you think Whole Foods will undergo further changes?

Leading means creating a vision for the organization and communicating, guiding, training, coaching, and motivating others to work effectively to achieve the organization's goals and objectives. Researchers have spent a considerable amount of time studying motivation, given the direct relationship between motivation and output. This subject is explored further in Chapter 11. The trend is to empower employees and give them as much freedom as possible to become self-directed and self-motivated. Empowerment will be further discussed in Chapter 12, Human Resource Management. This function was once known as *directing;* that is, telling employees exactly what to do. In many smaller firms, that is still the role of managers. In most large modern firms, however, managers no longer tell people exactly what to do because knowledge workers and other employees often know how to do their jobs better than the manager.[15] Nonetheless, leadership is necessary to keep employees focused on the right tasks at the right time along with training, coaching, motivating, and the other leadership tasks.[16]

© Creatas/photolibrary RF

Planning is what helps managers understand the environment in which their businesses must operate. When people's tastes and preferences for restaurant meals change, food service managers must respond with menu alternatives. What changes have occurred in your preferences?

Controlling involves establishing clear standards to determine whether an organization is progressing toward its goals and objectives, reporting the results achieved, rewarding people for doing a good job, and taking corrective action if work is not proceeding according to plan. Basically, it means measuring whether what actually occurs meets the organization's goals.

controlling
A management function that involves establishing clear standards to determine whether or not an organization is progressing toward its goals and objectives, rewarding people for doing a good job, and taking corrective action if they are not.

The four functions—planning, organizing, leading, and controlling—are the heart of management, so let's explore them in more detail. The process begins with planning; we'll look at that right after the Progress Assessment.

PROGRESS ASSESSMENT

- What is the definition of management used in this chapter?
- What are the four functions of management?

LO3

Relate the planning process and decision making to the accomplishment of company goals.

Planning and Decision Making

Planning, the first managerial function, involves setting the organizational vision, values, goals, and objectives. Executives rate planning as the most valuable tool of their workbench. Part of the planning process involves the creation of a vision for the organization. A **vision** is more than a goal; it is a broad explanation of why the organization exists and where it is trying to head.[17] A vision gives the organization a sense of purpose and a set of values that unite workers in a common destiny.[18] **Values** are a set of fundamental beliefs that guide a business in the decisions it makes. Values guide strategic planning through to day-to-day decisions by being mindful of how all stakeholders will be treated. Vision informs values, and together they unite workers in a common purpose. Managing an organization without first establishing a vision can be counterproductive. It is like getting everyone in a rowboat excited about going somewhere, but not telling them exactly where. The boat will just keep changing directions rather than speeding toward an agreed-upon goal.

vision
An encompassing explanation of why the organization exists and where it is trying to head.

values
A set of fundamental beliefs that guide a business in the decisions it makes.

mission statement
An outline of the fundamental purposes of an organization.

Top management usually sets the vision for the organization and then works with others in the organization to establish a mission statement. A **mission statement** is an outline of the organization's fundamental purposes and it should address:

- the organization's self-concept;
- the organization's philosophy and goals;
- long-term survival;
- customer needs;
- social responsibility; and
- the nature of the organization's product or service.

goals
The broad, long-term accomplishments an organization wishes to attain.

objectives
Specific, measurable, short-term statements detailing how to achieve the organization's goals.

Figure 8.2 contains the mission statements for a number of well-known businesses. How well do their mission statements address all of the issues listed above?

The mission statement becomes the foundation for setting specific goals and selecting and motivating employees. **Goals** are the broad, long-term accomplishments an organization wishes to attain. Goals need to be mutually agreed on by workers and management. Thus, goal setting is often a team process.

Objectives are specific, short-term statements detailing *how to achieve* the organization's goals. One of your goals for reading this chapter, for example, may be to learn basic concepts of management. An objective you could use to achieve this goal is to answer the chapter's Progress Assessment questions correctly. Objectives must be measurable. For example, you can measure your progress in answering questions by determining what percentage you answer correctly over time.

Planning is a continuous process. It is unlikely that a plan that worked yesterday would be successful in today's market. Most planning follows a pattern. The procedure you would follow in planning your life and career is basically the same as that used by businesses for their plans. Planning answers two fundamental questions for businesses: What is the gap between where an organization is now and where it wants to be? and then, How can we get there from here?

FIGURE 8.2

SAMPLE COMPANY MISSION STATEMENTS

Maple Leaf Sports and Entertainment Ltd.'s mission: "Bring the world to its feet."
Google's mission: "To organize the world's information and make it universally accessible and useful."
Nike's mission: "To bring inspiration and innovation to every athlete* in the world. *If you have a body, you are an athlete."
Starbuck's mission: "To inspire and nurture the human spirit—one person, one cup and one neighborhood at a time."
Loblaw Companies Ltd.'s mission: "Live Life Well - Supports the needs and well-being of Canadians."
FGL Sports' mission: "To help Canadians live healthy, active lives."

Sources: According to the websites of MLSE, http://mlse.com/our-company/our-mission/; Google, https://www.google.com/about/our-company/; Nike, https://about.nike.com/; Starbuck's, https://www.starbucks.ca/about-us/company-information/mission-statement; Loblaw Companies Ltd., https://www.loblaw.ca/en/about-us/mission---values.html; and FGL Sports, http://www.fglsports.com/corporateMission.html. All accessed July 7, 2018.

1. *What is the situation now?* What are the success factors affecting the industry participants and how do we compare? What is the state of the economy and other environments? What opportunities exist for meeting people's needs? What products and customers are most profitable? Who are our major competitors? What threats are there to our business?

These questions frame the **SWOT analysis.**[19] This is an analysis of an organization's **S**trengths, **W**eaknesses, **O**pportunities, and **T**hreats—how can strengths be used and capitalized on, how can weaknesses be improved, how can opportunities be exploited, and how can threats be mitigated. A company begins such a process by soliciting input from all key stakeholders in order to create a general review of the business situation. Then it identifies its internal strengths and weaknesses, relative to its competitors.

SWOT analysis
A planning tool used to analyze an organization's strengths, weaknesses, opportunities, and threats.

These strengths and weaknesses are for the most part internal and therefore within the control of the organization. They include elements that are referred to as PRIMO-F: people, resources, innovation and ideas, marketing, operations, and finance. Next, a business environment analysis (you were introduced to some elements, such as the legal environment, in Chapter 1) is conducted. Opportunities and threats in the marketplace are identified—and, while they cannot always be controlled or anticipated, they most definitely affect the organization. Opportunities and threats include concepts referred to as PESTLE: political, economic, social, technological, legal, and environmental.

Figure 8.3 lists some of the potential issues companies consider when conducting a SWOT analysis: What external success factors affect the industry? How does our organization measure up to other organizations? What are our social objectives? What are our personal development objectives? What can we do to survive and prosper during a

FIGURE 8.3

SWOT ANALYSIS

This matrix identifies potential strengths, weaknesses, opportunities and threats organizations may consider in a SWOT analysis.

Potential Internal STRENGTHS	Potential Internal WEAKNESSES
• an acknowledged market leader • core competencies in key areas • proven and respected management team • well-conceived functional area strategies • cost advantages • better advertising campaigns	• no clear strategic direction • weak market image • subpar profitability • obsolete facilities • lack of managerial depth and talent • too narrow a product line
Potential External OPPORTUNITIES	**Potential External THREATS**
• ability to serve additional customer groups • expand product lines • ability to grow due to increases in market demands • falling trade barriers in attractive foreign markets • ability to transfer skills/technology to new products • complacency among rival firms	• recession and changing (negative) economic conditions • rising sales of substitute products (by competitors) • costly regulatory requirements • entry of low-cost foreign competitors • changing buyer needs and tastes

recession? A SWOT analysis is framed by the vision and when completed may result in the vision being revisited. All of the data are gathered and organized to reflect where a company is today and where a company would like to be. Differences between the two represent gaps. These gaps should then be addressed in the planning described next.

2. How can we get there from here? This is the most important part of planning. It takes four forms: strategic, tactical, operational, and contingency planning. See Figure 8.4 for a visual of this. Notice the continuous connection between the four forms. Not only does this illustrate the relationship between them, but also that planning is a continuous process where each of the forms is informed by another of the forms.

strategic planning
The process of determining the major goals of the organization and the policies and strategies for obtaining and using resources to achieve those goals.

Strategic planning outlines how the company will meet its objectives and goals. It provides the foundation for the policies, procedures, and strategies for obtaining and using resources to achieve those goals.[20] Policies are broad guides to action, and strategies determine the best way to use resources. At the strategic planning stage, top managers of the company decide which customers to serve, what goods or services to sell, and the geographic areas in which the firm will compete.[21]

For example, in response to the economic slump that impacted global and North American markets in 2008, Taco Bell introduced a "value menu" of items like cheese roll-ups and bean burritos with low prices. It also went after the "fourth-meal" (late-night) crowd and introduced several low-calorie, low-fat Fresco items. However, Blockbuster was not as successful in fighting off the introduction of new technology offered by Netflix and Hulu, making its brick and mortar stores obsolete.

In today's rapidly changing environment, strategic planning is becoming more difficult because changes are occurring so quickly that plans—even those set for just months into the future—may soon be obsolete. Think of how the used car dealership had to adjust the price for small fuel-efficient cars when the price of gas went from a dollar per litre to nearly two dollars and then dropped back to the dollar and a half range again.

FIGURE 8.4

PLANNING FUNCTIONS

Very few firms bother to make contingency plans. If something changes the market, such companies may be slow to respond. Most organizations do strategic, tactical, and operational planning.

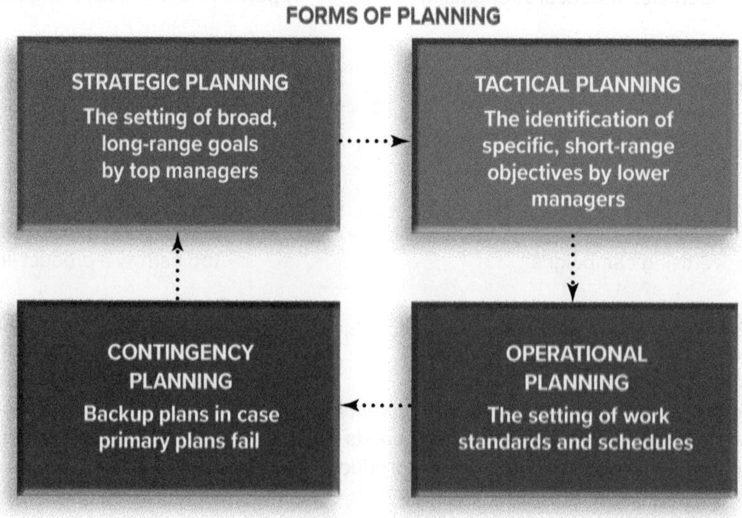

Clearly, some companies are making shorter-term plans that allow for quick responses to customer needs and requests. The goal is to be flexible and responsive to the market.[22]

Even though top managers are responsible for strategic planning, it is important for them to listen to those who might have the best strategic insights—employees. Employees whose ideas about strategy are ignored might leave. For example, when John Lasseter worked as a young animator for Disney, he lobbied the company to take computer animation seriously. He believed that animation technology would be central to Disney's future. The company didn't agree and fired him. Lasseter then joined Lucasfilm's growing computer graphics team. Later Disney realized that Lasseter was right and tried to lure him back, but it was too late. Lucasfilm became Pixar, the powerhouse animation company that created the *Toy Story* series, *Finding Nemo,* and many others. Two decades later Disney bought Pixar for $7.4 billion and made Lasseter chief creative officer.[23]

Clearly, some companies are making plans that allow for quick responses to customer needs and requests. The goal is to be flexible and responsive to the market. The Adapting to Change box talks about how some managers partner with robots to develop strategic plans.

Adapting *to* CHANGE

Will Strategy Robots Replace Managers?

Some machines can beat humans in just about any game, recommend cancer cures and diabetes treatments, manufacture products, make insurance underwriting and bank credit decisions, and a multitude of other tasks. But can machines produce strategic plans? Is there a robot capable of making big strategic plans, such as a plan for what a car company should do now that there is an increasing number of teens less interested in driving, ride services like Uber and Lyft are becoming increasingly popular, and self-driving cars are likely to be in our future? Well, robots aren't ready yet to make those "big-picture" decisions, but experts say their time may come.

© Juan Carlos Baena/Alamy

In fact, some computers now can handle more specific strategic problems. For example, IBM uses an algorithm rather than depending solely on human judgment to evaluate potential acquisition targets. Netflix uses analytics for its movie recommendation engine as well as to help decide what programs to create. Amazon uses 21 data systems to optimize supply chains, forecast inventory, forecast sales, optimize profits, and recommend purchases. All of the systems are tightly integrated with each other and human strategists.

Yes, humans still play a vital role in designing experiments and reviewing data traces in order to plan the evolution of the machines. For now, there is still a level of reasoning only human strategists can do. This ability to think strategically will be even more prized in this era of strategic human–machine partnerships.

Sources: Martin Reeves and Daichi Ueda, "Designing the Machines That Will Design Strategy," *Harvard Business Review,* April 18, 2016; Thomas H. Davenport, "Rise of the Strategy Machines," *Sloan Management Review,* Fall 2016; Tim O'Reilly, "Managing the Bots That Are Managing the Business," *Sloan Management Review,* Fall 2016; Landon Thomas, Jr., "At BlackRock, Machines Are Rising Over Managers to Pick Stocks," *The New York Times,* March 28, 2017.

tactical planning
The process of developing detailed, short-term statements about what is to be done, who is to do it, and how it is to be done.

Tactical planning is the process of developing detailed, short-term statements about what is to be done, who is to do it, and how it is to be done. Tactical planning is normally the responsibility of managers or teams of managers at *lower* levels of the organization, whereas strategic planning is the responsibility of the *top* managers of the firm (e.g., the president and vice-presidents of the organization). Tactical planning, for example, involves setting annual budgets and deciding on other details and activities necessary to meet the strategic objectives. If the strategic plan of a truck manufacturer, for example, is to sell more trucks in northern Canada, the tactical plan might be to fund more research of northern truck drivers' wants and needs, and to plan advertising to reach those customers.

operational planning
The process of setting work standards and schedules necessary to implement the company's tactical objectives.

Operational planning is the process of setting work standards and schedules necessary to implement the company's tactical objectives. Whereas strategic planning views the organization as a whole, operational planning focuses on the specific responsibilities of supervisors, department managers, and individual employees. Operational plans can include operational budgets. You will read about budgets in more detail in Chapter 17. The operational plan is the department manager's tool for daily and weekly operations. An operational plan could also include, say, the specific dates for certain truck parts to be completed and the quality specifications those parts must meet. You will read about operations management in more detail in Chapter 10.

contingency planning
The process of preparing alternative courses of action that may be used if the primary plans do not achieve the organization's objectives.

Contingency planning is the process of preparing alternative courses of action that may be used if the primary plans do not achieve the organization's objectives. The economic and competitive environments change so rapidly that it is wise to have alternative plans of action ready in anticipation of such changes. For example, if an organization does not meet its sales goals by a certain date, the contingency plan may call for more advertising or a cut in prices at that time.

Some companies see opportunities where others see threats. Morneau Shepell Inc. provides global benefits consulting, administration systems, and outsourcing services. Morneau Shepell believes that most companies view contingency planning solely as a tool to prevent operational shutdowns. A company should be able to mitigate the potential damage and financial loss resulting from an unforeseen emergency or catastrophe, but it encourages companies to re-evaluate their thinking regarding contingency planning and the importance of anticipating health care–related emergencies (HREs). For example, at the time of the widespread SARS epidemic in 2003, a survey to examine how Canadian businesses were managing the health crisis found only 11 percent of the employers had a human resource policy to address HREs. The benefits of an HRE contingency plan include ensuring business continuity, reducing risk to employees and their dependents, maintaining productivity, and minimizing the possibility of litigation.[24]

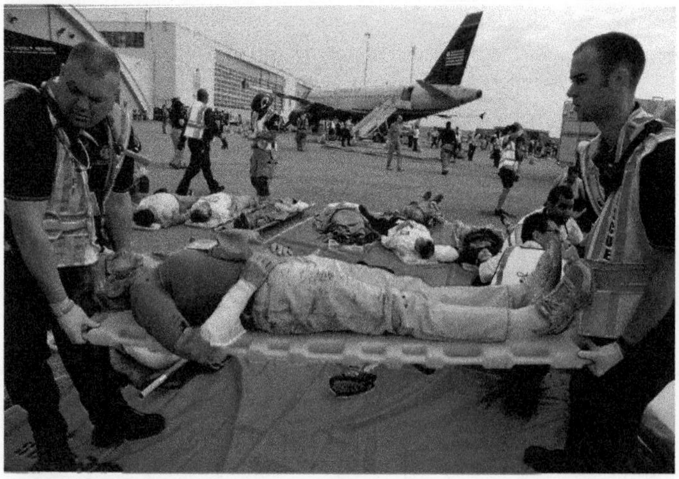

Organizations of all kinds need contingency plans for unexpected events. Here, airport first responders participate in a drill with volunteers who are pretending to be victims in a simulated airplane crash. What contingency plans are you aware of on your campus or at work?

Crisis planning is a part of contingency planning. **Crisis planning** involves reacting to sudden changes in the environment.[25] For example, many cities and businesses have developed plans to respond to terrorist attacks. You can imagine how important such plans would be to hospitals, airlines, the police, and public transportation authorities. In short, crisis planning is a critical component of contingency planning that requires understanding and acceptance throughout the whole organization. You will read more about risk management in Online Supplement 2.

crisis planning
Involves reacting to sudden changes in the environment.

Instead of creating detailed strategic plans, the leaders of market-based companies (companies that respond quickly to changes in competition or to other environmental changes) often simply set direction. They want to stay flexible, listen to customers, and seize opportunities—expected or not. Think of how stores selling to teenagers must adapt to style changes.[26] The opportunities, however, must fit into the company's overall goals and objectives; if not, the company could lose its focus.

Before we consider decision making, let us summarize some of the points in this chapter. A vision ("WHERE we are going . . ."), in combination with values (HOW we will treat our stakeholders . . .), and the mission statement ("Our purpose IS . . ."), provides direction for the company. A company's objectives (WHAT we want to accomplish) are linked to its strategy (HOW we will accomplish the objectives). So, there is a progression from vision and values, to mission, to objectives, and to strategy. Once the strategy has been established, plans must be developed and implemented to ensure that objectives are met. There is never a strategy without there first being an objective. A SWOT analysis alone has little effect unless you match it to the company's strategy and plan.

Clearly, then, much of management and planning requires decision making. The Spotlight on Small Business box illustrates how one unique small business handles planning and decision making.

Decision Making: Finding the Best Alternative

All management functions require decision making. **Decision making** is choosing among two or more alternatives. It sounds easier on paper than it is in practice. In fact, decision making is the heart of all management functions. The *rational decision-making* model is a series of steps that managers often follow to make logical, intelligent, and well-founded decisions.[27] These steps can be thought of as the six Ds of decision making:

decision making
Choosing among two or more alternatives.

1. Define the situation.
2. Describe and collect needed information.
3. Develop alternatives.
4. Decide which alternative is best.
5. Do what is indicated (begin implementation).
6. Determine whether the decision was a good one and follow up.

Spotlight *On* SMALL BUSINESS

I'd Rather Be Blue

Some of the best-managed organizations can be found in the most unusual situations. Consider, for example, three entrepreneurs whose product involved shaving their heads, slathering themselves with blue paint, and drumming on homemade instruments such as PVC pipe. Enter the Blue Man Group. The original Blue Men—Matt Goldman, Phil Stanton, and Chris Wink—manage an organization of over 500 employees, 70 of whom appear nightly as Blue Men in cities around the world. Their Megastar World Tour included a number of shows in central Canada featuring their unique music, comedy, and multimedia theatrics.

Like the founders of any other company, the Blue Man Group creators knew they had to tinker with their product if they wanted to expand and be successful. Planning and organization were critical. The partners locked themselves away for several days to write a detailed 132-page Blue Man operating manual. Writing the manual made the partners realize the vast market potential for their concept, but it also taught them the importance of managing the product's growth and everyday operations. The three leaders also knew they needed to think strategically about how to build their business and maintain audience interest. The result was their first tour in Latin America and expansion into other areas including albums, film scores, orchestra performances, and advertising campaigns.

In 2017, the Montreal-based circus group, Cirque du Soleil, acquired Blue Man Productions in an effort to diversify its entertainment offerings. Given Blue Man's origins as street performers, it should be a great fit!

© 360b / Shutterstock.com

Sources: Mark Rendell, "Cirque du Soleil Acquires Blue Man Group Production Company," *The Globe and Mail*, July 16, 2017; "Blue Man Group to Launch First Latin American Tour this Summer," BroadwayWorld.com, May 1, 2015, http://www.broadwayworld.com/brazil/article/Blue-Man-Group-to-Launch-First-Latin-American-Tour-This-Summer-20150501#; Liz Welch, "How We Did It: The Blue Man Group," *Inc.*, August 2008; and Blue Man Group, www.blueman.com, accessed January 29, 2009.

problem solving
The process of solving the everyday problems that occur. Problem solving is less formal than decision making and usually calls for quicker action.

brainstorming
Generating as many solutions to a problem as possible in a short period of time with no censoring of ideas.

Managers do not always go through this six-step process. Sometimes decisions have to be made *on the spot*—when little information is available. Managers must make good decisions in all such circumstances.

Problem solving is the process of solving the everyday problems that occur. It is less formal than the decision-making process and usually calls for quicker action to resolve everyday issues. Problem-solving teams are made up of two or more workers who are given an assignment to solve a specific problem (e.g., Why are customers not using our service policies?). Problem-solving techniques that companies use include **brainstorming**, which involves generating as many solutions as possible in a short period of time with no censoring of ideas, and **PMI**, which includes listing all the **p**luses for a solution in one column, all the **m**inuses in another, and the **i**nteresting points for each solution in a third column.

PMI is a tool developed by Edward de Bono as part of his work on lateral and creative thinking strategies. You can practise using the PMI system on almost all of your decisions. For example, should you stay home and study tonight? You would list all benefits of your choice (Pluses) in one column: better grades, improved self-esteem, more responsible, and so forth. In the other column, you would put the negatives (Minuses): boredom, less fun, etc. In the third column you would write down the outcomes of taking the action, which often helps to clarify your decision. We hope that the pluses outweigh the minuses most of the time, and that you study often, but sometimes it is best to go out and have fun. In that case, the Interesting would be having fun in a way that would not hurt your grades or job prospects.

PMI
A creative thinking strategy that lists all the pluses, minuses, and interesting points for a solution in separate columns.

PROGRESS ASSESSMENT

- What is the difference between goals and objectives?
- What does a company analyze when it does a SWOT analysis?
- What is the difference between strategic, tactical, and operational planning?
- What are the six Ds in decision making?

Organizing: Creating a Unified System

LO4

Describe the organizing function of management.

After managers have planned a course of action, they must organize the firm to accomplish their goals. Operationally, organizing means allocating resources (such as funds for various departments), assigning tasks, and establishing procedures for accomplishing the organizational objectives. When organizing, a manager develops a framework that relates all workers, tasks, and resources to each other. That framework is called the *organizational structure.* In Chapter 9, we will look at examples of several organizational structures and will review some of the challenges in developing an organization structure.

Most organizations draw a diagram showing these relationships. This tool is called an organization chart. An **organization chart** is a visual device that shows relationships among people and divides the organization's work; it shows who is accountable for the completion of specific work and who reports to whom. Figure 8.5 shows a simple one. Each rectangle indicates a position (and usually who holds this position) within the organization. The chart plots who reports to whom (as indicated by the lines) and who is responsible for each task. For example, in Figure 8.5, manager C is the finance manager, and this middle manager reports directly to the president. Reporting directly to the finance manager are three first-line supervisors and in turn, three employees report directly to each of these first-line supervisors. The corporate hierarchy illustrated on the organization chart includes top, middle, and first-line managers. The problems involved in developing an organization structure will be discussed later in the text. For now, it is important to know that the corporate hierarchy usually includes three levels of management (see Figure 8.6).

organization chart
A visual device that shows relationships among people and divides the organization's work; it shows who is accountable for the completion of specific work and who reports to whom.

Top management (the highest level of management) consists of the president and other key company executives who develop strategic plans. Terms you are likely to see

top management
Highest level of management, consisting of the president and other key company executives, who develop strategic plans.

FIGURE 8.5

TYPICAL ORGANIZATION CHART

This is a snapshot of a rather standard chart with managers for major functions and supervisors reporting to the managers In this example, each supervisor manages three employees.

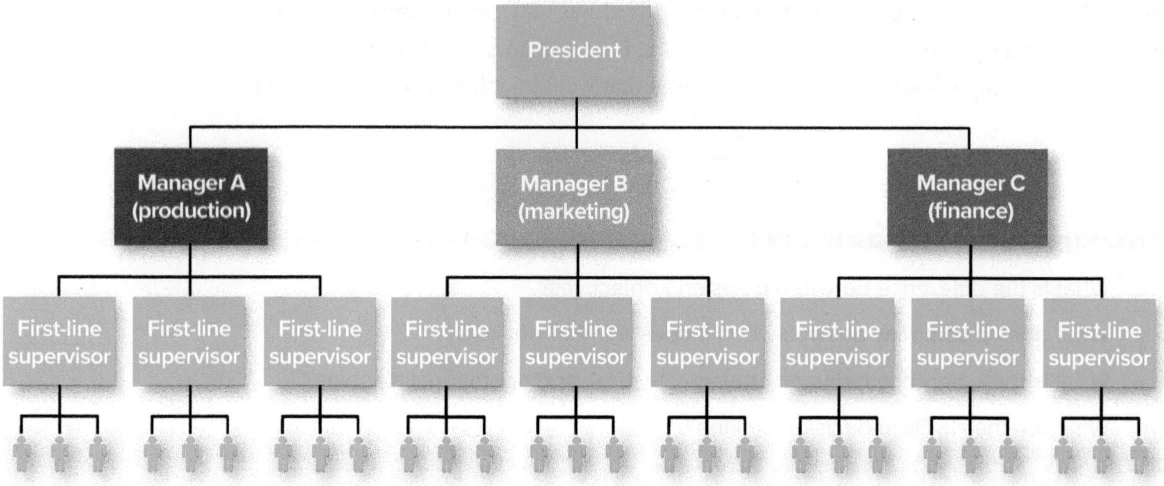

FIGURE 8.6

LEVELS OF MANAGEMENT

This figure shows the three levels of management. In many firms, there are several levels within middle management. Many firms have eliminated middle-level managers because fewer staff are needed to oversee self-managed teams and higher skilled employees.

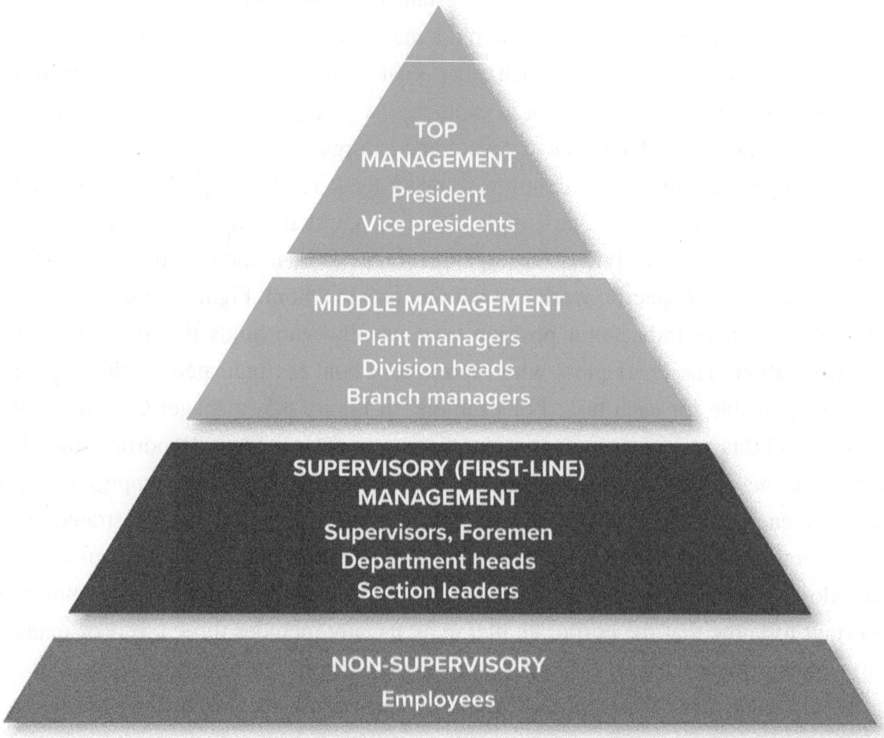

often are chief executive officer (CEO), chief operating officer (COO), chief financial officer (CFO), and chief information officer (CIO), or in some companies, chief knowledge officer (CKO). The CEO is often the president of the firm and is responsible for all top-level decisions in the firm. The CEO and president are the same person in a majority of large companies, such as United Parcel Services, John Deere, and General Electric.

CEOs are responsible for introducing change into an organization.[28] The COO is responsible for putting those changes into effect. His or her tasks include structuring work, controlling operations, and rewarding people to ensure that everyone strives to carry out the leader's vision. Today, many companies are eliminating the COO function as a cost-cutting measure and assigning that role to the CEO. The CFO is responsible for obtaining funds, planning budgets, collecting funds, and so on. The CIO or CKO is responsible for getting the right information to other managers so they can make correct decisions. CIOs are more important than ever to the success of their companies given the crucial role that information technology serves in every aspect of business. Many companies are simplifying their executive committee by combining some of the positions, like COO and CFO, which they believe provides better focus.[29]

Loblaw Companies Limited has been making significant changes in its operations over the past few years. Faced with the growing presence of Walmart and general merchandising distribution problems, which resulted in significant losses for a few years, they are looking to Galen Weston Jr., the executive chairman and president, to implement a series of strategic initiatives to restore their former glory. Loblaws is refocusing on its strong brands, including President's Choice, re-pricing some staple products to provide best-value-for-money, and improving efficiencies in its supply chain. While profits slowly improve the company is still involved in a major overhaul of its infrastructure, which included a decrease of top management jobs at its head office and an increase of supervisory management positions at new store openings.[30]

Middle management includes general managers, division managers, and branch and plant managers (in your post-secondary institution, deans and department/area heads) who are responsible for tactical planning and controlling. Many firms have eliminated some middle managers through downsizing, and have given the remaining managers more employees to supervise.

Supervisory management includes those who are directly responsible for supervising workers and evaluating their daily performance; they are often known as first-line managers (or supervisors) because they are the first level above workers.[31]

middle management
The level of management that includes general managers, division managers, and branch and plant managers, who are responsible for tactical planning and controlling.

supervisory management
Managers who are directly responsible for supervising workers and evaluating their daily performance.

Tasks and Skills at Different Levels of Management

Few people are trained to be good managers. Usually a person learns how to be a skilled accountant or sales representative or production-line worker, and then—because of his or her technical skills—is selected to be a manager. Once someone becomes a manager she or he spends more time supporting those people they supervise, showing them how to do things, helping them, supervising them, and generally being very active in the operating task. Robert Katz developed a model to explain the types of skills necessary to be a good manager, and the mix of these skills through the various management levels.

The further up the managerial ladder a person moves, the less important his or her original job skills become. At the top of the ladder, the need is for people who are

technical skills
The ability to perform tasks in a specific discipline or department.

human relations skills
The ability to communicate and motivate, enabling managers to work through and with people.

conceptual skills
The ability to picture the organization as a whole and the relationships among its various parts.

visionaries, planners, organizers, coordinators, communicators, morale builders, and motivators.[32] Figure 8.7 shows that a manager must have three categories of skills:

1. **Technical skills** involve the ability to perform tasks in a specific discipline (such as selling a product or developing software) or department (such as marketing or information systems).
2. **Human relations skills** involve communication and motivation; they enable managers to work through and with people. Such skills also include those associated with leadership, coaching, morale building, delegating, training and development, and help and supportiveness.
3. **Conceptual skills** involve the ability to picture the organization as a whole and the relationships among its various parts. Conceptual skills are needed in planning, organizing, controlling, systems development, problem analysis, decision making, coordinating, and delegating (see the Reaching Beyond our Borders box for more insight about skills training for top managers).

While it is not specifically stated, you can see how time-management skills are a necessary component of each one of these categories of skills. Successful managers effectively handle the daily points of contact that require their attention. This includes a high volume of phone calls, interruptions, meetings, and e-mails.

Looking at Figure 8.7, you will notice that first-line managers need to be skilled in all three areas. However, most of their time is spent on technical and human relations tasks (assisting operating personnel, giving directions, etc.). First-line managers spend little time on conceptual tasks. Top managers, in contrast, need to use few technical skills. Instead, almost all of their time is devoted to human relations and conceptual tasks. A person who is competent at a low level of management may not be competent at higher levels, and vice versa. The skills needed are different at each level of management.

FIGURE 8.7

SKILLS NEEDED AT VARIOUS LEVELS OF MANAGEMENT

All managers need human relations skills. At the top, managers need strong conceptual skills and rely less on technical skills. First-line managers need strong technical skills and rely less on conceptual skills. Middle managers need to have a balance between technical and conceptual skills.

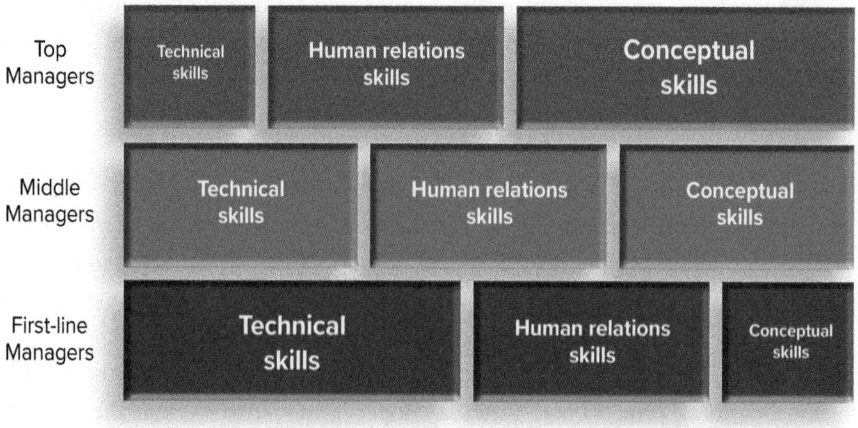

Reaching *Beyond* OUR BORDERS

Back to School for Top Managers

As the overseer of an organization's "big picture," CEOs need to have strong conceptual skills. In today's global market, the scope of those skills is expanding rapidly as businesses increasingly focus on globalization in their long-term planning.

The shift from a country-focused company to a global-focused company increases the CEO "to-do" list. Business leaders need to study a country's political, legal, and regulatory systems and the impact of each system upon important business functions such as supply chains, capital markets, and the productivity of human resources. It's also critical to thoroughly understand a nation's culture and respect its strengths and challenges.

There isn't a single global market, but rather a complex network of globally connected "local markets." Such "local markets" require their own set of local training, development, and assessment standards. Aligning a company's business applications across such diverse networks is no simple task. However, leaders at companies such as Coca-Cola, Nestlé, and IBM have done a noteworthy job.

© Rawpixel/Shutterstock

Samuel Palmisano, former CEO of IBM, perhaps summed up the global management challenge best in his book *Adapting from Re-Think: A Path to the Future.* In it he states, "The fundamental question for companies is not whether to compete globally, but how to compete globally." That's the challenge CEOs will have to answer company-by-company as they refine their conceptual skills.

Sources: Josh Bersin, "The World Is Not Global, It's Local," *Forbes*, April 23, 2013; Samuel J. Palmisano, "The New Era for Global Enterprise," *Bloomberg Businessweek*, March 28, 2014; and Rana Foroohar, "Globalization in Reverse," *Time*, April 7 2014.

Staffing: Getting and Keeping the Right People

The right kind of incentive is needed to get the right kind of people to staff an organization. For example, Google's gourmet chefs cook up free lunches, dinners, and snacks for employees. Would such an incentive appeal to you? How important to you is pay relative to other incentives?

staffing
A management function that includes hiring, motivating, and retaining the best people available to accomplish the company's objectives.

Staffing is recruiting, hiring, motivating, and retaining the best people available to accomplish the company's objectives. Today, staffing is critical, especially in the Internet and high-tech areas. At most high-tech companies, like Google, Sony, and Microsoft, the primary capital equipment is brainpower. A firm with innovative and creative workers can go from start-up to major competitor in just a few years.[33]

Many people are not willing to work at companies unless they are treated well and get fair pay. They may leave to find a better balance between work and home.[34] Staffing is becoming a large part of each manager's assignment, and all managers need to co-operate with the human resource department of her or his organization in order to attract and maintain effective workers. Chapter 12 is devoted to human resource issues, including staffing.

LO5

Explain the differences between leaders and managers, and describe the various leadership styles.

Leading: Providing Continuous Vision and Values

In business literature there's a trend toward separating the notion of management from that of leadership. One person might be a good manager but not a good leader. Another might be a good leader without being a good manager. One difference between managers and leaders is that managers strive to produce order and stability, whereas leaders embrace and manage change. Leadership is creating a vision for others to follow, establishing corporate values and ethics, and transforming the way the organization does business to improve its effectiveness and efficiency. Good leaders motivate workers and create the environment for workers to motivate themselves.[35] Management is the carrying out of the leadership's vision.[36]

Leaders must therefore:

- *Communicate a vision and rally others around that vision.* The leader should be openly sensitive to the concerns of followers, give them responsibility, and win their trust. A successful leader must influence the actions of others. Ellen Kullman took the reins at DuPont in the middle of a crisis. Nonetheless, she set the tone for growth and prosperity in the future.
- *Establish corporate values.* These values (as discussed earlier in this chapter) include a concern for employees, for customers, for the environment, and for the quality of the company's products. When companies set their business goals, they are defining the values of the company as well. The most important trait that others look for in a leader is honesty, followed by forward looking vision.
- *Promote corporate ethics.* Ethics include an unfailing demand for honesty and an insistence that everyone in the company is treated fairly. That is why we stress ethical decision making throughout this text (as covered in the Making Ethical Decision boxes within each chapter). Many business people have made the news by giving away huge amounts to charity, thus setting a model of social concern for their employees and others.[37]

Making ETHICAL DECISIONS

What Do You Tell the Team?

First-line managers assist in the decisions made by their department heads. The department heads retain full responsibility for the decisions—if a plan succeeds, it's their success; if a plan fails, it's their failure. Now imagine this: As a first-line manager, you have new information that your department head hasn't seen yet. The findings in this report indicate that your manager's recent plans are sure to fail. If the plans do fail, the manager will probably be demoted, and you're the most likely candidate to fill the vacancy. Will you give your department head the report? What is the ethical thing to do? What might be the consequences of your decision?

© stockbroker/123RF

- *Embrace transformational change.* A leader's most important job may be to transform the way the company does business so that it is more effective (does things better) and efficient (uses fewer resources to accomplish the same objectives).[38] The Seeking Sustainability box illustrates how management can provide leadership in the area of sustainability.
- *Stress accountability and responsibility.* One thing we have learned from the global recession of 2008–09 is that leaders need to be responsible for their actions and held accountable for their actions. A key word that has emerged from the crisis is transparency. **Transparency** is the presentation of a company's facts and figures in a way that is clear, accessible, and apparent to all stakeholders. Governments are trying to make companies (and themselves) more transparent so that everyone is more aware of what is happening to the economy and to specific businesses and government agencies.[39]

transparency
The presentation of a company's facts and figures in a way that is clear, accessible, and apparent to all stakeholders.

All organizations need leaders, and all employees can help lead. You do not have to be a manager to perform a leadership function. That is, any employee can motivate others to work well, add to a company's ethical environment, and report ethical lapses when they occur.

Over the past 10 years, there has been an increasing trend in compensation packages that involve share ownership for top executives. These packages have been justified as necessary

Seeking SUSTAINABILITY

Leadership in Sustainability

Sustainability was introduced and defined in Chapters 1 and 5. Sustainability has now become a leadership issue for business. This is due, in part, to the fact that customers make purchase decisions based on the sustainable practices of a business, and companies realizing that through sustainable practices they can also reduce their costs if they implement sustainable practices.

Leadership is shown by making sustainability part and parcel of how a business operates. Leadership opportunities can be found from how a business sources its inputs, to how it produces the goods or services, to how it distributes and services products. Furthermore, standards are emerging that measure sustainability, including measures of energy efficiency, carbon emissions, water usage, and labour practices (examples were discussed in Chapter 5).

As businesses become more mature in their view of sustainability they have moved from initially wanting to protect their value through compliance with regulations to embedding real, measurable, ongoing commitments to sustainability that they believe will differentiate them in the market.

The Network for Business Sustainability is a community of managers and researchers who advance the "profits, people, and planet" approach. Leaders from companies with a strong sustainability reputation share their insights with leaders from other organizations.

How might each management function (planning, organizing, leading, controlling) be applied to sustainability?

Sources: Tima Bansal, "Sustainability is not a buzzword. It's the future for Canadian business," *The Globe and Mail*, April 23, 2015, http://www.theglobeandmail.com/report-on-business/careers/leadership-lab/sustainability-is-not-a-buzzword-its-the-future-for-canadian-business/article23990341/; PwC, www.pwc.com/ca/en/sustainability/publications.jhtml; Sustainability Advantage, www.sustainabilityadvantage.com/; Simply Sustain, www.simplysustain.com/a/Sustainability/Ourviews/tabid/57/Default.aspx; and Network for Business Sustainability, https://nbs.net/.

autocratic leadership A style that involves making managerial decisions without consulting others.

participative (democratic) leadership A style that consists of managers and employees working together to make decisions.

free-rein leadership A style that involves managers setting objectives and employees being relatively free to do whatever it takes to accomplish those objectives.

to attract and keep good leaders, but some critics argue that they actually inhibit leadership. McGill University's Henry Mintzberg has been vocal in his disagreement with the increasing CEO compensation packages. In his view, many CEOs focus solely on the short-term increase in the share value of the company and their bonuses. "Find me a chief executive who refuses those bonuses, who takes the long-term view and says his team will share the spoils of their mandate in 10 years' time, and I'll show you a leader," he said.[40] Do you agree that top executives should receive such lucrative packages in today's environment?

Leadership Styles

Nothing has challenged researchers in the area of management more than the search for the "best" leadership traits, behaviours, or styles. Thousands of studies have tried to identify characteristics that distinguish leaders. Intuitively, you would conclude about the same thing they did; leadership styles are hard to pin down. Some leaders are well groomed and tactful, while others are unkempt and abrasive—yet the latter may be just as effective as the former.

Just as no one set of traits describes a leader, no one style of leadership works best in all situations. Even so, we can look at a few of the most commonly recognized leadership styles (see Figure 8.8) and see how they may be effective:

© Tiffany Brown/Redux

Tony Hsieh, CEO of Zappos.com, views culture as his company's top priority. He believes that all other aspects of business fall easily into place as long as employees are happy and motivated by their work. Hsieh got rid of middle managers and allowed employees to make more decisions on their own. Do you think you would thrive in a self-managed workplace?

1. **Autocratic leadership** involves making managerial decisions without consulting others. Such a style is effective in emergencies and when absolute "followership" is needed—for example, when fighting fires. Autocratic leadership is also effective sometimes with new, relatively unskilled workers who need clear direction and guidance. Former Los Angeles Lakers Coach Phil Jackson used an autocratic leadership style to take the team to three consecutive National Basketball Association championships in his first three seasons. By following his leadership, a group of highly skilled individuals became a winning team. Do you think he is using the same leadership style as president as he did as coach? What kind of leadership do you see being used most successfully in baseball, football, and other areas? Can you think of a situation where Jackson's leadership style makes sense?
2. **Participative (democratic) leadership** consists of managers and employees working together to make decisions. Research has found that employee participation in decisions may not always increase effectiveness, but it usually increases job satisfaction.[41] Many large organizations like Google, Apple, IBM, Cisco, and AT&T, and most smaller organizations have been highly successful using a democratic style of leadership that values traits such as flexibility, good listening skills, and empathy. Employees meet to discuss and resolve management issues by giving everyone an opportunity to contribute to decisions.
3. **Free-rein leadership** involves managers setting objectives and employees being relatively free to do whatever it takes

FIGURE 8.8

VARIOUS LEADERSHIP STYLES

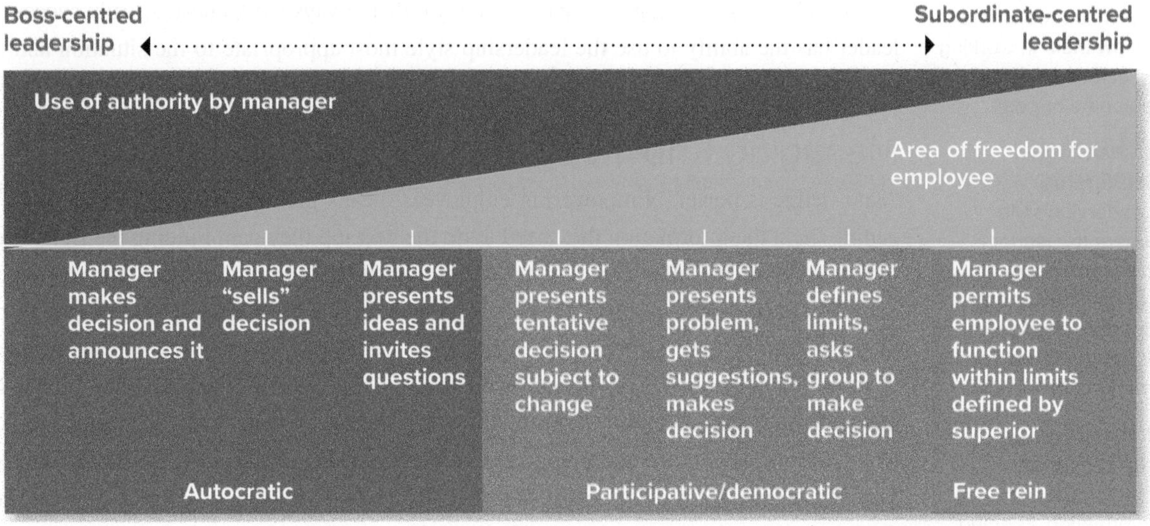

Source: Robert Tannenbaum; Warren Schmidt, "How to Choose a Leadership Pattern," *Harvard Business Review*. (May/June 1973).

to accomplish those objectives. Free-rein leadership is often the most successful leadership style in organizations in which managers supervise doctors, professors, engineers, or other professionals. The traits needed by managers in such organizations include warmth, friendliness, and understanding. More and more firms are adopting this style of leadership with at least some of their employees.

Individual leaders rarely fit neatly into just one of these categories. Researchers illustrate leadership as a continuum with varying amounts of employee participation, ranging from purely boss-centred leadership to subordinate-centred leadership

Other research has identified two other styles that can be included in this discussion. **Transformational leadership** occurs when visionary leaders can influence others to follow them in working to achieve a desired outcome or goal. This leadership style works best in situations where dramatic organizational change is required. Can you think of leaders who have been transformational for their organization?

Transactional leadership is associated with employees who are motivated by a system of reward. Here the leader is given power to assign tasks and their successful completion earns rewards and reinforcement. The difference between this style and the autocratic style is that with the former the source of motivation is a reward, while with the latter it is punishment.

Which leadership style is best? Research suggests that it depends largely on a combination of factors such as organizational goals and values, those being led, and the situation. A manager may be autocratic but friendly with a new trainee, democratic with an experienced

Alan Mulally, former CEO of Ford Motors, managed to lead the U.S. auto manufacturer back to profitability after the global economic recession—without a government financial bailout. The reason for this success was the leadership style of the most authoritarian CEO that Ford has seen since its founder, Henry Ford. When an organization is under extreme pressure, why might autocratic leadership be necessary?

transformational leadership
Leadership style that occurs when leaders can influence others to follow them in working to achieve a desired outcome or goal.

transactional leadership
Leadership style where the leader is given the power to assign tasks and their successful completion leads to rewards and reinforcement.

knowledge management
Finding the right information, keeping the information in a readily accessible place, and making the information known to everyone in the firm.

employee, and free-rein with a trusted long-term supervisor. No single leadership trait is effective in all situations nor is there one leadership style that will always be effective. A successful leader in one organization may not be successful in another organization.

There's no such thing as a leadership style that always works best. A truly successful leader has the ability to use the leadership style most appropriate to the situation and the employees involved.

Managing Knowledge

"Knowledge is power." Empowering employees means giving them knowledge—that is, getting them the information they need to do the best job they can. Finding the right information, keeping the information in a readily accessible place, and making the information known to everyone in the firm constitutes **knowledge management**. For example, Canadian Tire was the first major Canadian retailer to use an Internet-based eLearning program. eLearning is an online training and education program that delivers product knowledge and skills training on everything from plumbing to paint mixing. The program is credited with improved customer and employee satisfaction levels. According to Janice Wismer, former vice-president of human resources, "People say the lessons have increased their confidence, that they're happier working here because the company is committing to their growth and development."[42] This is good news for store sales.

Today there is no shortage of information to manage. In fact, the amount of data gathered has grown so much that the term *big data* has become a popular term to describe the vast collection of available information. These data are collected from both traditional sources like sales transactions and digital sources like social media from both inside and outside the company.

The first step to developing a knowledge management system is determining what knowledge is most important. Do you want to know more about your customers? Do you want to know more about competitors? What kind of information would make the company more effective or more efficient or more responsive to the marketplace? Once you have decided what you need to know, you set out to find answers to those questions.

Knowledge management tries to keep people from reinventing the wheel—that is, duplicating the work of gathering information—every time a decision needs to be made. A company really progresses when each person in the firm asks continually, "What do I still not know?" and "Whom should I be asking?" It is just as important to know what is not working as what is working. Employees and managers now have e-mail, text messaging, and other means of keeping in touch with each other, with customers, and with other stakeholders. The key to success is learning how to process that information effectively and turn it into knowledge that everyone can use to improve processes and procedures. That is one way to

At fast food chains, the typical approach for managers is to supervise and direct employees rather than empower employees. What do you think are some of the consequences for managers who do not empower their staff with decision-making authority?

enable workers to be more effective. (Recall that there is a brief discussion in Appendix A: Using Technology to Manage Information, about information technology and knowledge management.) See the Adapting to Change box for an example of how GM used social media to manage information customers needed during a time of crisis for the company.

Adapting *to* CHANGE

Using Social Media During the Worst of Times

When a company struggles with a recall of 1.6 million of their products that are linked to 13 deaths, managers naturally expect a harsh backlash from consumers. This was the situation Mary Barra faced, just a few short weeks after being named CEO of General Motors (GM). GM was forced to recall 2006 Saturn Ions and five other models because of a defective ignition switch that, if bumped or weighed down by a heavy key ring, could turn off, shutting down the engine and disabling the car's air bags.

To make matters worse for the company, investigations indicated that there were employees within the company who knew about the defective switch years ago; yet the problem was not corrected. At the deadline for submitting claims for compensation in early 2015, over 4000 claims had been submitted for review to receive funds from the Victim Compensation Fund.

Barra knew it was impossible to undo the damage already done. She decided the best path was to try to redefine GM as an open, transparent, listening organization that customers could trust. One of her first moves was appointing a vehicle-safety czar whose job is to quickly identify and resolve any safety issues facing the company. She also wanted worried owners of recalled vehicles to know that GM was listening and ready to address their concerns. To achieve this, GM's social media group was deployed to reach out to impacted customers to explain their cars were drivable while they waited for repairs so long as extra items were not attached to their key rings. Despite such assurances, GM provided more than 6000 loaner cars to customers who were skeptical about their car's safety. The company's social media staffers also set up dealership appointments with frustrated owners to have the problem fixed.

© Michael Spooneybarger/Reuters

CEO Barra's overriding concern was that the recall not permanently tarnish GM's image going forward. The company had made strong financial progress since emerging from bankruptcy and a government bailout. She knew that when it came to social media like Facebook and Twitter, a customer's perception of a brand is influenced by what an organization does and other people's opinion of it. Therefore, GM's social media commitment was to search for complaints, respond quickly, and solve the problems. Professor Roland Rust from the University of Maryland, an expert in managing brand crises, believed GM's responsiveness online was "absolutely the right thing to do." According to Rust, "If they didn't respond to customers, then those customers are going to continue to flame them." Mary Barra certainly hopes he is right and GM's response was on target. For right now, it remains to be seen whether GM can repair its internal quality-control issues and whether consumers will trust its products again.

Sources: James Healey, "GM victims' fund closes with 51 deaths – so far," *USA Today*, February 2, 2015, http://www.usatoday.com/story/money/2015/02/02/gm-ignition-switch-recall-death-victims-compensation/22741027/; "GM ignition-switch victims accepting offers, Feinberg says," *Automotive News*, January 30, 2015, http://www.autonews.com/article/20150130/OEM11/150139985/gm-ignition-switch-victims-accepting-offers-feinberg-says; Vince Bond Jr., "GM Uses Social Media to Respond to Customer Gripes," *Automotive News*, March 8, 2014; Lindsay Gellman, "Companies Turn to Social-Media Coaches," *The Wall Street Journal*, March 26, 2014; and Vindu Goel, "G.M. Uses Social Media to Manage Customers and Its Reputation," *The New York Times*, March 23, 2014.

PROGRESS ASSESSMENT

- What are some characteristics of leadership today that make leaders different from traditional managers?
- Explain the differences between autocratic and democratic leadership styles.
- What is the first step in developing a knowledge management system?

Controlling: Making Sure It Works

LO6

Summarize the five steps of the control function of management.

The control function involves measuring performance relative to the planned objectives and standards, rewarding people for work well done, and then taking corrective action when necessary. Thus, the control process (see Figure 8.9) is the heart of the management system because it provides the feedback that enables managers and workers to adjust to any deviations from plans and to changes in the environment that have affected performance. Controlling consists of five steps:

1. Establish clear performance standards. This ties the planning function to the control function. Without clear standards, control is impossible.
2. Monitor and record actual performance (results).

FIGURE 8.9

THE CONTROL PROCESS

The control process is based on clear standards. Without such standards, the other steps are difficult, if not impossible. With clear standards, performance measurement is relatively easy and the proper action can be taken.

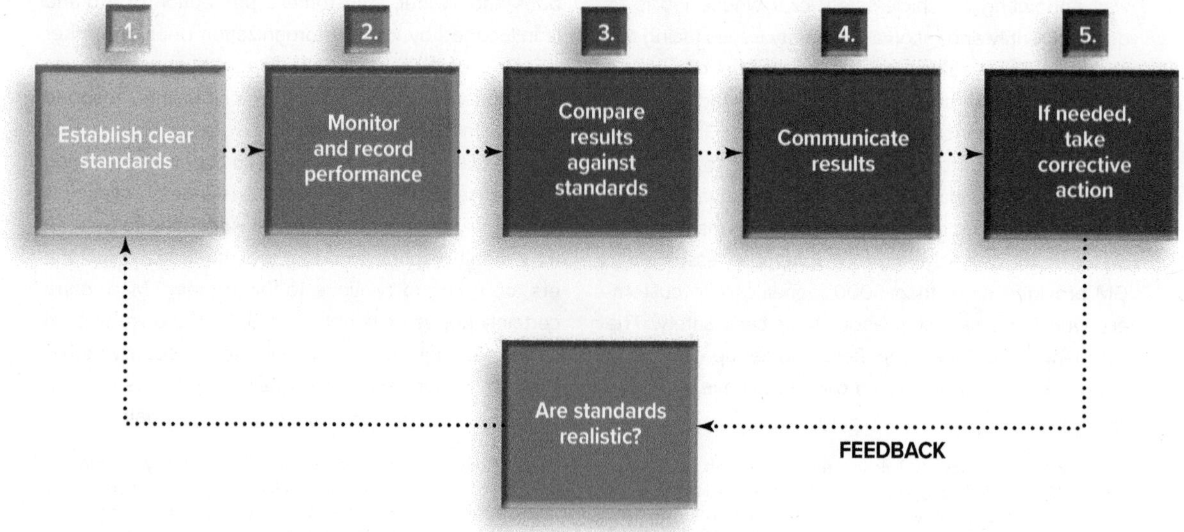

3. Compare results against plans and standards.
4. Communicate results and deviations to the employees involved.
5. Take corrective action when needed and provide positive feedback for work well done.

This control process is ongoing throughout the year. Continuous monitoring ensures that if corrective action is required, there is enough time to implement changes. When corrective action is necessary, the decision-making process is a useful tool to apply (recall the six Ds of decision making). Simply, managers are encouraged to review the situation and, based on collected information, develop alternatives with their staff and implement the best alternative. Or, in some circumstances, if significant changes have occurred, management can implement a contingency plan (as discussed earlier in the chapter). The focus is to meet the standards that were initially established during the planning stage or the standards that have since been modified. Since this process is continuous, it may take several attempts before standards are successfully met.

The control system's weakest link tends to be the setting of standards. To measure results against standards, the standards must be specific, attainable, and measurable. Vague goals and standards such as "better quality," "more efficiency," and "improved performance" are not sufficient because they do not describe what you are trying to achieve. For example, let's say you are a runner and you want to improve your distance. When you started your improvement plan last year, you ran 2 kilometres a day. Now you run 2.1 kilometres a day. Did you meet your goal? You did increase your distance, but certainly not by very much. A more appropriate goal statement would be: To increase running distance from 2 kilometres a day to 4 kilometres a day by January 1. It is important to establish a time period for when specific goals are to be met. Here are examples of goals and standards that meet these criteria:

- Cut the number of finished-product rejects from 10 per 1000 to 5 per 1000 by March 31.
- Increase the number of times managers praise employees from 3 per week to 12 per week by the end of the quarter.
- Increase sales of product X from $10,000 per month to $12,000 per month by July 31.

One way to make control systems work is to establish clear procedures for monitoring performance. Accounting and finance are often the foundation for control systems because they provide the numbers management needs to evaluate progress. We shall explore both accounting and finance in detail later in the text.

A Key Criterion for Measurement: Customer Satisfaction

Traditional measures of success are usually financial: that is, they define success in terms of profits or return on investment. Certainly these measures are still important, but they are not the whole purpose of a firm. Other purposes may include pleasing customers

external customers
Dealers, who buy products to sell to others, and ultimate customers (or end users), who buy products for their own personal use.

© Jared Siskin/Patrick McMullan/Getty Images

One way colleges and universities measure their performance is to track the number of students who complete their degrees or who graduate within a certain number of years. What are some of the factors that could affect the achievement of this performance standard, and how do post-secondary administrators take corrective action when necessary?

(including both external and internal customers). **External customers** include dealers, who buy products to sell to others, and ultimate customers (also known as end users) such as you and me, who buy products for their own personal use. **Internal customers** are individuals and units within the firm that receive services from other individuals or units. For example, the field salespeople are the internal customers of the marketing research people who prepare research reports for them.

One goal today is to go beyond simply satisfying customers to "delighting" them with unexpectedly good products and services. We'll discuss management in more detail in the next few chapters. Let's pause now, review, and do some exercises. Management is doing, not just reading.

internal customers Individuals and units within the firm that receive services from other individuals or units.

PROGRESS ASSESSMENT

- What are the five steps in the control process?
- What is the difference between internal and external customers?

SUMMARY

LO1 **Describe the changes occurring today in the management function.**

Many managers are changing their approach to corporate management.

What reasons can you give to account for these changes in management?

Business people are being challenged to be more ethical and to make their accounting practices more visible to investors and the general public. Change is happening faster than ever, and global competition is just a click away. Managing change is an important element of success, particularly in light of today's emphasis on speed in the global marketplace. National borders mean much less now compared to the past, and co-operation and integration among companies have greatly increased. Within companies, knowledge workers are demanding managerial styles that allow for freedom, and the workforce is becoming increasingly diverse, educated, and self-directed.

How are managers' roles changing?

Leaders of Fortune 100 companies today tend to be younger, more of them are female, and fewer of them are educated at elite universities. They appreciate that many of their employees know more about technology and other practices than they do. Therefore, they tend to put more emphasis on motivation, teamwork, and co-operation. Managers in the future are likely to assume completely new roles in the firm. No matter what, managers will be taking a leadership role in adapting to climate change. Further, they'll be doing more expansion overseas.

LO2 **Describe the four functions of management.**

Managers perform a variety of functions.

What are the four primary functions of management?

The four primary functions are (1) planning, (2) organizing, (3) leading, and (4) controlling.

Describe each of the four functions.

Planning includes anticipating trends and determining the best strategies and tactics to achieve organizational goals and objectives. Organizing includes designing the structure of the organization and creating conditions and systems in which everyone and everything works together to achieve the organization's goals and objectives. Leading involves creating a vision for the organization and guiding, training, coaching, and motivating others to work effectively to achieve the organization's goals and objectives. Controlling involves establishing clear standards to determine whether an organization is progressing toward its goals and objectives, rewarding people for doing a good job, and taking corrective action if they are not.

LO3 **Relate the planning process and decision making to the accomplishment of company goals**

The planning function involves the process of setting objectives to meet the organizational goals. Goals are broad, long-term achievements that organizations aim to accomplish.

What are the four types of planning, and how are they related to the organization's goals and objectives?

Strategic planning is broad, long-range planning that outlines the goals of the organization. Tactical planning is specific, short-term planning that lists organizational objectives. Operational planning is part of tactical planning and involves setting specific timetables and standards. Contingency planning involves developing an alternative set of plans in case the first set does not work out.

What are the steps involved in decision making?

Decision making is choosing among two or more alternatives and it is the heart of all management functions. The six Ds of decision making are (1) define the situation, (2) describe and collect needed information, (3) develop alternatives, (4) decide which alternative is best, (5) do what is indicated (begin implementation), and (6) determine whether the decision was a good one and follow up.

LO4 **Describe the organizing function of management.**

Organizing means allocating resources (such as funds for various departments), assigning tasks, and establishing procedures for accomplishing the organizational objectives.

What are the three levels of management in the corporate hierarchy?

The three levels of management are (1) top management (highest level consisting of the president and other key company executives who develop strategic plans); (2) middle management (general managers, division managers, and plant managers who are responsible for tactical planning and controlling); and (3) supervisory management (first-line managers/supervisors who evaluate workers' daily performance).

What skills do managers need?

Managers must have three categories of skills: (1) technical skills (ability to perform specific tasks such as selling products or developing software), (2) human relations skills (ability to communicate and motivate), and (3) conceptual skills (ability to see organizations as a whole and how all the parts fit together). Managers at different levels need different skills.

LO5 **Explain the differences between leaders and managers, and describe the various leadership styles.**

Executives today must be more than just managers; they must be leaders as well.

What's the difference between a manager and a leader?

A manager plans, organizes, and controls functions within an organization. A leader has vision and inspires others to grasp that vision, establishes corporate values, emphasizes corporate ethics, and does not fear change.

Which leadership style is most effective?

Figure 8.8 shows a continuum of leadership styles ranging from boss-centred to subordinate-centred leadership. The most effective leadership style depends on the people being led and the situation.

LO6 **Summarize the five steps of the control function of management.**

The control function of management involves measuring employee performance against objectives and standards, rewarding people for a job well done, and taking corrective action if necessary.

What are the five steps of the control function?

Controlling incorporates (1) setting clear standards, (2) monitoring and recording performance, (3) comparing performance with plans and standards, (4) communicating results and deviations to employees, and (5) providing positive feedback for a job well done and taking corrective action if necessary.

What qualities must standards possess to be used to measure performance results?

Standards must be specific, attainable, and measurable.

KEY TERMS

CAREER EXPLORATION

If you are interested in pursuing a career in management, here are a few to consider. Find out about the tasks performed, skills needed, pay, and opportunity outlook in these fields through Internet sites that include the Government of Canada Job Bank, Workopolis, Monster, CareerBuilder, Glassdoor, and Indeed, as well as through the Career Centre at your school.

- **Administrative services manager**—plans, directs, and coordinates supportive services of an organization; maintains facilities and supervises activities that include record keeping, mail distribution, and office upkeep.
- **Construction manager**—plans, coordinates, budgets, and supervises construction projects from start to finish.
- **Emergency management director**—prepares plans and procedures for responding to natural disasters or other emergencies.
- **Food service manager**—responsible for the daily operation of restaurants and other establishments that prepare and serve food and beverages.
- **Computer and information technology (IT) manager**—plans, coordinates, and directs computer-related activities in an organization.

CRITICAL THINKING

Many students say they would like to be a manager someday. Here are some questions to get you thinking like a manager.

1. Would you like to work for a large firm or a small business? Private or public? In an office or out in the field? Give your reasons for each answer.
2. What type of leader would you be? What type of a leader would you most enjoy working with?
3. Do you see any problems with a participative (democratic) leadership style? Can you see a manager getting frustrated when he or she exercises less control over others?
4. Can someone who is trained to give orders (like a military sergeant) be retrained to be a participative leader? How? What problems may emerge?

DEVELOPING CAREER SKILLS

Key: ● **Team** ★ **Analytic** ▲ **Communication** ⊡ **Technology**

★▲ 1. Allocate some time to do some career planning by doing a SWOT analysis of your present situation. Choose one career you are interested in and answer the following questions: What does the marketplace for your chosen career(s) look like today? What skills do you have that will make you a winner in that type of career? What weaknesses might you target to improve? What are the threats to that career choice? What are the opportunities? Prepare a two-minute presentation for the class.

●★▲ 2. Bring several decks of cards to class and have the class break up into teams of four or so members. Each team should then elect a leader. Each leader should be assigned a leadership style: autocratic, participative, or free-rein. Have each team try to build a house with a given design. The team that completes the task the quickest wins. Each team member should then report his or her experience under that style of leadership.

★▲ 3. In class, discuss the advantages and disadvantages of becoming a manager. Does the size of the business make a difference? What are the advantages of a career in a profit-seeking business versus a career in a non-profit organization?

★▲ 4. Review Figure 8.8 and discuss managers you have known, worked for, or read about who have practised each style. Students from other countries may have interesting experiences to add. Which management style did you like best? Why? Which were most effective? Why?

★▲ 5. Because of the illegal and unethical behaviour of a few managers, managers in general are under suspicion for being greedy and dishonest. Discuss the fairness of such charges, given the thousands of honest and ethical managers, and what could be done to improve their opinion of managers among the students in your class.

ANALYZING MANAGEMENT DECISIONS

Leading in a Leaderless Company

In an issue of *BusinessWeek* devoted to the future of business, writer John Byrne speculated about the future of leadership. He said that the twenty-first century would be unfriendly to leaders who try to run their companies by sheer force of will, and that success would come instead to companies that are "leaderless"—or companies whose leadership is so widely shared that they resemble ant colonies or beehives. In a world that is becoming more dependent on brainpower, having teams at the top will make more sense than having a single top manager. The Internet enables companies to act more like beehives because information can be shared horizontally rather than sent up to the top manager's office and then back down to lower organizational levels again. Decisions can be made instantly by the best people equipped to make them. One of the best examples of this is Wikipedia.

In the past, uniform thinking from the top could cripple an organization. Today, however, team leadership is ideally suited for the new reality of fast-changing markets. Urgent projects often require the coordinated contribution of many talented people working together. Such thinking does not happen at the top of the organization; it takes place lower down the organization among the workers.

In the future, therefore, managers are more likely to be chosen for their team experience and their ability to delegate rather than to make all key decisions themselves. Companies in the future, it is said, will be led by people who understand that in business, as in nature, no one person can be in control.

Sources: John A. Byrne, "The Global Corporation Becomes a Leaderless Corporation," *BusinessWeek,* August 30, 1999, 88–90; and Etienne C. Wenger and William M. Synder, "Communities of Practice: The Organizational Frontier," *Harvard Business Review,* January–February 2000, 139–145.

Discussion Questions

1. What would you look for on a resumé that would indicate that a job candidate was a self-motivated team player? Are you that type? How do you know?
2. Given your experience with managers in the past, what problems do you see for managers who let employees decide for themselves the best way to do things and give them the power to obtain needed equipment?
3. What would happen if all businesses in your area had their employees interact with customers to hear their comments and complaints? Would that be an effective or ineffective approach? Why?
4. What are the various ways you can think of for companies to pay bonuses to team members? One way is to divide the money equally. What are other ways? Which would you prefer as a team member?

CHAPTER 9

Structuring Organizations for Today's Challenges

LEARNING OBJECTIVES

After you have read and studied this chapter, you should be able to:

LO1 Outline the basic principles of organization management.

LO2 Compare the organizational theories of Henri Fayol and Max Weber.

LO3 Evaluate the choices managers make in structuring organizations.

LO4 Contrast the various organizational models.

LO5 Identify the benefits of inter-firm co-operation and coordination.

LO6 Explain how organizational culture can help businesses adapt to change.

PROFILE

GETTING TO KNOW: DENISE MORRISON, CEO, CAMPBELL SOUP COMPANY

Since 1869, the Campbell Soup Company has been one of America's most iconic brands. Its products are familiar not only to millions of consumers, but also to art lovers around the world, thanks to Andy Warhol's legendary paintings of the company's soup cans. As a result, Campbell must walk a fine line between catering to people's prior expectations and updating the business to reflect current trends.

It's CEO Denise Morrison's job to keep the company on this narrow path. After earning the top position in 2011, she went on to oversee a major operational transformation that replaced Campbell's unhealthy ingredients with sustainable ones. This required far more effort than a standard rebranding project: she and her colleagues had to evaluate every aspect of the business and how it could be changed for the better.

Fortunately, Morrison has been training for enormous tasks like this one since she was a child. Her father, a top executive at companies like AT&T, encouraged his four daughters to get a head start on their careers. "He was talking to us at a very early age that he thought the world was going to open up for women and he wanted us to be

© Andrew Cutraro/Redux

prepared," said Morrison. "So, he taught us business." Each night he brought products home for his daughters to discuss at the dinner table. During these family focus groups, Morrison learned how to evaluate items and communicate her thoughts to her peers. Their father also placed a "job jar" in the house containing all the chores that needed to get done that week. His daughters had to decide among themselves who got assigned which chore, teaching them valuable lessons about negotiation and goal achievement.

This homegrown expertise proved to be essential for Morrison's future accomplishments. Her first taste of success came at Boston College, where she graduated magna cum laude with degrees in economics and psychology. She then landed a job at Procter & Gamble, soon followed by a series of other senior roles at Nabisco, Nestlé, and Kraft. After building extensive experience in the food industry, Morrison took a position at Campbell as president of global sales. She moved on to chief operating officer in 2010 and then became CEO a year later.

As she climbed up the corporate ladder, Morrison took careful notice of how the food industry was changing. By the 2010s consumers started to move away from processed, unhealthy options and toward organic cuisine. This "seismic shift" in people's preferences convinced Morrison that Campbell had to change with the times. "We believe that we need to participate in this, so you can either lead change or be a victim of it," said Morrison. "I'd much rather lead it."

In order to achieve this goal, she knew the company had to radically alter its operational structure. So along with acquiring healthy brands like Bolthouse Farms, Morrison closed down five underperforming plants while improving others. The company also had to find several new suppliers as it made the switch to sustainable ingredients. After that, Campbell then needed to determine how these added costs would affect production as a whole. So far, the company has spent about half a decade refining this process and will likely continue to do so for years to come. Thankfully for Campbell, Morrison remains determined to see this monumental chore through to the end. "We're talking, thinking and acting differently about the food we make," said Morrison. "We will be more honest about what goes in our food, how we made our food."

This chapter is about changing and adapting organizations to today's markets, as Denise Morrison is doing at Campbell. Most managers never face challenges that big, but there are plenty of opportunities in every firm to use the principles of organizing to manage—and benefit from—change.

Sources: "How Campbell Soup and Panera See Shifting Consumer Tastes," *The Wall Street Journal,* October 16, 2016; Jane M. Von Bergen, "Campbell Soup CEO Knew as a Child She Wanted to Be the Boss," *Seattle Times,* July 10, 2016; Jennifer Kaplan, "Campbell to Cut Artificial Flavors, Colors by End of 2018," *Bloomberg Businessweek,* July 22, 2015; Denise Morrison, "CEO of Campbell Soup: The Biggest Challenge of Leading an Iconic Food Brand," *Fortune,* October 27, 2015; "Denise M. Morrison: President and Chief Executive Officer," Campbellsoupcompany.com, accessed September 2017.

LO1

Outline the basic principles of organization management.

Everyone's Reorganizing

You don't have to look far to find examples of companies reorganizing.[1] A. G. Lafley, CEO of legendary Procter & Gamble, transformed the company into one of the most innovative firms in the world. Some entrepreneurial companies are organizing globally from the start, and succeeding. Other organizations have been declining, including some builders within the housing market.[2] Clearly the challenge to reorganize is strong.[3]

Few firms have established as strong an image as Starbucks, but even that company had to restructure to keep its customer base. As the company expanded its menu to include more sandwiches, one of the unexpected results was a change in the smell of the stores (the odour of burning cheese was overwhelming the smell of coffee). The company restored the stores' aroma by cutting back on sandwiches for a while. Many stores had to be closed and other stores were remodelled to recapture the feel of a Milan coffee bar. In the end, Starbucks regained its market image and is prospering again.

Adjusting to changing markets is a normal function in a capitalist economy. There will be big winners, like Amazon, Google and Facebook, and big losers as well.[4] The key to success is remaining flexible enough to adapt to the changing times.[5] Often that means going back to basic organizational principles and rebuilding the firm on a sound foundation.[6] This chapter will begin by discussing such basic principles.

Building an Organization from the Bottom Up

The principles of management are much the same, no matter the size of the business. Management, as you learned in Chapter 8, begins with planning. Let's say, for example, that you and two of your friends plan to start a lawn-mowing business. One of the first steps is to organize your business. *Organizing,* or structuring, begins with determining what work needs to be done (mowing, edging, trimming, etc.) and then dividing up tasks among the three of you; this is called a *division of labour.* One of you, for example, might have a special talent for trimming bushes, while another is better at mowing. The success of a firm often depends on management's ability to identify each worker's strengths and assign the right tasks to the right person. Often a job can be done quickly and well when each person specializes. Dividing tasks into smaller jobs is called *job specialization.* For example, you might divide the mowing task into mowing, trimming, and raking.

© Huntstock/age fotostock RF

The principles of organization apply to businesses of all sizes. Structuring the business, making an appropriate division of labour using job specialization and departmentalization, establishing procedures, and assigning authority are tasks found in most firms. How do these principles operate at your current or most recent job?

If your business is successful, you will probably hire more workers to help. You might then organize them into teams or departments to do the various tasks. One team, for example, might mow the lawn while another team uses blowers to clean up the leaves and cut grass. If you are really successful over time, you might hire an accountant to keep records for you, various people to do your marketing (e.g., advertising), and repair people to keep the equipment in good shape.

You can see how your business might evolve into a company with several departments: operations (all tasks related to mowing the lawns), marketing, accounting, and maintenance. The process of setting up individual departments to do specialized tasks is called *departmentalization.* Finally, you would need to assign authority and responsibility to people so that you could control the whole process. If something went wrong in the accounting department, for example, you would know who was responsible.

Structuring an organization, then, consists of devising a division of labour (sometimes resulting in specialization), setting up teams or departments to do specific tasks (e.g., human resources and accounting), and assigning responsibility and authority to people. It also includes allocating resources (such as funds for various departments), assigning specific tasks, and establishing procedures for accomplishing the organizational objectives. Right from the start, you have to make some ethical decisions about how you will treat your workers (see the Making Ethical Decisions box).

Finally, as you learned in Chapter 8, you may develop an *organization chart* that shows relationships among people: it shows who is accountable for the completion of specific work and who reports to whom. Finally, you have to monitor the environment (environmental factors were discussed in Chapter 1) to see what competitors are doing and what customers are demanding. Then, you must adjust to the new realities. For example, a major lawn care company may begin promoting its services in your area. You might have to make

Making ETHICAL DECISIONS

Safety and Environmental Concerns Versus Profit

Imagine that you have begun a successful lawn-mowing service in your neighbourhood. To get some input on what is needed, you observe other lawn-mowing services in the area. Several seem to hire untrained workers, many of them from other countries. The companies pay the workers minimum wage or slightly more, and often provide no safety equipment. Workers do not have ear protection against the loud mowers and blowers, and many do not wear goggles when operating the shredder. Very few workers wear masks when spraying potentially harmful fertilizers.

You are aware that there are many hazards connected with yard work. You also know that safety gear can be expensive and that workers often prefer to work without such protection. You are interested in making as much money as possible, but you also are concerned about the safety and welfare of your workers. Furthermore, you are aware of the noise pollution caused by blowers and other equipment and would like to keep noise levels down, but quiet equipment is expensive.

The corporate culture you create as you begin your service will last for a long time. If you emphasize safety and environmental concern from the start, your workers will adopt your values. On the other hand, you can see the potential for making faster profits by ignoring as many safety rules as you can and by paying little attention to the environment. What are the consequences of each choice? Which will you choose?

© Yuriy Vlasenko/Shutterstock

some organizational changes to offer even better service at competitive prices. What would be the first thing you would do if you began to lose business to competitors?

LO2

Compare the organizational theories of Henri Fayol and Max Weber.

The Changing Organization

Never before in the history of business has so much change been introduced so quickly—sometimes too quickly, as we saw with the 2011 earthquake and tsunami in Japan. As you learned in earlier chapters, much of that change is due to the dynamic business environment, including heightened global competition, a stagnating economy, faster technological change, and pressure to preserve the natural environment.[7]

Equally important to many businesses is the change in customer expectations. Consumers today expect high-quality products and fast, friendly service—at a reasonable cost. Doug Rauch, former President of Trader Joe's grocery chain, views employees and customers as two wings of a bird: you need both of them to fly. They go together—if you take care of your employees, they'll take care of your customers. When your customers are happier and they enjoy shopping, it also makes your employees' lives happier, so it's a virtuous cycle.[8]

Managing change, then, has become a critical managerial function. It may sometimes include redesigning the whole organizational structure. For example, in 2015 technology giant Google restructured its organization into a conglomerate called Alphabet. Alphabet consists of independent units including Google (the search engine and related businesses such as Gmail and YouTube), Calico (health care), Verily ("smart" contact lens), Deep Mind (artificial intelligence), and several others. These smaller units have more flexibility to listen to customers and adapt accordingly.[9] Such change may occur in non-profit and government organizations as well as businesses.

Many organizations in the past were designed more to facilitate management than to please the customer. Managers were typically the only members of an organization who had some level of training, and possessed most of the knowledge needed to run the business. Companies designed many rules and regulations to give managers control over employees. As you will learn later, that is called *bureaucracy.* Where did bureaucracy come from? What are the alternatives? To understand where we are, it helps to know where we have been.

The Development of Organizational Design

Until the twentieth century, most businesses were rather small, the processes for producing goods were relatively simple, and organizing workers was fairly easy. Organizing workers is still not too hard in most small firms, such as a lawn-mowing service or a small shop that produces custom-made boats. Not until the 1900s and the introduction of *mass production* (efficiently producing large quantities of goods) did business production processes and organizations become complex. Usually, the bigger the plant, the more efficient production became.

economies of scale
The situation in which companies can reduce their production costs if they can purchase raw materials in bulk and develop specialized labour, resulting in the average cost of goods going down as production levels increase.

Business growth led to what was called **economies of scale**. This term refers to the fact that companies can reduce their production costs if they can purchase raw materials in bulk. The average cost of goods decreases as production levels rise. The cost of building a car, for example, declined sharply when automobile companies adopted mass production and GM and Ford built huge factories.[10] Over time, such innovations became less meaningful as other companies copied their processes. You may have noticed the benefits of mass production in housing and computers.[11]

During the era of mass production, organization theorists emerged. In France, Henri Fayol published his book *Administration industrielle et générale* in 1919. It was popularized in North America in 1949 under the title *General and Industrial Management.*

FAYOL'S PRINCIPLES OF ORGANIZATION

In France, economic theoretician Henri Fayol published his book *Administration industrielle et générale* in 1919. Fayol introduced various management principles, including the following:

- *Unity of command.* Each worker is to report to one, and only one, boss. The benefits of this principle are obvious. What happens if two different bosses give you two different assignments? Which one should you follow? To prevent such confusion, each person should report to one manager. (later we'll discuss an organizational plan that seems to violate this principle.)
- *Hierarchy of authority.* All workers should know to whom they should report. Managers should have the right to give orders and expect others to follow. (In Chapter 12 we will talk about a change to this concept, called *empowerment.*)
- *Division of labour.* Functions are to be divided into areas of specialization such as production, marketing, and finance. This principle is now being questioned or modified, as you'll read later, and cross-functional teams are gaining more emphasis.
- *Subordination of individual interests to the general interest.* Workers are to think of themselves as a coordinated team. The goals of the team are more important than the goals of individual workers. Have you heard this concept applied to professional hockey and football teams? Did you see this principle at work in the last Stanley Cup playoff?
- *Authority.* Managers have the right to give orders and the power to enforce obedience. Authority and responsibility are related: whenever authority is exercised, responsibility arises. This principle is also being modified as managers are beginning to empower employees.
- *Degree of centralization.* The amount of decision-making power vested in top management should vary by circumstances. In a small organization, it is possible to centralize all decision-making power in the top manager. In a larger organization, however, some decision-making power, for both major and minor issues, should be delegated to lower-level managers and employees.
- *Clear communication channels.* All workers should be able to reach others in the firm quickly and easily.
- *Order.* Materials and people should be placed and maintained in the proper location.

Public Domain

Henri Fayol introduced several management principles still followed today, including the idea that each worker should report to only one manager and that a manager, in turn, should have the right to give orders for others to follow and the power to enforce them. Which of Fayol's principles have you observed?

- *Equity.* A manager should treat employees and peers with respect and justice.
- *Esprit de corps.* A spirit of pride and loyalty should be created among people in the firm.

These principles became synonymous with the concept of management. Organizations were designed so that no person had more than one boss, lines of authority were clear, and everyone knew to whom they were to report. Naturally, these principles tended to be written down as rules, policies, and regulations as organizations grew larger. That process of rulemaking often led to rather rigid organizations that did not always respond quickly to consumer requests. So, where did the idea of bureaucracy come from? We talk about that next.

MAX WEBER AND ORGANIZATIONAL THEORY

Sociologist Max Weber (pronounced "Vay-ber") was writing about organization theory in Germany around the same time Fayol was writing his books in France. Weber's book *The Theory of Social and Economic Organizations,* like Fayol's, also appeared in North America in the late 1940s. He promoted the pyramid-shaped organization structure that became very popular in large firms. Weber put great trust in managers and felt that the firm would do well if employees simply *did what they were told.* The less decision making employees had to do, the better. Clearly, this is a reasonable way to operate if you are dealing with relatively uneducated and untrained workers. (Where are you likely to find such workers today?) Often, such workers were the only ones available at the time Weber was writing; most employees did not have the kind of educational background and technical skills that today's workers generally have.

© Interfoto/Alamy Images

Max Weber promoted an organizational structure composed of middle managers who implement the orders of top managers. He believed workers were best managed if managers or supervisors gave them strict rules and regulations to follow and monitored their performance. What industries or businesses today would benefit by using such controls?

Weber's principles of organization were similar to Fayol's. In addition, Weber emphasized:

- Job descriptions;
- Written rules, decision guidelines, and detailed records;
- Consistent procedures, regulations, and policies; and
- Staffing and promotion based on qualifications.

Weber believed that large organizations demanded clearly established rules and guidelines that were to be followed precisely. In other words, he was in favour of *bureaucracy.* Although his principles made a great deal of sense at the time, the practice of establishing rules and procedures was so rigid in some companies that it became counterproductive. However, some organizations today still thrive on Weber's theories.[12] United Parcel Service (UPS), for example, still has written rules and decision guidelines that enable the firm to deliver packages quickly because employees do not have to pause to make decisions—procedures are clearly spelled out for them.

Other organizations are not as effective because they do not allow employees to respond quickly to new challenges. That is clearly the case with disaster relief in many areas, as was the case when Hurricane

Katrina hit New Orleans. Later, we shall explore what can be done to make organizations more responsive. First, let's look again at some basic terms and concepts.

Turning Principles into Organizational Design

Following the concepts of theorists like Fayol and Weber, managers in the latter part of the 1900s began designing organizations so that managers could *control* workers. Many organizations are still organized that way, with everything set up in a hierarchy. A **hierarchy** is a system in which one person is at the top of the organization and there is a ranked or sequential ordering from the top down of managers and others who are responsible to that person. Since one person cannot keep track of thousands of workers, the top manager needs many lower-level managers to help. The **chain of command** is the line of authority that moves from the top of the hierarchy to the lowest level.

hierarchy
A system in which one person is at the top of the organization and there is a ranked or sequential ordering from the top down of managers who are responsible to that person.

chain of command
The line of authority that moves from the top of a hierarchy to the lowest level.

Some organizations have a dozen or more layers of management between the chief executive officer (CEO) and the lowest-level employees. If employees want to introduce work changes, they ask a supervisor (the first level of management), who asks his or her manager, who asks a manager at the next level up, and so on. It can take weeks or months for a decision to be made and passed from manager to manager until it reaches employees. At pharmaceutical company Pfizer, for example, there were once 17 layers in the hierarchy between the chief executive and the lowest employee.

Max Weber used the word *bureaucrat* to describe a middle manager whose function was to implement top management's orders. Thus, **bureaucracy** came to be the term used for an organization with many layers of managers.

bureaucracy
An organization with many layers of managers who set rules and regulations and oversee all decisions.

When employees in a bureaucracy of any size have to ask managers for permission to make a change, the process may take so long that customers become annoyed. Has this happened to you in a department store or some other organization? Since many customers want efficient service—and they want it *now*—slow service is simply not acceptable in many of today's competitive firms.

Some companies are reorganizing to let employees make decisions on their own to please the customer no matter what. Home Depot has adopted this approach to win more customers from competitors. Nordstrom, a fashion specialty retailer, empowers employees to accept a return from a customer without managerial approval, even if the item was not originally sold at that store.[13] As you will see in Chapter 12, giving employees such authority and responsibility to make decisions and please customers is called *empowerment.* Remember that empowerment works only when employees are given the proper training and resources to respond. Can you see how much training would help first responders in crisis conditions?

It is important to note that well-run bureaucratic organizations can be extremely effective in certain contexts—when there is little innovation in the marketplace, consistency in demand, low-skilled workers, and adequate time to weigh the consequences of decisions.

PROGRESS ASSESSMENT

- What do the terms "division of labour" and "job specialization" mean?
- What are the principles of management outlined by Fayol?
- What did Weber add to Fayol's principles?

LO3

Evaluate the choices managers make in structuring organizations.

Decisions to Make in Structuring Organizations

Henry Mintzberg, an expert on management and business, supports the current view that there is no single structure that will lead to success for all organizations. "Structure should reflect the organization's situation—for example, its age, size, type of production system, and the extent to which its environment is complex and dynamic. Small businesses with up to five employees do not need to spend time on how to structure themselves. However, the effectiveness of larger organizations or those experiencing significant change is impacted by structure. As well, a firm's design decisions (such as span of control, centralization versus decentralization, and matrix structures) need to work within the chosen structure and design."[14] These design decisions will be discussed in this chapter. Mintzberg has also written a book on MBA programs entitled *Managers Not MBAs,*[15] which is an insightful review of the soft practice of managing and management development.

When designing responsive organizations, firms have to make decisions about several organizational issues: (1) centralization versus decentralization, (2) span of control, (3) tall versus flat organization structures, and (4) departmentalization. Their specific choices are based upon a process called change management. This strategic approach begins by preparing for the change, then managing the change, and concludes with re-enforcing the change. Given the risk involved with this type of change, a formal process increases the likelihood of success.

Choosing Centralization Versus Decentralization of Authority

centralized authority An organization structure in which decision-making authority is maintained at the top level of management at the company's headquarters.

Centralized authority occurs when decision-making authority is maintained at the top level of management at the company's headquarters. For example, Burger King has a globally centralized structure in which most major decisions are made by a core management team. While this organizational structure has the advantage of providing strong global control, it limits the flexibility to immediately respond to regional or local market changes and trends.[16]

McDonald's believes that purchasing, promotion, and other such decisions are best handled centrally. There's usually little need for each McDonald's restaurant in Canada to carry different items, although, as you have read, the restaurants' menus are often quite different in other countries. The company leans toward centralized authority. Today's rapidly changing markets and global differences in consumer tastes tend to favour some decentralization and thus more delegation of authority, even at McDonald's. Its restaurants in England offer tea, those in France offer a Croque McDo (a hot ham-and-cheese sandwich), those in Japan sell rice, and those in China offer taro and red bean desserts.[17]

decentralized authority An organization structure in which decision-making authority is delegated to lower-level managers more familiar with local conditions compared to headquarters' management.

Decentralized authority occurs when decision-making authority is delegated to lower-level managers and employees who are more familiar with local conditions compared to headquarters' management.

Roots customers in Kelowna, for example, are likely to demand clothing styles different from those in Charlottetown or Lethbridge. It makes sense, therefore, to give store managers in various cities the authority to buy, price, and promote merchandise appropriate for each area. Such delegation of authority is an example of decentralized management. Magna International has a decentralized operating structure. Magna's manufacturing divisions operate as independent profit centres aligned by geographic region in each of the company's product areas. This decentralized structure prevents bureaucracy and makes Magna more responsive to customer needs and changes within the global automotive industry as well as within specific regions.[18] Figure 9.1 lists some advantages and disadvantages of centralized versus decentralized authority.

Choosing the Appropriate Span of Control

Span of control refers to the optimum number of subordinates a manager supervises or should supervise. There are many factors to consider when determining span of control. At lower levels, where work is standardized, it is possible to implement a wide span of control (15 to 40 workers). For example, one supervisor can be responsible for 20 or more workers who are assembling computers or cleaning up movie theatres. However, the number gradually narrows at higher levels of the organization because work is less standardized and there's more need for face-to-face communication. Variables in span of control include the following:

span of control
The optimum number of subordinates a manager supervises or should supervise.

- *Capabilities of the manager.* The more experienced and capable the manager, the broader the span of control can be. (A large number of workers can report to that manager.)
- *Capabilities of the subordinates.* The more subordinates need supervision, the narrower the span of control should be. Employee turnover at fast-food restaurants, for example, is often so high that managers must constantly be training new people and thus need a narrow span of control.
- *Geographical closeness.* The more concentrated the work area, the broader the span of control can be.
- *Functional similarity.* The more similar the functions, the broader the span of control can be.
- *Need for coordination.* The greater the need for coordination, the narrower the span of control might be.
- *Planning demands.* The more involved the plan, the narrower the span of control might be.

FIGURE 9.1

ADVANTAGES AND DISADVANTAGES OF CENTRALIZED VERSUS DECENTRALIZED MANAGEMENT

	ADVANTAGES	DISADVANTAGES
Centralized	• Greater top-management control • More efficiency • Simpler distribution system • Stronger brand/corporate image	• Less responsiveness to customers • Less empowerment • Interorganizational conflict • Lower morale away from headquarters
Decentralized	• Better adaptation to customer wants • More empowerment of workers • Faster decision making • Higher morale	• Less efficiency • Complex distribution system • Less top-management control • Weakened corporate image

- *Functional complexity.* The more complex the functions, the narrower the span of control might be.

Other factors to consider include the professionalism of superiors and subordinates and the number of new problems that occur in a day.

The trend today is to expand the span of control as organizations adopt empowerment, reduce the number of middle managers, and hire more educated and talented lower-level employees. Information technology makes it possible for managers to handle more information, so the span can be broader still.[19] More companies could expand the span of control if they trained their employees better and were willing to trust them more. Figure 9.2 lists some advantages and disadvantages of a narrow versus a wide span of control.

tall organization structure
An organization structure in which the pyramidal organization chart would be quite tall because of the various levels of management.

flat organization structure
An organization structure that has few layers of management and a broad span of control.

Choosing Between Tall and Flat Organization Structures

In the early twentieth century, organizations grew bigger and bigger, adding layer after layer of management to create **tall organization structures**. Some organizations had as many as 17 levels, and the span of control was small (few people reported to each manager).

Imagine how a message might be distorted as it moved up through each level of managers, management assistants, secretaries, assistant secretaries, supervisors, trainers, and so on. The cost of all of these managers and support people was quite high, the paperwork they generated was enormous, and the inefficiencies in communication and decision making often became intolerable.

More recently, organizations have adopted **flat organization structures** with fewer layers of management (see Figure 9.3) and a broad span of control (many people reporting to each manager). Flat structures can respond readily to customer demands because lower-level employees have authority and responsibility for making decisions,

FIGURE 9.2

ADVANTAGES AND DISADVANTAGES OF A NARROW VERSUS A WIDE SPAN OF CONTROL

The flatter the organization the wider the span of control.

	ADVANTAGES	DISADVANTAGES
Narrow	• More control by top management • More chances for advancement • Greater specialization • Closer supervision	• Less empowerment • Higher costs • Delayed decision making • Less responsiveness to customers
Wide	• Reduced costs • More responsiveness to customers • Faster decision making • More empowerment	• Fewer chances for advancement • Overworked managers • Loss of control • Less management expertise

FIGURE 9.3

NARROW VERSUS WIDE SPAN OF CONTROL

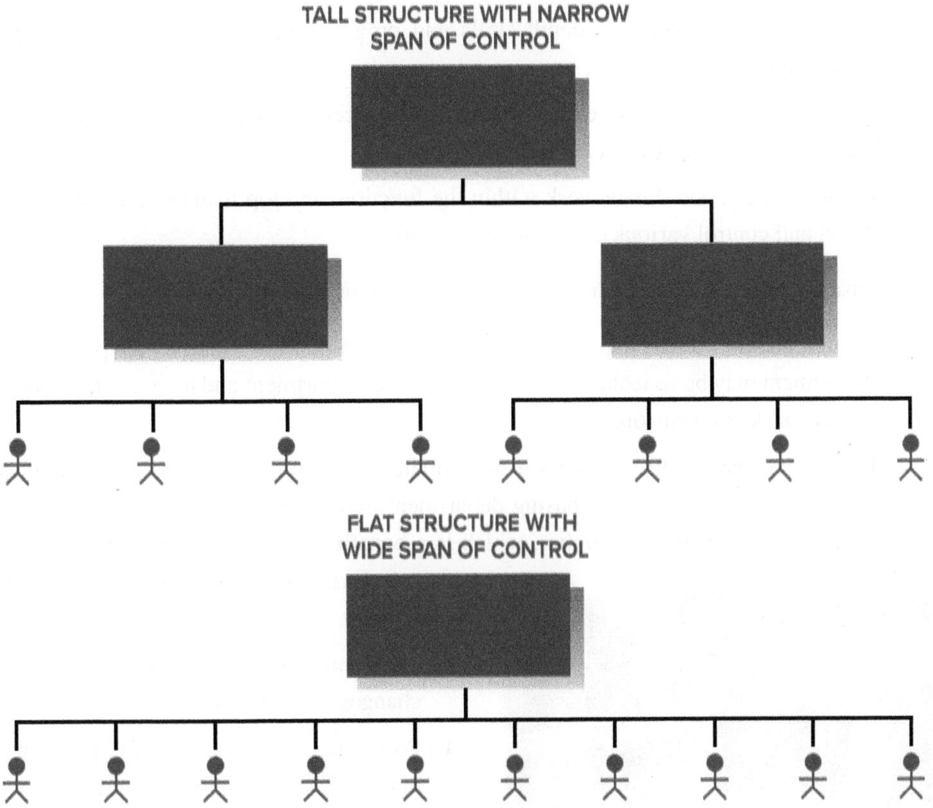

This figure describes two ways to structure an organization with the same number of employees. The tall structure with a narrow span of control has two managers who supervise four employees each. Changing to a flat surface with a wide span of control, the company could eliminate two managers and perhaps replace them with one or two employees, but the top manager would have to supervise ten people instead of two.

and managers can be spared certain day-to-day tasks. In a bookstore with a flat organizational structure, employees may have authority to arrange shelves by category, process special orders for customers, and so on.

Large organizations use flat structures to try to match the friendliness of small firms, whose workers know customers by name. The flatter organizations became, the broader the span of control, which means the elimination of some management positions.

© Luke Sharrett/Bloomberg/Getty Images

A broad span of control allows one supervisor to be responsible for many workers whose work tasks are predictable and standardized. In addition to assembly lines, can you think of other management situations that might benefit from a broad span of control? What about in a service industry?

Weighing the Advantages and Disadvantages of Departmentalization

Departmentalization divides an organization into separate units. The traditional way to departmentalize organizations is by *function,* such as design, production, marketing, and accounting. Departmentalization groups workers according to their skills, expertise, or

departmentalization Dividing an organization into separate units.

resource use so that they can specialize and work together more effectively. It may also save costs and improve efficiency. Other advantages of departmentalization include the following:

1. Employees can develop in-depth skills and progress within a department as they master those skills.
2. The company can achieve economies of scale by centralizing all the resource needs and locating various experts in a specific area.
3. Employees can coordinate work within the function, and top management can easily direct and control various departments' activities.

Disadvantages of departmentalization by function include the following:

1. Communication across departments may be problematic. For example, the production department may be so isolated from the marketing department and as a result, does not get feedback from customers.
2. Employees may identify with their department's goals rather than the organization's goals. For example, the purchasing department may save money buying a huge volume of goods from one supplier, which is a benefit to the department, but the high cost of storing the goods hurts the overall profitability.
3. The company's response to external changes may be slow.
4. People may not be trained to fulfill multiple managerial responsibilities and as a result they tend to become narrow specialists.
5. Department members may engage in groupthink (they think alike) and may need input from outside the department to become more creative.

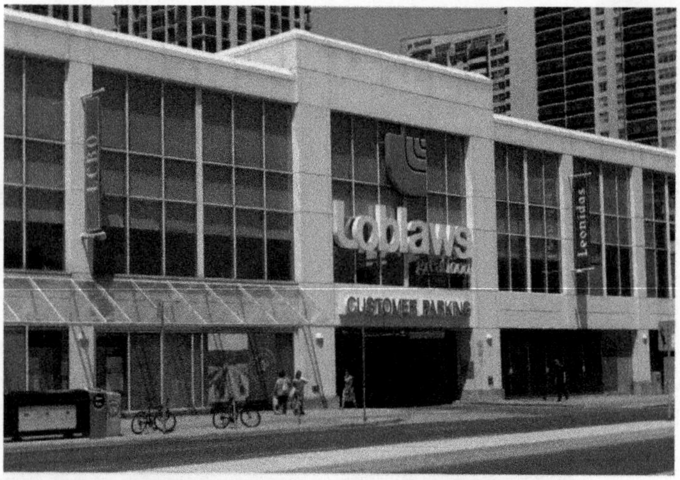

© mikecphoto / Shutterstock.com

Loblaw Companies Limited, Canada's largest food distributor, operates a number of supermarket chains across Canada including Atlantic Cash & Carry, Dominion, Fortinos, Loblaws, Provigo, and Real Canadian Superstore. The company also acquired T&T Supermarket, which has stores based in Vancouver. The company has operated since the 1960s and developed many excellent brands, including the President's Choice line of products. Since 2006, Loblaws has gone through a series of senior management shake-ups as it responds to growing competition from major U.S. merchandisers. Consolidating its distribution centres resulted in serious problems with its supply chain, costing millions of dollars. Loblaws continued to work on this issue over the next five years. How well do you think Loblaws performs today? Has the company's move to a more "responsive organization structure" fostered effective competition with the foreign retail Goliaths?

LOOKING AT ALTERNATIVE WAYS TO DEPARTMENTALIZE

Functional separation is not always the most responsive form of organization. So what are the alternatives? Figure 9.4 shows five ways a firm can departmentalize. One way is by product. A book publisher might have a trade book department (for books sold to the general public), a textbook department, and a technical book department, each with separate development and marketing processes. Such product-focused departmentalization usually results in positive customer relations.

Some organizations departmentalize by customer group. A pharmaceutical company

FIGURE 9.4

WAYS TO DEPARTMENTALIZE

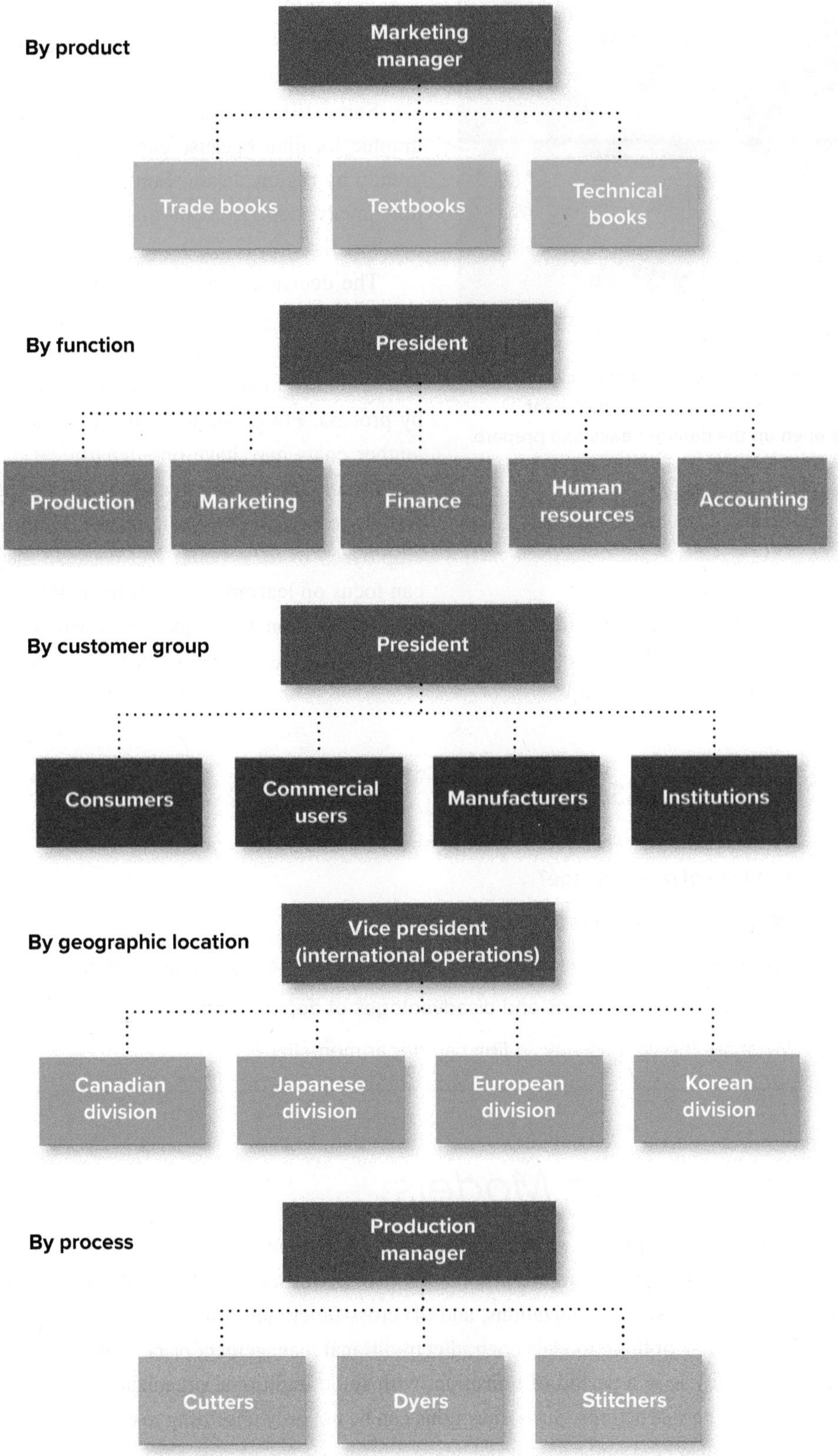

A computer company may want to departmentalize by geographic location, a manufacturing company by function, a pharmaceutical company by customer group, a leather manufacturer by process, and a publisher by product. In each case the structure must fit the firm's goals.

© Amy Sancetta/AP Images

After the material for footballs has been cut and sewn in the Wilson Sporting Goods factory, it moves on to the lacing department where workers like this one open up the deflated balls and prepare them for lacing. What are the advantages and disadvantages of departmentalizing by process similar to Wilson?

might have one department for the consumer market, another that calls on hospitals (the institutional market), and another that targets doctors. You can see how the customer groups might benefit from having specialists satisfying their needs.

Some firms group their units by geographic location because customers vary so greatly by region. Japan, Europe, and Korea may involve separate departments with obvious benefits.

The decision about how to departmentalize depends greatly on the nature of the product and the customers. A few firms find that it is most efficient to separate activities by process. For example, a firm that makes leather coats may have one department cut the leather, another dye it, and a third sew the coat together. Such specialization enables employees to do a better job because they can focus on learning a few critical skills.

Some firms use a combination of departmentalization techniques; they would be called *hybrid forms.* For example, a company could departmentalize by function, by geography, and by customer groups.

PROGRESS ASSESSMENT

- What is bureaucracy? What challenges do bureaucratic organizations face in a time of rapid change?
- Why are organizations becoming flatter?
- What are some reasons for having a narrow span of control in an organization?
- What are the advantages and disadvantages of departmentalization?
- What are the various ways a firm can departmentalize?

LO4

Contrast the various organizational models.

Organization Models

Now that we have explored the basic issues of organizational design, let's look in depth at four ways to structure an organization: (1) line organizations, (2) line-and-staff organizations, (3) matrix-style organizations, and (4) cross-functional self-managed teams. You will see that some of these models contradict traditional management principles. The business community is in a period of transition, with some traditional organizational models giving way to new structures. Such transitions can be not only unsettling to employees and managers but also be fraught with problems and errors.

Line Organizations

A **line organization** has direct two-way lines of responsibility, authority, and communication running from the top to the bottom of the organization, with everyone reporting to only one supervisor. The military and many small businesses are organized in this way. For example, the locally owned pizza parlour has a general manager and a shift manager. All general employees report to the shift manager, and he or she reports to the general manager or owner.

line organization
An organization that has direct two-way lines of responsibility, authority, and communication running from the top to the bottom of the organization, with all people reporting to only one supervisor.

A line organization does not have any specialists who provide managerial support. For example, there would be no legal department, accounting department, human resource department, or information technology (IT) department. Line organizations follow all of Fayol's traditional management rules. Line managers can issue orders, enforce discipline, and adjust the organization as conditions change.

In large businesses, a line organization may have the disadvantages of being too inflexible, of having few specialists or experts to advise people along the line, and of having lengthy lines of communication. Thus a large line organization may be unable to handle complex decisions relating to thousands of products and tons of paperwork. Such organizations usually turn to a line-and-staff form of organization.

Line-and-Staff Organizations

To minimize the disadvantages of simple line organizations, many organizations today have both line and staff personnel. A couple of definitions will help. **Line personnel** are responsible for directly achieving organizational goals and include production workers, distribution people, and marketing personnel. **Staff personnel** advise and assist line personnel in meeting their goals and include those in marketing research, legal advising, information technology, and human resource management.

line personnel
Employees who are part of the chain of command that is responsible for achieving organizational goals.

staff personnel
Employees who advise and assist line personnel in meeting their goals.

See Figure 9.5 for a diagram of a line-and-staff organization. One important difference between line and staff personnel is authority. Line personnel have formal authority to make policy decisions. Staff personnel have the authority to advise the line personnel and influence those decisions, but they cannot make policy changes themselves. The line manager may choose to seek or to ignore the advice of staff personnel.

Many organizations have benefitted from the expert staff advice on safety, legal issues, quality control, database management, motivation, and investing. Staff positions strengthen the line positions and are similar to having well-paid consultants on the organization's payroll.

Matrix-Style Organizations

Both line and line-and-staff organization structures suffer from inflexibility. Both allow for established lines of authority and communication, and work well in organizations with stable environments and slow product development (such as firms selling household appliances). In such firms, clear lines of authority and relatively fixed organization structures are assets that ensure efficient operations.

Today's economy, however, is dominated by high-growth industries like telecommunications, nanotechnology, robotics, and biotechnology, where competition is brisk and the life cycle of new ideas is short. Emphasis is on product development, creativity, special projects, rapid communication, and interdepartmental teamwork. From those changes

FIGURE 9.5

A SAMPLE LINE-AND-STAFF ORGANIZATION

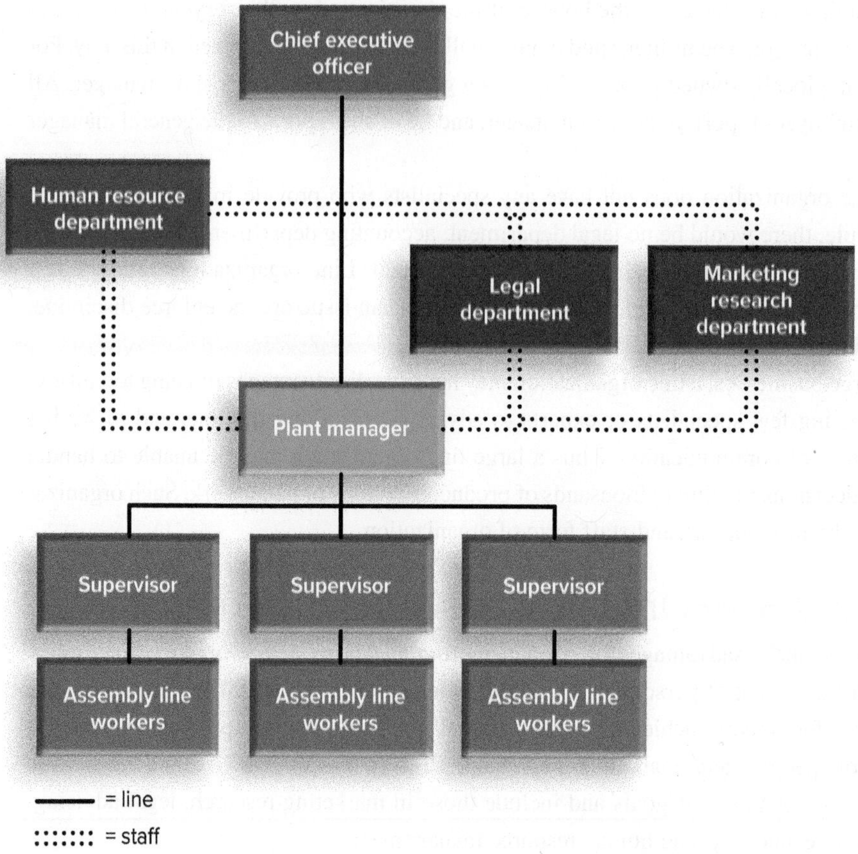

matrix organization
A system in which specialists from different parts of the organization are brought together to work on specific projects but still remain part of a line-and-staff structure.

grew the popularity of the **matrix organization**, in which specialists from different parts of the organization work temporarily on specific projects but still remain part of a line-and-staff structure (see Figure 9.6.). In other words, a project manager can borrow people from different departments to help design and market new product ideas.[20]

The matrix structure was developed in the aerospace industry and is now familiar in banking, management consulting firms, accounting firms, advertising agencies, and school systems. Matrix structure advantages include:

- Gives managers flexibility in assigning people to projects.
- Encourages inter-organizational co-operation and teamwork.
- Generates creative solutions for product development problems.
- Makes efficient use of organizational resources.

Matrix structure disadvantages include:

- Is costly and complex.
- Confuses employees about where their loyalty belongs—with the project manager or their functional unit.

FIGURE 9.6

A MATRIX ORGANIZATION

In a matrix organization, project managers are in charge of teams comprised of members of several departments. In this case, Project manager 2 supervises Employees A, B, C, and D. These employees are accountable not only to Project manager 2 but also to the head of their individual departments. For example, Employee B, a market researcher, reports to Project manager 2 and to the Vice president of marketing.

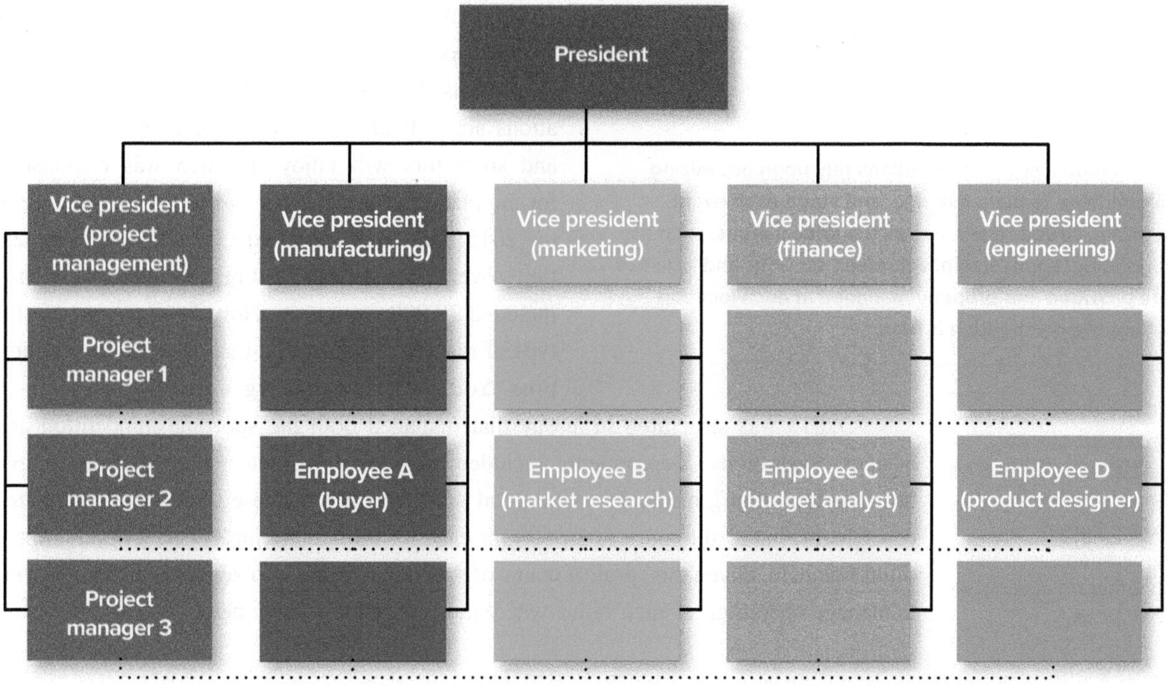

- Requires effective interpersonal skills as well as co-operative employees and managers to avoid communication problems.
- Provides only a temporary solution to a long-term problem.

If you are thinking that matrix organizations violate some traditional managerial principles, you are right. Normally a person cannot work effectively for two bosses. Who has the real authority? Which directive has first priority?

In reality, however, the system functions more effectively than you might imagine. To develop a new product, a project manager may be given temporary authority to "borrow" line personnel from production, marketing, and other line functions. The employees work together to complete the project and then return to their regular positions. Thus, no one really reports to more than one manager at a time.

A potential problem with matrix management, however, is that the project teams are not permanent. They form to solve a problem or develop a new product, and then they disband. There is little chance for cross-functional learning because teams work together for such a short period of time.

In the future, decision making will be distributed throughout the organization so that people can respond rapidly to change, says the *Harvard Business Review.* Global teams

© PCN Photography/Alamy

International sport competitions rely upon organizing committees to plan, manage, and stage each event. A matrix structure ensures all the critical areas, such as marketing, sponsorship, volunteer, security, and logistics are provided and properly managed at each location where the competition is held.

will collaborate on the Internet for a single project and then disband. It is likely younger employees who play online games will feel quite comfortable working in such groups.

Matrix organizations are also an effective structure in the world of international sport events. The 2015 Pan Am/Parapan Am Games Organizing Committee (TO2015) is an example of a project-based organization. When a major international sporting event is awarded to a city, an organizing committee is formed to serve as the event host. The host committee operations are critical for a successful event that athletes and spectators will enjoy. TO2015 was responsible for the planning, organizing, financing, and staging of the 2015 Pan Am/Parapan Am Games. The organization's overall budget was $1.4 billion and its workforce included 20 000 volunteers. How do you structure this type of massive organization that lasts for such a short time? You design a matrix organization.

cross-functional, self-managed teams Groups of employees from different departments who work together on a long-term basis.

TO2015 was structured in a way that managed both the sporting competition and business operations. Departments included marketing, volunteers, ceremonies, logistics (transportation), medical services, and security. Each of these areas were centralized departments but also important aspects for each location, or venue, where a sport competition was held. Given this, project teams of specialists from each department were formed to manage operations at each venue where the competitions were held.

Cross-Functional, Self-Managed Teams

One solution to the disadvantage of the temporary nature of matrix teams is to establish *long-lived teams* and to empower them to work closely with suppliers, customers, and others to quickly and efficiently bring out new, high-quality products while giving great service.

Cross-functional, self-managed teams are groups of employees from different departments who work together on a long-term basis (as opposed to the temporary teams established in matrix-style organizations).[21] Usually the teams are empowered to make decisions without management approval.[22] The barriers among design, engineering, marketing, distribution, and other functions are reduced when interdepartmental teams are created. One Smooth Stone is a corporate events company. They put together large, one-time functions for corporate clients. They have a team of highly skilled and trained staff that go from the planning and

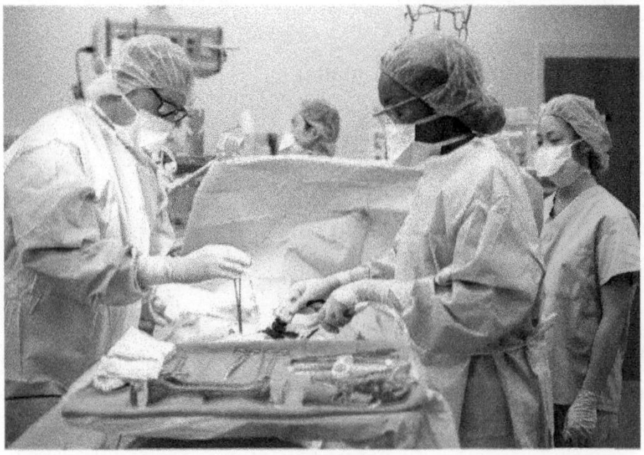

© monkeybusinessimages/Getty Images RF

You can think of a team of medical specialists in an operating room as a cross-functional, self-managed team. Doctors, nurses, technicians, and anesthesiologists from different departments and areas in the hospital work together to complete successful operations. What kinds of tasks do cross-functional, self-managed teams complete in an office or retail environment?

execution of one corporate function to another. Sometimes the self-managed teams are inter-firm. Toyota, for example, works closely with teams at other firms to produce its cars.

Figure 9.7 lists the advantages and disadvantages of these four types of organizations.

Cross-functional teams should be empowered and collaborative. They work best when leadership is shared. An engineer may lead the design of a new product, but a marketing expert may take the leadership position once it's ready for distribution. See the Adapting to Change box to learn about how some organizations are taking self-management to a new level.

GOING BEYOND ORGANIZATIONAL BOUNDARIES

Cross-functional teams work best when the voice of the customer is prioritized, especially in product development tasks.[23] Suppliers and distributors should be on the team as well. A self-managed team that includes customers, suppliers, and distributors goes beyond organizational boundaries. When suppliers and distributors are in other countries,

FIGURE 9.7

TYPES OF ORGANIZATIONS

Each form of organization has its advantages and disadvantages.

	ADVANTAGES	DISADVANTAGES
Line	• Clarifies responsibility and authority • Simplifies structure and easy understand • Establishes one supervisor for each person	• Is too inflexible • Limits number of specialists to advise workers • Extends lines of communication • Hinders ability to quickly handle complex questions
Line and Staff	• Provides expert advice from staff to line personnel • Establishes lines of authority • Encourages co-operation and better communication at all levels	• Risks overstaffing • Risks overanalyzing • Blurs lines of communication • Increases staff frustrations because of lack of authority
Matrix	• Is flexible • Encourages co-operation among departments • Produces creative solutions to problems • Allows organization to take on new projects without adding to the organizational structure • Provides for more efficient use of organizational resources	• Is costly and complex • Confuses employees • Requires effective interpersonal skills and co-operative managers and employees • Inhibits employee evaluation and reward systems
Cross-Functional, Self-Managed Teams	• Enhances interdepartmental coordination and co-operation • Enables quicker response to customers and market conditions • Increases employee motivation and morale	• Confuses responsibility and authority • Generates a perceived loss of control by management • Inhibits employee evaluation and reward systems • Requires self-motivated and highly trained workers

Adapting *to* CHANGE

Going Bossless

Why stop at self-managed teams? Why not apply self-management principles to the whole organization? That's what companies like Zappos, Morning Star, and W.L. Gore have done. Using an organizational structure known as *holacracy,* these companies have eliminated hierarchies (aka bosses) altogether.

In holacratic organizations, authority and decision making are given to "circles" (think of circles as teams of teams) throughout the organization. A circle is a group of "roles" working toward the same purpose that is formed or dissolved as the organization's needs change. A role is a set of responsibilities for certain outcomes or processes. Roles can be created, revised, or abolished as needed. Individuals usually have more than one role, in multiple circles.

As new goals and tasks develop, individuals create circles to deal with them. For example, a St. Louis television station mobilized temporary teams to add community voices to stories about major events, such as the financial crisis and the events in Ferguson. When the goals are reached, the circles disband.

It would be impossible to keep track of who's doing what where and when without technology. Systems such as GlassFrog or holaSpirit are used to list the purpose, accountability, and decision rights of every circle and every role. This information is available for everyone to see.

Self-management isn't appropriate for all organizations, or for all workers. When Zappos offered severance packages to all employees who didn't think self-management was a good fit for them, 18 percent accepted the offer. What do you think it would be like to work in an organization with no bosses?

Sources: Ethan Bernstein, John Bunch, Niko Canner, and Michael Lee, "Beyond the Holacracy Hype," *Harvard Business Review,* July–August 2016; Erik Roelofsen and Tao Yue, "Case Study: Is Holocracy for Us?" *Harvard Business Review,* March–April 2017.

cross-functional teams may share market information across national boundaries. Government coordinators may assist such projects, letting cross-functional teams break the barriers between government and business. Cross-functional teams are only one way in which businesses can interact with other companies. In the next section we look at other ways that organizations manage their various interactions.

PROGRESS ASSESSMENT

- What is the difference between line and staff personnel?
- What management principle does a matrix-style organization challenge?
- What is the main difference between the structure of a matrix-style organization and the use of cross-functional teams?

Managing Interactions Among Firms

LO5

Identify the benefits of inter-firm co-operation and coordination.

Whether it involves customers, suppliers, distributors, or the government, **networking between firms** is using communications technology and other means to link organizations and allow them to work together on common objectives. Let's explore this concept further.

networking between firms Using communications technology and other means to link organizations and allow them to work together on common objectives.

Virtual Organizations

Networked organizations are so closely linked by the Internet that each can find out what the others are doing in real time. **Real time** simply means the present moment or the actual time in which something takes place. The Internet has allowed companies to send real-time data to organizational partners as they are developed or collected.[24] The result is transparency. Transparency occurs when a company is so open to other companies working with it that the once-solid barriers between them become see-through and electronic information is shared as if the companies were one. With this integration, two companies can work as closely as two departments once did in traditional firms. As part of the movement to increase corporate social responsibility (as discussed in Chapter 5) many businesses want to ensure that their suppliers are meeting certain standards. The Seeking Sustainability box below describes the approach taken by Loblaw Companies Limited.

Seeking SUSTAINABILITY

Ethical Consumerism

Like many companies, Loblaws is working closely with its suppliers to align its values in areas from labour conditions to animal welfare. The year 2016 marked the 10th corporate social responsibility (CSR) report by the company. Its CSR focuses primarily upon three pillars—environment, sourcing, and community. The company documents its strategies and achievements in its Corporate Social Responsibility Report. Highlights from the 2016 report include the following future targets:

- Reduce operational carbon footprint 20 percent by 2020 and 30 percent by 2030.
- Transition all shell eggs to cage-free by year-end 2025.
- Disclose on the Loblaws corporate website the list of offshore apparel factories we do direct business with, and update the list twice a year.
- Raise and donate $3 million to various charities as part of our "Save It Forward" program in discount stores by year-end 2018.

To ensure these practices continue, Loblaws now requires all existing and new suppliers to be subject to, at a minimum, an annual Corporate Social Responsibility Audit. Loblaws engages qualified auditors to review all the processes and records of their suppliers. These auditors then report to Loblaws on the results of their investigation. This transparency on the part of Loblaws' suppliers is repeated in many industries so that retailers can demonstrate their social responsibility to consumers. Loblaws' purpose, *Live Life Well,* demonstrates how the company thinks about CSR!

© Image Source/age fotostock

Source: "2016 Corporate Social Responsibility Report," Loblaws, http://www.loblaw.ca/en/responsibility/reports.html.

real time
The present moment or the actual time in which something takes place; data sent over the Internet to various organizational partners as they are developed or collected are said to be available in real time.

virtual corporation
A temporary networked organization made up of replaceable firms that join and leave as needed.

Can you see the implications for organizational design? Most organizations are no longer self-sufficient or self-contained. Rather, they are part of a vast network of global businesses that work closely together (see the Spotlight on Small Business box below for more discussion). An organization chart showing what people do within any one organization is simply not complete, because the organization is part of a much larger system of firms. A modern chart would show people in different organizations and indicate how they are networked. This is a relatively new concept, however, and very few such charts are yet available.

Networked organization structures tend to be flexible.[25] A company may work with a design expert from a different company in Italy for a year and then not need that person anymore. It may hire an expert from a company in another country for another project. Such a temporary network, made of replaceable firms that join and leave as needed, is called a **virtual corporation** (see Figure 9.8).

People who work within a virtual organization still need to communicate. Many options help ensure co-workers may collaborate and co-operate even though they may be in

Spotlight *On* SMALL BUSINESS

Canadian Virtual Assistant Association

As a new graduate looking for work, how can you create the best opportunity to find a job? The answer is to make yourself, and your skills, available to as many employers as possible. That is the goal of a virtual assistant (VA). VAs are typically self-employed and provide professional administrative, technical, and creative services. Their clients need the expertise but want to save the cost of hiring a permanent employee to work "in house."

The Canadian Association of Virtual Assistants (CAVA) helps people establish and build their personal business. It provides a forum for independent professionals to network and obtain support as they develop their business. CAVA's mission seeks to establish global connection between and among VAs and clients.

Various websites, such as People Per Hour, help VAs find and bid on contracts, but competition is fierce so many VAs gravitate to sites like Time Etc. where the work is found for you. Time Etc. founder Barnaby Lashbrooke believed an online clearinghouse that matched clients with needs to professionals with skills filled an important gap. "The responsibility of having to find new business is what puts some people off. Being a VA requires being proactive, but many VAs find they have excellent contacts who are more than willing to recommend them, or keep them on part time" There are many other VA services that connect companies to highly effective remote professionals.

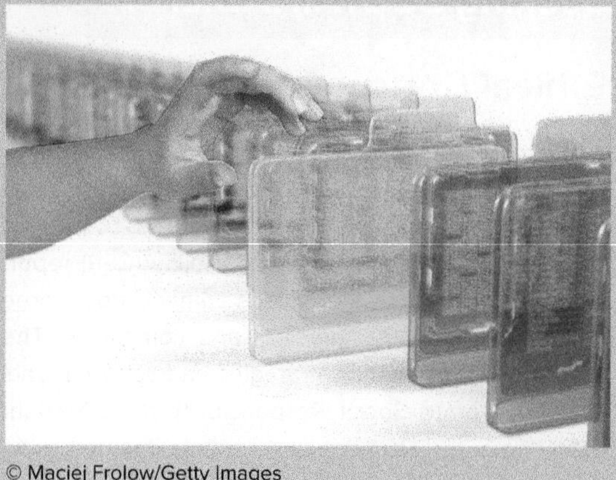

© Maciej Frolow/Getty Images

"The world is your oyster" is a saying often told to new graduates when they finish their education and enter the workforce. With the growth of virtual organizations, this saying has never been so true.

Sources: Alison Coleman, "How to set-up a home-based virtual assistant business," *The Guardian*, April 23, 2015, http://www.theguardian.com/small-business-network/2013/nov/25/virtual-assistant-small-business; "What is CAVA?" Canadian Association of Virtual Assistants, http://canadianava.org/what-is-cava/, accessed May 9, 2015; Sara Angeles, "10 virtual assistant services for your business," Business News daily, February 5, 2014, http://www.businessnewsdaily.com/5878-virtual-assistant-services.html.

FIGURE 9.8

A VIRTUAL CORPORATION

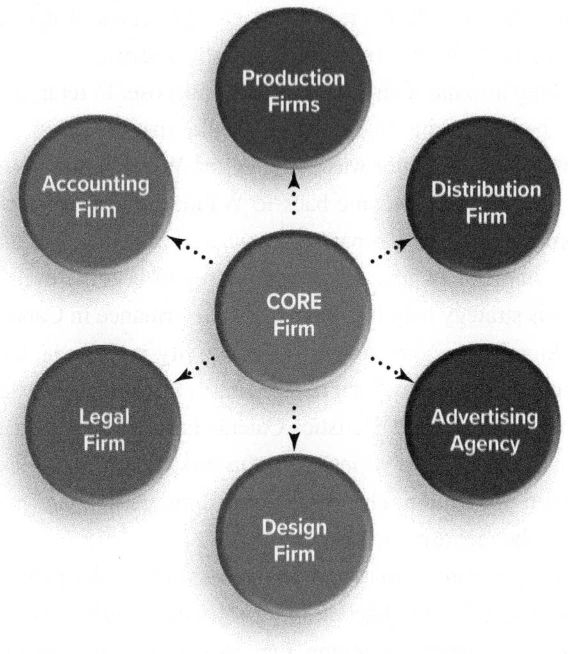

A virtual corporation has no permanent ties to the firms that do its production, distribution, legal, and other work. Such firms are very flexible and can adapt to changes in the market quickly.

different physical locations. Simple information-sharing platforms such as Dropbox have expanded into virtual private networks to share knowledge. For example, the life sciences industry has a large number of multi-partner virtual organizations that use online collaboration platforms to connect pharmaceutical executives and life sciences researchers.[26] When knowledge sharing reaches a point where face-to-face communication is needed, employees turn to online tools such as Skype and GoToMeeting for business web conferencing. Business leaders are always searching for new virtual team members and these practices help ensure a virtual organization can be successful.

Benchmarking and Core Competencies

Historically, organizations have tried to do all functions themselves. Each had its own department for accounting, finance, marketing, production, and so on. As we have noted, today's organizations look to other organizations to help in areas where they do not generate world-class quality.

benchmarking Comparing an organization's practices, processes, and products against the world's best.

Benchmarking compares an organization's practices, processes, and products against the world's best. As one example, K2 Skis is a company that makes skis, snowboards, in-line skates, and related products. It studied the compact-disc industry and learned to use ultraviolet inks to print graphics on skis. It went to the aerospace industry to get piezoelectric technology to reduce vibration in its snowboards (the aerospace industry uses the technology for wings on planes). It learned from the cable television industry how to braid layers of fibre-glass and carbon, and adapted that knowledge to make skis. Wyeth, a pharmaceutical company, benchmarked the aerospace industry for project management, the shipping industry for standardization of processes, and computer makers to learn the most efficient way to make prescription drugs. As another example, Suncor, one of Canada's largest emitters of greenhouse gases, continually benchmarks its environmental and social progress.[27] By doing so, they are able to evaluate their performance in reducing their impact in various areas such as greenhouse gas emissions, water, land and tailings, and improve their impact on biodiversity and renewable energy.

Benchmarking also has a direct competitive purpose. In retailing, Sam Walton used to do competitive benchmarking regularly. He would visit the stores of competitors and see what, if anything, the competitor was doing better. When he found something better—say, a pricing program—he would come back to Walmart and make the appropriate changes. Target may compare itself to Walmart to see what, if anything, Walmart does better. Target will then try to improve its practices or processes to become even better than Walmart. How well did this strategy help the company's performance in Canada?

Benchmarking has become a significant activity in Canada. Governments and large and small companies are all involved in procedures to discover and apply the best practices available. Industry Canada and Statistics Canada have accumulated extensive statistics on the use of benchmarking in a variety of industries. Some examples are breweries, flour mixing and cereal production, electronic computing, paperboard manufacturing, musical instruments, and the recording industry.

If an organization cannot do as well as the best in, say, shipping, it will try to outsource the function to an organization like UPS or FedEx that specializes in shipping. Remember, outsourcing means assigning one or more functions, such as accounting, production, security, maintenance, and legal work, to outside organizations. Even small firms are getting involved in outsourcing. We have already discussed some problems associated with outsourcing, especially when companies outsource to other countries. Jobs are lost in Canada and this has a negative impact on our economy. Some functions, such as information management and marketing, may be too important to assign to outside firms. In that case, the organization should benchmark the best firms and restructure its departments to try to be equally good. It is important to remember that companies in other countries often outsource their functions to companies in Canada. We call that *insourcing* and it is the basis of many jobs.[28]

core competencies
Those functions that an organization can do as well as or better than any other organization in the world.

When a firm has completed its outsourcing process, the remaining functions are the firm's **core competencies**, those functions that the organization can do as well as or better than any other organization in the world. For example, Nike is great at designing and marketing athletic shoes. Those are its core competencies. It outsources the manufacturing of those shoes, however, to other companies that can make shoes better and less expensively than Nike itself can.[29] Similarly, Dell is best at marketing computers and outsources most other functions, including manufacturing and distribution, to others. Canadian banks, such as the Royal Bank of Canada, have been criticized for outsourcing jobs in areas such as information technology and finance operations.[30]

© Jens Kalaene/picture-alliance/dpa/AP Images

Nike's core competencies are designing and marketing athletic shoes. The company outsources other functions (i.e., manufacturing) to other businesses that assemble shoes better and cheaper than Nike could do on its own. What are the advantages of focusing on the company's core competencies? What are the disadvantages?

After you have structured an organization, you must keep monitoring the environment (including customers) to learn what changes are needed. Dell, for example, recently reversed its practice of outsourcing customer support and now offers a premium service that enables Canadian customers to access tech support in North America. The following section discusses organizational change in more detail.

Adapting to Change

Once you have structured an organization, you must be prepared to adapt that structure to changes in the market. That is not always easy to do.[31] Over time an organization can get set in its ways. Employees have a tendency to say, "That's the way we've always done things. If it isn't broken, don't fix it." Managers also get complacent. They may say that they have 20 years' experience when the truth is that they have had one year's experience 20 times. Do you think that slow adaptation to change was a factor in the decline of the manufacturing sector in Canada?

Introducing change is one of the hardest challenges facing any manager. Nonetheless, change is what is happening at General Motors (GM), Ford, Facebook, and other companies eager to become more competitive. If you have old facilities that are no longer efficient, you have to unload or update them. That is exactly what GM and other companies are doing.[32] In fact, they have asked the government to lend them billions of dollars to help.[33]

The Internet has created new opportunities, not only to sell to customers directly but also to ask them questions and provide them with any information they want. To win market share, companies must coordinate the efforts of their tradiitonal departments and their Internet staff to create friendly, easy-to-manage interactions. Young people today are called **digital natives** because they grew up with the Internet and cell phones. Using these devices is second nature to them. On the other hand, companies often need to retrain older employees to be more tech-savvy. While the ease and immediacy of communication created by technology may be powerful, there are disadvantages to being constantly connected to work (see the Adapting to Change box).

digital natives
Young people who grew up using technology including the Internet and electronic devices such as cell phones.

Although Target is a highly centralized organization, the company tries to respond to changes in consumer preferences, in part by keeping in touch with an enormous web of people of all ages, interests and nationalities—its "creative cabinet"—via the Internet. The members of the "cabinet," who never meet so they cannot influence each other, evaluate various new initiatives and recommend new programs to help Target determine out what belongs on store shelves.

But when Target entered the highly competitive Canadian retail market, it faced many challenges that ultimately led to failure. Why didn't the centralization and "cabinet" structure that proved so effective for Target in other markets work for the company in Canada? As soon as Target Canada opened its doors the losses mounted to $1 billion in the first year. In less than two years, the doors closed at 133 stores and 17 000 employees were laid off.[34] It seemed the senior executives didn't know how to communicate with the front-line staff. Even though staff knew all the customer complaints about the lack of product on the shelves and the over-pricing, the centralized structure made it difficult to respond. Management couldn't connect to the staff in the stores, many of whom described the atmosphere as ". . . akin to swimming with smiling sharks."[35] The next section, about restructuring in ways to empower employees, provides insight about the Target Canada story.

Adapting *to* CHANGE

When Open Communication Should Not Be So Open

People today use technology to text, tweet, surf the web, and run apps as they go about their personal lives and, in many cases, their business lives. In fact, many companies provide work-issued smartphones, tablets, and other mobile technology to their employees. The blending of mobile technology and work has been a boon to employees and businesses in many ways, particularly in terms of speed, reach, and efficiency. Unfortunately, it has also encroached on the traditional boundaries between work and home.

According to a survey conducted by Right Management, a career and outplacement service, more than one-third of employees receive work-related e-mails after work hours. According to Monika Morrow, senior vice president at Right Management, "The boundaries of the workplace are expanding and now reach deeper into employees' lives. Workers can no longer leave the office at the office." While no one disputes the value of technology, many believe its use has gone overboard and is affecting employees' quality of life. Companies such as Volkswagen, PricewaterhouseCoopers, and shipping company PBD have heard the complaints and created both formal and informal rules regarding e-mail.

© almagami/ Alamy RF

The e-mail encroachment problem is not just in Canada. France is considering legislation that would block work e-mails and phone calls, and legally give employees at least 11 hours of daily rest free from mobile technology. What do you think would be the impact upon businesses of imposing a similar law in Canada?

Sources: Scott Sayare, "In France, a Move to Limit Off-the-Clock Work Emails," *The New York Times*, April 11, 2014; Chris Baysden, "Why You're Never Safe from More Work—Even After Hours," *CGMA Magazine*, July 4, 2013; and Cecilia Kang, "Firms Tell Employees: Avoid After-Hours E-Mail," *The Washington Post*, September 21, 2012.

Companies that are the most successful in adapting to change have these common traits: (1) listening to customers, (2) inspiring managers who drive new ideas throughout the organizations, and (3) having experience almost going out of business.[36] Of course, adapting to change is difficult, but not changing can be disastrous.

Restructuring for Empowerment

restructuring
Redesigning an organization so that it can more effectively and efficiently serve its customers.

inverted organization
An organization that has contact people at the top and the chief executive officer at the bottom of the organization chart.

To empower employees firms must reorganize dramatically to make front-line workers their most important people. **Restructuring** is redesigning an organization so it can more effectively and efficiently serve its customers. Until recently, department-store clerks, bank tellers, and front-desk staff in hotels were not considered key employees. Instead, managers were considered more important, and they were responsible for directing the work of the front-line people. The organization chart in a typical firm looked much like the pyramid in Figure 9.9.

A few service-oriented organizations have turned the traditional organization pyramid structure upside down. An **inverted organization** has contact people (like nurses) at the top and the chief executive officer (like the hospital CEO) at the bottom. Management

FIGURE 9.9

COMPARISON OF A TRADITIONAL ORGANIZATION STRUCTURE AND AN INVERTED ORGANIZATION STRUCTURE

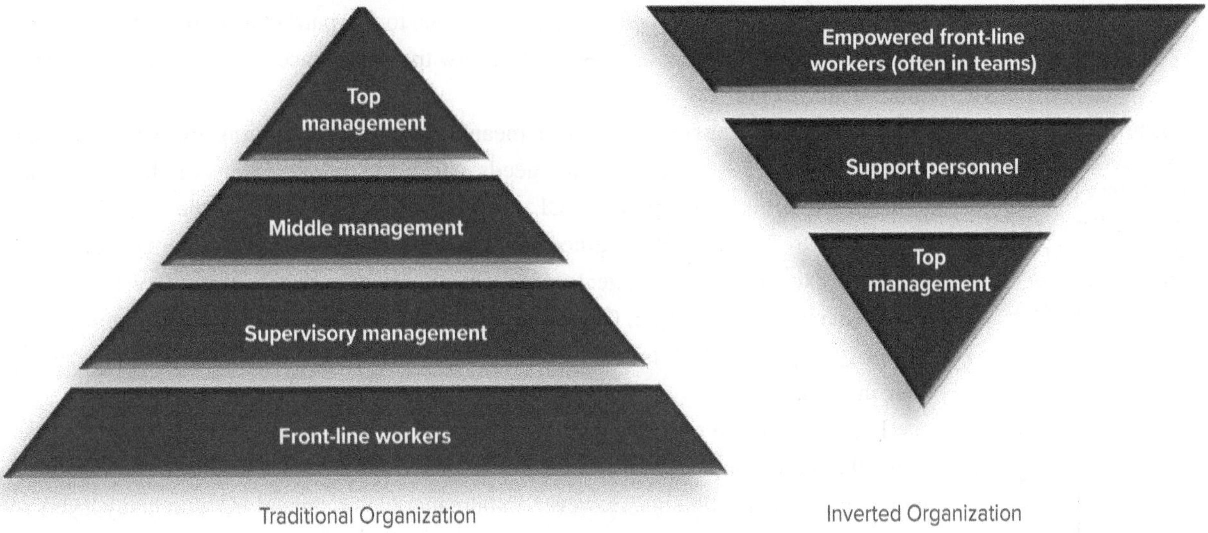

layers are few, and the manager's job is to *assist* and *support* front-line people, not boss them around. Figure 9.9 illustrates the difference between an inverted and a traditional organizational structure.

A good example of an inverted organization is NovaCare, a diversified health care company.[37] At its top are some 5000 physical, occupational, and speech therapists. The rest of the organization is structured to serve those therapists. Managers consider the therapists to be their bosses, and the manager's job is to support the therapists by arranging contacts with nursing homes, handling accounting and credit activities, and providing training.

Companies based on this organization structure support front-line personnel with internal and external databases, advanced communication systems, and professional assistance. Naturally, this means that front-line people have to be better educated, better trained, and better paid than in the past. It takes a great deal of trust for top managers to implement such a system—but when they do, the payoff in customer satisfaction and in profits is often well worth the effort.[38]

In the past, managers controlled information—and that gave them power. In more progressive organizations everyone shares information, often through an elaborate database system, *among* firms as well as *within* them. No matter what organizational model you choose or how much you empower your employees, the secret to successful organization change is to focus on customers and give them what they want.

The Restructuring Process

It is not easy to move from an organization dominated by managers to one that relies heavily on self-managed teams. How you restructure an organization depends on the status of the present system. If the system already has a customer focus but is not working well, a total quality management approach may work.

total quality management (TQM) Striving for maximum customer satisfaction by ensuring quality from all departments.

Total quality management (TQM) is the practice of striving for maximum customer satisfaction by ensuring quality from all departments. TQM calls for *continual improvement of present processes.* Processes are sets of activities joined together for a reason, such as the process for handling a customer's order. The process may consist of receiving the order in the mail, opening it, sending it to someone to fill, putting the order into a package, and sending it out. In Chapter 10 we will review the importance of quality control in operations management.

continuous improvement (CI) Constantly improving the way the organization operates so that customer needs can be better satisfied.

Continuous improvement (CI) means constantly improving the way the organization operates so that customer needs can be satisfied. Many of the companies spotlighted in this book practice CI. No matter what the size of the organization it is possible to innovate. Re-engineering and change is not the sole domain of small, nimble organizations and large companies also demonstrate a propensity for change management.[39] For example, Canadian companies such as HootSuite and Shopify continuously improve products and constantly challenge employees to be creative despite their increase in size.

It is possible, in an organization with few layers of management and a customer focus, that new computer software and employee training could lead to a team-oriented approach with few problems. However, in bureaucratic organizations with many layers of management, TQM is not useful. Continual improvement does not work when the whole process is incorrect. When an organization needs dramatic changes, only re-engineering will do.

re-engineering The fundamental rethinking and radical redesign of organizational processes to achieve dramatic improvements in critical measures of performance.

Re-engineering is the fundamental rethinking and radical redesign of organizational processes to achieve dramatic improvements in critical measures of performance. Note the words *radical redesign* and *dramatic improvements.* Stanfield's, a Canadian clothing manufacturer based in Nova Scotia, was established in 1856. A "Made in Canada" philosophy is important to the company, both for its brand and its customers. Stanfield's has faced many challenges that prompted it to re-engineer in order to remain competitive.[40] Jon Stanfield, the fifth-generation family member who currently serves as president, recognized the need to adapt: "We have re-engineered the factory as far as making it more efficient and cutting waste to deal with the competitive pressures that occurred during the Free Trade Agreements and then subsequently the North American Free Trade Agreement." Changes have occurred in many areas including revised packaging to develop better supplier relations and energy consumption technology to reduce the company's carbon footprint.

Can you see how re-engineering is often necessary to change a firm from a managerial orientation to one based on self-managed teams? Re-engineering may also be necessary to adapt an organization to fit into a virtual network. Remember, re-engineering involves radical redesign and dramatic improvements. Not all organizations need such dramatic change. In fact, because of the complexity of the process, many re-engineering efforts fail. In firms where re-engineering is not feasible, restructuring may do. As discussed earlier in this chapter, restructuring involves making relatively minor changes to an organization in response to a changing environment. For example, many firms have added an Internet marketing component to the marketing department. That is a restructuring move, but it is not drastic enough to be called re-engineering.

Creating a Change-Oriented Organizational Culture

Any organizational change is bound to cause some stress and resistance among members. Firms adapt best when their culture is change-oriented. **Organizational (or corporate) culture** is the widely shared values within an organization that foster unity and co-operation to achieve common goals. Usually the culture of an organization is reflected in its stories, traditions, and myths.

© Onoky/SuperStock

Empowering employees who deal directly with customers to solve problems without needing a manager's approval makes a higher level of customer service possible and also helps employees develop. What kind of guest issues do you think a front-line hotel employee should be allowed to solve on his or her own?

Each McDonald's restaurant has the same feel, look, and atmosphere; in short, each has a similar organizational culture. It is obvious from visiting almost any McDonald's that the culture emphasizes quality, service, cleanliness, and value.

An organizational culture can also be negative. Have you ever been in an organization where you feel that no one cares about service or quality? The clerks may seem uniformly glum, indifferent, and testy. The mood pervades the atmosphere and patrons become unhappy or upset. It may be hard to believe that an organization, especially a profit-making one, can be run so badly and still survive. Clearly then, when you search for a job, study the organizational culture to see whether you will thrive in it.

LO6

Explain how organizational culture can help businesses adapt to change.

organizational (or corporate) culture
Widely shared values within an organization that provide coherence and co-operation to achieve common goals.

Mintzberg notes that culture affects the way in which employees are chosen, developed, nurtured, interrelated, and rewarded. The kinds of people attracted to an organization and the way they can most effectively deal with problems and each other are largely a function of the culture an organization builds and the practices and systems that support the culture.[41]

Some of the best organizations have cultures that emphasize service to others, especially customers. The atmosphere reflects friendly, caring people who enjoy working together to provide a good product at a reasonable price. Companies that have such a culture have less need for close supervision of employees. That usually means fewer policy manuals, organization charts, and formal rules, procedures, and controls. The key to a productive culture is mutual trust. You receive such trust by giving it. The very best companies stress high moral and ethical values such as honesty, reliability, fairness, environmental protection, and social involvement. One such example is TD Bank Group. They have been recognized for multiple years as one of the best workplaces in Canada. The Careers section of their home page provides numerous employee video testimonials on the culture that contributes to this success.[42]

Thus far, we have been talking as if organizational matters were mostly controllable by management. The fact is that the formal organization structure is just one element of the

© Geber86/Getty Images RF

The informal organization is the system that develops as employees meet and form relationships. The grapevine, or the unofficial flow of information among employees, is the nerve centre of the informal organization. How does the informal organization affect the work environment? How might it affect organizational performance?

total organizational system. In the creation of organizational culture, the informal organization is of equal or even greater importance. Let's explore this notion next.

The Informal Organization

All organizations have two organizational systems. The **formal organization** details lines of responsibility, authority, and position. It is the structure shown on organization charts. The other is the **informal organization**, the system that develops spontaneously as employees meet and form cliques, relationships, and lines of authority outside the formal organization. It is the human side of the organization that does not show on any organization chart.

No organization can operate effectively without both types of organization. The formal system is often too slow and bureaucratic to let the organization adapt quickly although it does provide helpful guides and lines of authority for routine situations.

formal organization
The structure that details lines of responsibility, authority, and position; that is, the structure shown on organization charts.

informal organization
The system of relationships and lines of authority that develops spontaneously as employees meet and form power centres; that is, the human side of the organization that does not appear on any organization chart.

The informal organization is often too unstructured and emotional to allow careful, reasoned decision making on critical matters. It is extremely effective, however, in generating creative solutions to short-term problems and creating camaraderie and teamwork among employees.[43]

In any organization, it is wise to learn quickly who is important in the informal organization. Following formal rules and procedures can take days. Who in the organization knows how to obtain resources immediately without the normal procedures? Which administrative assistants should you see if you want your work given first priority? Answers to these questions help people work effectively in many organizations.

The informal organization's nerve centre called the *grapevine,* is the system through which unofficial information flows between and among managers and employees. Key people in the grapevine usually have considerable influence.

In the old "us-versus-them" system of organizations, where managers and employees were often at odds, the informal system hindered effective management. Within a more open organization, managers and employees work together to set objectives and design procedures. The informal organization is an invaluable managerial asset that can promote harmony among workers and establish the corporate culture.[44]

As effective as the informal organization may be in creating group co-operation, it can still be equally powerful in resisting management directives. Employees may form unions, go on strike together, and generally disrupt operations. Learning to create the right corporate culture and to work within the informal organization is a key to managerial success.

PROGRESS ASSESSMENT

- What is an inverted organization?
- Why do organizations outsource functions?
- What is organizational culture?

SUMMARY

LO1 **Outline the basic principles of organization management.**

The basic principles of organization are much the same regardless of the size of the business.

What is happening today to Canadian businesses?

Canadian businesses are adjusting to changing markets. This is a normal function in a capitalist economy. There will be big winners, like Google and Facebook, and big losers, like Target (in Canada). The key to success is remaining flexible and adapting to the changing times.

What are the principles of organization management?

Structuring an organization means devising a division of labour (sometimes resulting in specialization), setting up teams or departments, and assigning responsibility and authority. It includes allocating resources (such as funds), assigning specific tasks, and establishing procedures for accomplishing the organizational objectives. Managers also have to make ethical decisions about how to treat workers.

LO2 **Compare the organizational theories of Henri Fayol and Max Weber.**

Until the twentieth century, most businesses were rather small, the processes of producing goods were rather simple, and organizing workers was fairly easy. Not until the early 1900s and the introduction of mass production did businesses become complex. During this era, business theorists emerged.

What were Fayol's basic principles?

Fayol introduced principles such as unity of command, hierarchy of authority, division of labour, subordination of individual interests to the general interest, authority, clear communication channels, order, and equity.

What principles did Weber add?

Weber added principles of bureaucracy such as job descriptions, written rules and decision guidelines, consistent procedures, and staffing and promotions based on qualifications.

LO3 **Evaluate the choices managers make in structuring organizations.**

What are the four issues in structuring organizations?

Issues involved in structuring and restructuring organizations are (1) centralization versus decentralization, (2) span of control, (3) tall versus flat organization structures, and (4) departmentalization.

What are the latest trends in structuring?

Departments are often replaced or supplemented by matrix organizations and cross-functional, self-managed teams that decentralize authority. The span of control becomes larger as employees become self-directed. Another trend is to eliminate managers and flatten organizations.

LO4 **Contrast the various organizational models.**

Organizational design is the coordination of workers so that they can best accomplish the firm's goals. New forms of organization are emerging that enable firms to be more responsive to customers.

What are the two major organizational models?

Two traditional forms of organization are (1) line organizations and (2) line-and-staff organizations. A line organization has clearly defined responsibility and authority, is easy to understand, and provides each worker with only one supervisor. The expert advice of staff assistants in a line-and-staff organization helps in areas such as safety, quality control, computer technology, human resource management, and investing.

What are the key alternative forms to the major organizational models?

Matrix organizations assign people to projects temporarily and encourage inter-organizational co-operation and teamwork. Cross-functional self-managed teams have all the benefits of the matrix style and are long term.

LO5 **Identify the benefits of inter-firm co-operation and coordination.**

Networking is using communications technology and other means to link organizations and allow them to work together on common objectives.

What are the major concepts involved in inter-firm communications?

Communications technology allows firms to work together on common objectives. A virtual corporation is a networked organization of replaceable firms that join and leave as needed. Benchmarking tells firms how their performance measures up to that of their competitors in specific functions. The business may then outsource to companies that perform its weaker functions more effectively and efficiently. The functions that remain within the organization are the firm's core competencies.

What is an inverted organization?

An inverted organization places employees at the top of the hierarchy; managers are at the bottom to train and assist employees.

LO6 **Explain how organizational culture can help businesses adapt to change.**

Organizational (or corporate) culture may be defined as widely shared values that foster unity and co-operation to achieve common goals.

What is the difference between the formal and informal organization of a firm?

The formal organization details lines of responsibility, authority, and position. It is the structure shown on organization charts. The informal organization is the system that develops spontaneously as employees meet and form cliques, relationships, and lines of authority outside the formal organization. It is the human side of the organization. The informal organization is an invaluable managerial asset that often promotes harmony among workers and establishes the corporate culture. As effective as the informal organization may be in creating group co-operation, it can still be equally powerful in resisting management directives.

KEY TERMS

benchmarking 341
bureaucracy 325
centralized authority 326
chain of command 325
continuous improvement (CI) 346
core competencies 342
cross-functional, self-managed teams 336
decentralized authority 326
departmentalization 329
digital natives 343
economies of scale 322
flat organization structure 328
formal organization 348
hierarchy 325
informal organization 348
inverted organization 344
line organization 333
line personnel 333
matrix organization 334
networking between firms 339
organizational (or corporate) culture 347
real time 339
re-engineering 346
restructuring 344
span of control 327
staff personnel 333
tall organization structure 328
total quality management (TQM) 346
virtual corporation 340

CAREER EXPLORATION

If you are interested in pursuing a career in organizational management, here are a few to consider. Find out about the tasks performed, skills needed, pay, and opportunity outlook in these fields through Internet sites that include the Government of Canada Job Bank, Workopolis, Monster, CareerBuilder, Glassdoor, and Indeed, as well as through the Career Centre at your school.

- **Top executive—**works in nearly every industry in both large and small businesses and non-profit organizations, ranging from companies in which there is only one employee to firms with thousands of employees.
- **Management analyst—**proposes ways to improve an organization's efficiency.

CRITICAL THINKING

Now that you have learned some of the basic principles of organization, pause and think about where you have already applied such concepts yourself or when you have been part of an organization that did.

1. Did you find a division of labour necessary and helpful?
2. Were you assigned specific tasks or left on your own to decide what to do?
3. Were promotions based strictly on qualifications, as Weber suggested? What other factors may have been considered?
4. What problems seem to emerge when an organization expands in size?
5. What organizational changes might you recommend to Canadian manufacturers, such as the auto companies, airlines, and technology firms?

DEVELOPING CAREER SKILLS

Key: ● **Team** ★ **Analytic** ▲ **Communication** ⊡ **Technology**

●▲ 1. There is no better way to understand the effects of having many layers of management on communication accuracy than to play the game of Message Relay. Choose seven or more members of the class and have them leave the classroom. Then choose one person to read the following paragraph and another student to listen. Call in one of the students from outside and have the "listener" tell him or her the information contained in the paragraph.

Then bring in another student and have the new listener repeat the information to him or her. Continue the process with all those who left the room. Do not allow anyone in the class to offer corrections as each listener becomes the storyteller in turn. In this way, all students can hear how the facts become distorted over time. The distortions and mistakes are often quite humorous, but they are not so funny in organizations such as Ford, which once had 22 layers of management.

Here is the paragraph:

Dealers in the Maritimes have received more than 130 complaints about steering on the new Commander and Roadhandler models of our minivans. Apparently, the front suspension system is weak and the ball joints are wearing too fast. This causes slippage in the linkage and results in oversteering. Mr. Berenstein has been notified, but so far only 213 of 4300 dealers have received repair kits.

★ **2.** Describe some informal groups within an organization with which you are familiar (at school, at work, etc.). What have you noticed about how those groups help or hinder progress in the organization?

▲ **3.** Imagine that you are working for Kitchen Magic, an appliance manufacturer that produces, among other things, dishwashers for the home. Imagine further that a competitor introduces a new dishwasher that uses sound waves to clean dishes. The result is a dishwasher that cleans even the worst burned-on food and sterilizes the dishes and silverware as well. You need to develop a similar offering fast, or your company will lose the market. Write an e-mail to management outlining the problem, explaining your rationale for recommending the use of a cross-functional team to respond quickly, and identifying the type of skills you need.

●★▲ **4.** Divide the class into teams of five. You are a producer of athletic shoes and you have been asked to join a virtual network. How might you minimize the potential problems of joining? Begin by defining a virtual corporation and listing its advantages and disadvantages. Each team should report its solutions to the class.

●★▲ **5.** A growing number of work groups, including management, are cross-functional and self-managed. To practice working in such an organization, break into groups of five or so students, preferably with different backgrounds and interests. Each group must work together to prepare a report on the advantages and disadvantages of working in teams. Many of the problems and advantages of cross-functional, self-managed teams should emerge in your group as you try to complete this assignment. Each group should report to the class how it handled the problems and benefitted from the advantages.

ANALYZING MANAGEMENT DECISIONS

IBM Is Both an Outsourcer and a Major Outsource for Others

Few companies are better known for their manufacturing expertise than IBM. Nonetheless, even IBM has to adapt to today's dynamic marketplace. In the area of personal computers, for example, IBM was unable to match the prices or speed of delivery of mail-order firms such as Dell Computer. Dell built machines after receiving orders and then rushed the computers to customers. IBM, in contrast, made machines ahead of time and hoped that the orders would match its inventory.

To compete against firms like Dell, IBM had to custom-make computers for its business customers, but IBM was not particularly suited to do such work. To address this issue IBM entered into a relationship with

Lenovo whereby Lenovo became the manufacturer of IBM personal computers and over time replaced IBM in the personal computer market.

IBM's long-range strategy was to move away from hardware toward software development. It acquired PricewaterhouseCoopers to put more emphasis on services rather than hardware. As a result, IBM dominated the IT industry. They offered outsourcing for IT infrastructure, application development, and IT support services. They spent over $6 billion annually on research and development and held the most patents of any U.S. technology company.

While growing this side of their business they outsourced a number of jobs to India in sales, semiconductor, and finance groups, resulting in the layoff of 4600 U.S.-based employees in these positions in 2009.

Today IBM continues to face many challenges. While revenues from cloud computing have helped the company, major competitors such as Amazon, Google, and Microsoft have gained ground in this area. The drop in server hardware sales led IBM to sell this part of its business to Lenovo and focus upon business acquisitions to capitalize on growth within cloud computing. While generating profit for the company, the switch to acquisitions led to a de-emphasis upon innovation.

Despite explicitly stating three strategic areas—clients, innovation, and trust—decision making was driven by a desire to earn more for shareholders. This focus upon investment returns, referred to as "Roadmap 2015," led to massive cost-cutting measures that created high costs for the company and led to further employee layoffs.

Nevertheless, the company still finds ways to innovate. IBM Research has defined the future of information technology with more than 3000 researchers in 12 labs located across 6 continents. IBM inventors received over 5000 patents in 2017, marking the company's 25th consecutive year of patent leadership.

Sources: "IBM Breaks Records to Top U.S. Patent List for 25th Consecutive Year," *Canada NewsWire,* January 8, 2018; "IBM Reveals Five Innovations That Will Help Change Our Lives in the Next Five Years," *Canada NewsWire,* January 5, 2017; Steve Denning, "Why IBM is in decline," *Forbes,* May 30, 2014, http://www.forbes.com/sites/stevedenning/2014/05/30/why-ibm-is-in-decline/; Julie Bort, "IBM CEO Ginni Rometty is a year away from delivering on a plan that has tied her hands for years," *Business Insider,* May 22, 2014, http://www.businessinsider.com/ibm-ginni-rometty-and-2015-road-map-2014-5; Michael Useem and Joseph Harder, "Leading Laterally in Company Outsourcing," *Sloan Management Review,* Winter 2000, 25–36; Alison Overholt, "In the Hot Seat," *Fast Company,* January 2003, 46; "IBM Outsourcing Thousands of Jobs to India," Exposing the Elitist Agenda Blog, www.peacerebelgirl.wordpress.com/2009/03/26/ibm-outsourcing-thousands-of-jobs-to-india/, March 26, 2009; and "IBM Outsourcing with Big Blue," www.itouotsourcinghq.com/it-outsourcing-to-ibm, April 12, 2011.

Discussion Questions

1. What does it say about today's competitive environment when leading companies such as IBM give up competing in an area of their business that they dominated for many years and expand significantly into a related area of business they have only been involved in for a relatively short period of time?
2. In what ways does this example demonstrate an organization's ability and/or inability to adapt to change?

CHAPTER 10

Producing World-Class Goods and Services

LEARNING OBJECTIVES

After you have read and studied this chapter, you should be able to:

LO1 Describe the current state of Canadian manufacturing and how companies are becoming more competitive.

LO2 Describe the evolution from production to operations management.

LO3 Describe operations management planning issues, including facility location, facility layout, materials requirement planning, purchasing, just-in-time inventory control, quality control.

LO4 Identify various production processes and describe techniques that improve productivity, including computer-aided design and manufacturing, flexible manufacturing, lean manufacturing, mass customization, robotics, and 3D printing.

LO5 Explain the use of PERT and Gantt charts to control manufacturing processes.

PROFILE

GETTING TO KNOW: SHAHID KHAN, OWNER, FLEX-N-GATE

At just 16 years old, Shahid Khan moved to Champaign, Illinois, ready to live the American Dream. However, the young Pakistani immigrant quickly lost his confidence when he discovered an enormous blizzard had hit his new Midwestern home. To make matters worse, the dorms at the University of Illinois hadn't opened yet, forcing Khan to pay $3 for a room and a meal at the local YMCA. With precious little money to his name, he began to worry about how he would survive the next four years at college.

His fears subsided the next morning when he discovered a notice about an opening for a dishwashing job in the YMCA kitchen. With a starting salary of $1.20 per hour, Khan was shocked that he could recoup his losses from the previous night so quickly. "It's like, wow," said Khan. "If you put the $1.20 per hour in terms of Pakistan, you're making more than 99% of the people over there. I'm breathing oxygen for the first time." The new opportunities fuelled Khan's enthusiasm for his work and after

© Michael Hickey/Getty Images

graduating he landed a job overseeing production for a local aftermarket auto parts company called Flex-N-Gate. At first Khan couldn't believe the inefficient manufacturing methods the company used to make its bumpers, which sometimes involved welding together as many as 15 different parts. Using his engineering expertise, Khan refined the process to make it less complicated. His hard work paid off in the form of a revolutionary new product: a bumper stamped from a single piece of steel that managed to slim down the rear end of a truck.

After seven years in the aftermarket business, Khan realized that the value-focused industry didn't provide much room for innovation. If Khan wanted his product to succeed, he knew he had to sell directly to automakers instead of to consumers. So, armed with little more than a post office box and a small business loan, Khan started his own company. Within two years he earned enough money to buy the failing Flex-N-Gate from his old boss, giving him additional revenue streams as well as an established brand name. While business boomed at first, sales eventually ground to a halt when its biggest client, General Motors, passed off his bumper design to their large-scale suppliers.

Other entrepreneurs would have reacted angrily to such a slight, but Khan remained positive. "It really was the right thing for them," he says. "We had no business going from making 200 bumpers a day to making 40 000." Plus, his dealings with GM put him in contact with executives at Isuzu, one of Japan's biggest auto companies. Khan travelled to Japan in the early 1980s in a last-ditch effort to win clients. His timing couldn't have been better. Japanese car companies had been preparing to enter the American market, but needed more domestic suppliers to fuel their growth. Khan fit this need perfectly thanks to his manufacturing experience and his game-changing bumper design. Soon Flex-N-Gate was manufacturing parts for Toyota, Isuzu, and Mazda. As these brands grew into some of the biggest names on the American market, Khan's company grew right along with them. By 2011, two-thirds of cars and trucks sold in America used Flex-N-Gate parts. And since Khan is the sole shareholder, all profits from the company's sales go to him. He's now worth about $7 billion.

In 2012 he used some of that immense wealth to purchase the Jacksonville Jaguars, fulfilling a personal dream to own a NFL franchise. Although the Jaguars haven't exactly been Super Bowl contenders in recent years, Khan is confident that someday the team will become another one of his comeback stories.

By setting Flex-N-Gate on the path to productivity, Shahid Khan made a fortune while also creating thousands of jobs. It has also earned him great respect in the auto industry. In this chapter you'll learn about how other company leaders thrive and survive in the production and operations sector. You'll also find out why Canada is generally moving from a production-based economy to a service economy.

Sources: P. R. Sanjai, Jie Ma, and John Lippert, "NFL's Jaguars Billionaire Rises From Dishwasher to Takata Suitor," *Bloomberg,* September 28, 2016; Brent Snavely, "Shahid Khan's Advice to Engineers: 'Make Sure You Make Money'," *Detroit Free Press,* April 12, 2016.

LO1

Describe the current state of Canadian manufacturing and how companies are becoming more competitive.

Canada Today

Canada is a large industrial country with many major industries. We are one of the largest producers of forest products in the world, with plants in nearly all provinces turning out a vast array of wood, furniture, and paper products. There are giant aluminum mills in Quebec and British Columbia, automotive-related manufacturing plants in Ontario and Quebec, and aircraft plants in Ontario, Quebec, and Manitoba. Oil, natural gas, and coal are produced in Alberta, Saskatchewan, Newfoundland and Labrador, Nova Scotia, and British Columbia, and a vast array of metals and minerals come from all parts of Canada.

These are only some of the thousands of components, products, and natural resources produced or processed in Canada. Given that most of our industry is focused on natural resources we can experience significant growth in times when world economies are growing, offset by an equally large retraction when world economies are stagnant or in recession. Such has been the case over the past 7 to 10 years. What happens in the United States, along with world economies including China and India, has a dramatic impact on Canada, as was discussed in Chapter 3.

Canada is facing some serious challenges to its ability to remain a modern, competitive industrial country. Today's business climate is characterized by constant and restless change and dislocation, as ever-newer technologies and increasing global competition force companies to respond quickly to these challenges. Many factors account for our difficulties in the world's competitive race. Among them are inadequate improvement in productivity and unrelenting competition from the United States, Japan, Germany, and more recently from India, China, and other Southeast Asian countries; inadequate education and retraining programs for our workforce; our "branch plant economy," whereby many subsidiaries are owned by foreign parent companies and profits are mostly returned to these foreign-based companies rather than invested in Canada; and a lack of money spent on research and development. Where Canada used to be able to rely on a lower-valued Canadian dollar compared to the U.S. dollar to sustain our exports, an exchange rate closer to parity negates this advantage. Figure 10.1 lists priorities that could improve Canada's competitiveness.

FIGURE 10.1

MAKING CANADA MORE COMPETITIVE

The Canadian Manufacturing Coalition published a report identifying priorities that would make our country more competitive.

1. Retain and attract investment to expand manufacturing capacity through new domestic and foreign sources of capital in order to expand existing facilities and create new facilities.
2. Manufacture more products and technologies in Canada in ways to improve demand for for Canadian-made products.
3. Accelerate adoption of new technologies and processes so that Canadian manufacturers can improve efficiency, improve environmental performance and increase competitiveness.
4. Sell more to customers in Canada and around the world by promoting products that are designed, engineered, and manufactured in Canada.

Source: "Industrie 2030: Manufacturing, Growth, Innovation and Prosperity for Canada," Canadian Manufacturing Coalition, 2016, accessed August 26, 2017, http://www.industrie2030.ca/download.php?id=77/download.

Despite these challenges, Canada still ranks fairly well in world competitiveness (see the Reaching Beyond Our Borders box in this chapter). However, one cannot expect this to continue, as other countries are becoming stronger and more competitive. In response, the federal government's innovation strategy focuses on research and development as a way to improve our competitiveness. Let us look at research and development next.

Research and Development

According to the *Canadian Oxford Dictionary*, **research and development (R&D)** is defined as work directed toward the innovation, introduction, and improvement of products and processes. When evaluating why some companies are more competitive than others, the terms *technology* and *innovation* often come up. What do these terms mean?

research and development (R&D) Work directed toward the innovation, introduction, and improvement of products and processes.

The Centre for Canadian Studies at Mount Allison University, in co-operation with the Canadian Heritage Canadian Studies Programme, produces the *About Canada* series. Innovation in Canada is the focus of one of these documents.

> *Technology is know-how, knowing how to make and use the tools for the job. It's the combination of technology with markets that creates innovation and gives a competitive edge. An innovation is a new product or process that can be purchased. Put another way, an idea may lead to an invention, but it cannot be called an innovation until it is commercialized. When technological know-how is developed, sold, distributed, and used, then it becomes an innovation.*[1]

In the Survey of Innovation conducted by Statistics Canada, respondents indicated that the three most important objectives of innovation are to improve product quality, to increase production capacity, and to extend product range. Since that time, the Science, Innovation, and Electronic Information Division (SIEID) of Statistics Canada has piloted a greater number of surveys that focus on the importance of innovation. SIEID believes that innovation and the adoption and dissemination of innovative technologies and processes are vital to economic growth and development. It continues to elaborate by stating that, through innovation, new products are introduced in the market, new production processes are developed and introduced, and organizational changes are made. Through the adoption of newer, more advanced technologies and practices, industries can increase their production capabilities, improve their productivity, and expand their lines of new goods and services.[2]

Private industry, Canadian universities, hospitals, and government laboratories are key contributors to R&D in Canada. In 2014, Canada dropped out of the world's top-ten list for R&D spending.[3] Future R&D expansion in Canada will depend upon three key drivers: revenues and profitability, government policy, and corporate strategy.[4]

Figure 10.2 outlines Canada's top ten corporate R&D spenders. In 2015, the Top 100 Corporate R&D spending rose 6.9 percent from 2014.[5] Two companies with a significant decline in R&D spending were Syncrude Canada Ltd. and Cenovus Energy Inc. Offsetting the steep declines was the significant increase in R&D by Open Text Corporation and Mitel Networks Corporation.

Based on its research, what does RE$EARCH Infosource Inc. forecast? First, the financial crisis in 2008–2009 was a logical reason for a decline in R&D spending.

However, given the decrease in manufacturing and the increase in the service industry, it will be difficult to reverse the trend. Manufacturing typically needs to invest in R&D and has been supported by government in the past, however a similar R&D environment does not traditionally exist in the service sector.

FIGURE 10.2

CANADA'S TOP CORPORATE R&D SPENDERS

Rank			R&D Expenditures			Revenue	Research Intensity	
2015	2014	Company	FY2015 $000	FY2014 $000	% Change 2014–2015	FY2015 $000	R&D as % of Revenue	Industry
1	1	Bombardier Inc.	$2,293,988	$2,022,340	13.4	$23,236,536	9.9	Aerospace
2	3	Magna International Inc.	$ 639,350	$ 585,385	9.2	$41,089,746	1.6	Automotive
3	2	Blackberry Limited	$ 599,710	$ 785,300	−23.6	$ 2,761,992	21.7	Communication/ Telecom Equipment
4	4	BCE Inc.	$ 530,300	$ 546,000	−2.9	$21,514,000	2.5	Telecommunication Services
5	7	Canadian Natural Resources Limited	$ 527,000	$ 450,000	17.1	$12,795,000	4.1	Energy/Oil and Gas
6	5	Pratt & Whitney Canada Corp.	$ 518,000	$ 542,000	−4.4	nd		Aerospace
7	6	IBM Canada Ltd.	$ 477,000	$ 466,000	2.4	nd		Software & Computer Services
8	13	Valeant Pharmaceuticals International Inc.	$ 427,597	$ 271,707	57.4	$13,357,940	3.2	Pharmaceuticals/ Biotechnology
9	8	Rogers Communication Inc.	$ 425,287	$ 418,000	1.7	$13,414,000	3.2	Telecommunication Services
10	12	Constellation Software Inc.	$ 349,325	$ 287,518	21.5	$ 2,350,646	14.9	Software & Computer Services

Notes: nd = Not disclosed

Source: © RE$EARCH Infosource Inc.

Canada's Evolving Manufacturing and Services Base

Over the previous two decades, foreign manufacturers captured huge chunks of the North American market for basic products such as steel, cement, machinery, and farm equipment using the latest in production techniques. That competition forced companies to greatly alter their production techniques and managerial styles. Many firms are now as good as or better than competitors anywhere in the world. What have Canadian manufacturers done to regain a competitive edge? They have emphasized the following:

- Focus on customers;
- Maintain close relationships with suppliers and other companies to satisfy customer needs;
- Practise continuous improvement;
- Focus on quality;
- Save on costs through site selection;
- Rely on the Internet to unite companies; and
- Adopt production techniques such as enterprise resource planning, computer-integrated manufacturing, flexible manufacturing, and lean manufacturing.

As you may recall from Figure 1.8 in Chapter 1, the goods-producing sectors employ 21.2 percent of Canada's working population. R&D spending by businesses is also critical to our economy, as the business enterprise sector contributed 46 percent of total R&D expenditure in 2014.[6] This sector is highly innovative and technology-driven. It continues to invest in facilities increasing production agility, expanding automation capabilities, and facilitating new product introductions.[7]

As we progress through this chapter, you will see that operations management has become a challenging and vital element of Canadian business. The growth of Canada's manufacturing base will likely remain a major business issue in the near future. There will be debates about the merits of moving production facilities to foreign countries. Serious questions will be raised about replacing workers with robots and other machinery. Major political decisions will be made regarding protection of Canadian manufacturers through quotas and other restrictions on free trade. Concerns about the impact of manufacturing on our environment will result in the development of new green technologies (as discussed in the Seeking Sustainability box in this chapter). Regardless of how these issues are decided, however, there will be many opportunities along the way.

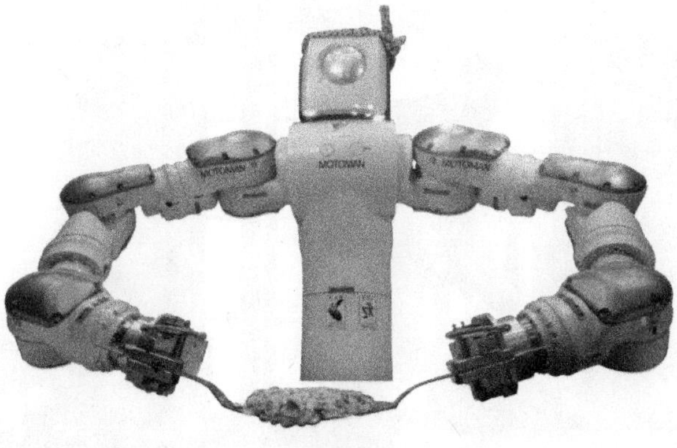

© Kim Kyung-Hoon/Reuters/Landov

Each year companies discover new ways of automating that eliminate the need for human labour. This robot demonstrates an ability to cook *Okonomiyaki*, a Japanese pancake. The robot can take verbal orders from customers and use standard kitchen utensils. Do you think the robot has a better chance to get your order right compared to a human cook?

The service sector will also continue to get attention as it continues to become a larger part of the overall economy. Service productivity is an important issue, as is the blending of service and manufacturing through the Internet. Since many of tomorrow's graduates will likely find jobs in the service sector, it is important to understand the latest operations management concepts and how they apply to the service sector.

LO2

Describe the evolution from production to operations management.

PROGRESS ASSESSMENT

- What are some challenges that Canada is facing in its ability to remain a competitive country?
- How is innovation related to research and development?

production
The creation of finished goods and services using the factors of production: land, labour, capital, entrepreneurship, and knowledge.

production management
The term used to describe all of the activities that managers do to help their firms create goods.

From Production to Operations Management

Production is the creation of goods and services using the factors of production: land, labour, capital, entrepreneurship, and knowledge (see Chapter 1). Production has historically meant *manufacturing* and the term **production management** has described the management activities that helped firms create goods. But the nature of business has changed significantly in the last 20 years or so as the service sector, including Internet services, has grown dramatically. As discussed in Chapter 1, Canada is a service economy—that is, one dominated by the service sector. This can be a benefit to future graduates because many of the top-paying jobs are in legal services, medical services, entertainment, broadcasting, and business services such as accounting, finance, and management consulting.

© Mark Edward Atkinson/Getty Images RF

Operations management for services is all about enriching the customer experience. Hotels, for instance, have responded to the needs of business travellers with in-room Internet access and other kinds of office-style support, as well as stored information about the preferences of frequent guests. What other amenities do hotels provide for business people on the go?

Operations management is a specialized area in management that converts or transforms resources (including human resources) into goods and services. It includes inventory management, quality control, production scheduling, follow-up services, and more. In an automobile plant, operations management transforms raw materials, human resources, parts, supplies, paints, tools, and other resources into automobiles. It does this through the processes of fabrication and assembly.

In a college or university, operations management takes inputs—such as information, professors, supplies, buildings, offices, and computer systems—and creates

Seeking SUSTAINABILITY

Carbon Capture and Storage

One of Canada's primary resources is its fossil fuels. Abundant supplies of oil, natural gas, and coal make this country one of the world's most attractive energy centres for continuing investment and development. However, with this economic opportunity comes a challenge, to mitigate greenhouse gas (GHG) emissions and their impact on climate change. More and more evidence is being gathered by the scientific community that supports the claim that global emissions growth could bring rapid climate change. The challenge is to reduce GHG emissions while continuing economic progress.

© wloven/iStock/Thinkstock

Carbon dioxide capture and storage (CCS) is one way to address the carbon challenge. With CCS, carbon dioxide emissions from large industrial facilities are separated from the plant's process or exhaust system, compressed, and injected deep underground.

CCS can be built as an add-on to existing fossil energy infrastructure or incorporated into new and future facilities. The main components of this operation are: capture, transportation, and storage. Once the carbon dioxide is captured at a plant, it needs to be transported to a location with the appropriate geological formation. These stable sedimentary rock formations, that formerly securely held vast oil and gas reserves, can now be used to hold carbon dioxide, which is injected into the underground space.

Both the federal and a number of provincial governments are financially supporting the development of CCS and introducing legislation to reduce GHG emissions. A total of $3 billion in funding for CCS has been provided by all levels of government during the past few years.

Carbon dioxide capture and storage is used by SaskPower where a large-scale CCS operation was built for a coal-fired power plant in Estevan, Saskatchewan. The project cost $1.4 billion and officials claim the GHG reduction is equivalent to removing a quarter of a million cars from the road.

While you may initially assume the most important area for CCS is in manufacturing, there are a variety of industries that can benefit from CCS. According to the Integrated CO_2 Network, approximately 24 percent of GHG emissions are generated from personal transportation and residential areas. Do you believe CSC technology will expand beyond large industry to also help Canadians make their everyday living more GHG efficient?

Source: "A Strategic Investment," Integrated CO_2 Network, 2015, http://www.ico2n.com/, accessed May 10, 2015; "Carbon capture history made in Saskatchewan, besting once ambitious Alberta," CBC News, October 3, 2014, http://www.cbc.ca/news/canada/calgary/carbon-capture-history-made-in-saskatchewan-besting-once-ambitious-alberta-1.2786478; "Quick Facts on CO_2 Capture and Storage in Canada," Natural Resources Canada, www.CO²network.gc.ca; and Rachel Pulfer, "Burying King Coal," *Canadian Business*, April 28, 2008, 21–22.

services that transform students into educated people. It does this through a process called education.

Some organizations—such as factories, farms, and mines—produce mostly goods. Others—such as hospitals, schools, and government agencies—produce mostly services. Still others produce a combination of goods and services. For example, an automobile manufacturer not only makes cars but also provides services such as repairs, financing, and insurance. Wendy's provides goods such as hamburgers and fries, but customers also receive services such as order taking, order filling, food preparation, and cleanup.

operations management
A specialized area in management that converts or transforms resources (including human resources) into goods and services.

Reaching *Beyond* OUR BORDERS

How Does Canada Shape Up as an International Competitor?

How does Canada rank when compared to other industrialized countries? Canadian businesses have been criticized for not being more productive as productivity contributes to competitiveness. Analysts are concerned that an under-investment in innovation and technology will have a negative impact on the long-term productivity of Canadian businesses. In order to remain competitive with other countries in the world, Canada needs to invest in R&D and higher education.

Assessing international competitiveness is complex and open to varying opinions. There are several indexes that attempt to measure competitiveness, and different criteria and weightings are used by the agencies that produce them. You will notice the importance of economic conditions and the role of government when evaluating a country's attractiveness. Let us consider two popular rankings.

The prestigious World Economic Forum produces the annual Global Competitiveness Report. The Growth Competitiveness Index is based on estimates of each country's ability to grow over the next five to ten years. Thus, economic conditions and institutions (e.g., government and financial markets) are reviewed. It was determined that Canada's future competitiveness and productive potential would benefit by improving the sophistication and innovative potential of the private sector with greater R&D spending and producing goods and services higher on the value chain.

The International Institute for Management Development (IMD) produces the World Competitiveness Yearbook, which ranks the ability of a nation to provide an environment that sustains the competitiveness of enterprises. The ranking considers four criteria: economic performance, government efficiency, business efficiency, and infrastructure. In the past it was determined that while Canada ranks well on government policies conducive to competitiveness, Canada would rank higher if it had a more enterprising business community.

There is no single authority on ranking a country's competitiveness. These two examples highlight how different criteria are considered by different organizations. What should be of interest is that the criteria incorporate some of the concepts that are discussed in this text (e.g., economic performance). As a business student, be assured that the concepts that you are learning are in fact incorporated in business decision making.

© Shutterstock / cybrain

Year	Canada's Rank, WEF's Growth Competitiveness Index	Canada's Rank, IMD's World Competitiveness Ranking
2017	15	12
2016	13	10
2015	15	5
2014	15	7
2013	14	7
2012	14	6
2011	12	7
2010	10	7
2009	10	8
2008	13	8
2007	12	10
2006	14	5
2005	15	3

The business environment is clearly influenced by factors such as economic performance and government policies. Canada's ranking is influenced not only by what happens domestically, but also by what happens internationally. Our fall in the rankings is influenced by our strengths and weaknesses (as assessed by the organizations listed above) and measured against the strengths and weaknesses of other countries. As other countries improve their competitiveness, this will contribute to Canada's fall in the rankings if we do not improve accordingly.

Sources: "The 2017 IMD World Competitiveness Ranking," IMD, accessed August 27, 2017, https://www.imd.org/globalassets/wcc/docs/release-2017/2017-world_competitiveness_ranking.pdf; "IMD World Competitive Yearbook, 2015," imd.org, accessed August 27, 2017, http://www.imd.org/news/IMD-releases-its-2015-World-Competitiveness-Ranking.cfm; "The Global Competitiveness Report, 2016-2017—Canada," World Economic Forum, http://www3.weforum.org/docs/GCR2016-2017/05FullReport/TheGlobalCompetitivenessReport2016-2017_FINAL.pdf; "The Global Competitiveness Report, 2015-2016—Canada," World Economic Forum, accessed August 27, 2017, http://www3.weforum.org/docs/gcr/2015-2016/Global_Competitiveness_Report_2015-2016.pdf; David Parkinson, "Canada slips a notch in global competitiveness ranking," *The Globe and Mail*, September 3, 2014, http://www.theglobeandmail.com/report-on-business/economy/canada-slips-a-notch-in-global-competitiveness-ranking/article20313100/; "The Global Competitiveness Report 2014-2015 – Canada," World Economic Forum, 2014, accessed May 10, 2015, http://www3.weforum.org/docs/GCR2014-15/Canada.pdf; "Canada falls to 15th in global competitiveness ranking," CBC News, September 3, 2014, http://www.cbc.ca/news/business/canada-falls-to-15th-in-global-competitiveness-ranking-1.2754078; "IMD releases its 25th anniversary World Competitiveness Rankings," IMD, May 29, 2013, http://www.imd.org/news/World-Competitiveness-2013.cfm.

Operations Management in the Service Sector

Operations management in the service industry is all about creating a good experience for those who use the service.[8] For example, in a Hilton hotel operations management includes smooth-running elevators, fine restaurants, comfortable beds, and a front desk that processes people quickly. It may also include fresh-cut flowers in lobbies and dishes of fruit in every room.

Along with these classic amenities, Hilton must also stay innovative so it can cater to the ever-changing needs of its guests. Most business travellers today expect in-room WiFi as well as work centres that provide all the resources of a modern office. Hilton provides these services and also develops new features that could someday become standard in their hotels. One such innovation is keyless room entry. Rather than give guests a keycard they can easily lose, Hilton is creating a system that would allow guests to use their smartphone to enter their room.[9]

Another ambitious Hilton project is Connie, a two-foot tall front desk robot that can answer guests' basic questions.[10] Named after company founder Conrad Hilton, the robot uses IBM's Watson system to learn new information and tasks. So while Connie is currently capable of little more than providing directions to the gym, someday it could be the centre of operations at every Hilton hotel. The company tests all these new ideas at a hotel located near its headquarters.[11] This allows Hilton to observe the ways that guests react to new features and how it affects overall operations.

Operations management is responsible for locating and providing such amenities to make customers happy. In short, pleasing customers by anticipating their needs has become the quality standard for hotels like Hilton, as it has for many other service businesses. But knowing customer needs and satisfying them are two different things. That is why operations management is so important: it is the implementation phase of management that allows companies to turn their ideas into actual goods and services.

Can you see the need for better operations management in airports, hospitals, government agencies, schools, and non-profit organization such as the Red Cross? The opportunities seem almost unlimited. Although manufacturing still needs innovation, much of the future of Canada's economic growth is in these service areas.

Measuring Quality in the Service Sector

There's strong evidence that productivity in the service sector is rising, but productivity measures do not capture improvements in quality. In an example from health care, positron emission tomography (PET) scans are much better than X-rays, but the quality difference is not reported in productivity figures. The traditional way to measure productivity involves tracking inputs (worker hours) compared to outputs (dollars). Notice that there is no measure for quality improvement. When new information systems are developed to measure the quality improvement of goods and services—including the speed of their delivery and customer satisfaction—productivity in the service sector will go up dramatically.

Using computers is one way in which the service sector is improving productivity, but not the only one. Think about labour-intensive businesses such as fast-food restaurants, where automation plays a big role in controlling costs and improving service. Today, at Burger King, for example, customers fill their own drink cups from pop machines, which allows workers to concentrate on preparing the food. And because the people working at the drive-up window now wear headsets instead of using stationary mikes, they are no longer glued to one spot and can do four or five tasks while taking an order.

Most of us have been exposed to similar productivity gains in banking. For example, people in most cities no longer have to wait in long lines for tellers to help them deposit and withdraw money. Instead, they use automated teller machines (ATMs), which usually involve little or no waiting and are available 24 hours a day.

© vasabii/iStock/Thinkstock

Information Mapping helps leading organizations focus on improving performance through better written communication. Clients, including Citizenship and Immigration Canada and the Ontario Pension Board, have increased productivity through better implementation of policies and procedures.[12] What types of measures could you implement to track whether a company's efforts to manage customer complaints were effective?

Another service that was once very slow was grocery store checkout. The system of marking goods with universal product codes (UPC) enables computerized checkout and allows cashiers to be much more productive than before. Now, many stores have set up automated systems that enable customers to go through the checkout process on their own. Some grocery chains, such as Longo's, are implementing Internet services that allow customers to place orders online and receive home delivery. The potential for productivity gains in this area are enormous.

In short, operations management has led to tremendous productivity increases in the service sector but there is still a long way to go to capture potential improvements. Also, service workers are losing jobs to machines just as manufacturing workers did. The secret to obtaining and holding a good job is to acquire appropriate education and training. Such education and training must go on for a lifetime to keep up with the rapid changes that are happening in all areas of business. That message cannot be repeated too frequently.

LO3

Describe operations management planning issues, including facility location, facility layout, materials requirement planning, purchasing, just-in-time inventory control, and quality control.

PROGRESS ASSESSMENT

- Explain the difference between production management and operations management.
- What is the biggest issue with productivity in the service sector?

Operations Management Planning

Operations management planning helps solve many of the problems in the service and manufacturing sectors. These include facility location, facility layout, and quality control. The resources used in the two sectors may be different, but the management issues are similar.

Facility Location

facility location The process of selecting a geographic location for a company's operations.

Facility location is the process of selecting a geographic location for a company's operations. In keeping with the need to focus on customers, one strategy is to find a site that makes it easy for consumers to use the company's services and to communicate about their needs. For example, German food company Dr. Oetker's opened a new pizza plant in London, Ontario, because the location provided skilled workers and a close proximity to consumers in Canada and the United States.[13] Flower shops and banks are putting facilities in supermarkets so that their products are more accessible than they are in freestanding facilities. You can find a McDonalds' inside some Walmart stores and there are Tim Hortons outlets in some gas stations. Customers can buy gas and their meals, all in one location.

The ultimate in convenience is never having to leave home to get goods and services. That is why there is so much interest in online banking, shopping, education, and other services. **E-commerce** (a topic discussed earlier in Chapter 1) uses Facebook and other social media to make transactions even easier. For brick-and-mortar businesses to beat such competition, they have to choose good locations and offer outstanding service. Study the location of service-sector businesses—such as hotels, banks, athletic clubs, and supermarkets—and you will see that the most successful ones are conveniently located. Google builds large data centres in jurisdictions that give tax breaks and have lower cost electricity readily available. They are also located near bodies of water for cooling their servers.

e-commerce The buying and selling of goods and services over the Internet.

FACILITY LOCATION FOR MANUFACTURERS

A major issue of the recent past has been the shift of manufacturing organizations from one city or province to another in Canada, or to other foreign sites. In the past few years several prominent plant closures impacted the Canadian processed food industry. For example, Kellogg Canada closed its cereal plant in London, Ontario, and Heinz closed its tomato-processing plant in Leamington, Ontario.[14] Such shifts sometimes result in pockets of unemployment in some geographic areas and lead to tremendous economic growth in others that benefit from these shifts. The Making Ethical Decisions box considers some of the issues surrounding such moves.

Making ETHICAL DECISIONS

Do We Stay or Do We Go?

Suppose the hypothetical company ChildrenWear Industries has long been the economic foundation for its hometown. Most of the area's small businesses and schools either supply materials the firm needs for production or train its future employees. ChildrenWear has learned that if it were to move its production facilities to Asia it could increase its profits by 15 percent.

Closing operations in the company's hometown would cause many of the town's other businesses, such as restaurants, to fail, which would leave a high percentage of the town's adults unemployed, with no options for re-employment within the local community. As a top manager at ChildrenWear, you must help decide whether the plant should be moved. What alternatives do you have? What are the consequences of each? Which will you choose?

© Christopher Penler/iStock/Thinkstock

Inexpensive resources are another major reason for moving production facilities. Companies usually need water, electricity, wood, coal, and other basic resources. By moving to areas where natural resources are inexpensive and plentiful, firms can significantly lower not only the cost of buying such resources but also the cost of shipping finished products. Often the most important resource is people, so companies tend to cluster in a location where smart and talented people are readily available. Witness the Ottawa area, also known as Silicon Valley North.

Time-to-market is another decision-making factor. As manufacturers attempt to compete globally, they need sites that allow products to move quickly, so that they can offer fast delivery to customers. Thus, access to highways, rail lines, waterways, and airports is critical. Information technology (IT) is also important to quicken response time, so many firms are seeking countries with the most advanced information systems.

Another way to work closely with suppliers in order to satisfy your customers' needs is to locate your production facilities near supplier facilities. This option cuts the cost of distribution and makes communication easier.

Many businesses are building factories in foreign countries to get closer to their international customers. That is a major reason why the U.S. automaker General Motors builds cars in Oshawa, Ontario, and Japanese automaker Toyota builds cars in Cambridge, Ontario. Japanese-based automaker Honda opened an engine factory plant in Alliston, Ontario, in 2008, close to its two assembly plants. Honda Canada president Hiroshi Kobayashi told a news conference that this site selection "supports Honda's global strategic manufacturing focus of bringing manufacturing and sales operations to the local market." In 2014, Honda announced it will make a $857 million investment to expand the plant in Alliston, Ontario, to upgrade vehicle assembly and engine manufacturing. When firms select foreign sites, they consider whether they are near airports, waterways, and highways so that raw materials and finished goods can be moved quickly and easily.

Businesses also study the quality of life for workers and managers. Are there good schools nearby? Is the weather nice? Is the crime rate low? Does the local community welcome new businesses? Do the chief executive and other key managers want to live there? Sometimes a region with a high quality of life is also an expensive one, which complicates the decision. In short, facility location has become a critical issue in operations management.

Sources: David Simchi-Levi, James Paul Peruvankal, Narenda Mulani, Bill Read, and John Ferreira, "Is It Time to Rethink Your Manufacturing Strategy?" *MIT Sloan Management Review,* Winter 2012; Gary Norris, "Honda Putting New Assembly Plant in U.S.; Ontario Gets $154M Engine Factory," Canadian Business Online, May 17, 2006, www.canadianbusiness.com/markets/headline_news/article.jsp?content=b051777A; and Canadian Press, "Honda to invest $857M in Ontario plant to build next generation of Civic car," *Financial Post,* November 6, 2014, http://business.financialpost.com/news/transportation/honda-to-invest-857-million-in-alliston-operations-ontario-kicks-in-10.

Why would companies spend millions of dollars to move their facilities from one location to another? In making these decisions they consider labour costs; availability of resources, including labour; access to transportation that can reduce time-to-market; proximity to suppliers; proximity to customers; crime rates; quality of life for employees; cost of living; and the need to train or retrain the local workforce.

© Gino de Graff/Alamy RF

Facility location is a major decision for manufacturing and other companies that must take into account the availability of qualified workers; access to suppliers, customers, transportation, and local regulation including zoning and taxes. How has the growth of Internet commerce affected company location decisions?

Even though labour is becoming a smaller percentage of total cost in highly automated industries, availability of low-cost labour or the right kind of skilled labour remains a key reason many producers move their plant to Malaysia, China, India, Mexico, and other countries. Some of these firms have been charged with providing substandard working conditions, exploiting children, or both in the countries where some manufacturers have set up factories. Others, such as Grupo M, a textile products and services company in the Dominican Republic, are being used as role models for global manufacturing. Grupo M provides its employees with higher pay relative to local businesses, transportation to and from work, daycare centres, discounted food, and health clinics. Its operations are so efficient that it can compete in world markets and provide world-class services to its employees.

OUTSOURCING

The previous chapter noted that many companies now try to divide their production between core competencies, work they do best in-house, and outsourcing, using outside companies with expertise to service specific functional areas. The result is intended to achieve the best-quality products at the lowest possible costs.

Outsourcing goods and services has become a hot practice in North America. Software development, call-centre jobs, and back-office jobs have been moving to developing countries for some time. The range of jobs now shifting to these countries expands beyond manufacturing to also include accounting, financial analysis, medical services, architecture, aircraft maintenance, law, film production, and banking activities.[15]

Based on a survey of its over 120 000 members and affiliates, the International Association of Outsourcing Professionals has found that increasing business flexibility is the most prominent reason for outsourcing.[16] According to Jerome Thirion with KPMG Canada, consumer-facing companies may renew approximately one-third of a product line on an annual basis in order to remain competitive.[17] In these situations, it makes better economic sense to work with an outsourcer who can adapt to a company's changing production needs.

© Agencja Fotograficzna Caro / Alamy Stock Photo

A great deal of Germany's economic success is attributed to the strength of its industrial sector, consisting of a longstanding group of small manufacturers, many of which have been in business for centuries. At the core of this manufacturing juggernaut is the Mittelstand, consisting of family-owned, small to midsize companies that account for 52 percent of the country's economic output and supply almost two-thirds of the nation's jobs. The Mittelstand are able to build Germany's economy, especially its exports, without moving facilities to other countries.

In the manufacturing sector, employment continues to drop lower and lower through outsourcing. However, outsourcing is expected to also expand in other industries in the future. The survey also found the demand for outsourcing higher-skill activities as opposed to lower-skilled activities rose 6 percent from the previous year. In the past outsourcing was driven by a need for cheap labour but it is now more often that labour expertise is the key reason.[18]

Another industry where significant outsourcing happens is software R&D. For Canadian companies needing software, hourly rates outside of Canada are much lower. Keep in mind that while outsourcing may look good on paper financially, if a company does not do its homework, outsourcing can become a problem due to language and cultural differences, differences in expectations, etc. A Canadian organization, the Centre for Outsourcing Research and Education (CORE), has been formed to provide organizations with the knowledge and skills to manage outsourcing activities.[19] More than just a cost-saving tool, outsourcing is being used as a strategic tool to focus scarce human capital on core business activities.

Future global outsourcing trends are uncertain, but the overall volume of outsourcing by companies around the world is expected to grow. Both private and public sectors need to invest in areas that improve Canada's attraction as a viable and affordable outsourcing destination.[20]

TAKING OPERATIONS MANAGEMENT TO THE INTERNET

Many rapidly growing companies do very little production themselves. Instead, they outsource engineering, design, manufacturing, and other tasks to other companies that specialize in those functions. They create new relationships with suppliers over the Internet, making operations management an *inter-firm* process in which companies work closely together to design, produce, and ship products to customers.

Many manufacturing companies are developing Internet-focused strategies that will enable them and others to compete more effectively in the future.[21] These changes have a dramatic effect on operations managers as they adjust from a one-firm system to an inter-firm environment and from a relatively stable environment to one that is constantly changing and evolving. This linking of firms is called *supply chain management.* We will briefly introduce you to this concept later in the chapter. Manufacturing companies are developing Internet-focused strategies that will enable them and others to compete more effectively in the future.

FACILITY LOCATION IN THE FUTURE

The use of information technology (IT) such as computers, modems, e-mail, voice mail, text messaging, teleconferencing, etc. gives employees the flexibility to choose where they work while at the same helps keeps the firm in the competitive mainstream (see also the discussion on virtual organizations in Chapter 9). **Telecommuting**, working from home via computer, is a major trend in business. Companies that no longer need to locate near sources of labour will be able to move to areas where land is less expensive and the quality of life may be higher. Furthermore, more salespeople are keeping in touch with the company and its customers through videoconferencing apps like Skype and Adobe Connect.[22]

One strong incentive for a business to locate in a particular city, province, or territory is the tax situation. Some provincial and local governments have higher taxes than others, yet many compete fiercely by offering companies tax reductions and other support, such as zoning changes and financial aid, in order to convince the company to locate within its boundaries. The previously mentioned Honda plant expansion in Alliston included a provincial government grant of up to $85.7 million. Have you seen advertisements for entrepreneurs to locate in your hometown?

© Lee Brown/Alamy

In 2013, the Canadian Auto Workers (CAW) and Communications, Energy, and Paperworkers Union of Canada (CEP) merged to form a new union called Unifor. The organization, which represents Canada's biggest private sector union and spans approximately 20 sectors, still represents workers in automotive manufacturing. Many jobs have been lost in this sector due to imports and the global financial crisis. What priorities do you think Unifor should focus upon to help its members who face the challenges of a changing global marketplace?[24]

Facility Layout

Facility layout is the physical arrangement of resources, including people, to most efficiently produce goods and provide services to customers. Facility layout depends greatly on the processes that are to be performed. For services, the layout is usually designed to help the consumer find and buy services, including on the Internet. Some stores have added kiosks that enable customers to search for goods online and place orders or make returns and credit payments in the store. In short, the facilities and Internet capabilities of service organizations are becoming more customer-oriented.

telecommuting
Working from home via computer.

facility layout
The physical arrangement of resources (including people) in the production process.

Similar to manufacturers, some service-oriented organizations, such as hospitals, use layouts that improve the efficiency. For manufacturing plants, facilities layout has become critical because the possible cost savings are enormous.

Many companies are moving from an *assembly-line layout,* in which workers do only a few tasks at a time, to a *modular layout,* in which *teams* of workers combine to produce more complex units of the final product.[23] There may have been a dozen or more workstations on an assembly line to complete an automobile engine in the past, but all of that work may be done in one module today.

When working on a major project, such as a bridge or airplane, companies use a *fixed-position layout* that allows workers to congregate around the product to be completed.

A *process layout* is one in which similar equipment and functions are grouped together. The order in which the product visits a function depends on the design of the item. This allows for flexibility. The Igus manufacturing plant in Cologne, Germany, can shrink or expand in a flash. Its flexible design keeps it competitive in a fast-changing market. Because the layout of the plant changes so often, some employees use scooters to more efficiently provide needed skills, supplies, and services to multiple

© Lipo Ching/MCT/Landov

At Cisco Systems, work spaces in some offices are fluid and unassigned, so employees with laptops and mobile phones can choose where to sit when they arrive each day. What do you think are some of the advantages of such nontraditional facility layouts? Are there any disadvantages?

workstations. A fast-changing plant needs a fast-moving employee base to achieve maximum productivity. Figure 10.3 illustrates typical layout designs.

Materials Requirement Planning (MRP)

Materials requirement planning (MRP) is a computer-based operations management system that uses sales forecasts to ensure that needed parts and materials are available at the right time and place. In a diner, for example, employees could enter the sales forecast into the computer, which would specify how many eggs and how much coffee to order, and then print out the proper scheduling and routing sequence. The same can be done with orders for the seats and other parts of an automobile. In the next section, you will read how just-in-time inventory control has a similar objective.

Enterprise resource planning (ERP), a newer version of MRP, combines the computerized functions of all the divisions and subsidiaries of the firm—such as finance, human resources, and order fulfillment—into one integrated software program that uses a single database (see Figure 10.4). The result is shorter time between orders and payment, less staff to do ordering and order processing, reduced inventories, and better customer service. For example, the customer can place an order, either through a customer service representative or online, and immediately see when the order will be filled and how much it will cost. The representative can instantly see the customer's credit rating and order history, the company's inventory, and the shipping schedule. Everyone else in the company can see the new order as well; thus when one department finishes its portion of the task, the order is automatically routed via the ERP system to the next department. The customer can see exactly where the order is at any point by logging into the system.

materials requirement planning (MRP)
A computer-based production management system that uses sales forecasts to make sure that needed parts and materials are available at the right time and place.

enterprise resource planning (ERP)
A computer application that enables a firm to manage all of its operations (finance, requirements planning, human resources, and order fulfillment) on the basis of a single, integrated set of corporate data.

By entering customer and sales information in an ERP system, a manufacturer can generate the next period's demand forecast, which in turn generates orders for raw materials, production scheduling, and financial projections.

ERP software enables the firm to monitor quality and customer satisfaction as it is happening. ERP systems are going global now that the Internet is powerful enough to handle the data flows. At the plant level, dynamic performance monitoring enables plant operators to monitor the use of power, chemicals, and other resources and to make needed adjustments. In short, flows to, through, and from plants have become automated.

Some firms are providing a service called sequential delivery. These firms are suppliers that provide components in an order sequenced to their customers' production process. For example, Ford's seat supplier loads seats onto a truck such that, when off-loaded, the seats are in perfect sequence for the type of vehicle coming down the assembly line.

While ERP can be an effective tool, it also can have its problems. The Royal Canadian Mint had difficulties extracting and manipulating data from its integrated software system.

FIGURE 10.3

TYPICAL LAYOUT DESIGNS

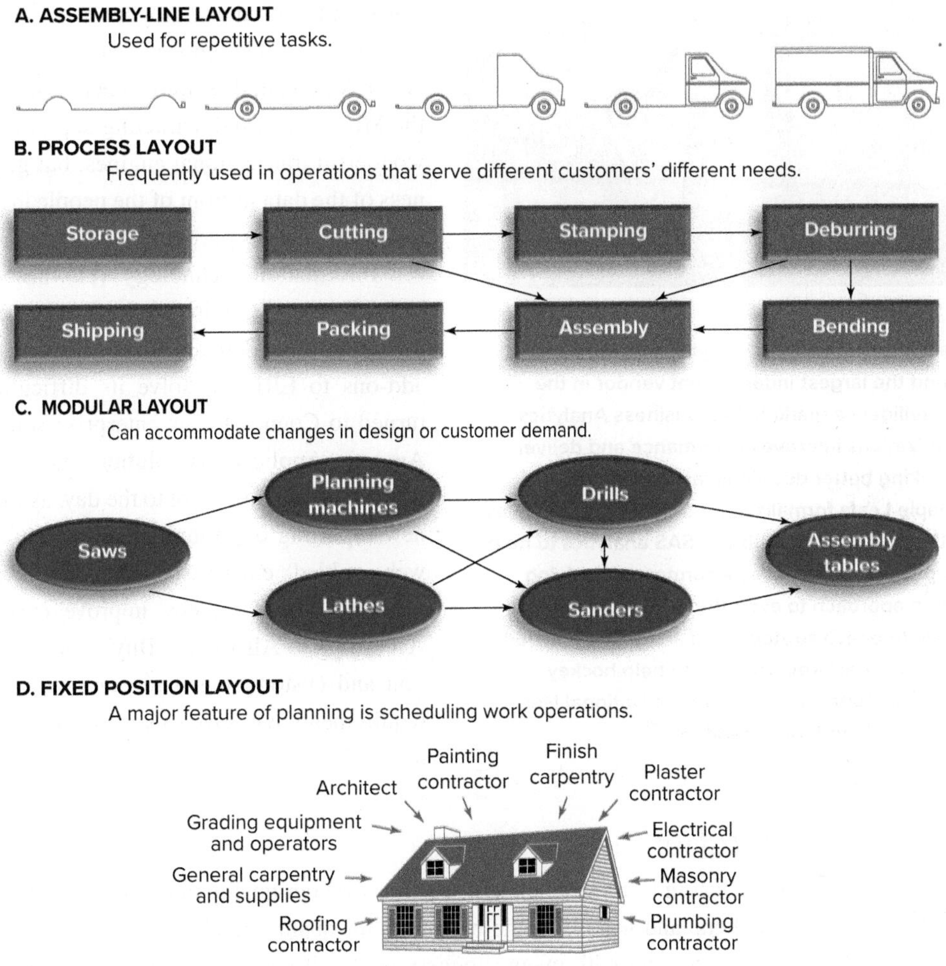

FIGURE 10.4

ENTERPRISE RESOURCE PLANNING

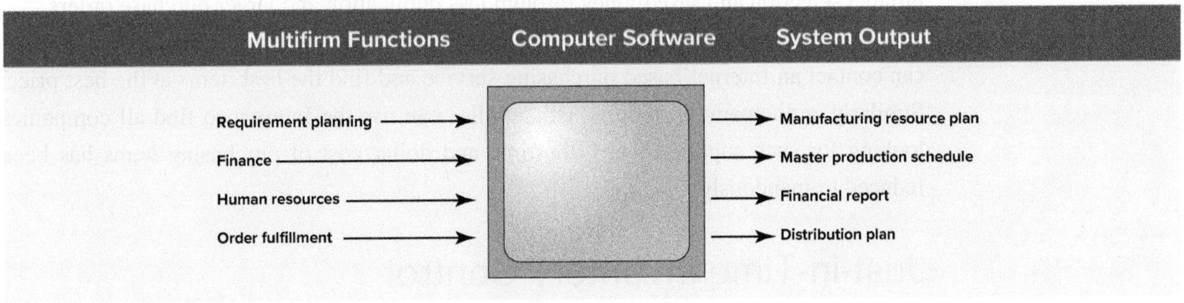

Courtesy of SAS Institute

SAS is the leader in business analytics software and services, and the largest independent vendor in the business intelligence market. SAS Business Analytics helps organizations improve performance and deliver value by making better decisions faster. SAS and the Toronto Maple Leafs formalized a partnership for hockey analytics that will see the Club use SAS analytics to help analyze aspects of the team's performance; applying a data-driven approach to everything from player performance to on-ice strategy. The analysis will include the use of player performance data to help hockey executives make better decisions at the National Hockey League entry draft and trade deadline.[29]

Departments operated independently, and because it took so long to produce reports for analysis, employees did not trust the reliability of the information once it was in their hands. "Anyone who has used an ERP system knows that reporting can be problematic," says Azfar Ali Khan, director of operations and systems at the Mint's sales and marketing departments. "They're wonderful transactional engines, but getting the richness of the data in front of the people in a context they can understand is particularly challenging."[25]

Information technology (IT) has had a major influence on the entire production process, from purchasing to final delivery. Many IT advances have been add-ons to ERP. To solve its difficulties, the Mint turned to Cognos for its enterprise solution. Cognos' Analytic Applications solution made it possible for users to access data right to the day, as well as to create new reporting opportunities. The Mint's self-service, web-enabled, enterprise-wide solution allowed it to act quickly and thereby improve customer service. According to Ali Khan, "Buying a prepackaged solution and customizing it to our own unique business requirements has saved us a lot of time and a lot of money."[26]

Purchasing

purchasing The functional area in a firm that searches for quality material resources, finds the best suppliers, and negotiates the best price for goods and services.

Purchasing is the function that searches for high-quality material resources, finds the best suppliers, and negotiates the best price for quality goods and services. In the past, manufacturers dealt with many suppliers so that if one could not deliver, the firm could get materials from a different supplier. Today, however, manufacturers rely more heavily on just one or two suppliers, because the relationship between suppliers and manufacturers is much closer than before.[27] Producers share a great deal of information and consequently, they want as few suppliers as possible knowing their business. The Hudson's Bay Company shifted to single merchandise buyers for a growing number of departments at its Bay, Saks Fifth Avenue, and Home Outfitters chains. This move was designed to help improve product selection and save money through less duplication and larger purchase orders.[28]

The Internet has transformed the purchasing function. A business looking for supplies can contact an Internet-based purchasing service and find the best items at the best price. Similarly, a company wishing to sell supplies can use the Internet to find all companies looking for such supplies. Thus, the time and dollar cost of purchasing items has been reduced tremendously.

Just-in-Time Inventory Control

One major cost of production is holding parts and other items in storage for later use. Storage not only subjects such items to obsolescence, pilferage, and damage, but also requires construction and maintenance of costly warehouses. To cut such costs, many companies have implemented a concept called **just-in-time (JIT) inventory control**. JIT systems keep a minimum of inventory on the premises and delivers parts, supplies, and other needs just in time to go on the assembly line. To work effectively, however, the process requires an accurate production schedule (using ERP) and excellent coordination with carefully selected suppliers, who are usually connected electronically so they know what is needed and when.

© Alistair Berg/Getty Images

Huge warehouses such as the one depicted in the photo would become a thing of the past if all companies implemented just-in-time (JIT) inventory control. What are the advantages and disadvantages of having large amounts of inventory available?

Sometimes the supplier builds new facilities close to the main producer to minimize distribution time. JIT runs into problems when suppliers are farther away. Weather may delay shipments, for example, as happened when weather (earthquakes and the resulting tsunami) disrupted the supply chain of materials from Japan to Canada in 2011.

Delays require that companies adjust their JIT schedules. Today, the longer delays at border crossings due to increased traffic and security measures have forced companies to do just that. Other limitations are that JIT works best with standard products, needs a high and stable demand to justify the cost and savings, and requires extremely reliable suppliers.

just-in-time (JIT) inventory control
A production process in which a minimum of inventory is kept on the premises and parts, supplies, and other needs are delivered just in time for use on the assembly line.

JIT systems ensure that the right materials are at the right place at the right time at the cheapest cost in order to meet both customer and production needs. That is a key step in modern production innovation.

Quality Control

Maintaining **quality** means consistently producing what the customer wants while reducing errors before and after delivery to the customer. In the past, firms often conducted quality control at the end of the production line. Products were completed *and then tested* for quality. This resulted in several problems, including the need to:

1. Utilize extra workers and resources to inspect work.
2. Correct the mistake or scrap the product if an error was found, resulting in higher costs.
3. Risk customer dissatisfaction if she or he found the mistake, and decided to buy from another firm thereafter.

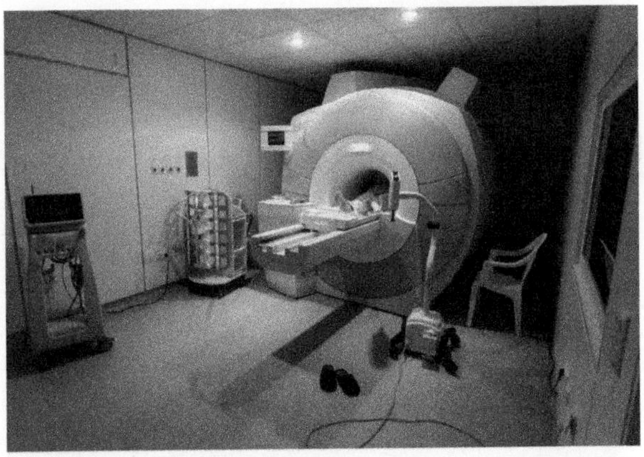

© Shutterstock / zlikovec

What happens when you combine the zeal of technical innovators with the Six Sigma discipline of a large company like General Electric? You get a medical breakthrough. Janet Burki and her 280-person operations team developed the world's fastest CT scanner. It works ten times faster than other systems and produces clear 3-D images of the beating heart. Can you see how efforts to build in quality lead to better (and faster) products?

Such problems led to the realization that quality is not an outcome; it is a never-ending process of continually improving what a company produces. Quality

quality
Consistently producing what the customer wants while reducing errors before and after delivery to the customer.

Six Sigma quality
A quality measure that allows only 3.4 defects per million events.

control should be part of the operations management planning process rather than simply an end-of-the-line inspection.

Companies have turned to the use of modern quality control standards, such as Six Sigma. **Six Sigma quality**, which sets a benchmark of just 3.4 defects per million opportunities, detects potential problems to prevent their occurrence. That is important to a company that makes 4 million transactions a day, like some banks. The Spotlight on Small Business box explores how small businesses can apply Six Sigma to their operations.

Statistical quality control (SQC) is the process some managers use to continually monitor all phases of the production process and assure quality is built into the product from the beginning. **Statistical process control (SPC)** is the process of testing statistical

Spotlight *On* SMALL BUSINESS

Meeting the Six Sigma Standard

Six Sigma is a quality measure that allows only 3.4 defects per million opportunities. Here is how Six Sigma works: If you can make it to the level of one sigma, two out of three products will meet specifications. If you can reach the two sigma level, then more than 95 percent of products will qualify. But when you meet Six Sigma quality, as we have said, you have only 3.4 defects in a million opportunities (which means that 99.99966 percent of your products will qualify), a quality standard that approaches perfection. Service organizations are also adopting Six Sigma standards through the elimination of any activity involved with the service they provide that does not add value to the customer.

It is one thing for Motorola (often cited as the driving force behind the development of this standard) or General Electric (GE) to reach for such standards given their vast resources, but what about a small company like Dolan Industries? Dolan is a 41-person manufacturer of fasteners. It spent a few years trying to meet ISO 9000 standards, which are comparable to Six Sigma. Dolan had to do that because its customers were demanding that level of quality.

Small companies can successfully implement Six Sigma if the owner is committed, the company has a routine core of work that can benefit from the standard, and the company's culture is open to change. Any change that is part of a Six Sigma project should not be so significant that any problem would have a major

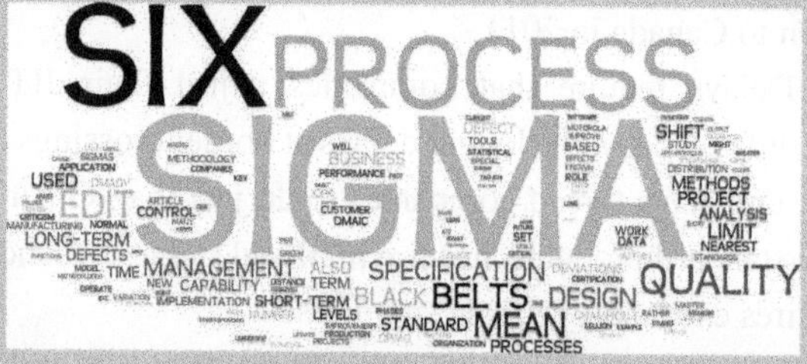

© MacXever/iStock/Thinkstock

impact on customer relations. While the management buy-in for a Six Sigma initiative may be easier in a small business, resource commitment and employee training are more challenging compared to large companies. As a general rule, a small business can begin deploying Six Sigma when one employee can devote one day per week to this work, which represents 0.5 to 1 percent of employee hours (i.e., a minimum of 20 employees is required, which results in combined work hours of 800—based on 8 hour days). They should invest in software and books on the subject, access outside expertise, and pursue each project aggressively—completing most projects in four to six weeks.

While Six Sigma techniques can result in specific improvements, the true value of working toward the standard comes from an organization-wide culture shift. No matter what the size of the organization, there is much to be gained from finding cost-effective methods to deliver quality goods and services.

Sources: Charles Waxer, "Is Six Sigma Just for Large Companies? What about small companies?" iSix Sigma, 2015, http://www.isixsigma.com/new-to-six-sigma/getting-started/six-sigma-just-large-companies-what-about-small-companies/, accessed May 11, 2015; Virginia Galt, "There's heavy demand in all sectors for 'lean' *specialists*," *The Globe and Mail*, August 15, 2013, http://www.theglobeandmail.com/report-on-business/careers/career-advice/life-at-work/heavy-demand-for-lean-specialists/article13795394/; and "Training," Six Sigma Canada Inc., http://www.sixsigmacanada.net/training/, accessed May 15, 2015.

samples of product components at each stage of production and plotting the test results on a graph. Managers can thus see and correct any deviation from quality standards. Making sure products meet standards all along the production process reduces the need for a quality-control inspection at the end because mistakes are caught much earlier in the process. Consequently, SQC and SPC save companies much time and money. Some companies use a quality-control approach called the Deming cycle (after the late W. Edwards Deming, the father of the movement toward quality).[30] Its steps are: Plan, Do, Check, Act (PDCA). Again, the idea is to find potential errors *before* they happen. Deming's approach, including implementing standards, was used for many years before the International Organization for Standardization (ISO), which we will talk about shortly, came into being.

statistical quality control (SQC)
The process some managers use to continually monitor all phases of the production process to assure that quality is being built into the product from the beginning.

statistical process control (SPC)
The process of testing statistical samples of product components at each stage of the production process and plotting those results on a graph. Any variances from quality standards are recognized and can be corrected if beyond the set standards.

Businesses are getting serious about providing top customer service, and many are already doing it. But while physical goods can be designed and manufactured to near perfection, there's no similar process that can be applied to services. Service organizations find it difficult to provide outstanding service every time because the process is so labour intensive. Physical goods (e.g., a gold ring) can be designed and manufactured to near perfection. However, it is hard to reach such perfection when designing and providing a service experience such as a dance on a cruise ship or a cab drive through Vancouver.

QUALITY AWARD: THE CANADA AWARDS FOR EXCELLENCE[31]

Excellence Canada is the leading authority in Canada on organizational excellence based on quality systems, innovation, and healthy workplace criteria. The *Canada Awards for Excellence (CAE)* are presented annually to private, public, and not-for-profit organizations that have demonstrated continual innovation and sustainable improvement across all business drivers and all departments, including: Leadership and Governance, Corporate Social Responsibility, Planning and Strategy, People Engagement, Psychological and Physical Health & Safety, Customer Experience, Process and Project Management, and relationships with Partners and Suppliers.

The award has honoured hundreds of Canadian organizations, including Manulife Investment, Toronto East General Hospital, Hill & Knowlton Strategies Canada, and the Peel Regional Police. Recent recipients also include Ceridian HCM Canada, British Columbia Pension Corporation, the Canadian Forces Housing Agency, and the Toronto Transit Commission,

CAE awards categories are: Excellence, Innovation and Wellness; Healthy Workplace; and Mental Health at Work. For more information, visit the Excellence Canada website.

EXCELLENCE • CANADA
improving performance, recognizing excellence | améliorer le rendement, reconnaître l'excellence

Courtesy of Excellence Canada

Excellence Canada (formally the National Quality Institute) is an independent, not-for-profit organization founded by Industry Canada. It helps companies understand and apply a focus on excellence through the adoption of the Excellence, Innovation and Wellness Standard. This approach will help companies reduce waste and costs while improving productivity and competitiveness. Do you see how this framework incorporates principles discussed in this textbook?

ISO 9000 AND ISO 14000 SERIES AND STANDARDS

The International Organization for Standardization (ISO) is a worldwide federation of national standards bodies from more than 160 countries that set the global measures for the quality of individual products.[32] ISO is a nongovernmental organization established in 1947 to promote the development of world standards to facilitate the international exchange of goods and services (ISO is not an acronym. It comes from the Greek word *isos,* meaning equal). Within the ISO 9000 series are specific standards, such as ISO 9001. **ISO 9001** is the common name given to quality management and assurance standards. A more recent standard that focuses upon sustained success, ISO 9004:2018, primarily targets the strategic and operational management of organizations.[33]

ISO 9001
The common name given to quality management and assurance standards.

The standards require that a company must determine customer needs, including regulatory and legal requirements, and make communication arrangements to handle issues such as complaints. Other standards involve process control, product testing, storage, and delivery. Improving quality is an investment that can pay off in better customer relations and higher sales.

It is important to know that ISO did not start as a quality certification, the way many people think. In the beginning, it simply meant that your process was under control. In short, it looked to see that companies were consistently producing the same products each time. There is a difference between consistency (flawed products every time) and quality (products free from defects). Today, ISO has developed over 22 000 international standards and includes 162 member countries.[34]

What makes ISO 9001 so important is that the European Union (EU) demands that companies that want to do business with the EU be certified by ISO standards. Some major Canadian companies are also demanding that suppliers meet these standards. Several accreditation agencies in Europe and in North America will certify that a company meets the standards for all phases of its operations, from product development through production and testing to installation.

SNC-Lavalin Group Inc., one of the leading groups of engineering and construction companies in the world, has met such standards. It provides engineering, procurement, construction, project management, and project financing services to a variety of industry sectors in more than 120 countries. The Quality Policy at SNC-Lavalin is to "achieve client satisfaction through the careful management of our work processes, with due attention to value creation through scope, schedule, cost control, and with emphasis on safety and the environment." To best serve its various stakeholders, the company has implemented Client Satisfaction and Continual Improvement Programs in every division, business unit, geographic office, and subsidiary. These programs are based on the applicable requirements of ISO 9001 International Standard for Quality Management Systems.[35]

Another series, the ISO 14000 series, deals with environmental management, Within this series, **ISO 14001** is a collection of specific standards that address the best practices for managing an organization's impact on the environment. As an environmental management system, it does not prescribe a performance level. Requirements for certification include having an environmental policy, having specific improvement targets, conducting audits of environmental programs, and maintaining top management review of the processes.

ISO 14001
A collection of the best practices for managing an organization's impact on the environment.

Certification in both ISO 9001 and ISO 14001 would show that a firm has a world-class management system in both quality and environmental standards. In the past, firms assigned employees separately to meet each set of standards. Today, ISO 9001 and ISO

14001 standards have been blended so that an organization can work on both at once. ISO is now working on ISO 26000 standards, which are designed to give guidance on social responsibility.[36]

More recently, consumers have begun to support companies that produce environmentally friendly goods (as discussed earlier in Chapter 5). As a result, businesses have begun to re-examine their operations in order to create sustainable production processes. In 2002, William McDonough and Dr. Michael Braungart published the book *Cradle to Cradle: Remaking the Way We Make Things* which discusses the need to shift from a linear cradle-to-grave production process to an endless, eco-effective production process.[37] The sustainability advocates gifted the licence to provide Cradle to Cradle (C2C) certification to the non-profit organization called the Cradle to Cradle Products Innovation Institute. The Cradle to Cradle Certified Mark demonstrates a manufacturer's commitment to sustainability.

You know C2C certification has made an impact when you see a major multi-national manufacturer such as Nike take notice. The company responded to the sustainable manufacturing movement through its "Nike Considered" design ethos where the company adopts a sustainable approach to its footwear innovation. Its product redesign included the Nike Trash Talk shoe, which is endorsed by former NBA player Steve Nash, that is manufactured from leather waste and scrap-ground foam, and environmentally-preferred rubber made with fewer toxins.[38] The company continued this trend through its Nike Free footwear line which has reduced waste by nearly 2 million pounds through its Nike Flyknit technology.[39] The company has made a commitment to develop a closed-loop business model that includes reusing, reducing, and composting materials in order to decrease its waste production.[40]

Supply Chain Management

Before we discuss this next topic, it is important to introduce some terms. **Logistics** involves those activities that focus on getting the right amount of the right products or services to the right place at the right time at the lowest possible cost. A **supply chain** is a sequence of firms that perform activities required to create and deliver a good or service to consumers or industrial users. Some companies have been successful in attracting more customers due to their supply chain management efficiencies. **Supply chain management** is the integration and organization of information and logistics activities *across* firms in a supply chain for the purpose of creating and delivering goods and services that provide value to customers. The Adapting to Change box highlights how one company created a unique business that resolved a logistics issue in their supply chain.

Facilities in supply chain management include factories, processing centres, warehouses, distribution centres, and retail outlets (Figure 10.5). Functions and activities include forecasting, purchasing, inventory management, information management, quality assurance, scheduling, production, delivery, and customer service. Today, the major factors contributing to the importance of supply chain management include: (1) the need for improvement to remain competitive, (2) the increase in outsourcing, (3) shorter product life cycles and increased customization, (4) globalization, (5) the growth of technology and e-commerce, (6) the increase in complexity through JIT inventory, and (7) the need for better management of inventories. When implementing supply chain management, firms try to improve quality, reduce costs, increase flexibility and speed, and

logistics
Those activities that focus on getting the right amount of the right products or services to the right place at the right time at the lowest possible cost.

supply chain
The sequence of firms that perform activities required to create and deliver a good or service to consumers or industrial users.

supply chain management
The integration and organization of information and logistics activities across firms in a supply chain for the purpose of creating and delivering goods and services that provide value to customers.

Adapting to CHANGE

Your Own Farm in a Box

Imagine sitting in your favourite restaurant in Calgary in the middle of winter with a 12-inch snowfall coming your way. You crave some of the fresh, locally grown produce you enjoy so much in the warmer months. Unfortunately, it's winter so it probably won't be on the menu. Well, crave no more. Help is on the way thanks to a couple of entrepreneurs.

Brad McNamara and Jon Friedman could not get the results they wanted growing produce in a rooftop greenhouse. Frustrated, Jon came up with the idea that using a shipping container to grow produce might be more appropriate. Thanks to his insight, Freight Farms' customers can now grow leafy greens, vine crops, and mushrooms hydroponically in insulated, climate-controlled containers. The company uses 320-square-foot shipping containers that are retrofitted and converted into modular, stackable farms that can produce 900 heads of leafy greens per container each week. The entire hydroponic system is simple enough that it can be digitally monitored and controlled from a smartphone. The weekly output from one of Freight Farms containers is approximately equivalent to the annual yield of a one-acre farm.

© Freight Farms

The immediate goal of Freight Farms is to create an appropriate infrastructure that fosters local food economies. The company targets small and medium-sized food distributors such as wholesalers and restaurants with revenues between $3 million and $75 million. The result is a simpler and shorter supply chain for getting food from "farm to table."

Friedman and McNamara also want to attract non-profit groups involved in food distribution in depressed or disaster-relief areas as buyers for their $60,000 farms-in-a-box. But they don't want to stop here. While attracting enough customers to make local farming a cost-effective option is the key goal of Freight Farms today, the founders have a much broader objective for the future. Predicting a global food shortage in 2050, they believe Freight Farms is the first step in the redesign of the global food system. Bon Appetit!

Sources: Jeremy Quittner, "A One-Acre Farm in a 320-Square-Foot Box," *Inc.*, March 2013; Peter Cohan, "Grow Produce Anywhere in Freight Farms' $60,000 Shipping Container," *Forbes*, June 27, 2013; and Leon Neyfakh, "If Urban Farming Took Off, What Would Boston Look Like?" *The Boston Globe*, January 19, 2014.

improve customer service while at the same time reduce the number of suppliers used. Two examples follow:

- The Coca-Cola Company sought to streamline and simplify its supply chain through a number of measures. Historically, the company has worked with independent bottlers to produce and distribute its products. That changed in 2010 when Coca-Cola purchased its largest bottler and began to reduce its bottling operations. Since 2010, the company's bottling plant network has dropped from 353 ownerships to 73 ownerships with only 100 plants. This change is even more difficult given Coca-Cola's entire line includes 3500 products. In order to respond to changes, the planners are constantly adjusting the supply chain through one guiding principle—DOIP (Demand, Operations, and Inventory Planning). Given Coca-Cola's global reach, operation management is a critical part of the company's success. Their mantra—"There is a person at the end of our supply chain"—clearly highlights this priority.[41]

FIGURE 10.5

SUPPLY CHAIN MANAGEMENT

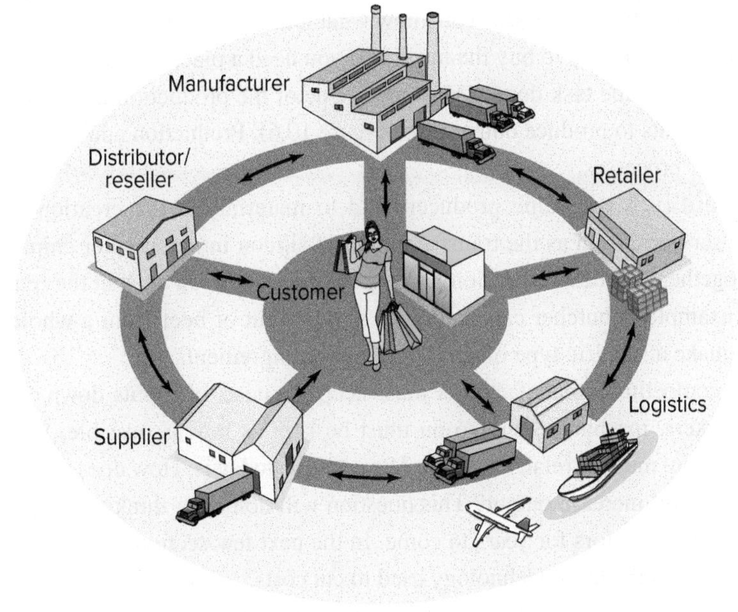

This is an image of supply chain management showing the interrelationships between all of the types of firms involved in the provision of a good or a service to a customer.

- Source for Sports is a national brand with over 150 independently owned and operated sport retailers across Canada. Its approach is to enable independents to purchase products at a cheaper price than if stores owners had to buy products on their own. No two stores are alike and therefore operations management is an important part of making this approach a success. In order to build retailer–supplier collaboration, the company adopted a big data analytics platform, called Askuity. The software will help the head office be more responsive to supply needs for each store and better manage the availability of stock as products change from one season to the next. For example, Askuity will identify which types of hockey equipment sold the best at different times of the season, which in turn improves purchase and distribution planning the following year.[42]

PROGRESS ASSESSMENT

- Can you name and define three functions that are common to operations management in both the service and the manufacturing sectors?
- What are the major criteria for facility location?
- What is the difference between materials resource planning (MRP) and enterprise resource planning (ERP)?
- What is just-in-time inventory control?
- What is involved in implementing each of the following: Six Sigma, SQC, SPC, ISO 9000, and ISO 14000?

LO4

Identify various production processes and describe techniques that improve productivity, including computer-aided design and manufacturing, flexible manufacturing, lean manufacturing, mass customization, robotics, and 3D printing.

Production Processes

Common sense and some experience have already taught you much of what you need to know about production processes. You know what it takes to write a term paper or prepare a dinner. You need money to buy the materials, you need a place to work, and you need to be organized to get the task done. The same is true of the production process in industry. It uses basic inputs to produce outputs (see Figure 10.6). Production adds value, or utility, to materials or processes.

form utility
The value added by the creation of finished goods and services.

Form utility is the value producers add to materials in the creation of finished goods and services, such as the transformation of silicon into computer chips or putting services together to create a vacation package. Form utility can exist at the retail level as well. For example, a butcher can produce a specific cut of beef from a whole cow or a baker can make a specific type of cake out of basic ingredients.

To be competitive, manufacturers must keep the costs of inputs down. That is, the costs of workers, machinery, and so on must be kept as low as possible. Similarly, the amount of output must be relatively high. The question today is: How does a producer keep costs low and still increase output? This question will dominate thinking in the manufacturing and service sectors for years to come. In the next few sections, we explore production processes and the latest technology used to cut costs.

Manufacturers use several different processes to produce goods. Andrew S. Grove, chairman of computer chip manufacturer Intel, offers a great analogy to explain production:

> Imagine that you're a chef . . . and that your task is to serve a breakfast consisting of a three-minute soft-boiled egg, buttered toast, and coffee. Your job is to prepare and deliver the three items simultaneously, each of them fresh and hot.

process manufacturing
That part of the production process that physically or chemically changes materials.

assembly process
That part of the production process that puts together components.

Grove says this task encompasses the three basic requirements of production: (1) to build and deliver products in response to the demands of the customer at a scheduled delivery time, (2) to provide an acceptable quality level, and (3) to provide everything at the lowest possible cost.

Let's use the breakfast example to understand process and assembly. **Process manufacturing** physically or chemically changes materials. For example, boiling physically changes the egg. Similarly, process manufacturing turns sand into glass or computer chips. The **assembly process** puts together components (eggs, toast, and coffee) to make a product

FIGURE 10.6

THE PRODUCTION PROCESS

The production process consists of taking the factors of production and using the inputs to produce goods, services, and ideas. Planning, routing, scheduling, and the other activities are the means to accomplish the objective—output.

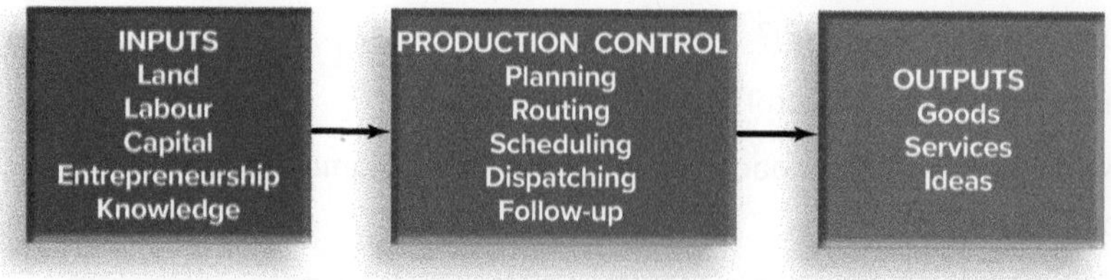

(breakfast). Cars are made through an assembly process that puts together the frame, engine, and other parts.

Production processes are either continuous or intermittent. A **continuous process** is one in which long production runs (lots of eggs) turn out finished goods over time. As the chef, you could have a conveyor belt that lowers eggs into boiling water for three minutes and then lifts them out. A three-minute egg would be available whenever you want. A chemical plant, for example, is run on a continuous process.

© ChameleonsEye / Shutterstock.com

Production lines allow for the efficient and speedy production of goods that are consistent in size, weight, colour, and other measures of quality. How many products can you think of that are likely made on a production line?

It usually makes more sense when responding to specific customer orders to use an **intermittent process**. Here the production run is short (one or two eggs) and the producer adjusts machines frequently to make different products (like the oven in a bakery or the toaster in the diner). Manufacturers of custom-designed furniture would use an intermittent process.

continuous process
A production process in which long production runs turn out finished goods over time.

intermittent process
A production process in which the production run is short and the machines are changed frequently to make different products.

An example of a product that uses both long and short production runs is Kodiak boots. In 2006, the company re-established production in Canada after a nine-year absence. "At the end of the day, we're going to service customers a lot better through this core Canadian production," says Kevin Huckle, president of Kodiak Group Holdings Inc., which plans to do a third of its production in Canada. Domestic production offers quick, efficient service for Canadian retailers, who may require only small numbers of boots, but need them in a hurry. With Asian production, he has to contract for long production runs—more than 1200 pairs—and has to carry a high volume of inventory. With domestic manufacturing, the plant keeps enough materials available for relatively short runs. Because of automation and location, it can turn around Canadian production orders in 21 days, compared with 90 days for orders in Asia. While Canadian workers gained jobs from this manufacturing facility re-location, there are also times when a move isn't as beneficial. In 2014, Kodiak announced it would relocate its Terra Nova Shoes plant in Harbour Grace, Newfoundland, to Cambridge, Ontario. The result was a loss of 80 jobs in Harbour Grace.[43] At the same time, the company obtained support from the Southwestern Ontario Development Fund, a Government of Ontario program, to expand its Cambridge, Ontario, plant operation and in turn create 80 additional jobs.[44]

Today, many new manufacturers use intermittent processes. Computers, robots, and flexible manufacturing processes allow firms to turn out custom-made goods as fast as mass-produced goods were produced. We'll discuss how they do that in more detail in the next few sections as we explore advanced production techniques and technology.

Improving Production Techniques and Cutting Costs

The ultimate goal of operations management is to provide high-quality goods and services instantaneously in response to customer demand. As we stress throughout this text, traditional organizations were simply not designed to be so responsive to the customer. Rather, they were designed to make goods efficiently (inexpensively). The idea behind mass production was to make a large number of a limited variety of products at very low cost.

© Philip Friedman/Studio D

Bakers, like Duff Goldman of Charm City Cakes, add form utility to materials by transforming basic ingredients into special customized cakes. Can you see how the production of such cakes involves both process manufacturing and assembly processes?

Over the years, low cost often came at the expense of quality and flexibility. Furthermore, suppliers did not always deliver when they said they would, so manufacturers had to carry large inventories of raw materials and components to keep producing. Such inefficiencies made Canadian companies vulnerable to foreign competitors that were using more advanced production techniques and less expensive labour.

As a result of global competition, companies have had to make a wide variety of high-quality, custom-designed products at very low cost. Clearly, something had to change on the production floor to make that possible. Several major developments have made companies more competitive: (1) flexible manufacturing, (2) lean manufacturing, (3) mass customization, (4) robotics, (5) computer-aided design and manufacturing, and (5) 3D printing and additive manufacturing.

Flexible Manufacturing

Flexible manufacturing means designing machines to do multiple tasks so they can produce a variety of products. Allen-Bradley, part of Rockwell Automation, uses flexible manufacturing to build motor starters. Orders come in daily, and within 24 hours the company's 26 machines and robots manufacture, test, and package the starters—which are untouched by human hands. Allen-Bradley's machines are so flexible that managers can include a special order, even a single item, in the assembly without slowing down the process. Did you notice that this product was made without any labour? One way to compete with cheap labour in other facility locations is to have as few workers as possible.

flexible manufacturing
Designing machines to do multiple tasks so that they can produce a variety of products.

Lean Manufacturing

Lean manufacturing is the production of goods using less of everything compared to mass production: less human effort, less manufacturing space, less investment in tools, and less engineering time to develop a new product.[45] A company becomes lean by continuously increasing its capacity to produce high-quality goods while decreasing its need for resources.[46] Here are some characteristics of a lean company:

lean manufacturing
The production of goods using less of everything compared to mass production.

- Takes half the human effort.[47]
- Has half the defects in the finished product or service.
- Requires one-third the engineering effort.
- Uses half the floor space for the same output.
- Carries 90 percent less inventory.

Technological improvements are largely responsible for the increase in productivity and efficiency of Canadian plants. That technology made labour more productive and made it possible to pay higher rates. On the other hand, employees can get frustrated by innovations (e.g., they must learn new processes), and companies must constantly train and retrain employees to stay competitive. The need for additional productivity and efficiency has never been greater. The solution to the economic crisis depends on such innovations. One step in the process is to make products more individualistic. The next section discusses how that happens.

Mass Customization

To *customize* means to make a unique good or provide a specific service to an individual. Although it once may have seemed impossible, **mass customization**, which means tailoring products to meet the needs of a large number of individual customers, is now practised widely. The National Bicycle Industrial Company in Japan made 18 bicycle models in more than 2 million combinations, each designed to fit the needs of a specific customer. The customer chose the model, size, colour, and design. The retailer took various measurements from the buyer and faxed the data to the factory, where robots handled the bulk of the assembly. Thus, flexible manufacturing (discussed earlier) is one of the factors that makes mass customization possible.

mass customization Tailoring products to meet the needs of individual customers.

More and more manufacturers are learning to customize their products. The fashion startup Proper Cloth uses software called Smart Sizes to custom-design shirts for online shoppers.[48] At General Nutrition Center (GNC), health-minded buyers can customize their own vitamin plans. For those with more of a sweet tooth, you can even buy custom-made M&M's in colours of your choice. General Nutrition Center (GNC) stores feature machines that enable shoppers to custom-design their own vitamins, shampoo, and lotions. The Custom Foot stores use infrared scanners to precisely measure each foot so that shoes can be made to fit perfectly.

One unique way of using mass customization can be seen at Moniker Guitars.[49] The company follows Nike's model called NikeiD that allows consumers to customize their shoes. This customer customization is also the basis of Moniker's guitar business. By using online design tools and advanced manufacturing techniques, Moniker can produce top-quality, personalized guitars for what a guitar player would pay for a generic model.

Today, Moniker's website guides guitar pickers through a number of steps to customize their instruments using colour and graphics, as well as hardware and pickups. The company uses PPG paint on its guitars—the same paint used for Lamborghini and Ferrari automobiles. If polka dots are your passion, or tiger stripes turn you on, Moniker will deliver. According to founder Kevin Tully, "Every design is different. You never paint the same guitar twice. Every day is a new project. I love it."

Mass customization can be used in the service sector as well. Capital Protective Insurance (CPI) uses the latest computer software and hardware to sell customized risk-management plans to companies. Health clubs offer unique fitness programs for individuals,

Not only can you customize the colours of your M&M's, you can also have personal messages and/or images imprinted on them. What other customized products can you think of?

travel agencies provide vacation packages that vary according to individual choices, and some schools allow students to design their own majors. Actually, it is much easier to custom-design service programs than it is to custom-make goods, because there is no fixed tangible good that has to be adapted. Each customer can specify what he or she wants, within the limits of the service organization—limits that seem to be ever widening.

Robotics

Mass customization is easy for industrial robotics where machines can work 24 hours a day, seven days a week, with great precision. Robots have completely changed manufacturing by improving productivity while also reducing the number of jobs available to humans.[50] Along with assembly line jobs in factories, robots have also begun to take over in service businesses as well. At Aloft Hotels, a robot butler called Botlr roams the halls delivering room service to guests.[51] Even Wall Street financial analysts have had to start competing for jobs with robots.[52] In other words robots are slowly but surely either helping people perform better or are replacing them completely. Soon we may be entering what could be known as the robot economy.[53] Many people think that China is so successful because of cheap labour, but China may soon be the world's largest robot market.[54]

computer-aided design (CAD)
The use of computers in the design of products.

computer-aided manufacturing (CAM)
The use of computers in the manufacturing of products.

Current studies predict that almost a quarter of automated tasks will be performed by robots in the next decade.[55] The adoption of robotics in manufacturing is strongly influenced by the cost of labour compared to the cost of robotic labour. As the cost of robot technology drops and the cost of employees rises, Canada's manufacturing sectors are poised for some drastic changes. How do you think robotics will impact the workplace in the future?

© Benoit Decout/REA/Redux

3D tools allow designers to create cloth prototypes without a pattern's traditional stages (seaming, trying on, alternations, etc.). What advantages might this technology offer to small manufacturing companies?

Computer-Aided Design and Manufacturing

One development that has changed production techniques is the use of computers to design products. Called **computer-aided design (CAD)**, businesses ranging from construction companies to carmakers to video game designers depend on 3D modelling software to create new products.[56]

The next step was to bring computers directly in the production process with **computer-aided manufacturing (CAM)**. CAD/CAM, the use of both computer-aided design and computer-aided manufacturing made it possible to custom-design products to meet the needs of small markets with very little increase in cost. A manufacturer programs the computer to make a simple design change, and that change is directly incorporated into production. In the clothing industry, a computer program establishes a pattern and cuts the cloth automatically, even adjusting to a specific person's dimensions to create custom-cut clothing at little additional cost. In food service, CAM supports on-site, small-scale, semi-automated, sensor-controlled baking in fresh-baked cookie shops to make consistent quality easy to achieve. The latest CAM technology includes 3D printers that make a product layer by layer until it appears as a finished good.

CAD has doubled productivity in many firms. But in the past CAD machines could not talk to CAM machines directly. Today, however, software programs unite CAD with CAM: the result is **computer-integrated manufacturing (CIM)**. The software is expensive, but it cuts as much as 80 percent of the time needed to program machines to make parts.

computer-integrated manufacturing (CIM) The uniting of computer-aided design with computer-aided manufacturing.

3D Printing and Additive Manufacturing

One of the most exciting production processes to emerge in recent years has been 3D printing. During this advanced procedure also known as additive manufacturing, a product is created one layer at a time by a nozzle similar to those found in inkjet printers. So far manufacturers have largely used 3D printing to create prototype models or molds for other industrial projects.[57] But experts claim that 3D printing could someday revolutionize the production of all sorts of items. The Adapting to Change box looks at some of these potential developments and how they could affect several industries.

Adapting *to* CHANGE

The Vast Possibilities of 3D Printing

As 3D printers become more reliable and affordable, many commentators hail the process as the future of all sorts of industries. These experts claim that 3D printing will change everything from manufacturing to medicine to fashion. Of course, no one can predict the future. While the possibilities of "additive manufacturing" are vast, only time will tell which methods succeed and which fail.

So far, 3D printing has shown the most promise when used in factories. Manufacturers have used the process for years to create molds for parts or to develop prototypes. At the same time, though, factories couldn't produce working parts from 3D printers since the machines could only use plastic. Now, engineers have developed 3D printers that can create objects out of strong carbon fibre material or even metal. As additive manufacturing becomes more efficient, these advancements could completely transform production.

3D printing could also prove to be revolutionary for the medical industry. Along with producing models that help with organ transplants, additive manufacturing could be used to design better medicines or improve medical imaging.

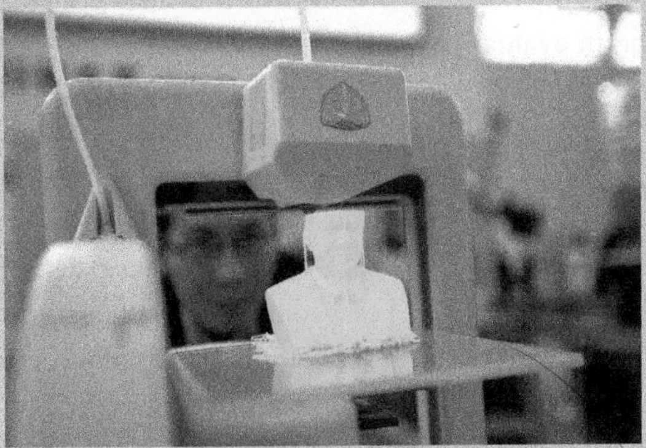

© Imaginechina/AP Images

Even the fashion industry sees a bright future in 3D printing. The footwear company Feetz, for instance, depends on additive manufacturing to produce a line of customizable shoes. Some clothing makers claim that the 3D printer could be just as transformative to the industry as the sewing machine. In fact, one day your favourite outfit could emerge from a 3D printer installed in your house. Still, no one knows for sure if 3D printing will live up to this enormous promise. Stay tuned to see how this advanced process improves in your lifetime.

Sources: Ted Mann, "3-D Printing Expands to Metals, Showing Industrial Promise," *The Wall Street Journal,* November 11, 2016; Constance Gustke, "Your Next Pair of Shoes Could Come From a 3-D Printer," *The New York Times,* September 14, 2016; Bhaskar Chakravorti, "3 Ways in Which a 3D Printer May One Day Save Your Life," *The Washington Post,* March 7, 2016.

PROGRESS ASSESSMENT

- What are three basic requirements of production?
- Define and differentiate the following: process manufacturing, assembly process, continuous process, and intermittent process.
- How does flexible manufacturing differ from lean manufacturing?
- What are CAD, CAM, and CIM?

Control Procedures: PERT and Gantt Charts

LO5

Explain the use of PERT and Gantt charts to control manufacturing processes.

program evaluation and review technique (PERT)
A method for analyzing the tasks involved in completing a given project, estimating the time needed to complete each task, and identifying the minimum time needed to complete the total project.

critical path
In a PERT network, the sequence of tasks that takes the longest time to complete.

Gantt chart
Bar graph showing production managers what projects are underway and what stage they are in at any given time.

Operations managers must ensure products are manufactured and delivered on time, on budget, and to specification. How can managers be sure all will go smoothly and be completed by the required time? One popular technique for monitoring the progress of production was developed in the 1950s for constructing nuclear submarines: the **program evaluation and review technique (PERT)**. PERT users analyze the tasks to complete a given project, estimate the time needed to complete each, and compute the minimum time needed to complete the whole project.

The steps used in PERT are (1) analyze and sequence tasks that need to be done, (2) estimate the time needed to complete each task, (3) draw a PERT network illustrating the information from steps 1 and 2, and (4) identify the critical path. The **critical path** is the sequence of tasks that takes the longest time to complete. We use the word *critical* because a delay anywhere along this path will cause the project or production run to be late.

Figure 10.7 illustrates a PERT chart for producing a music video. The squares indicate completed tasks, and the arrows indicate the time needed to complete the next task. The path from one completed task to another illustrates the relationships among tasks; the arrow from "set designed" to "set materials purchased" indicates we must design the set before we can purchase the materials. The critical path, indicated by the bold black arrows, indicates producing the set takes more time than auditioning dancers, choreographing dances, or designing and making costumes. The project manager now knows it is critical that set construction remain on schedule if the project is to be completed on time, but short interruptions in dance and costume preparation are unlikely to delay it.

A PERT network can be made up of thousands of events over many months. Today, a computer is utilized to create this complex procedure. Another, more basic strategy manufacturers use for measuring production progress is a Gantt chart. A **Gantt chart** (named for its developer, Henry L. Gantt) is a bar graph, now also prepared by computer, that clearly shows what projects are underway and how much of the project has been completed at any given time. Figure 10.8, a Gantt chart for a doll manufacturer, shows that the dolls' heads and bodies should be completed before the clothing is sewn. It also shows that at the end of week 3, the dolls' bodies are ready, but the heads are about half a week behind. Using a Gantt-like computer program, a manager can trace the production process minute by minute to determine which tasks are on time and which are behind, so that adjustments can be made to allow the company to stay on schedule.

FIGURE 10.7

PERT CHART FOR A MUSIC VIDEO

The minimum amount of time it will take to produce this video is 15 weeks. To get that number, you add the week it takes to pick a star and a song to the four weeks to design a set, the two weeks to purchase set materials, the six weeks to construct the set, the week before rehearsals, and the final week when the video is made. That is the critical path. Any delay in that process will delay the final video.

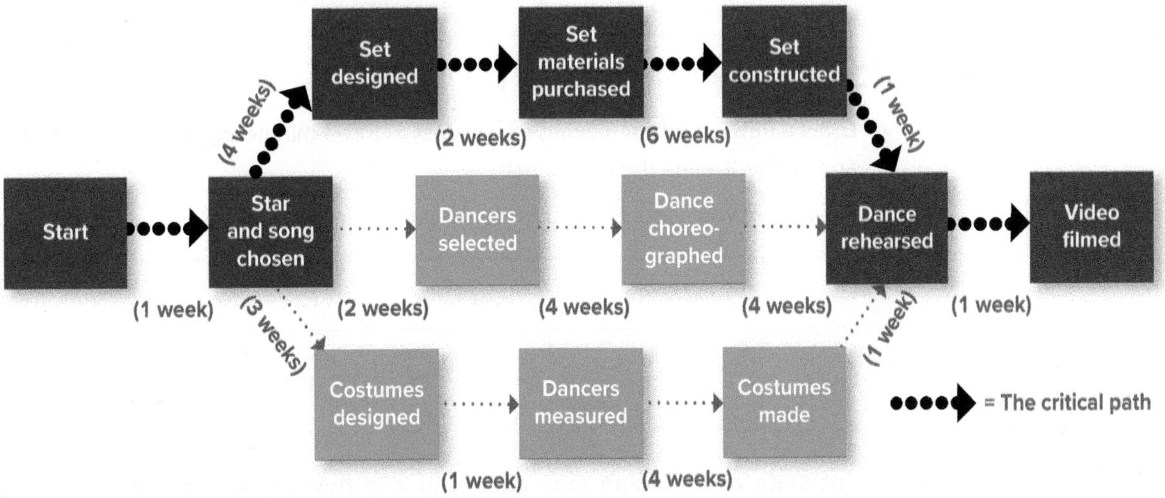

FIGURE 10.8

GANTT CHART FOR A DOLL MANUFACTURER

A Gantt chart enables a production manager to see at a glance when projects are scheduled to be completed and what the current status is. For example, the dolls' heads and bodies should be completed before the clothing is sewn, but they could be a little late as long as everything is ready for assembly in week 6. This chart shows that at the end of week 3, the dolls' bodies are ready, but the heads are about half a week behind.

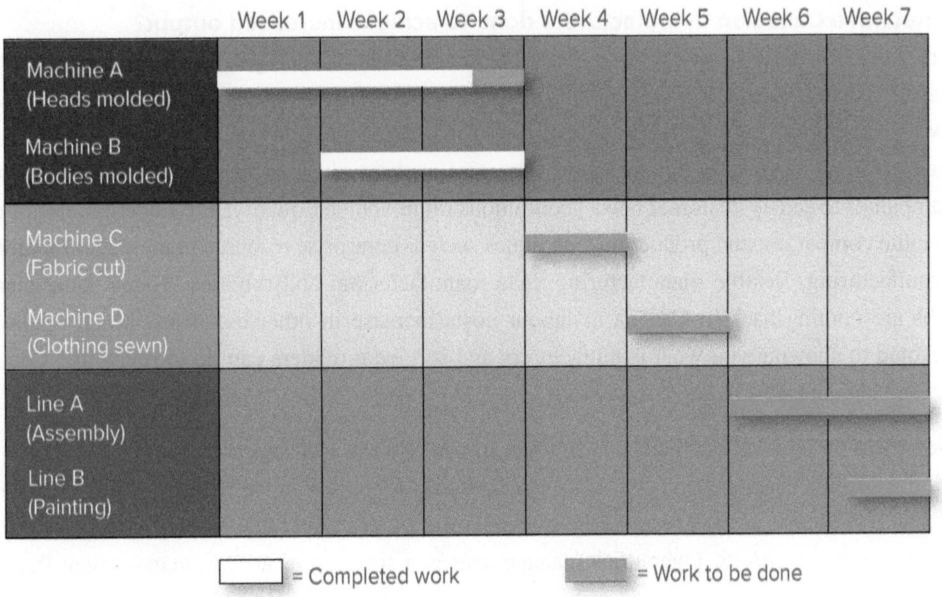

Preparing for the Future

Canada is a major industrial country, but competition is growing stronger each year. Tremendous opportunities for careers in operations management exist as both manufacturing and service companies fight to stay competitive. Students who can see future trends and have the skills to own or work in tomorrow's highly automated factories and modern service facilities will benefit.

PROGRESS ASSESSMENT

- Draw a PERT chart for making a breakfast of three-minute eggs, buttered toast, and coffee. Define the critical path.
- How could you use a Gantt chart to keep track of production?

SUMMARY

LO1 **Describe the current state of Canadian manufacturing and how companies are becoming more competitive.**

Canada's industrial profile results in significant swings in activity and a number of challenges are faced in an increasingly competitive global environment. Activity in the manufacturing sector has declined which has also led to job loss. Even though manufacturing companies offer fewer jobs, they have become more productive, meaning that they need fewer employees to do the same amount of work.

Where is most of Canada's industry focused?

Most of our industry is focused on natural resources, which results in significant progress when world economies are growing, but is offset by significant retraction when the world economies are stagnant.

What have Canadian manufacturers done to achieve increased output?

Activity in Canada's manufacturing sector has declined since its height. The result has been fewer jobs in manufacturing. Even though manufacturing companies offer fewer jobs, they have become more productive, meaning that they need fewer employees to do the same amount of work. Canadian manufacturers have increased output by emphasizing strategies such as close relationships with suppliers and other companies to satisfy customer needs; continuous improvement; quality; site selection; use of the Internet to unite companies; and production techniques such as enterprise resource planning, computer-integrated manufacturing, flexible manufacturing, lean manufacturing, and robotics. Today some manufacturing jobs are coming back to Canada as labour costs increase in other countries. Much of this chapter is devoted to showing you what manufacturers and service providers can do to revive the Canadian economy to become world-class competitors.

LO2 **Describe the evolution from production to operations management.**

Production management consists of all the activities managers do to help their firms create goods. To reflect the change in importance from manufacturing to services, the term *production* is often replaced by the term *operations*. Operations management is a specialized area in management that converts or transforms resources (including human resources) into goods and services.

What kinds of firms use operations managers?

Firms in both the manufacturing and the service sectors use operations managers.

Why is productivity so hard to measure?

The traditional way to measure productivity involves tracking inputs (worker hours) compared to outputs (dollars). Quality improvements are not weighed. New information systems must be developed to measure the quality of goods and services, the speed of their delivery, and customer satisfaction.

LO3 **Describe operations management planning issues including facility location, facility layout, materials requirement planning, purchasing, just-in-time inventory control, quality control, and supply chain management.**

Issues involved in both the manufacturing and the service sectors include facility location, facility layout, materials requirement planning, purchasing, just-in-time inventory control, quality control, and supply chain management.

What is facility location and how does it differ from facility layout?

Facility location is the process of selecting a geographic location for a company's operations. Facility layout is the physical arrangement of resources (including people) to produce goods and services effectively and efficiently.

Why is facility location so important, and what criteria are used to evaluate different sites?

The very survival of manufacturing depends on its ability to remain competitive, and that means either making inputs less costly (reducing costs of labour and land) or increasing outputs from present inputs (increasing productivity). Labour costs and land costs are two major criteria for selecting the right sites. Other criteria include whether (1) resources are plentiful and inexpensive, (2) skilled workers are available or are trainable, (3) taxes are low and the local government offers support, (4) energy and water are available, (5) transportation costs are low, and (6) the quality of life and quality of education are high.

What relationship do materials requirement planning (MRP) and enterprise resource planning (ERP) have with the production process?

MRP is a computer-based operations management system that uses sales forecasts to make sure the needed parts and materials are available at the right time and place. Enterprise resource planning (ERP), a newer version of MRP, combines the computerized functions of all the divisions and subsidiaries of the firm—such as finance, material requirements planning, human resources, and order fulfillment—into an integrated software program that uses a single database. The result is a shorter period of time between orders and payment, less staff to complete orders and order processing, reduced inventories, and better customer service for all the firms involved.

What is just-in-time (JIT) inventory control?

JIT involves having suppliers deliver parts and materials just in time to go on the assembly line so they do not have to be stored in warehouses.

What are the latest quality control concepts?

Six Sigma quality (just 3.4 defects per million products) detects potential problems before they occur. Statistical quality control (SQC) is the process that some managers use to continually monitor all processes in production to ensure that quality is being built into the product from the beginning. Statistical process control (SPC) tests statistical samples of product components at each stage of the production process and plots the results on a graph so managers can recognize and correct deviations from quality standards.

What quality standards do firms use in Canada?

International standards that Canadian firms strive to meet include ISO 9000, ISO 9001, and ISO 14001. The first two are European standards for quality and the last is a collection of the best practices for managing an organization's impact on the environment.

LO4 **Identify various production processes and describe techniques that improve productivity, including computer-aided design and manufacturing, flexible manufacturing, lean manufacturing, mass customization, robotics, and 3D printing.**

There are several different processes that manufacturers use to produce goods along with varying techniques to improve productivity.

What is process manufacturing, and how does it differ from assembly processes?

Process manufacturing physically or chemically changes materials. Assembly processes put together components.

Are there other production processes?

Production processes are either continuous or intermittent. A continuous process is one in which long production runs turn out finished goods over time. An intermittent process is an operation where the production run is short and the machines are changed frequently to manufacture different products.

What is flexible manufacturing?

Flexible manufacturing involves designing machines to produce a variety of products.

What is lean manufacturing?

Lean manufacturing is the production of goods using as little of the needed inputs as possible compared to mass production: less human effort, less manufacturing space, less investment in tools, and less engineering time to develop a new product.

What is mass customization?

Mass customization means making custom-designed goods and services for a large number of individual customers. Flexible manufacturing makes mass customization possible. Given the exact needs of a customer, flexible machines can produce a customized good as fast as mass- produced goods were once made. Mass customization is also important in service industries.

How do CAD/CAM systems work?

Design changes made in computer-aided design (CAD) are instantly incorporated into the computer-aided manufacturing (CAM) process. The linking of the two systems—CAD and CAM—is called computer-integrated manufacturing (CIM).

How do robotics help make manufacturers more competitive?

Industrial robotics can work 24 hours a day, seven days a week, with great precision. Most of the jobs they replace are dirty or so repetitive that robots are necessary, or at least helpful.

What is 3D printing and what are its uses?

3D printing (also known as additive manufacturing) is technology that creates a product one layer at a time by a nozzle similar to those found in inkjet printers. Today 3D printing is largely used to create prototype models or molds for other industrial projects.

LO5 **Explain the use of PERT and Gantt charts to control manufacturing processes**

Operations managers must ensure their products or services are provided on time and on budget.

Is there any relationship between a PERT chart and a Gantt chart?

Figure 10.7 shows a PERT chart. Figure 10.8 shows a Gantt chart. Whereas PERT is a tool used for planning, a Gantt chart is a tool used to measure progress.

KEY TERMS

assembly process 380
computer-aided design (CAD) 384
computer-aided manufacturing (CAM) 384
computer-integrated manufacturing (CIM) 385
continuous process 381
critical path 386
e-commerce 365
enterprise resource planning (ERP) 370
facility layout 369
facility location 365
flexible manufacturing 382
form utility 380
Gantt chart 386
intermittent process 381
ISO 9001 376
ISO 14001 376
just-in-time (JIT) inventory control 373
lean manufacturing 382
logistics 377
mass customization 383
materials requirement planning (MRP) 370
operations management 360
process manufacturing 380
production 360
production management 360
program evaluation review technique (PERT) 386
purchasing 372
quality 373
research and development (R&D) 357
Six Sigma quality 374
statistical process control (SPC) 374
statistical quality control (SQC) 374
supply chain 377
supply chain management 377
telecommuting 368

CAREER EXPLORATION

If you are interested in pursuing a career in production, here are a few to consider. Find out about the tasks performed, skills needed, pay, and opportunity outlook in these fields through Internet sites that include the Government of Canada Job Bank, Workopolis, Monster, CareerBuilder, Glassdoor, and Indeed, as well as through the Career Centre at your school.

- **Production, planning and expediting clerks**—Coordinate and expedite the flow of work and materials within or between departments according to production schedule.
- **First-line supervisors**—Directly supervise and coordinate the activities of production and operating workers, such as inspectors, precision workers, machine setters and operators, assemblers, fabricators, and plant and system operators.
- **Industrial production managers**—oversee the daily operations of manufacturing and related plants. They coordinate, plan, and direct the activities used to create a wide range of goods, such as cars, computer equipment, or paper products.
- **Producers and directors**—create motion pictures, television shows, live theatre, commercials, and other performing arts productions.

CRITICAL THINKING

1. Workers on the manufacturing floor are being replaced by robots and other machines. On the one hand, that is one way in which companies compete with cheap labour from other countries. On the other hand, automation eliminates many jobs. Are you concerned that automation may increase unemployment or under-employment in Canada and around the world? Why or why not?
2. Computer-integrated manufacturing (CIM) has revolutionized the production process. What will such changes mean for the clothing industry, the shoe industry, and other fashion-related industries? What will they mean for other consumer and industrial goods industries? How will you benefit as a consumer?
3. One way to create new jobs in Canada is to have more innovation from new graduates of engineering and the sciences. How can Canada motivate more students to study in those areas?

DEVELOPING CAREER SKILLS

Key: ● **Team** ★ **Analytic** ▲ **Communication** ⊡ **Technology**

●★▲ 1. Choosing the right location for a manufacturing plant or a service organization is often critical to its success. Form small groups and have each group member pick one manufacturing plant or one service organization in town and list at least three reasons why its location helps or hinders its success. If its location is not ideal, what location would be a better one?

●★▲ 2. In teams of four or five, discuss the need for better operations management in the airline industry. Have the team develop a report listing (1) problems team members have encountered in travelling by air, and (2) suggestions for improving operations so such problems will not occur in the future.

★▲ 3. Discuss some of the advantages and disadvantages of producing goods overseas using inexpensive labour. Summarize the moral and ethical issues of this practice.

★▲ 4. Think of any retail outlet (e.g., bookstore or food outlet) or service centre (e.g., library, Registrar's Office) at your university or college and redesign the layout (make a pencil sketch) to more effectively serve customers and allow employees to be more effective and efficient.

★▲ 5. Think about recent experiences you have had with service organizations and select one in which you had to wait for an unreasonable length of time to get what you wanted. Describe what happens when customers are inconvenienced, and explain how management could make the operation more efficient and customer-oriented.

●★▲ 6. In teams of four or five, have each team build a PERT chart for a business of their choosing. First have each team identify all the tasks involved in producing the good or providing the service and then organize the tasks into a chart. Have teams identify the critical path and identify the minimum amount of time it will take to produce the good or provide the service to customers.

ANALYZING MANAGEMENT DECISIONS

Why Big Companies Fail to Innovate

Matthew Kiernan, based in Unionville, Ontario, is a management consultant whose views command attention. He has a PhD degree in strategic management from the University of London and was a senior partner with an international consulting firm, KPMG. Subsequently, he founded his own firm, Innovest Group International, with staff operating out of Geneva, Switzerland; London, United Kingdom; and Toronto, Canada. He was also a director of the Business Council for Sustainable Development based in Geneva.

His book *Get Innovative or Get Dead* took aim at big corporations for their poor record on innovation. Any five-year-old could tell you that companies must innovate to survive, he said, so what's the problem? According to Kiernan, it is one thing to understand something in your head but quite another thing to really feel it in your gut. This is further complicated by the difficulty of getting a big company to shift gears, to turn its culture around so that innovation becomes the norm rather than the special effort. Look back at the discussion on innovation at the beginning of the chapter to re-visit its importance in our increasingly competitive world.

Kiernan called for a company to develop a style and atmosphere that favours individual risk-taking, similar to the intrapreneurial approach discussed in Chapter 7. That means that if a team tries something that does not work, you do not shoot it down. Encouraging innovation, which inevitably involves taking risks with the unknown, means accepting the fact that it may take two or three attempts before something useful is developed. Recently, Matthew has applied this principle to sustainable development, including the topic of carbon finance.

The 3M company is often used as a great example of a company that encourages creativity. Its policy dictates that 30 percent of annual sales come from products less than four years old. However, 3M was not always that progressive. When the now legendary Post-it Notes were first developed by an employee, he had a hard time getting the company to see the potential in his idea. This ultimately triggered a major change in the company's policy. Kiernan pointed out that most companies give lip service to the necessity of innovation but do not act in a credible way as far as their employees are concerned. If you mean business, you must take that "bright guy out of the basement, [the one] everybody knows is a genius, but whose last two enterprise efforts came to grief, and visibly promote him."

Discussion Questions

1. Why do large companies find it difficult to innovate? Is it because they are big or because they are afraid of the unknown? Explain.
2. Do smaller companies do better at innovation? Is that because most of them are private companies and not accountable to outside stakeholders? Explain.
3. Do some research on 3M and find out how this large company encourages innovation and what it means to them.

RUNNING CASE

Leadership, Benchmarking, and Operations Management Planning at Fox 40 International Inc.

For successful Canadian entrepreneur and inventor Ron Foxcroft, it all started in 1982 when he purchased Fluke Transport, a Southern Ontario trucking business. The company slogan—If It's On Time . . . It's A "FLUKE"—was soon recognized throughout North America. Over the years, Ron diversified into new ventures and the Foxcroft Group of Companies now includes Fluke Transportation Group, Fluke Warehousing Inc., Foxcroft Capital Corp., Fox 40 International Inc., and Fox 40 USA Inc.

The formation of Fox 40 International Inc. (Fox 40) is the result of a dream for a pealess whistle. When developing his first whistle, Ron was motivated by his knowledge and experience as an international basketball referee. Frustrated with faulty pea whistles, he spent three years of development with design consultant Chuck Shepherd, resulting in the creation of the Fox 40® Classic Whistle. (The whistle was named for Ron and that he was 40 when he applied for the patent.)

Introduced in 1987, this finely tuned precision instrument does not use a pea to generate sound. In fact, there are no moving parts. The patented design moves the air blast through three tuned chambers. This whistle, and all the subsequent whistles that have been introduced, is 100 percent constructed of high-impact ABS plastic so it is impervious to moisture. Wet or dry, Fox 40 Pealess Whistles cannot be overblown and never fail—the harder you blow, the louder the sound! They can be heard for miles and work in all conditions. They are faultless, reliable, and trusted.

Fox 40, a proudly Canadian company, dominates the global whistle industry. Tens of thousands of Fox 40 Whistles are produced monthly for shipment to 140 countries. A mould may be made offshore due to the cost savings (at least $100,000); however, Fox 40 owns all of its moulds. Approximately 90 percent of the company's products are made in Canada with select components coming from overseas markets. Final assembly occurs in Canada. While the first product was the Fox 40® Classic Whistle, the company now has over 900 active stock-keeping units (SKUs). Its product mix includes 19 Whistles Styles (e.g., Fox 40 electronic whistle); Lanyards & Attachments (e.g., flex coils); additional brands that include Fox 40 Gear; SmartCoach Coaching Boards; SICK Self Impression Custom Kit, and Heat Alert Mouthguards; Marine & Outdoor Products (e.g., Xplorer LED Light); Pink Products; and Logo Imprinted Products.

Leadership at Fox 40 is very much a reflection of the vision of the company's founder and CEO, Ron Foxcroft, along with Dave Foxcroft, President and COO. Over the past 25 years of growth, Ron and Dave continue to appreciate that success is very much related to both customers and employees. The importance of satisfying customer needs is central to all they do. As Ron states, "no one (i.e., any employee) needs permission to satisfy a customer." Every employee will do whatever it takes. One of the company's values is to respond to any customer question in 12 seconds, either with an answer or a commitment to, "I don't know but will find out." This vision is also reflected in a firm belief that any employee should be prepared to do any job, except take out the garbage; that is Ron's job.

They also know their vision can only be continually and consistently fulfilled if it is embodied by every employee. So, when hiring staff, Fox 40 knows the importance of hiring the right kind of people; honesty and integrity being key and a very much a reflection of how Ron and Dave behave. Starting in entry-level positions, each employee's strengths and weaknesses are assessed through the assignment of tasks with specific time lines. Performance is monitored not only by management, but by peers. Strengths are channelled to customer satisfaction issues. Weaknesses are discussed and plans for improvement are identified. Senior management are directly accessible to any customer and to any employee. Ron and Dave embody the importance of front-line interaction. For example, Ron is the first person at work every day and both of them come and leave through the front doors, passing through the main areas of the company's facility to their offices.

Fox 40 embodies benchmarking by comparing itself to the very best. Much of the research and development is focused on "not" robbing and duplicating what very successful companies have done. One method is to look to companies that started with a single, simple, product and then have expanded through the addition of complementary products. Gillette started with a shaving blade, added shaving cream, and then deodorant. Wrigley's started with gum. There is also a focus on brand recognition and so they look to market leaders in this area, including Coke. When making decisions on potentially entering a market new to them, the Foxcrofts are guided by a belief that no market is worth considering unless they believe they can become the number one company, in terms of sales, in the new market. They expect to be able to sell to all customers in any market they enter.

When planning facility location, key factors are once more impacted by customers and employees. With sales in 140 countries, both men know the overriding perception of their customers of the importance of "Made in Canada." So, that is an overarching criterion. The large number of global customers supports a focus on logistics. Transportation infrastructure, including highways, shipping, airlines and close proximity to the border, are also important. The majority of employees work in distribution and rely on public transportation to get to work. This is an equally important criterion. For their large customer base in the United States, they have chosen to do customs clearing, so they have a distribution centre in that country, located in Niagara Falls, New York, which is very close to their facilities in Hamilton, Ontario.

The importance of employee input also plays out in terms of layout decisions. The company has recently moved to a new location. Their entire location is very clean and has "hospital operating room" white walls as Dave is a strong proponent of "employees act their environment."

Sources: Ron Foxcroft, CEO of Fox 40 International Inc. and Chairman and CEO of Fluke Transportation, in-person interview, September 22, 2017, Hamilton; and Dave Foxcroft, President and COO, Fox 40 International Inc., in-person interview, May 22, 2012, Hamilton.

Discussion Questions

1. The leadership of Ron and Dave Foxcroft has been influenced by Donald Cooper, former founder and president of Cooper Sporting Goods. Research Donald Cooper's leadership ideas including his concept of "front-line interaction."
2. Access the company's online sites for Fox40, Gillette, and Wrigley. Compare the product offerings of all three companies and comment on how Fox40 has benchmarked itself to the other two companies.
3. Fox 40 has just relocated its business to 340 Grays Road, Hamilton, Ontario. Referring to the above discussion, identify the specifics that supported a move to this location.

PART 4

CHAPTER 11

Motivating Employees

LEARNING OBJECTIVES

After you have read and studied this chapter, you should be able to:

LO1 Explain Taylor's theory of scientific management, and describe the Hawthorne studies and their significance to management.

LO2 Identify the levels of Maslow's hierarchy of needs and apply them to employee motivation. Contrast this with the motivators and hygiene factors identified by Herzberg.

LO3 Differentiate between McGregor's Theory X and Theory Y.

LO4 Explain the key principles of goal-setting, expectancy, reinforcement, and equity theories.

LO5 Show how managers put motivation theories into action through such strategies as job enrichment, open communication, and job recognition.

LO6 Show how managers personalize motivation strategies to appeal to employees around the globe and across generations.

PROFILE

GETTING TO KNOW: LISA LISSON, PRESIDENT, FEDERAL EXPRESS CANADA (FEDEX)

Lisa Lisson, President of FedEx Express Canada (FedEx), leads a team of more than 5000 employees in 63 facilities. They serve shipping needs from coast-to-coast, to the United States, and internationally to 211 countries. There are over 1000 FedEx drop-off locations in Canada and the three call centres (Vancouver, Toronto, and Montreal) respond to 36 500 calls a day.

As a student studying at the University of Guelph for a Bachelor of Commerce degree with a major in marketing, "I knew I wanted to work in the corporate environment," says Lisson. After graduation,

© FedEx

she targeted FedEx as a potential employer. "What I loved about what I read is they talked about this thing called PSP. The philosophy is people, service, profit. . . . Treat your people well with utmost respect and they in turn will provide service to your customers that's exceptional, which will deliver profit to your shareholders and then you can reinvest back in the people." Lisson joined the company as a junior marketing specialist in 1992. She quickly progressed and in 2003 was appointed Vice-President of Sales, Marketing, and Corporate Communications. In 2006, Lisson gained responsibility for improving the FedEx customer experience in Canada. Four years later, she became the first Canadian to be appointed president of FedEx.

Under her leadership, FedEx has implemented critical improvements to the operation of the sales team, resulting in significant revenue growth for the company. She also drove the introduction of *fedex.ca,* shipping and tracking software, and led initiatives to increase brand awareness and market share for FedEx. Lisson also launched a full range of new domestic and international products reinforced with award-winning advertising and new methods for measuring customer satisfaction. In the annual internal opinion survey, Lisson's own employees have ranked her above the country average in each year that she has been a manager.

In an *Undercover Boss Canada* episode, Lisson wanted to ensure that employees had the tools they needed to succeed—and that FedEx not only delivered to its customers, but also to its valuable employees. Lisson disguised herself as new employee Suzanne, a mother of two re-entering the workforce. The employees she met were all real people, survivors who had come through very difficult life challenges and chosen to move forward with remarkable optimism and hope. And they did so in a corporate culture that supported them—by creating a "second family" for them. It was a powerful lesson for Lisson: if you hire the right people, train them well, engender a strong sense of belonging, listen to their ideas, and expect high standards, you will achieve business success.

Says Lisson, "Going undercover was a life-changing experience for me on so many levels but, more importantly, it reinforced my strong belief in the importance of being a leader who knows the front line. Unless you walk in someone else's shoes and experience what they do, you never actually know. I encourage every FedEx manager—in fact, any manager of any company—to get out on the front line and burn the shoe leather. Go and spend a day doing what your employees do and experience what they experience day in and day out. And do it often. I always say that it's my front-line teams who create my "to-do" list.

As a single mother with a high-stress job, she believes in maintaining a healthy work–life balance. Under her leadership, FedEx employees have ranked FedEx Express Canada one of the best places to work in Canada. She has also helped make the company one of the most respected brands in Canada. On advancing women into leadership: "I mentor many young women who often tell me they can have it all—a family and a great career—just not at the same time. I'm a widow and I'm raising four young children, so I'm living proof that you can have it all at the same time. You can be a devoted mom and a successful, senior leader."

In this chapter, you will learn about the theories and practices managers like Lisa Lisson use in motivating their employees to focus on goals common to them and the organization. This includes being introduced to some motivation theories. As you read through this chapter, consider situations in which you have been involved. Did you witness some of the theories being applied? Looking back, could some of these situations have been handled differently to better motivate the audience?

Sources: "FedEx Canada History," Federal Express Canada Corp., 2017, http://www.fedex.com/ca_english/about/overview/fastfacts/canadahistory.html; "5:30 Club: Lisa Lisson, president of FedEx Express Canada," University of Guelph, February 11, 2015, https://www.uoguelph.ca/business/530-club-lisa-lisson-president-fedex-express-canada; "FedEx Express Facts - Canada," Federal Express Canada Corp., 2015, http://www.fedex.com/ca_english/about/overview/fastfacts/expressfactscanada.html; Angus Gillespie, "Lisa Lisson - FedEx President Triumphs Over Personal Tragedy," *The Canadian Business Journal,* September 12, 2014, http://www.cbj.ca/LISA_LISSON_FEDEX_PRESIDENT_TRIUMPHS_OVER_PERSONAL_TRAGEDY/; "Canada's Most Powerful Women: Top 100 – Current Winners, LISA LISSON PRESIDENT, FEDEX EXPRESS CANADA Bio," WXN, 2014, https://www.wxnetwork.com/TOP-100/TOP-100-WINNERS/; Lisa Lisson, "Uncovering the Heart of FedEx," FedEX Express Canada, May 21, 2012, http://blog.fedex.designcdt.com/blog/uncovering-heart-fedex?page=2; Heather Connelly, "Undercover Analysis: Episode 10; FedEx CEO Lisa Lisson," *Financial Post,* April 6, 2012, http://business.financialpost.com/2012/04/06/undercover-analysis-episode-10-fedex-ceo-lisa-lisson/; and "FedEX," Undercover Boss Canada, 2012, www.wnetwork.com/Shows/Undercover-Boss-Canada.aspx.

The Value of Motivation

motivation
The overall desire to excel.

"If work is such fun, how come the rich don't do it?" quipped comedian Groucho Marx. Well, the rich do work—Bill Gates did not make his billions playing computer games. And workers can have fun—if managers make the effort to motivate them. **motivation** refers to the overall desire to excel.[1] This is the extent to which persistent effort is directed toward a goal as a motivated person usually works "hard," "keeps at" his or her work, and directs his or her behaviour toward appropriate outcomes.[2] Have you heard the motivation myths listed in Figure 11.1?

It is difficult to overstate the importance of workers' job satisfaction as this contributes to motivation. Happy workers lead to happy customers, and happy customers lead to successful businesses. On the other hand, unhappy workers are likely to leave. When that happens, the company usually loses more than an experienced employee. It can also lose the equivalent of six to nine months' salary to cover the costs of recruiting and training a replacement. Other costs of losing employees are even greater: loss of intellectual capital, decreased morale of remaining workers, increased employee stress, increased employee gossip, decreased customer service, interrupted product development, and a poor reputation.[3]

Although it is costly to recruit and train new workers, it's also expensive to retain those who are disengaged. The word *engagement* is used to describe employees' level of motivation, passion, and commitment. Engaged employees work with passion and feel a connection to their company.[4]

Disengaged workers have essentially checked out; they plod through their day putting in time, but not energy. Not only do they act out their unhappiness at work, but disengaged employees undermine the efforts of engaged employees.

■ **FIGURE 11.1**

MOTIVATION MYTHS

Money is the only effective motivator. In some situations, money is one of the best methods to motivate people. In others, it is entirely ineffective. Most importantly, it is certainly not the only motivator. What will motivate always depends on the people and the situation.

Everyone is motivated by the same things I am. Although many people share common needs and desires, different people in different situations are motivated by an extraordinary range of factors, including financial gain, recognition, esteem, personal achievement, desire for equity, need to belong, fear, freedom, involvement, interesting work, and so on. What motivates one may not motivate another, and the same factor that motivates a person in one situation may not motivate that same person in a different situation.

Punishment does not motivate. Although rarely the first choice to influence behaviour, punishment, or the threat of it, can be an effective motivator. The problem, however, is that this type of motivation tends to be short term and rarely is associated with getting people to do more than the minimum. Its appropriateness will depend on the situation. In some cases, it may be the only or most effective consequence available, and thus it is important to learn how to most fairly administer punishment.

Low performance is always attributable to low motivation. Any performance is a function of motivation, ability, and the opportunity to perform. So, although low motivation is a common cause of low performance, it is certainly not the sole cause. Low performers may well lack the ability or the opportunity to achieve high performance.

Lack of motivation stems largely from lazy and apathetic people. That is sometimes the case, of course, but more often it is the situation that lacks sufficient incentives to energize people. People labelled as unmotivated in one situation (say their job) are sometimes highly engaged and committed in another case (for example, as a Little League coach). The managerial challenge is to discover what brings out the effort in your people and to influence what you can.

Smart people don't need to be motivated. This is a dangerous myth that can have consequences well beyond what a manager may realize. Because smart people have high ability, their motivation is key to obtaining high levels of performance. A smart, but unmotivated person may still perform at an acceptable level, but that person is capable of much more and ultimately will probably become disillusioned with the job and leave it—leaving a hole bigger than will be immediately obvious to most managers.

Source: Timothy T. Baldwin, William H. Bommer, and Robert S. Rubin, *Managing Organizational Behavior, What Great Managers Know and Do,* 2nd ed. (New York: McGraw-Hill Irwin, 2013), 198.

Motivating the right people to join the organization and stay with it is a key function of managers. Top-performing managers are usually surrounded by top-performing employees. It is no coincidence that geese fly faster in formation than alone. Although the desire to perform well ultimately comes from within, good managers stimulate people and bring out their natural drive to do a good job. People are willing to work, and work hard, if they feel that their work makes a difference and is appreciated.[5]

intrinsic reward
The good feeling you have when you have done a job well.

extrinsic reward
Something given to you by someone else as recognition for good work; extrinsic rewards include pay increases, praise, and promotions.

People are motivated by a variety of things, such as recognition, accomplishment, and status. An **intrinsic reward** is the personal satisfaction you feel when you perform well and achieve goals. The belief that your work makes a significant contribution to the organization or society is a form of intrinsic reward. An **extrinsic reward** is something given to you by someone else as recognition for good work. Pay increases, praise, and promotions are examples of extrinsic rewards.[6] Although ultimately motivation—the drive to satisfy a need—comes from within an individual, there are ways to stimulate people that bring out their natural drive to do a good job.

Image courtesy of DAC Group. Used with permission.

Selected as one of Canada's 100 Best Small and Medium Employers, DAC Group is a digital performance marketing agency that seeks employees with technical skills, industry passion, and the curiosity to learn. New-grad recruiters (above) look to hire "geeks with personalities." Would you be motivated if you worked for a company like this whose work space includes gaming stations, lounge areas, and calming rooms?[7]

© Shutterstock / ProStockStudio

Intrinsic (inner) rewards include the personal satisfaction you feel for a job well done. People who respond to such inner promptings often enjoy their work and share their enthusiasm with others. Are you more strongly motivated by your own desire to do well, or by extrinsic (external) rewards like pay and recognition?

This chapter will help you understand the concepts, theories, and practice of motivation. We begin with a look at some traditional theories of motivation. Why should you bother to know about these theories? Because sometimes "new" approaches are not really new; variations of them have been tried in the past. Knowing what has gone before will help you see what has worked and what has not. First we discuss the Hawthorne studies because they created a new interest in worker satisfaction and motivation. Then we'll look at some assumptions about employees that come from the traditional theorists. You will see the names of these theorists over and over in business literature and future courses: Taylor, Mayo, Maslow, Herzberg, and McGregor. Finally, we'll introduce modern motivation theories and show you how managers apply them.

Ultimately, the goal of this chapter is to provide you with information needed to motivate different types of people, to do different types of things, in different circumstances.[8] The question, "How do you motivate people?" should be expanded to "*How do you motivate who, to do what, and under what circumstances?*" as effective motivation strategies always depend on the people involved, their history, and the context.[9]

LO1

Explain Taylor's theory of scientific management, and describe the Hawthorne studies and their significance to management.

Frederick Taylor: The Father of Scientific Management

Several nineteenth-century thinkers presented management principles, but not until the early twentieth century did there appear any significant works with lasting implications. *The Principles of Scientific Management* was written by American efficiency engineer Frederick Taylor and published in 1911, earning Taylor the title "father of scientific management." Taylor's goal was to increase worker productivity to benefit both the firm and the worker. The solution, he thought, was to scientifically study the most efficient ways to do things, determine the one "best way" to perform each task, and then teach people those methods. This became known as **scientific management**. Three elements were basic to Taylor's approach: time, methods, and rules of work. His most important tools were observation and the stopwatch. Taylor's thinking is behind today's measure of how many burgers McDonald's expects its cooks to flip.

scientific management Studying workers to find the most efficient ways of doing things and then teaching people those techniques.

A classic Taylor story involves his study of men shovelling rice, coal, and iron ore with the same type of shovel. Believing that different materials called for different shovels, he proceeded to invent a wide variety of sizes and shapes of shovels and, with stopwatch in hand, measured output over time in what were called **time-motion studies**. These were studies of the tasks performed to complete a job and the time needed to do each task. Sure enough, an average person could shovel 25 to 35 tons more per day using the most efficient motions and the proper shovel. This finding led to time-motion studies of virtually every factory job. As the most efficient ways of doing things were determined, efficiency became the standard for setting goals.

time-motion studies Studies, begun by Frederick Taylor, of which tasks must be performed to complete a job and the time needed to do each task.

Taylor's scientific management became the dominant strategy for improving productivity in the early 1900s. Hundreds of time-motion specialists developed standards in plants throughout the country. One follower of Taylor was Henry L. Gantt, who developed charts by which managers plotted the work of employees a day in advance down to the smallest detail. Engineers Frank and Lillian Gilbreth used Taylor's ideas in a three-year study of bricklaying. They developed the **principle of motion economy**, which showed that every job could be broken down into a series of elementary motions. They then analyzed each motion to make it more efficient.

Some interpreted scientific management as viewing people largely as machines that needed to be properly programmed. There was little concern for the psychological or human aspects of work. Taylor believed that workers would perform at a high level of effectiveness—that is, be motivated—if they received high enough pay. While Taylor did not use this comparison to machines, he had very precise ideas about how to introduce his system: "It is only through enforced standardization of methods, enforced adoption of the best implements and working conditions, and enforced co-operation that this faster work can be assured. And the duty of enforcing the adoption of standards and enforcing this co-operation rests with management alone."[10] A crusader for better working conditions and pay for the working class, Taylor believed that the resulting improved productivity should then benefit both the workers and the company.

Some of Taylor's ideas are still being implemented. Some companies continue to emphasize conformity to work rules rather than creativity, flexibility, and responsiveness. For example, United Parcel Service (UPS) tells drivers how to get out of their trucks (with the right foot first), how fast to walk (three feet per second), how many packages to pick up and deliver a day (average of 125 to 175 in off-peak seasons), and how to hold their keys (teeth up, third finger). Drivers use a handheld computer called Delivery Information Acquisition Device to scan bar codes on packages. This lets a customer check online and know exactly where a package is at any given moment. If a driver is considered slow, a supervisor rides along, prodding the driver with stopwatches and clipboards. UPS has training centres in nine U.S. cities with simulators that teach employees how to properly lift and load boxes, drive their trucks proficiently, and even lessen the risk of slipping and falling when carrying a package.[11]

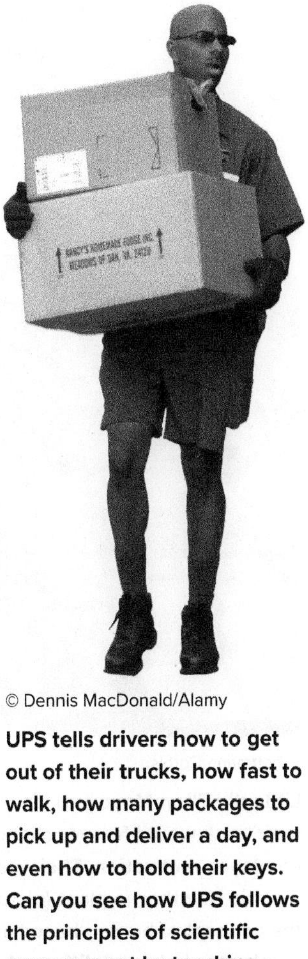

© Dennis MacDonald/Alamy

UPS tells drivers how to get out of their trucks, how fast to walk, how many packages to pick up and deliver a day, and even how to hold their keys. Can you see how UPS follows the principles of scientific management by teaching people the one "best way" to perform each task?

principle of motion economy
Theory developed by Frank and Lillian Gilbreth that every job can be broken down into a series of elementary motions.

The benefits of relying on workers to come up with solutions to productivity problems have long been recognized, as we shall discover next.

Elton Mayo and the Hawthorne Studies

One study, inspired by Frederick Taylor's research, began at the Western Electric Company's Hawthorne plant in Cicero, Illinois. The study began in 1927 and ended six years later. Let's see why it was one of the major studies in management literature.

Elton Mayo and his colleagues from Harvard University went to the Hawthorne plant to test the degree of lighting associated with optimum productivity. In this respect, their research was a traditional scientific management study. The idea was to keep records of the workers' productivity under different levels of illumination. But the initial experiments revealed what seemed to be a problem. The researchers had expected productivity to fall as the lighting was dimmed. Yet the experimental group's productivity went up regardless of whether the lighting was bright or dim, and even when the lighting was reduced to about the level of moonlight.

In a second series of 13 experiments, a separate test room was set up where researchers could manipulate temperature, humidity, and other environmental factors. Productivity went up each time; in fact, it increased by 50 percent overall. When the experimenters repeated the original condition, they expected productivity to fall to original levels; however, productivity increased yet again. The experiments were considered a total failure at this point. No matter what the experimenters did, productivity went up. What was causing the increase?

Little did Elton Mayo and his research team know that their work would forever change managers' beliefs about employee motivation. Their research at the Western Electric Hawthorne plant (pictured here) gave birth to the concept of human-based motivation by showing that employees behaved differently simply because they were involved in planning and executing the experiments.

In the end, Mayo guessed that some human or psychological factor was at play. He and his colleagues interviewed the workers, asking about their feelings and attitudes toward the experiment. The answers began a profound change in management thinking that has had repercussions today. Here is what the researchers concluded:

- The workers in the test room thought of themselves as a social group. The atmosphere was informal, they could talk freely, and they interacted regularly with their supervisors and the experimenters. They felt special and worked hard to stay in the group. This motivated them.
- The workers were included in the planning of the experiments. For example, they rejected one kind of pay schedule and recommended another, which was adopted. They believed that their ideas were respected and they felt engaged in managerial decision making. This, too, motivated them.
- No matter the physical conditions, the workers enjoyed the atmosphere of their special room and the additional pay for being more productive. Job satisfaction increased dramatically.

Researchers now use the term **Hawthorne effect** to refer to the tendency for people to behave differently when they know they are being studied. The Hawthorne study's results encouraged researchers to study human motivation and the managerial styles that lead to greater productivity. Research emphasis shifted from Taylor's scientific management toward Mayo's new human-based management.

Mayo's findings led to completely new assumptions about employees. One was that pay is not the only motivator. In fact, money was found to be a relatively ineffective motivator. New assumptions led to many theories about the human side of motivation. One of the best-known motivation theorists was Abraham Maslow, whose work we discuss next.

Hawthorne effect
The tendency for people to behave differently when they know they are being studied.

LO2

Identify the levels of Maslow's hierarchy of needs and apply them to employee motivation. Contrast this with the motivators and hygiene factors identified by Herzberg.

Abraham Maslow's Hierarchy of Needs

Psychologist Abraham Maslow believed that to understand motivation at work, one must understand human motivation in general. It seemed to him that motivation arises from need. That is, people are motivated to satisfy unmet needs. Needs that have been satisfied no longer provide motivation.

He thought that needs could be placed on a hierarchy of importance. Figure 11.2 shows **Maslow's hierarchy of needs**, whose levels—from lower to higher—are as follows:

- *Physiological Needs.* Basic survival needs, such as the need for food, water, and shelter.
- *Safety Needs.* The need to feel secure at work and at home.
- *Social Needs.* The need to feel loved, accepted, and part of the group.

Maslow's hierarchy of needs
Theory of motivation that places different types of human needs in order of importance, from basic physiological needs to safety, social, and esteem needs to self-actualization needs.

FIGURE 11.2

MASLOW'S HIERARCHY OF NEEDS

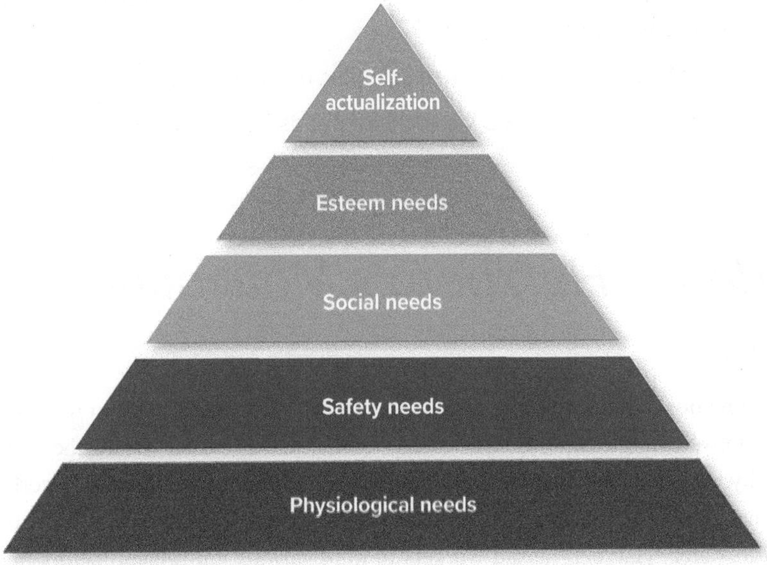

Maslow's hierarchy of needs is based on the idea that motivation comes from need. If a need is met, it is no longer a motivator, so a higher-level need becomes the motivator. Higher-level needs demand the support of lower-level needs. This chart shows the various levels of need. Do you know where you are on the chart right now?

- *Esteem Needs.* The need for recognition and acknowledgement from others, as well as self-respect and a sense of status or importance.
- *Self-Actualization Needs.* The need to develop to one's fullest potential.

When one need is satisfied, another higher-level need emerges and motivates us to do something to satisfy it. The satisfied need is no longer a motivator. For example, if you just ate a full-course dinner, hunger would not (at least for several hours) be a motivator, and your attention may turn to your surroundings (safety needs) or family (social needs). Of course, lower-level needs (perhaps thirst) may re-emerge at any time they are not met and take your attention away from higher-level needs (perhaps the need for recognition or status).

To compete successfully, firms must create a work environment that includes goals such as social contribution, honesty, reliability, service, quality, dependability, and unity—for all levels of employees. Chip Conley of Joie de Vivre, a chain of of more than 20 boutique hotels, thinks about higher-level needs such as meaning (self-actualization) for all employees, including lower-level workers. Half his employees are housekeepers who clean toilets all day. How does he help them feel they are doing meaningful work? One technique is what he calls the George Bailey exercise, based on the main character in the movie *It's a Wonderful Life.* Conley asks small groups of housekeepers what would happen if they weren't there every day. Trash would pile up, bathrooms would be full of wet towels, and let's not even think about the toilets. Then he asked them to come up with some other name for housekeeping. They offer suggestions like "serenity keepers," "clutter busters," or "the peace-of-mind police." In the end, these employees have a sense of how the customer's experience would not be the same without them. This gives meaning to their work that helps satisfy higher-level needs.[12]

PROGRESS ASSESSMENT

- What are the similarities and differences between Taylor's time-motion studies and Mayo's Hawthorne studies?
- How did Mayo's findings influence scientific management?
- Draw a diagram of Maslow's hierarchy of needs. Label and describe the parts.

Frederick Herzberg's Motivating Factors

Another direction in managerial theory is to explore what managers can do with the job itself to motivate employees. In other words, some theorists ask, "Of all the factors controllable by managers, which are most effective in generating an enthusiastic work effort?"

In the mid-1960s, psychologist Frederick Herzberg conducted the most-discussed study in this area. Herzberg asked workers to rank various job-related factors in order of importance relative to motivation. The question was: "What creates enthusiasm for workers and makes them work to full potential?" The most important motivating factors were:

1. Sense of achievement.
2. Earned recognition.
3. Interest in the work itself.
4. Opportunity for growth.
5. Opportunity for advancement.
6. Importance of responsibility.
7. Peer and group relationships.
8. Pay.
9. Supervisor's fairness.
10. Company policies and rules.
11. Status.
12. Job security.
13. Supervisor's friendliness.
14. Working conditions.

motivators
In Herzberg's theory of motivating factors, job factors that cause employees to be productive and that give them satisfaction.

hygiene (maintenance) factors
In Herzberg's theory of motivating factors, job factors that can cause dissatisfaction if missing but that do not necessarily motivate employees if increased.

Factors receiving the most votes all clustered around job content. Workers like to feel that they contribute to the company (sense of achievement was number 1). They want to earn recognition (number 2) and feel that their jobs are important (number 6). They want responsibility (which is why learning is so important), and to earn recognition for that responsibility by having a chance for growth and advancement. Of course, workers also want the job to be interesting. Is this the way you feel about your work?

Workers did not consider factors related to the job environment to be motivators. It was interesting to find that one of those factors was pay. Workers felt that the *absence* of good pay, job security, and friendly supervisors could cause dissatisfaction, but their presence did not motivate employees to work harder; it just provided satisfaction and contentment. Would you work harder if you were paid more?

Herzberg concluded that certain factors, which he called **motivators**, made employees productive and gave them satisfaction. These factors, as you have seen, mostly related to job content. Herzberg called other elements of the job **hygiene (maintenance) factors (or maintenance factors)**. These related to the job environment and could cause dissatisfaction if missing but would not necessarily motivate employees if increased. See Figure 11.3 for a list of both motivators and hygiene factors.

© Jetta Productions/Getty Images

Herzberg believed that motivational factors such as recognition increase worker performance. How do you think Herzberg's motivational factors encourage workers to a higher level of performance on the job?

Herzberg's motivating factors led to the following conclusion—the best way to motivate employees is to

FIGURE 11.3

HERZBERG'S MOTIVATORS AND HYGIENE FACTORS

There's some controversy over Herzberg's results. For example, sales managers often use money as a motivator. Recent studies have shown that money can be a motivator if used as part of a recognition program.

Motivators	Hygiene (Maintenance) Factors
(These factors can be used to motivate workers.)	(These can cause dissatisfaction, but changing them will have little motivational effect.)
Work itself Achievement Recognition Responsibility Growth and advancement	Company policy and administration Supervision Working conditions Interpersonal relations (co-workers) Salary, status, and job security

make their jobs interesting, help them achieve their objectives, and recognize their achievements through advancement and added responsibility.[13] A review of Figure 11.4 shows the similarity between Maslow's hierarchy of needs and Herzberg's motivating factors.

Look at Herzberg's motivating factors, identify those that motivate you, and rank them in order of importance to you. Keep them in mind as you consider jobs and careers.

FIGURE 11.4

COMPARISON OF MASLOW'S HIERARCHY OF NEEDS AND HERZBERG'S MOTIVATING FACTORS

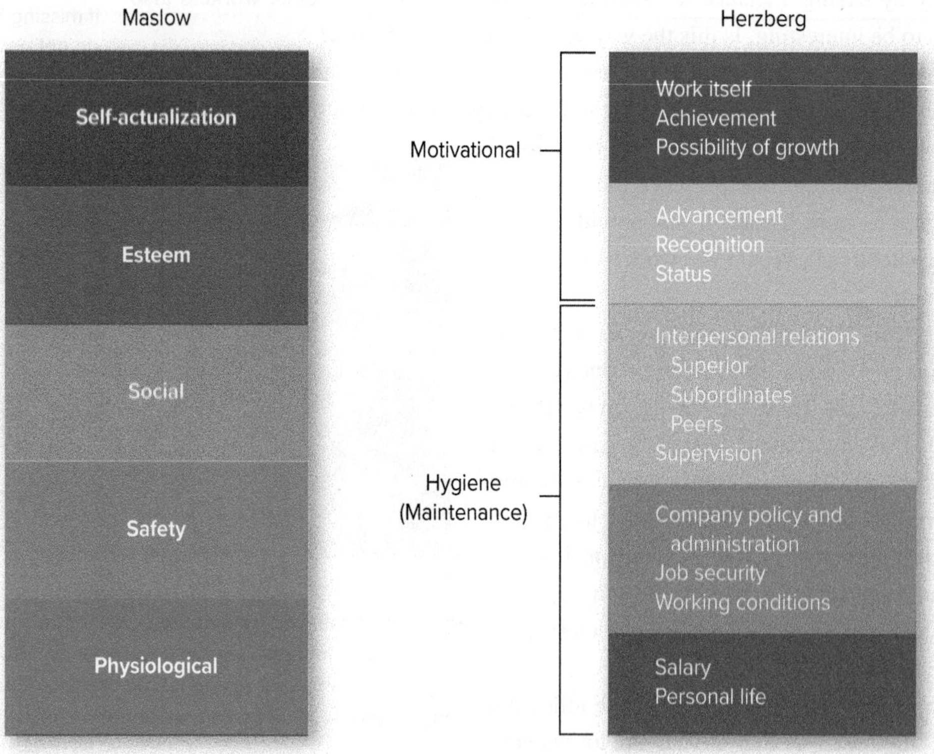

What motivators do your job opportunities offer you? Evaluating your job offers in terms of what is really important to you will help you make a wise career choice. This technique was used by Lisa Lisson, the focus of this chapter's profile.

Applying Herzberg's Theories

Improved working conditions (such as better wages or increased security) are taken for granted after workers get used to them. This is what Herzberg meant by hygiene (maintenance) factors: their absence causes dissatisfaction, but their presence (maintenance) does not motivate. The best motivator for some employees is a simple and sincere "Thanks, I really appreciate what you're doing."

Each year, Canadian Pacific Railway Ltd.'s Holiday Trains make stops in communities raising food and cash donations for local food banks. Free concerts and seasonal festivities are offered from the travelling stage. Can you think of other company examples of community involvement?

Mediacorp Canada Inc. annually publishes a list of Canada's Top 100 Employers. Companies are evaluated on eight key areas: (1) physical workplace; (2) work atmosphere and social; (3) health, financial, and family benefits; (4) vacation and time off; (5) employee communications; (6) performance management; (7) training and skills development; and (8) community involvement.[14] For example, Air Canada offers its employees discounted seats on available flights, "work trading" opportunities that can include a long-term special assignment training other employees, acting as brand ambassadors at major conferences, and trying out other roles (e.g., moving from a call centre to the airport or from economy to premium check-in). Employees can also recognize other staff through Air Canada's online SHINE system.[15] The Seeking Sustainability box highlights Vancity, an organization that has been recognized not only as one of Canada's Top 100 Employers, but also as #1 among Canada's Top 50 Socially Responsible Corporations.

Douglas McGregor's Theory X and Theory Y

LO3

Differentiate between McGregor's Theory X and Theory Y.

The way managers go about motivating people at work depends greatly on their attitudes toward workers. Management theorist Douglas McGregor observed that managers' attitudes generally fall into one of two entirely different sets of managerial assumptions, which he called Theory X and Theory Y.

Theory X

The assumptions of Theory X management are:

- The average person dislikes work and will avoid it if possible.
- Because of this dislike, workers must be forced, controlled, directed, or threatened with punishment to make them put forth the effort to achieve the organization's goals.

Seeking SUSTAINABILITY

Values Drive Vancity's Initiatives

Vancouver City Savings Credit Union (Vancity) is Canada's largest community credit union with $25.6 billion in assets, 523 000 member owners, and 59 branches in Metro Vancouver, the Fraser Valley, Victoria, Squamish, and Alert Bay. A financial co-operative, Vancity's triple-bottom line business model is driven by its vision to redefine wealth and focus on building healthy communities that are financially, socially, and environmentally sustainable. For example, the company allocates 30 percent of its net earnings to be shared with its members, communities, and employees.

The company believes in impact investing and lending. Providing credit is the biggest way to help members and their communities thrive and prosper. Deposits are invested in local businesses, organizations, and initiatives that create positive impacts in the community, such as creating jobs, reducing greenhouse gases, and fighting homelessness. "If you're a business, not-for-profit, First Nation government, social enterprise, co-operative, or strata," asserts the website, "and you're looking to finance a green building project, energy-efficiency upgrade, or innovative environmental or clean technology initiative, then we want to talk to you." The Green Business program provides support in the forms of financing (eco-efficiency and micro-loans for green business start-up and expansion), grants, partnerships, and learning, networking, resources, and events.

Skwachàys Lodge
New opportunities through authentic partnerships.
Community building and business success with our First Peoples.

© Vancity

You have learned a little about Vancity and its value-driven business model. Visit its site to read stories of impact investing in the energy and environment fields. Would you like to work for an organization that is committed to addressing climate change?

Sources: "Vancity at a Glance," Vancouver City Savings Credit Union, 2017, https://www.vancity.com/AboutVancity/VisionAndValues/Glance/?xcid=about_megamenu_glance; and "Energy and environment," Vancouver City Savings Credit Union, 2017, https://www.vancity.com/BusinessBanking/Financing/SpecializedSectorSolutions/EnergyEnvironment/.

- The average worker prefers to be directed, wishes to avoid responsibility, has relatively little ambition, and wants security.
- Primary motivators are fear and money.

The natural consequence of these assumptions is a manager who is very busy and who watches people closely, telling them what to do and how to do it. Motivation is more likely to take the form of punishment for poor work rather than reward for good work. Theory X managers give their employees little responsibility, authority, or flexibility. Taylor and other theorists who preceded him would have agreed with Theory X. Time-motion studies calculated the one best way to perform a task and the optimal time to devote to it. Researchers assumed workers needed to be trained and carefully watched to see that they conformed to standards.

Some managers and entrepreneurs still suspect that employees cannot be fully trusted and need to be closely supervised.[16] No doubt you have seen such managers in action. How did they make you feel? Were these managers' assumptions accurate regarding the workers' attitudes?

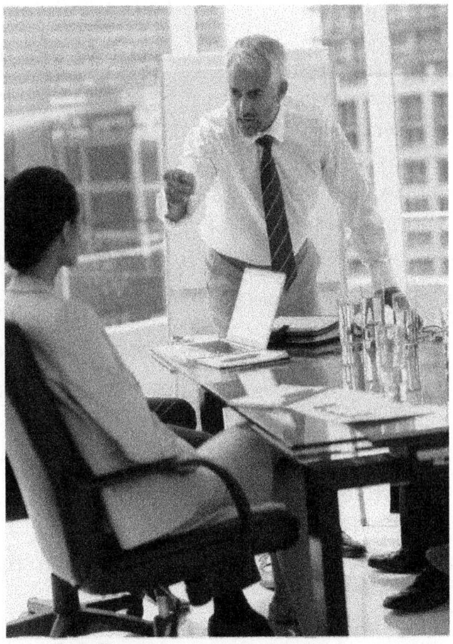

© Wavebreakmedia Ltd/Thinkstock

Theory X managers come in all sizes and shapes. Such managers may have an in-your-face style. Would you prefer to work for a Theory X or a Theory Y manager?

Theory Y

Theory Y makes entirely different assumptions about people:

- Most people like work; it is as natural as play or rest.
- Most people naturally work toward goals to which they are committed.
- The depth of a person's commitment to goals depends on the perceived rewards for achieving them.
- Under certain conditions, most people not only accept responsibility, but also seek it.
- People are capable of using a relatively high degree of imagination, creativity, and cleverness to solve problems.
- In industry, the average person's intellectual potential is only partially realized.
- People are motivated by a variety of rewards. Each worker is stimulated by a reward unique to that worker (e.g., time off, money, recognition, etc.).

Rather than authority, direction, and close supervision, Theory Y managers emphasize a relaxed managerial atmosphere in which workers are free to set objectives, be creative, be flexible, and go beyond the goals set by management. (Figure 11.5 compares both Theories X and Y.) A key technique in meeting these objectives is *empowerment,* which

FIGURE 11.5

A COMPARISON OF THEORIES X AND Y

Theory X	Theory Y
1. Employees dislike work and will try to avoid it.	1. Employees view work as a natural part of life.
2. Employees prefer to be controlled and directed.	2. Employees prefer limited control and direction.
3. Employees seek security, not responsibility.	3. Employees will seek responsibility under proper work conditions.
4. Employees must be intimidated by managers to perform.	4. Employees perform better in work environments that are non-intimidating.
5. Employees are motivated by financial rewards.	5. Employees are motivated by many different needs.

includes giving employees the authority to make decisions and the tools to implement the decisions they make. For empowerment to be a real motivator, management should follow these three steps:

1. Find out what people think the problems in the organization are.
2. Let them design the solutions.
3. Get out of the way and let them put those solutions into action.

Often employees complain that although they are asked to engage in company decision making, their managers fail to actually empower them to make decisions. Have you ever worked in such an atmosphere? How did that make you feel?

goal-setting theory The idea that setting ambitious but attainable goals can motivate workers and improve performance if the goals are accepted, accompanied by feedback, and facilitated by organizational conditions.

management by objectives (MBO) A system of goal setting and implementation that involves a cycle of discussion, review, and evaluation of objectives among top and middle-level managers, supervisors, and employees.

PROGRESS ASSESSMENT

- Explain the distinction between what Herzberg called motivators and hygiene factors.
- Briefly describe the managerial attitudes behind Theories X and Y.
- Which of the theories introduced so far resonates the most with you? Explain.

LO4

Explain the key principles of goal-setting, expectancy, reinforcement, and equity theories.

Goal-Setting Theory and Management by Objectives

Goal-setting theory says setting ambitious but attainable goals can motivate workers and improve performance if the goals are accepted, accompanied by feedback, and if conditions in the organization pave the way for achievement. All organization members should have some basic agreement about both overall goals and specific objectives for each department and individual. Thus, there should be a system to engage everyone in the organization in goal setting and implementation.

© Sam Edwards/Getty Images

When applying MBO, managers provide direction to their employees. For their part, employees are asked to participate in the process and to take responsibility for the outcome. Would you prefer a manager that helps you or coaches you to success?

The late management expert Peter Drucker developed such a system in the 1960s. "Managers cannot motivate people; they can only thwart people's motivation because people motivate themselves," he said. Managers, he believed, can only create the proper environment for the seed to grow. Called **management by objectives (MBO)**, Drucker's system of goal setting and implementation involves a cycle of discussion, review, and evaluation of objectives among top- and middle-level managers, supervisors, and employees. It calls on managers to formulate goals in co-operation with everyone in the organization, to commit employees to those goals, and then to monitor results and reward accomplishments.

MBO is most effective in relatively stable situations when managers can make long-range goals and implement them with few changes. Managers must also understand the difference between helping and coaching subordinates. *Helping* means working with the subordinate and doing part of the work, if necessary. *Coaching* means acting as a resource—teaching, guiding, and recommending—but not participating actively or doing the task. The central idea of MBO is that employees need to motivate themselves.

Employee input and expectations are important. Problems can arise when management uses MBO as a strategy for forcing managers and workers to commit to goals that are not agreed on together but are instead set by top management.[17]

Victor Vroom identified the importance of employee expectations and developed a process called expectancy theory. Let's examine this concept next.

Meeting Employee Expectations: Victor Vroom's Expectancy Theory

According to Victor Vroom's **expectancy theory**, employee expectations can affect motivation. That is, the amount of effort employees exert on a specific task depends on their expectations of the outcome. Vroom contends that employees ask three questions before committing their maximum effort to a task: (1) Can I accomplish the task? (2) If I do accomplish it, what is my reward? (3) Is the reward worth the effort? See Figure 11.6 for a summary of this process.

expectancy theory
Victor Vroom's theory that the amount of effort employees exert on a specific task depends on their expectations of the outcome.

Think of the effort you might exert in your class under the following conditions. Suppose your instructor says that to earn an A in the course you must achieve an average of 90 percent on coursework plus jump two metres high. Would you exert maximum effort toward earning an A if you knew you could not possibly jump two metres high? Suppose your instructor said that any student can earn an A in the course but you know that this instructor has not awarded an A in 25 years of teaching. If the reward of an

FIGURE 11.6

EXPECTANCY THEORY

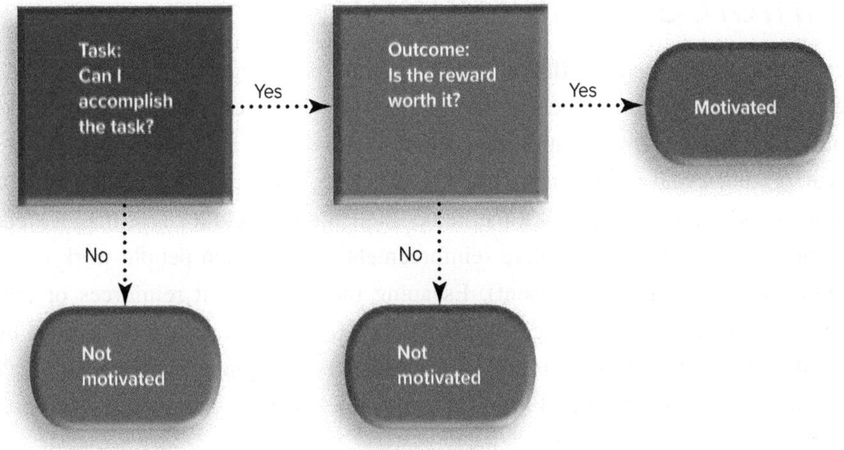

The amount of effort employees exert on a task depends on their expectations of the outcome.

© LWA/Larry Williams/Getty Images

Performance feedback is crucial for the motivation of employees. The feedback session is also ideal for setting goals. Have you experienced a feedback session?

A seems unattainable, would you exert significant effort in the course? Better yet, let's say that you read online that businesses prefer hiring C-minus students to hiring A-plus students. Does the reward of an A seem worth it? Now think of similar situations that may occur on the job.

Expectancy theory does note that expectations vary from individual to individual. Employees establish their own views of task difficulty and the value of the reward.[18] Researchers David Nadler and Edward Lawler modified Vroom's theory and suggested that managers follow five steps to improve employee performance:[19]

1. Determine what rewards employees value.
2. Determine each employee's desired performance standard.
3. Ensure that performance standards are attainable.
4. Guarantee rewards tied to performance.
5. Be certain that employees consider the rewards adequate.

Now that we have covered several theories, you may have realized that they try to explain all behaviour, by all people, all of the time. But this is impossible given the complexity of human behaviour. The value of being briefly introduced to different theories (you will discuss these theories in more detail in an Organizational Behaviour course) is that each theory offers some piece of the puzzle. No theory is complete, as people are very complex and our attempts to theorize about behaviour will never be complete. Successful leaders are sensitive to the differences between their employees and what motivates them. A starting point is understanding these theories.

Reinforcing Employee Performance: Reinforcement Theory

reinforcement theory
The concept that positive and negative reinforcers motivate a person to behave in certain ways.

According to **reinforcement theory**, positive reinforcers, negative reinforcers, and punishers motivate a person to behave in certain ways. In other words, motivation is the result of the carrot-and-stick approach whereby individuals act to receive rewards (i.e., the carrot) and avoid punishment (i.e., the stick). Positive reinforcements are rewards such as praise, recognition, and a pay raise. Punishment includes reprimands, reduced pay, and layoffs or firing. Negative reinforcement occurs when people work to escape the punishers (i.e., the punishment). Escaping the punishment reinforces or rewards the positive behaviour. A manager might also try to stop undesirable behaviour by not responding to it. This response is called *extinction* because managers hope the unwanted behaviour will become extinct. Figure 11.7 illustrates how a manager can use reinforcement theory to motivate workers.

FIGURE 11.7

REINFORCEMENT THEORY

Managers can either add or subtract stimuli (positive reinforcement, negative reinforcement, or punishers) to increase desired behaviour or decrease undesired behaviour.

	ADD STIMULI	SUBTRACT STIMULI
Increase Behaviour	Positive Reinforcement: Jill gets praise (the reinforcement added) for turning in her reports on time (target behaviour to increase).	Negative Reinforcement: Jack is on probation (punishment that will be removed) until such time as he can turn in three reports on time (target behaviour to increase).
Decrease Behaviour	Punishment: Jack gets written up (the punisher) for turning in his reports late (target behaviour to decrease).	Extinction: Jill does not get praise (reinforcement is removed) when her reports are turned in late (target behaviour to decrease), no matter how well done they are.

Source: Casey Limmer, MSW, LCSW, Washington University.

Treating Employees Fairly: Equity Theory

Equity theory looks at how employees' perceptions of fairness affect their willingness to perform. It assumes employees ask, "If I do a good job, will it be worth it?" and "What's fair?" Employees try to maintain equity between what they put into the job and what they get out of it, comparing those inputs and outputs to those of others in similar positions. Workers find comparative information through personal relationships, professional organizations, and other sources.

equity theory
The idea that employees try to maintain equity between inputs and outputs compared to others in similar positions.

When workers perceive inequity, they will try to re-establish fairness in a number of ways. For example, suppose that you compare the grade you earned on a term paper with your classmates' grades. If you think you received a lower grade compared to the students who put out the same effort as you, you may (1) reduce your effort on future class projects, or (2) rationalize the difference by saying, "Grades are overvalued anyway!" If you think that your paper received a higher grade than comparable papers, you will probably (1) increase your effort to justify the higher reward in the future, or (2) rationalize by saying, "I'm worth it!"

© Hill Street Studios/Blend Images LLC

If you attend class regularly but do not do well on your first midterm exam, how do you react? Do you stop going to class regularly as you do not think that it is worthwhile? Or, do you go and speak with your instructor to find out how to improve for the next exam?

In the workplace, perceived inequity may lead to lower productivity, reduced quality, increased absenteeism, and voluntary resignation.

Remember that equity judgments are based on perception and are therefore subject to error. When workers overestimate their own contributions—as happens often—they feel *any* rewards given out for performance are inequitable.[20] Sometimes organizations try to deal with this by keeping employee salaries secret, but secrecy may make things worse. Employees are likely to overestimate the salaries of others, in addition to overestimating their own contributions. A recent study showed workers often estimate their own productive hours as 11 percent higher than their average co-worker.[21] The best remedy is generally clear and frequent communication. Managers must communicate as clearly as possible both the results they expect and the outcomes that will occur.[22]

PROGRESS ASSESSMENT

- Explain goal-setting theory.
- Evaluate expectancy theory. When could expectancy theory apply to your efforts or lack of effort?
- Describe reinforcement theory. What are examples of positive and negative reinforcers?
- Explain the principles of equity theory.

LO5

Show how managers put motivation theories into action through such strategies as job enrichment, open communication, and job recognition.

Putting Theory into Action

Now that you know what a few theorists have to say about motivation, you might be asking yourself "So what? What do all of these theories have to do with what really goes on in the workplace today?" Let's look at how companies put the theories into action through job enrichment, open communication, and job recognition.

Motivating Through Job Enrichment

job enrichment
A motivational strategy that emphasizes motivating the worker through the job itself.

Managers have extended both Maslow's and Herzberg's theories through **job enrichment**, a strategy that motivates workers through the job itself. Work is assigned so that individuals can complete an identifiable task from beginning to end and are held responsible for successful achievement. Job enrichment is based on Herzberg's higher motivators, such as responsibility, achievement, and recognition.[23] It stands in contrast to *job simplification,* which produces task efficiency by breaking a job into simple steps and assigning people to each. Review Maslow's and Herzberg's work to see how job enrichment grew from those theories.

J. Richard Hackman and Greg R. Oldham proposed the Job Characteristics Model, which defines core job characteristics that have a certain psychological impact on workers. In turn, the psychological states induced by the nature of the job lead to certain outcomes that are relevant to the worker and the organization.[24] Put another way, when people are matched to a job that really "fits" them, most of the problems associated with "unmotivated" or "lazy" people disappear.[25] Those who advocate job enrichment believe that five characteristics of work are important in motivation and performance:

1. *Skill Variety.* The extent to which a job demands different skills.
2. *Task Identity.* The degree to which the job requires doing a task with a visible outcome from beginning to end.

3. *Task Significance.* The degree to which the job has a substantial impact on the lives or work of others in the company.
4. *Autonomy.* The degree of freedom, independence, and discretion in scheduling work and determining procedures.
5. *Feedback.* The amount of direct and clear information that is received about job performance.

© Sipa/Newscom

Here a worker in Baccarat's factory puts the finishing touches on a crystal vase. One of the hallmarks of job enrichment is the worker's ability to perform a complete task from beginning to end. Why do you think this might be more motivating than simply adding a few parts to a product on an assembly line?

Variety, identity, and significance contribute to the meaningfulness of the job. Autonomy gives people a feeling of responsibility, and feedback contributes to a feeling of achievement and recognition.[26]

One type of job enrichment is **job enlargement**, which combines a series of tasks into one challenging and interesting assignment. Maytag, the home appliance manufacturer, redesigned its washing machine production process so that employees could assemble an entire water pump instead of just adding a single part. **Job rotation** also makes work more interesting and motivating by moving employees from one job to another. One problem, of course, is the need to train employees to do several different operations. However, the resulting increase in employee motivation and the value of having flexible, cross-trained employees offsets the costs.

job enlargement
A job-enrichment strategy that involves combining a series of tasks into one challenging and interesting assignment.

job rotation
A job-enrichment strategy that involves moving employees from one job to another.

Figure 11.8 summarizes the theories discussed throughout this chapter. Review the motivation myths in Figure 11.1. Is it clearer now why these are myths?

Motivating Through Open Communication

Communication and information must flow freely throughout the organization when employees are empowered to make decisions—they can't make these decisions in a vacuum. It is crucial for people to be able to access the knowledge they need when they need it. The entire organization must be structured so that managers and employees can talk to one another. Procedures for encouraging open communication include the following:[27]

- *Create an organizational culture that rewards listening.* Top managers must create places to talk, and they must show employees that talking with superiors matters—by providing feedback, adopting employee suggestions, and rewarding upward communication—even if the discussion is negative. Employees must feel free to say anything they deem appropriate and believe their opinions are valued.
- *Train supervisors and managers to listen.* Most people receive no training in how to listen, in school or anywhere else, so organizations must do such training themselves or hire someone to do it.
- *Use effective questioning techniques.* We get information through questioning. Different kinds of questions yield different kinds of information. Closed questions that generate yes/no answers do not encourage the longer, more thoughtful responses that

FIGURE 11.8

SUMMARY OF MOTIVATION THEORIES

Theory Name	Description
Scientific Management	Studying workers to find the most efficient ways of doing things and then teaching workers those techniques.
The Hawthorne Effect	The tendency for people to behave differently when they know they are being studied.
Hierarchy of Needs	People are motivated to satisfy unmet needs. Needs are placed in order of importance, from basic physiological needs to safety, social, and esteem needs to self-actualization needs.
Theory of Motivating Factors	Motivators are job factors that cause employees to be productive and that give them satisfaction. Hygiene (maintenance) factors are job factors that can cause dissatisfaction if missing but that do not necessarily motivate employees if increased.
Theory X and Theory Y	Theory X managers believe workers dislike work and will avoid it. Theory Y managers believe people like working and will accept responsibility.
Goal-Setting Theory	Setting ambitious but attainable goals can motivate workers and improve performance if the goals are accepted, accompanied by feedback, and if conditions in the organization pave the way for achievement.
Management by Objectives	A system of goal setting and implementation that involves a cycle of discussion, review, and evaluation of objectives among top- and middle-level managers, supervisors, and employees.
Expectancy Theory	The amount of effort employees exert on a specific task depends on expectations of the outcome.
Reinforcement Theory	Positive and negative reinforcers motivate a person to behave in certain ways.
Equity Theory	Employees try to maintain equity between inputs and outputs compared to others in similar positions.
Job Enrichment	Emphasizes motivating the worker through the job itself by considering five characteristics (skill variety, task identity, task significance, autonomy, and feedback). Examples of job enrichment include job enlargement and job rotation.

open questions do. Appropriate personal questions can create a sense of camaraderie between employees and managers.

- *Remove barriers to open communication.* Separate offices, parking areas, bathrooms, and dining rooms for managers only set up barriers. Other barriers are different dress codes and different ways of addressing one another (like calling workers by their first names and managers by their last). Removing such barriers may require imagination and managers' willingness to give up special privileges.

- *Avoid vague and ambiguous communication.* Passive voice appears weak and tentative. Statements such as "Mistakes were made" leave you wondering who made the mistakes. Hedging is another way managers send garbled messages. Terms like *possibly* and *perhaps* sound wishy-washy to employees who need more definitive direction.
- *Make it easy to communicate.* Encouraging organization members to eat together at large lunch tables, allowing employees to gather in conference rooms, having organizational picnics and athletic teams, and so on can help workers at all levels mix with one another.
- *Ask employees what is important to them.* Managers should not wait until the exit interview to ask an employee, "What can I do to keep you?" At that point it is too late. Instead they should have frequent *stay interviews* to find out what matters to employees and what they can do to keep them on the job.

The Adapting to Change box discusses how some organizations utilize "happiness meters" to learn how they can identify and address workplace issues in order to keep employees engaged.

Adapting *to* CHANGE

Employee Engagement's Mood Ring

Have you ever wondered what was going on in someone else's head? Managers always want to know. They need to know what keeps employees going, what causes them to disengage, and, ultimately, what makes workers happy. Though they may not be able to read exactly what is in their employees' heads, they now have more tools to help track employee moods.

Apps from companies like Culture Amp and Talmetrix allow managers to ask questions on the fly and employees can quickly give feedback through a mobile app. Although some managers may call them "happiness meters," they are much more than that. They help managers monitor moods, yes, but they can also help discover what employees really want and what is important to the workplace culture as a whole. Some managers, who had previously assumed their employees wanted enhancements to the games in the break room, found their employees actually craved more responsibilities and greater roles in the strategic planning process. Not knowing what the employees were looking for almost led to another foosball table. Oops!

© Shutterstock / racorn

Managers won't always know what motivates and engages their employees unless they ask. Apps like this are already helping to increase employee engagement. How's that? Didier Elzinga, cofounder of Culture Amp, says, "Every person is important. People feel they can make a positive difference." When employees feel important to the company, that gets the ball rolling. From there, they feel like they're being listened to and will work harder to prove they are worthy of the attention.

Sources: "JumpStart Inc. Announces Investment in Talmetrix," Yahoo! Finance, February 28, 2017; Megan Rose Dickey, "Culture Amp Launches Its Own Take on Performance Reviews," TechCrunch, August 17, 2016; Kate Rockwood, "Tracking the Mood of Your Employees," *Inc.*, June 2016; "BlackbookHR Becomes Talmetrix," Business Wire, September 20, 2016; Ian Davies, "Three Ways Technology is Transforming Talent Management in 2016," *Forbes*, March 17, 2016; and Heather Clancy, "This Startup Helps Airbnb and Slack Measure What Employees Think," *Fortune*, March 7, 2016.

© Raymond Boyd/Getty Images

In the car business nothing works like the "wow" factor. At Ford, the 400-member Team Mustang group was empowered to create the "wow" response for the company's sleek Mustang convertible. The work team, suppliers, company managers, and even customers worked together to make the Mustang a winner in the very competitive automobile market.

Applying Open Communication in Self-Managed Teams

At Ford Motor Company, a group known as Team Mustang set the guidelines for how production teams should be formed. Given the challenge to create a car that would make people dust off their old "Mustang Sally" records and dance into showrooms, the 400-member team was also given the freedom to make decisions without waiting for approval from headquarters. Everyone worked under one roof in an old warehouse where drafting experts sat next to accountants, and engineers next to stylists. Budgetary walls between departments were knocked down as department managers were persuaded to surrender some control over their subordinates on the team.

When the resulting Mustang convertible displayed shaking problems, engineers were so motivated to finish on time and under budget that they worked late into the night, sleeping on the floor when necessary. Senior Ford executives were tempted to intervene, but they stuck with their promise not to meddle. Working with suppliers, the team solved the shaking problem and still came in under budget and a couple of months early. The new car was a hit with drivers and sales soared.[28]

To implement such teams, managers at most companies must reinvent work. This means respecting workers, providing interesting work, developing workers' skills, allowing autonomy, decentralizing authority, and rewarding good work. In the process of reinventing work, it is essential that managers behave ethically toward all employees. The Making Ethical Decisions box illustrates a problem managers may face when filling temporary positions.

Recognizing a Job Well Done

A recent survey indicated that more than half of employees who voluntarily left their jobs did so because of lack of appreciation.[29] Letting people know you appreciate their work

Making ETHICAL DECISIONS

Motivating Temporary Employees

Say that you work as a manager for Highbrow's, a rather prestigious department store. Each year, to handle the large number of holiday shoppers, you must hire temporary employees. Because of store policy and budget constraints, all temporaries must be discharged on January 10. As you interview prospective employees, however, you give the impression that the store will hire at least two new full-time retail salespeople for the coming year. You hope that this will serve to motivate the temporary workers and even foster some competition among them. You also instruct your permanent salespeople to reinforce the falsehood that good work during the holiday season is the path to full-time employment. Is this an ethical way to try to motivate your employees? What are the dangers of using a tactic such as this?

is usually more powerful than giving a raise or bonus alone.[30] More and more recent graduates report salary is not their ultimate motivator. Yes, they needed enough money to cover their basic needs. However, the majority of participants rated career advancement opportunities as well as interesting and challenging work to be the most important things.[31]Clearly, providing advancement opportunities is important in attracting and retaining valuable and engaged employees.

© Shotshop GmbH/Alamy RF

Rather than giving out boring certificates or plaques to exceptional employees, Caribou Coffee uses watermelons to show appreciation. Employees can win one of these juicy prizes by hitting a personal goal, excelling on a company project, or simply by using their "melon." What role do you think these awards play in motivating the winners to continue their outstanding performance?

Promotions are not the only way to celebrate a job well done. Recognition can be as simple as noticing positive actions out loud, making employees feel their efforts are worthwhile and valued enough to be noticed. For example: "Sarina, you didn't say much in the meeting today. Your ideas are usually so valuable; I missed hearing them." This comment lets Sarina know her ideas are appreciated, and she will be more likely to participate fully in the next meeting.

Here are just a few examples of ways managers have raised employee spirits without raising paycheques:

- FedEx Office sent high-achieving employees to Disneyland *and* put the company's top executives in those employees' places while they were gone.
- Walt Disney World offers more than 150 employee recognition programs. The Spirit of Fred Award is named after an employee named Fred, who makes each award (a certificate mounted and varnished on a plaque) himself. Fred's name became an acronym for Friendly, Resourceful, Enthusiastic, and Dependable.
- Maritz Motivation Solutions has a Thanks a Bunch program that gives flowers to a selected employee in appreciation of a job well done. That employee passes the bouquet to someone else who helped. The idea is to see how many people are given the flowers throughout the day. The bouquet comes with thank-you cards that are entered into a draw for awards like binoculars and jackets.
- Hewlett-Packard (HP) bestows its Golden Banana Award for a job well done. The award started when an engineer burst into his manager's office saying he had found the solution to a long-standing problem. In his haste to find something to give the employee to show his appreciation, the manager grabbed a banana from his lunch and said, "Well done! Congratulations!" The Golden Banana is now one of the most prestigious honours awarded to an inventive HP employee.

Giving valued employees prime parking spots, more vacation days, or more flexible schedules may help them feel their work is appreciated, but sometimes nothing inspires workers like the prospect of a payout down the road. Companies that offer a small equity stake or stock options often have a good chance of developing loyal employees. The Spotlight on Small Business offers examples of what a number of small businesses have done to motivate employees.

The same things do not motivate all employees. After the Progress Assessment, we'll explore how employees from different cultures and generations are motivated.

Spotlight *On* SMALL BUSINESS

Motivators for Small Businesses

The competition to attract and retain top-notch workers is "job one" for all businesses big or small. But how can small companies compete against the likes of Apple and Amazon? Wouldn't any talented person choose to work for one of these big name employers that offer such perks as onsite gourmet meals, putting greens, gymnasiums, and massages?

It's true small businesses cannot offer the money, benefits, or glory of working for one of the corporate heavyweights. But they can offer more intangible benefits such as collaborative management, less bureaucracy, more work–life balance, a sense of independence, and sometimes even potential ownership. Many small businesses strive to create an upbeat, relaxed company culture that encourages employees to bond with one another rather than compete against each other for the next promotion. By instilling the idea that the business' culture belongs to the employees, culture can equal perks, fun, and happiness. Small businesses also can take advantage of motivating employees with open communication and broad responsibility on the job. Individual workers can have more say in the company and not feel like just another drone in a giant corporate beehive.

© Caiaimage/Glow Images

This doesn't mean small businesses can't also try their hand at the innovative perks department. Here are some examples:

- Vigilant Global provides free breakfast and lunch to its staff, "smoothie stations," and two games rooms.
- Cisco Systems Canada Co. offers employees up to five paid personal days each year in addition to four weeks of starting vacation.
- Bigcommerce offers employees a weekly boot camp with a certified trainer.
- Zoosk invites employees to bring their dogs to work.

Not only do businesses hope these methods help employees bond with their colleagues, they also hope they become productive workers. Do you think such workplaces might appeal to you? Why?

Sources: "Canada's Top 100 Employers (2018)," *The Globe and Mail* and Mediacorp Canada Inc., 2017, 7; "Canada's 100 Best Small & Medium Employers - Eat well: Vigilant Global goes all-out on perks," *The Globe and Mail* and Mediacorp Canada Inc., March 2015, 61; Michael Fertik, "How to Cultivate the Culture That Makes Your Company Succeed," *Inc.*, February 2014; Laura Garnett, "3 Questions That Will Motivate Your Employees," *Inc.*, February 2014; and Gene Marks, "Startup Perks Wal-Mart and Amazon Can Never Offer," *Entrepreneur*, October 22, 2013.

PROGRESS ASSESSMENT

- Explain job-enrichment theory.
- What procedures can firms implement to encourage open communication?
- List examples of ways managers can improve motivation without raising paycheques.

Personalizing Motivation

LO6

Show how managers personalize motivation strategies to appeal to employees around the globe and across generations.

Managers cannot use one motivational formula for all employees. They have to get to know each worker personally and tailor the motivational effort to the individual. This is further complicated by the increase in global business and the fact that managers now work with employees from a variety of cultural backgrounds. Cultural differences also exist between generations raised in the same country. Let's look at how managers personalize their strategies to appeal to employees around the globe and across generations.

Motivating Employees Around the Globe

Different cultures experience motivational approaches differently; therefore, managers study and understand these cultural factors in designing a reward system. In a *high-context culture,* workers build personal relationships and develop group trust before focusing on tasks. In a *low-context culture,* workers often view relationship building as a waste of time that diverts attention from the task. Koreans, Thais, and Saudis tend to be high-context workers who may view their North American colleagues as insincere due to their need for data and quick decision making (low-context culture).

Hershey solved a cross-cultural problem with a recognition program for its 21 000 employees in 17 countries, all of whom use a wide variety of languages and currencies. Globoforce Ltd. revamped and introduced a new rewards program for Hershey called SMILES that automatically adjusts for differences created by cultural preferences, tax laws, and even local standards of living. The points-based system allows for rewards to be redeemed for thousands of products and gift card options, depending on where the employee is based. The system allows for both managers and employees to send SMILES and in the program's first week, almost 9 percent of the entire company was recognized for good work—some employees recognized for the very first time.[32]

Understanding motivation in global organizations and building effective global teams is still a new task for most companies. Developing group leaders who are culturally astute, flexible, and able to deal with ambiguity is a challenge businesses face in the twenty-first century. See the Reaching Beyond Our Borders box for more about managing culturally diverse employees.

© Nasi Sakura/Purestock/Superstock

There's no magic formula to successfully motivating every worker. Each generation of employees has different attitudes about what is important to them in seeking a balance between a successful career and happy private life. What expectations do you have of your potential supervisor and company?

Motivating Employees Across Generations[33]

Age is among the most frequently used demographic characteristic to determine the size and lifestyles of groups of individuals. The terms "cohort" and "generation" are often used interchangeably to refer to such groups. Determining the size of these groups is challenging as the year spans are widely debated.

Reaching *Beyond* OUR BORDERS

Beyond Just Knowing Cross-Cultural Differences

© Wavebreakmedia Ltd | Dreamstime.com

As companies today become more global and employees more diverse than ever before, managers are well aware of their need to develop cross-cultural competencies. This means not only understanding different languages, but also understanding different food choices, customs, how people want to be addressed, how much space should be between people, and particularly, how employees expect to be managed.

Many companies do a respectable job in developing cultural intelligence in managers before they move to different global assignments. For example, IBM works closely with leaders in business, government, academia, and community organizations before entering a new market. Why then do seasoned managers, who appreciate diversity and are schooled in cross-cultural differences, often have problems motivating employees in their new global environment?

According to Professor Andrew Molinsky of Brandeis University's International Business School, the problems occur because of what he refers to as "cultural code-switching." This problem appears when managers are aware of how they should approach and deal with global employees, but deep down they lack the ability to adapt their behaviour to the situation. When this happens, their behaviour seems inauthentic to global employees, and therefore not effective. An example would be an American executive giving feedback to Japanese employees. The American's natural style is to "tell-it-like-it-is," but Japanese workers expect a much more indirect approach. That may be difficult for the American to do. What managers need to develop is "global dexterity," the ability to shift one's own cultural behaviour in a way that's effective and appropriate in the global setting. It always helps to know what to do, but it's even more important to know how to do it.

Sources: Samuel J. Palmisano, "The Former CEO of IBM on Working at a Global Scale," *Fast Company*, April 10, 2014; Dan Schawbel, "Andy Molinsky: How to Adapt to Cultural Changes in Foreign Countries," *Forbes*, April 10, 2013; and Andrew Molinsky, Thomas H. Davenport, Bala Iyer, and Cathy Davidson, "Three Skills Every 21st-Century Manager Needs," *Harvard Business Review*, February 2012.

Figure 11.9, for example, contrasts two Canadian sources. Environics Research Group, co-founded by Michael Adams, is a leading public opinion and market research firm. David Foot, Professor Emeritus of Economics at the University of Toronto, and founder of Footwork Consulting Inc., is a demographics expert. Foot explores how changing demographics is redefining society's needs. While Adams and Foot are best-selling authors, each has a different perspective on the impact of demographics. "Demography is not destiny," writes Adams. Contrast this with "Demographics explains about two-thirds of everything," according to Foot. For the purposes of this discussion, the Environics terms will be used

Members in each generation are linked through shared life experiences in their formative years—usually the first 10 years of life. The beliefs that you accept as a child affect how you view risk and challenge, authority, technology, relationships, and economics. Companies need to understand each generational cohort because they have unique workplace expectations, needs, and goals and as a result, the management styles and recruiting techniques required to successfully engage with them will vary.[34]

FIGURE 11.9

TWO EXAMPLES OF GENERATIONAL COHORT TERMS

Year Born (Environics Research Group)	Term	Year Born (Footwork Consulting Inc.)
1946 to 1964	Baby Boomers	
	Baby Boomers	1947 to 1966
1965 to 1976	Generation X	
	Generation X (subset of Baby Boomers)	1961 to 1966
	Baby Bust	1967 to 1979
1977 to 1994	Generation Y/Millennials/Echo Boomers	
	The Baby-Boom Echo	1980 to 1995
1995 to Present	Generation Z	
	The Millennium Busters	1996 to 2010

Sources: Based on "Generations Variables - 2013," Environics Analytics, 2012, http://www.environicsanalytics.ca/docs/default-source/2014-variables/generations-variables---2013.pdf; and Colonel James C. Taylor, "Whither march the cohorts: The validity of generation theory as a determinant of the sociocultural values of Canadian Forces personnel," Canadian Forces College, June 2008, http://www.cfc.forces.gc.ca/259/281/280/taylor.pdf, 6.

Some generalities apply to these different groups. Baby Boomers were raised in families that experienced unprecedented economic prosperity, secure jobs, and optimism about the future. Gen Xers were raised in dual-career families with parents who focused on work. As children, some attended day care or became latchkey kids. (Latchkey kids are school-aged children of working parents who must spend part of the day unsupervised at home.[35]) Their parents' layoffs added to their insecurity about a lifelong job.

Across Canada, there are 10 million Millennials (also known as Gen Y), and they are forecasted to represent 75 percent of the Canadian workforce by the year 2028.[36] Millennials were raised by indulgent parents, and most do not remember a time without cell phones, computers, and electronic entertainment. Gen Z is also a big group; there are 2 billion worldwide, 7 million in Canada and 20 million in the United States.[37] They are growing up in an era of global economic turmoil and climate change. According to social researcher Mark McCrindle, "They are the most connected, educated, and sophisticated generation in history. They don't just represent the future, they are creating it."[38]

The main constant in the lives of Gen Xers, Millennials, and Gen Zers is inconstancy. Consider the unprecedented change in the past 20 years in every area (i.e., economic, technological, scientific, social, and political). Gen Xers, Millennials, and Gen Zers expect change. It is the absence of change that they find questionable.

How do generational differences among these groups affect motivation in the workplace? Boomer managers need to be flexible with their Gen X and Millennial employees, or they will lose them. Gen X employees need to use their enthusiasm for change and

© Pressmaster/Shutterstock

Future managers are influenced by their experiences as children. When in a management position, these experiences can even affect who they hire, fire, or promote.

streamlining to their advantage. Although many are unwilling to pay the same price for success their parents and grandparents did, their concern about undue stress and long hours does not mean they lack ambition. They want economic security as much as older workers, but they have a different approach to achieving it. Rather than focusing on job security, Gen Xers tend to focus on career security instead and are willing to change jobs to find it.

Many Gen Xers are now managers themselves, responsible for motivating other employees. In general, they are well equipped to motivate people. They usually understand that there is more to life than work, and they think a big part of motivating is letting people know you recognize that fact. Gen X managers tend to focus more on results than on hours in the workplace. They tend to be flexible and good at collaboration and consensus building. They often think in broader terms than their predecessors because the media has exposed them to problems around the world. They also have a big impact on their team members. They are more likely to give them the goals and outlines of the project and leave them alone to do their work.

Perhaps the best asset of Gen X managers is their ability to give employees feedback, especially positive feedback. One reason might be that they expect more of it themselves. One new employee was frustrated because he had not received feedback from his boss since he was hired—two weeks earlier. In short, managers need to realize that young workers demand performance reviews and other forms of feedback more than the traditional one or two times a year.

As Millennials entered the job market, they created a workplace very generationally diverse. As a group, Millennials tend to share a number of characteristics: they're often impatient, skeptical, blunt, expressive, and image-driven. Like any other generation, they can transform their characteristics into unique skills. For example, Millennials tend to be adaptable, tech-savvy, able to grasp new concepts, practised at multitasking, efficient, and tolerant.[39] They tend to place a higher value on work–life balance, expect their employers to adapt to them (not the other way around), and are more likely to rank fun and stimulation in their top-five ideal job requirements.[40]

Many Millennials are not rushing to find lifetime careers after graduation. They tend to "job surf" and aren't opposed to living with their parents while they test out jobs. Some of this career postponement isn't by choice as much as a result of the state of the economy. The recession hurt younger workers more deeply than other workers. Today, Millennials are less likely to be employed than Gen Xers or Boomers were at the same age. Downturns in the economy have increased competition for jobs as younger workers struggle to enter the job market, Boomers try to make up lost retirement savings, and Gen Xers fight to pay mortgages and raise families. *The Gen Z and Gen Y Workplace Expectations Study,* counter to previous research, found that Millennials now prioritize money over meaningful work because the economy and student loans have forced them to do so.[41]

As Millennials assume more responsibility in the workplace, they sometimes must manage and lead others far older than themselves. How can young managers lead others who may have more experience than they do? Perhaps the three most important things to keep in mind are to be confident, to be open-minded, and to solicit feedback regularly.[42] Just remember that asking for input and advice is different from asking for permission or guidance.[43]

© Cultura Limited/Getty Images RF

Each generation is motivated by different things. Companies need to provide mentoring, feedback, and meaningful projects if they want to reach Gen Zers and retain them.[46] What does effective mentoring and feedback look like to you?

As Gen Zers enter the workplace, they are likely to be more cautious and security-minded, but inspired to improve the world. Since they've seen the effects of an economic downturn first-hand, they are more aware of troubling times. Given the young nature of this cohort (between 0 to 23 years of age when this chapter was written), research is not conclusive as Gen Zers are still developing. A study titled, *Meet Generation Z: Forget everything you learned about Millennials,* reported that 60 percent of Gen Zers want jobs that have a social impact, compared with 31 percent of Millennials. It called Gen Zers entrepreneurial (72 percent want to start their own businesses), community-oriented (26 percent already volunteer), and prudent (56 percent said they were savers, not spenders). Gen Z is also seen to be more tolerant than Millennials of racial, sexual, and generational diversity, and less likely to subscribe to traditional gender roles.[44]

The Gen Z and Gen Y Workplace Expectations Study found that Gen Z appears to be more entrepreneurial, loyal, open-minded, and less motivated by money than Millennials. (The latter could be that Gen Z has not experienced workforce challenges to the extent of the earlier cohort.) The study confirms that Canadian Gen Zers want their managers to engage them to do their best work by assigning meaningful projects, while secondly serving as mentors and providing regular feedback so that they have a better transition into the work force. Gen Z can also be defined by its potential loyalty to future employers. While Millennials expect to work for five companies in their lifetime, Gen Zers expect to work for fewer than four. In response, companies should stress the benefits of loyalty and longevity and reward those who serve longer and accomplish more.[45]

© theartofphoto/123RF

Gen Zers may be more entrepreneurial than Millennials due to the amount of information and people accessible at a younger age. Is there more pressure on this generation to succeed? What might success mean for Gen Zers?

It is important for managers of all ages to be aware that employees of different generations communicate differently. The Traditionalists, the generation that lived through the Great Depression and World War II, prefer to communicate face-to-face. Their second choice is by phone, but recordings often frustrate them. Boomers generally prefer to communicate in meetings or conference calls. Gen Xers generally prefer e-mail and will choose meetings only if there are no other options. Millennials most often use technology to communicate, particularly through social media.[47] Gen Zers are starting to trend back toward face-to-face meetings and shy away from phone calls.[48]

In every generational shift, the older generation tends to say the same thing about the new: "They break the rules." The Traditionalists said it of the Baby Boomers. Boomers look at Gen Xers and say, "Why are they breaking the rules?" And now Gen Xers are looking at Millennials and Gen Zers and saying, "What's wrong with these kids?" And you know that this will be the same for the next generation someday.

One thing in business is likely to remain constant: much motivation will come from the job itself rather than from external punishments or rewards. Managers need to give workers what they require in order to do a good job: the right tools, the right information, and the right amount of co-operation. Motivation does not have to be difficult. It begins with acknowledging a job well done—and especially doing so in front of others. After all, as we said earlier, the best motivator is frequently a sincere "Thanks, I really appreciate what you're doing."

PROGRESS ASSESSMENT

- What is the difference between a high-context culture and a low-context culture?
- Compare how motivation strategies may differ for Millennials versus Gen Zers.
- Why is it important to adjust motivational styles to individual employees?
- Are there any general principles of motivation that today's managers should follow?

SUMMARY

LO1 **Explain Taylor's theory of scientific management, and describe the Hawthorne studies and their significance to management.**

Human efficiency engineer Frederick Taylor was one of the first people to study management and has been called the father of scientific management. He conducted time-motion studies to learn the most efficient way of doing a job and then trained workers in those procedures.

What led to the more human-based managerial styles?

The greatest impact on motivation theory was generated by the Hawthorne studies in the late 1920s and early 1930s. In these studies, Elton Mayo found that human factors such as feelings of involvement and participation led to greater productivity gains than did physical changes in the workplace.

LO2 **Identify the levels of Maslow's hierarchy of needs and apply them to employee motivation. Contrast this with the motivators and hygiene factors identified by Herzberg.**

Abraham Maslow studied basic human motivation and found that motivation was based on needs. He said that a person with an unfilled need would be motivated to satisfy it and that a satisfied need no longer served as motivation.

What levels of need did Maslow identify?

Starting at the bottom of Maslow's hierarchy of needs and going to the top, the levels of need are physiological, safety, social, esteem, and self-actualization.

How can managers use Maslow's theory?

Managers can recognize what unmet needs a person has and design work so that it satisfies those needs.

What is the difference between Frederick Herzberg's motivators and hygiene factors?

Herzberg found that while some factors motivate workers (motivators), others cause job dissatisfaction if missing but are not motivators if present (hygiene or maintenance factors).

What are the factors called motivators?

The work itself, achievement, recognition, responsibility, growth, and advancement are motivators.

What are the hygiene (maintenance) factors?

Company policies, supervision, working conditions, interpersonal relations, and salary are examples of hygiene factors.

LO3 **Differentiate between McGregor's Theory X and Theory Y.**

Douglas McGregor held that managers will have one of two opposing attitudes toward employees. They are called Theory X and Theory Y.

What is Theory X?

Theory X assumes that the average person dislikes work and will avoid it if possible. Therefore, people must be forced, controlled, and threatened with punishment to accomplish organizational goals.

What is Theory Y?

Theory Y makes entirely different assumptions about people. It assumes that people like working and will accept responsibility for achieving goals if rewarded for doing so.

LO4 **Explain the key principles of goal-setting, expectancy, reinforcement, and equity theories.**

More modern motivation theories include goal-setting, expectancy, reinforcement, and equity theories.

What is goal-setting theory?

Goal-setting theory is based on the notion that setting ambitious but attainable goals will lead to high levels of motivation and performance if the goals are accepted, accompanied by feedback, and facilitated by organizational conditions. Management by objectives (MBO) is a system of goal setting and implementation. It includes a cycle of discussion, review, and evaluation by objectives among top and middle-level managers, supervisors, and employees.

What are the key elements involved in expectancy theory?

According to Victor Vroom's expectancy theory, employee expectations can affect an individual's motivation. Expectancy theory centres on three questions employees often ask about performance on the job: (1) Can I accomplish the task? (2) If I do accomplish it, what is my reward? and (3) Is the reward worth the effort?

What are the variables in reinforcement theory?

Positive reinforcers are rewards like praise, recognition, or pay raises that a worker might strive to receive after performing well. Negative reinforcers are punishments such as reprimands, pay cuts, layoffs, or firing that a worker might be expected to try to avoid.

According to equity theory, employees try to maintain equity between inputs and outputs compared to other employees in similar positions. What happens when employees perceive that their rewards are not equitable?

If employees perceive that they are under-rewarded, they will either reduce their effort or rationalize that it is not important. If they perceive that they are over-rewarded, they will either increase their effort to justify the higher reward in the future or rationalize by saying, "I'm worth it!" Inequity leads to lower productivity, reduced quality, increased absenteeism, and voluntary resignation.

LO5 **Show how managers put motivation theories into action through such strategies as job enrichment, open communication, and job recognition.**

Job enrichment describes efforts to make jobs more interesting.

What characteristics of work affect motivation and performance?

The job characteristics that influence motivation are skill variety, task identity, task significance, autonomy, and feedback.

Name two forms of job enrichment that increase motivation.

Job-enrichment strategies include job enlargement and job rotation.

How does open communication improve employee motivation?

Open communication helps both managers and employees understand the objectives and work together to achieve them.

How can managers encourage open communication?

Top managers can create an organizational culture that rewards listening, train supervisors and managers to listen, use effective questioning techniques, remove barriers to open communication, avoid vague and ambiguous communication, and actively make it easier for all to communicate.

What are some job recognition techniques that managers can consider?

Letting people know you appreciate their work is usually more powerful than giving a raise or bonus alone. Job recognition techniques can include noticing positive actions out loud, offering perks like Netflix memberships, and bestowing awards.

LO6 **Show how managers personalize motivation strategies to appeal to employees around the globe and across generations.**

Managers cannot use one motivational formula for all employees.

What is the difference between high-context and low-context cultures?

In high-context cultures people build personal relationships and develop group trust before focusing on tasks. In low-context cultures, people often view relationship building as a waste of time that diverts attention from the task.

How are Generation X managers likely to be different from their Baby Boomer predecessors?

Baby Boomers tend to be willing to work long hours to build their careers and often expect their subordinates to do likewise. Gen Xers may strive for a more balanced lifestyle and are likely to focus on results rather than on how many hours their teams work. Gen Xers tend to be better than previous generations at working in teams and providing frequent feedback. They are not bound by traditions that may constrain those who have been with an organization for a long time and are willing to try new approaches to solving problems.

What are some common characteristics of Millennials?

Millennials tend to be adaptable, tech-savvy, able to grasp new concepts, practised at multi-tasking, efficient, and tolerant. They often place a higher value on work–life balance, expect their employers to adapt to them, and are more likely to rank fun and stimulation in their top five ideal job requirements.

What will employers need to do to hire or engage with Gen Z?

Employers will need to emphasize incentives for loyalty and training and development over money. Companies need to provide mentoring, feedback, and meaningful projects if they want to reach Gen Z and retain these employees.

KEY TERMS

equity theory 413
expectancy theory 411
extrinsic reward 399
goal-setting theory 410
Hawthorne effect 403
hygiene (maintenance) factors 405
intrinsic reward 399
job enlargement 415
job enrichment 414
job rotation 415
management by objectives (MBO) 410
Maslow's hierarchy of needs 403
motivation 398
motivators 405
principle of motion economy 401
reinforcement theory 412
scientific management 401
time-motion studies 401

CAREER EXPLORATION

If you are interested in pursuing a career that involves motivating others, here are a few to consider. Find out about the tasks performed, skills needed, pay, and opportunity outlook in these fields through Internet sites that include the Government of Canada Job Bank, Workopolis, Monster, CareerBuilder, Glassdoor, and Indeed, as well as through the Career Centre at your school.

- **Coach—**teaches amateur or professional athletes the skills they need to succeed at their sport.
- **Elementary, middle, and high school principal—**manages all school operations, including daily school activities; coordinates curricula; oversees teachers and other school staff; and provides a safe and productive learning environment for students.
- **Sales manager—**directs organizations' sales teams, sets sales goals, analyzes data, and develops training programs for organizations' sales representatives.

CRITICAL THINKING

1. This text introduced you to the theory of scientific management. What do you think are problems that would arise as a result of breaking jobs into a series of discrete steps and treating people as cogs in a wheel? How can you motivate employees if this is how they are managed?
2. Your job right now is to finish reading this chapter. How strongly would you be motivated to do that if you were sweating in a room at 40 degrees Celsius? Imagine your roommate has turned on the air-conditioning. Once you are more comfortable, are you more likely to read? Look at Maslow's hierarchy of needs to see what need would be motivating you at both times. Now recall a situation in your home, school, or work life in which you were

feeling particularly motivated to do something. Which of the needs identified by Maslow motivated you then?

3. Humanistic management is an approach to management theory based on the idea of human needs and human values.[49] Further investigate this theory. How does this contrast with scientific management? What are advantages and disadvantages for employers and employees?

DEVELOPING CAREER SKILLS

Key: ● **Team** ★ **Analytic** ▲ **Communication** ⊡ **Technology**

★▲ 1. Talk with several of your friends about the subject of motivation. What motivates them to work hard or not work hard on projects in teams? How important is self-motivation to them?

★▲ 2. Speak to a manager in the workplace. Find out what this manager does to motivate his or her direct reports.

★▲ 3. Think of all of the groups with which you have been associated over the years—sports groups, friendship groups, and so on—and try to recall how the leaders of those groups motivated the group to action. What motivational tools were used and to what effect? Discuss your answers in class.

●★▲ 4. Partner with two of your classmates and discuss motivation. Herzberg concluded that pay was not a motivator. If you were paid to get better grades, would you be motivated to study harder? In your employment experiences, have you ever worked harder to obtain a raise or as a result of receiving a raise? Do you agree with Herzberg?

●★▲ 5. Partner with two of your classmates and discuss the recent managerial idea to let employees work in self-managed teams. There is no reason why such teams could not be formed in schools as well as businesses. Discuss the benefits and drawbacks of dividing your class into self-managed teams for the purpose of studying, completing assignments, and so forth.

ANALYZING MANAGEMENT DECISIONS

Motivation Tips for Tough Times

With company cutbacks, layoffs, and economic uncertainty weighing heavily on everybody, it is no wonder some employees are dragging their feet into work. But according to Steven Stein, Toronto-based psychologist and entrepreneur, there are ways to lift and maintain motivation, even in tough times. In *Make Your Workplace Great: The 7 Keys to an Emotionally Intelligent Organization,* he offers these valuable tips for motivating employees.

- *What motivates your workers.* You may be surprised to discover how small changes, such as those in job design or reporting systems, can motivate certain people. It might not take much, but the only way to discover what your employees want, and how they react to change, is to ask them.
- *Offer ongoing feedback.* No time is better than now to open up lines of communication with your employees, if you have not already. Whether you offer feedback formally or informally, it is important to regularly let your staff know how they are doing, where they are performing well, and where there is room for improvement.
- *Emphasize personal accountability.* Self-management can be highly motivating, and if you are short-staffed, it can make a lot of sense, too. Most people will work much harder for their own

sense of accomplishment than they will because they were told to do something.

- *Involve everyone in decision making.* By involving workers in certain company decisions, especially those that involve them directly, you are much more likely to get support for your initiatives. And you may even get some creative input along the way as your front-line staff might have knowledge about the impact of certain decisions that you may not be aware of.
- *Be flexible.* Time is an important commodity for people today, especially if they are taking on more work than usual. By giving your employees the opportunity to juggle their time around critical personal or family events and responsibilities, you will increase their motivation.
- *Celebrate employee and company success.* It is important to stop and recognize successes, whether individual, team, or organizational. Let everybody see that hard work is recognized and worth carrying out.

Source: "Business Owners Try to Motivate Employees," *The Wall Street Journal,* January 14, 2012, http://online.wsj.com/article/SB10001424052748704362004575000911063526360.html; and "Great Ideas: Motivation Tips for Tough Times," *PROFIT,* June 4, 2009, www.canadianbusiness.com/entrepreneur/human_resources/article.jsp?content=20090603_115416_7820.

Discussion Questions

1. What other suggestions might you add to this list?
2. If you are employed now (or have been in the past), how has your supervisor motivated you? If you have never been employed before, how might a supervisor motivate you?
3. Apply each one of these tips to group work. How might you implement these suggestions so that group members, including yourself, are motivated to do well in the assigned work?

CHAPTER 12

Human Resource Management: Finding and Keeping the Best Employees

LEARNING OBJECTIVES

After you have read and studied this chapter, you should be able to:

LO1 Explain the importance of human resource management as a strategic contributor to organizational success, and summarize the five steps in human resource planning.

LO2 Describe methods that companies use to recruit new employees, and explain some of the issues that make recruitment challenging.

LO3 Outline the six steps in selecting employees, and illustrate the use of various types of employee training and development methods.

LO4 Trace the six steps in appraising employee performance, and summarize the objectives of employee compensation programs.

LO5 Describe the ways in which employees can move through a company: promotion, reassignment, termination, and retirement.

LO6 Illustrate the effects of legislation on human resource management.

PROFILE

GETTING TO KNOW: LINDA HASENFRATZ, CEO, Linamar Corporation

In today's business world, the prospect of lifetime employment at a single company is becoming increasingly unlikely. Thanks to a sluggish economy and never-ending technological innovation, workers no longer have much of a chance to stay in one place until their retirement. As staff sizes rise and fall with the global marketplace, many companies continue to require a skilled and flexible workforce of people. Workers in turn may require specialized training and flexible schedules to help balance work and life.

Linamar Corporation, Canada's second-largest auto-parts maker, is a diversified global manufacturing company of highly engineered products. With more than 25 700 employees in 17 countries,

Courtesy Linamar Corporation. Used with permission.

Linamar generated sales of $6 billion in 2016 with a goal to grow to $20 billion by 2030.

Founded by Frank Hasenfratz in the 1960s, daughter Linda Hasenfratz became the CEO in 2002 after rotating through various positions throughout the company. She started on the shop floor running a machine and learning the business from the bottom up. Hasenfratz then worked in different plants and in different areas, such as engineering, accounting, estimating, quality assurance, and factory management. This was followed by five years as an executive. Under her leadership, the company has recorded double-digit annual growth. Such growth requires skilled workers to run the company's 59 manufacturing locations, 6 R&D centres, and 21 sales offices around the world.

Linamar's human resource practices include a company goal to have equivalent representation to its overall demographic at every level. With this in mind, the percentage of women in the company should be reflected by the same percentage at every level of management. In another example, a five-year management-training program develops promising employees to become plant general managers. After a rigorous screening process, trainees spend two years rotating through different departments, then another three years in mid-level management positions that expose them to materials, accounting, and quality management. The program aims to mirror an entrepreneur's experience. Says Hasenfratz, "As an entrepreneur, you initially have to do everything: You are the salesperson, the person running the machine, the delivery person. As a consequence, you become very familiar with the company."

Hasenfratz's focus on innovation, financial performance, and her ability to find opportunities during a recession contributed to her recognition as the first female EY Entrepreneur of the Year. "I'm a big believer in the competitiveness of our manufacturers," says Hasenfratz. "I think we have an incredible employee base in Canada—skilled trades, engineers, machinists, metallurgists, technologists, quality assurance—great technical people who have the ability to innovate, which is the key to competitiveness."

In this chapter, you will learn how businesses of all sizes recruit, manage, and make the most of their employees. Training and development programs like the ones at Linamar are just one important area of human resource management.

Sources: Greg Keenan, "Linamar Corp. to create 1,500 jobs at new innovation, research centre," *The Globe and Mail,* August 21, 2018, sec. B, p. 1; "Linamar to Acquire the MacDon Group of Companies, a Global Harvesting Specialist, to Further Diversity & Grow," Linamar Corp., December 14, 2017, http://www.linamar.com/sites/default/files/press/MacDon%20-%20Press%20Release%20-%2014dec17.pdf; Trevor Cole, "Auto-parts magnate Linda Hasenfratz on NAFTA, Trump and sexism in the boardroom," *ROB Magazine,* July 6, 2017, https://www.theglobeandmail.com/report-on-business/rob-magazine/auto-parts-magnate-linda-hasenfratz-on-nafta-trump-and-sexism-in-theboardroom/article35509156/; "Linamar Delivers Record 2014 Sales & Earnings on Nearly 50% Earnings Growth," Linamar Corp., 4 March 2015, http://www.linamar.com/sites/default/files/q4_2014_press_release.pdf; Joanna Pachner, "A Second-Generation Success Story: Linda Hasenfratz at Linamar," PROFITguide.com, January 15, 2015, http://www.profitguide.com/manage-grow/leadership/a-second-generation-success-story-linda-hasenfratz-at-linamar-73054/3; Mary Teresa Bitti, "Linamar chief Linda Hasenfratz continues to prove she belongs at the top," *Financial Post,* December 15, 2014, http://business.financialpost.com/2014/12/15/linamar-chief-linda-hasenfratz-continues-to-prove-she-belongs-at-the-top/; and Joanna Pachner, "Linda Hasenfratz's bet on auto manufacturing is paying off—big time," *Canadian Business,* November 27, 2014, http://www.canadianbusiness.com/lists-and-rankings/richest-people/linda-hasenfratz-linamar-ceo/.

LO1

Explain the importance of human resource management as a strategic contributor to organizational success, and summarize the five steps in human resource planning.

human resource management (HRM) The process of determining human resource needs and then recruiting, selecting, developing, motivating, evaluating, compensating, and scheduling employees to achieve organizational goals.

Working with People Is Just the Beginning

Students often say they want to go into human resource management because they want to "work with people." Human resource managers do work with people, but they are also deeply involved in planning, record keeping, and other administrative duties. This chapter will discuss what else human resource management is all about.

Human resource management (HRM) is the process of determining human resource needs and then recruiting, selecting, developing, motivating, evaluating, compensating, and scheduling employees to achieve organizational goals (see Figure 12.1). For many years, human resource management was called "personnel" and involved clerical functions such as screening applications, keeping records, processing the payroll, and finding new employees when necessary. The roles and responsibilities of HRM have evolved primarily because of two key factors: (1) organizations' recognition of employees as their ultimate resource and (2) changes in laws that rewrote many traditional practices. Let's explore both.

Developing the Ultimate Resource

One reason the role of human resource management has grown is that the shift from traditional manufacturing industries to service and high-tech manufacturing industries requires businesses to hire workers with highly technical job skills. This shift means that many workers must be retrained for new, more challenging jobs. People truly are the ultimate resource. They develop the ideas that eventually become the products that satisfy consumers' wants and needs. Take away their creative minds and leading firms such as Linamar, Cirque du Soleil, Apple, Google, and Disney would be nothing.

In the past, human resources were plentiful, so there was little need to nurture and develop them. If you needed qualified people, you simply hired them. If they did not work out, you fired them and found others. Most firms assigned the job of recruiting, selecting, training, evaluating, compensating, motivating, and, yes, firing people to the functional departments that employed them, like accounting and marketing. Today, the job of human resource management has taken on an increased role in the firm since *qualified* employees are much scarcer due to an increase in the number of jobs that require advanced or specialized training. This shortage of qualified workers makes recruiting and retaining people more important and more difficult.[1] In fact, the human resource function has become so important that it is no longer the responsibility of just one department; it is a responsibility of *all* managers. What are some human resource challenges all managers face? We'll outline a few next.

Human Resource Challenges

Many of the changes that have had the most dramatic impact on business are the changes in the labour force. The ability to compete in global markets depends on new ideas, new products and services, and new levels of productivity—in other words, on people with good ideas. These are some of the challenges and opportunities in human resources (HR):[2]

- Uncertainty in global politics and increased attention on hiring immigrants.
- Technology, such as talent networks, crowdsourcing, and internal social networks.

FIGURE 12.1

HUMAN RESOURCE MANAGEMENT (HRM)

As this figure shows, HRM is more than hiring and firing personnel. All activities are designed to achieve organizational goals within the laws that affect human resource management. (Note that human resource management includes motivation, as discussed in Chapter 11, and employee–management relations, which will be discussed in Chapter 13.)

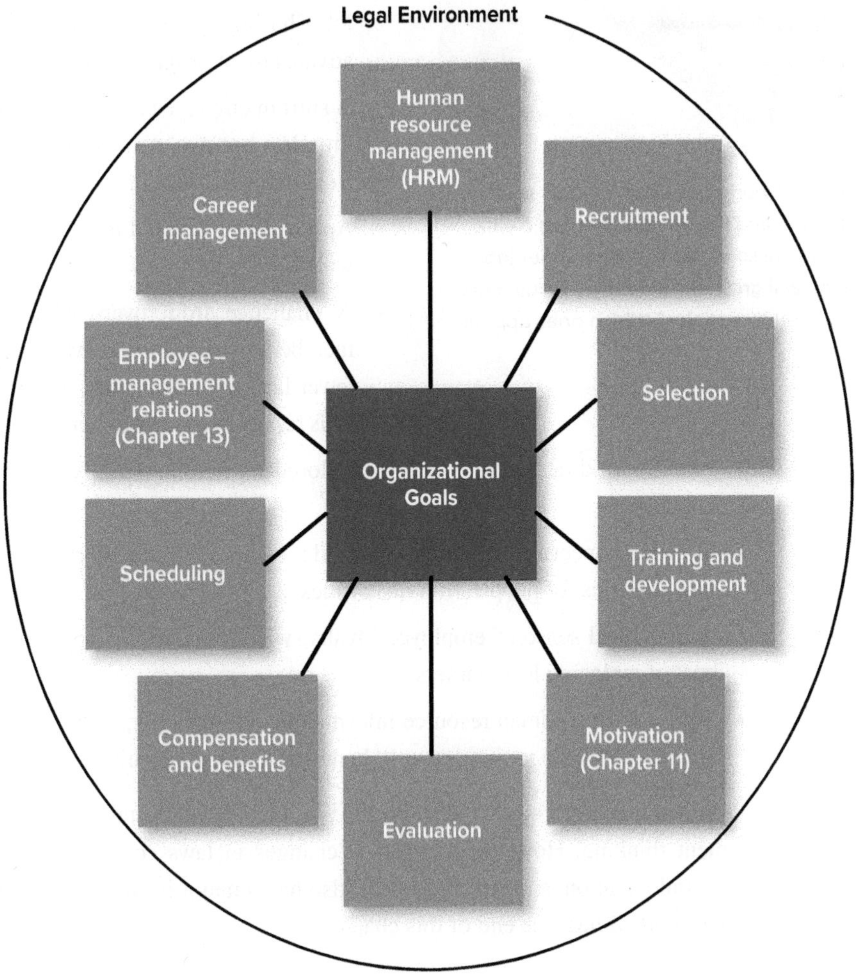

- Multigenerational workforce where older Millennials and Gen Xers hold management positions, while Gen Zers are entering the workforce and many Baby Boomers are delaying retirement (discussed in more detail later in the chapter).
- Shortages of trained workers in growth areas such as computer technology, biotechnology, robotics, green technology, and the sciences.
- Large numbers of skilled and unskilled workers from declining industries, such as steel and automobiles, who are unemployed or underemployed and need retraining. *Underemployed workers* are those who have more skills or knowledge than their current jobs require or those with part-time jobs who want to work full-time.

© Pedro Castellano/Getty Images RF

Firms face a shortage of workers skilled in areas such as sustainable engineering and the development of clean energy sources like these solar panels. What other job markets do you think will grow as companies focus more on environmentally friendly policies? Which ones appeal to you?

- A growing percentage of new workers who are undereducated and unprepared for jobs in the contemporary business environment.
- A shortage of workers in skilled trades due to the retirement of aging Baby Boomers.
- An increasing number of both single-parent and two-income families, resulting in a demand for job sharing, parental leave, and special career advancement programs for women.
- A shift in employee attitudes toward work. Leisure time has become a much higher priority, as have flextime and a shorter workweek.
- An increased demand for temporary and part-time workers.
- A challenge from overseas labour pools whose members work for lower wages and are subject to fewer laws and regulations than Canadian workers. This results in many jobs being outsourced overseas.
- An increased demand for benefits tailored to the individual yet cost-effective to the company.
- Growing concerns over health care, elder care, child care, workplace harassment, and opportunities for people with disabilities.
- A decreased sense of employee loyalty, which increases employee turnover and the cost of replacing lost workers.
- Implementing human resource information systems (e.g., technology that helps manage HR activities such as payroll, benefits, training, recruiting, and so forth).

Given the issues mentioned, you can see why HRM has taken a central place in management thinking. However, significant changes in laws covering areas such as hiring, safety, unionization, and equal pay have also had a major influence. We will consider laws affecting HRM near the end of this chapter.

Determining a Firm's Human Resource Needs

All management, including HRM, begins with planning. The five steps in the human resource planning process are:

1. *Preparing a human resource inventory of the organization's employees.* This inventory should include ages, names, education, capabilities, training, specialized skills, and other relevant information (e.g., such as languages spoken). It reveals whether the labour force is technically up to date and thoroughly trained.
2. *Preparing a job analysis.* A **job analysis** is a study of what is done by employees who hold various job titles. It is necessary to recruit and train employees with the necessary

job analysis
A study of what is done by employees who hold various job titles.

FIGURE 12.2

JOB ANALYSIS

A job analysis yields two important statements: job descriptions and job specifications. Here you have a job description and job specifications for a sales representative position.

Job Analysis	
Observe current sales representatives doing the job. Discuss job with sales managers. Have current sales representatives keep a diary of their activities.	
Job Description (about the job)	**Job Specifications** (about the person)
Primary objective is to sell the company's products to stores in Territory D. Duties include servicing accounts and maintaining positive relationships with clients. Responsibilities include: • introducing the new products to store managers in the area • helping the store managers estimate the volume to order • negotiating prime shelf space • explaining sales promotion activities to store managers • stocking and maintaining shelves in stores that wish such service	Characteristics of the ideal person qualifying for this job include: • bilingual • self-motivated • positive attitude • strong written and communication skills • have a valid driver's licence • two years of sales experience • a diploma or degree in Business

skills to do the job. The results of job analysis are two written statements: job descriptions and job specifications. A **job description** specifies the objectives of the job, the type of work to be done, the responsibilities and duties, the working conditions, and the relationship of the job to other functions. **Job specifications** are a written summary of the minimum qualifications (e.g., education and skills) required of workers to do a particular job. In short, job descriptions are statements about the job, whereas job specifications are statements about the person who does the job. A PWC report highlights that the hardest skills to find are those that can't be performed by machines. Ranked in order of importance of skill, they are problem solving, adaptability, leadership, creativity and innovation, and emotional intelligence.[3] If you do not have these skills, how can you develop them and demonstrate them in the next few years? See Figure 12.2 for a hypothetical job description and job specifications.

job description
A summary of the objectives of a job, the type of work to be done, the responsibilities and duties, the working conditions, and the relationship of the job to other functions.

job specifications
A written summary of the minimum qualifications required of workers to do a particular job.

3. *Assessing future human resource demand.* Because technology changes rapidly, effective human resource managers are proactive; that is, they forecast the organization's requirements and train people ahead of time or ensure trained people are available when needed.[4]

4. *Assessing future human resource supply.* The labour force is constantly shifting: getting older, becoming more technically oriented, and becoming more diverse. Some workers will be scarcer in the future, like biomedical engineers and robotic repair workers, and others will be oversupplied, like assembly-line workers.

5. *Establishing a strategic plan.* The plan must address recruiting, selecting, training, developing, appraising, compensating, and scheduling the labour force.[5] Because the first four steps lead up to this one, we'll focus on them in the rest of the chapter.

Some companies use advanced technology to perform the human resource planning process more efficiently. HRIS (Human Resource Information System) is software that uses multiple tools and processes to manage an organization's employees and databases. HRIS (such as Salesforce, IBM Kenexa, and Sage People) helps businesses of all sizes perform basic HR functions ranging from recruitment to retirement, For example, IBM manages its global workforce of about 100 000 employees and 100 000 subcontractors with a database that matches employee skills, experiences, schedules, and references with jobs available. If a client in Nova Scotia has a month-long project requiring a consultant who can speak English and French, has an advanced degree in engineering, and has experience with Linux programming, IBM can find the best-suited consultant available and put him or her in touch with the client.

LO2

Describe methods that companies use to recruit new employees, and explain some of the issues that make recruitment challenging.

Recruiting Employees from a Diverse Population

recruitment
The set of activities used to obtain a sufficient number of the right people at the right time.

Recruitment is the set of activities for obtaining the right number of qualified people at the right time. Its purpose is to select those who best meet the needs of the organization. You might think a continuous flow of new people into the workforce makes recruiting easy. On the contrary, it has become very challenging. In fact, 45 percent of CEOs surveyed say that attracting and retaining talent is their biggest challenge.[6] Here are several reasons why:

- Some organizations have policies that demand promotions from within, operate under collective labour agreements (to be discussed in Chapter 13), or offer low wages, which makes recruiting and keeping employees difficult or subject to outside influence and restrictions.[7]
- There are legal guidelines that surround hiring practices. The Canadian Human Rights Act requires that employers provide equal employment opportunities. For example, a human rights complaint could be made if an employer said that he would not hire a woman or a visible minority for a particular job, regardless of that person's competency. The Canadian Human Rights Act protects those who work for federally regulated organizations or service providers (e.g., chartered banks and airlines). Other employees are protected by provincial or territorial jurisdiction.
- An emphasis on corporate culture, teamwork, and participative management makes it important to hire people who not only are skilled but also fit in with the culture and leadership style of the organization. For example, in order to find out if its new hires fit the company culture, VinoPRO has its newbies play a game to see who makes the most sales. How the employees react (e.g., excitement, fear, or all-out aggression) will determine whether their new bosses believe they will thrive or not.[8]
- Sometimes people with the necessary skills are not available; consequently, workers must be hired and then trained internally.

Human resource managers turn to many sources for assistance (see Figure 12.3). *Internal sources* include employees who are already within the firm (and may be transferred or promoted) and employees who can recommend others to hire. For example, Montreal, Quebec-based accounting firm Richter LLP offers referral bonuses up to $4,000 to employees when they successfully recruit a new candidate.[9] Using internal sources is less expensive than recruiting from outside the company and it helps maintain employee morale. Review the Making Ethical Decisions box for a dilemma that can apply to hiring from within.

Using internal sources is less expensive than recruiting from outside and helps maintain employee morale. Managers in the Government of Canada start the recruiting process by looking inside the federal

© Darryl Estrine/Getty Images

Human resource managers today have the opportunity to recruit people from a wide range of cultural and ethnic backgrounds. What are some of the advantages of a diverse workforce?

FIGURE 12.3

SOURCES OF RECRUITMENT

Internal sources are often given first consideration. So it is useful to get a recommendation from a current employee of the firm for which you want to work. School placement offices are also an important source. Be sure to learn about these services early so that you can plan an employment strategy throughout your academic career.

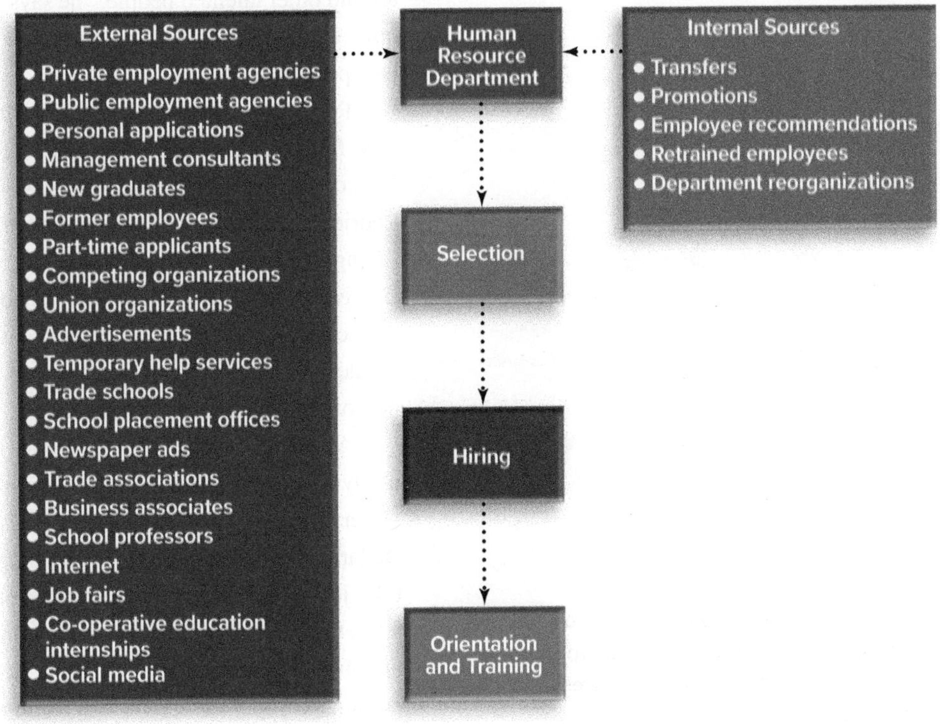

Making ETHICAL DECISIONS

Recruiting Employees from Competitors

As the human resource director for Technocrat, Inc., it is your job to recruit the best employees. Your most recent human resource inventory indicates that Technocrat currently has an abundance of qualified designers and that several lower-level workers will soon be eligible for promotions to designer positions. Despite the surplus of qualified designers within the firm, you are considering recruiting a designer who is now with a major competitor. Your thinking is that the new employee will be a source of information about the competition's new products. What are your ethical considerations in this case? Will you lure the employee away from the competition even though you have no need for a designer? What will be the consequences of your decision?

service to find individuals with the skill set and experience that they need. (An exception is for Post Secondary Recruitment.) It is easier to hire within because most federal public servants understand the culture, the environment, and the expectations of departments.[10]

However, it isn't always possible to find qualified workers within the company, so human resource managers also use *external sources.* Examples include advertisements, public and private employment agencies, college placement bureaus, management consultants, online sites, professional organizations, referrals, online and walk-in applications, and social media. Rohit Gupta, president of Edmonton, Alberta-based Rohit Group of Companies says the key to the company's success is the talented people it has managed to attract by utilizing a wide range of recruitment sources that include post-secondary institutions, industry associations, and online tools. "We know talented people like to be around other talented people," he says. "So retention is quite easy when you make sure you are bringing in the best people."[11]

© Universum

There are seven career types. To learn which one you are and suggested employers based on career type, complete the *From Learning to Work Survey* at careertest.universumglobal.com.

Popular recruiting Internet sites include Workopolis, Monster, CareerBuilder, Glassdoor, and Indeed. Passion Inc. was founded by brothers Mark and Nathan Laurie from their student residence with $500 in savings and the dream of graduating from Dalhousie University debt free.[12] Have you visited Jobpostings.ca, one of Passion's divisions? Resources include Career Guides and Career Planning. You can also find information on companies and salaries.

At L'Oréal Canada, social media has been particularly successful when it comes to attracting students. "Everyone is digital nowadays," says VP Catherine Bédard, "but at L'Oréal we're going much further than just using LinkedIn—many of our employees are attracted from YouTube or Instagram. When we're at job fairs on campus, you have so many students coming to you with a C.V. and asking you to employ them. Instead of taking their résumé, we ask them to

Spotlight *On* SMALL BUSINESS

Competing Through Social Media

Most small business owners would agree that attracting top-quality employees is one of their major challenges. Unfortunately, competing for the cream of the crop is difficult when you can't afford expensive recruiters or pay gold-plated benefits to lure qualified workers. Despite these hurdles, small businesses can compete through social media.

Social media play a crucial role in the hiring process today. More than 94 percent of recruiters say they use LinkedIn to recruit new candidates and 70 percent of job seekers say they use social media to find jobs. Talented Millennials usually value professional development more than employer loyalty, so it is important that businesses make their hiring policies and work culture attractive to draw the best talents. For example, Google makes its workplace culture known by talking about its fun atmosphere and its interesting perks such as free gourmet food, sports complexes, on-site laundry, and so on.

Of course, it's always better to have someone else sing your praises. Businesses should encourage their current employees to talk on social media about why they love working for the company. It helps give employees an incentive to bring in new talent. Some companies, such as the Business Development Bank of Canada, offer employees a referral fee for recommendations.

Here's how managers can use social media networks to target potential hires:

- LinkedIn—It can be expensive to post jobs on LinkedIn. If cost is a problem, there is a cheaper solution. Join groups that have potential candidates and be active in group discussions. Once you build a good-sized network, post your openings on the status box.
- Facebook—Use Facebook Directory to search for relevant users, pages, groups, and applications. You can post jobs for free in Facebook Marketplace. Obviously, make sure your business has an active Facebook page.
- Twitter—Tweet about your job opening. Expand your network by building relationships with candidates and clients on the site. Make sure your tweet can be found by using the most relevant hashtags. Many recruiters use #NAJ (need a job?). Look at the posts, tweets, or recommendations of candidates to get an idea of how well they might fit your organization.

Using social media in the hiring process is one of the most cost-effective ways of attracting talent to a company. Have you found a job through social media?

© pictafolio/Getty Images

Sources: "Canada's Top Employers (2017)," *The Globe and Mail* and Mediacorp Canada Inc., Special Annual Edition insert, p. 6; Whitney Headen, "Social Recruiting: How I Used Social Media To Build A Business From Scratch," *Forbes*, July 24, 2017; Monty Majeed, "How to Use Social Media for Hiring," *Your Story*, September 2016; and David Port, "Staffing Made Easy (or Easier)," *Entrepreneur*, February 2016.

go on YouTube and post a clip explaining why they're such a good fit for L'Oréal and why they're interested in working for us." It's a win–win strategy—not only do the videos let the L'Oréal team see the creativity and eligibility of a student in a short clip, but as more videos make it online, the company's employer branding improves.[13]

Recruiting qualified workers may be particularly difficult for small businesses with few staff members and less-than-competitive compensation to attract external sources.

Online sites like LinkedIn have helped firms by attracting millions of visitors per day. The Spotlight on Small Business box offers suggestions for how businesses can use social media for hiring.

PROGRESS ASSESSMENT

- What is human resource management?
- What are the five steps in human resource planning?
- What factors make it difficult to recruit qualified employees?
- State five sources of internal and external recruitment.

LO3

Outline the six steps in selecting employees, and illustrate the use of various types of employee training and development methods.

Selecting Employees Who Will Be Productive

selection
The process of gathering information and deciding who should be hired, under legal guidelines, to serve the best interests of the individual and the organization.

Selection is the process of gathering information and deciding who should be hired, under legal guidelines, to serve the best interests of the individual and the organization. Selecting and training employees are extremely expensive processes in some firms. Just think of what is involved: advertising or recruiting agency fees, interview time, medical exams, training costs, unproductive time spent learning the job, possible travel and moving expenses, and more. It can cost 75 percent of the employee's annual salary to recruit, process, and train even an entry-level worker, and more than 200 percent a year's salary for a top manager.[14]

A typical selection process involves six steps:

1. *Obtaining complete application forms.* Although employment laws limit the kinds of questions that can appear, applications help reveal the applicant's educational background, work experience, career objectives, and other qualifications directly related to the job.
2. *Conducting initial and follow-up interviews.* A staff member from the human resource department often screens applicants in a first interview. If the interviewer considers the applicant a potential employee, the manager who will supervise the new employee may interview the applicant as well. It is important that managers prepare adequately for the interview to avoid selection decisions they may regret. No matter how innocent the intention, missteps such as asking about pregnancy or child care could later be evidence if that applicant files discrimination charges. In the past, an employer might have asked if the applicant had children to determine whether the applicant could work shift work or on weekends. Today, the applicant would be asked if working shift work or on weekends would be a problem (without asking about children), as this is a relevant job-related question.

Depending on the job, it is not uncommon to be involved in several interviews, one or more of which may be a panel interview. How would you prepare differently if this was the case?

Adapting *to* CHANGE

Let's Face It

What you say online goes into the virtual world and stays there. Your social media and digital footprint is a critical part of your public identity. The online personality you project reflects to potential employers who you really are. Sixty percent of employers say they use social media to screen prospective hires and evaluate a person's fit with a company's culture. What this means to you is that your social media footprint could be a selling tool in your job search—or could end up costing you a job.

© Bloomua/Shutterstock.com

The growing use of social media background checks has created a new set of candidate disqualifiers. Forty-six percent of employers say they've eliminated candidates because of provocative or inappropriate photographs, video, or information; 43 percent because of information about drinking or drug use; and 33 percent because of discriminatory comments about race, religion, and gender. Do you think that it is unethical that potential employers access your social media?

It's best to use social media to your advantage. Many companies admit to hiring a candidate because of the professional image they conveyed on social media. If you have reservations about posting something, the best advice is, don't.

Sources: Roy Maurer, "Know before You Hire," Society for Human Resource Management, January 25, 2017; and "How to Use Social Media for Applicant Screening," Society for Human Resource Management, August 16, 2016.

3. *Giving employment tests.* Organizations often use tests to measure basic competency in specific job skills like welding or firefighting, and to help evaluate applicants' personalities and interests. There are many employment test software options available, such as Wonscore and Pairin Pre-employment Test Selection. The tests should always be directly related to the job. Employment tests have been legally challenged as potential means of discrimination. Some companies test potential employees in assessment centres where they perform actual job tasks. Such testing can make the selection process more efficient and will generally satisfy legal requirements.
4. *Conducting background investigations.* Most organizations now investigate a candidate's work record, school record, credit history, and references more carefully than in the past to help identify those most likely to succeed. It is simply too costly to hire, train, and motivate people only to lose them and have to start the process over. Services such as BackCheck allow prospective employers to not only conduct speedy background checks of criminal records, driving records, and credit histories, but also to verify work experience and professional and educational credentials.[15] Statistics reveal that up to 50 percent of resumés contain one or more major misrepresentations so this is a critical step in the selection process.[16] The Adapting to Change box discusses how companies use social media to screen job applicants and weed out those with undesirable traits.

5. *Obtaining results from physical exams.*[17] There are obvious benefits to hiring people who are physically and mentally healthy. Testing is sometimes requested from job applicants. An estimated 10 percent of Canadian worksites having drug testing programs where drug testing is primarily conducted to ensure a safe work environment. Yet, drug and alcohol testing is controversial. According to Ryan Anderson, an employment lawyer with Mathews Dinsdale & Clark LLP, "Testing for drug and alcohol use in the workplace may reduce risks in some circumstances, it also raises concerns regarding privacy, unlawful discrimination and the reasonable exercise of management rights."
6. *Establishing trial (probationary) periods.* Often, an organization will hire an employee conditionally to let the person prove his or her value on the job. After a specified probationary period (perhaps three months or a year), the firm can either permanently hire or discharge that employee on the basis of supervisors' evaluations.[18] Some businesses include co-workers' evaluations as well. Whole Foods' new store employees must win the approval of two-thirds of their departmental co-workers in order to stay on past their 90-day trial period.[19] Although such systems make it easier to fire inefficient or problem employees, they do not eliminate the high cost of turnover.

The selection process is often long and difficult, but it is worth the effort to select new employees carefully because of the high cost of replacing them. Care helps ensure that new employees meet all requirements, including communication skills, education, technical skills, experience, personality, and health. Finally, where a company has a collective labour agreement (a union contract with its employees) the selection process must also follow the provisions of that agreement. This is discussed in more detail in the next chapter.

contingent workers
Workers who do not have regular, full-time employment.

Hiring Contingent Workers

A company with employment needs that vary—from hour to hour, day to day, week to week, and season to season, or project to project—may find it cost-effective to hire contingent workers. **Contingent workers** are workers who do not have regular, full-time employment. Such workers include part-time workers (according to Statistics Canada, this includes "employed persons who usually work less than 30 hours per week, at their main or only job"), temporary workers (workers paid by temporary employment agencies), seasonal workers, independent contractors, interns, co-op students, and freelancers.

© Ken Gillespie Photography/Alamy

Seasonal businesses depend on hiring contingent workers to help them through the limited time they are operational. What are the advantages and disadvantages of hiring contingent workers for employers? What are the advantages and disadvantages for contingent workers?

Clear Stream Energy Services in Sherwood Park, Alberta, relies heavily on contract workers, who make up 35 percent of its workforce, due to the nature of its project-based work, said JoAnne Mather, Vice-President of HR, Health and Safety and Environment. The 2000-employee oilfields services company doesn't know what projects it will be awarded from year to year, so it has many contractors in its database it can call upon. "Some of the work is 20 days, some can be two months . . . and the only way to get those folks is to engage them in a contract because you can't offer them the traditional, long-term employment relationship," she said. "The work is so variable so a contract situation is what works."[20]

According to staffing company Randstad Canada, if you add up all the contingent workers, freelancers, independent contractors and consultants, you are talking about 20 to 30 percent of the Canadian workforce being "non-traditional workers" already.[21] That percentage is only going higher as 85 percent of the companies surveyed by Randstad figure that they will increasingly move to an "agile workforce" over the next few years.[22]

Hiring contingent workers is so common today that some have called this a *gig economy.* A gig describes a single project or task for which a worker is hired, often through a digital marketplace, to work on demand. Some gigs are types of short-term jobs, and some workers look at gigs as self-employment options. When one gig is over, workers who need to earn a steady income must find another. Sometimes, that means juggling multiple jobs at once. There are two key reasons for the rise of the gig economy: (1) workers want diversity and flexibility in their roles and the ability to showcase their skills, and (2) employers have shifted from "I need to hire a person" to "I need to complete a task."

Companies may hire contingent workers when full-timers are on some type of leave (such as parental leave), when there is a peak demand for labour or products (like the holiday shopping season), or when quick service to customers is a priority. Companies also tend to hire more contingent workers in an uncertain economy, particularly when they are available and qualified, and when the jobs require minimal training.

Contingent workers receive few benefits; they are rarely offered health insurance, vacation time, or company pensions. They also tend to earn less than permanent workers do. On the positive side, some on temporary assignments may be offered full-time employment. Managers see using temporary workers as a way of weeding out poor workers and finding good hires. Experts say temps are filling openings in an increasingly broad range of jobs, from unskilled manufacturing and distribution positions to middle management. Increasing numbers of contingent workers are educated professionals such as accountants, attorneys, and engineers.

Many companies include college and university students in their contingent workforce plan. Working with temporary staffing agencies, companies have easier access to workers who have already been screened. Of course, temp agencies benefit students as well. Once the agencies have assessed the workers, their information is entered into their databases. Then when students are coming back in town for vacations or whatever,

© Ian Allenden/Alamy RF

Traditionally, unpaid internships have been a great way for young people to gain work experience. What are the advantages and disadvantages for both employees and employers? Under what conditions are unpaid internships illegal in Canada? Is it ethical for companies to use unpaid interns if they know they will not have any jobs to offer at the end of the internships or if the unpaid internships replace paid jobs? Why or why not?

they can call the agency and ask them to put their names into the system for work assignments. There is no need to spend time searching for openings or running around town for interviews. In an era of rapid change and economic uncertainty, some contingent workers have even found that temping can be more secure than full-time employment.

PROGRESS ASSESSMENT

- What are the six steps in the selection process?
- How can you use social media to your best advantage when searching for a job?
- Who is considered a contingent worker, and why do companies hire such workers?

training and development
All attempts to improve productivity by increasing an employee's ability to perform. Training focuses on short-term skills, whereas development focuses on long-term abilities.

orientation
The activity that introduces new employees to the organization; to fellow employees; to their immediate supervisors; and to the policies, practices, values, and objectives of the firm.

Training and Developing Employees for Optimum Performance

The term **training and development** includes all attempts to improve productivity by increasing an employee's ability to perform. A well-designed training program often leads to higher retention rates, increased productivity, and greater job satisfaction. Employers find that spending money on training is usually money well spent. *Training* focuses on short-term skills, whereas *development* focuses on long-term abilities. Both include three steps: (1) assessing organization needs and employee skills to determine training needs; (2) designing training activities to meet identified needs; and (3) evaluating the training's effectiveness. As technology and other innovations change the workplace, companies must offer training programs that often are quite sophisticated. Some common training activities are employee orientation, on-the-job training, apprenticeships, off-the-job training, online training, vestibule training, and job simulation. Management development will be discussed in a separate section.

© M. Spencer Green/AP Images

At FedEx, time is money. That's why the company spends six times more on employee training than the average firm. Does the added expense pay off? You bet. FedEx enjoys a remarkably low 4 percent employee turnover rate. Should other companies follow FedEx's financial commitment to training? Explain.

Orientation is the activity that initiates new employees to the organization; to fellow employees; to their immediate supervisors; and to the policies, practices, values, and objectives of the firm. Orientation programs range from informal talks to formal activities that last a day or more and often include scheduled activities to various departments and required reading of company handbooks. For example, at online retailer Zappos, every new employee must spend two weeks answering customer calls, two weeks learning in a classroom, and a week shipping boxes in the company's fulfillment centre.[23]

Courtesy of LiUNA. Used with permission

The Labourers' International Union of North America (LiUNA) is the most progressive, aggressive, and fastest growing union representing construction workers in all sectors of construction, waste management workers, show service workers, health-care workers, and manufacturing and building supply workers in Canada. Here at the LiUNA Local 183 Training Centre, Asphalt Program, the class is building additional parking spaces at the Vaughan, Ontario training site. Have you considered an apprentice program?

On-the-job training lets the employee learn by doing, or by watching others for a while and then imitating them, right at the workplace. Salespeople, for example, are often trained by watching experienced salespeople perform (often called *shadowing*). Naturally, this can be either quite effective or disastrous, depending on the skills and habits of the person being watched. On-the-job training is the easiest kind of training to implement when the job is relatively simple (such as clerking in a store) or repetitive (such as collecting refuse, cleaning carpets, or mowing lawns). More demanding or intricate jobs require a more intense training effort. Technology makes cost-effective on-the-job training programs available 24 hours a day. Online systems can monitor workers' input and give them instructions if they become confused about what to do next.

In **apprentice programs**, a trainee works alongside an experienced employee to master the skills and procedures of a craft. Some apprentice programs involve classroom training. Labour unions in skilled crafts, such as bricklaying and plumbing, require a new worker to serve as an apprentice for several years to ensure excellence among their members as well as to limit entry to the union. Workers who successfully complete an apprenticeship earn the classification *journeyman.* As Baby Boomers retire from skilled trades such as pipefitting, welding, and carpentry, shortages of trained workers are developing. Skills Canada, a group that promotes careers in skilled trades and technologies, estimates almost half of new jobs created in the next decade will be in skilled trades, but only 26 percent of young people are considering that type of career.[24] Apprentice programs may be shortened to prepare people for skilled jobs in changing industries, such as auto repair and aircraft maintenance, that require increased knowledge of computer technology.

Off-the-job training occurs away from the workplace and consists of internal or external programs to develop any of a variety of skills or to foster personal development. Training is becoming more sophisticated as jobs become more sophisticated. Furthermore, training is expanding to include education (e.g., through a PhD, a postgraduate doctoral degree) and personal development. Subjects may include time management, stress management, health and wellness, physical education, nutrition, and even art and languages.

Online training demonstrates how technology is improving the efficiency of many off-the-job training programs. Online training's key advantage is the ability to provide a large number of employees with consistent content tailored to specific training needs at convenient times. Both non-profit and profit-seeking businesses make extensive use of online training. Most colleges and universities offer a wide variety of online classes, sometimes called *distance learning.* Technology giants like EMC and large manufacturers like Timken use the online training tool GlobeSmart to teach employees how to operate in different cultures.[25]

on-the-job training
Training at the workplace that lets the employee learn by doing or by watching others for a while and then imitating them.

apprentice programs
Training programs during which a learner works alongside an experienced employee to master the skills and procedures of a craft.

off-the-job training
Internal or external training programs away from the workplace that develop any of a variety of skills or foster personal development.

online training
Training programs in which employees complete classes via the Internet.

vestibule training
Training done in schools where employees are taught on equipment similar to that used on the job.

job simulation
The use of equipment that duplicates job conditions and tasks so that trainees can learn skills before attempting them on the job.

Vestibule training (or *near-the-job training*) is done in classrooms with equipment similar to that used on the job so that employees learn proper methods and safety procedures before assuming a specific job assignment. Computer and robotics training is often completed in a vestibule classroom.

Job simulation is the use of equipment that duplicates job conditions and tasks so that trainees can learn skills before attempting them on the job. It differs from vestibule training in that it duplicates the *exact* combination of conditions that occur on the job. This is the kind of training given to astronauts, airline pilots, army tank operators, ship captains, and others who must learn difficult procedures off the job. Virtual reality devices are used in medical facilities where doctors in training practice their skills before working with real life patients.[26]

Management Development

Managers often need special training. To be good communicators, they need to learn listening skills and empathy. They also need time management, planning, and human relations skills.

management development
The process of training and educating employees to become good managers, and then monitoring the progress of their managerial skills over time.

Management development, then, is the process of training and educating employees to become good managers and then monitoring the progress of their managerial skills over time. Management development programs are widespread, especially at colleges, universities, and private management development firms. Managers participate in role-playing exercises, solve various management cases, and attend films and lectures to improve their skills.

Management development is increasingly being used as a tool to accomplish business objectives. General Electric's and Procter & Gamble's management teams were built with significant investment in their development.[27] Most management training programs include several of the following:[28]

© Patrick T. Fallon/Bloomberg/Getty Images

On simulated training courses like this one, firefighters learn how to deal with the dangers of a burning building while remaining out of harm's way. This allows firefighters to learn all the fine details about their jobs so they'll be ready when the real thing happens. What other professions do you think could benefit from simulation training?

- *On-the-job coaching.* A senior manager assists a lower-level manager by teaching needed skills and providing direction, advice, and helpful feedback.
- *Understudy positions.* Job titles such as *undersecretary* and *assistant* are part of a relatively successful way of developing managers. Selected employees work as assistants to higher-level managers and participate in planning and other managerial functions until they are ready to assume such positions themselves.
- *Job rotation.* Managers are often given assignments in a variety of departments so that they can learn about different functions of the organization. Such job rotation gives them the broad picture of the organization they need to succeed. The chapter profile highlights Linamar's program. Job rotation is also valuable when starting out. For example, Loblaw Companies Limited created Grad@Loblaw, a rotational program for new graduates that covers multiple streams including store

management, supply chain, merchandising, marketing, IT, finance, and HR.[29]

- *Off-the-job courses and training.* Managers periodically go to classes or seminars off-site to hone technical and human relations skills. McDonald's Corporation has its own Hamburger University. Managers and potential franchisees attend six days of classes and complete a course of study equivalent to 36 hours of business-school credit.[30]

© Wavebreakmedia Ltd/Thinkstock

Management development can include on-the-job and off-the-job training. The activities will vary depending on the person being developed and the purpose of the program.

EMPOWERING WORKERS

Historically, many managers gave explicit instructions to workers, telling them what to do to meet the goals and objectives of the organization. The term for such an approach is *directing*. In traditional organizations, directing involves giving assignments, explaining routines, clarifying policies, and providing feedback on performance. Many organizations still follow this model, especially in firms such as fast-food restaurants and small retail establishments where the employees do not have the skills and experience needed to work on their own, at least at first.

Progressive managers, such as those in many high-tech firms and Internet companies, are less likely than traditional managers to give specific instructions to employees. Rather, they are more likely to empower employees to make decisions on their own. Empowerment means giving employees the *authority* (the right to make a decision without consulting the manager) and *responsibility* (the requirement to accept the consequences of one's actions) to respond quickly to customer requests. Managers are often reluctant to give up the power they have to make such decisions; thus, empowerment is often resisted. In those firms that are able to implement the concept, the manager's role is becoming less that of a boss and director and more that of a coach, assistant, counsellor, or team member.

Cisco Canada has been listed on Aon Hewitt's *Best Employers in Canada* study. "Cisco has a culture of improvement," says David Clarkson, Director of Human Resources. He attributes the company's success to employee engagement, where hiring those with the right approach to life is essential. "We're looking for candidates with enthusiasm—they need to be passionate about something in their lives," says Clarkson. "We find that same passion often carries over into their work." Willa Black, Cisco Canada's Vice-President, states that employees are self-starters who don't need to be micromanaged: "We communicate from the top down—as well as from the bottom up and the middle out. But employees control their own destiny. They know what they need to do to succeed as individuals as well as how to help the company succeed."[31]

© Stuart Miles/Shutterstock

Have you worked for a manager that acted less like a boss and more like a coach? Looking ahead, will you ask about the level of empowerment in any future jobs? Is this autonomy important to you?

© Caiaimage/Sam Edwards/Getty Images

Networking provides you with an array of personal contacts on whom you can call for career advice and help. Have you begun creating your network yet? Are you part of someone else's network?

Networking

Networking is the process of establishing and maintaining contacts with key managers in your own organization and other organizations, and using those contacts to weave strong relationships that serve as informal development systems. Of equal or greater importance may be a **mentor**, a corporate manager who supervises, coaches, and guides selected lower-level employees by introducing them to the right people and generally acting as their organizational sponsor. In most organizations, informal mentoring occurs as experienced employees assist less experienced workers. However, many organizations formally assign mentors to employees considered to have strong potential.[32] Some companies, such as Sodexo Canada, also think globally. It organizes an international mentorship program that pairs new graduates with overseas mentors for a week in that country.[33]

networking
The process of establishing and maintaining contacts with key managers within and outside the organization, and using those contacts to weave strong relationships that serve as informal development systems.

mentor
An experienced employee who supervises, coaches, and guides lower-level employees by introducing them to the right people and generally being their organizational sponsor.

Companies have found that mentoring programs provide a number of benefits: (1) improved recruiting and retention, (2) more engaged employees, (3) cost savings, and (4) increased skills and better attitudes.[34] Randstad Canada's survey, *From Y to Z – A Guide to the Next Generation of Employees,* reports that Gen Y (also known as Millennials) and Gen Z not only welcome a mentoring approach to support their advancement, it's one of their highest priorities.[35] As a result, managers should keep the communication lines open so employees can ask questions and receive constructive advice. As well, employees should be encouraged to attend webinars, take part in industry networking activities, and do some job shadowing. Finally, managers should show these younger generations how their work fits into the big picture and brings value to the team and to the organization.[36] As discussed in Chapter 11, each generation is motivated by different approaches. A targeted training and development program is one way to communicate that these employees are valuable resources.

It's also important to remember that networking and mentoring go beyond the business environment. For example, school is a perfect place to begin networking. Associations you nurture with instructors, with local business people through internships, and especially with your classmates might provide you with a valuable network you can turn to for the rest of your career.

Diversity in Management Development

As women moved into management, they also learned the importance of networking and of having mentors. Unfortunately, women often have more difficulty than men in networking or finding mentors, since most senior managers are male. More women are now entering established networking systems or, in some instances, creating their own. Some examples of organizations include the Canadian Women's Business Network, Women's Enterprise Centre, and Canadian Association of Women Executives & Entrepreneurs.

Selected as one of Canada's Best Diversity Employers, TD Bank has a formal diversity strategy targeted to women, those with disabilities, visible minorities, Aboriginal people, and the lesbian, gay, bisexual and transgender (LGBT) peoples. Specific initiatives include the following:[37]

- TD employs a Manager of Aboriginal Talent Acquisition that is responsible for establishing relationships with schools, student centres, and Aboriginal community organizations, as well as working with its Bank's Aboriginal Circle and Aboriginal Banking Unit to support recruitment and employee referrals;
- As a result of employee and customer feedback, TD Bank works to further incorporate diverse groups in advertising materials; and
- Maintaining 11 regional LGBT employee resource groups across Canada and the enterprise-wide LGBTA Pride Network with nearly 3000 members.

Courtesy of CIBC. Used with permission

One of Canada's Best Diversity Employers, CIBC has a diversity and inclusion program with a focus on attracting, motivating, and retaining a qualified workforce that represents the diversity of its clients and communities. Would you seek out a company that has been recognized for its diversity initiatives?

Companies that take the initiative to develop female and minority managers understand three crucial principles: (1) grooming women and minorities for management positions is not about legality, morality, or even morale but rather about bringing more talent in the door—the key to long-term profitability; (2) the best women and minorities will become harder to attract and retain, so the companies that commit to development early have an edge; and (3) having more women and minorities at all levels lets businesses serve their female and minority customers better. If you do not have a diversity of people working in the back room, how are you going to satisfy the diversity of people coming in the front door?

performance appraisal
An evaluation that measures employee performance against established standards in order to make decisions about promotions, compensation, training, or termination.

PROGRESS ASSESSMENT

- What are the five steps in the selection process?
- List four benefits to companies that provide mentoring programs.
- Can you name and describe four training and four development techniques?

LO4

Trace the six steps in appraising employee performance, and summarize the objectives of employee compensation programs.

Appraising Employee Performance to Get Optimum Results

Managers must be able to determine whether their workers are doing an effective and efficient job, with a minimum of errors and disruptions. They do this by using a **performance appraisal**, an evaluation that measures employee performance against established standards in order to make decisions about promotions, compensation, training, or termination. Performance appraisals have six steps:

1. *Establishing performance standards.* This is a crucial step. Standards must be understandable, subject to measurement, and reasonable. Both managers and subordinates must accept them.
2. *Communicating standards.* It's dangerous to assume that employees know what is expected of them. They must be told clearly and precisely what the standards and expectations are and how to meet them.
3. *Evaluating performance.* If the first two steps are done correctly, performance evaluation is relatively easy. It is a matter of evaluating the employee's behaviour to see whether it matches standards.
4. *Discussing results.* Employees often make mistakes and fail to meet expectations at first. It takes time to learn a job and do it well. Discussing an employee's successes and areas that need improvement can provide managers an opportunity to be understanding and helpful and guide the employee to better performance. The performance appraisal can also allow employees to suggest how a task could be done better. Figure 12.4 illustrates how managers can make performance appraisals more meaningful.
5. *Taking corrective action.* As part of the performance appraisal, a manager can take corrective action or provide corrective feedback to help the employee perform better. The key word is *perform.* The primary purpose of an appraisal is to improve employee performance, if possible.
6. *Using the results to make decisions.* Decisions about promotions, compensation, additional training, or firing are all based on performance evaluations. (Be aware that sometimes new hires and promotions are also influenced by other factors such as a family connection or whether the employee is particularly liked by his or her supervisor. Make sure that decisions are based on the performance evaluation.) An effective performance-appraisal system is also a way of satisfying legal requirements about such decisions.

FIGURE 12.4

CONDUCTING EFFECTIVE APPRAISALS AND REVIEWS

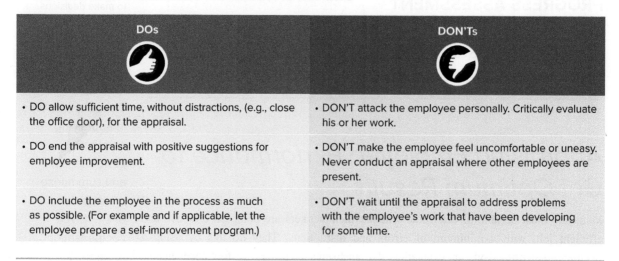

DOs	DON'Ts
• DO allow sufficient time, without distractions, (e.g., close the office door), for the appraisal.	• DON'T attack the employee personally. Critically evaluate his or her work.
• DO end the appraisal with positive suggestions for employee improvement.	• DON'T make the employee feel uncomfortable or uneasy. Never conduct an appraisal where other employees are present.
• DO include the employee in the process as much as possible. (For example and if applicable, let the employee prepare a self-improvement program.)	• DON'T wait until the appraisal to address problems with the employee's work that have been developing for some time.

Managing effectively means getting results through top performance. That's what performance appraisals are for all levels of the organization, including at the top, where managers benefit from performance reviews by their subordinates and peers. In the *360-degree review,* for example, management gathers opinions from those around the employee, including those under, above, and on the same level, to get an accurate, comprehensive idea of the worker's abilities.

Many companies such as General Electric, Kimberly-Clark, and Coca-Cola are moving away from formal annual reviews toward *continuous performance reviews.* This performance management strategy allows workers to receive and give continuous, real-time feedback via mobile apps that are focused on helping employees meet goals—or leave the company faster. These strategies are particularly welcomed by Millennial workers who demand more feedback, more coaching, and a better idea of their career paths.[38]

PROGRESS ASSESSMENT

- What is the primary purpose of a performance appraisal?
- What are the six steps in a performance appraisal?
- Why can employers and employees find the appraisal process so difficult?

Compensating Employees: Attracting and Keeping the Best

Companies do not just compete for customers; they also compete for employees. Compensation is one of the main tools companies use to attract (and retain) qualified employees, and one of their largest operating costs. The long-term success of a firm—perhaps even its survival—may depend on how well it can control employee costs and optimize employee efficiency. Service organizations like hospitals, hotels, and airlines struggle with high employee costs since these firms are *labour intensive* (the primary cost of operations is the cost of labour). Manufacturing firms in the auto and steel industries have asked employees to take reductions in wages (called givebacks) to make the firms more competitive. (We discuss this in Chapter 13.) Those are just a few reasons compensation and benefit packages require special attention. In fact, some experts believe that determining how best to compensate employees is today's greatest human resource challenge.

A carefully managed and competitive compensation and benefits program can accomplish several objectives:

- Attract the kinds of people the organization needs, and in sufficient numbers.
- Provide employees with the incentive to work efficiently and productively.
- Keep valued employees from going to competitors or starting competing firms.
- Maintain a competitive position in the marketplace by keeping costs low through high productivity from a satisfied workforce.
- Provide employees with some sense of financial security through fringe benefits (to be discussed soon) such as insurance and retirement benefits.

© Mayuree Moonhirum/Shutterstock RF

Competitive compensation and benefit programs can have a tremendous impact on employee efficiency and productivity. Sometimes businesses reward exceptional performance by handing out bonuses. Does your instructor ever award bonuses for exceptional performance in class?

Pay Systems

Many companies still use the pay system known as the Hay system, devised by Edward Hay. This compensation plan is based on job grades, each of which has a strict pay range. The system is set up on a point basis with three key factors considered: knowledge, problem solving, and accountability.

The most commonly used pay structure today is market-based.[39] Companies that use *market-based pay structures* compensate people relative to the market value of their job, regardless of their level in the organization. Companies research what other firms are paying and decide to pay either the same, more, or less. The market may suggest, for example, that certain information technology workers should be paid more than their managers because there is a high demand and short supply of skilled tech workers.[40]

The way an organization chooses to pay its employees can have a dramatic effect on efficiency and productivity. Managers therefore look for a system that compensates employees fairly. Figure 12.5 outlines some of the most common pay systems. Which do you think is the fairest?

Compensating Teams

Thus far we have talked about compensating individuals. What about teams? Since you want your teams to be more than simply a group of individuals, would you still compensate them like individuals? Measuring and rewarding individual performance on teams, while at the same time rewarding team performance, is tricky—but it can be done. Professional football players, for example, are rewarded as a team when they go to the playoffs and to the Super Bowl, but they are paid individually as well. Companies are now experimenting with and developing similar incentive systems.

Jay Schuster, coauthor of a study of team pay, found that when pay is based strictly on individual performance, it erodes team cohesiveness and makes the team less likely to meet its goals as a collaborative effort. Skill-based pay and gain-sharing systems are the two most common compensation methods for teams.

Skill-based pay rewards the growth of both the individual and the team. Base pay is raised when team members learn and apply new skills. Baldrige Award winner Eastman Chemical Company rewards its teams for proficiency in technical, social, and business knowledge skills. A cross-functional compensation policy team defines the skills. The drawbacks of skill-based pay are twofold: the system is complex, and it is difficult to relate the acquisition of skills directly to profit gains. The advantages of skill-based pay include improved employee skills and job satisfaction.[41]

Most *gain-sharing systems* base bonuses on improvements over previous performance. Nucor Steel, one of the largest U.S. steel producers, calculates bonuses on quality—tonnes of steel that go out the door with no defects. There are no limits on bonuses a team can earn. One of the drawbacks of basing bonuses on improving previous performance is that

FIGURE 12.5

PAY SYSTEMS

Salary	Fixed compensation computed on weekly, bi-weekly, or monthly pay periods (e.g., $400 per week or $1500 per month). Salaried employees do not receive additional pay for any extra hours worked.
Hourly wage or daywork	Wage based on number of hours or days worked. Used for most blue-collar and clerical workers. Often employees must punch a time clock when they arrive at work and when they leave. Hourly wages vary greatly. This does not include benefits such as retirement systems, which may add 30 percent or more to the total package.
Piecework system	Wage based on the number of items produced rather than by the hour or day. This type of system creates powerful incentives to work efficiently and productively.
Commission plans	Pay based on some percentage of sales. Often used to compensate salespeople, commission plans resemble piecework systems.
Bonus plans	Extra pay for accomplishing or surpassing certain objectives. There are two types of bonuses: monetary and cashless. Money is always a welcome bonus. Cashless rewards include written thank-you notes, appreciation notes sent to the employee's family, movie tickets, flowers, time off, gift certificates, shopping sprees, and other types of recognition.
Profit-sharing plans	Annual bonuses paid to employees based on the company's profits. The amount paid to each employee is based on a predetermined percentage. Profit-sharing is one of the most common forms of performance-based pay.
Gain-sharing plans	Annual bonuses paid to employees based on achieving specific goals such as quality measures, customer satisfaction measures, and production targets.
Cost-of-living allowances (COLAs)	Annual increase in wages based on increases in the Consumer Price Index. This is usually found in union contacts.
Stock options	Right to purchase shares in the company at a specific price over a specific period of time. Often this gives employees the right to buy shares cheaply despite huge increases in the price of the share. For example, if over the course of his employment a worker received options to buy 10 000 shares of the company stock at $10 each and the price of the share eventually grows to $100, he can use those options to buy the 10 000 shares (now worth $1 million) for $100,000.

workers may improve just enough to meet the target, but not by much. Since their target for the next year will be to beat this year's performance, they don't want to risk setting a new goal they won't be able to reach.[42]

It is important to reward individual team players also. Outstanding team players—those who go beyond what is required and make an outstanding individual contribution—should be separately recognized with cash or non-cash rewards. A good way to compensate for uneven team participation is to let the team decide which members get what type of individual award. After all, if you really support the team process, you need to give teams the freedom to reward themselves.

© Fredrick Kippe/Alamy

According to a Randstad Canada study on Gen Y and Gen Z, one in three (32 percent) say health insurance is the most important employee benefit they expect. Other benefits include work flexibility (29 percent), training and development (17 percent), individual performance bonuses (10 percent), a stock purchase plan and profit-sharing program (4 percent), and tuition reimbursement (4 percent).[48] Do you agree with this order? What are ways that companies can highlight their benefit plans when recruiting?

Fringe Benefits

Fringe benefits include sick-leave pay, vacation pay, pension plans, and health plans that represent additional compensation to employees beyond base wages. They may be divided into three categories. Federal and provincial legislation (which varies somewhat from province to province) require compulsory deductions from employees' pay cheques, employer contributions, or both. These *statutory benefits* include the Canada/Quebec Pension Plan, employment insurance, and workers' compensation. The second category consists of *legally required benefits,* including vacation pay, holiday pay, overtime pay, and unpaid maternity leave with job protection. The third category includes *all other benefits* and stems from voluntary employer programs and from collective labour agreements. Some are paid by the employer alone and others are jointly paid by the employer and employee. Among the most common are bonuses, company pension plans, and group insurance.

fringe benefits
Benefits such as sick-leave pay, vacation pay, pension plans, and health plans that represent additional compensation to employees beyond base wages.

Benefits in recent years have grown faster than wages and can't really be considered fringe anymore. According to the Conference Board of Canada, the average cost of providing benefits for employees is $8,330 per full-time equivalent.[43] Farrah Press, VP of Sales and Marketing at Executive Link, states that companies can be widely different in the scope of the plans they can offer. "A large, publicly traded company can offer a more competitive plan than a small private company because the former can afford to and because it has a larger base of employees."[44] "How much you spend depends on the demographics of your company," says Chris Gory, the president of Insurance Portfolio Financial Services Inc., a Toronto-based independent insurance brokerage specializing in employee benefits coverage. "I work with a lot of startups where the average age is between 25 and 32. These employees tend to use a lot of paramedical treatments (massage, chiropractic, and acupuncture treatments, for example) and not as much prescription drug or disability coverage."[45]

Benefits policies can have a significant impact on attracting and retaining high-performing employees.[46] Benefits will not replace performance incentives as motivators, but especially for older generations, health and pension benefits can make a great difference in corporate loyalty.[47] Health-care costs—particularly drug and dental-care costs—are expected to continue to rise as people spend more on health care as they age. The government, which already spends a large percentage of its revenue on health care, will likely continue to shift costs to private plans by limiting and eliminating health services. As a result, employers are trying to control costs in various ways and are making cuts where possible.

For example, two Coburg, Ontario, Tim Hortons franchisees faced public, government, and head office outrage when they cut workers' benefits to offset higher wage costs in response to an increase in the province's minimum wage.[49] In reaction, there were boycotts and protests across the province.[50] Why do you think there was backlash when the franchisees had the legal right to make these changes? Were people outraged because this was undermining the philosophy behind an increase in minimum wage (e.g., supporting minimum-wage workers in Ontario that were struggling to make ends meet)? Do you think the fact that the franchisees were the children of the company's billionaire co-founders contributed to this reaction?[51] Are you surprised to learn that the negative reaction, coupled with franchisee dissatisfaction with Tim Hortons' management and hefty cost-cutting measures, contributed to a drop from 4th place to 50th in an annual ranking of the most-admired companies in Canada?[52] "In the traditional media era the crisis could have been limited geographically," says Christian Bourque, the executive vice president of Leger, the producer of this survey, "but these are different times. At the pace at which bad news hits social media, is then reinterpreted by the masses through the endless game of shares, reputation volatility is clearly upon us."[53]

The workers at DreamWorks Studios who helped create Kung Fu Panda enjoy perks like free breakfast and lunch, afternoon yoga classes, free movie screenings, on-campus art classes, and monthly parties. How might fringe benefits like these affect employee performance?

Fringe benefits can include recreation facilities, company cars, country club memberships, discounted massages, special home-mortgage rates, paid and unpaid sabbaticals, day care services, and executive dining rooms. Increasingly, employees want dental care, mental health care, wellness programs, elder care, legal counselling, eye care, and even short workweeks.[54] Two newer employee benefits are aimed at Millennials: help paying off student loan debt and low-cost loans.[55]

Understanding that it takes many incentives to attract and retain the best employees, companies offer soft benefits. *Soft benefits* help workers maintain the balance between work and family life that is often as important to hardworking employees as the nature of the job itself. These perks include on-site haircuts and shoe repair, concierge services, and free breakfasts. Freeing employees from errands and chores gives them more time for family—and work. Biotechnology firm, Genentech, offers free car washes, Facebook offers free housing for interns, and American Express gives five months of paid parental leave.[56] Varafin Inc., based in St. John's, Newfoundland, offers employees a flexible "no limit" vacation policy.[57] Would you value such benefits?

At one time, most employees sought benefits that were similar. Today, however, some may seek child care benefits while others prefer attractive pension plans. To

Canada's Top 100 Employers

Published annually, *Canada's Top 100 Employers* highlights employers that lead their industries in providing the best benefits and working conditions. You can also read about Canada's top employers for young people. Would you consider these resources when looking for a job?

Reaching *Beyond* OUR BORDERS

Cultural Challenges Working Worldwide

Human resource management of a global workforce begins with understanding the customs, laws, and local business needs of every country in which the organization operates. Country-specific cultural and legal standards can affect a variety of human resource functions:

- *Compensation.* Salaries must be converted to and from foreign currencies. Often employees with international assignments receive special allowances for relocation, children's education, housing, travel, or other business-related expenses.

© JohnnyGreig/Getty Images RF

- *Health and pension standards.* There are different social contexts for benefits in other countries. In the Netherlands, for example, the government provides retirement income and health care.
- *Paid time off.* Four weeks of paid vacation is the standard of many European employers. But many other countries lack the short-term and long-term absence policies offered in Canada, including sick leave, personal leave, family leave, and medical leave. Global companies need a standard definition of *time off.*
- *Taxation.* Each country has different taxation rules, and the payroll department must work within each country's regulations.
- *Communication.* When employees leave to work in another country, they often feel disconnected from their home country. Technology helps keep these faraway employees in direct contact.

Human resource policies at home are influenced more and more by conditions and practices in other countries and cultures. Human resource managers need to sensitize themselves and their organizations to the cultural and business practices.

Sources: Diana Coker, "Efficient Millennial Employees: Crucial Part of Global Workforce," *The HR Digest*, February 12, 2017; and Elaine Varelas, "Tomorrow's Leadership Trends: Bridging the Global Generation Gap in Human Resources," *Human Resources Today*, January 5, 2017.

cafeteria-style fringe benefits
Fringe benefits plan that allows employees to choose which benefits they want up to a certain dollar amount.

address such growing demands, over half of all firms offer **cafeteria-style fringe benefits**, in which employees can choose the benefits they want up to a certain dollar amount. Such plans let human resource managers equitably and cost-effectively meet employees' individual needs by allowing them choice.[58]

As the cost of administering benefits programs has increased, many companies have outsourced this function. Managing benefits can be complicated when employees are located in other countries. HR challenges faced by global businesses are discussed in the Reaching Beyond Our Borders box. To put it simply, benefits are often as important to recruiting top talent as salary and may even become more important in the future.

Scheduling Employees to Meet Organizational and Employee Needs

Workplace trends and the increasing costs of transportation have led employees to look for scheduling flexibility. Flextime, telecommuting, and job sharing are important benefits employees seek with choice being influenced by the type of job, employers' needs, and

FIGURE 12.6

A FLEX-TIME EXAMPLE

At this company, employees can start work anytime between 6:30 and 9:30 a.m. They take a half hour for lunch anytime between 11:00 a.m. and 2:00 p.m., and can leave between 3:00 and 6:30 p.m. Everyone works an eight-hour day. The blue arrows show a typical employee's flextime day.

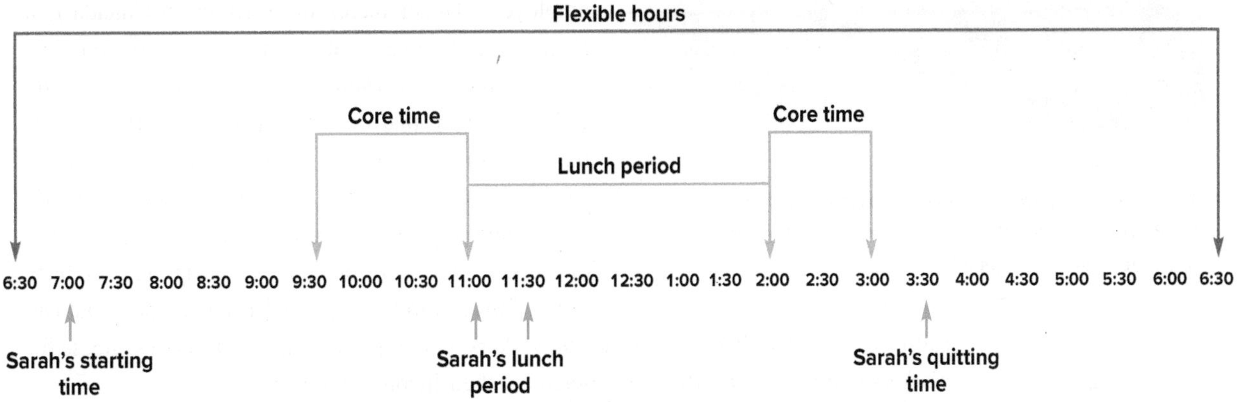

each individual's needs. In fact, 76 percent of Gen Xers surveyed say they look for jobs that allow flexible work schedules and 66 percent of Millennials say they left jobs that didn't support flexible schedules.[59]

Flex-Time Plans

A **flex-time plan** gives employees some freedom to choose which hours to work as long as they work the required number of hours or complete their assigned tasks. The most popular plans allow employees to come to work between 7:00 and 9:00 a.m. and leave between 4:00 and 6:00 p.m. Flex-time plans generally incorporate core time. **Core time** refers to the period when all employees are expected to be at their job stations. For example, an organization may designate core time as 9:00 and 11:00 a.m. and 2:00 and 4:00 p.m. During these hours, all employees are required to be at work, as highlighted in Figure 12.6. Flex-time allows employees to adjust to work–life demands. Two-income families find them especially helpful. Companies that use flex-time say it boosts employee productivity and morale.

flex-time plan
Work schedule that gives employees some freedom to choose when to work, as long as they work the required number of hours.

core time
In a flex-time plan, the period when all employees are expected to be at their job stations.

Flex-time is not for all organizations, however. It doesn't suit shift work, like fast-food or assembly-line processes in manufacturing, where everyone on a given shift must be at work at the same time. Another disadvantage is that managers often have to work longer hours to assist and supervise in organizations that may operate from 6:00 a.m. to 6:00 p.m. Flex-time also makes communication more difficult since certain employees may not be there when others need to talk to them. Furthermore, if not carefully supervised, some employees could abuse the system, causing resentment among others.

Another option is a **compressed workweek**. An employee works the full number of hours, but in fewer than the standard number of days. For example, an employee may work four 10-hour days and then enjoy a long weekend instead of working five 8-hour days

compressed workweek
Work schedule that allows an employee to work a full number of hours per week but in fewer days.

© georgerudy/123RF

Do you know of any retailers that use on-call scheduling? Would this practice discourage you from working for an employer that employs it?

with a traditional weekend. There are obvious advantages of compressed workweeks, but some employees get tired working such long hours, and productivity can decline. Others find the system of great benefit, however, and are enthusiastic about it. Nurses often work compressed weeks.

Flexible scheduling isn't always a benefit to employees. Under increasing scrutiny in Canada is a flexible scheduling strategy used by some retailers called *on-call scheduling* or *in-demand scheduling.* Using software that determines hourly staffing needs based on sales and traffic information, employers can call in or cancel workers with little notice. Based on this technology, chain retailers can adjust the number of workers on the floor quickly during slow or busy times. This flexibility is great for the company but can cause stress on the lives and pay of the workers. On-call scheduling makes it a struggle for workers to arrange their lives or supplement their incomes with second jobs.[60]

Telecommuting

Providing employees with the ability to choose their work location is another opportunity for organizations to demonstrate flexibility. This can include home-based work or working from a client's site. *Telecommuting* (also known as *telework*), can save employers money as the company can get by with less office space. One study also found workers were more productive, got more done, worked longer hours, took fewer breaks, and used less sick time than in-office workers. Home-based workers were also happier and quit less than those who went into the office regularly.[61]

More than 1.7 million paid Canadians employees work from home at least once a week.[62] Home-based workers can choose their own hours, interrupt work for child care or other tasks, and take time out for personal reasons. Working at home isn't for everyone. It requires discipline to stay focused on the job and not be easily distracted.

© stockbroker/123RF

Rising gas prices, technology, and the push for work–life flexibility have all contributed to an increase in telecommuting. What do you think would be your biggest challenge if you worked from home?

Many large companies offer "hotelling" (being assigned to a desk through a reservation system) or "hot-desking" (sharing a desk with other employees who work at different times) as alternatives. Hot-desking can lead to more collaboration since workers get to know more people throughout the organization than they would have at a fixed desk.[63] American Express Canada has moved to a hotelling-style environment where employees are assigned one of four work styles. The majority reserve desks online or work at one of the building's many informal work spaces.[64]

Seeking SUSTAINABILITY

How Employers Can Support Work–Life Balance

Do you find it difficult to balance the different roles in your life? If so, you're not alone as 58 percent of Canadians report "overload" as a result of the pressures associated with work, home and family, friends, physical health, and volunteer and community service. Kevin O'Leary, Chairman of O'Leary Financial Group, agrees that finding the right balance between work and living a life outside of work can be difficult, especially for entrepreneurs. "Unfortunately, this is one of the great sacrifices entrepreneurs have to make because if you're not spending 25 hours a day on your business, your competitor is. And it's not just the Canadian competitor, it's a global competitor," said O'Leary. He says that finding the right partner in life who is willing to ride the journey with you is also important.

Not all employees will have the same work–life balance issues. Baby Boomers will most likely have different issues than Millennials. Age, culture, gender, family and marital status, caregiver demands, socio-economic status, and other factors affect an employee's work–life balance. Those same factors can also influence how individuals are affected by demands. Everyone responds differently to stress. What creates a serious problem for one employee may not be felt in the same way by colleagues.

© Sirikul Thirasuntrakul | Dreamstime.com

To help employees achieve/maintain a sense of work–life balance, Health Canada suggests that employers:

- Identify ways of reducing employee workloads. Employees should be asked for suggestions as they often are in the best position to identify ways of streamlining work.
- Reduce reliance on both paid and unpaid overtime by employees.
- Recognize and reward overtime work.
- Reduce job-related travel time for employees.
- Make alternative work arrangements more widely available within the organization. These might include flextime or the opportunity to work at home for part of the work week.
- Give employees the opportunity to say "no" when asked to work overtime. Saying "no" should not be a career-limiting move. Employees should not have to choose between having a family and career advancement.

More organizations are creating health and welfare committees that are responsible for recognizing health and safety concerns and identifying solutions. Wellness program options include flexible work arrangements such as those discussed in this chapter, leaves of absence and vacation, education and training opportunities, encouraging fitness and healthy living, providing supportive managers, and incorporating other management approaches.

There are many benefits for companies that invest in work–life balance initiatives. These include a reduction in absenteeism, an increase in productivity, decreased stress, and stronger working relationships. In addition, such initiatives help to attract new employees and retain current ones as employees are drawn to organizations that help them find balance and personal satisfaction.

Sources: William Kee, "For entrepreneurs there is no work–life balance: Kevin O'Leary," BNN.ca, March 27, 2015, http://www.bnn.ca/News/2015/3/27/Life-is-very-Darwinian-OLeary.aspx; "Work–Life Balance," Workplace Mental Health Promotion, February 15, 2015, http://wmhp.cmhaontario.ca/workplace-mental-health-core-concepts-issues/issues-in-the-workplace-that-affect-employee-mental-health/work-life-balance; Canadian Mental Health Association, 2015, http://www.cmha.ca/mental-health/your-mental-health/worklife-balance/; and "Workplaces that Work," HRCouncil.ca, [n.d.], http://hrcouncil.ca/hr-toolkit/workplaces-health-safety.cfm.

Job-Sharing Plans

job sharing
An arrangement whereby two part-time employees share one full-time job.

Job sharing lets two or more part-time employees share one full-time job. For instance, students may work only after school hours and parents with small children may work only during school hours, and older workers can work part-time before fully retiring or after retiring. Benefits of job sharing include:

- Employment opportunities for those who cannot or prefer not to work full-time.
- An enthusiastic and productive workforce.
- Reduced absenteeism and tardiness.
- The ability to schedule part-time workers into peak demand periods (e.g., financial institutions on payday).
- Retention of experienced employees who might otherwise have retired.

Disadvantages include having to hire, train, motivate, and supervise at least twice as many people and perhaps prorate some fringe benefits. But firms are finding that the benefits outweigh the disadvantages.

Implementing workplace alternative work arrangements, such as flextime, telecommuting, and job sharing, more widely and where appropriate, would contribute to a better work–life balance. The Seeking Sustainability box offers additional suggestions for employers.

PROGRESS ASSESSMENT

- Can you name and describe four alternative compensation systems?
- What advantages do compensation plans such as profit-sharing offer an organization?
- What are the benefits and challenges of flextime? Telecommuting? Job sharing?

LO5

Describe the ways in which employees can move through a company: promotion, reassignment, termination, and retirement.

Career Management: Up, Over, and Out

Employees do not always stay in the position they were hired to fill. They may excel and move up the corporate ladder or fail and move out the front door. Employees can also be reassigned or retire. Of course, some choose to move themselves by going to another company.

Promoting and Reassigning Employees

Many companies find that promotion from within the company improves employee morale. It is also cost-effective in that the promoted employees are already familiar with the corporate culture and procedures and don't need to spend valuable time on basic orientation.

In the new, flatter corporate structures identified in Chapter 9, there are fewer levels for employees to reach than in the past. Thus they often move *over* to a new position rather than *up* to a new one. Such lateral transfers allow employees to develop and display new skills and to learn more about the company overall. Reassignment is one way of motivating experienced employees to remain in a company that offers limited upward advancement opportunities.

© Steve Cole/Getty Images

When there is a downturn in the economy, managers sometimes terminate employees. Do you think they will rehire full-time employees when the economy recovers? Why or why not? What alternatives do employers have?

Terminating Employees

We have seen that the relentless pressure of global competition, shifts in technology, increasing customer demands for greater value, and uncertain economic conditions have human resource managers struggling to manage layoffs and firings. For terminated senior managers, companies usually pay for private-agency career counselling.

Even if the economy is booming, many companies are hesitant to hire or rehire workers full-time. Why is that the case? One reason is that the cost of terminating employees is prohibitively high in terms of lost training costs and possible damages and legal fees for wrongful discharge suits. (This is also why it is critical to have a good system of verbal and written notices and record keeping to deal with poorly performing employees.) As a result, many companies are either using temporary employees or outsourcing certain functions.

Retiring Employees

Companies looking to downsize sometimes offer early retirement benefits to entice older (and more expensive) workers to retire. Such benefits can include one-time cash payments, known in some companies as *golden handshakes.* The advantage early retirement benefits have over layoffs or firing is the increased morale of remaining employees. Retiring senior workers earlier also increases promotion opportunities for younger employees.

Losing Valued Employees

In spite of a company's efforts to retain them, some talented employees will choose to pursue opportunities elsewhere. Knowing their reasons for leaving can be invaluable in preventing the loss of other good people in the future. One way to learn the reasons is to have an outside expert conduct an *exit interview.* Outsiders can provide confidentiality and anonymity that earns more honest feedback than employees are comfortable giving in face-to-face interviews with their supervisors. Online systems can capture, track, and statistically analyze employee exit interview data to generate reports that identify trouble areas. Such programs can also coordinate exit interview data with employee satisfaction surveys to predict which departments should expect turnover to occur.

Offboarding is the process surrounding employee exits. Whether employees are fired, resigning or retiring, there are things that need to be done before they leave. This includes managing payments, insurance, and benefits; conducting exit interviews; collecting work and documents; and returning anything owned by the company.

Attracting and retaining the best employees is the key to success in the competitive global business environment. Changes in laws have also had a major influence. Let's look at this next.

LO6

Illustrate the effects of legislation on human resource management.

Laws Affecting Human Resource Management[65]

The Charter of Rights and Freedoms, which is part of the Constitution of Canada, guarantees equality before the law for every Canadian. The Human Rights Act seeks to provide equal employment opportunities without regard to race and colour, national or ethnic origin, religion, age, sex, sexual orientation, marital status, family status, disability, or pardoned convictions. Human rights legislation requires that every employer ensure equal opportunities and that there is no discrimination. This legislation affects nearly every human resource function (which includes planning, recruiting, selection, training, and compensation) and it has made managing these activities more complicated. This is true in both a non-union environment, which is governed by these laws and regulations, and a union environment, which must also reflect the conditions outlined in the labour contract (to be discussed in Chapter 13).

Since Canada is a confederation of provinces and territories, jurisdiction over many aspects of our lives is divided between the federal and provincial governments. The federal government legislates on national issues (e.g., employment insurance) and it has jurisdiction over certain types of businesses that are deemed to be of a national nature. Federally regulated businesses and industries are defined by the Canada Labour Code. The Canada Labour Code applies to approximately 18 000 employers and 900 000 of their employees, accounting for 6 percent of all Canadian workers. Examples of organizations that are regulated under federal jurisdiction include banks, insurance companies, communications companies, interprovincial transportation companies (e.g., airlines, rail, and trucking companies), many First Nation activities, and most federal Crown corporations.

© Khakimullin Aleksandr/Shutterstock

Older employees are guaranteed protection against age discrimination in the workplace. Coupled with the elimination of a mandatory retirement age, these employees have more opportunities to retire later. What are workplace benefits in keeping these workers?

Provincial or territorial labour laws outline employment standards that apply to the majority (94 percent) of employees. This includes employment standards in areas such as minimum wage, hours of work, overtime, statutory holidays, parental leave, employment of people under 18 years of age, and discrimination in the workplace.

What all of this means is that there are hundreds of laws and regulations at different levels of government that apply to all aspects of human resource management. Furthermore, these laws are constantly being revised because of the changing social and political environments, as well as rulings by human rights commissions and courts. One of the most regulated areas involves discrimination.

Pay Equity[66]

Pay equity refers to equal pay for work of equal value. It compares the value of male and female jobs by objectively evaluating the jobs in terms of four neutral factors: skill, effort, responsibility, and working conditions. If a female job is approximately equal in value to a higher-paying job done mainly by men, the female job gets the same wages as the male job.

pay equity Equal pay for work of equal value.

The **gender wage gap** is the difference between wages earned by men and wages earned by women. On average, Canadian women earn less than men. The persistent wage gap that women face, combined with fewer hours of work (women are more likely to work part-time then men), make for a significant earnings gap. In Canada, estimates for the pay equity gap vary from 8 to 50 percent, and it depends on what is being measured.[67] For example, Statistics Canada states that women continue to earn on average 74 cents for every dollar men earn.[68] Historical factors that have contributed to the gender wage gap include the following:

gender wage gap The difference between wages earned by men and wages earned by women.

- Women choosing or needing to leave and re-enter the workforce to meet family caregiving responsibilities, resulting in a loss of seniority, advancement opportunities, and wages.
- Occupational segregation in historically undervalued and low-paying jobs, such as child care and clerical work.
- Women are overrepresented in low-paying occupations and underrepresented in high-paying ones.
- Traditionally lower levels of education (although this is becoming less of a factor as more women graduate from all levels of education).
- Less unionization among female workers.
- Discrimination in hiring, promotion, and compensation practices in the workplace.

Today, women are more educated, they are working in greater numbers and for longer hours, they are having fewer children, and they are taking less time away from work. Despite these changes, women's hourly wages continue to fall below men's wages at all levels of education. Generally speaking, the wage gap between men and women has been narrowing as education level rises.

© Monalyn Gracia/Fancy/age fotostock RF

Studies have shown that women's jobs with the same value as men's work are underpaid. What actions can you take once you are in the workforce to close this gap?

Canada has a variety of pay equity laws and policies that differ depending on where one works. For some organizations,

© michaeljung/Shutterstock

The Employment Equity Act promotes equitable representation for women, Aboriginal peoples, persons with disabilities, and visible minorities who work in federally regulated workplaces. If you belong to one of these groups, would you consider employment in these workplaces? If you do not belong to one of these groups, would employment equity programs discourage you from applying to these workplaces?

legislation has been difficult to implement. How do you define equal (or comparable) value? For example, which job has more value, that of a nurse or that of a trash collector? As well, officials cite budget cutbacks and the huge costs of making up for past inequitable compensation to female employees as the reasons for delaying the implementation of this legislation. As you can imagine, this is not an issue that can easily be resolved.

Employment Equity[69]

A well-known 1980s case of discrimination highlights a major problem and how it was solved. A group of women accused Canadian National Railway Company (CNR) of not hiring them because they were women. CNR, like many other companies, did not hire women for jobs that were thought to be traditional men's jobs, those for which heavy physical labour was required. In this case, the jobs involved maintenance and repairs of the tracks. The Canadian Human Rights Commission ruled in favour of the women. CNR appealed the decision and the courts ruled against CNR all the way to the Supreme Court of Canada.

employment equity Employment activities designed to increase employment opportunities for four groups (women, Aboriginal people, persons with disabilities, and members of visible minorities) given past discrimination.

Employment equity refers to employment activities designed to increase employment opportunities for four groups given past discrimination toward the designated groups. These four groups are (1) women; (2) Aboriginal peoples (people who are Indian, Inuit, or Métis); (3) persons with disabilities; and (4) members of visible minorities (people, other than Aboriginal peoples, who are non-Caucasian in race or non-white in colour). Employment equity programs are developed by employers to remedy past discrimination or to prevent discrimination in the future. Employment equity "encourages the establishment of working conditions that are free of barriers, corrects the conditions of disadvantage in employment, and promotes the principle that employment equity requires special measures and the accommodation of differences for the four designated groups in Canada." Introduced in 1986, the Employment Equity Act applies to federally regulated industries, Crown corporations, and other federal organizations with 100 employees or more, as well as portions of the federal public administration. At the provincial level, these programs are implemented almost exclusively on a voluntary basis.

How did this apply in the CNR example? The Canadian Human Rights Commission ordered CNR to develop a plan that would result in more women than men being hired for such jobs until the balance was more even. Specifically, women had to be hired for one in four non-traditional or blue-collar jobs in its St. Lawrence region until women held 13 percent of such jobs. When a man and a woman were equally qualified, the woman was expected to be selected until the balance was achieved.

Interpretation of the employment equity law eventually led employers to actively recruit and give preference to women and minority group members. Employment equity, for many employers, has become mostly a reporting function. They keep track of the numbers of employees that belong to these groups, and they try to remove any discrimination from hiring procedures, including trying to advertise positions more widely. As you might expect, interpretation of the law is often controversial and enforcement is difficult. Questions persist about the effect the program could have in creating a sort of reverse discrimination in the workplace.

Reverse discrimination has been defined as discriminating against members of a dominant or majority group (say, whites or males) usually as a result of policies designed to correct previous discrimination against minorities or disadvantaged groups. Charges of reverse discrimination have occurred when companies have been perceived as unfairly giving preference to women or minority group members, for example, in hiring and promoting. The Canadian Charter of Rights and Freedoms specifically allows for employment equity as a method to overcome long-standing discrimination against specific groups. Although preferential treatment will always raise questions of fairness, the Canadian Human Rights Act declares employment equity programs non-discriminatory if they fulfill the spirit of the law. This continues to be a controversial issue today.

reverse discrimination Discriminating against members of a dominant or majority group (say, whites or males) usually as a result of policies designed to correct previous discrimination against minority or disadvantaged groups.

Laws that Protect the Disabled

Legislation protects people with disabilities. Businesses cannot discriminate against people on the basis of any physical or mental disability. Employers are required to give disabled applicants the same consideration for employment as people without disabilities. Employers used to think that being fair meant treating everyone the same, but *accommodation* means treating people *according to their specific needs.* That can include putting up barriers to isolate people readily distracted by noise, reassigning workers to new tasks, and making changes to supervisors' management styles. Accommodations are not always expensive; for example, an inexpensive headset can allow someone with cerebral palsy to talk on the phone.

Effects of Legislation

Clearly, laws and regulations affect all areas of human resource management. It should be apparent that a career in this field offers a challenge to anyone willing to put forth the effort. Figure 12.7 lists some sites that you may consult to learn about some of the topics discussed in this chapter. In summary:

- Employers must know and act in accordance with the legal rights of their employees or risk costly court cases.
- Legislation affects all areas of human resource management, from hiring and training to compensation.
- Managers must be sensitive not only to legal requirements, but also to union contracts and social standards and expectations, which can be even more demanding.
- Court cases demonstrate that it is sometimes legal to implement special employment policies (e.g., employment equity) and training to correct past discrimination.
- New court cases and legislation change human resource management almost daily. The only way to keep current is to read business literature and stay familiar with emerging issues.

FIGURE 12.7

HUMAN RESOURCE INFORMATION SITES

Human Resource Sites	URL
Benefits Canada	www.benefitscanada.com
Chartered Professionals in Human Resources	www.chrp.ca
Canadian HR Reporter	www.hrreporter.com
Canadian Human Rights Reporter	www.cdn-hr-reporter.ca
The Conference Board of Canada	www.conferenceboard.ca
Human Resources Professionals Association	www.hrpa.ca
Society for Human Resource Management	www.shrm.org
Government Sites	**URL**
Canadian Human Rights Commission	www.chrc-ccdp.ca
Government of Canada	www.canada.gc.ca
Statistics Canada	www.statcan.gc.ca

PROGRESS ASSESSMENT

- Name three areas of human resource management responsibility that are affected by government legislation.
- Explain what employment equity is and give one example of it.
- What are ways employers can accommodate people with disabilities?

SUMMARY

LO1 Explain the importance of human resource management as a strategic contributor to organizational success, and summarize the five steps in human resource planning.

Human resource management is the process of evaluating human resource needs, finding people to fill those needs, and getting the best work from each employee by providing the right incentives and job environment, all with the goal of meeting organizational objectives.

What are current challenges and opportunities in human resource management?

Many current challenges and opportunities arise from changing demographics: more women, minorities, immigrants, and older workers in the workforce. Others include a shortage of trained workers and an abundance of unskilled workers, skilled workers in declining industries requiring retraining, changing employee work attitudes, and complex laws and regulations.

What are the five steps in human resource planning?

The five steps are (1) preparing a human resource inventory of the organization's employees; (2) preparing a job analysis; (3) assessing future demand; (4) assessing future supply; and (5) establishing a strategic plan.

LO2 **Describe methods that companies use to recruit new employees, and explain some of the issues that make recruitment challenging.**

Recruitment is the set of activities used to obtain a sufficient number of the right people at the right time.

What methods do companies use to recruit new employees?

Recruiting sources are classified as either internal or external. Internal sources include hiring from within the firm (e.g., transfers and promotions) and employees who recommend others to hire. External recruitment sources include advertisements, public and private employment agencies, school placement offices, management consultants, professional organizations, referrals, walk-in applications, and the Internet.

Why has recruitment become more challenging?

Legal restrictions complicate hiring practices. Finding suitable employees can also be made more difficult if companies are considered unattractive workplaces.

LO3 **Outline the six steps in selecting employees, and illustrate the use of various types of employee training and development methods.**

Selection is the process of gathering and interpreting information to decide which applicants should be hired.

What are the six steps in the selection process?

The steps are (1) obtaining complete application forms; (2) conducting initial and follow-up interviews; (3) giving employment tests; (4) conducting background investigations; (5) obtaining results from physical exams; and (6) establishing a trial period of employment.

What are some employee training methods?

After assessing the needs of the organization and the skills of the employees, training programs are designed that may include the following activities: orientation, on-the-job training, apprentice programs, off-the-job training, online training, vestibule training, and job simulation.

What methods are used to develop managerial skills?

Management development methods include on-the-job coaching, understudy positions, job rotation, and off-the-job courses and training.

How does networking fit in this process?

Networking is the process of establishing contacts with key managers within and outside the organization to get additional development assistance.

LO4 **Trace the six steps in appraising employee performance, and summarize the objectives of employee compensation programs.**

A performance appraisal is an evaluation of the performance level of employees against established standards to make decisions about promotions, compensation, training, or termination.

What are the six steps in appraising employee performance?

The six steps are (1) establish performance standards; (2) communicate those standards; (3) evaluate performance; (4) discuss results; (5) take corrective action when needed; and (6) use the results for decisions about promotions, compensation, training, or termination.

What are examples of compensation systems?

Compensation systems include salary systems, hourly wages, piecework, commission plans, bonus plans, profit-sharing plans, and stock options. The most common compensation systems appropriate for teams are skill-based and gain-sharing compensation programs. Managers also reward outstanding individual performance within teams.

What are objectives of employee compensation programs?

Compensation is one of the main tools that companies use to attract and retain qualified employees. These programs can attract the right kinds of people the organization needs and in sufficient numbers. They provide employees with the incentive to work efficiently and productively. They also provide employees with some sense of financial security through fringe benefits.

What are fringe benefits?

Fringe benefits include such items as sick leave, vacation pay, pension plans, and health plans that provide additional compensation to employees beyond base wages. Cafeteria-style fringe benefits plans let employees choose the benefits they want, up to a certain dollar amount.

LO5 **Describe the ways in which employees can move through a company: promotion, reassignment, termination, and retirement.**

Employees do not always stay in the position they were hired to fill.

How can employees move within a company?

Employees can be moved up (promotion), over (reassignment), or out (termination or retirement) of a company. Employees can also choose to leave a company to pursue opportunities elsewhere.

LO6 **Illustrate the effects of legislation on human resource management.**

There are many laws that affect human resource management.

What do the Charter of Rights and Freedoms and the Human Rights Act guarantee?

The Charter of Rights and Freedoms guarantees equality before the law for all Canadians. The Human Rights Act seeks to provide equal employment opportunities without regard to race and colour, national or ethnic origin, religion, age, sex, sexual orientation, marital status, family status, disability, or pardoned convictions.

What areas does the federal government legislate?

The federal government legislates on national issues and it has jurisdiction over certain types of businesses that are deemed to be of a national nature (e.g., banking, air transportation, and many First Nation activities). Federal labour laws apply to 6 percent of all Canadian employees.

What are some examples of employment laws?

Pay equity, employment equity, and laws that protect the disabled are highlighted in this chapter.

KEY TERMS

apprentice programs 447
cafeteria-style fringe benefits 458
compressed workweek 459
contingent workers 444
core time 459
employment equity 466
flex-time plan 459
fringe benefits 456
gender wage gap 465
human resource management (HRM) 434
job analysis 436
job description 437
job sharing 462
job simulation 448
job specifications 437
management development 448
mentor 450

networking 450
off-the-job training 447
online training 447
on-the-job training 447
orientation 446
pay equity 465
performance appraisal 451
recruitment 438
reverse discrimination 467
selection 442
training and development 446
vestibule training 448

CAREER EXPLORATION

If you are interested in pursuing a career in the field of human resource management, here are a few to consider. Find out about the tasks performed, skills needed, pay, and opportunity outlook in these fields through Internet sites that include the Government of Canada Job Bank, Workopolis, Monster, CareerBuilder, Glassdoor, and Indeed, as well as through the Career Centre at your school.

- **Training and development manager**—plans, directs, and coordinates programs to enhance the knowledge and skills of an organization's employees; oversees a staff of training and development specialists.
- **Compensation manager**—plans, develops, and oversees programs to determine how much an organization pays its employees and how employees are paid.
- **Benefits manager**—plans, directs, and coordinates retirement plans, health insurance, and other benefits that an organization offers its employees.
- **Human resource manager**—plans, directs, and coordinates the administrative functions of an organization; oversees the recruiting, interviewing, and hiring of new staff; consults with top executives on strategic planning; and serves as a link between an organization's management and its employees.

CRITICAL THINKING

1. Does human resource management interest you as a career? What are your experiences working with human resource professionals?
2. If you were a human resource manager, how would you address the brain drain that occurs as knowledgeable workers retire?
3. What effects have dual-career families had on the human resource function? How about single-parent families? Are there any similarities?
4. What problems can arise when family members work together in the same firm?
5. Imagine that you must delete a position due to budgetary (not performance) reasons. What effect might the dismissal have on remaining employees? Explain how you would tell the affected employee and your remaining subordinates.
6. What are some implications for employers as a result of legalized recreational marijuana? What changes should employers be making to their alcohol and drug policies?

DEVELOPING CAREER SKILLS

Key: ● **Team** ★ **Analytic** ▲ **Communication** ⊡ **Technology**

⊡★ 1. Look for job listings online and find at least two positions that you might like to have when you graduate. List the qualifications specified in each of the ads and identify methods the companies might use to determine how well applicants meet each of those qualifications.

★▲ 2. Choose one of these positions: a human resource manager notifying employees of mandatory drug testing or an employee representative protesting such testing. Write a memorandum supporting your position.

★● **3.** Consider the following occupations: doctor, car salesperson, computer software developer, teacher, and assembly worker. In a team of three students, identify the method of compensation you think is appropriate for each. Explain your answer.

★▲ **4.** Recall any on-the-job and off-the-job training sessions you've experienced. Write a brief critique of each. How would you improve each? Share your ideas with the class.

●□ ★▲ **5.** The federal government's Temporary Foreign Worker Program touches on both immigration and employment as it permits Canadian employers to hire foreign nationals to fill temporary labour and skill shortages when qualified Canadian citizens or permanent residents are not available.[70] In a group, investigate program advantages and disadvantages to the Canadian economy. Which industries employ these temporary foreign workers? Where in Canada do they work? What are some recent program changes as a result of abuse allegations? Share your information with the class.

ANALYZING MANAGEMENT DECISIONS

Dual-Career Planning

Carey Moler is a 32-year-old account executive for a communications company. She is married to Mitchell Moler, a lawyer. Carey and Mitchell did not make any definite plans about how to juggle their careers and family life until Carey reached age 30. Then they decided to have a baby, and career planning took on a whole new dimension. A company named Catalyst talked to 815 dual-career couples and found that most of them, like the Molers, had not made any long-range career decisions regarding family lifestyle.

From the business perspective, such dual-career families create real concerns. There are problems with relocation, with child care, and so on that affect recruiting, productivity, morale, and promotion policies.

For a couple such as the Molers, having both career and family responsibilities is exhausting. But that is just one problem. If Carey is moving up in her firm, what happens if Mitchell gets a terrific job offer a thousand kilometres away? What if Carey gets such an offer? Who is going to care for the baby? What happens if the baby becomes ill? How do they plan their vacations when there are three schedules to balance? Who will do the housework? Dual careers require careful planning and discussion, and those plans need to be reviewed over time. A couple that decides at age 22 to do certain things may change their minds at age 30. Whether or not to have children, where to locate, how to manage the household—all such issues and more can become major problems if not carefully planned.

The same is true for corporations. They too must plan for dual-career families as well as single-parent families. They must give attention to job sharing, flextime, parental leave policies, transfer policies, nepotism rules (i.e., rules about hiring family members), and more.

Discussion Questions

1. In addition to the examples stated above, what other issues can you see developing because of dual-career families? How is this affecting children in such families?
2. What kind of corporate policies need changing to adapt to these new realities?
3. What are the advantages of dual careers? What are the disadvantages? What can couples do to minimize the problems of dual careers? How can a couple reap the rewards?

CHAPTER 13

Dealing with Employee–Management Issues

LEARNING OBJECTIVES

After you have read and studied this chapter, you should be able to:

LO1 Trace the history of organized labour in Canada.

LO2 Discuss the major legislation affecting labour unions.

LO3 Describe the collective bargaining process.

LO4 Outline the objectives of labour unions.

LO5 Describe the negotiation tactics used by labour and management during conflicts.

LO6 Explain some of today's employee–management issues.

PROFILE

GETTING TO KNOW: GERALD (GERRY) VARRICCHIO, REGIONAL ORGANIZING DIRECTOR FOR CENTRAL AND EASTERN CANADA, LABOURERS' INTERNATIONAL UNION OF NORTH AMERICA (LIUNA)

The Labourers' International Union of North America (LiUNA) is the most progressive, aggressive, and fastest growing union of construction workers, waste management workers, show service workers, and health-care workers in Canada. Although LiUNA began in 1903 as a construction union, its members now work in many types of factories and processing plants. They also work in stores, hotels, restaurants, banquet centres, hospitals, long-care facilities, and offices. An international union with members both in Canada and the United States, LiUNA has over half a million members. In Canada it represents 110 000 members and retirees with affiliates from coast to coast, and the Canadian arm of LiUNA is proud to be a part of one of North America's oldest and most powerful unions.

Gerry Varricchio is an International Representative with LiUNA and a labour organizer. He specializes in the construction industry in the province of Ontario, though he regularly runs campaigns in

Source: Courtesy of LiUNA. Used with permission.

the industrial sector. As the Regional Organizing Director for the LiUNA Central and Eastern Canada Region, Varricchio works with LiUNA's District Councils and Local Unions across Ontario and the Atlantic Provinces. Together, they develop and implement LiUNA's regional and local union organizing plans. This includes training and hiring union organizers as required to meet the needs of each of the organizing plans across the region.

As Regional Organizing Director for CECOF (the Central and Eastern Canada Organizing Fund), Varricchio has 85 regional organizers reporting to him. Contrast this to 1993 when he was the sole regional organizer employed. LiUNA is a highly motivated and powerful unit dedicated to organizing the unorganized and to preserving work for its members, while keeping management competitive. To achieve this goal, Varricchio's vision encompasses a joint, co-operative effort between labour and management. As a result of LiUNA's organizing initiatives through CECOF, and the efforts of Varricchio and the affiliates, LiUNA has the distinct honour of being the most prolific union organizer in Canada.

Varricchio started his working life on the tools, first as a carpenter, and then as a member of LiUNA Local 1089 in his hometown of Sarnia, Ontario, working in "Chemical Valley." He was elected to the LiUNA Local 1089 executive board and as a delegate to the LiUNA Ontario Provincial District Council in 1985, and re-elected every four years subsequently. Experiencing his own health issues as a result of chemical spills in the workplace, Varricchio was personally aware of the difficulties faced in the work environment, including health and safety issues. He recognized early on that some of the major protections for workers are accessible only through unionization. Consequently, when offered a job in 1987 by the LiUNA Ontario Provincial District Council as an organizer, Varricchio jumped at the chance.

In addition to his organizing duties on behalf of LiUNA, Varricchio also serves as a Trustee on the Local 1089 Training and Rehabilitation Trust Fund and on the Benefits Trust Fund. One accomplishment is that he pioneered the first union benefit plan that integrates a registered educational scholarship plan for members and their children into a union benefit trust plan as part of the standard benefit package.

Throughout the past 31 years, Varricchio has adapted to the demands of the workplace. He was at the forefront in introducing the process of "top-down" organizing, a system of engaging the employer in the initial stages of organizing, with the intent of levelling the playing field for all of the employers in the industry. This reassures individual employers who believe that the presence of a union in the workplace will lead to inequalities in terms of bid power and limit their access to future contracts. Varricchio has expressed this as follows: "Unions have a dual responsibility—to ensure that their members are getting the best wage and benefit packages and working conditions available in the marketplace, and equally as important, to ensure that their contractual employers not only remain competitive, but have a labour partner that can assist them in expanding their business and market share."

Managers in both profit-seeking and nonprofit organizations address labour-relations challenges every day. This chapter discusses some of these employee–management relations and issues. When asked what his thoughts are for the future of labour–management relations, Varricchio points out that the labour–management community is at the mercy of the political climate, both federally and provincially as well as to evolving social and cultural influences across the country. It is important for labour and management to partner together to achieve common goals and look out for each other's interests. "Perhaps in spite of the adversarial beginnings between unions and employers and the prejudices that have evolved over time," says Varricchio, "the true business value of unions will be recognized and utilized when it is most needed."

Source: Gerry Varricchio, Regional Organizing Director for the Central and Eastern Canada Organizing Fund, The Labourers' International Union of North America, interview, January 15, 2018, Hamilton.

Employee–Management Issues

Unfortunately, the relationship between managers and employees isn't always trouble-free. Management's responsibility to produce a profit by maximizing productivity sometimes means making hard decisions, which aren't always popular with employees. Employees have long been concerned about fairness, income equality, and workplace security. Like other managerial challenges, employee–management issues require open discussion, goodwill, and compromise. In this chapter, we will look at several key workplace issues that impact the manager's job and workplace environment. This includes unions, harassment, executive compensation, child care, and elder care.

© UFCW

The United Food and Commercial Workers (UFCW) union offers a Young-Workers Internship Program to young members interested in becoming more involved in their union, organizing, labour history, globalization, and more.[4] Would you consider applying for this program? How could the knowledge gained help you during your working career?

One of the major issues in employee–management relations involves labour unions. Labour (the collective term for non-management workers) is interested in fair and competent management, human dignity, and a reasonable share of the wealth its work generates. (One could argue that management is also interested in these same ideals.) A **labour union** is an employee organization whose main goal is representing its members in employee–management negotiations of job-related issues.

According to Statistics Canada, private-sector employees include those who work as employees of a private firm or business.[1]

Public sector employees are those who work for a local, provincial, or federal government; for a government service or agency; for a Crown corporation; or for a government funded establishment such as a school (including universities) or hospital.[2] We often think of union members as workers in the private sector. In fact, union membership in the private sector stands at 16.4 percent compared to 75.5 percent in the public sector.[3]

Workers originally formed unions to protect themselves from intolerable work conditions and unfair treatment, and also to secure some say in the operation of their jobs. As the number of private-sector union members grew, workers gained more negotiating power with managers and more political power. For example, labour unions were largely responsible for the establishment of minimum-wage laws, overtime rules, workers' compensation, severance pay, child-labour laws, job safety regulations, and more. Although labour unions have lost a great deal of the economic and political power they once had, and membership has declined, they still play a significant role in many sectors in some parts of the country.[5]

labour union An employee organization whose main goal is representing its members in employee–management negotiation of job-related issues.

Labour Unions Yesterday and Today

Are labour unions essential today? This is a very political subject with strongly-held opposing positions. An electrician carrying a picket sign in Sudbury, Ontario, would say yes and elaborate on the dangers to a free society if employers continue to try to bust or break apart unions. A small manufacturer would disagree then complain about being restricted by union wage and benefit obligations in an increasingly competitive global economy.

Historians generally agree that today's unions are an outgrowth of the economic transition caused by the Industrial Revolution of the 19th and early 20th centuries. Workers who once toiled in the fields, dependent on the mercies of nature for survival, found themselves relying on the continuous roll of factory presses and assembly lines for their living. Making the transition from an agricultural economy to an industrial economy was quite difficult. Over time, workers in businesses learned that strength through unity (unions) could lead to improved job conditions, better wages, and job security. These improvements did not come easily or quickly. Even today, while both sides have a vested interest in seeing their organizations thrive, the needs and desires of both sides can sometimes be wholly different.

Today's critics of organized labour maintain that few of the inhuman conditions once dominant in Canada exist in the modern workplace. They argue that organized labour is an industry in itself, and protecting workers has become secondary. Some workplace analysts maintain that the current legal system and changing management philosophies minimize the possibility that sweatshops (workplaces of the late 19th and early 20th centuries with unsatisfactory, unsafe, or oppressive labour conditions) could reappear in Canada.

While the technological achievements of the Industrial Revolution brought countless new products to market and reduced the need for physical labour in many industries, they also put pressure on workers to achieve higher productivity in factory jobs that called for long hours and low pay. Can you see how these conditions made it possible for labour unions to take hold by the turn of the 20th century?

"In a perfect world," states Gerry Varricchio, Regional Organizing Director for Central and Eastern Canada for the Labourers' International Union of North America (LiUNA), "labour and management partner together to achieve common goals and look out for each other's interests. Unfortunately, human nature being what it is, greed, incompetence, and self-serving interests of players from one side or the other, or both, can supersede the common good thereby creating conflict and negative perceptions about unions. In any market, competing on a level playing field is extremely important to the success and future growth of a business. The most effective vehicle available to business to create and sustain such a level playing field, is a union. Through the unionized collective bargaining process, competing firms are obligated to follow the same standards and rules."[6]

Let's look at the history of labour unions to see how we got to where we are today.

LO1

Trace the history of organized labour in Canada.

The Early History of Organized Labour

craft union
An organization of skilled specialists in a particular craft or trade; typically local or regional.

The presence of formal labour organizations in Canada dates back to the 1800s. Early unions on the wharves of Halifax, St. John's, and Quebec during the War of 1812 existed to profit from labour scarcity. Others, such as the Montreal shoemakers or the Toronto printers of the 1830s, were craft unions. A **craft union** is an organization of skilled specialists in a particular craft or trade, typically local or regional. These unions were formed to address fundamental work issues of pay, hours, conditions, and job security—many of the same issues that dominate labour negotiations today. By forming a union, these skilled workers hoped to protect their craft and status from being undermined.

Many of the early labour organizations were local or regional in membership. Also, most were established to achieve some short-range goal (e.g., a pay increase) and disbanded after attaining a specific objective. This situation changed dramatically in the late nineteenth century with the expansion of the Industrial Revolution and the emergence of modern industrial capitalism. The system of producing the necessities of society in small, home-based workplaces gave way to production in large factories driven by steam and later electricity. Enormous productivity increases were gained through mass production and job specialization. However, this brought problems for workers in terms of productivity expectations, long hours of work, low wages, and unemployment.

© TorontoPlaques.com

Workers' protests were recorded as early as the 1850s, but it was the need for a shorter work week that sparked Toronto, Ontario printers to walk off the job on March 25, 1872. A crowd of 10 000 supporters rallied at Queen's Park even though union activity was illegal. Prime Minister John A. Macdonald introduced the Trade Union Act on April 18, 1872, legalizing and protecting unions.[7]

Workers were faced with the reality that production was vital. Those who failed to produce, or stayed home because they were ill or had family problems, lost their jobs. Over time, the increased emphasis on production led firms to expand the hours of work. The length of the average workweek in 1900 was 60 hours, compared to 40 hours today, but an 80-hour workweek was not uncommon for some industries. Wages were low and child labour was widespread. Minimum-wage laws and unemployment benefits were non-existent, which meant that periods of unemployment were hard on families who earned subsistence wages. As you can imagine, these were not short-term issues that would easily go away. The workplace was ripe for the emergence of labour organizations.

The struggle for more humane working conditions and wages was not an easy one because before 1872, it was illegal to attempt to form a union in Canada. The pioneers in the early struggles were treated as common criminals. They were arrested, beaten, and often shot. The Winnipeg General Strike of 1919 is Canada's best known general strike, where almost 30 000 workers left their jobs. A charge by police into a crowd of protesters resulted in 30 casualties, including one death.[8]

As the years progressed, more unions were formed and more employees joined them. Other types of unions—such as industrial unions—were created to represent certain workers. An **industrial union** is one that consists of unskilled and semi-skilled workers in mass-production industries such as automobile manufacturing and mining.

Long after it was no longer illegal, the idea of workers forming unions to protect their interests was still regarded with suspicion by employers and governments in Canada. Democratic rights for all was still a weak concept, and the idea of people getting together to fight for their rights was not accepted as it is today. The union movement was greatly influenced by immigrants from Europe (especially Britain), who brought with them the ideas and experiences of a more advanced and often more radical background. The growing union movement in the United States also influenced Canada. Many Canadian unions started as locals of American unions, and this relationship continues today. As democracy gradually gained strength, the union movement grew with it. Its participation, in turn, helped democracy sink deeper, wider roots in Canada.

© Tibor Kolley/CP Images

A legal holiday since 1894, Labour Day is a celebration of workers and their families. (Here you see workers participating in a Labour Day parade.) It was inspired by the first significant workers' demonstration in 1872 where, accompanied by four bands, unionists marched through the streets of Toronto. Leaders demanded better conditions for all workers, as well as the release of 24 union members who were imprisoned for going on strike. About 10 000 Torontonians turned out that day to see the parade and listen to the speeches.

The Structure of Labour Unions in Canada[9]

The organizational structure of unions in Canada is quite complex. There are 776 unions in Canada. The four types of unions and the percentage of workers they represent are as follows: national (69.7 percent), international, (24.9 percent), independent local (3.9 percent), and directly chartered (1.5 percent). Let's consider these four types next.

The most basic unit is an **independent local organization** (also called the *union local, local,* or *local union*), which is a union that is not formally connected or affiliated with any other labour organization. One local usually represents one school, government office, or a specific factory or office of a company. However, that local can also cover several small companies or other work units.

Contrast this with a **directly chartered union**, which is a union that is directly affiliated to a labour congress. A directly chartered union pays per capita dues directly to the congress and it receives services from the congress. Examples of labour congresses include the Canadian Labour Congress (CLC) and the Confédération des syndicats nationaux (CSN).

Labour congresses are also known as *union centrals.* While directly chartered unions are represented by labour congresses, unions in general can also affiliate with labour congresses for assistance at national and international levels. The main functions of these

industrial union
Consists of unskilled and semi-skilled workers in mass-production industries such as automobile manufacturing and mining.

independent local organization
A union that is not formally connected or affiliated with any other labour organization; also called the union local, local, or local union.

© Denphumi/Shutterstock

The CLC and its affiliated unions have been promoting the creation of green jobs for decades. This requires a change in how we produce, transport, and consume goods.[10] Consider how it proposes to do this by reading, "Making the Shift to a Green Economy" at canadianlabour.ca. Does this issue resonate with you?

labour congresses has been to coordinate the activities of member unions when representing the interests of labour to local, provincial, and federal governments as well as to organized labour on the world scene. For example, the CLC is Canada's largest labour organization. It brings together dozens of national and international unions, provincial and territorial federations of labour, and community-based labour councils to represent 3.3 million workers. It lobbies the different levels of government on social and economic issues, human rights and equality, workplace issues, international issues, and environmental issues.

While a local can be an independent organization within a specific geographic area, it is usually part of a larger structure, namely one that is provincial or regional in focus, or a **national union**, which is a union that only represents workers in Canada. Two examples that will be discussed shortly include the Canadian Union of Public Employees and Unifor.

An **international union** has its headquarters outside of Canada (usually the United States). For example, Teamsters Canada represents more than 125 000 members in Canada and it is affiliated with the Washington, D.C.-based International Brotherhood of Teamsters.

directly chartered union
A union that is directly affiliated to a labour congress to whom it pays per capita dues and receives services.

national union
A union that only represents workers in Canada.

international union
A union that has its headquarters outside of Canada (usually the United States).

LiUNA's International Office is headquartered in Washington, D.C. In Canada, it is represented by Regional Offices in the Pacific Northwest and Central and Eastern Canada. Consider LiUNA Local 1089, based in Sarnia, Ontario. Local 1089 is affiliated with LiUNA by charter with its International through the LiUNA Central and Eastern Canada regional office, located in Hamilton, Ontario. It is also affiliated to LiUNA's provincial council, the LiUNA Ontario Provincial District Council. You can read more about LiUNA in the chapter profile and throughout this chapter.

Figure 13.1 charts the structure of the international union of LiUNA. Based in the United States, it is structured under a governing constitution, which is reviewed and amended every five years at a constitutional convention. This convention brings together elected delegates from every local union and district council in North America. Along with constitutional resolutions, the convention also elects the General Executive Board, which is composed of the general president, general secretary treasurer, and fourteen regional vice presidents. The international union issues and holds the charters of all local unions and district councils that operate under the rule of the LiUNA Constitution. District councils are composed of elected delegates from local unions within a state, states, province, or provinces. These councils are responsible for collective bargaining and are the holders of "bargaining rights" on behalf of their members. LiUNA also has established national labour–management funds that are directed toward training, health and safety, and the promotion of unionized construction and positive labour–management relations. The funds are referred to as the Tri-Funds. These unique funds, which are supported by joint contributions, provide a broad range of services to both labour and management.

FIGURE 13.1

THE STRUCTURE OF THE LABOURERS' INTERNATIONAL UNION OF NORTH AMERICA (LiUNA)

Elections are democratic at LiUNA as LiUNA members vote for representation at each level of the union's structure. At the local union level, members of the local union elect their local union Executive Board and Officers. Each local then elects district council delegates. These delegates elect the District Council Executive Board. At the local union level, members also elect convention delegates, who in turn attend the union's General Convention, which is held every five years. At the general convention, each delegate votes to elect the General President (equivalent of a CEO) and the General Secretary Treasurer (equivalent of a CFO) and their International Vice Presidents. At this convention, the delegates also vote on constitutional changes and amendments.

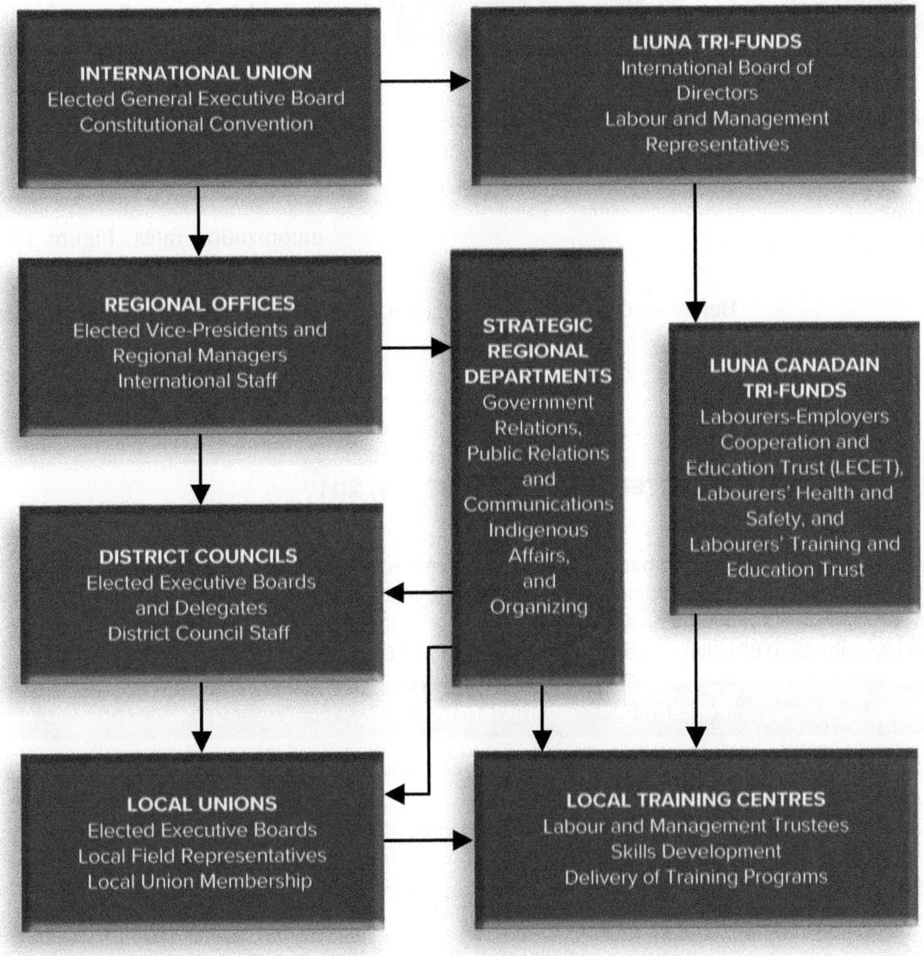

Union Coverage

unionization rate (union density)
A number of employed individuals who are union members as a proportion of the total number of employed individuals.

Union activity can be measured in two ways: the unionization rate and the coverage rate. The **unionization rate**, also known as *union density,* refers to the number of employed individuals who are union members as a proportion of the total number of employed individuals.[11]

© Christopher Futcher/Getty Images

Union members can include bricklayers, teachers, journalists, professional athletes, retail store clerks, and airline pilots. Can you think of a profession that would not benefit from union representation?

The **coverage rate** refers to the proportion of employed individuals, both union members and non-unionized employees, who are covered by a collective agreement, as a percentage of all employees.[12] While Canada's unionization rate is 28.8 percent, its coverage rate is 30.4 percent (approximately 4.7 million workers).[13] According to Statistics Canada, "a union member today is slightly more likely to be a woman, and working in an office, school or hospital, while factory workers, miners and other blue collar trades have seen their union membership fall over the past quarter century."[14]

Full-time employment, longer job tenure, larger firms, higher educational attainment, and better wages are associated with higher unionization rates. Figure 13.2 summarizes union coverage by selected characteristics.

Before we discuss labour legislation, let us consider two unions that are often in the news.

FIGURE 13.2

UNION COVERAGE BY SELECTED CHARACTERISTICS, 2017

Union coverage measures union members and persons who are not union members but are covered by collective agreements as a percentage of all employees. For example, full-time employees (31.8 percent) are more likely to be covered by a collective agreement than are part-time employees (24.0 percent). Full-time employees have a higher average hourly wage ($30.69) than do part-time employees ($24.63).

Characteristic	Percentage	Characteristics	Percentage
Public sector	75.5	No degree, certificate, or diploma	20.0
Private sector	16.4	University degree	34.3
Age 15 to 24	15.6	Workplace size: less than 20 employees	13.7
Age 45 to 54	37.8	Workplace size: more than 500 employees	55.8
Men	28.7	Least unionized industry—agriculture	4.4
Women	32.2	Most unionized industry—educational services	72.7
Goods-producing sector	27.4	Most unionized province—Newfoundland and Labrador	38.7
Services-producing sector	31.2	Least unionized province—Alberta	25.0

Source: Compiled from CANSIM tables 282-0220 to 282-0225, Statistics Canada, January 5, 2018.

Canada's Largest Unions

Canada's largest union is the Canadian Union of Public Employees (CUPE). Unifor is Canada's largest private-sector union. Let's briefly look at each next.

coverage rate
A measure of the proportion of employed individuals, both union members and non-unionized employees, who are covered by a collective agreement.

CUPE[15]

Formed in 1963, CUPE has over 650 000 members and more than 70 offices across Canada. It represents workers in health care, emergency services, education, early learning and child care, municipalities, social services, libraries, utilities, transportation and airlines. Collectively, the payroll for CUPE members is over $21.8 billion. CUPE has more than 2636 locals and chartered organizations across the country ranging in size from 20 to 20 000 members. More than 70 percent of CUPE's 3946 collective agreements are with locals of 100 members or less.

UNIFOR[16]

Unifor represents more than 315 000 workers. It was formed during the 2013 Labour Day weekend when the Canadian Auto Workers (CAW) and the Communications, Energy, and Paperworkers (CEP) unions merged. Like its name, it is a union for everyone—workers, the unemployed, and those that are self-employed. Its diverse membership includes workers in nearly every industry including communications, resources, manufacturing, and services. There are 750 local unions of all sizes operating under the Unifor banner.

PROGRESS ASSESSMENT

- Why were unions originally formed?
- What are the four types of labour organizations? Describe each one.
- Summarize union coverage by selected characteristics.
- Name Canada's two largest unions.

Labour Legislation

LO2

Discuss the major legislation affecting labour unions.

The growth and influence of organized labour in Canada have depended primarily on two major factors: the law and public opinion. As with other movements that promoted greater fairness and equity in our society—such as women's right to vote, equal rights for minorities and women, and protection for children—when support for employees' rights became widespread in Canada, laws were passed to enforce them. Today we have laws establishing minimum wage, paid minimum holidays and vacation, maximum hours, overtime pay, health and safety conditions, workers' compensation, employment insurance, the Canada/Quebec Pension Plan, and a host of other rights. It is strange to realize that at one time or another, these were all on the agenda of unions and were opposed by employers and governments for many years. They often denounced these demands as radical notions.

The effect of unions goes far beyond their numbers. Companies that want to keep unions out often provide compensation, benefits, and working conditions that match or exceed those found in union plants or offices. Thus, the levels established by unions spill over to non-union companies.

© Finnbarr Webster/Alamy

The Supreme Court of Canada struck down a federal law that forbade the Royal Mounted Police from unionizing, saying it violated the Canadian Charter of Rights and Freedom. The Court suggested forming a traditional union as one option that would restore the employees' collective bargaining rights.[21] Do you think that all workers should have the right to unionize?

Unions are regulated by federal and provincial legislation, and they are required by law to be democratic and financially accountable to their members. In addition, all unions have constitutions that must be registered with government labour boards.[17]

The federal government has control over specified fields of activity that are national in nature. As stated in Chapter 12, such activities apply to approximately 6 percent of Canadian workers.[18] The major legislation that governs labour–management relations for these employees is the Canada Labour Code, which is administered by Employment and Social Development Canada. It is also responsible for the Employment Equity Act as well as other legislation on wages and working conditions.

Provincial or territorial laws apply to the rest of the Canadian workforce. As you can imagine, these laws vary and it is the responsibility of businesses to know the rights of their workers and vice versa. For example, Bill 148, the Ontario Government's Fair Workplaces, Better Jobs Act, 2017 incorporated a number of changes to the Employment Standards Act, the Labour Relations Act, and the Occupational Health and Safety Act. These changes impacted minimum wage, overtime, vacation pay, public holiday pay, leave of absences, personal emergency leaves, temporary agency help and difference in pay based on employment status.[19]

Keep in mind, the Supreme Court of Canada can still intervene in provincial jurisdictions. For example:[20]

> Saying it was unconstitutional, the Supreme Court of Canada struck down a controversial Saskatchewan law that prevented public-sector employees from striking. In the absence of employer and union agreements, the law had permitted the provincial government to decide which workers were considered essential and therefore could not strike. The Supreme Court affirmed the principle that any labour-relations scheme that gives management a final authoritative say over the conditions of its workers was not appropriate. The ruling will affect public service unions in provinces across the country that have essential services laws for health-care workers.

Workplace Laws[22]

Legislation protects workers against health and safety hazards in the workplace. According to CCOHS (Canadian Centre for Occupational Health and Safety), employees have the following three basic rights: (1) the right to refuse unsafe work; (2) the right to participate in the workplace health and safety activities through the Health and Safety Committee or as a worker health and safety representative; and (3) the right to know, or the right to be informed about, actual and potential dangers in the workplace.

For example, the *right to refuse unsafe work* entitles a worker to step away from work that he or she believes is unsafe. This right allows the worker to have the refused work investigated, and repaired if it is dangerous. During this time, the worker receives pay and is protected from an employer's possible reprisal, since it is illegal for an employer to fire or discipline a worker who refuses work that he or she believes is unsafe.

By knowing about workplace hazards, workers can ensure that employers make work safer, provide protection to workers, and give training so that workers can work with the smallest possibility of injury or illness. Accidents at work are caused by a complex combination of unsafe employee behaviour and unsafe working conditions. It is estimated that about three Canadian workers die every working day from an occupational injury or disease. There is growing emphasis on the health and safety of young workers as about one in seven young workers is injured on the job.

Canada's unions are calling on the federal government to do more to address workplace harassment and violence as these can also lead to worker deaths, as well as significant mental and physical injuries. "Workplace harassment and violence are often overlooked hazards of the job," said Hassan Yussuff, President of the CLC. "In the era of #metoo and #timesup, we need to talk about the negative, even deadly, impacts these hazards can have in the workplace." These topics are discussed in more detail next.

Know Your Rights Workshop
"A unique training course, on workplace rights"

© UFCW

Recognizing that new and young workers are particularly vulnerable in the workplace, UFCW Canada representatives and member activists run Know Your Rights Workshops. Topics covered include human rights, employment standards, labour rights, and health and safety. Would you be interested in attending such a workshop?

Sexual Harassment

The Supreme Court of Canada defines **sexual harassment** as unwelcome conduct of a sexual nature that detrimentally affects the work environment or leads to adverse job-related consequences for the victims of the harassment.[23] Managers and workers are now much more sensitive to sexual comments and behaviour than they were in the past. Conduct on the job can be considered illegal under specific conditions:[24]

- An employee's submission to such conduct is explicitly or implicitly made a term or condition of employment, or an employee's submission to or rejection of such conduct is used as the basis for employment decisions affecting the worker's status. A threat like "Go out with me or you're fired" or "Go out with me or you'll never be promoted here" constitutes *quid pro quo sexual harassment.*
- The conduct unreasonably interferes with a worker's job performance or creates an intimidating, hostile, or offensive work environment. This hostile work environment is the more common type of sexual harassment in the workplace.

sexual harassment
Unwelcome conduct of a sexual nature that detrimentally affects the work environment or leads to adverse job-related consequences for the victims of the harassment.

According to Daniel Lublin, Partner at Whitten & Lublin, Employment & Labour Lawyers, "Once an employer is made aware of a complaint, it is required to investigate and ensure that the workplace, broadly defined, is free from harassment."[25] Many companies

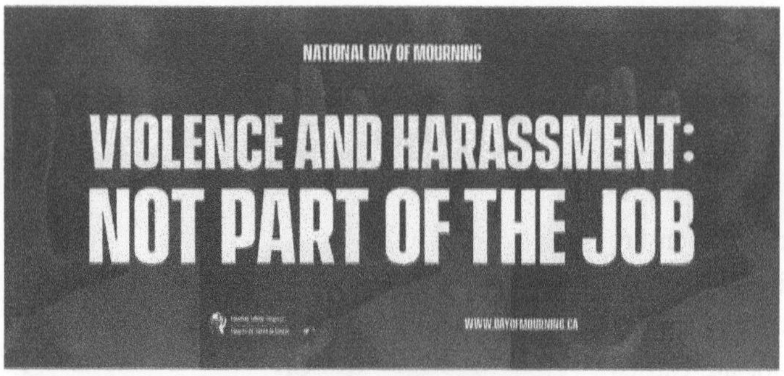

© Canadian Labour Congress (CLC)

April 28 is Canada's national Day of Mourning. Over 900 Canadian workers die each year due to an unsafe workplace, and more than 240 000 workers experience lost time due to workplace injuries or disease. How can workers and employers work together to ensure they do not become statistics on this day?

have set up rapid, effective grievance procedures and react promptly to allegations of harassment. Such efforts may save businesses millions of dollars in lawsuits and make the workplace more productive and harmonious.

Violence and Bullying in the Workplace[26]

Employers and managers must be vigilant about potential violence in the workplace. CCOHS defines **workplace violence** as any act in which a person is abused, threatened, intimidated or assaulted in his or her employment. Violence can occur within a traditional workplace, at off-site, business-related functions (e.g., conferences), at social events, etc. Rumours, swearing, verbal abuse, pranks, arguments, property damage, vandalism, sabotage, pushing, theft, physical assaults, psychological trauma, anger-related incidents, rape, arson, and murder are all examples of workplace violence.

workplace violence Any act in which a person is abused, threatened, intimidated, or assaulted in his or her employment.

© jayfish/Alamy

Unwelcome sexual advances, requests for sexual favours, and other verbal or physical conduct are illegal. Although most employees are aware of sexual harassment policies in the workplace, they are often not certain what sexual harassment actually means. Should companies train employees about the dos and don'ts of acceptable sexual conduct on the job?

Certain work factors, processes, and interactions can put people at increased risk from workplace violence. Examples include working with the public; handling money, valuables, or prescription drugs (e.g. cashiers); carrying out inspection or enforcement duties (e.g. government employees); providing service, care, advice, or education (e.g. health-care providers); and working in premises where alcohol is served. Risk of violence may be greater at certain times of the day or night (e.g., late hours of the night or early hours of the morning) or year (e.g., during the holidays and during performance appraisals).

Workplace design (e.g., positioning office furniture so that the employee is closer to a door or exit than the client and so that the employee cannot be cornered), *administrative practices* (e.g., keeping cash register funds to a minimum), and *work practices* (e.g., do not enter any situation or location where you feel threatened or unsafe) are preventative measures that have helped curtail workplace violence. Other examples include holding focus groups that invite employee input, hiring managers with strong interpersonal skills, and employing skilled consultants to deal with any potential for workplace violence.

The Spotlight on Small Business shares suggestions on what employers can do to limit potential liability in the areas of workplace harassment and violence.

Spotlight *On* SMALL BUSINESS

Helping Reduce Harassment and Violence in the Workplace

© Shutterstock/create jobs 51

Robinson Heeney LLP, a Toronto-based employment law firm, was founded in 2011 by lawyers Kevin Robinson and James Heeney. The firm provides advice to both employers and employees on all aspects of employment law. The firm also provides third-party workplace investigations and training services.

Partner James Heeney has been named by *Canadian HR Reporter* as a leading employment lawyer in Toronto. His employer-side practice focuses on providing strategic advice and litigation support in the areas of employment agreements, policy manuals, terminations, and human rights issues. On the employee side of his practice, Heeney routinely advises clients on both unionized and non-unionized issues relating to executive compensation, employment contracts, terminations, and human rights.

Why take on the challenge of starting your own business? Heeney was motivated to create a firm focused on integrity and exceptional legal advice, while still ensuring it was provided in a manner that was cost effective, timely, and practical. He wanted to influence an organization that ranked a good work environment as one of its top priorities. While he admits that running a business is not easy, there is certainly more satisfaction out of its successes. "No one wants to work long hours, but it is easier when it happens and you know it's to build your own business," says Heeney. "Many of my clients are long standing and I am so proud to be able to say that."

One area in which Heeney advises his clients is anti-harassment legislation. The courts provide anti-harassment protections throughout Canada for both complainants and respondents. Whether a province has harassment legislation or not, the courts will find employers liable where an inappropriate workplace investigation occurs or where harassment isn't addressed. An employee found to have been terminated for requesting that an employer comply with the harassment and violence provisions, for example, may be entitled to back wages and to being reinstated in his or her job. These are significant remedies which can be costly to businesses.

In Ontario, the Occupational Health and Safety Act provides protections to employees regarding workplace violence and harassment. (Similar legislation exists in Quebec, Manitoba, and Saskatchewan.) All employers, regardless of size, are required to actively adopt policies and training designed to prevent workplace harassment and violence. Employees who feel there has been a breach of the harassment and violence provisions in their workplace can file a complaint with the Ontario Labour Relations Board, and the Board has extraordinary powers when it feels a breach has occurred. New legislation under Bill 132 not only requires the above protections, but it also puts an obligation on employers to conduct an investigation that is appropriate in the circumstances. It also allows the Ministry of Labour to order the employer to retain an independent investigator at its own expense.

Heeney recommends the following tips on what businesses can do to limit an employer's potential liability:

1. *Take complaints seriously.* When complaints are filed by an employee, ensure that they are given serious consideration.
2. *Acknowledge receipt of the complaint.* Make sure that when complaints are filed you acknowledge to the employee that the complaint has been received and will be investigated.
3. *Perform an unbiased investigation.* Advise the employee alleged to have committed wrongdoing that there is a complaint. Conduct an unbiased investigation and then make the decision.
4. *Report back with your findings.* Advise both sides of the findings, and in writing.
5. *Avoid retaliation.* Always advise all parties that they will not be subjected to retaliation for participating in the investigation.

"Preparing for changes in legislation can be a lengthy and detailed process for employers," counsels Heeney, "particularly for smaller businesses with limited resources. However, the changes to the legislation are an essential step in ensuring that employers are doing their part in reducing the risk of violence and harassment in their workplaces and to avoiding possible fines and liability."

Sources: James Heeney, Partner, Robinson Heeney LLP, interview, January 9, 2018, 416-646-5169; "James Heeney, Partner," Robinson Heeney LLP, 2018, http://www.robinsonheeney.com/toronto-employment-lawyers/lawyers_jheeney/; James Heeney, "Don't get blindsided by workplace harassment, violence laws," CBC News, September 30, 2011, www.cbc.ca/news/business/smallbusiness/story/2011/09/30/f-smallbiz-james-heeney.html; and James Heeney, "Is your business ready for new harassment and violence legislation?," CBC News, May 28, 2010, www.cbc.ca/money/smallbusiness/story/2010/05/28/f-james-heeney-workplace-harassment.html.

bullying
Acts or verbal comments that could mentally hurt or isolate a person in the workplace.

labour relations board (LRB)
An organization created by the federal or provincial government to administer labour relations legislation.

WORKPLACE BULLYING

CCOHS defines **bullying** as acts or verbal comments that could "mentally" hurt or isolate a person in the workplace. The Workplace Bullying Institute maintains that bullying is four times more common than sexual harassment on the job.[27] Zogby International research estimates that 35 percent of workers have been bullied at work.[28]

Unfortunately, employers and managers often discount or deny bullying, and often refer to it simply as personality conflicts or management styles. By trivializing bullying, an organization can suffer reduced employee morale and productivity, increased turnover, and in some cases, even legal problems.

Although "schoolyard" bullying tends to be physical in nature, workplace bullying involves more psychological and verbal abuse. Also, the targets of workplace bullying are often the strongest employees (who are considered threats to the bully), not the weakest. The majority of bullies are supervisors or managers but can also be fellow workers.[29] Men far outnumber women as workplace bullies, but women tend to bully other women more frequently than men. Bullying is increasingly becoming a major problem in the workplace and can be directed at employees at all levels of the organization.[30] To be an effective leader, a manager must be aware of what bullying is, learn the signs of bullying, and most importantly take corrective action to end it. By ignoring workplace bullying, companies may lose their most productive or promising employees.

© Shutterstock/Kzenon

Examples of bullying include spreading malicious rumours, gossip, or innuendo; excluding or isolating someone socially; intimidating a person; undermining or deliberately impeding a person's work; constantly changing work guidelines; establishing impossible deadlines that will set up the individual to fail; yelling or using profanity; and criticizing a person persistently or constantly. What can an employee do if he or she is being bullied?

Labour Relations Boards[31]

To enforce labour legislation, the federal and provincial governments have created **labour relations boards (LRBs)**. These agencies investigate violations of the law and have the power to determine: (1) whether a person is an employee for the purposes of the law;

(2) whether an employee is a member of a trade union; (3) whether an organization is an appropriate bargaining agent for bargaining purposes; (4) whether a collective agreement is in force; and (5) whether any given party is bound by it.

An LRB functions more informally than a court but it has the full authority of the law. In all jurisdictions, the LRB's decision is final and binding and cannot be appealed except on procedural matters.

PROGRESS ASSESSMENT

- What two major factors have contributed to the growth and influence of organized labour in Canada?
- What three basic rights do employees have in the workplace?
- What are examples of sexual harassment, workplace violence, and bullying?
- How do LRBs regulate labour–management relations?

The Collective Bargaining Process

LO3 Describe the collective bargaining process.

The LRB oversees **collective bargaining**, which is the entire process whereby union and management representatives negotiate a contract for workers. Collective bargaining includes more than the contract itself. Collective bargaining determines how unions are selected, actions that are allowed during the period prior to certification, certification, and ongoing contract negotiations. Collective bargaining also determines behaviour while a contract is in force and during a breakdown in negotiations for a contract renewal, as well as decertification. **Certification** is a formal process whereby a union is recognized by the LRB as the bargaining agent for a group of employees. **Decertification** is the process by which workers can take away a union's right to represent them.

collective bargaining
The process whereby union and management representatives negotiate a contract for workers.

certification
Formal process whereby a union is recognized by the Labour Relations Board (LRB) as the bargaining agent for a group of employees.

decertification
Process by which workers can take away a union's right to represent them.

The whole bargaining process and the important certification procedure are shown in Figure 13.3. As you can see, the process is regulated. This process is also democratic and, as in any election, the minority has to accept the majority's decision. All parties involved have to follow a strict procedure to ensure that everybody is playing by the rules. For example, did you know that it is illegal for employers to fire employees for union activities?

Objectives of Organized Labour

LO4 Outline the objectives of labour unions.

The objectives of labour unions shift with social and economic trends. For example, in the 1970s the primary objective of unions was to obtain additional pay and benefits for their members. Throughout the 1980s, objectives shifted toward issues related to job security and union recognition. Today, we are seeing increasing emphasis on skills upgrading as the basis of job security. In some industries, union jobs have been declining due to outsourcing and offshoring.

Unions recognize that they must work closely with management if jobs are going to be kept within Canada. Having a skilled and productive workforce is one major way to do this. "Unions have a dual responsibility—to ensure that their members are getting the best wage and benefit packages and working conditions available in the marketplace, and equally

FIGURE 13.3

STEPS IN COLLECTIVE BARGAINING

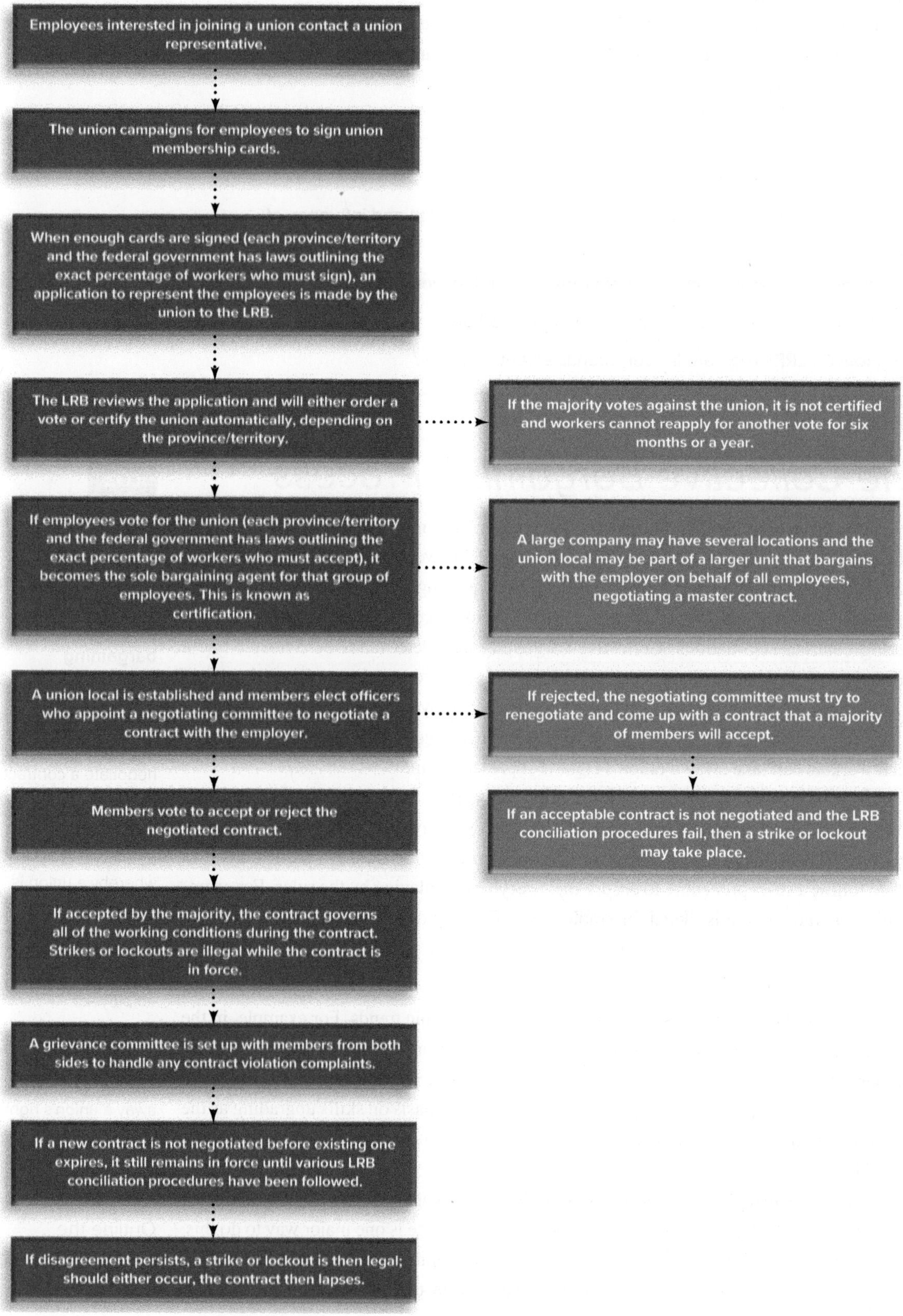

as important, to ensure that their contractual employers not only remain competitive, but have a labour partner that can assist them in expanding their businesses and market share," says Varricchio. "Through the union structure and the collective bargaining process, employers can level off labour costs across entire markets and create optimum standards in training and health and safety practices that can be properly enforced through their collective agreements."[32]

© Shutterstock/AlexLMX

In the 1990s and 2000s, unions focused on job security, but the issue of global competition and its effects often took centre stage. Unions were a major opponent of NAFTA as they feared that this would lead to job losses. Fast forward 20 years to the renegotiation of NAFTA. Representatives from public- and private-sector unions urged the federal government to ensure that any new trade deals were fair and would protect workers' rights, public services, the government's right to regulate in the public's interest, and the environment.[34] What was the outcome of this renegotiation?

The **negotiated labour–management agreement**, informally referred to as the **labour contract**, sets the tone and clarifies the terms and conditions under which management and the union will function over a specific period. However, it doesn't necessarily end negotiations between them because there are sometimes differences concerning interpretations of the agreement. "Common sense and good business practice dictates the importance of having a binding written contract between parties engaged in any business transaction, thereby protecting the interests of all parties involved," says Varricchio. "Such a contract spells out the responsibilities and obligations of both parties, itemizes the compensation package agreed to for services rendered or products purchased, and identifies a mechanism to be employed to settle differences in the event either party violates the terms of the mutually agreed-to contract. How much more important is it to have such a contract between an employer and his/her employees protecting the interests of everyone, especially in an environment where the dynamics between many different personalities could adversely impact the productivity of the workforce and the business?"[33]

labour contract (negotiated labour–management agreement)
Informal name for negotiated labour-management agreement, which is an agreement that sets the tone and clarifies the terms and conditions under which management and labour agree to function over a period of time.

Figure 13.4 lists topics commonly negotiated by management and labour. Unions attempt to address their most pressing concerns in the labour contract, such as job security and outsourcing. Negotiations can cover a wide range of work topics, and it can take a long time to reach an agreement. To save jobs, for example, some unions have granted management concessions, or **givebacks**, of previous gains. (Review the Analyzing Management Decisions discussion near the end of the chapter for more on this topic.) Both public- and private-sector unions face challenges as they try to maintain remaining wage and fringe benefits achieved in past negotiations.

givebacks
Concessions made by union members to management; gains from previous labour negotiations are given back to management to help employers remain competitive and thereby save jobs.

Labour unions generally insist that contracts contain a **union security clause** stipulating that employees who benefit from a union must either officially join or at least pay dues to the union. There are basically four types of agreements:

1. A **closed shop agreement** specifies that workers have to be members of a union before being hired for a job. In effect, hiring is done through the union.
2. In a **union shop agreement**, the employer is free to hire anybody but the recruit must then join the union within a prescribed period (usually 30, 60, or 90 days).

union security clause
Provision in a negotiated labour–management agreement that stipulates that employees who benefit from a union must either officially join or at least pay dues to the union.

closed shop agreement
Clause in a negotiated labour–management agreement that specifies workers need to be members of a union before being hired.

union shop agreement
Clause in a negotiated labour–management agreement that says workers do not have to be members of a union to be hired, but must agree to join the union within a prescribed period.

agency shop (Rand formula) agreement
Clause in a negotiated labour–management agreement that says employers may hire non-union workers; employees are not required to join the union but must pay union dues.

open shop agreement
Clause in a negotiated labour–management agreement that says employees are free to join or not join the union and to pay or not pay union dues.

checkoff
A contract clause requiring the employer to deduct union dues from employees' pay and remit them to a union.

FIGURE 13.4

ISSUES IN A NEGOTIATED LABOUR–MANAGEMENT AGREEMENT

Labour and management often meet to discuss and clarify the terms that specify employees' functions within the company. The topics listed in this figure are typically discussed during these meetings.

1. Management rights
2. Union recognition
3. Union security clause
4. Strikes and lockouts
5. Union activities and responsibilities
   a. Dues checkoff
   b. Union bulletin boards
   c. Work slowdowns
6. Wages
   a. Wage structure
   b. Shift differentials
   c. Wage incentives
   d. Bonuses
   e. Piecework conditions
   f. Tiered wage structures
7. Hours of work and time-off policies
   a. Regular hours of work
   b. Holidays
   c. Vacation policies
   d. Overtime regulations
   e. Leaves of absence
   f. Break periods
   g. Flextime
   h. Mealtime allotments
8. Job rights and seniority principles
   a. Seniority regulations
   b. Transfer policies and bumping
   c. Promotions
   d. Layoffs and recall procedures
   e. Job bidding and posting
9. Discharge and discipline
   a. Suspension
   b. Conditions for discharge
10. Grievance procedures
    a. Arbitration agreement
    b. Mediation procedures
11. Employee benefits, health, and welfare

3. The **agency shop agreement** states that employers may hire workers who are not required to join the union but the workers must pay a special union fee or regular union dues. Based on the **Rand formula** devised by Supreme Court Justice Rand in 1946, employees in a unionized environment have to fund the bargaining and administration of the collective agreement.[35] Labour leaders believe that such fees or dues are justified because the union represents all workers in collective bargaining, not just its members.
4. An **open shop agreement** gives workers the option to join or not join the union if one exists. A worker who does not join cannot be forced to pay a fee or dues.[36]

Regardless of which hiring condition prevails, the labour contract usually contains **checkoff** as a standard clause. Checkoff requires the employer to deduct union dues from employees and to pay and remit them to the union (except for non-members in an open shop). Otherwise, it would be harder to collect union dues individually.

"A collective agreement provides protection if an employer wishes to discharge an employee," states employment lawyer, Aaron Rousseau, Partner of Rousseau Mazzuca LLP. "In the absence of a collective agreement, employers can fire non-union employees for almost any reason so long as the employees are given reasonable notice, or payment in lieu of notice. In a union environment, the employer needs to prove misconduct on the part of the employee before he or she can be fired."[37] Review Figure 13.5 for some additional advantages of joining a union. Note the disadvantages as well.

© Mike Kemp/Blend Images

Future contract negotiations will likely focus on evolving workplace issues such as child and elder care, worker retraining, two-tiered wage plans, drug testing, and other such work-related issues. Job security will remain a top union priority due to job losses from outsourcing, offshoring, and free trade agreements. Can you think of other issues?

Resolving Labour–Management Disputes

The negotiated labour–management agreement becomes a guide to work relations between management and the union. However, it does not necessarily end negotiations between them because sometimes there are differences concerning interpretations of the agreement. For example, managers may interpret a certain clause in the agreement to mean that they are free to select who works overtime. Union members may interpret the same clause to mean that managers must select employees for overtime on the basis of employee seniority. If the parties can't resolve such disagreements, grievances may be filed.

A **grievance** is a charge by employees that management is not abiding by or fulfilling the terms of a negotiated labour–management agreement as they perceive it. Overtime rules, promotions, layoffs, transfers, and job assignments are generally sources of employee grievances. Handling grievances demands a good deal of contact between union officials and managers. Grievances, however, do not imply that the company has broken the law or the labour agreement. In fact, the vast majority of grievances are negotiated and resolved by **shop stewards** (union officials who work permanently in an organization and represent employee interests on a daily basis) and supervisory-level managers. However, if a grievance is not settled at this level, formal grievance procedures will begin. Figure 13.6 illustrates the steps a formal grievance could follow.

grievance
A charge by employees that management is not abiding by or fulfilling the terms of the negotiated labour–management agreement.

shop stewards
Union officials who work permanently in an organization and represent employee interests on a daily basis.

FIGURE 13.5

SOME ADVANTAGES AND DISADVANTAGES OF JOINING A UNION

Union Advantages	Union Disadvantages
Members are generally better protected when disputes arise	Promotion and pay may be determined by seniority
Usually receive higher wages and better benefit coverage	Negotiated compensation usually leads to higher production costs
Better negotiating power as a group rather than as an individual	You may not be agree with all of the union's decisions (e.g., to go on strike)

Source: "Joining a union in Canada," Working in Canada, accessed April 29, 2018, www.workingin-canada.com/jobs/job-tools/joining-a-union.

■ FIGURE 13.6

GRIEVANCE RESOLUTION PROCESS

The grievance process may move through several steps before the issue is resolved. At each step, the issue is negotiated between union officials and managers. If no resolution is achieved, an outside arbitrator may be mutually agreed on. If so, the decision by the arbitrator is binding (legally enforceable).

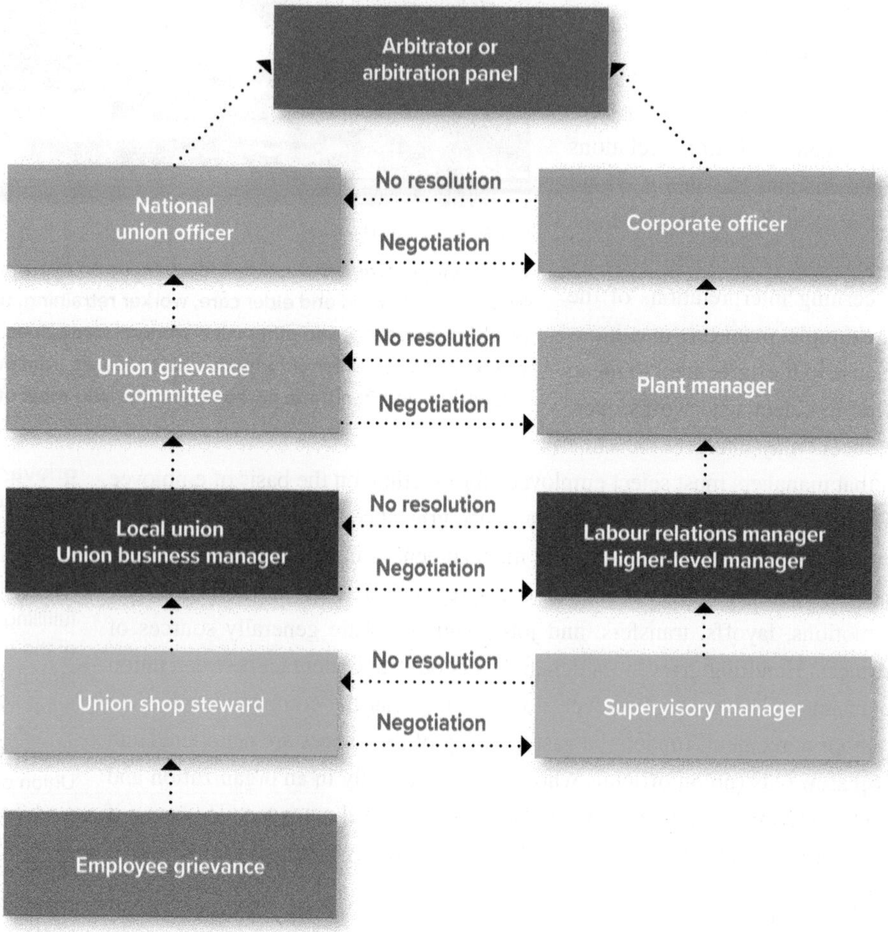

Conciliation, Mediation, and Arbitration

bargaining zone
Range of options between the initial and final offer that each party will consider before negotiations dissolve or reach an impasse.

During the contract negotiation process, there is generally a **bargaining zone**, which is the range of options between the initial and final offers that each party will consider before negotiations dissolve or reach an impasse. If labour and management negotiators aren't able to agree on alternatives within this bargaining zone, conciliation is the next necessary step. In their legislation, all jurisdictions provide for conciliation and mediation services.[38]

Conciliation is the use of a government-appointed third party (usually through the Ministry of Labour) to explore solutions to a labour–management dispute.[39] If conciliation fails, the union is then in a legal position to strike and the employer is also in a legal position to declare a lockout.

Mediation is the use of a third party, called a *mediator,* who encourages both sides in a dispute to consider negotiating and often makes suggestions for resolving the matter. Keep in mind that mediators evaluate facts in the dispute and then make suggestions, not decisions. Elected officials (current and past), attorneys, and professors often serve as mediators in labour disputes. In 2011, the National Football League and the Players Association asked for the assistance of a federal mediator in their attempt to forge a new contract. The National Hockey League made the same request during the labour dispute in 2012.[40]

A more extreme approach used to resolve conflicts is **arbitration**, which is an agreement to bring in an impartial third party (a single arbitrator or arbitration panel) to render a binding decision in a labour dispute. Arbitration may be *voluntary,* where both sides decide to submit their case to an arbitrator. Arbitration may also be *compulsory,* where a decision is imposed by the government (e.g., by Parliament or a provincial legislature). Compulsory arbitration usually occurs in a major or prolonged strike with serious consequences for the public. Usually, non-grievance arbitration (say, for contract disputes) is voluntary and grievance arbitration is compulsory. Employees who are designated as providing essential services (e.g., police, firefighters, and hospital employees) usually do not have the right to strike as stated in their collective agreements, and their disputes must be settled through binding arbitration.[41] While binding arbitration may result in a new collective agreement, it can leave contentious issues unresolved.

Both mediation and arbitration can be difficult, lengthy, and costly procedures, especially when both sides are locked into rigid positions. That is why negotiators from both sides usually try to settle their differences before resorting to these steps.

© THE CANADIAN PRESS/Richard Buchan

Do you recall when the 12 000 Ontario colleges' professors, instructors, counsellors and librarians were on strike for five weeks? They were legislated back to work and outstanding issues were sent to binding arbitration. About 27 500 of the roughly 250 000 full-time students withdrew and received a tuition refund rather than finish their semester on a condensed timeline.[42] Should educational-services employees be designated as essential services?

© TeerawatWinyarat/iStock/Thinkstock

With changes to collective bargaining laws, the federal government now has the right to decide whether labour disputes are solved by conciliation, arbitration, or strike. Smaller unions that have picked arbitration in the past could be forced to go on strike in the event of an impasse.[43] What can these smaller unions do to strengthen their positions in such negotiations?

conciliation
The use of a government-appointed third part to explore solutions to a labour–management dispute.

mediation
The use of a third party, called a mediator, who encourages both sides in a dispute to continue negotiating and often makes suggestions for resolving the dispute.

arbitration
An agreement to bring in an impartial third party (a single arbitrator or a panel of arbitrators) to render a binding decision in a labour dispute.

PROGRESS ASSESSMENT

- In the collective bargaining process, what happens after certification?
- What issues are included in a negotiated labour-management agreement?
- What are the differences between conciliation, mediation, and arbitration?

Negotiation Tactics

If labour and management cannot reach an agreement through collective bargaining and negotiations break down, either side, or both, may use specific tactics to enhance their negotiating position and perhaps sway public opinion. Be aware that the great majority of labour negotiations end successfully without the disruption of a strike or lockout. Remember that mediation and arbitration are always available to the parties in dispute. They may take advantage of these procedures before, during, or after any of these tactics are exercised. Let us look at some examples next.

LO5

Describe the negotiation tactics used by labour and management during conflicts.

Union Tactics

Unions primarily use strikes and boycotts to get desired changes. A **strike** occurs when workers collectively refuse to go to work. Strikes have been the most potent union tactic. They attract public attention to a labour dispute and can cause operations in a company to slow down or totally cease. Besides refusing to work, strikers may also *picket* the company, walking around carrying signs and talking with the public and the media about the issues in the dispute. Unions also use picketing as an informational tool before going on strike. Strikes sometimes lead to the resolution of a labour dispute; however, they also have generated violence and extended bitterness. Often after a strike is finally settled, labour and management remain openly hostile toward each other and mutual complaints of violations of the negotiated labour–management agreement continue.

© The Canadian Press/Dave Chidley

For one month, GM CAMI's 2800 assembly factory workers in Ingersoll, Ontario, went on strike largely over job security issues. The strike was costing GM $5 million a day and had the strike continued much longer, the plant would have been closed.[44] If you were an employee, would you be willing to take such a risk? What can other unions learn from this strike?

Prior to the actual strike, union leaders call for a *strike vote,* which is a secret ballot authorizing the union leadership to call a strike. This democratic vote is necessary if a potential strike is to be considered legal. If the union gets a strong mandate—say, more than 80 percent in favour of a strike—it can use this as a lever to convince management to accept its demands without actually going on strike.

Union tactics include rotating strikes—on and off or alternating among different plants or cities—rather than a full-fledged strike in which all employees are off the job for the duration. With rotating strikes, employees still get some pay, which is not the case in an all-out strike. Many unions build up a strike fund from union dues and use it to give their members strike pay, but that is usually a fraction of their normal wages. Sometimes, in important or long-lasting strikes, other unions will give moral or financial aid.

Unions also attempt boycotts as a means to obtain their objectives in a labour dispute. Boycotts can be classified as primary or secondary. A **primary boycott** occurs when organized labour encourages both its members and the general public not to buy the products or services of a firm engaged in a labour dispute. A **secondary boycott** is an attempt by labour to convince others to stop doing business with a firm that is the subject of a primary boycott. For example, a union can initiate a secondary boycott against a supermarket chain because the chain carries goods produced by a company that is the target of a primary boycott.

© Keith Dunne

Striking Labatt's brewery workers in St. John's, Newfoundland, launched a boycott campaign asking the public to stop buying products produced at the site.[45] Would striking employees influence your purchasing decisions?

Sabotage (where workers damage machines), *sit-ins* (where workers occupy the workplace and refuse to move), or *work-to-rule* (where workers follow the operating rules of the workplace in every detail to slow down the work) are other tactics that have been used by unions. Why might unions prefer these tactics to going on strike?

strike
A union strategy in which workers refuse to go to work.

primary boycott
When a union encourages both its members and the general public not to buy the products of a firm involved in a labour dispute.

Management Tactics

Like labour unions, management also uses specific tactics to achieve its workplace goals. A **lockout** is an attempt by management to put pressure on union workers by temporarily closing the business. When workers don't work, they don't get paid; however, without products and services, there are no profits. Management most often uses injunctions and strikebreakers to counter labour demands it sees as excessive.

An **injunction** is a court order directing someone to do something or to refrain from doing something. Management has sought injunctions to order striking workers back to work, limit the number of pickets that can be used during a strike, or otherwise deal with actions that could be detrimental to the public welfare. For a court to issue an injunction, management must show just cause, such as the possibility of violence or the destruction of property.

Sometimes, a company may try to bring in replacement workers. Known as **strikebreakers** (called *scabs* by unions), they are workers who are hired to do the jobs of striking employees until the labour dispute is resolved. Why do you think strikebreakers have been a particular source of hostility and violence in labour relations? Read the Making Ethical Decisions box on this issue for further insight.

© Allison Joyce/Getty Images

Were you impacted by the 2012–2013 National Hockey League (NHL) lockout that lasted almost four months? Here you see fans protesting the lockout outside of the NHL offices. What were the starting and ending positions of the NHL and the NHL Players Association?

Making ETHICAL DECISIONS

Walking a Fine Line

Your wallet is almost empty, and bills for school expenses, food, and other expenses keep piling up. You read last weekend that Shop-Till-You-Drop, a local grocery chain in your town, is looking for workers to replace striking members of United Food and Commercial Workers (UFCW). The workers are striking because of a reduction in health insurance benefits and reduced payment to their pensions.

© Rubberball/Getty Images

Several classmates at your school are UFCW members employed at Shop-Till-You-Drop stores, and many other students at your school are supporting the strike. The stores also employ many people from your neighbourhood whose families depend on the income and benefits. Shop-Till-You-Drop argues that the company has made a fair offer to the union workers, but with the increasing cost of health care and other benefits, the workers' demands are excessive and could force the company into bankruptcy.

Shop-Till-You-Drop is offering replacement workers an attractive wage rate and flexible schedules to cross the picket line and work during the strike. The company has even suggested the possibility of permanent employment, depending on the results of the strike. As a struggling student, you could use the job and the money for tuition and expenses. Will you cross the picket line and apply? What could be the consequences of your decision? Is your choice ethical?

secondary boycott
An attempt by labour to convince others to stop doing business with a firm that is the subject of a primary boycott.

lockout
An attempt by management to put pressure on unions by temporarily closing the business.

injunction
A court order directing someone to do something or to refrain from doing something.

strikebreakers
Replacement workers hired to do the jobs of striking employees until the labour dispute is resolved.

Legislation

Under the Labour Relations Code, essential services legislation restricts the right to strike for various levels of civil servants and quasi-government employees such as hospital workers and electric and telephone utility workers. The provinces and the federal government forbid some employees under their jurisdiction from striking. In other cases, certain minimum levels of service must be provided. For example, the Ontario government designated the Toronto Transit Commission as an essential service based on the argument that the city could not afford another transit strike or lockout. The last one cost Toronto's economy an estimated $50 million a day.[46] Essential services designation means that in the event that a new agreement cannot be reached, unresolved issues will go to arbitration unless the government imposes a new contract unilaterally.

Federal or provincial governments have the power to end a particular strike or lockout by passing back-to-work legislation. **Back-to-work legislation** is a special law passed by the federal or provincial government that orders an end to a labour–management dispute in an industry the government decides is essential to the operation of the economy. Such legislation has been used to end strikes by teachers, nurses, postal workers, bus drivers, and others. Typically, back-to-work legislation is imposed only after some time has passed, further efforts at reaching a settlement have failed, there is considerable public pressure to end the dispute, or the service provided by striking workers is deemed essential to the economy or public safety. On some occasions, it has been introduced as a pressure tactic to get negotiations to move faster.

Union supporters believe that back-to-work legislation is a denial of the legal right to strike; therefore, to a certain extent it is a restriction of the democratic rights of individuals. Consequently, there is often much controversy about such legislation. It is rarely used to deal with strikes against private businesses. If union members remain on strike after they have been legislated back to work, they are engaging in an illegal strike and are subject to punishment (e.g., substantial fines), as are all lawbreakers.

© The Canadian Press/Sean Kilpatrick

Here Air Canada workers demonstrate against back-to-work legislation in 2011.[47] Under what circumstances do you feel the government should impose back-to-work legislation?

PROGRESS ASSESSMENT

- How have union objectives changed over time?
- What are the major tactics used by unions and by management to assert their power in contract negotiations?
- When is back-to-work legislation used?

back-to-work legislation
A special law passed by the federal or provincial government that orders an end to a labour–management dispute in an industry the government decides is essential to the operation of the economy.

The Future of Unions and Labour–Management Relations

Unions in the future will be quite different from those in the past. To grow, unions will have to include more white-collar, female, and foreign-born workers. The traditional manufacturing base that unions depended on for growth needs to give way to organizing efforts in industries like health care, information technology, agriculture, and financial services.[48] Perhaps what's even more concerning to labour unions is that union membership is highest among workers 45–54 years old and lowest among workers 15–24 years old.[49] Many unions have taken on a new role in assisting management in training workers, redesigning jobs, and assimilating the changing workforce. They help recruit and train foreign workers, unskilled workers, and others who need special help in adapting to the job requirements of the service and knowledge-work economy.

© Shutterstock/Rawpixel.com

Students are a source of membership for unions. What does a union need to do to gain your support? What messages would resonate with you?

© Liuna!

LiUNA members live in every community across Canada. They build highways and bridges, waterways and dams, hospitals, schools and government institutions. They make streets, communities, cities and provinces work. From low rise to high rise construction, pouring concrete to landscaping homes, LiUNA members literally and figuratively build Canada. Do you see any signs of LiUNA's work in your community?

According to The Conference Board of Canada, "Wages continue to be the top bargaining issue for both management and unions. After this, top priorities for unions include a reduction of precarious employment and improved health and safety provisions for their members. Top priorities for employers include flexible work practices, and improving productivity and business competitiveness."[50]

Joseph S. Mancinelli, LiUNA International Vice President and Regional Manager for Central and Eastern Canada, understands these challenges and opportunities. According to Mancinelli, to meet such challenges, "Pensions, level of skills, quality of work, productivity, and safety in the workplace are our priority. Meeting these challenges cannot be addressed through adversarial conflict, but rather in a new era of unionism, through good relations with our employer partners. Good relations are paramount in ensuring such progress and evolution. Working closely with our employer partners can produce more benefits for our members, our employers, and the entire construction industry. LiUNA has an established labour–employer co-operation trust specifically set up for both parties to work together, outside of the bargaining table, to find creative and innovative solutions and initiatives that result in positive outcomes for both labour and management. LiUNA is proud of this strong partnership which we have developed and honed over the years to procure work opportunities. Concurrently, LiUNA has actively pursued public–private partnerships (P3s). Through the successful $7 billion Labourers' Pension Fund of Central and Eastern Canada, sound, financially viable partnerships have evolved resulting in excellent returns on pension fund dollars and employment opportunities for our members. LiUNA partners with numerous construction companies to fund and build projects across the country also furthering strong labour–management relations while procuring work for our members, and the growth of our pension fund. LiUNA has built a legacy of meeting its challenges head on, always putting the best interests of our members first."[51]

Both public- and private-sector union members face challenges as they try to maintain remaining wage and fringe benefit gains achieved in past negotiations. With provinces and cities facing serious debt problems, government officials are trying to cut costs, particularly labour costs. However, provinces with public-sector unions face limitations in cutting labour costs because of prior agreements with the unions. How organized labour and management handle challenges identified throughout this textbook may well define the future of labour unions. After the Progress Assessment, we will look at other issues facing employees and managers in the 21st century.

PROGRESS ASSESSMENT

- What types of workers should unions target in order to grow?
- What are future priorities for unions and for employers?
- What behaviour should be evident in a new era of unionism?

Controversial Employee–Management Topics

Today, the government is taking a more active role in requiring businesses to provide workers with certain benefits and assurances. Employees are raising questions of fairness, income inequality, and workplace security. Let's look at several key workplace issues, starting with executive compensation.

Executive Compensation

Cristiano Ronaldo kicks and dribbles his way to $88 million a year, Dwayne Johnson "rocks" his way to $64 million a year, Taylor Swift sings her way to $170 million a year, and Dr. Phil counsels his way to over $88 million a year.[52] Is it out of line, then, for some of Canada's top executives to make millions of dollars in annual compensation (e.g., salary, bonuses, and incentives)? Chapter 2 explained that the free-market system is built on incentives that allow top executives to make large amounts of money. Today, however, the government, shareholders, unions, and employees are challenging this principle and arguing that executive compensation has gotten out of line.

In theory, CEO compensation and bonuses are determined by the firm's profitability or an increase in its share price. The logic of this assumption was that as the fortunes of a company and its shareholders grew, so would the rewards of the CEO. Today, however, executives generally receive *stock options* (the ability to buy company stock at a set price at a later date) and *restricted stock* (stock issued directly to the CEO that cannot be sold for usually three or four years) as part of their compensation.[53] Today, stock and stock options account for over 50 percent of a CEO's compensation.[54] The Adapting to Change box discusses questions about the value of using performance-based pay for executives.

© Frederick M. Brown/Getty Images

USA Today listed Disney as one of the eight U.S. companies that most owed their employees a raise. The average Disney World cast member earned $9.48 an hour in 2017. Meanwhile Disney's chair and CEO Robert Iger enjoyed a total compensation package of approximately $44 million. Corporate boards of directors determine executive compensation. Do you think this is a fair system of compensation for CEOs? Do you think workers should have input?

LO6

Explain some of today's employee–management issues.

What is even more frustrating to those who question how much chief executives are paid is that the CEOs are often rewarded richly if their company does not meet expectations, or they leave under pressure.[55] Target Canada's failed expansion into Canada, in addition to the company's credit card data breach, contributed to Gregg Steinhafel's exit as Target Corporation's CEO. Estimated by *Fortune Magazine* to be $61 million, his overall severance package included severance pay of $15.9 million, stock options, and pension and deferred compensation. Contrast this to the $70 million Target made available for designated employee trust funds offered to the 17 600 workers that were laid off due to the closure of its 133 Canadian stores.[56] Some CEOs are also awarded fat retainers, consulting contracts, and lavish perks when they retire.

The late management consultant Peter Drucker criticized executive pay levels and he suggested that CEOs should not earn more than 20 times the salary of the company's lowest-paid employee.[57] Noted economist Thomas Piketty agrees and believes this income

Adapting to CHANGE

Paying for Underperforming

When it comes to paying CEOs, it's not unusual for companies to tie 60–80 percent of their compensation to performance. The idea sounds logical and simple. Companies set a target for profits and if the firm beats the target, the CEO gets a bigger payout. If he or she falls short, the CEO gets less or maybe nothing. The message is concise and direct: the boss makes money only if the company does well. Unfortunately, recent research on executive compensation has found that the nature of CEOs' work is not really suited to performance-based pay. In fact, performance-based pay can actually have dangerous outcomes for companies that implement it. The suggestion offered is not to pay CEOs less (even though many argue that should be the case); the argument is that CEOs are better compensated using a fixed salary system.

© Bank of Canada

Researchers sifting through pay data from 750 companies found that when a company sets a profit target, firms tend to either hit the target exactly or beat it by just a penny per share. As they dug deeper into the data, they found that firms that just barely beat the profit target were more likely to have cut research spending, cut overhead expenses and jobs, cut advertising, and/or used accrual accounting to boost revenues to hit the target number. They also found evidence that when a firm had a strong year, a lower profit was often reported by charging expenses against this year's profit or using accounting tactics to lower the company's profit. Why? Because the current year's results become the baseline for next year's bonus plan, and the idea is to keep the profit target low making it easier to achieve next year's goal.

Additional research suggests that performance-based pay is best suited for jobs with routine tasks; the job of a top manager is certainly not a routine one. Top managers need to be innovative and creative, open to learning about workplace changes, and able to develop new solutions for the many challenges they regularly face. If CEOs' financial rewards are linked to particular performance measures, it can draw their attention away from long-term results that would benefit the company more.

Sources: Peter Coy, "Heresy! Stop Paying CEOs Performance Bonuses," *Bloomberg Businessweek*, February 26, 2016; David Nicklaus, "Professors Explore Dark Side of Performance-Based Pay," *St. Louis Post-Dispatch*, April 5, 2016; Dan Cable and Freek Vermeulen, "Stop Paying Executives for Performance," *Harvard Business Review*, February 2016; Theo Francis and Joann S. Lublin, "Should Bar Be Lifted on CEO Bonuses?" *The Wall Street Journal*, June 2, 2017.

inequality is harmful and unnecessary, "When you pay $10 million instead of $1 [million], you don't have necessarily better performance or much higher productivity. . . . So I think there is really very little evidence that we need to pay people 100 times or 200 times the average wage to get them to work." Unfortunately, not many companies agree and few have placed such limits on executive compensation.[58]

According to the Canadian Centre for Policy Alternatives (CCPA), the average Canadian CEO salary among the top 100 highest-paid executives on the S&P/TSX Composite Index topped $10.4 million, which is 209 times the annual wage of an average Canadian at $49,738.[59] (Valeant Pharmaceuticals International's CEO, Joseph Papa, ranked number one with a total pay package of $83 million.[60]) Compare this to the average CEO of a Fortune 500 company that makes over 344 times the average salary of workers in his or her company.[61] Another area that concerns the CCPA is Canada's low-wage problem. Read the Seeking Sustainability box for a discussion on the living wage.

Seeking SUSTAINABILITY

The Living Wage: Why Minimum Wage Is Not Enough

The minimum (hourly) wage refers to the legal minimum all employers must pay their workers. It varies across Canada and even within some provinces, depending on the job. For example, in Quebec, the minimum wage is $12.00 but if gratuities apply to the role, the wage is $9.80. In recent years, there has been a rise in the living wage movement due to a recognition of Canada's low-wage problem. A significant proportion of full-time workers earn significantly less than a middle-class wage, and struggle to make ends meet.

With a higher standard than the minimum wage, a living wage is calculated as the hourly rate at which a household (e.g., a family of four with two parents working full-time at this hourly rate) can pay for necessities, support the healthy development of their children, escape severe financial stress, and participate in the social, civic, and cultural lives of their communities. The living wage varies across communities. For example, in 2018 the living wage in metro Vancouver was $20.91, in contrast to British Columbia's minimum wage of $11.35.

The Community Social Planning Council of British Columbia believes that the difference between the minimum and the living wage is the result of public policy failure to provide inputs such as universal affordable child care, affordable rental and social housing, affordable enrolment in health care, and affordable transportation. If there were adequate universal supports for low-income families in these areas, their struggles to make ends meet would be significantly reduced, which would be reflected in a lower living wage. Do you agree with this assessment?

According to a Canadian Centre for Policy Alternatives (CCPA) report, many workers do not earn a living wage because of discrimination. Female workers and those who are not Caucasian, immigrants, Aboriginal people, those living with disabilities, or similarly disadvantaged people are all segregated into low-wage

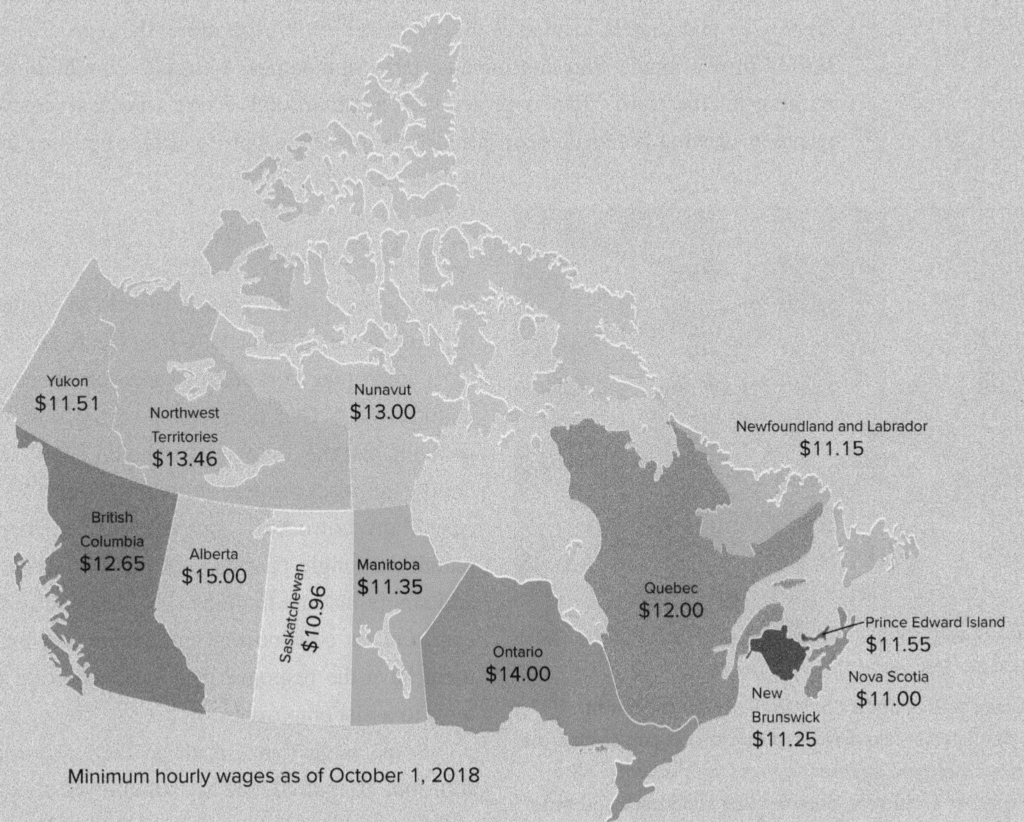

Minimum hourly wages as of October 1, 2018

Source: Data based on: "Payroll Legislation," Payworks Inc., accessed May 1, 2018, http://www.payworks.ca/payroll-legislation/MinimumWage.asp.

jobs. As a result, the CCPA calls on governments and employers to deliver more equitable compensation incomes for vulnerable workers.

Economists who support higher minimum wages believe that increases can be positive for both workers and employers in reducing turnover and raising productivity. For example, two-thirds of U.K. living-wage employers report significant positive impacts on recruitment, retention, and absenteeism.

Living wages are adopted voluntarily by employers and some examples include Vancity, the Canadian Cancer Society, and the Hamilton-Wentworth District School Board. What are employer reservations for a living wage policy? How can employees influence a living wage policy in their place of employment? What is the government's role, if any, in influencing living wage policies?

Sources: "Canadian Living Wage Framework," Living Wage Canada, accessed May 2, 2018, http://www.livingwagecanada.ca/index.php/about-living-wage/about-canadian-living-wage-framework/; "Minimum Wage by Province," Retail Council of Canada, accessed May 2, 2018, http://www.retailcouncil.org/quickfacts/minimum-wage; "Payroll Legislation," Payworks Inc., accessed May 2, 2018, http://www.payworks.ca/payroll-legislation/MinimumWage.asp; Iglika Ivanova, Seth Klein and Tess Raithby, "Working for a Living Wage: Making Paid Work Meet Basic Family Needs in Metro Vancouver," Canadian Centre for Policy Alternatives, April 25, 2018, https://www.policyalternatives.ca/sites/default/files/uploads/publications/BC%20Office/2018/04/BC_LivingWage2018_final.pdf; Andrew Jackson, "Why paying a living wage makes good business sense," *The Globe and Mail,* March 26, 2017, https://www.theglobeandmail.com/report-on-business/economy/economy-lab/why-paying-a-living-wage-makes-good-business-sense/article5152175/; and Mary Cornish, "A Living Wage As a Human Right," Canadian Centre for Policy Alternatives, October 5, 2012, https://www.policyalternatives.ca/publications/reports/living-wage-human-right.

Still, it's important to remember that some executives are responsible for multibillion-dollar corporations, work 70-plus hours a week, and often travel excessively. Many have turned potential problems at companies into successes and reaped huge benefits for employees and shareholders as well as themselves. Furthermore, there are few seasoned, skilled professionals who can manage large companies, especially troubled companies looking for the right CEO to accomplish a turnaround. There's no easy answer to the question of what is fair compensation for executives, but it's a safe bet the controversy will not go away.

© Ed Murray/The Star Ledger/The Image Works

On-site day care is not a common employee benefit. Although it is often expensive to operate, it can contribute to greater employee satisfaction and productivity. Who should pay for employee benefits like child care and elder care? Should it be the employee or the company or both?

Child Care

Today women make up almost half (47.7 percent) of the workforce in Canada.[62] Child care is an increasingly important workplace issue as absences related to child care cost Canadian businesses millions of dollars annually and the issue of who should pay for employee child care raises a question that often divides employees. Many coworkers oppose child care benefits for parents or single parents, arguing that single workers and single-income families should not subsidize child care. Others contend that employers and the government have the responsibility to create child care systems to assist employees.

Some large firms, such as IBM and Johnson & Johnson, offer child care as an employee benefit. Some additional child-care benefits provided by employers include:

- Discount arrangements with national child-care chains.
- Vouchers that offer payments toward child care the employee selects.
- Referral services that help identify high-quality child-care facilities to employees.
- On-site child-care centres where parents can visit children at lunch or during lag times throughout the workday.
- Sick-child centres to care for moderately ill children.

Increasing numbers of single-parent and two-income households ensure that child care will remain a key employee–management issue even as businesses face the growing challenge of elder care.[63]

Elder Care

Nearly one in six Canadians (16.1 percent of the population at approximately 5.8 million) is at least 65 years old with Canada now having more seniors than children aged 1 to 14 years (16 percent).[64] The likelihood that a Canadian aged 65 will live to 90 has also increased significantly. While Baby Boomers will not have to concern themselves with finding child care for their children, they will confront another problem: how to care for older parents and other relatives. In the future, more workers are expected to be involved in the time-consuming and stressful task of caring for an aging relative. Companies are seeing reduced productivity, and increased absenteeism and turnover from employees who are responsible for aging relatives.[65]

Employees with elder-care responsibilities need information on medical, legal, and insurance issues, as well as the full support of their supervisors and company. Such caregivers may require flextime, telecommuting, part-time employment, or job sharing. Some firms offer employee assistance programs. Such elder-care management services can include a needs assessment program for the employee, and health-spending accounts in which employees can put aside pre-tax income for elder-care expenses. However, the number of companies offering elder care benefits still lags behind the number offering child care benefits and small businesses lag considerably behind large companies in providing elder care benefits. Unfortunately, the government does not provide much relief as heavy financial burdens for care are placed on family caregivers.

© Radius Images/Alamy

Canadians are living longer which means that they will likely require elder care in addition to providing elder care for older parents or relatives. Do you have a relative that requires elder care? What support is available for the person receiving care as well as for the care provider? Is this level of care sustainable?

As more experienced and high-ranking employees begin caring for older parents and relatives, the costs to companies will rise even higher. This argument makes sense, since older, more experienced workers (who are most affected by elder care issues) often hold jobs more critical to the company than those held by younger workers (who are most affected by child-care problems). Firms now face the fact that transfers and promotions are often out of the question for employees whose elderly parents or relatives need ongoing care.

Unfortunately, as Canadians age, the elder-care situation will grow considerably worse, meaning this employee–management issue will persist well into the future.

PROGRESS ASSESSMENT

- How does top-executive pay in Canada compare with the pay of average workers?
- How does the living wage compare to the minimum wage?
- What are some of the issues related to child care and elder care, and how are companies addressing these issues?

You and Unions

Do you think that unions are still necessary? We are fortunate to be living in a democratic country where free and private enterprise is the vital feature of our economic system. We believe that all citizens have the right to do what they can, within legal and ethical limits, to better themselves. Improving your financial situation is an admired goal, and those who do so are usually seen as good examples.

If you select the entrepreneurial route, you will try to build a successful company by providing a necessary service or product in a manner that your customers appreciate. If you are successful, you will ultimately accumulate profits, personal wealth, and financial security for yourself and your family. One of the costs of doing business that you will be keeping an eye on is wages, salaries, and benefits paid to employees. Will you consider unions nothing but a hindrance?

Suppose that you do not see yourself as an entrepreneur and instead go the employee route. Imagine yourself ten years down the road: you have a partner and two children and are now working for a large company in a non-managerial role. Will you seek the best salary you can possibly get? How about working hours? Your partner also works and you need flexible arrangements to be able to spend time with your children and deliver them to school and various other activities. How about overtime demands on the job that cut into time with your family? Will you have adequate, affordable child care?

Firms that have healthy employee–management relations have a better chance to prosper than those that don't. Taking a proactive approach is the best way to ensure positive employee–management work environments. The proactive manager anticipates potential sensitive issues and works toward resolving them before they get out of hand—a good lesson for any manager.

SUMMARY

LO1 **Trace the history of organized labour in Canada.**

Organized labour in Canada dates back to the 1800s. Early unions on the wharves of Halifax, St. John's, and Quebec existed during the War of 1812 to profit from labour scarcity. Craft unions represented shoemakers and printers. Many of the early labour organizations were local or regional in nature.

Describe some of the main objectives of labour and whether they were achieved.

Unions hoped to improve workers' poor conditions and wages by forming unions that would fight for workers' rights. This has largely been achieved, and many early demands are now entrenched in law.

Describe some of the unions in existence today.

CUPE and Unifor are two of the largest unions in Canada. They represent workers from different industries in the economy. Many unions in Canada are national in nature. Many also belong to international organizations. The Canadian Labour Congress, which represents 3.3 million unionized workers, is the largest labour congress in Canada.

LO2 **Discuss the major legislation affecting labour unions.**

Much labour legislation has been passed by federal and provincial governments.

What is the major piece of labour legislation?

The Canada Labour Code outlines labour legislation as it applies to federal government employees, who represent approximately 6 percent of all workers in Canada. Each provincial jurisdiction in Canada has its own labour legislation and employment standards that apply to workers within its borders.

What are workplace rights?

All workers in Canada have the right to work in a safe and healthy environment. Workplace laws include the right to participate in the workplace health and safety activities, and the right to know about actual and potential dangers in the workplace. A safe and healthy workplace environment also includes one that is free of sexual harassment, violence, and bullying.

LO3 **Describe the collective bargaining process.**

Collective bargaining is the process by which a union represents employees in relations with their employer.

What is included in collective bargaining?

Collective bargaining includes how unions are selected, the period prior to a vote, certification, ongoing contract negotiations, and behaviour while a contract is in force.

What are the steps in the collective bargaining process?

Refer to Figure 13.3 for the steps in the collective bargaining process.

LO4 **Outline the objectives of labour unions.**

The objectives of labour unions shift in response to changes in social and economic trends.

What is the purpose of the negotiated labour–management agreement?

Informally referred to as the labour contract, the labour–management agreement sets the tone and clarifies the terms and conditions under which management and the union will function over a specific period.

What topics typically appear in labour–management agreements?

Labour–management agreements may include issues such as management rights, union security clauses, hours of work, vacation policies, job rights and seniority principles, and employee benefits. See Figure 13.4 for a more detailed list.

LO5 **Describe the negotiation tactics used by labour and management during conflicts.**

If negotiations between labour and management break down, either or both sides may use certain tactics to enhance their positions or sway public opinion.

What are the tactics used by unions in conflicts?

Unions primarily use strikes and boycotts.

What are the tactics used by management in conflicts?

Management can use lockouts, injunctions, and strikebreakers.

LO6 **Explain some of today's employee–management issues.**

Some employee–management issues are executive compensation, child care, and elder care.

What is a fair wage for executives?

The market and the businesses in it set executives' salaries. What is fair is open to debate.

How are some companies addressing the child-care issue?

Responsive companies are providing child care on their premises, discounts with child-care chains, vouchers to be used at the employee's chosen care centre, and referral services.

What problems do companies face with regard to elder care?

Companies are seeing reduced productivity and increased absenteeism and turnover from employees who are responsible for aging relatives. As more experienced and high- ranking employees begin caring for elders, the costs to companies will rise even higher since older workers often hold jobs more critical to the company than those held by younger workers.

KEY TERMS

agency shop (Rand formula) agreement 492
arbitration 495
back-to-work legislation 498
bargaining zone 494
bullying 488
certification 489
checkoff 492
closed shop agreement 491
collective bargaining 489
conciliation 495
coverage rate 482
craft union 478
decertification 489
directly chartered union 479
givebacks 491
grievance 493
independent local organization 479
industrial union 479
injunction 497
international union 480
labour relations board 488
labour union 476
lockout 497
mediation 495
national union 480
negotiated labour–management agreement (labour contract) 491
open shop agreement 492
primary boycott 497
Rand formula (agency shop agreement) 492
secondary boycott 497
sexual harassment 485
shop stewards 493
strike 496
strikebreakers 497
union security clause 491
union shop agreement 491
unionization rate (union density) 481
workplace violence 486

CAREER EXPLORATION

If you are interested in pursuing a career in employee–management relations, here are a few to consider. Find out about the tasks performed, skills needed, pay, and opportunity outlook in these fields through Internet sites that include the Government of Canada Job Bank, Workopolis, Monster, CareerBuilder, Glassdoor, and Indeed, as well as through the Career Centre at your school.

- **Labour relations specialist**—interprets and administers labour contracts regarding issues such as wages and salaries, health care, pensions, and union and management practices.

- **Human resource specialist—**recruits, screens, interviews, and places workers; handles other human resource work, such as those related to employee relations, compensation and benefits, and training.
- **Arbitrator and mediator—**facilitates negotiation and dialogue between disputing parties to help resolve conflicts outside of court.

CRITICAL THINKING

1. Do you believe that union shop agreements are violations of a worker's freedom of choice in the workplace? Do you think open shop agreements unfairly penalize workers who pay dues to unions they have elected to represent them in the workplace?
2. Why are unionization rates much higher in the public sector than in the private sector? Are you more or less attracted to the public sector as a result of this coverage?
3. Do you agree that back-to-work legislation is a denial of the legal right to strike; therefore, to a certain extent it is a restriction of the democratic rights of individuals? Factor in the rights of employers in your answer.
4. If a company provides employer-paid child care services to workers with children, should those who don't have children or don't need child care services be paid extra?

DEVELOPING CAREER SKILLS

Key: ● **Team** ★ **Analytic** ▲ **Communication** ⊡ **Technology**

●⊡★▲ 1. With several classmates, investigate the emerging role of employee associations and professional associations as replacements for labour unions. What are the advantages and disadvantages of each of these three models? Which model provides the greatest legal protection in case of a disagreement between labour and management? Share your findings with the class.

★▲ 2. Do businesses and government agencies have a duty to provide additional benefits to employees beyond fair pay and good working conditions? Propose a benefits system that you consider fair and workable for employees and employers.

●★▲ 3. Debate the following statement with several classmates: "Non-union firms are better managed (or perform better) than unionized firms." To get a better feeling for the other side's point of view, take the opposite side of this issue from the one you normally would. Consider such questions as: Do unions serve a purpose in some industries? Do unions make Canada less competitive in global markets?

●★▲ 4. Compile a list of two or three employee–management issues not covered in the chapter. Compare your list with those of several classmates and see which issues you selected in common and which are unique to each individual. Pick an issue you all agree will be important in the future and discuss its likely effects and outcomes.

●⊡★▲ 5. With a classmate, investigate which unions have been in the news over the past six months. What were the issues? Were these issues resolved? Share this information with the class.

ANALYZING MANAGEMENT DECISIONS

Plant Closings, Unions, and Concessions

Over the past decade, the Canadian economy has witnessed a series of plant closing or lockout actions taken by foreign companies against employees in Canada. Plants and offices have laid off thousands of people or closed because of bankruptcy, consolidation, or transfer of operations to other lower-wage countries. In some cases, management advised unions that the only way that they could avoid closing would be substantial concessions in wages and other changes in existing contracts.

American-based heavy equipment maker Caterpillar Inc. ended a one-month standoff with locked-out workers by closing its 62-year-old Electro-Motive plant in London, Ontario, eliminating about 450 manufacturing jobs that mostly paid twice the rate of a U.S. counterpart. Caterpillar spokesman Rusty Dunn summed up the reasoning as follows: "All facilities must achieve competitive costs, quality, and operating flexibility to remain viable in the global marketplace. Expectations at the London plant were no different."

The closing angered former CAW president Ken Lewenza. Caterpillar had demanded pay cuts of 50 percent in many job categories, elimination of a defined-benefit pension plan, reductions in dental and other benefits, and the end of a cost-of-living adjustment. "I've never had a situation where I've dealt with such an unethical, immoral, disrespectful, highly profitable company like Caterpillar," said Lewenza. During bargaining he told the company's negotiators: "If it's in your business plan to close us, don't punish us, let's work out a closure agreement. They said, 'We have no intention of closing the facility.'"

In another industry, negotiations were long and hard won. Workers at international mining giant Vale in Ontario approved a new labour agreement, ending a year-long strike in 2010. Vale said it needed to cut labour costs to keep its operations competitive, but workers argued the Brazilian company made billions of dollars a year and did not need concessions from workers. The strike was bitter at times, with the union accusing Vale of bad faith bargaining and the company taking the union to court over a variety of alleged incidents on the picket lines. The output from the Canadian operations—which account for more than 10 percent of the world's nickel supply—was significantly decreased during the strike. The agreement resulted in more than 3000 workers receiving a raise and a big signing bonus. However, it also saw new employees placed on a defined-contribution pension plan as opposed to the existing defined-benefit plan. Defined-contribution plans depend on market returns and do not guarantee a steady income, unlike defined-benefit plans.

Givebacks are not being asked just by foreign-owned companies. For example, since Air Canada came out of bankruptcy protection in 2004, it received concessions in the areas of wages, jobs, and pensions from its unions as part of its restructuring conditions. Eight years later, union members grew tired of givebacks and voted to go on strike. The federal government stepped in and threatened the unions with back-to-work legislation before imposing binding arbitration in some instances.

Keep in mind that non-unionized employees also saw tens of thousands of jobs eliminated. For example, in 2001 Nortel Networks Corporation had more than 90 000 employees worldwide. Ten years later, and after a couple of rounds of bankruptcy, no one had a job. Nortel's union and former employees failed to persuade an Ontario appeals court they were entitled to retirement and severance payments. No employees are safe as companies try to remain competitive in the marketplace.

Union leaders and their members are in a quandary when faced with such decisions. Sometimes they think management is bluffing. Sometimes they are reluctant to give up contract conditions they fought long and hard for. Accepting wage cuts or benefit reductions when the cost of living continues to rise is not easy. Agreeing to staff reductions to save other jobs is also a tough decision. Unions worry about where these concessions will end. Will there be another round of layoffs or even worse in a few months?

These examples highlight some of the dilemmas facing unions and employers. The business environment demands that companies become more efficient and productive. However, this will not happen unless there is mutual respect between management and labour.

Sources: James R. Hagerty, "Caterpillar Closes Plant in Canada After Lockout," *The Wall Street Journal,* 4 February 4, 2012, http://online.wsj.com/article/SB10001424052970203889904577200953014575964.html; Greg Keenan, "Caterpillar pulls plug on London plant," *The Globe and Mail,* February 3, 2012, www.theglobeandmail.com/globe-investor/caterpillar-pulls-plug-on-london-plant/article544321/; "Timeline: Nortel—The rise and fall of a telecom giant," Global News, January 18, 2012, www.globalnews.ca/timeline+nortel+-+the+rise-+and+fall+of+a+telecom+giant/6442560329/story.html; "Ont. Vale workers vote to approve new contract," The Canadian Press, January 13, 2010, www.ctvnews.ca/ont-vale-workers-vote-to-approve-new-contract-1.530694; Brent Jang, "Air Canada, Union at Odds Over Proposed Moratorium on Pension Payments," *The Globe and Mail,* May 5, 2009, www.theglobeandmail.com/servlet/story/LAC.20090505.RAIRCANADA05ART1908/TPStory/Business; "Study: The Year in Review in Manufacturing," Statistics Canada, April 29, 2009, www.statcan.gc.ca/daily-quotidien/090429/dq090429b-eng.htm; Paul Kunert, "Nortel Networks Lays off 3,200 Staff," *Computer Weekly,* February 26, 2009, www.computerweekly.com/Articles/2009/02/26/235029/nortel-networks-lays-off-3200-staff.htm; "Air Canada: Fly it Right!" Canadian Auto Workers Union, 2009, www.caw.ca/en/7423.htm; and "Nortel Rebuilding and Hiring Again: CEO," CBC News, September 29, 2006, www.cbc.ca/money/story/2006/09/29/zafirovski-nortel.html.

Discussion Questions

1. What would you recommend to union workers whose employer is threatening to close down unless they agree to wage decreases or other concessions?
2. Is there some alternative to cutting wages or closing down? What is it?
3. Union workers often feel that the company is bluffing when it threatens to close. How can such doubts be settled so that more open negotiations can take place?
4. Does government have a right to interfere with organizations (i.e., union and employer) that have already negotiated a collective agreement and force them to renegotiate? Explain.

RUNNING CASE

Human Resources at Fox 40 International Inc.

For successful Canadian entrepreneur and inventor Ron Foxcroft, it all started in 1982 when he purchased Fluke Transport, a Southern Ontario trucking business. The company slogan—If It's On Time . . . It's A "FLUKE"—was soon recognized throughout North America. Over the years, Foxcroft diversified into new ventures and the Foxcroft Group of Companies now includes Fluke Transportation Group, Fluke Warehousing Inc., Foxcroft Capital Group, Fox 40 International Inc., and Fox 40 USA Inc.

The formation of Fox 40 International Inc. (Fox 40) is the result of a dream for a pealess whistle. When developing his first whistle, Ron was motivated by his knowledge and experience as an international basketball referee. Frustrated with faulty pea whistles, he spent three years of development with design consultant Chuck Shepherd, resulting in the creation of the Fox 40® Classic Whistle. Fast forward 25 years and Fox 40 dominates the global whistle industry.

Fox 40 is a privately held, family-run organization with Ron as the Chief Executive Officer and son, Dave, as the President and Chief Operating Officer. The company employs 35 individuals, and as many as 45 during peak seasons. You may be surprised to learn that there is no formal human resource department in this company. In fact, there are no layers of management. Among other reasons, this is to empower employees, regardless of position, to develop solutions to problems, with the goal of satisfying customers.

It is important to create a good working environment. Open communication is encouraged throughout the organization. There is an open-door policy within the three teams—Corporate, Product and Marketing, and Sales and Customer Service—and across the teams. Senior management is directly accessible by both employees and customers. The lack of internal titles is another signal that the owners do not stand on ceremony. Outside of the organization, however, employees have titles as this is expected by external stakeholders.

Hiring the right people is critical. According to Ron, "Managers hire people that are dumber than them, but owners hire people that are smarter than them." With this in mind, new hires are expected to contribute to the organization. There is a focus on hiring self-starters who require minimum supervision. Chemistry with current employees (i.e., organizational fit), strong communication skills, a customer-focus, enthusiasm, and honesty are required qualities. Initiative is expected and employees should have the courage to go to Ron or Dave with suggestions on how to make the company better. Examples can include improving processes, developing new products, or improving the customer experience.

For example, Dave and his team approached Ron with the idea to develop a new variation of the Fox 40 Classic. Ron struggled with this as the Fox 40 Classic was his first whistle and he was not convinced that this was the right direction. The team believed that there were some untapped opportunities. One advantage would be that a new whistle could be registered for an 18-year patent and trademark. Ron agreed and the Fox 40 Classic Eclipse was created. This whistle was re-engineered for maximum performance and style. The Fox 40 Classic Eclipse was also the first whistle to be developed using exclusive SpectraBurst™ glow-in-the dark colours that would last up to ten hours. Since its introduction in the marketplace, feedback has been tremendous.

At Fox 40, new hires start in entry-level positions. They should be prepared to do any job (except take out the garbage; this is the CEO's job). Orientation includes on-the-job training. As Dave says, "The best way to learn is by doing." Employees are assigned tasks with a timeline and their performance is monitored. During a performance review, discussions centre on finding opportunities that will tap into each employee's strengths while also discussing how to improve on any weaknesses.

Fox 40 is a non-unionized work environment. "We pay our employees fairly," says Ron. For the production staff, manufacturing output is tracked. Those that exceed their targets are also compensated with money and gift certificates that can be redeemed at local retailers.

Sources: Ron Foxcroft, CEO of Fox 40 International Inc. and Chairman and CEO of Fluke Transportation, in-person interview, September 22, 2017, Hamilton; and Dave Foxcroft, President and COO, Fox 40 International Inc., in-person interview, June 25, 2012, Hamilton.

Discussion Questions

1. Considering Douglas McGregor's research on managers' attitudes toward their workers. How would you categorize the management style described at Fox 40?
2. What pay systems does Fox 40 use for its production staff? (Hint: Review Figure 12.5 for some examples.)
3. What are some company advantages in not having a unionized workforce? What are some employee advantages in not belonging to a labour union?

PART 5

CHAPTER 14

Marketing: Helping Buyers Buy

LEARNING OBJECTIVES

After you have read and studied this chapter, you should be able to:

LO1 Define marketing and explain how the marketing concept applies to both for-profit and non-profit organizations.

LO2 Describe the four Ps of marketing.

LO3 Identify the steps in the marketing research process, and explain how marketers use environmental scanning to learn about the changing marketing environment.

LO4 Compare the consumer market to the business-to-business market.

LO5 Describe the market segmentation process, and the role of relationship marketing.

LO6 Explain how marketers meet the needs of the consumer market through the study of consumer behaviour.

PROFILE

GETTING TO KNOW: MICHELLE PHAN, FOUNDER, IPSY

When Michelle Phan began uploading makeup tutorials on YouTube in 2007, she never thought her videos would someday be the foundation of a multimillion-dollar business. But thanks to her determination and unique sense of style, Phan was able to transform her hobby into a successful company named ipsy. Valued at more than $500 million, the beauty start-up has become a marketing juggernaut thanks to its squad of social media influencers who shine spotlights on the latest products.

Phan and her more than 8 million YouTube subscribers form the core of this operation. She joined the video-sharing site at age 19 and mostly uploaded videos of dogs because they cheered her up. As time went by, though, she noticed that some of her videos about beauty tips were racking up

Source: © Katie Falkenberg/Los Angeles Times/Getty Images

tens of thousands of views. So along with producing more makeup-centric clips, Phan also applied for a new program that allowed YouTube creators to collect ad revenue from their videos. Although rejected at first, she eventually made it into the program and started earning 5 cents a day from ads. Of course, the laughable payday didn't faze Phan. She recognized that YouTube had the potential to be an enormously influential platform and wanted to get in on the ground floor. "I thought, if [YouTube] is going to be the global television of the future, I need to build my brand here," said Phan.

Plus, Phan gained immense personal satisfaction from making videos that allowed her to broadcast a different version of herself to the world. Whereas her on-screen persona seemed to have a perfect life, the off-screen reality was much different. Phan is the daughter of Vietnamese immigrants. Her father dropped out of her life for 10 years as he ran from debts brought on by his gambling problem. Her mother supported the family as a beautician, but they had little extra money to spend. So Phan learned from an early age how to make things happen for herself. For instance, when she needed a computer, she raised the cash by selling candy to her classmates. Then when she began making videos, she created a glamorous, confident persona that had it all. "I depicted myself as the girl I wanted to be, with money and a great family," said Phan. "I always had that yearning, that hunger, to one day be independent and be my own person and build my own world."

This world grew rapidly as her videos started bringing in millions of viewers. In 2011 she and a partner used this exposure to start ipsy, a beauty product subscription service. For $10 a month, subscribers receive a "Glam Bag" full of an ever-changing array of makeup and other beauty products. What's more, Phan developed an ingenious business model that allowed her to keep costs low. Rather than pay companies to stock its products, ipsy instead receives items for free in exchange for marketing exposure. Along with Phan, the company employs a staff of beauty vloggers (video bloggers) who feature the products in demonstration videos. These employees are then aided by thousands of independent vloggers who create content under the ipsy brand in exchange for mentoring and networking opportunities. Thanks to this army of influencers, the company has amassed 1.5 million subscribers and brought in hundreds of millions of dollars in venture capital investment.

For Phan, this is just the start of her story. As she maintains this growing beauty empire, she also plans to start a music label and a premium video company, and publish a comic book. The one component that will likely unite these varying ventures will be Phan's widespread marketing influence. As she once said: "Influence is the new power—if you have influence you can create a brand."

In this chapter you'll learn how master marketers like Michelle Phan identify their audience and figure out how to reach them. Whether through distribution, advertising, or publicity, successful marketing makes a connection with customers that they won't soon forget.

Sources: Michelle Phan, "Michelle Phan Relaunches Em Cosmetics and Explains Her Social Media Detox," *Teen Vogue*, April 11, 2017; Gillian Fuller, "Michelle Phan Returns To YouTube After A Yearlong Hiatus To Explain Why She Left," *Allure*, June 2, 2017.

LO1

Define marketing and explain how the marketing concept applies to both for-profit and non-profit organizations.

What is Marketing?

marketing
A set of business practices designed to plan for and present an organization's products or services in ways that build effective customer relationships.

The term marketing means different things to different people. Many think of marketing as simply "selling" or "advertising." Yes, selling and advertising are part of marketing, but it is much more. The Canadian Marketing Association defines **marketing** as a set of business practices designed to plan for and present an organization's products or services in ways that build effective customer relationships.[1] We can also think of marketing, more simply, as the activities buyers and sellers perform to facilitate mutually satisfying exchanges. A market (note that this is the core word in *marketing*) is defined as a group of people with unsatisfied wants and needs who have the resources and the willingness to buy. A market is, therefore, created as a result of this demand for goods and services. What marketers do at any particular time will depend on what needs to be done to fill customers' needs. This "find a need and fill it" concept is core to marketing.

In the past marketing focused almost entirely on helping the seller sell. That is why many people still think of it as mostly selling, advertising, and distribution *from the seller to the buyer.* Today, much of marketing is instead about *helping the buyer buy.*[2] Let's examine a couple of examples.

Today, when people want to buy a new or used car, they often go online first. They go to a website like Cars.ca to search for the vehicle they want. At other websites they compare prices and features. By the time they go to the dealer, they may know exactly which car they want and the best prices available. The websites have *helped the buyer buy.* Not only are customers spared searching one dealership after another to find the best price, but manufacturers and dealers are eager to participate so that they do not lose customers. The future of marketing is doing everything one can to help the buyer buy. The easier a marketer makes the purchase decision process, the more that marketer will sell.[3]

Let's look at another example. In the past, one of the few ways students and parents could find the school with the right "fit" was to travel from campus to campus, a gruelling and expensive process. Today, schools use podcasts, virtual tours, live chats, and other interactive technologies to make on-campus visits less necessary. Such virtual tours help students and their parents buy.

© Shutterstock/Zapp2Photo

Shoppers use different sources of information when making purchasing decisions. Would you use your smart phone with an augmented reality app to check the number of social media likes and sale prices when shopping for clothes?

Of course, helping the buyer buy also helps the seller sell. Think about that for a minute. In the vacation market, many people find the trip they want themselves. They go online to find the right spot, and then make choices, sometimes questioning potential sellers. In industries like this, the role of marketers is to make sure that a company's products or services are easily found online, and that the company responds effectively to potential customers. Websites like Expedia, Travelocity, and Priceline allow customers to find the best prices or set their own prices.

These are only a few examples of the marketing trend toward helping buyers buy. Consumers today spend hours searching the Internet for good deals. Wise marketers provide a wealth of information online and even cultivate customer relationships using blogs and social networking sites such as Facebook and Twitter.[4]

Online communities provide an opportunity to observe people (customers and others) interacting with one another, expressing their own opinions, forming relationships, and commenting on various goods and services. It is important for marketers to track what relevant bloggers are writing by doing blog searches using key terms that define their markets. Vendors who have text-mining tools can help companies measure conversations about their products and their personnel. Much of the future of marketing lies in mining such online conversations and responding appropriately. For example, marketers are learning why people shop online, put the goods into a shopping cart, but then end the sale before they give their credit card information.[5]

The Evolution of Marketing

What marketers do at any particular time depends on what they need to do to fill customers' needs and wants, which are continually changing. Let's take a brief look at how those changes have influenced the evolution of marketing. The evolution of marketing includes five eras, also known as orientations: (1) production, (2) sales, (3) marketing concept, (4) market orientation, and (5) social media marketing. Figure 14.1 highlights the timeline for these eras.

THE PRODUCTION ERA

From the time the first European settlers arrived in Canada until the start of the 1900s, the general philosophy of business was, "Produce as much as you can because there is a limitless market for it." Given the limited production capability and the vast demand for products in those days, that production philosophy was both logical and profitable, as demand exceeded supply. Business owners were mostly farmers, carpenters, and trade workers. They needed to produce more and more, so their goals centred on *production.*

FIGURE 14.1

MARKETING ERAS

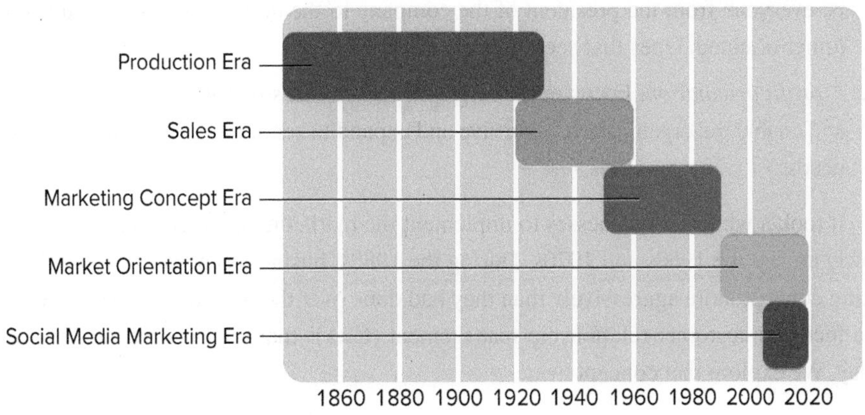

There are five different marketing eras in the history of North American business.

NOW! CROSLEY SHELVADOR®
GIVES YOU AUTOMATIC DEFROSTING
at the price of old-fashioned refrigerators!
YOU'LL NEVER DEFROST AGAIN!
PLUS—MORE FOOD AT YOUR FINGER TIPS!
CROSLEY
Better Products for Happier Living

© Interfoto/Alamy

During the Sales Era, the focus of marketing was on selling, with little service afterward and less customization. What economic and social factors made this approach appropriate for the time?

THE SALES ERA

By the 1920s, businesses had developed mass production techniques (such as automobile assembly lines), and production capacity often exceeded the immediate market demand. Therefore, the business philosophy turned from producing to *selling*. Most companies emphasized selling and advertising in an effort to persuade customers to buy existing products. Few offered extensive service after the sale.

THE MARKETING CONCEPT ERA

After World War II ended in 1945, returning soldiers started new careers and began families, sparking a tremendous demand for goods and services. The postwar years launched the sudden increase in the birth rate that we now call the baby boom, and also a boom in consumer spending. Competition for the customer's dollar was fierce. Businesses recognized that they needed to be responsive to customers if they wanted to get their business, and a philosophy called the marketing concept emerged in the 1950s.

The **marketing concept** had three parts:

marketing concept A three-part business philosophy: (1) a customer orientation, (2) a service orientation, and (3) a profit orientation.

1. *A customer orientation.* Find out what consumers want and provide it for them. (Note the emphasis on meeting consumer needs rather than on promotion or sales.) That is exactly what Cassandra Rush, founder of Sassy Cassy's Boots Inc. did when she started her company, which specialized in boots with varying calf sizes; "Every other boot company only does standard sizing for calves, which is about 15 inches around the calf of the leg," she said. "The market calls for bigger sizes because a lot of women can't zip up regular boots. My product is different because I offer different calf sizing so the boots are better customized to the woman's leg."[6]
2. *A service orientation.* Make sure everyone in the organization has the same objective: customer satisfaction. This should be a total and integrated organizational effort. That is, everyone from the president of the company to the delivery people should be customer oriented. Does that seem to be the norm today?
3. *A profit orientation.* Focus on those goods and services that will earn the most profit and enable the organization to survive and expand to serve more customers' wants and needs.

It took a while for businesses to implement the marketing concept. That process went slowly during the 1960s and 1970s. During the 1980s, businesses began to apply the marketing concept more aggressively than they had done over the preceding 30 years. That led to a focus on customer-relationship management (CRM) that has become very important today. We explore that concept next.

THE MARKET ORIENTATION ERA[7]

Many organizations transitioned from the marketing concept era to the market orientation era. Firms with a **market orientation** focus their efforts on (1) continuously collecting information about customers' needs and competitors' capabilities, (2) sharing this information throughout the organization, and (3) using the information to create value, ensure customer satisfaction, and develop customer relationships.

It is not surprising that organizations with a market orientation actually engage in **customer-relationship management (CRM)**—the process of building long-term relationships with customers by delivering customer value and satisfaction. Retaining customers over time, or managing the entire customer life cycle, is a cost-effective way for firms to grow in competitive markets. The idea is to enhance customer satisfaction and stimulate long-term customer loyalty. For example, most airlines offer frequent-flyer programs that reward loyal customers with free flights.

© WildPlay Elements Parks

WildPlay Element Parks is an aerial adventure company with locations in British Columbia, Ontario, and New York. The outdoor recreation company offers ways for people to have fun and challenge their self-perceived boundaries. WildPlay's nature-based activities for adults, teens, and kids include Bungy Jump, Primal Swings, tree-top Monkido Aerial Adventure courses, What's To Fear Jumps, and long Zip Line rides. Would you be interested in this experience? How would you share it with your friends via social media?

THE SOCIAL MEDIA MARKETING ERA[8]

Social media is the term commonly given to websites and online tools that allow users to interact with each other in some way—by sharing information, opinions, knowledge, and interests. As the name implies, social media involves the building of communities or networks, encouraging participation and engagement. There are two distinct dimensions to the **social media marketing** era:

1. Social media marketing is about consumer-generated online-marketing efforts to promote brands and companies for which they are fans (or conversely, negatively promoting brands and companies for which they are non-fans).
2. Social media marketing is the use by marketers of online tools and platforms to promote their brands or organizations. The most common tools or platforms used by both consumers and organizations are social networking sites (e.g., Facebook, LinkedIn, Instagram, and Twitter), blogs, wikis, podcasts, and other shared media sites such as YouTube.

It is the first dimension of social media marketing that is changing the rules of marketing and ushering in a new era of business. Social media creates a platform that empowers customers and provides them with an opportunity to communicate with an organization and with other customers. In fact, one author, Erik Qualman, suggests social media marketing is creating a new form of economy called *socialnomics,* where consumers will no longer search for products or services, but rather will find them via social media. He suggests that social media is transforming the way we live and the way organizations do business.

market orientation
Focusing efforts on (1) continuously collecting information about customers' needs and competitors' capabilities, (2) sharing this information throughout the organization, and (3) using the information to create value, ensure customer satisfaction, and develop customer relationships.

customer-relationship management (CRM)
The process of building long-term relationships with customers by delivering customer value and satisfaction.

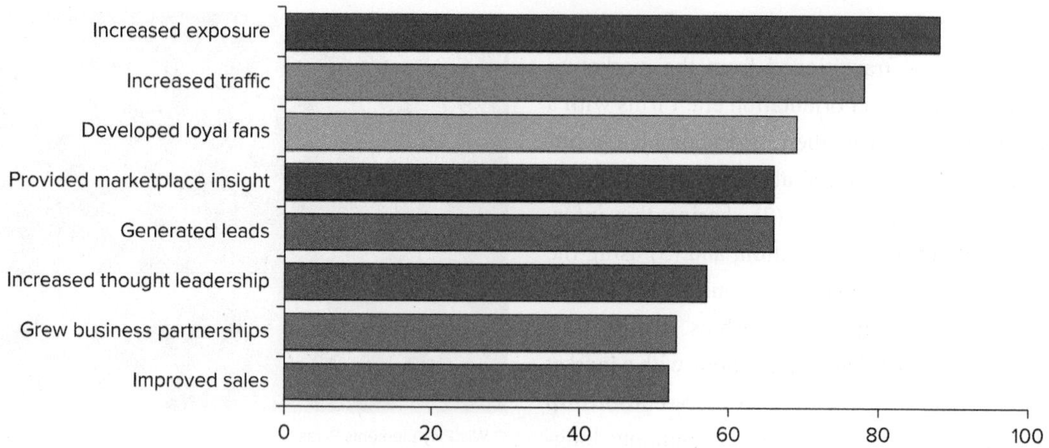

2017 Social Media Marketing Industry Report, SocialMediaExaminer.com

There are many benefits to social media marketing. Were you surprised by any of these statistics?

social media
The term commonly given to websites and online tools that allow users to interact with each other in some way—by sharing information, opinions, knowledge, and interests.

social media marketing
Consumer-generated online-marketing efforts to promote brands and companies for which they are fans (or conversely, negatively promoting brands and companies for which they are non-fans), and the use by marketers of online tools and platforms to promote their brands or organizations.

EMERGING: THE MOBILE/ON-DEMAND MARKETING ERA

The digital age is increasing consumers' power and pushing marketing toward being on demand, not just always "on." Consumers are demanding relevant information exactly when they want it, without all the noise of unwanted messages. Search technologies have made product information pervasive. Consumers share, compare, and rate experiences through social media and mobile devices make it all available 24/7.[9]

Developments such as inexpensive microtransmitters embedded in products will allow consumers to search by image, voice, or gestures. For example, if your friend has a product you like, you will be able to just tap it with your phone and instantly get product reviews, prices, and so on. If you can't decide what colour to buy, you can just send the photo to your Facebook friends who can vote for their favourite. After you buy it, you will get special offers from the manufacturer or its partners for similar products or services.

As digital technology continues to grow, consumer demands are likely to rise in four areas:[10]

1. *Now.* Consumers want to interact anywhere and anytime.
2. *Can I?* They want to do new things with different kinds of information in ways that create value for them. For example, a couple wanting to know if they can afford to buy a house for sale as they walk by could simply snap a photo and instantly see the sale price and other property information, while at the same time the device automatically accesses their financial information, contacts mortgage companies, and obtains mortgage pre-approvals.
3. *For me.* Consumers expect all data stored about them to be used to personalize what they experience.
4. *Simple.* Consumers expect all interactions to be easy.

Companies will be looking for employees who can improve the business' handling of social media and customer experiences. Maybe you will be one of them. The Adapting to Change box discusses a few of the challenges marketers face while using Snapchat.

Adapting *to* CHANGE

Snapping Up a Customer Base

Snapchat, one of the fastest-growing social networks, can be an extremely effective marketing tool. Millennials flock to the platform in droves, and it seems everyone loves the crazy filters the app offers—even celebrities. When Ariana Grande or Kylie Jenner use a sponsored filter, marketers have the opportunity to reach over 150 million users a day in a fun way that doesn't *look* like a sponsored advertisement.

Using Snapchat is quite the endeavour for a marketing team. When snaps expire and disappear quickly, how do you create a lasting memory? Some companies drop big money and create a really funny filter. Snapchat users are far more likely to use a filter that has a level of silliness than one that is plain and an obvious advertisement. Companies then can engage with their customers by creating a compilation video of people using the filter. Users love seeing themselves featured in the company's public feed and will work hard to find a way to be a part of it. This level of interaction doesn't come cheap, though. Before you start coming up with a killer campaign for your business, know that you could be dropping $500,000 for a weekday or $750,000 for a holiday!

Not all companies have embraced Snapchat yet and they could be missing out. Marketers may think Snapchat's user base is a younger demographic than their target markets. However, savvy marketing teams like L'Oréal, Burger King, and Amazon, are reaching audiences far and wide 24/7.

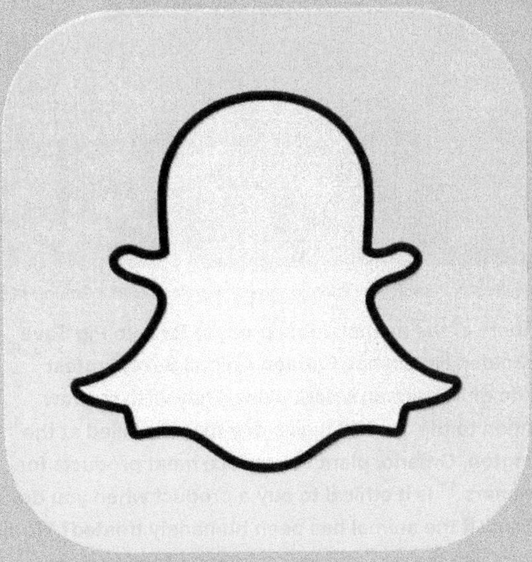

© tanuha2001/Shutterstock

Sources: Jillian Hausmann, "Millennials to Marketers: Some Advice on Using Snapchat," *Advertising Age*, April 4, 2016; Sujan Patel, "7 Brands That Are Killing It on Snapchat," *Entrepreneur*, February 6, 2017; Rachel Gee, "Snapchat Must Prove to Marketers It Has Mass Appeal," *Marketing Week*, February 6, 2017; "L'Oréal Is Benefitting from Higher Digital Spending," *Forbes*, February 8, 2017.

Non-Profit Organizations Prosper from Marketing

Even though the marketing concept emphasizes a profit orientation, marketing is a critical part of all organizations, including non-profits. Charities use marketing to raise funds for combating world hunger, for instance, or to obtain other resources. Canadian Blood Services uses promotion to encourage people to donate blood when local or national supplies run low. Greenpeace uses marketing to promote ecologically safe technologies. Environmental groups use marketing to try to cut carbon emissions. Churches use marketing to attract new members and to raise funds. Politicians use marketing to get votes.

Provinces and territories use marketing to attract new businesses and tourists. Some provinces, for example,

© Advertising Standards of Canada

Advertising Standards Canada (ASC), a non-profit organization, is committed to ensuring the integrity and viability of advertising in Canada through responsible industry self-regulation. Would you complain to ASC if you saw an ad that you thought was untrue?

© Nikki Wesley Pembleton | Photographer | Metroland Media Group, Halton

Members of the animal rights groups, Toronto Pig Save and Golden Horseshoe Farmed Animal Save, protest outside of a Fearman's pork plant. They wish to draw attention to the 10 000 pigs a day that are killed at the Burlington, Ontario, plant to produce meat products for consumers.[11] Is it ethical to buy a product when you do not know if the animal has been humanely treated? Would protests like the one above impact your food choices?

have competed to get automobile companies from other countries to locate plants in their areas. Schools use marketing to attract new students. Other organizations, such as arts groups, unions, and social groups, also use marketing. Organizations use marketing, in fact, to promote everything from environmentalism and crime prevention ("Take A Bite Out of Crime") to social issues ("Don't Drink and Drive").

The Marketing Mix

We can divide much of what marketers do into four factors called the four Ps to make them easy to remember. They are:

1. Product
2. Price
3. Place
4. Promotion

LO2

Describe the four Ps of marketing.

Managing the controllable parts of the marketing process, then, involves (1) designing a want-satisfying *product,* (2) setting a *price* for the product, (3) getting the product in a *place* where people will buy it, and (4) *promoting* the product. These four factors, highlighted in Figure 14.2, are called the **marketing mix** because businesses blend them in a well-designed marketing program.

FIGURE 14.2

MARKETING MANAGERS AND THE MARKETING MIX

Marketing managers must choose how to implement the four Ps of the marketing mix: product, price, place, and promotion. The goals are to please customers and make a profit.

The customer drives the marketing mix. The features and benefits of the product should meet, if not exceed, customer expectations. The price, place, and promotion is also driven by a desire to communicate with the customer in such a meaningful way that he or she seeks out the product (i.e., place) and is willing to purchase the product at the set price. These marketing decisions also need to achieve the organization's goals and objectives.

marketing mix
The ingredients that go into a marketing program: product, price, place, and promotion.

Applying the Marketing Process

The four Ps are a convenient way to remember the basics of marketing, but they do not include everything that goes into the marketing process for all products. One of the best ways to understand the entire marketing process is to take a product and follow the process that led to its development and sale. Figure 14.3 outlines some of these steps.

Imagine, for example, that you and your friends want to start a money-making business near your school. You noticed a lot of vegetarians among your friends. You do a quick survey in a couple of dorms and other campus clubs and find many vegetarians—and other students who like to eat vegetarian meals once in a while. Your preliminary research indicates some demand for fast, fresh, flavourful food that is preservative-free, chemical-free, cage-free, and antibiotic-free. You check the fast-food stores in the area and find that they offer little to no information about the meats and vegetables they use other than proclaiming them to be "fresh." And the vegetables are available only as salads.

You note the farm-to-table trend (documenting the food's path from its start at the farm to your plate on the table) has been growing nationwide. However, it appears in higher-level restaurants and some grocery stores in your area, but not in fast-food restaurants.

You've just performed the first few steps in the marketing process. You noticed an opportunity (a need for healthy, fresh, fast food near campus). You conducted some preliminary research to see whether your idea had any merit. And then you identified groups of people who might be interested in your product. They will be your *target market* (the people you will try to persuade to come to your restaurant).

Designing a Product to Meet Customer Needs

Once you have researched customer needs and found a target market (which we will discuss in more detail later) for your product, the four Ps of marketing come into play. You start by developing a product or products. A **product** is any physical good, service, or idea that satisfies a want or need plus anything that would enhance the product in the eyes of consumers, such as the brand name. In this case, your proposed product is a restaurant that would serve different kinds of fresh, fast, healthy meals at affordable prices, with the potential for providing these same foods online.

product
Any physical good, service, or idea that satisfies a want or need.

Many products today are not pure goods or pure services. Figure 14.4 illustrates the service continuum, which is a range from the tangible to the intangible or good-dominant to service-dominant offerings.[12] The service sector employs almost 79 percent of all working Canadians so there is a strong possibility that you will be employed in this sector.[13] While this text briefly introduces you to the concepts of marketing,

FIGURE 14.3

THE MARKETING PROCESS WITH THE FOUR PS

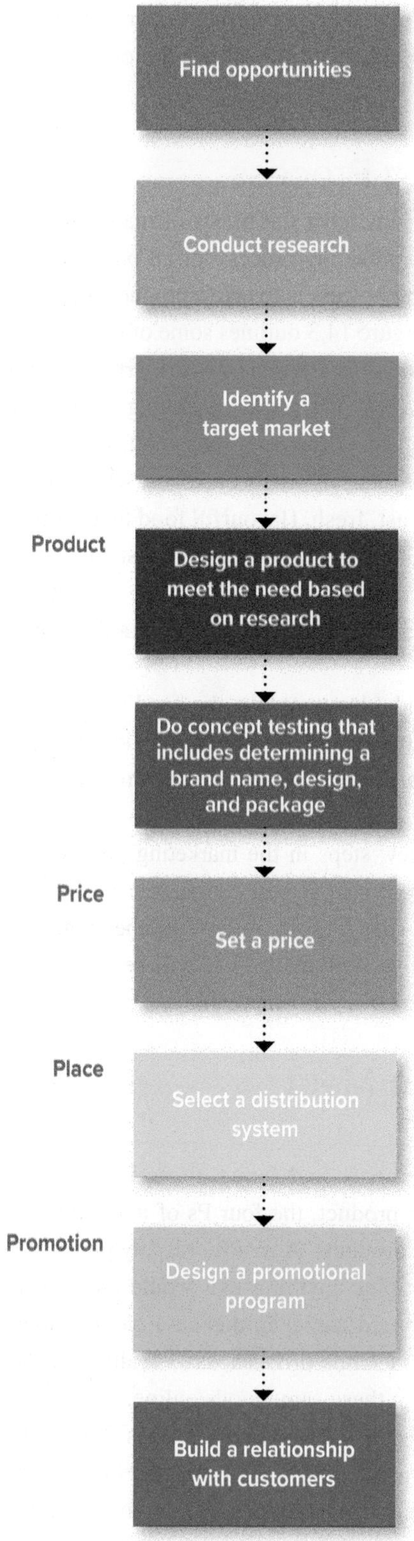

FIGURE 14.4

THE SERVICE CONTINUUM

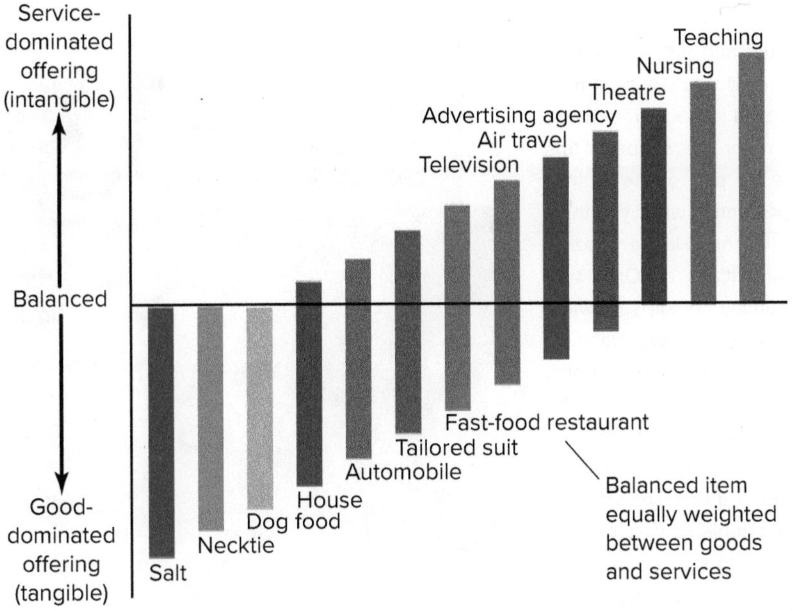

Products and services range from the tangible to the intangible.

services marketing is an area that warrants more attention as you pursue your studies in this discipline.

It is a good idea at this point to do *concept testing*. That is, you develop an accurate description of your restaurant and ask people, in person or online, whether the idea of the restaurant and the kind of meals you intend to appeal to them. If it does, you might go to a local farm that offers chemical-free produce to get the ingredients to prepare samples of salads, wraps, and bowls that you can take to consumers to test their reactions. The process of testing products among potential users is called **test marketing**. For example, you can test market your preservative-free dishes and learn how best to prepare them.[14]

test marketing
The process of testing products among potential users.

If customers like the products and agree that they would buy them, you have the information you need to find investors and a convenient location to open a restaurant. You'll have to think of a catchy name. (For practice, stop for a minute and try to think of one.) We'll use Harvest Gold with the tagline "Fresh from the Farm" in this text, although we're sure you can think of a better name. Meanwhile, let's continue with the discussion of product development.

You may want to offer some well-known brand names to attract people right away. A **brand name** is a word, letter, or group of words or letters that differentiates one seller's goods or services from those of competitors. Brand names of clean, organic juice products include Odwalla, Suja, and Naked. We'll discuss the product development process in detail in Chapter 15, in addition to the other Ps, and follow the Harvest Gold case to show you how all marketing and other business decisions tie together. For now, we're simply sketching the whole marketing process to give you an overall picture. So far, we've covered the first P of the marketing mix: product. After you read the Reaching

brand name
A word, letter, or group of words or letters that differentiates one seller's goods or services from those of competitors.

Reaching *Beyond* OUR BORDERS

Oreo: World's Favourite Cookie?

So, you've developed a product and you're ready to take it to the market. What should you call it? America's favourite cookie, Oreo, is said to be a great name because the two Os nicely mirror the shape of the cookie itself. Could the name be part of the charm? Think of other names that come to mind when you think of American products: Coke, Nike, and Häagen-Dazs.

For over 100 years, to Americans an Oreo was just an Oreo: two layers of crunchy cookie sandwiching a creamy vanilla centre. For many years, Nabisco, the maker of Oreos, followed the old adage "If it ain't broke, don't fix it." Today, however, if you visit the cookie aisle in your local supermarket, you may find tons of variations of Oreos such as red velvet, chocolate berry, and even Swedish Fish. If that isn't enough, you can also buy them in mini, double stuffed, or even super thin. Keep your eyes open for a candy bar next! Nabisco knew that to keep the brand vibrant and to reach different segments of the market, expanding its offerings was a good option.

It also knew it was a good decision to expand Oreos into global markets. Today, you can find Oreos in more than 100 countries across the globe. However, Nabisco understood that globally consumer tastes vary just like at home. What some people consider mouth-watering in one country will be frowned upon somewhere else. So with Oreos spanning the globe, additional variations on the original cookie-and-creme formula became even more extreme. China, for instance, prefers double fruit blueberry and strawberry-flavoured Oreos. In Indonesia, consumers prefer chocolate-and-peanut–flavoured soft Oreos. Argentines like their Oreos stuffed with banana and dulce de leche, a type of candied milk. What works overseas can even make its way back to North America. For example, new-product Oreo Thins was first introduced in China.

© Mark Lennihan/AP Images

Sources: Don Gil Carreon, "Mondelez Looks to Replicate China Success of Slim Oreos in U.S.," *Franchise Herald*, July 7, 2015; John Bruno Turiano, "Taste Test Tuesday: International Oreos and Kit Kats," *Westchester Magazine*, January 26, 2016; John Kell, "Mondelez Leans on Alibaba for E-Commerce Push in China," *Fortune*, April 7, 2016; Bonnie Burton, "Yes, Swedish Fish Oreo Cookies are Real and 'Potent'," *CNET*, August 11, 2016; Maya Salam, "When Just Vanilla Won't Do, How About a Blueberry Pie Oreo?" *The New York Times*, July 3, 2017.

Beyond Our Borders box that discusses how a well-known company promotes products in foreign markets, we'll consider price.

Setting an Appropriate Price

price
The money or other consideration (including other goods and services) exchanged for the ownership or use of a good or service.

After you've decided what products and services you want to offer consumers, you have to set appropriate prices. From a marketing viewpoint, **price** is the money or other consideration (including other goods and services) exchanged for the ownership or use of a good or service.[15] The price depends on a number of factors. In the restaurant business, the price could be close to what other restaurants charge to stay competitive. Or you might charge less to bring new customers in, especially at the beginning. Or you may offer high-quality products for which customers are willing to pay a little more (as Starbucks does). You also have to consider the costs of producing, distributing, and promoting the product, which all influence your price. We'll discuss pricing issues in more detail in Chapter 15.

Getting the Product to the Right Place

There are several ways you can serve the market for vegetarian meals. You can have people come in, sit down, and eat at the restaurant, but that's not the only alternative. Think of pizza. You could deliver the food to customers' dorms, apartments, and student unions. You may want to sell your products in supermarkets or health-food stores, or through organizations that specialize in distributing food products. Such intermediaries are the middle links in a series of organizations that distribute goods from producers to consumers. (The more traditional word for them is *middlemen.*) Getting the product to customers when and where they want it is critical to market success. We'll discuss the importance of marketing intermediaries and distribution in detail in Chapter 15.

© Mizina/Getty Images RF

A vegetarian restaurant might fill a popular need in the neighbourhood of many school campuses today. Is there one near your school? What can you tell about its application of the four Ps of marketing—product, price, place, and promotion?

Developing an Effective Promotional Strategy

The last of the four Ps of marketing is promotion. **Promotion** consists of all of the techniques sellers use to inform people and motivate them to buy their goods or services. They include advertising, personal selling, public relations, direct marketing, and sales promotion (such as coupons, rebates, and samples). We'll discuss promotion in detail in Chapter 15.

promotion
All of the techniques sellers use to motivate customers to buy their products.

Promotion often includes relationship building with customers. Among other activities, that means responding to suggestions consumers make to improve the products or their marketing, including price and packaging. For Harvest Gold, postpurchase, or after-sale, service may include refusing payment for meals that weren't satisfactory and stocking additional healthy products customers say they would like. Listening to customers and responding to their needs is the key to the ongoing process that is marketing.

PROGRESS ASSESSMENT

- What does it mean to "help the buyer buy"?
- State each marketing era and the emphasis for each.
- What are the three parts of the marketing concept?
- Describe each of the four Ps of the marketing mix.

LO3

Identify the steps in the marketing research process, and explain how marketers use environmental scanning to learn about the changing marketing environment.

Providing Marketers with Information

Every decision in the marketing process depends on information. When they conduct **marketing research**, marketers analyze markets to determine opportunities and challenges, and to find information they need to make good decisions.

marketing research The analysis of markets to determine opportunities and challenges, and to find the information needed to make good decisions.

Marketing research helps identify what products customers have purchased in the past, and what changes have occurred to alter what they want now and what they're likely to want in the future. Marketers also conduct research on business trends, the ecological impact of their decisions, global trends, and more. Businesses need information to compete effectively, and marketing research is the activity that gathers it. You have learned, for example, how important research is when thinking of starting a healthy fast-food restaurant. Besides listening to customers, marketing researchers also pay attention to what employees, shareholders, dealers, consumer advocates, media representatives, and other stakeholders have to say. As noted earlier, much of that research is now being gathered online through social media. Despite all that research, however, marketers still have difficulty understanding their customers as well as they should.[16]

The Marketing Research Process

A simplified marketing research process consists of at least four key steps:

1. Defining the question (the problem or opportunity) and determining the present situation
2. Collecting research data.
3. Analyzing the research data.
4. Choosing the best solution and implementing it.

The following sections look at each of these steps.

secondary data Information that has already been compiled by others and published in journals and books or made available online.

STEP 1: DEFINING THE QUESTION AND DETERMINING THE PRESENT SITUATION

Marketing researchers need the freedom to discover what the present situation is, what the problems or opportunities are, what the alternatives are, what information they need, and how to go about gathering and analyzing data.

© wdstock/Getty Images

Primary research can be used to collect information about customers' needs, wants, and buying habits. Which primary data source do you prefer when asked to answer questions about a product or product category you use?

STEP 2: COLLECTING DATA

Usable information is vital to the marketing research process. Research can become quite expensive, however, so marketers must often make a trade-off between the need for information and the cost of obtaining it. Normally the least expensive method is to gather information that has already been compiled by others and published in journals and books or made available online.

Such existing data are called **secondary data** since you aren't the first one to gather them. Figure 14.5 lists the principal sources of secondary marketing research

FIGURE 14.5

SELECTED SOURCES OF PRIMARY AND SECONDARY INFORMATION

Primary Sources	
Survey (e.g., phone, online, and mail) Personal interview	Focus group Observation
Secondary Sources	
Newspapers *The Globe and Mail* *The National Post* Local newspapers (e.g., *The Chronicle Herald*) **Internal Sources** Company records Balance sheets Income statements Prior research reports **Company Directories and Information** Canadian Business Database Mergent Online Business Source Complete Hoovers Infomart SEDAR Passport **General Sources** Internet searches Google-type searches Market news, company sites, etc.	**Trade Sources** Nielsen Canada Conference Board of Canada Dun & Bradstreet Canada Canadian Marketing Association Retail Council of Canada Advertising Standards Canada **Periodicals** *Journal of Marketing* *Journal of Consumer Research* *Journal of Small Business Management* *Marketing Magazine* *Advertising Age* *Maclean's* *Canadian Business* *PROFIT* **Databases** CANSIM (Statistics Canada) Canadian Business & Current Affairs Factiva LexisNexis Academic

information. Despite its name, *secondary* data is what marketers should gather *first* to avoid incurring unnecessary expense. To start your secondary data search about vegetarians, consider going online to learn about the farm-to-table movement and Canada's farm-to-table food scene.

Often, secondary data don't provide all the information managers need for important business decisions. To gather additional, in-depth information, marketers must do their own research. The results of such *new* studies are called primary data. **Primary data** are facts, figures, and opinions that you have gathered yourself (not from secondary sources such as books, journals, and newspapers). Four sources of primary data are surveys (also known as questionnaires), personal interviews, focus groups, and observation.

primary data
Data that you gather yourself (not from secondary sources such as books, journals, and newspapers).

Primary data can be gathered by developing a list of questions and conducting a survey. Surveys (telephone, online, and mail) and personal interviews are the most common forms of primary data collection. Surveys are best carried out by independent third parties so that the information gathered and the results reported can be as objective as possible. You can use the information to understand behaviours, perceptions, preferences, and opinions. While the information gathered is useful, there are some disadvantages to this method. Not everyone who is approached may be willing to answer your questions, respondents may not be truthful, and (for written surveys) not everyone can read and write.

© klenger/Getty Images

What do you think would be the best way to survey students about your potential new restaurant? Would you do a different survey after it had been open a few months? How could you help people find your restaurant? That is, how could you help your buyers buy? One question researchers pay close attention to is, "Would you recommend this product to a friend?"

To increase the response and accuracy rate, marketers use personal interviews. *Personal interviews* are a face-to-face opportunity to ask individuals prepared questions. While this research method can be more expensive than surveys, the interviewer has the opportunity to observe reactions and to dig a little deeper with the questions if the respondent wishes to add more information.

A **focus group** is a group of people who meet under the direction of a discussion leader to communicate their opinions about an organization, its products, or other given issues. These questions should be free of bias and participants should be encouraged to answer questions honestly without being influenced by the responses of others in the focus group. This text is updated periodically using many focus groups made up of faculty and students. They tell us, the authors, what subjects and examples they like and dislike, and the authors consider their suggestions for changes.

Observation involves watching how people behave, either mechanically (e.g., Nielsen Media Research's *people meter,* which is a box attached to television sets, cable boxes, and satellite dishes in selected households in Canada and the United States in order to determine the size of audiences watching television programs delivered by the networks) or in person.[17] Observation may provide insight into behaviours that consumers do not even know they exhibit while shopping by watching them in person or by videotaping them. For example, companies follow customers into supermarkets to record their purchasing behaviours for products such as meat, bread, and laundry detergent. These marketers may observe that consumers do not bend to look at products, that they compare prices, and that they handle products to assess their weight. In some circumstances, the speed of events or the number of events being observed make mechanical or electronic observation more appropriate than personal observation; retailers, for example, can use electronic cameras to count the number of customers entering or leaving a store.[18]

© Christopher Weddle/Centre Daily Times/TNS/Getty Images

The authors of this text, for example, do much research online as well as gather data from books, articles, databases, and other sources. Through focus groups, faculty and students tell us how to improve this book and its support materials. We listen carefully and make as many changes as we can in response. Suggestions have included adding more descriptive captions to the photos in the text and making the text as user-friendly as possible. How are we doing so far?

Social media is playing an important role in data mining as there is a lot of free and available information on Facebook, Twitter, blogs, and other social platforms.[19] It is now common for marketers such as Coca-Cola and WestJet Airlines to scan the web for posts that offer positive and negative comments on their companies and their products.[20] What are the advantages and disadvantages of this research? Do you agree that social media should complement traditional marketing research methods?

focus group
A small group of people who meet under the direction of a discussion leader to communicate their opinions about an organization, its products, or other issues.

observation
Involves watching, either mechanically or in person, how people behave.

big data
Large amounts of data collected from a variety of sources and analyzed with an increasingly sophisticated set of technologies.

STEP 3: ANALYZING THE RESEARCH DATA

Marketers must turn the data collected in the research process into useful information. Careful, honest interpretation of the data collected can help a company find useful alternatives to specific marketing challenges. For example, by conducting primary research, Fresh Italy, a small Italian pizzeria, found that its pizza's taste was rated superior to that of the larger pizza chains. However, the company's sales lagged behind the competition. Secondary research on the industry revealed that free delivery (which Fresh Italy did not offer) was more important to customers than taste. Fresh Italy now delivers—and has increased its market share.

Big Data, Data Analytics, and Data Mining[21] **Big data** is a vague term generally used to describe large amounts of data collected from a variety of sources and analyzed with an increasingly sophisticated set of technologies. The challenge facing managers is not data collection or even storage but how to efficiently transform the huge amount of data into useful information. This transformation is accomplished through the use of *data analytics.* (Recall from Appendix A that data analytics is the process of collecting, organizing, storing, and analyzing large sets of data in order to identify patterns and other information that helps business people make effective decisions now and in the future.[22]) Using specialized computer systems, meaning is extracted from raw data with conclusions drawn and patterns identified.[23]

In Appendix A, you were also introduced to data mining, as a component of data analytics. (Recall that *data mining* is a technique to find hidden patterns and previously unknown relationships among the data.) By extracting large amounts of hidden predictive information from large databases, one can find statistical links between consumer purchasing patterns and marketing actions. For example, companies put this new science into action by tracking what is selling where and who is buying the good or service. Would you have expected that men buying diapers in the evening sometimes buy a six-pack of beer as well? Supermarkets discovered this when they mined checkout data from scanners. So they placed diapers and beer near each other, then placed potato chips between them. This resulted in increased sales on all three items.

Still, data mining ultimately depends on humans—the marketing managers and researchers—and their judgements on how to select, analyze, and interpret the information. Additionally, new techniques and methods are always emerging and marketing researchers need to keep abreast of such developments. For example, the Internet and social media is exploding as information obtained via cookies, Facebook pages, Twitter accounts, and Google Ad Preferences is leading to one-to-one personalization and consumer targeting.

You may wish to consider a career in big data. Canada's Big Data Consortium estimates that Canada's big data talent gap is between 10 500 and 19 000

A wide variety of analytical tools is available for data scientists. Their work is also creating a new field of marketing research that focuses on data visualization, or the presentation of the results of the analysis. Are there any courses that you could take in your program that would support a career as a data scientist?

professionals with deep data and analytical skills, such as those required for roles like Chief Data Officer, Data Scientist, and Data Solutions Architect. The gap for professionals with solid data and analytical literacy to make better decisions is estimated at a further 150 000, such as those required for roles like Business Manager and Business Analyst.[24] What courses can you take in the next few years that would position you for such opportunities?

STEP 4: CHOOSING THE BEST SOLUTION AND IMPLEMENTING IT

After collecting and analyzing data, marketing researchers determine alternative strategies and make recommendations about which may be best and why. This final step in a research effort also includes following up on actions taken to see whether the results were what was expected. If not, the company can take corrective action and conduct new studies in its ongoing attempt to provide consumer satisfaction at the lowest cost. You can see, then, that marketing research is a continuous process of responding to changes in the marketplace and in consumer preferences.

In today's customer-driven market, ethics is important in every aspect of marketing. Ideally, companies should therefore do what is right as well as what is profitable. This step could add greatly to the social benefits of marketing decisions. See the Making Ethical Decisions box for such an example.

Making ETHICAL DECISIONS

No Kidding

Marketers have long recognized that children can be an important influence on their parents' buying decisions. In fact, many direct appeals for products are focused on children. Let's say that you have experienced a great response to a new high-fibre, high-protein cereal among health-conscious consumers. The one important group you have not been able to attract is children. Therefore, the product development team is considering introducing a child-oriented brand to expand the product line.

The new children's cereal may have strong market potential if you follow two recommendations of the research department. First, coat the flakes generously with sugar (significantly changing the cereal's nutritional benefits). Second, promote the product exclusively on children's TV programs. Such a promotional strategy should create a strong demand for the product, especially if you offer a premium (a toy or other "surprise") in each box. The consensus among the research department is that kids will love the new taste and parents will agree to buy the product because of their positive impression of your best-selling brand. The research director commented, "The chance of a parent actually reading our label and noting the addition of sugar is nil."

© Purestock/SuperStock

Would you introduce the children's cereal following the recommendations of your research department? What are the benefits of doing so? What are the risks involved in following these recommendations? What would you do if you were the marketing manager for this product?

The Marketing Environment

Marketing managers must be aware of the surrounding environment when making marketing mix decisions. **Environmental scanning** is the process of identifying the factors that can affect marketing success. Figure 14.6 should look familiar; it is a duplication of Figure 1.5. As introduced in Chapter 1, the business environment consists of six elements—global, technological, social, competitive, economic, and legal—that either help or hinder the development of businesses. It is helpful to review them strictly from a marketing perspective.

environmental scanning
The process of identifying the factors that can affect marketing success.

GLOBAL ENVIRONMENT

By going online, businesses can reach many of the world's consumers relatively easily and carry on a dialogue with them about the goods and services they want. The globalization process puts more pressure on those whose responsibility it is to deliver products to these global customers.

TECHNOLOGICAL ENVIRONMENT

The most important technological changes also relate to the Internet. Using customer databases, blogs, social networking sites, and the like, firms can develop products and

■ **FIGURE 14.6**

ENVIRONMENTAL SCANNING OF THE DYNAMIC BUSINESS ENVIRONMENT

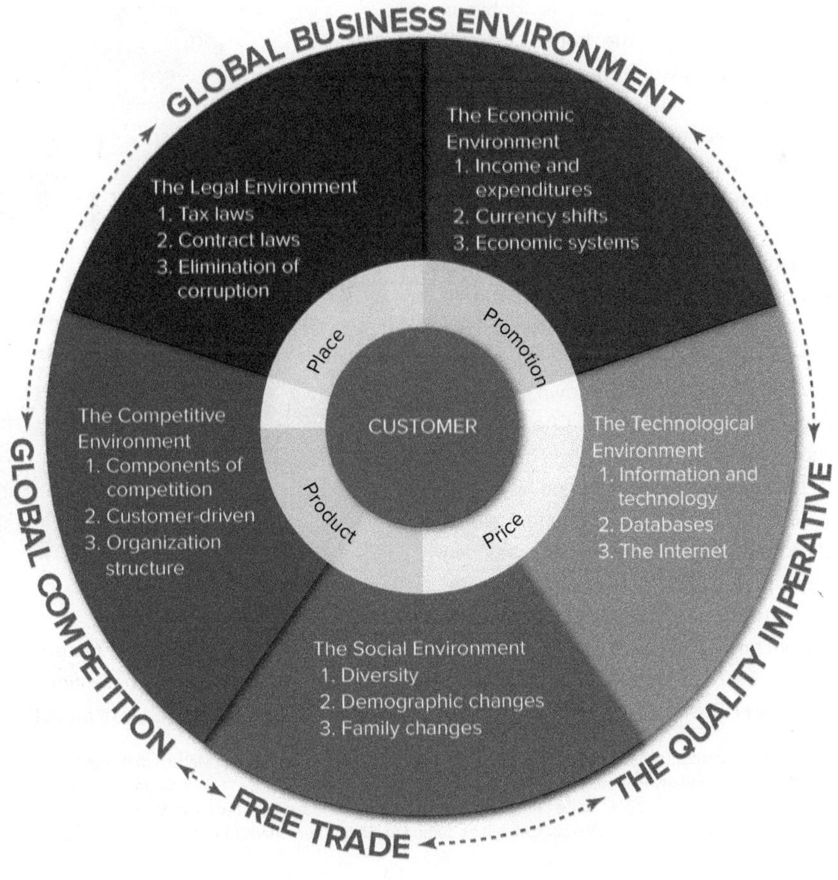

services that closely match customers' needs. As you read in Chapter 10, firms can now produce customized goods and services for about the same price as mass-produced goods. Thus, flexible manufacturing and mass customization are also major influences on marketers. Check out the Spotlight on Small Business box for an example. You can imagine, for example, using databases to help you devise custom-made salads and various dishes for your customers at Harvest Gold.

Internet of Things (IoT)
Refers to data-collecting technologies that connect ordinary objects to the Internet through sensors, cameras, software, databases, and massive data centres. Often, those technologies can communicate with one another.

The Internet of Things (IoT)[25] One growing area in technology is the Internet of Things (IoT), globally projected to grow to $457 billion by 2020 in comparison to $157 billion in 2016. The **Internet of Things (IoT)** is a system of machines or objects outfitted with data-collecting technologies so that those objects can communicate with one another. Businesses in the manufacturing, logistics and transportation, and utilities industries in particular are heavily investing in the IoT. Are you surprised to learn that improving customer experiences and safety are the two areas businesses are using data generated from IoT solutions most often today? Sensor applications of IoT include a smart home (e.g., a smart thermostat or fridge), wearables (e.g., an activity tracker such as a Fitbit), and a smart city (e.g., monitoring availability of parking spaces). Can you think of other applications?

Spotlight *On* SMALL BUSINESS

Creating Mass Appeal for a Custom Product

One item almost every person needs is footwear. Whether we're walking around the house, running to the store, or hitting the gym, having a little cushion under your feet is essential. ISlide founder, Justin Kittredge, knew just about all anyone could know when it came to footwear. He worked for Reebok for a decade and noticed a growth in the sandal market.

Kittredge broke out on his own in 2013 and revolutionized the custom footwear business. Interested customers can log onto the ISlide website and create their own design or choose from others' creations. Like what DJ Khaled is wearing? You can find his "Bless Up" sandals on the website. Or design your own, and who knows, you may find Ellen DeGeneres or Chelsea Handler wearing your creation.

Professional teams are also cashing in on ISlide—all 30 NBA teams reached a licensing agreement allowing ISlide rights to team logos. Small businesses can design their own promotional slides and have the products for sale on their site hours later. That sort of speed in the custom market was unheard of until ISlide came on the scene. Each pair is printed and shipped from a warehouse near Boston almost as fast as you can order it. As technological factors evolve, we may see even more mass customization available affordably in an increasing number of industries.

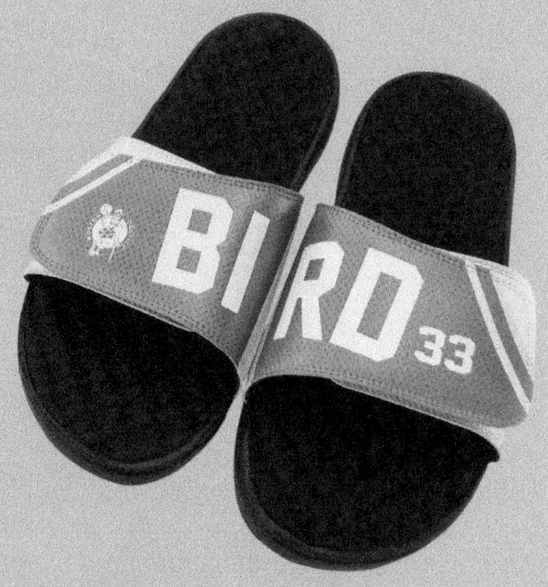

Courtesy of Islide

Sources: Ben Osborne, "NBA Grants Licensing Rights for All Teams to ISlide," *SLAM*, June 2, 2015; Melissa Malamut, "How DJ Khaled and Snapchat Made This Norwood Company Famous," Boston.com, June 18, 2016; Emily Sweeney, "Celebrity Sandals and Socks from New Kids, Aly Raisman," *Boston Globe*, October 16, 2016; Gayle Fee, "Norwood Sandal Maker Says 'No Thanks' to $500k from 'Shark Tank'," *Boston Herald*, October 18, 2016; Ky Trang Ho, "Major Brands, Celebrities Jump On ISlide After 'Shark Tank' Gave It The Boot," *Forbes*, March 5, 2017.

SOCIAL ENVIRONMENT

Marketers must monitor social trends to maintain their close relationship with customers since population growth and changing demographics can have an effect on sales. The fastest-growing segment of the Canadian population is the Baby Boomers who are approaching retirement. Looking ahead, the increase in the number of older adults creates growing demand for retirement communities, health care, prescription drugs, recreation, continuing education, and more. Do you see any evidence that older people would enjoy having more locally sourced, farm-fresh meals?

Other shifts in the Canadian population are creating new challenges for marketers as they adjust their products to meet the tastes and preferences of growing ethnicities. To appeal to diverse groups, marketers must listen better and be more responsive to unique ethnic needs. What might you do to appeal to specific ethnic groups with Harvest Gold?

© John Lund/Blend Images LLC

Shifts in the Canadian population are creating new opportunities for marketers as they adjust their products to meet the tastes and preferences of growing ethnic groups. To appeal to diverse groups, marketers must listen better and be more responsive to unique needs. What might you do to appeal to specific ethnic groups with Harvest Gold?

COMPETITIVE ENVIRONMENT

Of course, marketers must pay attention to the dynamic competitive environment. Brick-and-mortar companies must stay aware of online competition. For example, in the book business, Indigo Books & Music Inc. had to adjust to the reality of Amazon's huge selection of books at good prices. They are competing not only with Amazon.ca's huge selection of books at good prices in Canada but also with its U.S. counterpart, Amazon.com. Since consumers can literally search the world for the best buys online, marketers must continuously adjust their pricing, delivery, and services accordingly. What opportunities do you see for Harvest Gold to make use of the Internet and social media?

ECONOMIC ENVIRONMENT

When Canada experiences economic growth, customers are eager to buy expensive automobiles, watches, and vacations. But when the economy experiences slow growth, marketers have to adapt by offering products that are less expensive and more tailored to customers with modest incomes. You can see, therefore, that environmental scanning is critical to a company's success during rapidly changing economic times.

What economic changes are occurring around your school that might affect a new restaurant? How would an economic crisis or natural disaster, such as flood or drought, affect your area?

LEGAL ENVIRONMENT

Governments enact laws to protect consumers and businesses. Businesses must be aware of how these laws may impact their practices. For example, the Canadian Radio-television and Telecommunications Commission (CRTC) ruled that telecommunications provider, Northwestel, had to lower its rates for certain residential Internet services in the Yukon and the Northwest Territories. "Although we recognize the exceptional situation that exists in

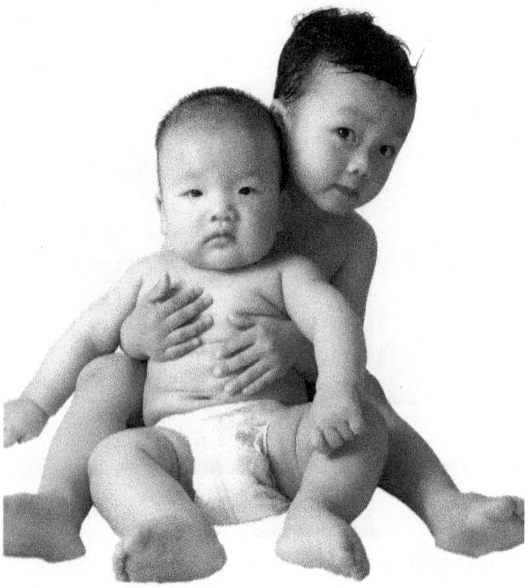

© NI QIN/E+/Getty Images RF

After more than 35 years of a strict one-child policy, China agreed to change the infamous regulation. The new law allows married couples to have two children if one of the spouses is an only child. This promises to have a big impact on businesses as the policy switch could mean 9.5 million additional babies coming into the Chinese market in five years.[27] What businesses would benefit from this law?

Northwestel's territory, we must not let these challenges hinder the development and affordability of telecommunications services in the North," said Jean-Pierre Blais, the CRTC's chairman. As part of this decision, Northwestel needed to have the CRTC's permission before any price hikes.[26]

A change in one environment can have an impact on another environment, or more. This is why marketers *continuously* scan the business environment to understand the impact of changes on their businesses. For example, a change in legislation that decreases barriers to entry will contribute to a more competitive marketplace as reflected in the increased number of competitors. Due to increased competition, prices could be lowered, and this could then be reflected in lower expenses as reflected in economic indicators.

PROGRESS ASSESSMENT

- What are the four steps in the marketing research process?
- What is environmental scanning? How often do marketers scan the business environment?
- What factors do you consider in environmental scanning?

LO4

Compare the consumer market to the business-to-business market.

Two Different Markets: Consumer and Business-to-Business

Marketers must know as much as possible about the market they wish to serve. As we defined it in Chapter 7, a market consists of people with unsatisfied wants and needs who have both the resources and the willingness to buy. There are two major markets in business: the consumer market and the business-to-business market.

consumer market All individuals or households that want goods and services for personal consumption or use.

The Consumer Market

The **consumer market** consists of all individuals or households that want goods and services for personal consumption or use and have the resources to buy them. The total potential global consumer market consists of the billions of people in global markets. Because consumer groups differ greatly in age, education level, income, and taste, a business usually cannot fill the needs of every group. It must decide which groups to serve, and then develop products and services specially tailored to their needs.

business-to-business (B2B) market All individuals and organizations that want goods and services to use in producing other goods and services or to sell, rent, or supply goods to others.

The Business-to-Business (B2B) Market

The **business-to-business (B2B) market** consists of all individuals and organizations that want goods and services to use in producing other goods and services or to sell, rent, or supply goods to others. So, businesses selling to other businesses. Oil-drilling bits, cash registers, display cases, office desks, public accounting audits, and business software are B2B goods and services. Traditionally, they have been known as *industrial* goods and services because they are used in industry.[28]

© praetorianphoto/Getty Images

Consumers purchase for personal use. When you go shopping for yourself, such purchases are captured under the consumer market. Are you planning on purchasing something soon for yourself?

B2B marketers include manufacturers; intermediaries such as wholesalers; institutions like hospitals, schools, and charities; and the government. The B2B market is larger than the consumer market because items are often sold and resold several times in the B2B process before they are sold to the final consumer. B2B marketing strategies also differ from consumer marketing because business buyers have their own decision-making process. Consider factors that make B2B marketing different from consumer marketing:

1. *Customers in the B2B market are relatively few.* There are far fewer B2B firms (e.g., construction or mining operations) compared to the almost 37 million potential customers in the Canadian consumer market.
2. *Business customers are relatively large.* Big organizations account for most of the employment, production of various goods and services, and purchases. Nonetheless, there are many small to medium-sized firms in Canada that together make an attractive market.
3. *B2B markets tend to be geographically concentrated.* Companies tend to locate close to their suppliers and customers. For example, diamond mines tend to be concentrated in Canada's Northwest Territories. Consequently, firms selling mining equipment may be concentrated close to these customers (or at least, within a reasonable distance).
4. *Business buyers are generally more rational and less emotional than ultimate consumers.* They use product specifications to guide buying choices and often more carefully weigh the total product offer, including quality, price, and service.
5. *B2B sales tend to be direct, but not always.* Tire manufacturers. for example, sell directly to auto manufacturers but use intermediaries, such as retailers, to sell to ultimate consumers.
6. *There is much more emphasis on personal selling in B2B markets.* Whereas consumer promotions are based on *advertising,* B2B sales are based on *selling.* There are fewer customers and they usually demand more personal service. As well, the quantities being purchased justify the expense of a sales force.

© RainerPlendl/Getty Images

Business customers, such as Ford Motor Company of Canada, are relatively large compared to consumer purchasers. Just think of the number of tires that are purchased by the company compared to your consumer tire purchase order. There are many job opportunities in the B2B market. Have you considered a career in this area of marketing?

FIGURE 14.7

COMPARING BUSINESS-TO-BUSINESS AND CONSUMER BUYING BEHAVIOUR

	Business-to-Business Market	Consumer Market
Market structure	Relatively few potential customers Larger purchases Geographically concentrated	Many potential customers Smaller purchases Geographically dispersed
Products	Require technical, complex products Frequently require customization Frequently require technical advice, delivery, and after-sale service	Require fewer technical products Sometimes require customization Sometimes require technical advice, delivery, and after-sale service
Buying procedures	Buyers are trained Negotiate details of most purchases Follow objective standards Formal process involving specific employees Closer relationships between marketers and buyers Buy from pre-approved suppliers	No special training Accept standard terms for most purchases Use personal judgment Informal process involving household members Impersonal relationships between marketers and consumers Buy from multiple sources

Figure 14.7 shows some of the differences between buying behaviour in the B2B market and the consumer market. B2B buyers also use the Internet to make purchases. You'll learn more about the business market in advanced marketing courses.

The important thing to remember is that the buyer's reason for buying—that is, the end use of the product—determines whether a product is a consumer product or a B2B product. A cup of yogourt that a student buys for breakfast is a consumer product. However,

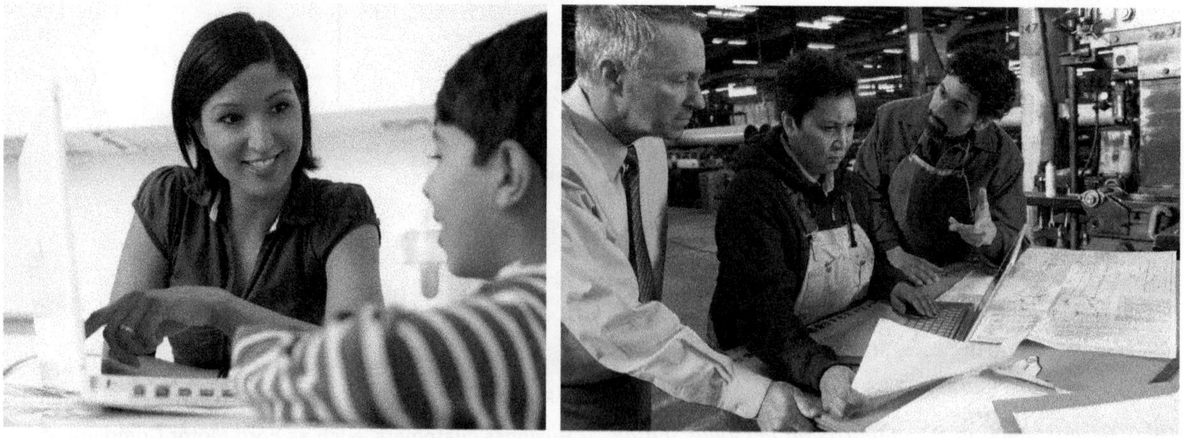

Many goods could be classified as consumer goods or business-to-business (B2B) goods, based on their uses. For example, a computer that a person uses at home for personal use would be a consumer good. But that same computer used in a business setting, such as a manufacturing plant or an accounting firm, would be classified as a B2B good. Can you think of other examples?

when Harvest Gold purchases the same cup of yogurt to sell to its breakfast customers, it has purchased a B2B product. This transaction between the yogourt manufacturer and the restaurant is considered a B2B transaction.

PROGRESS ASSESSMENT

- Define the terms consumer market and business-to-business (B2B) market.
- What are examples of B2B marketers?
- How does B2B marketing differ from consumer marketing?

Defining Your Market

LO5

Describe the market segmentation process, and the role of relationship marketing.

Before marketers develop a 4P marketing mix for each product, they need to know the details of their customers and how the product being sold will meet these customers' needs.

Market Segmentation: Segmenting the Consumer Market

You can appreciate the challenge a marketer may have in creating a product that will appeal to every Canadian. The starting point is **market segmentation**, which means dividing the total market into groups with similar characteristics. There are several ways a firm can segment the consumer market, as outlined in Figure 14.8. For example, rather than trying to sell a product throughout Canada, you might try to focus on just one or two regions of the country where you might be most successful. Dividing the market by geographic area (i.e., cities, counties, provinces, etc.) is called **geographic segmentation**.

market segmentation
The process of dividing the total market into groups with similar characteristics.

geographic segmentation
Dividing the market by geographic area.

Alternatively, you could aim your product's promotions toward people aged 25 to 45 who have some post-secondary training and have above-average incomes. Automobiles such as Lexus are often targeted to this audience. Segmentation by age, income, and education level are criteria for **demographic segmentation**. So are religion, ethnic origin, and occupation. Demographics are the most widely used segmentation variable, but not necessarily the best.[29]

demographic segmentation
Dividing the market by age, income, and education level.

You may want your ads to portray a target group's lifestyle. To do that, you would study the group's values, attitudes, and interests in a strategy called **psychographic segmentation**. If you decide to target Generation Z, you would do an in-depth study of their values and interests, like which TV shows they watch and which personalities they like the best. With that information you would develop advertisements for those shows using those stars. Some marketers prefer *ethnographic segmentation.* Basically, using such segmentation resembles using psychographic segmentation in that marketers talk with consumers and learn about the product from their perspective. Often customers have an entirely different view of your product than you do.[30]

psychographic segmentation
Dividing the market using the group's values, attitudes, and interests.

When marketers use a consumer's behaviour with or toward a product to segment the market, they are using **behavioural segmentation**.[31] Let us examine questions that

behavioural segmentation
Dividing the market based on behaviour with or toward a product.

FIGURE 14.8

CONSUMER MARKET SEGMENTATION

This table shows some of the consumer dimensions and variables that marketers use to select their markets. The aim of segmentation is to divide the market into smaller units.

Segmentation Base	Sample Variables	Possible Segments
Geographic Segmentation	Region	British Columbia, Prairies, Nunavut, Eastern Quebec, Prince Edward Island; Sydney, St. John's
	City or Area Size	Under 5000 5000–20 000 20 001–50 000 50 001–100 000 100 001–250 000 250 001–500 000 500 001–1 000 000 1 000 000+
	Density	Urban; suburban; rural
Demographic Segmentation	Age	Under 6; 6–11; 12–17; 18–24; 25–34; 35–49; 50–64; 65+
	Gender	Male; female
	Generational Cohort	Baby Boomer (1946 to 1964); Generation X (1965 to 1976); Generation Y/Millennials/Echo Boomers (1977 to 1994); Generation Z (1995 to present)
	Marital Status	Never married; married; separated; divorced; widowed
	Family Size	1–2; 3–4; 5+
	Education Attainment	0 to 8 years; some high school; high school graduate; some post-secondary; post-secondary certificate or diploma; bachelor's degree; above bachelor's degree
	Ethnic Origin	Canadian; English; French; Scottish; Irish; German; Italian; Chinese; First Nations; South Asian; Ukrainian; East Indian; Dutch; Polish; Jewish; Russian; Vietnamese
	Occupation	Professional; managerial; technical; clerical; labourer; sales; farmer; homemaker; self-employed; student; unemployed; retired; other
	Religion	Christian; Muslim; Hindu; Sikh; Buddhist; Jewish; no affiliation
Psychographic Segmentation	Personality	Gregarious; compulsive; extroverted; ambitious
	Social Class	Upper class; middle class; working class
	Lifestyle	Actualizers; Fulfillers; Achievers; Experiencers; Believers; Strivers; Makers; Survivors
Behavioural Segmentation	Benefits Sought	Convenience; quality; service; economy; luxury; safety; prestige; environmental impact
	Usage Rate	Light user; medium user; heavy user
	User Status	Non-user; ex-user; prospect; first-time user; regular user
	Loyalty Status	None; medium; strong

you might ask while considering a few variables of this segmentation strategy as it applies to Harvest Gold:

- *Benefits Sought*—What benefits of fresh, organic food might you talk about? Should you emphasize health benefits, taste, or something else?
- *Usage Rate*—In marketing, the **80/20 rule** says that 80 percent of your business is likely to come from 20 percent of your customers. Determine who the heavy users are of healthy food. Does your restaurant attract more men or more women? More students or more faculty and staff members? Are your repeat customers from the local community or are they commuters? Once you know your customer base, you can design your promotions to better appeal to that specific group or groups.

© Big Coat Media

On HGTV, you can watch Hilary Farr (interior designer on the left) and David Visentin (real estate agent on the right) compete on *Love It or List It*. She renovates the home so homeowners will "love it" and stay, while he tries to find these same homeowners a new home they love more than their renovated home. If he is successful, he will hear "list it" from them. When considering viewers for this show, what segmentation variables can you apply?

The best segmentation strategy is to use all the variables to come up with a consumer profile that represents a sizable, reachable, *and* profitable target market. That may mean not segmenting the market at all and instead going after the total market (everyone). Or it may mean going after ever-smaller segments. We'll discuss that strategy next.

80/20 rule
The axiom that 80 percent of your business is likely to come from 20 percent of your customers.

Target Marketing and Reaching Smaller Market Segments

Once one applies the consumer market segmentation bases to the total market, a marketer may end up with a number of potential market segments to consider. Due to limited resources, it is not feasible to consider all of them so a business goes to the trouble and expense of segmenting its markets when it expects that this will increase its sales, profit, and return on investment.[32] As a result, **target marketing** is the next step as it allows marketers to select which segment(s) an organization can serve profitably. For example, a shoe store may choose to sell only women's shoes, only children's shoes, or only athletic shoes. The issue is finding the right *target market*—the most profitable segment—to serve.

© Cosmo Condina/Alamy Stock Photo

Dangerous Lagoon is the largest exhibit at Ripley's Aquarium of Canada, and home to the longest moving sidewalk in North America. As you journey under the sea, you will see a wide array of species. Does the company have only one target market?

In the world of mass production following the Industrial Revolution, marketers responded by practising mass marketing. **Mass marketing** means developing products and promotions to please large

© Pat's Party Rental

Pat's Party Rentals provides everything one needs to ensure a successful event. Does this company practice mass marketing, niche marketing, or one-to-one marketing?

groups of people resulting in little market segmentation. The mass marketer tries to sell products to as many people as possible using mass media, such as TV, radio, and newspapers to reach them.[33] Although mass marketing led many firms to success, marketing managers often got so caught up with their products and competition that they became less responsive to the market. Airlines, for example, are so intent on meeting competition that they often annoy their customers.

Niche marketing is identifying small but profitable market segments and designing or finding products for them. Because it so easily offers an unlimited choice of goods, online retail transformed a consumer culture once based on big hits and best-sellers into one that supports more specialized niche products.

Historically, Canadian Tire tried to sell everything to everybody (mass marketing). As part of a three-year growth plan, Canadian Tire decided to target 30- to 49-year-olds with a focus on young families and products that appeal to them (niche marketing). For example, instead of ads featuring dad painting the deck, ads featured a father and his young son building a tree house.[34] With only 7.1 percent of Canadians identifying themselves as vegetarians, what types of vegetarian options do you think Harvest Gold might sell in its restaurants and online to this niche market?[35]

target marketing
Marketing directed toward those groups (market segments) an organization decides it can serve profitably.

mass marketing
Developing products and promotions to please large groups of people.

niche marketing
The process of finding small but profitable market segments and designing or finding products for them.

one-to-one marketing (micromarketing)
Developing a unique mix of goods and services for each individual customer.

micromarketing (one-to-one marketing)
Developing a unique mix of goods and services for each individual customer.

One-to-one marketing (also known as **micromarketing**) means developing a unique mix of goods and services for each *individual* customer. Travel agencies often develop such packages for individual customers, including airline reservations, hotel reservations, rental cars, restaurants, and admission to museums and other attractions. This is relatively easy to do in B2B markets where each customer may buy in huge volume. But one-to-one marketing is possible in consumer markets as well. Computer companies like HP and Apple can produce a unique computer system for each customer. Can you envision designing special Harvest Gold menu items for individual customers?

Positioning[36]

Next, **product positioning**, which refers to the place an offering occupies in customers' minds on important attributes relative to competitive products, is applied for each product. A **positioning statement**, which expresses how a company wants to be perceived by customers, can be useful with establishing a product's position relative to that of its competitors. For example, a positioning statement for 7-Up is as follows: "for non-cola consumers, 7-Up is a non-caffeinated soft drink that is light, refreshing, lemon-lime flavoured and, unlike colas, it has a crisp, bubbly, and clean taste."

The topics of market segmentation, target marketing, and positioning will be discussed in greater detail when you take a Marketing course. In the meantime, recognize that a product cannot usually be all things to all people. As a result, this process of

(1) applying market segmentation bases to arrive at potential market segments, (2) selecting the most profitable target market(s), and (3) developing the product positioning for each target market, is necessary before marketers can create a 4P marketing mix that will meet the wants and needs of each target market.

product positioning The place an offering occupies in customers' minds on important attributes relative to competitive products.

positioning statement Expresses how a company wants to be perceived by customers.

relationship marketing Marketing strategy with the goal of keeping individual customers over time by offering them products that exactly meet their requirements.

Building Marketing Relationships

Relationship marketing tends to lead away from mass production and toward custom-made goods and services. The goal is to keep individual customers over time by offering them new products that exactly meet their requirements. Technology and social media enable sellers to work with individual buyers to determine their wants and needs and to develop goods and services specifically designed for them, like hand-tailored shirts and unique vacations.

To build strong relationships, many firms undertake active CRM programs that identify and focus on building loyalty with the firm's most valued customers. CRM systems include a customer database or data warehouse where customer information (e.g., transaction, contact, preferences, and market segment) is input. Data are then analyzed and CRM programs are developed.[37] For example, a customer can deal with a salesperson in a store, online, or in a call centre. A customer's information can be quickly accessed via the CRM system that provides the information needed to address the purpose of the point of contact.

Firms sometimes reward dedicated customers with loyalty or CRM programs, such as points that customers can redeem for extra discounts or free services, advance notice of sale items, and invitations to special events sponsored by the company.[38] Loyalty programs include PC Optimum and SCENE, a partnership between Scotiabank and Cineplex Entertainment. What loyalty program cards do you have in your wallet?

Social media is a way that businesses can engage with their customers. G Adventures, a leading small-group adventure tour operator, has been chosen as Canada's favourite adventure tour operator in Baxter Travel Media's Agents' Choice Awards.[39] "Twitter has revolutionized our business," says founder Bruce Poon Tip. "Facebook has done the same thing. We have the ability to deliver our culture anywhere in the world now."[40]

Understanding consumers is so important to marketing that a whole area of marketing emerged called consumer behaviour. We explore that area next.

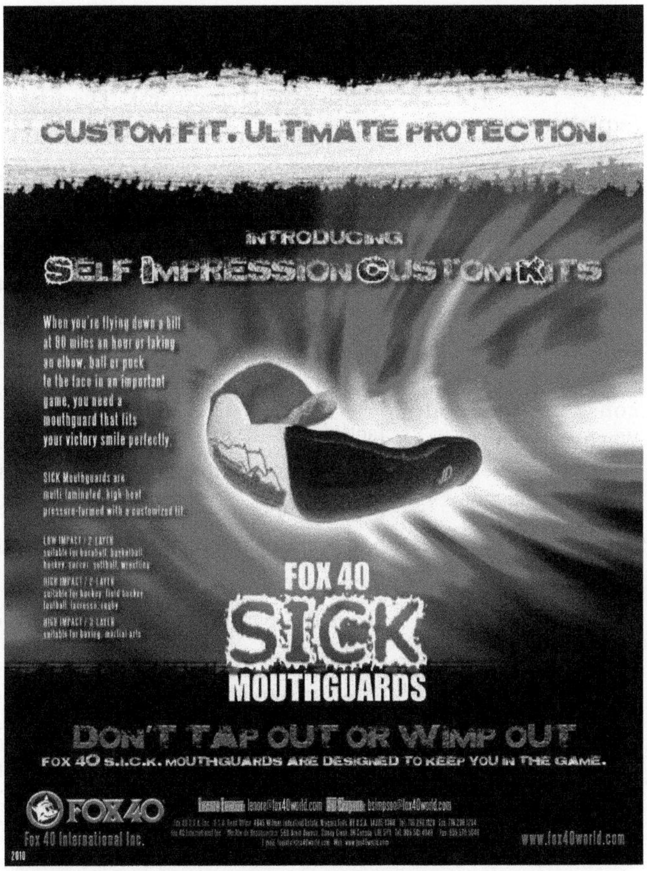

Courtesy of Fox 40 International Inc. Used with permission

There is a running case at the end of each text part and the focus is Fox 40 International Inc. What is the company's positioning statement in this ad?

© G Adventures

G Adventures offers small-group experiences. As the world's largest independent adventure travel company, it offers tours, safaris, and expeditions. Start with your travel style and then take it from there when targeting a location. Would you consider booking through this company?

PROGRESS ASSESSMENT

- Define market segmentation, target marketing, and positioning.
- Name and describe four ways to segment the consumer market.
- What are different target marketing approaches?
- What might be the product positioning for your favourite pair of shoes? What about one of your electronic items (e.g., computer, tablet, or phone)?

Consumer Behaviour

Marketing researchers investigate consumer-thought processes and behaviour at each stage in a purchase to determine the best way to help the buyer buy. This area of study in marketing is called **consumer behaviour**.

LO6

Explain how marketers meet the needs of the consumer market through the study of consumer behaviour.

consumer behaviour When marketing researchers investigate consumer thought processes and behaviour at each stage in a purchase to determine the best way to help the buyer buy.

Central to studying consumer behaviour is understanding the five steps of the decision-making process. The first step is *problem recognition,* which may occur when your computer breaks down and you realize you need a new one or it needs to be repaired. Let's assume you decide that you will purchase a new one. This leads to an *information search*—you look for ads about computers. You may consult secondary data sources like *Consumer Reports, CNET* or other online reviews from both experts and customers. And you'll likely seek advice from other people you know who have purchased computers. After compiling all this information, you *evaluate alternatives* and make a *purchase decision.* But your buying process doesn't end there. After the purchase, you may be asked to complete a *postpurchase evaluation* where you are asked to assess your satisfaction (or dissatisfaction) with your purchase. *Cognitive dissonance* is a type of psychological conflict that can occur after a purchase. Consumers who make a major purchase (e.g., computer) may have doubts (i.e., cognitive dissonance) about whether they got the best product at the best price. Marketers must reassure such consumers after the sale that they made a good decision. An auto dealer, for example, may send positive press articles about the particular car purchased, offer product guarantees, and provide certain free services.

Consumer behaviour researchers also study the various influences that affect consumer behaviour. In addition to the five steps of the decision-making process, Figure 14.9 shows several such influences: marketing mix variables (the four Ps); psychological influences, such as perception and attitudes; situational influences, such as the type of purchase and the physical surroundings; and sociocultural influences, such as reference groups and culture.

Consider some of these factors:[41]

- *Learning* creates changes in an individual's behaviour resulting from previous experiences and information. If you've tried a particular brand of shampoo and you don't like it, you've learned not to buy it again.

FIGURE 14.9

THE CONSUMER DECISION-MAKING PROCESS AND OUTSIDE INFLUENCES

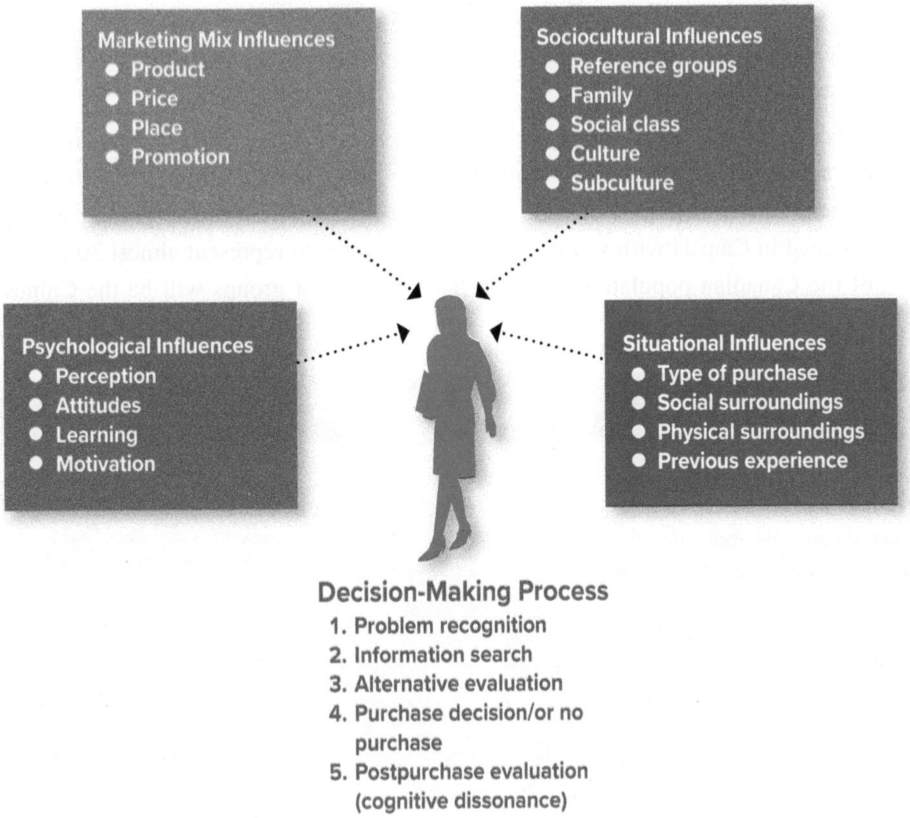

There are many influences on consumers as they decide which goods and services to buy. Marketers have some influence, but it is not usually as strong as sociocultural influences. Helping consumers in their information search and their evaluation of alternatives is a major function of marketing.

- *Reference group* is the group an individual uses as a reference point in forming beliefs, attitudes, values, or behaviour. A student who carries a briefcase instead of a backpack may see business people as his or her reference group.
- *Culture* is the set of values, attitudes, and ways of doing things transmitted from one generation to another in a given society. Attitudes toward work, lifestyles, and consumption are evolving. For example, there is a trend toward *value-consciousness* (the concern for obtaining the best quality, features, and performance of a product or service for a given price).

Another trend is *eco-consciousness* or *going green.* Canadians are more sensitive about the impact their consumption has on their natural environment, and they make their buying decisions accordingly. This may mean buying more environmentally safe or more environmentally friendly products, buying products that can be reused or recycled, or actually

© OJO Images Ltd/Alamy Stock Photo

Canadians are becoming increasingly health-conscious, creating opportunities for marketers that can develop products to address this change in buying behaviour. Do you think that Baby Boomers are driving this demand, or is it being driven by people of all ages? Do you see how Harvest Gold could profit from healthy takeout food that is quickly prepared?

green marketing The process of selling products and/or services based on their environmental benefits.

greenwashing When businesses try to make themselves or their products or services look green or socially responsible without the action to back it up.

reducing consumption altogether. The Seeking Sustainability box highlights some concerns that consumers have raised about "green" advertising claims. In the box, you will be introduced to the terms **green marketing**—the process of selling products and/or services based on their environmental benefits, and **greenwashing**—when businesses try to make themselves or their products or services look green or socially responsible without the action to back it up.

- *Subculture* is the set of values, attitudes, and ways of doing things that results from belonging to a certain ethnic group, religious group, or other group with which one closely identifies (e.g., teenagers). More than 100 different ethnic groups are represented in Canada with visible minorities projected to represent almost 30 percent of the Canadian population by 2031. The two largest groups will be the Chinese

Seeking SUSTAINABILITY

When Green Is Not Really Green

Companies are responding to concerns about the environment and global warming through a variety of ways. Green marketing refers to the process of selling products and/or services based on their environmental benefits. Such a product or service may be environmentally friendly in itself or produced and/or packaged in an environmentally friendly way. Green advertising is a useful way to communicate important information to consumers who want to make responsible and environmentally conscious choices between competing products that claim to respect the environment. The green marketing assumption is that potential consumers will view a product or service's "greenness" as a benefit and base their buying decisions accordingly. The not-so-obvious assumption of green marketing is that consumers will be willing to pay more for green products than they would for a less-green comparable alternatives.

Businesses are sometimes accused of greenwashing when they try to make themselves or their products or services look green or socially responsible without the action to back it up. An example of this is when a company spends more resources on advertising its sustainability attributes than resources spent on its sustainability programs. Other examples include vague and meaningless product claims like "environmentally friendly" that are not explained, or claims that are not backed up, such as shampoos and conditioners advertised as not having been tested on animals while offering no evidence or certification of such claims.

© Jakub Jirsák/iStock/Thinkstock

There are no laws specifically governing green claims. While CSA Group developed green guidelines, compliance is voluntary.

Studies confirm that job seekers are attracted to organizations with sustainable practices. Other studies show the same in relation to social practices more generally (e.g., community involvement and ethical governance). Not only may greenwashing hurt the company's image and bottom line, but if new employees find that the messages about sustainable practices that initially attracted them are really just a green veneer, many will become resentful and some will leave. Have you been attracted to companies with sustainable practices? Would you be turned off by companies that have been accused of greenwashing?

Sources: Susan Ward, "Green Marketing," About.com, http://sbinfocanada.about.com/od/marketing/g/greenmarketing, accessed April 5, 2015; "Three Reasons Job Seekers Prefer Sustainable Companies," Network for Business Sustainability, June 7, 2013, http://nbs.net/knowledge/three-reasons-job-seekers-prefer-sustainable-companies/; Rebecca Harris, "Greenwashing: Cleaning Up By 'saving the World'," *Marketing*, April 25, 2013, http://www.marketingmag.ca/brands/greenwashing-cleaning-up-by-saving-the-world-77259; and "SME Sustainability Roadmap," Industry Canada, September 30, 2011, https://www.ic.gc.ca/eic/site/csr-rse.nsf/eng/rs00182.html.

(from Hong Kong, mainland China, and Taiwan) and South Asians (from India, Pakistan, Sri Lanka, and Bangladesh).

Canadian companies engage in **ethnic marketing**—combinations of the marketing mix that reflect the unique attitudes, race or ancestry, communication preferences, and lifestyles of ethnic Canadians. Through its store concept, FreshCo, Sobeys has targeted the unique needs of the ethnic consumer. FreshCo is a value-driven concept with low prices, like No Frills or Food Basics, but with a focus on fresh produce, halal meats, and freshly baked breads. The international food aisles highlight Asian, West Indian, Middle Eastern, and Eastern European food products.

ethnic marketing Combinations of the marketing mix that reflect the unique attitudes, race or ancestry, communication preferences, and lifestyles of ethnic Canadians.

Similar to courses in business marketing, consumer behaviour is a long-standing part of a marketing curriculum. Do you think you will take this course in the future?

PROGRESS ASSESSMENT

- List the five steps in the decision-making process.
- Describe each of the four major influencers on the decision-making process.
- How is green marketing different from greenwashing?
- Why is ethnic marketing an important focus for companies?

Your Prospects in Marketing

There is a wider variety of careers in marketing than in most business disciplines. If you major in marketing, an array of career options will be available to you. You could conduct marketing research or get involved in product management. You could become a manager in a retail store. You could do marketing research or work in product management. You could go into selling, advertising, sales promotion, or public relations. You could work in transportation, storage, or international distribution. You could design websites. Think, for example, of the many ways to use social media and other technologies in marketing. These are just a few of the possibilities. As you read further into this topic in Chapter 15, consider whether a marketing career would interest you.

SUMMARY

LO1 **Define marketing and explain how the marketing concept applies to both for-profit and non-profit organizations.**

Marketing is the process of determining customer wants and needs and then providing customers with goods and services that meet or exceed these expectations.

How has marketing changed over time?

What marketers do at any particular time depends on what they need to do to fill customers' needs and wants, which continually change. The evolution of marketing includes five eras, also known as orientations: (1) production, (2) sales, (3) marketing concept, (4) market orientation, and (5) social media marketing.

What are the three parts of the marketing concept?

The three parts of the marketing concept are (1) a customer orientation, (2) a service orientation, and (3) a profit orientation (that is, market goods and services that will earn the firm a profit and enable it to survive and expand to serve more customers' wants and needs).

What kinds of organizations are involved in marketing?

All kinds of organizations use marketing, both for-profit and non-profit organizations. Examples of non-profit organizations include the provinces and other government agencies, charities (e.g., churches), politicians, and schools.

LO2 **Describe the four Ps of marketing.**

The marketing mix consists of the four Ps of marketing: product, price, place, and promotion.

What is required before marketers develop a product?

Once marketers have researched customer needs and found a target market, the four Ps come into play, starting with the development of a product. Recall that a product is any physical good, service, or idea which falls somewhere on the service continuum which is highlighted in Figure 14.4.

How do marketers implement the four Ps?

The idea is to design a product that people want, price it competitively, get it in a location where customers can find it easily, and promote it—considering advertising, personal selling, public relations, direct marketing, and sales promotion—so that customers know it exists. While this chapter briefly outlined these four Ps, they will be discussed in more detail in Chapter 15.

LO3 **Identify the steps in the marketing research process, and explain how marketers use environmental scanning to learn about the changing marketing environment.**

Marketing research is the analysis of markets to determine opportunities and challenges and to find the information needed to make good decisions.

What are the steps to follow when conducting marketing research?

The four steps are (1) define the problem or opportunity and determine the present situation, (2) collect data, (3) analyze the research data, and (4) choose the best solution and implement it.

What are different methods used to gather research?

Research can be gathered through secondary data (information that has already be compiled by others) and published in sources such as journals, newspapers, directories, databases, and internal sources. Primary data (data that you gather yourself) includes observation, surveys, interviews, and focus groups.

What is environmental scanning?

Environmental scanning is the process of identifying the trends that can affect marketing success. Marketers pay attention to all environmental trends that create opportunities and threats. Figure 14.6 shares the six environments—global, technological, social, competitive, economic, and legal—that are considered in environmental scanning.

What are some of the more important environmental trends in marketing?

The most important global and technological change is probably the Internet. Another is the growth of customer databases, with which companies can develop products and services that closely match the needs of customers. Marketers must also monitor social trends like population growth and shifts to maintain their close relationship with customers. Of course, marketers must also monitor the dynamic competitive environment and pay attention to the economic environment. Changes in laws can create opportunities and threats for business activities; thus, this is another important environment to scan.

LO4 **Compare the consumer market to the business-to-business market.**

The consumer market consists of all individuals or households that want goods and services for personal consumption or use and have the resources to buy them. The total potential global consumer market consists of the billions of people in global markets.

What types of businesses operate in the business-to-business (B2B) market?

The B2B market consists of manufacturers, intermediaries such as wholesalers, institutions (e.g., hospitals, schools, and charities), and the government.

What makes the business-to-business market different from the consumer market?

The number of customers in the B2B market is relatively small, and the size of business customers is relatively large. B2B markets tend to be geographically concentrated, and industrial buyers generally are more rational than ultimate consumers in their selection of goods and services. B2B sales tend to be direct, and there is much more emphasis on personal selling in B2B markets than in consumer markets.

LO5 **Describe the market segmentation process, and the role of relationship marketing.**

The process of dividing the total market into several groups whose members have similar characteristics is called market segmentation.

What are some of the ways that marketers segment the consumer market?

See Figure 14.8 for a summary of consumer segmentation variables. *Geographic* segmentation means dividing the market into different regions. Segmentation by age, income, and education level are methods of *demographic* segmentation. We study a group's values, attitudes, and interests using *psychographic* segmentation. *Behavioural* segmentation divides the market based on behaviour with or toward a product. Different variables of behavioural segmentation include benefits sought, usage rate, and user status. The best segmentation strategy is to use as many of these segmentation bases as possible to come up with a target market that is sizeable, reachable, and profitable.

What is the relationship between target marketing and product positioning?

Following market segmentation, marketers need to select the segment(s) that is (are) the most profitable. This is known as target marketing. Product positioning, which refers to the place an offering occupies in customers' minds on important attributes relative to competitive products, is then applied for each product. Market segmentation, target marketing, and positioning are necessary before marketers can create a 4P marketing mix for each target market that will meet their wants and needs.

What is the difference between mass marketing and relationship marketing?

Mass marketing means developing products and promotions to please large groups of people. Relationship marketing tends to lead away from mass production and toward custom-made goods and services. Its goal is to keep individual customers over time by offering them goods or services that meet their needs.

LO6 **Explain how marketers meet the needs of the consumer market through the study of consumer behaviour.**

Marketing researchers investigate consumer-thought processes and behaviour at each stage in a purchase to determine the best way to help the buyer buy. This area of study is called consumer behaviour.

What are the five steps of the decision-making process?

As listed on Figure 14.9, the five steps of the decision-making process are (1) problem recognition, (2) information search, (3) evaluate alternatives, (4) purchase decision, and (5) postpurchase evaluation.

What is cognitive dissonance?

Cognitive dissonance may occur in the postpurchase evaluation step. It is a type of psychological conflict that can occur after a purchase. If customers are satisfied with their purchases, they will not regret their purchases (i.e., experience cognitive dissonance).

What are some of the factors that influence the consumer decision-making process?

See Figure 14.9 for the four major influences on consumer decision making. Some specific factors include learning, reference group, culture, and subculture.

KEY TERMS

CAREER EXPLORATION

If you are interested in pursuing a career in marketing, here are a few to consider. Find out about the tasks performed, skills needed, pay, and opportunity outlook in these fields through Internet sites that include the Government of Canada Job Bank, Workopolis, Monster, CareerBuilder, Glassdoor, and Indeed, as well as through the Career Centre at your school.

- **Marketing research analyst**—studies market conditions to examine potential sales of a product or service; identifies what products people want, who will buy them, and at what price.
- **Graphic designer**—creates visual concepts, using computer software or by hand, to communicate ideas that inspire, inform, and captivate consumers; develops visuals for advertisements, brochures, magazines, and corporate reports.
- **Copywriter**—develops written content for advertisements, blogs, or other types of marketing media.
- **Sales manager**—directs sales teams, sets sales goals, analyzes data, and develops training programs for sales representatives.

CRITICAL THINKING

1. Which of your needs are not being met by businesses and/or non-profit organizations in your area? Are there enough people with similar needs to attract an organization that would meet those needs? How would you find out?
2. When businesses buy goods and services from other businesses, they usually buy in large volume. Salespeople in the business-to-business market usually are paid on a commission basis; that is, they earn a certain percentage of each sale they make. Why might B2B sales be a more financially rewarding career area than consumer sales?
3. Retailers such as the Hudson's Bay Company (HBC Rewards) and Shoppers Drug Mart (PC Optimum) offer loyalty programs. Are you encouraged to visit these retailers more often as a result of such programs? Do you buy more products as a result of such programs? Retailers also offer incentives to use their credit cards. For example, you may get 10 percent off your purchase if you open an HBC credit card account. Do you feel that companies are trying to bribe you to support their businesses, or do you think that these are good business practices? How effective is social networking in building loyalty? Explain.
4. Marketers must adapt as new technologies emerge. For example, younger consumers watch programs on the Internet and/or PVR, rather than during the scheduled television slots. Services such as Netflix, Crave TV, and Shomi also offer another programming alternative. What does this mean for traditional television advertisements (i.e., commercials)? How should marketers evaluate and plan a move to marketing through these newer alternatives as compared to scheduled television programming?

DEVELOPING CAREER SKILLS

Key: ● **Team** ★ **Analytic** ▲ **Communication** ⊡ **Technology**

★▲ 1. Think of an effective marketing mix for a new electric car or a brushless car wash for your neighbourhood. Be prepared to discuss your ideas in class.

●★▲ 2. Working in teams of five, think of a product your friends want but cannot get on or near campus. You might ask your friends at other schools what is available there. What kind of product would fill that need? Discuss your results in class and determine how you might go about marketing that new product.

★ 3. Business has fallen off greatly in your upscale restaurant due to the slow economy. List four things you can do to win back the loyalty of your past customers. Be prepared to discuss this in class.

●★▲ 4. Working in teams of four or five, list as many brand names of pizza as you can from pizza shops, restaurants, supermarkets, and so on. Merge your list with the lists from other groups or classmates. Then try to identify the target market for each brand. Do they all seem to be after the same market, or are there different brands for different markets? What are the separate appeals?

★▲ 5. Take a little time to review the concepts in this chapter as they apply to Harvest Gold, the restaurant we introduced in this chapter. Have an open discussion in class about (a) a different name for the restaurant, (b) a location for the restaurant, (c) a promotional program, and (d) a way to establish a long-term relationship with customers.

ANALYZING MANAGEMENT DECISIONS

Applying Customer-Oriented Marketing Concepts at Thermos

Thermos is the company made famous by its Thermos bottles and lunch boxes. Thermos also manufactures cookout grills. Its competitors include Sunbeam and Weber. To become a world-class competitor, Thermos completely reinvented the way it conducted its marketing operations. By reviewing what Thermos did, you can see how new marketing concepts affect organizations.

First, Thermos modified its corporate culture. It had become a bureaucratic firm organized by function: design, engineering, manufacturing, marketing, and so on. That organizational structure was replaced by flexible, cross-functional, self-managed teams. The idea was to focus on a customer group—for example, buyers of outdoor grills—and build a product development team to create a product for that market.

The product development team for grills consisted of six middle managers from various disciplines, including engineering, manufacturing, finance, and marketing. They called themselves the Lifestyle Team because their job was to study grill users to see how they lived and what they were looking for in an outdoor grill. To get a fresh perspective, the company hired Fitch, Inc., an outside consulting firm, to help with design and marketing research. Team leadership was rotated based on needs of the moment. For example, the marketing person took the lead in doing field research, but the R&D person took over when technical developments became the issue.

The team's first step was to analyze the market. Together, team members spent about a month on the road talking with people, videotaping barbecues, conducting focus groups, and learning what people wanted in an outdoor grill. The company found that people wanted a nice-looking grill that did not pollute the air and was easy to use. It also had to be safe enough for apartment dwellers, which meant that it had to be electric.

As the research results came in, engineering began playing with ways to improve electric grills. Manufacturing kept in touch to ensure that any new ideas could be produced economically. Design people were already building models of the new product. R&D people relied heavily on Thermos' strengths. The company's core strength was the vacuum technology it had developed to keep hot things hot and cold things cold in Thermos bottles. Drawing on that strength, the engineers developed a domed lid that contained the heat inside the grill.

Once a prototype was developed, the company showed the model to potential customers, who suggested several changes. Employees also took sample grills home and tried to find weaknesses. Using the input from potential customers and employees, the company used continuous improvement to manufacture what became a world-class outdoor grill.

No product can become a success without communicating with the market. The team took the grill on the road, showing it at trade shows and in retail stores. The product was such a success that Thermos is now using self-managed, customer-oriented teams to develop all of its product lines.

Discussion Questions

1. How could the growth of self-managed, cross-functional teams affect marketing departments in other companies? Do you believe that would be a good change or not? Explain.
2. How can Thermos now build a closer relationship with its customers using the Internet?
3. What other products might Thermos develop that would appeal to the same market segment that uses outdoor grills?

CHAPTER 15

Managing the Marketing Mix: Product, Price, Place, and Promotion

LEARNING OBJECTIVES

After you have read and studied this chapter, you should be able to:

LO1 Explain the concept of a total product offer, and summarize the functions of packaging.

LO2 Describe the product life cycle.

LO3 Identify various pricing objectives and strategies, and explain why non-pricing strategies are growing in importance.

LO4 Explain the concept of marketing channels, and the importance of retailing.

LO5 Define promotion, and list the five traditional tools that make up the promotion mix.

PROFILE

GETTING TO KNOW: MICHAEL DUBIN, CEO/CO-FOUNDER, DOLLAR SHAVE CLUB

There is no better way to get the attention of more and more people than to go viral on social media. That's not easy, though. With thousands of hours of content uploaded daily to YouTube alone, standing out in this vast crowd takes creativity and a unique message. It also helps to be funny. That's the strategy that Michael Dubin used when he launched Dollar Shave Club in 2012 with a short video he wrote, produced, and starred in. Millions of views later, he credits the clip with transforming his upstart company into the second-largest razor seller in the United States.

Dubin honed his business and comedy skills in New York. Arriving in the city after graduating from Emory University, he first worked as a page at NBC and then moved on to news writing and production. He shifted focus to marketing and digital media a couple of years later, creating content and videos for brands like Gatorade, Nintendo, and Ford. All the while Dubin took improv comedy classes in his

Source: Courtesy of Dollar Shave Club.

spare time at the famed Upright Citizens Brigade Theatre. He noticed how both businesspeople and improvisers worked together by identifying the best qualities of each individual in a group. "Whether it's an executive team or an improv comedy team, you need to know what you can expect from the other players or partners," said Dubin.

One thing he did not expect, however, was to receive a life-changing business offer at a holiday party. He had been talking with Mark Levine, the father of a friend's fiancee, about the downsides of buying razors. "I don't know how we got on the subject of shaving, but we started talking about what a rip-off it is," said Dubin. "For years, guys have been frustrated with the price of razors in the store and the experience of having to go to the store and find the razor fortress and have it unlocked. That whole thing is very unnecessary."

They developed a concept and called it Dollar Shave Club, a service that sends razors straight to customers' homes each month. Knowing that the company would need clear messaging and a reliable purchasing platform, Dubin withdrew $35,000 from his life savings to build the website. Along with this major investment, he also spent $4,500 to shoot an ad driven by his deadpan sense of humor. During the clip's one and a half minutes Dubin swears, rides a forklift, and whacks a length of packing tape with a machete as he explains Dollar Shave Club's business model. Before going online, Dubin used the video in meetings to win over investors. He also built relationships with bloggers and other online influencers so they would share the video when it hit the Internet. And share they did: as of this writing the company's first commercial has more than 25 million views on YouTube.

As the video went viral, DollarShaveClub.com crashed under the weight of all the new visitors. Since then, millions more have visited the site not only for the monthly razor service but also for other items like shaving cream, shampoo, and moist towelettes. But the company's biggest payday came in 2016 when Unilever bought the brand for $1 billion. Michael Dubin remains in charge and hopes one day that Dollar Shave Club will "own the entire bathroom."

Marketing begins with watching people to understand their needs. It then involves developing products that customers might want. One must develop a marketing mix that will resonate with the target market. Making such decisions is challenging, but if you are successful, you can make a lot of customers very happy. This is what marketing is all about.

Sources: Paul Ziobro, "How Michael Dubin Turned a Funny Video into $1 Billion," *The Wall Street Journal,* July 20, 2016; Jessica Naziri, "Dollar Shave Club Co-Founder Michael Dubin Had a Smooth Transition," *Los Angeles Times,* August 16, 2013; Mike Isaac and Michael J. De La Merced, "Dollar Shave Club Sells to Unilever for $1 Billion," *The New York Times,* July 20, 2016; Kris Frieswick, "The Serious Guy behind Dollar Shave Club's Crazy Viral Videos," *Inc.,* April 2016; Lucy Handley, "Michael Dubin: Shaving America," *CNBC,* June 21, 2017.

LO1

Explain the concept of a total product offer, and summarize the functions of packaging.

value
Good quality at a fair price.

Product Development and the Total Product Offer

Global managers continue to challenge Canadian managers with new products at low prices.[1] The best way to compete is to design and promote better products, meaning products that customers perceive to have the best **value**—good quality at a fair price. When customers calculate the value of a product, they look at the benefits and then subtract the cost (price) to see whether the benefits exceed the cost, including the cost of driving to the store (or shipping fees if they buy the product online). You may have noticed many restaurants pushed value and dollar menus when the economy slowed.

Whether customers perceive a product as the best value depends on many factors, including the benefits they seek and the service they receive. To satisfy customers, marketers must learn to listen better and constantly adapt to changing market demands.[2]

Marketers have learned that adapting products to new competition and new markets is an ongoing need. We're sure you've noticed menu changes at your local fast-food restaurants over time. An organization can't do a one-time survey of consumer wants and needs, design a group of products to meet those needs, put them in the stores, and then just relax. It must constantly monitor changing consumer wants and needs, and adapt products, policies, and services accordingly. For example, consumers are looking for healthier food choices today compared to in the past. Did you know that McDonald's now sells as much chicken as beef? It even incorporates chicken into its popular breakfast menu.[3] Following customer requests for smaller portions, McDonald's now offers value meals with a choice of sandwich size. It also transitioned some popular morning items into an all-day breakfast menu.

McDonald's and other restaurants are constantly trying new ideas. *Whopperito* or *Mac n' Cheetos,* anyone?[4] Taco Bell has gotten into the breakfast game. It rolled out a higher protein breakfast menu to compete with the current high-carbohydrate breakfast menus.[5] Have you noticed any other fast-food restaurants starting to create breakfast menus? Recall

(left) © Jeff Greenberg 2 of 6/Alamy; (right) The McGraw-Hill Companies, Inc./Christopher Kerrigan, photographer

How would you like a beer or glass of wine with your Big Mac? You can get both at this McDonald's in Paris (shown left). On the right, you see a McDonald's in Indonesia. Around the world, McDonald's adapts its architectural scheme, menus, and interior design to fit the tastes and cultural demands of each country.

Reaching *Beyond* OUR BORDERS

Playing with the Social Gaming Stars

Did you know that Ellen DeGeneres, Kim Kardashian, Nicki Minaj, and at least 30 other celebrities are competing in a new $200 million a year industry? They have created a new genre of gaming: social celebrity-driven mobile games.

Involving celebrities in our video game culture is nothing new. Michael Jackson had a partnership with Sega in 1990 in which players moonwalked through the levels. Many other celebrities lent their voices and likenesses to a multitude of games. But now, gaming is transitioning from our consoles to our phones. We're free to play wherever and whenever we want, and it's a big money business. Today, popular app developers use tried and proven games as the base, and then "turbocharge" them by inserting a popular celebrity with a massive social following.

© Cindy Ord/Getty Images

Take Kim Kardashian's app, for example. Titled *Kim Kardashian: Hollywood* and created by app developer Glu, the app actually had two previous lives (called *Stardom: The A List* and *Stardom: Hollywood*). Both were popular before Kardashian, bringing in about $2.5 million each through downloads and in-app purchases. However, they didn't have enough daily players. When Kardashian came in, she attracted a massive number of daily players—and more money. So far *Kim Kardashian: Hollywood* has brought in $160 million!

It's not just the app developers making all the money in these deals. *Forbes* estimated Kim Kardashian herself earned $45 million from her game. That has more celebrities wanting a piece of the action. Glu recently launched the app named *Nicki Minaj: The Empire* and is working on a game for Taylor Swift. Who do you think the next celebrity game star will be?

Sources: Natalie Robehmed, "Game Changers," *Forbes*, July 26, 2016; Michael Sylvain, "Why PewDiePie's New Game Is Proof We're All Doomed," *Rolling Stone*, October 7, 2016; Patrick Sietz, "Nicki Minaj No Match for Mario in Mobile Games," *Investor's Business Daily*, December 23, 2016; Chris Morrison, "Celebrity Branding: The Ultimate Built-In Marketing Tactic for a Mobile Game," Chartboost, accessed September 2017.

the Reaching Beyond Our Borders box about rolling out Oreo cookies in foreign markets in Chapter 14. But it isn't only food companies who must be creative. Every business must continually develop new offerings. Read the Reaching Beyond Our Borders box to discover more.

You can imagine what can happen when your product loses some of its appeal.[6] Zippo lighters, for example, lost market strength as people turn away from smoking cigarettes to using e-cigarettes.[7] Zippo then tried offering items such as knives, leather products, and even perfume.[8] They are no longer being sold. Zippo also introduced a clothing line that includes hoodies, ball caps, and jeans.

Product development, then, is a key activity in any modern business, anywhere in the world. There's a lot more to new-product development than merely introducing goods and services, however. What marketers do to create excitement for those products is as important as the products themselves.

Developing a Total Product Offer

total product offer (value package) Everything that customers evaluate when deciding whether to buy something; also called a *value package*.

value package (total product offer) Another name for total product offer, which is everything that customers evaluate when deciding whether to buy something.

From a strategic marketing viewpoint, a total product offer is more than just the physical good or service. A **total product offer**, also called a **value package**, consists of everything that customers evaluate when deciding whether to buy something. Thus, the basic good or service may be a washing machine, an insurance policy, or a beer, but the total product offer includes some or all of the *value enhancers* in Figure 15.1. You may hear some people call the basic product the "core product" and the total product offer the "augmented product." Can you see how sustainability can be part of the augmented product?[9]

When people buy a product, they may evaluate and compare total product offers on many dimensions. Some are tangible (the product itself and its package) while others are intangible (the producer's reputation and the image created by advertising). A successful marketer must think like a customer and evaluate the total product offer as a collection of impressions created by all of the factors listed in Figure 15.1. It is wise to talk with customers to learn which features and benefits are most important to them and which value enhancers they want or don't want in the final offering.[10] Frito-Lay, for example, had to drop biodegradable bags because they were too noisy. Marketers had not considered this dimension.

What questions might you ask customers when developing the total product offer for Harvest Gold? (Recall the business idea introduced in Chapter 14.) Remember,

FIGURE 15.1

POTENTIAL COMPONENTS OF A TOTAL PRODUCT OFFER

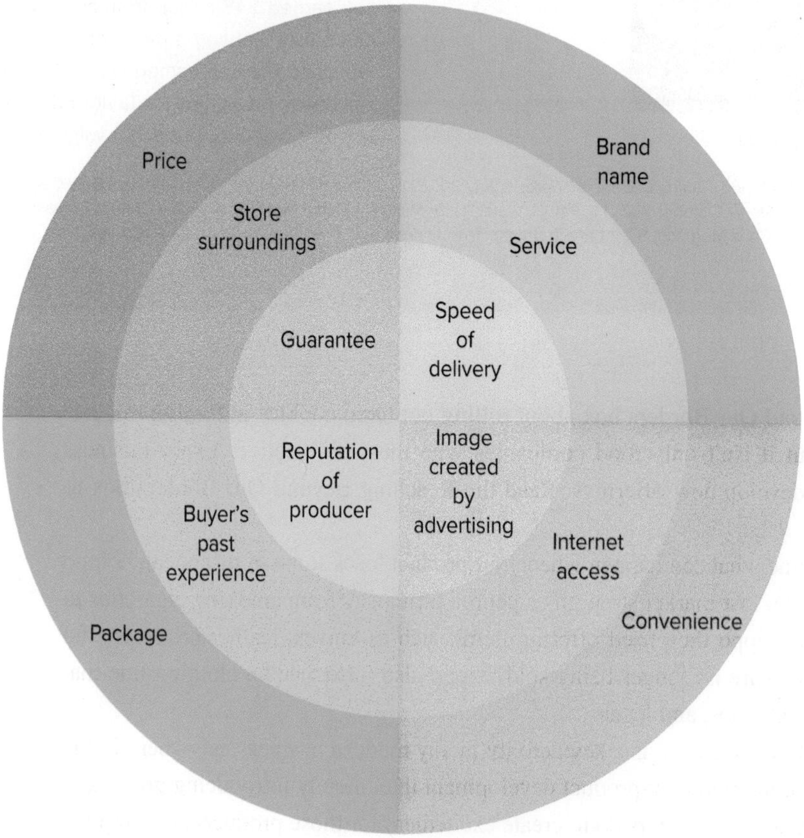

store surroundings are important in the restaurant business, as are the parking lot and the condition of the bathrooms.

Sometimes an organization can use low prices to create an attractive total product offer. For example, outlet stores offer brand-name goods for less. Shoppers like getting high-quality goods and low prices, but they must be careful. Outlets also carry lower-quality products with similar but not exactly the same features as goods carried in regular stores. Different consumers may want different total product offers, so a company must develop a variety of offerings.

© Erik Tham/Alamy

Apple, Samsung, and other smartphone makers are fighting for a greater share of the huge mobile market. Each continues to improve and add features hoping to win customers. What features would a smartphone company have to add to its product offer in order to convince you to switch phones?

Product Lines and the Product Mix

Companies usually don't sell just one product. A **product line** is a group of products that are physically similar or are intended for a similar market. They usually face similar competition. In one product line, there may be several competing brands. Notice, for example, Diet Coke, Diet Coke with Splenda, Diet Coke with Lemon, Diet Vanilla Coke, and Diet Cherry Coke. Now Coca-Cola is creating even more flavour options through its Coke Freestyle machines.[11] Makes it kind of hard to choose, doesn't it? Both Coke and Pepsi have added water and sports drinks to their product lines to meet new consumer tastes.

product line
A group of products that are physically similar or are intended for a similar market.

Procter & Gamble's (P&G) product lines include hair care, oral care, and household cleaners. In one product line, there may be several competing brands. For example, P&G has many brands in its laundry detergent product line, including Tide, Era, Downy, and Bold. All of P&G's product lines make up its **product mix**, the combination of product lines offered by an organization. The Spotlight on Small Business box shares how one product led to new product lines.

product mix
The combination of product lines offered by an organization.

Service providers have product lines and product mixes as well. Financial services firms, such as banks and credit unions, may offer a variety of services such as savings products (including chequing accounts and term deposits), credit products (including loans, mortgages, and credit cards), and a variety of other services (such as safety deposit boxes). TELUS combines services (plans) with goods (phones and accessories) in its product mix, with special emphasis on deals.[12]

Product Differentiation

Product differentiation is the creation of real or perceived product differences. Actual product differences are sometimes quite small, so marketers must use a creative mix of branding, pricing, advertising, and packaging (value enhancers) to create a unique, attractive image. Note the positive effect of developing brands like Uber, YETI, and Netflix.[13] Various bottled water companies, for example, have successfully achieved product differentiation. These companies made their bottled waters so attractive through pricing and promotion that some restaurant customers order water by brand name (e.g., Perrier).

product differentiation
The creation of real or perceived product differences.

Spotlight *On* SMALL BUSINESS

Made by Mommy

Imagine you're holding your 10-month-old baby and she will not stop grabbing at your necklace. Big and shiny, it's like you're wearing a baby magnet around your neck. But as much as she may love looking, grabbing, and chewing on it, metal and stones are not baby-friendly.

Photography by Raquel Langworthy, Courtesy of Chewbeads

Lisa Greenwald had the same issue. Her baby magnet was a brightly coloured necklace that her son, and all babies for that matter, just had to get in their mouths. She had her "aha" moment and Chewbeads were born. Developed in 2009, Lisa and her husband, Eric, went through many trials before creating their final product. Lisa wanted her necklaces to be gentle on babies' teeth and free of toxic chemicals. That turned out to be a more difficult task than they had originally thought. They found manufacturers who could make *parts* of Chewbeads, but never the whole product. After hiring a consultant, they were able to teach factory workers how to make the entire necklace.

Since its inception, Chewbeads has sold over 140 000 necklaces, keeping moms fashionable and babies happy for about $25. After a year of selling necklaces, Chewbeads started to branch out. The company now makes baby toys and stroller accessories and is working on a new bib. It looks like babies will have a lot to chew on for years to come.

Sources: Paula Andruss, "For the Mouths of Babes," *Entrepreneur,* April 2016; Adam Toren, "In Honor of Mother's Day Here Are 7 Mompreneurs Who Founded Million Dollar Businesses," *Fox Business,* May 6, 2016; Annie Pilon, "21 Successful Mom Entrepreneurs to Inspire You," *Small Business Trends,* May 5, 2016; Jo Piazza, "How Being A Mom Can Make You A Better Entrepreneur," *Forbes,* June 1, 2017.

There's no reason why you couldn't create a similar attractive image for Harvest Gold, your farm-to-table restaurant. Small businesses can often win market share with creative product differentiation. One yearbook entrepreneur competes by offering multiple clothing changes, backgrounds, and poses along with special allowances, discounts, and guarantees. His small business has the advantage of being more flexible in adapting to customer needs and wants, and he's able to offer attractive product options. He has been so successful that companies use him as a speaker at photography conventions. How could you respond creatively to the consumer wants of your Harvest Gold customers? Note the success that companies have had using the term *organic* or *natural* in their promotions.[14]

Packaging Changes the Product

We've said that consumers evaluate many aspects of the total product offer, including the brand. It's surprising how important packaging can be in such evaluations of various goods. Many companies have used packaging to change and improve their basic product. We have squeezable ketchup bottles that stand upside down; square paint cans with screw tops and integrated handles; plastic bottles for motor oil that eliminate the need for funnels; single-use packets of spices; and so forth. Another trend is packaging designed to evoke emotions by prompting customers to think of homemade treats. The goal is to have the customers' warm feelings about the homemade product transfer to the commercial product. For example, Peggy Jean's Pies uses jelly jars to ship its ready-to-eat pies and the package opened large markets.[15]

Packaging must perform the following functions:[16]

1. Attract the buyer's attention.
2. Protect the goods inside, stand up under handling and storage, be tamperproof, and deter theft.
3. Be easy to open and use.
4. Describe and give information about the contents.
5. Explain the benefits of the core product inside.
6. Provide information on warranties, warnings, and other customer matters.
7. Give some indication of price, value, and uses.

Courtesy of Thelma's Treats

Innovative packaging can make a great product look even better. Just ask the owners of Thelma's Treats, a bakery that packs all its delicious cookies into boxes resembling old-fashioned ovens. Can you think of any other food brands that use interesting packaging?

Packaging can also make a product more attractive to retailers. The Universal Product Codes (UPCs) on many packages help stores control inventory. They combine a bar code (black and white lines) and a preset number that gives the retailer information about the product's price, size, colour, and other attributes. Packaging changes the product by changing its visibility, usefulness, or attractiveness.

One relatively new packaging technology for tracking products is the radio frequency identification (RFID) chip, especially the ones made with nanoparticle powder. When attached to a product, the chip sends out signals telling a company where the product is at all times. RFID chips carry more information than bar codes, do not have to be read one at a time (whole pallets can be read in an instant), and can be read at a distance.[17]

bundling
Grouping two or more products together and pricing them as a unit.

THE GROWING IMPORTANCE OF PACKAGING

Today, packaging carries more of the promotional burden than in the past. Many products once sold by salespeople are now being sold in self-service outlets, and the package has acquired more sales responsibility.

Packaging may make use of a strategy called **bundling**, which combines goods and/or services for a single price. IcelandAir has bundled layover tours with an IcelandAir employee "stopover buddy" in its total product offer. Transatlantic passengers can opt to spend their layover seeing the sights of Reykjavik instead of just the airport.[18] Financial institutions are offering everything from financial advice to help in purchasing insurance, stocks, bonds, mutual funds, and

© Kristoffer Tripplaar/Alamy Stock Photo

The Heinz Dip & Squeeze® ketchup package allows customers a choice of peeling off the lid for dipping or tearing off the top for squeezing. It contains three times as much ketchup as traditional sachets and uses less packaging. Shaped like the iconic Heinz tomato ketchup glass bottles, the packets reinforce the Heinz Ketchup brand.

more. When combining goods or services into one package, marketers must not include so much that the price gets too high. It's best to work with customers to develop value enhancers that meet their individual needs.

PROGRESS ASSESSMENT

- What are some examples of value enhancers in a value package?
- What's the difference between a product line and a product mix?
- What functions does packaging perform?

brand
A name, symbol, or design (or combination thereof) that identifies the goods or services of one seller or group of sellers, and distinguishes them from the goods and services of competitors.

brand equity
The value of the brand name and associated symbols.

brand loyalty
The degree to which customers are satisfied, enjoy the brand, and are committed to further purchases.

Branding

A **brand** is a name, symbol, or design (or combination thereof) that identifies the goods or services of one seller or group of sellers, and distinguishes them from the goods and services of competitors. The word *brand* includes practically all means of identifying a product. Brand names you may be familiar with include Air Canada, Roots, President's Choice, Red Bull, Campbell Soup, Disney, and of course many more. Brand names give products a distinction that tends to make them attractive to consumers. Apple and Google now reign as brand champions—we're sure you understand why.[19]

Brand names give products a distinction that tends to make them attractive to customers. For the buyer, a brand name assures quality, reduces search time, and adds prestige to purchases. For the seller, brand names facilitate new-product introductions, support promotional efforts, add to repeat purchases, and differentiate products so that prices can be set higher.[20] Companies sue other companies for too closely matching brand names.

© Kristoffer Tripplaar/Sipa Press/Newscom

Athleisure powerhouse lululemon athletica got its name when its founder was looking for a unique name that couldn't be easily replicated in foreign markets. By creating a name that could be difficult to say in some countries, potential knockoffs could be avoided. For example, there is no Japanese phonetic sound for l, so the three ls in lululemon make it sound North American and authentic to Japanese consumers. Are there brand names that resonate with you?

Generating Brand Equity and Loyalty

A major goal of marketers in the future will be to reestablish the notion of brand equity. **Brand equity** is the value of the brand name and associated symbols. Usually the company cannot know the value of its brand until it sells it to another company. Canada's most valuable brands are RBC, TD, Bell, and Scotiabank.[21] Compare these to the world's most valuable brands of Amazon, Apple, Google, and Samsung.[22] Are you surprised by any of these results?

The core of brand equity is brand loyalty. **Brand loyalty** is the degree to which customers are satisfied, enjoy the brand, and are committed to further purchases. A loyal group of customers represents substantial value to a firm, and that value can be calculated. One way manufacturers are trying to create more brand loyalty is by focusing on sustainability.[23]

In the past, companies tried to boost their short-term performance by offering coupons and price discounts to move goods quickly. This eroded customers' commitment to brand names, especially of grocery products. Many consumers complain when companies drop brand names like Astro Pops or Flex shampoo. Such complaints show the power of brand names. Now companies realize the value of brand equity, and are trying harder to measure the earning power of strong brand names.[24]

Perceived quality is an important part of brand equity. A product that's perceived as having better quality than its competitors can be priced accordingly. The key to creating a perception of quality is to identify what consumers look for in a high-quality product, and then to use that information in every message the company sends out. Factors influencing the perception of quality include price, appearance, and reputation.

Trademarks of Canadian Tire Corporation, Limited use under licence

By creating the Canadian Tire Drivers Academy, Canadian Tire Corp., Ltd. hopes to strengthen its presence in the automotive market by fighting off competition and improving customer loyalty.[25] Would taking a course, such as beginner driver education or the car maintenance program, influence your loyalty? If one was available in your area, would you register for a course?

Brand Management

A **brand manager** (known as a *product manager* in some firms) has direct responsibility for one brand or product line. This individual also manages all the elements of the marketing mix: product, price, place, and promotion—throughout the life cycle of each product and service. Thus, you might think of the brand manager as the president of a one-product firm.

brand manager
The person in the company who has direct responsibility for one brand or one product line; called a product manager in some firms.

One reason many large consumer product companies created this position was to have greater control over new-product development and product promotion. Some companies have brand management *teams* to bolster the overall effort. In B2B companies, brand managers are often known as product managers.

LO2

Describe the product life cycle.

The Product Life Cycle

Once a product has been developed and tested, it goes to market. There it may pass through a **product life cycle** of four stages: introduction, growth, maturity, and decline as noted in Figure 15.2. This cycle is a *theoretical* model of what happens to sales and profits for a *product class* over time. However, not all individual products follow this life-cycle shape, and particular brands may act differently. For example, while frozen foods as a product class may go through the entire cycle, one brand may never get beyond the introduction stage. Some product classes,

Courtesy of Greenpeace. Used with permission

Greenpeace alleged that clothing from top brands such as Calvin Klein, H&M, Abercrombie & Fitch, and Ralph Lauren were tainted with hazardous chemicals.[26] As part of Greenpeace's Detox Campaign, Puma promised a toxin-free product and to eliminate toxins from its entire supply chain and life cycle by 2020; Nike and Adidas followed with their own initiatives.[27] What role do brand managers have in developing such programs? Do you seek out products that are sold by companies that support CSR initiatives?

product life cycle
A theoretical model of what happens to sales and profits for a product class over time; the four stages of the cycle are introduction, growth, maturity, and decline.

such as microwave ovens, stay in the introductory stage for years. Other products, like ketchup, become classics and never experience decline. Fad products (think Beanie Babies and mood rings) may go through the entire cycle in a few months. Still others may be withdrawn from the market altogether. Nonetheless, the product life cycle may provide some basis for anticipating future market developments and for planning marketing strategies.

Example of the Product Life Cycle

The product life cycle can give marketers valuable clues to successfully promoting a product over time. Some products, like crayons and sidewalk chalk, have very long product life cycles, change very little, and never seem to go into decline. Crayola's crayons have been popular for over 130 years! Mattel's Barbie is nearly 60 years old and is gearing up for another makeover.[28] How long do you think the new virtual video games will last?

As an example, let's consider the product life cycle of instant coffee. When it was introduced, most people did not like it as well as "regular" coffee, and it took several years for instant coffee to gain general acceptance (introduction stage). At one point, instant coffee became more popular, and new brands were introduced (growth stage). After a while, people became attached to one brand and sales levelled off (maturity stage). Sales then went into a slight decline when freeze-dried coffees were introduced (decline stage). Now freeze-dried coffee is, in turn, in the decline stage as consumers are buying fresh specialty beans from companies such as Second Cup and Starbucks and brewing them at home. It's extremely important for marketers to recognize what stage a product is in so that they can make intelligent and efficient marketing decisions about it.

Using the Product Life Cycle

Different stages in the product life cycle call for different marketing strategies. Figure 15.2 outlines some marketing mix decisions you might make. As you go through the figure, you will see that each stage calls for multiple marketing mix changes. Remember, these concepts are largely theoretical and you should use them only as guidelines. (We'll discuss the price strategies mentioned in the figure later in this chapter.)

Note that at the maturity stage, the product may reach the top in sales growth while profit is decreasing. At that stage, a marketing manager may decide to create a new image for the product to start a new growth cycle. For example, you may have noticed how Arm & Hammer baking soda gets a new image every few years to generate new sales. One year it's positioned as a deodorant for refrigerators and the next as a substitute for harsh chemicals in swimming pools. Knowing what stage in the cycle a product has reached helps marketing managers decide when such strategic changes are needed.

It was not until YouTube videos of people spinning them on their noses, foreheads and shoes that fidget spinners really took off.[29] Did you own this product? Can you think of other fad products that went viral quickly because of the Internet?

FIGURE 15.2

STAGES OF THE PRODUCT LIFE CYCLE

Profit levels start to fall before sales reach their peak. This is due to increasing price competition. When profits and sales start to decline, it is time to come out with a new product or to remodel the old one to maintain interest and profits. Note how stages of the product life cycle relate to a firm's marketing objectives and marketing mix actions.

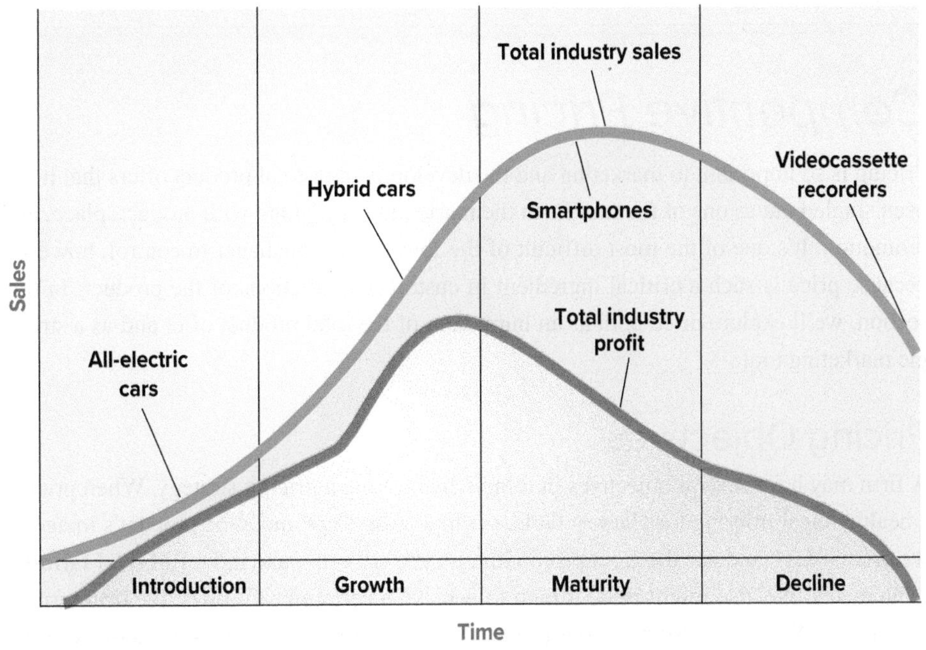

MARKETING OBJECTIVE	GAIN AWARENESS	STRESS DIFFERENTIATION	MAINTAIN BRAND LOYALTY	HARVESTING, DELETION
Competition	Few	More	Many	Reduced
Product	One	More versions	Full product line	Best sellers
Price	Skimming or penetration	Gain market share, deal	Defend market share, profit	Stay profitable
Place (distribution)	Limited	More outlets	Maximum outlets	Fewer outlets
Promotion	Inform, educate	Stress points of difference	Reminder-oriented	Minimal promotion

Source: Frederick G. Crane et al., *Marketing*, 9th Canadian ed. (Toronto: McGrawHill Ryerson, 2014), p. 285 with ISBN 9780070878693

PROGRESS ASSESSMENT

- What is a brand? What are the benefits of branding?
- What are the key components of brand equity?
- Explain the role of brand managers.
- What is the theory of the product life cycle? State the four stages.

LO3

Identify various pricing objectives and strategies, and explain why non-pricing strategies are growing in importance.

Competitive Pricing

Pricing is so important to marketing and the development of total product offers that it has been singled out as one of the four Ps in the marketing mix, along with product, place, and promotion. It's one of the most difficult of the four Ps for a manager to control, however, because price is such a critical ingredient in customer evaluations of the product. In this section, we'll explore price both as an ingredient of the total product offer and as a strategic marketing tool.

Pricing Objectives

A firm may have several objectives in mind when setting a pricing strategy. When pricing a healthy meal offering for Harvest Gold, we may want to promote the product's image. If we price it *high* and use the right promotion, maybe we can make it the BMW of farm-to-table meals. We also might price it high to achieve a certain profit objective or return on investment. We could also price our product *lower* than its competitors, because we want lower-income customers (like students) to afford this healthy meal. That is, we could have some social or ethical goal in mind. Low pricing may also discourage competition because it reduces the profit potential, but it may help us capture a larger share of the market.

A firm may have several pricing objectives over time, and it must formulate these objectives clearly before developing an overall pricing strategy. Popular objectives include the following:

1. *Achieving a target return on investment or profit.* Ultimately, the goal of marketing for profit-oriented firms is to make a profit by providing goods and services to others. Naturally, one long-run pricing objective of almost all firms is to optimize profit.
2. *Building traffic.* Supermarkets often advertise certain products at or below cost to attract people to the store. These products are called *loss leaders.* The long-run objective is to make profits by following the short-run objective of building a customer base.
3. *Achieving greater market share.* One way to capture a larger part of the market is to offer lower prices, low finance rates (like 0-percent financing), low lease rates, or rebates.
4. *Creating an image.* Certain watches (e.g., Rolex), perfumes, and other socially visible products are priced high to give them an image of exclusivity and status.
5. *Furthering social objectives.* A firm may want to price a product low so that people with little money can afford it. The government often subsidizes the price of farm products to keep basic necessities, like milk, affordable.

target costing
Designing a product so that it satisfies customers and meets the profit margins desired by the firm.

competition-based pricing
A pricing strategy based on what all the other competitors are doing. The price can be set at, above, or below competitors' prices.

A firm may have short-run objectives that differ greatly from its long-run objectives. Managers should understand both types at the beginning and put both into their strategic marketing plan. They should also set pricing objectives in the context of other marketing decisions about product design, packaging, branding, distribution, and promotion. All these marketing decisions are interrelated.

Intuition tells us the price charged for a product must bear some relationship to the cost of producing it. Prices usually *are* set somewhere above cost.[30] But as we'll see, price and cost are not always related. In fact, there are three major approaches to pricing strategy: cost-based, demand-based (target costing), and competition-based.

© Joshua Rainey | Dreamstime.com

One way companies have tried to increase profit is by reducing the amount provided to customers. Thus, cereal companies have cut the amount of cereal in a box, toilet paper companies are making their products smaller, and so on. Have you noticed this happening to products you buy?

COST-BASED PRICING

Producers often use cost as a primary basis for setting the price. They develop elaborate cost accounting systems to measure production costs (including materials, labour, and overhead), add in a margin of profit, and come up with a price. Picture the process in terms of producing a car. You add up all the various components (e.g., engine parts, body, tires, radio, windows, paint, and labour), add a profit margin, and come up with a price. The question is whether the price will be satisfactory to the market as well.[31] In the long run the market—not the producer—determines what the price will be (see Chapter 2). Pricing should take into account costs, but it should also include the expected costs of product updates, the marketing objectives for each product, and competitors' prices.[32]

DEMAND-BASED PRICING

Unlike cost-based pricing, **target costing** is demand-based.[33] That means we design a product so it not only satisfies customers but also meets profit margins we've set. Target costing makes the final price an *input* to the product development process, not an outcome of it. You first estimate the selling price people would be willing to pay for a product and then subtract your desired profit margin. The result is your target cost of production, or what you can spend to profitably produce the item.

COMPETITION-BASED PRICING

Competition-based pricing is a strategy based on what all the other competitors are doing. The price can be at, above, or below competitors' prices. Pricing depends on customer loyalty, perceived differences, and the competitive climate.[34]

© Heinz-Peter Bader/Reuters/Corbis

Shoppers around the world look for bargains, as these consumers in Austria are doing. How many different ways can marketers appeal to shoppers' desires to find the lowest price? Do online retailers adopt different pricing strategies?

© Sunil Kumar/Hemera/Thinkstock

Imagine how demand-based pricing is used for custom-made jewellery. Can you think of any other products where this approach is used?

price leadership
The strategy by which one or more dominant firms set the pricing practices that all competitors in an industry then follow.

break-even analysis
The process used to determine profitability at various levels of sales.

total fixed costs
All expenses that remain the same no matter how many products are made or sold.

variable costs
Costs that change according to the level of production.

Price leadership is the strategy by which one or more dominant firms set pricing practices that all competitors in an industry then follow. Examples include oil and gas companies, and some fast-food companies.[35]

Break-Even Analysis

Before you begin selling a new sandwich at Harvest Gold, it may be wise to determine how many sandwiches you would have to sell before making a profit. You'd then determine whether you could reach such a sales goal. **Break-even analysis** is the process used to determine profitability at various levels of sales. The break-even point is the point where revenue from sales equals all costs. The formula for calculating the break-even point is as follows:

$$\text{Break-even point (BEP)} = \frac{\text{Total fixed cost (FC)}}{\text{Price of one unit (P)} - \text{Variable cost (VC) of one unit}}$$

Total fixed costs are all expenses that remain the same no matter how many products are made or sold. Among the expenses that make up fixed costs are the amount paid to own or rent a factory or warehouse and the amount paid for business insurance. **Variable costs** change according to the level of production. Included are the expenses for the materials used in making products and the direct costs of labour used to make those products.

For producing a specific product, let's say you have a fixed cost of $200,000 (for mortgage interest, real estate taxes, equipment, and so on). Your variable cost (e.g., labour and materials) per item is $2. If you sold the products for $4 each, the break-even point would be 100 000 items. In other words, you would not make any money selling this product unless you sold more than 100 000 of them:

$$\text{BEP} = \frac{\text{FC}}{(\text{P} - \text{VC})} = \frac{\$200,000}{(\$4.00 - \$2.00)} = \frac{\$200,000}{(\$2.00)} = 100\,000 \text{ items}$$

Pricing Strategies for New Products

Let's say that a firm has just developed a new line of products, such as VR headsets. The firm has to decide how to price these units at the introductory stage of the product life cycle. A **skimming price strategy** prices a new product high, to recover research and development costs and to make as much profit as possible while there's little competition. Of course, those large profits will eventually attract competitors.

A second strategy would be to price new products low. Low prices will attract more buyers and discourage other companies from making these headsets because profits are slim. This **penetration price strategy** enables the firm to penetrate or capture a large share of the market quickly.

Retailer Pricing Strategies

Retailers use several pricing strategies. **Everyday low pricing (EDLP)** is the choice of Walmart. It sets prices lower than competitors and does not usually have special sales. The idea is to bring customers to the store whenever they want a bargain rather than waiting until there is a sale.

Department stores and some other retailers most often use a **high–low pricing strategy**. Regular prices are higher than at stores using EDLP, but during special sales they're lower. The problem with such pricing is that it encourages customers to wait for sales, thus cutting into profits. As online shopping continues to grow, you may see fewer stores with a high–low strategy because customers will be able to find better prices on the Internet.

Retailers can use price as a major determinant of the goods they carry. Some promote goods that sell for only $1 (e.g., Dollarama), or another amount (e.g., $10). Dollar stores have raised some of their prices to over one dollar because of rising costs.

Psychological pricing means pricing goods and services at price points that make the product appear less expensive than it is. A house might be priced at $299,000 because that sounds like a lot less than $300,000. Gas stations almost always use psychological pricing.

skimming price strategy
A strategy in which a new product is priced high to make optimum profit while there's little competition.

penetration price strategy
A strategy in which the product is priced low to attract many customers and discourage competitors.

everyday low pricing (EDLP)
Setting prices lower than competitors and then not having any special sales.

high–low pricing strategy
Set prices that are higher than EDLP stores, but have many special sales where the prices are lower than competitors.

How Market Forces Affect Pricing

Recognizing that different customers may be willing to pay different prices, marketers sometimes price on the basis of customer demand rather than cost or some other calculation. That's called *demand-oriented pricing* and it is reflected by movie theatres that charge lower prices on certain days (e.g., Cineplex on Tuesdays), and by retailers that offer discounts to seniors if they shop on certain days (e.g., Shoppers Drug Mart on the last Thursday of the month).

Today, marketers are facing a new pricing problem: customers comparing prices of products online. Priceline.com introduced customers to a "demand collection system," in which buyers post the price they are willing to pay and invite sellers to either accept or decline the price. Customers can get great prices on airlines, hotels, and other products by naming their price. They can also buy used goods online at sites such as eBay, Kijiji, or Craigslist. Clearly, price competition is going to heat up as customers have more access to price information from around the world. As a result, non-price competition is likely to increase.

© Rex Features/AP Images

Some products are priced high to create a high-status image of exclusivity and desirability. Jimmy Choo shoes fall into this category. What is the total product offer for a product like this?

Non-Price Competition

Marketers often compete on product attributes other than price. You may have noted that price differences are small with products like gasoline, candy bars, and even major products such as compact cars.

psychological pricing
Pricing goods and services at price points that make the product appear less expensive than it is.

You will not typically see price as a major promotional appeal on television. Instead, marketers tend to stress product images and customer benefits such as comfort, style, convenience, and durability.

Often marketers emphasize non-price differences because prices are so easy to match. In order to compete with bigger firms, many small organizations promote the services that accompany basic products rather than prices. Good service will enhance a relatively homogeneous product. Danny O'Neill, for example, is a small wholesaler who sells gourmet coffee to upscale restaurants. He has to watch competitors' prices *and* the services they offer so that he can charge the premium prices he wants. To charge high prices, he has to offer and then provide superior service. Larger companies often do the same thing.

Other strategies to avoid price wars include adding value (e.g., home delivery from a drugstore), educating customers on how to use the product, and establishing relationships. Customers will pay extra for goods and services when they have a friendly relationship with the seller. The services are not always less expensive, but they offer more value. Some airlines stress friendliness, large "sleeping" seats, promptness, abundant flights, and other such services. Many hotels stress "no surprises," business services, health clubs, and other extras.

PROGRESS ASSESSMENT

- Can you list four pricing objectives?
- What's a disadvantage of using a cost-based pricing strategy?
- How do you calculate a product's break-even point?
- Why is increasing focus being placed on non-price competition?

LO4

Explain the concept of marketing channels, and the importance of retailing.

The Importance of Channels of Distribution

marketing intermediaries
Organizations that assist in moving goods and services from producers to business and consumer users.

channel of distribution
A set of marketing intermediaries, such as agents, brokers, wholesalers, and retailers, that join together to transport and store goods in their path (or channel) from producers to consumers.

agents/brokers
Marketing intermediaries who bring buyers and sellers together and assist in negotiating an exchange but do not take title to the goods.

wholesaler
A marketing intermediary that sells to other organizations.

retailer
An organization that sells to ultimate consumers.

It's easy to overlook distribution and storage in marketing, where the focus is often on advertising, selling, marketing research, and other functions. But it doesn't take much to realize how important distribution is. Imagine the challenge Adidas faces of getting raw materials together, making millions of pairs of shoes, and then distributing those shoes to stores throughout the world. That's what thousands of manufacturing firms—making everything from automobiles to furniture and toys—have to deal with every day.[36] Imagine further that there has been a major volcano eruption or tsunami that has caused a disruption in the supply of goods. Distribution managers would need to deal with such issues.[37]

Managing the flow of goods has become one of the most important managerial functions for many organizations. **Marketing intermediaries** (once called *middlemen*) are organizations that assist in moving goods and services from producers to businesses (B2B) and from businesses to consumers (B2C). They're are called intermediaries because they're in the middle of a series of organizations that join together to push products through the channel of distribution. A **channel of distribution** consists of a whole set of marketing intermediaries (such as agents, brokers, wholesalers, and retailers) that join together to transport and store goods in their path (or channel) from producers to consumers.

Agents/brokers are marketing intermediaries who bring buyers and sellers together and assist in negotiating an exchange, but do not take title to the goods. That is, at no point do they own the goods (e.g, real estate agents)

A **wholesaler** is a marketing intermediary that sells to other organizations, such as retailers, manufacturers, and institutions (e.g., hospitals). Wholesalers are part of the B2B system. Because of high distribution costs, Walmart has been trying to eliminate independent wholesalers from its system and do the job itself. That is, Walmart provides its own warehouses and has its own trucks. It has over 150 distribution centres and 61 000 trailers to distribute goods to its stores.[38]

A **retailer** is an organization that sells to ultimate consumers (people like you and me) who buy for their own use. For consumers to receive the maximum benefit from marketing intermediaries, the various organizations must work together to ensure a smooth flow of goods and services to the customer.

Channels of distribution help ensure communication flows *and* the flow of money and title to goods. They also help ensure that the right quantity and assortment of goods will be available when and where needed. Figure 15.3 shows selected channels of distribution for both consumer and industrial goods.

© Graeme Robertson/eyevine/Redux

Distribution warehouses, such as Amazon's distribution centre, store goods until they are needed. Have you ever thought about the benefits of having food, furniture, clothing, and other needed goods close at hand?

Courtesy of Dougie Dog Diner Truck. Used with permission

Are food trucks a direct channel or an indirect channel? Some vendors use Twitter and other social media to reveal their current locations and build customer relationships. You might find cuisine such as specialty crepes, kimchi pork fries, osso bucco, banh mi, and Gruyère grilled cheese. Would a Harvest Gold truck make sense?

How Intermediaries Create Exchange Efficiency

When you consider that some manufacturers sell directly to customers, known as a *direct channel,* you may wonder why have intermediaries at all? The answer is that intermediaries perform certain marketing tasks—such as transporting, storing, selling, advertising, and relationship building—faster and more cheaply than most manufacturers could. Here's a simple analogy: You could personally deliver packages to people anywhere in the world, but usually you don't. Why not? Because it's generally cheaper and faster to

FIGURE 15.3

SELECTED CHANNELS OF DISTRIBUTION FOR CONSUMER AND INDUSTRIAL (B2B) GOODS AND SERVICES

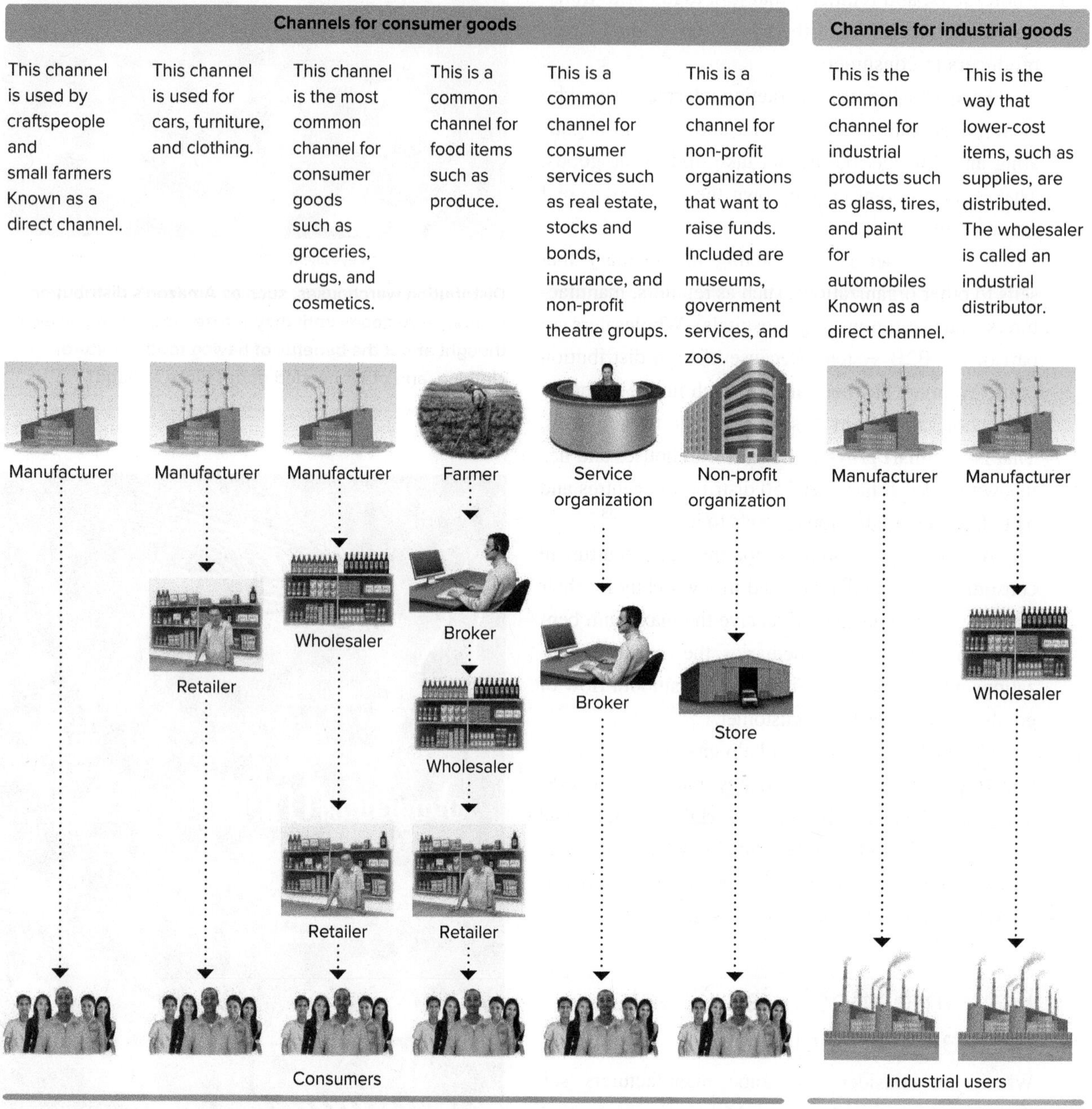

have them delivered by Canada Post or a private firm such as Purolator. If there is a channel member between the manufacturer and the customer, one has an *indirect channel.*

Channels for consumer goods
Channels for industrial goods
This channel is used by craftspeople and small farmers Known as a direct channel.
This channel is used for cars, furniture, and clothing.
This channel is the most common channel for consumer goods such as groceries, drugs, and cosmetics.
This is a common channel for food items such as produce.
This is a common channel for consumer services such as real estate, stocks and bonds, insurance, and non-profit theatre groups.
This is a common channel for non-profit organizations that want to raise funds. Included are museums, government services, and zoos.
This is the common channel for industrial products such as glass, tires, and paint for automobiles Known as a direct channel.
This is the way that lower-cost items, such as supplies, are distributed. The wholesaler is called an industrial distributor.
Manufacturer
Manufacturer
Manufacturer
Farmer
Service organization
Non-profit organization
Manufacturer
Manufacturer
Retailer
Wholesaler
Broker
Broker
Store
Wholesaler
Wholesaler
Retailer
Retailer
Consumers
Industrial users

While marketing intermediaries can be eliminated, their activities can't if customers are to have access to products and services. Intermediary organizations have survived because they have performed marketing functions faster and cheaper than others could.

PROGRESS ASSESSMENT

- What is a channel of distribution?
- What intermediaries are involved in a direct and indirect channel of distribution?
- Why do we need intermediaries? What are some examples?

Retail Intermediaries

Perhaps the most useful marketing intermediaries, as far as you are concerned, are retailers. Remember that retailers sell to ultimate consumers. They are the ones who bring goods and services to your neighbourhood and make them available day and night. Retailing is important to our economy. In 2017, retail trade generated over $588.8 billion and employed more than 2.1 million Canadians.[39] Internet-based sales from both store and non-store retailers was $15.7 billion.[40]

A CIBC report predicted that by 2020, the Canadian legal market for adult-use cannabis will approach $6.5 billion in retail sales, which would approach the wine market in scale and would be more than the amount of spirits sold.[41] Was this report accurate? What other retail businesses have been impacted by the growth in cannabis sales?

Figure 15.4 lists, describes, and gives examples of various kinds of retailers. For example, some retailers compete mostly on price while others, such as category killers, use variety as a competitive tool.

Retail Distribution Strategy

A major decision that marketers must make is selecting the right retailers to sell their products. Different products call for different retail distribution strategies.

Intensive distribution puts products into as many retail outlets as possible, including vending machines. Products that need intensive distribution include candy, gum, and popular magazines.

Selective distribution uses only a preferred group of the available retailers in an area. Such selection helps assure producers of quality sales and service. Manufacturers of appliances, furniture, and clothing use selective distribution.

Exclusive distribution is the use of only one retail outlet in a given geographic area. The retailer has exclusive rights to sell the product and is therefore likely to carry a large inventory, give exceptional service, and pay more attention to this brand than to others. Auto manufacturers usually use exclusive distribution, as do producers of specialty goods such as skydiving equipment.

intensive distribution
Distribution that puts products into as many retail outlets as possible.

selective distribution
Distribution that sends products to only a preferred group of retailers in an area.

exclusive distribution
Distribution that sends products to only one retail outlet in a given geographic area.

Non-Store Retailing

Nothing else in retailing has received more attention than online retailing.[42] Online retailing (e.g., Amazon) is just one form of non-store retailing. Other categories include telemarketing; vending machines, kiosks, carts, and pop-ups; direct selling; and multilevel marketing. Small businesses can use non-store retailing to open up new channels of distribution for their products.

FIGURE 15.4

TYPES OF RETAIL STORES

Type	Description	Example
Category killer	Sells a huge variety of one type of product to dominate that category of goods	Indigo Books & Music, Sleep Country Canada, Staples, Best Buy
Convenience store	Sells food and other often-needed items at convenient locations; may stay open all night	Circle K, 7-Eleven, Couche-Tard, On the Run
Department store	Sells a wide variety of products (clothes, furniture, and housewares) in separate departments	Hudson's Bay, Holt Renfrew Ogilvy
Discount store	Sells many different products at prices generally below those of department stores	Giant Tiger, Great Canadian Dollar Store
Off-price retailer (Outlet store)	Sells general merchandise directly from the manufacturer at a discount; items may be discontinued or have flaws ("seconds")	Marshalls, Winners, HomeSense, Saks OFF 5TH
Supercentre	Sells food and general merchandise at discount prices; no membership required	Real Canadian Superstore, Walmart Supercentre
Supermarket	Sells mostly food with other non-food products such as detergent and paper products	Loblaws, Metro, Sobeys
Warehouse club	Sells food and general merchandise in facilities that are usually larger than supermarkets and offers discount prices; membership may be required	Costco Wholesale, Wholesale Club

For grocery shopping, what if we just make a list and *click*? Easy for customers, but a tall task for companies like Amazon and Walmart. To deliver fresh food directly to customers, these companies have to figure out how to keep food cold continuously, manage large orders, and deliver at the right times. Non-perishable foods, on the other hand, would be much the same as shipping an average package.[44] Would you use this service if it were available in your area? How might this impact competitors that did not offer this service?

ELECTRONIC RETAILING

Online retailing consists of selling products to ultimate consumers online. **Social commerce** is a form of electronic commerce that involves using social media and user contributions to assist in the online buying and selling of products and services. Figure 15.5 shares a list of different types of social commerce.

Thanks to website improvements and discounting, online retail sales have risen dramatically over the last few years.[43] But getting customers is only half the battle. The other half is delivering the goods, providing helpful service, and keeping your customers. When electronic retailers fail to have sufficient inventory or fail to deliver goods on time (especially during holidays and other busy periods), customers give up and go back to brick-and-mortar stores.

Most online retailers offer e-mail order confirmation. But sometimes they are not as good as stores at handling complaints, accepting returns, and providing personal help. Some online sellers are improving customer service by adding help buttons and

FIGURE 15.5

TYPES OF SOCIAL MEDIA COMMERCE

Social commerce denotes a wide range of shopping, recommending, and selling behaviours. As these models are tested and proven to increase sales and customer satisfaction, more will be introduced.

1. **Peer-to-peer sales platforms** (eBay, Etsy, Amazon Marketplace, Getaround): Community-based marketplaces where individuals communicate and sell directly to other individuals.
2. **Social network-driven sales** (Facebook Marketplace, Twitter, Instagram, Pinterest): Sales driven by referrals from established social networks.
3. **Group buying** (Groupon, WagJag, LivingSocial): Products and services offered at a reduced rate if enough people agree to buy.
4. **Peer recommendations** (Amazon, Yelp): Sites that aggregate product or service reviews, recommend products based on others' purchasing history.
5. **User-curated shopping** (Fancy, Lyst, Styloko): Shopping-focused sites where users create and share lists of products and services that others can shop from.
6. **Crowdfunding/crowdsourcing** (Threadless, Kickstarter, Cut On Your Bias, Indiegogo): Consumers become involved directly in the production process through voting, funding, and collaboratively designing products.
7. **Social shopping** (ModCloth, Fab, Fancy): Shopping sites that includes chat and forum features for people to discuss and exchange advice and opinions.

Sources: "The 7 Types of Social Commerce," Conversity, accessed February 2017, conversity.com; Daniel Nations, "6 Social Shopping Websites You Need to Check Out," Lifewire, accessed February 2017, https://www.lifewire.com/top-social-shopping-websites-3486565.

monitoring their social media accounts to give customers real-time online assistance from a human employee.

Brick-and-mortar stores that add online outlets are called *brick-and-click* stores. They allow customers to choose which shopping technique suits them best. Most companies that want to compete in the future will likely need both a real store and an online presence to provide consumers with the options they want.[45]

online retailing
Selling products to ultimate consumers online.

social commerce
Using social media and user contributions to assist in the online buying and selling of products and services.

telemarketing
The sale of goods and services by telephone.

TELEMARKETING

Telemarketing is the sale of goods and services by telephone. Many companies use it to supplement or replace in-store selling and complement online selling. Many send a catalogue to consumers, who order by calling a toll-free number. Many electronic retailers provide a help feature online that serves the same function.

VENDING MACHINES, KIOSKS, CARTS, AND POP-UPS

Vending machines dispense convenience goods when customers deposit sufficient money in the machine. They carry the benefit of location—they're found in airports, schools, office buildings, service stations, and other areas where people want convenience items. In Japan, they sell everything from bandages and face cloths to salads and spiced seafood. North American vending machines are selling iPods, Bose headphones, sneakers, digital

© leaf/123RF

To reduce telemarketing calls, register your telephone number(s) on the National Do Not Call List. Examples of exemptions from this list include calls on behalf of Canadian registered charities, political parties, and calls from companies with whom you have an existing business relationship.[46] Do you dislike such calls?

cameras, and DVD movies. You can even find cars and trucks in some vending machines.[47] An ATM in Abu Dhabi dispenses gold.

Carts and kiosks have lower overhead costs than stores do, so they can offer lower prices on items such as T-shirts, purses, watches, and cell phones. You often see vending carts outside stores or along walkways in malls. Some mall owners love them because they're colourful and create a marketplace atmosphere. Kiosk workers often dispense coupons and helpful product information. You may have noticed airlines are using kiosks to speed the process of getting you on the plane. Most provide a boarding pass and allow you to change your seat.

Pop-up stores are quickly gaining in popularity around the country. Pop-ups are temporary outlets that remain open for a short amount of time in small spaces and offer items not found in traditional stores. For online business owners they can drum up new business, allow customers to see their goods in person, save on shipping expenses, and even "test drive" operating a brick-and-mortar store. Building owners also benefit from pop-ups because they can generate rent on a currently empty space.[48]

DIRECT SELLING

direct selling
Selling to customers in their homes or where they work.

Direct selling reaches consumers in their homes or workplaces. Businesses use direct selling to sell cosmetics, household goods, lingerie, clothes, and candles at house parties they sponsor. Because so many people work outside the home and aren't in during the day, companies that use direct selling are sponsoring parties at workplaces or at home on evenings and weekends. Some firms have dropped most of their direct selling efforts in favour of online selling.

MULTILEVEL MARKETING

Many companies have had success using multilevel marketing (MLM) and salespeople who work as independent contractors. Some of the best-known MLM companies include Avon and Thirty-One.[49] Salespeople earn commissions on their own sales, create commissions for the "upliners" who recruited them, and receive commissions from any "downliners" they recruit to sell. When you have hundreds of downliners—people recruited by the people you recruit—your commissions can be sizeable. Some people make tens of thousands of dollars a month this way. The main attraction of multilevel marketing for employees, other than the potential for making money, is the low cost of entry.[50] For a small investment, the average person can get started and begin recruiting others.

That doesn't mean you should get involved with such schemes. People question MLM because some companies using it have acted unethically. More often than not, people at the bottom buy the products themselves and sell a bare minimum, if anything, to others. In other words, be careful of multilevel schemes as a seller and as a buyer. But do not dismiss them out of hand, because some are successful. Potential employees must be very careful to examine the practices of such firms.

Choosing the Right Distribution Mode

As discussed in Chapter 10, a supply chain is a sequence of firms that perform activities required to create and deliver a good or service to consumers or industrial users. The supply chain is *longer* than a channel of distribution because it includes links from suppliers that provide raw materials to manufacturers, whereas the channel of distribution begins with manufacturers. Included in the supply chain are farmers, miners, suppliers of all kinds (e.g., parts, equipment, and supplies), manufacturers, wholesalers, and retailers.

As shown in Figure 15.6, channels of distribution are part of the overall supply chain. A key issue today is making the supply chain sustainable because so much of what affects the environment is caused by distribution.[51]

A primary concern of supply-chain managers is selecting a transportation mode that will minimize costs and ensure a certain level of service. (*Modes,* in the language of distribution, are the various means used to transport goods, such as by truck, train, plane, ship, and pipeline.) Generally speaking, the faster the mode of transportation, the higher the cost. The job of the supply-chain manager is to find the most efficient combination of these forms of transportation. Figure 15.7 shows the advantages and disadvantages of each mode.

FIGURE 15.6

THE SUPPLY CHAIN AND THE CHANNEL OF DISTRIBUTION

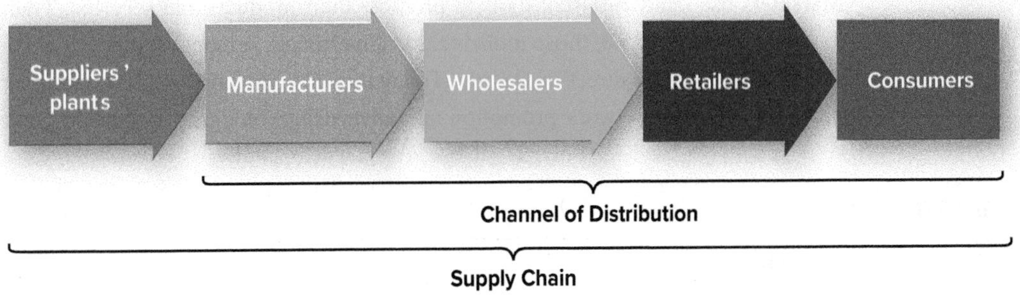

FIGURE 15.7

COMPARING TRANSPORTATION MODES

Combining trucks with railroads lowers cost and increases the number of locations reached. The same is true when combining trucks with ships. Combining trucks with airlines speeds goods long distances and gets them to almost any location.

Mode	Cost	Speed	On-Time Dependability	Flexibility Handling Products	Frequency of Shipments	Reach
Railroad	Medium	Slow	Medium	High	Low	High
Trucks	High	Fast	High	Medium	High	Highest
Pipeline	Low	Medium	Highest	Lowest	Highest	Lowest
Ships (water)	Lowest	Slowest	Lowest	Highest	Lowest	Low
Airplane	Highest	Fastest	Low	Low	Medium	Medium

Today, supply chains involve more than simply moving products from place to place; they involve all kinds of activities such as processing orders and taking inventory of products. In other words, logistics systems involve whatever it takes to see that the right products are sent to the right place quickly and efficiently.

PROGRESS ASSESSMENT

- What are some of the ways in which retailers compete?
- What kinds of products would call for each of the different distribution strategies: intensive, selective, and exclusive?
- Give examples of non-store retailing and describe each.
- Which transportation mode is fastest, which is cheapest, and which is most flexible?

Promotion and the Promotion Mix

LO5

Define promotion, and list the five traditional tools that make up the promotion mix.

Recall from Chapter 14 that promotion consists of all techniques that sellers use to motivate people to buy their products and services. Both profit-making and non-profit organizations use promotional techniques to communicate with people in their target markets about goods and services, and to persuade them to participate in a marketing exchange.[52] Marketers use many different tools to promote their products and services. Traditionally, as shown in Figure 15.8, those tools include advertising, personal selling, public relations, sales promotion, and direct marketing. Today they also include e-mail promotions, mobile promotions, social network promotion and advertising, blogging, podcasting, tweets, and

FIGURE 15.8

THE TRADITIONAL PROMOTION MIX

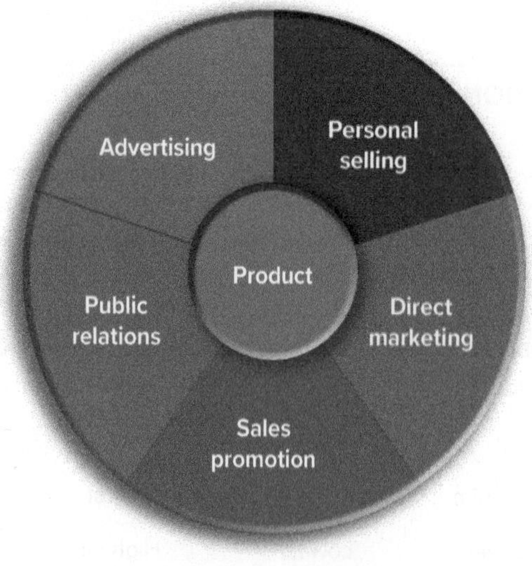

more.[53] The combination of promotional tools an organization uses is called its **promotion mix**. The product is shown in the middle of Figure 15.8 to illustrate that the product itself can also be a promotional tool, such as when marketers give away free samples.

Each target group calls for a separate promotion mix. For example, large homogeneous groups of customers (i.e., groups whose members share specific similar traits) are usually most efficiently reached through advertising. Large organizations are best reached through personal selling.

Integrated marketing communication (IMC) combines all of the promotional tools into one comprehensive and unified promotional strategy.[54] With IMC, marketers can create a positive brand image, meet the needs of customers, and meet the strategic marketing and promotional goals of the firm.

Digital marketing is the promotion of products or brands via one or more forms of electronic media.[55] Emphasis today is on integrating traditional media like TV with social media or integrating print media with websites.[56] Let us briefly explore each of the promotional tools.

promotion mix
The combination of promotional tools an organization uses.

integrated marketing communication (IMC)
A technique that combines all of the promotional tools into one comprehensive and unified promotional strategy.

digital marketing
The promotion of products or brands via one or more forms of electronic media.

Advertising: Informing, Persuading, and Reminding

Advertising is paid, non-personal communication through various media by organizations and individuals who are in some way *identified in the message*. Identification of the sender separates advertising from *propaganda,* which is nonpersonal communication that *does not have an identified sponsor.*

advertising
Paid, non-personal communication through various media by organizations and individuals who are in some way identified in the advertising message.

Ads are informative. Direct mail is full of information about products, prices, features, store policies, and more; so is newspaper advertising.[57] Newspaper advertising is down because fewer people are buying newspapers.[58] Instead, they're choosing to get their news on mobile devices. As a result, mobile advertising is growing very fast.[59]

The number of people who don't have a TV subscription with a cable, satellite, or telecommunications company is growing in Canada with more Canadians opting to consume content through online-streaming platforms such as Netflix or even from illegal downloads.[60] Can you see how this is a challenge for TV advertisers? Despite what you may read about the growth of alternative promotional tools, TV advertising is still a dominant medium.[61] Of course, TV is helped by the fact that many people post about what they have recently watched, making social media a "force multiplier" for TV.[62]

Figure 15.9 discusses the advantages and disadvantages of various advertising media. Note that newspapers, radio, and directories are usually attractive to local advertisers. The trend for local advertisements is moving more toward digital outlets. Some marketers even believe that digital advertisements will overtake the more traditional outlets for local markets in the near future.[63]

© Rita Newman/Anzenberger/Redux

Advertising seems to be everywhere as we go about our daily lives. How many advertisements, both digital and non-digital, can you spot in this photo? Can the noise created by so many ads interfere with the messages the advertisers are trying to communicate?

Marketers must choose which media can best be used to reach the audience they desire. Radio advertising, for example, is less expensive than TV advertising and often reaches people when they have few

FIGURE 15.9

ADVANTAGES AND DISADVANTAGES OF VARIOUS ADVERTISING MEDIA TO THE ADVERTISER

The most effective media are often very expensive. The inexpensive media may not reach your target market. The goal is to use the media that can reach your desired target market most efficiently.

Medium	Advantages	Disadvantages
Newspapers	Good coverage of local markets; ads can be placed quickly; high customer acceptance; ads can be clipped and saved	Ads compete with other features in paper; poor colour; ads get thrown away with paper (short lifespan)
Television	Uses sight, sound, and motion; reaches all audiences; high attention with no competition from other material	High cost; short exposure time; takes time to prepare ads; digital video recorders skip over ads
Radio	Low cost; can target specific audiences; very flexible; good for local marketing	People may not listen to ad; depends on one sense (hearing); short exposure time; audience can't keep ad
Magazines	Can target specific audiences; good use of colour; long life of ad; ads can be clipped and saved	Inflexible; ads often must be placed weeks before publication; cost is relatively high
Outdoor	High visibility and repeat exposures; low cost; local market focus	Limited message; low selectivity of audience
Direct mail	Best for targeting specific markets; very flexible; ad can be saved	High cost; customers may reject ad as junk mail; must conform to post office regulations
Directories (Yellow Pages–type print and online advertising)	Great coverage of local markets; widely used by customers	Competition with other ads; cost may be too high for very small businesses
Internet	Inexpensive global coverage; available at any time; interactive	Customers may leave the site before buying
Mobile advertising	Great reach among younger shoppers	Easy to ignore and avoid
Social media	Wonderful communication tools	Time drain

other distractions, such as while they're driving. Radio is especially effective at selling services people don't usually read about in print media—banking, mortgages, continuing education, and brokerage services, to name a few. On the other hand, radio has become so commercial-ridden that many people pay to switch to commercial-free premium services.

Mobile marketing via smartphones started out mostly as text messages, but now stores like Starbucks can send signals to your phone as you approach the store, reminding you to stop in for a latte. Kraft Foods developed iFood Assistant, an app that serves up recipes for users—recipes made with Kraft products. Other retailers use e-mail advertisements to build brand awareness and drive people to their stores or websites. Social media sites in general are growing so fast that some marketers can hardly keep up.

Adapting *to* CHANGE

Outdoor "Eyes" Are Watching You

© Michael Siluk/The Image Works

Have you ever felt that an ad was meant just for you? Drivers in Chicago, Dallas, and New Jersey certainly had that feeling—and for good reason. Billboard messages were tailored directly to them, simply because of the car they were driving. GM had cameras installed on billboards that were able to recognize passing vehicles' grilles. From there, the billboard displayed a message telling drivers why the Chevy Malibu was better than their own car. If there were no competitor cars on the road at that time, the digital screen would switch to a generic Malibu advertisement.

About 6400 traditional billboards have been converted into video screens and that number could be growing. Targeted billboards are not just tracking cars; some cities are involved in Clear Channel Outdoor's Radar program. Using data collected from nearby smartphones, digital billboards are prompted to show a message that's most appropriate for the current audience. Then the viewers could be tracked to see if they visit the store whose message was pushed to them. Not all campaigns involve prying eyes, though; interactive outdoor displays can be fun for people too. When a Harry Houdini television special was set to air, select bus shelters challenged folks to hold their breath for three minutes.

Out-of-home advertising and promotion is growing rapidly thanks to these technological innovations. It may still be low on advertising and promotional budgets, but creative minds are coming up with great ideas to make the messages more memorable than traditional media.

Sources: E.J. Schultz, "Technology Fuels Renaissance in Out-of-Home Advertising," *Advertising Age*, April 4, 2016; Robert Channick, "Hey, You in the Altima! Chevy Billboard Spots Rival Cars, Makes Targeted Pitch," *Chicago Tribune*, April 15, 2016; Sanjay Saloman, "Smartphone Tracking Could Let Highway Billboards Show You Personalized Ads," Boston.com, May 19, 2016; "LAMAR Deploys 'Smart' Digital Billboards Using Milestone IP Video," *Digital Signage Connection*, January 17, 2017.

Marketers also search for other places to put advertising, such as on video screens mounted on gas pumps. Have you noticed ads on park benches and grocery carts? You've certainly seen them on your favourite websites. The Adapting to Change box shows how companies are using technology in their outdoor advertisements.

Another way to get more impact from advertising is to appeal to the interest in green marketing among consumers and businesses. Review the Seeking Sustainability box for one such example.

GLOBAL ADVERTISING

Global advertising involves developing a product and promotional strategy that can be implemented worldwide. Global advertising that is the same everywhere can save companies money in research and design. In some cases, however, promotions tailored to specific countries or regions may be much more successful since each country or region has its own culture, language, and buying habits.

Problems can arise when marketers use one campaign in all countries. When a Japanese company named a popular drink, it came up with Pocari Sweat, not a good image for most English-speaking people. Canadians may have difficulty with Krapp toilet paper from Sweden. Clairol introduced its curling iron, the Mist Stick, to the German

Seeking SUSTAINABILITY

Corporate Knights and Sustainability

Corporate Knights has one of the world's largest circulation (125K+) magazines focused on the intersection of business and society. It claims to be the most prominent brand in the clean capitalism media space. "Clean capitalism" is defined as an economic system in which prices incorporate social, economic, and ecological benefits and costs, and companies know the full impacts of their actions. The vision is to provide information empowering markets to foster a better world. Rankings include the Best 50 Corporate Citizens in Canada and the Global 100 Most Sustainable Corporations.

Courtesy of Corporate Knights Magazine. Used with permission.

Recently, Larry Fink, CEO of BlackRock, the world's largest investment firm, sent a letter addressed to the CEOs of each corporation BlackRock invests in, encouraging them to make smarter business decisions. "Society is demanding that companies, both public and private, serve a social purpose. To prosper over time, every company must not only deliver financial performance, but also show how it makes a positive contribution to society. Companies must benefit all of their stakeholders, including shareholders, employees, customers and the communities in which they operate." This includes everything from rising CEO pay to water scarcity to the careful reconsideration of corporate supply chains.

The Top 30 under 30 Sustainability Leaders ranking is a collection of young entrepreneurs, activists, corporate professionals, and students eager to make the world a better place. The Millennial generation makes up an estimated 2.5 billion global citizens. The economic and political influence of Millennials is growing as they enter or move through the workforce toward their peak spending years. Following closely is Generation Z. The United Nations says youth from around the world must be an active part of all levels of decision making related to sustainable development as "it affects their lives today and has implications for their futures." Do any of the CK initiatives interest you? Are you inspired by the actions of these individuals? What can you do to make a difference, small or big?

Sources: "About Us," Corporate Knights Inc., accessed May 6, 2018, http://www.corporateknights.com/us/about-us/; "Just right," *Corporate Knights*, Spring 2018 Issue, April 19, 2018, http://www.corporateknights.com/magazines/2018-future-40-issue/just-right-15241107/; and CK Staff, "2015 Global 100 Results," Corporate Knights Inc., January 21, 2015, http://www.corporateknights.com/magazines/2015-global-100-issue/2015-global-100-results-14218559/.

market, not realizing that mist in German can mean "manure." Getting the words right in international advertising is tricky and critical, which calls for researching each country, designing appropriate ads, and testing them. In Canada we have regional differences (think differences between Montreal and Vancouver, for example) that are important enough to constitute separate market segments and may require their own promotions and advertising.

Many marketers today are moving from *globalism* (one ad for everyone in the world) to *regionalism* (specific ads for each country or for specific groups within a country). In the future, marketers will prepare more custom-designed promotions to reach smaller audiences—audiences as small as one person.

Personal Selling: Providing Personal Attention

Personal selling is the face-to-face presentation and promotion of goods and services, including the salesperson's search for new prospects and follow-up service after the sale. Effective selling isn't simply a matter of persuading others to buy. In fact, it's more accurately described today as helping others satisfy their wants and needs (again, helping the buyer buy).

It's costly for firms to provide customers with personal attention, so those companies that retain salespeople must train them to be especially effective, efficient, and helpful.[64] Given that perspective, you can see why salespeople use smartphones, tablets, and other technology to help customers search for information, design custom-made products, look over prices, and generally do what it takes to complete the order. The benefit of personal selling is having a person help you complete a transaction. The salesperson should listen to your needs, help you reach a solution, and do everything possible to make accomplishing it smoother and easier.

© Digital Vision/Photodisc/Thinkstock

You're familiar with all kinds of situations in which people apply personal selling. They sell all kinds of goods and services like food, clothing, automobiles, insurance, and real estate. What could they do to be more helpful to you, the customer?

THE BUSINESS-TO-CONSUMER (B2C) SALES PROCESS

Most sales to consumers take place in retail stores where knowing the product comes first. It is also important to understand as much as possible about the type of people who shop at a given store. Often the people who come to a store have already done some research online and know what they want.[65] The salesperson does need to focus on the customer and refrain from talking to fellow salespeople—or, worse, to friends on the phone. Have you ever experienced such rude behaviour from salespeople? What did you think? Did you complete the sale?

personal selling
The face-to-face presentation and promotion of goods and services.

The first formal step in the B2C sales process, then, is the *approach.* Sometimes, the second step of *ask questions* is also added to this first step. For example, many salespeople approach customers with an opening line like "May I help you?" but the answer too often is "No." A better approach is "How may I help you?" or simply "Welcome to our store." The idea is to show the customer that you are there to help and that you are friendly and knowledgeable.

Discover what the customer wants first, and then make a *presentation.* Show customers how your products meet their needs and answer questions that help them choose the right products for them.

© 4x6/Getty Images

The B2C sales process has five steps. Which step are you observing above?

Next comes the *close,* which can include a *trial close.* "Would you like me to put that on hold?" or "How will you be paying for that?" are two such

FIGURE 15.10

STEPS IN THE BUSINESS-TO-CONSUMER (B2C) SELLING PROCESS

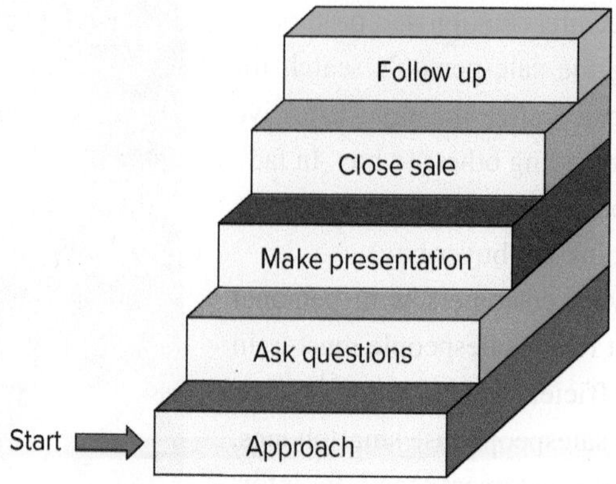

efforts. Selling is an art, and a salesperson must learn how to walk the fine line between being helpful and being pushy. Often individual buyers need some time alone to think about the purchase. The salesperson must respect that need but still be clearly available when needed.

After-sale *follow up* is an important but often neglected step. If the product is to be delivered, the salesperson should follow up to be sure it is delivered on time. The same is true if the product has to be installed. There is often a chance to sell more merchandise when a salesperson follows up on a sale. Figure 15.10 shows the B2C selling process.

PROGRESS ASSESSMENT

- What are the five traditional elements of the promotion mix?
- List examples of advertising medium.
- What are the five steps in the B2C selling process?

Public Relations: Building Relationships

public relations (PR) The function that evaluates public attitudes, changes policies and procedures in response to the public's requests, and executes a program of action and information to earn public understanding and acceptance.

Public relations (PR) is the function that evaluates public attitudes, changes policies and procedures in response to the public's requests, and executes a program of action and information to earn public understanding and acceptance. Recent events have emphasized the need for good public relations. Such events include Volkswagen's diesel emissions scandal, Samsung Galaxy 7 Note's battery problems, and the issues surrounding some politicians, key actors, and sports personalities.[66]

The PR department maintains close ties with company stakeholders (customers, media, community leaders, government officials, and other corporate stakeholders). Marketers are looking for alternatives to advertising. Public relations is a good alternative. As newspapers cut back on their reporting staff, people are looking for other sources of news information, including publicity releases. Linking up with bloggers has become an important way to keep company names in the news.

PUBLICITY: THE TALKING ARM OF PR

Publicity is the talking arm of PR and one of the major functions of almost all organizations. Suppose you want to introduce your restaurant, Harvest Gold, to consumers, but you have little money to promote it. You need to get some initial sales to generate funds. One effective way to reach the public is through publicity.

Publicity is any information about an individual, product, or organization that is distributed to the public through the media and that is not paid for, or controlled, by the seller. It takes skill to write interesting or newsworthy press releases that the media will want to publish. You may need to write different stories for different media.[67] One story may introduce the new owners. Another may describe unusual product offerings. If the stories are published, news about your restaurant will reach many potential consumers (and investors, distributors, and dealers) and you may be on your way to becoming a successful marketer. John D. Rockefeller (wealthy industrialist and philanthropist) once remarked, "Next to doing the right thing, the most important thing is to *let people know* that you are doing the right thing." What might Harvest Gold do to help the community and thus create more publicity?

© Jason Dawson/Rex/Shutterstock

Tens of thousands of people soaked themselves in freezing water to promote awareness for the disease ALS. From athletes and actors to ordinary people, videos of the Ice Bucket Challenge went viral for months and led to $115 million in donations to ALS research. What do you think made this promotion so successful?

Besides being free, publicity has several further advantages over other promotional tools like advertising. It may reach people who wouldn't read an ad. It may appear on the front page of a newspaper or in some other prominent position, or be given air time on a television news show. Perhaps the greatest advantage of publicity is its believability. When a newspaper or magazine publishes a story as news, the reader treats that story as news—and news is more believable than advertising. Review the Making Ethical Decisions box for a dilemma that you might face as a marketer when you consider publicity.

publicity
Any information about an individual, product, or organization that is distributed to the public through the media and that is not paid for or controlled by the seller.

Publicity has several disadvantages. Marketers have no control over whether, how, and when the media will use the story. The media aren't obligated to use a publicity release, most of which are thrown away. Furthermore, the media may alter the story so that it's not positive. There's good publicity (customers camp out all night to buy your products) and bad publicity (defective products are recalled). Also, once a story has run, it's not likely to be repeated. Advertising, in contrast, can be repeated as often as needed. One way to see that the media handle your publicity well is to establish a friendly relationship with media representatives and be open with them.

Sales Promotion: Giving Buyers Incentives

Sales promotion is the promotional tool that stimulates consumer purchasing and dealer interest by means of short-term activities See Figure 15.11 for business-to-consumer sales promotion examples.

sales promotion
The promotional tool that stimulates consumer purchasing and dealer interest by means of short-term activities.

Sales promotion programs are designed to supplement personal selling, advertising, PR, and other promotional efforts by creating enthusiasm for the overall promotional

Making ETHICAL DECISIONS

Is the Ad as Honest as the Product?

You are producing a high-fibre, nutritious cereal called Fiberrific and are having a modest degree of success. Research shows that your number of customers, or market segment, is growing but is still a relatively small percentage of breakfast cereal buyers. Generally, Fiberrific appeals mostly to health-conscious people aged 25 to 60. You are trying to broaden the appeal of your cereal to the under-25 and over-60 age groups. You know that Fiberrific is a tasty and healthy product that is good for customers. Joan, one of your managers, suggests that you stretch the truth a bit in your advertising and publicity material so that it will attract more consumers in the age groups you are targeting. After all, your product can't hurt anybody and is actually good for them.

© Shutterstock/Rido

Joan's idea is to develop two ads, each with two segments. The first segment of one ad would show two senior citizens. A woman is on a tennis court holding a racquet and talking across the net to a man. She is complaining that she seems to tire easily. The next segment would show the same two people, with the woman looking lively and saying that she tried this new breakfast cereal, Fiberrific, for two weeks and feels so energized, like a new person. A similar ad would be used to show two young men walking uphill and talking. The first segment would show the man wondering why he tires so easily and the second one would show the same scene, with one man now a little ahead of the other, looking lively and stating that he is amazed at the improvement in his energy and endurance after eating Fiberrific for only two weeks. Would you go along with Joan's suggestion? What is your decision based on? Explain.

© AF Archive/Alamy

Product placement is often subtle, like this out-of-focus 7-Eleven logo located just behind Superman. The goal is to influence the viewer to want that product. What product placements have you noticed in your favourite TV shows and movies?

program. Sales promotion can take place both within and outside the company. The most important internal sales promotion efforts are directed at salespeople and other customer-contact people, such as customer-service representatives and clerks. Internal sales promotion efforts include (1) sales training, (2) the development of sales aids such as audiovisual presentations and videos, and (3) participation in trade shows where salespeople can get leads. Other employees who deal with the public may also receive special training to improve their awareness of the company's offerings and make them an integral part of the total promotional effort.

After generating enthusiasm internally, marketers want to make distributors and dealers eager to help promote the product. Trade shows allow marketing intermediaries to see products from many different sellers and make comparisons among them. Today, virtual trade shows online (called webinars) enable buyers to see many products without leaving the office. Such promotions are usually interactive, so buyers can ask questions, and the information is available 24/7.

FIGURE 15.11

BUSINESS-TO-CONSUMER SALES PROMOTION TECHNIQUES

There are many kinds of business-to-consumer sales promotion techniques. Compare these with business-to-business sales promotion techniques such as trade shows, portfolios for salespeople, deals (e.g., price reductions), catalogues, and conventions.

Kind of Sales Promotion	Objectives	Advantages	Disadvantages
Coupons	Stimulate demand	Encourage retailer support	Consumers delay purchases
Deals	Increase trial; retaliate against competitor's actions	Reduce consumer risk	Consumers delay purchases; reduce perceived product value
Premiums	Build goodwill	Consumers like free or reduced-price merchandise	Consumers buy for premium, not product
Contests	Increase consumer purchases; build business inventory	Encourage consumer involvement with product	Require creative or analytical thinking
Sweepstakes	Encourage present customers to buy more; minimize brand switching	Get customer to use product and store more often	Sales drop after sweepstakes
Samples	Encourage new product trial	Low risk for consumer	High cost for company
Loyalty programs	Encourage repeat purchases	Help create loyalty	High cost for company
Point-of-purchase displays	Increase product trial; provide in-store support for other promotions	Provide good product visibility	Hard to get retailer to allocate high-traffic space
Rebates	Encourage customers to purchase; stop sales decline	Effective at stimulating demand	Easily copied; steal sales from future; reduce perceived product value
Product placements	Introduce new products; demonstrate product use	Positive message in a non-commercial setting	Little control over presentation of product

Source: Frederick G. Crane et al., Marketing, 9th Canadian ed. (Toronto: McGrawHill Ryerson, 2014), p. 477 with ISBN 9780070878693

After the company's employees and intermediaries have been motivated with sales promotion efforts, the next step is to promote to final consumers using samples, coupons, store demonstrations, rebates, displays, and so on. Sales promotion is an ongoing effort to maintain enthusiasm, so sellers use different strategies over time to keep the ideas fresh. For example, you can stimulate sales at Harvest Gold by putting coupons in the school paper and home mailers. Consider putting food displays in your Harvest Gold restaurant to show customers how attractive the products look. Sponsor in-store cooking demonstrations to attract new customers. Do you have any suggestions?

Direct Marketing

direct marketing
Any activity that directly links manufacturers or intermediaries with the ultimate customer.

Direct marketing includes any activity that directly links manufacturers or intermediaries with the ultimate consumer. It includes direct mail, catalogue sales, and telemarketing as well as online marketing. It uses direct communication with customers to generate a response in the form of an order, a request for further information, or a visit to a retail outlet.

Direct marketing has become popular because shopping from home or work is more convenient for consumers than going to stores. Instead of driving to a mall, people can shop online. Or they can browse catalogues and advertising supplements in the newspaper and magazines and then buy by phone, mail, or online. Interactive online selling provides increasing competition for retail stores. For example, clothing company L.L. Bean put pressure on rivals by eliminating shipping charges. That made the company even more attractive for people who like to shop by catalogue or online.

Direct marketing took on a new dimension with interactive video. Companies that use interactive video have become major competitors for those who market through static paper catalogues. For example, customers watching a video of a model moving and turning around in a dress get a much better idea of the look and feel of the outfit than simply seeing it in a printed photo.

PROGRESS ASSESSMENT

- What are the advantages and disadvantages of publicity versus advertising?
- What are the sales promotion techniques used to reach consumers? How do they differ when targeting businesses?
- Why has direct marketing become popular?

word-of-mouth promotion
A promotional tool that involves people telling other people about products they have purchased or services they have used.

viral marketing
Any strategy that encourages people to pass on a marketing message to others, creating exponential growth in the message's influence as the message reaches thousands to millions of potential customers.

Word of Mouth and Other Promotional Tools

Although word of mouth was not traditionally listed as one of the major promotional efforts (it was not considered to be manageable), it is now one of the most effective, especially online.[68] In **word-of-mouth promotion**, people tell other people about products they've purchased or services they've used. We've already discussed the role of social media in spreading word of mouth. Beyond word of mouth is customer participation, that is, getting customers to provide constructive suggestions and share their ideas on how to shape product and service offerings.[69]

Anything that encourages people to talk favourably about an organization can be effective word of mouth. Notice, for example, how stores use entertainers, banners, and other attention-getting devices to create word of mouth. Clever commercials can also generate word of mouth. The more that people talk about your products and your brand name, the more easily customers remember them when they shop, vote for you, etc.

One especially effective strategy for spreading positive word of mouth is to send testimonials to current customers. Most companies use these only in promoting to new customers, but testimonials are also effective in confirming customers' belief that they chose the right company. Therefore, some companies make it a habit to ask their satisfied customers for referrals.

Word of mouth is so powerful that negative word of mouth can hurt a firm badly. Criticism of a product or company can spread through online forums, social media, and websites. Addressing consumer complaints quickly and effectively is one of the best ways to reduce the effects of negative word of mouth.

What are some strategies for creating positive word of mouth about Harvest Gold? If your efforts are successful, your message may "go viral" and be seen by millions of consumers.[70] **Viral marketing** includes any strategy that encourages people to pass on a marketing message to others, creating exponential growth in the message's influence as the message can reach thousands, or even millions of potential customers.[71] Many viral marketing programs give away free products or services, often in exchange for valuable e-mail addresses. Free attracts attention; once you have consumers' attention they can see other products or services you offer and buy those.

Social Networking

We briefly touched on the importance of social media and advertising in the chapter. However, social media have a much greater role in promotion than just advertising. Marketers have quickly noticed how social media are changing the business environment. Companies utilize these tools to increase exposure for products or services, create loyalty among customers, drive traffic to the company website, and even to come up with new ideas.[72]

© Shutterstock/keport

"Fake news" is media that has been custom-made to fool you.[73] It's difficult to assess if the information is accurate or not when you see it in different media channels as it appears credible. What can you do to spot fake news? Are you more likely to believe something if you see it on social media?

© Taner Sumer/Alamy Stock Vector

Most Canadians are active on at least one social media platform, whether it be Snapchat, Twitter, Instagram, Facebook or any of the many sites adding users daily. How many platforms do you use? Would you want companies to engage with you on your platforms?

blog
An online diary (web log) that looks like a web page but is easier to create and update by posting text, photos, or links to other sites.

podcasting
A means of distributing multimedia digital files on the Internet for downloading to a portable media player.

One of the greatest advantages of social media platforms is that they offer easier two-way communication between businesses and customers. For example, companies like Nabisco and Travelocity can be in constant contact with customers and entertain them along the way. Nabisco is using celebrities to demonstrate the perfect way to dunk a cookie, which leads to Oreo fans creating their own dunk videos, and then posting them to the company's Facebook page.[74] Travelocity started #iWannaGo and many wannabe travellers tweeted to the company's @RoamingGnome handle their photos and their dreams of where they want to go and why. When people participate in these social media activities, they frequently continue interacting with the company and, more importantly, are likely to share branded content.[75]

Blogging

A **blog**—short for web log—is an online diary that looks like a web page but is easier to create and update by posting text, photos, or links to other sites. There are hundreds of millions of blogs online. How do blogs affect marketing? Running a blog is great way to interact with customers. Businesses can attract new customers when they coordinate their social media profiles with their blogs. As people click to a company's blog through the social media profile, it helps improve the company's website ranking. People love to share content they find relevant. In order for a blog to succeed, a business must take time to post and respond to the customers that leave comments. They can use some of the comments to help create new posts. They have to post consistently in order to be recognized by the search engines, and to keep customers coming back to the blog for new information. If the blog isn't kept updated, it will lose traffic and, therefore, its power as a promotional tool.

© monkeybusinessimages/iStock

Mobile marketing allows marketers to reach customers through text messaging. Have you received such promotional messages? For which products are they most effective? Would this be a good strategy for Harvest Gold?

Podcasting

Podcasting is a means of distributing multimedia digital files on the Internet for downloading to a portable media player. Podcasts are a great way to capture your existing and prospective customers' attention for an extended period of time by giving them something of value that is easy for them to understand. Companies have also found success in creating videos for YouTube.

Mobile Marketing

Most marketers make sure their media are viewable on mobile devices like tablets and smartphones. One key to success, therefore, is to keep the message brief because mobile users do not want to read through too much text. With mobile media, marketers can use text messaging to promote sweepstakes, send customers news or sports alerts, and give them company information. Companies can determine where you are and send you messages about restaurants and other services in your vicinity.

Managing the Promotion Mix: Putting it all Together

Each target group calls for a separate promotion mix. Advertising is most efficient for reaching large groups of customers whose members share similar traits. Personal selling is best for selling to organizations. To motivate people to buy now rather than later, marketers use sales promotions like sampling, coupons, discounts, special displays, and premiums. Publicity supports other efforts and can create a good impression among all customers. Word of mouth is often the most powerful promotional tool. Generate it by listening, being responsive, and creating an impression worth passing on to others that you spread through blogging, podcasting, and social media posting.

Courtesy of Outdoor Advertising Association of America

While most bus shelter ads aren't too special, Caribou Coffee designed its shelters in way that left commuters feeling all warm inside. The company installed heated bus shelters to promote a line of breakfast sandwiches. Do you think giving consumers experiences (like warmth on a cold day) is an effective way to remind them of a product?

Push and Pull Strategies

How do producers move products to consumers? In a **push strategy**, the producer uses advertising, personal selling, sales promotion, and all other promotional tools to convince *channel members* (e.g., wholesalers and retailers) to stock and sell merchandise, *pushing* products through the distribution system to the stores. If the push strategy works, consumers will walk into a store, see the product, and buy it.

A **pull strategy** directs heavy advertising and sales promotion efforts toward *consumers*. If the pull strategy works, consumers will go to the store and ask for the products. The store owner will order them from the wholesaler, who in turn will order them from the producer. Products are thus *pulled* through the distribution system. Of course, a company could use both strategies in a major promotional effort. Re-read the Adapting to Change box to see how companies are using technology in their pull strategy.

MARS Apprentice

MARS Apprentice is an annual undergraduate experiential learning program at the DeGroote School of Business, McMaster University. It centres around weekly case challenges in the fields of Marketing, Advertising, Retail, and Sales (MARS). Through program partners, student teams are introduced to real business challenges and each challenge week culminates in a boardroom assessment by senior industry professionals. Top-performing Apprentices are rewarded with cash prizes and internships. Here, teams had to design an incentive and rewards program to engage the field marketing representatives for Canadian Tire Bank. Do you have similar programs at your school?

push strategy
Promotional strategy in which the producer uses advertising, personal selling, sales promotion, and all other promotional tools to convince wholesalers and retailers to stock and sell merchandise.

pull strategy
Promotional strategy in which heavy advertising and sales promotion efforts are directed toward consumers so that they will request the products from retailers.

It has been important to make promotion part of a total systems approach to marketing. That is, promotion is part of supply-chain management. In such cases, retailers would work with producers and distributors to make the supply chain as efficient as possible. Then a promotional plan would be developed for the *whole system.* The idea would be to develop a total product offer that would appeal to everyone: manufacturers, distributors, retailers, and consumers.

PROGRESS ASSESSMENT

- What is viral marketing?
- Describe word-of-mouth promotion and list three other promotional tools.
- How does a push strategy differ from a pull strategy?

SUMMARY

LO1 **Explain the concept of a total product offer, and summarize the functions of packaging.**
A total product offer consists of everything that customers evaluate when deciding whether to buy something.

What's included in a total product offer?
A total product offer includes price, brand name, satisfaction in use, and more.

What are the functions of packaging?
The functions of packaging include the following: (1) attract the buyer's attention; (2) protect the goods inside, stand up under handling and storage, be tamperproof, and deter theft; (3) be easy to open and use; (4) describe the contents; (5) explain the benefits of the core product inside; (6) provide information about warranties, warnings, and other customer matters; and (7) indicate price, value, and uses.

LO2 **Describe the product life cycle.**
The product life cycle is a theoretical model of what happens to sales and profits for a product class over time.

What are the four stages in the product life cycle?
The four product life cycle stages are introduction, growth, maturity, and decline. Review Figure 15.2 for a discussion on how the stages of the product life cycle relate to a firm's marketing objectives and marketing mix actions.

LO3 **Identify various pricing objectives and strategies, and explain why non-pricing strategies are growing in importance.**
Pricing is one of the four Ps of marketing.

What are pricing objectives?
Pricing objectives include achieving a target profit, building traffic, increasing market share, creating an image, and meeting social goals.

What's the break-even point?

At the break-even point, total cost equals total revenue. Sales beyond that point are profitable.

What strategies can marketers use to determine a product's price?

For new products, a skimming price or a penetration price strategy is considered. Other strategies include cost-oriented pricing, demand-oriented pricing, and competition-oriented pricing.

Why do companies use non-price strategies?

Pricing is one of the easiest marketing strategies to copy. Therefore, often it is not a good long-run competitive tool. Instead, marketers may compete using non-price strategies that are harder to copy, including offering great service, educating customers, and establishing long-term relationships with customers.

LO4 **Explain the concept of marketing channels, and the importance of retailing.**

A channel of distribution consists of a set of marketing intermediaries, such as agents, brokers, wholesalers, and retailers, that join together to transport and store goods in their path (or channel) from producers to customers.

How do marketing intermediaries add value?

Intermediaries perform certain marketing tasks—such as transporting, storing, selling, advertising, and relationship building—faster and cheaper than most manufacturers could. Channels of distribution ensure communication flows and the flow of money and title to goods. They also help ensure that the right quantity and assortment of goods will be available when and where needed.

Why is retailing important?

A retailer is an organization that sells to ultimate consumers. Retailing is important to our economy. In 2017, retail trade generated over $588.8 billion and employed more than 2.1 million Canadians.

What is non-store retailing?

Non-store retailing is retailing done outside a traditional store. Non-store retailing includes electronic retailing; telemarketing; vending machines, kiosks, and carts; and direct selling. Telemarketing can also be used as part of direct marketing, which is a promotional tool.

LO5 **Define promotion, and list the five traditional tools that make up the promotion mix.**

Promotion is an effort by marketers to inform and remind people in the target market about products and to persuade them to participate in an exchange.

What are the five traditional promotional tools that make up the promotional mix?

The five traditional promotional tools are advertising, personal selling, public relations, sales promotion, and direct marketing. The product can also be a promotional tool which is why it's shown in the middle of Figure 15.8.

What are examples of other promotional tools?

In word-of-mouth promotion, people tell other people about products they have purchased. Other promotional tools include blogging, podcasting, and mobile marketing.

KEY TERMS

channel of distribution 571
competition-based pricing 567
digital marketing 579
direct marketing 588
direct selling 576
everyday low pricing (EDLP) 569
exclusive distribution 573
high–low pricing strategy 569
integrated marketing communication (IMC) 579
intensive distribution 573
marketing intermediaries 570
online retailing 574
penetration price strategy 568
personal selling 583
podcasting 590
price leadership 568
product differentiation 559
product life cycle 563
product line 559
product mix 559
promotion mix 579
psychological pricing 569
public relations (PR) 584
publicity 585
pull strategy 591
push strategy 591
retailer 571
sales promotion 585
selective distribution 573
skimming price strategy 568
social commerce 574
target costing 567
telemarketing 575
total fixed costs 568
total product offer (value package) 558
value 556
value package 558
variable costs 568
viral marketing 589
wholesaler 571
word-of-mouth promotion 588

CAREER EXPLORATION

If you are interested in pursuing a career in employee–management relations, here are a few to consider. Find out about the tasks performed, skills needed, pay, and opportunity outlook in these fields through Internet sites that include the Government of Canada Job Bank, Workopolis, Monster, CareerBuilder, Glassdoor, and Indeed, as well as through the Career Centre at your school.

- **Marketing manager**—estimates the demand for a product and identifies markets, as well as develops pricing strategies.
- **Brand manager**—creates and directs brand assets for a company or product.
- **Industrial designer**—develops the concepts for manufactured products for everyday use.
- **Cost estimator**—collects and analyzes data in order to estimate the time, money, materials, and labour required to manufacture a product.
- **Purchasing manager**—plans, directs, and coordinates the buying of materials, products, or services for wholesalers, retailers, or organizations.
- **Logistician**—analyzes and coordinates an organization's supply chain including how a product is acquired, distributed, allocated, and delivered.
- **Wholesale and manufacturing sales representative**—sells goods for wholesalers or manufacturers to businesses, government agencies, and other organizations.
- **Railroad worker**—ensures that passenger and freight trains run on time and travel safely.
- **Advertising sales agent**—sells advertising space to businesses and individuals; contacts potential clients, makes sales presentations, and maintains client accounts.
- **Public relations specialist**—creates and maintains a favourable public image for the organization they represent; designs media releases to shape public perception of the organization and to increase awareness of its work and goals.
- **Fundraising manager**—designs and coordinates campaigns that attract donations for the organizations.
- **Web developer**—designs and creates websites.

CRITICAL THINKING

1. What value enhancers affected your choice of school to attend? Did you consider size, location, price, reputation, library and research services, sports, courses offered, job placement opportunities (e.g., internship), and exchange opportunities? What factors were most important? Why? What schools were your alternatives? Why didn't you choose them?
2. What could you do to enhance the product offer of Harvest Gold, other than changing the menu from time to time? How could you use psychological pricing when making up the menu at Harvest Gold? Are you impressed by the use of celebrities in product advertisements? What celebrity could you use to promote Harvest Gold?
3. Many suggest that a scarce item in the future will be water. If you could think of an inexpensive way to get water from places of abundance to places where it is needed for drinking, farming, and other uses, such as fracking, you could become a wealthy marketing intermediary. Pipelines are an alternative, but could you also freeze the water and ship it by train or truck? Could you use ships to tow icebergs to warmer climates? What other means of transporting water might there be?
4. What kinds of problems can emerge if a firm doesn't communicate with environmentalists, the news media, and the local community? Do you know of any firms that aren't responsive to your community? What are the consequences?
5. As interactive communications between companies and customers grow, do you think traditional advertising will grow or decline? What will be the effect of this growth or decline on the price we pay for TV programs, newspapers, and magazines?
6. How have blogging, podcasting, and social media affected other media you use, like newspapers or television? Do you read print newspapers now or do you get your news some other way? Do you watch programs on TV or on other devices? How has the move away from print and network television affected advertising?

DEVELOPING CAREER SKILLS

Key: ● **Team** ★ **Analytic** ▲ **Communication** ⊡ **Technology**

★▲ 1. Look around your classroom and notice the different types of shoes students are wearing. What product qualities do you think they considered when they chose to purchase the shoes they're wearing? Then, ask them this question: How important were price, style, brand name, and colour? Describe the product offerings you would feature in a new shoe store designed to appeal to students.

●★▲ 2. In small groups, discuss the importance of price when buying the following products: clothes, milk, computers, haircuts, and rental cars. What non-price factors, if any, are more important than price? How much time did you spend evaluating factors other than price when making such purchases?

▲★ 3. In class, discuss the differences between wholesaling and retailing and why retailing has more appeal for students considering jobs. Since fewer students seek jobs in wholesaling than in retailing, do you think wholesaling jobs may be easier to get?

▲★ 4. Scan your local newspaper or search online for examples of publicity (e.g, stories of new products) and sales promotion (e.g., coupons, contests, and sweepstakes). Share your examples and discuss the effectiveness of such promotional efforts with the class.

●★▲ 5. In small groups, list six goods and services most students own or use and discuss promotional techniques that prompt you to buy them: advertising, personal selling, PR, sales promotions, direct marketing, social media, or word of mouth. Which seems most effective for your group? Why?

ANALYZING MANAGEMENT DECISIONS

Measuring Marketing Effectiveness

One of the major issues facing marketers today is measuring the effectiveness of various marketing campaigns. In the past, marketers set a budget for advertising, personal selling, and the like based on past sales or the need to push future sales. Measuring results has always been difficult and was given less attention. Now, however, marketers are demanding more accountability from their advertising agencies, their sales forces, and their website activities. They want to know who is receiving their messages and what the results are.

Many companies do not know how to establish such *metrics,* or measures of effectiveness. Digital media have more accurate metrics, and these are forcing marketers to find more reliable statistics for traditional marketing methods like TV advertising. Some companies have turned to the finance department to help develop metrics. The question often comes down to whether the measure should be of sales or of customer attitudes. Some 60 percent of marketers measure customer attitudes as a result of marketing campaigns, but fewer than 40 percent use the data for preparing their marketing budgets, preferring instead to rely on their own instincts.

Discussion Questions

1. You are planning a marketing campaign for Harvest Gold. How might you go about measuring the effectiveness of your advertising?
2. What would your reaction be if you found potential customers had heard about your restaurant but had not yet acted on that information and come in to buy?
3. Using your own reactions, discuss what marketing tools are most effective in reaching students and others. Talk with fellow students from different ethnic and age groups to determine whether their answers are different from yours and how.

RUNNING CASE

Marketing the Fox 40® Sonik Blast Whistle: Breaking the Sound Barrier!

For successful Canadian entrepreneur and inventor Ron Foxcroft, it all started in 1982 when he purchased Fluke Transport, a Southern Ontario trucking business. The company slogan—If It's On Time . . . It's A "FLUKE"—was soon recognized throughout North America. Over the years, Foxcroft diversified into new ventures and the Foxcroft Group of Companies now includes Fluke Transportation Group, Fluke Warehousing Inc., Foxcroft Capital Corp., Fox 40 International Inc., and Fox 40 USA Inc.

The formation of Fox 40 International Inc. (Fox 40) is the result of a dream for a pealess whistle. When developing his first whistle, Ron was motivated by his knowledge and experience as an international basketball referee. Frustrated with faulty pea whistles, he spent three years of development with design consultant Chuck Shepherd. They had about 25 prototypes but narrowed them down after two years to 14 prototypes, and then down to 2 prototype whistles that worked. This resulted in the Fox 40® Classic Whistle. (The Whistle was named for Ron and that he was 40 when he applied for the patent.)

Introduced in 1987, this finely tuned precision instrument does not use a pea to generate sound. In fact, there are no moving parts. The patented design moves the air blast through three tuned chambers. This whistle, and all the subsequent whistles that have been introduced, is 100 percent constructed of high-impact ABS plastic so it is impervious to moisture. Wet or dry, Fox 40 Pealess Whistles cannot be overblown and never fail—the harder you blow, the louder the sound! They can be heard for miles and work in all conditions. They are faultless, reliable, and trusted.

Fox 40, a proudly Canadian company, dominates the global whistle industry. Tens of thousands of Fox 40 Whistles are produced monthly for shipment to 140 countries. A mould may be made offshore due to the cost savings (at least $100,000); however, Fox 40 owns all of its moulds. Approximately 90 percent of the company's products are made in Canada with select components coming from overseas markets. Final assembly occurs in Canada. While the first product was the Fox 40® Classic Whistle, the company now has over 900 active stock-keeping units (SKUs). Its product mix includes 19 Fox 40 Whistles styles (e.g., Fox 40 electronic whistle); Lanyards & Attachments (e.g., flex coils); additional brands that include Fox 40 Gear; SmartCoach Coaching Boards; SICK Self Impression Custom Kit, and Heat Alert Mouthguards; Marine & Outdoor Products (e.g., Xplorer LED Light); Pink Products; and Logo Imprinted Products.

How did Ron tackle the $150,000 debt that he had incurred in developing the Fox 40® Classic Whistle? The answer is marketing. "I took the two whistles to the Pan Am Games in August 1987. I went upstairs in the dorm where the referees were living, and at 2 a.m., I blew the Whistle. Hundreds of referees opened the doors, standing there in their underwear, wondering what kind of whistle they heard. The next day, I got orders for 20 000 Whistles at $6.00 each in U.S. funds. That was $8.00 per Whistle in Canadian funds. My $150,000 debt was covered."

Over the years, Fox 40® has continued to introduce new whistles in its whistle product line. One example is the Fox 40® Sonik Blast. This whistle was in response to referee requests for a louder whistle in large stadiums. Let us consider how the four Ps of marketing were applied to this product.

Product: Introduced in 2010, the Fox 40® Sonik Blast is a two-chamber whistle that exceeds 120 decibels of sound. (This is louder than the Fox 40® Classic Whistle's 115 decibels of power.) It also has no down side, which means that it does not matter which side you put in your mouth as both sides are up. As a result, a referee (or anyone else that uses the whistle) does not have to think about which side of the whistle needs to go "up" before blowing it. To slow down counterfeiters, the cushioned mouth guard (CMG) feature became available at the same time. The CMG is a cushioned mouthgrip for better grip, better control, and a softer feel on one's teeth.

In support of its GREEN PLAN the company has changed its packaging. The packaging is made from recycled water and pop bottles that use virgin polyethylene terephthalate (PET). The switch to PET plastic for the blister is more environmentally friendly. There has also been a movement away from clam packaging.

This has been replaced with a packaging system that uses radio frequency (RF) and heat, known as RF/heat packaging, to seal the blister within two cards. The blister and cards can be separated and added to Blue Box recycling. An added benefit is that the packaging is tamper proof. Included in each package is print material that contains recyclable and/or recycled post-consumer waste material. This colourful cardboard communicates the product's brand name and benefits, head office location, and contact information.

According to Dave Foxcroft, President and COO, one advantage that the company has in manufacturing the whistles in Canada is that they can build to order products and different packages, given the market. Since different markets require different packages, the actual package will vary depending on the marketing channel. For example, the package and label for a Fox 40® Whistle sold in a Canadian Tire store may be different for a whistle that is targeted to referees in the sports aisle versus a whistle that is placed in the marine area. Lately, Dave has noticed that more distributors are moving away from these private labels (whereby Fox 40® manufactures the product with the distributor's name on it) and requesting that the whistles focus on the Fox 40® brand. These distributors were noticing that they were losing sales as customers were looking specifically for the Fox 40 brand and did not realize that the private labels were also Fox 40® Whistles.

The total product offer also includes the high level of service that employees provide to customers. "We stand out," states Ron. "When you call the company, you get a live person. You don't need to go through layers of management to get an answer. The employee can answer a question or find someone right away to answer the question. Customers will not get unanswered questions."

Price: Similar to the other whistles, the Fox 40® Sonik Blast is a premium-priced whistle. This is justified by the product's features, benefits, and high quality. When the Whistle was first introduced, an introductory promotional price was offered to the company's distributors, including trade show specials. The price Fox 40® charges to its distributors varies depending on several factors: the target market (e.g., sports or marine); the geographic market; and the volume purchased. For example, some global markets are driven by price versus quality. While the suggested retail price is $8.95, it is the distributors that ultimately set the price in their markets. According to Dave, "These distributors own their markets and they know the best price to charge in their specific area. Fox 40® provides its customers with the best products and the goal is that all of the channel members in the distribution channel are financially successful along the way."

Pricing decisions are influenced by many factors that impact costs. For example, Dave cites the ever-changing government regulations around the world in reference to colour, plastics, chemicals, etc. As a result, the Whistle is not the same today as it was 20 years ago due to product restrictions. According to Juliana Child, Manager, Marketing & Events, the company also considers the cost of new imprinting techniques that produce better quality logos. Given such changes, the costs and price are revised annually for imprinted products.

Place: The majority of sales are generated through an indirect channel of distribution. Fox 40® follows a B2B marketing channel structure that incorporates distributors between the company and its ultimate users. These distributors perform a variety of marketing channel functions including selling, stocking, and delivering the Fox 40® products.

Customers interested in buying Fox 40® products can do so directly from established distributors and retail partners or through online marketing channels such as Fox 40 Shop (fox40shop.com). If a customer chooses to purchase a product through this direct online site, a commission is paid to the local distributor or retail partner. The commission can be used toward future purchases. This unique arrangement is in recognition of the importance of this business-to-business relationship and the company's commitment to support its channel members. For those channel members that choose to join the site, Fox 40 communicates their information (e.g., name and location) in the package that includes the ordered product. This way, customers are made aware of local channel members for future purchases. Information is also sent to channel members about products that are being ordered by customers in their local area so that they can review products that they carry.

Promotion: The overall promotion budget is 12 percent of the previous year's sales. Money is directed primarily in the areas of advertising and sales. This budget is broken down as follows:

- 65 percent is allocated to direct sales (45 percent is for awareness and 25 percent includes online social media activities, support of the online site, fox40shop.com, etc.)

- 9 percent is allocated to research and development
- 6 percent is allocated to public relations (which includes community social responsibility initiatives)
- 20 percent is allocated to trade shows and customer visits

When the Fox 40® Sonik Blast was introduced, *public relations* activities included media releases that highlighted the features and benefits of the new product. Web blasts were sent to channel members in the different segments (i.e., marine, safety, etc.) via e-mail marketing tool, Constant Contact. Fox 40 also has a B2B online site where channel members can access information such as catalogues, product images, etc. While the paper catalogue continues to be available as it remains the company's best sales tool, the online site supports channel members.

Advertising is a large part of the promotional budget. While on occasion there may be ads that highlight only one whistle, the majority of ads highlight the family of Fox 40® Whistles. Advertising in trade magazines that target the company's different markets, such as *REFEREE Magazine,* occurred to promote the Fox 40® Sonik Blast. Social media initiatives were also created to introduce the new product. This included banner ads and Facebook advertising.

Product seeding was a *trade sales promotion* strategy that was targeted to channel members. This form of sampling meant getting the product into the hands of those that would actually use the whistle. For example, free Fox 40® Sonik Blast Whistles, with the distributor's contact information printed on them, were sent to approved distributors. These distributors were then encouraged to hand out the free whistles to users in their markets.

When you consider *personal selling* efforts, company representatives attend approximately 20 trade shows per year. The product was promoted at trade shows that target the sport, safety, outdoor, pet, and marine markets. Occasionally, a show promotion was offered but it was primarily the distributor that would offer the promotion. Distributor site visits around the world are also an ongoing aspect of the personal selling element of the promotion mix. These efforts are used to maintain and build long-term and profitable relationships with global distributors.

Increasingly, company attention is focusing on *direct marketing.* Information from current customers and prospects that is generated at trade shows is updated in the company's database. Personalized communications (i.e., e-blasts, letters, etc.) are created and sent out. This is followed by personal communication to confirm if a sale could be generated. There is a particular focus on current customers. As Ron states, "The best increase in sales is from within the company."

Fox 40 also runs a promotional products division. Approximately 65 percent of all whistles sold have another organization's logo on them. According to Juliana, since the Fox 40® brand is so well established, it can effectively be directed to promotional sales. This co-branding is another opportunity to link the Fox 40® brand with a company brand that is meaningful to the receiver of the whistle. Given the different package and imprint capabilities, the company can quickly fill personalized orders. Dave believes that this number will increase to 70 percent by mid-2013 as safety awareness is growing. "Organizations recognize the increasing importance of safety," says Dave. "These organizations want to associate themselves with a superior performing safety brand like Fox 40®."

Sources: Ron Foxcroft, CEO of Fox 40 International Inc. and Chairman and CEO of Fluke Transportation, in-person interview, September 22, 2017, Hamilton; Dave Foxcroft, President and COO, Fox 40 International Inc., in-person interview, June 25, 2012, Hamilton; "The Fox 40 pea-less whistle story," Canada.com, April 4, 2012, www.canada.com/sports/football/less+whistle+story/6410154/story.html; Kelley Horton, Vice President Sales, Fox 40 International Inc., interview, June 24, 2008; Juliana Child, Manager, Marketing & Events, Fox 40 International Inc., interview, June 24, 2008; and "Not An Inadvertent Whistle," *Referee,* July 2007, 45–47.

Discussion Questions

1. What new-product pricing strategy did Fox 40 International Inc. use for the Fox 40® Sonik Blast?
2. What retail distribution strategy do you think is used for the Fox 40® Sonik Blast? Justify your answer.
3. Which promotional strategy is the most effective when selling the Fox 40® Sonik Blast? Explain.

PART 6

CHAPTER 16

Understanding Accounting and Financial Information

LEARNING OBJECTIVES

After you have read and studied this chapter, you should be able to:

- **LO1** Describe the role that accounting and financial information play for a business and for its stakeholders.
- **LO2** Identify the different disciplines within the accounting profession.
- **LO3** List the steps in the accounting cycle, distinguish between accounting and bookkeeping, and explain how computers are used in accounting.
- **LO4** Explain how the major financial statements differ.
- **LO5** Demonstrate the application of ratio analysis in reporting financial information.

PROFILE

GETTING TO KNOW: SHELLY SUN, CEO, BRIGHTSTAR CARE

Shelly Sun never expected to start her own company. As a CPA (certified public accountant) with a master's degree in accounting from the University of Colorado, she was doing quite well in the private sector. In fact, at age 29 she was already a vice president at CNA Insurance. Her life changed when her family was trying with little success to find quality in-home care for an ailing grandmother. They tried a series of in-home care agencies, but none of them lived up to the quality and standards the family was seeking. As their quest continued, it became evident they had come upon a major gap in the health care sector: the need for better in-home health care. It was then she decided to take the plunge and start her own business, BrightStar Care.

Through her many years working in the corporate world as a CPA, Sun had the needed skills to focus on the essential financial aspects of her new business. The hours were long, but she knew if they offered other families the service they once sought, the payoff would be worth it. After three years, BrightStar Care had three successful company-owned locations.

Courtesy of BrightStar Care and Shelly Sun

Sun, however, believed the company's long-term success would come through franchising. Her accounting and numbers-oriented background helped her choose and mentor franchisees that would thrive in BrightStar's system. Today, BrightStar has over 300 locations that serve more than 15 000 families and that generate $400 million in systemwide revenue. The company remains on *Forbes* magazine's top-10 list of franchise opportunities under a $150,000 investment.

BrightStar's success has not caused Sun to slow down. She earned distinction as a Certified Franchise Executive and was named by the International Franchise Association (IFA) as Entrepreneur of the Year in 2009. In 2017, she was chairperson of the IFA's board of directors. She was featured on the CBS program *Undercover Boss* and published her first book *Grow Smart, Risk Less,* in which she shares her lessons and experiences of building a successful franchise.

Shelly Sun credits her knowledge of accounting for helping BrightStar Care survive during the tough times of the recession. By personally tackling her company's financial issues and working closely with franchisees to implement efficiencies and controls, the company survived the difficult times when franchise financing dried up. Sun strongly believes that developing a core competency such as accounting is a key to business or franchise success. As she readily admits, "Not a day goes by in running my company that I don't leverage some part of my accounting knowledge."

Controlling costs, managing cash flows, understanding profit margins and taxes, and reporting finances accurately are keys to survival for successful organizations like BrightStar Care. This chapter will introduce you to the accounting fundamentals and financial information critical to business success. The chapter also briefly explores the financial ratios that are essential in measuring business performance in businesses of all sizes.

Sources: BrightStar Care, *www.brightstarcare.com*, accessed October 2017; "BrightStar Founder Shelly Sun Lobbies Congress to Overturn NLRB's Joint-Employer Ruling," *Business Wire*, September 16, 2015; Kerry Pipes, "BrightStar Care's CEO Shelly Sun on Building and Leading a Growing Brand," *Franchising Update*, accessed October 2017.

The Role of Accounting Information

LO1

Describe the role that accounting and financial information play for a business and for its stakeholders.

Small and large businesses often survive or fail according to how well they handle financial procedures. Financial management is the heartbeat of competitive businesses, and accounting information helps keep the heartbeat stable. Accounting reports and financial statements reveal as much about a business' health as pulse and blood pressure readings tell us about a person's health.

You may think accounting is only for profit-seeking businesses. Nothing could be further from the truth. Accounting, often called the language of business, allows us to report financial information about non-profit organizations such as churches, schools, hospitals, and government agencies. Thus, you have to know something about accounting if you want to succeed in any type of business. It's almost impossible to understand business operations without being able to read, understand, and analyze accounting reports and financial statements.

By the end of this chapter, you should have a good idea of what accounting is, how it works, and the value it offers businesses. You should also know some accounting terms and understand the purpose of accounting statements. Your new understanding will pay off as you become more active in business, or will help you in simply understanding what is going on in the world of business and finance.

What Is Accounting?

accounting The recording, classifying, summarizing, and interpreting of financial events and transactions to provide management and other interested parties the information they need to make good decisions.

Accounting is the recording, classifying, summarizing, and interpreting of financial events and transactions in an organization to provide management and other interested parties the financial information they need to make good decisions about its operation. Financial transactions include buying and selling goods and services, acquiring insurance, paying employees, and using supplies. Once the business' transactions have been recorded, they are usually classified into groups that have common characteristics. For example, all purchases are grouped together, as are all sales transactions. The method used to record and summarize accounting data into reports is an *accounting system* (see Figure 16.1).

A major purpose of accounting is to help managers make well-informed decisions. Another is to report financial information about the firm to interested stakeholders, such as employees, owners, creditors, suppliers, unions, community activists, investors, and the government (for tax purposes). Review Figure 16.2 for an overview. Accounting is divided into five key areas. Let's look at those areas next.

FIGURE 16.1

THE ACCOUNTING SYSTEM

The inputs to an accounting system include sales documents and other records. The data are recorded, classified, and summarized. They are then put into summary financial statements, such as the income statement and balance sheet.

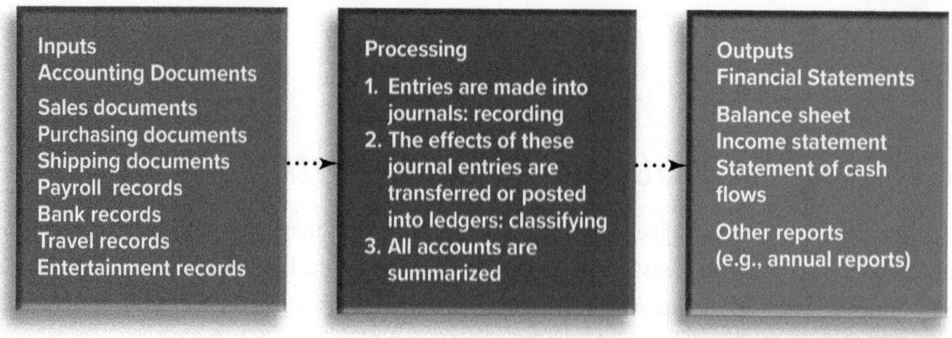

FIGURE 16.2

USERS OF ACCOUNTING INFORMATION AND THE REQUIRED REPORTS

Many types of organizations use accounting information to make business decisions. The reports needed vary according to the information each user requires. An accountant must prepare the appropriate reports.

Users	Type of Report
Government taxing authorities (e.g., Canada Revenue Agency)	Tax returns
Government regulatory agencies	Required reports
People interested in the organization's income and financial position (e.g., owners, creditors, financial analysts, and suppliers)	Financial statements found in annual reports (e.g., income statement, balance sheet, and statement of cash flows)
Managers of the firm	Financial statements and various internally distributed financial reports

Accounting Disciplines

LO2

Identify the different disciplines within the accounting profession.

As mentioned earlier, accounting allows us to report financial information about profit seeking as well as non-profit organizations, such as churches, schools, hospitals, and government agencies.[1] The accounting profession is divided into five key working areas: (1) managerial accounting, (2) financial accounting, (3) auditing, (4) tax accounting, and (5) government and not-for-profit accounting. All five areas are important, and all create career opportunities. Let's explore each in the following pages.

Managerial Accounting

managerial accounting Accounting used to provide information and analyses to managers inside the organization to assist them in decision making.

Managerial accounting provides information and analyses to managers *inside* the organization to assist them in decision making. Managerial accounting is concerned with measuring and reporting costs of production, marketing, and other functions; preparing budgets (planning); checking whether or not business units are staying within their budgets (controlling); and designing strategies to minimize taxes. If you are a business major, you'll likely take a course in managerial accounting.

Data within a company is often compared over a period of time to identify trends, or it is compared to other companies operating in the same industry when benchmarking a company's performance. For example, analysis of the accounts receivable (money that is owed to the company) will help in evaluating the credit policies of a company. Monitoring profit margins, unit sales, travel expenses, cash flow, inventory turnover, and other such data is critical to the success of a firm. Management decision making is based on such data.

Some of the questions managerial accounting reports are designed to answer include:

- What goods and services are selling the most and what promotional tools are working best?
- How quickly is the firm selling what it buys?

© Bill Pugliano/Getty Images

Assembling a truck engine requires many tools, parts, raw materials, and other components as well as labour costs. Keeping these costs at a minimum and setting realistic production schedules is critical to a business' survival. What other internal departments must management accountants team with to ensure the company's competitiveness?

- What is the appropriate allocation of expenses between products?
- Which expenses change with changes in revenue?
- How much tax is the firm paying and how can it minimize that amount?
- Will the firm have enough cash to pay its bills? If not, has it made arrangements to borrow that money?

Another aspect of managerial accounting concerns sustainability practices employed by business organizations. At the age of 23, CEO Anshula Chowdhury founded Social Asset Measurements Inc.[2] This business evolved into SAMETRICA whereby its Software-as-a-Service (SaaS) product helps organizations demonstrate their social value and supports informed decisions on how to invest and maximize the effects of their work.[3] See the Seeking Sustainability box for a discussion on what one company includes in its annual accountability report. With the growing emphasis on global competition, outsourcing, and organizational cost-cutting, managerial accounting is an area of importance in terms of anyone's career.

Financial Accounting

financial accounting Accounting information and analyses prepared for people outside the organization.

Financial accounting differs from managerial accounting in that the information and analyses it generates are for people primarily *outside* the organization. The information goes not only to company owners, managers, and employees but also to creditors and lenders, unions, customers, suppliers, government agencies, and the general public. External users are interested in questions like:

- Is the organization profitable? Should we invest in this company?
- Is it able to pay its bills?
- How much debt does it owe?
- If we lend money to this company, will it be able to pay it back?

annual report A yearly statement of the financial condition, progress, and expectations of an organization.

private accountant An accountant who works for a single firm, government agency, or not-for-profit organization.

public accountant An accountant who provides his or her accounting services to individuals or businesses on a fee basis.

These questions and others are often answered in the company's **annual report**, a yearly statement of the financial condition, progress, and expectations of an organization.

The annual reports of publicly traded companies are significantly more elaborate than for privately held companies for several reasons. First of all, securities commissions impose additional reporting requirements on publicly traded companies than for privately held companies. For publicly traded companies, many use their annual reports as public relations tools to communicate non-accounting information to stakeholders, such as shareholders, customers, the press, and others.[4] See Figure 16.3 for what can be found in an annual report.

It's critical for firms to keep accurate financial information. Some organizations employ a **private accountant** who works for a single firm, government agency, or nonprofit organization. For those firms that do not need a full-time accountant, independent accounting firms provide the services needed, for a fee. These **public accountants** provide

Seeking SUSTAINABILITY

Sustainability Reports

A sustainability report is a report published by a company or organization about the economic, environmental, and social impacts caused by its everyday activities. It also presents the organization's values and governance model, and demonstrates the link between its strategy and its commitment to a sustainable global economy. An increasing number of companies and organizations want to make their operations sustainable (i.e., last for a long time or indefinitely) and contribute to sustainable development. Sustainability reporting can help organizations to measure, understand, and communicate their economic, environmental, social, and governance performance.

More companies are committing to reporting their "green" initiatives via sustainability reports. For example, Mountain Equipment Co-op's (MEC) has a scorecard whereby it measures its performance in six key areas: products; responsible sourcing; operations; member experience and engagement; working at MEC; and financials.

Members are surveyed on issues such as product quality, functionality, and form; satisfaction; and product availability and advice provided. MEC reports on its promotion of recreation and leisure activity in Canada and its multi-million dollar contributions supporting community-based conservation ($3.66 million). There is also some comment on its own economic viability using accounting data (e.g., $465 million in annual sales), which we will talk about in this chapter.

© bubaone/iStock/Thinkstock

MEC takes issues surrounding sustainability very seriously. Why do you think companies like MEC are committing significant time and resources to these types of activities?

Source: "MEC at a Glance: Highlights of 2016–2017," Mountain Equipment Co-Op, accessed May 9, 2018, http://meccms.wpengine.com/wp-content/uploads/2017/06/MEC_2016-17_Annual-Report_Poster_Online_EN.pdf.

accounting services to individuals or businesses, such as designing an accounting system and analyzing the financial strength of an organization. Large accounting and auditing firms operate internationally to serve large, transnational companies.

Accountants know it's vital for users of a firm's accounting information to be assured the information is accurate. In Canada, the Accounting Standards Board (AcSB) has the authority to develop and establish accounting standards for use by all Canadian entities outside the public sector.[5] For example, it develops and maintains Canadian accounting standards to support the **international financial reporting standards (IFRS)**, which are the common set of accounting principles, standards and procedures that accountants and companies use to compile financial statements.[6] Publicly traded companies are required to follow IFRS, while private companies can follow IFRS or another set of standards called ASPE (accounting standard for private enterprises).[7] If accounting reports are prepared in accordance with IFRS or ASPE, users can expect the information to meet standards upon which accounting professionals have agreed.

international financial reporting standards (IFRS) The common set of accounting principles, standards, and procedures that accountants and companies use to compile financial statements.

This chapter focuses on the accounting and financial reporting standards used by publicly accountable enterprises; the accounting and financial reporting used by other types of organizations are covered in advanced accounting courses.[8]

FIGURE 16.3

ANNUAL REPORT INFORMATION

The annual reports of public companies are normally split into two sections. You may see photos of products, facilities, and personnel in the first section.

Section 1 (Non-Financial)

- A letter to shareholders from the chairperson and CEO
- Descriptions of the company's management philosophy
- Products, successes, and occasionally failures
- Exciting prospects and challenges for the future

→

Section 2 (Financial)

- Summarized financial data
- Management's discussion and analysis, covering financial condition and results of operations
- The basic financial statements
- Notes to the financial statements
- Report of independent accountants (auditor's opinion) and the management report

Source: Based on Robert Libby et al., *Financial Accounting,* 5th Canadian ed. (Canada: McGraw-Hill Ryerson Ltd., 2014), 301.

© Asia Images/Getty Images

Every public company is required to provide financial information. Users can access this information either from the company's website (e.g., Investor Relations) or from sites like SEDAR. This information varies from a quarterly set of financial statements with accompanying notes to annual reports with a breadth of financial information. Have you analyzed a company's annual report as an assignment?

Unfortunately, the accounting profession suffered a dark period in the early 2000s when accounting scandals at WorldCom, Enron, and Tyco raised public suspicions about the profession and corporate integrity in general. Arthur Andersen, a leading accounting firm, was forced out of business after being convicted of obstruction of justice for shredding records in the Enron case (the conviction was later overturned by the U.S. Supreme Court). Canadian companies are not immune either; Nortel (no longer in business) was investigated for its accounting practices related to large bonuses paid to senior management.

Scrutiny of the accounting industry intensified, however, and resulted in the U.S. Congress' passage of the Sarbanes-Oxley Act (referred to as Sarbox). Figure 16.4 lists some of the major provisions of Sarbox. This legislation created new government reporting standards for publicly traded companies. This Act also applies to any Canadian publicly traded company wishing to have its shares traded on an American stock exchange. In Canada, the Ontario Securities Commission introduced Bill 198. CEOs and CFOs of public companies are now required to certify reports. Auditors are now also required to be part of the Canadian Public Accountability Board Oversight Program, which reviews the audited financial statements of public companies. In addition, standards for the independence and education experience of Audit Committees were defined.

FIGURE 16.4

KEY PROVISIONS OF THE SARBANES-OXLEY ACT

- Prohibits accounting firms from providing certain non-auditing work (such as consulting services) to companies they audit.
- Strengthens the protection for whistleblowers who report wrongful actions of company officers.
- Requires company CEOs and CFOs to certify the accuracy of financial reports and imparts strict penalties for any violation of securities reporting (e.g., earnings misstatements).
- Prohibits corporate loans to directors and executives of the company.
- Establishes the five-member Public Company Accounting Oversight Board under the Securities and Exchange Commission (SEC) to oversee the accounting industry.
- Stipulates that altering or destroying key audit documents will result in felony charges and significant criminal penalties.

Like other business disciplines, accounting is subject to change. The accounting profession is feeling the impact of the global market. Reaching Beyond Our Borders box discusses a movement to globalize accounting procedures.

Reaching *Beyond* OUR BORDERS

Speaking a Universal Accounting Language

Throughout this text you've read about the tremendous impact of the global market. Companies like BlackBerry and Coca-Cola, for example, earn the majority of their revenues from global markets. Unfortunately, they face considerable accounting headaches since no global accounting system exists. This means they must adapt their accounting procedures to different countries' rules. Fortunately, a solution might be at hand. The Financial Accounting Standards Board (FASB) in the United States and the London-based International Accounting Standards Board (IASB) want that situation to change.

© Shutterstock / maxstockphoto

With over 120 countries permitting or requiring International Financial Reporting Standards (IFRS), the governing bodies of the accounting profession in the United States has proposed the integration of the U.S. accounting code with the IFRS used around the world. Many accountants support the shift to global standards for accounting and support the efforts of the FASB and IASB to work at convergence between the two systems.

In Canada, the AcSB has adopted the mandatory use of IFRS by all publicly accountable enterprises (PAEs). IFRS replaces previous Canadian generally accepted accounting principles as the acceptable set of accounting standards for PAEs. Canada Revenue Agency does not specify that financial statements must be prepared following any particular type of accounting principles or standards; however, the AcSB requires PAEs to use IFRS in the preparation of all interim and annual financial statements. Most private companies also have the option to adopt IFRS for financial statement preparation.

Sources: U.S. Securities and Exchange Commission, *www.sec.gov*, accessed October 2017; "International Financial Reporting Standards (IFRS)," Canada Revenue Agency, February 21, 2017, https://www.canada.ca/en/revenue-agency/services/tax/businesses/topics/international-financial-reporting-standards-ifrs.html; Michael Cohn, "Outgoing SEC Chair White, Keep on Converging Accounting Standards," *Accounting Today*, January 6, 2017; and Erich Knachel, "Revenue Recognition: The Clock Is Ticking," *CFO*, December 21, 2016.

© The Canadian Press/Christopher Katsarov

Auditor General Bonnie Lysyk warns about the Ontario Liberal government's projected deficit in her pre-election report on government finances; she believes that the projected deficit of $6.7 billion for 2018–2019 should actually be $11.7 billion.[12] The Premier called it a long-standing accounting dispute between her government and the auditor general.[13] What is the risk of understated deficits when government spends on new initiatives? How can a dispute like this be resolved?

Auditing

Reviewing and evaluating the records used to prepare a company's financial statements is referred to as **auditing**. Private accountants within the organization often perform internal audits to guarantee that the organization is carrying out proper accounting procedures and financial reporting. Public accountants also conduct independent audits of accounting information and related records. An **independent audit** is an evaluation and unbiased opinion about the accuracy of a company's financial statements. You may recall from Figure 16.3 that annual reports often include an auditor's unbiased written opinion.

All stakeholders, including the public, governments, financial institutions, and shareholders (owners) are interested in the results of these audits. Audits are required for all public corporations in Canada whose shares are traded in a public stock exchange.

After the accounting scandals of the early 2000s, the Sarbanes-Oxley Act put in place new rules around auditing and consulting to ensure the integrity of the auditing process. Auditing procedures, however, again came under fire in 2011, causing many to call for stricter controls over auditing procedures after analyzing the failure of Lehman Brothers in 2008 and the financial crisis that followed.[9]

In doing their job, auditors not only examine the financial health of an organization but also its operational efficiencies and effectiveness.[10] A relatively new area of accounting that focuses its attention on fraudulent activity is **forensic accounting**. This field of accounting gathers evidence for presentation in a court of law. This evidence comes from a review of financial and other records. Review Adapting to Change for a further discussion.

auditing
The job of reviewing and evaluating the records used to prepare a company's financial statements.

independent audit
An evaluation and unbiased opinion about the accuracy of a company's financial statements.

forensic accounting
A relatively new area of accounting that focuses its attention on fraudulent activity.

tax accountant
An accountant trained in tax law and responsible for preparing tax returns or developing tax strategies.

Tax Accounting

Taxes enable governments to fund roads, parks, schools, social services, police protection, and other functions. Federal and provincial governments require individuals and organizations to file tax returns at specific times and in precise formats. A **tax accountant** is trained in tax law and is responsible for preparing tax returns or developing tax strategies. Since governments often change tax policies according to specific needs or objectives, the job of the tax accountant is certainly challenging.[11] As the burden of taxes grows in the economy, the role of the tax accountant becomes increasingly valuable to the organization, individual, or entrepreneur.

Government and Not-for-Profit Accounting

Government and not-for-profit (non-profit) accounting supports organizations whose purpose is not generating a profit but rather serving ratepayers, taxpayers, and others according to a duly approved budget. The different levels of government require an accounting

Adapting *to* CHANGE

Accounting: CSI

Unfortunately, many companies lose money in the worst possible way—through fraud. Fraud is a major problem that impacts businesses both large and small. According to the Association of Certified Fraud Examiners, many large corporations lose almost 5 percent of their revenue each year due to fraud, and nearly half of all small businesses deal with financial fraud at some time in their business lives, often with very dire results.

© Pixattitude | Dreamstime.com

While SEC remains committed to fighting financial fraud and laws such as Sarbox promise stiff penalties, financial fraud marches on. The problem is, government and company auditors are not specifically trained in uncovering financial fraud. Their expertise is primarily to make sure accounting standards are being applied correctly and company financial statements are fairly stated. So, if auditors and chartered professional accountants (CPAs) are not prepared to search for and identify signs of financial fraud, "Who you gonna call?"

The answer is elementary. Meet the forensic accountant, the Sherlock Holmes of the accounting industry. While auditors search for accounting errors, forensic accountants search for crime-scene evidence. Forensic accountants sift through mountains of company information, trying to put together a paper trail to identify company rogues responsible for fraud. Their work is often long and arduous and can involve investigating inflated sales figures, money laundering, and inventory fraud. Jack Damico, founding partner of MDD Forensic Accountants, described his colleagues as "investigative accountants who look below the surface and read between the lines." If forensic accounting interests you, many schools offer advanced degrees and specialties in forensic accounting.

Sources: Bill Albert, "Alibaba: Digging into the Numbers," *Barron's*, February 20, 2016; Howard Scheck, "Risky Business: SEC Focuses on Internal Controls," *CFO*, November 16, 2016; The Association of Fraud Examiners, *www.acfe.com*, accessed October 2017.

system that helps taxpayers, special interest groups, legislative bodies, and creditors ensure that each level of government is fulfilling its obligations and making proper use of the funding with which it has been provided. Canada's auditor general regularly audits the federal government. CRA administers tax laws for the Government of Canada and for most provinces and territories, and it also administers various social and economic benefit and incentive programs delivered through the tax system.[14]

Not-for-profit organizations often require accounting professionals. Charities like the Canadian Cancer Society and the United Way of Canada, museums, universities and colleges, and hospitals all hire accountants to show contributors how their money is spent. During the recent recession, many businesses and individuals cut back on donations, making it more important than ever to account for every dollar contributed.[15]

government and not-for-profit (nonprofit) accounting Accounting system for organizations whose purpose is not generating a profit but rather serving ratepayers, taxpayers, and others according to a duly approved budget.

As you can see, financial and managerial accounting, auditing, tax accounting, and government and not-for-profit accounting each require specific training and skill. They also offer solid career opportunities. Looking ahead, the accounting profession is feeling the impact and challenge of the global market. Before we leave this section, let's look at Canada's accounting designations.

© Devin Komarniski

Did you know that 1 in 15 Aboriginal people in Canada is homeless, compared to around 1 in 128 of the general population? Bissell Centre advocates for Edmonton's Aboriginal community because this population disproportionately struggles with homelessness and poverty due to a history of systematic marginalization and discrimination.[17] Here you see some individuals celebrating National Aboriginal Day on June 21, the summer solstice. Have you considered working for a not-for-profit or government organization?

© Bernhard_Staehli/Getty Images

What role can accountants play to help organizations adapt to climate change? A new strategic initiative—sponsored by CPA Canada and Natural Resources Canada, and managed by the Network for Business Sustainability—says accountants are ideally positioned to be key contributors. As creators, enablers, preservers, and reporters of sustainable value, accountants can make their organizations' adaptation efforts more effective. Would working in this area of accounting interest you?

The Chartered Professional Accountant (CPA) Designation[16]

Canada has three legacy professional accounting designations. Accountants with any of these designations work in all areas of business. Each designation is as follows:

1. A *chartered accountant (CA)* has met the examination, education, and experience requirements of the Canadian Institute of Chartered Accountants (CICA). This includes passing the Uniform Final Evaluation (UFE), widely recognized as one of the most rigorous professional examinations in the world.
2. A *certified management accountant (CMA)* has met certain educational and experience requirements, passed a qualifying exam in the field, participated in a two-year professional development program, and was certified by the Management Accountants of Canada (CMA Canada).
3. *Certified general accountants (CGAs)* have met the examination, education, and experience requirements of the Certified General Accountants Association of Canada (CGA-Canada).

Chartered Professional Accountants of Canada (CPA Canada) was formed by the integration of the three organizations mentioned above, namely CICA, CMA Canada, and CGA-Canada. CPA Canada was created to unify Canadian provincial accounting bodies at the national level. All 40 of the accounting bodies in Canada have now either unified or are participating in discussions to unite under the CPA banner. The timing for integration and use of the CPA designation will vary from province to province because the profession is provincially regulated and mergers will occur at different times. As such, some of the provinces and regions will be represented by a merged CPA body, while others will be represented by the legacy bodies until an integrated CPA organization is in place. Once unification is completed the profession will move to 14 governing bodies and represent more than 200 000 members.

The **Chartered Professional Accountant (CPA) designation** is the internationally recognized Canadian accounting designation. One needs to have both an undergraduate degree and specific subject area coverage to be admitted to the new CPA Professional Education Program (CPA PEP). There is a different path for those who do not have an undergraduate degree.

This designation emerged from the belief that Canada needed a single, unified accounting profession. A combined Canadian accounting profession built on the strengths of the three legacy designations would be better positioned to represent its interests in Canada and abroad. "With unification, operations and governance will be simplified, efficiencies found, and the profession will speak with a stronger voice," explains Kevin Dancey, president and CEO of CPA Canada. A unified profession will best serve the public interest by establishing common codes of professional conduct, disciplinary systems, and licensing regimes. Dancey adds that with unification will come a nationally consistent regulatory framework that will facilitate labour mobility and the integration of foreign-trained professionals. "Unification will ease confusion about the legacy designations for employers," notes Dancey. "Soon, everyone will be operating under the CPA banner."

chartered professional accountant (CPA) designation The internationally recognized Canadian accounting designation.

PROGRESS ASSESSMENT

- What are the five key working areas of the accounting profession?
- What is the key difference between managerial and financial accounting?
- How is the job of a private accountant different from that of a public accountant?
- What ideas contributed to the creation of the CPA designation?

LO3

List the steps in the accounting cycle, distinguish between accounting and bookkeeping, and explain how computers are used in accounting.

The Accounting Cycle

The **accounting cycle** is a six-step procedure (see Figure 16.5) that results in the preparation and analysis of the major financial statements. It relies on the work of both the bookkeeper and an accountant. **Bookkeeping**, the recording of business transactions, is a basic part of financial reporting. Accounting, however, goes far beyond the mere recording of financial information. Accountants classify and summarize financial data provided by bookkeepers, interpret the data, and then report the information to management. They also

accounting cycle A six-step procedure that results in the preparation and analysis of the major financial statements.

bookkeeping The recording of business transactions.

FIGURE 16.5

STEPS IN THE ACCOUNTING CYCLE

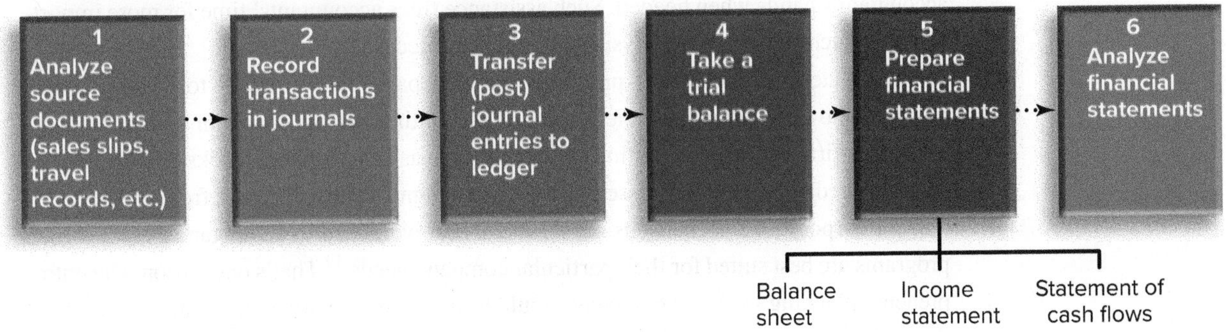
1 Analyze source documents (sales slips, travel records, etc.)
2 Record transactions in journals
3 Transfer (post) journal entries to ledger
4 Take a trial balance
5 Prepare financial statements
6 Analyze financial statements
Balance sheet
Income statement
Statement of cash flows

suggest strategies for improving the financial condition and prepare financial analyses and income tax returns.

A bookkeeper's first task is to divide all of the firm's transactions into meaningful categories, such as sales documents, purchasing receipts, and shipping documents, being very careful to keep the information organized and manageable. Bookkeepers then record financial data from the original transaction documents (sales slips and so forth) into a record book or computer program called a **journal**. The word *journal* comes from the French word *jour,* which means "day." Therefore, a journal is where the day's transactions are kept.

journal
The record book where accounting data are first entered.

It's quite possible to make a mistake when recording financial transactions, like entering \$10.98 as \$10.89. That's why bookkeepers record all transactions in two places, so they can check one list of transactions against the other to make sure both add up to the same amount. If the amounts are not equal, the bookkeeper knows there is a mistake. The practice of writing every transaction in two places is called **double-entry bookkeeping**. It requires two entries in the journal and in the ledgers (discussed next) for each transaction.

double-entry bookkeeping
The concept of every business transaction affecting at least two accounts.

Suppose a business wanted to determine how much it paid for office supplies in the first quarter of the year. Without a specific bookkeeping tool, that would be difficult—even with accurate accounting journals. Therefore, bookkeepers use a specialized accounting book or computer program called a **ledger**. In the ledger, they transfer (or post) information from accounting journals into specific categories so managers can find all the information about a single account, like office supplies or cash, in one place.

ledger
A specialized accounting book in which information from accounting journals is accumulated into accounts and posted so that managers can find all of the information about a specific account in one place.

The next step in the accounting cycle is to prepare a **trial balance**, a summary of all the financial data in the account ledgers that ensures the figures are correct and balanced. If the information in the account ledgers is not accurate, the accountant must correct it before preparing the firm's financial statements. Using the correct information, the accountant then prepares the firm's financial statements—including a balance sheet, an income statement, and a statement of cash flows—according to IFRS.

trial balance
A summary of all of the data in the account ledgers to show whether the figures are correct and balanced.

Using Technology in Accounting

A long while ago, accountants and bookkeepers needed to enter all of a firm's financial information by hand. The advent of adding machines and calculators made the job a bit simpler, but still generally required a paper entry. Toward the end of the 20th century, technology simplified the accounting process. Today, computerized accounting programs can post information from journals instantaneously, from remote locations to encrypted laptops or cell phones, making financial information available whenever the organization needs it. The company's sensitive financial information is safe and secure, but is in the accountant's hands when needed. Such assistance frees accountants' time for more important tasks such as financial analysis and financial forecasting.

Computerized accounting programs are also particularly helpful to small-business owners, who don't often have the variety of accounting personnel within their companies that larger firms enjoy. Accounting software—such as Intuit's QuickBooks—addresses the specific needs of small businesses that are often significantly different from the needs of a major corporation.[18] Small-business owners, however, need to understand exactly which programs are best suited for their particular company needs.[19] That's one reason why entrepreneurs planning to start a company should hire or consult with an accountant to identify the particular needs of the firm. They can then develop a specific accounting system that works with the accounting software they've chosen.

With sophisticated accounting software available and technology capabilities growing, you might wonder why you need to study and understand accounting. Without question, technology has greatly assisted business people and certainly eased the monotony of bookkeeping and accounting work. Unfortunately the work of an accountant requires training and very specific competencies that computers are not programmed to handle. It's the partnership of technology and an accountant's knowledge that helps a firm make the right financial decisions. After the Progress Assessment, we'll explore the balance sheet, income statement, and statement of cash flows. It's from the information contained in these financial statements that the accountant analyzes and evaluates the financial condition of the firm.

PROGRESS ASSESSMENT

- How is the job of the bookkeeper different from that of an accountant?
- What is the purpose of accounting journals and ledgers?
- Why does a bookkeeper prepare a trial balance?
- How has computer software helped businesses maintain and compile accounting information?

Understanding Key Financial Statements

LO4

Explain how the major financial statements differ.

financial statement
A summary of all of the transactions that have occurred over a particular period.

An accounting year is either a calendar or fiscal year. A calendar year begins January 1 and ends December 31. A fiscal year can begin at any date designated by the business. A **financial statement** is a summary of all the transactions that have occurred over a particular period. Financial statements indicate a firm's financial health and stability and are key factors in management decision making.[20] That is why shareholders, bondholders and financial services providers (people and institutions that lend money to the firm), unions, employees, and the CRA are all interested in a firm's financial statements. There are three key business financial statements:

1. The *balance sheet* reports the firm's financial position *on a specific date.*
2. The *income statement* summarizes revenues, cost of goods, and expenses (including taxes) for a specific period, and it highlights the total profit or loss the firm experienced *during that period.*
3. The *statement of cash flows* provides a summary of money coming into and going out of the firm. It tracks a company's cash receipts and cash payments.

© Dean Mitchell/Getty Images RF

Financial health and stability is important not only for businesses but also for your own life. Do you regularly assess your financial health? To learn more about managing personal finances, review Appendix B.

The differences among the financial statements can best be summarized this way: The balance sheet details what the company owns and owes on a certain day; the income statement shows the revenue a firm earned selling its products compared to its selling costs (profit or loss) over a specific period of time; and the statement of cash flows highlights the difference between cash coming in and cash going out of a business. To fully understand this important financial information, you need to know the purpose of an organization's financial statements. To help you with this task, we'll explain each statement in more detail. Before this, consider the fundamental accounting equation.

The Fundamental Accounting Equation

Imagine you don't owe anybody any money. That is, you have no liabilities (debts). In this case, your assets (cash and so forth) are equal to what you *own* (your equity). However, if you borrow some money from a friend, you have incurred a liability. Your assets are now equal to what you *owe* plus what you own. Translated into business terms, Assets = Liabilities + Owners' equity, which is the **fundamental accounting equation**. Different types of assets, liabilities, and owners' equity (which will be discussed later), are **accounts**.

fundamental accounting equation
Assets = Liabilities + Owners' Equity; this is the basis for the balance sheet.

accounts
Different types of assets, liabilities, and owners' equity.

In accounting, this equation must always be balanced. For example, suppose that you have $50,000 in cash and decide to use that money to open a small coffee shop. Your business has assets of $50,000 and no debts. The accounting equation would look like this:

Assets	=	Liabilities	+	Owners' equity
$50,000	=	$0	+	$50,000

Each business transaction impacts at least two accounts. Each entry has at least one debit and one credit. Debits or credits on their own are neither good nor bad, simply a mechanism for maintaining the balance of the accounting equation.

Referring back to our example, your business has $50,000 cash and $50,000 owners' equity (the amount of your investment in the business—sometimes referred to as net worth). However, before opening the business, you borrow $30,000 from a local bank. As a result, the accounting equation now changes. You have $30,000 of additional cash, but you also have a debt (liability) of $30,000. (Remember, in double-entry bookkeeping we record each business transaction in two places.)

Your financial position within the business has changed. The equation is still balanced but is changed to reflect the borrowing transaction:

Assets	=	Liabilities	+	Owners' equity
$80,000	=	$30,000	+	$50,000

This fundamental accounting equation is the basis for the balance sheet.

balance sheet (statement of financial position)
The financial statement that reports a firm's financial condition at a specific time and is composed of three major types of accounts: assets, liabilities, and owners' (shareholders' or stockholders') equity.

The Balance Sheet

A **balance sheet** (also known as the **statement of financial position**) is the financial statement that reports a firm's financial condition at a specific time. As highlighted in the sample balance sheet in Figure 16.6 (for our hypothetical restaurant, Harvest Gold, introduced in Chapter 14), assets are listed in a separate column from liabilities and owners'

FIGURE 16.6

SAMPLE HARVEST GOLD BALANCE SHEET

1. Current assets: Items that can be converted to cash within one year.
2. Fixed assets: Items such as land, buildings, and equipment that are relatively permanent.
3. Intangible assets: Items of value such as patents and copyrights that don't have a physical form.
4. Current liabilities: Payments that are due in one year or less.
5. Long-term liabilities: Payments that are not due for one year or longer.
6. Owners' equity: The value of what shareholders own in a firm (also called shareholders' equity).

HARVEST GOLD Balance Sheet December 31, 2018			
Assets			
1. Current assets			
Cash		$ 15,000	
Accounts receivable		200,000	
Notes receivable		50,000	
Inventory		335,000	
Total current assets			$ 600,000
2. Fixed assets			
Land		$ 40,000	
Building and improvements	$ 200,000		
Less: Accumulated depreciation	−90,000		
		110,000	
Equipment and vehicles	$ 120,000		
Less: Accumulated depreciation	−80,000		
		40,000	
Furniture and fixtures	$ 26,000		
Less: Accumulated depreciation	−10,000		
		16,000	
Total fixed assets			206,000
3. Intangible assets			
Goodwill		$ 20,000	
Total intangible assets			20,000
Total assets			$ 826,000
Liabilities and Owners' Equity			
4. Current liabilities			
Accounts payable		$ 40,000	
Notes payable (due June 2019)		8,000	
Accrued taxes		150,000	
Accrued salaries		90,000	
Total current liabilities			$ 288,000
5. Long-term liabilities			
Notes payable (due Mar. 2023)		$ 35,000	
Bonds payable (due Dec. 2028)		290,000	
Total long-term liabilities			325,000
Total liabilities			$ 613,000
6. Owners' equity			
Common stock (1 000 000 shares)		$ 100,000	
Retained earnings		113,000	
Total owners' equity			213,000
Total liabilities & Owners' equity			$ 826,000

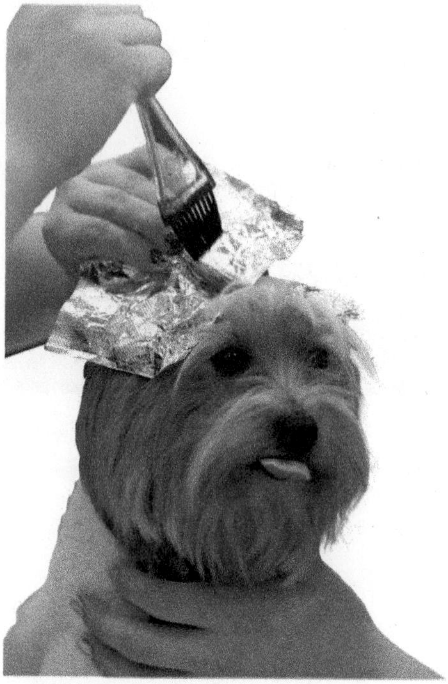

© Saxon Reed/AP Images

Service businesses, like dog groomers, rely on the same sets of financial statements as manufacturers like Ford and retailers like Best Buy. What are some of the assets and liabilities a typical service business like this one would carry on its balance sheet?

(or shareholders' or stockholders') equity. The assets are equal to or *balanced* with the liabilities and owners' equity.[21] The balance is that simple.

Let's say that you want to know what your financial condition is at a given time. Maybe you want to buy a house or car and therefore need to calculate your available resources. One of the best measuring sticks is your balance sheet. First, add up everything you own—cash, property, and money owed you. These are your assets. Subtract from that the money you owe others—credit card debt, IOUs, car loan, student loans, and the like. These are your liabilities. The resulting figure is your net worth, or equity. This is fundamentally what companies do in preparing a balance sheet: they follow the procedures set in the fundamental accounting equation. In that preparation, any company that is publicly traded is required to follow IFRS.[22]

Since it's critical that you understand the financial information on the balance sheet, let's take a closer look at what is in a business' asset account and what is in its liabilities and owners' equity accounts.

CLASSIFYING ASSETS

Assets are economic resources (things of value) owned by a firm. Assets include productive, tangible items, such as equipment, buildings, land, furniture, and motor vehicles, that help generate income, as well as intangible items with value, like patents, trademarks, copyrights, and goodwill. Goodwill represents the value attached to factors such as a firm's reputation, location, and superior products. Goodwill is included on the balance sheet when one firm acquires another firm and pays more for it than the value of its tangible assets. Even though intangible assets such as brand names (e.g., Roots, WestJet, and Via Rail) can be among the firm's most valuable resources, they are not listed on a company's balance sheet if they were developed within the company.[23]

assets
Economic resources (things of value) owned by a firm.

liquidity
The ease with which an asset can be converted into cash.

current assets
Items that can or will be converted into cash within one year.

fixed assets
Assets that are relatively permanent, such as land, buildings, and equipment.

Accountants list assets on the firm's balance sheet in order of their **liquidity**, or ease with which they can convert them to cash. Speedier conversion means higher liquidity. For example, an *account receivable* is an amount of money owed to the firm that it expects to receive within one year. It is considered a *liquid* asset because it can be quickly converted to cash. Land, however, is not considered a liquid asset because it takes time, effort, and paperwork to convert it to cash. It is considered a fixed or long-term asset. Assets are thus divided into three categories according to how quickly they can be turned into cash:

1. **Current assets** are items that can or will be converted into cash within one year. Current assets include cash, accounts receivable, and inventory.
2. **Fixed assets** are long-term assets that are relatively permanent, such as land, buildings, and equipment. They are acquired to produce products for a business. They

are not bought to be sold but to generate revenue. (On a balance sheet they are also referred to as capital assets or property, plant, and equipment.)

3. **Intangible assets** are long-term assets that have no physical form but do have value.[24] Patents, trademarks, copyrights, and goodwill are intangible assets.

intangible assets Long-term assets (e.g., patents, trademarks, and copyrights) that have no physical form but do have value.

LIABILITIES AND OWNERS' EQUITY ACCOUNTS

Liabilities are what the business owes to others—its debts. *Current liabilities* are debts due in one year or less. *Long-term liabilities* (also called non-current liabilities) are debts due in over one year. The following are common liability accounts recorded on a balance sheet. Look at Figure 16.6 again for these accounts:

liabilities What the business owes to others (debts).

1. **Accounts payable** are current liabilities or bills a company owes others for merchandise or services it purchased on credit but have not yet paid for. The longer you take to pay, the greater the risk that a supplier will no longer grant you credit.
2. **Notes payable** can be short-term or long-term liabilities (like loans from banks) that a business promises to repay by a certain date.
3. **Bonds payable** are long-term liabilities. This is money lent to the firm that must be paid back. (We will discuss bonds in Chapters 17.)

accounts payable Current liabilities or bills a company owes others for merchandise or services purchased on credit but not yet paid for.

notes payable Short-term or long-term liabilities that a business promises to repay by a certain date.

bonds payable Long-term liabilities that represent money lent to a firm that must be paid back.

As you saw in the fundamental accounting equation, the value of things you own (assets) minus the amount of money you owe others (liabilities) is called *equity*. The value of what shareholders own in a firm, minus liabilities, is called *shareholders' equity* (or *stockholders' equity*). Because shareholders are the owners of a firm, we call shareholders' equity **owners' equity**, or that amount of the business that belongs to the owners, minus any liabilities the business owes. This consists of all that the owners have invested in the company plus all profits that have accumulated since the business commenced but that have not yet been paid out to them. This figure always equals the book value of the assets minus the liabilities of the company.

owners' equity The amount of the business that belongs to the owners minus any liabilities owed by the business.

The owners' equity account will differ according to the type of organization. For sole proprietors and partners, owners' equity means the value of everything owned by the business minus any liabilities of the owner(s), such as bank loans. Owners' equity in these firms is called the *capital* account. In a sole proprietorship, it is called owner's or proprietor's equity or capital. In a partnership, owners' equity is called partners' equity or capital.

For corporations, it's called shareholders' equity and is divided in two separate accounts. The amount the owners (shareholders) invest is shown in one account, called common stock. The second account is **retained earnings**, which are accumulated earnings from the firm's profitable operations that remain in the business and are not paid out to shareholders in distributions of company profits. (Distributions of profits, called dividends, are discussed in Chapter 17). Take a few moments to review Figure 16.6 and see what facts you can determine about Harvest Gold from its balance sheet. Have some fun and estimate your own personal net worth, following the directions in Figure 16.7.

retained earnings The accumulated earnings from a firm's profitable operations that remains in the business and are not paid out to shareholders as dividends.

FIGURE 16.7

YOU INCORPORATED

How does You Inc. stack up financially? Take a little time to find out. You may be pleasantly surprised, or you may realize that you need to think hard about planning your financial future. Remember, your net worth is nothing more than the difference between what you own (assets) and what you owe (liabilities). Be honest, and do your best to give a fair evaluation of your private property's value.

ASSETS		LIABILITIES	
Cash	$ _______	Installment loans & interest	$ _______
Savings account	_______	Other loans & interest	_______
Chequing account	_______	Credit card accounts	_______
Home	_______	Mortgage	_______
Stocks & bonds	_______	Taxes	_______
Automobile	_______	Cell phone service	_______
TFSA & RRSP	_______	Other liabilities	_______
Personal property	_______		
Other assets	_______		
Total assets	$ _______	Total liabilities	$ _______
Determine your net worth:			
Total assets	$ _______		
Total liabilities	_______		
Net worth	$ _______		

PROGRESS ASSESSMENT

- What do we call the formula for the balance sheet? What three accounts does it hold?
- What does it mean to list assets according to liquidity?
- What is included in the liabilities section in the balance sheet?
- What is owners' equity, and how is it determined?

income statement (statement of earnings)
The financial statement that shows a firm's profit after costs, expenses, and taxes.

net income (or net loss)
Revenue left over (or depleted if a net loss) after all costs and expenses, including taxes, are paid.

The Income Statement

The financial statement that shows a firm's bottom line—that is its profit (or loss) after costs, expenses, and taxes—is the **income statement** (also known as the **statement of earnings**). The income statement summarizes all the resources, called *revenue,* that have come into the firm from operating activities, money resources the firm used up, expenses it incurred in doing business, and resources it has left after paying all costs and expenses, including taxes. See Figure 16.8 for an example. The resources (revenue) left over or depleted are referred to as **net income** or **net loss**.

FIGURE 16.8

SAMPLE HARVEST GOLD INCOME STATEMENT

1. Revenues: Value of what's received from goods sold, services rendered, and other financial sources.
2. Cost of goods sold: Cost of merchandise sold or cost of raw materials or parts used for producing items for resale.
3. Gross profit: How much the firm earned by buying or selling merchandise.
4. Operating expenses: Cost incurred in operating a business.
5. Net income after taxes: Profit or loss over a specific period after subtracting all costs and expenses, including taxes.

HARVEST GOLD Income Statement For the Year Ended December 31, 2018			
1. Revenues			
Gross sales		$720,000	
Less: Sales returns and allowances	$ 12,000		
Sales discounts	8,000	−20,000	
Net sales			$700,000
2. Cost of goods sold			
Beginning inventory, Jan. 1		$200,000	
Merchandise purchases	$400,000		
Freight	40,000		
Net purchases		440,000	
Cost of goods available for sale	$640,000		
Less ending inventory, Dec. 31		−230,000	
Cost of goods sold			410,000
3. Gross profit			$290,000
4. Operating expenses			
Selling expenses			
Salaries for salespeople	$ 90,000		
Advertising	18,000		
Supplies	2,000		
Total selling expenses		$110,000	
General expenses			
Office salaries	$ 67,000		
Depreciation	1,500		
Insurance	1,500		
Rent	28,000		
Light, heat, and power	12,000		
Miscellaneous	2,000		
		112,000	
Total operating expenses			222,000
Net income before taxes			$ 68,000
Less: Income tax expense			19,000
5. Net income after taxes			$ 49,000

cost of goods sold (cost of goods manufactured) A measure of the cost of merchandise sold or cost of raw materials and supplies used for producing items for resale.

gross profit (gross margin) How much a firm earned by buying (or making) and selling merchandise.

The income statement reports the firm's financial operations over a particular period of time, usually a year, a quarter of a year, or a month. It's the financial statement that reveals whether the business is actually earning a profit or losing money. The income statement includes valuable financial information for shareholders, lenders, potential investors, employees, and the government. Let's take a quick look at how to compile the income statement. Then we will discuss what each element in it means.

Revenue
− Cost of goods sold
= Gross profit (gross margin)
− Operating expenses
= Net income before taxes
− Taxes
= Net income or loss

REVENUE

Revenue is the monetary value of what a firm received for goods sold, services rendered, and other payments (such as rents received, money paid to the firm for use of its patents, interest earned, etc.). Be sure not to confuse the terms *revenue* and *sales;* they are not the same thing.[25] True, most revenue a business earns does come from sales, but companies can also have other sources of revenue. Also, a quick glance at the income statement shows you that *gross sales* refers to the total of all sales the firm completed. *Net sales* are gross sales minus returns, discounts, and allowances.

Lonnie McQuirter owns a gas station that works with local suppliers to provide customers with healthy, organic food instead of the typical convenience store fare. In 2007 he took out an $875,000 loan to purchase the property and gas pumps from BP. His business now brings in $11 million annually in gross revenue. What's the difference between revenue and profit?

COST OF GOODS SOLD

The **cost of goods sold** (also known as **cost of goods manufactured**) measures the cost of merchandise the firm sells or the cost of raw materials and supplies it used in producing items for resale. It makes sense to compare how much a business earned by selling merchandise and how much it spent to make or produce the merchandise. The cost of goods sold includes the purchase price plus any freight charges paid to transport goods, plus any costs associated with storing the goods.

In financial reporting, it doesn't matter when a firm places a particular item in its inventory, but it does matter how an accountant records the cost of the item when the firm sells it. Why? To understand, read the Spotlight on Small Business about two different inventory valuation methods, *LIFO* and *FIFO*.

When we subtract the cost of goods sold from net sales, we get the firm's gross profit or gross margin. **Gross profit** (or **gross margin**) is how much a firm earned by buying

Spotlight *On* SMALL BUSINESS

Out with the Old, In with the New

IFRS sometimes permit an accountant to use different methods of accounting for a firm's inventory. Two of the most popular methods are called FIFO and LIFO.

Let's look at a simple example. Say your bookstore buys 100 copies of a particular textbook in July at $150 a copy. When classes begin in September, the bookstore sells 50 copies of the text to students at $175 each. Since instructors intend to use the same book again next term, the bookstore places the 50 copies it did not sell in its inventory until then.

In late December, the bookstore orders 50 additional copies of the text to sell for the coming term.

© McGraw-Hill Education/Mark Dierker, photographer

However, the publisher's price of the book to the bookstore has increased to $175 a copy due to inflation and other increased production and distribution costs. The bookstore now has in its inventory 100 copies of the same textbook, purchased during two different buying cycles. If it sells 50 copies to students at $200 each at the beginning of the new term in January, what is the bookstore's cost of the book for accounting purposes? Actually, it depends.

The books sold are identical, but the accounting treatment could be different. If the bookstore uses a method called first in, first out (FIFO), the cost of goods sold is $150 for each textbook, because the textbook the store bought first—the first in—cost $150. The bookstore could use another method, however. Under last in, first out (LIFO), its last purchase of the textbooks, at $175 each, determines the cost of each of the 50 textbooks sold.

If the book sells for $200, what is the difference in gross profit (margin) between using FIFO and using LIFO? As you can see, the inventory valuation method used makes a difference in the profit margin. Eventually, when all 100 copies are sold the cumulative net income will be the same regardless of whether FIFO or LIFO is used. The choice between the two methods solely affects the timing of when the net income is realized.

(or making) and selling merchandise. In a service firm, there may be no cost of goods sold; therefore, gross profit could *equal* net sales. Gross profit, however, does not tell you everything you need to know about the firm's financial performance. To get that, you must also subtract the business' expenses.

OPERATING EXPENSES

In selling goods or services, a business incurs certain **operating expenses**, such as rent, salaries, supplies, utilities, and insurance. Other operating expenses that appear on an income statement, like *depreciation,* are a bit more complex. For example, have you ever heard that a new car depreciates in market value as soon as you drive it off the dealer's lot? The same principle holds true for assets such as equipment and machinery. **Depreciation** is the systematic write-off of the cost of a tangible asset over its estimated useful life. Under accounting rules set by IFRS and CRA (which are beyond the scope of this chapter), companies are permitted to recapture the cost of these assets (i.e., cars, computers, office and electronic equipment) over time by using depreciation as an operating expense.

operating expenses
Costs involved in operating a business, such as rent, utilities, and salaries.

depreciation
The systematic write-off of the cost of a tangible asset over its estimated useful life.

We can classify operating expenses as either selling or general expenses. *Selling expenses* are expenses related to the marketing and distribution of the firm's goods or services (such as advertising, salespeople's salaries, and supplies). *General expenses* are administrative expenses of the firm (such as office salaries, insurance, and rent). Accountants are trained to help you record all applicable expenses and find other relevant expenses you can deduct from your taxable income as a part of doing business.

NET PROFIT OR NET LOSS

After deducting all expenses, we can determine the firm's net income before taxes, also referred to as net earnings or net profit (refer to Figure 16.8). After deducting taxes, we get to the *bottom line,* which is the net income (or perhaps net loss) the firm incurred from revenue minus sales returns, costs, expenses, and taxes over a period of time. We can now answer the question "Did the business earn or lose money in the specific reporting period?"

As you can see, the basic principles of the balance sheet and income statement are already familiar to you. You know how to keep track of costs and expenses when you prepare your own budget. If your rent and utilities exceed your earnings, you know you're in trouble. If you need more money, you may need to sell some of the things you own to meet your expenses. The same is true in business. Companies need to keep track of how much money they earn and spend and how much cash they have on hand. The only difference is that companies tend to have more complex problems and a good deal more information to record than you do.

© Imaginechina/Corbis

Most businesses incur operating expenses that include rent, salaries, utilities, supplies, and insurance. What are some of the likely operating expenses for companies like Starbucks?

Users of financial statements are interested in how a firm handles the flow of cash coming into a business and the cash flowing out of the business. Cash flow problems can plague both businesses and individuals. Keep this in mind as we look at the statement of cash flows next.

The Statement of Cash Flows

The **statement of cash flows** (also known as the **cash flow statement**) reports cash receipts and cash disbursements related to the three major activities of a firm:

- *Operations* are cash transactions associated with running the business.
- *Investments* are cash used in or provided by the firm's investment activities.
- *Financing* is cash raised from taking on new debt or equity capital, or cash used to pay business expenses, past debts, or company dividends. We will discuss equity capital and dividends in Chapter 17.

statement of cash flows (cash flow statement)
A financial statement that reports cash receipts and cash disbursements related to a firm's three major activities: operations, investing, and financing.

Accountants analyze all changes in the firm's cash that have occurred from operating, investing, and financing in order to determine the firm's net cash position.[26] The statement of cash flows also gives the firm some insight into how to handle cash better so that no cash flow problems occur—such as having no cash on hand for immediate expenses.

Figure 16.9 shows a sample statement of cash flows, again using the example of Harvest Gold. As you can see, the statement of cash flows answers such questions as: How much cash came into the business from current operations, such as buying and selling goods and services? Did the firm use cash to buy stocks, bonds, or other investments (e.g., capital assets)? Did it sell some investments that brought in cash? How much money did the firm take in from issuing shares?

We analyze these and other financial transactions to see their effect on the firm's cash position. Managing cash flow can mean the success or failure of any business, which is why we analyze it in more depth in the next section.

THE NEED FOR CASH FLOW ANALYSIS

Cash flow, if not properly managed, can cause a business much concern. Understanding cash flow analysis is important and not difficult to understand. Let's say you borrow $100 from a friend to buy a used bike and agree to pay her back at the end of the week. You then sell the bike for $150 to someone else, who also agrees to pay you by the end of the week. Unfortunately, by the weekend, your buyer does not have the money as promised and says he will have to pay you next month. Meanwhile, your friend wants the $100 you agreed to pay her by the end of the week!

What seemed a great opportunity to make an easy $50 profit is now a cause for concern. You owe $100 and have no cash. What do you do? If you were a business, you might default on the loan and possibly go bankrupt, even though you had the potential for profits.

It's possible for a business to increase its sales and profits yet still suffer cash flow problems. **Cash flow** is simply the difference between cash coming in and cash going out of a business. Poor cash flow constitutes a major operating problem that many companies face. For example, Tesla is a fast-growing, innovative car manufacturer that has experienced much hype and growth over the past several years. Unfortunately, it also has faced some formidable cash flow problems that have raised eyebrows in the investment

cash flow
The difference between cash coming in and cash going out of a business.

FIGURE 16.9

SAMPLE HARVEST GOLD STATEMENT OF CASH FLOWS

1. Cash receipts from sales, commissions, fees, interest, and dividends. Cash payments for salaries, inventories, operating expenses, interest, and taxes.
2. Includes cash flows that are generated through a company's purchase or sale of long-term operational assets, investments in other companies, and its lending activities.
3. Cash inflows and outflows associated with the company's own equity transactions or its borrowing activities.

HARVEST GOLD
Statement of Cash Flows
For the Year Ended December 31, 2018

1. Cash flows from operating activities		
Cash received from customers	$700,000	
Cash paid to suppliers and employees	(567,000)	
Interest paid	(64,000)	
Income tax paid	(19,000)	
Interest and dividends received	2,000	
Net cash provided by operating activities		$52,000
2. Cash flows from investing activities		
Proceeds from sale of plant assets	$ 4,000	
Payments for purchase of equipment	(23,000)	
Net cash provided by investing activities		(19,000)
3. Cash flows from financing activities		
Proceeds from issuance of short-term debt	$ 2,000	
Payment of long-term debt	(8,000)	
Payment of dividends	(15,000)	
Net cash inflow from financing activities		(21,000)
Net change in cash and equivalents		$12,000
Cash balance (beginning of year)		(3,000)
Cash balance (end of year)		$15,000

Making ETHICAL DECISIONS

Would You Cook the Books?

You are the lone accountant employed by Fido's Feast, a small producer of premium dog food that sells directly online. The effects of the last recession are still plaguing the company. During that time, many of the company's customers became cost-conscious and switched to lower-cost brands. Fortunately, as the economy has improved many of the firm's long-standing customers are returning and things are looking up.

© Shutterstock/kitzcorner

The problem is the company's cash flow has suffered severely during the past few years, and the firm needs immediate funding to continue to pay its bills. The CEO has prepared a proposal to a local bank asking for a loan to keep the company afloat. Unfortunately, you know that Fido's financial statements for the past year will not show good results and expect the bank will not approve the loan on current financial information, even though the firm seems to be doing better.

Before you close the books for the end of the year, the CEO suggests you might "improve" the company's financial statements by treating the sales that were made at the beginning of January of the current year as if they were made in December of the past year.

You know that this is against the rules of the AcSB, and refuse to alter the information. The CEO warns that without the bank loan, the business is likely to close, and everyone will be out of a job. You know he's right, and also know that with the current economic downturn, finding a job will be tough for you and for others in the company. What are your alternatives? What are the likely consequences of each? What will you do?

community.[27] Cash flow problems are particularly difficult for small and seasonal businesses.[28] Accountants sometimes face tough ethical challenges in reporting the flow of funds into a business. Read the Making Ethical Decisions box to see how such an ethical dilemma can arise.

How do cash flow problems start? Often in order to meet the growing demands of customers, a business buys goods on credit (using no cash). If it then sells a large number of goods on credit (getting no cash), the company needs more credit from a lender (usually a bank) to pay its immediate bills. If a firm has reached its credit limit and can borrow no more, it has a severe cash flow problem. It has cash coming in at a later date, but no cash to pay current expenses. That problem could, unfortunately, force the firm into bankruptcy, even though sales may be strong—all because no cash was available when it was most needed. Cash flow analysis shows that a business' relationship with its lenders is critical to prevent cash flow problems.

© ImageShop/Corbis RF

Cash flow is the difference between money coming into and going out of a business. Careful cash flow management is a must for a business of any size, but it's particularly important for small businesses and for seasonal businesses like ski resorts. Have you read of any firms that were forced into bankruptcy because of cash flow problems?

Accountants can provide valuable insight and advice to businesses in managing cash flow, suggesting whether they need cash and how much. After the Progress Assessment, we'll see how accountants advise companies by analyzing the financial statements using ratios.

PROGRESS ASSESSMENT

- What are the key steps in preparing an income statement?
- What is the difference between revenue and income on the income statement?
- What is the connection between the income statement and the balance sheet?
- Why is the statement of cash flows important in evaluating a firm's operations?

LO5

Demonstrate the application of ratio analysis in reporting financial information.

Analyzing Financial Performance Using Ratios

The firm's financial statements—its balance sheet, income statement, and statement of cash flows—form the basis for financial analyses performed by accountants inside and outside the firm. **Ratio analysis** is the assessment of a firm's financial condition, using calculations and financial ratios developed from the firm's financial statements. Financial ratios are especially useful in comparing the company's performance to its financial objectives and to the performance of other firms in the industry.[29]

ratio analysis
The assessment of a firm's financial condition using calculations and interpretations of financial ratios developed from the firm's financial statements.

You probably are already familiar with the use of ratios in sports. For example, in basketball we express the number of shots made from the foul line with a ratio: shots made to shots attempted. In baseball we use the ratio number of hits to the number of at bats. You don't want to foul a player who shoots 85 percent from the foul line or pitch to a .375 hitter in a close game.

Whether ratios measure an athlete's performance or the financial health of a business, they provide valuable information. Financial ratios provide key insights into how a firm compares to other firms in its industry on liquidity, amount of debt, profitability, and overall business activity. Understanding and interpreting business ratios is important to sound financial analysis. Let's look briefly at four key types of ratios businesses use to measure financial performance.

Liquidity Ratios

As discussed earlier, *liquidity* refers to how fast an asset can be converted to cash. Liquidity ratios measure a company's ability to turn assets into cash to pay its short-term debts (liabilities that must be repaid within one year). These short-term debts are of particular importance to the firm's lenders who expect to be paid on time. Two key liquidity ratios are the current ratio and the acid-test ratio.

The *current ratio* is the ratio of a firm's current assets to its current liabilities. This information appears on the firm's balance sheet. Look back at Figure 16.6, Harvest Gold's balance sheet. The company lists current assets of \$600,000 and current liabilities of \$288,000, yielding a current ratio of 2.08. This means that Harvest Gold has \$2.08 of current assets for every \$1 of current liabilities. See the following calculation:

$$\text{Current ratio} = \frac{\text{Current assets}}{\text{Current liabilities}} = \frac{\$600{,}000}{\$288{,}000} = \$2.08$$

The question the current ratio attempts to answer is: "Is Harvest Gold financially secure for the short term (less than one year)?" It depends! Usually a company with a current ratio of 2 or better is considered a safe risk for lenders granting short-term credit, since it appears to be performing in line with market expectations. However, lenders will also compare Harvest Gold's current ratio to that of competing firms in its industry and to its current ratio from the previous year or so to note any significant changes.

Another key liquidity ratio, called the *acid-test* or *quick ratio,* measures the cash, marketable securities (such as stocks and bonds), and receivables of a firm, compared to its current liabilities. Again, this information is on a firm's balance sheet. See the following calculation:

$$\text{Acid-test ratio} = \frac{\text{Cash + Accounts Receivable + Marketable securities}}{\text{Current liabilities}}$$

$$= \frac{\$265{,}000}{\$288{,}000} = 0.92$$

This ratio is particularly important to firms with relatively large inventory, which can take longer than other current assets to convert into cash. It helps answer such questions as: "What if sales drop off and we can't sell our inventory? Can we still pay our short-term debt?" Though ratios vary among industries, an acid-test ratio between 0.5 and 1.0 is usually considered satisfactory, but bordering on cash flow problems. Therefore, Harvest Gold's acid-test ratio of 0.92 could raise concerns that perhaps the firm may not meet its short-term debt obligations and may have to go to a high-cost lender for financial assistance.

Leverage (Debt) Ratios

Leverage (debt) ratios measure the degree to which a firm relies on borrowed funds in its operations. A firm that takes on too much debt could experience problems repaying lenders or meeting promises made to shareholders. The *debt to owners' equity ratio* measures the degree to which the company is financed by borrowed funds that it must repay. Again, we can use data from Figure 16.6 to measure Harvest Gold's level of debt:

$$\text{Debt to owners' equity ratio} = \frac{\text{Total liabilities}}{\text{Owners' equity}} = \frac{\$613{,}000}{\$213{,}000} = 288\%$$

Anything above 100 percent shows that a firm has more debt than equity. With a ratio of 288 percent, Harvest Gold has a rather high degree of debt compared to its equity, which implies that lenders and investors may perceive the firm to be quite risky. However, *it is*

© ac productions/Blend Images LLC

Building luxury hotels, such as Chateau Frontenac in Quebec City, Quebec generally requires taking on a high degree of debt before the hotel ever earns its first dollar. Once opened, companies incur high daily expenses just to keep the business functioning efficiently. Do you see how monitoring the four key accounting ratios could be a major part of the accountants' jobs at hotels?

important to compare a firm's debt ratios to those of other firms in its industry because debt financing is more acceptable in some industries than in others. Comparisons with the same firm's past debt ratios can also identify possible trends within the firm or industry.

Profitability (Performance) Ratios

Profitability (performance) ratios measure how effectively a firm's managers are using its resources to achieve profits. Three of the more important ratios are earnings per share (EPS), return on sales, and return on equity.

EPS is a revealing ratio because earnings help stimulate the firm's growth and provide for shareholders' dividends. Companies report their quarterly EPS in two ways: basic and diluted. The *basic earnings per share (basic EPS) ratio* helps determine the amount of profit a company earned for each share of outstanding common stock. The *diluted earnings per share (diluted EPS) ratio* measures the amount of profit earned for each share of outstanding common stock, but also considers stock options, warrants, preferred stock, and convertible debt securities the firm can convert into common stock. For simplicity's sake, we will compute only the basic EPS for Harvest Gold:

$$\text{Basic earnings per share} = \frac{\text{Net income after taxes}}{\text{Number of common stock shares outstanding}}$$

$$= \frac{\$49{,}000}{\$1{,}000{,}000 \text{ shares}} = \$0.049 \text{ per share}$$

Another reliable indicator of performance is *return on sales,* which tells us whether the firm is doing as well as its competitors in generating income from sales. We calculate it by comparing net income to total sales. Harvest Gold's return on sales is 7 percent, a figure we must measure against similar numbers for competing firms to judge Harvest Gold's performance.

$$\text{Return on sales} = \frac{\text{Net income after tax}}{\text{Net sales}} = \frac{\$49{,}000}{\$700{,}000} = 7\%$$

The higher the risk of failure or loss in an industry, the higher the return investors expect on their investment as they expect to be well compensated for shouldering such odds. *Return on equity* indirectly measures risk by telling us how much a firm earned for each dollar invested by its owners. We calculate it by comparing a company's net income to its total owners' equity. Harvest Gold's return on equity looks reasonably sound since some believe anything over 15 percent is considered a reasonable return:

$$\text{Return on equity} = \frac{\text{Net income after tax}}{\text{Total owners' equity}} = \frac{\$49{,}000}{\$213{,}000} = 23\%$$

Remember that profits help companies like Harvest Gold grow. That is why profitability ratios are such closely watched measurements of company growth and management performance.

Activity Ratios

Converting the firm's inventory to profits is a key function of management. Activity ratios tell us how effectively management is turning over inventory.

The *inventory turnover ratio* measures the speed with which inventory moves through a firm and gets converted into sales. Idle inventory sitting in a warehouse earns nothing and costs money. The more efficiently a firm sells or turns its inventory, the higher its revenue. Harvest Gold's inventory turnover ratio is:

$$\text{Inventory turnover} = \frac{\text{Costs of goods sold}}{\text{Average inventory}} = \frac{\$410{,}000}{\$215{,}000} = 1.9 \text{ times}$$

The average inventory is calculated by adding the beginning and ending inventories and dividing by two.

A lower-than-average inventory turnover ratio often indicates obsolete merchandise on hand or poor buying practices. A higher-than-average ratio may signal lost sales because of inadequate stock. Of course, like other ratios, rates of inventory turnover vary from industry to industry.

Managers need to be aware of proper inventory control and anticipate inventory turnover to ensure proper performance. For example, have you ever worked as a food server in a restaurant? How many times did your employer expect you to *turn over* a table (keep changing customers at the table) in an evening? The more times a table turns, the higher the return to the owner.

Accountants and other finance professionals consider other ratios in addition to the ones we have discussed to learn more about a firm's financial condition. To review where the accounting information in ratio analysis comes from, see Figure 16.10 for a quick reference of the ratios we have discussed. Remember, financial analysis begins where the accounting statements end.

Inventory turnover is critical to just about any business, particularly restaurants that serve perishable items and that must turn over tables to keep the flow of food moving and profits up. (They are limited in their earnings potential by the number of seats they have.) Can you think of other businesses that need to watch their inventory turnover closely?

FIGURE 16.10

ACCOUNTS IN THE BALANCE SHEET AND INCOME STATEMENT

BALANCE SHEET ACCOUNTS			INCOME STATEMENT ACCOUNTS			
Assets	**Liabilities**	**Owners' Equity**	**Revenues**	**Cost of Goods Sold**	**Expenses**	
Cash	Accounts payable	Capital stock	Sales revenue	Cost of buying goods	Wages	Interest
Accounts receivable	Notes payable	Retained earnings	Rental revenue	Cost of storing goods	Rent	Donations
Inventory	Bonds payable	Common stock	Commissions revenue		Repairs	Licences
Investments	Taxes payable	Treasury stock	Commissions revenue		Repairs	Licences
Equipment			Royalty revenue		Travel	Fees
Land					Insurance	Supplies
Buildings					Utilities	Advertising
Motor vehicles					Entertainment	Taxes
Goodwill					Storage	

We hope that you can see from this chapter that there is more to accounting than meets the eye. It can be fascinating and it is critical to the firm's operations. It is worth saying once more that, as the language of business, accounting is a worthwhile language to learn.

PROGRESS ASSESSMENT

- What is the primary purpose of performing ratio analysis using a firm's financial statements?
- Describe the four main categories of financial ratios.
- Why is EPS a revealing ratio?

SUMMARY

LO1 **Describe the role that accounting and financial information play for a business and for its stakeholders.**

Financial information is critical to the growth and development of an organization.

What is accounting?

Accounting is the recording, classifying, summarizing, and interpreting of financial events that affect an organization. The methods used to record and summarize accounting data into reports are called an accounting system.

What role does accounting play?

Accounting provides the information to measure a firm's financial condition in support of managing a business.

LO2 **Identify the different disciplines within the accounting profession.**

The accounting profession covers five major areas: managerial accounting, financial accounting, auditing, tax accounting, and governmental and not-for-profit accounting.

How does managerial accounting differ from financial accounting?

Managerial accounting provides information (often of segments of a business) for planning and control purposes to managers within the firm to assist them in decision making. Financial accounting provides information in the form of the three basic financial statements to managers and external users of data such as creditors and lenders.

What is the difference between a private accountant and a public accountant?

A public accountant provides services for a fee to a variety of companies, whereas a private accountant works for a single company. Private and public accountants do essentially the same things, with the exception of independent audits. Private accountants do perform internal audits, but only public accountants supply independent audits.

LO3 **List the steps in the accounting cycle, distinguish between accounting and bookkeeping, and explain how computers are used in accounting.**

Many people confuse bookkeeping and accounting.

What are the six steps of the accounting cycle?

As illustrated in Figure 16.5, the six steps of the accounting cycle are (1) analyzing documents, (2) recording information into journals, (3) posting that information into ledgers, (4) developing a trial balance, (5) preparing financial statements (the balance sheet, income statement, and statement of cash flows), and (6) analyzing financial statements.

What is the difference between bookkeeping and accounting?

Bookkeeping is part of accounting and includes the mechanical part of recording data. Accounting also includes classifying, summarizing, interpreting, and reporting data to management.

How can computers help accountants?

Computers can record and analyze data and provide financial reports. Software can continuously analyze and test accounting systems to be sure they are functioning properly (e.g., the accounting equation is always in balance when recording each transaction). Computers can help decision making by providing appropriate information, but they cannot themselves make good financial decisions independently. Accounting applications and creativity are still human traits.

LO4 **Explain how the major financial statements differ.**

The major financial statements provide different information.

What is a balance sheet?

A balance sheet reports the financial position of a firm on a particular day. The fundamental accounting equation used to prepare the balance sheet is Assets = Liabilities + Owners' equity.

Explain how the major financial statements differ.

What is an income statement?

An income statement reports revenues, costs, and expenses for a specific period of time (e.g., for the year ended December 31, 2019). The formulas used in preparing the income statement are:

Revenue − Cost of goods sold = Gross margin

Gross margin − Operating expenses = Net income before taxes

Net income before taxes − Taxes = Net income (or Net loss)

What is a statement of cash flows?

Cash flow is the difference between cash receipts (money coming in) and cash disbursements (money going out). The statement of cash flows reports cash receipts and disbursements related to the firm's major activities: operations, investing, and financing.

What are LIFO and FIFO?

LIFO and FIFO are methods of transferring a cost of inventory sold to the income statement. FIFO means first in, first out; LIFO means last in, first out. The method an accountant uses to value the transfer, FIFO or LIFO, can affect a firm's net income.

LO5 **Demonstrate the application of ratio analysis in reporting financial information.**

Financial ratios are a key part of analyzing financial information.

What are the four key categories of ratios?

There are four key categories of ratios: liquidity ratios, leverage (debt) ratios, profitability (performance) ratios, and activity ratios.

What is the major value of ratio analysis to the firm?

Ratio analysis provides the firm with information about its financial position in key areas for comparison to similar firms in its industry and to its own past performance.

KEY TERMS

CAREER EXPLORATION

If you are interested in pursuing a career in finance, here are a few to consider. Find out about the tasks performed, skills needed, pay, and opportunity outlook in these fields through Internet sites that include the Government of Canada Job Bank, Workopolis, Monster, CareerBuilder, Glassdoor, and Indeed, as well as through the Career Centre at your school.

- **Auditor—**an accountant who is responsible for evaluating the validity and reliability of a company's financial statements.[30]
- **Bookkeeper—**an individual who records business transactions.
- **Chartered Professional Accountant (CPA)—**an accountant who has met education and work experience requirements, and has been certified by the Chartered Professional Accountants of Canada.
- **Forensic accountant—**an accountant who focuses on fraudulent activity.
- **Tax examiner—**an account who ensures that federal, provincial, and municipal governments get tax money due from businesses and citizens by reviewing tax returns, conducting audits, and identifying taxes owed.

CRITICAL THINKING

1. In business, hundreds of documents are received or created every day, so you can appreciate the valuable role an accountant plays. Can you see why most businesses hire people to do this work? Would it be worth the owner's time to do all the paperwork? Can you understand why most accountants find it easier to do this work on a computer?
2. As a potential investor in a firm or perhaps the buyer of a business, would it be advisable for you to evaluate the company's financial statements? Why or why not? What key information would you seek from a firm's financial statements?
3. Why must accounting reports be prepared according to specific procedures (e.g., IFRS)? Should we allow businesses some flexibility or creativity in preparing financial statements? Why or why not?
4. What value do financial ratios offer investors in reviewing the financial performance of a firm? Why is it important to remember financial ratios can differ from industry to industry?

DEVELOPING CAREER SKILLS

Key: ● **Team** ★ **Analytic** ▲ **Communication** ⊡ **Technology**

▲★ 1. Contact an accountant at a firm in your area, or talk with one in your school's accounting department. Ask what challenges, changes, and opportunities he or she foresees in the accounting profession in the next five years. List the forecasts on a sheet of paper and then compare them with the information gathered by your classmates.

★▲ 2. Place yourself in the role of a small-business consultant. One of your clients, Be Pretty Fashions, is considering opening two new stores. The fashion industry experiences continuous style changes. Prepare a formal draft memo to Be Pretty Fashions explaining the difficulties a firm experiences when it encounters the cash flow problems that typically occur in this industry. Think of a business option that Be Pretty Fashions could try to avoid cash flow problems.

★▲ **3.** You are a new board member for an emerging not-for-profit organization hoping to attract new donors. Contributors want to know how efficiently not-for-profit organizations use their donations. Unfortunately, your fellow board members see little value in financial reporting and analysis and believe the good works of the organization speak for themselves. Prepare a fact sheet convincing the board of the need for effective financial reporting with arguments about why it would help the organization's fundraising goals.

□★ **4.** Obtain the most recent annual report for a publicly traded Canadian company of your choice. (Hint: You can visit the company's website or SEDAR.) Using data from the annual report, try your hand at computing financial ratios, such as the current ratio, debt to owners' equity ratio, and return on sales for the firm. Next, obtain an annual report of one of the company's competitors and compute the same ratios for that company. What did you find?

□★ **5.** Obtain the most recent annual report for a publicly traded Canadian company of your choice. (Hint: You can visit the company's website or SEDAR.) Look over the firm's financial statements and see how they match the information in this chapter. Read the auditor's opinion (usually at the end of the report) and evaluate what you think are the most important conclusions of the auditors.

ANALYZING MANAGEMENT DECISIONS

Getting Through the Hard Times at Hard Rock

In the mid-1990s, the theme-dining business seemed like a path lined with gold. With regularity, celebrity stargazers, enthusiastic press from around the globe, and hungry customers gathered at the openings of theme restaurants such as Planet Hollywood and Motown Cafe. Unfortunately, the situation changed. In the late 1990s and early 2000s, Planet Hollywood filed for bankruptcy protection and Motown Cafe closed units across the country. Consumer boredom, a slowing economy, and a saturated market were blamed.

The changing "entertainment" market raised eyebrows at the granddaddy of theme restaurants, the Hard Rock Cafe (HRC). HRC knew that its market position was shaky due to increased competition and shifting consumer attitudes. The company also felt growing financial pressures and speculated that a change in financial management might be needed. HRC had operated with a traditional, competent accounting department that ensured that the company paid its bills, had money left at the end of the day, and could state how much it was earning. The problem was that HRC lacked the ability to analyze its financial information fully and use it to improve operations. To address these concerns, the company recruited a new CFO and dedicated itself to changing the financial reporting and information structure at the company.

Management believed that it had a tremendous undervalued asset—a premium global brand. The company dedicated itself to protecting and expanding that asset. However, it was evident that without revenue, brand loyalty did not matter. The company's CFO was astonished to find that HRC sold $180 million per year in merchandise (primarily its well-known T-shirts) in addition to food. Yet, there was no exact explanation how individual items contributed to the firm's profit. As a result, the decision was made to change the company's accounting and financial management systems.

To begin, the company piloted a food and beverage management system to track usage and item profitability. This system included information such as daily and seasonal buying patterns, profitability of one menu versus another, average weekly guest counts per restaurant, and specific cost of sales and profit margins per item. The company then shifted the responsibility of the firm's accountants. Instead of being responsible for profit-and-loss statements for a certain number of restaurants, company accountants now were responsible for one major financial category only, such as cost of goods sold, for all of the company's operations. The objective was to compile companywide information for sound financial decision making.

Hard Rock Cafe also broke down the barriers that existed between the finance and accounting departments as well as operations, merchandising, and marketing. Today, financial information is shared directly with managers who can execute the recommendations at the restaurant level. There are now over 192 locations, which include restaurants, hotels, casinos, and live music venues, in 60 countries around the world. It's hard to believe that it all started with the search for a good burger.

Sources: "Hard Rock History," Hard Rock Cafe International, Inc., accessed April 15, 2015, http://www.hardrock.com/corporate/history.aspx; "Rank Is Betting on Another Good Year," *Birmingham (UK) Post,* March 1, 2003, 15; Jon Griffin, "Rank Is Backing a Winner," *Evening Mail (UK)*, February 28, 2003, 26; and Larry Bleiberg, "Cafe Quest Has Retiree on a Roll," *Dallas Morning News,* March 15, 2000, 12G.

Discussion Questions

1. Why is it important for Hard Rock Cafe to know how different products contribute financially to overall company profits?
2. Do you think that Hard Rock Cafe's focus on improved financial reporting helped its company planning capabilities? How?
3. In terms of accounting principles, what would you need to remember when analyzing the financial performance of the Hard Rock Cafe, a U.S. business, to the Keg Steakhouse and Bar, a Canadian business?

CHAPTER 17

Financial Management

LEARNING OBJECTIVES

After you have read and studied this chapter, you should be able to:

LO1 Explain the role and responsibilities of financial managers.

LO2 Outline the financial planning process, and explain the three key budgets in the financial plan.

LO3 Explain why firms need operating funds.

LO4 Identify and describe different sources of short-term financing.

LO5 Identify and describe different sources of long-term financing.

PROFILE

GETTING TO KNOW: KATHY WALLER, EXECUTIVE VICE PRESIDENT/CFO, COCA-COLA

As executive vice president, chief financial officer (CFO), and president, Enabling Services, of The Coca-Cola Company, Kathy Waller knows a thing or two about the challenges of the beverage industry. Coca-Cola is the world's largest beverage company, with operations in over 200 countries where it produces more than 500 different brands. The company employs 39 000 people worldwide (if you include bottling operations, the Coca-Cola system employs almost 700 000). This makes Coca-Cola one of the top 10 employers globally. Throughout the world, Coke products are sold at 24 million retail customer outlets. While these statistics are impressive, think of the complications of dealing in a market this size where different countries' currencies, tax laws, economic trends, and consumer incomes vary significantly. Financial management is extremely challenging for even the smallest business let alone a company the size of Coca-Cola that has such a wide range of consumers, customers, and products. Well, welcome to her world.

Waller is responsible for leading Coca-Cola's Global Finance organization. She also is the key company representative dealing with Coke's

Courtesy of Kathy Waller and The Coca-Cola Company

Waller has a degree in history and an MBA concentrating in accounting and finance. After achieving her MBA, she worked for Deloitte, Haskins and Sells, a major public accounting firm, until deciding to transfer home to Atlanta. Shortly after transferring home, she joined Coca-Cola in 1987 as a senior accountant in the company's accounting research department.

Over her 30 years at Coke, Waller has worked in several different positions including as principal accountant for the Northeast Europe/Africa Group, financial services manager for the Africa group, chief of internal audit, and controller. In 2009, her training as a CPA came in handy. In 2014, she was promoted to executive vice president and CFO. And in 2017, she also became president of Enabling Services.

In addition to her CFO duties, Waller serves on the board of directors of Delta Air Lines and Monster Energy Company and is a member of the board of trustees of Spelman College, the University of Rochester (her alma mater), and the Woodruff Arts Center. She's also committed to using her 30-plus years of experience in business to assist women to advance in their careers. For example, she formerly served as the founding chair of Coca-Cola's Women's Leadership Council and was instrumental in developing Coke's highly successful Women in Leadership Global Program. She also serves on the board of Catalyst, a leading not-for-profit organization whose mission is to expand opportunities for women. Kathy Waller's advice to both women and men is to "dream, and dream big. There are no obstacles in your dreams so everything is possible and one day, you may find your dreams are within your reach. You never know what can happen until you try." She certainly can attest to what can happen.

Risk and uncertainty clearly define the role of financial management. In this chapter, you'll explore the role of finance in business. We'll discuss the challenges and the tools top managers like Kathy Waller use to attain financial stability and growth.

investors, lenders, and financial rating agencies. But her job doesn't stop there. As CFO she oversees Coke's tax, audit, mergers and acquisitions, accounting and financial controls, reporting and financial analysis, real estate, and risk management. As president of Enabling Services, she has responsibility for other key governance areas, specifically Global Technical and Integrated Services (Coke's global shared services operations), which includes procurement as well as employee services. Her job is to take all the varied and complicated pieces of Coke's financial puzzle and create a budget and financial plan that puts the company on the right financial path for the current year and the foreseeable future. She must also ensure the business has sufficient funds to invest in capital assets, brands, and/or other businesses to deliver the company's long-term growth targets. Waller's role is varied, but she would say she loves the challenge of putting all the pieces of the puzzle together.

Sources: "Our Company: Kathy N. Waller," The Coca-Cola Company, accessed May 14, 2018, https://www.coca-colacompany.com/our-company/senior-functional-leadership-kathy-n-waller; Monica Watrous, "Coca-Cola Transforms Leadership Team," *Food Business News,* March 23, 2017; and Christopher Seward, "Coca-Cola Names Kathy Waller as CFO," *Atlanta Journal Constitution,* April 24, 2014.

LO1

Explain the role and responsibilities of financial managers.

The Role of Finance and Financial Managers

finance
The function in a business that acquires funds for the firm and manages them within the firm.

financial management
The job of managing a firm's resources to meet its goals and objectives.

financial managers
Managers who examine the financial data prepared by accountants and recommend strategies for improving the financial performance of the firm.

The goal of this chapter is to answer two major questions: "What is finance?" and "What do financial managers do?" **Finance** is the function in a business that acquires funds for the firm and manages them within the firm. Finance activities include preparing budgets; completing cash flow analysis; and planning for the expenditure of funds on assets such as plant, equipment, and machinery. **Financial management** is the job of managing a firm's resources to meet its goals and objectives. Without a carefully calculated financial plan and sound financial management, a firm has little chance for survival, regardless of its products or marketing effectiveness. Let's briefly review the roles of accountants and financial managers.

We can compare an accountant to a skilled laboratory technician who takes blood samples and other measures of a person's health and writes the findings on a health report (in business, this process is the preparation of financial statements). A financial manager is like the doctor who interprets the report and makes recommendations that will improve the patient's health. In short, **financial managers** examine the financial data prepared by accountants and recommend strategies for improving the financial performance of the firm.

Clearly, financial managers can make sound financial decisions only if they understand accounting information. Think of Kathy Waller of Coca-Cola whom we met in the chapter opener and how she used her accounting background to grow in her career at Coca-Cola. That's why we examined accounting in Chapter 16. Similarly, since accounting and finance go together like a peanut butter and jelly sandwich, a good accountant needs to understand finance. In large and medium-sized organizations, both the accounting and finance functions are generally under the control of a chief financial officer (CFO). A CFO is generally the second-highest paid person in an organization and CFOs often advance to the top job of CEO.[1] However, financial management could also be in the hands of a person who serves as company treasurer or vice president of finance.[2] A comptroller is the chief *accounting* officer.

Figure 17.1 highlights a financial manager's tasks. As you can see, two key responsibilities are to obtain funds and to effectively control the use of those funds. Controlling funds includes managing the firm's cash, credit accounts (accounts receivable), and inventory. Finance is a critical activity in both profit-seeking and non-profit organizations.[3] The role of advising top management on financial matters has become even more important in recent years as risk has increased. Online Supplement 2, an online supplement to this text, is devoted to the subject of financial risk. Visit Connect to learn more about managing risk.

Finance is important no matter what the firm's size. As you remember from Chapter 7, financing a small business is essential if a firm expects to survive its important first five years. But the need for careful financial management remains a challenge that a business, large or small, private or public, must face throughout its existence.[4] For example, the Canadian divisions of General Motors and Chrysler received $13.7 billion in loans from the federal and Ontario governments because of severe financial problems.[5]

■ FIGURE 17.1

WHAT FINANCIAL MANAGERS DO

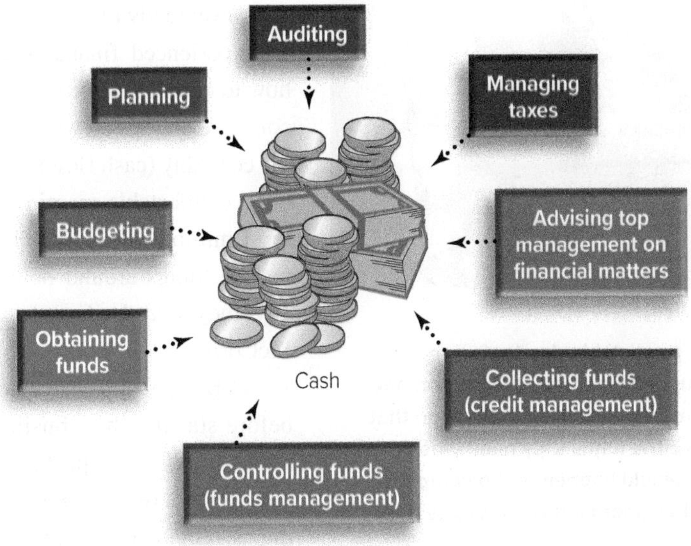

The Value of Understanding Finance

Three of the most common reasons a firm fails financially are:

1. Undercapitalization (insufficient funds to run a business)
2. Poor control over cash flow
3. Inadequate expense control

You can see all three in the following story.

Two friends, Elizabeth Bertani and Pat Sherwood, started a company called Parsley Patch on what can best be described as a shoestring budget. It began when Bertani prepared salt-free seasonings for her husband, who was on a no-salt diet. Her friend Sherwood thought the seasonings were good enough to sell. Bertani agreed, and Parsley Patch Inc. was born. The business began with an investment of $5000 that was rapidly depleted on a logo and label design. Bertani and Sherwood quickly learned the need for capital in getting a business going. Eventually, they invested more than $100,000 of their own money to keep the business from being undercapitalized.

Everything started well, and hundreds of gourmet shops adopted the product line. But when sales failed to meet expectations, the women decided the health-food market offered more potential because salt-free seasonings were a natural for people with restricted diets. The choice was a good one. Sales soared, approaching $30,000 a month. Still, the company earned no profits.

© B. O'Kane/Alamy

Michael Miller overhauled the underperforming Goodwill Industries operation in his area by treating the non-profit like a for-profit business. He trimmed operating expenses; compared sales by store, closing weak outlets and opening new ones in better locations; and cut distribution costs. Sales soared from $4 million to over $135 million, eliminating the need for outside funding.

© Shutterstock / Tyler Olson

Most businesses have predictable day-to-day needs, like the need to buy supplies, pay for utilities, and pay employees. Financial management is the function that helps ensure firms have the funds they need when they need them. What would happen to the company providing the work in this photo if it couldn't pay its employees?

Bertani and Sherwood weren't trained in monitoring cash flow or in controlling expenses. In fact, they had been told not to worry about costs, and they hadn't. They eventually hired a certified public accountant and an experienced financial manager, who taught them how to compute the costs of their products, and how to control expenses as well as cash moving in and out of the company (cash flow). Soon Parsley Patch was earning a comfortable margin on operations that ran close to $1 million a year. Luckily, the two owners were able to turn things around before it was too late. Eventually, they sold the firm to spice and seasonings giant McCormick.[6]

If Bertani and Sherwood had understood finance before starting their business, they might have been able to avoid the problems they encountered. The key word here is *understood.* Financial understanding is crucial to anyone who wants to start a business, invest in stocks and bonds, or plan a retirement plan. To put it simply, finance and accounting are two areas everyone in business needs to study and understand. Since we discussed accounting in Chapter 16, let's look more closely at what financial management is all about.

What is Financial Management?

Financial managers are responsible for paying a company's bills at the appropriate time and for collecting overdue payments to make sure the company does not lose too much money to bad debts (people or firms that do not pay their bills). Therefore, finance functions, such as buying merchandise on credit (accounts payable) and collecting payments from customers (accounts receivable), are key components of the financial manager's job (see Figure 17.1). While these functions are vital to all types of businesses, they are particularly critical to small and medium-sized businesses, which typically have smaller cash or credit cushions than large corporations.

It's also essential that financial managers stay abreast of changes or opportunities in finance, such as changes in tax laws, since taxes represent an outflow of cash from the business. Financial managers must also analyze the tax implications of managerial decisions to minimize the taxes the business must pay. Usually a member of a firm's finance department, the internal auditor, also checks the journals, ledgers, and financial statements the accounting department prepares, to make sure all transactions are in accordance with the international financial reporting standards (IFRS).[7] (Recall the brief discussion on IFRS in Chapter 16.) Without such audits, accounting statements would be less reliable. Therefore, it's important that internal auditors be objective and critical of any improprieties or deficiencies noted in their evaluations. Thorough internal audits assist the firm in financial planning, which we'll look at next.[8]

Financial Planning

LO2

Outline the financial planning process, and explain the three key budgets in the financial plan.

Financial planning means analyzing short-term and long-term money flows to and from a firm. One of the basic problems that financial managers face is how to determine the value today of cash flows that are expected in the future. This requires assessing the **time value of money**, which refers to the fact that a dollar in hand today is worth more than a dollar promised at some time in the future.[9] This is because you could earn interest on the dollar, for example, while you wait for a future dollar. Financial managers must evaluate this trade off between dollars today and dollars at some future time.

time value of money
A dollar in hand today is worth more than a dollar promised at some time in the future.

When considering money flows, financial managers also assess the costs and risks of accessing money whether it is from creditors (e.g., a loan through a financial institution) or from selling investors financial instruments, such as bonds and stocks (to be discussed later in this chapter.) This assessment includes understanding the **risk-return tradeoff**, which states that the level of return to be earned from an investment should increase as the level of risk increases and vice versa.[10] Understanding the risk-return tradeoff of all stakeholders contributes to stronger short-term and long-term finance decision making.

risk-return tradeoff
The principle that the level of return to be earned from an investment should increase as the level of risk increases and vice versa.

The overall objective of financial planning is to optimize the firm's profitability and make the best use of its money. Financial planning has three steps: (1) forecasting a firm's short-term and long-term financial needs; (2) developing budgets to meet those needs; and (3) establishing financial control to see whether the company is achieving its goals (see Figure 17.2). Let's look at each step and the role it plays in improving the organization's financial health.

Forecasting Financial Needs

Forecasting is an important part of any firm's financial plan. A **short-term forecast** predicts revenues, costs, and expenses for a period of one year or less. Part of the short-term forecast may be a **cash flow forecast**, which predicts the cash inflows and outflows in future periods, usually months or quarters. The inflows and outflows of cash recorded in the cash flow forecast are based on expected sales revenues and on various costs and expenses incurred, as well as when they are due for payment. The company's sales forecast estimates projected sales for a particular period. A business often uses its past financial statements as a basis for projecting expected sales and various costs and expenses.

short-term forecast
Forecast that predicts revenues, costs, and expenses for a period of one year or less.

cash flow forecast
Forecast that predicts the cash inflows and outflows in future periods, usually months or quarters.

A **long-term forecast** predicts revenues, costs, and expenses for a period longer than one year, and sometimes as long as 5 or 10 years. This forecast plays a crucial part in the company's long-term strategic plan, which asks questions such as these: "What business are we in? Should we be in it five years from now? How much money should we invest in technology and new plant and equipment over the next decade? Will we have cash available to meet long-term obligations?" Innovations in web-based software help financial managers address these long-term forecasting questions.[11]

long-term forecast
Forecast that predicts revenues, costs, and expenses for a period longer than one year, and sometimes as far as five or ten years into the future.

The long-term financial forecast gives top management, as well as operations managers, some sense of the income or profit of different strategic plans.[12] It also helps in preparing company budgets.

■ FIGURE 17.2

FINANCIAL PLANNING

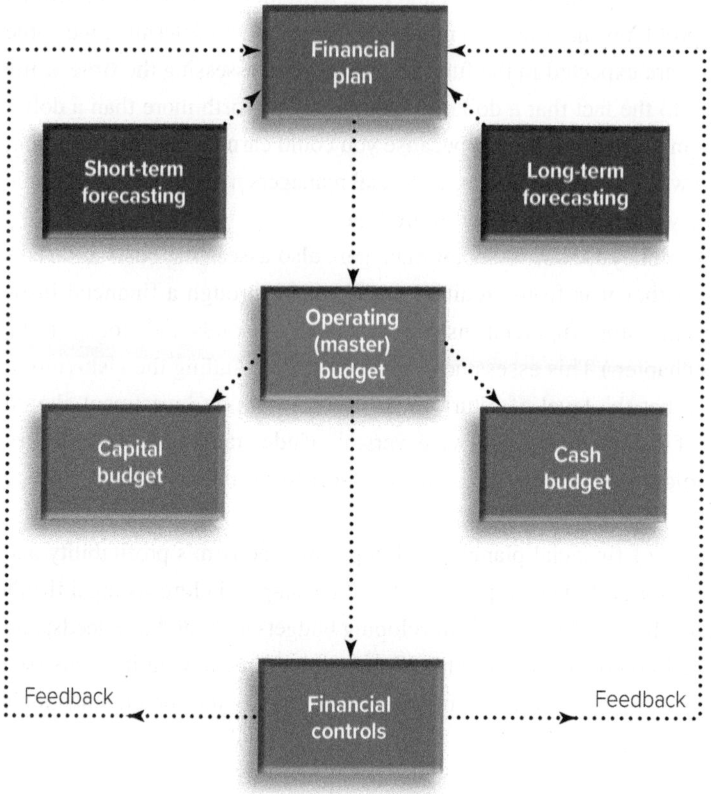

© AndrisTkachenko/iStock/Thinkstock

Special processing equipment turns an average potato into the chips and fries we consume. The firm's capital budget is the financial tool that controls business spending for expensive assets such as this processing equipment. Such major assets are referred to as capital assets or property, plant, and equipment. What items would be in your school's capital budget?

Working with the Budget Process

A **budget** sets forth management's expectations for revenues and, on the basis of those expectations, allocates the use of specific resources throughout the firm. As a financial plan, it depends heavily on the accuracy of a firm's balance sheet, income statement, statement of cash flows, and short-term and long-term financial forecasts. These all need to be as accurate as possible. To effectively prepare budgets, financial managers must take their forecasting responsibilities seriously. A budget becomes the primary guide for the firm's financial operations and expected financial needs.

There are usually several types of budgets established in a firm's financial plan. Three of the most common are:

- A capital budget.
- A cash budget.
- An operating or master budget.

A **capital budget** forecasts a firm's spending plans for major asset purchases that often require large sums of money, like property, buildings, and equipment.

A **cash budget** estimates cash inflows and outflows during a particular period, like a month or a quarter. It helps managers anticipate borrowing needs, debt repayment, operating expenses, and short-term investments, and is often the last budget prepared.[13] A sample cash budget for our restaurant example, Harvest Gold, is provided in Figure 17.3.

The **operating (master) budget** ties together the firm's other budgets and summarizes the business' proposed financial activities. More formally, it is presented to all the company's managers and estimates the costs and expenses needed to run the business, given all projected revenues. The firm's spending on supplies, travel, rent, technology, advertising, and salaries is determined in the operating budget, generally the most detailed budget a firm prepares.

Financial planning obviously plays an important role in the firm's operations and often determines what long-term investments it makes, when it will need specific funds, and how it will generate them. Once a company forecasts its short-term and long-term

budget
A financial plan that sets forth management's expectations, and, on the basis of those expectations, allocates the use of specific resources throughout the firm.

capital budget
A budget that forecasts a firm's spending plans for major asset purchases that often require large sums of money, like property, buildings, and equipment.

FIGURE 17.3

A SAMPLE CASH BUDGET FOR HARVEST GOLD

HARVEST GOLD Monthly Cash Budget	January	February	March
Sales forecast	$50,000	$45,000	$40,000
Collections			
Cash sales (20%)		$ 9,000	$ 8,000
Credit sales (80% of past month)		$40,000	$36,000
Monthly cash collection		$49,000	$44,000
Payments schedule			
Supplies and material		$11,000	$10,000
Salaries		12,000	12,000
Direct labour		9,000	9,000
Taxes		3,000	3,000
Other expenses		7,000	5,000
Monthly cash payments		$42,000	$39,000
Cash budget			
Cash flow		$7,000	$ 5,000
Beginning cash		−1,000	6,000
Total cash		$ 6,000	$11,000
Less minimum cash balance		−6,000	−6,000
Excess cash to market securities		$ 0	$ 5,000
Loans needed for minimum balance		0	0

cash budget
A budget that estimates a firm's cash inflows and outflows during a particular period (e.g. monthly or quarterly).

financial needs (Step 1) and compiles budgets to show how it will allocate funds (Step 2), the final step in financial planning is to establish financial controls (Step 3). Before we talk about those, however, Figure 17.4 challenges you to check your personal financial planning skill by developing a monthly budget for You Incorporated. In addition, you can review Appendix B—Managing Personal Finances—to learn more about financial planning.

FIGURE 17.4

YOU INCORPORATED MONTHLY BUDGET

In Chapter 16 you compiled a sample balance sheet for You Inc. Now, let's develop a monthly budget for You Inc. Be honest and think of everything that needs to be included for an accurate monthly budget for You! Much like a small business, when putting the monthly budget together, remember that the norm is to overestimate income and underestimate expenses. Often you need to revisit the budget a number of times before finalizing the numbers as you try to balance the income with the expenses.

	Expected	Actual	Difference
Monthly income			
Wages (net pay after taxes)			
Savings account withdrawals			
Family support			
Loans			
Other sources			
Total monthly income			
Monthly expenses			
Fixed expenses			
Rent or mortgage			
Car payment			
Life insurance			
Tuition or fees			
Other fixed expenses			
Subtotal of fixed expenses			
Variable expenses			
Food			
Clothing			
Entertainment			
Transportation			
Cell phone			
Utilities			
Publications			
Internet connection			
Cable television			
Other expenses			
Subtotal of variable expenses			
Total expenses			
Total monthly income – Total expenses = Cash on hand or Cash deficit			

Establishing Financial Controls

Financial control is a process in which a firm periodically compares its actual revenues, costs, and expenses with its budget. Most companies hold at least monthly financial reviews as a way to ensure financial control. Such control procedures help managers identify variances to the financial plan and allow them to take corrective action if necessary. Financial controls also help reveal which accounts, which departments, and which people are varying from the financial plan. Finance managers can judge whether these variances are legitimate and thereby merit adjustments to the plan. Shifts in the economy or unexpected global events can also alter financial plans. For example, a slowdown in the housing market or a slowdown in the global economy can cause many companies to consider adjusting their financial plans.[14]

operating (master) budget
The budget that ties together all of a firm's other budgets and summarizes the business' proposed financial activities.

financial control
A process in which a firm periodically compares its actual revenues, costs, and expenses with its projected ones.

PROGRESS ASSESSMENT

- Name three finance functions important to the firm's overall operations and performance.
- What are the three primary financial problems that cause firms to fail?
- How do short-term and long-term financial forecasts differ?
- What is the purpose of preparing budgets in an organization?
- Identify three different types of budgets and state the purpose of each budget.

The Need for Operating Funds

LO3

Explain why firms need operating funds

In business, the need for funds never seems to end. That is why sound financial management is essential to all businesses. And like our personal financial needs, the capital needs of a business change over time. Remember the example of Parsley Patch to see why a small business' financial requirements can shift considerably. The same is true for large corporations such as The Bank of Nova Scotia, Apple, and Nike when they venture into new-product areas or new markets. Virtually all organizations have operational needs for which they need funds. Key areas include:

- Managing day-to-day needs of the business.
- Controlling credit operations.
- Acquiring needed inventory.
- Making capital expenditures.

Let's look carefully at the financial needs of these key areas, which affect both the smallest and the largest of businesses.

Managing Day-to-Day Needs of the Business

If workers expect to be paid on Friday, they do not want to wait until Monday for their paycheques. If tax payments are due on the 15th of the month, the government expects the money on time. If the payment on a business loan is due on the 30th of this month, the lender doesn't mean the 1st of next month. As you can see, funds have to be available to meet the daily operational costs of a business.

Financial managers must ensure that funds are available to meet daily cash needs without compromising the firm's opportunities to invest money for its future. As mentioned earlier, money has *time value.*[15] In other words, if someone offered to give you $200 today or one year from today, you would benefit by taking the $200 today. Why? It's very simple. You could invest the $200 you receive today and over a year's time it would grow. The same is true in business; the interest a firm gains on its investments is important in maximizing the profit it will gain. That's why financial managers often try to minimize cash expenditures to free up funds for investment in interest-bearing accounts. They suggest the company pay its bills as late as possible (unless a cash discount is available for early payment). They also advise companies to try to collect what's owed them as fast as possible, to maximize the investment potential of the firm's funds.[16] Unfortunately, collecting funds as fast as possible can be particularly challenging especially during times when the economy slows down. Efficient cash management is particularly important to small firms since their access to capital is much more limited than larger businesses.

Controlling Credit Operations

Financial managers know that in today's highly competitive business environment, making credit available helps keep current customers happy and attracts new ones. Credit for customers can be especially important during tough financial times, like a recession, as lenders are more hesitant to approve loans.

The problem with selling on credit is that as much as 25 percent of the business' assets could be tied up in its credit accounts (accounts receivable). This forces the firm to use its own funds to pay for goods or services sold to customers who bought on credit. Financial managers in such firms often develop efficient collection procedures like offering cash or quantity discounts to buyers who pay their accounts by a certain (usually earlier) date. They also scrutinize old and new credit customers to see whether they have a history of meeting their credit obligations on time.

© ICP/age fotostock

It's difficult to think of a business that doesn't make credit available to its customers. However, collecting accounts receivable from some customers can be time-consuming and costly. Accepting credit cards, such as Visa, MasterCard, and American Express, can simplify transactions for sellers and guarantee payment. What types of products do you regularly purchase with a credit card?

One convenient way to decrease the time and expense of collecting accounts receivable is to accept bank credit cards such as MasterCard or Visa. The banks that issue these cards have already established the customer's creditworthiness, which reduces the business' risk. Businesses must pay a fee to accept credit cards, but the fees are usually offset by the benefits. In an effort to reduce those credit card costs as well as speed up the transaction process, many businesses today accept mobile payments like ApplePay and Android Pay.[17] For example, restaurants, supermarkets, and hotels have invested in mobile payment systems.[18] Mobile payment systems not only make transactions quick and simple, the processors usually charge lower fees than traditional credit card companies.

Acquiring Needed Inventory

As you read in Chapter 14, effective marketing requires focusing on the customer and providing high-quality service and readily available goods. A carefully constructed inventory policy helps manage the firm's available funds and maximize profitability.[19] For example, Dozzle's, an ice cream parlour, deliberately ties up fewer funds in its inventory of ice cream in the winter. It is obvious why; demand for ice cream is lower in the winter.

Just-in-time inventory control (see Chapter 10) and other such methods can reduce the funds a firm must tie up in inventory. Carefully evaluating its inventory turnover ratio (see Chapter 16) can also help a firm control the outflow of cash for inventory. A business of any size must understand that poorly managed inventory can seriously affect cash flow and drain its finances. The Making Ethical Decisions box raises an interesting question about sound financial management and inventory control in a critical industry.

Making Capital Expenditures

Capital expenditures are major investments in either tangible long-term assets such as land, buildings, and equipment, or intangible assets, such as patents, trademarks, and copyrights. In many organizations the purchase of major assets—such as land for future expansion, manufacturing plants to increase production capabilities, research to develop new product ideas, and equipment to maintain or exceed current levels of output—is essential. Expanding, however, into new markets can be expensive with no guarantee of success. Therefore, it's critical that companies weigh all possible options before committing a large portion of available resources.

capital expenditures Major investments in either tangible long-term assets, such as land, buildings, and equipment, or intangible assets, such as patents, trademarks, and copyrights.

Making ETHICAL DECISIONS

Not What the Doctor Ordered!

After earning your business degree, you are hired as a hospital administrator at a small hospital. Having studied finance, you know that efficient cash management is important to all firms in all industries to meet their day-to-day operations. One way to ensure such efficiency is to use a carefully planned and managed inventory control system that reduces the amount of cash an organization has tied up in inventory. You know that just-in-time inventory is a proven system that helps reduce the costs of managing inventory.

At a meeting of the hospital's executive committee, you recommend the hospital save money by using a just-in-time inventory system to manage its drug supply. You suggest discontinuing the hospital's large stockpile of expensive cancer treatment drugs that tie up a great deal of the hospital's cash, and order them only when they are needed. Several board members like the idea, but the doctors in charge of the hospital's cancer centre are outraged, claiming you are sacrificing patients' well-being for cash flow. After debate, the committee says the decision is up to you. What will you do? What could result from your decision?

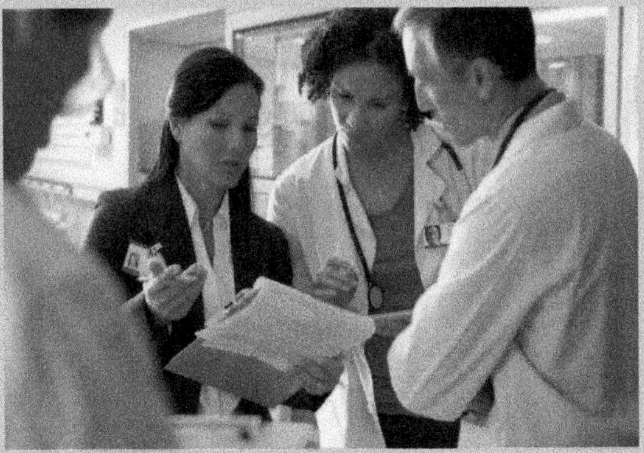

© SelectStock/Getty Images

debt financing Funds raised through various forms of borrowing that must be repaid.

equity financing Money raised from within the firm, from operations or through the sale of ownership in the firm.

short-term financing Borrowed funds that are needed for one year or less.

long-term financing Borrowed funds that are needed for a period more than one year.

Consider a firm that needs to expand its production capabilities due to increased customer demand. It could buy land and build a new plant, purchase an existing plant, or rent space. Can you think of financial and accounting considerations at play in this decision?

The need for operating funds raises several questions for financial managers: "How does the firm obtain funds to finance operations and other business needs? Will it require specific funds in the long or the short term? How much will it cost (i.e., interest) to obtain these funds? Will they come from internal or external sources?" We address these questions next.

Alternative Sources of Funds

We described finance earlier as the function in a business responsible for acquiring and managing funds. Sound financial management determines the amount of money needed and the most appropriate sources from which to obtain it. While in Chapter 7 you were introduced to financing sources, such as angel investors and crowdfunding, in this chapter we will highlight how a firm can raise needed capital by borrowing money (debt), selling ownership (equity), or earning profits (retained earnings).

Debt financing refers to funds raised through various forms of borrowing that must be repaid. **Equity financing** is money raised from within the firm, from operations or through the sale of ownership in the firm (stock). Firms can borrow funds either short-term or long-term. **Short-term financing** refers to funds needed for one year or less. **Long-term financing** refers to funds needed for more than one year (usually 2 to 10 years). Figure 17.5 highlights why firms may need short-term and long-term funds.

We'll explore the different sources of short-term and long-term financing next. Let's first pause to check your understanding by completing the Progress Assessment.

FIGURE 17.5

WHY FIRMS NEED FUNDS

Short-Term Funds	Long-Term Funds
Monthly expenses	New-product development
Unanticipated emergencies	Replacement of capital equipment
Cash flow problems	Mergers or acquisitions
Expansion of current inventory	Expansion into new markets (domestic or global)
Temporary promotional programs	New facilities

PROGRESS ASSESSMENT

- Money has time value. What does this mean?
- Why is accounts receivable a financial concern to a firm?
- What's the primary reason an organization spends a good deal of its available funds on inventory and capital expenditures?
- What is the difference between debt and equity financing?

Obtaining Short-Term Financing

LO4

Identify and describe different sources of short-term financing.

The bulk of a finance manager's job does not relate to obtaining long-term funds. In small businesses, for example, long-term financing is often out of the question. Instead, day-to-day operations call for the careful management of *short-term* financial needs. Firms may need to borrow short-term funds for purchasing additional inventory or for meeting bills that come due unexpectedly. Like an individual, a business, especially a small business, sometimes needs to secure short-term funds when its cash reserves are low. Let's consider how it does so.

Trade Credit

trade credit
The practice of buying goods and services now and paying for them later.

promissory note
A written contract with a promise to pay.

Trade credit is the practice of buying goods or services now and paying for them later. It is the most widely used source of short-term funding, the least expensive, and the most convenient. Small businesses rely heavily on trade credit from firms such as Purolator, just as do large firms such as the Hudson's Bay Company. When a firm buys merchandise, it receives an invoice (a bill) much like the one you receive when you buy something with a credit card. As you'll see, however, the terms businesses receive are often different than those on your monthly statement.

Business invoices usually contain terms such as *2/10, net 30.* This means the buyer can take a 2 percent discount for paying the invoice within 10 days. Otherwise the total bill (net) is due in 30 days. Financial managers pay close attention to such discounts because they create opportunities to reduce the firm's costs. Think about it for a moment: If terms are 2/10, net 30, the customer will pay 2 percent more by waiting an extra 20 days to pay the invoice. If the firm *can* pay its bill within 10 days, it is needlessly increasing its costs by not doing so.

Some suppliers hesitate to give trade credit to an organization with a poor credit rating, no credit history, or a history of late payments. They may insist the customer sign a **promissory note**, a written contract with a promise to pay a supplier a specific sum of money at a definite time. Promissory notes are not as rigid as formal loan contracts and are negotiable. The supplier can sell them to a bank at a discount (the amount of the promissory note less a fee for the bank's services in collecting the amount due), and the business is then responsible for paying the bank.

© Piet Mall/Getty Images

One thing you can never have too much of is cash. Financial managers must make certain there is enough cash available to meet daily financial needs and still have funds to invest in its future. What does it mean when we say cash has a time value?

Family and Friends

Firms often have several bills coming due at the same time with no sources of funds to pay them. Many small firms obtain short-term funds by borrowing money from family and friends. Such loans can create problems, however, if all parties do not understand cash flow. That's why it's sometimes better to go to a commercial bank that fully understands the business' risk and can help analyze its future financial needs rather than to borrow from friends or relatives.[20]

Entrepreneurs appear to be listening to this advice. According to the National Federation of Independent Business, entrepreneurs today are

© Peter Foley/EPA/Redux

Did you ever wonder how retailers get the money to buy all of the items available during the holiday season? Department stores and other large retailers make extensive use of commercial banks and other lenders to borrow the money needed to buy merchandise to stock their shelves. How do stores benefit from using this type of financing?

relying less on family and friends as a source of borrowed funds than they have in the past.[21] If an entrepreneur decides to ask family or friends for financial assistance, it's important that both parties (1) agree to specific loan terms, (2) put the agreement in writing, and (3) arrange for repayment in the same way they would for a bank loan. Such actions help keep family relationships and friendships intact.

Commercial Banks

Banks, being sensitive to risk, generally prefer to lend short-term funds to larger, established businesses. Imagine the different types of business people who go to banks for a loan, and you'll get a better idea of the requests bankers evaluate. Picture, for example, a farmer going to the bank in the spring to borrow funds for seed, fertilizer, supplies, and other needs that will be repaid after the fall harvest. Or consider a local toy store buying merchandise for holiday sales. The store borrows the money for such purchases in the summer and plans to pay it back after the holidays. Restaurants often borrow funds at the beginning of the month and then repay the funds at the end of the month.

How much a business borrows and for how long depends on the kind of business it is and how quickly it can resell the merchandise it purchases with a bank loan or use it to generate funds. In a large business, specialists in a company's finance and accounting departments do a cash flow forecast. Small-business owners generally lack such specialists and monitor cash flow themselves.

During difficult economic times, such as a recession, bank loans can virtually disappear, even for well-organized small businesses. What's important for a small firm to remember is if it gets a bank loan, the owner or person in charge of finance should keep in close touch with the bank and send regular financial statements to keep the bank up-to-date on its operations. The bank may spot cash flow problems early or be more willing to lend money in a crisis if the business has established a strong relationship built on trust and sound management.

Different Forms of Short-Term Loans

secured loan
A loan backed by collateral, something valuable such as property.

Banks and other financial institutions offer different forms of short-term loans. A **secured loan** is backed by *collateral,* something valuable such as property. If the borrower fails to pay the loan, the lender may take possession of the collateral. An automobile loan is a secured loan. If the borrower doesn't repay it, the lender will repossess the car. Inventory of raw materials, like coal, copper, and steel, often serve as collateral for business loans. Collateral removes some of the bank's risk in lending the money.

Accounts receivable are company assets often used as collateral for a loan. The process is called *pledging* and it works as follows: A percentage of the value of a firm's accounts receivable pledged (usually about 75 percent) is advanced to the borrowing firm.

© benedek/iStock/360/Getty Images RF

A secured loan is backed by collateral, a tangible item of value. A car loan, for instance, is a secured loan in which the car itself is the collateral. What is the collateral in a mortgage loan?

As customers pay off their accounts, the funds received are forwarded to the lender in repayment of the funds that were advanced.

An **unsecured loan** is more difficult to obtain because it does not require any collateral. Normally, lenders give unsecured loans only to highly regarded customers—long-standing businesses considered financially stable.

If a business develops a good relationship with a bank, the bank may open a **line of credit** for the firm. This is a given amount of unsecured short-term funds a bank will lend to a business, provided the funds are readily available. A line of credit is *not* guaranteed to a business. However it speeds up the borrowing process since a firm does not have to apply for a new loan every time it needs funds.[22] As a business matures and becomes more financially secure, banks will often increase the line of credit.

If a business is unable to secure a short-term loan from a bank, the financial manager may seek short-term funds from **commercial finance companies**. These non-deposit-type organizations make short-term loans to borrowers who offer tangible assets like property, plant, and equipment as collateral. Commercial finance companies will often make loans to businesses that cannot get short-term funds elsewhere. Since commercial finance companies assume higher degrees of risk than commercial banks, they usually charge higher interest rates. The Adapting to Change box highlights online lenders, another high-cost option of securing short-term financing.

unsecured loan
A loan that does not require any collateral.

line of credit
A given amount of unsecured funds a bank will lend to a business.

commercial finance companies
Organizations that make short-term loans to borrowers who offer tangible assets as collateral.

EVALUATING CREDITWORTHINESS[23]

Whether you are a business or a consumer, each time you apply to borrow money, you build a credit history. When you apply for credit, lenders consider your financial track record, along with information about your employment and other debts and assets you have. This information is captured in your **credit profile**, which is your financial reputation. It reflects your financial track record based on your borrowing history (e.g., applications for credit as well as credit repayment).

When considering a credit application (e.g., a loan or revolving credit agreement), a lender will consider creditworthiness. Creditworthiness is determined by the **4 Cs of credit**—character, capacity, capital, and conditions. (These 4Cs can also apply to you.) Let's briefly consider each next.

Character includes factors such as business size, location, number of years in business, business structure, number of employees, history of principals, appetite for sharing information about itself, media coverage, liens, judgements or pending lawsuits, stock performance, and comments from references.

Capacity considers the ability of the business to pay its bills (i.e., its cash flow). It also includes the structure of the company's debt—whether secured or unsecured—and the existence of any unused lines of credit. Any defaults must also be identified.

credit profile
A borrower's financial track record in the form of borrowing history.

4 Cs of credit
A business' creditworthiness is determined by its character, capacity, capital, and conditions.

Adapting *to* CHANGE

Financing Just a Click Away

Coming up with a great idea is only the first step in getting a business off the ground. Entrepreneurs need money to turn their ideas into reality. Unfortunately, most traditional lenders (banks) are not very receptive to new businesses. Online business lenders in the financial technology (fintech) world are filling a major gap for small businesses often overlooked by the major banks. Small business owners, however, should take the time to research these various platforms to ensure they fit the company's needs.

One of the biggest attractions of online lenders is the speed in which they can process an application. While banks can take weeks to process a business loan application, most online providers can process in one to two days of the application. Sound good? In fact, it's probably *too* good. Before entering into any loan agreement with an online lender, it's vital to do research into the lender's reputation and the loan's fine print.

If you find a barrage of critical reviews online or evidence of negative press about the company, it's best to seek out other lending options. The loan's fine print also deserves a thorough evaluation (if possible with the help of an attorney). For example, with many online loans you can expect a high interest rate that will accrue daily the minute you take out the loan. It's likely rates could be as high as 300 percent. It's also important to remember the loan is generally linked to your bank account through a direct deposit. This permits the lender to collect payments via automatic withdrawal from your account. If you fail to keep a constant balance in your bank account, you run the risk of being assessed possible overdraft penalties. If you do experience problems paying off the loan, online lenders are not as co-operative or flexible in setting up affordable repayment plans. The best advice is be careful and be wise of online lenders bearing gifts.

© iStock/Getty Images RF

Sources: "Geoff Williams, "What You Should Know about Online Lending Services," *U.S. New & World Report,* July 26, 2016; James Rufus Koren, "As Troubles Pile Up, Online Lenders Pull Back," *Los Angeles Times,* May 9, 2016; "This Is the Latest Threat to Online Lenders," Reuters, June 10, 2016; Michael Corkery, "As Lending Club Stumbles, Its Entire Industry Faces Skepticism," *The New York Times,* May 9, 2016; Peter Rudegeair, "On Deck Capital, a Fallen Fintech Star, to Focus on Turning a Profit," *The Wall Street Journal,* May 8, 2017; Clare O'Hara, "New online lenders make it easier to get small business loans," *The Globe and Mail,* May 15, 2018, https://www.theglobeandmail.com/report-on-business/small-business/sb-money/new-online-lenders-make-it-easier-to-get-small-businesses-loans/article26092911/; and Patricia Meredith and James Darroch, "The forces of change are trumping banks and regulators," *The Globe and Mail,* May 15, 2018, https://www.theglobeandmail.com/business/commentary/article-the-forces-of-change-are-trumping-banks-and-regulators/.

Capital assesses whether a company has the financial resources to repay its creditors. This information is obtained from financial records. In general, this portion of the credit report is the one most closely reviewed by the credit analyst. Heavy weighting is given to such balance sheet items as working capital, net worth, and cash flow.

Conditions includes the external factors surrounding the business under consideration, including influences such as market fluctuations, industry growth rate, legal factors (e.g., political and legislative), and currency rates.

A credit bureau agency takes several elements of your credit profile and identifies a score that rates your creditworthiness on a scale. Your *credit score* may influence the interest rate that you pay and help determine whether lenders approve you for credit (e.g., a credit card or a car loan).

The 4Cs are also taken into consideration by other service providers, such as insurance companies, to set premiums. More than ever, lenders input scores and ratings that summarize the 4 Cs into a financial model to determine the risk of doing business with organizations and consumers.

© ximagination/123RF

To build a positive credit history, consider these dos and don'ts. Do pay your bills on time, pay at least the minimum amount, and check your credit profile for errors. Don't use credit you don't understand, wait to report problems, pay bills late, or exceed your credit limit. Request a free copy of your credit profile from a credit bureau agency, such as TransUnion or Equifax. Were you surprised by what was captured in your profile?

Factoring Accounts Receivable

One relatively expensive source of short-term funds for a firm is **factoring**, the process of selling accounts receivable (a firm's asset) for cash. Here is how it works: Let's say a firm sells many of its products on credit to customers, creating a number of accounts receivable. Some of these buyers may be slow in paying their bills, so a large amount of money is due the firm. A *factor* is a market intermediary (usually a financial institution such as a commercial bank) that agrees to buy the firm's accounts receivable, at a discount, for cash. The discount depends on the age of the accounts receivable, the nature of the business, and the condition of the economy. When it collects the accounts receivable that were originally owed to the firm, the factor keeps them. Even though factoring is an expensive way of raising short-term funds, it is popular among small businesses as some cannot qualify for a loan.

factoring
The process of selling accounts receivable for cash.

Commercial Paper

Often a corporation needs funds for just a few months and prefers not to have to negotiate with a commercial bank. One strategy available to larger firms is to sell commercial paper. **Commercial paper** consists of *unsecured* promissory notes, in amounts of $100,000 and up, that mature (come due) in a period of one month up to one year.[24] Commercial paper states a fixed amount of money the business agrees to repay to the lender (investor) on a specific date at a specified rate of interest.

commercial paper
Unsecured promissory notes of $100,000 and up that mature (come due) in one month up to one year.

Because commercial paper is unsecured, only financially stable firms (mainly large corporations with excellent credit reputations) are able to sell it. Commercial paper can be a quick path to short-term funds at lower interest than charged by commercial banks. Since most commercial paper matures in 30 to 90 days, it can be an investment opportunity for lenders who can afford to put up cash for short periods to earn some interest on their money.

Credit Cards

Credit cards provide a business with ready access to money that can save time and the likely embarrassment of being rejected for a bank loan.[25] Of course, in contrast to the convenience that credit cards offer, they can be costly. Interest rates can be exorbitant, and there can be penalties if users fail to make their payments on time. That's why it's important to understand the penalties and perks that come with different credit cards.[26]

Some credit card perks can help keep a small business afloat. For example, Joe Speiser found a cash-back card that helped put dollars back into his e-commerce company Petflow when it needed funds back in 2010. Today, he runs a $50 million business named Little Things.

Still, when dealing with credit cards, remember it's an expensive way to borrow money and credit cards are probably best used as a last resort. After checking your progress, we'll look into long-term financing options.

PROGRESS ASSESSMENT

- What does an invoice containing the terms "2/10, net 30" mean?
- What's the difference between trade credit and a line of credit?
- What's the key difference between a secured loan and an unsecured loan?
- What is factoring? What are some of the considerations involved in establishing the discount rate?

Obtaining Long-Term Financing

LO5

Identify and describe different sources of long-term financing.

In a financial plan, forecasting determines the amount of funding the firm will need over various periods and the most appropriate sources for obtaining those funds. In setting long-term financing objectives, financial managers generally ask three questions:

1. What are the organization's long-term goals and objectives?
2. What funds do we need to achieve the firm's long-term goals and objectives?
3. What sources of long-term funding (capital) are available, and which will best fit our needs?

© Steven Schleuning

Firms of all sizes, whether private or public, regardless of industry, require long-term financing. Here you see a tractor seeding a field. What other equipment do you think a farm may require?

Firms need long-term capital to purchase expensive assets such as plant and equipment, to develop new products, and perhaps finance their expansion. In major corporations, the board of directors and top management usually make decisions about long-term financing, along with finance and accounting executives. Pfizer, one of the world's largest research-based biomedical and pharmaceutical companies, spends over $8 billion a year researching and developing new products. The development of a single new drug could take 10 years and cost the firm over $1 billion before it brings in any profit.[27] Plus, the company loses its patent protection on a drug after 20 years. It's easy to see why high-level managers make the long-term financing decisions at Pfizer. Owners of small and medium-sized businesses are almost always actively engaged in analyzing their long-term financing decisions. As we noted earlier, long-term funding comes from two major sources: debt financing and equity financing. Let's look at these sources next.

Debt Financing

Debt financing is borrowing money a company has a legal obligation to repay. Firms can borrow either by getting a loan from a lending institution or by issuing bonds.

DEBT FINANCING BY BORROWING MONEY FROM LENDING INSTITUTIONS

Long-term loans are usually due within 3 to 7 years but may extend to 15 or 20 years. A **term-loan agreement** is a promissory note that requires the borrower to repay the loan, with interest, in specified monthly or annual instalments. A major advantage is that the loan interest is tax deductible.

term-loan agreement
A promissory note that requires the borrower to repay the loan in specified instalments.

Long-term loans are both larger and more expensive to the firm than short-term loans. Since the repayment period can be quite long, lenders assume more risk and usually require collateral, which may be real estate, machinery, equipment, company shares, or other items of value. Lenders may also require certain restrictions to force the firm to act responsibly. The interest rate is based on the adequacy of collateral, the firm's credit rating, and the general level of market interest rates. The greater the risk the lender takes in making a loan, the higher the rate of interest (recall the risk-return tradeoff).

DEBT FINANCING BY ISSUING BONDS

If an organization is unable to obtain its long-term financing needs by getting a loan from a lending institution, such as a bank, it may try to issue bonds. A **bond** is a corporate certificate indicating that an investor has lent money to a firm or a government. An organization that issues bonds, such as different levels of governments and corporations, has the legal obligation to make regular interest payments during the term of the bond and to repay the entire bond principal amount at a prescribed time.

bond
A corporate certificate indicating that an investor has lent money to a firm or a government.

Bonds are usually issued in units of $1000. The *principal* is the face value (dollar value) of a bond, which the issuing company is legally bound to repay in full to the bondholder on the **maturity date**. **Interest** is the payment the bond issuer makes to the bondholders to compensate them for the use of their money. If Harvest Gold issues a $1000 bond with an interest rate of 5 percent and a maturity date of 2025, the company is agreeing to pay a bondholder a total of $50 in interest each year until a specified date in 2025, when the full $1000 must be repaid. Maturity dates for bonds can vary. For example, in 2014 the federal government raised $2.5 billion worth of 50-year bonds in two rounds. The second round of bonds, with an interest rate of 2.76 percent, mature on December 1, 2064.[28] Firms such as Disney, IBM, and Coca-Cola have issued century bonds with 100-year maturity dates. Review the Seeking Sustainability box to learn more about the Ontario Government's Green Bonds.

maturity date
The exact date the issuer of a bond must pay the principal to the bondholder.

interest
The payment the bond issuer makes to the bondholders for use of the borrowed money.

Bond interest is sometimes called the *coupon rate,* a term that dates back to when bonds were issued as *bearer* bonds. The holder, or bearer, was considered the bond's owner. Back then, the company issuing the bond kept no record of changes in ownership. Bond interest was paid to whoever clipped the coupons attached to the bond and sent them to the issuing company for payment. Today, bonds are registered to specific owners and changes in ownership are recorded electronically.

Seeking SUSTAINABILITY

Buying Green Bonds

You may already be familiar with bonds. Maybe your community is building a new stadium or cultural centre and is selling bonds to finance the project. Businesses and governments compete when issuing bonds. Potential investors (individuals and institutions) measure the risk of purchasing a bond against the return the bond promises to pay—the interest—and the issuer's ability to repay when promised.

© Kletr/Shutterstock

On October 2, 2014, Ontario became the first province to launch Green Bonds through its $500 million bond sale. Since then, it has issued three more rounds of bonds totalling $2.55 billion. Ontario's Green Bonds are standard debt obligations of the Province and rank equally with Ontario's other bonds.

The size of each Green Bond issue is determined by market demand and Ontario's availability of suitable green projects in any given fiscal year. Categories of eligible projects that have environmental benefits include the following: clean transportation; energy efficiency and conservation; clean energy and technology; forestry, agriculture and land management; and climate adaptation and resilience.

Canadian green bond issuers include one federal agency (Export Development Canada); two provinces (Ontario and Quebec); and one city (Ottawa), with the City of Toronto planning one. Among corporations, TD Bank and Manulife Financial Corporation have issued green bonds. Why do you think other provinces and corporations have not followed with their own green bonds? If you were investing in bonds, would you find green bonds to be more attractive than standard bonds?

Sources: Mike Cherney, "$100 Billion in Bids for $46 Billion in Bonds," *The Wall Street Journal*, January 14, 2016; Christopher Whittall and Emese Bartha, "Italy Debuts 50-Year Bond to Strong Demand," *The Wall Street Journal*, October 5, 2016; Cordell Eddings, "Corporate Bond Sales Surge above $23 Billion as Apple Sells Debt," Bloomberg, February 16, 2016; Simon Constable, "The Case for Treasury Bonds," U.S. News and World Report, June 6, 2017; Barry Critchley, "$1 billion green bond offering Ontario's largest to date," *Financial Post*, January 30, 2018, http://business.financialpost.com/news/fp-street/1-billion-green-bond-offering-ontarios-largest-to-date; Barry Critchley, "Canada slow to embrace green bond market, even though investors are eager to buy," *Financial Post*, May 7, 2018, http://business.financialpost.com/news/fp-street/canada-slow-to-embrace-green-bond-market-even-though-investors-are-eager-to-buy-them; "Province of Ontario Green Bonds," Ontario Financing Authority, accessed May 23, 2018, https://www.ofina.on.ca/greenbonds/; and "Ontario Green Bond Q&A's," Ontario Financing Authority, accessed May 23, 2018, https://www.ofina.on.ca/pdf/green_bond_qa.pdf.

Like other forms of long-term debt, the interest rate paid on a bond varies according to factors such as the general level of market rates, the reputation of the company issuing the bond, and the going interest rate for government bonds or bonds of similar companies. Once an interest rate is set for a corporate bond issue (except in the case of what is called a *floating-rate bond*), it cannot be changed. Though bond interest is quoted for an entire year, it is usually paid in two instalments.

Bond-rating organizations assess the creditworthiness of a corporation's bond issue. Independent rating firms, such as Dominion Bond Rating Service and Standard & Poor's Rating Services, rate bonds according to their degree of risk.[29] Bond ratings can range from the highest quality to junk bonds. Naturally, the higher the risk associated with the bond issue, the higher the interest rate the organization must offer investors. Investors should not assume high levels of risk if they do not feel that the potential return is worth it.

© Adam Bettcher/Getty Images

Major League Baseball is a big business, and building a new stadium requires big dollars. When the Minnesota Vikings needed financing to replace its old stadium with a new state-of-the-art facility, the city of Minneapolis and the state issued bonds that helped finance the construction of the Vikings' new home. What organizations in your community have issued bonds, and for what purpose?

Advantages and Disadvantages of Issuing Bonds Bonds offer long-term financing advantages to an organization:

- Bondholders are creditors of the firm, not owners. They seldom vote on corporate matters; thus, management maintains control over the firm's operations.
- Bond interest is a business expense and as a result, it is tax-deductible for the firm.
- Bonds are a temporary source of funding. They are eventually repaid and the debt obligation is eliminated.
- Bonds can be repaid before the maturity date if they are *callable,* which permits the bond issuer to pay off the bond's principal before its maturity.

unsecured bonds (debenture bonds) Bonds that are unsecured (i.e., not backed by any collateral such as equipment).

Bonds also have financing drawbacks:

- Bonds increase debt (long-term liabilities) and may adversely affect the market's perception of the firm.
- Paying interest on bonds is a legal obligation. If interest is not paid, bondholders can take legal action to force payment.
- The face value of the bond must be repaid on the maturity date. Without careful planning, this obligation can cause cash flow problems when the repayment comes due.

© Stockbyte/Getty Images

To make bonds more attractive, decisions are made on the best combination of features before new bonds are issued. After all, new bonds will be competing against not only other new bond issues, but also against current bonds in the marketplace, both domestically and internationally. What special bond features would make a bond more attractive to a potential investor?

Different Classes of Bonds Corporations can issue two different classes of corporate bonds. **Unsecured bonds**, usually called **debenture bonds**, are not backed by any specific collateral (such as land or equipment). Only firms with excellent reputations and credit ratings can issue debenture bonds, due to the lack of security they provide investors. **Secured bonds**, sometimes called **mortgage bonds**, are backed by collateral, such as land or buildings, that is pledged to bondholders if interest or principal is not paid when promised. A corporate bond issuer can choose to include different bond features. For example, *convertible* bonds may be converted to common shares.

secured bonds (mortgage bonds)
Bonds that are secured (i.e., backed by collateral such as land).

sinking fund
A reserve account in which the issuer of a bond periodically retires some part of the bond principal prior to maturity so that enough capital will be accumulated by the maturity date to pay off the bond.

Now you understand that bonds are issued with an interest rate, are unsecured or secured by some type of collateral, and must be repaid at their maturity dates. This repayment requirement often leads companies (or governments) to establish a reserve account called a **sinking fund**. Its primary purpose is to ensure that enough money will be available to repay bondholders on the bond's maturity date. Firms issuing sinking-fund bonds periodically *retire* (set aside) some part of the principal prior to maturity so that enough funds will accumulate by the maturity date to pay off the bond. Sinking funds are generally attractive to both issuing firms and investors for several reasons:

- They provide for an orderly retirement (repayment) of a bond issue.
- They reduce the risk the bond will not be repaid.
- They support the market price of the bond because they reduce the risk the bond will not be repaid.

PROGRESS ASSESSMENT

- What are the major forms of debt financing available to a firm?
- What does it mean when a firm states that it is issuing a 9 percent debenture bond due in 2030?
- What are advantages and disadvantages of bonds?

Equity Financing

Rather than obtaining a long-term loan from a lending institution or selling bonds to investors, a firm may look at equity financing. Equity financing makes funds available when the owners of the firm sell shares of ownership (including selling shares to venture capitalists) or when they reinvest earnings. Let's look more closely at each of these options.

EQUITY FINANCING BY SELLING STOCK (SHARES)

stocks (shares)
Shares of ownership in a company.

initial public offering (IPO)
The first public offering of a corporation's stock.

stock certificate
Evidence of stock ownership that specifies the name of the company, the number of shares it represents, and the type of stock being issued.

Stock (shares) represent ownership in a company. Both common and preferred shares (to be discussed soon) form the company's *capital stock,* also known as the company's *equity capital.* The key thing to remember about stocks is that stockholders (also known as shareholders) become owners in the organization. Generally, the corporation's board of directors decides the number of shares of stock that will be offered to investors for purchase.

An **initial public offering (IPO)** occurs the first time a corporation offers to sell new stock to the general public. After this initial sale, the *secondary market* handles the trading of these securities between investors, with the proceeds of the sale going to the investor selling the stock, not to the corporation whose stock is sold. For example, Cara Operations Ltd. raised $200 million through its IPO in 2015 with a share price of $23. The share price went as high as $33 in its first day of trading on the Toronto Stock Exchange (secondary market), benefitting investors who may have chosen to sell their shares for a profit.[30] What is the share price now? Are investors happy with their return to date?

A **stock certificate** represents stock ownership. It specifies the name of the company, the number of shares owned, and the type of stock it represents. Companies, however, are not required to issue paper stock certificates to owners since stock is generally held electronically.

Stock certificates sometimes indicate a stock's *par value,* which is a dollar amount assigned to each share of stock by the corporation's charter. Today, since par values do not reflect the market value of the stock (what the stock is actually worth), most companies issue stock with a very low par value or no par value.

Dividends are part of a firm's profits that may be (but is not required to be) distributed to shareholders as either cash payments or additional shares of stock.[31] Dividends are declared by a corporation's board of directors and are generally paid quarterly.[32] For example, the Board of Directors of Sun Life Financial Inc. approved a common-share dividend increase of 4 percent (or 2 cents per share), resulting in a dividend of $0.475 cents per common share.[33]

© EPA/ANDREW GOMBERT/The Canadian Press

When Canada Goose issued its IPO in 2017, the company raised more than $340 million by selling 20 million shares.[35] The day was not without controversy as PETA protested outside of the New York Stock Exchange. Would such protests discourage you from buying the company's products? Can you see why issuing stock can be an appealing option for financing a company's growth?

Advantages and Disadvantages of Issuing Stock Some advantages to a firm of issuing stock include:

- As owners of the business, shareholders never have to be repaid.
- There is usually no legal obligation to pay dividends to stockholders; therefore, the firm can reinvest income (retained earnings) to finance future needs.
- Selling stock can improve the condition of a firm's balance sheet since issuing stock creates no debt. (A corporation may also buy back its stock to improve its balance sheet and make the company appear stronger financially.[34])

dividends
Part of a firm's profits that may be distributed to shareholders as either cash payments or additional shares of stock.

Disadvantages of issuing stock include:

- As owners, stockholders (usually only common shareholders) have the right to vote for the company's board of directors. (Typically one vote is granted for each share of stock.) Issuing new shares of stock can thus alter the control of the firm.
- Dividends are paid from profit after taxes and thus are not tax deductible.
- The need to keep stockholders happy can affect managers' decisions.

Companies can issue two classes of stock: common and preferred. Let's see how these two forms of equity financing differ.

Issuing Shares of Common Stock **Common stock** is the most basic form of ownership in a firm. In fact, if a company issues only one type of stock, by law it must be common stock. Holders of common stock have the right to (1) elect members of the company's board directors, and vote on important issues affecting the company, and (2) share in the firm's profits through dividends, if approved by the firm's board of directors. Having voting rights in a corporation allows common stockholders to influence corporate policy because the board members they elect both choose the firm's top management as well as make major policy decisions.

common stock
The most basic form of ownership in a firm; it confers voting rights and the right to share in the firm's profits through dividends, if offered by the firm's board of directors.

Common stockholders also have a *pre-emptive right* to purchase new shares of common stock that may be issued via an IPO before anyone else. This allows common stockholders to maintain their proportional share of ownership in the company.

preferred stock
Stock that gives its owners preference in the payment of dividends and an earlier claim on assets than common shareholders if the company is forced out of business and its assets are sold.

Issuing Shares of Preferred Stock Owners of **preferred stock** enjoy a preference in the payment of company dividends and must be paid their dividends in full before any common stock dividends can be distributed; hence, the term *preferred.* They also have a prior claim on company assets—before common shareholders—if the firm is forced out of business and its assets sold. Normally, however, preferred shareholders do not get voting rights in the firm.

Preferred stock may be issued with a par value that becomes the base for a fixed dividend the firm is willing to pay. For example, if a preferred share's par value is $50 a share and its dividend rate is 4 percent, the dividend is $2 a share ($50 times 4 percent = $2). An owner of 100 shares would receive a fixed yearly dividend of $200 if dividends are declared by the board of directors.

Preferred stock are therefore quite similar to bonds; both have a face (or par) value and both have a fixed rate of return. Also, like bonds, rating services assess preferred shares according to risk. So how do bonds and preferred shares differ? Remember that companies are legally bound to pay bond interest and to repay the face value (denomination) of the bond on its maturity date. In contrast, even though preferred share dividends are generally fixed, they do not legally have to be paid. Also, shares (preferred or common) never have to be repurchased by the issuing company. Though both bonds and stock can increase in market value, the price of stock generally increases at a higher percentage than bonds. Of course, the market value of both could also go down. Figure 17.6 compares features of bonds and stock.

FIGURE 17.6

COMPARISON OF BONDS AND STOCK OF PUBLIC COMPANIES

The different features help both the issuer and the investor decide which vehicle is right for each of them at a particular time.

	Bonds	Common Stock	Preferred Stock
Interest (Bonds) or Dividends (Stock)			
Must be paid	Yes	No	Depends
Pays a fixed rate	Yes	No	Usually
Deductible from issuer's income tax	Yes	No	No
Canadian investor pays reduced tax rate	No	(if issuing company is Canadian) Yes	Yes
Bond or Stock			
Has voting rights	No	Yes	Not normally
May be traded on the stock exchange	Yes	Yes	Yes
Can be held indefinitely	No	Yes	Depends
Is convertible to common shares	Maybe	No	Maybe

EQUITY FINANCING FROM VENTURE CAPITAL

The hardest time for a business to raise money is when it is just starting up or just beginning to expand. A start-up business typically has few assets and no market track record, so the chances of borrowing significant amounts of money from a bank are slim.

Recall from Chapter 7 that venture capitalists are a potential source of funds. **Venture capital** is money that is invested in new or emerging companies that some investors—venture capitalists—believe have great profit potential. Venture capital helped firms like Intel and Apple get started, and it helped Facebook and Google expand and grow. Venture capitalists invest in a company in return for part ownership of the business. They expect higher-than-average returns and competent management performance for their investment. See the Spotlight on Small Business about a recent venture capital firm that hopes to "court" new investments.

venture capital
Money that is invested in new or emerging companies that are perceived as having great profit potential.

EQUITY FINANCING FROM RETAINED EARNINGS

You probably remember from Chapter 16 that the profits the company keeps and reinvests in the firm are called *retained earnings*. Retained earnings are often a major source

Spotlight *On* SMALL BUSINESS

Looking for a Slam Dunk

After being drafted to the NBA directly from high school, Kobe Bryant spent the next two decades perfecting his skills on the hardcourt with the Los Angeles Lakers. In his 20-year career, he was an 18-time all-star and a key part of the Lakers' five NBA championships. Unfortunately, not even a player of Kobe's ability could play basketball forever. He hung up his number 24 Lakers jersey at the end of the 2016 season. However, he is far from pulling up a rocking chair and relaxing.

Six-foot-six Bryant teamed up with five-foot-seven entrepreneur, scientist, and investor Jeff Stibel to start a $100 million venture capital fund, Bryant Stibel. The fund intends to invest primarily in technology, media, and data companies with a focus on those in the sports and wellness fields. Since meeting in 2013, the partners have invested in 15 companies including the legal service website, LegalZoom, and sports website, The Players Tribune. Now that the new partnership has officially jumped into the competitive world of venture capital, the partners expect to become much more active.

The former Lakers star promises to bring his intensely competitive work ethic to the world of venture capital. He vows to devote the same obsession he displayed on the basketball court to learning about potential start-ups seeking funding. Billionaire investor Chris Sacca believes Kobe has a very unique personality similar to successful entrepreneurs like Uber founder Travis Kalanick. Whether Kobe Bryant will pivot and become a venture capital all-star remains to be seen. Keep your eyes on the scoreboard for his future three-pointers.

© Harry How/Getty Images

Sources: Danielle Wiener-Bronner, "Kobe Bryant Reveals His $100 Million Venture Capital Fund," *CNNMoney,* August 26, 2016; Emily Jane Fox, "Kobe Bryant Launches $100 Million Venture-Capital Fund," *Vanity Fair,* August 22, 2016; Lucinda Stern, "Kobe Bryant Just Started a Venture Capital Fund," *Fortune,* August 22, 2016; Dennis Berman, "Kobe Bryant and Jeff Stibel Unveil $100 Million Venture Capital Fund," *The Wall Street Journal,* August 22, 2016; Katilin Ugolik, "Kobe Bryant Reinvents Himself as a Venture Capitalist," *Institutional Investor,* September 17, 2016; Kathleen Elkins, "Kobe Bryant and Ex-NFL Player Agree on What Pro Athletes Should Do after Retiring," *CNBC,* August 24, 2017.

of long-term funds, especially for small businesses since they often have fewer financing alternatives, such as selling bonds or stock, than large businesses do. However, large corporations also depend on retained earnings for long-term funding. In fact, retained earnings are usually the most favoured source of meeting long-term capital needs. A company that uses them saves interest payments, dividends (payments for investing in stock), and any possible underwriting fees for issuing bonds or stock. Retained earnings also create no new ownership in the firm, as stock does.

Suppose you want to buy an expensive personal asset such as a new car. Ideally you would go to your personal savings account and take out the necessary cash. No hassle! No interest! Unfortunately, few people have such large amounts of cash available. Most businesses are no different. Even though they would like to finance long-term needs from operations (retained earnings), few have the resources available to accomplish this.

Comparing Debt and Equity Financing

leverage
Raising needed funds through borrowing to increase a firm's rate of return.

cost of capital
The rate of return a company must earn in order to meet the demands of its lenders and expectations of its equity holders.

Figure 17.7 compares debt and equity financing options. Raising funds through borrowing to increase the firm's rate of return is referred to as **leverage**. Though debt increases risk because it creates a financial obligation that must be repaid, it also enhances a firm's ability to increase profits. Debt can be good; leverage is favourable when the uses to which debt can be put generate returns greater than the interest expense associated with the debt.[36] Recall that two key jobs of the financial manager or CFO are forecasting the firm's need for borrowed funds and planning how to manage these funds once they are obtained.

Firms are concerned with the cost of capital. **Cost of capital** is the rate of return a company must earn in order to meet the demands of its lenders and expectations of its equity holders (shareholders or venture capitalists). If the firm's earning are greater than the interest payments on borrowed funds, business owners can realize a higher

FIGURE 17.7

DIFFERENCES BETWEEN DEBT AND EQUITY FINANCING

	Type of Financing	
	Debt	**Equity**
Management influence	There's usually none unless special conditions have been agreed on.	Common shareholders have voting rights.
Repayment	Debt has a maturity date.	Stock has no maturity date.
	Principal must be repaid.	The company is never required to repay equity.
Yearly obligations	Payment of interest is a contractual obligation.	The firm is not usually legally liable to pay dividends.
Tax benefits	Interest is tax deductible.	Dividends are paid from after-tax income and aren't deductible.

FIGURE 17.8

USING LEVERAGE (DEBT) VERSUS EQUITY FINANCING

Harvest Gold wants to raise $200,000 in new capital. Compare the firm's debt and equity options. Return on equity is calculated by dividing operating profit by total shareholders' equity.

Additional Debt		Additional Equity	
Shareholders' equity	$500,000	Shareholders' equity	$500,000
Additional equity	–	Additional equity	$200,000
Total equity	$500,000	Total equity	$700,000
Bond @ 8% interest	$200,000	Bond interest	–
Total shareholders' equity	$500,000	Total shareholders' equity	$700,000
Year-End Earnings			
Gross Profit	$100,000	Gross Profit	$100,000
Less bond interest ($200,000 times 8%)	–$16,000	Less interest	–
Operating Profit	$84,000	Operating Profit	$100,000
Return on equity ($84,000 ÷ $500,000)	16.8%	Return on equity ($100,000 ÷ $700,000)	14.3%

rate of return than if they had used equity financing. Figure 17.8 shows an example, again involving our restaurant example, Harvest Gold (introduced in Chapter 14). If Harvest Gold needed $200,000 in new financing, it could consider debt by selling bonds or equity through offering stock. Comparing the two options in this situation, you can see that Harvest Gold would benefit by selling bonds since the company's earnings are greater than the interest paid on borrowed funds (bonds). However, if the firm's earnings were less than the interest paid on borrowed funds (bonds), Harvest Gold could lose money. It's also important to remember that bonds, like all debt, have to be repaid at a specific date.

Individual firms must determine exactly how to balance debt and equity financing by comparing the costs and benefits of each. Leverage ratios (discussed in Chapter 16) can also give companies an industry standard for this balance, to which they can compare themselves. Still, debt varies considerably among major companies and industries. Social media leader Facebook, for example, has no long-term debt and more than $20 billion in cash available. Similarly, tech companies Microsoft, Apple, and Alphabet have very little debt and huge piles of cash.[37] On the other hand, oil companies Exxon, BP, and Shell together have over $184 billion of debt on their balance sheets.[38] According to Standard & Poor's and Moody's Investors Service (firms that provide corporate and financial research), the debt of large industrial corporations and utilities typically ranges between 30 and 35 percent of the companies' total assets. The amount of debt obviously varies considerably from firm to firm.

© Shutterstock / Monkey Business Images

CFA candidates report dedicating in excess of 300 hours of study to prepare for each exam. Are there any courses that you can take at your school that will help you when it is time to study for a CFA exam?

Your Prospects in Finance[39]

A career in finance can include analyst positions (e.g., research and corporate finance), management positions (e.g., relationship, portfolio, and risk), financial consultants, investment bankers, chief information officer (CIO) positions, and more. This chapter's Career Exploration highlights a few more examples. Are any of these of interest to you?

In Chapter 16, you were introduced to the chartered professional accountant (CPA) designation. Another well-known finance designation is the chartered financial analyst (CFA) designation. Administered through the CFA Institute, it has become the most respected and recognized investment designation in the world. Graduation requires successful completion of three levels. Level I focuses on a basic knowledge of the topic areas and simple analysis using investment tools. Level II emphasizes the application of investment tools and concepts with a focus on the valuation of all types of assets. Level III focuses on synthesizing all of the concepts and analytical methods in a variety of applications for effective portfolio management and wealth planning. Would you consider this designation as a way to round out your studies and experience? Regardless of your career choice, an understanding of finance will support sound decision making.

PROGRESS ASSESSMENT

- What are the major forms of equity financing available to a firm?
- Name at least two advantages and two disadvantages of issuing stock as a form of equity financing.
- What are the major differences between common shares and preferred shares?
- In what ways are preferred shares similar to bonds? How are they different?

SUMMARY

LO1 **Explain the role and responsibilities of financial managers.**

Finance comprises those functions in a business responsible for acquiring funds for the firm, managing funds within the firm (e.g., preparing budgets and doing cash flow analysis), and planning for the expenditure of funds on various assets.

What are the most common ways in which firms fail financially?

The most common financial problems are (1) undercapitalization, (2) poor control over cash flow, and (3) inadequate expense control.

What do financial managers do?

Financial managers plan, budget, control funds, obtain funds, collect funds, conduct audits, manage taxes, and advise top management on financial matters.

LO2 **Outline the financial planning process, and explain the three key budgets in the financial plan.**

Financial planning involves forecasting short-term and long-term needs, budgeting, and establishing financial controls.

What are the three budgets in a financial plan?

The capital budget is the spending plan for expensive assets, such as property, plant, and equipment. The cash budget is the projected cash inflows and outflows for a period and the balance at the end of a given period. The operating (master) budget summarizes the information in the other two budgets. It projects dollar allocations to various costs and expenses given various revenues.

LO3 **Explain why firms need operating funds.**

During the course of a business' life, its financial needs shift considerably.

What are firms' major financial needs?

Businesses need financing for four major tasks: (1) managing day-to-day needs of the business, (2) controlling credit operations, (3) acquiring needed inventory, and (4) making capital expenditures.

How can a firm access operating funds?

A firm can raise needed capital by borrowing money (debt), selling ownership (equity), or earning profits (retained earnings).

LO4 **Identify and describe different sources of short-term financing.**

Short-term financing raises funds to be repaid in less than one year.

What are major forms of short-term financing?

Sources of short-term financing include trade credit, family and friends, commercial banks and other financial institutions, short-term loans, factoring accounts receivable, commercial paper, and credit cards.

Why should businesses use trade credit?

Trade credit is the least expensive and most convenient form of short-term financing. Businesses can buy goods today and pay for them sometime in the future.

What is a line of credit and a revolving credit agreement?

A line of credit is an agreement by a bank to lend a specified amount of money to the business at any time, as long as certain conditions are met. A revolving credit agreement is a line of credit that guarantees a loan will be available—for a fee.

What is the difference between a secured loan and an unsecured loan?

An unsecured loan has no collateral backing it. Secured loans have collateral backed by assets, such as accounts receivable, inventory, or other property of value.

Is factoring a form of secured loan?

No, it is not. Factoring means selling accounts receivable at a discounted rate to a factor (an intermediary that pays cash for those accounts and keeps the funds it collects on them).

What is commercial paper?

Commercial paper is a corporation's unsecured promissory note maturing in 270 days or less.

LO5 **Identify and describe different sources of long-term financing.**

Long-term financing raises funds that will be repaid over a period greater than one year.

What are the major sources of long-term financing?

Debt financing involves borrowing from lending institutions, and the issuance of bonds to investors. Equity financing is obtained through the sale of company stock, which includes selling to venture capitalists, and taking funds from the firm's retained earnings.

What is leverage and how do firms use it?

Leverage is borrowing funds to invest in expansion, major asset purchases, or research and development. Firms measure the risk of borrowing against the potential for higher profits.

KEY TERMS

4 Cs of credit 651
bond 655
budget 642
capital budget 643
capital expenditures 647
cash budget 643
cash flow forecast 641
commercial finance companies 651
commercial paper 653
common stock 659
cost of capital 662
credit profile 651
debenture bonds (unsecured bonds) 657
debt financing 648
dividends 659
equity financing 648
factoring 653
finance 638
financial control 645
financial management 638
financial managers 638
initial public offering (IPO) 658
interest 655
leverage 662
line of credit 651
long-term financing 648
long-term forecast 641
maturity date 655
mortgage bonds (secured bonds) 657
operating (master) budget 643
preferred stock 660
promissory note 649
risk-return tradeoff 641
secured bonds (mortgage bonds) 657
secured loan 650
short-term financing 648
short-term forecast 641
sinking fund 658
stock certificate 658
stocks (shares) 658
term-loan agreement 655
time value of money 641
trade credit 649
unsecured bonds (debenture bonds) 657
unsecured loan 651
venture capital 661

CAREER EXPLORATION

If you are interested in pursuing a career in finance, here are a few to consider. Find out about the tasks performed, skills needed, pay, and opportunity outlook in these fields through Internet sites that include the Government of Canada Job Bank, Workopolis, Monster, CareerBuilder, Glassdoor, and Indeed, as well as through the Career Centre at your school.

- **Financial examiner**—ensures compliance with laws governing financial institutions and transactions; reviews balance sheets, evaluates the risk level of loans, and assesses bank management.
- **Tax preparer**—helps individual and small-business clients complete and file their tax returns; assists with tax planning.
- **Financial manager**—produces financial reports, directs investment activities, and develops strategies and plans for the long-term financial goals of the organization.
- **Cost estimator**—collects and analyzes data in order to estimate the time, money, materials, and labour required to manufacture a product, construct a building, or provide a service.

- **Personal financial planner—**provides advice on investments, insurance, mortgages, savings, estate planning, taxes, and retirement to help others manage their finances.
- **Appraiser and assessor of real estate—**provide an estimate of the value of land and the buildings on the land usually before it is sold, mortgaged, taxed, insured, or developed.
- **Financial analyst—**provides guidance to individuals making investment decisions and assesses the performance of stocks, bonds, and other types of investments.

CRITICAL THINKING

1. Budgets are designed to keep decision makers informed of progress compared to company plans. An important theme of this book is the need for managers to be flexible so that they can adapt quickly to rapidly changing conditions. This often means modifying previous plans. How do managers stay within the confines of budgets when they must shift gears to accommodate a rapidly changing world?
2. What are the primary sources of short-term funds for new business owners? What are the major sources of long-term funds?
3. Why does a financial manager need to understand the accounting information if the firm has a trained accountant on its staff?
4. Why do firms generally prefer to borrow funds to obtain long-term financing rather than issue shares of stock?

DEVELOPING CAREER SKILLS

Key: ● **Team** ★ **Analytic** ▲ **Communication** ⊡ **Technology**

▲★ 1. Contact a lending officer at a local bank in your community or visit the bank's website to review the bank's policies on providing a business line of credit and a revolving line of credit. Under what circumstances would a business qualify for either form of short-term financing?

●★▲ 2. One of the most difficult concepts to get across to small-business owners is the need to take all the trade credit they can get. For example, the credit terms 2/10, net 30 can save businesses money if they pay their bills in the first 10 days. Work with a group of classmates to build a convincing financial argument for using trade credit.

⊡★ 3. Go online and check the capitalization required to open a franchise of your choice, like Subway or McDonald's. Does the franchisor offer financial assistance to prospective franchisees? Evaluate the cost of the franchise versus its business potential using the risk/return trade-off discussed in this chapter.

⊡★▲ 4. Factoring accounts receivable is a form of financing used since the days of Babylonian King Hammurabi approximately 4000 years ago. Today it is still a source of short-term funds used by small businesses. Visit 21stfinancialsolutions.com to get more in-depth information about factoring and be prepared to discuss the pros and cons of factoring to the class.

⊡★ 5. Go to your school's website and see whether its operating budget is online. If not, go to the campus library and see if the reference librarian can help you access this information. Try to identify major capital expenditures your school has planned for the future.

ANALYZING MANAGEMENT DECISIONS

Making Dreams Come True

Carlos Galendez had big dreams but very little money. He worked more than 10 years washing dishes and then as a cook for two major restaurants, all the while saving enough money to start his own Mexican restaurant. Finally, his dream came true. Galendez opened his restaurant, Casa de Carlos, with a guaranteed loan. His old family recipes and appealing Hispanic decor helped the business gain immediate success. He repaid his small-business loan within 14 months and immediately opened a second location, and then a third. Casa de Carlos became one of the largest Mexican restaurant chains in the area.

Galendez decided that the company needed to go public to help finance expansion. He believed that continued growth was beneficial to the company, and that offering ownership was the way to bring in loyal investors. Nevertheless, he wanted to make certain that his family maintained a controlling interest in the firm's stock. Therefore, in its IPO, Casa de Carlos offered to sell only 40 percent of the company's available shares to investors. The Galendez family kept control of the remaining 60 percent.

As the public's craving for Mexican food grew, so did the fortunes of Casa de Carlos. By early 2007, the company enjoyed the enviable position of being light on debt and heavy on cash. But the firm's debt position changed dramatically when it bought out Captain Ahab's Seafood Restaurants. Two years later, it expanded into the full-service wholesale distribution of seafood products with the purchase of Ancient Mariner Wholesalers.

The firm's debt increased, but the price of its stock was up and all of its business operations were booming. Then tragedy struck the firm when Carlos Galendez died suddenly from a heart attack. His oldest child, Maria, was selected to take control as CEO. Maria Galendez had learned the business from her father, who had taught her to keep an eye out for opportunities that seemed fiscally responsible. Even so, the fortunes of the firm began to shift. Two major competitors were taking market share from Casa de Carlos, and the seafood venture began to flounder (pun intended). Also, consumer shifts in eating habits and the recession encouraged consumers to spend less, causing the company some severe cash flow problems. It was up to Maria Galendez as CEO to decide how to get the funds the firm needed for improvements and other expenses. Unfortunately, several local banks would not expand the firm's credit line, so she considered the possibility of a bond or stock offering to raise capital for the business. Her decision could be crucial to the future of the firm.

Discussion Questions

1. What advantages do bonds offer a company such as Casa de Carlos? What disadvantages do bonds impose?
2. What would be the advantages and disadvantages if the company sold new stock to investors?
3. Are any other options available to Maria Galendez?
4. What choice would you make and why?

CHAPTER 18

The Canadian Financial System

LEARNING OBJECTIVES

After you have read and studied this chapter, you should be able to:

LO1 Explain what money is and what makes it useful.

LO2 List the three components of the Canadian financial system, and explain how it is regulated.

LO3 Discuss the role that financial institutions play in providing services.

LO4 Describe the role of the financial markets.

LO5 Outline the role of the clearing and settlement systems.

PROFILE

GETTING TO KNOW: JIM CRAMER, HOST, CNBC'S MAD MONEY

You probably wouldn't say that listening to financial experts drone on about the economy and stock market is entertaining. Many expert commentators, while qualified and credible, have a style that could best be described as dry or flat-out boring. Well, if dry or boring is not your style, check out *Mad Money* hosted by Jim Cramer. Cramer could never be accused of droning; instead he rants, yells, and screams as he recommends certain investments and disses others. Since 2005, he has been on a mission to educate investors about the investments they own or perhaps plan to buy.

Cramer's path to *Mad Money* was as wild and chaotic as his actions on his TV show. He earned a BA magna cum laude from Harvard and began working as a reporter for several different newspapers. After his home was burglarized and his bank account wiped out, he hit a financial low and even lived in his car for several months. Thanks to friends and family, he sprung back from this setback and entered Harvard Law School. It was during law school that Cramer revived his love for stock trading. As a child he memorized stock symbols and had a fantasy stock portfolio. At Harvard he began trading for real using money

© Gregg DeGuire/FilmMagic/Getty Images

he earned working as a researcher for a law professor. He became a "go-to" guy for stock tips, often leaving them on his phone's answering machine. A friend asked him to manage a $500,000 portfolio. Within two years, his friend's investments were worth $650,000.

After law school, Cramer spent a brief time working as a lawyer, but his passion was finance. He became a stockbroker at Goldman Sachs Private Wealth Management where he worked for three years until he left to start his own hedge fund Cramer & Co. (A hedge fund is an alternative investment option available only to sophisticated investors such as institutions and high-wealth individuals.) His tremendous personal drive and countless hours spent researching led to enormous rewards for Cramer and his clients. Cramer & Co. regularly boasted annual returns of 24 percent for investors, and Cramer routinely made $10 million or more a year.

Unfortunately, the rigors and pressures of the hedge fund business took their toll on Cramer and his family. After 14 years he retired from the fund. His partner Jeff Berkowitz took over the firm and renamed it Cramer, Berkowitz, and Co. But don't get the impression Cramer slowed down. For starters, he wrote three books and became more active on the online investment site TheStreet.com which he cofounded. In 2005, CNBC approached him about hosting *Mad Money*, a program that would focus on stocks and investing. The show's primary objective was to educate and entertain investors about the market. After a very short time, CNBC knew it had chosen the right person for the job.

Despite the frenetic pace of *Mad Money*, Cramer's intentions are serious. His objective is to educate investors about the stocks they own, the importance of dividends, and other key elements of successful investing. He knows if you don't make the presentation interesting, no one will listen. He has never been accused of not being interesting. To fully understand finance, you need to know the basics of securities markets, how they help businesses gain needed funding, and how investors can build their financial future. In this chapter you'll learn about how securities markets achieve both objectives.

The Canadian financial system includes financial institutions, the financial markets, and clearing and settlement systems. Professionals like Jim Cramer have played a role in the dollar value growth of investments in the financial markets. It's through the financial system that most commercial activity (e.g., saving; borrowing; investing; and buying and selling by means of debit and credit cards, cheques, and e-money) is carried out. Read further to learn how governments, corporations, and individuals benefit from the stability of the Canadian financial system.

Sources: "Jim Cramer Host of *Mad Money*," CNBC, accessed October 2017; Jim Cramer, *TheStreet.com*, accessed October 2017.

© Shutterstock/Paisit Teeraphatsakool

Arguments for moving away from cash include combating illegal activity and the underground economy, creating more efficient monetary policy, and reducing transaction costs.[5] What other benefits come to mind?

Why Money is Important

You may recall from Chapter 4 that the Bank of Canada's (BoC) role is to promote the economic and financial well-being of Canada. It does this by administering Canada's monetary policy, bank notes, financial system, funds management, and retail debt.[1] In this chapter, you will learn more about some of these topics.

LO1

Explain what money is and what makes it useful.

Two of the most critical issues in Canada today, economic growth and the creation of jobs, depend on the ready availability of money. Money is so important to the economy that many institutions have evolved to manage it and make it available when needed. Today, you can get cash from an automated teller machine (ATM) almost anywhere in the world, and most organizations will accept a cheque, credit card, debit card, or smart card for purchases. Some businesses will even accept digital currencies, an online version of money. Behind the scenes is a complex system of banking that makes the free flow of money possible. Each day, over $5 trillion is exchanged in the world's currency markets.[2] Therefore, what happens to any major country's economy has an effect on the Canadian economy and vice versa.

Some countries like Sweden are moving toward a cashless economy; however, this is unlikely to be the case in Canada. While BoC data shows Canadians are using cash less often to actually pay for things—down to roughly 44 percent of all transactions—there's currently $80 billion worth of Canadian coins and bank notes in circulation, and the amount of cash is growing at a pace of between four and seven percent per year.[3] Let's start at the beginning by discussing exactly what the word *money* means.

What is Money?

money
Anything that people generally accept as payment for goods and services.

barter
The direct trading of goods and services for other goods and services.

Money is anything that people generally accept as payment for goods and services. In the past, objects as diverse as salt, feathers, fur pelts, stones, rare shells, tea, and horses have served as money. In fact, until the 1880s, cowrie shells were one of the world's most popular currencies.

Barter is the direct trading of goods or services for other goods and services. Strict laws in Europe limited the number of coins people could bring to the colonies in the New World. Thus, colonists were forced to barter for goods. For example, they might trade cotton and tobacco for shoes and lumber.

Though barter may sound like something from the past, many people have discovered the benefits of bartering online.[4] One entrepreneur describes his bartering experience as follows: "Last year we bartered the creation of a full-colour graphic novel in exchange for a new website design. . . . The value of the trade was $50,000. We provided three months of writing services to provide the graphic novel story line . . . and then five months of illustration. In exchange, they helped us to define, design, and then program our new website."

Today, some people barter goods and services the old-fashioned way.[6] In Siberia, for example, people have bought movie tickets with two eggs, and in Ukraine people have paid their energy bills with sausages and milk. Today you can go to a *barter exchange* where you can put goods or services into the system and get trade credits for other goods and services that you need.[7] The barter exchange makes it easier to barter because you do not have to find people with whom to barter. The exchange does that for you.

© Loop Images/David Cheshire/Getty Images

Although people have long used barter to exchange goods without money, one problem is that objects like chickens and eggs are harder to carry around than a $10 bill. What other drawbacks does bartering have?

The problem with traditional barter is that eggs and milk are difficult to carry around. Most people need some object that's portable, divisible, durable, and stable so that they can trade goods and services without carrying the actual goods around with them. One solution is coins and paper bills. The five standards for a useful form of money are:

- *Portability.* Coins and paper money are a lot easier to take to market than pigs, eggs, milk, or other heavy products. While it is portable, Desjardins' senior economist Hendrix Vachon recommends that Canada eliminate the nickel and move to 10-, 20-, and 50-cent coins. "Due to the gradual increase in the cost of living and decreased buying power of small coins, the time will come when the nickel will have to be taken out of circulation," he says.[8] Do you agree with him?
- *Divisibility.* Different-sized coins and bills can represent different values. Because silver is now too expensive, today's coins are made of other metals, but the accepted face values remain.
- *Stability.* When everybody agrees on the value of coins, the value of money is relatively stable. Due to its stability, much of the world has used the U.S. dollar as the measure of value. If the value of the dollar fluctuates too rapidly, the world may turn to some other form of money, such as the euro, for the measure of value.
- *Durability.* Coins last for thousands of years, even when they've sunk to the bottom of the ocean, as you've seen when divers find old coins in sunken ships.
- *Uniqueness.* It's hard to counterfeit, or copy, elaborately designed and minted coins. With the latest colour copiers, people are able to duplicate the look of paper money relatively easily. Thus, the government has gone to extra lengths to ensure that Canadian dollars are readily identifiable. Security features include raised ink, transparent text, metallic portraits, a transparent window, the display of small numbers, use of hidden numbers, and a maple leaf border.[9]

© Bank of Canada

Canada's Frontiers series banknotes are printed on polymer, which lasts at least 2.5 times longer than paper notes, reducing processing, replacement costs, and environmental impact.[10] How do these banknotes reflect the five standards of money?

Coins and paper money simplify exchanges. Most countries have their own currencies, and they are all about equally portable, divisible, and durable. However, they are not always equally stable.

Electronic Money

Electronic money (e-money) is a newer form of money. You can make online payments using PayPal, Google Wallet, or your bank's website or app. You can use Apple Pay on your smartphone to pay in brick-and-mortar stores.

digital currency
Electronic money that is not available as bills or coins.

cryptocurrencies
A type of digital currency created using computer algorithms.

Digital currency is electronic money. It's not available as bills or coins. **Cryptocurrencies** are a type of digital currency created using computer algorithms. They use cryptography for security, making it tougher to forge, easier to cut across international boundaries, and able to be stored on your hard drive instead of in a bank. See the Adapting to Change box for more about digital currencies.

PROGRESS ASSESSMENT

- Explain why money is important to the economy.
- List the five characteristics of useful money.
- What are advantages and disadvantages of cryptocurrencies?

LO2

List the three components of the Canadian financial system, and explain how it is regulated.

The Canadian Financial System[11]

The financial system makes a vital contribution to the welfare of Canadians. The system includes (1) financial institutions, (2) the financial markets, and (3) clearing and settlement systems. It is through the financial system that most commercial activity (e.g., saving, borrowing, investing, and buying and selling by means of debit and credit cards, cheques, and e-money) is carried out.

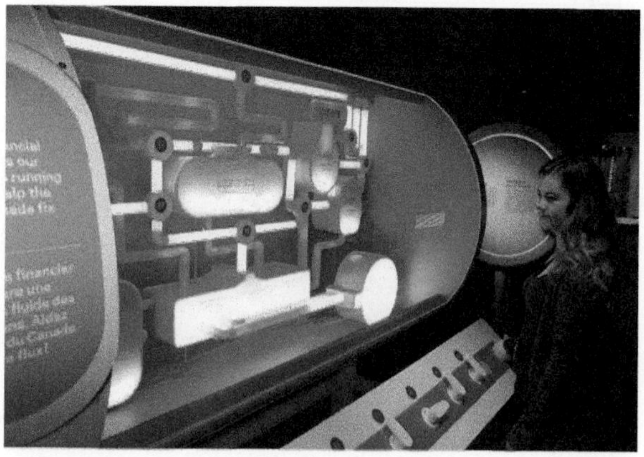

© Bank of Canada

At the Bank of Canada Museum, you can learn about your role in the economy as well as Canada's role in the world economy and how the BoC helps it all run smoothly. At the liquidity exhibit, one can place liquidity where it's needed by routing money from the BoC to commercial banks. Do hands-on exhibits interest you as a learning tool?

With a focus on promoting a stable and efficient financial system in Canada, the BoC provides liquidity to the financial system, gives policy advice to the federal government on the design and development of the system, oversees major clearing and settlement systems, and provides banking services to these systems and their participants. It also contributes to international discussions on important financial system issues.

The International Monetary Fund has concluded that the system "is mature, sophisticated, and well-managed," that "financial stability is underpinned by sound macroeconomic policies and strong prudential regulation and supervision," and that "deposit insurance and arrangements for crisis management and failure resolution are well-designed." Let's consider how the financial system is regulated.

Adapting to CHANGE

What's in Your Wallet?

No single organization, such as a central bank, creates digital currencies. Digital currencies are based on a decentralized, peer-to-peer (P2P) network. The "peers" in this network are the people who take part in digital currency transactions, and their computers make up the network.

To use digital currencies, you need to create a digital currency wallet to store and transfer digital currencies. You can store your wallet yourself or have a wallet provider manage your digital currency for you. You need a "public key" and a "private key" to use your wallet. Keys are made up of a random sequence of numbers and letters. Public keys are used to identify your wallet. Private keys are used to unlock your wallet and access your money. Private keys should be kept secret. All transactions are recorded to a public ledger or "blockchain." The blockchain may include information such as transaction amounts, wallet addresses, and the public keys of the sender and recipient.

Digital currencies have some notable disadvantages:

- Digital currencies are not legal tender in Canada as only the Canadian banknotes and coins are considered official currency in Canada.
- Digital currencies are not supported by any government or central authority, such as the BoC.
- Financial institutions (e.g., banks and credit unions) don't manage or oversee digital currency.
- Digital currencies can be difficult to buy and use as you may not be able to exchange them easily for cash or to purchase goods and services.
- Merchants don't have to accept digital currencies as payment, and they don't have to exchange digital currencies for traditional currencies, such as the Canadian dollar.
- Digital currencies may be vulnerable to fraud, theft, and hackers.

© Shutterstock/REDPIXEL.PL

- Transactions aren't reversible.
- Digital currencies can be risky investments because their value can change quickly and can be difficult to predict.

Cryptocurrencies like Bitcoin, Ethereum, Ripple, and EOS are attractive to users because there's no central authority that regulates the currency (recall that the BoC regulates currency in Canada, for example). Transactions involve two people anywhere in the world with no middlemen (e.g., a financial institution), government regulations, or transaction fees involved. In fact, you do not even have to give your name.

Launched in 2009, Bitcoin remains the most popular cryptocurrency today. Yet, it is not yet generally accepted and has been the subject of over 40 thefts already (some for over a million dollars).

Whether cryptocurrencies achieve a level of stability or just become interesting financial case studies for the digital age remains to be seen. Efforts will continue to be made to create a cashless society using some form of currency other than the bills and coins we use now.

Sources: "All CryptoCurrencies," Investing.com, accessed June 4, 2018, https://ca.investing.com/crypto/currencies; "Digital currency," Government of Canada, January 19, 2018, https://www.canada.ca/en/financial-consumer-agency/services/payment/digital-currency.html; Nathaniel Popper, "Identity Thieves Hijack Cellphone Accounts to Go After Virtual Currency," *The New York Times*, August 21, 2017; and Sunny Freeman, "What Is Bitcoin? 11 Things You Need to Know About the Digital Currency," *Huffington Post*, January 26, 2014.

Regulating the Financial System[12]

Regulating the Canadian financial system is a systemwide approach that is the shared responsibility of the Department of Finance, the BoC, and other federal financial regulatory authorities (to be discussed shortly). Ultimately, it is the Minister of Finance who is responsible for the financial system.

Due to its important role in the economy, the financial system is heavily regulated. Regulation is designed to ensure the integrity, safety, and soundness of financial institutions and markets. In addition, they protect investors, depositors, and policyholders. Keep in mind, though, that these compliance requirements require a lot of time and money for companies in this industry to complete.

In Canada, there is no single body that regulates the financial system. It is a responsibility shared among different organizations and levels of government. As highlighted in Figure 18.1, financial institutions may be regulated at either the federal or the provincial level, or jointly, and in some instances may depend on the jurisdiction under which the company is incorporated or registered.

For institutions under provincial jurisdiction, the province(s) in which a company is incorporated or registered is (are) responsible for regulating the company's overall powers. As at the federal level, provinces are supported by agencies and organizations that supervise the ongoing operations of these institutions.

For institutions under federal responsibility, the Department of Finance is charged with overseeing their overall powers—in other words, what they can and cannot do. The Department of Finance relies on three federal agencies to supervise the ongoing operations of these institutions and their compliance with legislation. Let us briefly consider each agency.

OFFICE OF THE SUPERINTENDENT OF FINANCIAL INSTITUTIONS (OSFI)[13]

OSFI, whose purpose is "to contribute to public confidence in the Canadian financial system," regulates and supervises more than 400 federally regulated banks and insurance companies and 1200 pension plans. It monitors the day-to-day operations of financial institutions with respect to their financial soundness.

FIGURE 18.1

REGULATORY RESPONSIBILITY FOR FINANCIAL INSTITUTIONS

Financial Institution	Federal	Provincial	Depends on Jurisdiction
Banks	✓		
Securities Commissions		✓	
Credit Unions		✓	
Caisses Populaires		✓	
Insurance Providers			✓
Trust and Loan Companies			✓
Cooperative Credit Associations			✓

Source: Based on data "Regulation of the Canadian Financial System," Bank of Canada, April 2012, http://www.bankofcanada.ca/wp-content/uploads/2010/11/regulation_canadian_financial.pdf.

CANADA DEPOSIT INSURANCE CORPORATION (CDIC)[14]

CDIC oversees the deposit insurance system, which protects deposits that Canadians have in their federal financial institutions. Since it was created in 1967, CDIC has dealt with 43 member failures affecting some 2 million Canadians. No one has lost a dollar of deposits under CDIC protection.

CDIC guarantees deposits up to $100,000 (principal and interest), in Canadian dollars, in each member institution; however, it does not cover all deposits. For example, foreign-currency accounts, stocks, bonds, and mutual funds are not covered. (Look for a further discussion later on in this chapter.) If you own digital currency, it's your responsibility to protect your digital currency wallet. Federal or provincial deposit insurance plans don't cover digital currency. If the currency exchange or wallet provider that has your digital currency fails or goes bankrupt, your funds won't be protected.

Some CDIC members have subsidiaries that are CDIC members in their own right. As a result, depending on how deposits are registered, you can be protected for more than $100,000.

Courtesy of Canada Deposit Insurance Corporation

CDIC is funded primarily by premiums paid by banks and trust companies that belong to this program. Membership sign decals must be displayed prominently at a member institution's entrance. Have you seen this sign in your local or online financial institution?

FINANCIAL CONSUMER AGENCY OF CANADA (FCAC)[15]

FCAC monitors financial institutions to ensure that they comply with federal consumer protection measures, which range from disclosure requirements to complaint-handling procedures. FCAC also provides information, and in some cases, online tools to support Canadians.

In a recent report, FCAC published its review of domestic banks' retail sales practices. The report found that bank cultures strongly anchored in sales can increase the risks of mis-selling to consumers and of bank employees breaching market conduct obligations. It proposed a number of measures banks can take to reduce these risks. Do you have more confidence in the Canadian financial system now knowing a little more of the purpose of these three agencies?

After the Progress Assessment, let's consider financial institutions, one area of Canada's financial system. This will be followed by a discussion on the financial markets, and then the clearing and settlement systems.

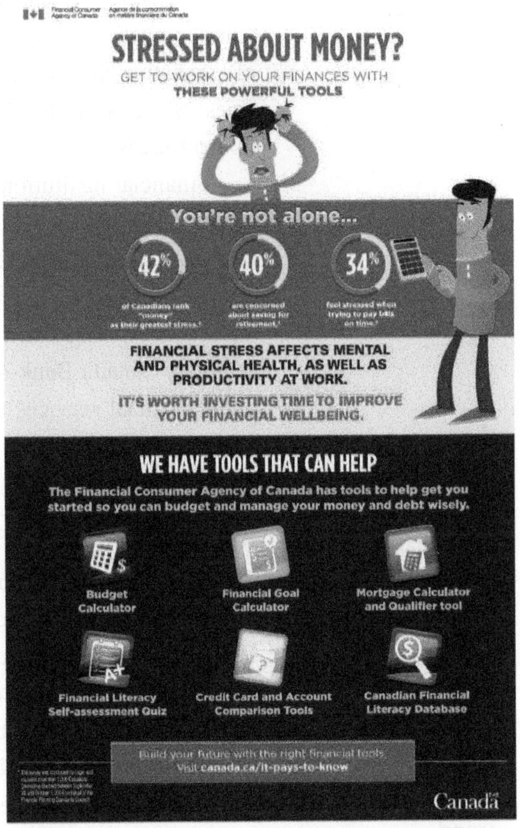

Stressed About Money?, canada.ca/it-pays-to-know, Financial Consumer Agency of Canada, 2018. Reproduced with the permission of the Minister of Public Services and Procurement Canada 2018.

Do you see how these FCAC tools may help you throughout your life? Which tools are most relevant to you now?

Canada Deposit Insurance Corporation (CDIC) Oversees the deposit insurance system, which protects deposits that Canadians have in their federal financial institutions.

PROGRESS ASSESSMENT

- What three areas does the Canadian financial system oversee?
- Give three examples of financial institutions. Include which level of government regulates each example.
- Describe the roles of three federal agencies: OSFI, CDIC, and FCAC.

LO3

Discuss the role that financial institutions play in providing services.

The Canadian Financial System: Financial Institutions

Until the middle of the 1980s, Canada had a "four-pillar system" that included (1) banks, (2) trust companies, (3) insurance companies, and (4) securities dealers. Regulation was designed to foster competition within each pillar, but not among them. Changes in regulations have eliminated many of the old barriers that prohibited financial institutions from competing in each other's business, and consequently, the four pillars. As a result of legislative changes in 1992, the banks were allowed to own insurance, trust, and securities subsidiaries and vice versa. Today, most of Canada's large banks have subsidiaries in these areas[16]

Financial institutions include commercial banks, credit unions, trust and loan companies, insurance companies, and non-banks.[17] These financial institutions support both businesses and consumers. Today, it is increasingly difficult to distinguish firms by type of function, as financial institutions have become highly competitive. For example, we see non-traditional financial services providers—such as Canadian Tire Bank and Walmart Canada Bank—taking advantage of changes in the regulatory environment to offer financial services to their customer base. Next, consider some of the competitors in this business.

commercial bank A profit-seeking organization that receives deposits from individuals and corporations in the form of chequing and savings accounts and then uses some of these funds to make loans.

spread The difference between the interest a bank earns on loans extended to customers and the interest paid to depositors and other creditors for the use of their money.

Commercial Banks

The banks that are probably the most familiar to you are commercial banks. A **commercial bank** is a profit-seeking organization that receives deposits from individuals and corporations in the form of chequing and savings accounts, and uses these funds to make loans. It has two types of customers, depositors and borrowers, and is equally responsible to both.

Figure 18.2 highlights how banks make money, how revenues are utilized, and the distribution of net income. Net interest income is generated from what is known as the *spread.* The **spread** is simply the difference between the interest a bank earns on loans extended to customers and the interest paid to depositors and other creditors for the use of their money.[18] Are you surprised to learn that 45 percent of bank revenue earned is net interest income while only 5 percent is generated from service charges?[19]

According to the Canadian Bankers Association (CBA), the major domestic banks offer a full range of banking, investment, and financial services. They have extensive, nationwide distribution networks and also are active in the United States, Latin America, the Caribbean, Asia, and other parts of the world. Many large international banks have a

FIGURE 18.2

HOW BANKS MAKE MONEY AND DISTRIBUTE NET INCOME

The majority of Canadians are shareholders in Canadian banks either directly through share ownership or indirectly through pension and mutual funds, including the Canada Pension Plan. Do you own such investments?

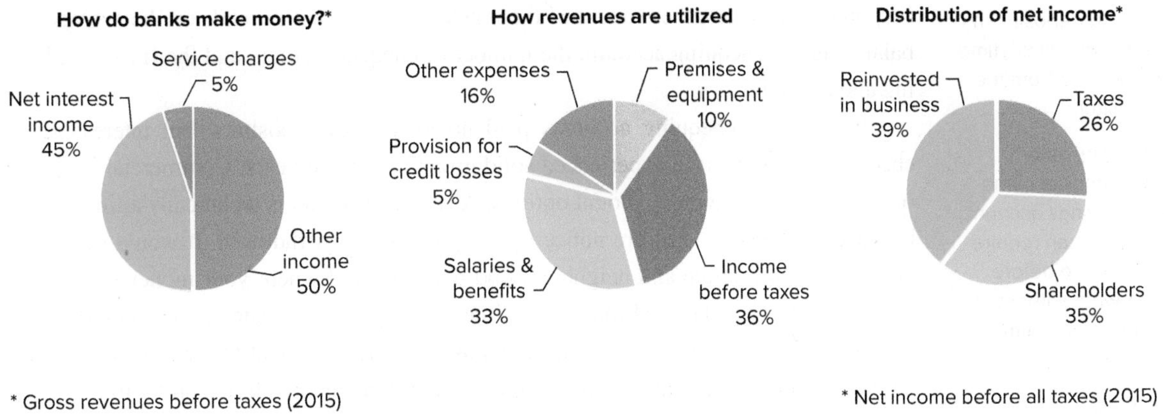

Source: "Focus: Bank Revenues and Profits," Canadian Bankers Association, accessed June 6, 2018, https://www.cba.ca/bank-revenues-and-earnings-profits.

presence in Canada—through a subsidiary, representative office, or branch of the parent bank. Most specialize in corporate and investment banking (e.g., niche financing) and have only one or two offices/branches.[20]

Review Figure 18.3 for a list of Canada's top five banks. The domestic operations of these five banks accounts for more than half of the industry's revenues with the four largest banks deriving a third or more of their revenues from outside Canada.[21]

FIGURE 18.3

CANADA'S BIG FIVE BANKS IN 2017

Ranking	Bank Name	Total Assets (C$ billions)
1	Toronto-Dominion Bank (TD)	1,279.0
2	Royal Bank of Canada (RBC)	1,212.9
3	Bank of Nova Scotia (Scotiabank)	915.3
4	Bank of Montreal (BMO)	709.6
5	Canadian Imperial Bank of Commerce (CIBC)	565.3

Source: Based on data from "Top 10 Banks in Canada," Banks around the World, accessed June 4, 2018, http://www.relbanks.com/north-america/canada.

SOME SERVICES PROVIDED BY COMMERCIAL BANKS

Individuals and corporations that deposit money in a chequing account can write personal cheques to pay for almost any purchase or transaction. The technical name for a chequing account is a **demand deposit** because the money is available on demand from the depositor. Some banks impose a service charge for cheque-writing privileges or demand a minimum deposit. They might also charge a small handling fee for each cheque written. For corporate depositors, the amount of the service charge often depends on the average daily balance in the chequing account, the number of cheques written, and the firm's credit rating and credit history.

demand deposit
The technical name for a chequing account; the money in a demand deposit can be withdrawn anytime on demand from the depositor.

time deposit
The technical name for a savings account; the bank can require prior notice before the owner withdraws money from a time deposit.

certificate of deposit
A time-deposit (savings) account that earns interest to be delivered at the end of the certificate's maturity date; also called a Guaranteed Investment Certificate (GIC).

In the past, chequing accounts paid no interest to depositors, but interest-bearing chequing accounts have experienced solid growth in recent years. Commercial banks also offer a variety of savings account options. A savings account is technically a **time deposit** because the bank can require notice before you make a withdrawal. It would be wise for you to compare online and neighbourhood banks to find where your money can earn the most interest. The Making Ethical Decisions box explores an issue that you could face.

A **certificate of deposit** is a time-deposit (savings) account that earns interest, to be delivered on the certificate's maturity date. Some financial institutions refer to certificates of deposit as *Guaranteed Investment Certificates* or *GICs*. The depositor agrees not to withdraw any of the funds in the account until then. The longer the term deposit is to be held by the bank, the higher the interest rate. The interest rates also depend on economic conditions.

Banks offer a variety of products and services. Examples include credit cards and loans for creditworthy customers, life insurance, brokerage services, financial counselling, automatic bill payments, safe-deposit boxes, registered retirement savings accounts, traveller's cheques, automated teller machines (ATMs), and overdraft protection. The latter means preferred customers can automatically get loans when they've written cheques exceeding their account balance.

Making ETHICAL DECISIONS

An Open and Shut Option?

You work at a large bank in the new accounts department where you open accounts for new customers. The bank has a policy that pays bonuses related to the number of new accounts opened. Your manager tells you that many of the accounts are for small depositors. He suggests that when opening a new savings account for customers, you can add another account, such as a credit card, without them being aware of it.

You know that opening an account without the approval of the customer is not proper, but you also know the person may never know who opened it. Anyway, your manager suggested it and bonus money sounds good. What are your alternatives? What would you do? Is that the ethical thing to do?

© YinYang/Getty Images

Today, banks are continually trying to improve services to mobile users, especially Millennials. Having been in an Internet and personal computer world their entire lives, Millennials are very adept at mobile banking. They use technology to deposit cheques, pay bills, track expenses, and transfer money.[22]

© SOPA Images Limited/Alamy Stock Photo

This is not your traditional ATM. When this chapter was written, Canada had 540 crypto ATMs.[25] How many are there in Canada now? If you have seen a crypto ATM, have you used it?

MANAGING YOUR PERSONAL FINANCES

Studying business prepares you for finding and keeping a good job. You already know that one of the secrets to finding a well-paying job is to have a good education. With your earnings, you can take vacations, raise a family, make investments, buy the products you want, and give generously to others. Money management, however, is not easy. You have to earn the money in the first place. Then you have to learn how to save money, spend money wisely, and insure yourself against any financial and health risks. Review Appendix B at the end of this chapter for a discussion on managing your personal finances.

credit union
A non-profit, member-owned financial co-operative that offers a full variety of banking services to its members.

trust company
A financial institution that can administer estates, pension plans, and agency contracts, in addition to other activities conducted by banks.

Credit Unions and Trust Companies

There are over 300 credit unions serving over 5.5 million Canadians.[23] A **credit union** is a non-profit, member-owned financial co-operative that offers a full variety of banking services to its members. They include interest-bearing chequing accounts at relatively high rates, short-term loans at relatively low rates, financial counselling, life insurance policies, and a limited number of home mortgage loans. (Recall some of the key differences between co-operatives and for-profit organizations from our Chapter 6 discussion.) They are organized by government agencies, corporations, unions, and professional associations. Caisses populaires, one example, are located predominantly in Quebec. Today, credit unions are growing in popularity.

You might want to visit a local credit union to see whether you are eligible to belong, and then compare the rates to those at local banks. Credit unions often have fewer branches than banks and less access to ATMs. It is best to determine what services you need and then compare those services to the same services offered by banks.[24]

© Lee Brown/Alamy Stock Photo

Credit unions are member-owned financial co-operatives that offer their members a wide range of banking services. If you do not belong to a credit union, what would a credit union need to offer you to get you to switch?

A **trust company** is a financial institution that over the years conducted activities similar to those of banks. How they differ is that trust companies have a fiduciary role. Due to this role, trust companies can administer estates, pension plans, and agency contracts, which banks cannot do as it was originally considered a conflict of interest for banks. Changes in regulations over the years have seen trust companies expand their quasi-banking operations—designed originally to attract savings and term deposits to fund mortgage lending—into complete banking facilities for both individuals and businesses.[26]

Other Financial Institutions: Non-Banks

non-banks
Financial organizations that accept no deposits but offer many services provided by regular banks.

There are also a variety of other institutions called non-banks. **Non-banks** are financial organizations that accept no deposits but offer many services provided by regular banks. Non-banks include life insurance companies, pension funds, brokerage firms, commercial finance companies, and corporate financial services.

Life insurance companies provide financial protection for policyholders, who periodically pay premiums. In addition, insurers invest the funds they receive from policyholders in corporate and government bonds. Today, insurance companies often provide long-term financing for real estate development projects.

pension funds
Amounts of money put aside by corporations, non-profit organizations, or unions to cover part of the financial needs of their members when they retire.

Pension funds are amounts of money put aside by corporations, non-profit organizations, or unions to help fund their members' financial needs when they retire. Contributions to pension funds are made by employees, employers, or both. To generate additional income, pension funds typically invest in low-return, but safe, corporate stocks or other conservative investments, such as government securities and corporate bonds.

As competition between banks and non-banks has increased, the differences between them have become less apparent. The diversity of financial services and investment alternatives non-banks offer has led banks to expand their own services. Some banks acquired *brokerage firms* to offer full-service financial assistance, such as when CIBC acquired Merrill Lynch Canada's retail brokerage firm in 2001. In addition, CIBC also bought Merrill's Canadian mutual fund and securities services businesses, beating out rivals reported to have included TD, Scotiabank, National Bank, and a group of Merrill insiders backed by the Caisse de dépôt et placement du Québec.[27]

Commercial and consumer finance companies offer short-term loans to businesses or individuals who cannot meet the credit requirements of regular banks, such as new businesses, or those who have exceeded their credit limit and need more funds. Be careful when borrowing from such institutions as their interest rates can be quite high.

Financial institutions are facing increased competition from financial technology or "fintech" firms. In addition to partnering with these companies, financial institutions have ramped up their hiring of in-house IT workers to upgrade their own technological infrastructure.[28] The Spotlight on Small Business highlights a fintech that hopes to become the Millennials' lender of choice.

Using Technology to Improve Efficiency

Imagine the cost to a financial institution of approving a written cheque, physically processing it, and mailing it back to you. Such transactions are processed by the third component of the financial system, the clearing and settlement systems. This can all be expensive, so it should not be a surprise that financial institutions continue to look for ways to make the system more efficient.

Spotlight *On* SMALL BUSINESS

Becoming Your Best Friend in Banking

The willingness of Millennials to embrace banking alternatives led to the development of SoFi, a fintech firm. Started in 2011, SoFi originally provided student loan refinancing. Today, the company boasts 225 000 members with roughly $15 billion in loans. SoFi hopes to become the bank of choice to Millennials and do to banks what Amazon has done to bookstores and Uber has done to taxi service.

After experiencing rapid growth with student loan refinancing, SoFi moved into mortgages and personal loans after members requested help with other aspects of their financial lives. In addition to providing personal loans and mortgages, SoFi distinguishes itself by offering its members social events, job placement, wealth management, and the ability to pause loan payments if they lose their jobs. A borrower who wants to start a new business can even apply to have loan payments suspended for 6 months (with a possible extension to 12 months) to devote his or her time and energy to the business. SoFi believes that traditional banks have lost sight of building professional and personal relationships with their customers. It believes that financial services and transactions should go beyond a pure transactional relationship and work to improve the lives of customers. According to SoFi, "It's all about money, career, and relationships."

© vladwel/Shutterstock RF

SoFi has excelled at developing new products by carefully listening to its customers and adapting its services to their needs. The company generates its fees by selling loans to third-party investors (mainly hedge funds) and sales of loans to banks. At present, despite providing traditional banking functions, the company is not subject to many of the strict banking rules traditional banks must follow. However, expectations are SoFi and other fintech lenders will face increased regulatory scrutiny in the future.

Sources: Andy Kessler, "The Uberization of Banking," *The Wall Street Journal*, May 1, 2016; Leena Rao, "This Bank Wants to Be Your Best Friend," *Fortune*, March 15, 2016; Ainsley O'Connell, "Club SoFi," *Fast Company*, August 2016; Murray Newlands, "SoFi Is Dominating the Finance Space: Here's What They Are Planning Next," *Forbes*, November 23, 2016; Peter Rudegeair, "Online Lender SoFi Takes Step Toward Becoming a Bank," *The Wall Street Journal*, June 12, 2017.

One solution was to issue credit cards to reduce the flow of cheques, but they too have their costs: there's still paper to process. Accepting credit cards costs retailers a bit over 2 percent of the amount charged. In the future we'll see much more electronic rather than physical exchange of money, because it is the most efficient way to transfer funds.

If you must use a credit card, be sure to search for one that offers the best deal for you. Some offer cash back, others offer free travel, and so forth. Don't just sign up for whatever card is offering free T-shirts on campus. Do your research.

electronic funds transfer (EFT) system A computerized system that electronically performs financial transactions such as making purchases, paying bills, and receiving paycheques.

In an **electronic funds transfer (EFT) system**, messages about a transaction are sent from one computer to another. Thus, organizations can transfer funds more quickly and economically than with paper cheques. EFT tools include electronic cheque conversion, debit cards, smart cards, direct deposits, and direct payments.

Courtesy of Pacsafe, www.pacsafe.com

RFID chips in credit cards allow consumers to pay for products with just a wave of a hand. But they're also easier for hackers to access, leading some people to keep their cards in RFID-blocking holders like this one. How do you make sure that your identity and finances are secure?

A **debit card** serves the same function as a cheque—it withdraws funds from a chequing account. When the sale is recorded, the debit card sends an electronic signal to the financial institution, automatically transferring funds from your account to the seller's. A record of transactions immediately appears online. Debit transactions surpassed credit years ago and continue to grow.

Debit cards may not offer the same protection as credit cards. If someone steals your credit card, for example, Visa markets a zero liability policy. (Be aware that the financial institution that approved the credit card may still hold you liable if it is proven that you did not maintain the confidentiality and safekeeping of your credit card and electronic signature.[29]) The same holds for debit card losses; the Canadian Code of Practice for Consumer Debit Card Services maintains that you will be responsible if you have contributed to the unauthorized use of your debit card (e.g., writing your Personal Identification Number [PIN] on or near your card or choosing an unacceptable PIN selected from your name, telephone number, date of birth, address, or social insurance number).[30] You should review the Cardholder Agreement for details.

Payroll debit cards are an efficient way for some firms to pay their workers, and are an alternative to cash for those who don't qualify for a credit or debit card—the so-called unbanked. Employees can access funds in their accounts immediately after they are posted, withdraw them from an ATM, pay bills online, or transfer funds to another cardholder. The system is much cheaper for companies than issuing cheques, and more convenient for employees.[31]

A **smart card** is an electronic funds transfer tool that combines a credit card, debit card, phone card, driver's licence card, and more. Smart cards replace the typical magnetic strip on a credit or debit card with a microprocessor. The card can then store a variety of information, including the holder's bank balance. Merchants can use this information to verify the card's validity and spending limits, and transactions can debit up to the amount on the card.

debit card
An electronic funds transfer tool that serves the same function as cheques: it withdraws funds from a chequing account.

smart card
An electronic funds transfer tool that is a combination credit card, debit card, phone card, driver's licence card, and more.

Some smart cards have embedded radio frequency identification (RFID) chips that make it possible to enter buildings and secure areas and to buy gas and other items with a swipe of the card. A biometric function lets you use your fingerprint to boot up your computer. Students are using smart cards to open locked doors to dorms and identify themselves to retailers near campus and online. The cards also serve as ATM cards.

For many, the ultimate convenience in banking is automatic transactions such as direct deposit and direct payments. A *direct deposit* is a credit made directly to a chequing or savings account in place of a paycheque. The employer contacts the financial institution and orders it to transfer funds from the employer's account to the worker's account. Individuals can use direct deposits to transfer funds to other accounts, such as from a chequing account to a savings or retirement account.

A *direct payment* is a preauthorized electronic payment. Customers sign a separate form for each company whose bill they would like to automatically pay from their chequing or savings account on a specified date. The customer's financial institution completes each transaction and records it on the customer's monthly statement.

ONLINE BANKING

Financial institutions allow customers to access their accounts online, and most have bill-paying capacity. Thus, you can complete your financial transactions from home using your telephone, computer, or mobile device to transfer funds from one account to another, pay your bills, and check the balance in each of your accounts. You can apply for a car loan or mortgage and get a response while you wait. Buying and selling stocks and bonds is also easy.

Internet banks, such as Scotiabank-owned Tangerine and CIBC-owned Simplii Financial offer online banking only. They can offer customers slightly higher interest rates and lower fees because they do not have the overhead costs traditional financial institutions have with branches. While many consumers are pleased with the savings and convenience, not all are happy with the service. Why? Some are nervous about security. People fear putting their financial information into cyberspace, where others may see it despite all the assurances of privacy.

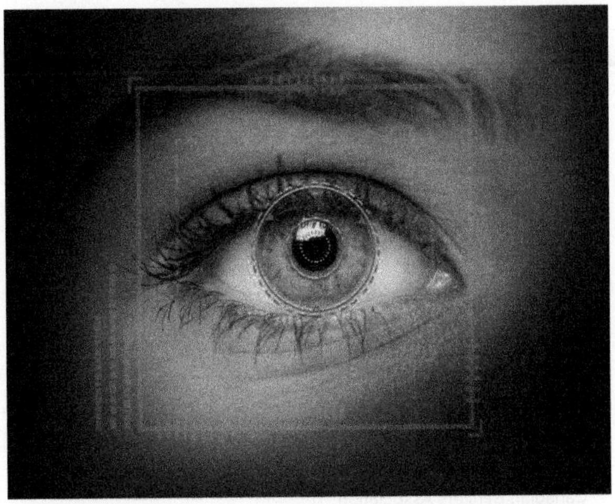

© Shutterstock/rimom

The Bank of Montreal became the first bank to offer a biometric identification program for corporate credit card users (Selfie Pay). Tangerine offers the first banking app using eye verification (Eye Verify).[35] Would you be comfortable using a biometric identification program? Would the availability of one encourage you to switch financial institutions?

LOOKING AHEAD

Canadians are embracing new technologies in their daily lives, and value innovative ways to make their banking more accessible and convenient. Examples include the increasing use of online and mobile banking, with payments quickly evolving as mobile wallets and "tap and go" contactless payments become more widely available.[32] Results from a Payments Pulse Survey shares that although users of electronic payment tools, such as e-wallets, almost unanimously applaud their convenience, few Canadians (13 percent) have adopted such innovations to date. Approximately 50 percent of respondents were willing to let go of cash and even more were willing to let go of cheques (66 percent).[33] What is your position on e-wallets, cash, and cheques?

Neil Parmenter, president and CEO of the CBA, recognizes that the CBA's immediate challenge will be managing the digital transformation: "Among other challenges, customers are being tempted away by new and nimble digital competitors with low overhead and sometimes lighter regulatory burdens. Consequently, banks are scrambling to adopt new technologies and ways of doing business to avoid the fate of slow-footed incumbents in other, already disrupted industries."[34]

With this in mind, the CBA is advocating for a *digital ID* in Canada. A federated digital ID framework—one interconnected network—would need to be developed in collaboration with Canada's banks, telecommunications companies, law enforcement, and government. With a digital ID, Canadians could identify themselves to government, businesses and each other electronically, with ease and security, and without the need to

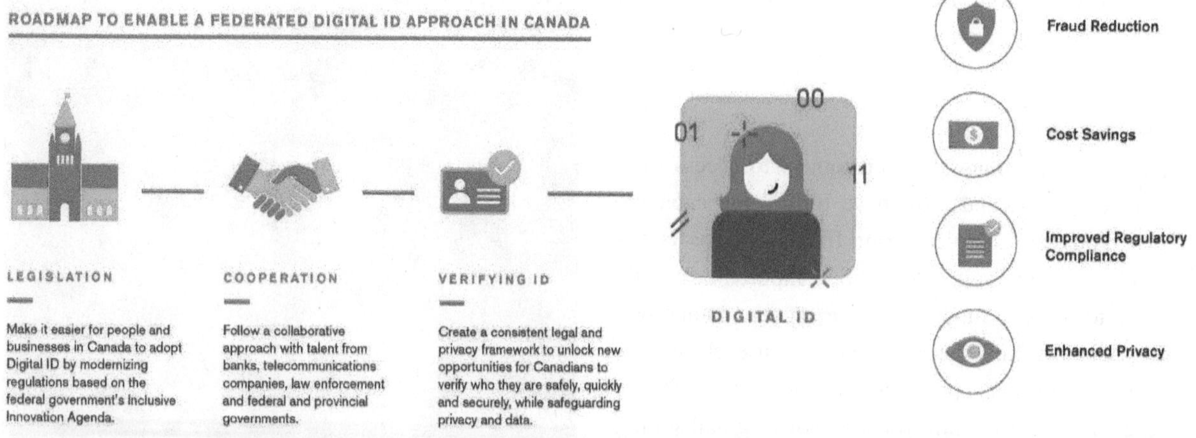

CBA believes that collaboration is crucial to enable Canada's participation in a digital economy as a way to improve innovation and growth while creating a stronger and safer way to manage Canadians' identities.[37] Do you have any concerns about having a digital ID? Can you think of any immediate benefits?

present physical documents when doing business with the public and private sectors.[36] What are your thoughts on this?

After the Progress Assessment, let's learn about financial markets, another area of Canada's financial system.

PROGRESS ASSESSMENT

- What components of the financial services industry were known as the four pillars?
- Contrast credit unions and caisses populaires, and list some non-bank competitors.
- How does a debit card differ from a smart card?
- Describe a digital ID. What would be benefits of a digital ID?

LO4

Describe the role of the financial markets.

The Canadian Financial System: Financial Markets[38]

Financial markets consist of markets for money, bonds, equities, derivatives, and foreign exchange. It is mainly through the financial markets that the BoC's key policy rate influences interest rates and the exchange rate. This, in turn, helps the BoC achieve its monetary policy objectives. The BoC is also involved in financial markets through auctions of government securities. On rare occasions, the BoC may also intervene in the foreign exchange market on behalf of the government to promote orderly markets for the Canadian dollar.

A **security** is a negotiable financial instrument that represents some type of financial value. It is a transferable certificate of ownership of an investment product such as a note, bond, stock, futures contract, or option. You will learn about futures contracts and options in a financial management course.

security
A negotiable financial instrument that represents some type of financial value.

The Canadian government closely regulates who can sell securities, including stocks and bonds. If you wish to engage in such transactions, look for a registered securities dealer. A **securities dealer or investment dealer** is a firm that trades securities for its clients and offers investment services. These dealers have passed background checks and a series of extremely challenging examinations. You can verify an individual's credentials by going to the Investment Industry Regulatory Organization of Canada, which is also the licensing authority for securities dealers.

securities dealer or investment dealer
A firm that trades securities for its clients and offers investment services; also known as an investment dealer.

Linking back to a discussion earlier in this chapter, the BoC Governor Stephen Poloz objects to the term cryptocurrencies. "They are crypto but they aren't currencies . . . they aren't assets for the most part . . . I suppose they are securities technically . . . There is no intrinsic value for something like bitcoin so it's not really an asset one can analyze. It's just essentially speculative or gambling." Do you agree?

The Function of Securities Markets

Financial markets include securities markets. *Securities markets*—financial marketplaces for stocks, bonds, and other investments—serve two major functions. First, they assist businesses in finding long-term funding to finance capital needs, such as expanding operations, developing new products, or buying major goods and services. (Recall this discussion in Chapter 17.) Second, they provide private investors a place to buy and sell securities (investments), such as stocks and bonds, that can help them build their financial future.

Securities markets are divided into primary and secondary markets. *Primary markets* handle the sale of *new* securities. This is an important point to understand. Corporations make money on the sale of their securities (stock) only once—when they sell it on the primary market.[39] As introduced in Chapter 17, the first public offering of a corporation's stock is called an initial public offering (IPO). After the IPO, the *secondary market* handles the trading of these securities between investors, with the proceeds of the sale going to the investor selling the stock, not to the corporation whose stock is sold.

© Carrie Devorah/WENN.com/Newscom

David and Tom Gardner, the Motley Fools, are passionate about spreading the message that securities markets can provide opportunities for all. The brothers have built their careers on providing high-quality financial information to investors regardless of education or income. Would you consider them as a source of information?

For example, imagine your restaurant, Harvest Gold, has grown into a chain and your products are available in many retail stores throughout the country. You want to raise additional funds to expand further. If you offer 1 million shares of stock in your company at $10 a share, you can raise $10 million at this initial offering. However, after the initial sale, if Shareholder Jones decides to sell 100 shares of her Harvest Gold stock to Investor Liu, Harvest Gold collects nothing from that transaction. Liu buys the stock from Jones, not from Harvest Gold. It is possible, however, for companies like Harvest Gold to offer (new) additional shares of stock for sale to raise additional capital.

As mentioned in Chapter 17, we can't overemphasize the importance of long-term funding to businesses. Given a choice, businesses normally prefer to meet their long-term financial needs by using retained earnings or borrowing funds either from a lending institution (e.g., bank or credit union) or corporate bond issue. However, if long-term funds are not available from retained earnings or lenders, a company may be able to raise capital by issuing corporate stock. (Recall that selling stock in the corporation is a form of *equity financing* and issuing corporate bonds is a form of *debt financing.*) These sources of equity and bond financing are not available to all companies, especially small businesses.

investment bankers
Specialists who assist in the issue and sale of new securities.

institutional investors
Large organizations—such as pension funds, mutual funds, and insurance companies—that invest their own funds or the funds of others.

stock exchange
An organization whose members can buy and sell (exchange) securities for companies and investors.

Let's imagine you need further long-term financing to *expand* operations at Harvest Gold. Your chief financial officer (CFO) says the company lacks sufficient retained earnings and she doesn't think it can secure the needed funds from a lending institution. She suggests that you offer shares of stock or issue corporate bonds to private investors to secure the funding. She warns, however, that issuing shares of stock or corporate bonds is not simple or automatic. To get approval for stock or bond issues you must make extensive financial disclosures and undergo detailed scrutiny by a securities exchange. Because of these requirements, your CFO recommends that the company turn to an investment banker for assistance. Let's see why.

The Role of Investment Bankers

Investment bankers are specialists who assist in the issue and sale of new securities. These large financial firms can help companies like Harvest Gold prepare the extensive financial analyses necessary to gain securities commission approval for bond or stock issues. Investment bankers can also *underwrite* new issues of stocks or bonds.[40] That is, the investment banking firm buys the entire stock or bond issue at an agreed-on discount, which can be quite sizeable, and then sells the issue to private or institutional investors at full price.

Institutional investors are large organizations—such as pension funds, mutual funds, and insurance companies—that invest their own funds or the funds of others. Because of their vast buying power, institutional investors are a powerful force in securities markets.

Before we look at how investors buy securities, it's important to understand stock exchanges—the places where stocks and bonds are traded.

© John Angelillo/UPI/Newscom

The TSX and the MX are not the only fish in the stock exchange sea. Exchanges like the New York Stock Exchange (NYSE), pictured here, are located throughout the world. Today, stocks are bought and sold primarily through electronic networks.

Stock Exchanges

A **stock exchange** is an organization whose members can buy and sell (exchange) securities for companies and investors. The Toronto Stock Exchange (TSX) and the Montréal Exchange (MX) are just two examples of securities markets in Canada. Most trading today takes place on computers that can transact thousands of stock trades within seconds.

Thanks to expanded communications and the relaxation of many legal barriers, investors can buy securities from companies almost anywhere in the world. If you uncover a foreign company you feel has great potential for growth, you can purchase shares of its stock with little difficulty from Canadian brokers who have access to foreign stock exchanges. Foreign investors can also invest in Canadian securities, and large foreign stock exchanges, like those in New York, London, and Tokyo. Other major stock exchanges are located in Shanghai, Sydney, Hong Kong, and São Paolo. As global markets continue to expand, stock exchanges have become active in Africa.[41]

Not all securities are traded on registered stock exchanges. The **over-the-counter (OTC) market** provides companies and investors with a means to trade stocks not listed on the large securities exchanges. The OTC market is a network of several thousand brokers who maintain contact with one another and buy and sell securities through a nationwide electronic system. Trading is conducted between two parties directly, instead of through an exchange like the TSX. In addition to the OTC market, stocks can be traded through **alternative trading systems (ATSs)** —automated trading systems that bring together dealers and institutional investors who trade large quantities of stocks.[42]

over-the-counter (OTC) market
An exchange that provides companies and investors with a means to trade stocks not listed on the national exchanges.

alternative trading systems (ATSs)
Automated trading systems that bring together dealers and institutional investors who trade large quantities of stocks.

Securities Regulations

As mentioned earlier in the text, one of the reasons why private corporations become public corporations is to raise capital to expand their existing operations. Companies seeking public financing must issue a prospectus. A **prospectus** is a condensed version of economic and financial information that a company must make available to investors before they purchase the security. The prospectus must be approved by the securities commission in the province or territory where the public funding is being sought.

A **securities commission** is a provincial or territorial government agency, such as the Ontario Securities Commission, that administers and enforces rules around how securities are issued, bought, and sold.[43] The Canadian Securities Administrators (CSA) is an umbrella organization of Canada's ten provincial and three territorial securities regulators whose objective is to improve, coordinate, and harmonize regulation of the Canadian capital markets.[44]

prospectus
A condensed version of economic and financial information that a company must make available to investors before they purchase a security.

securities commission
A provincial or territorial government agency that administers and enforces rules around how securities are issued, bought and sold.

For years, the federal government has been working toward the creation of a national securities regulator. Citing that Canada is the only industrialized country without a national regulator, it believes that "by pooling provincial, territorial and federal jurisdiction and expertise, Canada could have a world-leading securities regulatory regime that contributes to a stronger national economy and allows Canada to better compete in global capital markets. Businesses would be able to raise funds throughout Canada more quickly and at lower cost, which would stimulate investment. Businesses would also benefit from more expedited regulatory decisions."[45] Not all of the provinces and territories agree as to date, only six governments—Yukon, British Columbia, Saskatchewan, Ontario, New Brunswick, and Prince Edward Island—have joined the federal government in this Cooperative System.[46] Have more provinces and territories joined since this text was published?

PROGRESS ASSESSMENT

- Describe the financial markets in Canada.
- What are two main functions of securities markets?
- Compare primary and secondary markets.
- What is the purpose of a stock exchange? Name a Canadian stock exchange.
- Describe the role of securities commissions.

How Investors Buy Securities

stockbroker
A registered representative who works as a market intermediary to buy and sell securities for clients.

Investing in bonds, stocks, or other securities is not difficult. First, you decide what bond or stock you want to buy. After that, you find a registered brokerage firm authorized to trade securities to execute your order. A **stockbroker** is a registered representative who works as a market intermediary to buy and sell securities for clients. Stockbrokers place an order and negotiate a price. After the transaction is completed, the trade is reported to your broker, who notifies you. Today, large brokerage firms maintain automated order systems that allow brokers to enter your order the instant you make it. The order can be confirmed in seconds.

A broker can also be a source of information about what stocks or bonds would best meet your financial objectives, but it's still important to learn about stocks and bonds on your own since investment analysts' advice may not always meet your specific expectations and needs.[47]

Investing Through Online Brokers

Investors can also choose from multiple online trading services to buy and sell stocks and bonds. BMO InvestorLine, TD Direct Investing, and Scotia iTRADE are some examples. Investors who trade online are willing to do their own research and make investment decisions without the direct assistance of a broker. This allows online brokers to charge much lower trading fees than traditional stockbrokers. The leading online services do provide important market information, such as company financial data, price histories of a stock, and analysts' reports. Often the level of information services you can get depends on the size of your account and your level of trading.

© Shutterstock/Matej Kastelic

Based on your knowledge level now, would you prefer to work with a stockbroker or invest through an online broker? What services would you value the most in order to trade securities?

Whether you decide to use an online broker or to invest through a traditional stockbroker, remember that investing means committing your money with the hope of making a profit. The dot-com bubble in the early 2000s and the financial crisis that began in 2008 proved again that investing is a risky business. Therefore, the first step in any investment program is to analyze your level of risk tolerance. Other factors to consider include your desired income, cash requirements, and need to hedge against inflation, along with the investment's growth prospects.

You are never too young or too old to invest, but you should first ask questions and consider investment alternatives. Let's take a look at several strategies.

Choosing the Right Investment Strategy

Investment objectives change over the course of a person's life. A young person can better afford to invest in high-risk investment options such as stocks than can a person nearing retirement. Younger investors generally look for significant growth in the value of their investments over time. If stocks go into a tailspin and decrease in value, a younger person has time to wait for stocks to rise again. Older people, perhaps on a fixed income, lack the luxury of waiting, and may be more inclined to invest in bonds that offer a steady return as a protection against inflation.

Consider five key criteria when selecting investment options:

1. *Investment risk.* The chance that an investment will be worth less at some future time than it's worth now.
2. *Yield.* The expected rate of return on an investment, such as interest (bonds) or dividends (stocks), usually over a period of one year.
3. *Duration.* The length of time your money is committed to an investment.
4. *Liquidity.* How quickly you can get back your invested funds in cash if you want them.
5. *Tax consequences.* How the investment will affect your tax situation.

What is important in any investment strategy is the risk-return tradeoff, a concept introduced in Chapter 17. Setting investment objectives such as *growth* (choosing stocks you believe will increase in price) or *income* (choosing bonds that pay interest and/or stocks that pay consistent dividends) should set the tone for your investment strategy.

Reducing Risk by Diversifying Investments

diversification Buying several different investment alternatives to spread the risk of investing.

Diversification involves buying several different types of investments to spread the risk of investing. For example, an investor may put 25 percent of his or her money into Canadian stocks that have relatively high risk but strong growth potential, another 25 percent in conservative government bonds, 25 percent in dividend-paying stocks that provide income, 10 percent in an international mutual fund (mutual funds will be discussed later), and the rest in the bank for emergencies and other possible investment opportunities. By diversifying with such a *portfolio strategy* or *allocation model,* investors decrease the chance of losing everything they have invested.[48]

Both stockbrokers and certified financial planners are trained to give advice about the investment portfolio that would best fit each client's financial objectives. However, the more investors themselves read and study the market, the higher their potential for gain. A short course in investments can also be useful. Stocks and bonds are investment opportunities individuals can use to enhance their financial future. The Reaching Beyond Our Borders box discusses growing opportunities investors can find in global stocks. After the Progress Assessment, we will consider investing in stocks, bonds, mutual funds, and exchange-traded funds.

Reaching *Beyond* OUR BORDERS

Global Stocks: Love Them or Leave Them

Concerns about the ups and downs of Canadian stocks may keep you from even thinking about investing in global stocks. If you also read the news about conflicts in Eastern Europe and the Middle East, and natural disasters in Japan and Indonesia, the thought of investing globally may grow even less attractive. Your inclination may be to forget about global stocks and play it safe with what may seem to be relatively secure Canadian securities. However, financial analysts generally recommend investing in some global stocks in order to diversify your investments.

Let's consider market facts that support their recommendation. If you research respected blue-chip stocks, like Scotiabank and Coca Cola, you will find they earn a large portion of their revenue from global markets. Economists also project developing economies in areas such as Asia and Africa will grow at a much faster pace than Canada.

Given the potential return, you would be remiss to not at least explore the opportunities that exist in global markets. However, like any investments, set your long-term financial goals and stay abreast of the daily news. Keep the following suggestions in mind as you consider global investments:

- Invest in familiar global companies with a solid reputation and record of performance. Companies like Honda (Japan), Nestlé (Switzerland), Samsung (South Korea), and Siemens (Germany) come to mind.

© Rtbilder | Dreamstime.com

- Invest in only global stocks listed on Canadian or U.S. exchanges. These companies must comply with Canadian and U.S. accounting standards, and rules of the securities exchanges such as the TSX and the U.S. Securities Exchange Commission (SEC).
- Investing in mutual funds and exchange-traded funds (ETFs) offers a wide range of global opportunities. Many funds and ETFs have a mix of Canadian and foreign stocks. Others may focus strictly on specific countries, such as China, on entire regions, such as Africa, Asia, Europe, or Latin America, or on the entire world. Mutual funds and ETFs will be discussed shortly.
- Investing in stocks from countries with a history of currency problems or political instability might be investments you want to avoid.

Sources: Selena Maranjian, "Foreign Stocks with Dividends," The Motley Fool, January 2, 2014; Robert Schmansky, "How Much Should You Invest in International Stock Mutual Funds?" *Forbes*, August 8, 2013; and John Waggoner, "Investing: Simplify Life, Go Global, with Funds," *USA Today*, March 14, 2013.

PROGRESS ASSESSMENT

- What is a key advantage and disadvantage of investing through a stock broker?
- What is a key advantage and disadvantage of investing through an online broker?
- List the five key criteria when selecting investment options.
- What is the benefit of diversifying investments?

Investing in Stocks and Bonds

Buying stocks make investors part owners of a company who participate in its success. Shareholders can also lose money if a company doesn't do well or the overall stock market declines.

Investors looking for guaranteed income and limited risk often turn to government bonds for a secure investment. These bonds have the financial backing and full faith and credit of the government. Corporate bonds are a bit riskier and challenging. Taxes are another consideration when evaluating bonds and stocks. Bond interest is fully taxable in the hands of the bond holder, while dividend income qualifies for tax credits.

Investing in Stocks

Stock investors are often called bulls or bears according to their perceptions of the market. *Bulls* believe that stock prices are going to rise; they buy stock in anticipation of the increase. A bull market is when overall stock prices are rising. *Bears* expect stock prices to decline and sell their stocks in anticipation of falling prices. That's why when stock prices are declining, the market is called a bear market.

The market price and growth potential of most stocks depend heavily on how well the corporation is meeting its business objectives. A company that achieves its objectives offers great potential for **capital gains**, the positive difference between the price at which you bought a stock and what you sell it for. For example, an investment of $2250 in 100 shares of McDonald's when the company first offered its stock to the public in 1965 would

capital gains
The positive difference between the purchase price of a stock and its sale price.

Investing in the stock market has never been for the faint of heart. The market seems to have continuous steep climbs and sharp falls. Do you have the risk tolerance to survive the market swings?

have grown to 74 360 shares (after the company's 12 stock splits) and be worth approximately $10.6 million as of the market close on May 3, 2017. Now that's a lot of Big Macs!

Investors often select stocks depending on their investment strategy. Stocks issued by higher-quality companies, such as BCE Inc. and the Canadian National Railway Company, are referred to as *blue-chip stocks* (a term derived from poker where the highest-value chip is the blue chip). These stocks generally pay regular dividends and experience consistent stock price appreciation.

Stocks in corporations in emerging fields such as technology, biotechnology, or Internet-related firms, whose earnings are expected to grow at a faster rate than other stocks, are referred to as *growth stocks*. While riskier, growth stocks may offer the potential for high returns. Stocks of public utilities are considered *income stocks* because they usually offer investors a higher dividend yield that generally keeps pace with inflation. There are even *penny stocks*, representing ownership in companies that compete in high-risk industries like oil exploration. Penny stocks sell for less that $2 (some analysts say less than $5) and are considered very risky investments.[49]

When purchasing stock, investors have choices when placing orders to buy. A *market order* tells a broker to buy or sell a stock immediately at the best price available. A *limit order* tells the broker to buy or sell a stock at a specific price, if that price becomes available. Let's say a stock is selling for $40 a share. You believe the price will eventually go higher but could drop to $36 first. You can place a limit order at $36, so your broker will buy the stock at $36 if it drops to that price. If the stock never falls to $36, the broker will not purchase it for you.

STOCK SPLITS

Brokers prefer to make stock purchases in *round lots* of 100 shares at a time. Investors, however, usually cannot afford to buy 100 shares, and therefore often buy in *odd lots*, or fewer than 100 shares at a time. High per-share prices often induce companies to declare **stock splits**, in which they issue two or more shares for every one that is outstanding. If Harvest Gold stock were selling for $100 a share, the firm could declare a two-for-one stock split. Investors who owned one share of Harvest Gold would now own two, each worth only $50 (half as much as before the split).

stock splits
An action by a company that gives shareholders two or more shares of stock for each one they own.

Stock splits cause no change in the firm's ownership structure and no immediate change in the investment's value. Investors generally approve of stock splits, however, because they believe demand for a stock may be greater at $50 than at $100, and the price may then go up in the near future. A company cannot be forced to split its stock, and today stock splits are becoming less common.[50] Legendary investor Warren Buffett's firm, Berkshire Hathaway, has never split its class A stock even when its per-share price surpassed $218,000.[51]

STOCK INDEXES

Stock indexes measure the trend of different stock exchanges. Every country with a stock exchange has such indexes. The prices of company shares fluctuate constantly. Some may be rising over a certain period and others may be falling. Various indexes have been developed to give interested parties useful information about significant trends, and more indexes are being developed. Another use of an index is as an investment vehicle. Investors who do not have the time or expertise to actively manage their investments are choosing to be passive investors by investing in index funds.

S&P/TSX Composite Index[52] The largest Canadian index is the S&P/TSX Composite Index. Reviewed quarterly, the Index is the principal market measure for the Canadian equities market as it contains both common stocks and income trust units of the largest companies on the TSX. The Index represents 11 categories of securities: financial, energy, materials, industrial, consumer discretionary, telecommunication services, health care, consumer staples, utilities, information technology and real estate.

Since the Index has many financial and energy constituents, its performance heavily reflects how those industries are doing, and disturbances in the economy or oil price dips can have a big impact. "Our energy sector has been, and still is, one of our more important natural resources exports," Bipan Rai, executive director of foreign exchange at CIBC Capital Markets, said. "As a result, our currency trades according to how well that export is doing."

Staying abreast of what is happening in the market will help you decide what investments seem most appropriate to your needs and objectives. Remember two key investment realities: your personal financial objectives will change over time, and markets can be volatile.

© Lloyd Sutton/Alamy

Over one hundred products can be manufactured from one oil barrel. Oil provides fuel for our cars, trucks, planes, and heating oil. Crude oil is also used in plastic, clothing, furniture, insulation, kitchen items, cars, and food (e.g., fertilizers). This means that the world's dependence on oil is expected to continue into the near future. Do you see why the price of oil is followed closely?

UNDERSTANDING STOCK QUOTATIONS

Publications like the *Globe and Mail,* the *Financial Post,* and possibly your local newspaper carry information concerning stocks and other investments. Financial websites like Yahoo! Finance Canada carry up-to-the-minute information about companies that is much more detailed and only a click away. Look at Figure 18.4 to see an example of a stock quote from MSN Money for Microsoft. Microsoft trades on the NASDAQ exchange under the symbol MSFT. Preferred stock is identified by the letters *pf* following the company symbol. Corporations can have several different preferred stock issues.

Information provided in the quote includes the highest and lowest price the stock traded for that day, the stock's high and low over the past 52 weeks, the dividend paid (if any), the stock's dividend yield (annual dividend as a percentage of the stock's price per share), important ratios like the price/earnings (P/E) ratio (the price of the stock divided by the firm's per-share earnings), and the earnings per share.[53] Investors can also see the number of shares traded (volume) and the total market capitalization of the firm. More technical features, such as the stock's beta (which measures the degree of the stock's risk), may also appear. Figure 18.4 illustrates the stock's intraday trading (trading throughout the current day), but you can also click to see charts for different time periods. Similar information about bonds, mutual funds, and other investments is also available online.

Investing in Bonds

Investors looking for guaranteed income and limited risk often turn to government bonds for a secure investment. These bonds have the financial backing and full faith and credit of

FIGURE 18.4

UNDERSTANDING STOCK QUOTATIONS

Microsoft Corporation (MSFT)
NasdaqGS - NasdaqGS Real Time Price. Currency in USD

71.74 −0.74 (−1.01%)
As of 3:24PM EDT. Market open.

Previous Close	72.4700	Market Cap	552.559B
Open	71.90	Beta	1.44
Bid	71.94 x 100	PE Ratio (TTM)	31.66
Ask	71.94 x 3900	EPS (TTM)	2.27
Day's Range	71.56 - 72.19	Earnings Date	Oct 30, 2017
52 Week Range	55.6100 - 74.4200	Dividend & Yield	1.56 (2.14%)
Volume	15,191,793	Ex-Dividend Date	2017-08-15
Avg. Volume	25,006,690	1y Target Est	80.19

Trade prices are not sourced from all markets.

the government. Corporate bonds are a bit riskier and challenging. Taxes are another consideration when evaluating bonds and stocks. Again, bond interest is fully taxable in the hands of the bond holder, while dividend income qualifies for tax credits.

First-time corporate bond investors often ask two questions. The first is, "If I purchase a corporate bond, do I have to hold it until the maturity date?" No, you do not. Bonds are bought and sold daily on major securities exchanges (the secondary market we discussed earlier). However, if you decide to sell your bond to another investor before its maturity date, you may not get its face value. If your bond does not have features that make it attractive to other investors, like a high interest rate or early maturity, you may have to sell at a *discount,* which is a price less than the bond's face value. But if other investors do highly value it, you may be able to sell your bond at a *premium,* which is a price above its face value. Bond prices generally fluctuate inversely with current market interest rates. This means *as interest rates go up, bond prices fall, and vice versa.* Like all investments, however, bonds have a degree of risk.

The second question is, "How can I assess the investment risk of a particular bond issue?"[54] Standard & Poor's and Moody's Investors Service rate the risk of many corporate and government bonds. In evaluating the ratings, recall the risk-return tradeoff: The higher the risk of a bond, the higher the interest rate the issuer must offer. Investors will consider a bond that is considered risky only if the potential return (interest) is high enough. Remember that investors have many investment options besides stocks and bonds. Let's consider mutual funds next.

PROGRESS ASSESSMENT

- What is a bull market? What is a bear market?
- Compare blue-chip stocks to penny stocks.
- Why do companies sometimes split their stock?
- What do stock indexes measure?
- Under what conditions would a bond be sold for a discount?

Investing in Mutual Funds and Exchange-Traded Funds

mutual fund
A organization that buys stocks and bonds and other investments, then sells shares in those securities to the public.

A **mutual fund** buys stocks, bonds, and other investments, and then sells shares in those securities to the public. A mutual fund is like an investment company that pools investors' money and then buys stocks or bonds, for example, in many companies in accordance with the fund's specific purpose. Mutual fund managers are specialists who pick what they consider to be the best securities available and help investors diversify their investments.

Mutual fund companies such as Mackenzie Financial Ltd., AGF Management Ltd., and Manulife Financial Corp. are regulated by provincial securities commissions. According to the Investment Funds Institute of Canada, assets under management are over $1.4 trillion.[55] Mutual funds account for 31 percent of Canadians' financial wealth with research showing that to meet their financial goals, Canadians have greater confidence in mutual funds (86 percent) than other financial products such as GICs (59 percent), bonds (51 percent) and stocks (64 percent).[56]

Mutual funds provide professional investment management and help investors diversify their investments in exchange for fees. One fee is the Management Expense Ratio (MER) and it represents the costs associated with owning a mutual fund. It reflects how much a fund pays in management fees and operating expenses (including taxes) on an annual basis.[57] Stated as a percentage per year, it is calculated and charged

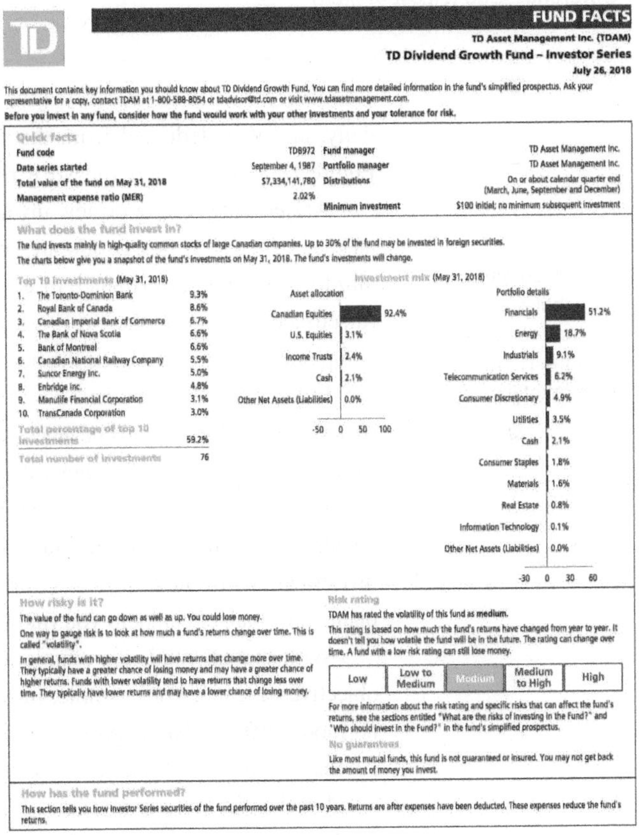
FUND FACTS

TD Asset Management Inc. (TDAM)

TD Dividend Growth Fund – Investor Series

July 26, 2018

This document contains key information you should know about TD Dividend Growth Fund. You can find more detailed information in the fund's simplified prospectus. Ask your representative for a copy, contact TDAM at 1-800-588-8054 or tdadvisor@td.com or visit www.tdassetmanagement.com.

Before you invest in any fund, consider how the fund would work with your other investments and your tolerance for risk.

Quick facts

Fund code	TDB972	Fund manager	TD Asset Management Inc.
Date series started	September 4, 1987	Portfolio manager	TD Asset Management Inc.
Total value of the fund on May 31, 2018	$7,334,141,780	Distributions	On or about calendar quarter end (March, June, September and December)
Management expense ratio (MER)	2.02%	Minimum investment	$100 initial; no minimum subsequent investment

What does the fund invest in?

The fund invests mainly in high-quality common stocks of large Canadian companies. Up to 30% of the fund may be invested in foreign securities.

The charts below give you a snapshot of the fund's investments on May 31, 2018. The fund's investments will change.

Top 10 investments (May 31, 2018)

1.	The Toronto-Dominion Bank	9.3%
2.	Royal Bank of Canada	8.6%
3.	Canadian Imperial Bank of Commerce	6.7%
4.	The Bank of Nova Scotia	6.6%
5.	Bank of Montreal	6.6%
6.	Canadian National Railway Company	5.5%
7.	Suncor Energy Inc.	5.0%
8.	Enbridge Inc.	4.8%
9.	Manulife Financial Corporation	3.1%
10.	TransCanada Corporation	3.0%
	Total percentage of top 10 investments	59.2%
	Total number of investments	76

Investment mix (May 31, 2018)

Asset allocation

Canadian Equities	92.4%
U.S. Equities	3.1%
Income Trusts	2.4%
Cash	2.1%
Other Net Assets (Liabilities)	0.0%

Portfolio details

Financials	51.2%
Energy	18.7%
Industrials	9.1%
Telecommunication Services	6.2%
Consumer Discretionary	4.9%
Utilities	3.5%
Cash	2.1%
Consumer Staples	1.8%
Materials	1.6%
Real Estate	0.8%
Information Technology	0.1%
Other Net Assets (Liabilities)	0.0%

How risky is it?

The value of the fund can go down as well as up. You could lose money.

One way to gauge risk is to look at how much a fund's returns change over time. This is called "volatility".

In general, funds with higher volatility will have returns that change more over time. They typically have a greater chance of losing money and may have a greater chance of higher returns. Funds with lower volatility tend to have returns that change less over time. They typically have lower returns and may have a lower chance of losing money.

Risk rating

TDAM has rated the volatility of this fund as **medium**.

This rating is based on how much the fund's returns have changed from year to year. It doesn't tell you how volatile the fund will be in the future. The rating can change over time. A fund with a low risk rating can still lose money.

Low	Low to Medium	Medium	Medium to High	High

For more information about the risk rating and specific risks that can affect the fund's returns, see the sections entitled "What are the risks of investing in the Fund?" and "Who should invest in the Fund?" in the fund's simplified prospectus.

No guarantees

Like most mutual funds, this fund is not guaranteed or insured. You may not get back the amount of money you invest.

How has the fund performed?

This section tells you how Investor Series securities of the fund performed over the past 10 years. Returns are after expenses have been deducted. These expenses reduce the fund's returns.

Mutual funds range from very conservative funds that invest only in government securities to others that specialize in emerging biotechnology firms, Internet companies, foreign companies, precious metals, and other investments with greater risk. Some funds will have a mix of investments like stocks and bonds. Are you surprised by this fund's portfolio details? What is the MER for this fund?

FIGURE 18.5

HOW THE MER MAY AFFECT THE RETURN ON YOUR INVESTMENT

Set at a percentage of the fund's value, the MER is paid even if the fund does not make money (i.e., does not have a positive annual return). It is deducted before calculating the investor's return.

	Fund A	Fund B	Fund C
Your Total Investment ($1,000 a year for 10 years)	$10,000	$10,000	$10,000
Target Annual Return	5.0%	5.0%	5.0%
MER	0%	1%	3%
Investor's Return (after MER)	5%	4%	2%
Fund Value after 10 Years (assume achieved the target annual return of 5%)	$13,207	$12,486	$11,169
Difference (due to cost of MER)	N/A	–$721	–$2,038

daily, and it is deducted from the fund's assets before returns are calculated.[58] Review Figure 18.5 to learn how the MER may affect the return on your investment.

index funds
Specialized mutual funds that are constructed to aim to equal the performance of a market index.

At one time, young or new investors were advised to buy a type of mutual fund called an index fund.[59] **Index funds** are specialized mutual funds that are constructed with the aim to equal the performance of a market index, such as the S&P/TSX Composite Index (discussed earlier) or the S&P 500.[60] The S&P 500, for example, includes 500 leading companies and is considered the best market gauge of large-cap stocks in the United States.

Index funds are very low cost, easy to obtain, and can be held by investors for a long period of time. Index funds have also matched or beat the performance of higher-priced funds managed by professional money managers. Today, index funds are recommended for all levels of investors. An index fund may focus on large companies, small companies, emerging countries, or real estate (real estate investment trusts or REITs). One way to diversify your investments is by investing in a variety of index funds. A stockbroker, certified financial planner, or banker can help you find the option that best fits your investment objectives.

With mutual funds it's simple to change your investment objectives if your financial objectives change. For example, moving your money from a bond fund to a stock fund is no more difficult than making a phone call, clicking a mouse, or tapping your cell phone. Another advantage of mutual funds is that you can generally buy directly from the fund and avoid broker fees or commissions. It's important to check the long-term performance of the fund's managers; the more consistent the performance of the fund's management, the better. Also, check for fees and charges of the mutual fund because they can differ significantly. A *load fund,* for example, charges investors a commission to buy or sell its shares; a *no-load fund* charges no commission.[61] Mutual funds called *open-end funds* will accept the investments of any interested investors. *Closed-end funds,* however, limit the number of shares; once the fund reaches its target number, no new investors can buy into the fund.

A growth area for mutual funds is socially responsible investing (SRI). To learn more, review the Seeking Sustainability box.

Seeking SUSTAINABILITY

Socially Responsible Investing (SRI)

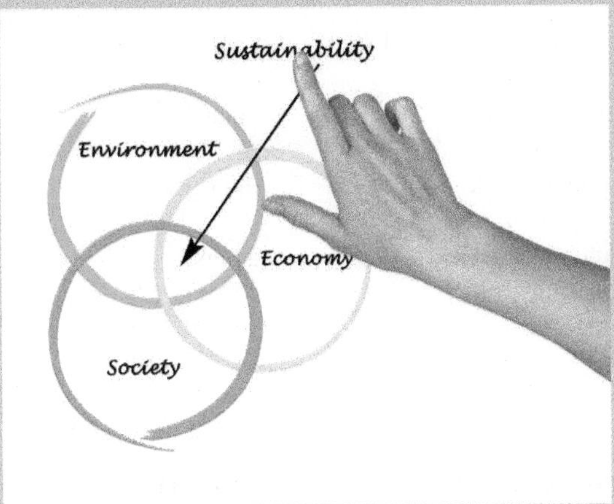

© Vaeenma I Dreamstime.com

Socially responsible investing (SRI) is the integration of environmental, social and governance (ESG) factors into the selection and management of investments. There is a growing body of evidence that responsible investments (RIs) meet, and often exceed, the performance of traditional investments and have a positive societal impact; thus, buyers don't have to choose one over the other and can therefore choose investments that are consistent with both their financial goals and personal values. Common themes for SRIs include avoiding investment in companies that produce or sell addictive substances (like alcohol, gambling, and tobacco), and seeking out companies engaged in environmental sustainability and alternative energy/clean technology efforts.

Eighty-two percent of Canadian investors say they have some understanding of what sustainable investing (SI) is, but that level of understanding varies. Sixty-eight percent of Canadians say that SI has become more important to them in the past five years with Millennials having the strongest feelings about SI. Although younger investors typically do not have significant wealth, they are having a growing influence over household investment decisions. This younger generation of investors will be an increasingly important demographic for the investment industry going forward, as they are set to inherit billions over the next few decades.

Consider that SRI assets total over $1.5 trillion, representing 38 percent of the Canadian investment industry. In two years, SRI mutual funds grew by 24 percent, reaching over $8 billion in assets. SRIs can be made in individual companies or through socially conscious mutual funds or ETFs (e.g., iShares Jantzi Social Index Fund). Newer SRI mutual funds, products, and strategies include:

- Fossil-fuel–free and low carbon funds.
- Green funds that focus on solutions.
- Green bonds (discussed in Chapter 17).
- Impact funds.
- ESG funds that incorporate engagement with companies about environmental, social, and governance issues.

Resources and investment products that cater to SRI for Canadian investors include:

- Sustainalytics, a leading global provider of ESG research, ratings, and analytics serving asset managers, asset owners, and other institutional investors.
- *Corporate Knights*, which covers the best and worst ideas in SRI, and produces special reports on corporate citizens.
- Some mutual fund companies (e.g., Ethical Funds) which offer specific products that might interest you. Investments are available for purchase through a discount broker or a financial adviser.

Is this an area of investing that interests you? Would you seek out RI if you had money to invest?

Sources: "Responsible Investment: Growing Market, Growing Opportunities," Responsible Investment Association, accessed June 6, 2018, https://www.riacanada.ca/wp-content/uploads/2012/08/Advisor-Handout-v2.pdf; "Canadian RI Assets Surpass $1.5 Trillion: Canadian RI Trends Report," Responsible Investment Association, accessed June 6, 2018, https://www.riacanada.ca/trendsreport/; "Socially Responsible Investment (SRI)," Investing Answers, accessed June 6, 2018, http://www.investinganswers.com/financial-dictionary/stock-market/socially-responsible-investment-sri-2578; "National leader in responsible investment Michael Jantzi joins Tides Canada Board of Directors," Sustainalytics, May 2, 2018, https://www.sustainalytics.com/press-release/national-leader-in-responsible-investment-michael-jantzi-joins-tides-canada-board-of-directors/; Doug Watt, "Invest your conscience," *MoneySense*, October 2, 2017, http://www.moneysense.ca/save/investing/sustainability-no-longer-an-obscure-investment-consideration-study/; and Bruce Sellery, "Guide to socially responsible investing," *MoneySense*, August 27, 2012, http://www.moneysense.ca/columns/guide-to-socially-responsible-investing.

FIGURE 18.6

COMPARING INVESTMENTS

Investment	Degree of risk	Expected income	Possible growth (capital gain)
Bonds	Low	Secure	Little
Preferred Stock	Medium	Steady	Little
Common Stock	High	Variable	Good
Mutual Funds	Medium	Variable	Good
ETFs	Medium	Variable	Good

exchange-traded funds (ETFs) Collections of stocks that are traded on exchanges but are traded more like individual stocks than like mutual funds.

Exchange-traded funds (ETFs) resemble both stocks and mutual funds. They are collections of stocks, bonds, and other investments that are traded on securities exchanges, but are traded more like individual stocks than like mutual funds.[62] Mutual funds, for example, permit investors to buy and sell shares only at the close of the trading day. ETFs can be purchased or sold at any time during the trading day just like individual stocks. There are over $151 billion in ETF assets under management in Canada.[63]

The key points to remember about mutual funds and ETFs is that they offer small investors a way to spread the risk of owning stock, bonds, and other securities while having their investments managed by a financial specialist for a fee. Financial advisors put mutual funds and ETFs high on the list of recommended investments, particularly for small or first-time investors.

Consider Figure 18.6 as it evaluates bonds, stocks, mutual funds, and ETFs according to risk, income, and possible investment growth (capital gain).

After the Progress Assessment, consider the third component of Canada's financial system, the clearing and settlement systems.

financial market infrastructure (FMI) A system that facilitates the clearing, settling, or recording of payments, securities, derivatives, or other financial transactions among participating entities; also called a clearing and settlement system.

PROGRESS ASSESSMENT

- What are advantages and disadvantages of mutual funds?
- Describe socially responsible investing.
- What are ETFs? How do they differ from mutual funds?

LO5

Outline the role of the clearing and settlement systems.

The Canadian Financial System: Clearing and Settlement Systems[64]

A **financial market infrastructure (FMI)** is a system that facilitates the clearing, settling, or recording of payments, securities, derivatives, or other financial transactions among participating entities. It is also called a "clearing and settlement system." FMIs play an important role in enhancing financial stability by enabling consumers and firms to safely and efficiently purchase goods and services, make financial investments, and transfer funds.

Under the Payment Clearing and Settlement Act, the BoC is responsible for the oversight of FMIs that have the potential to pose systemic or payments system risk. It is therefore essential that FMIs incorporate appropriate risk-control mechanisms so that systemic risk is adequately controlled. There are three types of FMIs:

1. Payment systems that facilitate the transfer of funds.
2. Central counterparties (CCPs) become the buyer to every seller and the seller to every buyer of a financial contract to ensure that, even if a buyer or a seller fails to meet its obligation to the CCP, obligations will be met on all contracts.
3. Securities settlement systems facilitate the transfer of securities and other financial assets. These systems often operate in conjunction with central securities depositories which provide securities accounts, central safekeeping, and asset services. Securities settlement systems may provide additional securities clearing and settlement services, such as CCP clearing services.

In summary, economic growth and the creation of jobs depend on the ready availability of money. Given this importance, the BoC plays a pivotal role in overseeing the Canadian financial system. The three components—financial institutions, the financial markets, and clearing and settlement systems—are connected and they work together to support the welfare of Canadians.

PROGRESS ASSESSMENT

- What is the third component to the Canadian financial system?
- What is the BoC's responsibility under the Payment Clearing and Settlement Act?
- List three types of FMIs.

SUMMARY

LO1 **Explain what money is and what makes it useful.**

Money is anything that people generally accept as payment for goods and services.

What are the five standards for a useful form of money?

The five standards are portability, divisibility, stability, durability, and uniqueness.

What are cryptocurrencies?

Digital currency is electronic money. It's not available as bills or coins. Cryptocurrencies are a type of digital currency created using computer algorithms.

LO2 **List the three components of the Canadian financial system, and explain how it is regulated.**

The financial system makes a vital contribution to the welfare of Canadians.

What are the three components of the Canadian financial system?

The financial system includes financial institutions, the financial markets, and clearing and settlement systems. It is through the financial system that most commercial activity is carried out.

How is the financial system regulated?

Due to its important role in the economy, the financial system is heavily regulated by different organizations and levels of government. Organizations include the Bank of Canada (BoC), OSFI, and CDIC. Ultimately, it is the Minister of Finance who is responsible for the financial system. Review Figure 18.1 for some examples of regulatory responsibility.

LO3 **Discuss the role that financial institutions play in providing services.**

Financial institutions include commercial banks, credit unions, trust and loan companies, insurance companies, and non-banks.

How are commercial banks important players in the financial system?

Commercial banks serve millions of customers that include individuals, small and medium-sized businesses, large corporations, governments, institutional investors, and non-profit organizations. Based on assets, the five largest Canadian banks represent upwards of 80 percent of the national financial institution market.

How do credit unions differ from commercial banks?

A credit union is a non-profit, member-owned financial co-operative that offers a full variety of banking services to its members. Credit unions often have fewer branches than banks and less access to ATMs.

What are some non-banks?

Non-banks include life insurance companies that lend out their funds, pension funds that invest in stocks and bonds and make loans, brokerage firms that offer investment services, and commercial finance companies that offer short-term loans to those who do not meet the credit requirements of banks.

LO4 **Describe the role of the financial markets.**

Financial markets consist of markets for money, bonds, equities, derivatives, and foreign exchange.

What is the link between the BoC and financial markets?

It is mainly through the financial markets that the BoC's key policy rate influences interest rates and the exchange rate. This, in turn, helps the BoC achieve its monetary policy objectives. The BoC is also involved in financial markets through auctions of government securities. On rare occasions, the BoC may also intervene in the foreign exchange market on behalf of the government to promote orderly markets for the Canadian dollar.

Explain the different options discussed in this chapter for investing in securities.

The options include stocks, bonds, mutual funds, and ETFs. Review Figure 18.6 as it evaluates these options according to risk, income, and possible investment growth (capital gain).

LO5 **Outline the role of the clearing and settlement systems.**

A clearing and settlement system, also called a financial market infrastructure (FMI), plays an important role in enhancing financial stability by enabling consumers and firms to safely and efficiently purchase goods and services, make financial investments, and transfer funds.

Who is responsible for FMIs?

The BoC is responsible for the oversight of FMIs that have the potential to pose systemic or payments system risk.

List three examples of FMIs.

Three examples of FMIs are payment systems, central counterparties, and securities settlement systems.

KEY TERMS

alternative trading systems (ATSs) 689
barter 672
capital gains 693
Canada Deposit Insurance Corporation (CDIC) 677
certificate of deposit 680
commercial bank 678
credit union 681
cryptocurrencies 674
debit card 684
demand deposit 680
digital currency 674
diversification 691
electronic funds transfer (EFT) system 683
exchange-traded funds (ETFs) 700
financial market infrastructure (FMI) 700
index funds 698
institutional investors 688
investment bankers 688
money 672
mutual fund 697
non-banks 682
over-the-counter (OTC) market 689
pension funds 682
prospectus 689
securities commission 689
securities dealer or investment dealer 687
security 687
smart card 684
spread 678
stock exchange 688
stock splits 694
stockbroker 690
time deposit 680
trust company 681

CAREER EXPLORATION

If you are interested in pursuing a career in finance, here are a few to consider. Find out about the tasks performed, skills needed, pay, and opportunity outlook in these fields through Internet sites that include the Government of Canada Job Bank, Workopolis, Monster, CareerBuilder, Glassdoor, and Indeed, as well as through the Career Centre at your school.

- **Personal financial advisor—**provides investment advice on investments, mortgages, insurance, registered educational savings plans (RESPs), estate planning, taxes, and retirement to help individuals manage their finances.
- **Investment banker—**connects businesses that need money to finance their operations with investors who are interested in providing that funding; assists with company mergers and acquisitions.
- **Stockbroker—**sells securities and commodities directly to individual clients; advises clients on appropriate investments based on their needs and financial understanding.
- **Financial analyst—**provides guidance to businesses and individuals making investment decisions; assesses the performance of stocks, bonds, and other types of investments.

CRITICAL THINKING

1. Imagine that you have just inherited $50,000 and you want to invest it to meet two financial goals: (a) to save for your wedding, which you plan to have in two years, and (b) to save for your retirement several decades from now. How would you invest the money? Explain your answer.
2. The overnight bank rate, set by the Bank of Canada, is currently very low. What circumstance(s) would cause the Governor of the Bank of Canada to raise this rate? What impact would this increase have on individuals and businesses with debt?
3. Do you keep your savings in a bank, a credit union, a *caisse populaire,* or some combination? Have you compared the benefits you could receive from each? Where would you expect to find the best loan rates?

4. If you were thinking of investing in the securities market, would you prefer individual stocks, mutual funds, or ETFs? Explain your choice by comparing the advantages and disadvantages of each.

DEVELOPING CAREER SKILLS

Key: ● **Team** ★ **Analytic** ▲ **Communication** ⊡ **Technology**

●★⊡▲ 1. In a small group, discuss the following: What services do you use from financial institutions? Does anyone use online or mobile banking? What seem to be the pros and cons of online banking? What about mobile banking? Use this opportunity to compare the rates and services of various local banks and credit unions.

★▲ 2. Poll the class to see who uses a bank, a credit union, a caisse populaire, or a combination of these. Have class members compare the services at each (e.g., interest rates on savings accounts, the services available, and loan rates). If anyone uses an online service, see how those rates compare. If no one uses a credit union, a caisse populaire, or an online bank, discuss the reasons.

●★▲ 3. In small groups discuss when and where you use cheques, credit cards, debit cards, and cash. Do you often write cheques for small amounts? Would you stop if you calculated how much it costs to process each cheque? Have you switched to using your debit card as a result? Discuss your findings with the class.

●⊡★▲ 4. See whether others in the class are interested in forming an investment group. If so, each member should choose one stock and one mutual fund or ETF. Record each student's selections and the corresponding prices. In two weeks, measure the percentage of change in the investments and discuss the results.

★▲ 5. Write a one-page paper on the role of the World Bank and the International Monetary Fund in providing loans to countries. (Recall that you were introduced to these institutions in Chapter 3.) Is it important for Canadian citizens to lend money to people in other countries through such organizations? Why or why not? Be prepared to debate the value of these organizations in class.

ANALYZING MANAGEMENT DECISIONS

Financial Crisis—Banking Disaster

The year 2011 was characterized by a sluggish economy and high unemployment, when millions of Americans lost their homes and businesses closed. How did this happen? Back in 2008, there was a global banking crisis that was the worst since the Great Depression of the 1930s. Several major American investment banks went bankrupt, markets plummeted around the world, and there was a global recession. The causes of the crisis included failures in financial regulations in some countries, such as the United States, reckless behaviour by financial firms, excessive borrowing by households and investment banks, and a lack of accountability and ethics at many levels.

Back even further, in 2000, the tech bubble burst. Share prices in high-tech companies fell dramatically and major financial frauds were discovered, including Worldcom, Enron, and Global Crossings. Governments wanted to keep consumers spending to head off an economic slowdown, so they chose to dramatically cut interest rates by over 5 percent, down to near 1 percent. Given this historic low cost of credit, consumers borrowed money, lots of it. By far the most significant borrowing related to home loans, that is, mortgages. By 2007, household debt rose to 127 percent of disposable income in the United States and Canadian household debt was climbing also. Home mortgages resulting from the housing boom became the biggest financial bubble in history. As more and more homes were purchased, housing costs rose rapidly.

While everyone wants a home, the reality is that not everyone can afford the cost of buying one. But with relatively cheap mortgage interest, many were buying homes, from first-time homeowners to long-time homeowners who wanted bigger and fancier houses. And banks were writing up mortgages for people who would not normally qualify. Banks typically look at the income of the borrower and assess the ability of the borrower to make the mortgage payments. But this criterion was overlooked more and more because the banks and everyone else believed that the prices of houses would continue to rise. These mortgages were called subprime mortgages. In 2004, subprime mortgages made up 10 percent of all mortgages. By 2006, this percentage doubled.

These riskier mortgages became an international problem. After mortgages were written, the banks sold them to investment banks. The investment banks in turn bundled these mortgages into securities, selling them in the open market to investors. They were called mortgage-backed securities, or MBSs.

MBSs have been traded since the 1980s as a safe investment, as only low-risk conventional mortgages were bundled. With the rapid increase in mortgages being written, more and more MBSs appeared. Investors liked the increasing return that was promised given the higher and higher percentage of sub-prime mortgages that made up the newer MBSs. And bank lenders wrote riskier and riskier mortgages because investment banks demanded them and the banks were passing on the risk to investment banks and investors. Given the involvement of banks, investment banks, and investors, it was very difficult to know where the risk was. Investors relied on ratings agencies, specifically Moody's and Standard and Poor's, for advice on safe investments. And these agencies were more than willing to oblige. Between 2000 and 2006 the number of AAA ratings exploded. MBSs were rated as AAA even though they consisted of a higher percentage of subprime mortgages.

The potential return from MBSs convinced the investment banks to request that the limits on the amount of money they could borrow to buy these securities be raised. In 2004, the SEC relaxed limits on leverage and these banks were allowed to take on as much risk as they liked. By 2007, the five largest investment banks increased their leverage significantly; they believed that housing prices would continue to go up and that MBSs were a good source of income.

In 2007, the real estate bubble burst and the growing recession left many homeowners unable to pay their mortgages, especially subprime mortgages. The number of foreclosures jumped 79 percent. As housing prices fell, many homeowners found themselves "underwater," with mortgages higher than the value of their homes. The financial incentive to pay their mortgages was gone, so they defaulted. The value of MBSs plummeted, leaving both investment banks and investors with hundreds of billions of dollars of defaulted mortgages with little chance of recouping the value of the mortgages. All the major investment banks were impacted; some consolidated, while others failed.

Many countries and international companies, including Canadian banks and investors, had invested in the U.S. housing market through MBSs. They were all affected. Foreign markets collapsed, and the crisis went global.

As we look back on this time period, we realize that this financial crisis was the largest the world had ever experienced. Not since the Great Depression of the 1930s have we seen, on a global scale, rising unemployment, many failed businesses, plummeting consumer wealth, declining international trade, and the near-collapse of foreign governments, especially in Europe. At the writing of this text, we still do not fully comprehend the long-term impact of this crisis.

Discussion Questions

1. What does "household debt increasing to 127 percent of disposable income" mean, and what is the implication for homeowners?
2. How is a subprime mortgage different from a conventional mortgage, and why were banks so willing to approve this type of mortgage?
3. Why did the returns from MBSs continue to rise?
4. Why did the housing bubble burst?

RUNNING CASE

Accounting, Financial Management, and Risk Management at Fox 40 International Inc.

For successful Canadian entrepreneur and inventor Ron Foxcroft, it all started in 1982 when he purchased Fluke Transport, a Southern Ontario trucking business. The company slogan—If It's On Time . . . It's A "FLUKE"—was soon recognized throughout North America. Over the years, Foxcroft diversified into new ventures and the Foxcroft Group of Companies now includes Fluke Transportation Group, Fluke Warehousing Inc., Foxcroft Capital Corp., Fox 40 International Inc., and Fox 40 USA Inc.

The formation of Fox 40 International Inc. (Fox 40) is the result of a dream for a pealess whistle. When developing his first whistle, Ron was motivated by his knowledge and experience as an international basketball referee. Frustrated with faulty pea whistles, he spent three years of development with design consultant Chuck Shepherd. They had about 25 prototypes but narrowed them down after two years to 14 prototypes, and then down to two prototype whistles that worked. This resulted in the Fox 40® Classic Whistle. (The whistle was named for Ron and that he was 40 when he applied for the patent.)

Introduced in 1987, this finely tuned precision instrument does not use a pea to generate sound. In fact, there are no moving parts. The patented design moves the air blast through three tuned chambers. This whistle, and all the subsequent whistles that have been introduced, is 100 percent constructed of high-impact ABS plastic so it is impervious to moisture. Wet or dry, Fox 40 Pealess Whistles cannot be overblown and never fail—the harder you blow, the louder the sound! They can be heard for miles and work in all conditions. They are faultless, reliable, and trusted.

Fox 40, a proudly Canadian company, dominates the global whistle industry. Tens of thousands of Fox 40 Whistles are produced monthly for shipment to 140 countries. A mould may be made offshore due to the cost savings (at least $100,000); however, Fox 40 owns all of its moulds. Approximately 90 percent of the company's products are made in Canada with select components coming from overseas markets. Final assembly occurs in Canada. While the first product was the Fox 40® Classic Whistle, the company now has over 900 active stock-keeping units (SKUs). Its product mix includes 19 whistles styles (e.g., Fox 40 electronic whistle); lanyards & attachments (e.g., flex coils); additional brands that include Fox 40 Gear; SmartCoach Coaching Boards; SICK Self Impression Custom Kit, and Heat Alert Mouthguards; marine and outdoor products (e.g., Xplorer LED Light); Pink products; and logo imprinted products.

Let's consider the nature of Fox 40's financial statements and the scope of the business. The company has close to 200 accounts in its general ledger, of which 70 are expense accounts. There are over 3000 products grouped into 12 product lines. The product lines are then grouped in the income statement into three markets: Domestic, Export USA, and Export International. Expenses are grouped into three departments: sales and marketing, production and distribution, and general management administration. When comparing these statistics to the financial statements of Harvest Gold, you should appreciate the increased complexity of Fox 40's operations. Even with this level of complexity, Fox 40 prepares monthly financial statements by the 12th to the 15th of the following month. For CEO Ron Foxcroft, with all the financial data available, he first looks at the bottom line—the net profit as reflected in the income statement.

Foxcroft is also concerned with profitability by product, which is reflected in a product's gross margin. There is an expected range in gross margins between 40 percent to 60 percent. He is also focused on how well receivables and inventory are managed. The expectation is that the accounts receivable turnover is 8, which translates into average days credit sales in receivables of 45. Meanwhile, inventory turnover will range from 1 to 12 depending on the product. This translates into average inventory by product being sold between 30 days to 1 year.

The company's lenders closely monitor the debt-to-equity ratio and debt-service coverage ratio. The latter ratio compares the cash flow to the principal and interest payments on bank loans. Bank balances are managed daily, and transfers can be made between any of the associated company bank accounts to ensure that sufficient funds are available to cover operating requirements and to properly manage the various operating lines.

Financial planning is managed through a set of monthly budgeted financial statements for their fiscal year, which starts July 1. When comparing actual to budgeted performance, any variance of more than 3 percent on a product line and any negative variance on expense items is investigated. Sales meetings are held every other week and current monthly sales are always discussed.

The majority of Fox 40's approximately 200 credit customers are Canadian businesses. Their terms range from 15 to 90 days. New international customers are required to pay in advance for their purchases until Fox 40 has experience in dealing with a particular customer. After a good relationship has been established, about 25 percent of these customers are given credit. Export Development Corporation (EDC), introduced in Chapter 4, insures these credit sales.

Operating lines are in place and inventory and receivables are pledged as collateral. These lines are set up with the bank, which the company has been with for 20 years. In fact, the company has worked with the same bank manager during this time. Long-term financing is arranged through the same bank for certain capital assets, such as moulds and dies used to manufacture many of the company's products, and leasehold improvements for office and assembly space in the buildings. In addition, there is a relatively small amount of long-term leasing arrangement. In addition, the company's financing needs are met in part through investments by the shareholders.

Risks are twofold in nature. One risk relates to major receivables defaulting, which occurs when a credit customer goes bankrupt. The second risk relates to the economy in general, when a downturn occurs. The former is managed through the rigour employed from the decision to first grant a customer credit, to regularly reviewing each credit customer's account. According to Foxcroft, since this last happened in 2008 and 2009, "our company has to be able to 'turn-on-a-dime'." In terms of the second risk, Fox 40 frequently monitors sales and quickly makes decisions on controlling costs when they see sales contracting.

Source: Ron Foxcroft, CEO of Fox 40 International Inc. and Chairman and CEO of Fluke Transportation, in-person interview, September 22, 2017, Hamilton.

Discussion Questions

1. A ratio mentioned above is the debt-service coverage, which is not covered in Chapter 16. Based on the definition provided above in this case, why would a lender be interested in this ratio? Would the lender be looking for the cash flow to be more than, equal to, or less than interest payments?
2. Why are the financial controls for expenses so tight that every negative dollar variance needs to be investigated while on sales there is a leeway of 3 percent?
3. When compared to domestic credit customers, why are international credit customers less creditworthy? Consider that there are a limited number of international credit customers and the fact that EDC insures credit sales to international customers.
4. What does it mean for Fox40 to be able to "turn-on-a-dime" if the economy experiences a downturn? What would be an example of a decision that could be made in such a situation?

APPENDIX B

Managing Personal Finances

PROFILE

GETTING TO KNOW: ALEXA VON TOBEL, FOUNDER/CEO, LEARNVEST

Alexa von Tobel fully understands the importance of financial planning and wants to communicate its importance to the masses. von Tobel is a certified financial planner (CFP) and founder and CEO of LearnVest, a personal financial planning website. After graduating from Harvard College, she worked at Morgan Stanley before becoming head of business development at former file-sharing service Drop.io. From there, she attended Harvard Business School until she took a leave of absence to launch LearnVest with a vision of bringing financial planning to women. She eventually broadened her mission and expanded to other plan-needy consumers.

von Tobel found money is a leading cause of stress. LearnVest offers financial planning services with reasonable flat rates that vary with the customer's financial needs. The company also charges no percentage fees and does not require minimum balances.

von Tobel proposes a simple 50/20/30 plan that anyone can follow to help build a firm financial future. The 50/20/30 formula suggests that 50 percent of your take-home pay goes to pay for essentials (rent/mortgage, utilities, groceries, transportation); 20 percent goes to your future (savings for emergencies, debt repayment, retirement funds); and 30 percent goes to your lifestyle (travel,

© Lisa Lake/Getty Images

shopping, restaurants, etc.). She warns younger people, particularly 20- and 30-somethings, to not make big mistakes like accumulating too much credit card debt and paying bills late. It helps to remember her advice, "Money is a tool that allows you to live your richest life. And remember, you can take out a loan for college, but you can't take out a loan for retirement."

Alexa von Tobel doesn't suggest how you should live and what you should buy; she only wants to help you think about why you are buying something and its financial ramifications. It's also important to remember that a good financial plan should encompass where you stand today, what you hope to accomplish this year and in the future. Evidently her planning skills did not go unnoticed. In 2015, von Tobel sold LearnVest to Northwestern Mutual for $250 million. Her book *Financially Fearless* is a good investment to consider. In this appendix, we'll take a look at ways that will help you keep your finances in order.

Sources: Leena Rao, "Northwestern Mutual Acquires LearnVest, the Financial Planning Startup," *Fortune,* March 25, 2015; Alexa von Tobel, "6 of the Smartest Things You Can Do with Your Money in 2016," *Fortune,* January 2, 2016; Adam Bryant, "Alexa von Tobel of LearnVest; What's Your Weakness?" *The New York Times,* April 16, 2015; Alexandra Macon, "Meet the Woman Who Makes Financial Planning Refreshingly Easy," *Vogue,* March 23, 2017; LearnVest, Inc., www.learnvest.com accessed October 2017.

The Need for Personal Financial Planning

financial literacy
Having the knowledge, skills, and confidence to make responsible financial decisions.

The secret to success is to have capital, or money. With capital, you can pay off loans, take nice vacations, raise a family, invest in stocks and bonds, buy the goods and services you want, give generously to others, and retire with enough money to see you through. Money management, however, is not easy. You have to earn the money in the first place. Your chances of becoming wealthy are much greater if you choose to become an entrepreneur. That is one of the reasons why we have put so much emphasis on entrepreneurship throughout the text, including a chapter on the subject. Of course, there are risks in starting a business, but the best time to take risks is when you are young.

After you earn money, you have to learn how to spend it wisely, save some, and insure yourself against the risks of serious accidents, illness, or death. We shall discuss each of these issues in this appendix so that you can begin making financial plans for the rest of your life.

You'll likely need some help. **Financial literacy** is defined as having the knowledge, skills, and confidence to make responsible financial decisions. The Financial Consumer Agency of Canada (FCAC) has developed a national strategy for financial literacy with goals and priorities in working to strengthen the financial literacy of Canadians at different stages of their lives.[1] Through the Canadian Financial Literacy Database, one can find resources, events, tools and information on budgeting, money management, insurance, saving, investing, and taxes that

November is financial literacy month in Canada. With this in mind, what workshops are being offered on campus?

are offered by public, private, and non-profit providers of financial education.[2] Take some time to review this tool as it can help you better understand financial matters and improve your money management skills. Since financial literacy is important to your fiscal health, you may even enjoy taking an entire class on it.[3] Check your school to see what is available.

Financial Planning Begins with Making Money

You already know that one of the secrets to finding a good-paying job is having a good education. This is still true, although what you major in does matter.[4] Throughout history, an investment in business education has paid off regardless of the state of the economy or political ups and downs. Education has become even more important since we entered the information age. One way to become financially stable, therefore, is to finish school. Make sure you investigate all the financial help available to you.

Making money is one thing; saving, investing, and spending it wisely is something else. Following the advice in the next section will help you become one of those with enough to live in comfort throughout your life.[5]

Six Steps to Controlling Your Assets

The only way to save enough money to do all of the things you want to do in life is to spend less than you make. Although you may find it difficult to save today, it is both possible and imperative if you want to accumulate enough to be financially secure. The following are six steps you can take today to get control of your finances.

STEP 1: TAKE AN INVENTORY OF YOUR FINANCIAL ASSETS

To take inventory, you need to develop a balance sheet for yourself, like the one in Chapter 16. Remember, a balance sheet starts with the fundamental accounting equation: Assets = Liabilities + Owners' Equity. List your tangible assets (such as an iPad, TV, DVR player, computer, cell phone, car, jewellery, clothes, and savings account) on one side, and your liabilities (such as rent, credit card debt, auto and education debt, and any other debt) on the other side.

Assign a dollar value to each of your assets, based on its current value, not what you originally paid for it. If you have debts (liabilities), subtract them from your assets to get your net worth. If you have no debts, your assets equal your net worth. If your liabilities exceed the value of your assets, you are *not* on the path to financial security. You may need more financial discipline in your life.

Let's also create an income statement for you. At the top of the statement is revenue (all the money you take in from your job, investments, and so on). Subtract all your costs and expenses to get net income or profit. Software programs like Quicken and websites like Dinkytown and NerdWallet have a variety of tools that can easily help you with these calculations.

Now is an excellent time to think about how much money you will need to accomplish all your goals. The more clearly you can visualize your goals, the easier it is to begin saving for them.

STEP 2: KEEP TRACK OF ALL YOUR EXPENSES

Do you occasionally find yourself running out of cash? If you experience a cash flow problem, the only way to trace where the money is going is to keep track of every cent you spend. Keeping records of your expenses can be tedious, but it's a necessary step if you want to learn discipline. Actually, it could turn out to be enjoyable because it gives you such a feeling of control.

Here's what to do: List *everything* you spend as you go through the day. That list is your journal. At the end of the week, transfer your journal entries into a record book or computerized accounting program. The Royal Bank of Canada has developed the online Spend-o-meter tool as a way to highlight how some expenses can add up monthly and yearly. For example, if you buy two magazines a week, it is estimated that you will spend $624 per year. A tip to save money is to subscribe to your favourite magazine since it is less expensive than buying off the shelf each month. Alternatively, share a subscription with a friend to save even more. Going to two movies per month will cost you $360 per year. To cut down on this cost, you can stream directly to your device. To estimate some of your expenses, check out this tool. Were you surprised by some of the calculations?

© Purestock/SuperStock

Do you currently keep track of your expenses? If not, will you consider starting to do so now? You may be surprised to learn where you spend your money.

Develop spending categories (accounts) to make your task easier and more informative. You can have a category called "Food" for all of the food you bought from the grocery or convenience store during the week. You might want a separate account for meals eaten away from home because you can dramatically cut these costs if you make your meals at home. Other accounts could include rent, insurance, automobile repairs, gasoline, clothing, utilities, toiletries, entertainment, and donations to charity. Most people also like to have a category called "Miscellaneous" for impulse items like candy and lattes. You won't believe how much you fritter away on miscellaneous items unless you keep a *detailed* record for at least a couple of months.

Develop your accounts on the basis of what's most important to you or where you spend the most money. Once you've recorded all of your expenses for a few months, you'll easily see where you are spending too much and what you have to do to save more. You can even use an app, like Splurge Alert, that's designed to help curb mindless spending behaviours.

STEP 3: PREPARE A BUDGET

Once you know your financial situation and your sources of revenue and expenses, you're prepared to make a personal budget. Remember, budgets are financial plans and a recent survey showed more than half of adults don't keep track of theirs![6] A household budget includes rent or mortgage, utilities, food, clothing, vehicles, furniture, insurance, medical care, and taxes.

You'll need to choose how much to allow for expenses such as eating out, entertainment, cell phone use, and so on. Keep in mind that what you spend now reduces what you can save later. Choosing *not* to spend that $5 a day for coffee or cigarettes adds up to about $35 a week, $140 a month, and $1700 a year. Keep this up during four years of school and you'll have about $7,000 by graduation. And that's before adding any interest your money will earn. If you invest the savings in a mutual fund earning 6 percent

© Gail Vaz-Oxlade

Gail Vaz-Oxlade's money jar system as a way to manage money. That is, you stop spending when there is no more money in the jar. This is especially helpful for those who need to see their money in order to understand how much they have to spend. Would this system work for you?

compounded annually, you would double your money every 12 years. The Rule of 72 says that your money doubles every 12 years at 6 percent. You do that calculation by dividing the percentage earned into 72 (72 divided by 6 = 12).

Running a household is similar to running a small business. It takes the same careful record keeping, the same budget processes and forecasting, and the same control procedures. Sometimes it also creates the same need to borrow funds or rely on a credit card and become familiar with interest rates. The time you spend practising budgeting techniques will benefit you throughout your life.

Gail Vaz-Oxlade, financial expert and TV host of *Til Debt Do Us Part, Princess,* and *Money Moron,* recommends the money jar system as a way to manage money. Of your total income, 35 percent should go to housing, 15 percent to transportation, 25 percent on "life" (everything from groceries, pets, kids, etc), 15 percent to debt and 10 percent to savings. If you walk most places or have no debt, obviously these will change—but savings in your budget should go to savings, not just be spent because you have it.[7]

STEP 4: PAY OFF YOUR DEBTS

The first thing to do with the money remaining after you pay your monthly bills is to pay off your debts, starting with those carrying the highest interest rates. Credit card interest, for example, is calculated daily and charged monthly, at a yearly rate—typically 19.99 percent for most rewards credit cards in Canada.[8] Check credit card statements and other mailings carefully to make certain the charges are accurate.

Try to make more than the minimum payment as the longer you carry debt, the more interest you will pay. For example, assume the following conditions: your credit card debt is $9500; your credit card interest rate is 18 percent; and your monthly minimum payment (usually 3 percent of the balance) is $285. If you only made the minimum payment, it would take you 22 years and five months to pay off your debt completely, and you will have paid $9298 in interest, for a total debt repayment of $18,798.[9]

STEP 5: START A SAVINGS PLAN

It's important to save some money each month in a separate account for large purchases you're likely to make (such as a car or house). Then, when it comes time to make that purchase, you'll have the needed cash. Save at least enough for a significant down payment so that you can reduce the finance charges you'll pay to borrow the rest.

The best way to save money is to pay yourself first. David Chilton, Canadian author of *The Wealthy Barber,* has sold over 2 million copies of his self-published book reinforcing this advice. His key advice is to invest 10 percent of what you earn for long-term growth by

FIGURE B.1

ANNUAL RATE OF RETURN: HOW MONEY GROWS

This chart illustrates how the $5,000 would grow at various rates of return. Recent savings account interest rates have been low (less than 2 percent), but in earlier years, they've been over 5 percent.

Time	2%	5%	8%	11%
5 years	$5,520	$ 6,381	$ 7,347	$ 8,425
10 years	6,095	8,144	10,795	14,197
15 years	6,729	10,395	15,861	23,923
20 years	7,430	13,266	23,305	40,312
25 years	8,203	16,932	34,242	67,927

paying yourself first and live within your means.[10] "It's crucial to understand that wealth flows from savings, not from income," says Chilton. He suggests that when you get an unexpected windfall or a raise at work, or you take on a part-time job to generate more income, it's important to put away at least 10 to 15 percent of your income. Life happens, and money might not come as easily down the road. A divorce, a bad investment return, or an illness can leave you financially crippled if you haven't planned ahead.[11]

You can arrange with your financial institution to deduct a certain amount every two weeks or once a month. You will be pleasantly surprised when the money starts accumulating and earning interest over time. This **compound interest**, which is "interest on the interest" is the reason many investors are so successful.[12] With some discipline, you can eventually reach your goal of financial security. It is not as difficult as you may think. Figure B.1 illustrates how $5000 grows over various periods, and at different rates of return. For example, assuming a 2 percent rate of return and no taxes, you would see $5000 grow to $5520 in five years. The calculation is broken down as follows: Year 1: $5100 ($5000 × 1.02%); Year 2: $5202 ($5100 × 1.02%); Year 3: $5306.04 ($5202 × 1.02%); Year 4: $5412.16 ($5306.04 × 1.02%); and Year 5: $5520.04 ($5412.16 × 1.02%). The earlier you start to save, the bigger the impact of compound interest, resulting in higher savings.

compound interest Interest calculated on your interest.

STEP 6: BORROW ONLY TO BUY ASSETS THAT INCREASE IN VALUE OR GENERATE INCOME

Don't borrow money for ordinary expenses; you'll only get into more debt that way.[13] If you have budgeted for emergencies, such as car repairs, you should be able to stay financially secure. In general, it's recommended that you save the equivalent of 3 to 6 months of your regular expenses and once you reach this goal, consider saving 3 to 6 months of your income.[14] Keep this money in highly liquid accounts, such as a bank account or a cashable term deposit.

Only the most unexpected of expenses should cause you to borrow. It is hard to wait until you have enough money to buy what you want, but learning to wait is a critical part of self-discipline. Of course, you can always try to produce more income by working overtime or by taking on other jobs for extra income.

If you follow these six steps, not only will you have money for investment, but you'll have developed most of the financial techniques needed to become financially secure. If you find it hard to live within a budget at first, remember the payoff is well worth the effort.

Building Your Financial Base

The path to financial success is to have capital (money) to invest, yet many students today graduate with debt. As you've read, accumulating capital takes discipline and careful planning. With the money you save, however, you can become an entrepreneur, one of the fastest ways to wealth.

Living frugally is extremely difficult for the average person. Most people are eager to spend their money on a new car, furniture, electronics, clothes, entertainment, and the like. They look for a fancy apartment with all the amenities. A capital-generating strategy may require foregoing most (though not all) of these purchases to accumulate investment money. It might mean living like a frugal student in a relatively inexpensive apartment furnished in hand-me-downs from parents, friends, Kijiji, resale shops, etc.

Tax-Free Savings Account (TFSA)
An investment option into which Canadian residents 18 years of age or older who have a valid social insurance number can contribute up to $5,500 annually; the amount contributed as well as the income earned in the account is tax free, even when it is withdrawn.

For five or six years, you can manage with the old stereo, a used car, and a few nice clothes. The strategy is sacrifice, not luxury. It's important not to feel burdened by this plan; instead, feel happy knowing your financial future will be more secure. That is the way the majority of millionaires got their money. If living frugally seems too restrictive for you, you can still save at least a little. It is better to save a smaller amount than none at all.

A great strategy for couples is to try to live on one income and to save the other. The longer you wait to marry, the more likely it will be that one of you can be earning enough to do that, as a college or university graduate. If the second spouse makes $35,000 a year *after taxes,* saving that income for five years quickly adds up to $175,000 (plus interest).

© stockbroker/123RF

It's wise to plan your financial future with the same excitement and dedication you bring to other aspects of your life. If you get married, for example, it's important to discuss financial issues with your spouse. Conflicts over money are a major cause of divorce, so agreeing on a financial strategy before marriage is very important. Do you know people who fight over how money is spent?

Tax-Free Savings Account (TFSA)[15]

What do you do with the money you accumulate? Where do you invest this money? In Chapter 18, some options discussed included depositing money into a savings account or a term deposit (also known as a certificate of deposit). Also consider a **Tax-Free Savings Account (TFSA)**, where Canadian residents who are 18 years of age or older and who have a valid social insurance number are eligible to contribute up to $5,500 annually. (This annual allowable contribution amount may change from year to year.) You can carry your unused contribution room forward. For example, the total contribution limit since the TFSA was launched in 2009 would be $57,500 in 2018. This is good news for the 90 percent of TFSA holders who don't max out their TFSAs.

The initial amount contributed as well as the income earned in the account (e.g., interest income) is tax free, even when it is withdrawn. Generally, the types of investments that will be permitted in a TFSA include cash, mutual funds, securities listed on a designated stock exchange, term deposits, bonds, and certain shares of small business corporations.

One strategy is to save your money in a TFSA and when you accumulate enough to make a large purchase (e.g., home or a trip) you withdraw the money and pay for the purchase. Let us look at real estate next as an investment option.

© karen roach/Shutterstock

One purpose of planning your personal finances is to have enough money for retirement. Before that time arrives, however, you will have other reasons to save, such as for a trip, car, or house purchase. The TFSA is an ideal savings vehicle to protect your investments until you need to cash them in. If you do not have a TFSA, do you plan to open one?

Real Estate

What do you do with the money you accumulate? According to a Royal LePage Peak Millennial survey, 86 percent of those between the ages of 25 and 30 still view real estate as a good investment.[16] And for good reason. Real estate is likely to provide several investment benefits. First, a home is the one investment that you can live in. Second, once you buy a home, the payments are relatively fixed (though taxes and utilities may go up). As your income rises, mortgage payments get easier to make, but renters often find that rents go up at least as fast as income. On the other hand, the changes in home prices have made it more important than ever for you to check whether it is better to own or rent.[17]

Paying for a home has historically been a good way of forcing yourself to save.[18] You must make the payments every month. Those payments are an investment that can prove to be very rewarding over time. A home is also a good asset to use when applying for a business loan.

Many people take huge risks by buying too much home for their income. Furthermore, people sometimes take out interest-only (e.g., a secured line of credit where the minimum monthly payment is the interest) or other loans that are very risky. The suggestion, "Don't buy a home that costs more than two and a half times your annual income," still stands as a good strategy. Buy for the long term, and stay within your means. What has happened to housing prices in your area over the last couple of years? Lower prices may mean an opportunity if the market gains strength.

Some couples have used the seed money accumulated from saving one income (in the strategy outlined earlier) to buy two attached homes (a duplex) so that they can live in one part and rent out the other. The rent they earn covers a good part of the payments for both homes so the couple can live comfortably, yet inexpensively, while their investment in a home appreciates.[19] In this way, they accumulate capital, and as they grow older, they pull far ahead of their peers in terms of financial security. As capital accumulates and values rise, they can sell, and then buy an even larger apartment building or a single-family home. Many have made fortunes in real estate in just this way.

Today, some people are making additional income by renting unused housing space on Airbnb.[20] Of course, it all depends on how valuable your space is. An apartment in Toronto or Vancouver may bring in some real income if you rent it while away. Such rentals are part

© Blend Images/Alamy RF

Buying a home has usually been a very good and safe investment. But sometimes housing prices can rise fast, especially in large metropolitan areas such as Vancouver, Toronto, and Montreal. What has contributed to this increase in prices? What has happened to housing prices in your area over the last few years?

of a "shared economy" that is emerging. That is, people are learning to share cars, homes, bicycles, driveways, and tools as a way of saving some money.[21]

Once you understand the benefits of home ownership versus renting, you can decide whether those same principles apply to owning the premises where you set up your own business—or owning your own equipment, vehicles, and the like. Furthermore, you may start thinking of real estate as a way to earn a living. You could, for example, buy older homes, fix them up, and sell them—a path many have taken to attain financial security.

To find out more, look for mortgage affordability calculators online. Many financial institutions in Canada offer this free service on their websites. You may also consider using an online calculator to consider the cost differences between renting and buying a home.

The Stock Market

You have learned that one place to invest the money you have saved is in a home. What are some other good places to save your money? For a young person, one of the *worst* places to keep long-term investments is a bank through a savings account or term deposit. (This is different for your emergency funds.) Online banks usually pay higher interest than your local bank, but even their rates are relatively *low*.

One of the best places to invest over time has been the stock market. The stock market does tend to go up and down, but over a longer period of time it has proven to be one of the best investments. Remember, the greater the risk, usually the greater the return. When stock prices are low, that's the time to *buy*. When stocks collapse, it's an opportunity to get into the stock market—not avoid it. The average investor buys when the stock market is high and sells when it is low. Clearly, that's not a good idea. It takes courage to buy when everyone else is selling. In the long run, however, this **contrarian approach** to investing is the way the rich get richer. (Of course, you'll need to do your research to determine the health and potential of any companies or sectors in which you're interested in investing.)

contrarian approach Buying stock when everyone else is selling or vice versa.

A stockbroker can be a source of information about what investments would best meet your financial objectives. However, it's still important to learn about stocks and bonds on your own since investment analysts' advice may not always meet your specific expectations and needs.[22] Today, some investors are taking advantage of having their investment decisions managed by robots. Read the Adapting to Change box for more about robo-advisors.

Chapter 17 introduced you to stocks and bonds. There are tools that track the performance of such investments over time. For example, the Andex Chart summarizes the performance of some key indices such as the S&P/TSX Composite (the Canadian stock market), the S&P 500, U.S. small stocks, Canadian bonds, fixed-term investments, Canadian Treasury bills, and the cost of living.[23] As you can see in Figure B.2, this chart captures historical performances that have been impacted by trends in the business environment. Bonds, for example, have traditionally lagged behind stocks as a long-term investment.

No one knows what will happen in the future and this is where doing your homework and knowing your risk tolerance is very important when making financial investments.

Learning to Manage Credit

Credit cards are an important element in your personal financial system, even if you rarely use them. First, you may have to own a credit card to buy certain goods or even rent a car, because some businesses require one for identification and to ensure payment. Second, you can use a credit card to keep track of purchases. A credit card gives you records of purchases over time for your income tax returns (if you drive for work) and financial planning purposes. Third, a credit card is more convenient than cash or cheques. You can carry less cash and easily cancel a stolen card to protect your account. Most of our phones now have capabilities for managing data for your credit, debit, loyalty, membership, and gift cards through Apple Wallet and Android Pay.[24] The most secure cards will be PIN and chip cards, since such cards are much less prone to identity theft.[25]

If you do use a credit card, you should pay the balance in full during the period when no interest is charged. Not having to pay 18 percent interest, as an example of the interest charged, is as good as earning 18 percent tax free. You may want to choose a card that pays you back in cash (e.g., *Scotia Momentum*® no-fee VISA credit card) or offers paybacks like credits toward the purchase of gas (e.g., Canadian Tire Financial Service's *Gas Advantage*™ *MasterCard*®), or frequent-flier air miles. The value of these givebacks can vary. Some cards have no annual fees while others offer lower interest rates. To learn more about credit cards that will best suit your needs, visit the Financial Consumer Agency of Canada's website and look for the Credit Card Comparison Tool.

The danger of a credit card is the flip side of its convenience. It's too easy to buy things you wouldn't buy if you had to pay cash, or to pile up debts you can't repay. If you aren't the type who can stick to a financial plan or household budget, it may be better not to have a credit card at all. Imagine a customer who has a $10,000 balance on his or her credit

Adapting *to* CHANGE

R2-D2 to the Investor's Rescue

Investors' frustrations with the advice and financial results from traditional investment advisors have moved some people toward a new type of money manager—robots. To be honest, robo-advisors are not actual robots. Robo-advisors are automated online tools that use advanced algorithms that make investment suggestions, manage money, rebalance a client's portfolio, and perhaps even shift investments to save taxes. Since hitting the money management scene in 2008, robo-advisors have attracted roughly $67 billion under management. Some analysts even suggest robo-advisors could displace traditional financial advisors in the future.

Originally, robo-advisors' target customers were Millennials, who were interested in saving money, and grew up on technology. Millennials were often overlooked by traditional financial advisors since they lacked the minimum investment (usually $50,000) needed to interest the human financial advisors. In contrast, robo-advisors don't require minimum amounts. Also their fees are significantly lower. At Wealthfront, robo-advisors charge nothing for the first $10,000 invested and then 0.25 percent on all investments after that. Traditional, human advisors often charge in excess of 1 percent annually.

Today robo-advisors are reaching beyond Millennial investors. Older, higher-net-worth individuals are attracted to the bargain-basement fees and the simplicity of opening robo-advisor accounts. With robo investing, you tell the robots what your risk tolerance is and what your financial goals are, and the rest is handled by the robo-advisor using its algorithms. In general, your account will be invested in conservative exchange-traded funds (ETFs) and high-rated bond issues. The robo-advisor will rebalance your account when it decides it's appropriate, and some will make beneficial trades to minimize taxes.

It's fair to say that robo-advisors cannot do the same things that human financial professionals can do. Human financial managers, especially certified financial planners (CFPs), are schooled in estate planning, mortgage refinancing, and trust investments, as well as any personal issues you may have such as planning your children's education. Yet old-school financial advisors realize robo-advisors are changing the money management landscape. Michael Spellacy, PwC Global wealth management leader, warns, "The traditional financial advisor model is under assault. Financial advisors have to ask themselves, what's my differentiation and how will I be a better financial advisor to my customers?" It's very possible the future of financial management will embrace a hybrid model: part robo-advisor, part human advisor.

© Palto/Shutterstock RF

Sources: Lisa Kramer and Scott Smith, "Can Robo Advisers Replace Human Advisers?" *The Wall Street Journal*, February 29, 2016; Larry Light, "Here's Why the Most Talked-about Way to Invest Right Now Could Be a Huge Mistake," *Fortune*, March 5, 2016; Tom Anderson, "Returns Vary Widely for Robo Advisors with Similar Risk," Charles Schwab Personal Finance, September 2016; John Divine, "How Robo Advisors Will Impact the Future," U.S. News & World Report, September 29, 2016; Richard Eisenberg, "Robo-Advisors: Not Just for Millennials Anymore?" *Forbes*, December 6, 2016; Katie Brockman, "Battle of the Robots: Which Robo-Advisor Is Right for You?" The Motley Fool, August 4, 2017.

card with a 16 percent interest rate and pays the minimum monthly payment established by the credit card company (e.g., 4 percent). How long will it take to pay off the debt, and what would the cost for interest be? The answers are 14 years and nearly $5000—and that's without using the card again to purchase so much as a candy bar.

FIGURE B.2

THE ANDEX CHART SUMMARIZES THE PERFORMANCE OF SOME KEY INDICES.

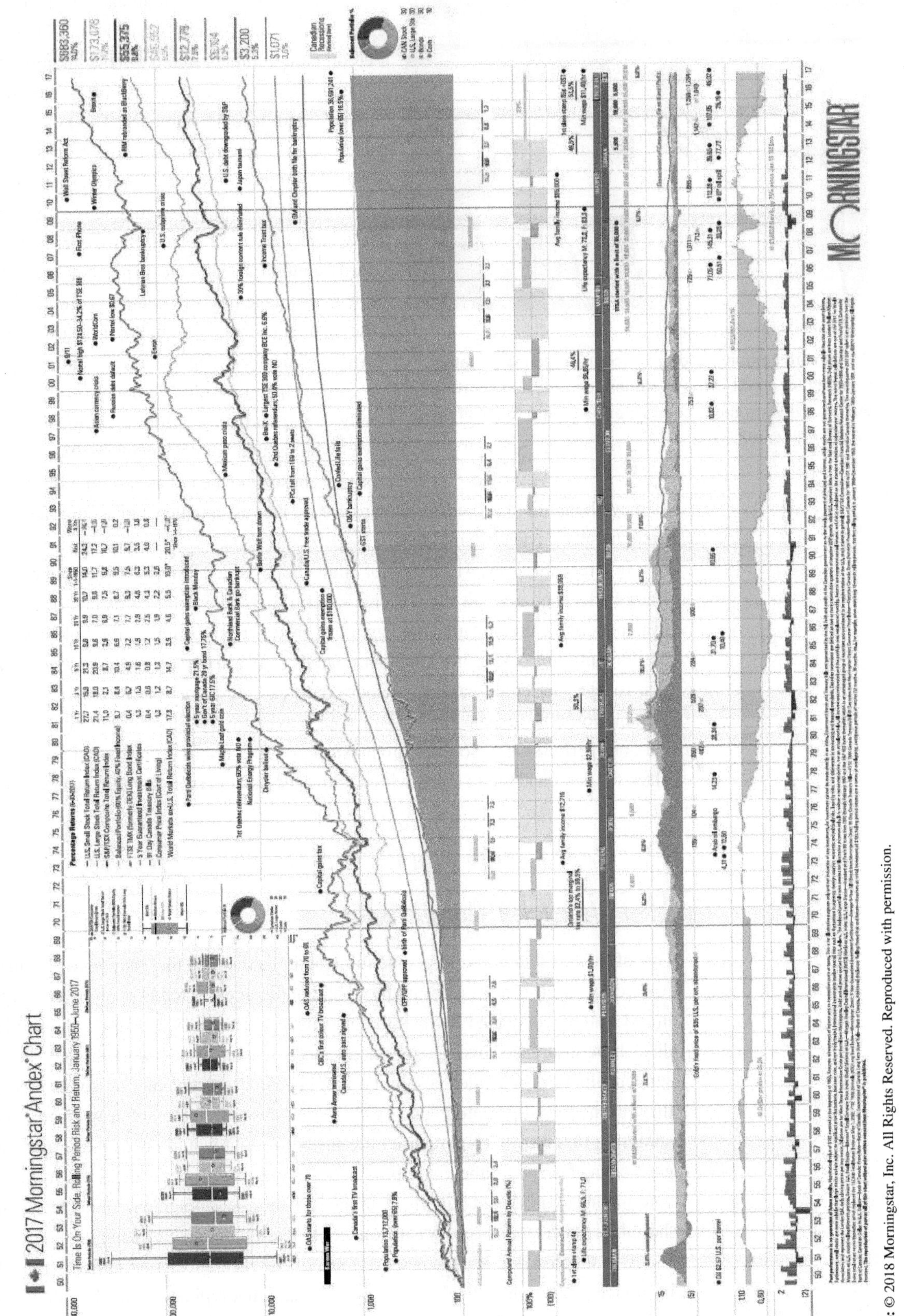

© UpperCut Images/SuperStock

Credit card companies often encourage young people to apply for credit cards at student centres and sports events. Why are these companies so willing to qualify you for a credit card?

Another danger of credit cards is the issue of hacking. Stores like Wendy's and Home Depot have had credit card numbers stolen.[26] This identity theft results in people getting access to customers' e-mail addresses, names, and account numbers. The newer credit cards use both a chip embedded in the card and a customer PIN. Though studies are showing fewer fraudulent activities with chip versus magnetic strip cards, not all problems have been solved. Since current chip-enabled cards contain a magnetic strip, they are still vulnerable. It may take up to 10 years to completely phase out the magnetic strip. Time will tell if these cards will cut down on the losses due to stolen credit card numbers.[27]

Some people would be better off with a *debit* card only. Debit cards don't allow you to spend more than what you have in your financial institution, a great benefit for those who are not as careful with their spending as they should be. Furthermore, there are no interest payments or annual fees, other than account-specific fees, if applicable.

In a recent survey, 41 percent of adults believed a debit card could protect them from fraud better than a credit card.[28] That's not true. While debit cards can protect you from overspending, a credit card offers greater consumer protection as the holder would be liable for only up to $50 in fraudulent charges.[29] If a federally regulated financial institution issued your credit card, then your credit card agreement must explain the maximum amount you'll be responsible for—or your maximum liability—if your card is used without your permission.[30] So there are no surprises, be sure to discuss what protections are in place for debit and credit cards with a knowledgeable person at your financial institution.

Protecting Your Financial Base: Buying Insurance

One of the last things young people think about is the idea that they may become sick, get injured, or die. It is not a pleasant thought, but the unexpected happens every day. According to a study conducted by investment firm, Edward Jones, less than one-third of Canadians have insurance coverage for unexpected financial crises, whether they are caused by sudden illness or extended disability. Twenty-three percent of Canadians answered that they are not at all prepared financially if they pass away too soon, with only 16 percent admitting that they have purchased life insurance that would cover their remaining mortgage payments should they ever pass away.[31] To protect your loved ones from the loss of your income, you should buy life insurance. An online supplement to this text is devoted to the subject of financial risk. Visit Connect to learn more about managing risk.

term insurance
Pure insurance protection for a given number of years.

The simplest and least expensive form of life insurance is **term insurance**. It is pure insurance protection for a given number of years that typically costs less the younger you are when you buy it. When your term expires, you would need to renew the policy, and the premium can then rise. Compare prices through a service like Insurance-Canada.ca.

FIGURE B.3

WHY BUY TERM INSURANCE?

Insurance Needs in Early Years Are High	Insurance Needs Decline as You Grow Older
1. Children are young and need money for education.	1. Children are grown.
2. Mortgage is high relative to income.	2. Mortgage is low or completely paid off.
3. Often there are auto payments and other bills to pay.	3. Debts are paid off.
4. Loss of income would be disastrous.	4. Insurance needs are few.
	5. Retirement income is needed

How much insurance do you need? The answer depends on the objectives that you have. For an idea, complete a life insurance needs calculator, such as the Kanetix.ca Life Insurance Needs Calculator. This tool is designed to give you an estimate of how much life insurance you'll need to ensure that your family is covered in the event of your death. Keep in mind that this calculator should not be considered as a replacement for consultation with a qualified insurance professional.[32] Figure B.3 summarizes why you should buy term insurance.

Even stay-at-home parents should carry life insurance. It was recently reported that a stay-at-home parent's work was equal to a $118,905 salary.[33] How much insurance do you need? It depends on your age, income, number of dependents, savings, debts and how secure you want to leave your dependents. A suggestion is to apportion your coverage so that a spouse earning 60 percent of the income carries 60 percent of the insurance.

Multi-year level-premium insurance guarantees that you'll pay the same premium for the life of the policy. Recently, 40 percent of new term policies guaranteed a set rate for 20 years or more. Some companies allow you to switch your term policy for a more expensive whole or universal life policy.

Whole life insurance combines pure insurance and savings so you are buying both insurance and a savings plan. This may be a good idea for those people who have trouble saving money. A universal life policy lets you choose how much of your payment should go to insurance and how much to investments. The investments in such plans traditionally are very conservative but pay a steady interest rate.

whole life insurance
Life insurance that combines pure insurance and savings.

Variable life insurance is a form of whole life insurance that invests the cash value of the policy in stocks or other high-yielding securities. Death benefits may thus vary, reflecting the performance of the investments.

variable life insurance
A form of whole life insurance that invests the cash value of the policy in stocks or other high-yielding securities.

Life insurance companies recognized people's desire to earn higher returns on their insurance (and to protect themselves against running out of money before they die) and began selling annuities. An **annuity** is a contract to make regular payments to a person for life or a fixed period. With an annuity, you are guaranteed to have an income until you die or for the agreed upon time.

annuity
A contract to make regular payments to a person for life or a fixed period.

There are two kinds of annuities: fixed and variable. *Fixed annuities* are investments that pay the policyholder a specified interest rate. They are not as popular as *variable annuities,* which provide investment choices identical to mutual funds. Such annuities are becoming more popular than term or whole life insurance. But buyers must be careful in selecting an insurance company and choosing the investments made with their money.

Before buying any insurance, it is wise to consult with both an insurance agent and a financial advisor. They can help you make the wisest decision about insurance based on your overall needs.

Disability Insurance

Your chances of becoming disabled at an early age are much higher than your chances of dying from an accident. It's a good idea to supplement Canada's public health coverage with **disability insurance** that pays part of the cost of a long-term illness or an accident. Disability insurance replaces part of your lost income, and, in some cases, pays disability-related expenses not covered by health insurance. Call an insurance agent or check online for possible quotes for such insurance. The cost is relatively low to protect yourself from losing your income for an extended period of time.

Homeowner's or Renter's Insurance

You may be surprised how much it would cost to replace all the things you own. As you begin to accumulate possessions, you may want to have apartment or homeowner's insurance that covers any losses. Specify that you want *guaranteed replacement cost.* That means that the insurance company will give you whatever it costs to buy all of those things new. It costs a little bit more than a policy without guaranteed replacement, but you will get a lot more if you have a loss.[34]

The other option is insurance that covers the *depreciated cost* of the items. For example, a sofa you bought five years ago for $600 may be worth $150 now. That current value is what you would get from insurance, not the $700 or more you may need to buy a brand-new sofa. If your computer is stolen, you might only get a couple hundred dollars for it rather than its replacement cost.

Most policies don't cover expensive items like engagement and wedding rings. You can buy a *rider* to your policy that will cover them at a reasonable cost.

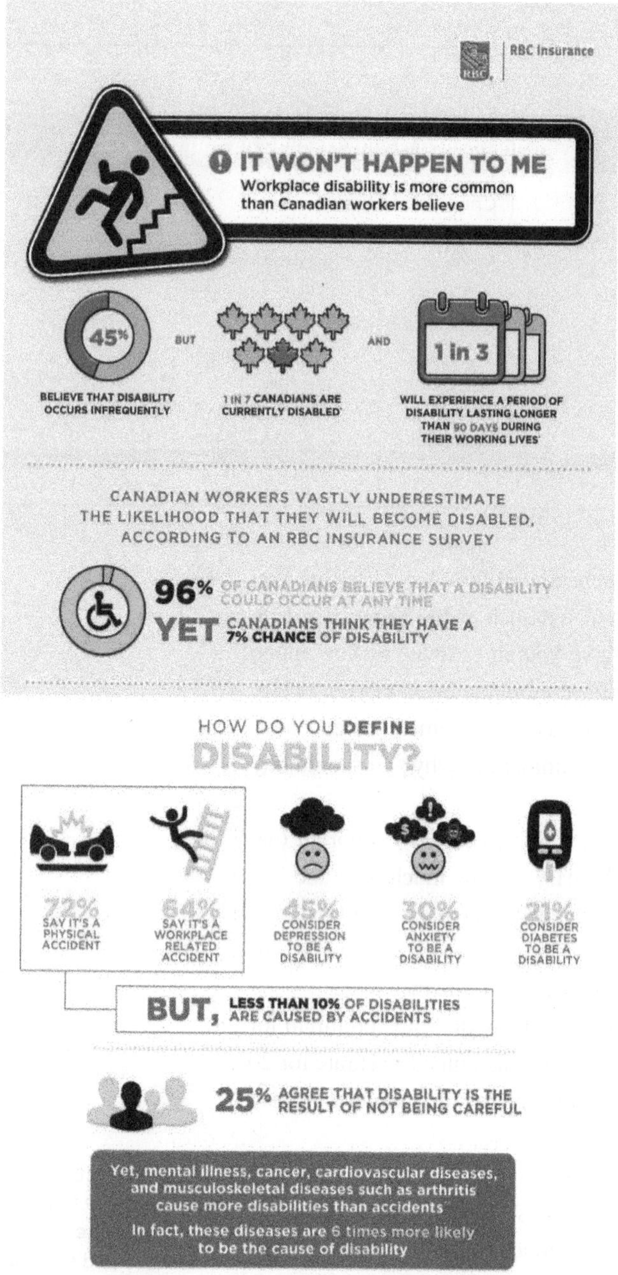

Reproduced with permission of RBC Insurance Services Inc.

In Canada, 65 percent of individuals end up with unexpected and uncovered illnesses, and 47 percent of these individuals do not have enough medical care insurances or savings to cover their expenditures.[35] Does your school offer disability insurance? Is this something that you will seek out once you work full time?

disability insurance
Insurance that pays part of the cost of a long-term illness or an accident.

Other Insurance: Car and Liability Insurance

You should buy insurance for your car. Consider selecting a large deductible of $1000 or so to keep the premiums low, and pay for small damages on your own. Be sure to include insurance against losses from uninsured motorists. You will also need liability insurance to protect yourself against being sued by someone you accidentally injure.

Often you can get a discount by buying all your insurance (e.g., life, disability, homeowners, automobile, etc.) with one company. This is called an **umbrella policy**. Look for other discounts such as for safe driving, good grades, using snow tires, and more.

umbrella policy
A broadly based insurance policy that saves you money because you buy all your insurance from one company.

Planning Your Retirement

It may seem a bit early to be planning your retirement; however, not doing so would be a big mistake. Successful financial planning means long-range planning, and retirement is a critical phase of life. What you do now could make a world of difference in your quality of life when you retire. If you think that it is too early, as a minimum you can start to gather information.

How much do you need for retirement? The answer is that it depends on factors such as your age, your spending patterns, your health, if you have any debt, etc. For example, retirement length has a big impact on when you can retire. According to Statistics Canada, workers in economic regions that had a higher unemployment rate were expected to retire two years earlier (62.7 years), on average, than workers in economic regions with a lower unemployment rate (64.2 years).[36] Canadians are living longer than past generations so it is wise budget for 30 years of retirement or more.[37]

The Three Pillars Approach[38]

Retirement income in Canada is shared among the government, individuals, and their employers. Income may come from what is commonly referred to as the *three pillars approach.* Pillar 1 consists of the federal Old Age Security (OAS) program. Retirement income from Pillar 2 consists of income from the Canada Pension Plan (CPP) and the Québec Pension Plan (QPP). Government pensions were designed to replace only 40 percent of pre-retirement income for individuals who were earning the average national wage. Pillar 1 represents 15 percent and Pillar 2 represents 25 percent of pre-retirement income.

You can see how Pillar 3 at 60 percent, or more if one does not qualify for OAS or CPP/QPP, has some heavy lifting to do. It consists of income generated from private savings and retirement savings plans, with the most common being employer-sponsored, registered pension plans (RPPs) and registered retirement savings plans (RRSPs).

© Fuse/Getty Images RF

If you plan to relax and travel when you retire, you need to begin saving now. What are your retirement goals, and what resources will you need to accomplish them?

The retirement income system in Canada is based on both public (Pillars 1 and 2) and private (Pillar 3) retirement savings plans. Almost all of today's seniors receive income from Canada's public pensions. Let's briefly consider each of these three pillars next.

PILLAR 1: OAS PENSION PROGRAM[39]

The OAS program is one of the cornerstones of Canada's retirement income system. Payment amounts for the OAS benefits (Guaranteed Income Supplement, Allowance and Allowance for the Survivor) are based on your marital status and level of income.

This program is financed from general tax revenues collected by the Government of Canada. All benefits payable under the Old Age Security Act are adjusted four times a year if there are increases in the cost of living, as measured by the consumer price index (CPI).

OAS generates a pension at age 65 if one has lived in Canada for at least 10 years since the age of 18. Between April to June 2018, the basic OAS pension benefit was $589.59 regardless of marital status. If the pensioner's income, however, exceeds $123,019 in 2018, he or she will have to repay all of the OAS benefits received that year. This is commonly referred to as the "claw back" or the OAS "pension recovery tax."

PILLAR 2: CPP/QPP[40]

The CPP operates throughout Canada, except in Quebec, where the Québec Pension Plan (QPP) provides similar benefits. Established in 1966, the CPP provides basic benefits when a contributor to the Plan becomes disabled or retires. At the contributor's death, the Plan provides benefits to his or her survivors.

The CPP is a "contributory" plan. This means that all its costs are covered by the financial contributions paid by employees, employers, and self-employed workers, and from revenue earned on CPP investments. Though the standard age is 65, one can take a reduced benefit as early as 60 or an enhanced benefit as late as 70.

According to Doug Runchey of DR Pensions Consulting, "People who join the workforce late or drop out for a period of time, who retire early or who have low incomes, may not hit the maximum annual pensionable earnings level often enough over the years to get the highest possible CPP retirement benefit." To be eligible for the maximum benefit, one must make 39 years of contributions to the CPP at the maximum level. In 2018, this maximum monthly benefit per retired recipient (age 65) was $1,134.17. Approximately 6 percent of recipients receive the maximum while on average, Canadians receive 56.6 percent of the maximum.

PILLAR 3: PRIVATE RETIREMENT PLANS

Based on the values noted earlier, between OAS and the CPP/QPP, the government(s) will pay out a maximum of approximately $1,724 a month to an eligible 65-year-old. This is not a lot of money, which is why you need to take charge of saving for retirement.

Financial experts recommend that we need 70 percent of our pre-retirement income in order to have a comfortable retirement.[41] As a result, the third pillar must make up what is not covered by public pensions. This third pillar considers money that you have saved, a potential stream of income (e.g., from a part-time job or investment income), and private retirement plans. Private retirement plans include voluntary, employer, and union-sponsored pension and retirement plans, such as RPPs, and personal plans, such as RRSPs.[42] Let's consider each one next.

RPPs[43] **Registered pension plans (RPPs)** are established by employers or unions for employees. These private pension plans are employer-specific and, if applicable, are introduced during an employee's orientation period. With an RPP, both the employer and employee typically contribute to the plan. In Canada, RPPs cover just over 6.2 million workers, which is 37.8 percent of all employees. This means that there is a good chance that you may not have an RPP when you retire.

© kali9/E+/Getty Images

You would agree that individuals who work for employers that offer RPPs have a financial advantage over those that do not have access to RPPs. What can individuals who do not have RPPs do to compensate for a weak Pillar 3?

RRSPs[44] As you read above, a minority of working Canadians have access to a RPP. Consequently, the majority of Canadians need to proactively consider other personal investment strategies such as RRSPs. A **registered retirement savings plan (RRSP)** is a federally-regulated, tax-sheltered savings plan designed to encourage Canadians to save for their retirement. Any earnings from cash or investments held within an RRSP are not taxed until they are withdrawn. An RRSP lets you save for retirement and save taxes at the same time. Not only do you avoid paying income tax on the money you contribute, but you postpone paying tax on your investment earnings until you take the money out of your plan later on. And because you'll earn interest on the interest, the tax-free compounding will make a huge difference in the amount of money you'll be able to save for retirement. You, your spouse, or a common-law partner can establish and contribute to an RRSP.

registered pension plans (RPPs) Pension plans established by employers or unions for employees.

registered retirement savings plan (RRSP) A federally-regulated, tax-sheltered savings plan designed to encourage Canadians to save for their retirement.

The exact amount you're entitled to contribute for the tax year is shown in a separate section of the Notice of Assessment you receive from Canada Revenue Agency after you file last year's tax return. The amount you're allowed to deduct for tax purposes is referred to as your *contribution room* or *deduction room.* The dollar limit (or maximum) that you can contribute for any tax year is 18 percent of your earned income from the previous year (up to a certain limit), minus any "pension adjustment" (if applicable, this refers to the amount of a work pension that you may have built up in the pension plan during the year), plus any unused contributions from previous years.

You may deduct the entire amount from your taxable income when you make the contribution. The amount of tax you save will depend on your marginal tax rate. For tax planning purposes, the **marginal tax rate** is defined as the rate of tax payable on the last dollar earned. The marginal tax rate varies from province to province, and it increases as your income rises. Your tax rate tells you how much money you get to keep if you make an extra dollar, or how much you save in taxes by reducing your taxable income by a dollar. The higher your income, the more tax you will save by contributing to your RRSP.

Consider Figure B.4, which lists a snapshot of the combined federal and Ontario marginal tax rates for our example. Your friend has earned \$25,000 and you have earned \$75,000. A \$1000 investment into an RRSP would save your friend \$200.50 (\$1000 × 20.05%) and would save you \$296.50 (\$1000 × 29.65%) in tax. Despite investing the same \$1000, everyone derives different tax benefits depending on each person's marginal tax rate.

marginal tax rate The rate of tax payable on the last dollar earned.

■ FIGURE B.4

SNAPSHOT OF COMBINED FEDERAL AND ONTARIO MARGINAL TAX RATES FOR 2018

Taxable Income	Marginal Tax Rates
first $42,960	20.05%
over $42,960 up to $46,605	24.15%
over $46,605 up to $75,657	29.65%
over $75,657 up to $85,923	31.48%
over $85,923 up to $89,131	33.89%
over $89,131 up to $93,208	37.91%

Source: "Ontario Personal Tax Rates," TaxTips.ca, May 23, 2018, https://www.taxtips.ca/taxrates/on.htm.

The annual RRSP contribution deadline is 60 days after the end of the year (i.e., March 1). You can buy an RRSP at any financial institution or through a broker or financial advisor.

When you start contributing to your RRSP earlier in life, you'll allow more time for the income earned in your RRSP to compound. (Recall the compound interest discussion in Chapter 17.) You may also find that you can make a smaller total investment in your RRSP, and still be further ahead. While this sounds straightforward, 32 percent of Canadians between the ages of 45 and 64 have nothing saved for retirement.[45]

According to a CIBC report, the average amount of personal savings Canadians estimate they'll need to retire comfortably is $756,000. Unfortunately, this estimation is not based on fundamentals, such as how much money one can expect from an employer and the government, as well as one's various personal savings vehicles. One should consider this information first. Once those numbers are calculated, the next step should be to determine how they stack up against fixed costs, and then what's left over can go toward other lifestyle choices.[46] Like any savings program, retirement planning requires discipline.

There are other uses for RRSP money, other than for retirement. Two plans allow you to withdraw money from your RRSP without penalty, assuming that you pay back these funds within a certain period of time. For example, the Home Buyers' Plan allows you to withdraw up to $25,000 from your RRSP to buy or build a home for yourself or for a related person with a disability. The Lifelong Learning Plan allows you to withdraw up to $20,000 from your RRSP to finance training or education for you, your spouse, or common-law partner.

Contributing to an RRSP is one of several strategies that Canadians can pursue when planning for retirement. There are free online programs that will help you determine how much you need to save in your RRSP to achieve your retirement goals. Figure B.5 summarizes Canada's three pillar approach.

FIGURE B.5

CANADA'S RETIREMENT INCOME SYSTEM: THE THREE PILLARS APPROACH

Pillar 1 (15%) OAS Program	Pillar 2 (25%) CPP/QPP	Pillar 3 (60%) Private Retirement Plans
Payments are based on eligibility (lived in Canada for at least 10 years after the age of 18), marital status, and income level.	Compulsory, contributory public pension plans that provide benefits based on earnings for retirement.	Voluntary, private employer, and union-sponsored pension and retirement plans that include RPPs and RRSPs.

Financial Planners

If the idea of developing a comprehensive financial plan seems overwhelming, relax. Help is available from financial planners. Financial planners assist in developing a comprehensive program that covers investments, taxes, insurance, and other financial matters. Be careful, though—anybody can claim to be a financial planner today as there isn't one professional credential or one certification governing the industry of financial planners.[47] It's often best to find a person who has earned the distinction of being a Certified Financial Planner® (CFP) or a similar designation. Unfortunately, many so-called financial planners are simply insurance salespeople. For a list and description of financial designations, as well as advice on finding an advisor, visit Financial Advisors Association of Canada at www.advocis.ca.

It pays to shop around for financial advice. Ask your friends and family. Find someone who understands your situation and is willing to spend some time with you. Financial planning covers all aspects of investing, all the way to retirement and death. Financial planners can advise you on the proper mix of investments, insurance, and retirement planning.

Estate Planning

Your retirement may be far away, but it is never too early to begin thinking about estate planning, or making financial arrangements for those who will inherit from you. You may even help your parents or others to do such planning. An important first step is to select a guardian for your minor children. That person should have a genuine concern for your children as well as a parental style and moral beliefs you endorse.

Also ensure that you leave sufficient resources to rear your children, not only for living expenses but also for school and other major expenses. Often life insurance is a good way to ensure such a fund. Be sure to discuss all these issues with the guardian, and choose a contingent guardian in case the first choice is unable to perform the needed functions.

© Yellow Dog Productions/Getty Images

You do not have to be working full time before you meet with a financial planner. If you do know where to start, ask your banker for a recommendation. Don't be surprised if you learn that he or she may have some financial planner training .

Making ETHICAL DECISIONS

Money Going Up in Smoke

You recently received news that your Uncle Alex passed away after a long battle with lung cancer. To your surprise, he left you $25,000 in his will, saying you were his favourite nephew. You remember your uncle as a hardworking man who loved baseball and liked nothing better than to watch you pitch for your school team. Unfortunately, he started smoking as a young man and became a heavy chain smoker. His doctors said that smoking was the primary cause of his lung cancer.

After receiving the inheritance, you wonder where to invest the money. Your old teammate, Jack, a financial advisor, recommends that you buy stock in a well-known multinational firm that offers a good dividend and has solid global growth potential. He tells you the firm's major product is tobacco, but assures you it produces other products as well. You know Jack has your best interests at heart. You also believe Uncle Alex would like to see the money he left you grow. However, you wonder if a company that markets tobacco is an appropriate place to invest the inheritance from Uncle Alex. What are the ethical alternatives in this situation? What are the consequences of the alternatives? What will you do?

© Shutterstock/Roman Sigaev

It is never too early to begin thinking about estate planning, although this may be decades away. You may need to contact a lawyer or a financial planner, or both, to help you prepare the paperwork and do the planning necessary to preserve and protect your investments for your beneficiaries. Two important documents are a will and a power of attorney.

will
A document that names the guardian for your children, states how you want your assets distributed, and names the executor for your estate.

executor
An individual who assembles and values your estate, files income and other taxes, and distributes assets when you pass away.

A second step is to prepare a **will**, a document that names the guardian for your children, states how you want your assets distributed, and names the executor for your estate. An **executor** assembles and values your estate, files income and other taxes, and distributes assets. This document takes effect when you pass away. The Making Ethical Decisions box describes a personal stock investment decision.

A third step is to prepare a durable power of attorney. This document gives an individual you name the power to take over your finances if you become incapacitated. A *durable power of attorney for health care* delegates power to a person you name to make health care decisions for you if you are unable to make such decisions yourself. A **power of attorney**, which can take effect when you are alive, is a written document in which you appoint someone else to act on your behalf on matters that you specify. This can be made to start immediately, or upon mental incapacity.[48] Rules regulating powers of attorney tend to vary significantly from province to province.

Other steps to follow are beyond the scope of this text. You may need to contact a financial planner/attorney to help you do the paperwork and planning to preserve and protect your investments for your children and spouse and others. But it all begins with a strong financial base.

power of attorney
A written document in which you appoint someone else to act on your behalf on matters that you specify; this can be made to start immediately, or upon mental incapacity.

KEY TERMS

Endnotes

Chapter 1

1. Yuri Ostrovsky and Marc Frenette, *The Cumulative Earnings of Postsecondary Graduate Over 20 Years: Results by Field of Study.* Catalogue no. 11-626-X, Statistics Canada, October 2014. Accessed March 15, 2015. http://www.statcan.gc.ca/pub/11-626-x/11-626-x2014040-eng.htm.
2. Marc Frenette, *An Investment of a Lifetime: The Long-Term Labour Market Premiums Associated with a Postsecondary Education.* Catalogue no. 11F0019M. Statistics Canada, February 2014. Accessed March 15, 2015. http://www.statcan.gc.ca/pub/11f0019m/11f0019m2014354-eng.htm.
3. U.S. Census Bureau, www.census.gov, accessed May 2014.
4. Mary Gooderham, "Interest-rate hikes require a nimble approach to financing: Small firms can't coast along on low rates any more, but those in need of cash have additional loan options today," *The Globe and Mail,* October 2, 2017.
5. Jim McElhatton, "Community Colleges Seen as Essential," *The Washington Times,* April 14, 2008.
6. Lisa Philipps, "The best way to improve access to postsecondary education isn't through tax policy," *The Globe and Mail,* September 21, 2017.
7. Innovation, Science and Economic Development Canada Small Business Branch, *Key Small Business Statistics,* June 2016. Accessed May 19, 2018. https://www.ic.gc.ca/eic/site/061.nsf/vwapj/KSBS-PSRPE_June-Juin_2016_eng-V2.pdf/$file/KSBS-PSRPE_June-Juin_2016_eng-V2.pdf.
8. Ibid.
9. "Business Insolvencies," *Small Business Quarterly,* Industry Canada, May 2008, www.ic.gc.ca/epic/site/sbrp-rppe.nsf/vwapj/SBQ_May2008_Eng.pdf/$FILE/SBQ_May2008_Eng.pdf.
10. Fareed Zakaria, "Switched-On Highways," *Newsweek,* January 19, 2009.
11. Chris Horwood, "Tesla: An exciting company—but is it a winning investment?" *The Globe and Mail,* March 20, 2018.
12. "Cost of Living Comparison Between Canada and Japan," Numbeo.com, June 20, 2018, www.numbeo.com/cost-of-living/compare_countries_result.jsp?country1=Canada&country2=Japan.
13. Jonathan Clements, "Down the Tube: The Sad Stats on Happiness, Money and TV," *The Wall Street Journal,* April 2, 2008.
14. Pete Engardio, "The Future of Outsourcing," *BusinessWeek,* January 30, 2006, 50–58.
15. John R. Baldwin and Wulong Gu, "Outsourcing and Offshoring in Canada," Statistics Canada, May 2008, www.statcan.ca/english/research/11F0027MIE/11F0027MIE2008055.pdf.
16. Erin White, "Smaller Companies Join the Outsourcing Trend," *The Wall Street Journal,* May 8, 2006, B3.
17. Baldwin and Gu, "Outsourcing and Offshoring in Canada."
18. Pete Engardio and Bruce Einhorn, "Outsourcing Innovation," *BusinessWeek,* March 21, 2005, 84–94.
19. Ibid.
20. 2014 Global Outsourcing and Insourcing Survey Results: Executive Summary. Deloitte Consulting LLP, May 2014. http://www2.deloitte.com/us/en/pages/strategy/articles/2014-global-outsourcing-and-insourcing-survey.html.
21. "Ford to Pay Full Wages to Some New Hires Under Two-Tier Wage Deal," The Associated Press, February 4, 2015. http://www.cbc.ca/news/business/ford-to-pay-full-wages-to-some-newer-hires-under-two-tier-pay-deal-1.2945228.
22. Jeff Beer, "The Real Reason Rogers and Bell Bought MLSE," *Canadian Business,* January 2012, http://www.canadianbusiness.com/business-strategy/the-real-reason-rogers-and-bell-bought-mlse/; Sean Fitz-Gerald, "MLSE Deal: What the Rogers and Bell Buyout Means for Fans," *National Post,* December 19, 2011, http://news.nationalpost.com/2011/12/09/rogers-bell-buy-majority-stake-in-mlse/; "Rogers, Bell Finalize MLSE Purchase," *Toronto Star,* August 22, 2012, http://www.thestar.com/sports/leafs/ 2012/08/22/rogers_bell_finalize_mlse_purchase.html.
23. Steve Hamm, "When the Bottom Line Is Ending Poverty," *BusinessWeek,* March 10, 2008.
24. "Key Facts about Canada's Charities," Imagine Canada, http://www.imaginecanada.ca/resources-and-tools/research-and-facts/key-facts-about-canada%E2%80%99s-charities.
25. "Canada's top 100 non-profit organizations (registered charities)," *The Globe and Mail,* February 5, 2015, updated June 19, 2017, http://www.theglobeandmail.com/report-on-business/rob-magazine/top-100-non-profit-organizations-registered-charities/article17298702/.
26. "2013 Corporate Profile," Tim Hortons, http://www.timhortons.com/ca/en/corporate/profile.php.
27. Jamie Sturgeon, "It's official, Tim Hortons, Burger King become one," *Global News,* December 12, 2014, http://globalnews.ca/news/1724238/its-official-tim-hortons-burger-king-become-one/.
28. Frederick G. Crane et al., *Marketing,* 8th Canadian ed., (Canada: McGraw-Hill Ryerson, 2011), 92.
29. Ibid.
30. Claire Brownell, "One in five executives thinks corruption is widespread in Canada's business world, EY report shows," *The Financial Post,* June 11, 2014.
31. Annys Shin, "Economic Picture Bleak in Fed Report," *The Washington Post,* January 15, 2009.
32. "The Origins of the Financial Crisis: Crash Course," *The Economist,* September 7, 2013, http://www.economist.com/news/schoolsbrief/21584534-effects-financial-crisis-are-still-being-felt-five-years-article.
33. "'Sense of Urgency,' as Premiers Meet with Central Banker," *CBC News,* July 18, 2008, www.cbc.ca/canada/saskatchewan/story/2008/07/18/premiers-economy.html.
34. Brenda Bouw, "New Anti-Spam Law a 'Big Deal' for Small Business," *The Globe and Mail,* March 2014, http://www.theglobeandmail.com/report-on-business/small-business/sb-digital/biz-categories-technology/businesses-rush-to-comply-with-tough-new-anti-spam-law/article17609044/.
35. Frederick G. Crane et al., *Marketing,* 8th Canadian ed. (Toronto: McGraw-Hill Ryerson Ltd., 2011), 86.
36. Richard Stengel, "Made in America, Again," *Time,* April 22, 2013.
37. Laura Weber, "Elance Taps Growing Demand for Freelancers," *The Wall Street Journal,* 4 February 2014; Ari Levy, "Elance Merges with oDesk to Enlarge Service for Freelancers," *Bloomberg BusinessWeek,* 18 December 2013; and Patrick Clark, "What Elance-oDesk Merger Means for Freelancers," *Bloomberg BusinessWeek,* 19 December 2013.
38. Sharaz Kahn, "Wearable intelligence coming to a workplace near you," *The Globe and Mail,* Case Study published February 3, 2015; updated March 27, 2018, accessed June 22, 2018, http://www.theglobeandmail.com/report-on-business/small-business/sb-tools/sb-how-to/wearable-intelligence-coming-to-a-workplace-near-you/article22746277/; www.vivametrica.com; "Start-up of the Week – Vivametrica," *Calgary Herald,* November 28, 2014, http://calgaryherald.com/technology/startup-of-the-week-vivametrica.
39. "Digital Technology and Internet Use, 2013," Statistics Canada, June 11, 2014, http://www.statcan.gc.ca/daily-quotidien/140611/dq140611a-eng.pdf.
40. Hollie Shaw, "Amazon is Canada's top e-commerce site; New analysis $3.5B in sales last year, up from 2014's $2B," *National Post,* 27 June 2017.

41. "How to Get the Most from Kijiji and Craigslist," *Toronto Star,* January 18, 2012, http://www.thestar.com/business/personal_finance/spending_saving/2012/01/18/how_to_get_the_most_from_kijiji_and_craigslist.html.
42. Hal Lawton. "Celebrating Small Businesses & Entrepreneurship on eBay," eBay North America, May 1, 2017, https://www.ebayinc.com/stories/news/celebrating-small-businesses-entrepreneurship-on-ebay/.
43. "Numbers," *Time,* May 5, 2008.
44. Nicole LaMarco, "What is the Difference Between E-Business and E-Commerce?" Chron, June 29, 2018, https://smallbusiness.chron.com/difference-between-e-business-e-commerce-2639.html.
45. Robert Hackett, "Apple Responds to Hacker's Threat to Wipe Hundreds of Millions of iPhones," *Fortune,* March 22, 2017.
46. Martha C. White, "This Year's Spike in Online Fraud," *Money,* November 2016; Lo Bénichou, "How to Protect Your Digital Self," *Wired,* July 6, 2017.
47. "Privacy Legislation in Canada," Office of the Privacy Commissioner of Canada, December 5, 2008, www.priv.gc.ca/fs-fi/02_05_d_15_e.cfm.
48. Lisa Gerstner, "What You Need to Know about Identity Theft," Kiplinger's Personal Finance, June 2013.
49. Crane et al., *Marketing,* 18.
50. "Use of Social Media Among Canada's Small Business Owners Up 42 Percent from 2012," BMO Financial Group, October 25, 2013, http://newsroom.bmo.com/press-releases/bmo-report-use-of-social-media-among-canada-s-sma-tsx-bmo-201310250906689001.
51. "Crowdsourcing to stand out from the masses," Canada Business Network, March 9, 2015, http://www.canadabusiness.ca/eng/blog/entry/5012/.
52. Ivor Tossel, "Don Tapscott: Let's Crowdsource Canada," *The Globe and Mail,* February 20, 2013, http://www.theglobeandmail.com/report-on-business/economy/canada-competes/don-tapscott-lets-crowdsource-canada/article8897102/.
53. Crane et al., *Marketing,* 90.
54. For the Purpose of this discussion, Environics Analytics demographic terms and time periods are used. See Chapter 11, Figure 11.9 for more details.
55. Adapted from "Population Projections for Canada, Provinces and Territories 2009–2036," Cat. No. 91-520-X, June 2010.
56. *Boom, Bust & Echo: Profiting from the Demographic Shift in the 21st Century,* Footwork Consulting Inc., 2008, www.footwork.com/21c.asp.
57. "Population projections," *The Daily,* Statistics Canada, December 15, 2015, http://www.statcan.gc.ca/daily-quotidien/051215/dq051215b-eng.htm.
58. "Global Talent Risks – Seven Responses," World Economic Forum, 2011, http://www.bcg.com/documents/file69643.pdf, accessed June 18, 2018; http://www.bcg.com/media/PressReleaseDetails.aspx?id=tcm:12-69648.
59. "Facts and Figures 2010 – Immigration overview: Permanent and Temporary residents," Citizenship and Immigration Canada, August 30, 2011, www.cic.gc/english/resources/statistics/facts2010/permanent/01.asp; "Census Snapshot – Immigration in Canada: A portrait of the foreign-born population, 2006 Census," Statistics Canada, November 21, 2008, www.statcan.gc.ca/pub/11-008-x/2008001/article/10556-eng.htm#1.
60. "Backgrounder – 2014 Immigration Levels Planning: Public and Stakeholder Consultations," Statistics Canada, June 21, 2013, http://www.cic.gc.ca/english/department/media/backgrounders/2013/2013-06-21.asp#role.
61. Andrea Cooper, "The Influencers," *Entrepreneur,* March 2008.
62. Charrnchai Athitchitskul, "Towards a Sustainable Society," *Global Management Review,* 5, no. 4, August 2011, 1–28.
63. "Gross domestic product at basic prices, manufacturing and construction industries," Statistics Canada, December 23, 2011, www40.statcan.gc.ca/l01/cst01/manuf10-eng.htm.
64. *Manufacturing Our Future: A manufacturing action plan for Canada,* Canadian Manufacturers and Exporters Association, March 2012, http://www.cme-mec.ca/download.php?file=h8q5gph6.pdf.
65. Ibid.
66. "Canadian Manufacturing Today: Cautiously Optimistic: BDOs perspective on CMEs 2014 Management Issues Survey," BDO Canada LLP, http://www.cme-mec.ca/_uploads/_media/51wjbzblm.pdf.
67. Ibid.
68. Deborah Aarts. "Canada's Fastest Growing Company is Built for Growth," ProfitGuide.com, June 12, 2014, accessed June 24, 2018, http://www.profitguide.com/small-business/canadas-fastest-growing-company-is-built-for-growth-66142.
69. International Humanistic Management Associations, accessed May 2018, http://humanisticmanagement.international.com.
70. Domenec Melé. "Understanding humanistic management," *Humanistic Management Journal,* September 2016, pages 33–55.
71. Michael Pirson, *Humanistic Management: Protecting Dignity and Promoting Well-Being,* Cambridge University Press, 2017.

Appendix A

1. Kristina McElheran and Erik Brynjolfsson, "The Rise of Data-Driven Decision Making Is Real but Uneven," *Harvard Business Review,* February 3, 2016; Gency Warren, "Why Data-Driven Decisions are Crucial to Your Performance," Raving Consulting, September 17, 2017.
2. Ryan Mulcahy, "Business Intelligence Definition and Solutions," *CIO,* September 1, 2017.
3. Scott Anthony, "Kodak's Downfall Wasn't about Technology," *Harvard Business Review,* July 15, 2016; Tendayi Viki, "On the Fifth Anniversary Of Kodak's Bankruptcy, How Can Large Companies Sustain Innovation?" *Forbes,* January 19, 2017.
4. Chad Quinn, "The New Value of CIOs in 2016," *CIO,* 4 January 2016; Rob Preston, "Top 10 Strategic CIO Priorities For 2017," *Forbes,* January 17, 2017.
5. Hamza Shaban, "An Amazon Echo recorded a family's conversation, then sent it to a random person in their contacts, report says," *The Washington Post,* May 24, 2018, accessed May 26, 2018, https://www.washingtonpost.com/news/the-switch/wp/2018/05/24/an-amazon-echo-recorded-a-familys-conversation-then-sent-it-to-a-random-person-in-their-contacts-report-says/?noredirect=on&utm_term=.7ee1bc4e0c01.
6. "Are any Canadian companies using RFID?" November 20, 2013, *RFID Journal,* http://www.rfidjournal.com/blogs/experts/entry?10828.
7. Ibid.
8. Michael Corkery, "Goodbye, Password: Banks Opt to Scan Fingers and Faces Instead," *The New York Times,* June 21, 2016; Ben Dickson, "Unlocking the Potential of Eye Tracking Technology," *TechCrunch,* February 19, 2017.
9. Jonathan Vanian, "Big Data and Data Analytics Are Becoming One in the Same," *Fortune,* January 13, 2016; Michael S. Malone, "The Big Data Future Has Arrived," *The Wall Street Journal,* February 22, 2016; Gil Press, "6 Predictions For The $203 Billion Big Data Analytics Market," *Forbes,* January 20, 2017.
10. Mark Buchanan, "Battling the Tyranny of Big Data," *Bloomberg,* January 13, 2017.
11. Ryan Kh, "How Does Big Data Change Social Media Marketing Strategies?" *Social Media Today,* February 29, 2016; Michael Schrage, "How the Big Data Explosion Has Changed Decision Making," *Harvard Business Review,* August 25, 2016; Rob Marvin and Alyson Behr, "The Best Social Media Management & Analytics Tools of 2017," *PC Magazine,* September 1, 2017.
12. Bernard Marr, "Big Data-Driven Decision-Making at Domino's Pizza," *Forbes,* April 6, 2016; Brian Barrett, "How Domino's Put Automagic Pizza on Every Device. Like, Every Device," *Wired,* April 29, 2016; Abigail Stevenson, "Domino's CEO Reveals How It Smoked the Pizza Competition Last Quarter," *CNBC,* March 6, 2017.
13. "A Guide for Intranet Managers: 5 Simple Tips for Reviving an Ailing Sharepoint Intranet," Cambridge Network, February 28, 2017.
14. Max Eddy, "The Best VPN Services of 2017," *PC World,* February 28, 2017.

15. Eric Griffin, "The Fastest ISPs of 2017: Canada," *PC Magazine,* June 19, 2017, accessed May 27, 2018, https://www.pcmag.com/article/353971/the-fastest-isps-of-2017-canada.
16. Ibid.
17. SpeedTest Global Index, April 2018, accessed May 27, 2018, from http://www.speedtest.net/global-index/canada#mobile.
18. Ookla Net Index, accessed May 15, 2015, http://www.netindex.com/download/2,7/Canada/.
19. Mike Snider, "How Net Neutrality Could Get Reversed (and What That Means to You)," *USA Today,* February 7, 2017.
20. Tim Smart, "Protecting the Open Internet," *US News and World Report,* February 25, 2016; Nikhil Reddy, "Net Neutrality in 2017—What You Should Know," *Huffington Post,* August 28, 2017.
21. AJ Dellinger, "Is Net Neutrality Dead? What the Internet Will Look Like without Open Internet Rules, Title II," *International Business Times,* February 9, 2017.
22. Libby Watson, "AT&T Charges Ahead with Fiber Internet While Google Languishes," *Gizmodo,* March 24, 2017.
23. Vijay Prabhu, "Internet2 Is the Alternate Internet Which Gives a Speed of 10 to 100 Gigabits per Second," *TechWorm,* February 7, 2016.
24. "The Internet2 Community: Enabling the Future," Internet2, accessed June 2018, www.internet2.edu/about-us/.
25. "About Us," Hootsuite, accessed May 27, 2018, https://hootsuite.com/about/#.
26. Chris O'Brien, "What Hootsuite founder Ryan Holmes learned from his own social media fail: 'Own it. Apologize.'" *Venture Beat,* August 27, 2017, accessed May 27, 2018 https://venturebeat.com/2017/08/27/what-hootsuite-founder-ryan-holmes-learned-from-his-own-social-media-fail-own-it-apologize/.
27. "Enterprise," Hootsuite, accessed 27 May 2018, https://hootsuite.com/plans/enterprise.
28. Julie Jargon, "McDonald's Goes Digital to Draw Youth," *The Wall Street Journal,* 14 October 2016; "McDonald's Wins Back Millennials," *Warc,* October 17, 2016; Mac Hogan, "McDonald's Customers Are Fed Up with Not Being Able to Order McFlurries," *CNBC,* January 19, 2017; Brian Sozzi, "Social Media Blows Up as McDonald's Gives Away Iconic Big Mac Sauce in Bottles," *The Street,* January 28, 2017.
29. Randy Hlavac, "Because We're Happy: Using Social Media to Turn Audiences Around," *Forbes,* June 3, 2014.
30. Amol Sharma and Jessica E. Vascellaro, "Companies Eye Location-Services Market," *The Wall Street Journal,* November 28, 2009.
31. Shabana Arora, "Recommendation Engines: How Amazon and Netflix Are Winning the Personalization Battle," *MarTech Advisor,* June 28, 2016; Klint Finley, "Amazon's Giving Away the AI behind Its Product Recommendations," *Wired,* May 16, 2016; Michael Schrage, "Great Digital Companies Build Great Recommendation Engines," *Harvard Business Review,* August 1, 2017.
32. Tim Sandle, "Op-Ed: How Will Web 3.0 Turn Out?" *Digital Journal,* July 23, 2016; Vangie Beal, "Web 3.0," Webopedia, accessed October 2017, https://www.webopedia.com/TERM/W/Web_3_point_0.html .
33. Martin Zwillig, "When Will Siri Be Able to Make That Romantic Dinner Reservation for You?" *Entrepreneur,* January 6, 2016; Daniel Nations, "What Is Web 3.0 and Is It Here Yet?" *Lifewire,* March 22, 2017.
34. "Fundamentals: What Is Semantic Technology?" Ontotext, accessed June 19, 2018, https://ontotext.com/knowledgehub/fundamentals/semantic-web-technology/.
35. Global Newswire, "Introducing aia from Amdocs: Bringing Real-Time Intelligence to the Heart of a Communications Business," *The New York Times,* February 27, 2017.
36. Sheila Kloefkorn, "The Five Most Important Website Design Trends That Will Emerge in 2017," *Forbes,* December 21, 2016; Brian Rashid, "5 Essential Reasons You Should Be Using A Responsive Website Design Now," *Forbes,* June 13, 2017.
37. Elizabeth Reade, "When Virtual Reality Meets Education," *TechCrunch,* January 23, 2016; Aaron Burch, "The Top 10 Companies Working on Education in Virtual Reality and Augmented Reality," Touchstone Research, June 2, 2016; Brian Crecente, "The State of Virtual Reality," *Polygon,* June 8, 2017.
38. Andrew Meola, "What Is the Internet of Things (IoT)?" *Business Insider,* December 19, 2016; Matt Burgess, "What Is the Internet of Things? Wired Explains," *Wired* UK, February 16, 2017.
39. Joanna Stern, "Google Home vs. Amazon Echo: Which Robot Do You Let into Your Life?" *The Wall Street Journal,* November 7, 2016; Lee Bell, "The Best Wearable Tech and Fitness Gadgets of 2017," *Forbes,* April 3, 2017.
40. Tim Greene, "John Deere Is Plowing IoT into Its Farm Equipment," *Network World,* May 17, 2016; Thor Olavsrud, "Teradata Accelerators Help Put IoT on the Fast Track," *CIO,* August 24, 2016; John Carpenter, "'The Old John Deere' Makes Way for New Tech with Precision Farming Platforms," *Forbes,* March 13, 2017.
41. Kate Gerwig, "IT Priorities 2017 Survey: Virtualization Gains in Networking Plans," *TechTarget,* March 14, 2017.
42. Eric Griffith, "What Is Cloud Computing?" *PC Magazine,* May 3, 2016.
43. Quentin Hardy, "Why the Computing Cloud Will Keep Growing and Growing," *The New York Times,* December 25, 2016.
44. Robert Kruk, "Public, Private and Hybrid Clouds: What's the Difference?" *Techopedia,* February 22, 2017; Andy Patrizio, "Hybrid Cloud Computing," *Datamation,* April 3, 2017.
45. Source: Irving Wladawsky-Berger, "The Transformative Power of Cloud Computing," *The Wall Street Journal,* December 16, 2016; Lauren Fish, "Top 5 Benefits of Cloud Computing," *Microsoft UK Small and Medium Business Blog,* July 18, 2016; Cynthia Harvey, "Cloud Computing," *Datamation,* March 27, 2017.
46. Priya Viswanathan, "Cloud Computing and Is It Really All That Beneficial?" *Lifewire,* February 1, 2017.
47. Elizabeth Weise, "Amazon Makes It Easy to Order Automatically," *USA Today,* January 20, 2016; Loretta Chao and Steven Norton, "Race for Web Sales Leaves Some in the Dust," *The Wall Street Journal,* January 29, 2016; Daniel Newman, "Top Five Digital Transformation Trends in Retail," *Forbes,* March 14, 2017.
48. Karen Turner, "Hacked Dropbox Login Data of 68 Million Users Is Now for Sale on the Dark Web," *The Washington Post,* September 6, 2016.
49. Jaikumar Vijayan, "MSSPs Add Advanced Threats as Managed Security Services Gain Hold," *TechTarget,* April 4, 2017; "2017 MSP 500: Managed Security 100," *CRN,* February 14, 2017.
50. Kate Conger, "Yahoo Discloses Hack of 1 Billion Accounts," *TechCrunch,* December 14, 2016; Brian Fung, "Why Verizon Is Still Buying Yahoo on Sale, Despite That Epic Security Breach," *The Washington Post,* February 21, 2017.
51. Evan Koblentz, "Deceptive Networking Lures Hackers with Decoy Data," *TechRepublic,* January 23, 2017.
52. "Cybercrime: an overview of incidents and issues in Canada," 2014, Royal Canadian Mounted Police, accessed May 17, 2015, http://www.rcmp-grc.gc.ca/pubs/cc-report-rapport-cc-eng.pdf.
53. "Fraud Facts—Recognize, Reject, Report Fraud," Competition Bureau Canada, February 22, 2018, accessed May 27, 2018, http://www.competitionbureau.gc.ca/eic/site/cb-bc.nsf/eng/04334.html#sec02.
54. Armina Ligaya, "'Grasping in the Dark': How Canada's 'undercounting' of cybercrime costs may be leaving us vulnerable," June 9, 2014, *The Financial Post,* http://business.financialpost.com/fp-tech-desk/grasping-in-the-dark-how-canadas-undercounting-of-cybercrime-costs-may-be-leaving-us-vulnerable?__lsa=89cc-2e21.
55. Luke Graham, "Cybercrime Costs the Global Economy $450 Billion: CEO," *CNBC,* February 7, 2017.
56. Treena Hein, "Barbarians Inside the Gates," *tq Magazine,* Summer 2006, 28.
57. Ibid.
58. Jason Markusoff, "How MacEwan University got duped out of $11.8 million by scammers," *Maclean's,* August 31, 2017, accessed May 27, 2018, https://www.macleans.ca/news/canada/how-macewan-university-got-duped-out-of-11-8-million-by-scammers/.
59. Lee Rainie, "The State of Privacy in Post-Snowden America," Pew Research Center, September 21, 2016; Timothy H. Edgar, "Why the NSA Should Thank Edward Snowden," *Fortune,* October 3, 2017.

60. Abby Ohlheiser, "Erasing Yourself from the Internet Is Nearly Impossible. But Here's How You Can Try," *The Washington Post,* February 10, 2017.
61. Shan Li, "Target Hires New Security Chief from General Motors after Security Breach," *Los Angeles Times,* 11 June 2014.
62. "Platform for Privacy Preferences," www.w3.org/P3P, accessed June 2014.
63. Donovan Vincent, "Ontario's welfare computer glitches are not the first," January 25, 2015, *Toronto Star,* http://www.thestar.com/news/canada/2015/01/25/ontarios-welfare-computer-glitches-are-not-the-first.html.
64. Mallory Schlossberg, "This Model Who Couldn't Get an Internship in Fashion Is Becoming an Icon for an Industry Most Retailers Ignore," *Business Insider,* January 19, 2016; Chantal Fernandez, "Chiara Ferragni Opens Milan Boutique, Gabi Gregg and Nicolette Mason's New Brand," *Business of Fashion,* July 24, 2017.

Chapter 2

1. Jeff Gray, "Canadian Documentary Warns Tax Havens Threaten Democracy," *The Globe and Mail,* March 11, 2015, http://www.theglobeandmail.com/report-on-business/industry-news/the-law-page/canadian-documentary-warns-tax-havens-threaten-democracy/article23409274/.
2. Romain Hatchuel, "The Coming Global Wealth Tax," *The Wall Street Journal,* January 15, 2014.
3. Benjamin Auslin, "Economics Shouldn't Be and Elective", *The Wall Street Journal,* March 3, 2017.
4. Richard Blackwell, "Green energy sector jobs surpass total oil sands employment," *The Globe and Mail,* December 2, 2014, http://www.theglobeandmail.com/report-on-business/industry-news/energy-and-resources/green-energy-sector-jobs-surpass-oil-sand-employment-total/article21859169/.
5. "Ballard Closes Technology Solutions Transaction with Volkswagen Group," Ballard Power Systems, February 23, 2015, http://www.ballard.com/about-ballard/newsroom/news-releases/2015/02/23/ballard-closes-technology-solutions-transaction-with-volkswagen-group.
6. Roger Lowenstein, "Macro Master," *The Wall Street Journal,* December 4, 2013.
7. Glen Hodgson, "Canada's debt levels are relatively healthy, but some provinces are worrisome," *The Globe and Mail,* May 17, 2017.
8. Andrea Gunn, "Canada to Double Protected Areas," *Chronicle-Herald,* November 7, 2017.
9. "The Canadian Aquaculture Industry—A success story," Canadian Aquaculture Industry Alliance, http://www.aquaculture.ca/files/CanAquacultureFacts-08.pdf.
10. Ed Feulner, "The Slow Fade of Economic Freedom," *The Washington Times,* January 14, 2014.
11. Greg Ip, "For Economy Aging Population Poses Double Whammy," *The Wall Street Journal,* August 3, 2016; John Authers, "Demographics and Market: The Effects of Aging," *Financial Times,* October 15, 2016; Prashanth Perumal, "Robots Might Be Saving the World From a Demographic Disaster," *Business Insider,* March 8, 2017.
12. Gordan Harris and Glen Miller, "How Aging Boomers Will Disrupt Canada's Demographic 'Crisis'," *The Globe and Mail,* February 4, 2015, http://www.theglobeandmail.com/globe-debate/how-aging-boomers-will-disrupt-canadas-demographic-crisis/article22780291/.
13. Randall Stephenson, "A Business Shortlist for Growth," *The Wall Street Journal,* January 15, 2015.
14. Ed Feulner, "The Slow Fade of Economic Freedom," *The Washington Times,* January 14, 2014.
15. Dennis Rasmussen, "The Problem of Inequality, According to Adam Smith," *The Atlantic,* June 9, 2016.
16. Ibid.
17. Sara Mojtehedzadeh, "Toronto now Canada's inequality capital, United Way study shows," *The Toronto Star,* February 27, 2015, http://www.thestar.com/news/gta/2015/02/27/toronto-now-canadas-inequality-capital-united-way-study-shows.html.
18. Charles Lane, "The Politics of Inequality," *The Washington Post,* December 10, 2013.
19. "The Philanthropic," *Forbes,* December 2, 2013.
20. Chase Petersen-Withorn, "Buffet Just Donated Nearly $2.9 Billion to Charity," *Forbes,* July 14, 2016; Laura Lorenzetti, "17 More Billionaires Join Buffet and Gates Giving Pledge This Year," *Fortune* June 1, 2016; Kerry A. Dolan, "Big Philanthropy Gets a Boost: 14 Titans from 7 Countries Join the Gates-Buffet Giving Pledge," *Forbes,* May 30, 2017.
21. Jeff Kehoe, "Can Capitalism Be Redeemed?" *Harvard Business Review,* July-August, 2016; Lauren Gensler, "Rising Income Inequality is Throwing the Future of Capitalism into Question, Says World Economic Forum," *Forbes,* January 11, 2016.
22. John Mackey and Raj Sisodia, *Conscious Capitalism,* (Boston, MA: Harvard Business Review Press, 2013).
23. Mark Benioff, "Salesforce CEO Mark Benioff: How Business Leaders Can Help Narrow Income Inequality," *Fortune,* January 17, 2017.
24. Peter Coy, "The Sting of Long-Term Unemployment," *Bloomberg Businessweek,* February 11, 2013.
25. "Bill Gates No Longer Tops World's-Richest List," *The Chronicle of Philanthropy,* March 6, 2008, http://philanthropy.com/news/philanthropytoday/4105/bill-gates-no-longer-tops-worlds-richest-list.; Laura Lorenzetti, "17 More Billionaires Join Buffet and Gates Giving Pledge This Year," *Forbes,* June 1, 2016.
26. "Global Citizenship," Cirque du Soleil, accessed June 26, 2018, www.cirquedusoleil.com/en/about/global-citizenship/community.aspx.
27. Darren Heitner, "Sports industry expected to reach $73.5 billion by 2019," *Forbes,* October 21, 2015, accessed May 22, 2018, https://www.forbes.com/sites/darrenheitner/2015/10/19/sports-industry-to-reach-73-5-billion-by-2019/#24fc09c31b4b.
28. Stefan Szymanski. "What sports capitalism can teach us about real world fair play," *CNN,* January 24, 2014, accessed May 22, 2018, https://www.cnn.com/2014/01/24/business/davos-sports-capitalism-real-world/index.html.
29. Tim Mak, "Hockey economics: how a freer market in hockey could lead to more Canadian teams," Fraser Institute, Summer 2011, accessed May 22, 2018, https://www.fraserinstitute.org/sites/default/files/hockey-economics_csr-summer-2011.pdf.
30. Marjory Abrams, "The Economy in a Nutshell," *Bottom Line Personal,* May 1, 2008.
31. Brian M. Carney, "Europe Hasn't Outgrown 'That '70s Show'," *The Wall Street Journal,* May 9, 2005, A23.
32. Laura D'Andrea Tyson, "How Europe Is Revving Its Engine," *BusinessWeek,* February 21, 2005, 24.
33. "Population and Dwelling Count Highlight Tables, 2016 Census," Statistics Canada, August 28, 2017, http://www12.statcan.gc.ca/census-recensement/2016/dp-pd/hlt-fst/pd-pl/Table.cfm?Lang=Eng&T=101&S=50&O=A.
34. Matthew Coutts, "Complacency Hurts Nation: Think-Tank; Quality of Life Declining, Report Warns," *National Post,* June 30, 2008, A4.
35. Ibid.
36. "Economic Concepts—Unemployment Rate," Government of Canada, May 4, 2007, http://canadianeconomy.gc.ca/english/economy/unemployment2.html.
37. Ibid.
38. Ibid.
39. "Classification of Labour Status," Statistics Canada, July 21. 2011, http://www.statcan.gc.ca/pub/71-543-g/2014001/part-partie2-eng.htm.
40. David Pilling, "Japan Still in Grip of Deflation as Prices Fall," *Financial Times,* April 27, 2005, 7.
41. Kalen Smith, "What is Deflation: Definitions, Causes and Effects," *Money Crashers,* accessed September 2017; George Melloan, "Rising Global Debt and the Deflation Threat," *The Wall Street Journal,* March 8, 2016; David Nicholas, "Stagflation? Probably Not Now," *St. Louis Post-Dispatch,* August 18, 2017.

42. Carol Goar, "Worried Economists Tell Flaherty to Stop Starving the Economy," *The Toronto Star,* February 11, 2014, http://www.thestar.com/opinion/commentary/2014/02/11/worried_economists_tell_flaherty_to_stop_starving_the_economy_goar.html.
43. Consumer Price Index, Statistics Canada, CANSIM, table 326-0020 and Catalogue nos. 62-001-X and 62-010-X. Last modified: 2018-01-26.
44. The Human Development Report 2016: Human Development for Everyone, United Nations, 2016, http://hdr.undp.org/sites/default/files/2016_human_development_report.pdf.
45. Victor Zarnowitz and Dara Lee, "Can U.S. Business Cycles Still Be Dated by Monthly Coincident Indicators Alone?" *Business Cycle Indicator,* March 2005, 3–4.
46. "Business Cycle," Wikimedia Foundation Inc., August 18, 2008, http://en.wikipedia.org/wiki/Business_cycle.

Chapter 3

1. Robert J. Thomas, Joshua Bellin, Claudy Jules, and Nandani Lynton, "Developing Tomorrow's Global Leaders," *Sloan Management Review,* Fall 2013; and Gregory C. Unruh and Angel Cabera, "Join the Global Elite," *Harvard Business Review,* May 2013.
2. "U.S. and World Population Clock," U.S. Census Bureau, June 2018, http://www.census.gov/popclock/; and "Canada's Population Estimates: First Quarter, 2018," Statistics Canada, accessed June 27, 2018, https://www150.statcan.gc.ca/n1/daily-quotidien/180614/dq180614c-eng.pdf.
3. Russell Flannery, "What Can Be Done about the Big U.S. Trade Deficit with China?" *Forbes,* 3 August 2013; and Paul Davidson, "U.S. Trade Deficit Drops to 4-Year Low," *USA Today,* 7 January 2014.
4. "Trade Data Online," Industry Canada. February 6, 2018, http://www.ic.gc.ca/eic/site/tdo-dcd.nsf/eng/Home.
5. "TSN shut out as Rogers signs 12-year $5.2B NHL deal, CBC job cuts loom after losing editorial control of HNIC," *National Post,* November 26, 2013, http://news.nationalpost.com/2013/11/26/nhl-rogers-reach-12-year-5-2-billion-broadcast-deal-that-would-see-cbc-keep-hockey-night-in-canada/.
6. "Rogers and TSN Acquire Premier League TV Rights in Canada in 3-Year Deal," Word Soccer Talk, October 29, 2012, http://worldsoccertalk.com/2012/10/29/rogers-and-tsn-acquire-premier-league-tv-rights-in-canada-in-3-year-deal/.
7. Major League Baseball International, www.mlb.com, accessed September 2017.
8. "Why Is American Football Going Big in Britain?" *The Economist,* September 28, 2016; Kevin Seifert, "How American Football Is Becoming a Worldwide Sport," ESPN, May 6, 2016; National Basketball Association, www.nba.com, accessed September 2017.
9. Richard Sandomir, "NBC Retains Rights to Premier League in Six-Year Deal," *The New York Times,* August 10, 2015; The Associated Press, "NBC Moves 130 Premier League Games to Streaming Service," *The New York Times,* August 11, 2017.
10. "Profile," Bombardier Inc., 2015, http://ir.bombardier.com/en/profile.
11. Ibid.
12. "Hargrove calls for help from feds after another round of Chrysler cuts," CBC News, July 24, 2008, http://www.cbc.ca/news/business/hargrove-calls-for-help-from-feds-after-another-round-of-chrysler-cuts-1.731263; Nicolas Van Praet, "Polywheels grinds to halt in Oakville," *Financial Post,* July 10, 2008; "Auto parts maker slashing 2,000 jobs," CTV News, July 3, 2008, https://toronto.ctvnews.ca/toronto-area-auto-parts-maker-slashing-2-000-jobs-1.306460.
13. Kristine Owrami, "'We're fighting an uphill battle': When automakers' promises end, Canada may have to say goodbye," *Financial Post,* August 23, 2014, http://business.financialpost.com/2014/08/23/were-fighting-an-uphill-battle-when-automakers-promises-end-canada-may-have-to-say-goodbye/.
14. Matthew J. Slaughter, "Exports Sagging? Try Some Free Trade," *The Wall Street Journal,* January 23, 2013.
15. Robert Skidelsky, "In a World Based on Free Trade, Love Will Cost You," *Global Times,* January 23 2014.
16. David Parkinson, "Canada's Trade Surplus Narrows to $99 million in October," *The Globe and Mail,* December 5, 2014, http://www.theglobeandmail.com/report-on-business/canadas-trade-surplus-narrows-to-99-million-in-october/article21966651/.
17. Michael McCrae, "Canada will double diamond production in four years," Mining.com, October 13, 2014, http://www.mining.com/chart-of-the-day-canada-on-track-to-double-diamond-production-over-the-next-four-years-97740/.
18. "Key Small Business Statistics," Industry Canada, August 2013, https://www.ic.gc.ca/eic/site/061.nsf/vwapj/KSBS-PSRPE_August-Aout2013_eng.pdf/$FILE/KSBS-PSRPE_August-Aout2013_eng.pdf.
19. "Canada's young entrepreneurs increasingly drive export trade: CIBC Poll," *CIBC,* October 5, 2017, accessed May 20, 2018, https://www.newswire.ca/news-releases/canadas-young-entrepreneurs-increasingly-drive-export-trade-cibc-poll-649539863.html.
20. "Canada's State of Trade 2011," Foreign Affairs and International Trade Canada, 2011, www.international.gc.ca/economist-economiste/assets/pdfs/SoT_2011_e.pdf; "Importing into Canada," Foreign Affairs and International Trade Canada, May 26, 2010, www.international.gc.ca/controls-controles/about-a_propos/impor/canada.aspx?menu_id=1&view=d; "Canada's Merchandise and Service Trade, 2007," adapted from Statistics Canada website "Exports of Goods on a Balance-of-Payments Basis, by Product," Statistics Canada, August 13, 2008, www40.statcan.ca/l01/cst01/gblec04.htm; "Imports of Goods on a Balance-of-Payments Basis, by Product," Statistics Canada, August 13, 2008, www40.statcan.ca/l01/cst01/gblec05.htm; and "Canada's Balance of International Payments," Statistics Canada, May 29, 2008, www40.statcan.ca.libaccess.lib.mcmaster.ca/l01/cst01/econ01a.htm?sdi=services.
21. "Canada's State of Trade: Trade and Investment Update 2012 - Table 2-1 World Merchandise Trade by Region and Selected Countries (US$ billions and %)," Foreign Affairs and International Trade Canada, September 13, 2012, http://www.international.gc.ca/economist-economiste/assets/pdfs/performance/SoT_2012/SoT_2012_Eng.pdf, 16 and 23; and "Canada's State of Trade 2011," 35.
22. "Canada's State of Trade: Trade and Investment Update 2014," Foreign Affairs, Trade, and Development Canada, accessed March 27, 2015, http://www.international.gc.ca/economist-economiste/performance/state-point/state_2014_point/index.aspx?lang=eng#2.0.
23. "Less dependent on Uncle Sam," *The Globe and Mail,* February 6, 2012, B10.
24. "Canada's State of Trade: Trade and Investment Update—2009," Foreign Affairs and International Trade Canada, 2009, www.international.gc.ca/economist-economiste/assets/pdfs/DFAIT_SoT_2009_en.pdf; "Seizing Global Advantage: A Global Commerce Strategy for Securing Canada's Growth & Prosperity," Foreign Affairs and International Trade Canada, 2008, www.international.gc.ca/commerce/assets/pdfs/GCS-en.pdf; "A Global Commerce Strategy for Securing Canada's Growth and Prosperity, A Message from the Minister," Foreign Affairs and International Trade Canada, August 12, 2008, www.international.gc.ca/commerce/strategy-strategie/minister-ministre.aspx; Jim Middlemiss, "Canada Readying to Ride the Tiger," *Financial Post,* May 28, 2008, www.financialpost.com/reports/legal/story.html?id=546037; "International Science and Technology Partnerships Program—ISTPP," Foreign Affairs and International Trade Canada, June 5, 2007, www.infoexport.gc.ca/science/istpp-en.htm.
25. "Global Markets Action Plan," Foreign Affairs, Trade and Development Canada, accessed March 27, 2015, http://international.gc.ca/global-markets-marches-mondiaux/plan.aspx?lang=eng#message.

26. *License Global,* www.licensemag.com, accessed September 2017.
27. "About Us," Yogen Fruz, 2015, www.yogenfruz.com/home/en/about-us.
28. "History and Company Facts," BeaverTails Pastry, 2015, www.beavertailsinc.com.
29. "'YumBrands' world hunger relief efforts result in record breaking $37 million in cash and food donations," *The Wall Street Journal,* January 9, 2014.
30. AnnaLisa Kraft, "Crazy Food you can't get here," *The Motley Fool,* January 4, 2014.
31. "Global Contract Pharmaceutical Manufacturing Market Worth $84 Billion by 2020—Increasing Demand for Generic Drugs—Research and Market," *The Business Wire,* May 10, 2016.
32. "FouFou Dog," *PROFIT,* 2009, http://list.canadianbusiness.com/rankings/hot50/2008/DisplayProfile.aspx?profile=32; Jerry Langton, "Canine Couture," *Toronto Star,* November 17, 2008, www.thestar.com/Business/SmallBusiness/article/538014; "About Us," FouFou Dog, 2009, www.foufoudog.com/about.html.
33. Hugo Martin and Julie Makinen, "Shanghai Disney Opens Next Week, and It's Working Hard to Avoid Cultural Faux Pas," *Los Angeles Times,* June 9, 2016; Julie Lasky, "At Shanghai Disney Resort, Mulan, Mickey and Dumplings," *The New York Times,* July 4, 2017.
34. Alby Gallum, "European hotel chain coming to River North," *Crane Chicago Business,* January 24, 2014.
35. "Pepsi announces plans for $5 billion investment in Mexico," *The Wall Street Journal,* January 24, 2014.
36. Valerie Dumont and Souyma Sharma, "How to Reduce International Joint Venture Risk," *CFO,* March 28, 2016; David B. Nast, "Joint Ventures: Risks and Rewards," *Huffington Post,* July 5, 2017.
37. Ha Hoang and Frank T. Rothaermel, "How to Manage Alliances Strategically," *Sloan Management Review,* Fall 2016; Katie Fehrenbacher, "Why Tesla Is Partnering with Panasonic on Solar Tech," *Fortune,* October 17, 2016; Stephanie Vozza, "How Uber, Adidas, and Tesla Use Strategic Relationships to Get Ahead," *Fast Company,* May 3, 2017.
38. Nestlé SA, www.nestle.com, accessed September 2017.
39. Shuli Rodal, Peter Franklyn, Peter Glossop, Michelle Lally, Riyaz Dattu, Jaime Auron, Gajan Sathananthan, "Foreign investment in Canada: Osler Fall 2017 update," *Osler,* 5 October 2017, accessed https://www.osler.com/en/resources/cross-border/2017/foreign-investment-in-canada-osler-fall-2017-upda.
40. Investment Canada Act, accessed May 2017 https://www.ic.gc.ca/eic/site/ica-lic.nsf/eng/Home
41. Steven Chase, "Ottawa approves sale of B.C. retirement-home chain to Chinese group with murky ownership," *The Globe and Mail,* February 21, 2017, accessed May 26, 2018 https://www.theglobeandmail.com/news/politics/ottawa-approves-sale-of-bc-retirement-home-chain-to-chinese-group-with-murky-ownership/article34107591/.
42. Reuters, "CNOOC completes contentious $15.1-billion acquisition of Nexen," *Financial Post,* February 25, 2013, accessed May 26, 2018, http://business.financialpost.com/commodities/energy/cnooc-completes-contentious-15-1-billion-acquisition-of-nexen.
43. "China, Foreign Ownership & B.C. Resources," *BCBusiness,* July 11, 2011, accessed May 26, 2018, https://www.bcbusiness.ca/china-foreign-ownership-bc-resources.
44. Robert Fife and Steven Chase, "U.S. rebukes Canada over Chinese takeover of Norsat," *The Globe and Mail,* June 13, 2017, accessed May 26, 2018, https://www.theglobeandmail.com/news/politics/us-rebukes-canada-over-chinese-takeover-of-norsat/article35294914/.
45. Andrew Coyne, "The good and bad reasons to block the Aecon sale and why we should be prepared to accept them," *The National Post,* May 25, 2018, accessed May 26, 2018, http://nationalpost.com/news/canada/aecon-decision-was-right-and-for-the-right-reason.
46. Mark Srite, "Levels of Culture and Individual Behavior: An Integrative Perspective," *Journal of Global Information Management,* April 1, 2005.
47. Spin Master Toys, Our Story, accessed May 26, 2017, http://www.spinmaster.com/our-story.php?userLoc=us; Spin Master Corporation Business Segment Report 2017, accessed May 26, 2017, http://www.spinmaster.com/download/SM_2017_Business_Segment_Report.pdf.
48. Susan Bergfield, "4 Countries Walmart Can't Conquer," *MSN Money,* October 15, 2013; Walter Loeb, "Walmart: What Happened in India?" *Forbes,* October 16, 2013; and Agustino Fontevecchia, "IBM Falls Off Cliff as Q3 Sales Fall on Services and Hardware Weakness," *Forbes,* October 16, 2013.
49. Jonathan Gregson, "The World's Richest and Poorest Countries," *Global Finance,* February 13, 2017.
50. Preetika Rana, "L'Oréal Shrinks Packages in India," *The Wall Street Journal,* June 9, 2016; Jamie Matusow, "Innovation and Sustainability Drive L'Oréal's Packaging," *Beauty Packaging,* January 30, 2017.
51. "In Dollars They Trust," *The Economist,* April 27, 2013.
52. Michelle Higgins, "The Greenback Is Losing Universal Appeal," *The New York Times,* February 10, 2008.
53. Simon Kennedy, "Developed Economies Seen Fighting Off Emerging Market Contagion," *Bloomberg BusinessWeek,* January 27, 2014.
54. Taos Turner, Ken Parks, and Juan Foreno, "Crisis Squeeze Two Latin Leaders," *The Wall Street Journal,* January 26, 2014; and Jonathan Gilbert, Simon Romero, and William Neuman, "Erosion of Argentine Peso Sends a Shudder Through Latin America," *The New York Times,* January 24, 2014.
55. Rick Gladstone, "How Venezuela Fell into Crisis, and What Could Happen Next," *The New York Times,* May 27, 2016; Patrick Gillespie and Rhonny Zamora, "Venezuela's Hyperinflation Is Jaw-Dropping. See for Yourself," *CNN,* August 3, 2017.
56. Christina LeBeau, "Rules of the Trade," *Entrepreneur,* February 2014.
57. World Trade Organization, www.wto.org, accessed September 2017.
58. Alexandra Wrage, "What Companies Can't Do about Corruption," *Forbes,* January 24, 2014.
59. United States Department of Commerce, International Trade Administration – Fact Sheet, accessed June 27, 2018, http://enforcement.trade.gov/download/factsheets/factsheet-multiple-certain-crystalline-silicon-photovoltaic-products-ad-cvd-final-121614.pdf.
60. Richard Blackwell, "Tariffs on Chinese solar panels may hurt Canadian renewables industry," *The Globe and Mail,* March 8, 2015.
61. John Cotter, "Agriculture Minister Gerry Ritz threatens tariffs on U.S. goods over meat labeling laws," *Huffington Post,* December 29, 2014, accessed June 27, 2018, http://www.huffingtonpost.ca/2014/12/29/country-of-origin-laws-gerry-ritz_n_6389276.html.
62. "Controlled Products," Foreign Affairs, Trade and Development Canada, February 2, 2012, www.international.gc.ca/controls-controles/prod/index.aspx?menu_id=1&view=d.
63. "Exporting," Foreign Affairs, Trade and Development Canada, February 2, 2012, www.international.gc.ca/controls-controles/about-a_propos/expor/before-avant.aspx?lang=eng&view=d.
64. "Canadian Sanctions Related to North Korea," Foreign Affairs, Trade and Development Canada, November 13, 2013, http://www.international.gc.ca/sanctions/certificates_permits-certificats_permis.aspx?lang=eng.
65. "The Hidden Persuaders: Protectionism Can Take Many Forms, Not All of Them Obvious," *The Economist,* October 13, 2013.
66. "Canadian beef banned in Peru, Taiwan, and Belarus over mad cow case," CBC.ca, February 23, 2015, http://www.cbc.ca/news/canada/calgary/canadian-beef-banned-in-peru-taiwan-and-belarus-over-mad-cow-case-1.2968050.
67. World Trade Organization, www.wto.org, accessed September 2017 .
68. Canada takes U.S. to WTO in wide-ranging trade complaint. *CBC News,* January 10, 2018, accessed May 21, 2018, http://www.cbc.ca/news/business/canada-united-states-trade-complaint-1.4480738.
69. "Life After Doha," *The Economist,* December 14, 2013.
70. Judy Bottoni, "NAFTA, Trump and Canada: A guide to the trade file and what it could mean for you," *The Globe and Mail,* March 12,

2018, accessed May 26, 2018 from https://www.theglobeandmail.com/news/politics/trump-nafta-canada-mexico-trudeau/article33715250/.

71. Peter Armstrong, "Why the USMCA likely won't unleash a wave of pent-up business investment," CBC News, October 4, 2018. Accessed October 4, 2018, from https://www.cbc.ca/news/business/free-trade-usmca-nafta-armstrong-1.4848650.
72. Robert Fife and Adrian Morrow, "Canada, U.S. Reach Tentative NAFTA Deal; Trump Approves Pact," *The Globe and Mail,* September 30, 2018. Accessed October 1, 2018, from https://www.theglobeandmail.com/politics/article-canada-us-reach-outline-of-nafta-deal-pending-approval-of-trump/.
73. "Who are the Real Winners and Losers in the USMCA Deal?" CBC Radio. October 2, 2018. Accessed October 4, 2018, from https://www.cbc.ca/radio/thecurrent/the-current-for-october-2-2018-1.4846662/who-are-the-real-winners-and-losers-in-the-usmca-deal-1.4846675.
74. Blayne Haggart, "NAFTA Has Been Replaced But At What Cost to Canada?" *The Conversation,* October 1, 2018. Accessed October 4, 2018, from https://theconversation.com/nafta-has-been-replaced-but-at-what-cost-to-canada-104174?utm_medium=email&utm_campaign=Latest%20from%20The%20Conversation%20Canada%20for%20October%202%202018&utm_content=Latest%20from%20The%20Conversation%20Canada%20for%20October%202%202018+CID_5f28f994ece37c7a20dbf6fd4f21d988&utm_source=campaign_monitor_ca&utm_term=NAFTA%20has%20been%20replaced%20but%20at%20what%20cost%20to%20Canada.
75. Neil Macdonald, "With Its New Trade Deal, Canada Surrenders Sovereignty to a Bully," CBC News, October 1, 2018. Accessed October 2, 2018, from https://www.cbc.ca/news/opinion/canada-usmca-1.4845494.
76. Emma Ross Thomas, "EU Says Spain Should Improve Bank Monitoring as Bailout Ends," *Bloomberg BusinessWeek,* January 29, 2014; and Juergen Baetz, "EU Seeks to Make Mega-Banks Less Risky," *Bloomberg BusinessWeek,* January 29, 2014.
77. Steve Erlanger, "Britain Votes to Leave the EU; Cameron Plans to Step Down," *The New York Times,* June 23, 2016; Alex Hunt and Brian Wheeler, "Brexit: All You Need to Know about the UK Leaving the EU," *British Broadcasting Corporation,* March 14, 2017.
78. "Canadian-European Union: Comprehensive Economic and Trade Agreement," Foreign Affairs, Trade and Development Canada, accessed March 27, 2015, http://international.gc.ca/trade-agreements-accords-commerciaux/agr-acc/ceta-aecg/understanding-comprendre/overview-apercu.aspx?lang=eng.
79. Ibid.
80. "Trade and Investment Agreements," Global Affairs Canada, August 1, 2018, https://www.international.gc.ca/trade-commerce/trade-agreements-accords-commerciaux/agr-acc/index.aspx?lang=eng; "Canada–India Joint Study Group Report: Exploring the Feasibility of a Comprehensive Economic Partnership Agreement," Global Affairs Canada, February 14, 2013, modified October 24, 2017, accessed June 27, 2018, http://international.gc.ca/trade-commerce/trade-agreements-accords-commerciaux/agr-acc/india-inde/cepa-apeg/study-etude.aspx?lang=eng&_ga=2.170934432.1005374630.1530127003-1717544845.1530127003.
81. Jamil Anderlini and Lucy Hornby, "China Overtakes U.S. as World's Largest Goods Trader," *Financial Times,* January 10, 2014.
82. Liyan Qi and Grace Zhu, "China's Capital Inflows, Foreign Direct Investment Rose in 2013," *The Wall Street Journal,* January 16, 2014.
83. www.goldmansachs.com, accessed April 2014; and Morris Beschloss, "Will China Overtake U.S. GDP World Leadership by 2028?" *The Desert Sun (Gannett*), January 23, 2014.
84. Samuel Shen and Norihiko Shirozu, "China Auto Market Seen Cruising to Another Strong Year," Reuters, January 12, 2014.
85. "China's total number of cinema screens now exceeds the US," *PwC,* June 16, 2017, https://www.pwccn.com/en/press-room/press-releases/pr-160617.html.
86. "Profile, Strategy and Market," Bombardier Inc., February 2015, http://ir.bombardier.com.
87. "Can India Become a Great Power?" *The Economist,* March 30, 2013; and Philip Stephens, "India Still a Contender in the Asian Race," *Financial Times,* January 30, 2014.
88. Paul Hannon, "EBRD Reduces Investment in Russia," *The Wall Street Journal,* January 15, 2014; Mark Adomanis, "Russia's Economic Performance Is Actually Very Similar to Other East European Countries," *Forbes,* January 20, 2014.

Chapter 4

1. "Trade and Investment Agreements," Global Affairs Canada, 2017, https://www.international.gc.ca/trade-commerce/trade-agreements-accords-commerciaux/agr-acc/index.aspx?lang=eng.
2. "Crown Corporations - Links," Treasury Board of Canada Secretariat, 2018, accessed August 1, 2018, https://www.tbs-sct.gc.ca/gov-gouv/rc-cr/links-liens-eng.asp.
3. Nicholas Van Preet, "Quebec turns to pension giant Caisse to help fund transit projects," *The Globe and Mail,* January 12, 2015, http://www.theglobeandmail.com/report-on-business/quebec-turns-to-pension-giant-caisse-to-help-fund-transit-projects/article22421827/; "Investment -Overall Portfolio," Caisse de dépôt et placement du Québec, accessed May 30, 2018 https://www.cdpq.com/en/investments/overall-portfolio.
4. Konrad Yakabuski, "Privatization won't save provincially owned utilities," *The Globe and Mail,* July 7, 2017, B4.
5. Tamar Harris, "Hydro One undergoing 'intense transformation'," *The Windsor Star,* May 31, 2017, A10.
6. "Where Our Legal System Comes From," Department of Justice Canada, March 11, 2015, http://www.justice.gc.ca/eng/csj-sjc/just/03.html.
7. Eugene A. Forsey, *How Canadians Govern Themselves,* 6th ed., Government of Canada, 2005, www.parl.gc.ca/information/library/idb/forsey/index-e.asp; "Canada Health Transfer," Department of Finance Canada, December 19, 2011, www.fin.gc.ca/fedprov/cht-eng.asp.
8. "Federal Support to Provinces and Territories, 2017-2018," Finance Canada, https://www.fin.gc.ca/fedprov/mtp-eng.asp; "Future Cost of health Care in Canada, 2000–2020," Conference Board of Canada, 2011, accessed April 4, 2015, http://www.teamgrant.ca/M-THAC%20Greatest%20Hits/Bonus%20Tracks/FutureHealth.pdf.
9. "Consolidated text - The Canadian Free Trade Agreement (2017)," Canadian Free Trade Agreement, accessed May 30, 2018, https://www.cfta-alec.ca/canadian-free-trade-agreement/.
10. Jeff Gray, "Hershey, Cadbury lose bid to keep documents secret," 11 February 11, 2015, *The Globe and Mail,* http://www.theglobeandmail.com/report-on-business/industry-news/the-law-page/hershey-cadbury-lose-bid-to-keep-documents-secret/article22925825/; Peter Taylor, "How Canada's Competition Bureau makes products more expensive," *MoneySense,* March 25, 2015, http://www.moneysense.ca/spend/price-fixing-of-consumer-products; "Chocolate price fixing costs candy makers $23M," CBC News, September 17, 2013, http://www.cbc.ca/news/business/chocolate-price-fixing-costs-candy-makers-23m-1.1857642.
11. The Canadian Press, "HBC says Competition Bureau's mattress pricing probe has cost it $425K US," CBC News, November 22, 2017, accessed May 31, 2018, http://www.cbc.ca/news/business/hbc-competition-bureau-mattress-probe-cost-1.4414122.
12. Forsey, *How Canadians Govern Themselves;* "What the world can learn from Canada's P3 record," Canadian Council for Public-Private Partnerships, February 2015, http://www.pppcouncil.ca/news/551-report-what-the-world-can-learn-from-canadas-p3-record.html; "The P3 Pulse: National and Community Opinions on Public- Private Partnerships in Canada," Canadian Council for Public- Private Partnerships, April 10, 2014, http://www.pppcouncil.ca/resources/issues/public-opinion-and-communications.html.
13. "Canadian PPP Project database," Canadian Council for Public-Private Partnerships, P3 Spectrum, accessed May 31, 2018, http://www.pppcouncil.ca/web/News_Media/2017/Introducing_P3_SPECTRUM_-_Canada_s_Comprehensive_Source_for_P3_Project_Info.aspx?WebsiteKey=712ad751-6689-4d4a-aa17-e9f993740a89 and http://p3spectrum.ca/project/.

14. Trevor Tombe, "The good—and the bad—in Canada's provincial trade deal," Maclean's, 8 April 2017, accessed May 31, 2018 from https://www.macleans.ca/economy/economicanalysis/the-good-and-the-bad-in-canadas-provincial-trade-deal/. ; "Canada's evolving internal market: an agenda for a more cohesive economic union," Canada's Public Policy Forum, October 2013, http://www.ppforum.ca/sites/default/files/PPF%20AIT%20final%20report.pdf; Patrick Grady and Lathleen Macmillan, "Inter-provincial barriers to labour mobility in Canada: policy, knowledge gaps and research issues," Working Paper Series, Industry Canada, 2007, https://www.ic.gc.ca/eic/site/eas-aes.nsf/vwapj/wp200710.pdf/$file/wp200710.pdf, downloaded 5 April 2015; "Improving Internal Trade: A Bold Approach," Certified General Accountants Association of Canada, 2008, www.cga-canada.org/en-ca/DiscussionPapers/ca_rep_internal_trade_position-paper2008.pdf; "Overview of the Agreement on Internal Trade, 2009."
15. Forsey, *How Canadians Govern Themselves.*
16. "Bank of Canada," Historica Canada, accessed May 31, 2018, http://www.thecanadianencyclopedia.ca/en/article/bank-of-canada/; and "About the Bank," Bank of Canada, accessed May 31, 2018, https://www.bankofcanada.ca/about/.
17. "Canada's Money Supply," Bank of Canada, accessed May 24, 2018, https://www.bankofcanada.ca/wp-content/uploads/2010/11/canada_money_supply.pdf; and "Canada's Money Supply," Government of Canada, accessed May 24, 2018, http://publications.gc.ca/site/eng/9.843795/publication.html.
18. "The European Union's Quantitative Easing Options," *The Economist,* December 10, 2016; Claire Jones, "Crunch Looms on QE as European Central Bank Meets," *Financial Times,* October 18, 2016; Nina Adam and Paul Hannon, "Germany's Rising Inflation May Boost Calls to Halt ECB Stimulus," *The Wall Street Journal,* January 30, 2017.
19. "How Monetary Policy Works: The Transmission of Monetary Policy," Bank of Canada, accessed May 24, 2018, http://www.bankofcanada.ca/wp-content/uploads/2010/11/how_monetary_policy_works.pdf; and "The Bank's History," Bank of Canada, accessed May 24, 2018, https://www.bankofcanada.ca/about/history/.
20. "The Canadian Financial System," Bank of Canada, accessed May 24, 2018, http://www.bankofcanada.ca/wp-content/uploads/2010/11/canadian_financial_system.pdf; and "Financial System," Bank of Canada, accessed May 24, 2018, http://www.bankofcanada.ca/core-functions/financial-system/.
21. "Annual Financial Report of the Government of Canada: Fiscal Year 2016–2017," Department of Finance, September 19, 2017, accessed May 24, 2018, https://www.fin.gc.ca/afr-rfa/2017/report-rapport-eng.asp.
22. Milagros Palacios, Feixue Ren, and Charles Lammam, "Taxes versus the Necessities of Life: The Canadian Consumer Tax Index 2017 Edition," The Fraser Institute, August 2017, https://www.fraserinstitute.org/sites/default/files/canadian-consumer-tax-index-2017.pdf.
23. Ibid.
24. Elliot Ferguson, "Report distracts from problematic tax system: Pro," The Whig-Standard, April 27, 2012, www.thewhig.com/ArticleDisplay.aspx?e=3545447.
25. Ibid.
26. "Fraser Institute says reforming tax rate structure would boost economy," Lambton Shield, April 24, 2018, https://lambtonshield.com/fraser-institute-says-reforming-tax-rate-structure-boost-economy/.
27. Jessica Vomiero, "Canadian students owe $28B in government loans, some want feds to stop charging interest," Global News, May 21, 2018, https://globalnews.ca/news/4222534/canadian-student-loans-government-interest/.
28. Murray Brewster, "Federal government's total 'market debt' now tops $1 trillion, documents show," CBC News, March 26, 2018, http://www.cbc.ca/news/politics/federal-market-debt-1.4590441.
29. "Table 191-0002: Central government debt," Statistics Canada, May 22, 2018, http://www5.statcan.gc.ca/cansim/a26?lang=eng&id=1910002; and Craig Alexander, "Canadian voters should be concerned about government deficit spending," *The Globe and Mail,* April 5, 2018, https://www.theglobeandmail.com/business/commentary/article-canadian-voters-should-be-concerned-about-government-deficit-spending/.
30. "The Cost of Government Debt in Canada, 2017," Fraser Institute, January 19, 2017, https://www.fraserinstitute.org/studies/cost-of-government-debt-in-canada-2017.
31. Vincent McDermott, "Fort McMurray wildfire finally extinguished after 15 months," *Edmonton Journal,* September 1, 2017, http://edmontonjournal.com/news/local-news/fort-mcmurray-wildfire-finally-extinguished-after-15-months.
32. Jason Kirby, "A Burden to Future Taxpayers," *Maclean's,* December 5, 2017, https://www.macleans.ca/economy/economicanalysis/the-most-important-economic-charts-to-watch-in-2018/#aaronwudrick.
33. "Federal Support to Provinces and Territories," Department for Finance Canada, accessed May 31, 2018, https://www.fin.gc.ca/fedprov/mtp-eng.asp.
34. "Canadian Subsidy Directory - 2018 edition," Canadian Publications, 2018, http://www.grantscanada.org/.
35. "2017 Report on Angel Investing in Canada: The First Funders of Innovation," National Angel Capital Organizations, May 31, 2018, https://www.nacocanada.com/cpages/angel-activity-report.
36. "Aboriginal Business and Entrepreneurship Development," Indigenous and Northern Affairs Canada, accessed May 31, 2018, http://www.aadnc-aandc.gc.ca/eng/1375201178602/1375202816581.
37. Phillipe Karam, "Energy Subsidy Reform Lessons and Implications," International Monetary Fund, November 2013, http://www.oecd.org/gov/budgeting/Doha%202013%20-%208%20presentations%20in%20ENGLISH.pdf.
38. "Energy Subsidy Reform: Lessons and Implications," International Monetary Fund, January 28, 2013, http://www.imf.org/external/np/pp/eng/2013/012813.pdf.
39. Derek Wong, "Fossil fuel subsidies nearly $800 per Canadian, says the IMF," Toronto Sustainability Speaker Series, April 17, 2013, http://ecoopportunity.net/2013/04/fossil-fuel-subsidies-nearly-800-per-canadian-says-the-imf/.
40. Jehan Sauvage, "Through the looking glass: transparency and fossil-fuel subsidies," OECD, Trade and Agriculture Directorate, November 2013, http://www.oecd.org/gov/budgeting/Doha%202013%20-%208%20presentations%20in%20ENGLISH.pdf.
41. "Unpacking Canada's Fossil Fuel Subsidies," Global Subsidies Initiative - International Institute for Sustainable Development, accessed May 31, 2018, https://www.iisd.org/faq/unpacking-canadas-fossil-fuel-subsidies/.
42. "Federal Support to Provinces and Territories," Department for Finance Canada, accessed May 31, 2018, https://www.fin.gc.ca/fedprov/mtp-eng.asp.
43. "Preparing to sell to the Government," Government of Canada, accessed June 28, 2018, www.canadabusiness.ca/eng/page/2757/.
44. "Overview," MERX, 2018, https://www.merx.com/English/NonMember.asp?WCE=Show&TAB=1&PORTAL=MERX&State=5&hcode=9W6WLXToZAbWNQRpWOPMTg%3d%3d.
45. "About NRC," National Research Council Canada, accessed June 28, 2018, http://www.nrc-cnrc.gc.ca/eng/about/index.html.
46. "Corporate overview," National Research Council Canada, accessed May 31, 2018, https://www.nrc-cnrc.gc.ca/eng/about/corporate_overview/index.html
47. "Glossary of Key Terms: Minority Government," British Columbia Referendum Office, 2009, www.gov.bc.ca/referendum_info/first_past_the_post_bc_stv/glossary.html.
48. "Paper trail: the decline of Canada's forestry industry," *The Globe and Mail,* December 5, 2014, http://www.theglobeandmail.com/report-on-business/economy/paper-trail-the-fall-of-forestry/article21967746/.

Chapter 5

1. Brent Jang, "WestJet Admits Spying," globeandmail.com, 9 May 29, 2006, accessed June 29, 2018, https://www.theglobeandmail.com/report-on-business/westjet-admits-to-spying/article20411712/.

2. Ibid.
3. The Canadian Press. "Volkswagen reaches $290M Canadian diesel settlement," *The Star*, January 12, 2018, accessed May 21, 2018, https://www.thestar.com/business/2018/01/12/volkswagen-reaches-290m-canadian-diesel-settlement.html.
4. Laura Payton, "Conservatives deny party focus of robocalls probe," CBC News, April 17, 2012, www.cbc.ca/news/politics/story/2012/04/17/pol-robocalls-guelph-investigation-extends.html.
5. Ibid.
6. "Key facts in Canada's robocalls controversy," CBC News, August 14, 2014, http://www.cbc.ca/news/politics/key-facts-in-canada-s-robocalls-controversy-1.2736659.
7. Ottawa Citizen Editorial Board, "Editorial: Elections Canada should re-open robocalls investigation," *Ottawa Citizen*, August 15, 2014, accessed June 29, 2018, http://ottawacitizen.com/news/national/editorial-elections-canada-should-re-open-robocalls-investigation.
8. "Current land claims," Government of Ontario, https://www.ontario.ca/page/current-land-claims, accessed June 29, 2018; Brian Hutchison, "Supreme Court B.C. land-claim ruling has staggering implications for Canadian resource projects," *The National Post*, June 26, 2014, http://news.nationalpost.com/news/canada/supreme-court-b-c-land-claim-ruling-has-staggering-implications-for-canadian-energy-projects.
9. Pallavi Guniganti, "Ethics' Place in Education," *University Wire*, April 16, 2002.
10. Jahnabi Barooah, "The Golden Rule in World Religions (Quotes)," *Huffington Post*, www.huffingtonpost.com, accessed April 2014.
11. Turnitin, www.turnitin.com, accessed April 2014; and "Turnitin for iPad Surpasses 100,000 Downloads," *The Sacramento Bee*, January 14, 2014.
12. Thomas Ehrlich and Ernestine Fu, "Cheating in Schools and Colleges," *Forbes*, August 22, 2013.
13. Aaron Hutchins, "Universities' new rules for cheating," Maclean's, March 30, 2017, accessed May 21, 2018, https://www.macleans.ca/education/universities-new-rules-for-cheating/.
14. Rebecca Heilweil, "Harvard Rescinds Admissions To 10 Students For Offensive Facebook Memes," *Forbes*, June 5, 2017, accessed May 27, 2018, https://www.forbes.com/sites/rebeccaheilweil1/2017/06/05/harvard-rescinds-10-admissions-offer-for-offensive-facebook-memes-ollowing-commencement-speaker-zuckerberg/#5ff7c5553dbd; Valery Strauss, "Harvard yanks acceptances from at least 10 students — and everybody has an opinion," *The Washington Post*, June 6, 2017, accessed May 27, 2018, https://www.washingtonpost.com/news/answer-sheet/wp/2017/06/06/harvard-yanks-acceptances-from-at-least-10-students-and-everybody-has-an-opinion/?utm_term=.70c4d265a953.
15. Kenneth Blanchard and Norman Vincent Peale, *The Power of Ethical Management* (New York: William Morrow, 1996).
16. Christopher McLaverty and Annie McKee, "What You Can Do to Improve Ethics at Your Company," *Harvard Business Review*, December 29, 2016 and "National Business Ethics Survey," Ethics and Compliance Initiative, ethics.org, accessed January 2017.
17. "A brief history of SNC-Lavalin," CBC News, April 30, 2012, accessed June 29, 2018, https://www.cbc.ca/news/business/a-brief-history-of-snc-lavalin-1.1154986.
18. Ibid.
19. Graeme Hamilton, "RCMP charges SNC-Lavalin with fraud and corruption linked to Libyan projects," *The Financial Post*, February 19, 2015, accessed June 29, 2018, https://business.financialpost.com/news/rcmp-charges-snc-lavalin-with-fraud-and-corruption-linked-to-libyan-projects.
20. Jason Markusoff, "Loblaws' price-fixing may have cost you at least $400," Maclean's, January 11, 2018, accessed May 27, 2018, https://www.macleans.ca/economy/economicanalysis/14-years-of-loblaws-bread-price-fixing-may-have-cost-you-at-least-400/.
21. "Packaged Bread Price Fixing Class Action," strosbergco.com, accessed May 27, 2018, https://www.strosbergco.com/class-actions/bread/.
22. IANS, "Now, Apple says 'slowing-down' of older iPhones was not intentional," *The Economic Times*, February 1, 2018, accessed May 28, 2018, https://economictimes.indiatimes.com/magazines/panache/now-apple-says-slowing-down-of-older-iphones-was-not-intentional/articleshow/62738624.cms.
23. Jean Eaglesham, "CFTC Whistles Up Few Whistleblowers," *The Wall Street Journal*, February 9, 2016; Neil Weinberg, "JPMorgan Whistle-Blowers Set to Reap Record $61 Million Bounty," *Bloomberg*, July 20, 2017; Jean Eaglesham, "CFTC Whistles Up Few Whistleblowers," *The Wall Street Journal*, February 9. 2016; Paul K. McMasters, "Inside the First Amendment: Blowing the Whistle Can Also Blow a Career," *Gannett News Service*, January 16, 2006; Guillermo Contreras, "San Antonio Whistleblower Doubly Rewarded in Exposing HealthSouth Fraud," *San Antonio Express News*, January 14, 2005; and Scott Green, "A Look at the Causes, Impact and Future of the Sarbanes-Oxley Act," *Journal of International Business and Law*, Vol. 3: Issue 1, 2004, http://scholarlycommons.law.hofstra.edu/jibl/vol3/iss1/.
24. Rob Ferguson, "ORNGE: Proposed bill would block ombudsman oversight," Queen's Park Bureau, April 27, 2012, accessed June 29, 2018, www.thestar.com/news/canada/politics/article/1169002–ornge-proposed-bill-would-block-ombudsman-oversight; James Wood, "Alberta's lack of whistleblower law criticized," FAIR, March 19, 2012, http://fairwhistleblower.ca/content/albertas-lack-whistleblower-law-criticized; Kevin Donovan; "$25M in ORNGE money unaccounted for," *The Toronto Star*, February 24, 2012, www.thestar.com/news/canada/politics/article/1136628–25m-in-ornge-money-unaccounted-for; Kevin Donovan, "Whistleblower warned Ministry about ORNGE in 2008," Federal Accountability Initiative for Reform, February 3, 2012, http://fairwhistleblower.ca/content/ministry-was-warned-about-ornge-spending-four-years-ago-whistleblower-says; "Federal Conservatives broke their whistleblower protection and open government election promises, as the Afghan prisoner scandal makes clear," Democracy Watch, 2010, www.dwatch.ca/camp/OpEdNov2509.html; David Hutton and Gerard Seijts, "Canada needs whistleblowers to protect stimulus package," *The Hill Times*, February 16, 2009, http://fairwhistleblower.ca/news/articles/2009-02-16_Canada_needs_whistleblowers_to_protect_stimulus_package.html; "Ontario passes whistleblower law," Canadian Press, December 13, 2006, www.thestar.com/news/article/148456—ontario-passes-whistleblower-law; and "Providing real protection for whistleblowers," Treasury Board of Canada Secretariat, April 11, 2006, accessed June 29, 2018, www.tbs-sct.gc.ca/faa-lfi/fs-fi/16/09fs-fi-eng.asp.
25. "Canadian whistleblower on why he exposed 'problematic' Facebook data misuse by Trump consulting firm," CBC News, March 18, 2018, accessed May 21, 2018, http://www.cbc.ca/news/technology/cambridge-analytica-facebook-review-data-users-1.4581847.
26. John Ounpuu, "Facebook controversy offers a serious warning for Canadian businesses," *The Globe and Mail*, April 16, 2018.
27. John S. McClenahen, "Defining Social Responsibility," *Industry Week*, March 1, 2005.
28. Julie Irwin, "Ethical Consumerism Isn't Dead, It Just Needs Better Marketing," *Harvard Business Review*, January 12, 2015, accessed May 27, 2018, https://hbr.org/2015/01/ethical-consumerism-isnt-dead-it-just-needs-better-marketing.
29. Alvina Gillani and Smirti Kutaula, "An introduction to the special issue: ethical consumerism and sustainability," *Management Decisions*, 2018, Volume 56, Issue 3, pages 511–514.
30. Zoe McKnight, "Some ideas for ethical shopping: More people buying to suit the different philosophies of conscientious commerce," *Toronto Star*, December 17, 2016, E1.
31. Bill Saporito, "The Conscious-Capitalism Debate," *Inc.*, March 2016; Tim Worstall, "No Surprise at All—Corporate Social Responsibility Reduces Profits," *Forbes*, June 3, 2017.
32. Rachel Emma Silverman, "Workplace Democracy Catches On," *The Wall Street Journal*, March 28, 2016; Joshua Clark Davis, "So Much for 'Conscious Capitalism'," *Slate*, June 19, 2017.
33. Ivan Widjaya, "Corporate Social Responsibility: How it Affects Employee Satisfaction," Small Business Trends, May 13, 2016, accessed June 29, 2018, https://smallbiztrends.com/2016/05/corporate-social-responsibility.html.

34. Canadian Tire Corporation Ltd., "Canadian Tire Corporation, in Support of Jumpstart, Commits $50 Million Over Five Years to Get More Canadian Kids with Disabilities into Sport and Play," September 19, 2017, accessed May 21 2018, https://www.newswire.ca/news-releases/canadian-tire-corporation-in-support-of-jumpstart-commits-50-million-over-five-years-to-get-more-canadian-kids-with-disabilities-into-sport-and-play-645804003.html.
35. Logistics Cluster, www.logcluster.org, accessed September 2017.
36. Patagonia, www.patagonia.com, accessed September 2017.
37. Xerox, www.xerox.com, accessed September 2017.
38. Sarah Halzack, "Paid Time Off for Volunteering Gains Traction as Way to Retain Employees," *The Washington Post,* August 11, 2013.
39. David A. Kaplan, "Inside Mars," *Fortune,* February 4, 2013.
40. "Corporate Responsibility," Toronto Dominion Bank, accessed June 29, 2018, http://www.td.com/corporate-responsibility/community/index.jsp.
41. "Canada's big banks saw profits up in 2014, warn challenges ahead," CTV News, December 5, 2015, http://www.ctvnews.ca/business/canada-s-big-banks-saw-profits-up-in-2014-warn-challenges-ahead-1.2135107.
42. Debbie Haski-Leventhal, *MBA Students around the World and Their Attitudes towards Responsible Management, Second Annual Study* (Macquarie Graduate School of Management, University of Sydney, New South Wales, 2013); Debbie Haski-Leventhal and Mehrdokht Pournader, "Business Students Willing to Sacrifice Future Salary for Good Corporate Social Responsibility: Study," *The Conversation,* February 21, 2017.
43. "Corporate Social Responsibility," Wikipedia, accessed June 29, 2018, https://en.wikipedia.org/wiki/Corporate_social_responsibility#Nature_of_business.
44. Bryan Nella, "Consumer Study: Food, Apparel, & Pharmaceutical Industries Face Uphill Battle to Ensure Responsible Overseas Production," Gt Nexus, gtnexus.com accessed January 2017.
45. Kenny Kline, "How This Fashion Startup Is Blending Ethics with Profit," *Inc.*, August 18, 2016; Kelsey Chong, "Millennials and the Rising Demand for Corporate Social Responsibility," *Berkeley MBA Blog,* January 20, 2017.
46. Kris Hudson, "Oh, Give Me a Home Where the Prairie Dogs Roam—in Boulder," *The Wall Street Journal,* May 20, 2006, http://www.wsj.com/articles/SB114808815360858621.
47. Eric Gneckow, "'Socially Responsible Investing Steps Toward Mainstream," *North Bay Business Journal,* January 6, 2014; "Earl Jones gets 11 years for $50M Ponzi scheme," *The Gazette,* February 16, 2010, www.montrealgazette.com/news/Earl+Jones+gets+years+swindling/2567329/story.html; Sidhartha Banerjee, "Disgraced Financier Lived Lavishly," The Canadian Press, July 30, 2009, www.thestar.com/news/canada/article/673888; "Trustee Sues Madoff's Wife for $45M," CBS News, July 29, 2009, www.cbsnews.com/stories/2009/07/29/business/main5196249.shtml?source=related_story&tag=related; "Nortel May Lose NYSE Listing," CBC News, December 11, 2008, www.cbc.ca/mobile/text/story_news-technology.html?/ept/html/story/2008/12/11/nortellisting.html; Steven Skurka, "Black vs. Drabinsky: Two Trials, Two Very Different Systems," *National Post,* June 4, 2009; "Livent Sentencing Hearing Postponed," The Canadian Press, June 3, 2009, www.thestar.com/article/644834; Joe Schneider, "Drabinsky Sentence Bid Would Draw Laughs in U.S., Lawyer Says," Bloomberg.com, August 4, 2009, accessed June 29, 2018, https://www.bloomberg.com/news/articles/2009-08-04/drabinsky-sentence-bid-would-draw-laughs-in-u-s-lawyer-says; Stephen Payne, "Investors Oppose SEC Proposal on Shareholder Rights," *Oil & Gas Investor,* 1 January 2008; and Robert Kuttner, "Dishonest Capitalism Won't Go Unpunished," *BusinessWeek,* May 23, 2005, 32.
48. Rick Tetzell, "Great Strides," *Fast Company,* February 2016; Constance Gustke, "The Truth Is Finally Starting to Emerge About Socially Responsible Investing," CNBC, June 16, 2017.
49. Jeff Gray and Jacquie McNish, "Mitchell Finkelstein passed deal tips to fraternity friend, OSC rules," *The Globe and Mail,* March 25, 2015, http://www.theglobeandmail.com/report-on-business/industry-news/the-law-page/osc-rules-finkelstein-fed-tips-to-friend-on-corporate-deals/article23610690/; Tara Perkins, "Andrew Rankin Gets 6 Months in Canada's 1st Stock-Tipping Conviction," CBC News, April 10, 2005, www.cbc.ca/cp/business/051027/b1027100.html; "Former RBC Dominion Securities Exec Faces Insider Trading Charges," CBC News, 5 February 2004, http://www.cbc.ca/news/business/former-rbc-dominion-securities-exec-faces-insider-trading-charges-1.496642; Karen Howlett, "OSC lays charges in trading scandal," *The Globe and Mail,* February 5, 2004, updated April 19, 2018, accessed June 29, 2018, https://www.theglobeandmail.com/report-on-business/osc-lays-charges-in-trading-scandal/article18258997/.
50. Bill Catlette and Richard Hadden, *Contented Cows Still Give Better Milk* (Jacksonville, FL: Contented Cow Partners, 2012); Contented Cow Partners, www.contentedcows.com, accessed September 2017.
51. Bourree Lam, "What Costco's New Wages Say about the Health of the American Economy," *The Atlantic,* March 5, 2016; Niall McCarthy, "Costco Named America's Best Employer 2017," *Forbes,* May 10, 2017.
52. Julie Kantor, "High Turnover Costs Way More Than You Think," *Huffington Post,* February 11, 2016; Heather Boushey and Sarah Jane Glynn, "There Are Significant Business Costs to Replacing Employees," Center for American Progress, November 16, 2012, accessed June 29, 2018, https://www.americanprogress.org/issues/economy/reports/2012/11/16/44464/there-are-significant-business-costs-to-replacing-employees/; Jack Altman, "How Much Does Employee Turnover Really Cost?" *Huffington Post,* January 18, 2017.
53. "2014 Global Fraud Study," Association of Certified Fraud Examiners, accessed June 29, 2018, http://www.acfe.com/rttn/docs/2014-report-to-nations.pdf.
54. Marina Strauss, "Theft by retail workers on the increase: study," *The Globe and Mail,* October 30, 2012, updated May 9, 2018, accessed June 29, 2018, https://www.theglobeandmail.com/report-on-business/theft-by-retail-workers-on-increase-study/article4781854/.
55. Marina Strauss, "Foot-dragging in garment factory reform draws ire of Loblaw's Weston," *The Globe and Mail,* September 18, 2013, accessed June 29, 2018, http://www.theglobeandmail.com/report-on-business/international-business/asian-pacific-business/foot-dragging-in-garment-factory-reform-draws-ire-of-loblaws-weston/article14403359/; "Loblaw Companies Limited updated statement on Bangladesh," Loblaw Companies limited: Company Statements, April 23, 2014, accessed June 29, 2018, http://media.loblaw.ca/English/media-centre/company-statements/company-statements-details/2014/Loblaw-Companies-Limited-updated-statement-on-Bangladesh/default.aspx.
56. Heather Green and Kerry Capell, "Carbon Confusion," *BusinessWeek,* March 6, 2008.
57. "Maple Leaf's Commitment to Animal Care, Pledges Principles and Actions that will Advance the Five Freedoms," Maple Leaf Foods Inc., accessed May 27, 2018, http://www.mapleleaffoods.com/news/maple-leafs-commitment-to-animal-care-pledges-principles-and-actions-that-will-advance-the-five-freedoms/; Megan Griffith-Greene, "Maple Leaf Foods 'disturbed' by supplier turkey farm video, promises action," March 16, 2014, CBC News, accessed May 27, 2018, http://www.cbc.ca/news/business/maple-leaf-foods-disturbed-by-supplier-turkey-farm-video-promises-action-1.2574599.
58. "About Us," The Organic Box, accessed June 29, 2018, https://www.theorganicbox.ca/about-us/.
59. "Walkerton Report Blames Province Water Managers," January 18, 2002, CBC News, https://www.cbc.ca/news/canada/walkerton-report-blames-province-water-managers-1.303975.
60. Eric Pfeiffer, "BP oil spill two-year anniversary marked by somber statistics," The Sideshow, April 20, 2012, http://news.yahoo.com/blogs/sideshow/bp-oil-spill-two-anniversary-marked-somber-statistics-185242840.html; "BP oil disaster largely blamed on cement failure," The Associated Press, September 14, 2011, www.cbc.ca/news/world/story/2011/09/14/

bp-offshore-oil-spill-report.html; Sylvia Pfeifer and Sheila McNulty, "BP oil spill confirmed as 'world's worst'," *The Financial Times*, August 3, 2010, www.ft.com/cms/s/0/3e40d4ac-9e5d-11df-a5a4-00144feab49a.html#axzz1uZlfDvgn; Jim MacDonald, "Syncrude Charged after 500 Ducks Perished on Oilsands Pond," The Canadian Press, February 9, 2009, www.thestar.com/article/584719; "About Imagine Canada," Imagine Canada, accessed June 29, 2018, http://www.imaginecanada.ca/who-we-are/about-imagine-canada; "Home," Jantzi Research, 2005, www.jantziresearch.com; "Our Site Overview," Province of Nova Scotia: Sydney Tar Ponds Agency, 2004, www.gov.ns.ca/stpa; Chris Sebastian, "Canada Getting Tough on Spills," *Times Herald*, May 12, 2004, www.thetimesherald.com/news/stories/20040512/localnews/403633.html; Pat Currie, "All's Not Well in This Valley," *Lake Ontario Waterkeeper*, April 3, 2004, www.waterkeeper.ca/lok; "The Great Lakes Atlas," The United States Environmental Protection Agency, 2003, www.epa.gov/glnpo/atlas; "Tar Ponds in Sydney, Nova Scotia," PageWise Inc., 2002, http://tntn.essortment.com/tarpondssydney_rhxq.htm; and "Sydney Nova Scotia Tar Ponds Move Closer to Cleanup" Ellicott, www.dredge.com/casestudies/enviro8.htm

61. Erin Pottie, "Sydney tar ponds lawsuit quashed by Supreme Court," *Herald News*, January 16, 2015, http://thechronicleherald.ca/novascotia/1263229-sydney-tar-ponds-lawsuit-quashed-by-supreme-court.
62. Associated Press, "Judge's decision could cost BP $13bn for Deepwater Horizon oil spill," *The Guardian*, January 15, 2015, http://www.theguardian.com/business/2015/jan/15/bp-13bn-cost-deepwater-horizon-oil-spill.
63. "Just What Is a Carbon Tax?" CBC News, September 29, 2008, www.cbc.ca/news/canadavotes/story/2008/09/19/f-carbontaxprimer.html; "Carbon Taxes: Cash Grab or Climate Saviour?" CBC News, June 19, 2008, www.cbc.ca/canada/story/2008/06/18/f-carbon-tax.html; and "B.C. Carbon Tax Kicks in on Canada Day," CBC News, July 1, 2008, www.cbc.ca/canada/british-columbia/story/2008/06/30/bc-carbon-tax-effective.html.
64. Timothy Slaper and Tanya Hall, "The triple bottom line: what is it and how does it work?" Indiana Business Research Centre, Indiana University Kelley School of Business, http://www.ibrc.indiana.edu/ibr/2011/spring/pdfs/article2.pdf, accessed April 25, 2015.
65. Ibid.
66. Ibid.
67. "Canadian RI assets surpass $1.5 trillion: 2016 Canadian RI trends report," Responsible Investment Association, accessed June 6, 2018, https://www.riacanada.ca/trendsreport/.
68. Ethisphere, www.ethisphere.com, accessed September 2017
69. "Defining Sustainability," Sustainability Reporting Program, 2000, www.sustreport.org/background/definitions.html; "Introducing Revive," Green Solutions North American, Inc., 2009, http://revive-d.com/revive_overview.cfm; and "Loblaws, Sobeys put a wrap on plastic bags," The Canadian Press, November 27, 2008, www.cbc.ca/consumer/story/2008/11/27/loblaw-sobeys-bags.html.
70. "Envirotech Savings Calculator," Envirotech Office Systems, accessed July 27, 2015, http://www.envirotechoffice.com/why-envirotech/remanufactured-products.
71. "Fair trade – An alternative economic model," CBC News, April 23, 2007, www.cbc.ca/news/background/fair-trade/.
72. Ibid.
73. "Fairtrade Canada – What is Fair Trade," Fairtrade Canada, accessed April 25, 2015, http://fairtrade.ca/en/about-fairtrade/what-fair-trade.
74. "Socially Conscious Consumer Trends: Fair Trade," Market Analysis Report, Agriculture and Agri-Food Canada, April 2012, http://www5.agr.gc.ca/resources/prod/Internet-Internet/MISB-DGSIM/ATS-SEA/PDF/6153-eng.pdf.
75. Roberta Rampton and Krista Hughes, "Obama Puts Nike in Trade Spotlight Despite Sweatshop Stigma of Past," Reuters, May 6, 2015; Karen McVeigh, "Cambodian Female Workers in Nike, Asics and Puma Factories Suffer Mass Faintings," *The Guardian*, June 24, 2017.

Chapter 6

1. Media Kit, Abeego, http://abeego.com/pages/media-kit, accessed March 19, 2015.
2. "Should You Incorporate? - Proprietorship," Canadian Tax and Financial Information, Taxtips.ca, accessed June 30, 2018, https://www.taxtips.ca/smallbusiness/incorporate.htm.
3. "Canadian government spending tens of millions on Facebook ads, boosted posts," The Canadian Press, May 23, 2018, http://www.theguardian.pe.ca/news/business/canadian-government-spending-tens-of-millions-on-facebook-ads-boosted-posts-212149/.
4. Elaine Pofeldt, "Going It Alone," *Inc.*, February 2014.
5. "Proprietorship," World Wide Web
6. "SR&ED Claims for Partnerships Policy," Canada Revenue Agency, December 18, 2014, http://www.cra-arc.gc.ca/txcrdt/sred-rsde/clmng/clmsfrprtnrshpsplcy-eng.html#s3_1.
7. "Sole proprietorship, partnership, corporation or co-operative?" Canada Business Network, October 13, 2017, https://canadabusiness.ca/starting/before-starting-your-business/corporation-partnership-or-sole-proprietorship/.
8. Deborah Aarts, "The Smart Way to Run a Business With Your Spouse," May 16, 2016, *Profit Guide*, http://www.profitguide.com/manage-grow/leadership/w100-lulu-cohen-farnell-real-food-for-real-kids-working-with-your-spouse-103028.
9. Pia Silva, "Business Partners and Still Married: Here's What We've Learned," *Forbes*, February 13, 2017; and Kala Vijayraghavan and Devina Sengupta, "How Married Business Partners Make It Work," *The Economic Times*, June 16, 2016.
10. Bureau of Labor Statistics, www.bis.gov, accessed March 2014.
11. "matt & nat: Fashioning success with style - Inder Bedi wins BDC's Young Entrepreneur Award for Québec," Cision Communications Cloud, October 16, 2007, accessed June 30, 2018, http://www.newswire.ca/news-releases/matt--nat-fashioning-success-with-style---inder-bedi-wins-bdcs-young-entrepreneur-award-for-quebec-534488671.html.
12. Paula Andruss, "Divide & Conquer," *Entrepreneur*, April 2013.
13. "Should You Incorporate - Partnership," Canadian Tax and Financial Information, Taxtips.ca, accessed June 30, 2018, https://www.taxtips.ca/smallbusiness/incorporate.htm.
14. Ibid.
15. "About Us," The Jim Pattison Group, accessed October 15, 2017, http://www.jimpattison.com/about/our-story/.
16. Elizabeth Thompson, "Why Morneau wants to tighten rules on private companies," CBC News, July 28, 2017, http://www.cbc.ca/news/politics/taxation-companies-rules-morneau-1.4225139.
17. "Differences Between Private and Public Corporation," LawDepot.com, accessed 2015, http://wiki.lawdepot.ca/wiki/Differences_Between_Private_and_Public_Corporations.
18. Susan Ward, "Corporate Tax Advantages - Canadian-Controlled Private Corporation," The Balance, November 7, 2016, updated February 16, 2018, accessed June 30, 2018, https://www.thebalance.com/controlled-private-corporation-advantages-2948059.
19. "McCain Business Empire has Deep Roots," CBC.ca, March 19, 2004, accessed June 30, 2018, http://www.cbc.ca/news/business/mccain-business-empire-has-deep-roots-1.518215.
20. Jamie Sturgeon, "It's official, Tim Hortons, Burger King become one," Global News, December 12, 2014, http://globalnews.ca/news/1724238/its-official-tim-hortons-burger-king-become-one/; "The Story of Tim Hortons," Tim Hortons, 2012, www.timhortons.com/ca/en/about/index.html; and Josh Fineman and David Scanlan, "Tim Hortons Shares May Rise After Raising $671 Million in IPO," *Bloomberg*, March 24, 2006, www.bloomberg.com/apps/news?pid=newsarchive&sid=aq7mLjay_GVs&refer=us.
21. Nellie Akalp, "Top Reasons to Incorporate Your Business," *Small Business Trends*, February 3, 2014.
22. "The Basics of Corporate Structure," Investopedia.com, 2008, www.investopedia.com/articles/basics/03/022803.asp.
23. "Carol Hymowitz, "Not Going Anywhere," *Bloomberg BusinessWeek*, May 27–June 2, 2013.

24. Jim Combs and Dave Ketchen, "The Downside of Independent Boards," *The Wall Street Journal,* May 16, 2017; Olivia Oran, "U.S. Banks Set Director Pay Ceilings to Avoid Lawsuits," *St. Louis-Post Dispatch,* September 2, 2016; "How Do Boards Avoid Mistakes and Find Solutions?" *The Board Room Magazine,* August 26, 2016; and Theo Francis and Joann S. Lublin, "Investors Scrutinize Board Tenures," *The Wall Street Journal,* March 24, 2016.
25. "Booster Juice," Canadian Franchise Association, 2017, http://lookforafranchise.ca/browse-franchises/food-quick-service-restaurants/booster-juice/.
26. "Franchising Fast Facts," Canadian Franchise Association, 2017, https://www.cfa.ca/wp-content/uploads/2017/03/CFA_AR2017_FranchisingFacts.pdf.
27. Ibid.
28. "What We Offer: Operations," Boston Pizza International, accessed October 31, 2017, http://www.bostonpizzafranchise.com/en/about-bp/what-we-offer.html.
29. Kate Rogers, "Here's Where America's Billion-Dollar Franchising Industry is Growing Fastest," CNBC, January 24, 2017; and Jason Daley, "How Franchises Grow Fast," *Entrepreneur,* February 2016.
30. Ceren Cubukcu, "Franchise vs. Start-up: What is Best for You?" *Entrepeneur,* November 12, 2016.
31. "College Pro Painters," Canadian Franchise Association, accessed March 25, 2018, https://lookforafranchise.cfa.ca/browse-franchises/painting-services/college-pro-painters/.
32. "Boston Pizza International Inc.," Canadian Franchise Association, accessed March 25, 2018, https://lookforafranchise.cfa.ca/browse-franchises/food-restaurants-dining-rooms/boston-pizza-international-inc/.
33. Andrew Seid, "The Basics of Franchise Royalty Payments," *The Balance,* July 27, 2017 and Toni Kaiser, "Royalties 101: Daring to Touch the Sacred Cow," *Franchise Times,* May 2016.
34. Hollie Shaw, "Tim Hortons franchisees sue corporate parent for $850M, alleging bullying and intimidation," *Financial Post,* October 6, 2017, http://business.financialpost.com/news/retail-marketing/tim-hortons-franchisees-sue-corporate-parent-for-850m-alleging-bullying-and-intimidation.
35. "The Selection Process," Canadian Tire Corporation, Ltd., accessed October 31, 2017, http://corp.canadiantire.ca/EN/JOINOURTEAM/RETAILOWNERSHIP/Pages/TheSelectionProcess.aspx.
36. "We're Not Your Parents' Real Estate Company," PropertyGuys.com, accessed November 3, 2017, http://propertyguys.com/site/about/.
37. "2016 Top Home-Based Franchises," *Entrepreneur,* accessed September 2017.
38. Matt Rosenberg, "Number of McDonald's Restaurants Worldwide," ThoughtCo., March 3, 2017, https://www.thoughtco.com/number-of-mcdonalds-restaurants-worldwide-1435174.
39. Boyd Farrow, "Found in Translation," *Entrepreneur,* July-August 2017.
40. "About Us," Yogen Früz, accessed 3 November 3, 2017, www.yogenfruz.com/home/en/about-us.
41. "Co-operatives in Canada," Canadian Co-operative Association, accessed November 3, 2017, http://www.cooperativedifference.coop/co-operatives-in-canada/; "What is a Co-operative?" CoopZone Developers' Network Co-operative, accessed November 3, 2017, http://coopzone.coop/en/what; "The Co-Operative Advantage," CoopZone Developers' Network Co-operative, accessed November 3, 2017, http://www.coopzone.coop/about-co-operatives/co-operatives-in-canada/; "Co-Op Membership," Mountain Equipment Co-Operative, accessed November 3, 2017, http://www.mec.ca/AST/ContentPrimary/AboutMEC/AboutOurCoOp/CoOpFaqs.jsp; "The Gay Lea Story," Gay Lea Foods Co-operative Ltd., accessed November 3, 2017, http://www.gaylea.com/gay-lea-story/gay-lea-story/the-gay-lea-story; and Sara Mojtehedzadeh, "Ontario co-op movement could use a legislative leg-up," *The Toronto Star,* December 1, 2014, http://www.thestar.com/business/2014/12/01/ontario_coop_movement_could_use_a_legislative_legup.html#; and Blake Richards, "STATUS OF CO-OPERATIVES IN CANADA - Report of the Special Committee on Co-operatives," House of Commons, September 2012, http://www.parl.gc.ca/content/hoc/Committee/411/COOP/Reports/RP5706528/cooprp01/cooprp01-e.pdf?s1=pub&page=intro#ann.

Chapter 7

1. "A Definition of Entrepreneurship," Internet Center for Management and Business Administration, Inc., accessed November 5, 2017, www.quickmba.com/entre/definition/.
2. Ibid.
3. "The Co-Founder," Roots Canada, accessed November 5, 2017, http://about.roots.com/on/demandware.store/Sites-RootsCorporate-Site/default/Link-Page?cid=MSTR_CO_FOUNDERS; and Hollie Shaw, "Roots founders sell majority stake in iconic Canadian retailer to Searchlight Capital," *Financial Post,* October 26, 2015, http://business.financialpost.com/news/retail-marketing/roots-founders-sell-majority-stake-in-iconic-canadian-retailer-to-searchlight-capital.
4. Information accessed March 4, 2015, from the following company websites: http://www.leons.ca/shared/customerservice/aboutus.aspx; http://www.jimpattison.com/ and http://www.jimpattison.com/food/default.aspx; http://corp.canadiantire.ca/EN/AboutUs/Pages/default.aspx; http://www.mccain.com/GoodBusiness/Pages/History.aspx, http://www.mccain.com/GoodBusiness/business/Pages/default.aspx, and http://www.mccain.com/GoodBusiness/business/Documents/McCain%20Foods%20Fast%20Facts.pdf; http://www.irvingoil.com/who_we_are/our_leadership/ and http://www.irvingoil.com/who_we_are/; http://corporate.sobeys.com/at-a-glance/; https://www.jeancoutu.com/en/corpo/our-company/profile/; and Thomas Mulier and Tom Lavell, "Grocer Metro to buy pharmacy chain Jean Coutu in $4.5 billion deal," *Financial Post,* October 2, 2017, http://business.financialpost.com/news/retail-marketing/metro-inc-to-buy-jean-coutu-group-in-3-60-billion-deal.
5. "Who We Are?" Enactus Canada, accessed November 6, 2017, http://enactus.ca/who-we-are/our-mission/.
6. "Chronic Illness Led Emilie to Start Her Own Business," Female Entrepreneur Association, accessed September 2017; Jonathan Long, "60 Reasons Why Entrepreneurship is Amazing," *Entrepeneur,* accessed September 2017; Leigh Buchanan, "State of Entrepreneurship 2017: Growing Revenue, Growing Uncertainty," *Inc.,* December 2016/January 2017; Molly Petrilla, " 'Millennipreneurs' Are Starting More Businesses, Targeting Higher Profits," *Fortune,* February 20, 2016; and Steve Toback, "The Only Good Reason to Start a Business in 2016," *Fortune,* January 5, 2016.
7. "An Inside Look at How the W100 Innovate: No-stress nappies," PROFITGuide.com, accessed November 8, 2017, http://www.profitguide.com/manage-grow/innovation/w100-product-development-secrets-103044#621-an-inside-look-at-how-the-w100-innovate.
8. "Success Stories: Sweet Petite Confectioner," Futurpreneur Canada, 2017, http://www.futurpreneur.ca/en/success-stories/sweet-petite-confectioner/.
9. Ryan Westwood, "The Traits Entrepreneurs Need To Succeed," *Forbes,* January 9, 2017; "How Dreamers Become Doers," *Inc.,* September 2016; and Larry Kim, "Building a Business: 5 Things I Didn't Expect," *Inc.,* September 13, 2016.
10. "Dominion Lending Centres Chief Economist Comments on Bank of Canada Rate Hold," Dominion Lending Centres Inc., March 4, 2015, http://www.dominionlending.ca/about-dominion#mediakit; and "Startup Advice from Successful Entrepreneurs," PROFITguide.com, June 3, 2013, accessed July 3, 2018, https://www.canadianbusiness.com/innovation/startup-advice-from-successful-entrepreneurs/.
11. "Crazy Diamonds," *The Economist,* July 20, 2014.
12. "The World's Billionaires," *Forbes,* accessed September 2017.
13. Chuck Green, "When Entrepreneurs Don't Take No for an Answer," *The Wall Street Journal,* April 29, 2013; Lizette Chapman "Extreme Sports Get a Camera," *The Wall Street Journal,* January 20, 2013; Lisa Quast, "Turning Your Passion into Business," *Forbes,* September 2, 2013; and Gautam Gupta, "How to

Transform Your Passion into a Successful Business," *Entrepreneur,* November 20, 2013.
14. Susan Ward, "Statistics on Canadian Women in Business," The Balance, November 7, 2016, https://www.thebalance.com/statistics-on-canadian-women-in-business-2948029; "Key Small Business Statistics," Innovation, Science, and Economic Development Canada, vii, June 2016, https://www.ic.gc.ca/eic/site/061.nsf/vwapj/KSBS-PSRPE_June-Juin_2016_eng-V2.pdf/$file/KSBS-PSRPE_June-Juin_2016_eng-V2.pdf; and Josie L. Mousseau and Zoe Hawa, "Facts and Figures on Canadian Women Entrepreneurs," The Canadian Trade Commissioner Service, March 2014, http://www.owit-ottawa.ca/wp-content/uploads/2014/03/Facts-and-figures-on-women-entrepreneurs.pdf.
15. "Heather Reisman - Chief Executive Office of Indigo," Indigo Books & Music Inc., accessed 8 November 2017, https://www.chapters.indigo.ca/en-ca/our-company/management/; and "Annual Report 2017," Indigo Books & Music Inc., accessed 8 November 2017, https://static.indigoimages.ca/2017/corporate/Indigo-FY17-Q4-Report.pdf.
16. Ibid.
17. "Key Small Business Statistics," Industry Canada, June 2016, https://www.ic.gc.ca/eic/site/061.nsf/vwapj/KSBS-PSRPE_June-Juin_2016_eng-V2.pdf/$file/KSBS-PSRPE_June-Juin_2016_eng-V2.pdf.
18. Ibid., p. 2.
19. Hollie Shaw, "Nearly half of online purchases in Canada made at foreign retail sites: report," *Financial Post,* March 21, 2017, http://business.financialpost.com/news/retail-marketing/nearly-half-of-online-purchases-in-canada-made-at-foreign-retail-sites-report.
20. "Throw Things," www.throwthings.com, accessed March 2014.
21. 3M, www.3mc.om, accessed September 2017.
22. Howard Edward Haller, "Steve Jobs; The Ultimate Intrapreneur," Intrapreneurship Institute, accessed September 2017; Jules Schroeder, "Intrapreneurship: How Millennials Can Innovate and Influence Within Their Job," *Forbes,* March 27, 2017.
23. "About Canada Business Network," Government of Canada, March 6, 2015, http://www.canadabusiness.ca/eng/page/3711/; Humaira Irshad, "Business Incubation in Canada," Alberta Agriculture and Rural Development, June 14, 2014, http://www1.agric.gov.ab.ca/$Department/deptdocs.nsf/all/csi14921/$FILE/business-%20incubators%20.pdf; "Business Incubator FAQs," National Business Incubation Association, 2014, https://www.nbia.org/resource_library/faq/index.php#; National Business Association, downloaded March 2014, www.nbia.org; "Give It the Old College Try," *Inc.,* June 2013; Kristen Heredia, "DMZ Ranked Fifth Globally and First in Canada in University Business Incubator's Global Ranking, Digital Media Zone, June 24, 2014, http://digitalmediazone.ryerson.ca/dmznews/digital-media-zone-ryerson-university-ranked-fifth-globally-first-canada-university-business-incubators-global-ranking/; Alan Shepard, "University-based startup incubators to play a critical role in renaissance of Canadian city-states, *Financial Post,* November 13, 2013, http://business.financialpost.com/2013/11/13/university-based-startup-incubators-play-a-critical-role-in-renaissance-of-canadian-city-states/.
24. National Business Incubator Association, www.nbia.org, accessed September 2017.
25. "Key Small Business Statistics," Industry Canada, August 2013, https://www.ic.gc.ca/eic/site/061.nsf/vwapj/KSBS-PSRPE_August-Aout2013_eng.pdf/$FILE/KSBS-PSRPE_August-Aout2013_eng.pdf.
26. "Key Small Business Statistics," Innovation, Science and Economic Development Canada, June 2016, https://www.ic.gc.ca/eic/site/061.nsf/vwapj/KSBS-PSRPE_June-Juin_2016_eng-V2.pdf/$file/KSBS-PSRPE_June-Juin_2016_eng-V2.pdf.
27. CIBC, "Canada's young entrepreneurs increasingly drive export trade: CIBC Poll," CNW Group Ltd., October 5, 2017, http://www.newswire.ca/news-releases/canadas-young-entrepreneurs-increasingly-drive-export-trade-cibc-poll-649539863.html.
28. "Key Small Business Statistics," Industry Canada, August 2013, https://www.ic.gc.ca/eic/site/061.nsf/vwapj/KSBS-PSRPE_August-Aout2013_eng.pdf/$FILE/KSBS-PSRPE_August-Aout2013_eng.pdf.
29. Jonathan Chan, "Every Entrepreneur Will Fail--Here's How to Overcome Failure and Move On," *Foundr,* February 27, 2017; and Vivian Giang, "11 Famous Entrepreneurs Share How They Overcame Their Biggest Failures," *Fast Company,* May 1, 2014.
30. Neil Petch, "Five Signs You Are Headed for Startup Failure," *Entrepreneur,* January 15, 2017; and Jennifer Elsever, "The Unexpected Payoff of Failure," *Forbes,* April 1, 2016.
31. "Corporate Profile," BioSyent, 2015, http://www.biosyent.com/rx/corporate_profile/#.VPyukGB0wek; and "The PROFIT 500 Reveal Their Best Business Lessons," PROFITguide.com, June 12, 2014, http://www.profitguide.com/manage-grow/leadership/the-profit-500-reveal-their-best-business-lessons-66171.
32. "Company Profile," Running Room, 2015, http://www.runningroom.com/hm/inside.php?lang=1&id=3652; and "History," Running Room, 2012, www.runningroom.com/hm/inside.php?lang=1&id=3036.
33. "About Us - Our Story," The Running Room, accessed November 8, 2017, https://www.runningroom.com/hm/inside.php?id=3036.
34. Richard Blackwell, "Boomers will pass a small-business baton worth as much as $4-trillion," *The Globe and Mail,* November 10, 2015, https://beta.theglobeandmail.com/globe-investor/retirement/retire-planning/boomers-will-pass-a-small-business-baton-worth-as-much-as-4-trillion/article27196152/.
35. Jeff White, "How to Value a Business: The Ultimate Guide to Business Valuation," Fit Small Business, August 15, 2017; and Toni Ko, "How I Survived Selling My Company," *Inc.,* July-August 2016.
36. "Company Overview," CARA, accessed November 10, 2017, http://cara.investorroom.com/.
37. "Succession Planning," Family Business Institute, [2015?], http://www.familybusinessinstitute.com/index.php/Succession-Planning/; Dana Flavelle and Rita Trichur, "CanWest's newspaper empire for sale," *Toronto Star,* January 9, 2010, www.thestar.com/news/canada/article/748513-canwest-s-newspaper-empire-for-sale; "Leonard Asper stepping down from Canwest," *Financial Post,* March 4, 2010, www.financialpost.com/Leonard+Asper+stepping+down+from+Canwest/2640633/story.html; "Governance for the Family Business," KPMG in Canada, 2008, www.kpmg.ca/en/services/enterprise/issuesGrowthGovernance.html; and "Succession Planning for Family Business," BDO Canada LLP, [2012?], www.bdo.ca/library/publications/familybusiness/succession/planning1.cfm.
38. Heather Houle, "Matt & Nat," Prezi Inc., November 24, 2014, https://prezi.com/og1-0olednaw/matt-nat/.
39. "SME Profile: Canada Small Business Financing Program Borrowers (March 2016)," Government of Canada, accessed November 10, 2017, https://www.ic.gc.ca/eic/site/061.nsf/vwapj/SMEPCSBFPB-PPMEPFPME_2016-03_eng.pdf.
40. "FAQ: Difference between Angel Investors & Venture Capital," The Business Angel, 2017, http://www.thebusinessangel.org/difference-businessangel-venturecapital.html.
41. Ibid.
42. Ibid.; and "Venture Capitalists," Investopedia, accessed November 10, 2017, https://www.investopedia.com/terms/v/venture-philanthropy.asp.
43. Josh O'Kane, "New VC fund Disruption Ventures to focus entirely on firms led by women," *The Globe and Mail,* April 29, 2018, https://www.theglobeandmail.com/business/article-new-vc-fund-disruption-ventures-to-focus-entirely-on-firms-led-by/.
44. Jason Rowley, "Inside the Q2 2017 Global Venture Capital Ecosystem," *TechCrunch,* July 11, 2017; and Michael J. de la Merced, "After Belt Tightening, Venture Capitalists See More Promise in 2017," *The New York Times,* December 29, 2016.
45. "Definition of CROWDSOURCING," Merriam-Webster, Inc., 2015, http://www.merriam-webster.com/dictionary/crowdsourcing; "Crowdfunding," National Crowdfunding Association of Canada, 2015, http://ncfacanada.org/crowdfunding/; Tanya Prive, "What Is Crowdfunding And How Does It Benefit The Economy?"

Forbes, November 27, 2012, http://www.forbes.com/sites/tanyaprive/2012/11/27/what-is-crowdfunding-and-how-does-it-benefit-the-economy/; Mark Quinlan, "The pros and cons of crowd funding," CBC News, June 22, 2012, http://www.cbc.ca/news/canada/the-pros-and-cons-of-crowd-funding-1.1136449; Ruth Simon and Angus Loten, "Crowdfunding Gets State-Level Test Run," *The Wall Street Journal,* December 4, 2013; J. Craig Andersen, "Maine 'Crowd Investing' Bill Becomes Law," *Portland Press Herald,* March 6, 2014; and Nicole Fallon, "Equity Crowdfunding: 3 Facts Entrepreneurs Should Know," *Business News Daily,* March 21, 2014.

46. Geoffrey James, "How to Land a Career-Changing Job in Sales," *Inc.,* February 2, 2017; and Joe Robinson, "You're Going to Love Sales," *Entrepreneur,* February 2016.
47. Kate Ashford, "Why You Should Consider Working for A Small Company," *Forbes,* May 28, 2017; and Bill Saporito, "Do Workers Love Small Companies More?" *Inc.,* November 2015.
48. "The PROFIT 500 Reveal Their Best Business Lessons," PROFITguide.com, June 12, 2014, http://www.profitguide.com/manage-grow/leadership/the-profit-500-reveal-their-best-business-lessons-66171.
49. John Prusak, "FXR Racing's Milt Reimer Recognized as Powersports Industry Leader," Snow Goer, May 25, 2016, http://snowgoer.com/latest-news/fxr-racings-milt-reimer-recognized-as-powersports-industry-leader/; and John Lorinc, "A Global Business Built on Lateral Thinking," PROFITguide.com, August 5, 2014, http://www.profitguide.com/manage-grow/international-trade/a-global-business-built-on-lateral-thinking-68047.

Chapter 8

1. Christian Stadler and Davis Dyer, "Why Good Leaders Don't Need Charisma," *Sloan Management Review,* Spring 2013.
2. Rachel Feintzeig, "So Busy at Work, No Time to Do the Job," *The Wall Street Journal,* June 28, 2016; Michael Mankins, "How to Manage a Team of All-Stars," *Harvard Business Review,* June 6, 2017.
3. "The 23 Female CEOs Running Fortune 500 Companies," *San Jose Mercury News,* December 10, 2013.
4. David Malpass, "Five Big Steps Toward Global Growth," *Forbes,* February 10, 2014.
5. Katherine Duncan, "Command Performance," *Entrepreneur,* March 2013.
6. Steven Overly, "Going Green, Bit by Bit," *The Washington Post,* April 22, 2013.
7. Stephanie Marton, "The mysterious success of female-led firms," February 20, 2013, *Forbes,* http://www.forbes.com/sites/85broads/2013/02/20/the-mysterious-success-of-female-led-firms/.
8. Daniel Goleman, "The Focused Leader," *Harvard Business Review,* December 2013.
9. Lynda Gratton, "Rethinking the Manager's Role," *Sloan Management Review,* Fall, 2016; Brian Tracey, "Learning Leadership: Eight Key Skills that Make an Effective Manager," *Forbes,* March 13, 2017.
10. Marcus Buckingham, "What Great Managers Do," *Harvard Business Review,* March 2005, 70–79.
11. Elizabeth Fenner, "Happiness," *Fortune,* February 21, 2005, 36.
12. Kenneth R. Brousseau, Michael J. Driver, Gary Hourihon, and Rikard Larsson, "The Seasoned Executive's Decision-Making Style," *Harvard Business Review,* February 2006, 111–121.
13. Leigh Buchanan, "The Essential Management Book You're Not Reading," *Inc.,* December 2013–January 2014.
14. Lisa Baertlein, "Whole Foods' New, Cheaper Chain Launches Today," *Fortune,* May 25, 2016; Andrew Khouri, "Whole Foods to Open Lower-Priced 365 Store in Santa Monica," *Times,* May 16, 2017.
15. Roger L. Martin, "Rethinking the Decision Factory," *Harvard Business Review,* October 2013.
16. "What Is the Difference Between Management and Leadership?" *The Wall Street Journal,* accessed March 2014.
17. Interesting contrasts among purpose, mission, and vision can be found in: John Mackey and Raj Sisodia, *Conscious Capitalism* (Boston, MA: Harvard Business Review Press, 2013).
18. Eric Paley, "Go Beyond Visionary; Be a Leader," *Inc.,* February 2014.
19. "SWOT Analysis," www.MindTools.com, accessed September 2016.
20. Roger L. Martin, "The Big Lie of Strategic Planning," *Harvard Business Review,* February 2014.
21. Giovanni Gavetti and Jan W. Rivkin, "How Strategists Really Think," *Harvard Business Review,* April 2005, 54–63.
22. Greg Bensinger, "Amazon Plans to Compete with Paypal and Square in Retail Stores," *The Wall Street Journal,* January 30, 2014.
23. Teppo Felin, "When Strategy Walks Out the Door," *Sloan Management Review,* Fall, 2016: Terry Flores, "Disney-Pixar's John Lasseter to be Honored by Walt Disney Family Museum," *Variety,* August 16, 2017.
24. Anne Nicoll, "Beyond SARS: Developing Health Related Emergency Policies," Benefits and Pensions Online, June 2003, http://www.bpmmagazine.com/02_archives/2003/june/beyond_sars.html; "The New Contingency Plan—Health-Related Emergencies," May 27, 2003, www.morneausobeco.com/PDF/SARSCommuniqué_E.pdf
25. Gregory J. Millman and Samuel Rubenfeld, "For Corporate America, Risk Is Big Business," *The Wall Street Journal,* January 16, 2014.
26. Miriam Gottfried, "This Eagle Must Hunt Elsewhere," *The Wall Street Journal,* January 24, 2014.
27. Paul Rogers and Marcia Blenko, "Who Has the D?" *Harvard Business Review,* January 2006, 53–61.
28. Ram Charan, "The Secrets of Great CEO Selection," *Harvard Business Review,* December 2016; Mark Murphy, "CEOs Embarking on Change Management Know That Your Employees Don't Like Taking Risks," *Forbes,* March 26, 2017.
29. "Trends in Airline Governance, Management Structures and Mandates," June 14, 2011, www.iaaia.com/PDF/ent_trends_in_airline_governance_at_14-06-11.pdf.
30. Julia Hunter, "Loblaw Announces Leaner Head Office Structure," Loblaw Companies Limited, http://www.loblaw.ca/English/Media-Centre/news-releases/news-release-details/2012/Loblaw-Announces-Leaner-Head-Office-Structure1131481/default.aspx, accessed May 3, 2015; Sunny Freeman, "Loblaw Profits Jump 20 Per Cent But Still Hit by Infrastructure Overhaul," November 16, 2011, www.canadianbusiness.com/article/57306-loblaw-profits-jump-20-per-cent-but-still-hit-by-infrastructure-overhaul.
31. Andreas Priestland and Robert Hanig, "Developing First-Level Leaders," *Harvard Business Review,* June 2005, 113–120.
32. Robert Kutz, "Skills of an Effective Administrator," *Harvard Business Review,* Sept–Oct 1974, 90–101.
33. Sydney Finklestein, "Why Great Leaders Want Their Superstars to Leave," *The Wall Street Journal,* October 3, 2017; Mike Kappel, "Is it Really that Hard to Find Good Employees?" *Entrepreneur,* May 12, 2017.
34. "The 10 Best Companies to Work For in 2014," www.forbes.com, accessed March 2014.
35. Adam Bornstein and Jordan Bornstein, "What Makes a Great Leader?" *Entrepreneur,* March, 2016; Tony Schwartz, "How to Become a More Well-Rounded Leader," *Harvard Business Review,* July 21, 2017.
36. Amy C. Cooper, "Unite and Conquer," *Entrepreneur,* March 2013.
37. Kerry Dolan, "Billionaires, Led by Zuckerberg, Dig a Bit Deeper with 10 Biggest Charitable Gifts of 2013," www.forbes.com, 1 January 2014
38. Dorrie Clark, "How the Best Leaders Embrace Change," www.forbes.com, November 5, 2013
39. Barry Glassman, "In Business, Transparency Wins," *Forbes,* January 15, 2014.
40. Bertrand Marotte, "Management Guru Assails Excessive CEO Salaries," *The Globe and Mail,* May 8, 2003, B7.
41. Jim Pawlak, "Treating Employees as Assets, Not Expenses Boosts Profits," *Hartford Business Journal,* February 24, 2014.

42. Laura Bogomolny, "Most Innovative Exec/Canadian Tire—Janice Wismer," *Canadian Business,* 2004, www.canadianbusiness.com/allstars/best_innovative_exec.html.

Chapter 9

1. John Jullens, "How Emerging Giants Can Take On the World," *Harvard Business Review,* December 2013.
2. Jonathan House and Kathleen Madigan, "U.S. Factories Bounce Back in February," *The Wall Street Journal,* March 2, 2014.
3. Ann Hadley, "What Not to Do," *Entrepreneur,* September 2013.
4. Amol Sharma, Shalini Ramachandran, and Don Clark, "Amazon Joins the TV Crush," *The Wall Street Journal,* January 22, 2014.
5. Natalie Kaddas, "Being Flexible," www.huffingtonpost.com, November 23, 2013
6. Mary Jordan, "The Promise of a 'Made in America' Era," *The Washington Post,* May 1, 2013.
7. Fredrik Eliasson, "Emphasizing the Management in 'Change Management,'" *The Wall Street Journal,* January 24, 2014.
8. John Mackey and Raj Sisodia, *Conscious Capitalism* (Boston, MA: Harvard Business Review Press, 2013).
9. Austen Carr, David Lidsky, J.J. McCorvey, Harry McCraken and Harry Wilson, "Search for the Future," *Fast Company,* April 2016; Mark Bergen, "Alphabet" *Bloomberg,* September 1, 2017.
10. Jeff Bennett and John Kell, "GM Restores Annual Dividend as Sales Shine," *The Wall Street Journal,* January 15, 2014.
11. Rashik Parmar, Ian Mackenzie, David Cohn, and David Gann, "The New Patterns of Innovation," *Harvard Business Review,* January–February 2014.
12. Raymond Fisman and Tim Sullivan, "The Unsung Beauty of Bureaucracy," *The Wall Street Journal,* May16–17, 2014.
13. Sydney Hershman, "Nordstrom is Changing Its Popular Return Policy," *Essence,* February 1, 2017.
14. Henry Mintzberg and James Brian Quinn, *The Strategy Process: Concepts and Contexts* (New Jersey: Prentice Hall Inc., 1992).
15. Henry Mintzberg, *Managers not MBAs* (San Francisco: BerrettKoehler Publishers, 2004).
16. Nathaniel Smithson, "Burger King's Organizational Structure Analysis," Panmore Institute, February 6, 2017.
17. mcdonalds.com, accessed September 2017.
18. Magna International, "2014 Annual Report to Shareholders," 2014, http://www.magna.com/investors/financial-reports-public-filings.
19. Gary L. Neilson and Julie Wulf, "How Many Direct Reports?" *Harvard Business Review,* April 2012.
20. David Gann, Ammon Salter, Mark Dodgson and Nelson Phillips, "Inside the World of the Project Baron," *Sloan Management Review,* Spring 2012.
21. Jeff Weiss and Jonathan Hughes, "Want Collaboration?" *Harvard Business Review,* March 2005, 93–101.
22. Bill Fischer and Andy Boynton, "Virtuoso Teams," *Harvard Business Review,* July–August 2005, 117–21.
23. Braden Kowitz, "Why You Should Listen to the Customer," *The Wall Street Journal,* February 19, 2014.
24. Mary C. Lacity and Leslie P. Willcocks, "Outsourcing Business Processes for Innovation," *Sloan Management Review,* Spring 2013.
25. Rita Gunther McGrath, "Is Your Company Ready to Operate as a Market?" *Sloan Management Review,* Fall 2016; Josh Bersin, Tiffany McDowell, Amir Rahnema, Yves Van Durme, "The Organization of the Future: Arriving Now," *Deloitte University Press,* February 28, 2017.
26. David Raths, "KM infrastructure for the life sciences virtual organization," KKM World, March 1, 2015, http://www.kmworld.com/Articles/Editorial/Features/KM-infrastructure-for-the-life-sciences-virtual-organization-102166.aspx.
27. Suncor, Report on Sustainability 2014, http://sustainability.suncor.com/2014/en/goals/environment-and-social-progress-reports.aspx, accessed May 9, 2015.
28. Kasia Klimasinska, "Obama Budget Predicts Strongest U.S. Growth since 2005," *Bloomberg BusinessWeek,* March 4, 2014.
29. Dennis Green, "Trump's Policies Have Nike Facing One of Its Biggest Threats in History," *Business Insider,* January 26, 2017.
30. "Outsourcing bank jobs is common practice, say employees," CBC News, April 9, 2013, http://www.cbc.ca/news/canada/outsourcing-bank-jobs-is-common-practice-say-employees-1.1333814.
31. Robert I. Sutton and Huggy Rao, "Before You Make Any Changes, Ask These Questions," *Bloomberg BusinessWeek,* March 4, 2014.
32. Angela Charlton and Tom Krishner, "GM Sheds Money Drain, Gains Cash With Sale of European Unit," KWWL News, March 6, 2017
33. "How much did the GM Bailout Cost Taxpayers?" *Bloomberg,* September 20, 2016; Bill Vlasic & Neil E. Bodette, "Shell of Old GM Surfaces in Court Fight of Ignition Flaw," *The New York Times,* August 17, 2017; "Ottawa doesn't regret GM bailout," April 21, 2010, www.cbc.ca/news/canada/windsor/story/2010/04/21/wdr-detroit-gm-government-loans-100421.html.
34. Why did Target fail in Canada? It wasn't the U.S. Target," CBC News, January 15, 2015, http://www.cbc.ca/news/canada/manitoba/why-did-target-fail-in-canada-it-wasn-t-the-u-s-target-1.2901676.
35. Darah Hansen, "How to fix Target Canada's problems in six easy steps," *Canadian Business,* July 28, 2014, http://www.canadianbusiness.com/companies-and-industries/how-to-fix-target-canada/.
36. Dan Lyons, "How to Master Change," *Fortune,* December 1, 2016; Neale Godfrey, "Change or Be Left Behind: The Company of the Future," *Forbes,* April 9, 2017.
37. "About," Novocare Rehabilitation, accessed May 9, 2015, http://www.novacare.com/about/; David Ernst and James Bamford, "Your Alliances Are Too Stable," *Harvard Business Review,* June 2005, 133–141.
38. Michael E. Raynor and Mumtaz Ahmed, "Three Rules for Making a Company Truly Great," *Harvard Business Review,* April 2013.
39. Deborah Aarts, "Innovate at any size: we fetishize tiny startups, but lots of companies get big and keep their disruptive streak intact," *Canadian Business,* October 2014, 38.
40. Tracey Hilderley, "Keeping things comfortable for over 100 years," *Business in Focus,* May 9, 2014, http://www.businessinfocusmagazine.com/2012/11/keeping-things-comfortable-for-over-100-years/.
41. Henry Mintzberg and James Brian Quinn, *The Strategy Process: Concepts and Contexts* (New Jersey: Prentice Hall Inc., 1992).
42. www.td.com/careers
43. Alex (Sandy) Pentland, "The New Science of Building Great Teams," *Harvard Business Review,* April 2012.
44. Jay Rao and Joseph Weintraub, "How Innovative Is Your Company's Culture?" *Sloan Management Review,* Spring 2013.

Chapter 10

1. "*Innovation in Canada,*" Sackville: Centre for Canadian Studies at Mount Allison University, www.mta.ca/faculty/arts/canadian_studies/english/about/innovation/.
2. Innovation Analysis Bulletin, Vol. 6, No. 1, March 2004, www.statcan.gc.ca/pub/88-003-x/88-003-x2004001-eng.pdf.
3. "Canada's top 100 corporate R&D spenders," Canada's Innovation Leaders, Research Infosource Inc., November 17, 2016, https://researchinfosource.com/pdf/CIL%20Top%20100%20R%20and%20D%20Analysis.pdf.
4. Ibid.
5. Ibid.
6. "Spending on research and development, 2016," June 23, 2017, http://www.statcan.gc.ca/daily-quotidien/170623/dq170623c-eng.pdf.
7. "Canadian Manufacturing Today: Cautiously Optimistic," Canadian Manufacturers & Exporters, 2014, http://www.cme-mec.ca/_uploads/_media/51wjbzblm.pdf.
8. Andrea Petersen, "Checking In? Hidden Ways Hotels Court Guests Faster," *The Wall Street Journal,* April 12, 2012.
9. Julie Weed, "Hoteliers Comb the Ranks of Tech Workers to Gain an Edge," *The New York Times,* February 13, 2017.

10. Matthew Kronsberg, "Are High-Tech Hotels Alluring – or Alienating?" *The Wall Street Journal*, April 28, 2016.
11. Abha Bhattarai, "Hilton Tests Guest-Greeting Robots and Noise-Canceling Rooms," *The Washington Post*, January 15, 2016.
12. "The Method – before and after examples," Information Mapping Canada, 2014, accessed May 10, 2015, http://www.informationmapping.com/ca/the-method-ca/before-a-after-examples.
13. Eric Atkins, "Dr. Oetker's new pizza plant gives Ontario manufacturing a boost," *The Globe and Mail*, May 20, 2014, http://www.theglobeandmail.com/report-on-business/dr-oetker-builds-ontario-plant/article18748722/.
14. Dave Hall, "Kellogg, Heinz plant closures part of trend," *The Windsor Star*, December 10, 2013, http://blogs.windsorstar.com/business/kellogg-heinz-plant-closures-part-of-a-trend.
15. Dave Coles, "Sending jobs offshore hurts Canadian workers," *Times Colonist*, April 11, 2013, http://www.timescolonist.com/opinion/op-ed/comment-sending-jobs-offshore-hurts-canadian-workers-1.108110.
16. "Key Findings for the State of the Industry Survey 2014," International Association of Outsourcing Professionals, accessed July 9, 2018, www.iaop.org.
17. Diane Peters, "When does it pay to outsource your production?" *The Globe and Mail*, January 22, 2015, http://www.theglobeandmail.com/report-on-business/small-business/sb-growth/going-global/when-does-it-pay-to-outsource-your-production/article22565115/.
18. Amanda Lang, "Let's worry about skills, not outsourcing," *The Globe and Mail*, April 12, 2013, http://www.theglobeandmail.com/globe-debate/lets-worry-about-skills-not-outsourcing/article11084876/.
19. CORE Centre for Outsourcing Research and Education, www.core-outsourcing.org.
20. Danielle Goldfarb, "How Canada wins from global services outsourcing," C.D. Howe Institute, November 2004, accessed May 12, 2015, http://www.cdhowe.org/pdf/commentary_206.pdf.
21. John Greenough, "How the Internet of Things is revolutionizing manufacturing," *Business Insider*, October 12, 2016.
22. Juan Martinez and Molly K McLaughlin, "The Best Videoconferencing Software of 2016," *PC Magazine*, August 1, 2016.
23. Janet Bealer Rodie, "Brückner, M-Tec Partner to Provide Carpet Solutions," *Textile World*, May 1, 2005.
24. Tony Van Alphen, "CAW head Ken Lewenza resigns before historic union merger," *Toronto Star*, July 7, 2013, http://www.thestar.com/news/canada/2013/07/07/caw_head_ken_ lewenza_resigns_before_historic_union_merger.html.
25. "Royal Canadian Mint," Cognos, September 2003, www.cognos.com/products/applications/success.html
26. Ibid.
27. Gary Marion, "Do I Need fewer Suppliers or Just more of Them?" *The Balance*, November 18, 2016.
28. Daren Fonda, "Why the Most Profitable Cars Made in the U.S.A. are Japanese and German," *Time*, June 2003, A9–A13.
29. James Mirtle, "Maple Leafs bet big on Big Data with analytics partnership," *The Globe and Mail*, October 15, 2014, http://www.theglobeandmail.com/sports/hockey/maple-leafs-bet-big-on-big-data-with-analytics-partnership/article21119849/.
30. Davis Balestracci, "When Processes Moonlight as Trends," *Quality Digest*, June 2005, 18.
31. "More about NQI," National Quality Institute, 2011, www.nqi.ca; "Canada Awards for Excellence," National Quality Institute, 2011, www.nqi.ca; and "2016 Canada Awards for Excellence Recipients," Excellence Canada, accessed August 27, 2017, http://excellence.ca/en/awards/2016-cae-recipients/.
32. International Organization for Standardization, www.iso.org, accessed March 2017.
33. "Quality Management - Quality of an Organization - Guidance to Achieve Sustained Success," International Organization for Standardization, accessed August 1, 2018, https://www.iso.org/standard/70397.html.
34. "ISO Standards," International Organization for Standardization, https://www.iso.org/standards.html.
35. "Quality Policy," SNC-Lavalin Group Inc., www.snclavalin.com/en/6_0/6_10.aspx
36. "Extensive debate improves consensus on future ISO 26000 standard on social responsibility," International Organization for Standardization, June 4, 2009, www.iso.org/iso/pressrelease.htm?refid=Ref1229.
37. William McDonough and Michael Baungart, *Cradle to Cradle: Remaking the way we make things*, (New York: North Point Press, 2002).
38. Matthew Wheeland, "Design and performance reconsidered," *GreenBiz*, June 11, 2008, http://www.greenbiz.com/news/2008/06/11/design-and-performance-reconsidered.
39. "2015 Nike Free Collection: Five reasons less is more," Nike, http://news.nike.com/news/2015-nike-free-collection, accessed March 23, 2015.
40. "The future: closed-loop business model," Corporate Responsibility Report, FY2007-FY2009 Nike Inc. http://www.nikebiz.com/crreport/content/strategy/2-1-1-corporate-responsibility-strategy-overview.php?cat=cr-strategy, accessed May 17, 2015.
41. Robert Bowman, "The sign in the elevator banks at Coca-Cola Refreshments reads: 'There is a person at the end of our supply chain.' Well, that's a start," Supply Chain Brain, March 2, 2015, http://www.supplychainbrain.com/content/nc/general-scm/business-strategy-alignment/single-article-page/article/demand-planning-at-coca-cola-whats-the-secret-formula/.
42. Alicia Fiorletta, "Source for Sports streamlines supply chain with Askuity," Retail Touch Points, June 25, 2014, http://www.retailtouchpoints.com/features/retail-success-stories/source-forsports-streamlines-supply-chain-with-askuity; "Source for Sports – We Know Our Stuff," Source for Sports, 2015, accessed May 12, 2015 http://www.sourceforsports.com/AboutUs.aspx.
43. "Kodiak to close Terra Nova Shoes, move jobs to Ontario," CBC News, July 8, 2014, accessed July 9, 2018, https://www.cbc.ca/news/canada/newfoundland-labrador/kodiak-to-close-terra-nova-shoes-move-jobs-to-ontario-1.2699713.
44. "Three Cambridge Firms get $2 million in Provincial Funding," *Waterloo Region Record*, November 17, 2015.
45. Ann C. Logue, "Trimming the Fat," *Entrepreneur*, February 2014.
46. Steve Blank, "'Lean' Is Shaking Up the Entrepreneurial Landscape," *Harvard Business Review*, July–August 2013.
47. Dennis Sowards, "Lean Construction," *Quality Digest*, November 2007.
48. Max Berlinger, "A Custom Shirt is No Longer So Hard to Find," *The New York Times*, December 7, 2016.
49. Sandra Zaragoza, "Boston Duo Starts Customized Guitar Shop in Austin," *Austin Business Journal*, July 23, 2012; and Chris Raymond, "Design Your Own Guitar—This Startup Will Build It," *Popular Mechanics*, February 7, 2014.
50. Binyamin Applebaum, "Why Are Politicians So Obsessed with Manufacturing?" *The New York Times Magazine*, October 4, 2016, https://www.nytimes.com/2016/10/09/magazine/why-are-politicians-so-obsessed-with-manufacturing.html.
51. Emily Price, "You Rang? I Called the Hotel Room Service - And Got a Robot," *Fast Company*, February 27, 2017.
52. Nathaniel Popper, "The Robots Are Coming for Wall Street," *The New York Times*, February 25, 2016.
53. Jim Rock, "How Robots Will Reshape the U.S. Economy," TechCrunch, March 21, 2016.
54. David. Z. Morris, "iPhone Manufacturer FoxConn Aims for Full Automation of Chinese Factories," *Fortune*, December 31, 2016.
55. Tavia Grant, "Rise of machines: robots poised to transform global manufacturing," *The Globe and Mail*, February 10, 2015, http://www.theglobeandmail.com/report-on-business/rise-of-the-machines-robots-poised-to-transform-global-manufacturing/article22884032/.
56. Robb M. Stewart, "The Construction Business Goes Digital," *The Wall Street Journal*, September 18, 2016.
57. Ted Mann, "3-D Printing Expands to Metals, Showing Industrial Promise," *The Wall Street Journal*, November 11, 2016.

Chapter 11

1. Gary J. Bissonette, *Business,* 1st ed. (Toronto: McGraw-Hill Ryerson, 2012), 441.
2. Gary Johns and Alan M. Saks, *Organizational Behaviour,* 8th ed. (Toronto: Pearson Canada, 2011), 146.
3. Jack Altman, "How Much Does Employee Turnover Really Cost?" *Huffington Post,* January 18, 2017; and Julie Kantor, "High Turnover Costs Way More Than You Think," *Huffington Post,* February 11, 2016.
4. Marla Tabaka, "Want Smart, Happy, Loyal Employees? Give Them What They Crave," *Inc.,* October 11, 2016; Ryan Scott, "Employee Engagement Vs. Employee Experience," *Forbes,* May 4, 2017.
5. "Best Places to Work in 2017," *Forbes,* December 7, 2016; "The 100 Best Companies to Work for 2017," *Fortune,* March 9, 2017.
6. "Beyond the Cash Bonus," *Inc.,* November 2016; Tomas Chamorro-Premuzic and Lewis Garrad, "If You Want to Motivate Employees, Stop Trusting Your Instincts," *Harvard Business Review,* February 8, 2017.
7. "Canada's 100 Best Small & Medium Employers - DAC Group values 'geeks with personalities'," *The Globe and Mail* and Mediacorp Canada Inc., March 2015, p. 24.
8. Timothy T. Baldwin, William H. Bommer, and Robert S. Rubin, *Managing Organizational Behavior, What Great Managers Know and Do,* 2nd ed. (New York: McGraw-Hill Irwin, 2013), 198.
9. Ibid., 197.
10. Jay Velury, "Empowerment to the People," *Industrial Engineer,* May 1, 2005.
11. Ben Ames, "Technology Keeps UPS Drivers on Pace," *DC Velocity,* September 30, 2016; Matt McFarland, "UPS Is Training Drivers with Virtual Reality," *CNN,* August 15, 2017.
12. Peter High, "Standard International's CEO on the Future of Hospitality," *Forbes,* October 31, 2016; Joie de Vivre Hotels, accessed September 2017.
13. Victor Lipman, "Want to Develop Your Employees? A Simple Management Tool Can Help," *Forbes,* March 9, 2017.
14. "Canada's Top Employers (2018): Selection Process," *The Globe and Mail,* November 7, 2017, http://www.canadastop100.com/national/.
15. Ibid., 17.
16. Travis Bradberry, "Bad Manager Mistakes That Make Good People Quit," LinkedIn, January 30, 2017.
17. Erin Reid and Lakshmi Ramarajan, "Managing the High-Intensity Workplace," *Harvard Business Review,* June 2016; Dick Grote, "3 Popular Goal-Setting Techniques Managers Should Avoid," *Harvard Business Review,* January 2, 2017.
18. Kate Rockwood, "Want to Make Your Team Feel Great? Shower Them with Appreciation," *Inc.,* June 2016; John Rampton, "The Neuroscience of Motivation," *Mashable,* June 27, 2017.
19. David Nadler and Edward Lawler, "Motivation—a Diagnostic Approach," *Perspectives on Behavior in Organizations* (New York: McGraw-Hill, 1977).
20. David Nicklaus, "What Price Awards?" *St. Louis Post-Dispatch,* April 19, 2013.
21. Jae Yang and Janet Loehrke, "Lake Wobegon Effect," *USA Today,* May 12, 2016; Mark Murphy, "The Dunning-Kruger Effect Shows Why Some People Think They're Great Even When Their Work Is Terrible," *Forbes,* January 24, 2017.
22. Marcel Schwantes, "4 Communication Habits of Mentally Strong Leaders," *Inc.,* January 20, 2017.
23. Stephanie Vozza, "Surprising Work Tips," *Fast Company,* April 2016; Chris Dessi, "4 Powerful Ways to Be Happy with Your Career," *Inc.,* December 27, 2016; Miranda Brookins, "The Advantages & Disadvantages of Job Enrichment," *Houston Chronicle,* accessed September 2017.
24. Gary Johns and Alan M. Saks, *Organizational Behaviour,* 8th edition (Toronto: Pearson Canada, 2011), 194.
25. Baldwin, Bommer, and Rubin, *Managing Organizational Behavior, What Great Managers Know and Do,* 212.
26. Sheila Marikar, "Giving Employees the Tools to Excel Helps This Company Clean Up," *Inc.,* June 2016; John Brandon, "7 Ways to Motivate Your Team (Other Than Paying Them More)," *Inc.,* March 23, 2017.
27. Murray Newlands, "5 Proven Ways to Improve Your Company's Communication," *Forbes,* January 26, 2016; AJ Agrawal, "How to Perfect Communication in Your Company," *Inc.,* January 31, 2016; Catherine Ulrich, "The Easy Secret to Getting the Most Out of Your Team," *Fortune,* October 14, 2016; Tom Salonek, "5 Tips for More-Effective Business Communication," *The Business Journals,* April 7, 2017.
28. Richard Johnson, "Why Ford Stands By Its 'One Ford' Philosophy," *Automotive News,* March 7, 2017; Kenny Kline, "How to Communicate with Your Team More Effectively," *Inc.,* March 21, 2017.
29. Travis Bradberry, "9 Things That Make Good Employees Quit," *Huffington Post,* January 2, 2016; Shannon Gausepohl, "Why Your Best Employees Are Quitting (and 3 Ways to Keep Them)," *Business News Daily,* January 26, 2017.
30. Minda Zetlin, "Time Off Well Spent," *Inc.,* June 2016; Lolly Daskal, "9 Simple Ways You Can Make Your Employees Happy," *Inc.,* March 3, 2017; Jeff Haden, "To Be an Exceptional Boss, Here Are 11 Things You Must Give Your Employees," *Inc.,* March 27, 2017.
31. Tanya Hall, "10 Cheap and Simple Steps to Happy Employees," *Inc.,* January 20, 2017; Karen Higginbottom, "Employee Appreciation Pays Off," *Forbes,* March 3, 2017.
32. Globoforce, www.globoforce.com, accessed September 2017.
33. "Michael Adams," Environics Research Group, 2015, http://www.environics.ca/michael-adams; "Profile - David K. Foot," Footwork Consulting Inc., [n.d.], http://www.footwork.com/profile.asp; Colonel James C. Taylor, "Whither march the cohorts: The validity of generation theory as a determinant of the sociocultural values of Canadian Forces personnel," Canadian Forces College, June 2008, http://www.cfc.forces.gc.ca/259/281/280/taylor.pdf; John Markert, "Demographics of Age: Generational and Cohort Confusion," *Journal of Current Issues and Research in Advertising,* 26, no. 2 (Fall 2004), 1; and Dan Schawbel, "Employers, prepare to meet Gen Z," *The Globe and Mail,* September 2, 2014, http://www.theglobeandmail.com/report-on-business/careers/leadership-lab/employers-prepare-to-meet-gen-z/article20280755/.
34. Dan Schawbel, "Employers, prepare to meet Gen Z," *The Globe and Mail,* September 2, 2014.
35. "Latchkey child," Merriam-Webster, Inc., 2015, http://www.merriam-webster.com/dictionary/latchkey%20child.
36. Lisa Rochon, "Why the cities of the future belong to the millennial generation," *The Globe and Mail,* April 15, 2015, http://www.theglobeandmail.com/arts/why-the-cities-of-the-future-belong-to-the-millennial-generation/article11154532/; and Ray Williams, "Like it or not, Millennials will change the workplace," *Financial Post,* September 16, 2013, http://business.financialpost.com/2013/09/16/like-it-or-not-millennials-will-change-the-workplace/.
37. Anne Kingston, "Get ready for Generation Z," *Maclean's,* July 15, 2014, http://www.macleans.ca/society/life/get-ready-for-generation-z/.
38. Ibid.
39. Geoff Colvin, "Millennials Are Not Monolithic," *Fortune,* November 2016; Ryan Jenkins, "Why Millennials Will Matter More in 2017," *Inc.,* January 3, 2017.
40. Elizabeth Dukes, "3 Things Your Workplace Does That Millennials Hate," *Inc.,* March 7, 2017; Ayse Birsel, "What Millennials Want in a Workplace (Spoiler Alert: A Kitchen Is Involved)," *Inc.,* March 23, 2017; Rich Bellis, "Four Workplace Stereotypes Millennials (Like Me) Thoroughly Resent)," *Fast Company,* March 24, 2017.
41. Dan Schawbel, "Employers, prepare to meet Gen Z," *The Globe and Mail,* September 2, 2014, updated May 12, 2018, accessed July 11, 2018, https://www.theglobeandmail.com/report-on-business/careers/leadership-lab/employers-prepare-to-meet-gen-z/article20280755/.
42. Ryan Inzana, "Your New Office BFFs," *Money,* May 2013.
43. Lindsay Gellman, "Bosses Try to Decode Millennials," *The Wall Street Journal,* May 18, 2016; Shen Lu, "When Millennials Are the Boss," *CNN,* August 11, 2017.

44. Anne Kingston, "Get ready for Generation Z," Maclean's, July 15, 2014, https://www.macleans.ca/society/life/get-ready-for-generation-z/.
45. Dan Schawbel, "Employers, prepare to meet Gen Z."
46. Ibid.
47. Marina Khidekel, "The Misery of Mentoring Millennials," *Bloomberg BusinessWeek,* March 18–24, 2013.
48. Lisa Rabasco Roepe, "5 Ways Gen Z Can Ask Their Manager for Help with Communication Skills," *Forbes,* March 28, 2017; Deep Patel, "10 Ways to Prepare for Gen Z in the Workplace," *Forbes,* March 29, 2017.
49. Scott Thompson, "Challenges of Humanistic Management," *Houston Chronicle,* accessed May 13, 2018, http://smallbusiness.chron.com/challenges-humanistic-management-64545.html.

Chapter 12

1. Eric Garton, "HR's Vital Role in How Employees Spend Their Time, Talent, and Energy," *Harvard Business Review,* January 30, 2017.
2. Karen Higgenbottom, "Top Challenges Facing HR Directors of Global Firms in 2017," *Forbes,* December 28, 2016; Victoria Stilwell and Sarah McGregor, "On-Call, Temp Jobs Are the New Normal," *St. Louis Post-Dispatch,* June 3, 2016; Karsten Strauss, "10 Great 'Gig Economy' Jobs in 2017," *Forbes,* March 13, 2017.
3. "20th CEO Survey: 20 years inside the mind of the CEO . . . What's next?" PWC, 2017, https://www.pwc.com/gx/en/ceo-survey/2017/pwc-ceo-20th-survey-report-2017.pdf.
4. Peter Louch, "Workforce Planning Is Essential to High-Performing Organizations," *Society for Human Resource Planning,* accessed September 2017.
5. "Strategic Planning: How Can a Skills Inventory Be Used for Strategic HR Planning?" *Society for Human Resource Management,* accessed September 2017.
6. "The Secrets of Successful, Fast-Growing Businesses Today—and Plans for Tomorrow," *Inc.,* September 2016; Ellen Huet and Gerrit De Vynck, "America's Got No Talent," *Bloomberg Businessweek,* November 21, 2016; Forbes Human Resources Council, "Six Key Factors That Will Help You Retain Top Talent," *Forbes,* March 9, 2017.
7. Geoff Colvin, "Developing an Internal Market for Talent," *Fortune,* March 1, 2016; "The Surprising Benefits of Hiring Internally," *TRC Staffing Services,"* March 28, 2017.
8. Jeff Bercovici, "To Keep the Buzz Going, Be Sure to Hire People Who Fit In," *Inc.,* June 2016; Áine Cain, "An Ex-Apple Recruiter Says There's an Unexpected Dark Side to Hiring for 'Culture Fit'," *Business Insider,* September 1, 2017.
9. "Canada's 100 Best Small & Medium Employers—Richter LLP," *The Globe and Mail* and Mediacorp Canada Inc., March 2015, 7.
10. "Insider's Guide to Getting a Job in the Canadian Government," Government of Canada, 2018, https://canadiangovernmentjobs.ca/the-hiring-process-in-the-government-of-canada/.
11. "Canada's 100 Best Small & Medium Employers - Rohit Group's winning ways: challenge and teamwork," *The Globe and Mail* and Mediacorp Canada Inc., March 2015, 54.
12. "About Us," Passion Inc., January 24, 2018, https://www.jobpostings.ca/about-us.
13. Nicola Middlemiss, "Leveraging technology: because it's worth it," HRM Online, March 23, 2015, http://www.hrmonline.ca/hr-news/leveraging-technology-because-its-worth-it-189482.aspx.
14. Julie Kantor, "High Turnover Costs Way More Than You Think," *Huffington Post,* February 11, 2016; Heather Boushey and Sarah Jane Glynn, "There Are Significant Business Costs to Replacing Employees," Center for American Progress, accessed September 2017; Jack Altman, "How Much Does Employee Turnover Really Cost?" *Huffington Post,* January 18, 2017.
15. "Corporate Profile," BackCheck, 2018, http://www.backcheck.net/about.htm; Chad Brook, "Best Background Check Services 2017," *Business News Daily,* October 13, 2016; Antique Nguyen, "3 Background Check Compliance Tips for 2017," *PreCheck Blog,* February 15, 2017.
16. Kim Isaacs, "Lying on your Resume," Monster, accessed May 12, 2018, https://www.monster.ca/career-advice/article/lying-on-your-resume-canada.
17. Brian Thiessen, Damian Rigolo, and Shaun Parker, "Employer learnings from Suncor v Unifor," Osler, Hoskin & Harcourt LLP, 19 April 2017, https://www.osler.com/en/resources/governance/2017/random-drug-and-alcohol-testing-employer-learnin; Ryan Anderson, *"Can Employers Test for Drug & Alcohol Use in the Workplace?"* go2HR, 2017, https://www.go2hr.ca/legal/can-employers-test-for-drug-alcohol-use-in-the-workplace; and Scott MacDonald, "Drug Testing in the Canadian Workplace," HeretoHelp, 2015, http://www.heretohelp.bc.ca/visions/workplaces-vol5/drug-testing-in-the-canadian-workplace.
18. Jae Yang and Veronica Bravo, "Time Limit for New Hires," *USA Today,* May 3, 2016; "Probationary Employment Periods," *Inc.,* accessed September 2017.
19. Rachel Emma Silverman, "Workplace Democracy Catches On," *The Wall Street Journal,* March 28, 2016; Joshua Clark Davis, "So Much for 'Conscious Capitalism'," *Slate,* June 19, 2017.
20. Amanda Silliker, "More firms hiring contract workers," *Canadian HR Reporter,* May 7, 2012, http://www.hrreporter.com/articleview/13016-more-firms-hiring-contract-workers.
21. Linda Nazareth, "The gig economy is here – and we aren't ready," *The Globe and Mail,* October 20, 2017, https://www.theglobeandmail.com/report-on-business/rob-commentary/the-gig-economy-is-here-and-we-arent-ready/article36678505/.
22. Ibid.
23. Susan M. Heathfield, "20 Ways Zappos Reinforces Its Company Culture," *The Balance,* June 28, 2016; S. Chris Edmonds, "Are You Really Onboarding Your Employees the Best Way Possible?" *Forbes,* July 21, 2017.
24. "Mission Statement," Skills Canada, 2018, http://skillscompetencescanada.com/en/mission-statement/; "Skilled trades shortage costing Windsor-Essex $600M every year, says report," CBC News, June 20, 2017, http://www.cbc.ca/news/canada/windsor/skilled-trades-shortage-costing-windsor-essex-600m-every-year-says-report-1.4168822; and Susan Mas, "Shortage of skilled workers could jeopardize the economy," CBC News, June 25, 2014, http://www.cbc.ca/news/politics/shortage-of-skilled-workers-could-jeopardize-the-economy-1.2687365.
25. GlobeSmart, www.aperianglobesmart.com, accessed September 2017.
26. Tess Taylor, "4 Learning and Development Trends for HR Leaders to Watch in 2017," *HR Dive,* November 15, 2016; "6 Advantages of Training Simulations in the Workplace," *Designing Digitally,* June 20, 2017.
27. Lauren Weber and Rachel Louise Ensign, "Promoting Women Is Crucial," *The Wall Street Journal,* September 28, 2016; "How to Develop Future Leaders," *The Wall Street Journal,* accessed September 2017.
28. Lauren Weber and Rachel Louise Ensign, "Promoting Women Is Crucial," *The Wall Street Journal,* September 28, 2016; "Finding, and Keeping, the Right People," *Inc.,* September 2016; Eben Harrell, "Succession Planning: What the Research Says," *Harvard Business Review,* December 2016; Michael Corkery, "At Walmart Academy, Training Better Managers. But With a Better Future?" *The New York Times,* August 8, 2017.
29. "Canada's Top Employer for Young People," Mediacorp Canada Inc., 2015, http://www.eluta.ca/jobs-at-loblaws#young:young-more.
30. McDonald's, www.mcdonalds.com, accessed September 2017.
31. "Best Employers in Canada," Aon Hewitt, 2015, http://www.aon.com/canada/products-services/human-capital-consulting/consulting/best_employers/documents/casestudy_cisco.pdf.
32. Jeffrey Dauksevich, "How to Be an Effective Mentor," *Entrepreneur,* December 27, 2013; and John Brandon, "How to Maximize the Benefits of Mentoring," *Inc.,* January 2014.
33. "Creating Opportunity for Generation Next: This Year's 'Canada's Top Employers for Young People' are Announced," CNW Group Inc., April 24, 2014, http://www.newswire.ca/en/story/1345087/

creating-opportunity-for-generation-next-this-year-s-canada-s-top-employers-for-young-people-are-announced.

34. Harvey Meyer, "The Merits of Mentoring," *The Costco Connection,* July 2016; Anthony K. Tjan, "What the Best Mentors Do," *Harvard Business Review,* February 27, 2017.
35. "From Y to Z a guide to the next generation of employees," Randstad, 2015, http://w.randstad.ca/y2z/.
36. Ibid.
37. Richard Yerema and Kristina Leung, "Recognized as One of Canada's Top 100 Employers (2018)," Mediacorp Canada Inc., November 6, 2017, https://content.eluta.ca/top-employer-td-bank.
38. Rachel Emma Silverman, "GE Tries to Reinvent the Employee Review, Encouraging Risks," *The Wall Street Journal,* June 8, 2016; Lauren Weber, "Nowhere to Hide for 'Dead Wood' Workers," *The Wall Street Journal,* August 16, 2016; Dan Schawbel, "10 Workplace Trends You'll See in 2017," *Forbes,* November 1, 2016; Jeff Kauflin, "Hate Performance Reviews? Good News: They're Getting Shorter and Simpler," *Forbes,* March 9, 2017.
39. "More Organizations Shift to Market-Based Pay Structures," *Society for Human Resource Management,* shrm.org, accessed March 2017.
40. "Pay Structures," salary.com, accessed September 2017; "Building a Market-Based Pay Structure from Scratch," Society for Human Resource Management, October 27, 2016; Mykkah Herner, "Which Compensation Structure Is Right for Your Company?" *PayScale,* May 8, 2017.
41. "Advantages of Skill-Based Pay," *Human Resource Management Practice,* accessed September 2017.
42. David Nicklaus, "Professors Explore Dark Side of Performance-Based Pay," *St. Louis Post-Dispatch,* April 5, 2016; Chidiebere Ogbonnaya, Kevin Daniels and Karina Nielsen, "Research: How Incentive Pay Affects Employee Engagement, Satisfaction, and Trust," *Harvard Business Review,* March 15, 2017.
43. "Providing Employee Benefits Continues To Be A Significant Cost For Employers," The Conference Board of Canada, November 9, 2015, http://www.conferenceboard.ca/press/newsrelease/15-11-09/Providing_Employee_Benefits_Continues_To_Be_A_Significant_Cost_For_Employers.aspx?AspxAutoDetectCookieSupport=1.
44. Amanda Frank, "Do You Know How Much You're Paying for Health Benefits?" Monster.ca, accessed March 31, 2015, http://career-advice.monster.ca/salary-benefits/benefits-information/how-much-are-health-benefits-canada/article.aspx.
45. Catherine McIntyre, "How much should your company spend on employee benefits?" Canadian Business, November 8, 2016, http://www.canadianbusiness.com/innovation/how-much-should-employee-benefits-cost/.
46. Schwind et al., *Canadian Human Resource Management—A Strategic Approach,* 366.
47. Ibid.
48. "Younger Generations Expect Companies to Stimulate Economy and Close Gender Gap—But Don't Expect Their Loyalty," PRNewswire, February 26, 2015, http://www.prnewswire.com/news-releases/younger-generations-expect-companies-to-stimulate-economy-and-close-gender-gap---but-dont-expect-their-loyalty-294174141.html.
49. Tara Deschamps and Shawn Jeffords, "'Reckless': Tim Hortons blasts franchisees' cuts to paid breaks and benefits," *Financial Post,* January 8, 2018, http://business.financialpost.com/news/retail-marketing/tim-hortons-blasts-franchisees-cuts-to-paid-breaks-and-benefits-calling-them-reckless.
50. Jackie Dunham, "'They're vulnerable right now': Tim Hortons' brand reputation plummets," CTV News, April 5, 2018, https://www.ctvnews.ca/business/they-re-vulnerable-right-now-tim-hortons-brand-reputation-plummets-1.3872508.
51. Deschamps and Jeffords, *Financial Post,* January 8, 2018.
52. Dunham, CTV News, April 5, 2018.
53. Ibid.
54. Susan Johnston Taylor, "5 Employee Benefits Trends to Watch in 2017," *US News & World Report,* December 29, 2016; "2017 Compensation Best Practices Report," PayScale Human Capital, February 15, 2017, accessed September 2017, https://www.payscale.com/compensation-today/2017/02/payscales-2017-compensation-best-practices-report.
55. Theresa W. Carey, "Two New Employee Benefits Aimed at Millennials," *Barron's,* May 23, 2016; Rachel Emma Silverman, "Bosses Turn to Loans to Help Employees," *The Wall Street Journal,* June 1, 2016; Carla Fried, "Here's Why Employers May Want to Help Out on the Mountain of Student Loan Debt," *CNBC,* August 19, 2017.
56. Jeff Kauflin, "The Top 20 Employee Perks and Benefits for 2017," *Forbes,* February 9, 2017.
57. "Canada's 100 Best Small & Medium Employers," Verafin Inc.," 8.
58. National Legal and Research Group, "Cafeteria Plans: An Employer's Guide," Willis Towers Watson, accessed September 2017.
59. Kate Rockwood, "Blowing Up the Workweek," *Inc.,* December 2016–January 2017; Rachel Ritlop, "Millennials, Consider These 16 Companies If You're Looking For Work-Life Balance," *Forbes,* August 9, 2017.
60. Lauren Weber, "Regulators Investigate Retailers' Work Scheduling," *The Wall Street Journal,* April 13, 3016; Henry Grabar, "Malls and Restaurants Schedule Workers at the Last Minute. Oregon Just Made That Illegal," *Slate,* August 10, 2017; and Seres Lu, "On-call scheduling under increasing scrutiny in Canada," *The Globe and Mail,* March 25, 2017, https://www.theglobeandmail.com/report-on-business/on-call-scheduling-under-increasing-scrutiny-in-canada/article26240704/.
61. Sarah White, "Working from Home Can Benefit Employers as Much as Employees," monster.com, accessed September 2017.
62. Ross Marowits, "Telecommuting growing as companies look to save money, respond to employees," The Canadian Press, May 23, 2016, http://www.cbc.ca/news/business/telecommuting-growing-as-companies-look-to-save-money-respond-to-employees-1.3596420.
63. James Fettes, "Is Hot Desking Actually Any Good for Employee Productivity?" Australian Broadcasting Corporation, accessed March 2017.
64. Kristen Quan, "Amex Canada's Howard Grosfield," *Canadian Business,* April 2015, 18.
65. "Canadian pay equity requirements," Hay Group, 2018, http://www.haygroup.com/ca/services/index.aspx?id=43781; "Federally Regulated Businesses and Industries," Government of Canada, July 14, 2016, https://www.canada.ca/en/employment-social-development/programs/employment-equity/regulated-industries.html; Schwind et al., *Canadian Human Resource Management,* 136–141; and "Federal Labour Standards," Government of Canada, March 16, 2015, http://www.labour.gc.ca/eng/standards_equity/st/.
66. "Maclean's is asking men to pay 26% more for our latest issue," *Maclean's,* February 8, 2018, http://www.macleans.ca/society/why-macleans-is-asking-men-to-pay-26-more-for-our-latest-issue/; Catherine McIntyre, "Why do men make more money than women?" *Maclean's,* February 8, 2018, http://www.macleans.ca/society/why-do-men-make-more-money-than-women/; Catherine McIntyre, "These are the key numbers that explain the wage gap for women," *Maclean's,* February 28, 018, http://www.macleans.ca/society/pay-equity-statistics-canada/; "Study: Women in Canada: Women and paid work," Statistics Canada, March 8, 2017, http://www.statcan.gc.ca/daily-quotidien/170308/dq170308b-eng.pdf; Solomon Israel, "StatsCan on gender pay gap: Women earn 87¢ to men's $1," CBC News, March 8, 2017, http://www.cbc.ca/news/business/statistics-canada-gender-pay-gap-1.4014954; "What is the Gender Wage Gap?" Pay Equity Commission, 2018, http://www.payequity.gov.on.ca/en/GWG/Pages/what_is_GWG.aspx; and "Closing the Gender Pay Gap," Canadian Labour Congress, March 15, 2015, http://canadianlabour.ca/issues-research/closing-gender-pay-gap.
67. "Why Maclean's is asking men to pay 26% more for our latest issue," *Maclean's,* February 8, 2018, https://www.macleans.ca/society/why-macleans-is-asking-men-to-pay-26-more-for-our-latest-issue/.
68. Ibid.

69. "Equality and Inclusion," Government of Canada, October 18, 2016, https://www.canada.ca/en/services/jobs/workplace/human-rights.html; and Schwind et al., *Canadian Human Resource Management,* 147–151.
70. "Fact Sheet—Temporary Foreign Worker Program," Government of Canada, February 19, 2015, http://www.cic.gc.ca/english/resources/publications/employers/temp-foreign-worker-program.asp; and Bill Curry, "Everything you need to know about temporary foreign workers," *The Globe and Mail,* June 24, 2014, http://www.theglobeandmail.com/news/politics/temporary-foreign-workers-everything-you-need-to-know/article18363279/.

Chapter 13

1. "Table 282-0223 16: Labour Force Survey estimates (LFS), employees by union status, North American Industry Classification System (NAICS) and sex, Canada," Statistics Canada, January 5, 2018, http://www5.statcan.gc.ca/cansim/a26?lang=eng&id=2820223.
2. Ibid.
3. Ibid.
4. "Young Workers," UFCW Canada, 2018, http://ufcw.ca/index.php?option=com_content&view=article&id=2000:youth-homepage&catid=57:youth&Itemid=189&lang=en.
5. Jeff Cox, "Disorganized: Union Membership Hit an All-Time Low in 2016," CNBC, January 26, 2017.
6. Gerry Varricchio, Regional Organizing Director for the Central and Eastern Canada Organizing Fund, The Labourers' International Union of North America, interview, February 8, 2018, Hamilton.
7. "History of Labour in Canada," Canadian Labour Congress, accessed March 26, 2018, http://canadianlabour.ca/why-unions/history-labour-canada#short-week.
8. "Winnipeg General Strike," *The Canadian Encyclopedia,* accessed February 7, 2018, http://www.thecanadianencyclopedia.ca/en/article/winnipeg-general-strike/.
9. "Labour Organizations in Canada 2015," Government of Canada, August 19, 2016, https://www.canada.ca/en/employment-social-development/services/collective-bargaining-data/reports/union-coverage.html; "National Union Centrals," *The Canadian Encyclopedia,* accessed March 26, 2018, http://www.thecanadianencyclopedia.ca/en/article/union-centrals-national/; "What We Do," The Canadian Labour Congress, accessed March 26, 2018, http://canadianlabour.ca/about-clc/what-we-do; "Making the Shift to a Green Economy: A Common Platform of the Green Economy Network," The Canadian Labour Congress, May 2015, http://canadianlabour.ca/sites/default/files/media/GEN-Common-Platform-EN.pdf; "CLC accuses Unifor of leaving lobby group to raid another union," The Canadian Press, January 19, 2018, http://www.cbc.ca/news/business/clc-union-unifor-workers-1.4495389; and Gerry Varricchio and Lucy Faiella, The Labourers' International Union of North America, interview, February 8, 2018, Hamilton.
10. "Making the Shift to a Green Economy: A Common Platform of the Green Economy Network," The Canadian Labour Congress, May 2015, http://canadianlabour.ca/sites/default/files/media/GEN-Common-Platform-EN.pdf.
11. "Unionization rates falling," Statistics Canada, March 3, 2017, http://www.statcan.gc.ca/pub/11-630-x/11-630-x2015005-eng.htm#def1.
12. Ibid.
13. "Unionization rates falling," Statistics Canada, March 3, 2017, http://www.statcan.gc.ca/pub/11-630-x/11-630-x2015005-eng.htm#def1; and "Table 282-0078 4-Labour Force Survey estimates (LFS), employees by union coverage, North American Industry Classification System (NAICS), sex and age group," Statistics Canada, January 5, 2018, http://www5.statcan.gc.ca/cansim/a26?lang=eng&id=2820078.
14. Ibid.
15. "CUPE at a glance," Canadian Union of Public Employees, accessed March 26, 2018, http://cupe.ca/cupe-glance.
16. "About Unifor," Unifor, accessed March 26, 2018, https://www.unifor.org/en/about-unifor; and "FAQ," Unifor, accessed March 26, 2018, https://www.unifor.org/en/why-unifor/faq.
17. "Facts about unions," UFCW Canada, accessed March 26, 2018, http://www.ufcw.ca/index.php?option=com_content&view=article&id=29&Itemid=49&lang=en.
18. "Federally Regulated Businesses and Industries," Government of Canada, July 14, 2016, https://www.canada.ca/en/employment-social-development/programs/employment-equity/regulated-industries.html.
19. "A plan for fair workplaces and better jobs (Bill 148)," The Ontario Ministry of Labour, 2018, https://www.ontario.ca/page/plan-fair-workplaces-and-better-jobs-bill-148.
20. Mike Blanchfield, "Public Sector Workers' Right To Strike Protected By Constitution: Top Court," The Canadian Press, January 30, 2015, http://www.huffingtonpost.ca/2015/01/30/public-sector-workers-strike-supreme-court_n_6577280.html; and Mike Blanchfield, "Supreme Court strikes down law that prevents public sector strikes," *The Toronto Star,* January 30, 2015, http://www.thestar.com/news/canada/2015/01/30/supreme-court-strikes-down-law-that-prevents-public-sector-strikes.html.
21. James Fiz-Morris, "Ruling says union is one option, as federal government given a year to amend law," CBC News, January 16, 2015, http://www.cbc.ca/news/politics/rcmp-officers-have-right-to-collective-bargaining-supreme-court-rules-1.2912340.
22. "OH&S Legislation in Canada - Basic Responsibilities," Canadian Centre for Occupational Health and Safety, 2018, April 12, 2018, https://www.ccohs.ca/oshanswers/legisl/responsi.html.; "Right to refuse or to stop work where health and safety in danger," Ministry of Labour, 2018, https://www.ontario.ca/document/guide-occupational-health-and-safety-act/part-v-right-refuse-or-stop-work-where-health-and-safety-danger; Hermann Schwind et al., *Canadian Human Resource Management,* 11th ed. (Toronto: McGraw-Hill Ryerson, 2016), 551 and 555; "Statistics and Beyond," Canadian Centre for Occupational Health and Safety, April 26, 2018, https://www.ccohs.ca/events/mourning/; "Young Workers: Know Your Rights Workshop," UFCW Canada, 2018, http://www.ufcw.ca/index.php?option=com_content&view=article&id=2501:the-know-your-rights-workshop&catid=57:youth&Itemid=338&lang=en; and "Canada's unions call for better protections against workplace violence and harassment," Canadian Labour Congress, April 23, 2018, http://canadianlabour.ca/news/news-archive/canadas-unions-call-better-protections-against-workplace-violence-and-harassment.
23. "Definition of Sexual Harassment," Canadian Labour Relations, accessed May 2, 2018, http://www.canadianlabourrelations.com/definition-of-sexual-harassment.html.
24. Ibid.
25. Daniel Lublin, "What counts as workplace sexual harassment in Canada?" *The Globe and Mail,* November 30, 2017, https://www.theglobeandmail.com/report-on-business/careers/leadership-lab/what-counts-as-workplace-sexual-harassment-in-canada/article37137194/.
26. "Violence in the Workplace," Canadian Centre for Occupational Health and Safety, accessed May 2, 2018, http://www.ccohs.ca/oshanswers/psychosocial/violence.html; and "Bullying in the Workplace," Canadian Centre for Occupational Health and Safety, accessed May 2, 2018, https://www.ccohs.ca/oshanswers/psychosocial/bullying.html.
27. Christine Comaford, "75% of Workers Are Affected by Bullying—Here's What to Do about It," *Forbes,* August 27, 2016; and Philip Landau, "Bullying at Work: Your Legal Rights," *The Guardian,* March 29, 2017.
28. Margaret Jacoby, "8 Steps to Take to Stop Bullying in Your Workplace," *Huffington Post,* November 3, 2016; Gary Namie, "2017 WBI U.S. Survey: Reactions to Workplace Bullying of Employers and Witnesses," Workplace Bullying Institute, July 7, 2017.
29. Margaret Jacoby, "Workplace Bullying: Fact or Fiction?" *Huffington Post,* October 25, 2016; Pat McGonigle, "The 5 Kinds of Bullies at Work," KSDK, April 28, 2017.

30. Joyce E. A. Russell, "How to Recognize and Deal with Bullying at Work," *Los Angeles Times,* April 3, 2016; and Dr. Mary Lamia, "The Psychology of a Workplace Bully," *The Guardian,* March 28, 2017.
31. Hermann Schwind et al., *Canadian Human Resource Management,* 11th ed. (Toronto: McGraw-Hill Ryerson, 2016), 612.
32. Varricchio, interview, January 15, 2018.
33. Ibid.
34. "Canada's unions say NAFTA renegotiation is an opportunity for more fairness," Canadian Labour Congress, January 26, 2017, http://canadianlabour.ca/news/news-archive/canada%E2%80%99s-unions-say-nafta-renegotiation-opportunity-more-fairness.
35. "Rand Formula," The Canadian Encyclopedia, accessed April 28, 2018, http://www.thecanadianencyclopedia.ca/en/article/rand-formula/.
36. Aaron Rousseau, Founder and Lawyer, Rousseau Mazzuca LLP, interview, January 11, 2018.
37. Ibid.
38. Schwind et al., *Canadian Human Resource Management,* 622.
39. Ibid.
40. Ira Podell, "NHL Lockout 2012: Mediator Gets League, Union Back Together," Associated Press, January 5, 2013; and Mike Brehm and Kevin Allen, "NHL Lockout Ends at 113 Days: A Daily Look Back," *USA Today,* January 6, 2013.
41. "Essential services - Frequently Asked Questions," Government of Canada, March 3, 2015, https://www.canada.ca/en/treasury-board-secretariat/services/labour-management/essential-services.html; and "Strike and Lock-out: FAQ," Ontario Ministry of Labour, November 4, 2011, https://www.labour.gov.on.ca/english/lr/faqs/lr_faq3.php#do.
42. Allison Jones, "Arbitrator sets new contract for Ontario college faculty following strike," The Canadian Press, December 20, 2017, https://www.ctvnews.ca/canada/arbitrator-sets-new-contract-for-ontario-college-faculty-following-strike-1.3729643.
43. Steve Greenhouse, "Wage Strike Planned at Fast Food Outlets," *New York Times,* December 1, 2013.
44. Norman De Bono, "GM was within days of shutting Ingersoll plant for good when strike ended, sources say," *Financial Post,* October 18, 2017, http://business.financialpost.com/transportation/autos/gm-strike.
45. Cory Collins, "Labatt brewery strike escalates as union launches boycott," June 19, 2013, http://rabble.ca/news/2013/06/labatt-brewery-strike-escalates-union-launches-boycott.
46. "Ont. introduces TTC essential service legislation," CBC News, February 22, 2011, http://www.cbc.ca/news/canada/toronto/ont-introduces-ttc-essential-service-legislation-1.1063794.
47. "Government Intervention in the Economy: The End of Canadian Steelmaking," *The Marxist-Leninist Daily,* November 7, 2013, http://www.cpcml.ca/Tmld2013/D43127.htm.
48. Karla Thorpe, "The State of Canadian Unions—Down but Not Out," The Conference Board of Canada, January 31, 2013, http://www.conferenceboard.ca/topics/humanresource/commentaries/13-01-31/the_state_of_canadian_unions—down_but_not_out.aspx.
49. "Table 282-0220: Labour Force Survey estimates (LFS), employees by union status, sex, and age group, Canada and provinces," Statistics Canada, January 5, 2018, http://www5.statcan.gc.ca/cansim/a47.
50. "2018 To Be a Challenging Year for Both Sides of the Bargaining Table," The Conference Board of Canada, January 16, 2018, http://www.conferenceboard.ca/press/newsrelease/2018/01/16/2018-to-be-a-challenging-year-for-both-sides-of-the-bargaining-table?AspxAutoDetectCookieSupport=1#.
51. Joseph S. Mancinelli, LiUNA International Vice-President and Regional Manager for Central and Eastern Canada, The Labourers' International Union of North America, interview, February 8, 2018, Hamilton.
52. Zack O'Malley Greenberg, "Celeb 100: The Highest-Paid Celebrities of 2016," *Forbes,* July 11, 2016; Zack O'Malley Greenburg, "Full List: The World's Highest-Paid Celebrities 2017," *Forbes,* June 12, 2017.
53. Ian Salisbury, "The Completely Absurd and Infuriating Reason CEOs Get Paid So Much," *Time,* February 22, 2016; F. John Reh, "What You Need to Know about Restricted Stock Grants," *The Balance,* August 16, 2017.
54. Gretchen Morganstern, "Safety Suffers as Stock Options Propel Executive Pay Packages," *The New York Times,* September 11, 2015; Tim Mullaney, "Why Corporate CEO Pay Is So High and Going Higher," *CNBC,* accessed February 2017; Stephen Wilmot, "Better Ways to Measure Boss's Pay," *The Wall Street Journal,* July 4, 2017.
55. Jonathan R. Costa, "Target CEO's severance pay-out causes online outrage," *The Toronto Observer,* February 4, 2015, http://torontoobserver.ca/2015/02/04/target-ceos-severance-pay-out-causes-online-outrage/.
56. Damian Paletta, "5 Takeaways on Wealth and Inequality from Picketty," *The Wall Street Journal,* April 14, 2014.
57. Anders Melin and Caleb Melby, "Executive Pay," *Bloomberg,* February 15, 2017.
58. "Executives Got Biggest Raise Since 2013," *St. Louis Post-Dispatch,* May 24, 2017.
59. "Canada's Top 100 highest-paid CEOs," *Canadian Business,* January 2, 2018, http://www.canadianbusiness.com/lists-and-rankings/richest-people/canada-100-highest-paid-ceos/; and David Macdonald, "Climbing Up and Kicking Down: Executive Pay in Canada," Canadian Centre for Policy Alternatives, January 1, 2018, https://www.policyalternatives.ca/publications/reports/climbing-and-kicking-down.
60. Ibid.
61. Matthew T. Tice, "My Antibusiness Business Education," *The Wall Street Journal,* February 19, 2016; Ross Kerber and Peter Szekely, "CEO Pay Still Dwarfing Pay of U.S. Workers: Union Report," U.S. News and World Report, May 9, 2017.
62. "Women In The Workforce: Canada," Catalyst, September 7, 2017, http://www.catalyst.org/knowledge/women-workforce-canada.
63. U.S. Census Bureau, www.census.gov, accessed January 2017.
64. "Canada's population estimates: Age and sex, July 1, 2015," Statistics Canada, September 21, 2015, https://www.statcan.gc.ca/daily-quotidien/150929/dq150929b-eng.htm.
65. Lynn Feinberg and Rita Choula, "Understanding the Impact of Family Caregiving on Work," AARP Public Policy Institute, accessed September 2017.

Chapter 14

1. "Code of Ethics and Standards of Practice," Canadian Marketing Association, accessed May 2, 2018, www.the-cma.org/regulatory/code-of-ethics.
2. Amy Webb, "Virtually Convincing," *Inc.,* November 2016; Martin Holland, "The Future Of Marketing: What Should You Be Focusing On?" *Forbes,* July 11, 2017.
3. Iris Kuo, "How to Keep Them Coming Back," *Inc.,* April 2016; Jimmy Rohampton, "How Does Social Media Influence Millennials' Shopping Decisions?" *Forbes,* May 3, 2017.
4. Angela Ruth, "Six Social Media Marketing Trends to Stay on Top of in 2017," *Forbes,* February 6, 2017.
5. Jason Hidalgo, "Millennials Want It Quick and Affordable," *USA Today,* February 8, 2016; Rob Marvin, "The Best Social Listening and Influencer Identification Tools of 2017," *PC Magazine,* July 19, 2017.
6. Ryan Charkow, "5 young Canadian entrepreneurs reveal secrets to success," CBC News, October 6, 2011, www.cbc.ca/news/business/smallbusiness/story/2011/09/28/f-smallbiz-young-entrepreneurs.html.
7. Frederick G. Crane et al., *Marketing,* 10th Canadian ed. (Toronto: McGraw-Hill Ryerson, 2017), 13–14.
8. Ibid., 16-18; "Social Media Marketing Quick-Start Guide," Canadian Marketing Association, July 19, 2011, www.the-cma.org/Media/Default/Downloads/Library/2011/SocialMediaQSG.pdf; "YOUR TAKE – Mobile spa relies 100% on social media," CBC News, October 17, 2011, www.cbc.ca/news/business/smallbusiness/story/2011/10/17/

small-business-your-take-blog-goertzen.html; "Social Media Revolution 2015 #Socialnomics," YouTube.com, January 26, 2015, https://www.youtube.com/watch?v=jottDMuLesU; and Erik Qualman, *Socialnomics* (New York: Wiley, 2009).

9. Jillian Hausmann, "Millennial to Marketers: Some Advice on Using Snapchat," *Advertising Age,* April 4, 2016; Laurence Bradford, "7 Important Digital Skills All Marketers Should Master In 2017," *Forbes,* January 16, 2017.
10. "5 Trends in Consumer Demand for Digital Self-Service," Astute Solutions, July 31, 2016; Mayumi Negishi, "Consumer Demands To Bolster U.S. Jobs — WSJ," Fox Business, May 17, 2017.
11. Tim Whitnell, "Dozens protest outside Burlington pork processing plant," *Burlington Post,* July 2, 2015, https://www.insidehalton.com/news-story/5706765-dozens-protest-outside-burlington-pork-processing-plant/.
12. Crane et al., *Marketing,* 300.
13. "Employment by industry," Statistics Canada, January 5, 2018, http://www.statcan.gc.ca/tables-tableaux/sum-som/l01/cst01/econ40-eng.htm.
14. Angela Doland, "Pizza Hut's New Concept Restaurant in Shanghai Has Robots on Staff," *Advertising Age,* December 2, 2016; Andrew deGrandpre, "Dunkin' Donuts Testing Marketing Strategy That Sheds Name 'Donuts'," *The Washington Post,* August 4, 2017.
15. Crane et al., *Marketing,* 320.
16. Neil T. Bendle and Charan K. Bagga, "The Metrics That Marketers Muddle," *MIT Sloan Management Review,* Spring 2016; John Rampton, "8 Reasons Your Social Media Campaign Is Failing," *Forbes,* August 25, 2017.
17. Crane et al., *Marketing,* 205.
18. Ibid., 220.
19. Ibid., 193–194.
20. Ibid.
21. Ibid, 211–212.
22. Jonathan Vanian, "Big Data and Data Analytics Are Becoming One in the Same," *Fortune,* January 13, 2016; Michael S. Malone, "The Big Data Future Has Arrived," *The Wall Street Journal,* February 22, 2016; Gil Press, "6 Predictions For The $203 Billion Big Data Analytics Market," *Forbes,* January 20, 2017.
23. "What is Data Analytics?" Informatica, accessed May 4, 2018, https://www.informatica.com/ca/services-and-training/glossary-of-terms/data-analytics-definition.html#fbid=bvlhAJ6F0Bc.
24. "Closing Canada's Big Data Talent Gap," Canada's Big Data Consortium, October 2015, https://smith.queensu.ca/ConversionDocs/MMA/big-data-gap.pdf.
25. "50 Sensor Applications for a Smarter World," Libelium, accessed May 13, 2018, http://www.libelium.com/resources/top_50_iot_sensor_applications_ranking/; Bridget Botelho, "Explained: What is the Internet of Things?" IoTAgenda, accessed May 12, 2018, https://internetofthingsagenda.techtarget.com/feature/Explained-What-is-the-Internet-of-Things.; Louis Columbus, "2017 Roundup Of Internet Of Things Forecasts," *Forbes,* December 10, 2017, https://www.forbes.com/sites/louiscolumbus/2017/12/10/2017-roundup-of-internet-of-things-forecasts/#4e2e7bcb1480; Louis Columbus, "70% Of Enterprises Invest In IoT To Improve Customer Experiences," *Forbes,* November 4, 2017, https://www.forbes.com/sites/louiscolumbus/2017/11/04/70-of-enterprises-invest-in-iot-to-improve-customer-experiences/#61d86f0b622b; and "The 10 most popular Internet of Things applications right now," IOT Analytics, February 2, 2015, https://iot-analytics.com/10-internet-of-things-applications/.
26. "CRTC decision reduces some Northwestel internet rates for NWT, Yukon," *Nunatsiq News,* March 5, 2015, http://www.nunatsiaqonline.ca/stories/article/65674crtc_decision_to_lower_internet_rates_in_some_northern_communities/.
27. Susan Scutti, "One-Child Policy Is One Big Problem for China," *Newsweek,* January 23, 2014; Isabella Steger and Laurie Burkitt, "Chinese Couples—and Investors—Are Pregnant with Anticipation," *The Wall Street Journal,* November 19, 2013; and Ted Trautman, "The Year of the Lego," *The New Yorker,* November 11, 2013.
28. Jennifer Hakim, "The Real Differences between B2C and B2B Marketing," Chief Marketer, February 7, 2017.
29. Ernan Roman, "Stop (ONLY) Marketing to Millennials!" Customer Think, January 26, 2017; Charlotte Rogers, "The Shrinking and Emerging Demographics Marketers Need to Know," *Marketing Week,* March 13, 2017.
30. "Why Study Culture," *Forbes,* January 27, 2017.
31. Crane et al., *Marketing,* 226–227.
32. Crane et al., *Marketing,* 223.
33. Christina Binkley, "Fashion's Big Turning Point," *The Wall Street Journal,* February 11, 2016; Charlotte Rogers, "Is Digital an Effective Mass Market Medium?" *Marketing Week,* April 10, 2017.
34. Francine Kopun, "Canadian Tire announces 'generational shift' in new billion-dollar strategy," *The Toronto Star,* October 9, 2014, http://www.thestar.com/business/2014/10/09/canadian_tire_announces_ generational_shift_billiondollar_digital_and_expansion.html.
35. Aly Thomson, "Most vegans, vegetarians in Canada are under 35: survey," The Canadian Press, March 13, 2018, https://www.theglobeandmail.com/canada/article-most-vegans-vegetarians-in-canada-are-under-35-survey/.
36. Crane et al, *Marketing,* 248; and Dhruv Grewal et al., *Marketing,* 3rd Canadian ed. (Toronto: McGraw-Hill Ryerson, 2014), 189.
37. Grewal et al., *Marketing,* 490.
38. Ibid., 288.
39. "G adventures named Canada's favourite adventure travel tour operator," G Adventures, June 28, 2012, www.gadventures.com/press-releases/2012/Jun/28/g-adventures-named-canadas-favourite-adventure-travel-tour-operator/.
40. "Legends of the Small," Report on Small Business, *The Globe and Mail,* June 2012, p. 17.
41. Crane et al., *Marketing,* 125–134; and Grewal et al., *Marketing,* 91–92.

Chapter 15

1. Martha E. Mangelsdorf, "Getting Product Development Right," *MIT Sloan Management Review,* Spring 2016; Scott Roth, "The Challenges Of Product Development In A Connected World," *Forbes,* May 25, 2017.
2. Anne Marie Chaker, "To Appeal to Girls and Boys, Changing Superheros," *The Wall Street Journal,* June 22, 2016; Brent Lang, "The Reckoning: Why the Movie Business Is in Big Trouble," *Variety,* March 27, 2017.
3. Brian Sozzi, "You'll Never Believe McDonald's Newest Sandwich," *The Street,* January 8, 2017.
4. Hadley Malcolm, "Whopperito? Weird Food Gimmicks Draw New, Old Fans," *USA Today,* August 11, 2016; Jennifer Calfas, "They're Back: Mac N' Cheetos Returning to Burger King For A Limited Time," *Fortune,* May 11, 2017.
5. Julie Jargon, "Taco Bell Rolls Out New $1 Breakfast Menu as Battle for Breakfast Heats Up," *The Wall Street Journal,* March 11, 2016; Zlati Meyer, "Chick-Fil-A, Taco Bell Boast New Breakfast Options," *USA Today,* August 15, 2017.
6. Karen Kaplan, "As Popularity of E-Cigarette Rises, More People Are Able to Quit, Study Says," *LA Times,* September 13, 2016; Ronald Holden, "Red Delicious Apple Losing Its Appeal In Favor Of Jazzy Newcomers Like Cosmic Crisp," *Forbes,* August 27, 2017.
7. Ibid.; and Janet Morrissey, "Brands Expand Into New Niches With Care, but Not Without Risk," *The New York Times,* May 28, 2017.
8. "Colgate Ready Meals and Zippo Perfume: The World's Weirdest Off-Brand Products," *The Telegraph,* January 14, 2016; "Accessories," Zippo.com, accessed September 2017.
9. Andrew Winston, "How General Mills and Kellogg Are Tackling Greenhouse Gas Emissions," *Harvard Business Review,* June 1, 2016; Andrew Winston, "An Inside View of How LVMH Makes Luxury More Sustainable," *Harvard Business Review,* January 11, 2017.
10. Emma K. Macdonald, Hugh N. Wilson, and Umut Konus, "Better Customer Insight—In Real Time," *Harvard Business Review,* March 2013.

11. Mike Esterl, "Fast-Growing Diet Soda Taps into Cola Fatigue," *The Wall Street Journal,* July 22, 2016; Carole Duran, "A Coke Combo Takes New Meaning," *Reading Eagle,* July 28, 2016; Venessa Wong, "Coke Let People Make Any Flavor They Want, The People Demanded Cherry Sprite," BuzzFeed News, February 13, 2017.
12. TELUS, accessed May 6, 2018, https://www.telus.com.
13. "The Most Innovative Companies of 2016," *Fast Company,* March 2016; Ryan Caldbeck, "CircleUp25: The Most Innovative Consumer Brands of 2016," *Forbes,* July 28, 2016; John Clarke, "Yeti Coolers Are Hot! No Really, People Are Stealing Them," *The Wall Street Journal,* September 1, 2016; and Dan Solomon, "Instead of a Retail Flagship Store, Yeti Decided to Build A Brand Museum. Here's Why," *Fast Company,* February 20, 2017.
14. Anne Marie Chaker, "Packaged Foods' New Selling Point: Fewer Ingredients," *The Wall Street Journal,* August 10, 2016; Stephanie Schomer, "How a Packaging Overhaul Rescued This Protein Bar Company From Obscurity," *Inc.,* June 2017.
15. Lambeth Hochwald, "Play with Packaging," *Entrepreneur,* July 2016; "Iowa Entrepreneur: Thelma's Treats," Iowa Public Television, June 2, 2017.
16. "School of Packaging," Michigan State University, accessed September 2017.
17. Rick Lingle, "Packaging Machinery Attuned to the Functional Use of RFID," *Packaging Digest,* December 13, 2016; Mufassira Fathima, "How Smart Packaging Sensors Safeguard Foods and Drugs," *Packaging Digest,* April 13, 2017.
18. Anne Vandermey, "10-Hour Layover? Lucky You," *Fortune,* November 1, 2016; Miquel Ros, "Stopover Buddy Can Show You Local Sites During Layover," CNN, June 27, 2017.
19. Kurt Badenhausen, "The World's Most Valuable Brands," *Forbes,* May 11, 2016; Kurt Badenhausen, "Apple Heads The World's Most Valuable Brands Of 2017 At $170 Billion," *Forbes,* May 23, 2017.
20. Jessica Wohl, "How Marketers Can Win the Emoji Arms Race," *Advertising Age,* April 7, 2016; Matthew Campbell and Corinne Gretler, "Take Two Butterfingers and Call ME in the Morning," *Bloomberg Businessweek,* May 9, 2016; Sara Randazzo, "Craft Brewers Brawl over Catchy Labels as Puns Run Dry," *The Wall Street Journal,* July 11, 2016; and Denise Lee Yohn, "Why Your Company Culture Should Match Your Brand," *Harvard Business Review,* June 26, 2017.
21. "These are the most valuable brands in the world right now," Daily Hive, February 1, 2018, http://dailyhive.com/toronto/most-valuable-brands-in-world-2018.
22. Ibid.
23. Brian Hughes, "5 Reasons Why Sustainability and Social Issues Attract Customers," *Entrepreneur,* January 6, 2017.
24. Sharon Terlep, "Millennials Give Beauty Business a Makeover," *The Wall Street Journal,* May 4, 2016; Amanda Brinkman, "The Power Of Consistent Branding That Tells A Story," *Forbes,* February 15, 2017.
25. Akhila Vijayaraghavan, "Puma, Nike and Adidas Run Towards Toxin-Free Products With Greenpeace," Triple Pundit.com, September 7, 2011, www.triplepundit.com/2011/09/puma-nike-adidas-greenpeace/.
26. Ibid.
27. Paul Resnikoff, "15 Reasons Why You Should Never, Ever Buy a Streaming Service . . . ," Digital Music News, January 30, 2015, http://www.digitalmusicnews.com/permalink/2015/01/30/15-reasons-never-ever-buy-streaming-service.
28. Joseph Pisani, "The New Barbie Bunch," *St. Louis Post-Dispatch,* January 29, 2016; Paul Ziobro, "Mattel Reshapes Business; Barbie Gets New Chief," *The Wall Street Journal,* February 13–14, 2016; "Barbies That Look More Like Real Girls," *Time,* November 28–December 5, 2016; Paul Ziobro, "Mattel's Ken Doll Follows Barbie With a Full Makeover," *The Wall Street Journal,* June 20, 2017.
29. Joseph Pisani, "Fidget spinners: How they went from being a toy to help autistic kids to being a national phenomenon," *USA Today,* May 16, 2017, https://www.usatoday.com/story/tech/2017/05/16/fidget-spinners-how-they-went-being-toy-help-autistic-kids-being-national-phenom/101742758/.
30. Julie Wernau, "Higher Costs Bite Chocolate Makers," *The Wall Street Journal,* July 12, 2016; Jeff Daniels, "Global Food Prices Around Two-Year High in June as Meat, Dairy and Wheat Climb," CNBC, July 6, 2017.
31. Kelsey Gee, "Price Fixing Suits Weigh on Tyson," *The Wall Street Journal,* October 9, 2016; Alan Tovey, "Electric Vehicles to Cost the Same as Conventional Cars by 2018," *The Telegraph,* May 19, 2017.
32. Coeli Carr, "Is the Price Right?," *Inc.,* December 2016–January 2017.
33. Mike Snider, "Netflix Subscribers Soar Despite Price Hike," *USA Today,* October 18, 2016; Steven Bragg, "Target Costing," *Accounting Tools,* May 14, 2017.
34. Richard Kestenbaum, "Why Online Grocers Are So Unsuccessful and What Amazon Is Doing about It," *Forbes,* January 16, 2017.
35. Brad Tuttle, "Winners and Losers in the Latest Cheap Fast Food Battles," *Money,* February 5, 2016; Melanie Hammond, "The Pricing Strategy for Fast-Food Restaurants," Houston Chronicle, accessed September 2017.
36. "Adidas' High-Tech Factory Brings Production Back to Germany," *The Economist,* January 14, 2017.
37. Bill Conerly, "What Businesses Should Worry about in 2017: Labor, Trade, and Credit Availability," *Forbes,* January 12, 2017; Jennifer McKevitt, "Supply Chain Risks in 2017: Spotting Potential Disruptions Through Transparency, Data," Supply Chain Dive, January 19, 2017.
38. www.walmart.com, accessed September 2017.
39. "Retail trade, by province and territory," Statistics Canada, April 20, 2018, http://www.statcan.gc.ca/tables-tableaux/sum-som/l01/cst01/trad17a-eng.htm; "Number of employees of the retail trade industry in Canada from 2008 to 2017 (in millions)," Statista, accessed May 6, 2018, https://www.statista.com/statistics/454100/number-of-employees-of-the-retail-trade-industry-canada/.
40. "Retail trade, December 2017," Statistics Canada, accessed July 2018, https://www150.statcan.gc.ca/n1/daily-quotidien/180222/dq180222a-eng.htm.
41. "Canada's appetite for legal cannabis could be almost as big as it is for wine, CIBC says," CBC, May 9, 2018, https://ca.finance.yahoo.com/news/canada-apos-appetite-legal-cannabis-080000081.html.
42. Elizabeth Weise, "Amazon Makes It Easy to Order Automatically," *USA Today,* January 20, 2016; Loretta Chao and Steven Norton, "Race for Web Sales Leaves Some in the Dust," *The Wall Street Journal,* January 29, 2016; Daniel Newman, "Top Five Digital Transformation Trends In Retail," *Forbes,* March 14, 2017.
43. Laura Stevens, "Survey Shows Boost in Web Shopping," *The Wall Street Journal,* June 8, 2016; "National Retail Federation Estimates 8-12% U.S. E-Commerce Growth in 2017," *Business Insider,* February 10, 2017.
44. Greg Bensinger and Laura Stevens, "Amazon to Build Grocery Stores," *The Wall Street Journal,* October 12, 2016; Heather Haddon and Sarah Nassauer, "Grocers Forge Ahead Online," *The Wall Street Journal,* October 13, 2016; Heather Haddon, "Millennials Vex Grocers," *The Wall Street Journal,* October 31, 2016; Liz Welch, "The Next-Gen Health Club," *Inc.,* December 2016–January 2017; and Julie Jargon, Annie Gasparro and Heather Haddon, "For Amazon, Now Comes the Hard Part," *The Wall Street Journal,* June 18, 2017.
45. Greg Bensinger and Suzanne Kapner, "Online Stores Embrace Bricks," *The Wall Street Journal,* February 7, 2016; Suzette Parmley, "Online Retailer Warby-Parker Is on Fire, Opening a Full Store in Philly on Saturday and 24 More Nationwide," *The Philadelphia Inquirer,* January 27, 2017.
46. "Who Can Still Call You," Government of Canada, accessed May 6, 2018, https://www.lnnte-dncl.gc.ca/en/Consumer/WhoCanStillCallYou.
47. Russ Wiles, "Carvana Stays in the Fast Lane with $160m Funding Infusion," *USA Today,* August 12, 2016; Jennifer Calfas, "Singapore Is Now Home to the World's Tallest 'Car Vending Machine'," *Fortune,* May 16, 2017.
48. Karen Haywood Queen, "Here Today . . . ," *The Costco Connection,* October 2016; C.J. Hughes, "Pop Up Goes the Retail Scene as Store Vacancies Rise," *The New York Times,* May 30, 2017.

49. Ashley Renders, "Multi-Level Marketing," *Vice*, January 13, 2017.
50. Panos Mourdouktas, "How Many People Get Rich from Multilevel Marketing Networks?" *Forbes*, December 30, 2016; Michelle Celarier, "Trump's Great Pyramid," *Slate*, February 21, 2017.
51. Groupe Desgagnés Inc., "Another world first in sustainable transport: Desgagnés christens the M/T Mia Desgagnés - First polar-class dual-fuel product/chemical tanker," CISION, April 17, 2018, https://www.newswire.ca/news-releases/another-world-first-in-sustainable-transport-desgagnes-christens-the-mt-mia-desgagnes---first-polar-class-dual-fuel-productchemical-tanker-679996993.html; "Walmart Canada collaborates with Food-X to bring sustainable grocery delivery to Vancouver-area customers," CISION, February 21, 2018, https://www.newswire.ca/news-releases/walmart-canada-collaborates-with-food-x-to-bring-sustainable-grocery-delivery-to-vancouver-area-customers-674692763.html.
52. Suzanne Vranica, "Catch Me If You Can," *The Wall Street Journal*, June 22, 2016; Carl Hose, "Top Ten Promotional Strategies," Houston Chronicle, accessed September 2017.
53. E.J. Schultz, "Technology Fuels Renaissance in Out-of-Home Advertising," *Advertising Age*, April 4, 2016; John Lincoln, "3 Digital Marketing Strategies That Will Rule 2017," *Inc.*, February 1, 2017.
54. Christopher P. Skroupa, "Why Company Success Relies on Integrated Thinking," *Forbes*, January 18, 2017.
55. "Digital Marketing," SAS, accessed May 13, 2018, https://www.sas.com/en_ca/insights/marketing/digital-marketing.html.
56. Jeanine Poggi, "The Future of TV Advertising," *Advertising Age*, April 18, 2016; Amol Sharma, "Big Media Needs to Embrace Digital Shift—Not Fight It," *The Wall Street Journal*, June 22, 2016; Ahmad Kareh, "Seven Steps To A Better Integrated Marketing Communications Strategy," *Forbes*, March 16, 2017; and Christopher P. Skroupa, "Why Company Success Relies on Integrated Thinking," *Forbes*, January 18, 2017.
57. Etelka Lehoczky, "From Mail to Sale," *Inc.*, November 2016; Summer Gould, "Five Ways To Spice Up Your Direct Mail Marketing In 2017," *Forbes*, January 10, 2017.
58. Suzanne Vranica and Jack Marshall, "Newspaper Ad Woes Accelerate," *The Wall Street Journal*, October 21, 2016; Michael Barthel, "Despite Subscription Surges for Largest U.S. Newspapers, Circulation and Revenue Fall for Industry Overall," Pew Research Center, June 1, 2017.
59. Garett Sloane, "Are Snapchat Ads Worth the Effort?" *Advertising Age*, December 5, 2016; Sarah Frier, "Facebook Sales Top Estimates on Gains in Mobile Advertising," *Bloomberg*, February 1, 2017.
60. Lena H. Sun, "Captivating an Audience," *The Washington Post*, April 6, 2008.
61. Miriam Gottfried, "For Media Stocks, TV Advertising's Death Is Exaggerated," *The Wall Street Journal*, February 27, 2016; Davey Alba, "The TV Ad Isn't Going Anywhere—It's Going Everywhere," *Wired*, January 1, 2017.
62. Wayne Friedman, "TV Dominates Twitter Trending Topics in Prime Time," MediaPost, February 2, 2017.
63. Suman Bhattacharyya, "Digital Ads to Overtake Traditional Ads in U.S. Local Markets by 2018," *Advertising Age*, October 26, 2016; Lauren Johnson, "U.S. Digital Advertising Will Make $83 Billion This Year, Says EMarketer," Adweek, March 14, 2017.
64. Joe Robinson, "You're Going to Love Sales," *Entrepreneur*, February 2016.
65. Sharon Terlep, "P&G Seeks to Turn Tide by Direct Selling," *The Wall Street Journal*, July 20, 2016; Shep Hyken, "Ten Customer Service And Customer Experience Trends For 2017," *Forbes*, January 7, 2017.
66. Donovan Roche, "Lessons from Three of 2016's Biggest PR Fails," *Fast Company*, December 20, 2016; Lucy Handley, "United Airlines Isn't Alone: Here Are Some of the Worst PR Disasters of All Time," CNBC, April 12, 2017.
67. Robert Wynne, "How to Write a Press Release," *Forbes*, June 13, 2016; Hannah Fleishman, "How to Write a Press Release," HubSpot, August 10, 2017.
68. "Twitter Shows Influence of Word of Mouth on Movies," PR Newswire, January 19, 2017; Dr. Benjamin Ola. Akande, "The Importance of Word-of-Mouth," *Ladue News*, March 23, 2017.
69. Nathan Skid, "The Future of Customer Experience," *Advertising Age*, August 2, 2016; Woojung Chang and Steven A. Taylor, "The Effectiveness of Customer Participation in New Product Development: A Meta-Analysis," American Marketing Association, accessed September 2017.
70. Jack Neff, "The Big Agenda," *Advertising Age*, January 11, 2016; Charlie Riley, "Brand Hacking: Leveraging The Power Of Other Companies' Viral Marketing," *Forbes*, September 6, 2017.
71. Kim Garst, "Social Media Marketing World 2014," *Huffington Post*, April 9, 2014, http://www.huffingtonpost.com.
72. Ryan Holmes, "How Companies Will Use Social Media in 2017," *Fast Company*, January 1, 2016; Jefferson Graham, "Are Geofilters the New Hashtag?" *USA Today*, August 2, 2016; Jack Neff, "Marketers Embrace Facebook, Google Missionaries," *Advertising Age*, October 17, 2016; and Sophia Bernazzani, "7 Trends That Will Change Social Media in 2017," HubSpot, January 13, 2017.
73. Evan Annett, "What is 'fake news,' and how can you spot it? Try our quiz," *The Globe and Mail*, February 1, 2017, https://www.theglobeandmail.com/community/digital-lab/fake-news-quiz-how-to-spot/article33821986/.
74. Jessica Wohl, "Oreo Enlists Celebs to Demonstrate the Perfect Dunk in Latest Global Push," *Advertising Age*, February 8, 2017.
75. Josh Ames, "The Best—and Worst—Examples of Social Media Contests I've Seen," Spark Reaction Marketing, accessed September 2017, https://www.sparkreaction.com/blog/social-media-contests.

Chapter 16

1. Eric Sobota, "Doing Business with the Government: Administrative Challenges Faced by Nonprofits," *Nonprofit Quarterly*, June 14, 2014; John A. Byrne, "The GMAT: An Exam with Greater Profit Margins Than Apple," *Fortune*, February 17, 2014.
2. "Anshula Chowdhury," *Canadian Business*, April 2015, p. 7.
3. "Meet Our Companies: Success Story Sametrica," Ontario Centres of Excellence, 19 October 19, 2017, http://www.oce-ontario.org/meet-our-companies/success-story/2017/10/19/sametrica.
4. Robert Libby et al., *Financial Accounting*, 5th Canadian edition, (Canada: McGraw-Hill Ryerson Ltd., 2014), 301.
5. "About the AcSB," Financial Reporting & Assurance Standards Canada, http://www.frascanada.ca/accounting-standards-board/what-we-do/about-the-acsb/index.aspx, accessed May 10, 2018.
6. "Who we are," IFRS, accessed May 10, 2018, https://www.ifrs.org/about-us/who-we-are/.
7. Libby et al., *Financial Accounting*, 24.
8. Ibid., 19.
9. Madeline Farber, "Ernst & Young Was Just Fined $9.3 Million for Inappropriate Client Relationships," *Fortune*, September 20, 2016; Tatyana Shumsky, "Mistakes That Dog Financial Reporting," *The Wall Street Journal*, April 12, 2016; and Tom Hals, "Nine Years On, Another Lehman Brothers Bankruptcy," Reuters, September 1, 2017.
10. Michael Rapoport, "Auditors Count on Tech for Backup," *The Wall Street Journal*, March 8, 2016; Vipal Monga, "56% Share of North American Companies That Used a Third Party for Internal Audits," *The Wall Street Journal*, April 5, 2016; and Jason Zweig, "How a New Audit Rule Could Bring Sunshine to U.S. Markets," *The Wall Street Journal*, August 18, 2017.
11. Amrick Randhawa, "Don't Have a Tax Pro Yet? Time to Get Moving," *Entrepreneur*, February 12, 2014; Pamela Yip, "Be Picky When Choosing a Tax Preparer," *Dallas Morning News*, January 26, 2014.
12. "Ontario Liberals understating deficit by billions: auditor," CBC, April 25, 2018, http://www.cbc.ca/news/canada/toronto/ontario-pre-election-auditor-general-report-finances-1.4634542.
13. Matthew McClearn, "Ontario Liberals substantially understated deficits, province's Auditor-General warns," *The Globe and Mail*, April 25, 2018, https://www.theglobeandmail.com/canada/article-ontario-auditor-general-says-province-substantially-understating/.
14. "About the Canada Revenue Agency (CRA)," Government of Canada, August 23, 2017, http://www.cra-arc.gc.ca/gncy/menu-eng.html.
15. Gary Weiss, "Spotting Nonprofit Accounting Tricks," Barron's Penta, June 20, 2016; Shelley Elmblad, "Free and Low Cost

Accounting Software Options for Nonprofits," The Balance, August 27, 2017.

16. "Adapting to a changing climate: Getting more accountants engaged," CPA Canada, February 20, 2015, https://www.cpacanada.ca/en/connecting-and-news/news/professional-news/2015/February/adapting-to-climate-change-engaging-accountants; "CPA provincial and regional accounting bodies," CPA Canada, 2015, https://www.cpacanada.ca/en/the-cpa-profession/cpa-provincial-and-regional-accounting-bodies; "Uniting the Canadian accounting profession," CPA Canada, 2015, https://www.cpacanada.ca/en/the-cpa-profession/uniting-the-canadian-accounting-profession; "The new Canadian CPA: Bringing together three legacy accounting designations," Hays Canada, *Connected*, issue 6, October 2014, https://www.cpapro.ca/pdfs/hays_1242697.pdf; and "Become a CPA," CPA Canada, 2015, https://www.cpapro.ca/become-a-cpa.
17. "Happy National Aboriginal Day!" Bissell Centre, June 20, 2016, accessed July 18, 2018, https://bissellcentre.org/blog/2016/06/20/2016620happy-national-aboriginal-day/.
18. Pedro Hernandez, "Faster, Smarter Payments with QuickBooks Online," Small Business Computing.com, October 27, 2016; Intuit QuickBooks, www.quickbooks.com, accessed October 2017.
19. Sara Angeles, "Best Accounting Software for Small Business," Business News Daily, November 2, 2016; Kathy Yakal, "The Best Small Business Accounting Software of 2017," *PC Magazine*, August 24, 2017.
20. "Preparing Financial Statements," U.S. Small Business Administration, www.sba.gov, accessed October 2017; "Beginners Guide to Financial Statements," U.S Securities & Exchange Commission, www.sec.gov, accessed October 2017.
21. "How to Prepare a Balance Sheet," QuickBooks.com, accessed October 2017.
22. Catherine Clifford, "New Accounting Framework to Ease Burdens for Small Business," *Entrepreneur*, June 10, 2013.
23. J. B. Maverick, "How Do Intangible Assets Appear on a Balance Sheet?" Investopedia, accessed October 2017.
24. Vipal Monga, "Accounting's New Problem," *The Wall Street Journal*, March 22, 2016; Vipal Monga, "Financial Groups Roll Out New Valuation Standard," *The Wall Street Journal*, January 10, 2017.
25. John W. Schoen, "What's the Difference between Revenue and Income?" MSNBC.com, accessed October 2017.
26. Doug and Polly White, "Five Phases of Cash Flow," *Entrepreneur*, November 22, 2016; "How to Prepare a Cash Flow Statement," www.quickbooks.intuit.com, accessed October 2017.
27. Shawn Tully, "Why Tesla's Cash Crunch May Be Worse Than You Think," *Fortune*, September 2, 2016; Peter Cohan, "Four Reasons to Bet against Tesla," *Forbes*, September 2, 2016; Charley Grant, "Tesla Investors Still Need to Watch Their Wallets," *The Wall Street Journal*, November 18, 2016; Alex Eule, "Why 2017 Has Become a Crucial Year for Tesla," *Barron's*, January 11, 2017; Akin Oyedele, "Tesla Burns Through the Most Cash in Its History," *Business Insider*," August 2, 2017.
28. Thomas Smale, "5 Ways to Boost Your Business' Cash Flow," *Entrepreneur*, June 8, 2016; Carol Roth, "Why Your Business Needs Cash Flow Yoga," *Entrepreneur*, January 18, 2016; Karen Mills, "Here's How Big Government Could Help Small Businesses," *Fortune*, November 3, 2016; Emma Sheppard, "How Entrepreneurs Use Technology to Boost Cashflow," *The Guardian*, January 19, 2017.
29. "Financial Ratios Explanation," www.accountingcoach.com, accessed October 2017.
30. "What is an Auditor?" Reviso, accessed May 10, 2018, https://www.reviso.com/accountingsoftware/accounting-words/auditor.

Chapter 17

1. Joann S. Lublin, "CFO Searches Drag On as Demand Takes Off," *The Wall Street Journal*, February 9, 2016; Alix Stuart, "Quick CFO Exits Can Spell Trouble," *The Wall Street Journal*, August 2, 2016; "Coca-Cola Co Says Kathy Waller's Annual Base Salary for New Position to Be $850,000," Reuters, March 24, 2017.
2. Alix Stuart, "Finance Chiefs Collect Acronyms," *The Wall Street Journal*, June 7, 2016; "The Evolution of the Corporate Treasurer," Bloomberg Professional Services, March 15, 2017.
3. Alix Stuart, "Charities Exert Pull on CFOs," *The Wall Street Journal*, October 4, 2016; Amy West and Ronald Ries, "10 Challenges Facing Not-for-Profit CFOs," *The CPA Journal*, September 2017.
4. Warner Johnson, "How to Retain Young Finance Pros," *CFO*, December 8, 2016; "Fourteen Financial Mistakes All Entrepreneurs Should Avoid," *Forbes*, May 30, 2017.
5. Jason Fekete, "Auditor General: Multibillion-dollar auto sector bailout lacked proper oversight," *Ottawa Citizen*, November 25, 2014, http://ottawacitizen.com/news/politics/auditor-general-auto-sector-bailout-lacked-proper-oversight.
6. Robert Digitale, "Kelseyville company's salt-free spices revival," *The Press Democrat*, September 4, 2014, http://www.pressdemocrat.com/business/2669427-181/a-salt-free-spices-revival; McCormick, www.mccormick.com, accessed February 2014.
7. Justin Lahart, "Earnings: Not as Advertised," *The Wall Street Journal*, February 25, 2016; Michael Rapoport, "Auditors Count On Tech for Backup," *The Wall Street Journal*, March 8, 2016; Mike Hogan, "Defending the GAAP," *Barron's*, June 22, 2016; Terry Sheridan, "7 Top Priorities for Audit Committees in 2017," AccountingWEB, January 12, 2017.
8. Michael Rapoport, "Big Four Accounting Firms Show Fewer Problem Audits," *The Wall Street Journal*, December 12, 2016; Sean Allocca, "Audit Committees Face Expertise, Risk Management Challenges," *CFO*, January 11, 2017.
9. Stephen A. Ross et al., *Fundamentals of Corporate Finance*, 9th Canadian ed. (Toronto: McGraw Hill Ryerson Ltd., 2016), 147.
10. "Risk-return trade-off," Accounting Tools, May 13, 2017, https://www.accountingtools.com/articles/2017/5/13/risk-return-trade-off.
11. Robert Reiss, "Industry Leading CFOs Share Insights on How Digital Is Opening New Opportunities," *Forbes*, November 21, 2016; Heather Clancy, "CFOs Are Becoming Cloud Software Converts," *Fortune*, June 20, 2016; and Jeff Thomson, "The Seismic Shift in Finance, and How Workday's CFO is Capitalizing," *Forbes*, August 4, 2017.
12. Bill Fotsch and John Case, "Forecasting—The Secret to Controlling Your Business (and Engaging Employees Too)," *Forbes*, August 23, 2016; Rheaa Rao, "Executives Tend to Offer Precise Forecasts to Reassure Investors," *The Wall Street Journal*, May 31, 2017.
13. "Five of the Different Types of Budgets," The Finance Base, accessed October 2017.
14. David Charron, "What to Expect in the Housing Market in 2017," *The Washington Post*, December 27, 2016; John Minnich, "China's Economic Problems Will Come to a Head in 2017," *MarketWatch*, November 23, 2016; Gregor Stuart Hunter, "Why China's Recent Market Plunge Didn't Spark a Broader Selloff," *The Wall Street Journal*, January 18, 2017.
15. "Time Value of Money," Khan Academy, accessed October 2017; "What Is the Time Value of Money," The Motley Fool, accessed October 2017.
16. David Finkel, "7 Tips to Lower Your Outstanding Receivables and Collect More of What You Are Owed," *Inc.*, October 19, 2016; Larry Alton, "6 Steps to Successfully Collect on a Small Business Debt," Small Business Trends, May 24, 2017.
17. Elizabeth Weise, "Google Launches Android Pay," *USA Today*, May 28, 2015; "The Ultimate Guide to How and Where to Use ApplePay," *MacWorld*, April 29, 2016; Leena Rao, "ApplePay Now Accounts for Three-Fourths of Contactless Payments," *Fortune*, July 26, 2016; Irving Wladawsky-Berger, "Mobile Payments: A Long, Relentless War of Attrition," *The Wall Street Journal*, June 9, 2017.
18. Nancy Trejos, "Marriott to Let Guests Use ApplePay at Check-In," *USA Today*, 2016; Ryan Mac, "Apple Gunning for PayPal as It Introduces Apple Pay for Web," *Forbes*, June 16, 2016; "Mobile Payment Options Should Drive Growth For McDonald's, Burger King," *Forbes*, May 15, 2017.
19. Jason Kruger, "If You Don't Know Your Company's Inventory Turnover Ratio, You're in Trouble," *Fortune*, August 29, 2016; Ted

Needleman, "The Best Inventory Management Software of 2017," *PC Magazine,* August 29, 2017.
20. Caron Beesley, "6 Tips for Borrowing Start-Up Funds from Friends and Family," U.S. Small Business Administration, September 23, 2016; "The Ins and Outs of Raising Money from Friends and Family," *Entrepreneur,* accessed October 2017.
21. National Federation of Independent Business, www.nfib.com, accessed October 2017.
22. Jared Hecht, "The Perks of a Business Line of Credit," *Inc.,* September 1, 2016; Jared Hecht, "The Four Lines of Credit Now Available to Small Business," *Entrepreneur,* May 12, 2016; Jeff White, "Best Small Business Line of Credit 2017," Fit Small Business, July 13, 2017.
23. "I want to learn more about my credit profile," Canadian Bankers Association, accessed May 19, 2018, https://cba.ca/i-want-to-learn-more-about-my-credit-profile; "Understanding the Basics of Business Credit," Dun & Bradstreet, Inc., accessed May 19, 2018, https://iupdate.dnb.com/iUpdate/whatAre4Cs.htm.
24. "Commercial Paper," Rate Save Canada, accessed May 18, 2018, http://ratesavecanada.ca/investing.php topic=205&id=138&article=commercial-paper.
25. "The Basics of Using Credit Cards to Fund Your New Business," *Entrepreneur,* accessed October 2017.
26. Jared Hecht, "Using a Credit Card to Finance Your Business: Good Idea or Bad Idea?" *Inc.,* January 25, 2016; Diana Hembree, "Business Credit Cards Carry Hidden Risks," *Forbes,* August 28, 2017.
27. "Is the High Cost of Drugs to Offset R&D Spending Justified?" *Forbes,* March 23, 2016; Gonzalo Vina, "Returns on Big Pharma Research and Development Hit Six Year Low," *Financial Times,* December 12, 2016; Jason Gale and Marthe Forcade, "There's Big Money Again in Saving Humanity with Antibiotics," *Bloomberg Businessweek,* June 20, 2016; and Frank David, "Pharma's Not So Stingy With R&D After All," *Forbes,* May 14, 2017.
28. "Canada sells more 50-year bonds," CBC News, July 11, 2014, http://www.cbc.ca/news/business/canada-sells-more-50-year-bonds-1.2703972.
29. Timothy W. Martin, "What Crisis? Ratings Firms Thrive," *The Wall Street Journal,* March 11, 2016; Gretchen Morgenson, "Should Free Markets Govern the Bond Rating Agencies?" *The New York Times,* May 5, 2017.
30. "Cara shares jump 40% as parent of Harvey's and Swiss Chalet returns to TSX," *Financial Post,* April 10, 2015, http://business.financialpost.com/investing/cara-shares-jump-40-as-parent-of-harveys-and-swiss-chalet-returns-to-tsx; and Eric Lam, "Cara's a Beautiful Thing in Best IPO Debut Since 2007," Bloomberg L.P., April 10, 2015, http://www.bloomberg.com/news/articles/2015-04-10/cara-s-a-beautiful-thing-in-best-ipo-debut-since-2007.
31. Jeff Kornblau, "5 Dividend Aristocrats Where Analysts See Capital Gains," *Forbes,* January 18, 2017.
32. Jen Wieczner, "Microsoft Is the Best Dividend Stock on the Fortune 500," *Fortune,* June 21, 2016; Chris Davis, "Best Dividend Stocks for 2017," *Fortune,* December 6, 2016; Eric Ervin, "If These 4 Stocks Declared Dividends In 2017, It Could Mean Billions In Payouts," *Forbes,* January 26, 2017.
33. "Sun Life Financial increases Common Share dividend and declares dividends on Preferred Shares," CISION, May 8, 2018, https://www.newswire.ca/news-releases/sun-life-financial-increases-common-share-dividend-and-declares-dividends-on-preferred-shares-682104841.html.
34. "Common and Preferred Stock: What's the Difference," The Motley Fool, February 23, 2014.
35. Lauren Thomas, "Canada Goose closes its first day trading up more than 25%," CNBC, March 16, 2017, https://www.cnbc.com/2017/03/16/luxury-apparel-maker-canada-goose-shares-open-at-18-in-market-debut.html.
36. "Financial leverage," Accounting Tools, December 20, 2017, https://www.accountingtools.com/articles/2017/5/14/financial-leverage.
37. Chris Mathews, "Corporate America Is Drowning in Debt," *Fortune,* May 20, 2016; Paul R. La Monica, "Apple Has $246 Billion in Cash, Nearly All Overseas," CNN, February 1, 2017.
38. Selena Williams and Bradley Olsen, "Big Oil Companies Binge on Debt," *The Wall Street Journal,* August 26, 2016; Mark Fahey, "Corporate Debt Is at New Highs, and These Companies Owe the Most," CNBC, April 11, 2017.
39. "CFA Program," CFA Institute, accessed 22 May 2018, https://www.cfainstitute.org/programs/cfa; "CFA Program Course of Study," CFA Institute, accessed May 22, 2018, http://www.cfainstitute.org/programs/cfaprogram/courseofstudy/Pages/index.aspx; and "CFA Charter Factsheet," CFA Institute, accessed May 22, 2018, cfa-charter-factsheet.pdf.

Chapter 18

1. "Bank of Canada," Historica Canada, accessed May 31, 2018, http://www.thecanadianencyclopedia.ca/en/article/bank-of-canada/; and "About the Bank," Bank of Canada, accessed May 31, 2018, https://www.bankofcanada.ca/about/.
2. David Scott, "How Much Currency Is Traded Every Day," *Business Insider,* September 2, 2016; Andrea Wong and Vincent Cignarella, "It's 1980s All Over Again for FX Desks Looking at Trade Flow," *Bloomberg Businessweek,* February 10, 2017.
3. "Canada's nickel could soon be phased out like the penny, economist says," Canadian Press, February 2, 2018, https://globalnews.ca/news/4002870/canada-nickel-phased-out-penny/; and Andrew Russell, "Should Canada eliminate the nickel? New study says it will happen within 5 years," Global News, May 3, 2016, https://globalnews.ca/news/2677782/should-canada-eliminate-the-nickel-new-study-says-it-could-within-5-years/.
4. Sandeep Soni, "Bartering Is Back in Style! These Startups Tell Us How," *Entrepreneur,* December 16, 2016; "The Beauty of Bartering: A Smart Way to Start and Grow Your Business," *Entrepreneur,* October 19, 2016; and Hannah Wallace, "How to Barter Anything," Real Simple, accessed October 2017.
5. Russell, "Should Canada eliminate the nickel? New study says it will happen within 5 years."
6. Neal Godfrey, "Millennials Show Boomers the Benefits of Barter: Pass It On," *Forbes,* November 1, 2015; Natasha Burton, "Bartering in the Modern Day: How People Are Swapping Goods and Services . . . for Free," *Forbes,* July 20, 2015; Eli Newman, "Detroiters' Barter System Isn't Just About Kindness — It's A Necessity," NPR, July 29, 2017.
7. Jean Murry, "What is a Barter Exchange? How Does a Barter Exchange Work?" The Balance, June 16, 2016.
8. "Canada's nickel could soon be phased out like the penny, economist says," Canadian Press; and Russell, "Should Canada eliminate the nickel? New study says it will happen within 5 years."
9. "$5 Polymer Note," Bank of Canada, accessed June 3, 2018, https://www.bankofcanada.ca/banknotes/bank-note-series/frontiers/5-polymer-note/; "Security," Bank of Canada, accessed May 7, 2015, http://www.bankofcanada.ca/banknotes/bank-note-series/polymer/security/.
10. "Life-Cycle Assessment (LCA)," Bank of Canada, accessed June 3, 2018, https://www.bankofcanada.ca/banknotes/bank-note-series/frontiers/life-cycle-assessment-lca/.
11. "Laws, regulations and other obligations," Government of Canada, April 6, 2018, https://www.canada.ca/en/financial-consumer-agency/services/industry.html; and "Our History - Office of the Superintendent of Financial Institutions," Government of Canada, July 26, 2017, http://www.osfi-bsif.gc.ca/Eng/osfi-bsif/Pages/hst.aspx?pedisable=true; and "Regulation of the Canadian Financial System," Bank of Canada, April 2012, http://www.bankofcanada.ca/wp-content/uploads/2010/11/regulation_canadian_financial.pdf.
12. "The Scotiabank Story," Scotiabank, 2015, http://www.scotiabank.com/ca/en/0,476,00.html.
13. "About Us," Office of the Superintendent of Financial Institutions, April 20, 2017, http://www.osfi-bsif.gc.ca/Eng/osfi-bsif/Pages/default.aspx; Hamish Stewart, "The Bank of Canada could lead the way to a prosperous low-carbon economy," National Observer, May 28, 2018, https://www.nationalobserver.com/2018/05/28/opinion/bank-canada-could-lead-way-prosperous-low-carbon-economy.

14. "About deposit insurance," Canada Deposit Insurance Corporation, accessed June 4, 2018, http://www.cdic.ca/en/about-di/Pages/default.aspx; and "CDIC welcomes new measures to strengthen Canada's resolution regime," Canada Deposit Insurance Canada, May 18, 2017, http://www.cdic.ca/en/newsroom/newsreleases/Pages/cdic-welcomes-new-measures-to-strengthen-canadas-resolution-regime.aspx.
15. "Financial Consumer Agency of Canada," Government of Canada, May 30, 2018, https://www.canada.ca/en/financial-consumer-agency.html; and "Retail banking sales culture may raise risks for consumers: Financial Consumer Agency of Canada," Government of Canada, March 20, 2018, https://www.canada.ca/en/financial-consumer-agency/news/2018/03/retail-banking-sales-culture-may-raise-risks-for-consumers.html.
16. "Financial Institutions and Markets," Department of Finance Canada, November 14, 2014, http://www.fin.gc.ca/access/fininst-eng.asp.
17. "Banks Operating in Canada," Canadian Bankers Association, May 6, 2014, http://www.cba.ca/en/component/content/category/61-banks-operating-in-canada.
18. "Focus: Bank Revenues and Profits," Canadian Bankers Association, accessed June 6, 2018, https://www.cba.ca/bank-revenues-and-earnings-profits.
19. Ibid.
20. "Banks operating in Canada," Canadian Bankers Association, July 14, 2015, https://cba.ca/banks-operating-in-canada.
21. Richard Forbes, "Canadian Industrial Outlook: Banking - Winter 2018," 2, The Conference Board of Canada, April 4, 2018, https://www.conferenceboard.ca/temp/ba47a9f2-1208-4a31-93ea-1439ad18c3c8/9569_CIOS%20Banking_Winter2018.pdf.
22. Meghan Streit, "Money Lessons from Millennials," Erickson Tribune, October 2016; Boris Shiklo, "Mobile Banking: Exploring Trends For Market Leadership," *Forbes,* May 16, 2017.
23. "Credit Unions in Canada," Canadian Credit Union Association, accessed June 4, 2018, https://www.ccua.com/credit_unions_in_canada.
24. Kimberly Palmer, "The Pros and Cons of a Credit Union versus a Bank," U.S. News & World Report, June 6, 2015; Miriam Caldwell, "Advantages of Credit Unions," The Balance, May 14, 2017.
25. Tom Huddleston Jr., "This city's subway system just got new bitcoin ATMs — and it's not alone," CNBC, May 31, 2018, https://www.cnbc.com/2018/05/31/bitcoin-atms-in-america-and-around-the-world.html.
26. "Trust Company," The Canadian Encyclopedia, accessed June 4, 2018, http://www.thecanadianencyclopedia.ca/en/article/trust-company/.
27. Danielle Douglas, "Rise in Prepaid Credit Cards Entices Banks to Sponsor Them," *The Washington Post,* January 24, 2014.
28. *Forbes*, "Canadian Industrial Outlook: Banking - Winter 2018," 4.
29. Sean O'Shea, "Lost your credit card? Some Canadian banks may hold you fully liable," Global News, February 3, 2017, https://globalnews.ca/news/3227050/lost-your-credit-card-some-canadian-banks-may-hold-you-fully-liable/.
30. "Office of Consumer Affairs (OCA) - Debit Card Fraud - When would you be liable for losses?" Innovation, Science and Economic Development Canada, accessed 4 June 2018, http://www.ic.gc.ca/eic/site/oca-bc.nsf/eng/ca01836.html.
31. Aimee Picchi, "The Hidden Troubles with Payroll Cards," CBS News Moneywatch, May 20, 2016; Stacy Cowley, "Payroll Card Regulations in New York Are Struck Down," *The New York Times,* March 3, 2017.
32. "'Tap to pay' card security - An FAQ," Canadian Bankers Association, August 1, 2016, https://www.cba.ca/tap-to-pay-card-security-an-faq.
33. "Are Canadians ready to drop cheques and cash for digital/mobile alternatives?" CISION, May 9, 2017, https://www.newswire.ca/news-releases/are-canadians-ready-to-drop-cheques-and-cash-for-digitalmobile-alternatives-621720233.html.
34. Rudy Mezzetta, "Pulling focus: The banks' new strategy," Investment Executive, October 27, 2017, https://www.investmentexecutive.com/newspaper_/news-newspaper/pulling-focus-the-banks-new-strategy/.
35. "Canadian Bank Milestones," Canadian Bankers Association, accessed 4 June 4, 2018, https://www.cba.ca/Assets/CBA/Images/Article-detail-images/cba-anniversary-infographic-en.png.
36. "Canada needs a federated digital ID framework," Canadian Bankers Association, May 30, 2018, https://www.cba.ca/canada-needs-a-federated-digital-id-framework; and "Infographic: A Roadmap to Enable A Federated Digital ID Approach in Canada," Canadian Bankers Association, May 30, 2018, https://www.cba.ca/roadmap-to-enable-federated-digital-id-approach-in-canada.
37. Ibid.
38. "About Financial Markets," Bank of Canada, accessed June 4, 2018, https://www.bankofcanada.ca/markets/about-financial-markets/; "The Basics of Investing - Security," The Government of Canada, April 27, 2018, https://www.canada.ca/en/financial-consumer-agency/services/savings-investments/investing-basics.html; "Definition of securities/investment dealer," Super Brokers Inc., accessed June 5, 2018, https://www.superbrokers.ca/library/glossary/terms/securities_investment_dealer.php; Leslie McClintock, "How to Buy Corporate Bonds in Canada," Pocket Sense, April 19, 2017, https://pocketsense.com/buy-corporate-bonds-canada-1018.html; and Andrew Nelson, "Cryptocurrency Regulation in 2018: Where the World Stands Right Now," *Bitcoin Magazine,* February 1, 2018, https://bitcoinmagazine.com/articles/cryptocurrency-regulation-2018-where-world-stands-right-now/.
39. John Devine, "The Most Anticipated IPOs of 2017," *Money,* November 21, 2016; Jordan Novett, "This App Software Maker Filed to Raise $100 Million for an IPO," *Fortune,* December 29, 2016; Corrie Driebusch, "More Companies Test IPO Market," *The Wall Street Journal,* January 19, 2017.
40. "Careers in Investment Banking," Canadian Securities Institute, accessed June 5, 2018, https://www.csi.ca/student/en_ca/career/investment/index.xhtml.
41. Jake Bright, "Obama's Africa Trip Is All about Trade, Investment, and Tech," Fortune, July 23, 2015; Mathew A. Winkler, "Where's the Growth? Africa," *Bloomberg Businessweek,* November 10, 2015; and Ed Stoddard and TJ Strydom, "South Africa's Stock Market Defies Recession, Scales Record Highs," Reuters, July 31, 2017.
42. "Stock market basics," Ontario Securities Commission, accessed June 5, 2018, https://www.getsmarteraboutmoney.ca/invest/investment-products/stocks/stock-market-basics/.
43. "How Regulators Protect Investors," Ontario Securities Commission, accessed June 5, 2018, https://www.getsmarteraboutmoney.ca/protect-your-money/investor-protection/regulation-in-canada/how-regulators-protect-investors/.
44. "Overview," Canadian Securities Administrators, accessed June 5, 2018, https://www.securities-administrators.ca/aboutcsa.aspx?id=45.
45. "The Canadian Securities Transition Office," Government of Canada, http://csto-btcvm.ca/home.aspx, accessed May 8, 2015.
46. Ibid.
47. Jason Zweig, "Don't Let Others Sway You When Making Investment Decisions," *The Wall Street Journal,* January 21, 2017.
48. "The Case for Diversification," Charles Schwab Personal Finance, Summer 2016; Todd Schanel and Jackie Goldstick, "What Exactly Does Investment Diversification Really Mean?" CNBC, November 15, 2016; "The Pro's Guide to Diversification," Fidelity Investments Fidelity Viewpoints, November 8, 2016; Olivier Garret, "The Best Way To Diversify Your Portfolio In 2017," *Forbes,* February 2, 2017.
49. Alex Dumotier, "What Does 2017 Hold for Penny Stocks?" The Motley Fool, accessed October 2017.
50. Jason Zweig, "Death of the Stock Split: It's the Value That Matters," *The Wall Street Journal,* October 2, 2016; "Split Ends: A Wall Street Practice Is Dying Out," *The Economist,* September 24, 2016; David Nicklaus, "Splits: Goodbye, Good Riddance," St. Louis Post-Dispatch, November 14, 2016; Lu Wang, "Stock Split Is All But Dead and a New Study Says Save Your Tears," *Bloomberg Businessweek,* August 23, 2017.
51. Alan Elliott, "How to Sell Great Stocks: Why Big Stock Splits Usually Warn the End Is Near," *Investor's Business Daily,* October 11, 2016; Erik Holm, "Three Reasons Why Warren Buffett Never

Split Berkshire's $250,000 Stock," *The Wall Street Journal,* February 15, 2017.

52. Amanda Kay, "How is the S&P/TSX Composite Index Weighted?" Investing News, January 23, 2018, https://investingnews.com/daily/resource-investing/how-is-the-sptsx-composite-index-weighted/; Colibri Trader, "How to Trade the Oil and Canadian Dollar Relationship," FXStreet, July 12, 2017, https://www.fxstreet.com/analysis/how-to-trade-the-oil-and-canadian-dollar-relationship-201707121031; Patrick Cain, "Link between Canadian dollar and oil prices coming undone," Global News, August 22, 2016, https://globalnews.ca/news/2885196/link-between-canadian-dollar-and-oil-prices-coming-undone/; Khaleef Crumbley, "7 Important Uses For Crude Oil And Why It Matters," Bible Money Matters, accessed June 6, 2018, https://www.biblemoneymatters.com/7-important-uses-for-crude-oil-and-why-it-matters/; and Alexandria Arnold, "Crude Oil's Surge Is Putting the 'Petro' Back in Petrocurrencies," Bloomberg, May 20, 2018, https://www.bloomberg.com/news/articles/2018-05-20/crude-oil-s-surge-is-putting-the-petro-back-in-petrocurrencies.
53. "Everything You Need to Know about P/E Ratios," Money, accessed October 2017; Bob Bryan, "One Key Measure Shows the Stock Market Hasn't Been This Expensive in 13 Years," *Business Insider,* February 21, 2017.
54. Peter Coy, Sridhar Natarajan, and Michelle F. Davis, "The AAA Rating Club: Johnson & Johnson, Microsoft," *Bloomberg Businessweek,* May 15, 2016; Maurie Backman, "How to Invest in Bonds: A Step-by-Step Guide," The Motley Fool, May 7, 2017.
55. "IFIC Industry Overview," The Investment Funds Institute of Canada, April 2018, https://www.ific.ca/wp-content/uploads/2018/05/2018-4-Industry-Overview.pdf/19711/.
56. "Stats and Facts," The Investment Funds Institute of Canada, accessed June 6, 2018, https://www.ific.ca/en/info/stats-and-facts/.
57. "Understanding Management Expense Ratios," CI Investments, accessed June 6, 2018, http://www.ci.com/professionaldevelopment/files/mer-explained_e.pdf.
58. "About fees: Management expense ratios explained," Fidelity Investments, accessed June 6, 2018, https://www.fidelity.ca/fidca/en/valueofadvice/aboutfees.
59. Barbara Novick, "How Index Funds Democratize Investing," *The Wall Street Journal,* January 9, 2017.
60. Pat McKeough, "How to pick the best Canadian index funds," TSI Wealth Daily Watch, October 24, 2017, https://www.tsinetwork.ca/daily-advice/etfs/how-to-pick-the-best-canadian-index-funds/.
61. Daise Maxey, "New Rule Will Help No-Load Funds," *The Wall Street Journal,* November 7, 2016; Kent Thune, "The Best No-Load Mutual Fund Companies," The Balance, March 10, 2017.
62. "Exchange Traded Funds: Everything You Wanted to Know about Exchange Traded Funds but Were Scared to Ask," The Motley Fool, November 14, 2016.
63. "Industry Statistics," Canadian ETF Association, June 18, 2018, accessed July 19, 2018, http://www.cetfa.ca/files/1529346149_NEW%20CETFA%20-%20May%202018.pdf.
64. "Regulatory Oversight of Designated Clearing and Settlement Systems," Bank of Canada, accessed June 6, 2018, https://www.bankofcanada.ca/core-functions/financial-system/oversight-designated-clearing-settlement-systems/.

Appendix B

1. "Financial Consumer Agency of Canada," Government of Canada, May 23, 2018, https://www.canada.ca/en/financial-consumer-agency.html.
2. "Canadian Financial Literacy Database," Government of Canada, May 10, 2017, https://www.canada.ca/en/financial-consumer-agency/services/financial-literacy-database.html.
3. Jeff Charis-Carlson, "UI Students Help Local High Schools Think through Money Concerns," Iowa City Press-Citizen, January 3, 2017.
4. Jeff Kauflin, "The 20 College Majors with the Highest Starting Salaries," *Forbes,* October 17, 2016; Karsten Strauss, "College Degrees With the Highest (And Lowest) Starting Salaries In 2017," *Forbes,* June 28, 2017.
5. Jill Cornfield, "New Year's Resolutions That Help Your Retirement Savings," Bankrate, December 15, 2016.
6. Jae Yang and Paul Trap, "Forever in Debt," *USA Today,* January 20, 2016; Emmie Martin, "5 Things to Do in Your 20s to Get Out of Debt by 30," CNBC, July 11, 2017.
7. "Cash Jar/Envelope Budget Method (Gail Vaz-Oxlade Style)," SmartCanucks, January 5, 2013, https://smartcanucks.ca/gail-vaz-oxlade-cash-jar-envelope-budget-method/.
8. Alyssa Furtado, "Why Your Credit Card's Grace Period Is Your Best Friend," The HuffPost, May 10, 2017, https://www.huffingtonpost.ca/alyssa-furtado/credit-card-grace-period_b_16533976.html.
9. Scott Terrio, "Can it make sense to have savings as well as high-interest debt?" *MoneySense,* May 14, 2018, http://www.moneysense.ca/save/debt/pay-off-debt-quickly-savings/.
10. Ian McGugan, "David Chilton's rise from The Wealthy Barber to The Wealthy Dragon," *The Globe and Mail,* May 12, 2018, https://www.theglobeandmail.com/report-on-business/careers/careers-leadership/david-chiltons-rise-from-the-wealthy-barber-to-the-wealthy-dragon/article22612138/.
11. Krystal Yee, "5 essential money lessons from The Wealthy Barber Returns," *Canadian Living,* 2015, http://www.canadianliving.com/life/money/5_essential_money_lessons_ from_the_wealthy_barber_returns.php.
12. "What is Compound Interest?" The Motley Fool, accessed May 26, 2018, https://www.fool.com/knowledge-center/compound-interest.aspx.
13. Jae Yang and Paul Trap, "False Financial Belief," *USA Today,* May 9, 2016; Michelle Singletary, "The Debit Card Nightmare: a Number Is Stolen and Charges Pile Up," *The Washington Post,* July 25, 2017.
14. "Setting up an emergency fund," Government of Canada, November 21, 2017, https://www.canada.ca/en/financial-consumer-agency/services/savings-investments/setting-up-emergency-funds.html.
15. Dale Jackson, "Personal Investor: TFSA total contribution room increases another $5,500 in 2018," BNN Bloomberg, December 8, 2017, https://www.bnnbloomberg.ca/personal-investor-tfsa-contribution-limit-remains-at-5-500-in-2018-1.938436; "The Tax-Free Savings Account," Canada Revenue Agency, November 24, 2016, https://www.canada.ca/en/revenue-agency/services/tax/individuals/topics/tax-free-savings-account.html.
16. "Largest Cohort of Millennials Changing Canadian Real Estate, Despite Constraints of Affordability and Mortgage Regulation," Brookfield Real Estate Services Manager Limited, August 17, 2017, https://www.royallepage.ca/en/realestate/news/largest-cohort-of-millennials-changing-canadian-real-estate-despite-constraints-of-affordability-and-mortgage-regulation/.
17. Tara Siegal Bernard, "To Buy or Rent a Home? Weighing Which is Better," *The New York Times,* April 1, 2016; Ron Lieber, "All Our Best Advice on Deciding Whether to Rent or Buy a Home," *The New York Times,* June 4, 2017.
18. Cathie Ericson, "5 Habits to Start Now If You Hope to Buy a Home in 2017," Realtor.com, December 29, 2016; Wendy Connick, "How to Save Enough Money for a Down Payment on a Home," CNN, August 11, 2017.
19. "5 Reasons Your First Home Should Be a Duplex," *Forbes,* July 29, 2016; Steve Gillman, "We Invested in a Duplex. Here's What We've Learned So Far," The Penny Hoarder, July 10, 2017.
20. Dougal Shaw, "Could Your Unused Space Make You Money?" BBC News, December 16, 2016; James Dobbins, "Making a Living With Airbnb," *The New York Times,* April 7, 2017.
21. David Schrieberg, "Uber for Your Laundry Could Be the Next Sharing Economy Frontier," *Forbes,* December 18, 2016; Nathan Heller, "Is the Gig Economy Working?" *The New Yorker,* May 15, 2017.
22. Jason Zweig, "Don't Let Others Sway You When Making Investment Decisions," *The Wall Street Journal,* January 21, 2017.
23. "Detailed. Historical. Precise. Client conversation starters," Morningstar Canada, 2015, http://corporate.morningstar.com/ca/asp/subject.aspx?xmlfile=6775.xml.
24. David Nield, "Android Pay vs. Apple Pay: Who's Winning the Mobile Payment Battle?" T3, December 21, 2016; Donald Bush,

"The Future Of Mobile Wallets: The Sky's The Limit," *Forbes,* July 17, 2017.

25. Ellen Cannon, "After EMV Shift, Credit Card Transactions Still Not as Safe as Possible," NerdWallet, May 23, 2016; Sienna Kossman, "8 FAQs about EMV Credit Cards," www.creditcards.com, August 29, 2017.
26. Narayan Makaram, "'Threat Intelligence' Technology Can Fight Big Box Data Breaches," PaymentSource, December 29, 2016; Elizabeth Weise, "Why Our Credit Cards Keep Getting Hacked," *USA Today,* June 5, 2017.
27. "Security Expert: Chip-Enabled Credit Cards Don't Solve All Risks," Fox 25—Boston, December 15, 2016; Jeff Bukhari, "That Chip on Your Credit Card Isn't Stopping Fraud After All," *Fortune,* February 1, 2017.
28. Jae Yang and Paul Trap, "False Financial Belief," *USA Today,* May 9, 2016; Michelle Singletary, "The Debit Card Nightmare: a Number Is Stolen and Charges Pile Up," *The Washington Post,* July 25, 2017.
29. "Protection against unauthorized credit and debit transactions," Government of Canada, January 25, 2018, https://www.canada.ca/en/financial-consumer-agency/services/rights-responsibilities/protection-unauthorized-transactions.html.
30. Ibid.
31. Lyle Adriano, "Most Canadians are underinsured: Study," Insurance Business Canada, March 8, 2017, https://www.insurancebusinessmag.com/ca/news/breaking-news/most-canadians-are-underinsured-study-62245.aspx.
32. "Life Insurance News & Resources," Kanetix.ca Life Insurance, accessed May 27, 2018, https://www.kanetix.ca/life_cov_calc.
33. Barbara Marquand, "A New Parent's Guide to Life Insurance," NerdWallet, March 3, 2017.
34. Linda Ray, "What Does 'Guaranteed Replacement Cost' in a Homeowner's Insurance Policy Mean?" The Nest, accessed January 9, 2016.
35. "Disability Insurance," Onkar Supervisa Insurance, accessed May 28, 2018, http://onkarinsurance.ca/disability-insurance-edmonton/.
36. "Study: The local unemployment rate and retirement, 1991 to 2007," Statistics Canada, April 22, 2015, http://www.statcan.gc.ca/daily-quotidien/150422/dq150422a-eng.htm.
37. "Determining how much money you need for retirement," Government of Canada, November 1, 2017, https://www.canada.ca/en/financial-consumer-agency/services/retirement-planning/money-to-retire.html.
38. "A Complete Guide to Canada's Retirement Income System," Savvy New Canadians, accessed May 27, 2018, https://www.savvynewcanadians.com/a-complete-guide-to-canadas-retirement-income-system/; Jean-Claude Ménard, "Pillar integration, basic protection and replacement rates in four modern multi pillar pension systems – case of Canada," Office of the Superintendent of Financial Institutions Canada, November 4, 2014, http://www.osfi-bsif.gc.ca/Eng/oca-bac/sp-ds/Pages/jcm20141104.aspx; and Karim Moussaly, "Participation in Private Retirement Savings Plans, 1997 to 2008," Statistics Canada, March 2010, http://www.statcan.gc.ca/pub/13f0026m/13f0026m2010001-eng.pdf.
39. "Old Age Security payment amounts," Government of Canada, accessed May 28, 2018, https://www.canada.ca/en/services/benefits/publicpensions/cpp/old-age-security/payments.html#tbl1; Shane McNeil, "Government won't raise age of CPP, OAS eligibility: Families Minister," BNN, February 7, 2017, https://www.bnnbloomberg.ca/government-won-t-raise-oas-cpp-eligibility-families-minister-1.666405; Jason Heath, "How to reinstate OAS after it's clawed back," *MoneySense,* May 1, 2018, http://www.moneysense.ca/save/retirement/pensions/reinstate-oas-after-clawback/; and John Archer, "Government pensions: What (and when) to expect payments in 2018," *Montreal Gazette,* January 6, 2018, http://montrealgazette.com/news/local-news/government-pensions-what-and-when-to-expect-payments-in-2018.
40. "Canada Pension Plan - Overview," Government of Canada, accessed May 28, 2018, https://www.canada.ca/en/services/benefits/publicpensions/cpp.html; "Return on CPP contributions still meagre after expansion," Fraser Institute, accessed May 28, 2018, https://www.fraserinstitute.org/article/return-on-cpp-contributions-still-meagre-after-expansion; Rob Carrick, "Full CPP benefits are a tough goal to reach," *The Globe and Mail,* February 28, 2018, https://www.theglobeandmail.com/globe-investor/retirement/retire-lifestyle/full-cpp-benefits-are-a-tough-goal-to-reach/article38025370/; and Shane McNeil, "Government won't raise age of CPP, OAS eligibility: Families Minister," BNN, February 7, 2017, https://www.bnnbloomberg.ca/government-won-t-raise-oas-cpp-eligibility-families-minister-1.666405.
41. Erica Alini, "How much do you really need for retirement? We did the math," Global News, February 12, 2018, https://globalnews.ca/news/3981582/how-much-to-save-for-retirement-canada/.
42. "Canada's Retirement Income System: The Three Pillars," McCarthy Tétrault LLP, accessed May 28, 2018, https://www.actuaries.org/stjohns2016/presentations/Mon_Plenary_Bauslaugh.pdf.
43. "Pension plans in Canada, As of January 1, 2016," Statistics Canada, July 21, 2017, http://www.statcan.gc.ca/daily-quotidien/170721/dq170721d-eng.htm; and Moussaly, "Participation in Private Retirement Savings Plans, 1997 to 2008."
44. "Registered Retirement Savings Plan (RRSP)," Government of Canada, February 16, 2018, http://www.cra-arc.gc.ca/tx/ndvdls/tpcs/rrsp-reer/rrsps-eng.html; "What is the Home Buyers' Plan (HBP)?" Government of Canada, October 26, 2016, http://www.cra-arc.gc.ca/tx/ndvdls/tpcs/rrsp-reer/hbp-rap/menu-eng.html; "Lifelong Learning Plan (LLP)," Government of Canada, October 25, 2016, http://www.cra-arc.gc.ca/tx/ndvdls/tpcs/rrsp-reer/llp-reep/menu-eng.html; Pattie Lovett-Reid, "32% of Canadians are nearing retirement without any savings: Poll," BNN Bloomberg, February 8, 2018, https://www.bnnbloomberg.ca/32-of-canadians-are-nearing-retirement-without-any-savings-poll-1.991680; and Sarah Efron and Rob Gerlsbeck, "RRSP: Your top 20 questions answered," Breakfast Television, February 19, 2015, http://www.bttoronto.ca/2015/02/19/rrsp-your-top-20-questions-answered/.
45. Pattie Lovett-Reid, "32% of Canadians are nearing retirement without any savings: Poll," BNN Bloomberg, February 8, 2018, https://www.bnnbloomberg.ca/32-of-canadians-are-nearing-retirement-without-any-savings-poll-1.991680.
46. Ibid.
47. Guy Dixon, "Adviser, advisor or financial planner? Does the name matter?" *The Globe and Mail,* September 12, 2017, https://www.theglobeandmail.com/globe-investor/globe-advisor/adviser-advisor-or-financial-planner-does-the-name-matter/article36124697/.
48. "Power of Attorney FAQ - Canada," LawDepot, accessed May 27, 2018, https://www.lawdepot.ca/law-library/faq/power-of-attorney-faq-canada/#.Wws5cCbruSM.

Online Supplement 1

1. "The Canadian Judicial System," Supreme Court of Canada, 2015, accessed May 17, 2015, http://www.scc-csc.gc.ca/court-cour/sys-eng.aspx.
2. Henry C. Jackson, "House Votes to Increase Asbestos Claim Disclosure," *Bloomberg Businessweek,* November 13, 2013; and "W.R. Grace Emerges from Bankruptcy," *Bloomberg Businessweek,* February 3, 2014.
3. Mesothelioma Center, www.asbestos.com, accessed May 2014.
4. Joann Muller, "Toyota Halts Sales of Popular Models to Fix Seat Heaters," *Forbes,* January 30, 2014; and Ben Klayman, "Toyota Tells U.S. Agency Seat Issue Could Lead to Recall," *Chicago Tribune,* January 30, 2014.
5. Shaya Tayefe Mohajir, "Toyota Settlement: Orange County to Receive $16 Million over Acceleration, Braking Issues," *Huffington Post,* April 5, 2013; Jerry Hirsch, "NHTSA Opens Probe into Brake Failures of Toyota Camry Hybrid Sedan," *Los Angeles Times,* January 27, 2014; and Chris Woodward and Kevin Johnson, "Toyota to Pay $1.2 Billion to Settle Criminal Probe," *USA Today,* March 20, 2014.

6. Jeff Plungis, "GM Investigated over Ignition Recall Linked to 13 Deaths," *Bloomberg Businessweek*, February 27, 2014.
7. Larry Gordon, "Surgeon and Inventor Gives $50 Million for USC Building," *Los Angeles Times*, January 13, 2014.
8. "Competition Bureau – Our Legislation," Competition Bureau, 2015, accessed May 17, 2015, http://www.competitionbureau.gc.ca/eic/site/cb-bc.nsf/eng/h_00148.html.
9. "Competition Bureau – Canada's Anti-Span Law," Competition Bureau, 2015, accessed May 17, 2015, http://www.competitionbureau.gc.ca/eic/site/cb-bc.nsf/eng/03390.html.
10. "Software updates, installations now require consent," CBC News, January 15, 2015, http://www.cbc.ca/news/technology/software-updates-installations-now-require-consent-1.2901868.
11. Sharon Gaudin, "Antitrust Deal Leaves Google Unscathed," *Computerworld*, February 6, 2014.
12. "Global Banking Regulations and Banks in Canada," Canadian Bankers Association, March 13, 2015, http://www.cba.ca/en/media-room/50-backgrounders-on-banking-issues/667-global-banking-regulations-and-banks-in-canada.

Online Supplement 2

1. "Business Protection Lessons Learned: 25 Years After Hurricane Andrew," The Insurance Institute for Business & Home Safety, accessed May 13, 2018, https://disastersafety.org/ibhs/business-protection-lessons-learned-25-years-hurricane-andrew/.
2. John Bugalla and Emanuel Lauria, "When Enterprise Risk Management Gets Strategic," *CFO*, August 15, 2016; American Institute of Certified Public Accountants, www.aicpa.com, accessed October 2017.
3. Joanna Belbey, "Where Does Legal and Compliance Fit into the OCC Framework of Enterprise Risk Management?" *Forbes*, August 31, 2015; "Enterprise Risk Management (ERM) Program Communication – Not an Optional Activity," PwC, May 2017.
4. Raphael Satter, "Yahoo Issues Another Warning in Fallout from Hacking Attacks," *Boston Globe*, February 16, 2017.
5. Ryan Bort, "How Climate Changes Effect on Agriculture Can Lead to War," *Newsweek*, February 17, 2017.
6. Maria Armental, "Starbucks Again Misses Sales Target," *The Wall Street Journal*, July 22, 2016; "World Leaders Discuss Risks of Social Unrest from Advances in Technology," *Computer Weekly*, January 24, 2017.
7. Sy Mukherjee, "Employers Are Cutting Back on Some Wellness Programs," *Fortune*, June 20, 2016; Erika Fry, "Corporate Wellness Programs: Healthy or Hokey?" *Fortune*, March 15, 2017.
8. Patrick Morin, "A Tool to Build a Cyber Defense," *CFO*, February 24, 2016; Jeff John Roberts and Adam Lashinsky, "Hacked: How Business Is Fighting Back Against the Explosion in Cybercrime," *Fortune*, June 22, 2017.
9. Lisa Wirthman, "What Type of Insurances Should Small Business Explore?" *Forbes*, January 13, 2017.
10. "Johnson & Johnson Hopes to Reverse Baby Powder Lawsuits," Reuters, November 7, 2016; Margaret Cronin Fisk and Tim Bross, "J&J Loses Third Trial over Cancer Link to Talcum Powder," Bloomberg, October 27, 2016; Tiffany Hsu, "Risk on All Sides as 4,800 Women Sue Over Johnson's Baby Powder and Cancer," *The New York Times*, September 28, 2017.
11. Kim Lindros and Ed Tittel, "What Is Cyber Insurance and Why You Need It," CIO, May 4, 2016; Sonali Basak, "Is Equifax's Cyber Insurance Enough to Cover Breach?" *Insurance Journal*, September 11, 2017.
12. Matt Egan, "Fracking Fallout: 7.9 Million at Risk of Man-Made Earthquakes," CNNMoney, March 29, 2016; Judy Stone, "Fracking Is Dangerous to Your Health—Here's Why," *Forbes*, February 23, 2017.

Glossary

4 Cs of credit A business' creditworthiness is determined by its character, capacity, capital, and conditions.

80/20 rule The axiom that 80 percent of your business is likely to come from 20 percent of your customers.

absolute advantage The advantage that exists when a country has a monopoly on producing a specific product or is able to produce it more efficiently than all other countries.

accounting The recording, classifying, summarizing, and interpreting of financial events and transactions to provide management and other interested parties the information they need to make good decisions.

accounting cycle A six-step procedure that results in the preparation and analysis of the major financial statements.

accounts Different types of assets, liabilities, and owners' equity.

accounts payable Current liabilities or bills a company owes others for merchandise or services purchased on credit but not yet paid for.

administrative agencies Federal or provincial institutions and other government organizations created by Parliament or provincial legislatures with delegated power to pass rules and regulations within their mandated area of authority.

advertising Paid, non-personal communication through various media by organizations and individuals who are in some way identified in the advertising message.

agency shop (Rand formula) agreement Clause in a negotiated labour–management agreement that says employers may hire non-union workers; employees are not required to join the union but must pay union dues.

agents/brokers Marketing intermediaries who bring buyers and sellers together and assist in negotiating an exchange but do not take title to the goods.

alternative trading systems (ATSs) Automated trading systems that bring together dealers and institutional investors who trade large quantities of stocks.

angel investors Private individuals, often successful business people, who invest their own money into a potentially rewarding private company.

annual report A yearly statement of the financial condition, progress, and expectations of an organization.

annuity A contract to make regular payments to a person for life or a fixed period.

apprentice programs Training programs during which a learner works alongside an experienced employee to master the skills and procedures of a craft.

arbitration An agreement to bring in an impartial third party (a single arbitrator or a panel of arbitrators) to render a binding decision in a labour dispute.

articles of incorporation A legal authorization from the federal or provincial/territorial government for a company to use the corporate format.

assembly process That part of the production process that puts together components.

assets Economic resources (things of value) owned by a firm.

auditing The job of reviewing and evaluating the records used to prepare a company's financial statements.

autocratic leadership A style that involves making managerial decisions without consulting others.

Baby Boomers A demographic group of Canadians who were born in the period from 1946 to 1964.

back-to-work legislation A special law passed by the federal or provincial government that orders an end to a labour–management dispute in an industry the government decides is essential to the operation of the economy.

balance of payments The difference between money coming into a country (from exports) and money leaving the country (for imports) plus money flows from other factors such as tourism, foreign aid, military expenditures, and foreign investment.

balance of trade A nation's ratio of exports to imports.

balance sheet (statement of financial position) The financial statement that reports a firm's financial condition at a specific time and is composed of three major types of accounts: assets, liabilities, and owners' (shareholders' or stockholders') equity.

bankruptcy The legal process by which a person, business, or government entity unable to meet financial obligations is relieved of those obligations by a court that divides debtor assets among creditors, allowing creditors to get at least part of their money and freeing the debtor to begin anew.

bargaining zone Range of options between the initial and final offer that each party will consider before negotiations dissolve or reach an impasse.

barter The direct trading of goods and services for other goods and services.

behavioural segmentation Dividing the market based on behaviour with or toward a product.

benchmarking Comparing an organization's practices, processes, and products against the world's best.

big data Large amounts of data collected from a variety of sources and analyzed with an increasingly sophisticated set of technologies.

blog An online diary (web log) that looks like a web page but is easier to create and update by posting text, photos, or links to other sites.

bond A corporate certificate indicating that an investor has lent money to a firm or a government.

bonds payable Long-term liabilities that represent money lent to a firm that must be paid back.

bookkeeping The recording of business transactions.

boom A period that brings jobs, growth, and economic prosperity.

brain drain The loss of educated people to other countries.

brainstorming Generating as many solutions to a problem as possible in a short period of time with no censoring of ideas.

brand A name, symbol, or design (or combination thereof) that identifies the goods or services of one seller or group of sellers, and distinguishes them from the goods and services of competitors.

brand equity The value of the brand name and associated symbols.

brand loyalty The degree to which customers are satisfied, enjoy the brand, and are committed to further purchases.

brand manager The person in the company who has direct responsibility for one brand or one product line; called a product manager in some firms.

brand name A word, letter, or group of words or letters that differentiates one seller's goods or services from those of competitors.

breach of contract When one party fails to follow the terms of a contract.

break-even analysis The process used to determine profitability at various levels of sales.

broadband technology Technology that offers users a continuous connection to the Internet and allows users to send and receive mammoth files that include voice, video, and data much faster than ever before.

budget A financial plan that sets forth management's expectations, and, on the basis of those expectations, allocates the use of specific resources throughout the firm.

bullying Acts or verbal comments that could mentally hurt or isolate a person in the workplace.

bundling Grouping two or more products together and pricing them as a unit.

bureaucracy An organization with many layers of managers who set rules and regulations and oversee all decisions.

business Any activity that seeks to provide goods and services to others while operating at a profit.

business cycles (economic cycles) The periodic rises and falls that occur in economies over time.

business environment The surrounding factors that either help or hinder the development of businesses.

business incubators Centres that provide space, services, advice, and support to assist new and growing businesses to become established and successful.

business intelligence (BI) (or analytics) The use of data analytic tools to analyze an organization's raw data and derive useful insights.

business law Rules, statutes, codes, and regulations that are established to provide a legal framework within which business must be conducted and that are enforceable by court action.

business plan A detailed written statement that describes the nature of the business, the target market, the advantages the business will have in relation to competition, and the resources and qualifications of the owner(s).

business-to-business (B2B) market All individuals and organizations that want goods and services to use in producing other goods and services or to sell, rent, or supply goods to others.

cafeteria-style fringe benefits Fringe benefits plan that allows employees to choose which benefits they want up to a certain dollar amount.

Canada Deposit Insurance Corporation (CDIC) Oversees the deposit insurance system, which protects deposits that Canadians have in their federal financial institutions.

capital budget A budget that forecasts a firm's spending plans for major asset purchases that often require large sums of money, like property, buildings, and equipment.

capital expenditures Major investments in either tangible long-term assets, such as land, buildings, and equipment, or intangible assets, such as patents, trademarks, and copyrights.

capital gains The positive difference between the purchase price of a stock and its sale price.

capitalism An economic system in which all or most of the factors of production and distribution are privately owned and operated for profit.

cash budget A budget that estimates a firm's cash inflows and outflows during a particular period (e.g. monthly or quarterly).

cash flow The difference between cash coming in and cash going out of a business.

cash flow forecast Forecast that predicts the cash inflows and outflows in future periods, usually months or quarters.

cash flow statement (statement of cash flows) A financial statement that reports cash receipts and cash disbursements related to a firm's three major activities: operations, investing, and financing.

centralized authority An organization structure in which decision-making authority is maintained at the top level of management at the company's headquarters.

certificate of deposit A time-deposit (savings) account that earns interest to be delivered at the end of the certificate's maturity date; also called a Guaranteed Investment Certificate (GIC).

certification Formal process whereby a union is recognized by the Labour Relations Board (LRB) as the bargaining agent for a group of employees.

chain of command The line of authority that moves from the top of a hierarchy to the lowest level.

channel of distribution A set of marketing intermediaries, such as agents, brokers, wholesalers, and retailers, that join together to transport and store goods in their path (or channel) from producers to consumers.

chartered professional accountant (CPA) designation The internationally recognized Canadian accounting designation.

checkoff A contract clause requiring the employer to deduct union dues from employees' pay and remit them to a union.

civil law Legal proceedings that do not involve criminal acts.

claim A statement of a loss that the insured sends to the insurance company to request payment.

climate change The movement of the temperature of the planet up or down over time.

closed shop agreement Clause in a negotiated labour–management agreement that specifies workers need to be members of a union before being hired.

cloud computing A form of virtualization in which a company's data and applications are stored at offsite data centres that are accessed over the Internet (the cloud).

co-operative (co-op) An organization owned and controlled by people—producers, consumers, or workers—with similar needs who pool their resources for mutual gain.

collective bargaining The process whereby union and management representatives negotiate a contract for workers.

command economy An economy in which the government largely decides what goods and services are produced, who gets them, and how the economy will grow.

commercial bank A profit-seeking organization that receives deposits from individuals and corporations in the form of chequing and savings accounts and then uses some of these funds to make loans.

commercial finance companies Organizations that make short-term loans to borrowers who offer tangible assets as collateral.

commercial paper Unsecured promissory notes of $100,000 and up that mature (come due) in one month up to one year.

common law The body of law that comes from decisions handed down by judges; also referred to as unwritten law.

common market (trading bloc) A regional group of countries that have a common external tariff, no internal tariffs, and a coordination of laws to facilitate exchange; also called a trading bloc. An example is the European Union.

common stock The most basic form of ownership in a firm; it confers voting rights and the right to share in the firm's profits through dividends, if offered by the firm's board of directors.

communism An economic and political system in which the state (the government) makes all economic decisions and owns almost all of the major factors of production.

comparative advantage theory A theory that states that a country should sell to other countries those products that it produces most effectively and efficiently, and buy from other countries those products that it cannot produce as effectively or efficiently trade.

competition-based pricing A pricing strategy based on what all the other competitors are doing. The price can be set at, above, or below competitors' prices.

compliance-based ethics codes Ethical standards that emphasize preventing unlawful behaviour by increasing control and by penalizing wrongdoers.

compound interest Interest calculated on your interest.

compressed workweek Work schedule that allows an employee to work a full number of hours per week but in fewer days.

computer-aided design (CAD) The use of computers in the design of products.

computer-aided manufacturing (CAM) The use of computers in the manufacturing of products.

computer-integrated manufacturing (CIM) The uniting of computer-aided design with computer-aided manufacturing.

conceptual skills The ability to picture the organization as a whole and the relationships among its various parts.

conciliation The use of a government-appointed third part to explore solutions to a labour–management dispute.

consideration Something of value; it is one of the requirements of a legal contract.

consumer behaviour When marketing researchers investigate consumer thought processes and behaviour at each stage in a purchase to determine the best way to help the buyer buy.

consumer market All individuals or households that want goods and services for personal consumption or use.

consumer price index (CPI) A monthly statistic that measures the pace of inflation or deflation.

consumerism A social movement that seeks to increase and strengthen the rights and powers of buyers in relation to sellers.

contingency planning The process of preparing alternative courses of action that may be used if the primary plans do not achieve the organization's objectives.

contingent workers Workers who do not have regular, full-time employment.

continuous improvement (CI) Constantly improving the way the organization operates so that customer needs can be better satisfied.

continuous process A production process in which long production runs turn out finished goods over time.

contract A legally enforceable agreement between two or more parties.

contract law Set of laws that specify what constitutes a legally enforceable agreement.

contract manufacturing A foreign country's production of private-label goods to which a domestic company then attaches its brand name or trademark; also called outsourcing.

contrarian approach Buying stock when everyone else is selling or vice versa.

controlling A management function that involves establishing clear standards to determine whether or not an organization is progressing toward its goals and objectives, rewarding people for doing a good job, and taking corrective action if they are not.

cookies Pieces of information, such as registration data or user preferences, sent by a website over the Internet to a web browser that the browser software is expected to save and send back to the server whenever the user returns to that website.

copyright A form of intellectual property that protects a creator's rights to materials such as books, articles, photos, and cartoons.

core competencies Those functions that an organization can do as well as or better than any other organization in the world.

core time In a flex-time plan, the period when all employees are expected to be at their job stations.

corporate governance The process and policies that determine how an organization interacts with its stakeholders, both internal and external.

corporate philanthropy Dimension of social responsibility that includes charitable donations.

corporate policy Dimension of social responsibility that refers to the position a firm takes on social and political issues.

corporate responsibility Dimension of social responsibility that includes everything from hiring minority workers to making safe products.

corporate social initiatives Dimension of social responsibility that includes enhanced forms of corporate philanthropy that are more directly related to the company's competencies.

corporate social responsibility (CSR) A business' concern for the welfare of society.

corporation A legal entity with authority to act and have liability separate from its owners.

cost of capital The rate of return a company must earn in order to meet the demands of its lenders and expectations of its equity holders.

cost of goods sold (cost of goods manufactured) A measure of the cost of merchandise sold or cost of raw materials and supplies used for producing items for resale.

countertrading A complex form of bartering in which several countries may be involved, each trading goods for goods or services for services.

coverage rate A measure of the proportion of employed individuals, both union members and non-unionized employees, who are covered by a collective agreement.

craft union An organization of skilled specialists in a particular craft or trade; typically local or regional.

credit profile A borrower's financial track record in the form of borrowing history.

credit union A non-profit, member-owned financial co-operative that offers a full variety of banking services to its members.

criminal law Defines crimes, establishes punishments, and regulates the investigation and prosecution of people accused of committing crimes.

crisis planning Involves reacting to sudden changes in the environment.

critical path In a PERT network, the sequence of tasks that takes the longest time to complete.

cross-functional, self-managed teams Groups of employees from different departments who work together on a long-term basis.

crowdfunding Raising funds through the collection of small contributions from the general public (known as the crowd) using the Internet and social media.

crowdsourcing Using the expertise of a large group of people to solve a business problem.

Crown corporations Companies that are owned by the federal or a provincial government.

cryptocurrencies A type of digital currency created using computer algorithms.

culture The set of values, beliefs, rules, and institutions held by a specific group of people.

current assets Items that can or will be converted into cash within one year.

customer-relationship management (CRM) The process of building long-term relationships with customers by delivering customer value and satisfaction.

damages The monetary settlement awarded to a person who is injured by a breach of contract.

data analytics The process of collecting, organizing, storing, and analyzing large sets of data ("big data") in order to identify patterns and other information that is most useful to the business now and for making future decisions.

data mining A technique to find hidden patterns and previously unknown relationships among the data.

data processing (DP) Name for business technology in the 1970s; included technology that supported an existing business and was primarily used to improve the flow of financial information.

database An electronic storage file for information.

debenture bonds (unsecured bonds) Bonds that are unsecured (i.e., not backed by any collateral such as equipment).

debit card An electronic funds transfer tool that serves the same function as cheques: it withdraws funds from a chequing account.

debt financing Funds raised through various forms of borrowing that must be repaid.

decentralized authority An organization structure in which decision-making authority is delegated to lower-level managers more familiar with local conditions compared to headquarters' management.

decertification Process by which workers can take away a union's right to represent them.

decision making Choosing among two or more alternatives.

deficit Occurs when a government spends over and above the amount it gathers in taxes for a specific period of time (namely, a fiscal year).

deflation A situation in which prices are declining.

demand The quantity of products that people are willing to buy at different prices at a specific time.

demand deposit The technical name for a chequing account; the money in a demand deposit can be withdrawn anytime on demand from the depositor.

demographic segmentation Dividing the market by age, income, and education level.

demography The statistical study of the human population with regard to its size, density, and other characteristics, such as age, race, gender, and income.

departmentalization Dividing an organization into separate units.

depreciation The systematic write-off of the cost of a tangible asset over its estimated useful life.

depression A severe recession.

deregulation Government withdrawal of certain laws and regulations that seem to hinder competition.

devaluation Lowering the value of a nation's currency relative to other currencies.

digital currency Electronic money that is not available as bills or coins.

digital marketing The promotion of products or brands via one or more forms of electronic media.

digital natives Young people who grew up using technology including the Internet and electronic devices such as cell phones.

direct marketing Any activity that directly links manufacturers or intermediaries with the ultimate customer.

direct selling Selling to customers in their homes or where they work.

directly chartered union A union that is directly affiliated to a labour congress to whom it pays per capita dues and receives services.

disability insurance Insurance that pays part of the cost of a long-term illness or an accident.

disinflation A situation in which price increases are slowing (the inflation rate is declining).

diversification Buying several different investment alternatives to spread the risk of investing.

dividends Part of a firm's profits that may be distributed to shareholders as either cash payments or additional shares of stock.

double-entry bookkeeping The concept of every business transaction affecting at least two accounts.

dumping Selling products in a foreign country at lower prices than those charged in the producing country.

e-business Any information system or application that empowers business processes.

e-commerce The buying and selling of goods and services over the Internet.

economic cycles (business cycles) The periodic rises and falls that occur in economies over time.

economics The study of how society chooses to employ resources to produce goods and services and distribute them for consumption among various competing groups and individuals.

economies of scale The situation in which companies can reduce their production costs if they can purchase raw materials in bulk and develop specialized labour, resulting in the average cost of goods going down as production levels increase.

electronic funds transfer (EFT) system A computerized system that electronically performs financial transactions such as making purchases, paying bills, and receiving paycheques.

embargo A complete ban on the import or export of a certain product or the stopping of all trade with a particular country.

employment equity Employment activities designed to increase employment opportunities for four groups (women, Aboriginal people, persons with disabilities, and members of visible minorities) given past discrimination.

empowerment Giving front-line workers the responsibility, authority, and freedom to respond quickly to customer requests.

enterprise portal A centralized and secure online network for information and transactions.

enterprise resource planning (ERP) A computer application that enables a firm to manage all of its operations (finance, requirements planning, human resources, and order fulfillment) on the basis of a single, integrated set of corporate data.

entrepreneur A person who risks time and money to start and manage a business.

entrepreneurial team A group of experienced people from different areas of business who join together to form a managerial team with the skills needed to develop, make, and market a new product.

entrepreneurship Accepting the challenge of starting and running a business.

environmental scanning The process of identifying the factors that can affect marketing success.

equalization A federal government program for reducing fiscal disparities among provinces.

equity financing Money raised from within the firm, from operations or through the sale of ownership in the firm.

equity theory The idea that employees try to maintain equity between inputs and outputs compared to others in similar positions.

ethical consumerism A strategy where companies provide products that appeal to people's best selves.

ethics Standards of moral behaviour; that is, behaviour that is accepted by society as right versus wrong.

ethnic marketing Combinations of the marketing mix that reflect the unique attitudes, race or ancestry, communication preferences, and lifestyles of ethnic Canadians.

ethnocentricity An attitude that one's own culture is superior to all others.

everyday low pricing (EDLP) Setting prices lower than competitors and then not having any special sales.

exchange rate The value of one nation's currency relative to the currencies of other countries.

exchange-traded funds (ETFs) Collections of stocks that are traded on exchanges but are traded more like individual stocks than like mutual funds.

exclusive distribution Distribution that sends products to only one retail outlet in a given geographic area.

executor An individual who assembles and values your estate, files income and other taxes, and distributes assets when you pass away.

expectancy theory Victor Vroom's theory that the amount of effort employees exert on a specific task depends on their expectations of the outcome.

exporting Selling products to another country.

express warranties Specific representations by the seller that buyers rely on regarding the goods they purchase.

external customers Dealers, who buy products to sell to others, and ultimate customers (or end users), who buy products for their own personal use.

extranet A semi-private network that uses Internet technology and allows more than one company to access the same information or allows people on different servers to collaborate.

extrinsic reward Something given to you by someone else as recognition for good work; extrinsic rewards include pay increases, praise, and promotions.

facility layout The physical arrangement of resources (including people) in the production process.

facility location The process of selecting a geographic location for a company's operations.

factoring The process of selling accounts receivable for cash.

factors of production The resources used to create wealth: land, labour, capital goods, entrepreneurship, and knowledge.

federal budget A comprehensive report that reveals government financial policies for the coming year.

finance The function in a business that acquires funds for the firm and manages them within the firm.

financial accounting Accounting information and analyses prepared for people outside the organization.

financial control A process in which a firm periodically compares its actual revenues, costs, and expenses with its projected ones.

financial literacy Having the knowledge, skills, and confidence to make responsible financial decisions.

financial management The job of managing a firm's resources to meet its goals and objectives.

financial managers Managers who examine the financial data prepared by accountants and recommend strategies for improving the financial performance of the firm.

financial market infrastructure (FMI) A system that facilitates the clearing, settling, or recording of payments, securities, derivatives, or other financial transactions among participating entities; also called a clearing and settlement system.

financial statement A summary of all of the transactions that have occurred over a particular period.

fiscal policy The federal government's effort to keep the economy stable by increasing or decreasing taxes or government spending.

fixed assets Assets that are relatively permanent, such as land, buildings, and equipment.

flat organization structure An organization structure that has few layers of management and a broad span of control.

flex-time plan Work schedule that gives employees some freedom to choose when to work, as long as they work the required number of hours.

flexible manufacturing Designing machines to do multiple tasks so that they can produce a variety of products.

focus group A small group of people who meet under the direction of a discussion leader to communicate their opinions about an organization, its products, or other issues.

foreign direct investment (FDI) The buying of permanent property and businesses in foreign nations.

foreign subsidiary A company owned in a foreign country by the parent company.

forensic accounting A relatively new area of accounting that focuses its attention on fraudulent activity.

form utility The value added by the creation of finished goods and services.

formal organization The structure that details lines of responsibility, authority, and position; that is, the structure shown on organization charts.

franchise The right to use a specific business' name and sell its goods or services in a given territory.

franchise agreement An arrangement whereby someone with a good idea for a business sells the rights to use the business name and sell its goods and services in a given territory.

franchisee A person who buys a franchise.

franchisor A company that develops a product concept and sells others the rights to make and sell the products.

free trade The movement of goods and services among nations without political or economic barriers.

free-market economy An economy in which the market largely determines what goods and services are produced, who gets them, and how the economy grows.

free-rein leadership A style that involves managers setting objectives and employees being relatively free to do whatever it takes to accomplish those objectives.

fringe benefits Benefits such as sick-leave pay, vacation pay, pension plans, and health plans that represent additional compensation to employees beyond base wages.

fundamental accounting equation Assets = Liabilities + Owners' Equity; this is the basis for the balance sheet.

Gantt chart Bar graph showing production managers what projects are underway and what stage they are in at any given time.

gender wage gap The difference between wages earned by men and wages earned by women.

General Agreement on Tariffs and Trade (GATT) A 1948 agreement that established an international forum for negotiating mutual reductions in trade restrictions.

general partner An owner (partner) who has unlimited liability and is active in managing the firm.

general partnership A partnership in which all owners share in operating the business and in assuming liability for the business' debts.

Generation X A demographic group of Canadians who were born in the period from 1965 to 1976.

Generation Y (Millennials) A demographic group of Canadians who were born in the period from 1977 to 1994; the children of the Baby Boomers.

Generation Z A demographic group of Canadians who were born in the period from 1995 onward.

geographic segmentation Dividing the market by geographic area.

givebacks Concessions made by union members to management; gains from previous labour negotiations are given back to management to help employers remain competitive and thereby save jobs.

goal-setting theory The idea that setting ambitious but attainable goals can motivate workers and improve performance if the goals are accepted, accompanied by feedback, and facilitated by organizational conditions.

goals The broad, long-term accomplishments an organization wishes to attain.

goods Tangible products such as computers, food, clothing, cars, and appliances.

government and not-for-profit (non-profit) accounting Accounting system for organizations whose purpose is not generating a profit but rather serving ratepayers, taxpayers, and others according to a duly approved budget.

green marketing The process of selling products and/or services based on their environmental benefits.

greening The trend toward saving energy and producing products that cause less harm to the environment.

greenwashing When businesses try to make themselves or their products or services look green or socially responsible without the action to back it up.

grievance A charge by employees that management is not abiding by or fulfilling the terms of the negotiated labour–management agreement.

gross domestic product (GDP) The total value of goods and services produced in a country in a given year.

gross profit (gross margin) How much a firm earned by buying (or making) and selling merchandise.

hackers People who illegally access online information.

Hawthorne effect The tendency for people to behave differently when they know they are being studied.

hierarchy A system in which one person is at the top of the organization and there is a ranked or sequential ordering from the top down of managers who are responsible to that person.

high–low pricing strategy Set prices that are higher than EDLP stores, but have many special sales where the prices are lower than competitors.

human development index A measure of a country's progress that includes wealth, health, and education.

human relations skills The ability to communicate and motivate, enabling managers to work through and with people.

human resource management (HRM) The process of determining human resource needs and then recruiting, selecting, developing, motivating, evaluating, compensating, and scheduling employees to achieve organizational goals.

humanistic management A people-oriented management approach that emphasizes the dignity and well-being of employees.

hygiene (maintenance) factors In Herzberg's theory of motivating factors, job factors that can cause dissatisfaction if missing but that do not necessarily motivate employees if increased.

identity theft Obtaining an individual's personal information, such as Social Insurance Number and credit card numbers, for illegal purposes.

implied warranties Guarantees legally imposed on the seller.

import quota A limit on the number of products in certain categories that a nation can import.

importing Buying products from another country.

income statement (statement of earnings) The financial statement that shows a firm's profit after costs, expenses, and taxes.

independent audit An evaluation and unbiased opinion about the accuracy of a company's financial statements.

independent local organization A union that is not formally connected or affiliated with any other labour organization; also called the union local, local, or local union.

index funds Specialized mutual funds that are constructed to aim to equal the performance of a market index.

industrial design A form of intellectual property that protects the owner's exclusive right to use the visible features of a finished product that identify it.

industrial policy A comprehensive, coordinated government plan to guide and revitalize the economy.

industrial union Consists of unskilled and semi-skilled workers in mass-production industries such as automobile manufacturing and mining.

inflation A general rise in the prices of goods and services over time.

informal organization The system of relationships and lines of authority that develops spontaneously as employees meet and form power centres; that is, the human side of the organization that does not appear on any organization chart.

information systems (IS) Technology that helps companies do business; includes such tools as automated teller machines (ATMs) and voice mail.

information technology (IT) Technology that helps companies change business by allowing them to use new methods.

initial public offering (IPO) The first public offering of a corporation's stock.

injunction A court order directing someone to do something or to refrain from doing something.

insider trading An unethical activity in which insiders use private company information to further their own fortunes or those of their family and friends.

insourcing Assigning various functions that could go to an outside organization to employees in the company.

institutional investors Large organizations—such as pension funds, mutual funds, and insurance companies—that invest their own funds or the funds of others.

insurable interest The possibility of the policyholder to suffer a loss.

insurable risk A risk that the typical insurance company will cover.

insurance policy A written contract between the insured and an insurance company that promises to pay for all or part of a loss.

intangible assets Long-term assets (e.g., patents, trademarks, and copyrights) that have no physical form but do have value.

integrated marketing communication (IMC) A technique that combines all of the promotional tools into one comprehensive and unified promotional strategy.

integrity-based ethics codes Ethical standards that define the organization's guiding values, create an environment that supports ethically sound behaviour, and stress a shared accountability among employees.

intensive distribution Distribution that puts products into as many retail outlets as possible.

interest The payment the bond issuer makes to the bondholders for use of the borrowed money.

intermittent process A production process in which the production run is short and the machines are changed frequently to make different products.

internal customers Individuals and units within the firm that receive services from other individuals or units.

international financial reporting standards (IFRS) The common set of accounting principles, standards, and procedures that accountants and companies use to compile financial statements.

International Monetary Fund (IMF) An international bank that makes short-term loans to countries experiencing problems with their balance of trade.

international union A union that has its headquarters outside of Canada (usually the United States).

Internet of Things (IoT) Refers to data-collecting technologies that connect ordinary objects to the Internet through sensors, cameras, software, databases, and massive data centres. Often, those technologies can communicate with one another.

Internet2 The private Internet system that links government supercomputer centres and a select group of universities; it runs more than 22 000 times faster than today's public infrastructure and supports heavy-duty applications.

intranet A companywide network, closed to public access, that uses Internet-type technology.

intrapreneurs Creative people who work as entrepreneurs within corporations.

intrinsic reward The good feeling you have when you have done a job well.

inverted organization An organization that has contact people at the top and the chief executive officer at the bottom of the organization chart.

investment bankers Specialists who assist in the issue and sale of new securities.

Investment Canada Act Legislation that provide rules to review significant investment in Canada by non-Canadians.

invisible hand A phrase coined by Adam Smith to describe the process that turns self-directed gain into social and economic benefits for all.

involuntary bankruptcy Bankruptcy procedures filed by a debtor's creditors.

ISO 14001 A collection of the best practices for managing an organization's impact on the environment.

ISO 9001 The common name given to quality management and assurance standards.

job analysis A study of what is done by employees who hold various job titles.

job description A summary of the objectives of a job, the type of work to be done, the responsibilities and duties, the working conditions, and the relationship of the job to other functions.

job enlargement A job-enrichment strategy that involves combining a series of tasks into one challenging and interesting assignment.

job enrichment A motivational strategy that emphasizes motivating the worker through the job itself.

job rotation A job-enrichment strategy that involves moving employees from one job to another.

job sharing An arrangement whereby two part-time employees share one full-time job.

job simulation The use of equipment that duplicates job conditions and tasks so that trainees can learn skills before attempting them on the job.

job specifications A written summary of the minimum qualifications required of workers to do a particular job.

joint venture A partnership in which two or more companies (often from different countries) join to undertake a major project.

journal The record book where accounting data are first entered.

just-in-time (JIT) inventory control A production process in which a minimum of inventory is kept on the premises and parts, supplies, and other needs are delivered just in time for use on the assembly line.

knowledge management Finding the right information, keeping the information in a readily accessible place, and making the information known to everyone in the firm.

labour contract (negotiated labour–management agreement) Informal name for negotiated labour-management agreement, which is an agreement that sets the tone and clarifies the terms and conditions under which management and labour agree to function over a period of time.

labour relations board (LRB) An organization created by the federal or provincial government to administer labour relations legislation.

labour union An employee organization whose main goal is representing its members in employee–management negotiation of job-related issues.

law of large numbers Principle that if a large number of people are exposed to the same risk, a predictable number of losses will occur during a given period of time.

leading Creating a vision for the organization and guiding, training, coaching, and motivating others to work effectively to achieve the organization's goals and objectives.

lean manufacturing The production of goods using less of everything compared to mass production.

ledger A specialized accounting book in which information from accounting journals is accumulated into accounts and posted so that managers can find all of the information about a specific account in one place.

leverage Raising needed funds through borrowing to increase a firm's rate of return.

liabilities What the business owes to others (debts).

licensing A global strategy in which a firm (the licensor) allows a foreign company (the licensee) to produce its product in exchange for a fee (a royalty).

limited liability The responsibility of a business' owners for losses only up to the amount they invest; limited partners and shareholders have limited liability.

limited liability partnership (LLP) A partnership that limits partners' risk of losing their personal assets to only their own acts and omissions and to the acts and omissions of people under their supervision.

limited partner An owner (partner) who invests money in the business but does not have any management responsibility or liability for losses beyond the investment.

limited partnership A partnership with one or more general partners and one or more limited partners.

line of credit A given amount of unsecured funds a bank will lend to a business.

line organization An organization that has direct two-way lines of responsibility, authority, and communication running from the top to the bottom of the organization, with all people reporting to only one supervisor.

line personnel Employees who are part of the chain of command that is responsible for achieving organizational goals.

liquidity The ease with which an asset can be converted into cash.

lockout An attempt by management to put pressure on unions by temporarily closing the business.

logistics Those activities that focus on getting the right amount of the right products or services to the right place at the right time at the lowest possible cost.

long-term financing Borrowed funds that are needed for a period more than one year.

long-term forecast Forecast that predicts revenues, costs, and expenses for a period longer than one year, and sometimes as far as five or ten years into the future.

loss When a business's expenses are more than its revenues.

macroeconomics The part of economic study that looks at the operation of a nation's economy as a whole.

management The process used to accomplish organizational goals through planning, organizing, leading, and controlling people and other organizational resources.

management by objectives (MBO) A system of goal setting and implementation that involves a cycle of discussion, review, and evaluation of objectives among top and middle-level managers, supervisors, and employees.

management development The process of training and educating employees to become good managers, and then monitoring the progress of their managerial skills over time.

managerial accounting Accounting used to provide information and analyses to managers inside the organization to assist them in decision making.

marginal tax rate The rate of tax payable on the last dollar earned.

market People with unsatisfied wants and needs who have both the resources and the willingness to buy.

market orientation Focusing efforts on (1) continuously collecting information about customers' needs and competitors' capabilities, (2) sharing this information throughout the organization, and (3) using the information to create value, ensure customer satisfaction, and develop customer relationships.

market price The price determined by supply and demand.

market segmentation The process of dividing the total market into groups with similar characteristics.

marketing A set of business practices designed to plan for and present an organization's products or services in ways that build effective customer relationships.

marketing boards Organizations that control the supply or pricing of certain agricultural products in Canada.

marketing concept A three-part business philosophy: (1) a customer orientation, (2) a service orientation, and (3) a profit orientation.

marketing intermediaries Organizations that assist in moving goods and services from producers to business and consumer users.

marketing mix The ingredients that go into a marketing program: product, price, place, and promotion.

marketing research The analysis of markets to determine opportunities and challenges, and to find the information needed to make good decisions.

Maslow's hierarchy of needs Theory of motivation that places different types of human needs in order of importance, from basic physiological needs to safety, social, and esteem needs to self-actualization needs.

mass customization Tailoring products to meet the needs of individual customers.

mass marketing Developing products and promotions to please large groups of people.

materials requirement planning (MRP) A computer-based production management system that uses sales forecasts to make sure that needed parts and materials are available at the right time and place.

matrix organization A system in which specialists from different parts of the organization are brought together to work on specific projects but still remain part of a line-and-staff structure.

maturity date The exact date the issuer of a bond must pay the principal to the bondholder.

mediation The use of a third party, called a mediator, who encourages both sides in a dispute to continue negotiating and often makes suggestions for resolving the dispute.

mentor An experienced employee who supervises, coaches, and guides lower-level employees by introducing them to the right people and generally being their organizational sponsor.

micro-enterprise A small business defined as having one to four employees.

microeconomics The part of economic study that looks at the behaviour of people and organizations in particular markets.

micromarketing (one-to-one marketing) Developing a unique mix of goods and services for each individual customer.

micropreneurs Small-business owners with fewer than five employees who are willing to accept the risk of starting and managing the type of business that remains small, lets them do the kind of work they want to do, and offers them a balanced lifestyle.

middle management The level of management that includes general managers, division managers, and branch and plant managers, who are responsible for tactical planning and controlling.

mission statement An outline of the fundamental purposes of an organization.

mixed economies Economic systems in which some allocation of resources is made by the market and some by the government.

monetary policy The management of the money supply and interest rates.

money Anything that people generally accept as payment for goods and services.

money supply The amount of money the Bank of Canada makes available for people to buy goods and services.

monopolistic competition The market situation in which a large number of sellers produce very similar products that buyers nevertheless perceive as different.

monopoly A market in which there is only one seller for a product or service.

mortgage bonds (secured bonds) Bonds that are secured (i.e., backed by collateral such as land).

motivation The overall desire to excel.

motivators In Herzberg's theory of motivating factors, job factors that cause employees to be productive and that give them satisfaction.

multinational corporation An organization that manufactures and markets products in many different countries and has multinational stock ownership and multinational management.

mutual fund A organization that buys stocks and bonds and other investments, then sells shares in those securities to the public.

mutual insurance company A type of insurance company owned by its policyholders.

national debt (also known as public debt) The accumulation of the federal government's borrowing (deficits) over time.

National Policy Government directive that placed high tariffs on imports from the United States to protect Canadian manufacturing, which had higher costs.

national union A union that only represents workers in Canada.

negligence Part of tort law where behaviour does not meet the standard of care required and causes unintentional harm or injury.

negotiable instruments Forms of commercial paper (such as cheques) that are transferable among businesses and individuals and represent a promise to pay a specified amount.

net income (or net loss) Revenue left over (or depleted if a net loss) after all costs and expenses, including taxes, are paid.

networking The process of establishing and maintaining contacts with key managers within and outside the organization, and using those contacts to weave strong relationships that serve as informal development systems.

networking between firms Using communications technology and other means to link organizations and allow them to work together on common objectives.

niche marketing The process of finding small but profitable market segments and designing or finding products for them.

non-banks Financial organizations that accept no deposits but offer many services provided by regular banks.

non-profit organization An organization whose goals do not include making a personal profit for its owners or organizers.

notes payable Short-term or long-term liabilities that a business promises to repay by a certain date.

objectives Specific, measurable, short-term statements detailing how to achieve the organization's goals.

observation Involves watching, either mechanically or in person, how people behave.

off-the-job training Internal or external training programs away from the workplace that develop any of a variety of skills or foster personal development.

offshoring Sourcing part of the purchased inputs outside of the country.

oligopoly A form of competition in which just a few sellers dominate the market.

on-the-job training Training at the workplace that lets the employee learn by doing or by watching others for a while and then imitating them.

one-to-one marketing (micromarketing) Developing a unique mix of goods and services for each individual customer.

online retailing Selling products to ultimate consumers online.

online training Training programs in which employees complete classes via the Internet.

open shop agreement Clause in a negotiated labour–management agreement that says employees are free to join or not join the union and to pay or not pay union dues.

operating (master) budget The budget that ties together all of a firm's other budgets and summarizes the business' proposed financial activities.

operating expenses Costs involved in operating a business, such as rent, utilities, and salaries.

operational planning The process of setting work standards and schedules necessary to implement the company's tactical objectives.

operations management A specialized area in management that converts or transforms resources (including human resources) into goods and services.

organization chart A visual device that shows relationships among people and divides the organization's work; it shows who is accountable for the completion of specific work and who reports to whom.

organizational (or corporate) culture Widely shared values within an organization that provide coherence and co-operation to achieve common goals.

organizing A management function that includes designing the structure of the organization and creating conditions and systems in which everyone and everything work together to achieve the organization's goals and objectives.

orientation The activity that introduces new employees to the organization; to fellow employees; to their immediate supervisors; and to the policies, practices, values, and objectives of the firm.

outsourcing Assigning various functions, such as accounting, production, security, maintenance, and / or legal work, to outside organizations.

over-the-counter (OTC) market An exchange that provides companies and investors with a means to trade stocks not listed on the national exchanges.

overnight rate The interest rate at which major financial institutions borrow and lend one-day (or overnight) funds among themselves.

owners' equity The amount of the business that belongs to the owners minus any liabilities owed by the business.

participative (democratic) leadership A style that consists of managers and employees working together to make decisions.

partnership A legal form of business with two or more parties.

partnership agreement Legal document that specifies the rights and responsibilities of each partner.

patent A form of intellectual property that gives inventors exclusive rights to their inventions for 20 years.

pay equity Equal pay for work of equal value.

penetration price strategy A strategy in which the product is priced low to attract many customers and discourage competitors.

pension funds Amounts of money put aside by corporations, non-profit organizations, or unions to cover part of the financial needs of their members when they retire.

perfect competition The market situation in which there are many sellers in a market and no seller is large enough to dictate the price of a product.

performance appraisal An evaluation that measures employee performance against established standards in order to make decisions about promotions, compensation, training, or termination.

personal selling The face-to-face presentation and promotion of goods and services.

phishing E-mails embellished with a stolen logo from a well-known enterprise (often from financial institutions) that makes the messages look authentic, but which are used to collect personal data and use it to commit fraud.

planning A management function that includes anticipating trends and determining the best strategies and tactics to achieve organizational goals and objectives.

PMI A creative thinking strategy that lists all the pluses, minuses, and interesting points for a solution in separate columns.

podcasting A means of distributing multimedia digital files on the Internet for downloading to a portable media player.

positioning statement Expresses how a company wants to be perceived by customers.

power of attorney A written document in which you appoint someone else to act on your behalf on matters that you specify; this can be made to start immediately, or upon mental incapacity.

precedent Decisions judges have made in earlier cases that guide the handling of new cases.

preferred stock Stock that gives its owners preference in the payment of dividends and an earlier claim on assets than common shareholders if the company is forced out of business and its assets are sold.

premium The fee charged by an insurance company for an insurance policy.

price The money or other consideration (including other goods and services) exchanged for the ownership or use of a good or service.

price leadership The strategy by which one or more dominant firms set the pricing practices that all competitors in an industry then follow.

primary boycott When a union encourages both its members and the general public not to buy the products of a firm involved in a labour dispute.

primary data Data that you gather yourself (not from secondary sources such as books, journals, and newspapers).

prime rate The interest rate that banks charge their most creditworthy customers.

principle of motion economy Theory developed by Frank and Lillian Gilbreth that every job can be broken down into a series of elementary motions.

private accountant An accountant who works for a single firm, government agency, or not-for-profit organization.

private corporation Corporation that is usually controlled by a small number of shareholders and its shares are not listed on a stock exchange.

privatization The process of governments selling Crown corporations.

problem solving The process of solving the everyday problems that occur. Problem solving is less formal than decision making and usually calls for quicker action.

process manufacturing That part of the production process that physically or chemically changes materials.

producers' cartels Organizations of commodity-producing countries that are formed to stabilize or increase prices to optimize overall profits in the long run.

product Any physical good, service, or idea that satisfies a want or need.

product differentiation The creation of real or perceived product differences.

product liability Part of tort law that holds businesses liable for harm that results from the production, design, sale, or use of products they market.

product life cycle A theoretical model of what happens to sales and profits for a product class over time; the four stages of the cycle are introduction, growth, maturity, and decline.

product line A group of products that are physically similar or are intended for a similar market.

product mix The combination of product lines offered by an organization.

product positioning The place an offering occupies in customers' minds on important attributes relative to competitive products.

production The creation of finished goods and services using the factors of production: land, labour, capital, entrepreneurship, and knowledge.

production management The term used to describe all of the activities that managers do to help their firms create goods.

productivity The amount of output that is generated given the amount of input (e.g., hours worked).

profit The amount a business earns above and beyond what it spends for salaries and other expenses.

program evaluation and review technique (PERT) A method for analyzing the tasks involved in completing a given project, estimating the time needed to complete each task, and identifying the minimum time needed to complete the total project.

promissory note A written contract with a promise to pay.

promotion All of the techniques sellers use to motivate customers to buy their products.

promotion mix The combination of promotional tools an organization uses.

prospectus A condensed version of economic and financial information that a company must make available to investors before they purchase a security.

psychographic segmentation Dividing the market using the group's values, attitudes, and interests.

psychological pricing Pricing goods and services at price points that make the product appear less expensive than it is.

public accountant An accountant who provides his or her accounting services to individuals or businesses on a fee basis.

public corporation Corporation that has the right to issue shares to the public, so its shares may be listed on a stock exchange.

public relations (PR) The function that evaluates public attitudes, changes policies and procedures in response to the public's requests, and executes a program of action and information to earn public understanding and acceptance.

public-private partnerships (P3s or PPPs) A method of privatizing public services or public infrastructure.

publicity Any information about an individual, product, or organization that is distributed to the public through the media and that is not paid for or controlled by the seller.

pull strategy Promotional strategy in which heavy advertising and sales promotion efforts are directed toward consumers so that they will request the products from retailers.

purchasing The functional area in a firm that searches for quality material resources, finds the best suppliers, and negotiates the best price for goods and services.

pure risk The threat of loss with no chance for profit.

push strategy Promotional strategy in which the producer uses advertising, personal selling, sales promotion, and all other promotional tools to convince wholesalers and retailers to stock and sell merchandise.

quality Consistently producing what the customer wants while reducing errors before and after delivery to the customer.

quality of life The general well-being of a society in terms of its political freedom, natural environment, education, health care, safety, amount of leisure, and rewards that add to the satisfaction and joy that other goods and services provide.

Rand formula (agency shop agreement) Clause in a negotiated labour–management agreement that says employers may hire non-union workers; employees are not required to join the union but must pay union dues.

ratio analysis The assessment of a firm's financial condition using calculations and interpretations of financial ratios developed from the firm's financial statements.

re-engineering The fundamental rethinking and radical redesign of organizational processes to achieve dramatic improvements in critical measures of performance.

real time The present moment or the actual time in which something takes place; data sent over the Internet to various organizational partners as they are developed or collected are said to be available in real time.

recession Two or more consecutive quarters of decline in the GDP.

recovery When the economy stabilizes and starts to grow.

recruitment The set of activities used to obtain a sufficient number of the right people at the right time.

registered pension plans (RPPs) Pension plans established by employers or unions for employees.

registered retirement savings plan (RRSP) A federally-regulated, tax-sheltered savings plan designed to encourage Canadians to save for their retirement.

regulations Restrictions that provincial and federal laws place on businesses with respect to the conduct of their activities.

reinforcement theory The concept that positive and negative reinforcers motivate a person to behave in certain ways.

relationship marketing Marketing strategy with the goal of keeping individual customers over time by offering them products that exactly meet their requirements.

research and development (R&D) Work directed toward the innovation, introduction, and improvement of products and processes.

resource development The study of how to increase resources and the creation of the conditions that will make better use of those resources (e.g., recycling).

resources A general term that incorporates human resources, natural resources, and financial resources.

restructuring Redesigning an organization so that it can more effectively and efficiently serve its customers.

retailer An organization that sells to ultimate consumers.

retained earnings The accumulated earnings from a firm's profitable operations that remains in the business and are not paid out to shareholders as dividends.

revenue The total amount of money received during a given period for goods sold and services rendered, and from other financial sources.

reverse discrimination Discriminating against members of a dominant or majority group (say, whites or males) usually as a result of policies designed to correct previous discrimination against minority or disadvantaged groups.

risk The chance of loss, the degree of probability of loss, and the amount of possible loss (i.e., time and money).

risk management The process of understanding, costing, and efficiently managing unexpected levels of variability in the financial outcomes for a business.

risk-return tradeoff The principle that the level of return to be earned from an investment should increase as the level of risk increases and vice versa.

rule of indemnity Rule saying that an insured person or organization cannot collect more than the actual loss from an insurable risk.

sales promotion The promotional tool that stimulates consumer purchasing and dealer interest by means of short-term activities.

scientific management Studying workers to find the most efficient ways of doing things and then teaching people those techniques.

secondary boycott An attempt by labour to convince others to stop doing business with a firm that is the subject of a primary boycott.

secondary data Information that has already been compiled by others and published in journals and books or made available online.

secured bonds (mortgage bonds) Bonds that are secured (i.e., backed by collateral such as land).

secured loan A loan backed by collateral, something valuable such as property.

securities commission A provincial or territorial government agency that administers and enforces rules around how securities are issued, bought and sold.

securities dealer or investment dealer A firm that trades securities for its clients and offers investment services; also known as an investment dealer.

security A negotiable financial instrument that represents some type of financial value.

selection The process of gathering information and deciding who should be hired, under legal guidelines, to serve the best interests of the individual and the organization.

selective distribution Distribution that sends products to only a preferred group of retailers in an area.

self-insurance The practice of setting aside money to cover routine claims and buying only "catastrophe" policies to cover big losses.

services Intangible products (i.e., products that can't be held in your hand) such as education, health care, insurance, recreation, and travel and tourism.

sexual harassment Unwelcome conduct of a sexual nature that detrimentally affects the work environment or leads to adverse job-related consequences for the victims of the harassment.

shop stewards Union officials who work permanently in an organization and represent employee interests on a daily basis.

short-term financing Borrowed funds that are needed for one year or less.

short-term forecast Forecast that predicts revenues, costs, and expenses for a period of one year or less.

sinking fund A reserve account in which the issuer of a bond periodically retires some part of the bond principal prior to maturity so that enough capital will be accumulated by the maturity date to pay off the bond.

Six Sigma quality A quality measure that allows only 3.4 defects per million events.

skimming price strategy A strategy in which a new product is priced high to make optimum profit while there's little competition.

small business A business that is independently owned and operated, is not dominant in its field, and meets certain standards of size in terms of employees or annual revenues.

smart card An electronic funds transfer tool that is a combination credit card, debit card, phone card, driver's licence card, and more.

SMEs (small and medium-sized enterprises) Refers to all businesses with fewer than 500 employees.

social audit A systematic evaluation of an organization's progress toward implementing programs that are socially responsible and responsive.

social commerce Using social media and user contributions to assist in the online buying and selling of products and services.

social media The term commonly given to websites and online tools that allow users to interact with each other in some way—by sharing information, opinions, knowledge, and interests.

social media marketing Consumer-generated online-marketing efforts to promote brands and companies for which they are fans (or conversely, negatively promoting brands and companies for which they are non-fans), and the use by marketers of online tools and platforms to promote their brands or organizations.

socialism An economic system based on the premise that some, if not most, basic businesses should be owned by the government so that profits can be evenly distributed among the people.

sole proprietorship A business that is owned, and usually managed, by one person.

span of control The optimum number of subordinates a manager supervises or should supervise.

speculative risk A chance of either profit or loss.

spread The difference between the interest a bank earns on loans extended to customers and the interest paid to depositors and other creditors for the use of their money.

staff personnel Employees who advise and assist line personnel in meeting their goals.

staffing A management function that includes hiring, motivating, and retaining the best people available to accomplish the company's objectives.

stagflation A situation in which the economy is slowing but prices are going up regardless.

stakeholders All the people who stand to gain or lose by the policies and activities of a business.

standard of living The amount of goods and services people can buy with the money they have.

statement of cash flows (cash flow statement) A financial statement that reports cash receipts and cash disbursements related to a firm's three major activities: operations, investing, and financing.

statement of earnings (income statement) The financial statement that shows a firm's profit after costs, expenses, and taxes.

statistical process control (SPC) The process of testing statistical samples of product components at each stage of the production process and plotting those results on a graph. Any variances from quality standards are recognized and can be corrected if beyond the set standards.

statistical quality control (SQC) The process some managers use to continually monitor all phases of the production process to assure that quality is being built into the product from the beginning.

statutory law Federal and provincial legislative enactments, treaties of the federal government, and bylaws and ordinances—in short, written law.

stock certificate Evidence of stock ownership that specifies the name of the company, the number of shares it represents, and the type of stock being issued.

stock exchange An organization whose members can buy and sell (exchange) securities for companies and investors.

stock insurance company A type of insurance company owned by shareholders.

stock splits An action by a company that gives shareholders two or more shares of stock for each one they own.

stockbroker A registered representative who works as a market intermediary to buy and sell securities for clients.

stocks (shares) Shares of ownership in a company.

strategic alliance A long-term partnership between two or more companies established to help each company build competitive market advantages.

strategic planning The process of determining the major goals of the organization and the policies and strategies for obtaining and using resources to achieve those goals.

strict product liability Legal responsibility for harm or injury caused by a product regardless of fault.

strike A union strategy in which workers refuse to go to work.

strikebreakers Replacement workers hired to do the jobs of striking employees until the labour dispute is resolved.

supervisory management Managers who are directly responsible for supervising workers and evaluating their daily performance.

supply The quantity of products that manufacturers or owners are willing to sell at different prices at a specific time.

supply chain The sequence of firms that perform activities required to create and deliver a good or service to consumers or industrial users.

supply chain management The integration and organization of information and logistics activities across firms in a supply chain for the purpose of creating and delivering goods and services that provide value to customers.

surplus An excess of revenues over expenditures.

sustainability Social perspectives focus on quality of human life; economic views emphasize a steady-state economy.

sustainable development Implementing a process that integrates environmental, economic, and social considerations into decision making.

SWOT analysis A planning tool used to analyze an organization's strengths, weaknesses, opportunities, and threats.

tactical planning The process of developing detailed, short-term statements about what is to be done, who is to do it, and how it is to be done.

tall organization structure An organization structure in which the pyramidal organization chart would be quite tall because of the various levels of management.

target costing Designing a product so that it satisfies customers and meets the profit margins desired by the firm.

target marketing Marketing directed toward those groups (market segments) an organization decides it can serve profitably.

tariff A tax imposed on imports.

tax accountant An accountant trained in tax law and responsible for preparing tax returns or developing tax strategies.

Tax-Free Savings Account (TFSA) An investment option into which Canadian residents 18 years of age or older who have a valid social insurance number can contribute up to $5,500 annually; the amount contributed as well as the income earned in the account is tax free, even when it is withdrawn.

technical skills The ability to perform tasks in a specific discipline or department.

technology Everything from phones and copiers to computers, mobile devices, medical imaging machines, and the various software programs and apps that make business processes more effective, efficient, and productive.

telecommuting Working from home via computer.

telemarketing The sale of goods and services by telephone.

term insurance Pure insurance protection for a given number of years.

term-loan agreement A promissory note that requires the borrower to repay the loan in specified instalments.

test marketing The process of testing products among potential users.

time deposit The technical name for a savings account; the bank can require prior notice before the owner withdraws money from a time deposit.

time value of money A dollar in hand today is worth more than a dollar promised at some time in the future.

time-motion studies Studies, begun by Frederick Taylor, of which tasks must be performed to complete a job and the time needed to do each task.

top management Highest level of management, consisting of the president and other key company executives, who develop strategic plans.

tort A wrongful act that causes injury to another person's body, property, or reputation.

total fixed costs All expenses that remain the same no matter how many products are made or sold.

total product offer (value package) Everything that customers evaluate when deciding whether to buy something; also called a value package.

total quality management (TQM) Striving for maximum customer satisfaction by ensuring quality from all departments.

trade credit The practice of buying goods and services now and paying for them later.

trade deficit An unfavourable balance of trade; occurs when the value of a country's imports exceeds that of its exports.

trade protectionism The use of government regulations to limit the import of goods and services.

trade surplus A favourable balance of trade; occurs when the value of a country's exports exceeds that of its imports.

trademark A brand that has been given legal protection for the brand name, symbol, or pictorial design (or combination of these).

training and development All attempts to improve productivity by increasing an employee's ability to perform. Training focuses on short-term skills, whereas development focuses on long-term abilities.

transactional leadership Leadership style where the leader is given the power to assign tasks and their successful completion leads to rewards and reinforcement.

transfer payments Direct payments from governments to other governments or to individuals.

transformational leadership Leadership style that occurs when leaders can influence others to follow them in working to achieve a desired outcome or goal.

transparency The presentation of a company's facts and figures in a way that is clear, accessible, and apparent to all stakeholders.

trial balance A summary of all of the data in the account ledgers to show whether the figures are correct and balanced.

triple-bottom line (TBL, 3BL, or People, Planet, Profit) A framework for measuring and reporting corporate performance against economic, social, and environmental parameters.

trust company A financial institution that can administer estates, pension plans, and agency contracts, in addition to other activities conducted by banks.

umbrella policy A broadly based insurance policy that saves you money because you buy all your insurance from one company.

unemployment rate The percentage of the labour force that actively seeks work but is unable to find work at a given time.

uninsurable risk A risk that no insurance company will cover.

union security clause Provision in a negotiated labour–management agreement that stipulates that employees who benefit from a union must either officially join or at least pay dues to the union.

union shop agreement Clause in a negotiated labour–management agreement that says workers do not have to be members of a union to be hired, but must agree to join the union within a prescribed period.

unionization rate (union density) A number of employed individuals who are union members as a proportion of the total number of employed individuals.

United States-Mexico-Canada Agreement (USMCA) The agreement among three member-countries that coordinates trade. Replaces the NAFTA agreement.

unlimited liability The responsibility of business owners for all of the debts of the business.

unsecured bonds (debenture bonds) Bonds that are unsecured (i.e., not backed by any collateral such as equipment).

unsecured loan A loan that does not require any collateral.

value Good quality at a fair price.

value package (total product offer) Another name for total product offer, which is everything that customers evaluate when deciding whether to buy something.

values A set of fundamental beliefs that guide a business in the decisions it makes.

variable costs Costs that change according to the level of production.

variable life insurance A form of whole life insurance that invests the cash value of the policy in stocks or other high-yielding securities.

venture capital Money that is invested in new or emerging companies that are perceived as having great profit potential.

venture capitalists Individuals or companies that invest in new businesses in exchange for partial ownership of those businesses.

vestibule training Training done in schools where employees are taught on equipment similar to that used on the job.

viral marketing Any strategy that encourages people to pass on a marketing message to others, creating exponential growth in the message's influence as the message reaches thousands to millions of potential customers.

virtual corporation A temporary networked organization made up of replaceable firms that join and leave as needed.

virtual networking A process that allows software-based, networked computers to run multiple operating systems and programs, and share storage.

virtual private network (VPN) A private data network that creates secure connections, or "tunnels," over regular Internet lines.

virus A piece of programming code inserted into other programming to cause some unexpected and, for the victim, usually undesirable event.

vision An encompassing explanation of why the organization exists and where it is trying to head.

voluntary bankruptcy Legal procedures initiated by a debtor.

Web 2.0 The set of tools that allow people to build social and business connections, share information, and collaborate on projects online (including blogs, wikis, social networking sites and other online communities, and virtual worlds).

Web 3.0 A combination of technologies that adds intelligence and changes how people interact with the web, and vice versa (consists of the semantic web, mobile web, and immersive Internet).

whistleblowers People who report illegal or unethical behaviour.

whole life insurance Life insurance that combines pure insurance and savings.

wholesaler A marketing intermediary that sells to other organizations.

will A document that names the guardian for your children, states how you want your assets distributed, and names the executor for your estate.

word-of-mouth promotion A promotional tool that involves people telling other people about products they have purchased or services they have used.

workplace violence Any act in which a person is abused, threatened, intimidated, or assaulted in his or her employment.

World Bank An autonomous United Nations agency that borrows money from the more prosperous countries and lends it to less-developed countries to develop their infrastructure.

World Trade Organization (WTO) The international organization that replaced the General Agreement on Tariffs and Trade, and was assigned the duty to mediate trade disputes among nations.

Index

D

E

F

G

H

I

N

O

Q

R

S

W

Y

Z